BERLINGIERI ON
ARREST OF SHIPS

SHIPPING LAW LIBRARY

Series editors: M. T. Wilford and T. G. Coghlin

LLOYD'S SHIPPING LAW LIBRARY

The Ratification of Maritime Conventions
edited by The Institute of Maritime Law,
University of Southampton
(1990) (looseleaf)

*Contracts for the Carriage of Goods
by Land, Sea and Air*
by David Yates *et al.*
(1993) (looseleaf)

Marine Environment Law
by John H. Bates and Charles Benson
(1993) (looseleaf)

Voyage Charters
by Julian Cooke,
Timothy Young, Andrew Taylor,
John D. Kimball, David Martowski
and LeRoy Lambert
(1993)

Marine War Risks
second edition
and Supplement to the second edition
by Michael D. Miller
(1994)

Merchant Shipping Legislation
by Aengus R. M. Fogarty
(1994) (looseleaf)

Multimodal Transport
by Ralph De Wit
(1995)

*CMR: Contracts for the International
Carriage of Goods by Road*
third edition
by Andrew Messent
and David Glass
(2000)

Time Charters
fourth edition
by Michael Wilford, Terence Coghlin
and John D. Kimball
(1995)

The Law of Shipbuilding Contracts
second edition
by Simon Curtis
(1996)

The Law of Tug and Tow
by Simon Rainey
(1996)

Enforcement of Maritime Claims
second edition
by D. C. Jackson
(1996)

Laytime and Demurrage
fourth edition
by John Schofield
(2000)

London Maritime Arbitration
by Clare Ambrose
and Karen Maxwell
(1996)

EC Shipping Law
second edition
by Vincent Power
(1998)

*Limitation of Liability
for Maritime Claims*
third edition
by Patrick Griggs and Richard Williams
(1998)

Ship Sale and Purchase
third edition
by Iain Goldrein QC *et al.*
(1998)

*Shipping and the Environment—
Law and Practice*
by Colin de la Rue and
Charles B. Anderson
(1998)

Berlingieri on Arrest of Ships
third edition
by Francesco Berlingieri
(2000)

P. & I. Clubs—Law and Practice
third edition
by Steven J. Hazelwood
(2000)

Admiralty Jurisdiction and Practice
second edition
by Nigel Meeson
(2000)

BERLINGIERI ON
ARREST
OF SHIPS

A COMMENTARY ON THE
1952 AND 1999 ARREST CONVENTIONS

THIRD EDITION

BY

FRANCESCO BERLINGIERI

Former Professor of Maritime Law at the University of Genoa
Honorary President, Comité Maritime International
Advocate, Senior Partner, Studio Legale Berlingieri

FOREWORD BY PATRICK GRIGGS, PRESIDENT OF
THE COMITÉ MARITIME INTERNATIONAL

PUBLISHED UNDER THE AUSPICES OF
THE COMITÉ MARITIME INTERNATIONAL

LONDON   HONG KONG
2000

LLP Professional Publishing
(a trading division of Informa Publishing Group Ltd)
69–77 Paul Street
London EC2A 4LQ

EAST ASIA
LLP Asia
Sixth Floor, Hollywood Centre
233 Hollywood Road
Hong Kong

First published 1992
Second edition 1996
Third edition 2000

© Francesco Berlingieri 1992, 1996, 2000

British Library Cataloguing in Publication Data
A catalogue record for this book
is available from the
British Library

ISBN 1–85978–528–X

Text set in 10/12pt Times
by Interactive Sciences Ltd,
Gloucester
Printed in Great Britain by
Bookcraft [Bath] Ltd

Foreword

BY PATRICK GRIGGS, PRESIDENT
OF THE COMITÉ MARITIME INTERNATIONAL

In the four years which have passed since the Second Edition of this important work of reference was published, much has happened. In March 1999, at a Diplomatic Conference held under the auspices of IMO and UNCTAD in Geneva, the final text of a new Arrest Convention was adopted. This Convention was based upon a draft text prepared by the CMI and approved at its 33rd Conference in Lisbon in 1985. In the intervening years the IMO/UNCTAD Joint Intergovernmental Group of Experts met on numerous occasions to refine the Lisbon draft and to produce a text for submission to a Diplomatic Conference.

The one constant factor throughout the history of this new Convention has been the author of this book, Professor Francesco Berlingieri. He was President of the CMI at the time when the Lisbon draft was adopted and attended every meeting of the JIGE in an advisory capacity. He then attended the Diplomatic Conference in Geneva as leader of the CMI Observer Delegation. In brief there is no one better qualified to guide us through the complexities of the new Arrest Convention than the author of this book.

At this stage we cannot predict when the entry into force conditions of the 1999 Convention (Article 14) will be met (consent by 10 States is required) but when the Convention enters into force practitioners and academics alike will be well served not only by Professor Berlingieri's detailed analysis of the terms of the Convention but also by the inclusion as an appendix to this volume of the Travaux Préparatoires which includes the documentation produced by the CMI and by the JIGE. Increasingly, practitioners and courts are drawn to the Travaux Préparatoires to aid in the interpretation of the articles of a convention. All this valuable information has been carefully edited by the author and material is grouped on an article-by-article basis for ease of reference in Appendix II.III of book II (pages 379–564). Government lawyers charged with implementation of the Convention will also find this book invaluable.

A less energetic author might have felt that a detailed treatment of the 1999 Arrest Convention would, alone, be sufficient justification for a Third Edition. However, Professor Berlingieri has taken the opportunity offered by the publication of the Third Edition to overhaul the text of the section of the book which deals with the 1952 Arrest Convention. In updating this section of the book he has sent questionnaires to the CMI's affiliated Maritime Law Associations (or where there is no such Association he has consulted the relevant Government department). The material produced by this painstaking further research features in the substantially revised first part of the Third Edition (book I).

History tells us that the implementation of new conventions which are designed to replace earlier instruments is a slow process. We can therefore expect that even after the 1999 Convention has come into force there will be a long period during which the 1952 Convention will continue to apply in certain countries. For that reason this will remain, for many years, the first point of reference on matters concerning the arrest of ships for practising lawyers and academics, alike.

PATRICK GRIGGS

Acknowledgments

When I was requested to prepare a third edition of this book I thought that while maintaining the original layout, it was necessary, not only to review the information provided and the opinions expressed, but also to expand the information concerning the implementation of the 1952 Convention by as many Contracting States as possible as well as the interpretation of the most relevant provisions of the Convention. I therefore prepared a new questionnaire and circulated it amongst all Contracting States. In the States where there is a Maritime Law Association I sent the questionnaire to the Association while for the other States I sent it to the Department of the Government the address of which had been kindly provided by the UNCTAD Secretariat, to which I am greatly indebted. This initiative had only a limited success, particularly in respect of States where there is no Maritime Law Association. However many of the replies received are very exhaustive and have enabled me to expand significantly the information contained in the first and second editions. Here follows the list of the National Maritime Law Associations and of the persons in each Association who have replied to the Questionnaire. The only Contracting State where there is no Maritime Law Association from which I received replies is Haiti.

Belgium:	Association Belge de Droit Maritime (Mr Luc Keyzer)
Croatia:	Croatian Maritime Law Association (Mrs Pospišil-Miler, M Sc.)
Denmark:	Danish Branch of the CMI (Mr Jan Erlund and Mr Jesper Martens)
Finland:	Finnish Maritime Law Association (Professor Peter Wetterstein)
France:	Association Française du Droit Maritime (Professor Pierre Bonassies)
Germany:	German Maritime Law Association (Dr Hans-Heinrich Nöll)
Greece:	Greek Maritime Law Association (Professor Antonis Antapassis)
Haiti:	Autorité Portuaire Nationale (Mr Molière Frederic)
Italy:	Italian Maritime Law Association (Professor Francesco Berlingieri)
Netherlands:	Netherlands Maritime and Transport Law Association (Mr Taco van der Valk)
Nigeria:	Nigerian Maritime Law Association (Mr Louis N Mbanefo S.A.N.)

Norway:	Norwegian Maritime Law Association (Mr Karl-Johan Gombrii)
Poland:	Polish Maritime Law Association (Mr Przemysław Anders, LLM)
Slovenia:	Slovene Maritime Law Association (Dr Marko Pavliha)
Spain:	Asociacion Espanola de Derecho Maritimo (Ms Esther Zarza)
Sweden:	Swedish Maritime Law Association (Mr Lars Boman)
United Kingdom:	British Maritime Law Association (Professor Nicholas Gaskell, Mr Dimitrios Christodoulou and Mr Richard Shaw)

In view of the interest of the replies I have deemed it convenient, in addition to using the material provided in the commentary, to arrange all the replies under each question and to insert all such material in an annex—Annex II to the new edition.

I am greatly indebted to all those who have so kindly and so properly responded to the questionnaire.

This of course does not decrease the value of the information I had received in course of the preparation of the previous editions and my gratitude to all those who contributed is great.

In the second edition of this book I had added an Appendix in which I summarised the work in progress for the revision of the 1952 Convention, commenced by the CMI in 1983 and completed, in a preliminary stage, with the preparation of the draft of a new Convention—the "Lisbon Draft"—approved by the CMI Conference held in Lisbon in 1985. The work was then continued by the IMO-UNCTAD Joint Intergovernmental Group of Experts on Maritime Liens and Mortgages and Related Subjects and resulted in the adoption in March 1999 of the new Convention on Arrest of Ships.

I thought, therefore, that I should attempt to write an initial commentary of the new Convention, which could, however, be based only on its legislative history, of which I had a personal and direct knowledge, since I was the President of the CMI when the Lisbon Draft was prepared and approved and then I attended all sessions of the JIGE and the Diplomatic Conference as observer for the CMI. In order, however, to enable the future interpreters and commentators to acquire a direct knowledge of such legislative history, I collected all the travaux préparatoires which are now published as an annex—Annex III—to the commentary.

Francesco Berlingieri
Genoa, 20 December 1999

Glossary

I. INTERNATIONAL CONVENTIONS

Accession Convention: Convention on the Accession of the Kingdom of Denmark, Ireland the United Kingdom of Great Britain and Northern Ireland to the Convention on Jurisdiction and the Enforcement of Judgments in Civil and Commercial Matters and to the Protocol on its Interpretation by the Court of Justice, Luxembourg, 9 October 1978.

Arrest Convention 1952: International Convention Relating to the Arrest of Sea-Going Ships, Brussels, 10 May 1952.

Arrest Convention 1999: International Convention on Arrest of Ships, 1999.

Athens Convention 1974: Athens Convention Relating to the Carriage of Passengers and their Luggage by Sea 1974, Athens, 13 December 1974.

Civil Jurisdiction Convention 1952: International Convention on Certain Rules Concerning Civil Jurisdiction in Matters of Collision, Brussels, 10 May 1952.

CLC (Civil Liability Convention) 1969: International Convention on Civil Liability for Pollution Damage, Brussels, 29 November 1969.

CLC 1984 Protocol: Protocol of 1984 to Amend the International Convention on Civil Liability for Oil Pollution Damage 1969, London, 25 May 1984.

Collision Convention: Convention Internationale pour l'Unification de Certaines Règles en Matière d'Abordage, Brussels, 23 September 1910.

Collision Regulations: Convention on the International Regulations for Preventing Collisions at Sea 1972, London, 20 October 1972.

Convention on a Code of Conduct: Convention on a Code of Conduct for Liner Conferences, approved by the United Nations Conference of Plenipotentiaries on a Code of Conduct for Liner Conferences at Geneva, 6 April 1974.

Convention on Conditions for Registration of Ships 1986: United Nations Convention on Conditions for Registration of Ships, Geneva, February 1986.

Draft Articles: Draft Articles for a Convention on Arrest of Ships, prepared by the IMO and UNCTAD Secretariats, IMO Doc LEG/MLM 32, 15 June 1995 and UNCTAD Doc. TD/B/CN.4/GE/2/5.

EEC Jurisdiction Convention: Convention on Jurisdiction and the Enforcement of Judgments in Civil and Commercial Matters and Protocol on its Interpretation, Brussels, 27 September 1968.

Hague Rules: Convention Internationale pour l'Unification de Certaines Règles en Matière de Connaissement, Brussels, 25 August 1924.

ix

Hague-Visby Rules: Hague Rules as amended by the Protocol to Amend the International Convention for the Unification of Certain Rules of Law Relating to Bills of Lading, Signed at Brussels on 25 August 1924, Brussels, 23 February 1968.

Hamburg Rules: United Nations Convention on the Carriage of Goods by Sea 1978, Hamburg, 31 March 1978.

HNS Convention: International Convention on Liability and Compensation for Damage in Connection with the Carriage of Hazardous and Noxious Substances by Sea, 1996.

HSC Code: International Code of Safety for High Speed Craft, adopted by IMO Resolution MSC.36(63) on 20 May 1994.

IMO-UNCTAD Draft: Draft Articles for a Convention on Maritime Liens and Mortgages, Annex to the Final Report of the Joint Intergovernmental Group of Experts on Maritime Liens and Mortgages and Related Subjects, IMO Document JIGE (vi)/8 of 17 November 1989.

Immunity Convention 1926: Convention Internationale pour l'Unification de Certaines Règles Concernant les Immunités des Navires d'Etat, Brussels, 24 May 1926 and Protocole Additionnel à cette Convention, Brussels, 24 May 1934.

ISM Code: International Management Code for the Safe Operation of Ships and for Pollution Prevention, adopted by IMO Resolution A.741(18).

Limitation Convention 1957: International Convention Relating to the Limitation of Liability of Owners of Sea-Going Ships, Brussels, 10 October 1957.

LLMC (Limitation) Convention 1976: Convention on Limitation of Liability for Maritime Claims, 1976, London, 19 November 1976.

Lisbon Draft: Draft Revision of the International Convention for the Unification of Certain Rules Relating to the Arrest of Sea-Going Ships, done in Brussels, 10 May 1952, approved by the XXXIII International Conference of the Comité Maritime International, Lisbon 1985 (Lisboa II).

Load Line Convention: International Convention on Loadlines 1966, London, 5 April 1966.

Lugano Convention: Convention on Jurisdiction and the Enforcement of Judgments in Civil and Commercial Matters, Lugano, 16 September 1988.

MLM (Maritime Liens and Mortgages) Convention 1926: Convention Internationale pour l'Unification de Certaines Règles Relatives aux Privilèges et Hypothèques Maritimes, Brussels, 10 April 1926.

MLM (Maritime Liens and Mortgages) Convention 1967: International Convention for the Unification of Certain Rules Relating to Maritime Liens and Mortgages, done in Brussels, 10 May 1967.

MLM (Maritime Liens and Mortgages) Convention 1993: International Convention on Maritime Liens and Mortgages, 1993.

Memorandum of Understanding on Port State Control: 26 January 1982.

Multimodal Transport Convention 1980: United Nations Convention on International Multimodal Transport of Goods, Geneva, 24 May 1980.

Nuclear Ships Convention 1962: Convention on the Liability of Operators of Nuclear Ships, Brussels, 25 May 1962.

Off-Shore Mobile Craft (Draft) Convention: Draft International Convention on Off-Shore Mobile Craft approved by the XXXI International Conference of the Comité Maritime International Rio de Janeiro 1977, CMI Documentation, 1977, II.

Passengers Convention 1961: International Convention for the Unification of Certain Rules Relating to the Carriage of Passengers by Sea, Brussels, 29 April 1961.

Passengers' Luggage Convention 1967: International Convention for the Unification of Certain Rules Relating to the Carriage of Passengers' Luggage by Sea, Brussels, 27 May 1967.

Penal Jurisdiction Convention 1952: International Convention for the Unification of Certain Rules Relating to Penal Jurisdiction in Matters of Collision or Other Incidents of Navigation, Brussels, 10 May 1952.

Pollution Prevention: International Convention for the Prevention of Pollution from Ships, 1973 as modified by the Protocol of 1978.

Procedures for Port State Control: adopted by the Assembly of IMO on 23 November 1995.

Rhine Convention 1868: Revised Rhine Convention of 17 October 1968.

Salvage Convention 1910: Convention Internationale pour l'Unification de Certaines Règles en Matière d'Assistance et Sauvetage Maritimes, Brussels, 23 September 1910.

Salvage Convention 1989: International Convention on Salvage, 1989.

SOLAS Convention: International Convention for the Safety of Life at Sea 1974, London, 1st November 1974.

STCW Convention: International Convention on Standards of Training, Certification and Watchkeeping for Seafarers, 1978.

Stowaways Convention 1957: International Convention Relating to Stowaways, Brussels, 10 October 1957.

UNCLOS: United Nations Convention on the Law of the Sea, 1982.

II. INTERGOVERNMENTAL ORGANIZATIONS

CMI: Comité Maritime International

IMO: International Maritime Organization.

UNCTAD: United Nations Commission for Trade and Development.

III. INTERNATIONAL DOCUMENTS

Travaux Préparatoires: The Travaux Préparatoires of the 1910 Collision Convention and of the 1952 Arrest Convention, edited by F. Berlingieri, Genoa, 1997.

Procés-Verbaux: Conférence Internationale de Droit Maritime, Neuvième Session, Bruxelles, 1952, edited by the Ministère des Affaires Etrangères et du Commerce Extérieur of Belgium.

CMI Bulletin No. 96: Comité Maritime International, Bulletin No. 96, Conférence d'Oslo 1933, Antwerp 1934.

CMI Bulletin No. 102: Comité Maritime International, Bulletin No. 102, Conférence de Paris 1937, Antwerp 1938.

CMI Bulletin No. 104: Comité Maritime International, Bulletin No. 104, Conférence d'Amsterdam 1949, Antwerp 1951.

CMI Bulletin No. 105: Comité Maritime International, Bulletin No. 105, Conférence de Naples 1951, Antwerp 1952.

IV. NATIONAL ENACTMENTS

Australia

Admiralty Act: Admiralty Act 1988

Belgium

CCP: Code Judiciaire (Code of Civil Procedure)

Croatia

Maritime Code: Pomorski Zakonik, in force since 22 March 1994
Enforcement Proceedings Act: Ovzšni Zakon, in force since 11 August 1996

Denmark

Administration of Justice Act (Retsplejeloven): Act No. 90 of 11 April 1916 as amended by Act No. 159 of 15 March 1989.
Maritime Code Merchant Shipping Act: Act No. 56 of 1 April 1892 as amended by Act No. 159 of 15 March 1989.

Finland

Maritime Code: Merilaki, promulgated on 15 July 1994
Code of Judicial Procedure: Oikeudenkäymiskaari, promulgated on 31 December 1734

France

Code Disciplinaire et Pénal de la Marine Marchande: Loi du 17 décembre 1926 Portant Code Disciplinaire et Pénal de la Marine Marchande.
Decree 27.10.1967: Décret No. 67–957 of 27 October 1967 issued in connection with Loi No. 67–5 of 3 January 1967, portant Statut des Navires et Autres Bâtiments de Mer.
Decree 27.10.1971: Décret No. 67–967 du 27 octobre 1967 complétant la loi No. 67–5 du 3 janvier 1967 portant Statut des Navires et autres Bâtiments de Mer.
Law No. 61–1262 of 24.11.1961: Loi No. 61–1262 du 24 novembre 1961 relative à la police des épaves maritimes, modifiée par la loi No. 82–990 du 23 novembre 1982.
Law No. 77–530 of 26.5.1977: Loi No. 77–530 du 26 mai 1977 Relative à l'Obligation d'Assurance des Propriétaires de Navires pour les Dommages Résultant de la Pollution par les Hydrocarbures.
Law No. 83–583 of 5.7.1983: Loi No. 83–583 du 5 juillet 1983 réprimant la pollution des eaux de la mer par les hydrocarbures.

Germany

HGB: Handelsgesetzbuch of 10 May 1897, as amended.
ZPO: Zivilprozessordnung promulgated 1 January 1877, re-enacted 12 September 1950 as amended.

Ireland

Jurisdiction of Courts (Maritime Conventions) Act 1989: An Act to Give Force of Law to the International Convention Relating to the Arrest of Sea-Going Ships and the International Convention on Certain Rules Concerning Civil Jurisdiction in Matters of Collision both signed at Brussels on the 10th day of May 1952 and to provide for Matters consequent upon and otherwise related to the matters said.

Harbours Act 1946: An act to make further and better provision in relation to the membership of certain Harbour Authorities and to the management, control, operation and development of their harbours, to provide for the charging of rates by such provisions in relation to Pilotage Authorities and to provide for other matters connected with the matters aforesaid (2nd April 1946).

Merchant Shipping (Safety and Load Line Convention) Act 1933: An Act to make such provision as may be necessary to give full effect to the provisions of an International Convention for the Safety of Life at Sea signed in London on the 31st day of May 1929 and of an International Load Line Convention signed in London on the 5th day of July 1930 and to amend the Merchant Shipping Acts 1894 to 1921 insofar as is necessary to give effect to the said Conventions (3rd November 1933).

Mercantile Marine Act 1955: An Act to provide for the National Character, Ownership and Registration of Irish Ships, for the Mortgage, Sale, Transfer and Measurement of Tonnage of such Ships and to provide for other matters connected with the matters aforesaid (22nd December 1955).

Italy

CCP: Codice di Procedura Civile (Code of Civil Procedure).

CN: Codice della Navigazione (Navigation Code).

Law 25.10.1977, No. 880: Ratifica ed esecuzione di tre convenzioni internazionali firmate a Bruxelles il 10 maggio 1952 concernenti l'unificazione di alcune regole sul sequestro conservativo delle navi e sulla competenza civile e penale in caso di abbordaggio.

Law 26.11.1990 No. 353: Provvedimenti urgenti per il processo civile.

Implementation Rules: Disposizioni per l'Attuazione del Codice di Procedura Civile e Disposizioni Transitorie (Implementation and Transitional Rules of the Code of Civil Procedure) approved with Royal Decree 18 December 1941, No. 1368.

Netherlands

CCP: Wetboek van Burgerlijke Rechtsvordering (Code of Civil Procedure).

Transport Law: Chapter II, Book 8 (entitled "Verkeers middelen en Vervoer") of the Civil Code ("Burgerlijk Wetboet").

Nigeria

Admiralty Jurisdiction Decree: Decree No. 59 of 1991, in force since 30 December 1991

Admiralty Jurisdiction Procedure Rules, enacted in 1993 pursuant to the Admiralty Jurisdiction Decree.

Norway

Maritime Code: Lov 24 juni Nr. 39, 1994 om sjøfarten (sjøloven)
Act on Enforcement of Claims: Lov 26 juni Nr. 86, 1992 on tvangsfullbyrdelse og midlertidig sikring (tvangsfullbyrdelsesloven)
Civil Procedure Act: Lov 13 aug. Nr. 6, 1915 om rettergangsmåten for tvistemål (tvistemålsloven)

Portugal

CC: Codigo Civil.
CCP: Codigo de Processo Civil.
Law 4.9.1986, No. 35:
Law 21.10.1986, No. 352/86: Decreto-Lei No. 352/1986 on "Contrato de Transporte de Marcadorias por Mar".

Slovenia

Maritime and Internal Navigation Act:
Forced Execution and Security Act:
Civil Procedure Act:

South Africa

Admiralty Jurisdiction Regulation Act 105 of 1983: an Act to provide for the vesting of the powers of the admiralty courts of the Republic in the provincial and local divisions of the Supreme Court of South Africa, and for the extension of those powers; for the law to be applied by, and the procedure applicable in, those divisions; for the repeal of the Colonial Courts of Admiralty Act, 1890, of the United Kingdom, in so far as it applies in relation to the Republic; and for incidental matters.

Spain

CC: Codigo Civil (Civil Code).
CCP: Ley de Enjuciamiento Civil (Code of Civil Procedure) referred to in Spain as "LEC".
Decree No. 3384 of 1971: Decreto 3384/1971 de 28.10.1971. Reglamento de reconocimiento de buques y embarcaciones (Decree of Surveyance of vessels).
Law 8.4.1967, No. 1: Ley 1/67 de 8 de abril, sobre embargo preventivo de buques extrajeros en España (Arrest of foreign vessels in Spain Act).
Law 24.12.1962, No. 60: Ley 60/1962 de 24 de diciembre sobre No. Auxilios, Salvamentos, Remolques, Hallazgos y Extracciones Maritimas. Referred to in Spain as "LAS" (Maritime Assistance, Salvage, Towage, Findings and Extractions Act).
Official Journal: Boletin Oficial del Estado. Referred to in Spain as "BOE".
Reglamento del Registro Mercantil: Regulation approved by decree of 14 December 1956.
Regulations 20.4.1967: Decreto 984/67 de 20.4.1967, Reglamento para la aplicaciòn de la Ley de Auxilios y Salvamentos, etc. (Referred to in Spain as "Reglamento de la LAS").

Revenue Act: Real Decreto 1684/90, Estatuto General de Recaudaciòn". Referred to in Spain as "Estatuto General de Recaudaciòn" (General Rules for Collection of Revenue).

Sweden

Law on Arrest of Ships: Lag (1993:03) om Kvarstad på fartyg i internationella rättsförhållanden: (Law (1993:03) on Arrest of Ships in International Legal Relations).

Maritime Code: Sjölag 1994:009.

Code of Judicial Procedure: Rättgångsbalken.

United Kingdom

Administration of Justice Act 1956: 4&5 Eliz. 2, c. 46.

Civil Jurisdiction and Judgments Act 1982: 1982, c. 46.

Civil Procedure Rules: Supreme Court of England and Wales—County Courts. The Civil Procedure Rules 1998, 1998 No. 3132 (L. 17).

County Courts Admiralty Jurisdiction Amendment Act 1869:

Harbour, Pier and Docks Clauses Act 1847: 10 & 11 Vict., c. 27.

Merchant Shipping 1894 (also MSA): Merchant Shipping Act 1894 (57 & 58 Vict, c. 60). An Act to consolidate Enactments relating to Merchant Shipping.

MSA (Safety Convention) Act 1949: Merchant Shipping (Safety Convention) Act 1949 [12 & 13 Geo. 6, c.43]. An Act to enable effect to be given to an International Convention for the Safety of Life at Sea, signed in London, the 10th day of June 1948; etc.

MSA 1967: Merchant Shipping Act 1967, 1967, c. 26.

MSA (Merchant Shipping Act) 1995: 1995 c.21. An act to consolidate the Merchant Shipping Acts 1894 to 1994 and other enactments relating to merchant shipping [19 July 1995].

Perjury Act 1911: 1 & 2 GLD 5, c.6.

Port of London Act 1968: 1968, c. xxxii.

Practice Direction Admiralty: Supplementing Civil Procedure Rules Part 49 and replacing Order 75 of the Rules of the Supreme Court.

Prevention of Oil Pollution Act 1971: 1971, c. 60.

RSC: Rules of the Supreme Court.

Supreme Court Act 1981: Supreme Court Act 1981[1981, c. 54]. An Act to consolidate with amendments the Supreme Court of Judicature (Consolidation) Act 1925 and other enactments relating to the Supreme Court in England and Wales and the administration of justice therein, etc.

Supreme Court of Judicature (Consolidation) Act 1925: 15 & 16 Geo. 5. c. 49.

V. LAW REPORTS

Australia

ALJR: Australian Law Journal Reports, 1927—(current).

CLR: Commonwealth Law Reports, 1903—(current).

Belgium

JPA: Jurisprudence du Port d'Anvers, 1856—(current)

France

DMF: Le Droit Maritime Français, 1949—(current).

Germany

TransportR: Transportrecht: Zeitschrift für das gesamte Recht der Güterbeförder-
ung, der Spedition, der Versicherungen des Transports, der Personenbeförderung, der
Reiseveranstaltung.
NJW: Neue Juristiche Wochenschrift.
BGHZ: Amtliche Entscheidungssammlung des Bundesgerichtshofes in Zivilsachen.
RIW: Recht der Internationalen Wirtschaft.
Hansa: Zentralorgan für Schiffahrt, Schiffbau, Hafen.

Greece

C.L.R.: Commercial Law Review, (current) Epithcórisi Emporikoú Dikaíou (Com-
mercial Law Review), 1950—(current)
M.L.R.: Maritime Law Review (current) Epithcórisi Naftikioú Dikaíou (Maritime
Law Review), 1973—(current)
Piraiki Nomologia: 1979—(current)

Italy

Dir. Mar.: Il Diritto Marittimo, 1899—(current).
Foro Italiano: Il Foro Italiano, 1876—(current).
Giur. Comm.: Giurisprudenza Commerciale, 1974—(current)
Riv. Dir. Nav.: Rivista di Diritto della Navigazione, 1935–1972.

Netherlands

N.J.: Nederlandse Jurisprudentie, 1913—(current).
Schip en Schade, 1957—(current).

New Zealand

NZLR: New Zealand Law Reports, 1883—(current).

Nigeria

N.S.C.: Nigerian Shipping Cases, edited by Louis N. Mbanefo (six volumes),
1907–1997

Portugal

B.M.J.: Bolelim do Ministério de Justiça, 1947—(current)

Singapore

MLJ: Malaysian Law Journal.

South Africa

S.A.:   South African Law Reports, 1947—(current)

Spain

Anuario de Derecho Maritimo, 1981—(current)
La Ley: La Ley, Revista Jurídica Española de Doctrina, Jurisprudencia y Bibliografia, 1980—(current)

United Kingdom

A.C.:   Law Reports, Appeal Cases, House of Lords and Privy Council, since 1890.
All E.R.:   All England Law Report, 1936—(current).
Asp. M.L.C.:   Aspinall's Maritime Law Cases, 22 Volumes 1870–1943.
K.B.:   Law Reports, Kings Bench Division, 1900–1952.
L.M.C.L.Q.:   Lloyd's Maritime and Commercial Law Quarterly, 1974—(current).
Lloyd's Rep: Lloyd's Law Reports, 1951—(current).
Moo P.C.:   Moore's Privy Council Cases, 1836–1862.
P.D.:   Law Reports, Probate, Divorce, and Admiralty Division, 15 volumes, 1875–1890.
Q.B.:   Law Reports Queen's Bench Division, 1891–1901; and 1952—(current).
S.L.T.:   Scots Law Times, 1893—(current).

United States

A.M.C.:   American Maritime Cases, 1923—(current).
F.2d: Federal Reporter, Second Series, 1924—(current).
J.M.L.C.:   Journal of Maritime Law and Commerce, 1969—(current).
N.Y.2d: New York Reports, 1847—(current).
U.S.:   United States Supreme Court Reporter, 1882—(current).

CONTENTS

BOOK I   THE 1952 ARREST CONVENTION

1.   HISTORY OF THE CONVENTION

2.   THE SCOPE OF APPLICATION OF THE CONVENTION

6. PROCEDURE RELATING TO ARREST

APPENDICES

BOOK II   THE INTERNATIONAL CONVENTION
ON ARREST OF SHIPS, 1999

1.   HISTORY OF THE CONVENTION

2. SCOPE OF APPLICATION OF THE CONVENTION

3. THE NOTION OF ARREST AND CLAIMS IN RESPECT OF WHICH A SHIP MAY BE ARRESTED

4. SHIPS THAT MAY BE ARRESTED

5. PROCEDURE RELATING TO ARREST

APPENDICES

Table of Cases

TABLE OF CASES

TABLE OF CASES

TABLE OF CASES

UNITED STATES OF AMERICA

Table of Legislation

*References to the main text are to book and paragraph numbers, eg I.218 refers to paragraph 218 in Book I. References to Appendices are given as page numbers in **bold type**.*

Table of Conventions

References to the main text are to book and paragraph numbers, eg I.218 refers to paragraph 218 in Book I.
*References to Appendices are given as page numbers in **bold type**.*

Table of CMI (Comité Maritime International) Conferences

Table of Conventions—Travaux Préparatoires

This Table refers to page numbers only.

Miscellaneous Legislation, Etc

BOOK I

The 1952 Arrest Convention

BOOK II

The 1962 Arrest Convention

CHAPTER 1

History of the Convention

1. THE CMI CONFERENCE OF 1930 IN ANTWERP

I.1 In preparing for the Conference of the Comité Maritime International to be held in Antwerp in August 1930, the national associations were invited by the *Bureau Permanent* of the CMI to suggest new subjects for the study by the Comité. Three associations, the French, the German and the Italian, suggested as a new subject the arrest of ships.[1]

I.2 The French and the German associations considered the subject of arrest in connection with jurisdiction in case of collision.[2] The German Association produced a preliminary draft Convention on civil jurisdiction in the matter of collision wherein provisions were made on arrest of ships as security for collision claims.[3]

I.3 Furthermore, the German association, after having pointed out that arrest was closely linked not only with collision but also with maritime liens and hypothèques, in order to protect the holders thereof from arrest effected by other claimants, suggested four questions for discussion, viz. the following[4]:

1. Who is entitled to arrest a ship?
2. Which ships may be arrested?
3. Where can the arrest be made?
4. How can a ship be released from arrest?

I.4 During the Conference, Dr Sieveking for the German association[5] indicated that his country hesitated to ratify the 1926 Convention on Maritime Liens and Mortgages because the problem of arrest was not the subject of uniform regulation. Professor Francesco

---

1. Conference d'Anvers, 1930, CMI Bulletin No. 91, pp. 76 and 105.
2. CMI Bulletin No. 91, p. 105.
3. CMI Bulletin No. 91, p. 113. Art. VI of the draft provided as follows (translation of the original French text):

VI. Arrest of a ship on account of collision may be effected in any port located in a Contracting State.

Such arrest may be effected only with the permission of the competent authority designated by national law.

The authority mentioned in the preceding paragraph may order the applicant to provide security in respect of damages that may arise out of the arrest.

The owner of the ship may request that the ship be released from arrest against sufficient security.

The formalities that must be complied with for the validation of the arrest shall be governed by national law.

4. CMI Bulletin No. 91, p. 116.
5. CMI Bulletin No. 91, p. 508.

3

Berlingieri, Sr, for the Italian association, raised the question of liability for wrongful arrest.[6]

I.5 The proposal to take up the subject of arrest was supported by the Swedish and Japanese associations[7] and it was decided, following a suggestion by the President, to request the *Bureau Permanent* to carry out a preliminary investigation of the problem.[8]

2. THE PREPARATORY WORK FOR A DRAFT CONVENTION ON ARREST OF SHIPS

I.6 A questionnaire was then prepared by the Bureau Permanent with questions on the right of arrest, the forced sale of ships[9] and, finally, the unification of the law on arrest. Replies to the questionnaire were given by the national associations of Belgium,[10] France,[11] Germany,[12] Italy,[13] the Netherlands,[14] Norway,[15] Portugal,[16] Yugoslavia,[17] Sweden,[18] the United Kingdom[19] and the United States.[20]

I.7 The International Sub-Committee, which had meanwhile been constituted by the Bureau Permanent, at its meeting held in Antwerp on 19 November 1932 requested Mr Leopold Dor to prepare a preliminary draft convention. Such draft, accompanied by an explanatory report, was submitted to the International Sub-Committee at a subsequent meeting which was held in London on 16 May 1933.[21]

---

6. CMI Bulletin No. 91, p. 514.
7. CMI Bulletin No. 91, pp. 515 and 517.
8. CMI Bulletin No. 91, pp. 518 and 519.
9. CMI Bulletin No. 96, p. 23.
10. CMI Bulletin No. 96, pp. 86–91.
11. CMI Bulletin No. 96, pp. 127–149: including a preliminary draft Convention.
12. CMI Bulletin No. 96, pp. 21–26.
13. CMI Bulletin No. 96, pp. 39–47.
14. CMI Bulletin No. 96, pp. 29–32.
15. CMI Bulletin No. 96, pp. 60–61.
16. CMI Bulletin No. 96, pp. 94–99.
17. CMI Bulletin No. 96, pp. 49–52.
18. CMI Bulletin No. 96, pp. 55–58.
19. CMI Bulletin No. 96, pp. 201–210.
20. CMI Bulletin No. 96, pp. 68–79.
21. Here follows the text of the draft (CMI Bulletin No. 96, pp. 150–159):
Art. 1: All creditors of the owner of a ship within the jurisdiction of one of the Courts of a Contracting State may arrest such ship, even if it is ready to sail. The right of arrest may be exercised by any citizen of a Contracting State against any ship flying the flag of a Contracting State.
Art. 2: If the arrestor has not an enforceable title, arrest may not be effected without the authorization of a Court. The Court shall authorize the arrest upon simple verification of the claim being likely.
The Court may, however, require the arrestor to supply such security as it will deem reasonable in order to cover the damages suffered by the persons interested in case of wrongful arrest.
Art. 3: The arrest shall not affect the right of the owner to sell or mortgage the ship, subject, however, to the right of the arrestor to contest the operations thus made when intended to defraud his rights.
Art. 4: The Courts shall order the arrest released:
    1. When, after the arrest, those having an interest in the ship will prove that the arrest was not justified.
    2. When sufficient security is provided by the owner or for his account. However, the personal undertaking of the owner shall not, failing the agreement of the arrestor, be considered by the Court as a sufficient security for ordering the arrest released.
Art. 5: If the ship and the cargo are arrested at the same time, the Court, upon the request of release made by any interested party, shall allocate the amount of the security to be provided in proportion to the values of the properties arrested.

I.8 An amended draft was then prepared by Mr Dor, for consideration by the Conference of the CMI to be held in Oslo in August 1933.[22] The draft provided that any claimant having a claim against the owner of a vessel was entitled to arrest the vessel (Article 1), that security for damages could be required by the court (Article 2), that the court could, after the arrest, order the release of the vessel if the owner proved that the arrest was not justified, or if he provided satisfactory security (Article 3), that the arrestor might be held liable in damages for wrongful arrest (Article 5), and that the procedure of the arrest was governed by the *lex fori* (Article 6). The restriction of the right of arrest to claims against the owner was the subject of specific comments in the Report of the International Sub-Committee.[23] The rule on liability for wrongful arrest was strongly opposed by the British delegation and, in an attempt to offer a compromise solution, the entitlement of the owner of the ship to damages was limited to the case of *mauvaise foi* (bad faith).[24]

I.9 Only a few national associations submitted comments before the Oslo Conference. The British Association stated that a convention on arrest was of no particular interest in view of the fact that claimants had already the right to proceed *in rem* against the vessel in order to enforce a maritime claim.[25] The United States Association indicated that it did

---

Art. 6: The request of the owner to release the ship from arrest against security shall in no event be construed as an admission of his liability or a waiver of his right to the statutory limitation of liability.

Art. 7: In case an unjustified arrest is released, the arrestor shall be condemned to pay the cost of the security provided in order to release the ship. In case the unjustified arrest has been effected in bad faith, the arrestor may also be condemned to pay the damages caused by the arrest to all persons having an interest in the ship or in the cargo.

Art. 8: The procedure relating to the arrest of a ship as well as the issues that may arise in connection therewith, shall be governed by the law of the place of arrest.

Art. 9: This Convention shall not be applicable to warships, to ships employed in a public service and to postal ships.

Art. 10: The High Contracting Parties reserve the right to extend to nationals of non-Contracting States the benefit of the right of arrest provided by Art. 1.

22. In such amended draft (CMI Bulletin No. 96, pp. 182–192) the following changes were made:
   — The sentence in Art. 2 reading "The Court shall authorize the arrest upon simple verification of the claim being *likely*" was deleted.
   — Arts. 3 and 5 were both deleted.

23. The following statement was made in that respect in the Report (CMI Bulletin No. 96, p. 152):
   In our draft the right of arrest is granted only to the creditors of the owner of the ship. Some persons consider that such right could also be granted to the creditors of the operator who is not the owner and of the principal charterer. This approach has been adopted by the French Maritime Law Association in the Draft International Convention on Arrest. We confess that such idea seems to us to be difficult to understand. One can perfectly understand that the operator or the principal charterer may, to some extent, be treated as the owner of the ship, in particular in respect of the right to the limitation of liability. Moreover, this results from Art. 10 of the International Brussels Convention of 25 August 1924 on limitation of liability of owners of seagoing ships. But, we believe, it is impossible that a person may, in order to obtain security for his claim, arrest an asset belonging to a person other than his debtor. This is the reason why we believe that a ship may be arrested only by the creditors of her owner.

24. The following explanation was given in the Report (CMI Bulletin No. 96, p. 155):
   Article 7 raises a delicate question, namely that of the liability of the arrestor in case of wrongful arrest. We are convinced that, if the draft Convention will provide too hard sanctions, it will clash against the irreducible opposition of British interests, which may cause the failure of the future Convention.
   We have, therefore, drafted Art. 7 in such a way as to limit the liability of the arrestor in good faith to the payment of the cost of the security supplied by the owner in order to obtain the release.
   On the other hand, it is wholly natural that when the arrest is effected in bad faith, the creditor must be wholly responsible for all damages ensuing from his wrongful act and that he should indemnify not only the owner of the ship, but also the owners of the cargo for the damages thus caused to them.

25. CMI Bulletin No. 96, p. 185.

not favour the idea of a convention on arrest[26]; Japanese Association pointed out that a convention could apply only to foreign ships[27]; the Dutch Association supported the idea of a convention, though several amendments to the draft were suggested.[28]

3. THE CMI CONFERENCES OF 1933 IN OSLO AND OF 1937 IN PARIS

I.10 At the Oslo Conference the delegations of the United Kingdom and the United States refrained from taking any position in respect of the draft, thus showing their lack of interest in it. The delegations of Norway, Sweden and Germany stated that they could not accept the provision relating to damages for wrongful arrest. The delegation of the Netherlands suggested that the matter be left to the *lex fori*. The President of the Conference (Mr Alten), supported by the President of the CMI (Mr Franck), suggested that the draft should be resubmitted to the International Sub-Committee for further consideration.

I.11 During the debates it had emerged that there were two fundamental differences between the common and civil law systems. First, while in the civil countries a vessel could be arrested as security for any claim, whether or not of a maritime nature, in the common law countries (and more specifically in England) a vessel could only be arrested in the limited cases where claimants are entitled to enforce their claim by proceedings *in rem*. Secondly, while in civil law countries the arrestor, in case of wrongful arrest, could be held liable for the damages suffered by the owner of the vessel, in common law countries the owner could only claim the cost of the security, on the ground that he could always release the vessel from arrest by providing adequate security.[29]

I.12 The International Sub-Committee reconsidered the draft at a meeting held in Paris on 2 June 1936[30] and decided, in order to find a solution acceptable to all or almost all national associations, to restrict the scope of the Convention to some of the claims secured by a maritime lien under the 1926 Brussels Convention on Maritime Liens and Mortgages, viz. to the claims in respect of collision damage and salvage. Article 1 of the draft submitted to the Oslo Conference was amended accordingly, while all the other provisions were left practically unaltered, including Article 5, which dealt with damages for wrongful arrest, and which had given rise to many objections at Oslo.[31]

I.13 This new draft did not seem to have given rise to too favourable a reaction on the part of the national associations. While the UK and the US associations refrained from making any comment,[32] the Italian, Belgian and Swedish associations regretted the restricted scope of application of the new draft.[33] These views were confirmed during the

26. CMI Bulletin No. 96, p. 217.
27. CMI Bulletin No. 96, p. 212.
28. CMI Bulletin No. 96, pp. 218–221.
29. CMI Bulletin No. 96, p. 461.
30. On the history of the Convention from this stage onwards, see also A. Giannini, "Il Progetto del Comité Maritime International sul Sequestro Conservativo delle Navi" (Napoli 1951), [1951] I Riv. Dir. Nav. 155.
31. Art. 1 provided as follows (CMI Bulletin No. 102, p. 80):
Art. 1: Any creditor of the owner of a ship on account of collision, of damage caused by such ship, or of salvage services, may arrest such ship or another ship belonging to the same owner, even if ready to sail.
Such right may be exercised by all nationals of Contracting States against ships flying the flag of a Contracting State that will be in the jurisdiction of the Courts of one of the Contracting States.
32. CMI Bulletin No. 102, pp. 121, 130 and 136.
33. CMI Bulletin No. 102, pp. 121, 130 and 136.

Paris Conference of May 1937, when criticisms were also raised against the formulation of Article 5. The German delegate then suggested that, in order to reach some result, it might be advisable to confine the scope of the draft Convention to the arrest of the vessel involved in a collision, thus excluding salvage claims and, also, the arrest of sister ships. This suggestion was adopted.[34]

I.14 When Article 5 was examined, the suggestion was made to leave to the law of the court by which the arrest is granted the question of damages for wrongful arrest other than the cost of the bail. This suggestion met with the approval of the Conference.[35]

4. THE CMI CONFERENCES OF 1947 IN ANTWERP, OF 1949 IN AMSTERDAM AND OF 1951 IN NAPLES

I.15 After the war, at the first conference convened by the CMI in Antwerp in 1947, it was decided to submit to the Diplomatic Conference the draft convention approved by the Paris Conference in 1937.[36] However, the British and the Dutch Maritime Law Associations felt that the scope of the 1937 draft was too restricted and that further efforts should be made to reach wider uniformity on the subject of arrest of ships. Upon their instructions, two of their members (Mr Jan Asser and Mr Cyril Miller) prepared a new questionnaire in order to collect further information on the national laws in respect of arrest and recommended that an International Sub-Committee should be instructed to study this matter once more.

I.16 At the CMI Conference held in Amsterdam in 1949, Mr Asser summarised the result of the pre-war work[37] and Mr Miller gave a succinct and clear account of the

34. Art. 1 was redrafted as follows (CMI Bulletin No. 102, p. 340):
Art. 1: Any creditor of the owner of a ship, by reason of collision, may operate the provisional arrest of such ship, even when ready to sail.
This right may be exercised by the citizens of the Contracting States on the vessels flying the flag of one of the Contracting States which are found within the jurisdiction of the court of one of them.
35. Art. 5 was redrafted as follows (CMI Bulletin No. 102, p. 342):
Art. 5: In the event of an unlawful arrest, the arrestor shall be ordered to refund the cost of the guarantee furnished for obtaining the release of the arrest. The question whether the arrestor has to make good other damage resulting from unlawful arrest, shall be determined by the law of the place of arrest.
36. Although it was stated that the Paris draft would be submitted to the Diplomatic Conference (a decision in reality belonging to the Belgian Government), this was never done, because no diplomatic conference was held in 1950, as originally envisaged, and because a completely new draft was approved at the CMI Conference held in Naples in 1951.
37. Mr Asser's summary was the following (CMI Bulletin No. 104, p. 531):
A curious thing happened in regard to that (Leopold Dor's) draft. Article 1 of the first draft provided that each creditor of the owner of a ship may arrest her. According to the report presented by Maitre Dor on that occasion, this article was intended to mean that any ship might be arrested in respect of any debt of her owner whether maritime or non-maritime. In other words, this first draft reproduced what is called the Continental system of the law of arrest.
This draft met with a great deal of opposition on the part of the British delegates, who stated that they were reluctant to abandon, in favour of the Continental system, the British system of a very restricted possibility of arrest. As a result of this opposition, article I was redrafted several times the article was gradually amputated more and more and the text finally adopted at the Paris Conference stated no more than that: "Any creditor of an owner of a ship, by reason of collision, might operate the arrest of such ship". Consequently, whilst the first draft had incorporated the continental notion of the widest scope of arrest, providing for the arrest in respect of all claims, the final draft was based on the English conception of the action *in rem*, dealing merely with collision claims, the question of arrest in respect of all other claims being left to the respective municipal laws. So what was intended to be international uniformity became merely a reproduction of the law of England. If I may be permitted to say so, this was a rather meagre result.
Anyhow, the Bureau Permanent felt that it was a result hardly worthy of the dignity of being put before the

difference between the English and the continental system.[38] Neither Mr Asser nor Mr Miller mentioned the problem of liability for wrongful arrest. Mr Miller instead stated very clearly that the scope of any future uniform legislation should be confined to the arrest as a security measure (*saisie conservatoire*) and should not be extended to the seizure for the purpose of levying execution of a judgment (*saisie executoire*).[39]

I.17 The proposal of Mr Asser and Mr Miller initially met with some opposition. Then Mr Jean de Grandmaison presented on behalf of the French Association a compromise proposal based, he stated, on the system prevailing in Scotland and in the United States, viz. to limit the right of arrest to claims of a maritime nature but to allow the arrest of any ship in the same ownership.[40] Although the merits of this proposal were not discussed, the opposition to giving further consideration to the problem of arrest of ships was withdrawn and the following resolution was unanimously adopted[41]:

The Conference resolves to request the Bureau Permanent to appoint an International Sub-Committee to study all problems directly or indirectly appertaining to or connected with the international unification of the whole field of the law of arrest of ships to report thereon in good time before the next Conference of the Comité Maritime International and, if possible, to submit a draft Convention the Sub-Committee having free hand to consider and make such recommendations as it thinks proper.

I.18 The International Sub-Committee appointed by the *Bureau Permanent* of the CMI[42] prepared a new draft convention, accompanied by a report and a commentary. In

---

Diplomatic Conference, and it was therefore decided that a new effort should be made towards international uniformity in the whole field of the arrest of ships, whereupon Mr Miller and I were entrusted by the Bureau Permanent with the task of drafting a questionnaire.

38. Mr Miller so stated (CMI Bulletin No. 104, pp. 535–536):

Having studied the very careful and informative reports that we have received from other countries, it looks as if English law is in the minority as regards the differences between the laws of the various maritime countries. That is due, I think, to the fact that in English law this question of arrest is purely maritime; it is not part of our general law as it is in other countries. We make a distinction between arrest in maritime law and arrest of any other form of property. As regards arrest of any other form of property, we have no such procedure at all. Property in England can only be arrested after judgment has been given, and that, of course, is "*saisie-execution*". The only way in which an executor in England can obtain security before an action is brought is in a limited number of cases in which ships are involved. That is the first great difference.

The second difference—and it is one upon which the Conference may well desire to make a recommendation—is this: in England it is only possible to arrest by "*saisie conservatoire*" the particular ship with which the contemplated action is concerned. You cannot arrest, in the case of a collision, a vessel in the same ownership you must arrest the actual vessel which was in collision.

39. He so stated, in fact (CMI Bulletin No. 104, p. 535):

I particularly want to endorse what Mr Asser has said: that whatever we do about this subject we should confine ourselves to recommendations and deliberations upon the unification of the law relating to what we in England call "arrest" and what in the continental system is called "*saisie conservatoire*". We should not, I think, make any recommendations with regard to the other form of "*saisie*" ("*saisie executoire*"), which we in England call "attachment", because to do that would be to make recommendations upon a matter which is purely one of procedure, and it is quite impossible to attempt, and indeed undesirable, to unify the law of procedure. One has only to reflect that a procedure which is familiar and has been familiar to a French Court for centuries could not possibly be applied by a British Court, because it would be completely contrary to the procedure of that Court in which we British lawyers are all trained, whereas, with regard to substantive law, this can be changed, although I do not say it can be done easily. That is what the Comité Maritime is for. It can be changed without alteration in the procedure of the Court. That is why I endorse what Mr Asser has said. We would confine ourselves to "*saisie conservatoire*".

40. CMI Bulletin No. 104, pp. 545–550.

41. CMI Bulletin No. 104, pp. 559–560.

42. Consisting of A Franck, President, Martin Hill, Jean de Grandmaison, Carlo van den Bosch, Giorgio Berlingieri, N V Boeg, W Koelman, Kaj Pineus, Per Gram, John C Prizer, William Symmers, J A L M Loeff, Cyril Miller and J T Asser, Rapporteurs (CMI Bulletin No. 105, p. 1).

the draft the compromise suggested at the Amsterdam Conference of 1949 was adopted: arrest was permitted only in respect of the maritime claims described in Article 1, and in addition to the ship in respect of which the maritime claim arose, any other ship in the same ownership could be arrested. The problem of liability for wrongful arrest was solved by abandoning any attempt to provide uniform rules in that respect and merely inserting a private international law rule.

I.19 In the draft there was also provision in respect of the jurisdiction on the merits of the claim. The original text of the provision was to the effect that the courts of the State in which the ship was arrested always had jurisdiction to determine the merits of the dispute but then, following the strong opposition of the French Delegate, jurisdiction on the merits was attributed to the courts of the State where the arrest was made in only certain cases, viz.:

   (a) when the claimant has his domicile or his principal place of business in such State;

   (b) if the maritime claim has arisen in such State;

   (c) if the maritime claim has arisen in the course of the voyage during which the vessel is arrested;

   (d) if the claim is in respect of a collision;

   (e) if the claim is in respect of salvage.

The draft was thoroughly examined at the Conference held in Naples and, notwithstanding the criticisms raised by several delegations, was ultimately approved without too many substantial changes.

5. THE BRUSSELS DIPLOMATIC CONFERENCE, 2–10 MAY 1952

I.20 No significant changes were made either at the diplomatic conference held in Brussels in May 1952, when the Arrest Convention was approved with 13 votes in favour, none against and six abstentions. The questions most debated at the Conference were those relating to the liability for wrongful arrest, the requirement for the claimant to provide security and the extent to which the courts of the State where the ship is arrested should have jurisdiction to decide upon the merits.

CHAPTER 2

The Scope of Application of the Convention

6. INTRODUCTION

I.21 Four different rules are set out in Article 8 on the scope of application of the Convention.

I.22 The first rule, contained in paragraph (1), is to the effect that the provisions of the Convention apply to any vessel flying the flag of a Contracting State in the jurisdiction of any Contracting State.

I.23 The second rule, contained in paragraph (2), is to the effect that a ship flying the flag of a non-contracting State may be arrested in the jurisdiction of any Contracting State in respect of any of the maritime claims enumerated in Article 1 or of any other claim for which the law of the Contracting State permits the arrest.

I.24 The other two rules set out limits to the application of the Convention. The third rule, contained in paragraph (3), entitles a Contracting State wholly or partly to exclude from the benefits of the Convention any government of a non-contracting State or any person who does not, at the time of the arrest, have his habitual residence or principal place of business in that State.

I.25 The fourth rule, set out in paragraph (4), is to the effect that the provisions of the Convention do not modify or affect the domestic law of the respective Contracting States relating to the arrest of any ship within the jurisdiction of the State of her flag by a person who has his habitual residence or principal place of business in that State. Paragraph (5) contains a rule complementary to those in paragraphs (3) and (4). It provides that in case of subrogation or assignment, the person entitled to assert the claim is deemed to have the same habitual residence or principal place of business as the original claimant.

I.26 It is therefore necessary to clarify the notion of ship adopted in the Convention, the meaning of the words "flying the flag" (of a Contracting State or of a non-contracting State), the scope of application of the Convention in respect of ships flying the flag of a Contracting State and its scope of application in respect of ships flying the flag of a non-contracting State.

7. THE NOTION OF SHIP

I.27 The notion of ship, for the purpose of identifying the ships to which the Convention applies, may be considered with reference to the waters in which a ship is sailing or is intended to sail, and with reference to the size and other characteristics of the ship.

I.28 As regards the waters in which the ship is sailing or is intended to sail, three criteria have been adopted.

I.29 A. In some conventions a distinction is made between sea-going ships and ships of inland navigation. This is the case for the 1910 Collision Convention, where in Article 1 reference is made to a collision occurring between *navires de mer* (seagoing vessels)[1] or between *navires de mer* and *bateaux de navigation intérieure* (vessels of inland navigation); for the 1910 Salvage Convention, where in Article 1 reference is made to salvage services rendered to *navires de mer* or between *navires de mer* and *bateaux de navigation intérieure*; for the 1952 Civil Jurisdiction Convention where, similarly to the 1910 Collision Convention, reference is made in Article 1 to a collision occurring between seagoing vessels or between seagoing vessels and inland navigation craft; for the 1952 Penal Jurisdiction Convention wherein in Article 1 reference is made to a collision or other incident of navigation concerning a seagoing ship. In the 1976 LLMC Convention the benefit of limitation is granted to shipowners and salvors and the term shipowner is defined as "the owner, charterer, manager and operator of a sea-going ship". But the restriction of the scope of the LLMC Convention to owners, managers and operators of seagoing ships is impliedly negated by the provision in Article 15(2) according to which States Parties may regulate by specific provisions of national law the system of limitation of liability to be applied to ships intended for navigation on inland waterways. If, in fact, States do not avail themselves of the option granted to them, the Convention applies also to such ships and this deprives the term "seagoing" used in Article 1(2) of any significance.[2]

I.30 The basis of the distinction between sea-going ships and inland navigation vessels is not clearly indicated in any convention. The fact, however, that in the 1952 Civil Jurisdiction Convention reference is made in Article 1(1) to collision between seagoing

---

1. The expression "navire de mer" is not used in most of the recent conventions, such as the 1967 MLM Convention (Art. 1), the CLC 1969 (Art. 1(1)), the 1974 Athens Convention (Art. 1(3)), the 1986 Convention on Conditions for Registration of Ships (Art. 2), the 1989 Salvage Convention (Art. 1(b)) and the 1993 MLM Convention (Art. 1) (an exception is the 1976 LLMC Convention (Art. 1(2)). The reason is that the word "navire" connotes in French a sea-going ship, whilst the word used for inland navigation ships is "bateau" and the term used for all vessels is "bâtiment" (Rodière, *Droit Maritime-Le Navire*, Paris 1980, p. 4; Rémond-Gouilloud, *Droit Maritime*, 2nd Edition, Paris 1993, p. 36). In the conventions in which a definition of "seagoing ship" is given (e.g. the CLC 1969, the 1986 Convention on Conditions for Registration of Ships), in the French text the expression used is "bâtiment de mer". This gives rise to uncertainty when in the English text the word used is "ship" (and not "seagoing ship") and in the French text the words used are "navire de mer" as, for example, the 1989 Salvage Convention (Art. 1(b)). In fact the term "ship" can be deemed to include also inland navigation vessels. See, with reference to the definition of "ship" in the MSA 1894 (" 'ship' includes every description of vessel used in navigation not propelled by oars") *Corbett* v. *Pearce* [1904] 2 K.B. 422; *Weeks* v. *Ross*, 12 Asp. MLC 555, at p. 558. The same conclusion applies in respect of the definition of "ship" in s. 313 of the MSA 1995 (" 'ship' includes every description of vessel used in navigation").

2. The French text differs from the English and may be construed so to permit the extension, rather than the exclusion, of the Convention regime to ships intended for navigation on inland waterways. Whilst in fact the English text provides that "A State Party may regulate by specific provisions of national law the system of liability to be applied to vessels which are: a) according to the law of that State, ships intended for navigation on inland waterways; b) ships of less than 300 tons.", the French text provides that "Un Etat partie peut stipuler aux termes de disposition expresses de la légalisation nationale que le régime de la limitation de responsabilité s'applique aux navire qui sont: a) en vertu de la législation dudit Etat, des bateaux destinés à la navigation sur les voies d'eau intérieurs; b) des navires d'une jauge inférieure à 300 tonneaux". The French text, however, is clearly wrong, because the *extension* of the Convention regime to ships of less than 300 tons would be meaningless, since the Convention clearly applies to such ships. Furthermore, the subsequent sentence, according to which a State which makes use of the option provided for in this paragraph "shall inform the depositary of the limits of liability adopted in its national legislation or of the fact that there are none" would be meaningless, if the option were to *extend* the Convention regime to ships intended for navigation on inland waterways, rather than to *exclude* them from the application of the Convention regime.

THE NOTION OF SHIP

vessels or between seagoing vessels and inland navigation craft and then to a collision occurring within the limits of a port or in inland waters indicates that the place where the vessel lies at the relevant time is immaterial. A seagoing vessel remains such even if sailing in inland waters and an inland navigation vessel remains such even if at sea. The distinction, therefore, lies on the prevailing type of navigation for which the vessel is intended and the correctness of this conclusion is supported by the terminology used in the LLMC Convention where in Article 15(2) reference is made to "ships intended for navigation on inland waterways". Normally the distinction is evidenced by the register in which a vessel is registered, since different registers normally exist for seagoing vessels and inland navigation vessels.

I.31 B. In some other conventions reference is only made to "sea-going ships". For example, in the 1926 Convention on Immunity of State-Owned Ships reference is made in Article 1 to "navires de mer" (sea-going ships); in the CLC 1969 "ship" is defined (Article 1(1)) as "any sea-going vessel and any seaborne craft of any type whatsoever"; in the 1986 Convention on Conditions for Registration of Ships (Article 2) "ship" is defined as "any self-propelled sea-going vessel used in the international seaborne trade".

I.32 C. Reference to the size or characteristics of the ship is made for the first time in the 1969 CLC where, as previously stated, "any sea-borne craft" is included in the definition of ship, in addition to "any sea-going vessel". Similar, but more specific, is the definition of "ship" in the 1969 Intervention Convention where the notion of "sea-going vessel" is widened by the words "of any type whatsoever" and the notion of floating (and not sea-borne) craft is restricted by the exclusion of "an installation or device engaged in the exploration and exploitation of the resources of the seabed and the ocean floor and subsoil thereof".

I.33 Rather than an extension, a restriction of the notion of "ship" is made in the 1974 Passengers Convention where (Article 1(3)) air-cushion vehicles are excluded, in the 1976 LLMC Convention where (Article 15(5)) air-cushion vehicles and floating platform are excluded and in the 1986 Convention on Conditions for Registration of Ships where (Article 2) the notion of "ship" is restricted to self-propelled (sea-going) vessels of at least 500 tons used in international seaborne trade for the transport of goods, passengers or both. A different technique is used in the 1976 LLMC Convention where there is no definition of ship but there is a provision to the effect that the Convention does not apply to air-cushion vehicles and to floating platforms constructed for the purpose of exploring or exploiting the natural resources of the sea-bed or the subsoil thereof.

I.34 In the Arrest Convention reference to seagoing ships is made in the title, but nowhere else, nor is there a definition of ship. In all the provisions of the Convention reference is always made to a ship without any qualification. This is particularly significant in respect of Article 8 regulating the scope of application of the Convention, where in paragraph 1 it is provided that the Convention shall apply "to *any vessel* flying the flag of a Contracting State". The conclusion, therefore, seems to be that the Convention applies also to inland navigation vessels and such conclusion is supported by the reference in Article 7(1)(d) to the 1910 Collision Convention, which applies also to collisions between seagoing vessels and inland navigation vessels, and by the reference in Article 7(5) to the 1868 Rhine Convention only for the purpose of excluding the application of Article 7 to cases covered by such Convention, thereby implying that all other provisions apply also to inland navigation vessels.

I.35 The distinction between seagoing vessels and inland navigation vessels seems, therefore, to be immaterial.

I.36 As regards the size and characteristics of the ship, the following elements may be considered: (a) tonnage, (b) intended use, (c) propulsion, (d) other characteristics, (e) existence of a crew, (f) registration and (g) physical conditions of the ship.

(a) Tonnage

I.37 The tonnage does not seem to be relevant, since when it was intended to exclude ships under a certain tonnage from the scope of a convention, an express provision was made to this effect: the 1976 LLMC Convention (Article 15(2)) permits States Parties to regulate by specific provisions of national law the system of liability to be applied to ships of less than 300 tons; the 1986 Convention on Conditions for Registration of Ships does not apply to vessels of less than 500 tons.

(b) Intended use

I.38 Restrictions as to the use of the ship are made in the CLC 1969, where (Article 1(1)) reference is made to sea-going vessels and craft "actually carrying oil in bulk as cargo", and in the 1986 Convention on Conditions for Registration of Ships, where (Article 2) the ships must be used "in international seaborne trade for the transport of goods, passengers or both". In other conventions the restrictions arise out of the scope of the convention: this is the case for the conventions relating to the carriage of passengers or of goods. When no restriction is specifically provided or arises out of the scope of the convention, the use of the ship cannot be relevant. This is clearly so for the Arrest Convention, for most of the maritime claims enumerated in Article 1(1) can arise whatever the use of the ship, including pleasure.[3]

(c) Propulsion

I.39 Similar considerations apply in respect of the type of propulsion and the need for the ship to be self propelled. The fact that in other conventions craft which are not self-propelled are expressly excluded implies that when no such exclusion is made the convention applies to such craft when they come within its scope. The Arrest Convention therefore applies in respect of sailing ships or craft not self-propelled.

(d) Structure

I.40 There are today craft of a great variety of structures. Suffice it to consider the hydrofoils, the air-cushion vehicles,[4] the drilling platforms,[5] the storage tanks, the floating

---

3. Rodière, *Le Navire*, p. 7; du Pontavice, *Le Statut des Navires* (Paris, 1976), p. 324; Tassel, "Saisie Conservatoire du Navire" (1967) 1/1105 Jurisclasseur de Droit Commercial, p. 11 No. 73.

4. On the status of air-cushion vehicles see Rodière, *Le Navire, supra* note 1, p. 8; Tullio, "La natura giuridica dell'hovercraft" [1970] Rivista di Diritto della Navigazione, 205. In the United Kingdom the status of hovercraft is regulated by the Hovercraft Act 1968.

5. The drilling platforms are usually registered in ships registers. See Rodière, *Le Navire*, p. 10. In the Draft Convention adopted by the Comité Maritime International at Rio de Janeiro in 1977 off-shore mobile craft has been defined as follows:

In this Convention "craft" shall mean any marine structure of whatever nature not permanently fixed into the sea-bed which
(a) is capable of moving or being moved whilst floating in or on water, whether or not attached to the sea-bed during operations, and
(b) is used or intended for use in the exploration, exploitation, processing, transport or storage of the mineral resources of the sea-bed or its subsoil or in ancillary activities.

factories, the floating dry-docks, the floating hotels, the barges and the dredges. Also in this case the fact that in some conventions certain craft of a specific type of structure, such as the air-cushion vehicles and the drilling rigs, have been expressly excluded implies that where no such exclusion is made the convention applies.

I.41 In the case of the Arrest Convention there is, as it will be seen, an overriding condition for its application: the registration of the craft in a national register which enables such craft to fly the flag of the State in which such register is situated.

(e) Whether the ship or craft must be manned

I.42 Once it is accepted that any type of craft is included in the notion of ship for the purposes of the Arrest Convention, the requirement of the craft being manned must be excluded. There are in fact many types of craft that are not manned, or at least are not manned continuously. There are, also, ships and craft that, though normally manned, may be temporarily unmanned. Suffice it to mention a ship which is in drydock.

(f) Registration

I.43 Pursuant to Article 8, paragraphs (1) and (2), for the Convention to apply a ship must fly the flag of either a Contracting State or a non-contracting State. And since, as it will be seen,[6] the right to fly the flag of a State is linked with the registration of the ship in the ships register of such State, the Convention only applies to ships which are registered. If, therefore, a ship is deregistered by reason of her loss or for any other reason, the Convention no longer applies. On the other hand, the physical condition of the ship does not affect the application of the Convention, provided the ship continues to be registered.[7]

(g) Physical conditions of the ship

I.44 The physical conditions of the ship do not affect the application of the Convention. Therefore the Convention applies to ships which are not capable of sailing because they are stranded, sunken or damaged beyond repair. A similar problem has been considered with respect to the extinction of maritime liens and mortgages or *hypothèques* and the prevailing view has been that the security is not extinguished until the ship is physically in existence.[8]

It was then provided that the Conventions referred to in Arts. 2–7 applied to off-shore mobile craft. The Arrest Convention was referred to in Art. 4 which states as follows.

A State Party which is also a party to the International Convention for the unification of certain rules relating to the arrest of sea-going ships, dated May 10, 1952, shall apply the rules of that convention to craft to which they would not otherwise apply.

These provisions have been left unaltered in the revised draft approved by the CMI at Sydney in 1994.

6. See *infra*, section 8.

7. In France it was held that the special maritime rules on arrest of ships ceased to apply when a ship had become a wreck (*épave*): Cour d'Appel of Aix-en-Provence, 18 March 1983, *The "Balstar"* [1984] D.M.F. 608 with note by Bonassies. See also du Pontavice, *Le Statut des Navires* (Paris, 1976), No. 349.

8. See, for German law, Wüstendorfer, *Neuzeitliches Seehandelsrecht* (2nd Ed., Berlin, 1950), p. 97; Schaps-Abraham, *Das Deutsche Seerecht* (3rd Edn., Vol. I, Berlin, 1959), pp. 361 and 532; Abraham, "Das Schiffshypotek in deutschen and ausländischen Recht",' *Ubersee-Studien, Heft 20* (Stuttgart-Köln, 1950), p. 277 and, for Italy, F. Berlingieri Jr., *I Diritti di Garanzia Sulla Nave, l'Aeromobile e le Cose Caricate* (Milan, 1965), p. 456; Rubino, *l'Ipoteca Mobiliare e Immobiliare* (Milan, 1956), p. 508; Gaetano, *I Privilegi* (Turin, 1949), p. 61.

8. THE FLAG AS THE SYMBOL OF NATIONALITY

I.45 The scope of application of the Convention is established on the basis of the flag of the ship. Thus in Article 2 and Article 8(1) reference is made to ships flying the flag of a Contracting State, in Article 8(2) reference is made to ships flying the flag of a non-contracting State and in Article 8(4) the case of arrest of a ship within the jurisdiction of the flag State is considered.

I.46 The flag is the symbol of the nationality of the vessel and, therefore, reference to the flag must be taken to mean reference to the nationality.[9] Reference to the flag, as the connecting factor for the application of the Convention, is also made in the 1952 Penal Jurisdiction Convention (Article 1), in the 1957 Stowaways Convention (Article 2(1)), in the 1961 Passengers Convention (Article 2), in the 1962 Nuclear Ships Convention (Article XIII), in the 1974 Athens Convention (Article 2(1)) and in the LLMC Convention (Article 15(1)).

I.47 The equivalence between the nationality of a ship and the flag the ship is flying is affirmed by the 1986 Convention on Conditions for Registration of Ships. Article 4(2) of this Convention provides that "ships have the nationality of the State whose flag they are entitled to fly".

I.48 The nationality of a ship is that of the State in whose register of ships the ship is entered. Also, the identity between nationality and State of registration is clearly established by the Convention on Conditions for Registration of Ships. Article 9(6) of this Convention imposes certain obligations on the State of registration with respect to ships flying its flag. Equally, in Article 10 provisions are made in respect of the management of ship-owning companies from the State of registration with reference to ships flying its flag. Article 11(1) provides then that "a State of registration shall establish a register of ships flying its flag".

I.49 Although registration is normally the condition for a ship to acquire the nationality of the State in whose register of ships she is entered, it is possible that the nationality, and, therewith, the right to fly the flag, is acquired prior to the ship being entered in the register of ships. In many jurisdictions nationality is temporarily granted, prior to registration, by issuing a provisional certificate.

I.50 A ship may, however, have dual registration. This happens in the case of temporary suspension of the nationality following the registration of the ship in the register of the State where the bareboat charterer has its principal place of business for the purpose of enabling the ship to fly the flag of the charterer's State. The problem, therefore, arises whether, for the purposes of the Arrest Convention, the relevant flag is that of the State of temporary registration or that of the State of the underlying register.

I.51 There is no doubt that when reference was made in Article 8 of the Arrest Convention to ships flying the flag of a Contracting State and to ships flying the flag of a non-contracting State it was assumed that the flag was that of the State of registration. The arrest of a ship may, in fact, have a substantial bearing on the property of and charges on the ship, as registered in the ships register. Moreover, except and to the extent that Article 3(4) of the Convention permits the arrest of a ship in respect of claims for which a charterer is liable, and with the exclusion of claims secured by maritime liens, the

---

9. The nationality of the owners has been considered to be irrelevant by the Tribunal de Commerce of Le Havre in its judgment 4 March 1981 in *Aifanourios Shipping* v. *West of England* [1981] D.M.F. 740.

maritime claims for which a ship may be arrested are claims against the owner of the ship. If the relevant link for the application of the Convention is the flag of the ship, claimants lose the benefits of the Convention when the ship temporarily flies the flag of a non-contracting State, such as, for example, Cyprus, Liberia or Panama, depending on the interpretation of Article 8(2) and whether Contracting States have availed themselves of the exempting provisions of Article 8(3). Again, the owner of a ship registered in a Contracting State but temporarily flying the flag of a non-contracting State would, pursuant to Article 8(2), be subject to his ship being arrested as security also for non-maritime claims, if this is permitted by the *lex fori*.

I.52 Although these are certainly drawbacks, it is very difficult to ignore the text of the Convention, which makes reference to the flag. If, in fact, it is, on the basis of the text, impossible to exclude from the scope of Article 8(1) ships registered in non-contracting States temporarily flying the flag of a Contracting State, it seems rather difficult at the same time to apply this provision to ships registered in a Contracting State, but temporarily flying the flag of a non-contracting State.

I.53 The problem of temporary registration has been considered by the Genoa *Tribunale* in the case of a ship registered in Italy and temporarily flying the flag of the Bahamas. The court, by order of 24 March 1995 in *Lockwood & Carlysle and Others* v. *Sicilsud Leasing-The "Depa Giulia"*[10] in order to decide on its jurisdiction in respect of an application for the arrest of the ship, which, at that time, was in the port of Durban, considered first the regime of the Convention on the assumption (which is not correct) that the Bahamas was a party to the Convention and, secondly, the provisions of Italian law. It then made reference to Bahamian law in order to decide whether or not the claims in respect of which the arrest was applied for were secured by a maritime lien. The decision on this last issue was, however, reversed by the Tribunale of Genoa with the decree of 28 April 1995 which held that maritime liens continue to be governed by Italian law, as the law of the underlying register.[11]

9. SHIPS FLYING THE FLAG OF CONTRACTING STATES

I.54 All the provisions of the Convention apply to ships flying the flag of Contracting States and such application is exclusive of any domestic rule as respects the claims for which a ship may be arrested. Article 2 in fact provides that a ship flying the flag of one of the Contracting States may be arrested in the jurisdiction of any of the Contracting States in respect of any maritime claim but in respect of no other claim. Domestic rules are instead expressly referred to in Articles 5 and 6.

I.55 There are, however, two exceptions to the principle whereby the provisions of the Convention apply to all ships flying the flag of Contracting States. The first is set out in paragraph (3) of Article 8, which entitles Contracting States wholly or partly to exclude from the benefits of the Convention any Government of a non-contracting State or any person who does not, at the time of the arrest, have his habitual residence or principal

---

10. [1997] Dir. Mar. 1063.
11. [1997] Dir. Mar. 1082.

place of business in one of the Contracting States.[12] The second is set out in paragraph 4, which excludes from the scope of application of the Convention the arrest of a ship within the State of her flag by a person who has his habitual residence or principal place of business in that State.

(a) Exclusion of Governments of Non-contracting States and Persons who do not have their Habitual Residences or Principal Place of Business in a Contracting State

I.56 Paragraph (3) of Article 8 does not state whether its provisions apply to vessels flying the flag of Contracting States, to vessels flying the flag of non-contracting States or to both. The fact that the sentence starts with an adversative adverb ("Nevertheless") would in principle link this provision with that contained in the previous paragraph, which deals with vessels flying the flag of non-contracting States.[13] Of course, this solution would not be conceivable if paragraph (2) were to be construed so as to limit the application of the Convention to vessels flying the flag of a non-contracting State to Article 1(1). But, irrespective of whether or not the other provisions of the Convention apply to such vessels, there does not seem to be any doubt that paragraph (3) applies to vessels flying the flag of Contracting States. The purpose of this provision, which, albeit with varying formulations, exists in the great majority of the maritime conventions, is to exert pressure on non-contracting States for the ratification of the Convention, and this result would certainly not be achieved if the exclusion did not operate in respect of vessels flying the flag of Contracting States. This is the more so, because one of the "benefits" of the Convention, viz. the limitation of the right of arrest to maritime claims, is expressly excluded for vessels flying the flag of non-contracting States by paragraph (2). The "benefits" granted by the Convention to claimants that could be excluded pursuant to paragraph (3) differ according to the domestic law of the country where they may be invoked. In civil law countries they may consist in the possibility of arresting a vessel without having to prove that there is an actual need for a conservative measure,[14] in a

---

12. The nationality of one of the Contracting States is considered to be an implied additional requirement by La China, "Due Novità (d'Antica Data!) nel Campo del Diritto Processuale Civile Internazionale Marittimo: le Convenzioni di Bruxelles del 10 Maggio 1952" [1978] IV Foro Italiano 255. This view has no basis on the text of Art. 8.

13. But see, for a different view, *In the Matter of the M.V. "Kapitan Labunetz"* (Irish Supreme Court) [1996] Dir. Mar. 256.

14. This is a requirement, for example, in Italy (Tribunale of Genoa, 13 January 1990, *Compagnie Générale Maritime* v. *Ador Ter Mar S.r.l.–The "Pointe de Lasven" and "Audace A."* [1991] Dir. Mar. 408; Tribunale of Ancona, 16 January 1987, *Cingolani Fratelli Legnami Esotici* v. *Cichus Shipping Inc.—The "Eurohunter"* [1988] Dir. Mar. 214; Tribunale of Genoa, 11 May 1989, *Sean S.a.s.* v. *Mediterranean Shipping The "Rosa S"* [1990] Dir. Mar. 375; Tribunale of Genoa 15 March 1993, *International Marine Services Ltd.* v. *Empresa Cubana de Fletes—The "José Antonio Echeverria"*, [1995] Dir. Mar. 441; Tribunale of Genoa 11 January 1994, *Rimorchiatori Riuniti Porto di Genova S.r.l.* v. *Morfini Trasporti Marittimi S.r.l.–The "Ninfea"*, [1995] Dir. Mar. 1060; Tribunale of Genoa 1 March 1995, *Italbrokers S.p.A.* , [1995] Dir. Mar. 1073; Tribunale of Genoa 13 March 1995, *Italbrokers S.p.A.* v. *Black Sea Shipping Co.–The "Kapitan Smirnoff" and "Inzeheener Jermo-skin"*, [1995] Dir. Mar. 1090; Tribunale of Lecce 24 December 1994, *Cantiri Balsamo S.r.l.* v. *Sail Boat Enterprise—The "Felguera"*, [1996] Dir. Mar. 1064; Tribunale of Genoa 25 January 1997, *North Sea Petroleum GmbH—The "Dumbraveni"*, [1998] Dir. Mar. 1222; Tribunale of La Spezia 3 March 1998, *Valentyn Cher-noutsky* v. *Black Sea Shipping Co.–The "Pavel Mizikievich"*, [1998] Dir. Mar. 1269), except when a ship is arrested in order to enforce a maritime lien (Tribunale of Velletri, 3 November 1970, *Francesco and Roberto Spazzafumo* v. *Augusto and Arturo Carpignoli—The "Erminio Borio" and "Nunzia"* [1971] Dir. Mar. 50; Corte d'Appello of Trieste, 5 June 1963, *Sardamare* v. *Allami Biztosito Tarasag—The "Isola di Sardegna"* [1965] Dir. Mar. 142; Corte d'Appello of Lecce 12 January 1995, *Bibolini Società di Navigazione S.A.* v. *Impresa Fratelli*

simplified burden of proof and in the possibility of arresting a vessel ready to sail and of obtaining jurisdiction on the merits in the cases mentioned in Article 7(1). In common law countries they may consist in the possibility of arresting a sister ship.

I.57 The right granted to Contracting States by paragraph (3) is not a reservation, because permitted reservations are expressly set out in Article 10. Therefore, Contracting States are not required to give notice of their decision to avail themselves, wholly or partly, of the liberty granted by this paragraph at the time of ratification of or accession to the Convention. They may do so at any time in the implementing legislation.[15]

I.58 The provision whereby the claimants may be excluded from the "benefits" of the Convention, if interpreted in a strict sense, would mean that a Contracting State could apply the Convention when a ship flying the flag of a Contracting State is arrested in its jurisdiction but could exclude from its "benefits" any claimant who does not have his habitual place of business in a Contracting State. If, on the other hand, this provision were interpreted in a wide sense, it would mean that Contracting States could wholly exclude the application of the Convention in such cases. The strict interpretation seems to be the correct one, for it is in line with the sense of the words used. Furthermore, Contracting States would be in breach of their obligations under the Convention if they did not apply the Convention, or at least the provisions beneficial to the owners of a ship flying the flag of a Contracting State, only because the claimant does not have his habitual residence or principal place of business in a Contracting State.

I.59 The comparative analysis of the provisions of this nature contained in the other maritime conventions confirms this. Such provisions are of three types. In some conventions (1910 Collision Convention, Article 12; 1910 Salvage Convention, Article 15; 1926 Immunity Convention, Article 6; 1952 Civil Jurisdiction Convention, Article 8) the application of the uniform provisions to persons "belonging" to non-contracting States may be made conditional upon reciprocity. In other conventions (1924 Limitation Convention, Article 12; 1926 Maritime Liens and Mortgages Convention, Article 14) Contracting States are permitted generally not to apply the provisions of the convention to nationals of non-contracting States. In yet other conventions (1957 Limitation Convention, Article 7) Contracting States are permitted to exclude, wholly or partially, from the "benefits" of the convention non-contracting States or persons who are not ordinarily resident in a Contracting State or (1976 LLMC Convention, Article 15) simply to exclude wholly or partially from the application of the Convention persons who do not have their habitual residence in a Contracting State. Finally, the 1999 Arrest Convention (Article 10(1)) allows States Parties to exclude the application of the Convention to ships not flying the flag of a State Party.

I.60 While the provisions of the first and second type consider a global exclusion of the uniform rules, those of the last type, to which that in the Arrest Convention also belongs, consider a partial exclusion, or at least the possibility of a partial exclusion, either by referring to the exclusion from the "benefits" or by referring to the power to exclude the uniform rules "wholly or partially".

Barretta S.p.A.–The "Anna Bibolini", [1996] Dir. Mar. 175). It is also a requirement in Belgium (Verstrepen, "Arrest and Judicial Sale of Ships in Belgium" [1995] L.M.C.L.Q. 131, at 136) and in Denmark.

15. Tassel, "Saisie Conservatoire du Navire", *supra*, n. 3 is of the view that the power to decide on the exclusion belongs to the State and not to the court. This view is undoubtedly correct.

I.61 The replacement of the words "persons not belonging to a Contracting State" with "any person who has not . . . his habitual residence or principal place of business in one of the Contracting States" is due to the fact that in the draft approved at Naples there was, in Article 1, paragraph IV, the following definition of "person belonging to a Contracting State": " 'A person belonging to a Contracting State' shall mean a person having his domicile or principal place of business in one of the Contracting States." It was probably considered more appropriate to move the content of this definition (which now does not exist in the text of Article 1) to Article 8.

I.62 Contracting States may also exclude from the "benefits" of the Convention "any Government of a non-Contracting State" (the French text does not refer to governments, but simply to non-contracting States). This part of the provision did not exist in the draft approved at Naples, where[16] reference was made merely to "persons not belonging to a Contracting State". It was inserted at the Diplomatic Conference, but no explanation is given in the official report of the Conference.[17]

I.63 The reason for the addition of the reference to governments of non-contracting States is not clear, although governments could not, in the context of Article 8(3), be included in the word "person", notwithstanding the definition of "person" in Article 1(3), because of the reference to a person who does not have "his habitual residence or principal place of business in one of the Contracting States". Non-contracting States may have been referred to in their theoretical capacity as owners of ships, to the extent that such ships are not protected by immunity under the 1926 Immunity Convention. They may also have been referred to for the reason that certain provisions of the Convention may also apply to non-contracting States. This cannot be the case where the Convention imposes obligations on States, e.g. Articles 3, 4 and 5. There are, however, provisions that grant rights to States, such as Article 7(1), pursuant to which the courts of the State in which the arrest was made have jurisdiction to decide the case upon its merits in the examples set out therein. Pursuant to Article 8(3), the recognition of a judgment delivered in a non-contracting State may be refused if the jurisdiction of the courts of such State is based only on the provisions of Article 7(1).

I.64 From the replies to the Questionnaire[18] it appears that Germany and Haiti have availed themselves of this provision, while Belgium, Denmark, Finland, France, Greece, Italy, the Netherlands,[19] Nigeria, Norway, Poland, Sweden and the United Kingdom have not done so.

(b) Exclusion of the Arrest of Ships within the Jurisdiction of the Flag State by a Person having his Habitual Residence or Principal Place of Business in that State

I.65 While the exclusion from the benefits of the Convention of non-contracting States or persons who do not have their habitual residence or principal place of business in one

---

16. Art. 10, CMI Bulletin No. 105, p. 311 and *Travaux Préparatoires*, p. 446.
17. *Conférence Internationale de Droit Maritime, Neuvième Session, Bruxelles*, 1952 (hereinafter cited as "*Proces-verbaux*") pp. 116 and 117.
18. Appendix II, Question 15, pp. 284–286.
19. Judgment of the Gerechtshof (Court of Appeal) of Gravenhage 28 June 1985, *The "Alhena"* [1986] Schip en Schade 78.

of the Contracting States operates only if a Contracting State avails itself of the provision of paragraph (3), the exclusion of the application of the Convention provided for in paragraph 4 is operative without any implementing legislation. On the contrary, such legislation would be required for the uniform rules to apply also in the case mentioned in such paragraph.[20]

I.66 The reason for the exclusion set out in paragraph (4) is the lack of any foreign element in the situation referred to therein: the ship flies the flag of the State where the arrest is made and the arrestor has his habitual residence or principal place of business in that State. The theory whereby disputes that do not have a foreign element should be excluded from the scope of application of a private maritime law convention is clearly influenced by the approach adopted in respect of private international law rules, but is not justified in conventions aiming at the unification of substantive rules. This theory has in recent times been abandoned: reference is made in this respect to the 1967 and the 1993 Conventions on Maritime Liens and Mortgages, to the 1969 CLC, to the 1976 LLMC Convention and to the 1999 Arrest Convention.

I.67 While the wording used in this paragraph is similar, though not identical, to that used in the preceding paragraph, the 1976 LLMC Convention refers, in the corresponding provision, to nationality and not to the habitual residence or principal place of business. Article 15(3) of that Convention provides:

3. A State Party may regulate by specific provisions of national law the system of limitation of liability to be applied to claims arising in cases in which interests of persons who are nationals of other States Parties are in no way involved.

I.68 Although there was no need to use in paragraph (4) of the Arrest Convention a formula identical or similar to that used in paragraph (3), since the situations covered therein are totally different, it is probable that that was the reason for reference being made in paragraph (4) to habitual residence or principal place of business. It must also be considered that this formula is used in Article 7(1)(a) to found jurisdiction on the merits. The difference between Article 8(4), as well as Article 7(1)(a) and Article 8(3), is that, while in this latter paragraph there is an indication of the time when the habitual residence or principal place of business must be established, viz. the time of arrest, no such indication may be found in the two former provisions. However, at least insofar as Article 8(4) is concerned, it seems obvious that the relevant time is that of the arrest.

---

20. This, for example, was not done by France, Italy, the Netherlands, Poland, Portugal and Spain which gave the force of law to the Convention in its original text, without any implementing legislation (see *infra*, section 15). In Italy the provisions of the Convention were not applied by the Tribunale of Venice in a case where the ship was flying the Italian flag and the claimant was an Italian company (Tribunale of Ravenna, Order of 5 July 1990, *Padana Assicurazioni, petitioner* [1991] Dir. Mar. 129). It is worth noting that reference is made in that order to the nationality of the claimant (an insurance company), rather than to the claimant having its principal place of business in Italy. In Greece the courts have interpreted Art. 8(1) of the Convention as meaning that the Convention applies in the case of arrest of a ship flying the flag of a Contracting State in the jurisdiction of another Contracting State and not of the same Contracting State: Multi-Member First Instance Court of Piraeus, Decision No. 2511/1977 (1978) 6 Maritime Law Review 42; Single Member First Instance Court of Piraeus, Decision No. 849/1989 (1989) 18 Maritime Law Review 130, although in this case the claimant was a Greek national: the decision does not specify whether the claimant was also a resident of Greece. In Belgium the provisions of the Convention have been incorporated into Belgian law by Law of 4 December 1961 (Verstrepen, "Arrest and Judicial Sale of Ships in Belgium", *supra* n. 14, pp. 133 and 134.

I.69 The reference to the nationality of the ship creates, in cases of bareboat charter registration, the same problems previously considered in respect of Article 8(1) and (2)[21]: the provisions of the Convention apply to the arrest in State A, by a claimant who has his habitual residence or principal place of business in such State, of a ship whose underlying register is in such State but which is temporarily flying the flag of another State. They will not apply, unless otherwise provided by the domestic legislation, in respect of the arrest of a ship which is temporarily flying the flag of State A.

I.70 The reference to habitual residence and principal place of business may give rise to problems. In fact, the application of the Convention rules or, alternatively, of the domestic rules may be a determining factor regarding the entitlement of the claimant to arrest the ship. For example, in a civil law country a ship ready to sail may not be arrested. On the other hand, a ship may be arrested as security for any claim, whether maritime or not. The court of a Contracting State seised of the case has, therefore, to determine, when the ship is flying the flag of that State, whether or not the claimant has his habitual residence or principal place of business in such State. This is a question that is sometimes difficult to establish when a person has several domiciles or a company several places where it conducts its business.

I.71 The provision of paragraph (4) may give rise to difficulties where a ship is arrested by two claimants, one to whom the Convention applies and one to whom it does not, because the uniform rules and the national rules may be in conflict with one another.

I.72 Paragraph (5) of Article 8, added by the Diplomatic Conference of 1952, applies to both paragraphs (3) and (4) of Article 8 as well as to Article 7(1)(a). Therefore, the assignment of or subrogation to a claim cannot have the effect of modifying the scope of application of the Convention as established in respect of the original claimant.

I.73 Nothing is said in Article 8 about the time at which the nationality of the ship must be established. There seems, however, to be no doubt that the relevant time is when the arrest is made.

(c) Exclusion of the application of Article 7 to cases covered by the Rhine Navigation Convention of 1868

I.74 Reference to the Rhine Convention of 17 October 1868 is not made in Article 8, but in Article 7(5) which so provides:

This article shall not apply in cases covered by the provisions of the revised Rhine Navigation Convention of 17 October 1868.

I.75 The Rhine Convention, made at Mannheim on 17 October 1868 between the Great-Duchy of Bade, Bavière, France, the Great-Duchy of Hesse, The Netherlands and Prussia, was amended by the Amendment Convention made at Strasbourg on 20 November 1963 and by the Additional Protocols made at Strasbourg respectively on 25 October 1972, 17 October 1979 and 25 April 1989.

I.76 The Convention, which is presently in force, as amended, between Belgium, France, Germany, The Netherlands, Switzerland and the United Kingdom, sets out juris-

---

21. See *supra*, para. I.45–53.

diction rules in Articles 35–35ter. Pursuant to Article 34–II[22] the tribunals to be established in convenient places along the river or in the proximity of the river shall have civil jurisdiction on disputes relating to:

(a) the payment and amount of pilotage dues, crane dues, weighing and quay dues;

(b) the obstacles that individuals will create to the use of hauling paths;

(c) damage caused by the boatmen or the barges when berthing;

(d) claims against the owners of the horses employed for haulage of the boats in respect of damage caused to the land.

It appears, therefore, that there cannot be any conflict between Article 7 of the Arrest Convention and Article 34 of the Rhine Convention, since the claims mentioned in this latter provision differ from those mentioned in Article 7 of the Arrest Convention.

10. SHIPS FLYING THE FLAG OF NON-CONTRACTING STATES

I.77 The difference in the wording of paragraphs (1) and (2) of Article 8 has given rise to conflicting views in respect of the application of the Convention to ships flying the flag of non-contracting States.

I.78 The fact that in paragraph (1) there is a positive rule on the application of the Convention to ships flying the flag of a Contracting State and that in paragraph (2) it is provided only that ships flying the flag of non-contracting States may be arrested in the jurisdiction of any Contracting State in respect of any of the maritime claims enumerated in Article 1 (or of any other claim for which the law of the Contracting State permits arrest) has been invoked as clear evidence of the non-applicability of the provisions of the Convention—except Article 1(1)—to ships flying the flag of non-contracting States.[23]

I.79 On the other hand, the application of the Convention (except Article 2 whereby ships may be arrested only in respect of a maritime claim) also to ships flying the flags of

---

22. The English text of Article 34–II is a free translation. The original French text is the following:
    Art. 34
        Les tribunaux pour la navigation du Rhin seront compétents:
    I. En matière pénale pour instruire et juger toutes les contraventions aux prescriptions relatives à la navigation et à la police fluviale;
    II. En matière civile pour prononcer sommairement sur les contestations relatives:
    a. Au paiement et à la quotité des droits de pilotage, de grue, de balance de port et de quai;
    b. Aux entraves que des particuliers auraient mis à l'usage des chemins de halage;
    c. Aux dommage causés par les bateliers ou les flotteurs pendant le voyage ou en abordant;
    d. Aux plaintes portées contre les propriétaires des chevaux de trait, employés à la remonte des bateaux, pour dommages causés aux biens fonds.
23. *In the matter of the M.V. "Kapitan Labunets"* (Irish Supreme Court) [1996] Dir. Mar. 256; *Intergraan B.V.* v. *The Owners and All Persons Claiming an Interest in the M/T "Marshal Gelovani"* (Irish High Court-Admiralty) [1995] Dir. Mar. 256); the Italian Corte di Cassazione in a judgment of 25 May 1993, No. 5848, *Equinox Shipping Co. Ltd.* v. *Ryszard Lyko—The "Al Taif"* [1994] Dir. Mar. 157 held that Art. 7(1) does not apply to ships flying the flag of non-contracting States on the ground that Art. 8(1) provides that the provisions of the Convention apply to ships flying the flag of Contracting States without considering para. 2 at all.
    In the Netherlands the provisions of the Convention are not applied to ships flying the flag of a non-contracting State; the arrest of such ships is governed by the municipal rules, according to which a ship may be arrested as security for any type of claim. Also in Germany the arrest of ships flying the flag of non-contracting States is subject to ordinary German domestic rules.

non-contracting States has been upheld by several courts, even though no clear explanation seems ever to have been given.[24]

I.80 It appears advisable to start from the *travaux préparatoires* of the Convention in order to understand how paragraphs (1) and (2) of Article 8 came about.

I.81 Article 2 of the draft prepared by the CMI International Committee for consideration by the CMI Conference held in Naples in September 1951 provided thus[25]:

A ship flying the flag of one of the Contracting States may only be arrested in the jurisdiction of one of the Contracting States in respect of a maritime claim as defined in paragraph 1 of article 1.

This Convention shall apply to the arrest of any vessel flying the flag of a Contracting State; it shall, however, not apply to the arrest of a vessel in the jurisdiction of the State of her flag except where the claimant is a national of another Contracting State.

Article 10 of the draft in turn provided as follows[26]:

Any Contracting State may exclude wholly or partially from the benefits of this Convention any person who is not a national of a Contracting State.

24. The application of the Convention to ships flying the flags of non-contracting States has been affirmed in Portugal by Tribunal da Relaçao de Lisboa, May 1993, *Catonave-Proteçao Catodica Lda.* v. *Empresa de Navegacao Mercantil S.A., Merchem-Mercantil Chemical Navegaçao S.A. and Rio Fundo Navegacao S.A.,* unreported and in Spain, albeit not expressly, by the Tribunal Supremo with judgment 14 May 1992, *Pesqueros Bermeanos de Tunidos S.A.* v. *Angelos Rigopoulos,* [1994] Dir. Mar. 1075. The same view obtains in France: Cour d'Appel de Rouen 24 May 1995, *Lamyra Marine Co. Ltd.* v. *Compagnie Senegalaise de Navigation Maritime—The "Saint Pierre",* [1996] D.M.F. 489; Cour d'Appel de Douai 12 September 1996, *IMS* v. *Likeo Maritime—The "River Asab"* [1997] D.M.F. 36; Vialard, "La saisie conservatoire du navire pour dettes de l'affréteur à temps" [1985] D.M.F. 579, at p. 581; du Pontavice, *Le Statut des Navires* (Paris, 1976), p. 339. See also Tribunal de Commerce de Bordeaux, 28 July 1969, *The "Lady Laura"* [1970] D.M.F. 111. It seems to be settled today in France that the arrestor has the option to apply to the arrest of a vessel flying the flag of a non-contracting State either French domestic law or the Convention: Cour d'Appel de Aix-en-Provence 22 May 1997, *Flota Mercante Grancolombiana* v. *Nireus Navigation Co.–The "Mediterranea"* [1998] D.M.F. 692. In this latter case, all the provisions of the Convention are applicable. Also in Denmark and Sweden the uniform rules apply in all cases, irrespective of whether the ship flies the flag of a Contracting State or not.
   The question whether the Convention applies to ships flying the flag of non-Contracting States is not settled in Italy. The negative view has been held by the Corte di Cassazione with judgment 25 May 1993, *Equinox Shipping Co. Ltd.* v. *Ryszard Lyko—The "Al Taif"* [1994] Dir. Mar. 157 and by the Tribunal of Ravenna with judgment 12 February 1996, *Atlas Factoring Hizmetleri S.A.* v. *Turkay Denizcilik Ve Tikaret—The "Recai B"* [1998] Dir. Mar. 1165. The affirmative view has instead been unpheld by the majority of the lower Courts: Tribunale of Salerno 21 January 1997, *Mario Cirino Pomicino S.p.A.* v. *Liman Co. Ltd.–The "Komander",* [1998] Dir. Mar. 436; Tribunale of Naples 22 September 1995, *Mamidoil Jetoil Greek Petroleum Co. S.A.* v. *Alimar Shipping Co.–The "Carlo R."* [1997] Dir. Mar. 147; Tribunale of Messina 11 March 1995, *Smeb S.p.A.* v. *Black Sea Shipping Co.–Blasco-The "Kapitan Radionov"* [1995] Dir. Mar. 1075; Tribunale of Genoa, 20 May 1995, in *Uberseeschiffahrts-Agentur Transnautic GmbH & Co. K.G.* v. *Baltic Shipping Co.–The "Akademic Gorbunov"* [1995] Dir. Mar. 768); Tribunale of Ravenna, 24 January 1987, *Trademar Conasa S.A.* v. *Line Island Marine Co.–The "Eurobreeze"* [1988] Dir. Mar. 804.
   The negative view obtains instead in Ireland: *In the Matter of the M.V. "Kapitan Labunets" Constante Trading Limited* v. *The Owners and all Persons Claiming an Interest in the M.V. "Kapitan Labunets"* (Supreme Court), [1996] Dir. Mar. 256; *Intergraan B.V.* v. *The Owners and all Persons Claiming an Interest in the MT "Marshal Gelovani"* [1996] Dir. Mar. 266. Also in Germany the negative view probably obtains.
   On Art. 8 of the Convention, see also G. Berlingieri, La Conferenza di Napoli del Comité Maritime International" [1951] Dir. Mar. 574 at p. 589; F. Berlingieri, "Note sull'ambito di applicazione della Convenzione di Bruxelles del 1952 sul sequestro di navi e sulla sequestrabilità di navi non appartenenti al debitore" [1988] Dir. Mar. 804; Pasanisi, "Il Progetto di Convenzione Internazionale per la Unificazione delle Regole in Materia di Sequestro di Navi" [1952] Dir. Mar. 316; Chauveau, *Traité de Droit Maritime* (Paris, 1958), p. 164; Vincenzini, *Il Sequestro Conservativo di Nave Straniera* (Padova, 1988), p. 35; Vincenzini, "Il Sequestro Conservativo di Nave Straniera Secondo la Convenzione di Bruxelles del 10 Maggio 1952" [1987] 156 Rivista Diritto Processuale 167; Manca, *Commento alle Convenzioni Internazionali Marittime* (Milano, 1974).
   25. CMI Bulletin No. 105, p. 18 and *Travaux Préparatoires,* p. 463.
   26. CMI Bulletin No. 105, p. 21 and *Travaux Préparatoires,* p. 464. The original text is in French.

The British Maritime Law Association proposed the following amendment to Article 2[27]:

A ship flying the flag of one of the Contracting States may be arrested in the jurisdiction of any of the other Contracting States only in respect of a maritime claim and this Convention shall apply to the arrest of all ships flying the flag of any Contracting State. A ship flying the flag of a State which is not a party to this Convention may be arrested within the jurisdiction of any of the Contracting States by a claimant belonging to any of the Contracting States in respect of a maritime claim and in respect of any other claim in respect of which ships may be arrested under the existing law of the State but this Convention shall not apply to the arrest of any ship within the jurisdiction of her flag by a claimant who resides or has a place of business in that State.

It then explained as follows the reasons for its proposal:

There is no reason whatever why a vessel which is not flying the flag of a Contracting State should get better treatment, for example, in an English port than a vessel which flies the flag of a Contracting State. It is precisely thereto that the British amendment is directed. The original Article 2 had this effect when we considered it at Antwerp. Assuming, for instance, that one of the South American States (I will not venture to name any one) was not a signatory of the Convention, then a British ship in a British port could be arrested for a wider scope of maritime claims than could a ship belonging to that South American State, even though the creditor, the claimant, was a person belonging to one of the Contracting States.

We felt that that was very unfair. We felt that, if the law of our country was to be extended in the way the Convention suggests, that should apply to all vessels of whatever flag or whatever nationality.

I.82 It clearly appears, therefore, that the intention of the amendment was to apply the Convention to all ships, whether flying the flag of a Contracting State or not, but to restrict the application of the rule whereby ships can be arrested only in respect of a maritime claim to ships flying the flag of a Contracting State. This was how the amendment was interpreted by the other Delegations, and, in particular, by those who opposed it.[28]

I.83 Dean Ripert then suggested that one should deal in a separate Article with the scope of application of the Convention and to leave in Article 2 only the substantive rule

---

27. CMI Bulletin No. 105, p. 240 and *Travaux Préparatoires*, p. 438.
28. Mr Jean de Grandmaison stated (CMI Bulletin No. 105, p. 243 and *Travaux Préparatoires*, p. 440):
(Official translation)

   On their third point the British Association say that a ship flying the flag of a Contracting State can be arrested in a port of her own State for any of the maritime claims enumerated in Article 1 provided that the claimant resides or carries on business in a contracting State. We are in perfect agreement on the third point, but we disagree on the second. The second point is that a ship flying the flag of a State which is not one of the Contracting States can be arrested in the jurisdiction of any of the Contracting States by a claimant belonging to any Contracting State for at least any of the maritime claims enumerated in the Convention and for any other type of claim for which the existing domestic law of the arresting person permits the arrest of a ship.

   We object because we fail to see the reason for it. It seems obvious to us that a ship flying the flag of a non-contracting State will be arrested for any claims that arise under the domestic law of the *forum arresti*, but we do not understand how that ship can be arrested for a maritime claim within article 1 of the Convention if the particular claim is not a claim for which arrest is granted by the domestic law of the *forum arresti*—that means by the law of the State where the arrest is made. If the ship arrested does not belong to a Contracting State, then, in our opinion, the Convention cannot have any effect and the claimant cannot make use of this Convention. If the British Association intends that every Contracting State will amend its domestic law so that the right of arrest shall be given in respect of all the claims enumerated in article 1, we are of opinion that we must state clearly that we know how difficult it is to make such legal amendments in domestic laws, and therefore it is our opinion that this question of the purposes for which a ship of a non-contracting State can be arrested must be dropped and that the Convention must deal only with the right of arrest of ships flying the flags of Contracting States.

   Similar remarks were made by Mr. Bianchetti on behalf of the Italian delegation.

whereby ships flying the flags of Contracting States may only be arrested in respect of a maritime claim. He so stated in his speech[29]:

In Article 2 of this Convention there is a provision of fundamental importance: that is the provision whereby a ship of a Contracting State cannot be arrested in a port of another Contracting State except for one of the claims set out in the Convention.

This is a protective rule and for that reason this Convention is indivisible.

Such rule is not disputed by anybody and if we limit Article 2 to it it will be unanimously approved.

Unfortunately there is paragraph 2 which is wholly stranger to the question. That paragraph intends to deal with the question of the international application of the Convention, and you know that in preceding conventions that question has not always been happily solved, and this is so much so that in the Bill of Lading Convention, for example, the greatest doubts exist. It is, therefore, indispensable to solve it but that is another question and it would be convenient to appoint a committee consisting of the authors of the amendments so that they may agree on a text which will determine in which hypotheses the Convention will be applicable. We shall see then if it will be possible to apply it to ships of non-Contracting States and to which extent it must be applied, on account, for example, of the nationality of the claimant.

I.84 Dean Ripert's proposal was unanimously carried and a Committee was appointed by the Conference. The draft of the then Article 10 prepared by the Committee was worded as follows[30]:

The provisions of this Convention shall apply to any ship in the jurisdiction of any Contracting State.

A ship flying the flag of a non-Contracting State may be arrested in the jurisdiction of any Contracting State in respect of any of the maritime claims enumerated in Article 1 or of any other claim for which the law of the Contracting State permits arrest.

Nevertheless any Contracting State shall be entitled wholly or partially to exclude from the benefits of this Convention any person who is not a national of a Contracting State.

This Convention shall not apply to the arrest of a ship in the Contracting State whose flag she is flying by a claimant who has his domicile or principal place of business in that State.

I.85 It appears, therefore, that the draft already embodied the substance of Article 8 of the Convention.

I.86 A report on the work of the Committee was made at the Plenary Session by Dean Ripert who so stated in respect of paragraph (2)[31]:

The second paragraph covers the case of a ship flying the flag of a non-Contracting State who arrives in a port of a Contracting State.

We have decided that the Convention should permit the arrest of that ship, even though of a non-Contracting State. However, she may be arrested in respect of one of the claims enumerated in the Convention or pursuant to the domestic rules of that State.

Undoubtedly, from the international standpoint, it may appear somewhat excessive to apply an international convention even to ships flying the flag of a non-Contracting State, but if we were not to apply it, we would give them a particular advantage as compared to ships of Contracting States. This is why it must be decided that also such ships may be arrested by virtue of the Convention or of the domestic law.

I.87 This statement indicates that the British proposal and the arguments put forward by Mr Miller to support it were ultimately accepted by the Conference and that the

---

29. CMI Bulletin No. 105, pp. 147 and 248 and *Travaux Préparatoires*, p. 442. Original text in French. The English translation has been made by the author.
30. CMI Bulletin No. 105, pp. 309 and 310 and *Travaux Préparatoires*, p. 469.
31. CMI Bulletin No. 105, p. 310 and *Travaux Préparatoires*, p. 445. Original text in French. The English translation has been made by the author.

difference in the wording of paragraphs (1) and (2) was only due to the fact that ships flying the flag of non-contracting States can be also arrested in respect of any claim for which the *lex fori* permits arrest.

I.88 All the provisions of the Convention, except that restricting the right of arrest to maritime claims, should therefore apply to ships flying the flags of non-contracting States. The application to such ships of Article 1(1) only on the ground that this is the only provision expressly referred to in Article 8(2), would make no sense. In fact, this would bring about a result contrary to the clear intention which emerges from the *travaux préparatoires*: for example, in civil law countries, the claimant would not be able to invoke Article 7(1), whereby the court granting the arrest has jurisdiction on the merits in the cases specified therein and in common law countries—or in some of them[32]—the arrest of sister ships would not be permitted.

I.89 The principle that the provisions of the Convention apply also to ships flying the flag of a non-contracting State is settled in a significant number of contracting States[33]: Belgium, Denmark, Croatia, Finland, France, Germany, Haiti, Norway, Poland, Slovenia, Spain and Sweden. In Greece the affirmative view has been held by some judgments,[34] while the negative view has been held by other—and perhaps the majority of—judgments.[35]

I.90 In the Netherlands there have been several Court decisions to the effect that the owner of a ship registered in a non-contracting State cannot avail himself of the provisions of the Convention, such as those in Article 3(3) prohibiting re-arrest or arrest of a second ship.[36] It is thought that this implies generally that the provisions of the Convention do not apply to ships flying the flag of a non-contracting State, at least in so far as they increase the protection of the owner of the ship.

I.91 In some States where the Convention has not been given the force of law and its provisions have, in whole or in part, been incorporated in national enactments, such acts apply to all ships, irrespective of nationality. This is so in Nigeria and in the United Kingdom.[37]

I.92 As previously indicated Article 8(2) provides that ships flying the flag of non-Contracting States may be arrested in the jurisdiction of a Contracting State in respect of a maritime claim or of any other claim for which the law of that State permits arrest. In

---

32. For example, in Ireland. See *In the Matter of the MV "Kapitan Labunets"* (Irish Supreme Court) in [1996] Dir. Mar. 256.

33. See the replies to question 13 of the Questionnaire, Appendix II, pp. 280–282.

34. Nauples Court of Appeals 196/1972 Hellenic Jurists Journal 39, 730; PSFIC 595/1974 [1974] CLR 225; 864/1979 MLR 1981, 6.

35. Corinthe Single-member First Instance Court 23/1977, Commercial Law Review [1977] C.L.R., 95; Thessaloniki Single-member First Instance Court 3456/1980, [1980] C.L.R., 651. There is a number of judgments which did not apply the provisions of the Convention to the arrest of ships registered in non-contracting States without assigning any reason thereto: Crete Court of Appeals 56/1970 [1970] C.L.R., 485; PSFIC 1556/1973 [1973] C.L.R., 387; Patras SFIC 1042/1976 [1976] C.L.R., 409; PSFIC 2668/1976 [5] M.L.R., 242; 139/1983 [unpublished]; 769/1983 [11] M.L.R., 181; 1873/1983 [11] M.L.R., 452; Thessaloniki SFIC 4156/1983 [12] M.L.R., 18; PSFIC 1056/1983 [1983] Piraiki Nomologia, 173; 2384/1985 [14] M.L.R., 211; 869/1987 [1987] C.L.R., 466; 2075/1987 [16] M.L.R., 42; 2155/1990 [1991] C.L.R., 315.

36. President of the Arrondissementsrechtbank of Rotterdam 4 March 1983, *The "Kasamba"*, [1983] Schip en Schade 96 and, more expressly, Gerechtshof of Gravenhage 5 June 1987, *The "Spira"*, [1987] Schip en Schade 121, where the Court of Appeal held that the owner of a ship which is not flying the flag of a Contracting State cannot rely on article 3(3) which prohibits re-arrest. This principle has been stated in a more general way by the Supreme Court (Hoge Raad) in its judgment of 20 May 1993, *The "Kapitan Kanevskiy"*, [1994] Nederlandse Jurisprudentie Kort 329.

37. See the replies to Question 13 of the Questionnaire, Appendix II, p. 280–282.

several Contracting States where the general rule is that any asset of the debtor may be arrested, when the conditions required by the law materialise, in respect of any claim, the ratification of the Convention has been considered as having the effect of derogating to the general rule so that, outside its scope, the general rule continues to apply. This is so in France, Haiti, Italy, Slovenia and Spain. The position is similar in Sweden, but arrest is permissible only in respect of other claims secured by a maritime lien.

I.93 In Belgium instead also ships flying the flag of a non-Contracting State may be arrested only in respect of a maritime claim.

I.94 The position is different in all—or almost all—States who have not given force of law to the Convention but have translated its provisions into a national enactment, since such enactment is normally applicable in respect of all ships, of whatever nationality. This is the position in Denmark, Finland, Nigeria, Norway and the United Kingdom.

I.95 The question has been raised in France with respect to Article 8(2), namely whether the municipal law applicable is the law of the flag State or the law of the State where the arrest is made, and the view has been expressed that the first alternative is correct.[38] This view is clearly wrong for at least three reasons. First, because it would be against the global philosophy of the Convention to provide for the application of any law other than the *lex fori*; secondly, because "cet Etat" (that State) in the French text can only be the latter of the States previously mentioned in Article 8(2), i.e. the State in whose jurisdiction the ship has been arrested; thirdly, for the overwhelming reason that in the English text the words used are "Contracting State" and, therefore, such State must be that where the arrest is made, the other State mentioned being a non-contracting State.

---

38. Tassel, "Saisie Conservatoire du Navire", *supra*, note 3, at p. 5; Chauveau, *Traité de Droit Maritime* (Paris, 1958), No. 246. *Contra*, Achard, Notes on Cour de Cassation 18 Janvier 1983 [1984] D.M.F. 328 and on Cour d'Appel de Rouen 11 Mai 1984 [1985] D.M.F. 162. The law of the flag does not appear to have ever been applied by the French courts.

CHAPTER 3

Implementation of the Convention by Contracting States

11. METHODS OF IMPLEMENTATION

I.96 The methods of national implementation of international conventions differ from country to country and, sometimes, various methods are used on different occasions in the same country. In some countries, treaties, if self-executing, have the force of law as a consequence of their ratification, and they are therefore automatically incorporated in the national legal system.[1] In most countries, however, some sort of implementing legislation is required. This is so in the United Kingdom and in the countries of the Commonwealth.[2] This is also the case in a great many other countries, such as, for example, most of the civil law countries. The implementing legislation may vary from the promulgation or publication[3] to the enactment of a Convention,[4] to the translation of substantive provisions of the Convention into terms of national law,[5] and to the application of a Convention within the framework of a more general law.[6]

---

1. In the United States the 1910 Salvage Convention has been considered as self-executing and, therefore, treated as being part of national law pursuant to Art. VI, s. 2 of the Constitution. The Hague Rules have also been considered as self-executing, but in this respect the situation is far from clear owing to the enactment of the Carriage of Goods by Sea Act 1936. See F. Berlingieri, "Uniformity in Maritime Law and Implementation of International Conventions" (1989) JMLC 334–336.
2. In *Canada* v. *A. G. of Ontario (Labour Conventions)* [1937] A.C. 326, at pp. 347–348, Lord Atkins stated:

> Unlike some other countries, the stipulations of a treaty duly ratified do not within the Empire, by virtue of the treaty alone, have the force of law. If the national executive, the government of the day, decides to incur the obligations of a treaty which involve alterations of the law, they have to run the risk of obtaining the assent of Parliament to the necessary statute or statutes.

3. The promulgation, or publication, or executive order, of an international Convention, whatever theory concerning its legal character is accepted, has the effect of enacting the rules of the Convention into the national legal system.
4. The substantive provisions of a Convention may be enacted as part of national law through appropriate legislation. This method has been used, for example, in the United Kingdom in respect of the Hague Rules and the Hague-Visby Rules.
5. Legislation to give effect to a convention may take the form of rules whereby all or some substantive provisions of a convention are translated into terms of national law, or national law is amended so that it conforms with the terms of the convention. The first method was adopted by the United Kingdom in respect of the 1957 Brussels Convention on Limitation of Liability by the Merchant Shipping Act 1958, which amended s.503 of the Merchant Shipping Act 1894 so as to conform with the provisions of the 1957 Brussels Convention. The second method was adopted by the United Kingdom in respect of the 1910 Salvage Convention, which has been given effect by means of the Maritime Conventions Act 1911.
6. This method has been followed in the Scandinavian countries in respect of the Hague Rules and the Hague-Visby Rules and, as we shall see (*infra*, para. I.197), in the United Kingdom in respect of the Arrest Convention.

I.97 The method of implementation may affect the uniform interpretation of a convention. When in fact the provisions of a convention are translated into terms of national law the danger arises that they are interpreted on the basis of other (general or special) national rules rather than on the basis of the convention from which they originate, no account being taken anymore of the need for their uniform interpretation. This seems to be a real danger in some countries, such as Germany, where this type of implementation seems to cut away the link between the uniform rules and the convention from which they originate. The danger appears to be minor in common law countries, in which the principle seems to prevail whereby provisions of an international origin must be interpreted, when their formulation permits, so as to enable the State to fulfil its international obligations.[7]

12. HOW THE ARREST CONVENTION HAS BEEN IMPLEMENTED

I.98 In view of the variety of methods of implementation of international conventions, an analysis of the manner in which the Arrest Convention has been implemented in a number of Contracting States seems useful in order to find out to what extent the uniform rules are actually in force in each of the Contracting States. Such analysis will be conducted with reference to the Contracting States in respect of which it has been possible to obtain information.

---

7. In England see *Attorney-General for Canada* v. *Attorney-General for Ontario* [1937] A.C. 326; *The "Banco"* (C.A.) [1971] 1 Lloyd's Rep. 49 at p. 52; *The "Sandrina"* (H.L.) [1985] 1 Lloyd's Rep. 181, at p. 185. In Australia see *Minister for Immigration and Ethnic Affairs* v. *Teoh* (1995) 183 C.L.R. 273 at p. 287 cited by Mason, *Harmonization of Maritime Laws and the Impact of International Law or Australian Maritime Law*, F.S. Dethridge Memorial Address, Conference of the Maritime Law Association of Australia and New Zealand, Cairns, 30 September 1998 also published in [1999] Dir. Mar. 637. With specific reference to the Arrest Convention Brandon J. (as he then was) so stated in *The "Eschersheim"*, [1974] 2 Lloyd's Rep. 188, at p. 192:

> The second consideration is that the 1956 Act was passed for the purpose, among others, of giving effect to the adherence of the United Kingdom to the International Convention Relating to the Arrest of Seagoing Ships made at Brussels, Oct. 10, 1952. In such a case there is a presumption that the legislature, in giving effect to the Convention, intended to fulfil the international obligations of this country rather than to depart from them, and it follows that, where any provisions of the 1956 Act apparently intended to give effect to the Convention are capable of more than one meaning, the Court may look at the terms of the Convention in order to gain assistance, if possible, in deciding which meaning is to be preferred: *The Banco* [1971] P. 137; [1971] 1 Lloyd's Rep. 49, applying *Salomon* v. *Commissioners of Customs and Excise* [1967] 2 Q.B. 116; [1966] 2 Lloyd's Rep. 460 and *Post Office* v. *Estuary Radio* [1968] 1 Q.B. 470; [1967] 2 Lloyd's Rep. 299.

A partially different approach has however been adopted in Scotland by the Outer House of the Court of Session in *Landcatch Ltd.* v. *International Oil Pollution Compensation Fund and Braer Corporation* [1998] 2 Lloyd's Rep. 552. Lord Gill in fact so stated (at p. 566 and 567):

> The Court should start from the assumption that Parliament has accurately implemented the treaty obligations set out in the relevant Conventions. The sections should therefore be construed in the first instance without reference to the Conventions or other related sources such as travaux préparatoires. If the sections disclose a clear-cut meaning, then that is the meaning that they should be given, whether or not that meaning is at odds with the assumed purpose of the Convention. It is only if the statutory provisions are obscure or ambiguous that there is any need to resort to the Conventions themselves, or to any other secondary sources, as an aid to construction (*Salomon* v. *CEC* [1967] 2 Q.B. 116, Lord Justice Diplock at pp. 143–144). At that point, it becomes a matter for the Courts as to the weight to be given to the various secondary sources of assistance in the interpretation of the statutory provisions (*cf. Fothergill* v. *Monarch Airlines* [1981] A.C. 251, Lord Scarman at p. 295C).

The decision of the House of Lords in *Fothergill* v. *Monarch Airlines* [1980] 2 Lloyd's Rep. 295 is not directly relevant, because the Warsaw Convention as amended by the Hague Protocol has been given the force of law in England.

I.99 States that have given force of law to the Convention will be considered first. States that have ratified the Convention without giving it force of law, but enacting all or part of its provisions in their domestic legislation will be considered subsequently.

(a) States that have given force of law to the Convention

I.100 Amongst such States, some have merely given force of law to the Convention by an "order of execution" or by means of its publication in the national official journal; others have also enacted supplementary provisions.

States in the first group

I.101 Amongst the States of the first group there are Belgium, Croatia, France, Germany, Greece, Haiti, Italy, the Netherlands, Poland, Portugal and Slovenia.

BELGIUM

I.102 The Convention was ratified on 10 April 1961 pursuant to law 24 March 1961, published in the Belgian official journal on 19 July 1961 and the Convention acquired force of law in Belgium as from 10 October 1961. In order to avoid a possible conflict with the domestic law on arrest of ships in force at that time (law 4 September 1908) on 4 December 1961 a new law was enacted, incorporating the provisions of the Convention and replacing the previous legislation.

CROATIA

I.103 Croatia has succeeded to Yugoslavia as a party to the 1952 Arrest Convention as from 8 October 1991[8] and, therefore, the Convention has the force of law in Croatia. Most of the provisions of the Convention have also been incorporated in the Croatian Maritime Code of 1994. There are, therefore, two different regimes in force in Croatia: that of the 1952 Conventions which is applicable, except for claims in respect of disputes as to the title to or ownership of a ship,[9] to ships flying the flag of a Contracting State and the domestic regime, which is applicable in all situations outside the scope of application of the Convention. No rules for the implementation of the Convention have been enacted and, therefore, the arrest procedure is governed by the Maritime Code[10] and by the Enforcement Proceedings Act.[11]

FRANCE

I.104 The Convention was ratified on 25 May 1957 and then published by Decree of 4 January 1958, No. 14. Publication had the effect of enacting the rules of the Convention into the French legal system. There are, therefore, two different regimes in France, that of the Convention and that of the Decree of 27 October 1967. The former is applicable to

8. The notification of succession has been published in the Official Gazette of the Republic of Croatia (NN-MU 1/92 of 14 November 1992).
9. Reservation not to apply article 1(1)(o) had been made by Yugoslavia and is now applicable to Croatia. See CMI Yearbook 1998, p. 226.
10. See the replies of the Maritime Law Association of Croatia to the Questionnaire, Appendix II, p. 229.
11. See the replies of the Maritime Law Association of Croatia, *supra*, note 10.

ships flying the flag of a Contracting State, including French ships, unless the arrestor has his habitual residence or his principal place of business in France, and, if the arrestor so chooses, to ships flying the flag of a non-contracting State. The latter is applicable to French ships in the cases set out in Article 8(4) and to ships flying the flag of a non-contracting State where the arrestor elects to apply it.[12]

I.105 If a conflict between the scope of application of the two regimes were to arise, pursuant to Article 55 of the French Constitution the uniform rules would prevail.

GERMANY

I.106 The ratification of the Convention was approved by law on 21 June 1972 and the Convention was ratified on 6 October 1972. Pursuant to the ratification, its provisions acquired the force of law. No implementing legislation has been enacted, except that paragraph 482 of the *Handelsgesetzbuch* (Commercial Code), which prohibited the arrest of ships ready to sail, has been amended so as to authorise such arrest, provided the ship has not yet sailed.

I.107 When ratifying the Convention, Germany reserved the right not to apply Article 1(1)(o) and (p), as well as the right not to apply the provisions of Article 3(1) to the arrest of a ship within its jurisdiction for claims set out in Article 1(1)(q).

GREECE

I.108 The ratification of the Convention was authorised by law 4570/1966, by which the Convention in its original text became a part of the internal Greek legislation and thus was given the force of law.

I.109 No additional implementation rules have been enacted because any matters not directly regulated by the Convention are regulated by the Code of Civil Procedure in a satisfactory manner.

HAITI

I.110 The provisions of the Convention have been enacted in the domestic legal system by Decree of the Assemblée Nationale of 29 August 1953, published in the Official Journal No. 107 of 9 November 1953.

ITALY

I.111 When ratifying the Convention, Italy reserved the right not to apply Article 1(1)(o) and (p), as well as the right not to apply the provisions of Article 3(1) to the arrest of a ship within its jurisdiction for claims set out in Article 1(1)(q).

I.112 An executive order was issued with the Law of 25 October 1977, No. 880. The order had the effect of enacting the Convention, in its original English and French texts, into the Italian legal system, conditionally on its ratification. The instrument of ratification was deposited on 9 November 1979 and the Convention came into force on 9 May 1980.

I.113 Owing to the lack of any specific rules of implementation, there are doubts as to the manner in which certain rules of the Convention are enforced in practice in Italy. This

---

12. See *supra*, Chapter 2, note 24.

is the case for Article 2 of the Convention, which provides that a ship flying the flag of a Contracting State may be arrested in respect of any maritime claim. Under Italian law, arrest, either of a ship or of any other asset of the debtor, is conditional on the danger of the claimant being unable to enforce his claim after he has obtained an enforceable judgment (*periculum in mora*). As a general rule, therefore, an arrest cannot be granted if the debtor is financially sound. This rule, however, is not applied to maritime liens since arrest is the specific manner of enforcement of maritime liens. The question thus arises whether this exception may be extended to all the maritime claims listed in Article 1(1) of the Convention and the trend of case law seems to favour this solution.[13] The provision of Article 7(2), whereby if the court within whose jurisdiction the ship was arrested has no jurisdiction to decide upon the merits such court shall fix the time within which the claimant shall bring an action before a court having jurisdiction, has instead been recently implemented.[14] In fact Article 669*octies* or the Civil Procedure Code (CCP) provides that the order of arrest must set out a time limit, not to exceed 30 days, within which proceedings on the merits must be commenced and that if no time limit is fixed, such time limit shall be 30 days. Article 669*novies* CCP, in turn, provides that if proceedings on the merits are not commenced within the time limit fixed pursuant to Article 669*octies*, or if after such proceedings are commenced they are extinguished, the order of arrest becomes ineffective. It then provides that if a foreign court or an arbitration tribunal has jurisdiction on the merits, the order of arrest also becomes ineffective if the claimant does not request the enforcement of the foreign judgment or of the arbitration award within the time limits, if any, set out by statute or by an international convention. Since the Arrest Convention does not set out any time limit, but makes reference to the *lex fori*, Article 669*octies* CCP shall apply.

THE NETHERLANDS

I.114 When ratifying the Convention, the Netherlands reserved the right not to apply Article 1(1)(o) and (p), as well as the right not to apply the provisions of Article 3(1) to the arrest of a ship within its jurisdiction for claims set out in Article 1(1)(q).

I.115 The Convention has been implemented by giving it force of law. The instrument of ratification was deposited on 20 January 1983 and the Convention came into force on 20 July 1983. Pursuant to Article 94 of the Constitution, its provisions supersede those of the municipal law in case of a conflict.

I.116 No additional implementation rules have been enacted. It was in fact deemed that they were unnecessary, as the municipal law provided the complementary rules that were required.

POLAND

I.117 The instrument of ratification was deposited on 16 July 1976 and the Convention came into force on 16 January 1977 in its original text. No implementation rules were

---

13. This requirement was held not to apply by the Tribunale of Genoa on 20 May 1995 in *Uberseeschiffahrts-agentur Transnautic GmbH K.G.* v. *Baltic Shipping Co.* (*The "Akademic Gorbunov"*) [1995] Dir. Mar. 768; Tribunale of Genoa, 11 January 1994, *Rimorchiatori Riuniti Porto di Genova S.r.l.* v. *Morfini Trasporti Marittimi S.r.l.* (*The "Ninfea"*) unreported; Corte d'Appello of Lecce, 12 January 1995, *Bibolini Società di Navigazione S.p.A.* v. *Fratelli D. & G. Barretta S.n.c.* (*The "Anna Bibolini"*) [1995] Dir. Mar. 175.

14. The new provisions of the Italian CCP were enacted by law of 26 November 1990, No. 353 and came into force on 1 January 1993.

enacted and, therefore, arrest of ships is governed by the provisions of the Code of Civil Procedure.

PORTUGAL

I.118 The ratification of the Convention was authorised by Decree-Law No. 41.007 of 16 February 1957 and the instrument of ratification was deposited on 4 April 1957. The original text of the Convention was published in the *Official Journal*, together with the Decree whereby ratification was authorised and, therefore, the Convention has been enacted in Portugal in its original text.

I.119 No implementation rules were enacted. Consequently, the procedure of arrest of ships is governed by the general domestic rules on arrest.

SLOVENIA

I.120 The Convention has been given the force of law in Slovenia. In fact pursuant to Article 8 of the Constitution of the Republic of Slovenia international conventions ratified or acceded by Slovenia and which have been proclaimed in Slovenia have the force of law in their original text. Most of the provisions of the Convention have also been enacted in the Maritime and Internal Navigation Act of the former Yugoslavia, entered into force on 1 January 1978.[15] Two different legal regimes are therefore in force in Slovenia: the Convention of 1952 in respect of ships flying the flag of Contracting States, and the domestic regime in all cases falling outside the scope of application of the Convention, including ships flying the flag of non-Contracting States.

I.121 No implementation rules have been enacted. The arrest procedure is governed by the general domestic rules on arrest of the Maritime and Internal Navigation Act[16] and of the Forced Execution and Security Act as well as of the Civil Procedure Act.

States in the second group

I.122 Amongst the States of the second group there are Ireland and Spain.

IRELAND

I.123 Ireland acceded to the Convention on 17 October 1989 and gave it the force of law with the Jurisdiction of Courts (Maritime Conventions) Act 1989. This Act was brought into force on 17 April 1990 by Statutory Instrument No. 332 of 1989 signed by the Minister for Justice on 11 December 1989 pursuant to the powers vested in him by section 16(2) of the Act. Section 4(1) of the Act provides: "Subject to the provisions of this Part, the Convention shall have the force of law in the State and judicial notice shall be taken of it."

I.124 The provisions of Part I of the Act, therefore, if in conflict with those of the Convention have the effect of excluding the force of law of these latter provisions.

---

15. See the replies of the Maritime Law Association of Slovenia to the Questionnaire, Appendix II, pp. 230–231 and, in particular Art. 877 of the Maritime and Internal Navigation Act of the former Yugoslavia listing the maritime claims.

16. See the reply of the Maritime Law Association of Slovenia to question 2, *supra*, note 15.

I.125 The purpose of the relevant provisions of Part I, however, is that of interpreting the Convention[17] and all appear to be within the reasonable limits of the interpretation of the Convention.

I.126 A summary of such provisions may be of interest. Such summary is made, for convenience, with reference to the individual Convention rules the interpretation of which is given by the Act.

I.127 *The notion of ship.* As has been pointed out, there is no definition of "ship" in the Convention except that reference is made in the title to "sea-going ships".[18] Section 13 of the Act gives the following definitions of "ship" and "vessel" for the purposes of the Arrest Convention and of the Civil Jurisdiction Convention to which force of law has been given with the same Act, and of the Act itself:

"ship" includes every description of vessel used in navigation;
"vessel" includes any ship or boat, or any other description of vessel used in navigation.

I.128 The term "vessel" is used in the Civil Jurisdiction Convention while, as previously indicated, the term "ship" is used in the Arrest Convention. It would appear, therefore, that for the purpose of this latter Convention "ship" includes any ship or boat, or any other description of vessel used in navigation, wherever navigation takes place.

I.129 *Article 1(1)(c)* mentions, amongst the maritime claims, salvage. As it will be seen,[19] the notion of salvage may differ in the various jurisdictions. For example, it may or may not include the refloating of a sunken ship and of her cargo or the removal of wrecks; it may or may not include the finding of derelicts. Section 2(4) of the Act gives a very wide notion of salvage for the purpose of the Convention by providing that:

"salvage" includes a reference to such claims for services rendered in saving life from a ship or in preserving cargo, apparel or wreck as under sections 544 to 546 of the Merchant Shipping Act, 1894, are authorised to be made in connection with a ship (including the case of cargo or wreck salvage claims in respect of cargo or wreck found on land).

I.130 Article 1(1)(m) and (n) mention, amongst the maritime claims, wages of masters and master's disbursements. Section 2(4) of the Act provides that, unless the context otherwise requires, "master" includes every person (except a pilot) having command or charge of a ship. This is a very wide definition of "master", since it includes, for example, a custodian of a ship which is laid up afloat. It seems, however, that it is a convenient definition in respect of sub-paragraph (n), for there is no reason why the disbursements incurred by a custodian should not give rise, if unpaid, to a maritime claim. The situation is probably different in respect of wages: but recourse can be made to the phrase "unless the context otherwise requires" in order to restrict in this case the meaning of the word "master" to persons actually in the command of a ship.[20]

I.131 *Article 1(1)(o).* Pursuant to section 2(2)(a) of the Act this provision, wherein reference is made only to "disputes as to title and ownership" of the ship, must be construed as including disputes as to possession of the ship.[21]

---

17. This is expressly stated in the opening sentence of section 2 of the Act:
2(1). The provisions of this section shall apply for the purpose of interpreting the Convention.
18. *Supra*, para. I.34.
19. *Infra*, para. I.324.
20. *Infra*, para. I.372.
21. *Infra*, para. I.377.

I.132 *Article 1(1)(q)*. As it is known, in this sub-paragraph reference is made to the mortgage or hypothecation of a ship. Pursuant to section 2(2)(b) of the Act this provision must be construed as including the mortgage or hypothecation of any share in a ship. As it will be stated,[22] this is certainly the correct interpretation of Article 1(1)(q) of the Convention.

I.133 *Article 3(1)*. As it will be stated,[23] the moment that is relevant as regards the ownership of the sistership is that of the arrest. Section 3(a) of the Act provides that for the purpose of determining under Article 3(1) or 3(4) whether a right exists to arrest a sistership, its owner shall be deemed to be the owner at the time of the issue of proceedings against it.

I.134 *Article 3(2)*. The term "beneficial ownership" was never mentioned during the *travaux préparatoires* of the Convention. It was instead used in the English Administration of Justice Act, 1956 in the same provision (section 3(4)) in which the term "owner" is used. This is so also for the Supreme Court Act, 1981 (section 21(4)) and, therefore, the reason why different terms are used in the same provision is not clear. Section 3(b) of the Act settles this problem by providing that for the purpose of Article 3(2) of the Convention ownership shall be construed as including beneficial ownership.

I.135 *Articles 4, 5 and 7*. In Article 4 reference is made, in the English text of the Convention, to the "Court or . . . the appropriate judicial authority" and in the French text to the "Tribunal ou ... toute autre autorité judiciaire compétente". In Article 5 reference is instead made, in the English text to the "Court or *other* appropriate judicial authority", the French text remaining the same. Then in Article 7(1) reference is simply made to the "Tribunal" whilst in Article 7(2) reference is made once to the "Court" and another time to the "Court or other appropriate judicial authority". As it will be seen,[24] this different terminology may give rise to some uncertainties. Section 5(2) of the Act so provides:

(2) For the purpose of the application of the Convention to the State:
    (a) the expression "the Court or other appropriate judicial authority" where it occurs in the Convention means the High Court, and
    (b) "Courts" in Article 7(1) means the High Court.

I.136 *Article 7(2) and (3)*. Article 7(2) provides that if the Court within whose jurisdiction the ship was arrested has not jurisdiction on the merits, the security given to procure the release of the ship shall provide that it is given for the satisfaction of any judgment that may be pronounced and that the Court *shall* fix the time within which the claimant shall bring an action before a Court having such jurisdiction. Article 7(3) provides in turn that if the parties have agreed to submit the dispute to the jurisdiction of another Court or to arbitration, the Court (or other appropriate judicial authority) of the country in which the arrest is made *may* fix the time within which the claimant shall bring proceedings.[25]

I.137 Section 5(4) and (5) of the Act so provide:

(4) Where the High Court stays, declines or dismisses proceedings referred to in *subsection (1)* of this section on the ground that the dispute in question should be submitted to arbitration or be determined by the courts of another country the court may order that the ship arrested or, where bail or other security has been given to obtain release from arrest, the said bail or security, be retained for the purpose of satisfying (in part or in whole) any award or judgment which:

22. *Infra*, para. I.396.
23. *Infra*, para. I.422.
24. *Infra*, para. I.576–583.
25. *Infra*, para. I.717–736.

(a) is given in respect of the dispute in the arbitration or in the legal proceedings in the other country, and

(b) is enforceable in the State.

(5) Where the court makes an order under *subsection (4)* of this section it may attach such conditions to the order as it thinks fit, in particular conditions with respect to the institution or prosecution of the relevant arbitration or legal proceedings.

I.38 The wording of section (4) is due to the fact that the High Court has always original jurisdiction in respect of maritime claims. Also the provision in section (5), according to which the High Court *"may* attach such conditions to the order as it thinks fit", is due to the same reason. In fact the situation envisaged in Article 7(2) of the Convention of the Court of the place of arrest having no jurisdiction on the merits does not occur and, therefore, there are no cases where the High Court *must* fix the time for the commencement of proceedings on the merits.

I.139 The text of the Convention is set out in the First Schedule to the Act.

SPAIN

I.140 The Convention was ratified on 8 December 1953 and was published in the Spanish *Official Journal* of 5 January 1954.[26] It became part of the Spanish legal system upon the expiry of six months from the date of the deposit of the instrument of ratification (8 December 1953). Article 1(5) of the Civil Code in fact provides that the legal norms of an international treaty shall not be directly applicable in Spain unless they have become part of the national legal system through their integral publication in the *Official Journal*. The position, therefore, is the same as in France and Italy. However, it proved necessary to enact a subsequent law (Law of 8 April 1967, No. 2), promoted by the Spanish Maritime Law Association, with a view to making clear that the right of arrest exists, as respects maritime claims, on the basis of a mere allegation of a claim. In fact it had been held that the provision of the Convention had left unaffected the existing law in respect of the manner in which proof of claims must be provided for the purposes of arrest. Article 1400 of the Spanish Code of Civil Procedure provides that the claimant must produce a document evidencing the existence of the debt and then sets out the subjective conditions relating to the debtor which include his foreign nationality or, in case the debtor is Spanish, the lack of a domicile and of any of the assets specified therein.[27] Law 2/1967 states in the preamble that the provisions of the 1952 Convention have become part of Spanish national law and that it is necessary to enact rules ensuring the arrest of ships as

26. Information on the ratification by Spain of the Convention and on the relevant national laws has been kindly provided by Ms Esther Zarza.

27. Article 1400 of the Spanish Code of Civil Procedure (Ley de Enjuiciamento Civil) so provides:

Para decretar el embargo preventivo será necesario:

1° Que con la solicitud se presente un documento del que resulte la existencia de la deuda.

2° Que el deudor contra quien se pida se halle en uno de los casos siguientes:

Que sea extranjero no naturalizado en España.

Que, aunque sea español o extranjero naturalizado, no tenga domicilio conocido, o bienes raices, o un establecimiento agricolo, industrial o mercantil en el lugar donde corresponda demandarle en justicia el pago de la deuda.

Que, au teniendo las circunstancias que acaban de expresarse, haya desaparecido de su domicilio o establecimiento, sin dejar persona alguna al frente de él; y, si la hubiere dejado, que ésta ignore su residencia; o que se oculte, o exista motivo racional para creer que ocultará o malbaratará sus bienes en daño de sus acreedores.

security for maritime claims with the necessary rapidity[28] and further states that such rules are also required in respect of ships flying the flag of non party States.[29]

I.141 Article 1 of the law then provides that in order to order the arrest of a foreign ship in respect of a maritime claim as defined in Article 1 of the 1952 Brussels Arrest Convention the mere allegation of the right of claim in respect of which the arrest is requested suffices[30] and then provides that the Court shall in all cases require the claimant to provide security for damages. Article 2 provides that account shall be taken of the limits set out in article 3 of the Convention. Finally, pursuant to Article 3 the opposition to the arrest may only be grounded on the lack of any one of the requisites prescribed in the previous articles.[31] It would appear, therefore, that the allegation of the claim cannot be disputed in the course of the arrest proceeding, while the ownership of the ship by the person liable in respect of the claim may constitute the basis for an application that the arrest be lifted, unless Article 3(4) applies.

I.142 The fact, however, that Law 2/1967 applies only in respect of foreign ships, implies that the arrest of Spanish ships continues to be subject to the provisions of Article 1400 of the Spanish Code of Civil Procedure which restricts to very marginal cases the possibility of such arrest. This is in conflict with Article 8(4) of the Convention which excludes from its scope of application only the arrest of ships within the jurisdiction of the State of its flag by a person who has his habitual residence or principal place of business in that State. It follows that the provisions of the Convention may not apply in respect of the arrest in Spain of a Spanish ship by a claimant who has not his habitual residence or principal place of business in Spain.[32]

---

28. The statement made in the preamble is the following:
   El Convenio de Bruselas de 10 de mayo de 1952, al ser ratificado por España, impone sus normas como ley nacional; mas para que tenga plena efectividad es preciso acomodar las disposiciones procesales con el fin de que el embargo preventivo de buques en aseguramento de créditos maritimos pueda autorizarse con la rapidez necesaria. La presente Ley se limita a establecer las especialidades que a tal fin son necesarias, o sea los requisitos para que el embargo se produzca, las garantias que han de adoptarse para evitar toda pretensión infundada y los límites de la oposición.
29. The relevant part of the preamble is reproduced below:
   Si abundan las razones para adaptar nuestra legislación a los principios de rapidez y eficacia que inspiran el repetido Convenio de Bruselas, mayores son los motivos que aconsejan la adopción de una medida de carácter general que afecte a los buques que navegan bajo pabellón de paises no signatarios de aquel Convenio.
30. On this provision see the orders of the Audienca Territorial of Barcelona 26 November 1986, Anuario de Derecho Maritimo, vol. VI, p. 511 and 23 March 1987, Anuario de Derecho Maritimo, vol. VII, p. 695.
31. Here follows the text of the three articles of Law 2/1967:
   1. Para decretar el embargo preventivo de un buque extranjero por crédito maritimo que se define en el artículo 1° del Convenio de Bruselas de 10 de mayo de 1952, bastará que se alegue el derecho o créditos reclamados y la causa que los motive.
   El Juez exigirá en todo caso fianza en cantidad suficiente para responder de los daños perjuicios y costas que puedan ocasionarse. Esta fianza podra ser de cualquiera de las clases que reconce el derecho, incluso el aval bancario.
   2. Se tendrán en cuenta respecto a los buques objeto de embargo las limitaciones del articulo 3° del Convenio.
   3. Hecho el embargo, la oposición sólo podrá fundarse en el incumplimiento de alguno de los requisitos establecidos en los dos articulos anteriores.
32. This conclusion is not certain, since the Tribunal Supremo held with judgments of 13 April 1989 and 19 June 1990 (both cited in the judgment of the Audiencia Provincial de Las Palmas 1991, in Anuario de Derecho Maritimo, vol. XI, p. 1044) that the Convention applies in all cases where there is a "relación juridica de carácter internacional" and this is the case for the arrest in Spain of a Spanish ship by a foreign claimant.

(b) States that have incorporated the provisions of the Convention (or some of them) into their national legal system

I.143 These States include Denmark, Finland, Nigeria, Norway, Sweden and the United Kingdom. A summary of the relevant provisions of the domestic law of each of such States will be made hereafter with reference to the most relevant subjects under which the commentary of the Convention is arranged. Such summary does not intend to be a concise commentary on such laws—a task which would be beyond the scope of this book and the knowledge of the author. Its purpose is only to assess the extent to which the Convention has been implemented.

DENMARK

I.144 Denmark has implemented the Arrest Convention by incorporating some of its provisions into the Danish Merchant Shipping Act.

(A) Claims in respect of which a ship may be arrested

The rule whereby a ship may be arrested only in respect of a maritime claim is reproduced in section 92 of the Act, followed by a concise definition of arrest, qualified by the statement that the ship must be present.

(B) The individual maritime claims

I.145 The maritime claims enumerated in section 91 of the Act correspond to those of the Convention, the only difference being the addition to claims for pilotage[33] of claims for port, canal and other waterways dues[34] in respect of which a maritime lien is granted under the 1967 MLM Convention[35] ratified by Denmark, as well as under the 1993 MLM Convention.[36]

(C) The notion of arrest

I.146 Section 92 of the Act shortens the definition given in Article 1(2) of the Convention by stating that arrest shall mean the detention of a vessel without mentioning that the detention must take place by means of judicial process, it is thought because this is a general rule in Danish law as in a great many other national laws. There is added to the definition, however, the requirement that the vessel be "present", viz. within the jurisdiction of the Court. The purpose of this addition is to exclude from the scope of application of the rules enacted in order to implement the Convention the "documentary" arrest, effected by means of the endorsement of the warrant of arrest in the ships register.

(D) Ships that may be arrested

I.147 Section 93(1) of the Act, similarly to Article 3(1) of the Convention, merely states that the ship in respect of which the claim has arisen may be arrested. In the Convention

33. Article 1(1)(j) of the Convention.
34. Sec. 91(10) of the Danish Merchant Shipping Act.
35. Article 4(1)(ii) of the 1967 MLM Convention.
36. Article 4(1)(d) of the 1993 MLM Convention.

the fundamental rule according to which the ship must be owned by the person liable for the claim is drawn by implication from the reference to paragraph 4 of Article 3 which, as an exception, permits the arrest of a ship in respect of a claim against the bareboat charterer or, generally, a person other than the owner. The last sentence has been interpreted in such a way as to permit the arrest of a ship irrespective of whether the owner is liable for the claim or not. The only condition for the arrest is that the claim must have arisen in respect of the ship the arrest of which is applied for. This seemingly unrestricted right of arrest is, however, significantly limited by subsection 4, according to which a ship cannot be arrested if it is not possible to levy execution on that ship. It appears, therefore, that the Danish legislation has interpreted Article 3(1) and (4) of the Convention in a sound manner.

I.148 Arrest of sisterships is permitted as under the Convention. If the owner is liable for the claim the sistership must be a ship owned by him. If a person other than the owner is liable, the sistership must be a ship owned by the person liable.

(E) Re-arrest and multiple arrest

I.149 As under the Convention, the general rule set out in section 93(5) of the Act is that a ship cannot be arrested more than once for the same maritime claim. The exceptions are the same as under the Convention. Multiple arrest seems instead to be permissible, since section 93(1) provides that another ship owned by the owner of the ship to which the claim relates may *also* be arrested and section 93(2) provides that if the owner of the ship is not liable for a claim relating to the ship, such ship may be arrested *together with* another ship owned by the person liable. Under the Convention, instead, multiple arrest is subject to the same rules applicable to re-arrest. The difference, however, is not significant, because arrest of a second ship for the same claim, even if permissible, must be justified, and this will be so normally when the value of the ship that had been previously arrested is lower than the amount of the claim: this would be precisely a "good cause" permitting multiple arrest under the Convention.

(F) Security for damages

I.150 Section 94 of the Act provides that prior to issuing a warrant of arrest the Bailiff's Court may order the claimant to provide security for the damages the arrest may cause, stating that, as a general rule, such security should not exceed five days loss of hire. This provision is not in conflict with the Convention, which in Article 6 states that liability for wrongful arrest is subject to the *lex fori* and that the rules of procedure relating to the arrest are governed by the *lex fori*.

(G) Trading of a ship under arrest

I.151 The provision of Article 5 of the Convention is reproduced in section 95(2) of the Act.

(H) Release of the ship from arrest

I.152 Section 95(1) of the Act provides that the arrest may be avoided and the arrest already effected may be lifted if at the discretion of the Bailiff's Court satisfactory security is provided covering the amount of the claim together with interest and costs. This provision is in line with Article 5 of the Convention except that it does not appear to exclude its application in respect of disputes as to title to the ship and disputes between co-owners.

(I) Jurisdiction on the merits of the case

I.153 Section 246(a) of the Danish Administration Act, which is applicable pursuant to section 96 of the Merchant Shipping Act, provides that the Court of the place where the arrest has been effected, or would have been effected if security had not been provided to prevent the arrest, has jurisdiction on the merits of the case. This conforms with Article 7(1) of the Convention pursuant to which the Courts of the country in which the arrest was made have jurisdiction on the merits if the national law of that country gives such jurisdiction.

   I.154 Pursuant to section 634 the claimant must institute proceedings for the merits within one week after the arrest or within two weeks, if a foreign Court has jurisdiction and, pursuant to section 638 the Bailiff's Court may order the arrest to be lifted if proceedings for the merits are not commenced within the above time limits. This is in line with Article 7(2), (3) and (4) of the Convention except that the release of the ship from arrest is left to the discretion of the Court, while pursuant to Article 7(4) the defendant is entitled to obtain the release.

FINLAND

I.155 Finland, as all the Scandinavian countries, has given effect to the Convention by incorporating most of its provisions into its Maritime Code by means of Act 234/95. Since the relevant provisions of the Maritime Code correspond to those of chapter 4 of the Swedish Maritime Code, reference is made to the analysis of such latter provisions.[37]

NIGERIA

I.156 Prior to the enactment of the Admiralty Jurisdiction Decree, which came into force on 30 December 1991, the UK Administration of Justice Act 1956 was applicable in Nigeria[38] and, therefore, it could be said that Nigeria had thereby implemented the 1952 Convention, ratified on 7 November 1963.

   I.157 At present, in order to establish whether and to what extent Nigeria has implemented the Convention reference must be made to the aforesaid Admiralty Jurisdiction Decree.

(A) Claims in respect to which a ship may be arrested

I.158 The rule whereby a ship may only be arrested in respect of a maritime claim is the effect of an action *in rem* being permitted only for the enforcement of a maritime lien or of claims that are defined in the Act as "maritime claims". Pursuant to section 2(1) the term "maritime claim" includes "proprietary maritime claims" and "general maritime

---

37. See *infra*, para. I.188–196.
38. *American International Insurance Co.* v. *Ceekay Traders Ltd.* (1981) (Supreme Court of Nigeria), 2 N.S.C. 65.

claims".[39] There are, therefore, three categories of claims in respect of which a ship may be arrested:

  (a) the proprietary maritime claims[40] which, pursuant to section 2(2), include the claims relating to possession of a ship, title to or ownership of a ship or share in a ship, mortgage of a ship or of a share in a ship and correspond therefore to the maritime claims listed in Article 1(1) (o), (p) and (q) of the Convention;
  (b) the claims secured by a maritime lien which are the claims for salvage, damage done by a ship, wages of the master and crew and master's disbursements[41] which correspond to the maritime claims listed in Article 1(1) (a), (b), (c), (m) and (n) of the Convention;
  (c) the general maritime claims which are based on the general maritime claims enumerated in section 4(3) of the Australian Admiralty Act 1988.

(B) The individual maritime claims

I.159 The main differences between the maritime claims recognised in Nigeria and those set out in Article 1(1) of the 1952 Convention may be summarised as follows:

  (i) the "proprietary" claims include "claims" for the execution or satisfaction of a judgment;
  (ii) the claims for loss of life or personal injury are qualified in two ways: they are the claims arising out of a defect in the ship, apparel or equipment (section 2(3) (c) of the Act) and the claims arising out of an act or omission in the management of the ship by the owners, charterers, other persons in possession or control of the ship, persons for whose wrongful acts or omissions the owner is responsible (section 2(3)(d) of the Act)[42];
  (iii) the claims enumerated in Article 1(1)(k) of the Convention are described as a "claims in respect of goods, materials or services (including stevedoring services and lighterage services) supplied to a ship for its operation and maintenance" (section 2(3)(k) of the Act);
  (iv) dock charges and dues enumerated in Article 1(1)(l) are described as "claims in respect of a liability for port, harbour, canal or light tolls, charges and dues, or tolls charges or dues of any kind in relation to a ship";
  (vi) claims for insurance premiums or mutual insurance calls are listed amongst the "general maritime claims" and then, for reasons which are not clear, there are

---

39. This distinction between proprietary maritime claims and general maritime claims exists also in Australian law (section 4(1) of the Admiralty Act, 1988).
40. The enumeration of proprietary maritime claims in the Act corresponds to that in section 4(2) of the Australian Admiralty Act 1988.
41. Section 5(3) of the Act so provides:
  (3) In any case in which there is a maritime lien or other charge on any ship, aircraft or other property for the amount claimed, an action *in rem* may be brought in the Court against that ship, aircraft or property; and for the purpose of this subsection, "maritime lien" means a lien for:
  (a) salvage; or
  (b) damage done by a ship; or
  (c) wages of the master or a member of the crew of a ship; or
  (d) master's disbursements.
42. This description is based on that in section 20(2)(f) of the UK Supreme Court Act 1981 and on that of Section 4(3)(d) of the Australian Admiralty Act 1988.

also added claims for insurance premiums in respect of goods or cargoes carried by a ship.

(C) The notion of arrest

I.160 There is no express definition of arrest in the Act. Arrest is mentioned in connection with an action *in rem* which is brought in order to enforce a maritime claim. The notion of arrest is, however, wider than under the 1952 Convention, since there are included amongst the "proprietary claims", as previously stated, actions brought for the satisfaction or enforcement of a judgment and, amongst the "general maritime claims", actions brought for the enforcement of an arbitral award.

(D) Ships that may be arrested

I.161 There are three provisions in the Act relating to the arrest of the ship in respect of which the claim has arisen.

I.162 In two of them a ship may be arrested, irrespective of who is the owner. The first (section 5(2) of the Act) is related to disputes as to title to or possession of a ship, claims arising out of a mortgage and disputes between co-owners as to ownership, possession, operation or earnings of a ship. The second (section 5(3) of the Act) is related to claims secured by maritime liens.

I.163 The third provision (section 5(4) of the Act) applies generally to all other maritime claims and requires the existence of a specified link between the ship and the person liable for the claim both at the time when the cause of action arose and at the time when the action is brought. When the cause of action arose the person liable must have been the owner, charterer or in possession or control of the ship; at the time when the action is brought the person liable must be either the beneficial owner of the ship or the charterer of the ship under a charter by demise.[43] The wide typology of relationships at the time the cause of action arose is not in conflict with the Convention, which does not require any specific relationship between the ship and the person liable at that time. The much more restricted typology of relationships required at the time the action is brought is such as to reduce the scope of application of Article 3(4) of the Convention but, for the reasons stated when commenting on the Danish rules, in view of the uncertain construction of this latter provision, the Nigerian rules can hardly be stated to be in conflict with the Convention.

I.164 Sisterships may be arrested, as under the Convention, if they are fully owned by the person liable at the time the action is brought (section 5(4)(b) of the Act).

---

43. Section 5(4) of the Act, which reproduces almost literally section 21(4) of the English Supreme Court Act 1981, so provides:
    (4) In any other claim under section 2 of this Decree, where the claim arises in connection with a ship and the person who would be liable on the claim in an action *in personam* (in this Decree referred to as "the relevant person") was, when the cause of action arose, the owner or charterer of or in possession or in control of the ship in an action *in rem* may (whether or not the claim gives rise to a maritime lien on that ship) be brought against:
    (a) that ship, if at the time the action is brought the relevant person is either the beneficial owner of that ship as respects all the shares in it or the charterer of the ship under a charter by demise; or
    (b) any other ship of which, at the time when the action is brought, the relevant person is the beneficial owner as respects all the shares in the ship.

(E) Re-arrest and multiple arrest

I.165 The provision on re-arrest in section 6(2) of the Act is substantially the same as that in Article 3(3) of the Convention. There are separate provisions on multiple arrest in section 5(8),[44] (9) and (10). The general rule is that multiple arrest is prohibited. The exceptions are:

> (i) the release of the first ship because it had been invalidly arrested;
> (ii) the unlawful removal of the first ship from the custody of the Admiralty Marshal;
> (iii) the enforcement of a maritime claim secured by a maritime lien first on a sistership and then, for the balance of the claim, on the ship in respect of which the claim has arisen.

I.166 These provisions seem also to be in line with the rules of the Convention.

(F) Security for damages

I.167 No provision is made in this respect in the Act as in the Convention.

(G) Trading of a ship under arrest

I.168 No provision is made in this respect in the Act.

(H) Release of the ship from arrest

I.169 There is no express provision in the Act regulating the release of a ship from arrest against delivery of an appropriate security. However the rule set out in Article 5 of the Convention, whereby the Court shall permit the release of the ship upon sufficient security being furnished appears to exist in Nigeria, since implied reference is made to it in section 6(1) where it is provided that the Court may order re-arrest if default has been made in the performance of a guarantee given to procure the release of the ship from arrest.

(I) Jurisdiction on the merits of the case

I.170 The general rule is that the admiralty jurisdiction exists in respect of all ships, irrespective of the place of residence or domicile of the owners (and, it is thought, of the nationality of the ship) and of all maritime claims, wherever they have arisen (section 3).

I.171 The provisions of Article 7(2), (3) and (4) of the Convention are in part contained in section 10 of the Act. Section 10(1) states that if proceedings should be stayed or dismissed on the ground that the claim should be determined by a Court in a foreign country or by arbitration the Court may order that the proceeding be stayed on condition that the arrest should be maintained or satisfactory security for the satisfaction of the foreign judgment or the award be provided. Pursuant to section 10(2) the Court may impose any conditions as are just and reasonable, including a condition with respect to the instruction or prosecution of proceedings in the Court of the foreign country.

---

44. Corresponding to section 21(8) of the English Supreme Court Act 1981.

NORWAY

I.172 Norway has implemented the Convention[45] by incorporating some of its provisions into its Maritime Code of 1994 and into the Act on Enforcement of Claims. The scope of application of the special rules incorporated in the Code in order to implement the Convention is set out in section 91 of the Code by indicating the situations in which they do not apply. Such situations are the following:

(a) arrest of ships for which registration is not mandatory, viz. ships having a length of less than 15 metres;[46]

(b) arrest that does not entail the retention of the ship;[47]

(c) seizure of a ship in execution or satisfaction of a judgment;

(d) arrest securing claims for taxes and duties and other claims arising out of public law provisions or securing the implementation of public decisions.

I.173 Since in the Convention there is no definition of ship, the exclusion under (a) does not seem in conflict with the Convention. Some doubts arise, however, as to whether and in which manner this exclusion applies in respect of ships flying a foreign flag.

I.174 Also the exclusion under (b) is not in conflict with the provisions of the Convention, since the detention of the ship is an essential ingredient of the notion of arrest under the Convention.

I.175 This is the case also for the exclusion under (c), in view of the definition of arrest in the Convention.

I.176 As regards the exclusions under (d), it appears that the very wide description of the authorities that under Article 2 of the Convention may "arrest, detain or otherwise prevent the sailing" of ships may include also tax authorities[48] and, therefore, also the exclusions under (d) are not in conflict with the Convention.

(A) Claims in respect of which a ship may be arrested

I.177 Section 92 of the Code states, in line with the first sentence of Article 2 of the Convention, that a ship may only be arrested to secure a maritime claim.

(B) The individual maritime claims

I.178 The maritime claims enumerated in section 92 of the Act correspond to those of the Convention, except for the addition in subsection (c) of wreck removal to salvage and the exclusion of maritime liens from the scope of subsection (q), where reference is made to "any mortgage on or security in a ship".

I.179 Since normally wreck removal is effected for a public interest, this addition is permitted by Article 2 of the Convention. The exclusion of maritime liens is probably due

---

45. Norway has ratified the Arrest Convention on 1 November 1994 following the ratification of the Lugano Convention on Jurisdiction and the Enforcement of Judgments in Civil and Commercial Matters, article 54a of which requires ratification of the Arrest Convention. See Falkanger, "Arrest of Vessels — The Norwegian Rules based upon the Arrest Convention of 1952", Essays in Honour of Hugo Tiberg, Stockholm 1996, p. 209.

46. Falkanger, "Arrest of Vessels", *supra*, note 45, p. 214.

47. Examples of arrest of this type are given by Falkanger, "Arrest of Vessels", *supra* note 45, pp. 213 and 214.

48. See *infra*, section 15, para. I.274. On the exclusion under s. 91(d) see Falkanger, "Arrest of Vessels", *supra* note 45, p. 214.

to the fact that maritime liens would otherwise be included in the notion of "security", while in Article 1(1)(q) of the Convention reference is specifically made to mortgage or "hypothecation", viz. to registrable charges.

(C) The notion of arrest

I.180 Although in the Code there is no express definition of arrest, the principle that arrest must involve the detention of the ship is implied in the exclusion from the scope of the provisions in chapter 4 of the Code of arrest which does not entail the detention of the ship. The fact that the arrest is a detention "by judicial process" results clearly from the provisions of the Act on Enforcement of Claims.[49]

(D) Ships that may be arrested

I.181 As in Denmark, pursuant to section 93 of the Act the ship in respect of which the maritime claim has arisen may only be arrested if the claim may be enforced on such ship in accordance with the general provisions of the Enforcement of Claim Act, viz. when the ship is owned by the person liable, except for claims secured by maritime liens.[50] The comments made in respect of Danish law[51] apply also for Norway.

(E) Re-arrest and multiple arrest

I.182 The provisions of Article 3(3) of the Convention are reproduced in section 94 of the Act. Multiple arrest does not appear to be expressly regulated by Norwegian law.

(F) Security for damages

I.183 Pursuant to section 14(6) of the Act on Enforcement of Claims the Court may impose on the claimant the provision of security for damages in case of wrongful arrest as a condition for granting the arrest.[52]

I.184 Under Norwegian law in fact the claimant is liable for any loss suffered by the owner of the ship in case the arrest is proved to have been wrongful.[53]

(G) Trading of a ship under arrest

I.185 The provisions of Article 5 of the Convention in respect of the trading of the ship after arrest when the arrest has been effected for the claims enumerated in Article 1(1)(o) and (p) have not been reproduced in the Norwegian Code.[54] However section 95 of the Code provides generally that on application of the claimant the Court may permit the trading of the vessel, either in Norway or abroad, subject to the conditions prescribed by the Court.

---

49. See Falkanger, "Arrest of Vessels", *supra*, note 45, p. 210.
50. See Falkanger, "Arrest of Vessels", *supra*, note 45, p. 217 and 218.
51. See *supra*, para. I.172.
52. Section 14(6) of the Act on Enforcement of Claims. See Falkanger, "Arrest of Vessels", *supra*, note 45, p. 222.
53. Falkanger, "Arrest of Vessels", *supra*, note 45, p. 222.
54. See Falkanger, "Arrest of Vessels", *supra*, note 45, pp. 223 and 224.

(H) Release of the ship from arrest

I.186 There are no provisions in this respect in the Code and the general provisions set out in the Act on Enforcement of Claims apply.[55]

(I) Jurisdiction on the merits of the case

I.187 In Norway the Court of the place where the arrest has been granted has, pursuant to section 31 of the Civil Procedure Act, 1915, jurisdiction on the merits.[56]

SWEDEN

I.188 The Convention has been implemented by enacting in part its provisions in Law 1993:103 on arrest of ships in international legal relations (*Lag 1993:103 om kvarstad på fartyg i internationella rättsförhållanden*) which was subsequently incorporated in chapter 4 of the Swedish Maritime Code. Pursuant to section 1 the provisions of chapter 4 apply to the arrest of ships both of Swedish and foreign nationality except where the claimant has his habitual residence or principal place of business in Sweden and the ship is of Swedish nationality[57]: a provision in line with Article 8(4) of the Convention.

(A) Claims in respect of which a ship may be arrested

I.189 The Convention rule that ships may only be arrested in respect of maritime claims is set out in section 3 of chapter 4.

(B) The individual maritime claims

I.190 The maritime claims enumerated in section 3 of chapter 4 are the same as those enumerated in Article 1(1) of the Convention except for the claim under subparagraph (d). While the wording in the Convention is "agreement relating to the use or hire of any ship whether by charterparty or otherwise", the wording in section 3(4) is simply "demise charter agreement". This different wording, however, has no practical consequence, since, as it will be stated,[58] the word "hire" probably covers only bareboat (or demise) charters.

(C) The notion of arrest

I.191 In chapter 4 of the Code there is no definition of arrest but section 7 provides that a vessel under arrest "shall be prevented from sailing" and this provision is in line with

---

55. See Falkanger, "Arrest of Vessels", *supra*, note 45, pp. 221 and 222.
56. See Falkanger, "Arrest of Vessels", *supra*, note 45, p. 223.
57. In the Swedish reply to Question 2 of the Questionnaire (Annex II) attention is drawn to the fact that in the Swedish Maritime Code edited in Swedish and in English by the Alex Ax:son Johnsons Institut för Sjörätt och Transporträtt, in the English translation of section 1 first sentence the words "or in another country" (ett annat land) are missing after "are or may be adjudicated in Sweden". The first paragraph of section 1 should therefore read:

> The provisions in this chapter apply to arrest of vessels for civil claims which are or may be adjudicated in Sweden *or in another country* in the order prescribed for civil cases or in that prescribed for private claims pursued in criminal cases. The provisions do not, however, apply to arrest for claims concerning taxes and charges levied by the State or a municipality.

58. *Infra*, para. I.333.

the definition in Article 1(2) of the Convention, according to which arrest "means the detention of a ship". Section 2 provides that the general rules on arrest of ships shall apply unless otherwise provided in chapter 4. The rules in question are those set out in chapter 15 of the Code of Judicial Procedure wherein reference is made (sections 1 and 2) to the provisional attachment of property.

(D) Ships that may be arrested

I.192 Section 4 incorporates the provisions of Article 3(1) and (4) of the Convention by providing that the claimant may arrest the ship in respect of which the maritime claim arose or any other ship owned by the person who was the owner of that ship when the claim arose and by providing further that if a person other than the owner is liable the claimant may arrest the ship in respect of which the maritime claim arose or any other ship owned by the person liable. However, as in Denmark, arrest is permissible only if the claim may be enforced on the ship through its forced sale (section 5).[59] As already stated it can hardly be said that such provision is in conflict with the Convention.

(E) Re-arrest and multiple arrest

I.193 Section 6 sets out the same basic rules as Article 3(3) of the Convention except that it does not deal with multiple arrest.

(F) Security for damages

1.194 Section 6 of chapter 15 of the Code of Judicial Procedure provides that no "security measure"[60] may be granted unless the applicant deposits with the Court security for the loss that the opposing party may suffer. This provision is in no way in conflict with the Convention since pursuant to Article 6 all questions relating to liability for wrongful arrest shall be determined by the *lex fori* and this obviously includes also the provision of security for damages.

(G) Trading of a ship under arrest

I.195 Section 7 of chapter 4 incorporates the provision on the trading of the ship while under arrest of Article 5 of the Convention.

(H) Release of the ship from arrest

I.196 Section 8 of chapter 15 of the Code of Judicial Procedure provides that a security measure "shall be cancelled immediately if security satisfying the purpose of the security measure is furnished". This provision is in line with Article 5 of the Convention, the nature and amount of the security being left to the discretion of the Court.[61]

---

59. See the reply of the Danish MLA to Question 7 of the Questionnaire, *infra* Appendix II, p. 255.
60. Chapter 15 of the Code of Judicial Procedure is titled "Provisional attachment and other security measures" and its provisions apply to arrest of property generally (sections 1 and 2), other suitable security measures (section 3) and restoration of possession (section 4).
61. See the Swedish answer to Question 8 of the Questionnaire (Appendix II, p. 266).

UNITED KINGDOM

I.197 The United Kingdom has not given force of law to the Convention,[62] but has given in part effect to it by reproducing some of its provisions, though not literally, firstly in the Administration of Justice Act, 1956 and subsequently in the Supreme Court Act 1981 which has replaced in England the 1956 Act.[63]

I.198 In Scotland arrestment in admiralty is still governed by the provisions of the Administration of Justice Act 1956.[64]

I.199 Reference will, however, be made hereafter only to the Supreme Court Act 1981 (the "Act") and consequently the position that will be considered is that presently existing in England.

I.200 Arrest is available in England whenever an action *in rem* against a ship is available. According to section 20(7) of the Act Admiralty jurisdiction is exercisable in relation to all ships, whether British or not and whether registered or not and wherever the residence or domicile of their owners may be, in relation to all claims enumerated in section 20(2). In order to bring an action *in rem* against the ship in connection with which the claim arises it is necessary to issue an *in rem* claim in Admiralty Form No. ADM1[65] and to effect service thereof in one of the ways prescribed in rule 2.2 of the Practice Direction in Admiralty[66] and to this effect the ship must be within the jurisdiction of the High Court.[67]

(A) Claims in respect of which a ship may be arrested

I.201 The Supreme Court Act 1981 does not enumerate the claims in respect of which a ship may be arrested, but the claims in respect of which the High Court has Admiralty jurisdiction.

62. In *The "Maritime Trader"* [1981] 2 Lloyd's Rep. 153 Sheen J. stated (at p. 156): "Uniformity has not been achieved because Parliament did not enact the Convention." However, in consideration of the fact that the Administration of Justice Act 1956 and subsequently the Supreme Court Act 1981 were passed to give effect to the obligations in international law assumed with the ratification of the Convention, it was held in *The "Eschersheim"* [1976] 2 Lloyd's Rep. 1 that the construction of the Convention rules is relevant in the construction of the domestic rules. Lord Diplock stated (at p. 6):
  As the Act was passed to enable H. M. Government to give effect to the obligations in international law which it would assume on ratifying the convention to which it was a signatory, the rule of statutory construction laid down in *Salomon* v. *Customs and Excise Commissioners* [1966] 2 Lloyd's Rep. 460; [1967] 2 Q.B. 116 and *Post Office* v. *Estuary Radio Ltd.* [1968] 2 Q.B. 740 is applicable. If there be any difference between the language of the statutory provision and that of the corresponding provision of the convention, the statutory language should be construed in the same sense as that of the convention if the words of the statute are reasonably capable of bearing that meaning.
See also Jackson, *Enforcement of Maritime Claims*, 2nd Edition, London 1996, p. 82.
  It would appear, however, that the Arrest Convention has been subsequently incorporated into English municipal law through the 1968 EC Jurisdiction Convention (see *infra*, para. I.593, note 18). If this is correct, the consequence should be that to the extent that the provisions of the Supreme Court Act 1981 are in conflict with the provisions of the Convention the latter should prevail.
63. It has been stated (Jackson, *Enforcement of Maritime Claims, supra*, note 62, p. 21) that the provision in section 20(1)(c) whereby the Admiralty Court has "any other jurisdiction which it had immediately before the commencement of this Act" entails the incorporation of the Administration of Justice Act 1956 into the Act of 1981. It does not appear, however, that this provision has any material effect in so far as the Arrest Convention is concerned.
64. The law is currently under revision as a result of the Report on Diligence on the Dependence and Admiralty Arrestments, produced by the Scottish Law Commission (Scot Law Com. No. 164, 1998).
65. Rule 2.1(1) of the Practice Direction-Admiralty supplementing the Civil Procedure Rules and replacing, with modifications, Order 75 of the Rules of the Supreme Court.
66. See *infra*, para. I.646.
67. Jackson, *Enforcement of Maritime Claims, supra*, note 62, p. 205.

I.202 Arrest is not even mentioned in the Act. Reference to it was made in RSC Order 75 and is now made in the Practice Direction-Admiralty. Rules 6.1 and 6.4(2) so respectively provide:

6.1 Except as provided in this Practice Direction, the Claimant in a claim *in rem* and a judgment creditor in a claim *in rem* is entitled to have the property proceeded against arrested by the Admiralty Court by filing an application to arrest in Admiralty Form No. ADM4 (which shall also contain an undertaking) accompanied by a declaration in Admiralty Form No. ADM5 upon which the Admiralty Court will issue an arrest warrant.

6.4(2) Arrest is effected by service on the property of an arrest warrant in Admiralty Form No. ADM9 in the manner set out in paragraph 2.2(a) or, where it is not reasonably practicable to serve the warrant, by service of a notice of the issue of the warrant in that manner upon the property or by giving notice to those in charge of the property.

I.203 There is, therefore, a fundamental difference in the philosophy of the Act (as in the Administration of Justice Act 1956) and in that of the Convention: while the purpose of the former is to regulate the cases in which the High Court has Admiralty Jurisdiction, and the arrest of the ship against which *in rem* proceedings have been brought is only an interim relief,[68] the purpose of the Convention is to regulate the cases in which the arrest of a ship is permissible and jurisdiction on the merits is only a secondary effect, in certain cases, of the arrest.

I.204 This difference gives rise to a conflict between the Act and the Convention. While under the Convention jurisdiction on the merits is consequential upon the arrest,[69] under the Act jurisdiction is acquired through the service of the writ *in rem*, whether or not it is followed by the arrest of the ship.[70]

I.205 This conflict has not been cured by the decisions on the relationship between the Arrest Convention and the 1968 Civil Jurisdiction Convention[71] pursuant to which for the purposes of Article 57 of the 1968 Convention it is not sufficient that an action *in rem* be brought against the ship, but its arrest is required.[72] In fact this rule applies only in case the defendant is domiciled in a State party to the 1968 Convention, while the rule whereby Admiralty jurisdiction is acquired through the service of a writ *in rem* is of general application.

---

68. Jackson, *Enforcement of Maritime Claims*, *supra*, note 62, p. 300.

69. Article 7(1) of the Convention provides that the Courts of the country in which the arrest was made shall have jurisdiction to determine the case upon its merits if the domestic law of such country gives jurisdiction to such Courts or, in any event, in any of the cases subsequently enumerated.

70. Section 20(1) of the Act so provides:

20.(1) The Admiralty jurisdiction of the High Court shall be as follows, that is to say:
(a) jurisdiction to hear and determine any of the questions and claims mentioned in subsection (2);
(b) jurisdiction in relation to any of the proceedings mentioned in subsection (3);
(c) any other Admiralty jurisdiction which it had immediately before the commencement of this Act; and
(d) any jurisdiction connected with ships or aircraft which is vested in the High Court apart from this section and is for the time being by rules of court made or coming into force after the commencement of this Act assigned to the Queen's Bench Division and directed by the rules to be exercised by the Admiralty Court.

In South Africa instead the action *in rem* is instituted by the arrest of the relevant property (section 3(5) of the Admiralty Jurisdiction Act 105 of 1983).

71. *The "Deichland"* [1989] 2 Lloyd's Rep. 113 (C.A.); *The "Prinsengacht"* [1993] 1 Lloyd's Rep. 41; *The "Anna H"* [1995] 1 Lloyd's Rep. 11 (C.A.).

72. Jackson (*Enforcement of Maritime Claims*, *supra*, note 62, p. 307) is of the view that following the ratification by the United Kingdom of the 1968 Convention on jurisdiction and the enforcement of judgments in civil and commercial matters, as amended and of the 1988 Lugano Convention and the Civil Jurisdiction and Judgment Act 1982, jurisdiction depends on arrest.

(B) The individual claims in respect of which arrest is permitted

I.206 "Maritime claims" is not a term of art in English law and, therefore, in order to make a comparison between the claims for which arrest is permitted under the Act and the Convention maritime claims reference must be made to the claims in respect of which an action *in rem* may be brought.

I.207 These claims are indicated in section 21 of the Act which so provides in its relevant part:

21.   (1) Subject to section 22, an action *in personam* may be brought in the High Court in all cases within the Admiralty jurisdiction of that court.

(2) In the case of any such claim as is mentioned in section 20(2)(a), (c) or (s) or any such question as is mentioned in section 20(2)(b), an action *in rem* may be brought in the High Court against the ship, or property in connection with which the claim or question arises.

(3) In any case in which there is a maritime lien or other charge on any ship, aircraft or other property for the amount claimed, an action *in rem* may be brought in the High Court against that ship, aircraft or property.

(4) In the case of any such claim as is mentioned in section 20(2)(e) to (r), where:
    (a) the claim arises in connection with a ship; and
    (b) the person who would be liable on the claim in an action *in personam* ("the relevant person") was, when the cause of action arose, the owner or charterer of, or in possession or in control of, the ship,
an action *in rem* may (whether or not the claim gives rise to maritime lien on that ship) be brought in the High Court against:
    (i) that ship, if at the time when the action is brought the relevant person is either the beneficial owner of that ship as respects all the shares in it or the charterer of it under a charter by demise; or
    (ii) any other ship of which, at the time when the action is brought, the relevant person is the beneficial owner as respects all the shares in it.

I.208 Two categories of claims are mentioned in this provision: (i) the "questions and claims" enumerated in section 20(2) except one, and (ii) the claims secured by a maritime lien "or other charge".

(i) Questions and claims referred to in subsection (1)(a)

I.209 The questions and claims enumerated in section 1(2), are the following[73]:

    (a) any claim to the possession or ownership of a ship or to the ownership of any share therein;

This claim corresponds to that under Article 1(1)(o) of the Convention except that in the Convention no reference is made to possession. As it will be stated,[74] the wording of the Convention claim is definitely unsatisfactory and it may be said that the Act has cured an omission of some importance, even if it can hardly be said that the difference in the text is only a matter of interpretation.

    (b) any question arising between the co-owners of a ship as to possession, employment or earnings of that ship;

---

73. For an analysis of all such questions and claims see Jackson, *Enforcement of Maritime Claims, supra*, note 62, p. 45.
74. *Infra*, para. I.377–380.

I.210 This claim corresponds to that under Article 1(1)(p) of the Convention.

(c) any claim in respect of a mortgage of or charge on a ship or any share therein;

I.211 This claim corresponds to that under Article 1(1)(q) of the Convention, except that the word "hypothecation" has been replaced by "charge". In *The "St. Merriel"*[75] and in *The "Acrux"*[76] the word "charge" has been construed to mean a charge in the nature of a mortgage and it is worth mentioning that in the case of *The "Acrux"* the charge was an Italian "hypothèque". This construction is now supported by the addition in the 1999 Arrest Convention of the word "or other charge of the same nature" to "mortgage or hypothèque".

(d) any claim for damage received by a ship;

I.212 Reference to this kind of claim does not create any conflict with the Convention, because no action *in rem* may be brought in respect of this claim.[77]

(e) any claim for damage done by a ship;

I.213 This claim corresponds to that under Article 1(1)(a) of the Convention. The difference in wording (in the Convention reference is made to "damage by any ship in collision or otherwise") does not entail any difference in substance.

(f) any claim for loss of life or personal injury sustained in consequence of any defect in a ship or in her apparel or equipment, or in consequence of the wrongful act, neglect or default of:
   (i) the owners, charterers or persons in possession or control of a ship; or
   (ii) the master or crew of a ship, or any person for whose wrongful acts, neglects or defaults the owners, charterers or persons in possession or control of a ship are responsible,
being an act, neglect or default in the navigation or management of the ship, in the loading, carriage or discharge of goods on, in or from the ship, or in the embarkation, carriage or disembarkation of persons on, in or from the ship;

I.214 The description of this head of claim is much more detailed than that in Article 1(1)(b) of the Convention, where the loss of life or personal injury must either be caused by a ship or occur in connection with its operation.[78]

I.215 The words "caused by a ship" have been replaced by "in consequence of any defect in a ship or in her apparel or equipment". Although the wording of the Act is more restricted, it does not appear that in practice there is a difference in substance, because a claim in order to be successful must be related to a defect in the ship. Nor should the burden of proof be more difficult to meet, since it suffices for the claimant to allege that the event has been caused by a defect.

---

75. [1963] 1 All. E.R. 537.
76. [1965] 1 Lloyd's Rep. 565.
77. Section 21 of the Act sets out in subsections (2), (3) and (4) the claims in respect of which an action *in rem* may be brought in the High Court. Reference is made therein to all claims enumerated in section 20(2) except that under (d). On such claim see Jackson, *Enforcement of Maritime Claims, supra,* note 62, p. 21.
78. For a comment on this claim and a comparison with the corresponding claim under the Convention see Jackson, *Enforcement of Maritime Claims, supra,* note 62, p. 55.

I.216 The words "in connexion with the operation of the ship" have been replaced by a very detailed description of the event both from the subjective and the objective point of view. It is possible that the general description used in the Convention may cover some events that are not included in the description adopted in the Act.[79]

(g) any claim for loss of or damage to goods carried in a ship;

I.217 This claim corresponds to that under Article 1(1)(f). Section 24(1) of the Act provides in fact that the word "goods" includes baggage.

(h) any claim arising out of any agreement relating to the carriage of goods in a ship or to the use or hire of a ship;

I.218 Under this head of claim there are amalgamated the claims enumerated in Article 1(1)(d) and (e) of the Convention. The first part ("any agreement relating to the carriage of goods in a ship") corresponds to Article 1(1)(e) the words "any agreement" replacing the words "whether by charter party or otherwise". The second part ("the use or hire of a ship") corresponds to Article 1(1)(d) except that the words "whether by charter party or otherwise" have been omitted, but this does not change in any way the meaning of the phrase.

(j) any claim:
  (i) under the Salvage Convention 1989;
  (ii) under any contract for or in relation to salvage services; or
  (iii) in the nature of salvage not falling within (i) or (ii) above;
      or any corresponding claim in connection with an aircraft;

I.219 The corresponding provision of the Convention, in Article 1(1)(c), is much more concise since only salvage is mentioned. The reference to any claim under the 1989 Salvage Convention widens the scope of this head of claim, since it includes the special compensation of Article 14. The difference between the Convention and the Act would increase if the view taken in England in respect of the claims coming under section 1(1)(j) of the Administration of Justice Act 1956, where reference was made to "any claim in the nature of salvage", according to which claims for damages of the owner of the salved vessel against a negligent salvor[80] and claims of the salvor against the owner of the salved ship[81] fall outside the term "salvage", were still upheld. This view may well have been acceptable under the 1956 Act given the reference therein to claims *in the nature* of salvage, but would not be applicable in respect of the Convention, where reference is simply made to claims arising out of salvage, nor could it be applicable in respect of the Supreme Court Act as amended, for reference to claims "in the nature of salvage" is made therein in addition to claims under the 1989 Salvage Convention and under any contract for or in relation to salvage services.

I.220 Reference to aircraft is beyond the scope of the Convention but not in conflict with it.

(k) any claim in the nature of towage in respect of a ship or an aircraft;

79. See *infra*, the comment on Article 1(1)(b) of the Convention, in para. I.322.
80. The *"Jade"* [1974] 2 Lloyd's Rep. 188; [1976] 1 Lloyd's Rep. 81 (C.A.).
81. The *"Tesaba"* [1982] 1 Lloyd's Rep. 397. See the comments on this decision and on those relating to *The "Jade"* by Jackson, *Enforcement of Maritime Claims, supra*, note 62, p. 65.

I.221 Also in this case, the difference between the Act and the Convention Article 1(1)(i) is the addition in the Act of the words "in the nature of" which, as has been seen in respect of salvage, might restrict the scope of the claim.

   (l)   any claim in the nature of pilotage in respect of a ship or an aircraft;

I.222 The same comment applies here.

   (m) any claim in respect of goods or materials supplied to a ship for her operation or maintenance;

I.223 This claim corresponds to that under Article 1(1)(k) of the Convention except that in the Convention all claims enumerated in Article 1(1) are stated to be claims "arising out of" each individual head, while in the Act the words "in respect of" are used. The question arises whether these words should be given the narrow construction of the words "relating to"[82] or the wide construction of the words "arising out of".[83]

   (n)   any claim in respect of the construction, repair or equipment of a ship or in respect of dock charges or dues;

I.224 This claim corresponds to that under Article 1(1)(l) of the Convention except for the words "in respect of".

   (o)   any claim by a master or member of the crew of a ship for wages (including any sum allotted out of wages or adjudged by a superintendent to be due by way of wages);

I.225 Except for the words in brackets, this claim corresponds to that under Article 1(1)(m) of the Convention.

   (p)   any claim by a master, shipper, charterer or agent in respect of disbursements made on account of a ship;

I.226 The substance of this claim corresponds to that under Article 1(1)(n) of the Convention.

   (q)   any claim arising out of an act which is or is claimed to be a general average act;

I.227 Also in this case, as in several previous cases, the wording of the Act is more detailed than that of the Convention where in Article 1(1)(g) reference is simply made to general average. The words "an act which is or is claimed to be a general average act" seem to be redundant. In fact in all cases the mere allegation of a claim suffices.

   (r)   any claim arising out of bottomry;

I.228 This claim corresponds to that under Article 1(1)(h) of the Convention. It is worthwhile noting that here the words "arising out of" are used.

   (s)   any claim for the forfeiture or condemnation of a ship or of goods which are being or have been carried, or have been attempted to be carried, in a ship or

---

82. See *infra*, para. I.339 and I.340.
83. See *infra*, para. I.313–I.316.

for the restoration of a ship or any such goods after seizure, or for droits of Admiralty.

I.229 This head of claim has no corresponding head in the Convention, but seems to be permitted by Article 2 of the Convention.

(ii) Claims secured by a maritime lien or other charge

I.230 Section 21(3) by providing that an action *in rem* may be brought in any case in which there is a maritime lien does not add any new claim to those already considered. In fact all claims to which a maritime lien attaches are mentioned in section 21(2), with one insignificant exception: *respondentia*.

    (a) Bottomry is mentioned in subsection 2(r);

    (b) Damage caused by a ship is mentioned in subsection 2(e);

    (c) Salvage is mentioned in subsection 2(j)[84];

    (d) Seamen's wages are mentioned in subsection 2(o) where, however, reference is made to members of the crew. The view has been expressed[85] that the expression "members of the crew", which corresponds to that used in the Convention where reference is made to the crew, may be a narrower concept than "seamen", in which event the right of arrest would be granted to persons to whom it is not granted under the Convention. This opinion is clearly correct, since "seamen" indicates a category of workmen and a person is a seaman whether or not he is at any given time embarked on a ship, thus becoming a member of the crew of the ship on which he is embarked. A claim for wages may arise also when a seaman is not embarked on board a ship and, therefore, is not a member of a crew. Seamen in fact are nowadays frequently employed on a continuous basis and earn a salary even if they are temporarily ashore. If, however, a seaman earns a salary while ashore, one ingredient would be lacking for the arrest of a ship, since the claim would not arise in connection with a ship.

    (e) Master's wages and disbursements are mentioned in subparagraphs 2(o) and (p) respectively.

(C) The notion of arrest

I.231 There is no statutory definition of arrest in English law. The fact, however, that arrest implies the detention of a ship by judicial process results from rule 6.4(3) of the Practice Direction-Admiralty which so provides:

Property under arrest may not be moved without an order of the Admiralty Court and the property may be immobilised or otherwise prevented from sailing in such a manner as the Marshal or his substitute may decide is appropriate.

(D) Ships that may be arrested

I.232 A distinction is made in the Act between three types of claims:

    (i) Claims for which a ship may be arrested in consideration of the character of the claim.

---

84. Jackson (*Enforcement of Maritime Claims, supra*, note 62, p. 64–66) states that the claims mentioned in section 21(2)(j) cover an area which is wider than that in respect of which a maritime lien is granted.

85. Jackson, *Enforcement of Maritime Claims, supra*, note 62, p. 69.

I.233 These are the claims to the possession or ownership of a ship or to the ownership of any share therein (section 20(2)(a)), the claims in respect of a mortgage of or charge on a ship or any share therein (section 20(2)(c)), the questions arising between co-owners of a ship as to possession, employment or earnings of that ship (section 20(2)(b)) and the claims for the forfeiture or condemnation of a ship (section 20(2)(s)).

I.234 In respect of the first three heads of claim (the fourth is not considered by the Convention) no specific relationship between the person or persons against whom the claim is made or the question is raised and the ship is required other than that which results from the nature of the claim. No provision is made in this respect by the Convention. In any event the provisions of the Act are not in conflict with the underlying principles of the Convention.

(ii) Claims secured by a maritime lien.

I.235 Also in this case no particular relationship between the person liable and the ship is required under the Act and no special provision is made in the Convention in respect of such claims other than that of Article 9.[86] It is thought that the rule laid down in the Act is in line with the principles of the Convention,[87] in view also of the fact that pursuant to Article 9 of the Convention the proper law governing maritime liens is the *lex fori* where the 1926 MLM Convention is not applicable.

(iii) All other claims.

I.236 In respect of all other claims, enumerated in section 20(2) (d), (g), (h), (k), (l), (m), (n) and (q), the fundamental requisite is that the claim arises in connection with a ship. Reference is then made to the time when the cause of action has arisen and to the time when the action is brought: at the time when the cause of action has arisen the person liable (identified as the person who would be liable on the claim in an action *in personam*) must be the owner or charterer of, or in possession or in control of, the ship; at the time when the action is brought the person liable must be either the beneficial owner of that ship or the charterer of it under a charter by demise. English law, therefore, requires an objective and subjective connection with the ship at the time when the claim arises: the claim must be in connection with the ship against which the action *in rem* is brought and the person liable must be either the owner or a person who has the power to use the ship. The first requisite is also mentioned in Article 3(1) of the Convention; the second is not mentioned but is generally implied.[88]

I.237 As regards the time when the action is brought, the provisions of the Act are more restrictive than those of the Convention or, more precisely, ignore the last sentence of Article 3(4) which, as it will be stated,[89] is very difficult to understand.

I.238 In the Convention no indication is made about the time when either of the aforesaid relationships (ownership or charter by demise) must exist but it is thought that the relevant time is that when the arrest is effected. In the Act the relevant time is that when the action *in rem* is brought: a time, therefore, which precedes that of the arrest.

86. See *infra*, para. I.394–I.398.
87. See *infra*, para. I.392–I.406.
88. See *infra*, para. I.393.
89. See *infra*, para. I.502–I.523.

I.239 The answer to the question whether the provisions of the Act are in line with those of the Convention depends on the construction of the Convention which, as it will be stated[90] is certainly not easy.

I.240 As regards arrest of sisterships, section 21(4) provides that arrest is permitted of any other ship of which, at the time when the action is brought, the person liable is the beneficial owner as respects all shares in it. Two questions arise when comparing this provision with that in Article 3(1) of the Convention. The first concerns the notions of owner and of beneficial owner.

I.241 As it will be stated the notion of ownership in the Convention includes situations which in England would be qualified as beneficial ownership except probably the trust, which is not known in civil law countries.[91] The use of the expression "beneficial owner" does not seem therefore to create any material difference between English law and the Convention. The second question concerns the time when the (beneficial) ownership must be established. Although nothing is said in this respect in the Convention, it is thought that the relevant time is that of the arrest, while under the Act the relevant time is that when the action *in rem* is brought.

(E) Re-arrest and multiple arrest

I.242 Re-arrest is not mentioned in the Act but reference to it is now made in the Practice Direction-Admiralty. Rule 6.7(3) so provides:

Where in relation to a claim *in rem* security has been provided to obtain the release of property under arrest or to prevent the arrest of property the Admiralty Court may at any stage:

    (a) order that the amount of security be reduced, and may stay the claim pending compliance with such order;

    (b) order that the Claimant be permitted to arrest or re-arrest the property proceeded against for the purposes of obtaining further security, provided that the total security provided shall not exceed the value of the property at the time of the original arrest or at the time security was first given if the property was not arrested.

I.243 The need for further security[92] is certainly a "good cause", according to the language of the Convention, for the granting of the arrest or re-arrest.

I.244 Multiple arrest, which is permitted under Article 3(3) of the Convention in the same situations in which re-arrest is permitted, is instead expressly prohibited by section 21(8) of the Act which so provides:

Where, as regards any such claim as is mentioned in section 20(2)(e) to (r), a ship has been served with a writ or arrested in an action *in rem* brought to enforce that claim, no other ship may be served with a writ or arrested in that or any other action *in rem* brought to enforce that claim; but this subsection does not prevent the issue, in respect of any one such claim, of a writ naming more than one ship or of two or more writs each naming a different ship.

---

90. See *infra*, para. I.502–I.523.

91. On the notion of ownership and beneficial ownership in English law see Jackson, *Enforcement of Maritime Claims*, *supra*, note 62, pp. 198 and 199.

92. The situation where the amount of the claim subsequently appears greater than the security originally obtained was the example mentioned in the previous editions of this book: 1st edition, p. 107; 2nd edition, pp. 88 and 89. Such situation is now expressly mentioned in Article 5(1)(a) of the 1999 Convention (see *infra*, Book II, para. II.140–146), the text of which is very similar to that of rule 6.7(3) of the Practice Direction-Admiralty.

(F) Security for damages

I.245 Security for damages caused by a wrongful arrest is not mentioned in the Act or in the Practice Direction-Admiralty. The payment by the claimant of damages in favour of the owner or other person having an interest in the ship is, however, regulated by rule 6.3(3) of the Practice Direction for the case of arrest notwithstanding that a caveat against arrest has been filed.[93]

(G) Trading of a ship under arrest

I.246 No provision is made in this respect except that rule 6.4(3) of the Practice Direction-Admiralty by stating that the property under arrest may not be moved without an order of the Admiralty Court impliedly permits the Court to give such an order.

(H) Release of the ship from arrest

I.247 Article 5 of the Convention provides that the Court or other appropriate judicial authority shall permit the release of the ship upon sufficient bail or other security being furnished. Rule 6.6(1) of the Practice Direction-Admiralty provides that property will be released from arrest, *inter alia*, if the Admiralty Court orders release upon application made by any party. Although there is no express provision to the effect that the owner of the ship or any other party having an interest in it is entitled to obtain release by providing adequate security, this is implied in several provisions of the Practice Direction, such as rule 6.2(4) according to which the declaration to be filed in Admiralty Form No. ADM5 must contain, in every case, the amount of the security sought, if any and rule 6.7(3) wherein reference is made to the security provided to obtain the release of property under arrest and it is stated that the Admiralty Court may either order the amount of security to be reduced or that the claimant be permitted to arrest or re-arrest for the purposes of obtaining further security.

(I) Jurisdiction on the merits of the case

I.248 The jurisdiction of the High Court to determine the claims on the merits is, under the Act, the precondition for the commencement of an action *in rem* which, in turn, is the condition for the arrest of the property against which such action is brought. There is, therefore, a fundamental difference between English law and civil law, according to which the Court of the place where arrest is effected has always jurisdiction to grant the arrest, irrespective of its jurisdiction on the merits of the case.[94] This gap has been partly filled by section 26 of the Civil Jurisdiction and Judgment Act 1982, which so provides:

---

93. Rule 6.3(3) so provides:
   Property may be arrested notwithstanding that a caveat against arrest has been filed, but in such a case the Admiralty Court may if it considers that it is appropriate to do so, order that the arrest be discharged and that the party procuring the arrest do pay compensation to the owner of or other persons interested in the property arrested.
94. For a critical analysis of the English approach see Jackson, *Enforcement of Maritime Claims*, *supra*, note 62, p. 320. Professor Jackson raises the question whether an English Court could continue or allow an arrest after having declined jurisdiction on the merits and states that this problem has in part been cured by judicial creativity and is now in great part overcome by the Civil Jurisdiction and Judgment Act 1982, section 26 and possibly by the combined operation of the Brussels, Lugano and Arrest Convention.

26. (1) Where in England and Wales or Northern Ireland a court stays or dismisses Admiralty proceedings on the ground that the dispute in question should be submitted to arbitration or to the determination of the courts of another part of the United Kingdom or of an overseas country, the court may if in those proceedings property has been arrested or bail or other security has been given to prevent or obtain release from arrest:

    (a) order that the property arrested be retained as security for the satisfaction of any award or judgment which:

        (i) is given in respect of the dispute in the arbitration or legal proceedings in favour of which those proceedings are stayed or dismissed; and

        (ii) is enforceable in England and Wales or, as the case may be, in Northern Ireland; or

    (b) order that the stay or dismissal of those proceedings be conditional on the provision of equivalent security for the satisfaction of any such award or judgment.

(2) Where a court makes an order under subsection (1), it may attach such conditions to the order as it thinks fit, in particular conditions with respect to the institution or prosecution of the relevant arbitration or legal proceedings.

(3) Subject to any provisions made by rules of court and to any necessary modifications, the same law and practice shall apply in relation to property retained in pursuance of an order made by a court under subsection (1) as would apply if it were held for the purposes of proceedings in that court.

I.249 This provision is in line with Article 7(2) and (3) of the Convention except that pursuant to it the commencement of Admiralty proceedings seems to be a condition precedent for the issuance of an order thereunder. Probably the reason for this is that, as previously stated, a warrant of arrest cannot be issued if an action *in rem* has not been brought in the High Court.

CHAPTER 4

The Notion and Purpose of Arrest and Claims in Respect of which a Ship may be Arrested

13. THE NOTION OF ARREST

I.250 Article 1(2) gives the following definition of arrest:

"Arrest" means the detention of a ship by judicial process to secure a maritime claim, but does not include the seizure of a ship in execution or satisfaction of a judgment.

I.251 In the draft approved by the CMI Conference at Naples the definition of arrest was as follows: " 'Arrest' shall mean an arrest made to secure a claim."

I.252 However, while in the English title of the draft Convention the words "arrest of seagoing ships" were used, in the French title reference was made to the *saisie conservatoire de navires de mer* and it was clearly intended that the Convention should be confined to the arrest as a conservative measure.[1]

I.253 At the Diplomatic Conference the UK delegation[2] suggested that the word "arrest" (*saisie*) should be defined with greater precision by the Drafting Committee. The French delegation was of the view that that was not necessary.[3]

---

1. Mr J. T. Asser, one of the authors of the questionnaire circulated to the national associations prior to the CMI Naples Conference, stated in his report (CMI Bulletin No. 104, p. 534; *Travaux Préparatoires*, p. 248):

> However, if you permit, I should like to state briefly certain questions which, in the opinion of Mr. Miller and myself, deserve special consideration. In the first place we would suggest that, at least for the present, unification be limited to the provisional arrest, "*saisie conservatoire*", of ships and that questions pertaining to attachment, "*saisie exécutoire*", be left out.

Mr Cyril Miller, the second author of the questionnaire, in turn stated (CMI Bulletin No. 104, p. 535; *Travaux Préparatoires*, p. 248 and 249):

> I particularly want to endorse what Mr. Asser has said: that whatever we do about this subject we should confine ourselves to recommendations and deliberations upon the unification of the law relating to what we in England call "arrest" and what in the continental system is called "*saisie conservatoire*". We should not, I think, make any recommendations with regard to the other form of "*saisie*" ("*saisie exécutoire*"), which we in England call "attachment", because to do that would be to make recommendations upon a matter which is purely one of procedure, and it is quite impossible to attempt and indeed undesirable to unify the law of procedure. One has only to reflect that a procedure which is familiar and has been familiar to a French Court for centuries could not possibly be applied by a British Court because it would be completely contrary to the procedure of that court in which we British lawyers are all trained, whereas with regard to substantive law, this can be changed, although I do not say it can be done easily. That is what the Comité Maritime is for. It can be changed without alteration in the procedure of the Court. That is why I endorse what Mr. Asser has said. We would confine ourselves to "*saisie conservatoire*".

2. *Procès-verbaux*, p. 64; *Travaux Préparatoires*, p. 298.

3. The French Delegate, Mr de Grandmaison, stated (*Procès-verbaux*, p. 69; *Travaux Préparatoires*, p. 298):

> 6. With respect to the definition of the word "arrest" the French Delegation is of the view that it is not necessary to modify it, at least insofar as the French text is concerned. The draft convention concerns the conservative arrest of ships, and that excludes the other (types of) arrests considered by French law, such as the "*saisie exécution*" and the "*saisie arrêt*". If in the Convention only the term "*saisie*" (arrest) is used,

61

I.254 The Drafting Committee was then appointed under the chairmanship of Mr de Grandmaison and the definition of arrest was amended as now appears in Article 1(2). The purpose of the addition was to make the definition of arrest clearer by excluding from the scope of the Convention other types of attachment of a ship, which are available after an enforceable judgment is obtained. The substantial difference between arrest covered by the Convention and seizure excluded from its scope is that the former is a security measure which is requested before the claim is the subject of an assessment on its merits by a court. Its purpose is to preserve the security until a judgment on the merits is obtained and can be enforced; consequently, an alternative security may replace that of the ship herself. The seizure, on the other hand, is a manner of enforcing a judgment and satisfying the claim out of the proceeds of sale. In this event the assets of the debtor, including the ship or ships owned by him, are all liable to seizure irrespective of the nature of the claim, whether maritime or not.

I.255 The purpose of the definition is to exclude from the scope of the Convention all enforcement proceedings, irrespective as to whether the seizure of a ship is effected on the basis of a judgment or any other order issued by a Court. In this connection reference can be made to the definition of judgment in the 1968 Convention on Jurisdiction and the Enforcement of Judgments in Civil and Commercial Matters as well as in the 1988 Lugano Convention. Article 25 of both such Conventions provides as follows:

For the purposes of this Convention, "judgment" means any judgment given by a court or tribunal of a Contracting State, whatever the judgment may be called, including a decree, order, decision or writ of execution, as well as the determination of costs or expenses by an officer of the court.

I.256 Summary judgments and injunctions or similar orders issued in summary proceedings are, therefore, included in the notion of "judgment" for the purposes of Article 1(2) of the Arrest Convention.[4]

I.257 There are, however, other documents that may entitle a claimant to seize and sell a ship in a forced sale that cannot come under the notion of "judgment" however wide. These are, for example, in certain jurisdictions the promissory notes and the acknowledgments of debt made in the form of a notarial deed. Since the definition of "arrest" should be given a purposive rather than a literal interpretation it is thought that also a seizure effected on the basis of such document is outside the scope of the Arrest Convention because its purpose is not "to secure a maritime claim", but to obtain payment of a claim through the forced sale of a ship.

I.258 The definition of arrest is not, however, wholly satisfactory because in the legal systems where a distinction is drawn between arrest as a conservative measure and the arrest of property the title to or possession of which is in dispute,[5] the definition only

without adding thereto "*conservatoire*" (conservative) this is simply in order to lighten the text of the Convention. The definition given in Art. 1 does not allow any doubt as to the meaning of the word "*saisie*" (arrest). This is the "*saisie conservatoire*" (conservative arrest). If, however, the Assembly wants a more complete definition, the drafting Committee will have to take care of that.

4. In the Netherlands the president of the Arrondissementsrechtbank of Middelburg held with decision of 30 January 1992 in the case of *The "Kananga"* [1992] Schips en Schade 99, that a decision in a "Kort geding" procedure (corresponding to the French procedure "en référé") even if of a provisional character is an enforceable decision and, therefore, is excluded from the scope of the 1952 Arrest Convention.

5. This is the case, for example, in Italy, where a distinction is drawn between "conservative" arrest (*sequestro conservativo*) and "judicial" arrest (*sequestro giudiziario*). This latter type of arrest applies to cases where title to or possession of a property is in dispute and the arrest is subject to different rules.

In France the arrest in the aforesaid situations has been qualified as *saisie revendication* by Professor Chauveau who stated (*Traité de Droit Maritime* (Paris, 1958), p. 164):

applies to the first type of arrest. Among the "maritime claims" enumerated in Article 1(1) there are, in fact, included, in subparagraphs (o) and (p), disputes as to title and possession which, under the legal systems referred to above, are not, strictly speaking, "claims".[6] Similarly, the fact that in the French title of the Convention the words *saisie conservatoire* are used may create some uncertainty, even though in France the arrest of property when title or possession is in dispute is considered as a "conservative" measure in a wide sense.

I.259 The reference in the definition of arrest to the types of claim the arrest is intended to secure does not entirely exclude from the scope of the Convention arrest the purpose of which is to secure claims of a nature other than the maritime claims as defined in Article 1(1). In fact, when in Article 2 it is stated that a ship cannot be arrested in respect of other claims, the notion of arrest is necessarily wider and includes "the detention of a ship by judicial process", as the arrest is defined in Article 1(2) as a "conservative" measure generally. However, it does not include the detention of a ship by judicial process when such process is of a criminal, as opposed to a civil, nature.

I.260 The arrest of a ship ordered by a criminal court in connection with any type of crime (e.g. smuggling) is excluded from the scope of the Convention.[7]

If the right alleged is a property right (letters (o) and (p) of the Convention), the arrest acquires the nature of a "*saisie revendication*" and for that reason is subject to some particular rules.

It is probably more likely that the arrestor would first arrest the ship pursuant to the rules on "conservative" arrest—either uniform or domestic—and then request the recognition of his title to the vessel in the proceedings on the merits.

6. The Italian association made the following comments in its Report on the 1951 Draft (CMI Bulletin No. 105, pp. 67 and 68; *Travaux Préparatoires*, p. 276):

"Maritime claim"—states Art. 1 para. 1—means a claim arising out of one or more of the causes subsequently set out. The list of such causes, being sixteen in number (a–p) follows; but only thirteen or possibly fourteen consist of proper claims of the claimant whilst certainly two, namely those listed under (d) and (e) and maybe sometimes also that under (g), cannot be qualified as claims, but rather as possessory or property rights. In fact, there is no doubt that such are the disputes relating to the title to or property of a ship, and the disputes between co-owner of a ship in respect of the property or possession thereof, its operation or employment; such may be — in respect of possession — the disputes relating to the employment or affreightment of a ship.

And even if the English term "claim", which does not find an exact equivalent in Italian, lends itself to include also the disputes of the kind we have just referred to, its translation in French with the words "*créance maritime*" already stressed the lack of precision of the terminology.

In fact, in Italian law the disputes relating to the property or possession of movables or immovables do not create—that which is correct—credit rights, and that is the reason why such disputes cannot give rise to a conservative arrest, but to a different arrest, the judicial arrest.

In fact, there cannot be any doubt that the release of the arrest following a security cannot be accepted unless in respect of a conservative arrest.

The different nature of the arrest as security for a claim and as a means of detention of a property when title or possession are in dispute was recognised when, following the proposal of the Italian delegation, the release of the ship after the provision of security was excluded in respect of the "claims" enumerated in subparagraphs (d) and (e), now subparagraphs (o) and (p). See *infra*, section 20.

7. For example, in French law, a ship may be arrested by the customs authority when she has carried contraband. The provisions on such type of arrest in Arts. 324(1)(a), 326, 378 and 414 of the Code des Douanes have been held by the Cour d'Appel of Aix-en-Provence, in its judgment of 11 June 1974 in *Banque Maritime Turque* v. *Administration des Douanes* ([1975] D.M.F. 602) to give rise to the right of sale of the ship in accordance with the procedure set out in Art. 389 of such Code, which is independent from that of the Decree of 27 October 1967. See also du Pontavice, *Le Statut des Navires* (Paris, 1976), p. 322.

In Italy there are two kinds of criminal arrest. The first is the arrest of properties with which a crime has been committed, e.g. the ship in the case of contraband goods carried on board. The second is a "conservative" arrest, the main features of which are similar to those of civil arrest. Art. 189 of the criminal code provides that the assets of a person accused of a crime may be attached as security *inter alia* for fines, costs and damages due to the victims.

I.261 The arrest, as conceived and regulated by the Convention, is a judicial remedy. Article 1(2) refers, in fact, to the detention of a ship "by judicial process", and Article 4 provides that a ship "may only be arrested under the authority of a Court or of the appropriate judicial authority of the Contracting State in which the arrest is made". Thus, no ship flying the flag of a Contracting State may be arrested in another Contracting State, other than pursuant to an order of a court, or of the "appropriate judicial authority" of that State. In other Conventions, reference is made only to "a court".[8] The addition in this Convention of the words "or of the appropriate judicial authority" has been made with a view to including judicial authorities which may not qualify as "courts".[9] However, the words used are not entirely correct, for the court is also a judicial authority, and is the most typical judicial authority. The French text is more appropriate, and uses the words "*toute autre autorité judiciaire compétente*". It is to be noted that "appropriate" and competent do not have the same meaning.

I.262 The authority by which the arrest must be granted is a "judicial" authority, and therefore in a Contracting State ships flying the flag of another Contracting State may not be arrested pursuant to an order of an administrative authority, except in the cases mentioned in Article 2.

I.263 It is worth noting that if the word "judicial" had been omitted, as in the 1976 LLMC Convention (Article 11), the arrest by an administrative authority (such as the harbour master) would have been permissible.

14. THE PURPOSE OF THE ARREST

I.264 Originally, the purpose of the arrest, in the draft prepared by Leopold Dor and approved by the International Committee in 1933, was only to secure the payment of the claim of the arrestor. The notion and the purpose of the arrest were those prevailing in civil

---

8. See, for example, the 1952 Civil Jurisdiction Convention, Art. 1; the 1962 Nuclear Ships Convention, Art. X; the 1967 Convention on Maritime Liens and Mortgages Art. 11; the 1969 Civil Liability Convention, Arts. 9 and 10; the 1974 Athens Convention, Art. 17; the Hamburg Rules, Art. 21. In the 1993 Convention on Maritime Liens and Mortgages the word "court" was replaced by "competent authority".

9. This was the case, for example, in England, where the warrant of arrest, pursuant to Ord. 75, r. 5 was issued by the plaintiff and took effect upon its being stamped by an officer of the registry or district registry. In *The "Varna"* [1993] 2 Lloyd's Rep. 253 Scott L.J. stated (at p. 258):

Without carrying the analogy too far, the position under O. 75, r. 5 (post 1986) seems to me to be at least comparable. If the statutory requirements set out in r. 5 are complied with, if the requisite affidavit is filed complying with par. (9), a plaintiff is, in my opinion, entitled under r. 5 to issue a warrant of arrest. The warrant does not take effect, until the stamp is placed thereon in accordance with par. (8). The function of the stamping officer is, it seems to me, to ensure that the requirements of r. 5 have been complied with. If the requirements have not been complied with, the warrant will not be stamped.

The rules of practice then in force in England were taken into consideration when the reference in the first draft prepared by Léopold Dor in May 1933 to the "*autorisation du juge*" was replaced in the second draft submitted to the CMI 1933 Oslo Conference by "*autorisation de justice*". In his report (CMI Bulletin No. 96, p. 184; *Travaux Préparatoires*, p. 239) Dor stated:

However, it has been provided that the arrest can be effected on the basis of a judicial authorization, and not only on the basis of the authorization of the court.

This slight modification has been made in order to take into account the observation of Mr. Antoine Franck, who drew the attention to the fact that in certain countries, namely in England, the right of arrest may be granted by certain court officers, such as the Registrar, who are not strictly speaking judges.

At present, however, pursuant to the Practice Direction-Admiralty the arrest warrant is issued by the Admiralty Court on form no. ADM9 (see para. 6.1).

law countries and the words used in the French draft—*saisie conservatoire*—indicate this clearly.

I.265 As previously stated, the concern of the Committee had been to draw a clear distinction between arrest (*saisie conservatoire*) and seizure (*saisie exécution*).

I.266 Nor was there in the draft of 1933 any provision regulating jurisdiction on the merits in respect of the claim of the arrestor. This, however, did not give rise to any debate, but perhaps explains the lack of interest of the British Maritime Law Association, reference to which was made by Leopold Dor in his Report to the 1933 Oslo Conference.[10]

I.267 The clash between the civil and common law systems arose at that time with respect to the claims for which a ship could be arrested and to the liability for wrongful arrest.

I.268 The approach adopted at Oslo was totally changed at the CMI 1937 Paris Conference, when the International Committee submitted to the Conference a completely different draft, the scope of which was limited to the regulation of the arrest in respect of collision and salvage claims.[11] The change was interpreted as a replacement of the civil law system by that of common law.[12]

I.269 As previously indicated,[13] the International Committee appointed by the Bureau Permanent after the 1949 Amsterdam Conference adopted the English system whereby the arrest of a ship was permitted in respect of a specified number of maritime claims. The text considered by the Committee at its meeting in Antwerp in 1951, when the draft convention to be submitted to the CMI Conference to be held in Naples was prepared, also provided that the courts of the State in which the arrest is made would have jurisdiction to determine the case upon its merits. This provision, as that relating to the claims in respect of which a ship can be arrested, reproduced the English rule whereby jurisdiction

---

10. Léopold Dor stated in his report (CMI Bulletin No. 96, pp. 184 and 185; *Travaux Préparatoires*, p. 238):

> The draft International Convention on arrest does not seem to be favourably received by British Maritime circles as it appears from a letter addressed by Sir Norman Hill to the Comité Maritime International.
>
> During the discussion in London Sir Gonne St. Clair Pilcher stressed in fact that the question of arrest of ships does not attract any interest in anglo-saxon countries who know the *in rem* maritime proceedings.
>
> In any event, it appears that at least in England the right to arrest ships is widely granted without any other sanction in case of unjustified arrest, but the obligation for the arrestor to reimburse the cost of the security that the owner of the ship has been forced to provide in order to release the ship from arrest.
>
> In continental countries, on the contrary, the conservative arrest of ships has a considerable interest.
>
> In this respect the Committee took into consideration the draft and the remarkable report submitted by Mr. Lesueur on behalf of the French Maritime Law Association.

11. See *supra*, para. I.12.

12. The following comment on the Draft adopted by the CMI 1937 Conference is made in the report of the authors of the questionnaire submitted to the CMI 1949 Amsterdam Conference (CMI Bulletin No. 104, p. 531; *Travaux Préparatoires*, p. 248):

> This draft met with a great deal of opposition on the part of the British delegates, who stated that they were reluctant to abandon in favour of the Continental system the British system of a very restricted possibility of arrest. As a result of this opposition, article 1 was redrafted several times; the article was gradually amputated more and more and the text finally adopted at the Paris Conference stated no more than that: "Any creditor of an owner of a ship, by reason of a collision, might operate the arrest of such ship". Consequently, whilst the first draft had incorporated the continental notion of the widest scope of arrest, providing for the arrest in respect of all claims, the final draft was based on the English conception of the action *in rem*, dealing merely with collision claims, the question of arrest in respect of all other claims being left to the respective municipal laws. So what was intended to be international uniformity became merely a reproduction of the law of England. If I may be permitted to say so, this was a rather meagre result.

13. See *supra*, para. I.18.

is established with reference to the nature of the claim and may be invoked by an action *in rem* against the ship.

I.270 That provision, however, met with the strong opposition of the French and Italian associations and a "compromise" was then suggested by Dean Ripert. The "compromise", as will be seen later in further detail, consisted of providing that the courts of the State in the jurisdiction of which a ship is arrested have jurisdiction to determine the case upon its merits, if such jurisdiction is granted by the *lex fori* (as was the case in England) as well as with respect to certain specified claims.

I.271 Thus, with such "compromise" the English system was adopted, but its application was limited to some claims only. However, in respect of such claims the arrest became a means to establish jurisdiction on the merits in the State where the arrest was made.

I.272 In respect of such claims, therefore, the purpose of the arrest is two-fold: to obtain security for the claim, and to establish jurisdiction.[14]

15. ARREST OR DETENTION BY GOVERNMENTS AND PUBLIC AUTHORITIES

I.273 Article 2 of the Convention states in its latter part:

but nothing in this Convention shall be deemed to extend or restrict any right or powers vested in any Governments or their Departments, Public Authorities, or Dock or Harbour Authorities under their existing domestic laws or regulations to arrest, detain or otherwise prevent the sailing of vessels within their jurisdiction.

I.274 This provision did not exist in the draft approved by the CMI 1951 Naples Conference and was added during the 1952 Diplomatic Conference. The records of the Conference give no explanation for this provision, which was deemed to be self-explanatory. There would seem, however, to be a need for one or two observations. First, it must be noted that the authorities whose powers are unaffected by the provision are very widely described, viz. governments, their departments, public or private. Secondly, three different terms are used to describe the right or powers vested in such authorities, viz. to arrest, detain or otherwise prevent the sailing of ships. In view of the definition of arrest in Article 1(2), the aforesaid authorities may avail themselves of this provision not only for administrative or safety purposes, but also in order to secure payment of claims that may not be included in the list in Article 1(1), such as, for example, tonnage and similar dues.

I.275 This provision, therefore, is of a mixed nature. It is a substantive provision insofar as it excludes the applicability of the first part of Article 2 in respect of public authorities. It is a provision on the scope of application of the Convention insofar as it gives public authorities the right or power to detain or otherwise prevent the sailing of ships.

I.276 As previously stated, the arrest of a ship by a criminal court is outside the scope of the Convention and, therefore, the provisions of Article 2, according to which a ship

---

14. In *The "Deichland"* [1988] 2 Lloyd's Rep. 454 Sheen J. stated (at p. 458):

The special purpose of an action *in rem* is to induce the owner of the *res* to submit to the jurisdiction of this Court by acknowledging service of the writ and giving notice of intention to defend. Once the owner has done so the plaintiff has the advantage of being able to obtain a judgment *in personam*.

may only be arrested as security for a maritime claim, do not affect the "criminal" arrest even if this type of arrest is not included in the saving provision of Article 2.

I.277 The right of States to detain or otherwise prevent the sailing of ships may arise under international conventions or agreements and national law.

International Conventions and Agreements

I.278 The most far-reaching provisions are set out in the Memorandum of Understanding on Port State Control of 26 January 1982[15] and in the Procedures for Port State Control adopted by the Assembly of IMO on 23 November 1995.[16]

I.279 Section 2.3 of the Memorandum of Understanding provides that each national Authority will apply the instruments listed in section 2.1[17] which are in force and to which its State is a Party and section 3.1 provides that in fulfilling their commitments the Authorities will carry out inspections as indicated in that section.[18] Then section 3.7 so provides:

3.7. In the case of deficiencies which are clearly hazardous to safety, health or the environment, the Authority will, except as provided in 3.8., ensure that the hazard is removed before the ship is allowed to proceed to sea and for this purpose will take appropriate action, which may include detention.

As it will be seen, this provision is based on that of regulation 1/19(c) of SOLAS 1974, the scope of application of which is thus made much wider.

I.280 The IMO Procedures for Port State Control give the following definition of detention in paragraph 1.6.3.:

Detention: Intervention action taken by the port State when the condition of the ship or its crew does not correspond substantially with the applicable conventions to ensure that the ship will not sail until it can proceed to sea without presenting a danger to the ship or persons on board, or without presenting an unreasonable threat of harm to the marine environment.

They then set out detailed provisions in respect of the cases in which the Port State Control Officer (PSCO) must take action in order to detain a ship.

15. The full title of the Memorandum is "Memorandum of Understanding on Port State Control in Implementing Agreements on Maritime Safety and Protection of the Marine Environment". Parties to the Memorandum are Belgium, Denmark, Finland, France, Germany, Greece, Ireland, Italy, Netherlands, Norway, Portugal, Spain, Sweden and the United Kingdom. The Memorandum became effective on 1 July 1982.
16. Resolution A.787(19) of 23 November 1995.
17. The instruments listed in section 2.1 are the following:
— International Convention on Load Lines, 1966;
— International Convention for the Safety of Life at Sea, 1974;
— Protocol of 1978 relating to the International Convention for the Safety of Life at Sea, 1974;
— International Convention for the Prevention of Pollution from Ships, 1973, as modified by the Protocol of 1978 relating thereto;
— International Convention on Standards of Training, Certification and Watchkeeping for Seafarers, 1978;
— Convention on the International Regulations for Preventing Collisions at Sea, 1972;
— Merchant Shipping (Minimum Standards) Convention, 1976.
18. Section 3.1 so provides:
3.1. In fulfilling their commitments the Authorities will carry out inspections, which will consist of a visit on board a ship in order to check the certificates and documents relevant for the purposes of the Memorandum. In the absence of valid certificates or documents or if there are clear grounds for believing that the ship does not substantially meet the requirements of a relevant instrument, a more detailed inspection will be carried out. Inspections will be carried out in accordance with Annex I.

I.281 The International Convention for the Safety of Life at Sea, 1974 (SOLAS 1974) so provides in regulation 1/19(c) and (d):

(c) In the circumstances given in paragraph (b) of this regulation or where a certificate has expired or ceased to be valid, the officer carrying out the control shall take steps to ensure that the ship shall not sail until it can proceed to sea or leave the port for the purpose of proceeding to the appropriate repair yard without danger to the ship or persons on board.

(d) In the event of this control giving rise to an intervention of any kind, the officer carrying out the control shall forthwith inform, in writing, the Consul or, in his absence, the nearest diplomatic representative of the State whose flag the ship is entitled to fly of all the circumstances in which intervention was deemed necessary. In addition, nominated surveyors or recognized organizations responsible for the issue of the certificates shall also be notified. The facts concerning the intervention shall be reported to the Organization.

I.282 Paragraph (b) of regulation 1/19 provides that the certificates issued under regulation 12[19] or 13[20] shall be accepted by the competent authority of the port "unless there are clear grounds for believing that the condition of the ship or of its equipment does not correspond substantially with the particulars of any of the certificates or that the ship and its equipment are not in compliance with the provisions of regulation 11(a) and (b) of chapter 1".[21] If, therefore, any of the situations described in regulation 1/19 materialises, the competent authority of the port has the power to prevent the sailing of the ship.

I.283 The International Code of Safety for High Speed Craft (HSC Code) requires that High Speed Craft should not operate commercially unless a Permit to Operate and the High-Speed Craft Certificate are issued and valid (regulation 1.9) and then provides that regulation 1/19 of SOLAS 1974 shall apply.

I.284 The International Management Code for the Safe Operation of Ships and for Pollution Prevention (ISM Code) adopted by IMO Resolution A.741(18) requires that a Document of Compliance be issued to each company which complies with the requirements of the ISM Code and a Safety Management Certificate be issued to a ship to certify that the company and the shipboard management operate in accordance with the approved Safety Management System.[22] Although the ISM Code is not yet mandatory at an international level, most Governments have implemented the Code on a national basis by the deadline of 1 June 1998 as recommended by the IMO Resolution and, therefore, it is likely that possession of the documents required by the ISM Code be a condition for

---

19. The certificates mentioned in regulation 1/12 are the Passenger Ship Safety Certificate, the Cargo Ship Safety Construction Certificate, the Cargo Ship Safety Equipment Certificate, the Cargo Ship Safety Radiotelegraphy Certificate, the Cargo Ship Safety Radiotelephony Certificate and the Exemption Certificate.

20. Regulation 1/13 provides that a Contracting Government may, at the request of the Government of the State whose flag the ship is entitled to fly (called the "Administration") cause a ship to be surveyed and, if satisfied that the requirements of the regulations are complied with, shall issue certificates to the ship in accordance with the regulations.

21. Regulation 11(a) and (b) so provides:

(a) The condition of the ship and its equipment shall be maintained to conform with the provisions of the present regulations to ensure that the ship in all respects will remain fit to proceed to sea without danger to the ship or persons on board.

(b) After any survey of the ship under regulations 6, 7, 8, 9 or 10 of this chapter has been completed, no change shall be made in the structural arrangement, machinery, equipment and other items covered by the survey, without the sanction of the Administration.

22. Regulation 13.4 of the ISM Code so provides:

A certificate, called a "Safety Management Certificate" should be issued to a ship by the Administration or organizazion recognized by the Administration. The Administration should, when issuing a certificate, verify that the Company and its shipboard management operate in accordance with the approved SMS.

the sailing of a ship from the ports of a State in which the Code has been implemented.

I.285 A ship carrying oil in bulk as cargo to which the CLC 1969 is applicable may be prevented from sailing if insurance or other security as required by Article 7 of CLC is not in force.[23]

National laws

I.286 A summary of the law in a number of Contracting States regarding the right of arrest or detention of ships by public authorities follows.

DENMARK

I.287 A foreign ship in a Danish harbour or within Danish territorial waters can be detained by order of the Danish Maritime Authority if the continued sailing of the ship presents a hazard to the crew's health or safety due to defects or shortcomings with the hull, machinery, life-saving equipment, placing of ballast or cargo or manning.

I.288 The Danish maritime environmental authorities have the right to detain ships in Danish ports as security for the costs of prevention or clean-up of environmental damage in Danish waters caused by a ship.

FRANCE

I.289 Ships, French and foreign, may be detained without prior recourse to a court for violation of public duties, including the following:

  (i) Violation of customs rules and regulations.
  (ii) Non-compliance with safety and sanitary requirements.
  (iii) Violation of rules relating to safe navigation.

I.290 Pursuant to Article 83 of the *Code Disciplinaire et Pénal de la Marine Marchande*, a ship may be detained until payment of the sum necessary to ensure payment of the fine in cases of breach of the regulations or orders issued by the maritime authorities in connection with maritime navigation and of the Collision Regulations. Pursuant to Article 21 of the 1966 Load Line Convention, which is in force in France, the competent authorities of a Contracting State may prevent a ship from sailing until she can do so without danger to her passengers and crew.

  (iv) Non-compliance with rules and regulations relating to pollution.

I.291 Pursuant to Article 38 of the *Code Disciplinaire et Pénal de la Marine Marchande*, a tanker or other ship carrying hazardous or noxious substances, in case of failure to give advance notice of its entry into French territorial waters, may be detained until payment of the sum required to secure payment of the fine. Pursuant to section 13 of Law

---

23. Article 7(11) of CLC 1969 so provides:
    11. Subject to the provisions of this Article, each Contracting State shall ensure, under its national legislation, that insurance or other security to the extent specified in paragraph 1 of this Article is in force in respect of any ship, wherever registered, entering or leaving port in its territory, or arriving at or leaving an off-shore terminal in its territorial sea, if the ship actually carries more than 2,000 ton of oil in bulk as cargo.

No. 83–583 of 5 July 1983, a tanker may be "immobilised" (*immobilisé*) following a decision of the *Procureur de la République*, in cases of pollution of the sea, until security is provided for the payment of the fine. Pursuant to section 3 of Law No. 77–530 of 26 May 1977 whereby rules of implementation of the 1969 Civil Liability Convention have been enacted, a tanker carrying more than 2,000 tons of oil in bulk may not leave French territorial waters if it is not provided with a certificate of insurance or other financial security as required by Article 7(1) of the Convention.

(v) Failure to pay port dues.

GERMANY

I.292 No ship, whatever her flag, may be detained by public authorities unless the detention is, within a fixed period of time, authorised by an order of the court. Public authorities have, therefore, the power to detain a ship in a certain specified situation, but for a limited period of time.

GREECE

I.293 A foreign vessel may be detained by public authorities without a court decision if the ship does not comply with basic rules of safety of navigation (e.g. after a collision or grounding until the classification society allows sailing), for the purposes of investigation after a crime or accident or in respect of pollution fines until a bond is posted. Such detention is not an arrest within the meaning of the Convention and aims at satisfaction of public interests and not at providing security for private rights.

IRELAND

I.294 British legislation which applied to Ireland and which was enacted prior to 6 December 1921 (the date the treaty between Britain and Ireland was signed) continued in force until repealed. Consequently, legislation like the Merchant Shipping Act (MSA) 1894 is still in force in Ireland except for that part of it (e.g. Part I) which has been repealed. As a result there are many powers to arrest, detain or otherwise prevent the sailing of ships which are vested in non-judicial authorities. Examples are:

1. A receiver of wrecks has the same rights as a salvor to recover expenses due to him. It seems therefore that the section gives him a maritime lien (MSA 1894, section 567).
2. In some circumstances coastguard authorities have the same rights as receivers of wrecks (and therefore salvors) to recover from the owners of shipwrecked property remuneration for watching and protection (MSA 1894, section 568).
3. A harbour authority to which the Act applies can detain a ship to obtain payment or security for a claim for damage to a harbour, dock, pier or quay (Harbour Piers and Docks Clauses Act 1847, section 74).
4. A foreign ship which has caused damage in circumstances where the damage or injury was probably caused by the misconduct or want of skill of the master or crew may be detained by a court order pending proceedings that "may be instituted" for the damage (MSA 1894, section 688). Subsection (2), however,

appears to allow detention without any court order if there is a danger that the ship will leave the jurisdiction before an application can be made to the court.

5. A ship may be detained until outstanding rates on vessel and cargo have been paid (Harbours Act 1946, section 73).

6. Quite a number of sections of the Merchant Shipping (Safety and Load Line Conventions) Act 1933 provide for the detention of vessels for reasons of safety.

7. The Mercantile Marine Act 1955 provides for the forfeiture of Irish registered vessels if they come into the ownership of someone not qualified to own an Irish registered ship (section 22).

ITALY

I.295 Pursuant to Article 181 of the Navigation Code (CN) an Italian ship cannot sail from a port unless permission to sail has been granted by the port authority. Article 181, which is applicable also to foreign ships unless international Conventions provide otherwise (Article 185 CN), sets out the situations in which permission to sail cannot be granted, viz.:

   (i) failure by the master to comply with police duties;

  (ii) failure by the master or owner to comply with safety requirements;

 (iii) failure by the master to comply with orders of the port authority;

 (iv) failure by the master or the owner to comply with fiscal, sanitary or customs obligations;

  (v) failure to pay port dues;

 (vi) failure to provide bonds if required under statutory rules and regulations.

I.296 Article 646 CN provides that the competent court and, in case of urgency, the harbour master or the judicial police authority, may take the steps that are deemed advisable in order to prevent the vessel sailing. This rule is part of the title of the Code regulating arrest and seizure of ships and, therefore, recourse to it is made also in case of arrest, for example, when the court is closed.

THE NETHERLANDS

I.297 A foreign ship can be detained by the Dutch Shipping Inspectors (Nederlandse Scheepvaart Inspectie), without recourse to a court, if it is found that the ship does not comply with safety standards internationally accepted or agreed including, of course, those relating to seaworthiness and safety of human life.

PORTUGAL

I.298 Ships may be detained by the port authority without prior recourse to a court for various reasons, all of which are related to matters of public interest. These include breach of safety regulations in general, safety of human life in particular, and unseaworthiness of the ship.

SPAIN

I.299 Arrest or detention of a ship by order of an authority other than a judicial authority is permitted in a number of cases, including the following:

(i) failure to pay port dues and other similar dues: a ship may be arrested, pursuant to the provisions of the Revenue Act, by the Provincial Tax Office (Delegacion Provincial de Hacienda);

(ii) failure to comply with safety requirements: if a ship is not provided with the safety certificates required by the SOLAS Convention, Spanish maritime authorities shall not, pursuant to Article 1 of Decree No. 3384 of 1971, allow the ship to sail;

(iii) collision: the judicial authorities of the army may take urgent preventive measures such as the arrest of the ship presumably at fault in cases where national interest is involved; if it is found that no such interest is involved, the matter is then referred to the judicial authority;

(iv) salvage: a ship and cargo to which salvage services are rendered may be arrested by a judge competent for the conduct of proceedings for the assessment of salvage remuneration. Such judges do not belong to the judiciary, but are officials of the army called Juzgados Maritimos Permanentes, sitting in the main Spanish ports (Law of 24 December 1962, No. 60 and regulations approved by Decree of 20 April 1967, No. 984). Their decisions are subject to revision by the judiciary.

SWEDEN

I.300 Within Swedish territorial waters and harbours foreign ships can be detained by order of the proper Swedish authorities. The Swedish Maritime Administration has the power to detain a vessel if the vessel is unseaworthy or in other respects does not comply with the international rules and regulations relating to the safety of the vessel and crew. A vessel can be detained in connection with threatening violation of the laws on prevention of environmental damage and also as security for costs in connection with the breach of this legislation. The Swedish customs and police authorities also have the power to detain a vessel in the exercise of their duties in connection with crime and smuggling. A decision of detention enforced by a Swedish administration body can be appealed to a general Swedish court or to an administrative Swedish court depending upon the status of the relevant matter.

UNITED KINGDOM

I.301 Foreign ships may be detained by public authorities without prior recourse to a court for a number of purposes. These powers depend upon statute, and are not to be equated with arrest in the sense used by the Convention; they are given for the purposes of enforcing public law and not for the enforcement of private rights. Some public authorities have powers which depend on statutes relevant to that public authority only, and may not apply to another similar public authority in another part of the country.

I.302 Some examples can be given in connection with:

(i) Payment of dues: Harbours, Docks and Piers Clauses Act 1847, sections 44 and 47; Port of London Act 1968, sections 39 and 40; . . . and light dues Merchant Shipping Act (MSA) 1894, sections 650 and 651;

(ii) Safety requirements: MSA 1894, section 457; MSA (Safety Convention) 1949, section 23 and MSA (Load Lines) 1967, section 3(4);

(iii) Oil pollution measures: Prevention of Oil Pollution Act 1971, section 20;

  (iv) Payment of wreck removal: MSA 1894, sections 530 and 531;
  (v) Failure to carry required documents;
  (vi) Fees of coastguards and receivers of wrecks: MSA 1894, section 568(1);
 (vii) Customs' offences including drug offences;
(viii) Detention of a ship in port, or prohibition on her sailing, by the Secretary of
     State for Transport because she is not sufficiently seaworthy to go to sea: section
     30(A) MSA 1988 Merchant Shipping (Registration) Act 1933 *Ullapool Har-*
     bour Trustees v. *Secretary of State for Transport.*[24] Some of these powers carry
     the right of sale.

16. THE CLOSED LIST OF CLAIMS

I.303 As appears from the history of the Convention, there have been conflicting views among the CMI national associations regarding the type of claim in respect of which a vessel may be arrested.[25] The view of the associations of the civil law countries was that arrest should be permissible in respect of any claim; the view of the associations of the common law countries and particularly of the British association was that arrest, as in England, should be permitted only in respect of specific claims of a maritime nature.[26] As already indicated, the former view first prevailed but then the second was accepted to such an extent that in the draft approved at Paris in 1937 reference was made only to arrest in respect of claims arising out of a collision. At the Amsterdam Conference of 1949 the suggestion was made to reach a compromise by adopting the English approach whereby arrest is only permitted in respect of claims of a maritime nature and by permitting the arrest not only of the ship in respect of which the claim arose, but also of any other ship in the same ownership.[27] Once the principle that arrest should be permissible only in respect of claims of a maritime nature had been agreed, it would have been logical that the concept of "maritime claim" be discussed and clarified and that a thorough analysis be made of all claims which were deemed to fall under this general description. But almost no discussion took place and the list of claims submitted to the Naples Conference of 1951, inspired by the list of questions and claims in respect of which the English High Court was granted admiralty jurisdiction by section 22 of the Supreme Court of Judicature (Consolidation) Act 1925,[28] was adopted practically without any change, not even the

---

24. Reported in *The Times* 13 April 1995. The ships in question were Bulgarian.

25. For a summary of such views see Ripert, "Les Conventions de Bruxelles du 10 Mai 1952 sur l'Unification du Droit Maritime" [1952] D.M.F. 343, at p. 354.

26. That the list discussed and finally approved is a closed list has never been in dispute. See Pasanisi, "Il Progetto di Convenzione Internazionale per la Unificazione delle Regole in Materia di Sequestro di Navi" [1952] Dir. Mar. 316, at p. 318.

27. A summary of the compromise is made by Neill, L.J. in *The "Deichland"* [1989] 2 Lloyd's Rep. 113, at p. 117.

28. This was expressly stated in the report of the International Sub-Committee (CMI Bulletin No. 105, p. 5; *Travaux Préparatoires*, p. 274):

    The first paragraph of art. 1 gives a closed list of claims considered as "maritime claims". Such list is based on the types of claims submitted to the jurisdiction of the Admiralty Court of the High Court of Justice (Supreme Court of Judicature (Consolidation) Act 1925). The International Committee is of the view that the categories of claims mentioned in this paragraph practically include all maritime claims that may give rise to the arrest of a ship, whilst, reasonably, no other claim of a maritime nature could justify an arrest under the Convention which is envisaged.

    The fact that the list of maritime claims was based on that contained in s. 22 of the Supreme Court of Judicature (Consolidation) Act 1925 was considered by Lord Wilberforce in *Gatoil International Inc.* v.

changes that would have been required in order to include all claims secured by a maritime lien under the 1926 MLM Convention. In fact such proposal had been made by the Italian delegation,[29] but it was not adopted owing to the strong opposition of the British delegation on the mistaken ground that the United Kingdom was not likely to ratify the 1926 Convention on Maritime Liens and Mortgages.[30] Probably this result was also due to the previous proposal of the Norwegian delegation that the list of maritime claims be restricted to the claims for which a maritime lien was granted under the 1926 MLM Convention[31] which had been quite correctly opposed by the delegations of Belgium and France who feared an excessive reduction of the claims in respect of which arrest is permissible and, thus, an even greater departure from the civil law approach.[32]

Arkwright-Boston Manufacturers Mutual Insurance Co.—The "Sandrina" [1985] 1 Lloyd's Rep. 181, as a good reason for the use of the *travaux préparatoires* of the Convention in aid of the interpretation of ss. 1 and 47 of the Administration of Justice Act 1956. He stated (at p. 183):

> The situation is slightly more complex in that the list of maritime claims set out in Art. 1 of the Convention was, in fact, based on the list of such claims then applicable in England under the Supreme Court of Judicature (Consolidation) Act, 1925, s. 22 (see particularly sub-s. (1)(a)(xii)). This list was adopted, as part of a compromise, by the Brussels Convention, and was then made applicable (with minor variations) to England and to Scotland by s. 1 and s. 47 of the 1956 Act respectively. This derivation provides a clear justification for attributing to the provisions in the Scottish portion of the 1956 Act the meaning which they ought to receive under the Convention—if that can be ascertained.

This fact was also considered by Lord Brandon of Oakbrook in *The "River Rima"* [1988] 2 Lloyd's Rep. 193 as a basis for a different conclusion, viz. that Art. 1(1)(k) of the Convention should be interpreted in the light of the provisions of the Supreme Court of Judicature (Consolidation) Act 1925. He in fact stated (at p. 197):

> The significance of the historical background which I have outlined is this. Paragraph (m) of s. 20(2) of the 1981 Act was derived, through par. (m) of s. 1(1) of the 1956 Act, from par. (k) of art. 1(1) of the Convention. Paragraph (k) of art. 1(1) of the Convention was in turn derived from par. (vii) of s. 22(1)(a) of the 1925 Act. Since proceedings *in rem* in respect of a claim under par. (vii) of s. 22(1)(a) of the 1925 Act could only be brought against the particular ship in respect of which the claim arose, it was an essential ingredient of such a claim that it should relate to necessaries supplied to a particular ship, the identity of which had either been specified in the contract of supply, or at least notified to the supplier by the time when the necessaries came to be delivered under such contract.

29. The Italian delegate (Mr G. Berlingieri) stated (CMI Bulletin No. 105, p. 227; *Travaux Préparatoires*, p. 283: the following text is the translation from the original speech in French):

> I cannot, however, agree with what Mr. de Grandmaison said in respect of the difference existing between the list of claims set out in the Maritime Liens and Mortgages Convention and that set out in the draft convention on conservative arrest.
>
> If the list set out in Art. 1 includes maritime claims that are not privileged, it is impossible to deny that all privileged claims are maritime claims. And since it is intended to widen as much as possible that list of maritime claims, why not to add in this article the list of privileged claims?

Art. 9 of the Maritime Liens and Mortgages Convention in its last paragraph entitles Contracting Parties to provide in their domestic law as a cause of extension of the extinction period of privileged claims the fact that the ship has not been arrested in the territorial waters. That means that all privileged claims give automatically the right of arrest.

30. The British delegate (Sir Gonne St. Clair Pilcher) thus stated in fact (CMI Bulletin No. 105, p. 230; *Travaux Préparatoires*, p. 285):

> May I also add this, that, whilst it appears logical to marry this convention to the convention on mortgages and liens, or it may at any rate appear logical to do so, I venture to fear that it is almost impossible. I need not, I think, stress the reasons why it is impossible to introduce, at any rate into British legislation, a power of arrest which will follow exactly the existing convention on mortgages and liens. I think it is no secret to say that, whilst about twenty years ago the British Government were making promises to put the mortgages and liens convention into effect, they failed to do so because, for one reason at any rate, they found it extremely difficult to incorporate into British statutes the effect of the mortgages and liens convention.

31. CMI Bulletin No. 105, p. 217; *Travaux Préparatoires*, p. 280.

32. The Belgian delegate (Mr Koelman) stated (CMI Bulletin No. 105, p. 221; *Travaux Préparatoires*, p. 281):

> As regards the list of the claims, it obviously differs from that contained in the Convention on Maritime Liens and Mortgages. I think I can say that they are two things quite separate. The Convention on Maritime Liens and Mortgages deals with the privileged character of certain claims and provides that certain claims

I.304 While, however, it was right not to restrict maritime claims to claims secured by maritime liens, it was also right to include in the list of maritime claims all claims secured by maritime liens, for arrest is the ordinary means for their enforcement.

I.305 The fact, however, remains that the method adopted at Naples and then at Brussels leaves much to be desired. In general, a closed list is dangerous, for it is unlikely to be complete or, in any event, to continue to be complete in the light of new developments. It may suffice to refer to the 1969 Civil Liability Convention and to the 1989 Salvage Convention. In particular, the list appearing in the Arrest Convention was incomplete when the Convention was made because it did not include all maritime liens recognised by the 1926 Convention on Maritime Liens and Mortgages, and it also omitted some claims undoubtedly of a maritime nature.[33] The following claims giving rise to a maritime lien under the 1926 Convention on Maritime Liens and Mortgages, which is still in force in several maritime nations,[34] do not appear to be included:

(i) law costs due to the State (Article 2(1) of the 1926 Convention);

(ii) expenses incurred in the common interest of the creditors in order to preserve the vessel or to procure its sale and the distribution of the proceeds of sale (Article 2(1));

(iii) cost of watching and preservation from the time of the entry of the vessel into the last port (Article 2(1));

(iv) claims resulting from contracts entered into or acts done by the master, acting within the scope of his authority, away from the home port, when such contracts or acts are necessary for the preservation of the vessel or the continuation of the voyage (Article 2(5)).

I.306 The omission of claims under (i) above is not relevant, for pursuant to Article 2 of the Arrest Convention the right of governments and public authorities to arrest or detain vessels is not affected. The omission of claims under (ii) seems, on the contrary, to be relevant, and this is so also in respect of claims under (iii). The omission of claims under

---

shall be paid with priority. Here, the question is to establish in respect of which claims it is possible to effect the conservative arrest of a ship and in consideration of the relevant divergencies existing between anglo-saxon law and continental law, it is necessary that the list in Art. 1 be as extensive as possible. If such list was not necessary in the convention on maritime liens, it is indispensable here and it should be maintained.

The French delegate (Mr de Grandmaison) stated in turn (CMI Bulletin No. 105, p. 225; *Travaux Préparatoires*, p. 282):

On behalf of the French Delegation, I state that we are in total disagreement with the view expressed by the Honourable Mr. Alten. In fact, as the representative of the Belgian Delegation just stated, the Maritime Liens and Mortgages Convention dealt with the privileged character of certain claims and stated that certain claims shall be paid with priority over certain other claims.

But today this is not the question. The question is to know for which claim it will be permitted to the Court to effect the conservative arrest of a ship, and that simply gives to the claimant a security for the future. Therefore, one has not here to look for a privileged claim, but for a maritime claim, since the sacrifice that the continentals make is to waive the right of arrest for non maritime claims. Today we are presented with a draft convention that sets out claims which are all maritime. We cannot consider in detail all such list, but all claims for which the right of conservative arrest is provided are maritime claims.

33. Such as, for example, the claim in respect of insurance premiums, the inclusion of which was suggested by the Dutch association (CMI Bulletin No. 105, p. 79; *Travaux Préparatoires*, p. 277), and in respect of the commissions of shipbrokers and chartering brokers. It is worth noting that both these claims have been included in the new 1999 Arrest Convention in which, however, the closed list approach was adopted. See *infra*, Book II, para. II.88–96.

34. Algeria, Argentina, Belgium, Brazil, France, Haiti, Iran, Italy, Lebanon, Monaco, Poland, Portugal, Romania, Spain, Syrian Arab Republic, Turkey, Uruguay, Zaire.

(iv) is only partial, and relates to those claims which are not covered by subparagraphs (k), (l) and (n) of Article 1(1).

I.307 In addition to the maritime liens granted by international conventions, there may be maritime liens granted or recognised by national laws in respect of claims that are not listed in Article 1(1). The question arises, therefore, whether arrest would be permissible in respect of any such claim. This seems not to be the case in Belgium, Denmark, Finland, Italy, the Netherlands[35] and Norway while the solution is doubtful in Germany and Greece and is affirmative in Belgium and Spain.[36] The approach to the problem is different in the common law countries parties to the Convention, who, however, have not given force of law to it. In fact in such countries normally arrest is permissible in respect of all claims for which Admiralty jurisdiction is granted and, as it has been seen[37] such claims correspond, but are not identical, to those listed in Article 1(1) of the Convention. This is the case, for example, for the United Kingdom and Nigeria.[38]

I.308 Among the claims which might have been qualified as "maritime claims", in view of their connection with the operation of a ship, the following may be mentioned[39]:

(a) insurance premiums: the inclusion of insurance premiums was suggested by the Dutch association,[40] but such suggestion was not accepted[41] because it was not felt necessary to grant the right of arrest in respect of this type of claim[42];

(b) commissions and disbursements of insurance brokers;

(c) commissions of ship and chartering brokers;

(d) agency fees[43];

(e) stevedoring charges;

(f) pollution damage as defined in the 1969 Civil Liability Convention;

---

35. According to the information kindly provided by Mr. Taco van der Valk stevedoring companies claims for services rendered to owners are secured by a privilege on the ship pursuant to article 8:217 of the Dutch Civil Code but, even though they can enforce a judgment obtained against the owner on the ship and cause the ship to be sold in a forced sale, they cannot avail themselves of the arrest procedure, as a conservative measure.

36. This information is based on the replies to the Questionnaire published in Appendix II. See question 4, at pp. 241–244.

37. *Supra*, para. I.201–209.

38. See also the replies to question 4 of the Questionnaire, Appendix II, pp. 243–244.

39. For a detailed list of claims of a maritime nature not included in Art. 1(1) see La China, "Due Novità (d'Antica Data!) nel Campo del Diritto Processuale Civile Internazionale Marittimo: le Convenzioni di Bruxelles 10 Maggio 1952" [1978] IV Foro Italiano 255. All claims mentioned in the text are now mentioned in the 1999 Arrest Convention. See *infra*, Book II, para. II.88–II.96.

40. CMI Bulletin No. 105, p. 79; *Travaux Préparatoires*, p. 277.

41. For an analysis of the *travaux préparatoires* in this respect see Lord Wilberforce in *Gatoil International Inc.* v. *Arkwright-Boston Manufacturers Mutual Insurance Co.—The "Sandrina"* [1985] 1 Lloyd's Rep. 181, at pp. 185 and 186.

42. In *The "Sandrina"*, Lord Wilberforce stated (at p. 185):
The conclusion from the above is clear. The conference decided not to include premia on policies of insurance among the maritime claims justifying arrest. It did so, moreover, not because it thought that these premia were already covered (so that explicit reference was unnecessary), but because it considered it unnecessary as a matter of policy to provide for their protection by means of arrestment. The legislative intention is manifest: not by any provision in art. 1 to provide for the inclusion of premia among arrestable maritime claims.

43. The Juge des Saisies of Brussels by order of 24 October 1974 in *The "Corinthian Trader"* [1974] JPA 149, held that the claim of a maritime agent in respect of the claim for termination of the contract is not a maritime claim. M. Claringbould (Arrest of Ships–2, LLP 1986, p. 50) is instead of the view that agency fees should be treated as maritime claims.

(g) contract for the sale of a ship.[44]

I.309 The disadvantages of a closed list of maritime claims have been partly remedied in Denmark through the maintenance of the so-called "ship-register arrest" whereby the warrant of arrest is not executed on the ship, but is only endorsed in the ships register, thereby preventing the owner from selling or mortgaging the ship and thus securing the future enforcement on the ship of the claim of the arrestor. This type of arrest is in fact permissible also in respect of claims that are not maritime claims under the Convention, since it does not violate Article 2.

I.310 As it has been correctly pointed out by the Italian Association in its comments on the draft convention prepared by the CMI International Sub-committee prior to the 1951 Naples Conference,[45] the word "claim" and even more the word "créance" in the French text is not apt to describe some of the issues in respect of which arrest is permitted, and more precisely those under (o)—"disputes as to the title to or ownership of any ship" and (p)—"disputes between co-owners of any ship as to the ownership, possession, employment or earnings of that ship".

I.311 On the contrary the term "claim" is such as to include both claims arising out of a contract and claims in tort, such as the claims under (a) and, partly, under (b).[46]

17. THE INDIVIDUAL MARITIME CLAIMS

I.312 In order to specify the maritime claims in respect of which arrest is permissible the notion of "maritime claims" was restricted to such claims by means of a definition. Article 1 of the Convention in fact gives four definitions of varying importance, viz. those of "maritime claim", of "arrest", of "person" and of "claimant". The list of the maritime

---

44. In the Netherlands it has been decided that a claim under a contract of sale of a ship is not a maritime claim: President of the Arrondissementsrechtbank of Middleburg 22 August 1988—*The "Ypougon"* [1989] Ships en Schade 138; President of the Arrondissementsrechtbank of Groningen, 17 July 1989—*The "Hannelore Jürss"*, [1989] Kort Geding 319. The same decision was arrived at in France by the Cour d'Appel of Rouen with judgment of 15 April 1982, *The "GME Atlantico"* [1982] D.M.F. 744 and by the Tribunal de Commerce of Antibes with judgment 27 November 1998—*The "Turquoise"* [1999] DMF 917 and in Belgium by the Juge des Saisies by order of 15 July 1982, affirmed by the Cour d'Appel of Antwerp by order of 6 August 1982, both cited by Delwaide, "Saisie conservatoire des navires de mer en Belgique" [1984] DMF 248.

45. The Italian Association stated (CMI Bulletin No. 105, p. 67; *Travaux Préparatoires*, p. 276):
  "Maritime claim", it is stated in article 1(1), means a claim arising out of one or more of the causes subsequently listed. The list of such causes follows numbered sixteen (a–p); however, while certainly thirteen, or may be fourteen of such causes consist of real claims, certainly two, and more precisely those under (d) and (e), and may be sometime also those under (g), cannot be qualified as claims, but rather as possessory or real disputes. There is in fact no doubt that such are the disputes between co-owners of a ship in respect of title to, possession, employment, operation of a ship; such can be, in respect of possession, the disputes arising out of the employment or chartering of a ship. And even if the English term "claim", that does not have in Italian a precise corresponding term, lends itself to include also disputes such as those mentioned above, its French translation by the word "créance maritime" shows the lack of precision of the language.

46. The contractual or tort nature of the claim has been held to be irrelevant by the Cour d'Appel of Aix-en-Provence with judgment 16 October 1996, *S.A. Annico Maritime* v. *S.A. Horti International—The "Enarxis"*, [1997] DMF 603 and by the Tribunal of Genoa with judgment 3 December 1994, *A&B Trading and Financial* v. *Malta Cross Shipping & Co. Ltd.—The "Rijeka Express"*, [1996] Dir. Mar. 480. In *Samick Lines Co. v. Owners of the ship "Anthonis P. Lemos"*, (H.L.), [1985] 1 Lloyd's Rep. 283 it was held that claims in tort come under s. 20(2)(h) of the 1981 Act under which sub-paragraphs (d) and (e) of the Convention are merged.

claims in paragraph (1) of Article 1 is preceded by the following words: " 'Maritime claim' means a claim arising out of one or more of the following:".

I.313 The words in the French text of the Convention corresponding to "arising out of" are "ayant l'une des causes suivantes". The meaning of these words was considered in England by the House of Lords in *Samick Lines Co. Ltd.* v. *Owners of the Ship "Antonis P. Lemos"*[47] where the question at issue was whether a claim framed in tort by the subcharterers of the *Antonis P. Lemos* against that ship and her owners came within section 20(1)(h) of the Supreme Court Act 1981, in which Article 1(1)(d) and (e) of the Convention are combined as follows: "any claim arising out of any agreement relating to the carriage of goods in a ship or to the use or hire of a ship". The appeal against the judgment of the Court of Appeal by which it was held that the claim fell within paragraph (h) was dismissed unanimously by the House of Lords. Lord Brandon of Oakbrook considered whether these words should be given the narrow meaning of the expression "arising under" or the wider meaning of the expression "in connection with" and held that the second alternative was correct, on the ground, *inter alia*, that the expression "arising out of" is used in the Convention "in the wider of the two meanings of which it is capable."[48]

I.314 Owing to the manner in which the various maritime claims are formulated and to the variety of such claims, it was not easy to formulate the opening words of paragraph (1) of Article 1. A similar problem had to be faced in respect of the list of excepted perils in the Hague Rules. In the original English text of the Hague Rules 1921 (and subsequently in the unofficial translation of the Convention) in the opening sentence the expression "arising or resulting from" is used and then in subparagraph (q) the sentence begins with the words "any other cause",[49] thus clearly indicating that what is meant by "arising or resulting" is a causal relationship. In the Hague Rules, therefore, the excepted perils are relevant as the cause of the loss of or damage to the goods.

I.315 This is not the case, notwithstanding the use in the French text of the expression "*ayant l'une des causes suivantes*",[50] for the Arrest Convention, where probably an expression such as "in connection with" or "in respect of" would have been more correct.[51]

---

47. [1985] 1 Lloyd's Rep. 283.
48. At p. 290.
49. In the original French text of the 1924 Convention the expression used in the opening sentence of Art. 4(2) is "*résultant ou provenant*" and that used in subparagraph (q) is "*de toute autre cause ne provenant pas*".
50. The closed list of maritime claims was prepared by the International Committee appointed by the *Bureau Permanent* following the resolution approved by the CMI 1949 Amsterdam Conference (see section 4). In the original French text of Art. 1(1) the words used were "*allégation d'un droit ou d'une créance qui trouve son fondement dans l'une ou plusieurs des causes suivantes*".
51. It is worth noting that a different formulation was adopted in the 1967 Convention on Maritime Liens and Mortgages. Art. 4(1) in fact states: "The following claims shall be secured by maritime liens on the vessel" and then follows the list of the claims, for some of which the word "claims" is repeated and is linked to the description of the particular claim by the formula "in respect of" ("claims in respect of loss of life" and "claims in respect of loss of or damage to property").The word "claims" is instead always repeated in Art. 4(1) of the 1993 Convention on Maritime Liens and Mortgages and is linked to the description of the particular claim by the word "for" (e.g. "claims for wages" etc.; "claims for salvage") or by the formula "in respect of" ("claims in respect of loss of life" etc.).
The formula "in respect of" is also used in the 1976 Convention on Limitation of Liability for Maritime Claims, Art. 2(1), whilst in the 1957 Limitation Convention the formula "arising from" had been used. In England, in section 20(2)(m) of the Supreme Court Act 1991 the words "in respect of " are used in connection with the claims relating to goods and materials supplied to a ship. For their construction see *The "Kommunar"* [1997] 1 Lloyd's Rep. 1, at p. 5; *The "Edinburgh Castle"* [1999] 2 Lloyd's Rep. 362.

I.316 The view expressed by Lord Brandon that the expression "arising out of" must be given a wide meaning is, therefore, correct even though it does not justify, for the reasons indicated later,[52] the conclusion reached in the specific case.

(a) Damage caused by any Ship either in Collision or Otherwise

I.317 The British Association in its comments on the preliminary draft[53] said that it thought the words "or otherwise" were designed to cover all those situations where damage is caused by one ship to another without physical contact, either by wash or by creating a situation of damage through a negligent or hazardous manoeuvre, etc. On this assumption it agreed with the wording, and no further comment seems to have been made on this point.

I.318 It is worth noting that in the Administration of Justice Act 1956, whereby the United Kingdom gave effect, albeit in part only, to the Convention, the reference to collision is omitted and the wording used is "any claim for damage done by a ship". The wording is identical in the Supreme Court Act 1981, section 20(2)(e). The reference to collision is also omitted in the 1999 Arrest Convention, in which the wording used is "loss or damage caused by the operation of the ship".

I.319 In relation to this provision the House of Lords held in *The "Eschersheim"*[54] that, although the ship itself must be the actual instrument by which the damage was done, "physical contact between the ship, and whatever object sustains the damage is not essential".[55] This statement is particularly significant, for in the same judgment it was held that where any provision of the Act which appears to be intended to give effect to the Arrest Convention is capable of more than one meaning, the court may look at the Convention in order to gain assistance in deciding which meaning is to be preferred.

I.320 It is thought that the words "or otherwise" cover pollution damage as defined in the Protocol of 1992 to the Civil Liability Convention of 1969 and any damage caused by hazardous or noxious substances as defined in the HNS Convention of 1996.

I.321 The Cour d'Appel of Rouen in its judgment of 23 September 1992[56] held that the wording used in sub-paragraph (a) may include the costs incurred by the French Government for the removal of a number of containers stuffed with toxic products that had been washed overboard the *M/V Asilal* during a storm.

---

52. See *infra*, para. I.340.
53. CMI Bulletin No. 105, p. 44; *Travaux Préparatoires*, p. 277.
54. [1976] 2 Lloyd's Rep. 1.
55. Lord Diplock stated (at p. 8):
    The figurative phrase "damage done by a ship" is a term of art in maritime law whose meaning is well settled by authority: see *The Vera Cruz* (1884) 9 P.D. 96; *Currie* v. *M'Knight* [1897] A.C. 97. To fall within the phrase not only must the damage be the direct result or natural consequence of something done by those engaged in the navigation of the ship but the ship itself must be the actual instrument by which the damage was done. The commonest case is that of collision, which is specifically mentioned in the convention: but physical contact between the ship and whatever object sustains the damage is not essential—a ship may negligently cause a wash by which some other vessel or some property on shore is damaged.
    In Belgium the Cour d'Appel of Ghent in its judgment of 20 September 1994 in *The "Otrant Frigo"*, cited by Verstrepen, "Arrest and Judicial Sale of Ships in Belgium", [1995] LMCLQ 131, at p. 145, n. 104, held that damage done by a ship's crane to a crane ashore was covered by the words "or otherwise".
56. Cour d'Appel of Rennes, 23 September 1992, *Comanav* v. *Etat Francais—The "Azilal"* [1995] DMF 301.

(b) Loss of Life or Personal Injury caused by any Ship or occurring in connection with the Operation of any Ship

I.322 The words "caused by any ship" are not followed in this case by the additional words "either in collision or otherwise", but seem to cover the same types of occurrence; in addition they may cover events occurring on board when the ship is the actual instrument by which the damage was done, e.g. a block falling and killing a passenger. The second part of the sentence widens the scope of this particular maritime claim to situations where the ship is not the instrument of the occurrence, such as when a passenger is injured falling on a slippery deck, or when a passenger falls overboard due to the lack of an adequate rail.[57]

(c) Salvage

I.323 Claims arising out of salvage may include both claims of salvors for salvage reward, and claims of the owners of the salvaged vessel on account of damage or delay due to the negligence of the salvors.

I.324 The notion of salvage may not be the same in the jurisdictions of the States parties to the Arrest Convention. Traditionally, the notion of salvage was wider in common law jurisdictions than in civil law jurisdictions. In the former jurisdictions it included both services rendered to a ship afloat or aground and the refloating operations of a sunken ship and her cargo. In the latter jurisdictions instead it did not include the refloating of sunken ships, the removal of wrecks and the finding of derelicts. For example, in France law no. 61–1262 of 24 November 1961, as amended by law no. 82–990 of 23 November 1982, regulates the salvage of the "épaves maritimes" which include flotsam (*engins flottants*) ships in non-floating conditions (*en état de non-flottabilité*) abandoned by their crew as well as their provisions and their cargoes. Although the provisions of law no. 61–1262 are made subject to international conventions, it has always been settled in France that the 1910 Salvage Convention did not apply to the salvage of "épaves maritimes".[58] In Italy refloating of sunken ships, removal of wrecks and finding of derelicts are the subject of special rules different from those applicable to salvage and, therefore, are not included in the notion of salvage or, more precisely, of its equivalent in Italian legal terminology, identical to the French: "*assistenza e salvataggio*"/"*assistance et sauvetage*".

I.325 The definition of "vessel" for the purpose of determining the scope of application of the 1989 Salvage Convention has been discussed at some length within IMO's Legal Committee. In the CMI Montreal Draft[59] the following definition had been adopted:

"Vessel" means any ship, craft or structure capable of navigation, including any vessel which is stranded, left by its crew or sunk.

I.326 Objections were raised against the last part of this definition by France and Italy, and it was agreed to delete the words "including any vessel which is stranded, left by its crew or sunk". The deletion of these words has, however, not ensured clarity. In fact the

---

57. Verstrepen, "Arrest and Judicial Sale of Ships in Belgium", *supra*, note 55, p. 145, n. 105.

58. Ripert, *Droit Maritime*, IV edition, vol. III, Paris 1953, paragraph 2136, pp. 100 and 101; Rodière, *Traité Général de Droit Maritime, Evénements de Mer*, Paris 1972, p. 236.

59. CMI—Montreal II, article 1–1(2), page 40.

words "capable of navigation" may be interpreted as referring not as much to the vessel in the conditions in which she is at the time when the salvage services are rendered, but to the vessel in sound conditions; it is, in other words, a general definition of the characteristics of the *res* that may be the subject of the salvage services. That this must be the correct interpretation of the definition is confirmed by the fact that in the original text the (notion of) vessel "capable of navigation" *included* "any vessel which is stranded, left by its crew or sunk" and this indicated that also a stranded or sunken vessel was, for the purposes of the definition, treated as vessels "capable of navigation". Moreover, if the definition were strictly interpreted, a vessel which is aground would not be included.

I.327 It is thought that for the purpose of establishing the scope of the salvage services the definition of "property" in Article 1(c) is relevant,[60] particularly if it is considered in connection with the reservation permitted by Article 30 in respect of maritime cultural property of prehistoric, archaeological or historic interest situated on the sea-bed. In view of the wide definition of "property" as "any property not permanently and intentionally attached to the shoreline" and the limited possible exclusion, if a ship which is stranded or sunk and a wreck, could not come under the definition of "vessel", it would certainly come under the definition of "property".

I.328 Since the 1989 Salvage Convention is now in force between a relevant number of maritime States,[61] it is thought that the notion of salvage under that Convention is relevant, at least in the States Parties to both the Salvage and the Arrest Convention, for the purposes of the definition of the maritime claim under consideration.

I.329 Two further questions arise in respect of this maritime claim. The first is whether the claims to special compensation under Article 14 of the 1989 Salvage Convention may be treated as salvage claims. The second is whether the claims in respect of preventive measures under the Civil Liability Convention 1969 and under the HNS Convention 1996 may be so treated.

I.330 The first question should have a positive answer. In fact, the claim for special compensation is a claim of the salvor who has carried out (wholly or partly unsuccessfully) salvage operations. Therefore, the claim under Article 14 of the 1989 Salvage Convention should qualify as a claim in respect of salvage operations.

I.331 The second question, on the other hand, should have a negative answer. Measures taken after an incident causing pollution damage as defined in the Protocol of 1992 to the Civil Liability Convention 1969 or causing damage as defined in the HNS Convention 1996 has occurred to prevent or minimise such damage cannot qualify as salvage operations, for these operations, at least according to the classic notion of salvage, must relate to a ship or cargo in danger.

---

60. The definition is the following:
   "Property" means any property not permanently and intentionally attached to the shoreline and includes freight at risk.
   On such definition see Vincenzini, *International Salvage Law*, London 1997, p. 146; F. Berlingieri, "L'introduzione nell'ordinamento italiano della Convenzione del 1989 sul salvataggio: suoi effetti sulla normativa previgente", [1998] Dir. Mar. 1369.
61. The States Parties to the 1989 Salvage Convention are: Australia, Canada, China, Croatia, Denmark, Egypt, Georgia, Greece, Guyana, India, Iran, Ireland, Italy, Jordan, Marshall Islands, Mexico, Netherlands, Nigeria, Norway, Oman, Saudi Arabia, Sweden, Switzerland, United Arab Emirates, United Kingdom and United States.

(d) Agreement relating to the Use or Hire of any Ship whether by Charterparty or Otherwise

I.332 In order to establish the scope of this head of claim, it is necessary to consider also the two following heads, under (e) and (f) which relate respectively to agreements for the carriage of goods whether by charter party or otherwise and to loss of or damage to goods including baggage.

I.333 The heads of claim under (d) and (e) have two common elements: they both relate to an agreement, and identify such agreement with the phrase "whether by charter party or otherwise". The distinction lies in the description of the subject matter of the agreement: in subparagraph (d) it is the "use or hire" of a ship, while in sub-paragraph (e) it is the carriage of goods. Since a great many agreements for the hire of a ship are made for the carriage of goods, there is an overlapping between (d) and (e). For example, time and voyage charter-parties for the carriage of goods would come under the description of subparagraph (d) as well as under that of subparagraph (e).

I.334 Subparagraph (d), however, covers agreements for purposes other than carriage of goods, such as demise charters, where the owner does not undertake to perform the carriage but only to enable the charterer to employ the ship, as well as time or voyage charters for carriage of passengers, for the performance of a cruise, for rendering salvage[62] or towage services, for laying out cables or for drilling operations and for oil storage.

I.335 Reference to agreements for the "use" of a ship in addition to agreements for the "hire" of a ship, which existed in the UK Supreme Court of Judicature (Consolidation) Act 1925,[63] is probably meant to include agreements which do not provide for a payment in respect of the use of the ship, as is the case in a salvage agreement or a contract for carriage of goods or passengers without reward, as well as agreements connected with the use, or employment, of a ship, such as management agreements.[64]

---

62. The House of Lords in *The Escherscheim*, [1976] 2 Lloyd's Rep. 1, at p. 8 held, on the particular facts of the case, that a salvage agreement on Lloyd's form could be qualified as an agreement for the use or hire of a ship.

63. The English Supreme Court of Judicature (Consolidation) Act 1925, enumerated in s. 22(1)(a)(xii) the following three claims:

Any claim:

(1) arising out of an agreement relating to the use or hire of a ship; or

(2) relating to the carriage of goods in a ship; or

(3) in tort in respect of goods carried in a ship.

Neither under (1) nor under (2) was reference made to charterparties and, therefore, the words "use or hire" probably covered charterparties.

64. For a case of arrest of a vessel by the managers as security of their claim see *Stewart Chartering Ltd.* v. *Owners of the Ship "Peppy"* [1997] 2 Lloyd's Rep. 722. Even if in that case the arrest was held to be a repudiatory breach of the management agreement, it would appear that the claim of a manager, if grounded, is in English law a maritime claim. A contrary view was instead expressed in the Netherlands: President of the Arrondissementsrechtbank of Rotterdam 4 July 1996—*The "Olympian Duchess"*, [1997] Schip en Schade 100. In France the Cour d'Appel of Rouen in its judgment of 15 April 1982 in *Compania de Navegacion Pancarib* v. *Compagnie Générale Maritime* [1982] DMF 744, held that claims arising out of a sale contract were not covered by Art. 1(1)(d). In Greece the Single Member First Instance Court of Piraeus in Decision No. 3522/1984 (1985) 13 Maritime Law Review 44, held that the claim of the port authority of a French port against the owners of the ship for breach of a contract (non-continuation of voyages due to alleged repairs of the ship) which provided that the ship was permitted to carry passengers/tourists in a particular line from and to the port and the port authority undertook to cover any shortfall of the operational expenses of the ship is not a "maritime claim" (i.e. a claim arising out of an "agreement relating to the use or hire of any ship whether by charterparty or otherwise") because the French port authority did not have any claim from the use of the ship but expected profits from the tax and duties imposed on the passengers and cars moving through the port. In Belgium the Court of Appeal of Antwerp with judgment of 6 August 1982, *The "Ponte Pedrido"* (cited by Verstrepen,

I.336 The inclusion of these agreements is made possible by the very wide description of the type of contract—or document—evidencing the agreement realised with the words "whether by charter party or otherwise".

I.337 The French text does not correspond to the English text, since the word corresponding to "use" is "utilisation" and the word corresponding to "hire" is "location". In fact while "utilisation" can correspond to "use", or "employment", "location" has instead a much more restricted meaning, since it corresponds to contract by demise.

(e) Agreement relating to the Carriage of Goods in any Ship whether by Charterparty or Otherwise

I.338 The words "agreement relating to the carriage of goods . . . whether by charterparty or otherwise" seem to cover all contracts of affreightment with the exclusion of the bareboat charter, viz. time charterparties, trip charters, single and consecutive voyage charterparties, slot charters,[65] tonnage agreements and contracts of carriage under bills of lading or non-negotiable documents, such as waybills, usually in the liner trade. Claims arising out of any such agreement would seem to include those for any type of breach,[66] and thus also those for loss of or damage to goods. But since these latter claims are specifically covered by subparagraph (f), it would appear that subparagraph (e) covers all types of breach except those resulting in loss of or damage to goods. Surprisingly, no reference is made to contracts for the carriage of persons.

I.339 In England the significance of the words "relating to" was considered in *Gatoil Inc.* v. *Arkwright-Boston Manufacturers Mutual Insurance Co. (The "Sandrina")*[67] with reference to sections 1(1)(h) and 47(2)(e) of the Administration of Justice Act 1956[68] the

"Arrest and Judicial Sale of Ships", *supra*, note 14) held that a claim for loss of hire due to the repudiation of a sale agreement does not come under sub-paragraph (d). In England an agreement to refer disputes to arbitration was held not to be, itself, an "agreement in relation to the use or hire of a ship" under section 20(2)(h) of the Supreme Court Act 1981 for the purposes of the enforcement of an award by an action *in rem* on a ship owned by the debtor (*The "Bumbesti"*, [1999] 2 Lloyd's Rep. 481).

65. In *MSC Mediterranean Shipping Company S.A.* v. *The Owners of the Ship "Tychi"* [1999] 2 Lloyd's Rep. 11 the English Court of Appeal held that a slot charterer is a charterer for the purposes of s. 21(4) of the Supreme Court Act 1981. Clarke L.J. stated (at p. 21):
> It follows that the reasoning which leads to the conclusion that the voyage charterer of a ship is a charterer within section 21(4) also leads to the conclusion that the slot charterer is such a charterer.

He then stated (at p. 22):
> In my judgment a slot charter satisfies, for example, the characteristics of a charterparty identified by Hobhouse, J. in *The "Torenia"* [1983] 2 Lloyd's Rep. 210 at page 216. . . . In all these circumstances . . . I would hold that the expression "the charterer of the ship" can include a slot charterer and that a slot charterer can properly be described as the charterer of the ship.

66. In *The "Veliko Tirnovo"*, cited by Verstrepen, *Arrest and Judicial Sale of Ships in Belgium*, at p. 145, n. 108, the Juge des Saisies held that a claim for damages arising out of the issue of an antedated bill of lading was a maritime claim covered by subpara. (e).

67. [1985] 1 Lloyd's Rep. 181. For a comment on this judgment see D. C. Jackson, "Containers Supplied to a Ship for her Operation", [1988] 1 LMCLQ 423.

68. S. 47(2)(e) of the Administration of Justice Act 1956, which is in the part of the Act relating to Scotland, follows verbatim (except for the opening word "any") the terms of Art. 1(1)(e) of the Convention. Section 1(1)(h), which is in the part of the Act relating to England, combines paras. (d) and (e) of Art. 1(1) of the Convention by giving the following description of the claim: "any claim arising out of any agreement relating to the carriage of goods in any ship or to the use or hire of a ship." This formulation was maintained in s. 20(2)(h) of the Supreme Court Act 1981.

wording of which was criticised by Lord Wilberforce.[69] Lord Keith of Kinkel held that, while the meaning must be wider than would be conveyed by the particle "for", it would on the other hand be unreasonable to infer that it was intended to be sufficient that the agreement should be in some way connected, however remotely, with the carriage of goods in a ship or with the use or hire of a ship[70]: there should, in his view, be "some reasonably direct connection with such activities". Such a direct connection would exist, for example, in the case of an agreement for the cancellation of a contract for the carriage of goods in a ship or for the use or hire of a ship, but would not exist as regards the contract of insurance. A much wider meaning had been previously upheld by Sheen J. in *The "Sonia S"*[71] where it was decided that the claim for payment of container hire was a claim arising out of an agreement relating to the carriage of goods in a ship, because that was the purpose of hiring the containers and thus it was held that the claim came within paragraph (h) of section 20(2) of the 1981 Supreme Court Act, which corresponds to subparagraph (e) of Article 1(1) of the Convention. Although this decision was not taken to the Court of Appeal, in *The "Sandrina"* Lord Keith of Kinkel, after having expressed his opinion on the significance of the words "relating to", considered the decision in *The "Sonia S"* and stated[72]:

I consider that in *The "Sonia S"* [1983] 2 Lloyd's Rep. 63 there was likewise an insufficiently direct connection between the agreement for the hire of containers and the carriage of goods in a ship. There is clear fallacy in the reasoning of Mr Justice Sheen in the latter part of his judgment, where he equates the use to which the containers were to be put in *The "Eschersheim"* [1976] 2 Lloyd's Rep. 1; [1976] 1 W.L.R. 430. The salvage vessel there was a ship which was to be used under the salvage agreement. The containers were not a ship. In my opinion that decision was wrong and should be overruled.

I.340 The expression "relating to" was again considered by the House of Lords in *Samick Lines Co. Ltd.* v. *Owners of the Ship "Antonis P. Lemos"*[73] where Lord Brandon of Oakbrook stated that the narrow construction of this expression was based on English and Scottish authorities rather than on the arrangement or wording of Article 1(1) of the Convention, and that, in the absence of such authorities, it might not be right to give to the expression under consideration such a narrow construction.[74] However, while the English authority referred to by Lord Brandon, *The "Zeus"*,[75] may not be internationally relevant since it refers to the expression "relating to" as used in section 2 of the County Courts (Admiralty Jurisdiction) (Amendment) Act 1869, the Scottish authority considered

---

69. Lord Wilberforce stated (at pp. 182 and 183):
    Taking the statutory words by themselves, it is obvious enough that they are, in a legal sense, ambiguous, or as I would prefer to state it, loose textured. It is not possible to ascribe a precise or certain meaning to words denoting relationships without an indication what the criterion of relationship is to be. Must the agreement be directly "for" carriage of goods in a ship, or is it enough that it involves directly or indirectly, or that the parties contemplated that there would be, such a carriage as a consequence of the agreement? How close, in such a case, must the relationship be between the agreement and the carriage? Is any connection of a factual character between the agreement and some carriage in a ship sufficient? If not, what is the test of relevant connection? Even when par. (e) is read in conjunction with the other paragraphs in s. 47(2), the statute provides no guidance: the courts are left with a choice of a broad or a narrow interpretation.
70. This is the language used in section 1(1)(h) of the Administration of Justice Act 1956.
71. [1983] 2 Lloyd's Rep. 63.
72. [1985] 1 Lloyd's Rep. 181 at p. 188.
73. [1985] 1 Lloyd's Rep. 283.
74. At p. 289.
75. (1883) 13 P.D. 188.

by him, The *"Aifanourios"*,[76] is more directly relevant because it refers to section 47(2)(a) of the Administration of Justice Act 1956.

I.341 In New Zealand, where the head of claim under section 4(1)(h) of the Admiralty Act 1973 corresponds to that under section 1(1)(h) of the UK Administration of Justice Act, 1956, the High Court in *Reef Shipping Co. Ltd.* v. *The Ship "Fua Kavenga"*[77] followed the opinion of Lord Keith in *The "Sandrina"* and held that a "sufficiently direct connection existed in connection with a claim based on a guarantee given by the Government of Tonga for the performance of the obligations of the charterers under a charter by demise".

I.342 The need for a strict relationship between the claim and a particular ship was affirmed again, still in England, by the Admiralty Court in *The "Lloyd Pacifico"*.[78] This was a case involving an agreement for the carriage by Compania de Navegaçao Lloyd Brasileiro of a maximum of 8,000 containers containing cargoes of coffee or other cargoes to be agreed on the vessels that might be used by Lloyd Brasileiro in its liner service. The plaintiffs issued a writ *in rem* against the ship *Lloyd Pacifico* (and other ships), claiming damages for breach of contract in that the defendants had refused to carry more than 826 containers. Clarke J. stated, with reference to section 20(2)(h) of the Supreme Court Act 1981, which corresponds to Article 1(1)(e) of the Convention[79]:

The questions are thus, in my judgment, whether the contract relates to the use or hire of the *Lloyd Pacifico* or to the carriage of goods in *Lloyd Pacifico*. In my judgment, the claim cannot relate to the carriage of goods in an unidentified ship. I have reached that conclusion both on the ordinary and natural meaning of ss. 20 and 21 of the 1981 Act and on authority. The claim must arise out of an agreement relating to the use or hire of a ship or to the carriage of goods in a ship and the claim must arise in connection with a ship. The ship in the two sections is the same ship.

I.343 It was also considered whether claims in tort came under section 20(2)(h) under which subparagraphs (d) and (e) of the Convention are merged, and in *Samick Lines Co. Ltd.* v. *Owners of the Ship "Antonis P. Lemos"*[80] it was decided in the affirmative on the ground that the expression "arising out of" should be given a wide meaning. Although, as previously stated, this opinion is correct, it does not justify the conclusion reached by the House of Lords. In fact under subparagraphs (d) and (e) reference is made to agreements relating to the use or hire of a ship and to the carriage of goods respectively. Therefore, if the claims in respect of which the ship may be arrested are those arising out of agreements, claims in tort are excluded, because they do not arise out of an agreement. It is worth noting that reference to an agreement is made only in respect of the use or hire of a ship and of the carriage of goods, but not in respect of other claims, though normally based on contract, such as loss or damage to goods (subparagraph (f)), towage (subparagraph (i)), pilotage (subparagraph (j)), supply of goods or materials (subparagraph (k)) and construction, repair or equipment of a ship (subparagraph (l)). In particular, the lack of reference to an agreement is relevant in the present context in respect of claims for loss of or damage to goods, which, therefore, come under the Convention also if based on tort.

76. 1986 S.C. 346.
77. [1987] 1 NZLR 550.
78. [1995] 1 Lloyd's Rep. 54.
79. At p. 57.
80. [1985] 1 Lloyd's Rep. 283 (H.L.).

(f) Loss of or Damage to Goods including Baggage carried in any Ship

I.344 The interpretation of the words "loss or damage" has been considered with respect to the Hague Rules where they sometimes are qualified and sometimes they are not. They are qualified in Article 3(8) in which reference is made in the original French text to "perte ou dommage concernant des marchandises" translated "loss or damage to or in connection with goods" and in Article 4(5) in which reference is made in the original French text to "pertes ou dommage causés aux marchandises ou les concernant" also translated "loss or damage to or in connection with goods" although the French text differs from that in Article 3(8). They are not qualified in Articles 3(6), 4(1) and (2), but the reference in Article 3(6) to a loss or damage which is not apparent clearly indicates that such loss or damage must be a loss of or damage to goods.

I.345 In England in *G.H. Renton & Co. Ltd.* v. *Palmyra Trading Corporation*[81] Lord Morton of Henryton held[82] that the words "in connection with" in the phrase "loss or damage to or in connection with goods" in Article 3(8) of the Hague Rules were wide enough to cover, for example, the loss or damage sustained in having to bear the cost of transhipping the goods. The meaning of the words "loss or damage" was then considered by Devlin J. in *Anglo-Saxon Petroleum Co.* v. *Adamastos Shipping Co.*[83] in respect of Article 4(1) and (2) where they are not qualified. He said (at pp. 87 and 88):

The last question asks whether the words "loss or damage" in Sect. 4(1) and Sect. 4(2) of the Act relate only to physical loss of or damage to goods. The words themselves are not qualified or limited by anything in the section. The Act is dealing with responsibilities and liabilities under contracts of carriage of goods by sea, and clearly such contractual liabilities are not limited to physical damage. A carrier may be liable for loss caused to the shipper by delay or misdelivery, even though the goods themselves are intact. I can see no reason why the general words "loss or damage" should be limited to physical loss or damage.

I.346 In Italy, the Tribunale of Naples with judgment of 17 January 1951[84] held that the notion of "loss" in relation to the carriage of goods includes misdelivery.

I.347 It is not certain that the reasoning of Devlin J. in the *Anglo-Saxon Petroleum* case can apply to the provision in the Arrest Convention, since here the words are qualified by a reference to the goods, while in Article 4(1) and in Article 4(2) of the Hague Rules they are not. It is thought, however, that "loss" can, also in the Arrest Convention, be considered from the subjective standpoint and can, therefore, be related to the person entitled to the delivery of the goods. Misdelivery would, in such case, be included in the notion of loss.[85] It would be difficult, on the contrary, to include in the notion of "loss of or damage to goods" claims such as claims for the cost of transhipment as in the *Renton* v. *Palmyra* case.

I.348 This, however, would not exclude this type of claims from the scope of the Arrest Convention, since they would in any event come under the preceding subparagraph (e).

---

81. [1957] 2 Lloyd's Rep. 379 (H.L.).
82. At p. 390.
83. [1957] 1 Lloyd's Rep. 79.
84. *Sottocasa* v. *Tirrenia di Navigazione S.p.A.*, [1951] Dir. Mar. 512. For a discussion on this judgment and on the judgment in the case *Renton* v. *Palmyra* see Carver's *Carriage by Sea*, vol. 1, 13th Ed. London 1982, paragraphs 457 and 458.
85. French Cour de Cassation 3 February 1998, *Halic Denizcilik Ticaret Sanayi Turzim A.S.* v. *Banco Exterior Suiza-The "Yildiram"*, [1998] DMF 255.

I.349 In any event, this subparagraph is wider than the previous one in that it also covers tort claims.

I.350 The word "baggage", without any qualification, seems wide enough to cover both the "luggage" and "cabin luggage" as defined in Article 1(5) and (6) of the Athens Convention 1974.[86]

(g) General Average

I.351 While it is certain that claims for general average contribution come under this subparagraph,[87] it is doubtful whether other claims arising out of a general average act are also covered, particularly when the act is ultimately found not to be such. Probably the problem has no great practical importance, for these claims, at least insofar as damage to or loss of the cargo is concerned, would be covered by subparagraph (f).

(h) Bottomry

I.352 In the draft submitted at the CMI Conference in Naples, reference was also made to respondentia. Mr Miller, speaking for the sub-committee appointed by the Conference with the task of reviewing the list of the maritime claims, explained the deletion of that word[88] as follows:

In subclause (k) the words "or respondentia" are deleted. "Respondentia" is an anomaly which has been unknown to the law of the sea for very nearly a hundred years, as far as I can ascertain, so there is no point in keeping it in.

I.353 It is thought that this reasoning applies to "bottomry" as well.

(i) Towage

I.354 Any type of towage, whether deep-sea or port towage, is covered as well as claims such as damage done by the tug to the tow or vice versa, breach of contract, etc. It must be noted that sometimes reference is made to the nature of the event or to the type of service, as in this instance, and at other times to the type of contract under which the claim may arise. In view of the fact that here reference is made to the type of service, it may be doubted whether claims in respect of a towage contract which has not been executed are covered by this subparagraph.

---

86. A claim in respect of damage to goods carried under a bill of lading has been held to be a maritime claim for the purposes of Art. 7(1) by the Italian Supreme Court (Corte di Cassazione) in its judgment of 28 October 1987, No. 7972, in *S.r.l. Siamar and Nedlloyd Lijnen B.V.* v. *S.r.l. Spedimex* [1989] Dir. Mar. 149.

87. Tribunale of Ravenna, 24 January 1987, *Trademar Conasa S.A.* v. *Line Island Marine Co.—The "Euro-breeze"* [1988] Dir. Mar. 804; Tribunale of Genoa, 22 March 1994, *Galaxy Energy International Ltd.* v. *Dolphin Agenzia Marittima S.p.A.—The "Kapitan V. Trush"* [1994] Dir. Mar. 531; Cour d'Appel of Rouen, 19 June 1984, *Captain of the "Atlantic Mariner"* v. *Trademar Conasa* [1985] DMF 167.

The French Cour de Cassation has, however, held in its judgment of 23 November 1993, *Société Partenree-derei M/S Heidberg and Others* v. *Assurances Mutuelles Agricoles—The "Heidberg"* [1994] DMF 38, that the claim of the cargo insurer who has paid a provisional G.A. contribution is not a maritime claim. The reasons given by the Cour de Cassation are far from clear and are unconvincing.

88. CMI Bulletin No. 105, p. 236; Travaux Préparatoires, p. 287.

(j) Pilotage

I.355 Pilotage was not mentioned in the draft approved by the CMI at Naples. It was added at the Diplomatic Conference, following the proposal of the British delegation on the ground that in English law claims of pilots entitled them to arrest the ship. In this case too, as for towage, reference is made to the type of service giving rise to the claims, rather than to the claims themselves.[89]

(k) Goods or Materials wherever supplied to a Ship for her Operation or Maintenance

I.356 The corresponding head of claim under the English Administration of Justice Act 1956 and under section 20(2)(m) of the Supreme Court Act 1991, has been considered to be a new formulation of the claim for "necessaries" in respect of which the Admiralty jurisdiction was granted under section 6 of the Admiralty Court Act 1840, section 5 of the Admiralty Court Act 1861 and section 22 of the Supreme Court of Judicature (Consolidation) Act 1925. In *The "Fairport"* (No. 5)[90] Brandon J. stated that the claims under section 1(1)(m) of the Administration of Justice Act 1956 were certainly no narrower than the claims for necessaries in the previous Acts and on that basis held that since there was authority that the word "necessaries" covered payments made by way of advances to enable necessaries to be purchased, a similar construction should be given to subparagraph (m). The same reasoning was followed by Peter Gross, Q.C. in *The "Edinburgh Castle"*[91] where he considered to be "necessaries", and thus to come under section 20(2)(m) of the Supreme Court Act 1991, provisions for the passenger and the provision of services consisting in the provision of officers and crew.

I.357 There is no express reference to the origin of this head of claim in the *Travaux Préparatoires*. It is, however, conceivable that the CMI International Committee who drafted the list of maritime claims can have considered the maritime liens listed in Article 2 of the 1926 MLM Convention and more precisely the claims mentioned in Article 2(5), the unofficial English translation of which[92] is the following:

5. Claims resulting from contracts entered into or acts done by the master, acting within the scope of his authority, away from the vessel's home port, where such contracts or acts are necessary for the preservation of the vessel or the continuation of its voyage, whether the master is or is not at the same time owner of the vessel, and whether the claim is his own or that of shipchandlers, repairers, lenders, or other contractual creditors.

I.358 The words "wherever supplied" in subparagraph (k) have been in fact very likely included in order to make clear that, contrary to Article 2(5) of the 1926 MLM Convention, there is no need for this maritime claim to materialise, that goods and materials be

---

89. It may be interesting to note that slightly different language was used in England both in the Administration of Justice Act 1956 by which the Arrest Convention was enacted and in the Supreme Court Act 1981. This claim is in fact described in s. 1(1)(l) of the former and in s. 20(2)(l) of the latter as: "any claim in the nature of pilotage in respect of a ship or an aircraft."

90. [1967] 2 Lloyd's Rep. 162.

91. [1999] 2 Lloyd's Rep. 362, at p. 363.

92. The French text of article 2(5) of the 1926 MLM Convention is the following:

    5. Les créances provenant des contrats passés ou d'opérations effectuées par le capitaine hors du port d'attache, en vertu de ses pouvoirs légaux, pour les besoins réels de la conservation du navire ou de la continuation du voyage, sans distinguer si le capitaine est ou non en même temps propriétaire du navire et si la créance est la sienne ou celle des fournisseurs, réparateurs, prêteurs ou autres contractants.

THE INDIVIDUAL MARITIME CLAIMS

supplied away from the homeport. The maritime claim under consideration, considered jointly with that under subparagraph (l) in respect of construction, repair and equipment, is wider than the corresponding maritime lien under Article 2(5) of the 1926 MLM Convention not only because goods and materials may be supplied anywhere, thus also at the homeport, but, also, because they may be ordered by any person, including the owner himself, while for the maritime lien to arise under the 1926 MLM Convention they must be ordered by the master.[93]

I.359 Since the link between this maritime lien and the common law lien for necessaries[94] is undispensable, and is evidenced by the words "necessary for the preservation of the vessel or the continuation of the voyage", the precedents relating to the lien for necessaries as well as to the lien granted under the 1926 MLM Convention can be of avail in the interpretation of the maritime claims under Article 1(1)(k) of the Arrest Convention. It may be added that the concept of necessity is implied in subparagraph (k) in the word "for" (the operation and maintenance of the ship).[95]

I.360 It has been held that goods include bunker,[96] lubricating oil, stores,[97] food, drink and other consumables supplied for the use of the officers and crew and of the passengers.[98] Materials include spare parts and replacements of any kind[99] and equipment.[100]

I.361 The word "wherever" seems to indicate that the supply can also be made at the home port, so there is no requirement here that the supplies should be made for the preservation of the vessel or the continuation of the voyage, as in Article 2(5) of the 1926 Convention on Maritime Liens and Mortgages.

I.362 The word "supplied" does not necessarily refer to a sale, but may also include supply by way of hire[101] and, therefore, may include the lease of containers, provided the

---

93. On this provision see F. Berlingieri, *I diritti di garanzia sulla nave, l'aeromobile e le cose caricate*, Padova 1965, p. 214.

94. On the maritime lien for necessaries see in England Price, *The Law of Maritime Liens*, London 1940, p. 29 and, only in respect of the master's disbursements, Thomas, *Maritime Liens*, London 1980, p. 28. In the United States see Gilmore and Black, *The Law of Admiralty*, II Edition, Mineola, New York 1975, p. 657.

95. For a different view see D. C. Jackson, "Containers Supplied to a Ship for the Operation", *supra*, note 67.

96. Tribunale of Ravenna, 24 January 1987, *supra*, note 87; Tribunale of Bari 12 September 1997, *Shipoil S.A.—The "Bergamo"*, [1998] Dir. Mar. 172; Tribunale of Naples 22 September 1995, *Mamidoil Jetoil Greek Petroleum Co.—The "Carlo R."*, [1997] Dir. Mar. 147; Tribunale of Genoa 25 January 1997, *North Sea Petroleum GmbH* v. *Duplex Maritime Co. S.r.l.—The "Dumbraveni"*, [1998] Dir. Mar. 1222; Cour d'Appel of Antwerp, 16 January 1991, and Juge des Saisies of Antwerp, 6 June 1985, cited by Verstrepen, "Arrest and Judicial Sale of Ships in Belgium", *supra*, note 55, at p. 146, n. 110.

97. Tribunale of Venice 14 October 1998, *Sonino S.r.l. Provveditoria Marittima* v. *Star of Venice Navigation S.A.—The "Star of Venice"*, (unreported); Tribunale of Genoa 4 June 1997, *Italmare-Olivieri Ship Chandlers S.r.l.* v. *Adriatica Tankers Shipping Co. S.A.—The "Irene VII"*, [1998] Dir. Mar. 739. Cigarettes for the crew are treated as ship's stores, provided the quantity ordered is reasonable: Juge des Saisies of Antwerp, 1 February 1974, *The "Calypso IV"*, cited by Verstrepen, "Arrest and Judicial Sale of Ships in Belgium", *supra*, note 55, at p. 146, n. 110.

98. *The "Edinburgh Castle"*, [1999] 2 Lloyd's Rep. 362, at p. 363.

99. Tribunale of Genoa 4 June 1997, *Italmare-Olivieri Ship Chandlers S.r.l.* v. *Adriatic Tankers Shipping Co. S.A.—The "Irene VII"*, [1998] Dir. Mar. 739.

100. *The "Edinburgh Castle"*, [1999] 2 Lloyd's Rep. 362, at p. 363. It has also been held by the President of the Arrondissementsrechtbank of Gravenhage with decision of 29 November 1993 in *The "Ostsee"*, [1994] Nederlandse Jurisprudentie 30 that the lease of pipes to a dredger comes under the notion of supply of materials.

101. This was held in England in *The "River Rima"* [1988] 2 Lloyd's Rep. 193 at p. 195 by Lord Brandon of Oakbrook and in the Netherlands by the President of the Arrondissementsrechtbank of Gravenhage with decision of 29 November 1993, *supra*, note 100.

containers are intended for a particular ship and not for use by the shipowner on any ship owned or operated by him. This distinction was considered in England by the House of Lords in *The "River Rima"*.[102] In that case Tiphook Container Rental Co. Ltd. had leased a number of containers to Nigerian National Shipping Line Ltd. There was no term in the agreement relating to the use to which containers hired under it were to be put and, in particular, there was no provision that containers so hired should be used for the carriage of cargo on any ship of Nigerian National Shipping Line (NNSL), specified or unspecified. Tiphook began an action *in rem* against the *River Rima*, a ship owned by NNSL, and arrested her, claiming damages for conversion in respect of containers supplied to the *River Rima* and/or other sister ships. The Admiralty Court (Sheen J.) declared that the claim of Tiphook was within the Admiralty jurisdiction of the High Court by virtue of paragraph (m) of section 20(2) of the Supreme Court Act 1981, corresponding almost verbatim to Article 1(1)(k) of the Convention, and dismissed NNSL's application to set aside the writ.[103] On appeal by NNSL, the Court of Appeal held that the lease agreement was not sufficiently directly connected with the operation of ships.[104] The judgment of the Court of Appeal was upheld by the House of Lords, but on slightly different grounds. Lord Brandon of Oakbrook in fact, after having traced the historical background of section 20(2)(m) of the 1981 Act through section 1(1)(m) of the Administration of Justice Act 1956, Article 1(1)(k) of the Convention and section 22(1)(a) of the Supreme Court of Judicature (Consolidation) Act 1925 on which the list of maritime claims in the Convention was based, held[105]:

Since specification of the identity of the particular ship to which necessaries were supplied was an essential ingredient of a claim under par. (vii) of s. 22(1)(a) of the 1925 Act, it is to be inferred that it was also intended to be an essential ingredient of a claim under par. (k) of art. 1(1) of the Convention, which was derived from that earlier English provision.

I.363 He then added that this inference was reinforced by the terms of Article 3 of the Convention, which permits the arrest on a maritime claim of either the particular ship in respect of which the claim arose or a sister ship, pointing out that, therefore, it was intended that a maritime claim should arise in respect of a specified ship.

I.364 A different approach was followed instead by the District Court of Rotterdam in *The "River Jimini"*,[106] a ship also owned by NNSL, where the claim related to containers leased to them, intended for carriage on board that vessel or on board sister ships. However, the restricted approach of Lord Brandon seems to be correct. The relation of the maritime claim with a particular ship is indeed one of the essential ingredients of the structure of the Convention. Reference to it may also be found in Article 3(4), where reference is made to the situation where, in the case of a charter by demise of a ship, the charterer and not the registered owner is liable in respect of a claim relating to that ship, and in Article 7(1)(c) whereby jurisdiction on the merits of the court of the country in

---

102. [1988] 2 Lloyd's Rep. 193.

103. [1987] 2 Lloyd's Rep. 106, at pp. 107–110.

104. [1987] 2 Lloyd's Rep. 106, at pp. 110–114. A similar conclusion was reached in Greece by the Single Member First Instance Court of Piraeus in Decision No. 2956/1981 (1981) 3 Piraki Nomologia 364.

105. [1988] 2 Lloyd's Rep. 193, at p. 197. This judgment has been criticized by D. C. Jackson, "Containers Supplied to a Ship for her Operation", *supra*, note 67.

106. Judgment of 29 June 1984, [1984] Schip en Schaade 127, cited by Sheen J. in *The "River Rima"* [1987] 2 Lloyd's Rep. 106 at p. 108.

which the arrest is made is founded on the fact that "the claim concerns the voyage of the ship during which the arrest was made".

I.365 "Operation" is a much wider concept than "continuation of the voyage": thus bunker supplies under a contract made by the owner come within this concept.[107] In turn, "maintenance" is wider than "preservation", for maintenance includes work in excess of that strictly required for preservation. Even so, insurance premiums, which an insurance broker is legally liable to pay to the underwriter, whether or not his client has first paid him, are not costs of "operation or maintenance".

I.366 In the English case *Bain Clarkson Ltd.* v. *The Owners of the ship "Sea Friends"*,[108] a distinction is drawn between the costs of keeping a ship seaworthy to sail the seas and trade, and expenses made to protect the shipowner's financial interests. Sheen J. added:

Lord Wilberforce pointed out in *Gatoil International Inc.* v. *Arkwright Boston Manufacturers Mutual Insurance Co.* [1985] 1 Lloyd's Rep. 181; [1985] A.C. 255 that the point had arisen at the Diplomatic Conference in 1952; as a matter of policy insurance should not be included among the list of maritime claims . . . it would . . . be an odd result if they were included by a side-wind under paragraph (p) by the intervention of insurance brokers between the insurers and the shipowners.

(l) Construction, Repair or Equipment of any Ship or Dock Charges and Dues

I.367 Why claims of such a diverse nature have been put together is not easy to understand. The first group of claims relates to works, as opposed to supplies, and clearly aims at covering all kinds of work done on a ship, from her construction,[109] to any work done thereafter. Here there is no express limitation on the purpose, although repairs are done when something is damaged or not operational, and thus the purpose is to ensure the maintenance of the ship. The problem which arises is whether "repairs" must be restricted to the work done to make good damage, in which event it would not cover work done to improve the condition of a ship, or to effect her conversion into a ship of a different type.[110] Some works which do not come under the restricted definition of "repairs" would, however, be covered by the term "equipment", such as the installation of inert gas or segregated ballast systems on board a tanker.

I.368 The word "equipment" is used in Article 1(1)(l) of the 1952 Arrest Convention in the sense of work done on board with a view to providing the ship with the equipment required for her operation, rather than in the sense of providing the ship with supplies. It is worth noting that similar language is used in Article 3(1)(b) of the Hague Rules, wherein it is provided that the carrier shall exercise due diligence to: *convenablement*

---

107. Tribunale of Ravenna, 24 January 1987, *Trademar Conasa S.A.* v. *Line Island Marine Co.* [1988] Dir. Mar. 804. The court correctly stated that the claim for bunker supplies was a maritime claim even though, bunkers not being necessary for the continuation of the voyage, it was not secured by a maritime lien (Italy has ratified the 1926 Brussels Convention on Maritime Liens and Mortgages).

108. [1991] 2 Lloyd's Rep. 322.

109. Supplies effected and work done in respect of a ship under construction by subcontractors at the request of the builders have been held to give rise to a maritime claim by the Juge des Saisies of Dendermonde: order of 20 September 1982, *The "Flanders Harmony"*, cited by Verstrepen, "Arrest and Judicial Sale of Ships in Belgium", *supra*, note 55, at p. 146, n. 111.

110. For a wide interpretation of this provision, see Tribunale of Lecce, 24 December 1994, *Cantiri Balsamo* v. *Sail Boat Enterprise—The "Felguera"*, [1996] Dir. Mar. 1064.

armer, équiper et approvisionner le navire ("properly man, equip and supply the ship").

I.369 The words "dock charges and dues" did not exist in the draft approved by the CMI at Naples and were added at the Diplomatic Conference following the request of the British delegation, which explained such request as follows[111]:

It wishes also to add in subparagraph (n) that the builders or repairers of ships are entitled to include all repair costs.

I.370 By so stating, the British delegation meant dock charges, as appears from the subsequent intervention of the French Delegate Mr de Grandmaison who, speaking in support of the British proposal, stated[112]:

The French Delegation accepts the addition of "dock charges" to the list of maritime claims and is of the view that there is no possible conflict with the terms of Art. 9. The shiprepairer who pays, for example, the cost of drydock will be entitled to add to its claim such cost.

I.371 From the *travaux préparatoires* it would thus appear that claims in respect of dock charges were considered only if put forward by ship repairers.

(m) Wages of Masters, Officers or Crew

I.372 The problem that may arise in this connection is whether other emoluments and sums payable by the employer, such as taxes, social security and pension contributions, indemnities due to seamen in the event of the total loss of the vessel, etc., may be deemed to be included under this heading. The problem was examined in England in a number of cases, and it was held that the wages concept included emoluments such as victualling allowances and bonuses,[113] both the employer's and the employee's national insurance contributions[114] social benefit contributions[115] and insurance and pensions contributions.[116] "Severance pay" because the crew have lost their jobs has been held not to be a maritime claim.[117]

(n) Master's Disbursements, including Disbursements made by Shippers, Charterers or Agents on behalf of a Ship or her Owner

I.373 The final words of this subparagraph, although specifically referring to the disbursements made by shippers, charterers and agents, may also be utilised to establish the type of master's disbursements covered herein. Therefore, the disbursements made on behalf of a person other than the owner of the ship, such as the bareboat charterer or the time or

---

111. *Procès-verbaux*, p. 64; *Travaux Préparatoires*, p. 291.
112. *Procès-verbaux*, p. 69; *Travaux Préparatoires*, p. 293.
113. *The "Tergeste"*, 9 Asp. M.L.C. 346; *The "Elmville"* (No. 2), 10 Asp. M.L.C. 23.
114. *The "Gee Whizz"* [1951] 1 Lloyd's Rep. 145.
115. *The "Arosa Star"* [1959] 2 Lloyd's Rep. 396; *The "Arosa Kulm"* (No. 2) [1960] 1 Lloyd's Rep. 97.
116. *The "Fairport"* [1965] 2 Lloyd's Rep. 183; *The "Halcyon Skies"* [1976] 1 Lloyd's Rep. 461.
117. *The "Tacoma City"* [1990] 1 Lloyd's Rep. 408 and [1991] 1 Lloyd's Rep. 330.

voyage charterer, do not qualify as maritime claims unless made on behalf of the ship.[118]

I.374 The disbursements made on behalf of the ship (or, more correctly, in respect of the ship) seem to be of a different nature to those made on behalf of the owner, for otherwise there would have been no reason to refer to both.[119] If this is so, they should cover a more limited area and relate to the ship herself, and not to her operation, such as maintenance and repair costs. Disbursements made for the operation of the ship, such as harbour dues, agency fees, pilot fees, tug charges, stevedoring costs and the like, would not consequently be maritime claims unless made on behalf of the owner of the ship.

I.375 Such restricted interpretation of the notion of disbursements made on behalf of the ship seems to be supported by the fact that, if it were to include disbursements made for the running of the ship to the extent that this is at the charge of a charterer, it would make no sense to refer to disbursements made by charterers on behalf of the ship, for these would be made by them on their own behalf.

I.376 Agency fees and fees of the manager of a ship[120] are not disbursements, and therefore are not maritime claims[121] nor can claims of the owners against the agents come under this head of claim. A contrary view has been held by the Arrondissementsrechtbank of Rotterdam with decision 13 March 1987, in The "Ibn Badis"[122] which granted the arrest of a ship owned by the agent in respect of a claim of an owner for repayment of the balance of funds remitted to the agent.

(o) Disputes as to the title or to ownership of any ship

I.377 Any dispute about the title to a ship entails a dispute about property and vice versa.[123] When the property in the ship passes from the seller to the buyer, the title to the ship will be transferred to the buyer.

118. The French Cour de Cassation in its judgment of 10 May 1989 in *Delaware Shipping Corporation* v. *CNAN-The "Tabessa"* [1989] DMF 704 held that the claim of the owner against a port agent for the reimbursement of funds remitted to the agent is a maritime claim and entitled the owner to arrest a ship owned by the port agent. This judgment was strongly criticised—and quite rightly so—by Professor Bonassies ([1989] DMF 706) who pointed out that the Cour de Cassation had overlooked the fundamental principle whereby the claimant may arrest the ship "in respect of which the maritime claim arose" or a sister ship and that in the instant case that ship was the ship of the arrestor himself. In a similar case, the right of arrest was denied by the Tribunale of Genoa in its judgment of 21 April 1993 in *Empresa Cubana de Fletes* v. *International Maritime Services Ltd.—The "José Antonio Echeverria"* [1994] Dir. Mar. 449. In that case the claimant was the owner, who had a claim against the charterer for the payment of the freight and had applied for the arrest of a ship owned by the charterer.
119. See the UK Administration of Justice Act 1956, Part 1, s. 1(1)(p) and now the Supreme Court Act 1981, s. 20(2)(p) wherein reference is only made to disbursements made "on account of a ship".
120. Judgment of the President of the Arrondissementsrechtbank of Rotterdam 4 July 1996—The "Olympian Duchess" [1997] Schip en Schade 100.
121. See *contra* in England, The "Westport" [1966] 1 Lloyd's Rep. 342 and, in Greece, Single Member First Instance Court of Piraeus, Decision No. 8647/1979 (1985) 9 Maritime Law Review 6. In Italy, the Tribunale of Genoa in its judgment of 20 May 1995 in *Überseeschiffahrtsagentur Transnautic GmbH & Co. K.G.* v. *Baltic Shipping—The "Akademic Gorbunov"* [1995] Dir. Mar. 768, held that a claim of an agent for a substantial amount should be deemed to have arisen in connection with the agency relationship which existed between the owners and the agents, without considering how the claim had actually arisen.
122. [1987] Schip en Schade 123. This decision has been upheld by the Gerechtshof (Court of Appeal) of Gravenhage with judgment of 5 December 1989, [1990] Schip en Schade 75.
123. The claim of the owner of a ship sold in a forced sale contesting the validity of the sale was held not to be a maritime claim covered by sub-para. (o) by the Juge des Saisies of Antwerp in his order of 20 October 1980 in The "Jocelyne", cited by Verstrepen, "Arrest and Judicial Sale of Ships in Belgium", *supra*, note 55, at p. 146, n. 114.

I.378 The identity of the two terms is supported by the fact that in the French text reference is made only to *la propriété contestée d'un navire.*[124] Moreover, as regards disputes between co-owners, subparagraph (p) makes reference only to ownership.

I.379 Disputes about the ownership of shares in a ship are obviously included in this subparagraph, save disputes between co-owners, which are covered by the following subsection.

I.380 On the other hand, disputes about the possession of a ship do not seem to be covered by the language of this subparagraph, and the reference in the subsequent subparagraph to ownership and possession or earnings of a ship indirectly confirms this conclusion. If this is so, there seems to be an omission of some importance.

(p) Disputes between Co-owners of any Ship as to the Ownership, Possession, Employment or Earnings of that Ship

I.381 A preliminary remark which must be made in connection with this subparagraph is that the French text differs from the English text, for it is worded as follows:

La propriété contestée d'un navire ou sa possession ou son exploitation, ou les droits aux produits d'exploitation d'un navire en co-propriété.

I.382 The fact that in the first part of the French text reference is made generally to disputes as to ownership or possession of a ship, and only in the second part is reference made to a *navire en co-propriété*, may raise doubts whether the whole of this subparagraph refers to disputes between co-owners, as clearly appears from the English text. This seems the more reasonable solution to this language problem, for otherwise in the French text the first part of subparagraph (p) would cover the same ground as subparagraph (o). In any event, there remains an overlap between this and the preceding subparagraph since disputes between co-owners as to ownership are already covered in subparagraph (o). The disputes covered by this subparagraph must be between co-owners and not between partners or shareholders of a company. If, therefore, the operation of a ship is entrusted by the co-owners to a company formed between them for that purpose the dispute is not between co-owners. In the Netherlands the Gerechtshof (Court of Appeal) of Gravenhage in *The "Alhena"*[125] held that a claim of one company and its assignee against other company members of a joint venture for the operation of a shipping line did not fall under subparagraph (p).

(q) The Mortgage or Hypothecation of any Ship

I.383 The wording is not entirely correct, for the claim does not arise out of a mortgage, but out of the contract (e.g. loan agreement) in respect of which the mortgage is executed. It would have been more correct to refer to claims secured by a mortgage. This, however, would have created practical drafting difficulties, since the maritime claims are listed under the opening sentence of Article 1(1), which is worded: " 'Maritime Claim' means a claim arising out of one or more of the following:". A correct wording is used instead

---

124. In Part I, s. 1(1)(a) of the UK Administration of Justice Act 1956, as well as in s. 20(2)(a) of the Supreme Court Act 1981, reference is made to "possession or ownership".
125. Judgment of 28 June 1985, [1986] Schip en Schade 78.

in the French text of Article 7(1)(f) of the Convention, which provides: "Si la créance est garantie par une hypothèque maritime ou un mortgage sur le navire saisi".[126]

I.384 The word "hypothecation" is used in Article 1(1)(f), as in the unofficial translation of the 1926 Brussels Convention on Maritime Liens and Mortgages, whilst in subsequent conventions[127] the word *hypothèque* is used in the English text. The reason for this change is that the word "hypothecation" has a different meaning in English law, for it is used in respect of bottomry and respondentia.[128]

I.385 Another question to which this provision gives rise is whether the right of arrest is granted only in respect of mortgages and *hypothèques* or may be exercised also in respect of other charges, in addition to unregistered mortgages and *hypothèques*.

I.386 Finally, the present wording seems to include also claims arising out of the mortgages or hypothecation of any share in a ship.

I.387 In England, the contention of a mortgagee that the sale price of the bunkers should be included in the sale price of the ships and paid to them was rejected in *Den Norske Bank A/S* v. *The Owners of the Ships "Eurosun" and "Eurostar"*.[129]

---

126. See *infra*, para. I.866–I.867.

127. Maritime Liens and Mortgages Convention 1967, article 1; Maritime Liens and Mortgages Convention 1993, article 1.

128. In the Report entitled "Consideration of the scope of the revision of the International Convention relating to the Arrest of Sea-going Ships signed at Brussels, 10 May 1952" jointly prepared by the IMO and UNCTAD Secretariats in response to a request from the Joint Intergovernmental Group of Experts (Doc. IMO-LEG/MLM/22 of 20 June 1989 Doc. UNCTAD-TD/B/C.4/AC.8/22 of 8 August 1989) the following comments are made in respect of the wording of this maritime claim:

According to Article 1(q) of the Arrest Convention, a claim arising out of the mortgage or hypothecation of any ship is a "maritime claim" enabling the claimant to arrest the ship. It should be noted that the wording of Article 1 of the Draft Convention on Maritime Liens and Mortgages is "mortgages, 'hypothèques' and registrable charges of the same nature". It is, again, advisable to use the same wording in the Arrest Convention in order to enable the holders of registrable charges of the same nature as the mortgage or hypothèque to arrest the ship in respect of claims arising out of such charges. Furthermore, consideration should be given to the use of the term "hypothèque" in place of "hypothecation", which under English law had a different meaning and was used in relation to bottomry bond and respondentia.

129. [1993] 1 Lloyd's Rep. 106.

CHAPTER 5

Ships that may be Arrested

18. SUMMARY OF THE RULES OF ARTICLE 3

I.388 Pursuant to Article 4 of the Convention there are two basic requirements for the arrest of a ship. The first is that the claim must be related to a particular ship; the second is that the claim must be against the owner of that ship. The relationship between the claim and a ship is a fundamental condition for the arrest under the Convention. Lord Diplock so stated in *The "Eschersheim"*[1]:

It is clear that to be liable to arrest a ship must not only be the property of the defendant to the action but must also be identifiable as the ship in connection with which the claim made in the action arose (or a sister ship of that ship). The nature of the "connection" between the ship and the claim must have been intended to be the same as is expressed in the corresponding phrase in the convention "the particular ship in respect of which the maritime claim arose". One must, therefore, look at the description of each of the maritime claims included in the list in order to identify the particular ship in respect of which a claim of that description could arise.

I.389 Claims against a shipowner that relate to the maintenance and operation of his ships, but which are not related to a particular ship, cannot be secured by means of the arrest of one of the ships owned by him. If, for example, the owner purchases stores or spare parts for his fleet and uses them for one or more of his ships when the need arises, the claim of the supplier for the payment of such spare parts or stores has not arisen in respect of a particular ship. The same situation would exist in the case of a contract for the lease by a shipowner of a number of containers to be used on board the container ships he operates[2] and of a contract of affreightment, when the ships to be employed by the owner for the carriage of the agreed tonnage of cargo are not specified and the owner does not perform the contract. The question of the relationship between the claim and a particular ship has not arisen in respect of Article 3(1) but in respect of some specific maritime claims, such as those listed in Article 1(1)(e) and (f) and, therefore, reference has been made to the relevant judgments when dealing with those particular maritime claims.[3]

---

1. [1976] 2 Lloyd's Rep. 1 at p. 7.
2. In the United States, however, it has been held that the claim of a lessor of containers for accrued rental is secured by a maritime lien even when the containers are leased for use by an entire fleet: *Itel Containers International Corporation* v. *Atlanttrafik Export Service, Ltd.* [1987] A.M.C. 2721 and [1992] A.M.C. 622 *Thyssen Inc.* v. *S.S. Rio Capaya and Others* [1988] A.M.C. 1878. In Italy it has been held that the maritime lien securing claims of the flight personnel of an airline arises on all aircraft on which such personnel have been employed for the whole amount of the claim: Tribunale of Rome, 3 September 1985, *Istituto Mobiliare Italiano* v. *Aerolinee Itavia S.p.A.* [1986] Dir. Mar. 135.
3. *Supra*, para. I.339–I.343 and I.344–I.348.

I.390 The fact that the claim must relate to a particular ship does not entail that only the ship in respect of which the claim has arisen can be arrested. Under the sistership rule also other ships owned by the person liable may be arrested.

I.391 The second requirement, according to which the person liable must be the owner of the ship, is not absolute. Article 3(4) lays down exceptions to it in respect of claims against the demise charterer or other persons.

19. THE FUNDAMENTAL RULE: ARREST OF A SHIP WHEN THE OWNER IS LIABLE IN RESPECT OF THE MARITIME CLAIM RELATING TO THAT SHIP

I.392 Article 3(1) of the Convention provides:

Subject to the provisions of § 4 of this Article and of Article 10, a claimant may arrest either the particular ship in respect of which the maritime claim arose, or any other ship which is owned by the person who was, at the time when the maritime claim arose, the owner of the particular ship, even though the ship arrested be ready to sail; but no ship, other than the particular ship in respect of which the claim arose, may be arrested in respect of any of the maritime claims enumerated in Article 1, 1°, *(o), (p)* or *(q)*.

I.393 The rule that the arrest of a ship is permissible when the owner of that ship is liable in respect of a maritime claim relating to that ship is not expressly stated in this provision. From its wording it would instead appear that a ship may be arrested when the maritime claim has arisen in respect of that ship: a condition which is sufficient only when the claim is secured by a maritime lien.

I.394 The requirement that the owner must be the person liable (save when the claim is secured by a maritime lien) is, however, clearly implied by the provision according to which also a ship other than that in respect of which the maritime claim has arisen may be arrested when it was owned, at the time when the maritime claim has arisen, by the owner of the particular ship. The arrest of another ship in the same ownership would in fact be meaningless if the owner of the particular ship were not liable in respect of the maritime claim. It is also implied by the opening words of Article 3(1) "subject to the provisions of paragraph 4", that such provisions constitute an exception to the general rule laid down in paragraph 1. Since the exception consists in the right of arrest of a ship when the charterer by demise and not the owner is liable in respect of the maritime claim, the general rule must necessarily be that the arrest is only permissible when the owner of the ship is liable.

I.395 The link between the person liable and the ship in respect of which the maritime claim has arisen must continue to exist until the time when the arrest is made. The general rule is, in fact, that a claim is enforceable on the assets of the debtor and an exception to such rule is made only in respect of claims secured by a maritime lien.[4]

I.396 If in fact the claimant had the right to arrest the ship in the hands of a *bona fide* purchaser, the maritime claims would acquire one of the special features of the maritime

---

4. The arrest of a ship after its sale has been held not to be permissible in France by the Cour d'Appel of Montpellier with judgment 31 July 1996, *Sallyview Estates Ltd.* v. *S.A. Enjoy—The "Zaher V"*, [1997] DMF 31 on the strength of the provision in article 9, and in Italy by the Tribunale of Bari with judgment 12 September 1997, *Supoil S.A.*, [1998] Dir. Mar. 172. The opposite view has instead been held by the Cour d'Appel of Douai with judgment 12 September 1996, *IMS* v. *Likeo Maritime Co. Ltd. and Horizon Steamship Ltd.—The "River Asab"*, [1997] DMF 36. The arrest after the sale has been granted by the Cour d'Appel of Rouen with judgment 26 January 1995, *Compagnie Maritime Belge Transport-Italie* v. *Assurance Groupe de Paris—The "Merzario*

liens, viz. the so-called *droit de suite*, which is set out in Article 7(2) of the 1967 Convention on Maritime Liens and Mortgages and now in Article 8 of the 1993 International Convention on Maritime Liens and Mortgages.[5] This problem was raised during the Naples Conference by the British delegation, which drew the attention of the Conference to the fact that only four out of the maritime claims listed in Article 1(1) were maritime liens in English law and that only maritime liens followed the ship into the hands of a *bona fide* purchaser, while that was not the case for the other maritime claims. The view was then expressed that Article 3(1) as then drafted might be construed to extend to all maritime claims the peculiar characteristics of maritime liens and it was suggested that the matter might be taken care of by the Drafting Committee.[6]

I.397 The Drafting Committee thought that this question could be clarified by amending Article 11 (now Article 9), which at the time was drafted as follows[7]:

Nothing in this Convention shall be construed as creating a right of action, which, apart from the provisions of this Convention, would not arise under the law applied by the Court which had seisin of the case

by adding the words[8]:

nor as creating any maritime liens which do not exist under such law or under the Convention on Maritime Mortgages and Liens.

I.398 Probably because the British delegation had raised the question whether maritime claims not secured by maritime liens would follow the ship, in the French text reference was expressly made to the *droit de suite*. The addition was contained in a separate paragraph, while in the English text it was a continuation of the same paragraph, and was drafted as follows[9]:

La présente Convention ne confère aux demandeurs aucun droit de suite autre que celui accordé par la loi du lieu de la saisie ou par la Convention internationale sur les privilèges et hypothèques maritimes. (This Convention does not grant to claimants any *droit de suite* other than that granted by the law of the place of arrest or by the International Convention on Maritime Liens and Mortgages).

I.399 As is known, at the Diplomatic Conference the words "if the latter is applicable" (*"si celle-ci est applicable"*) were added at the end of the sentence.

Britannia", [1996] DMF 49 on the ground that the buyer had taken over the going concern of the seller. See also M. H. Claringbould, *Arrest of Ships–2*, LLP 1986, p. 51.

5. The views expressed in the text have been approved by the Scottish Law Commission in the "Report on Diligence on the Dependence and Admiralty Arrestment" (Scot Law Com. No. 164), p. 163.

6. Sir Gonne St. Clair Pilcher stated (CMI Bulletin No. 105, pp. 314 and 315):

In article I there are set out, as you know, a large number of claims which are called in the convention "maritime claims". Of those claims, some four only call for maritime liens . . . If, therefore, the effect of the convention article 1 and 3(1) is this, which I take it to be as at present drafted, that claims which are not true maritime liens under English law are still intended to follow the ship in the hands of a *bona fide* purchaser for value, then it is a distinction which the English delegation would, I think, find almost impossible to accept. I understand that in certain continental jurisdictions, the French jurisdiction, for example, all types of claims which are covered by the Mortgages and Liens Convention, some of which are maritime liens and some of which are not, follow the ship into the hands of a *bona fide* purchaser for value. Our law on that topic is peculiar and a little unusual. I gather that it is in fact peculiar to English law. Therefore the British Association would be glad if that matter might be taken care of in the drafting committee and if they might be permitted to suggest the introduction of some form of words which would safeguard their position and would not bring about the situation that partly does obtain in some of the continental countries and possibly America, whereby all maritime claims as such in article I of the convention follow into the hands of a *bona fide* purchaser for value.

7. CMI Bulletin No. 105, p. 21; *Travaux Préparatoires*, p. 451.

8. *Procès-verbaux*, p. 22; *Travaux Préparatoires*, p. 451 and 452.

9. *Procès-verbaux*, p. 12; *Travaux Préparatoires*, p. 450.

I.400 A further clarification of this question was suggested by the Finnish delegate at the Diplomatic Conference. He suggested that in order to avoid Article 3(1) being construed so as to give the claimant the right to follow the ship into the hands of a *bona fide* purchaser, there should be added in that paragraph a reference to Article 11.[10]

I.401 Although no comments were made on the amendment proposed by the Finnish Delegate, it appears that it was inserted in the text prepared by the Drafting Committee. Article 3(1), as submitted to the Plenary Conference and approved by it, read as follows[11]:

1. Subject to the provisions of paragraph 4 of this Article and of Article 10, a claimant may arrest either the particular ship in respect of which the maritime claim arose, or any other ship which is owned by the person who was, at the time when the maritime claim arose, the owner of the particular ship, even though the ship arrested be ready to sail but no ship, other than the particular ship in respect of which the maritime claim arose, may be arrested in respect of any of the maritime claims enumerated in Article (1)(1)(o), (p) or (q).

I.402 Article 10, reference to which was made in Article 3(1), was at that time Article 11, the numbering of the Articles having changed after the incorporation of Article 9 of the draft approved at Naples into Article 2. Article 9 provided[12]:

This Convention shall not apply to claims made by Governments or other Public Authority in respect of taxes, dues or penalties under any Statute or Regulation, and the Convention shall not affect any rights of Dock or Harbour Authorities under their existing domestic law against vessels or their owners.

I.403 Article 10 was approved by the plenary session of the Conference. But after the second paragraph of Article 6 had been deleted, President Lilar, when submitting Article 7 (which provided that the rules of procedure shall be governed by the law of the State in which the arrest is made or applied for) to the vote, stated that the text of Article 7 could be inserted into Article 6.[13]

I.404 Even if no express decision appears to have been taken on this suggestion of the President, Articles 6 and 7 were actually merged, and consequently Article 8 dealing with jurisdiction became Article 7, Article 9 dealing with the scope of application of the

---

10. The Finnish delegate so stated (*Procès-verbaux*, p. 75; *Travaux Préparatoires*, p. 321):

Mr. Anderson (Finland) submits to the Assembly a practical case relating to the application of Art. 3, para. 1: Ship A, belonging to B, is repaired by C in January 1952.

Payment is agreed to be made in February 1954. After repairs, B sells the ship to D. Payment not having been made, C arrests ship A in the hands of D in February 1954. Is Art. 3 applicable and is arrest possible?

If the ship is returned and if the arrest has caused expenses, who should bear them? He is of the view that it would be necessary to modify the text of Art. 3 so to make reference to Art. 11. If the amendment of Mr. Alten concerning this case is not accepted, he requests that reference be made in Art. 3, para. 1 to Art. 11; such reference could be worded as follows: "Without prejudice to paragraph 3, but subject to the provisions of Article 11".

At that time Art. 3(1) was drafted thus (*Procès-verbaux*, p. 20; *Travaux Préparatoires*, p. 319):

Without prejudice to the provisions of paragraph V of this Article a claimant may arrest either the particular ship in respect of which he alleges that a maritime claim arises or any other ship which is owned by the person who was, at the time when the maritime claim arose, the owner of the particular ship, even though the arrested ship may be ready to sail.

Para. V corresponded to the present para. (4) and, probably, there was a printing error in the summary of the statement of the Finnish delegate, where para. III should have read para. V.

11. *Procès-verbaux*, pp. 104 and 110; *Travaux Préparatoires*, p. 322.

12. *Procès-verbaux*, p. 21.

13. In the *Procès-verbaux* the statement of President Lilar is recorded as follows (*Procès-verbaux*, p. 114; *Travaux Préparatoires*, p. 396):

"President Lilar puts to the vote Article 7, that could be joined with Article 6, rather than having a separate number".

Convention became Article 8 and Article 10, which is that presently considered, became Article 9. Unfortunately, it was not realised that as a consequence of this change in the numbering of the Articles from 7 onwards, the reference in Article 3(1) to Article 10 should be changed to a reference to Article 9.

I.405 The conclusion is that the first part of Article 3(1) should read: "Subject to the provisions of paragraph 4 of this article and of article 9, a claimant may arrest either the particular ship", etc.[14]

I.406 There can be no doubt, therefore, that, unless the claim is secured by a maritime lien, the right of arrest of a ship in respect of a maritime claim exists only if that ship, at the time of the arrest, is still owned by the person who owned her when the maritime claim arose.[15]

I.407 This view is accepted in a number of Contracting States,[16] including Belgium,[17] Croatia,[18] Denmark, Finland, France, Germany, Greece,[19] Haiti,[20] Ireland, Italy, the

---

14. So has been held by the Cour d'Appel of Montpellier 31 July 1996, *Sallyview Estates Ltd.* v. *S.A. Enjoy—The "Zaher V"*, [1997] DMF 31.

15. One of the French delegates at the Diplomatic Conference (Mr de Grandmaison), though objecting to the proposal of creating a link between the Arrest Convention and the Maritime Liens and Mortgages Convention, and, in particular, of limiting the *droit de suite* to the maritime claims secured by maritime liens, so stated (*Procès-verbaux*, p. 107):

> Similarly, there is no reason to deal here with the *"droit de suite"*. There exists an extremely limited right in respect of the privileged claims and it is the Maritime Liens and Mortgages Convention that deals with it. It is not possible to revert to this question and to create here a *"droit de suite"* whatsoever.

16. See the replies to question 5 of the Questionnaire, Appendix II, pp. 245–249.

17. There are, however, decisions of the Belgian Courts cited by Verstrepen ("Arrest and Judicial Sale of Ships in Belgium", [1995] LMCLQ. 131 at p. 143, note 93) to the effect that arrest is permitted even if the ship is no longer owned by the person who owned her at the time the maritime claim arose. This view, according to Verstrepen (loc. cit.) is contrary to article 9 of the Convention.

18. Article 977 of the Maritime Code so provides in its relevant part (translation of the Croatian MLA: see reply to Question 5 of the Questionnaire, Appendix II, p. 245):

> Any ship may be arrested on which there exists the right of ownership, or which is owned by the same personal debtors, or which, for the claim for which arrest is sought, is encumbered by a maritime lien or a hypothec or another right of pledge based on a foreign law and for other claims as referred to in Article 878, Paragraph 2, of this Law which relates to the ship.

19. It would appear that this rule does not apply in Greece when a ship is sold as a part of a going concern, since in such case the purchaser is responsible for the debts arising out of the management of such concern. The sale of a ship as a going concern must, however, be considered separately, since in such case the subject matter of the sale is the going concern, and thus includes all rights and obligations that have arisen in connection with the operation of the ship and all contracts relating thereto, such as contracts of employment of the crew and contracts of affreightment. It was precisely on this basis that the Cour d'Appel of Rouen with judgment of 26 January 1995, *Compagnie Maritime Belge Transport-Italie* v. *Assurance Groupe de Paris—The "Merzario Britannia"*, [1995] DMF 49 held that claims against Merzario S.A. could be enforced on the *Merzario Britannia* after its sale. The Court so stated (at p. 52):

> Attendu que, contrairement à ce que soutient la société CMBT-I, la saisie n'a pas été en l'espèce autorisée sur la seule apparence du nom du navire, mais sur celle engendrée par le fait que la société CMBT-I à d'une façon plus large:
> — repris l'ensemble des activités de Merzario y compris les navires qui continuent à porter le nom de Merzario;
> — poursuivi l'exploitation des même lignes que Merzario, en coopération notamment avec la Compagnie UASC;
> Attendu d'ailleurs que les liens à tout le moins étroits entre la société CMBT-I et Merzario ont été postérieurement confirmés.

The transfer of all or part of the debts from seller to buyer is not uncommon in such particular case. For example, in Italy the transfer of a going concern (*cessione d'azienda*) entails, unless otherwise agreed, the transfer of all contracts made for the operation of the enterprise and the joint liability of transferor and transferee in respect of all debts (articles 2558 and 2560 Civil Code).

20. See the Haitian reply to Question 5 of the Questionnaire, Appendix II, p. 247.

Netherlands, Nigeria, Norway, Portugal, Slovenia,[21] Spain, Sweden[22] and the United Kingdom.

I.408 It must then be established when the passing of title must be deemed to have occurred in order that it becomes relevant vis-à-vis the arrestor. The relevant time may be the time when the transfer is perfected, the time when it becomes known to the arrestor or the time when it is endorsed in the ship register, irrespective of whether the arrestor is aware of the transfer or not. The solution should be the same as in the case of a conflict between the purchaser and the mortgagee to whom the vessel has been mortgaged by the seller or of a conflict between two buyers who have purchased the same vessel from its owner. In those cases the relevant time is normally that of the registration: if the mortgage is registered prior to the registration of the sale, it is enforceable against the buyer irrespective of the date of execution whilst if the sale is registered first, the mortgage cannot be registered any more; similarly, the buyer who first registers the purchase in the ship's register acquires title. In case of arrest the position can be different, since, at least in certain jurisdictions, the arrest is not endorsed in the ships register and, in any event, the endorsement may not be easy in respect of ships flying the flag of a State other than that in the jurisdiction of which the arrest is effected. But reference can always be made to the date of the registration of the sale. It is suggested, however, that whilst in respect of a mortgage or a sale constructive knowledge through registration is required for the protection of third parties, in respect of the arrest there is a factual knowledge resulting from the ship being unable to sail. On such assumption, the arrest would be valid if effected prior to the registration of the sale whilst it would not be valid, if effected subsequently.

I.409 This is so in France, where Article 93 of decree 27 October 1967 provides that none of the acts mentioned in Article 91 nos. 1–6 is effective[23] vis-à-vis third parties prior to its registration in the ships register[24] and none of the acts mentioned in Article 91 nos. 7 and

---

21. See the Slovenian reply to Question 5 of the Questionnaire, Appendix II, p. 248.
22. See the Swedish reply to Question 5 of the Questionnaire, Appendix II, p. 248.
23. The word used in article 93 is "opposable".
24. In article 93 reference is made to the "fiche matricule" which is the sheet of the register, called "fichier", in which the information relating to a given ship is endorsed. Article 90 of decree 27 October 1967 provides:

Les fichiers sont tenus par noms de navires. Une fiche matricule est affectée à chacun des navires.
Article 92 provides:
Sont mentionnés sur la fiche matricule:
1° Le cas échéant, les noms des gérants dans les conventions de copropriété pour l'application de l'article 15 de la loi n° 67–5 du 3 janvier 1967 portant statut des navires et autres bâtiments de mer;
. . . .
3° Les actes et contrats visés à l'article 10 de la loi précitée portant statut des navires et autres bâtiments de mer;
4° Les clauses des contrats visés à l'article 10, deuxième alinéa, de la loi précitée portant statut des navires et autres bâtiments de mer, donnant à l'affréteur la qualité d'armateur;
. . . .
7° Les hypothèques consenties sur tout ou partie du navire;
8° Les procès-verbaux de saisie.
Article 10 of law 67–5 of 3 January 1987 so provides:
Tout acte constitutif, translatif ou extinctif de la propriété ou de toute autre droit réel sur un navire francisé doit, à peine de nullité, être fait par écrit. Il en est de même des contrats d'affrètement à temps et des contrats d'affrètement coque nue conclus et des délégations de fret consenties pour une durée de plus d'un an dont la production peut aboutir à une pareille durée.

8 is effective vis-à-vis third parties prior to its registration in the special register of "hypothèques".[25] Amongst the acts mentioned in Article 91 nos. 1–6 there are the deeds of sale while the acts mentioned in Article 91 no. 8 are the "procès-verbaux de saisie". "Saisie" in French law includes arrest (*saisie conservatoire*) and seizure (*saisie exécution*) which are both covered by chapter VI of decree 27 October 1967 titled "Saisie de navires".

I.410 It follows, therefore, that a claimant may arrest the ship in respect of which the claim has arisen even if the ship is no longer owned by the person who is liable in respect of the claim, provided the arrest is registered prior to the registration of the sale.[26] Of course arrest is permissible also thereafter in respect of claims secured by a maritime lien, for which the claimant has a *droit de suite* that, under French law, may be exercised before the lapse of two months from the date of registration of the deed of sale.

I.411 The position is identical in Italy and similar in Spain.

I.412 In Italy Article 250 CN provides that for the purposes provided for in the Civil Code all acts creating, transferring or extinguishing title to or other real rights on ships are made public by means of registration in the ships register. Article 2644 Civil Code in turn provides that the acts listed in the preceding article (which include contracts of sale) have no effect vis-à-vis third parties who have acquired a right on the property. Article 684 CN in turn provides that the warrant of arrest after service shall be registered in the ships register. The controlling factor is, therefore, registration: if the arrest is registered prior to the registration of the sale, it is effective vis-à-vis the buyer; if the sale is registered first, the arrest (whether registered or not) is not effective.[27]

I.413 In Spain the transfer of title to and the constitution, modification and extinction of all charges (including, therefore, arrest (*embargo preventivo*)) on ships must, pursuant to Article 145 of the Reglamento del Registro Mercantil approved by decree of 14

---

25. Article 15 of decree 27 October 1967, reference to which is made in article 93, so provides:
   L'hypothèque est rendue publique par l'inscription sur un registre spécial tenu par le conservateur des hypothèques maritimes dans la circonscription duquel le navire est en construction ou dans laquelle le navire est inscrit, s'il est déjà pourvu d'un acte de francisation.

26. On the requirement of registration of the arrest see Cour d'Appel of Aix-en-Provence 25 February 1981, *S.té Transunt* v. *Baudoin Lefevre and Others—The "Patrick Victor"*, [1982] DMF 420, with a critical comment by Remond Gouilloud, centered, however, on the fact that the ship was a pleasure boat. Reference to this judgment is also made by Remond Gouilloud in her book *Droit Maritime*, II ed., p. 189 but rather in the sense of a critical comment of the law. Rodière, *Le Navire*, Paris 1980, p. 255 states that the procès-verbal of the "saisie conservatoire", contrary to that of the "saisie exécution" is not registrable. This statement, however, is in conflict with article 92 no. 8 of decree 27 October 1967 where reference is made generally to the "procès-verbaux de saisie". Nor can the provision of article 30 of decree 27 October 1967, whereby the saisie conservatoire "ne porte pas atteinte aux droits du propriétaire" (does not affect the rights of the owner) imply that the ship may be sold as if no arrest had been made. Rodière (*op. cit.*, p. 255) explains this provision as follows:
   Le saisi a donc la faculté de vendre son navire ou de l'aliéner de toute autre manière; il peut aussi le fréter, l'hypothéquer, etc. . . . On dira seulement que ces droits sont économiquement et pratiquement freinés par la saisie qui immobilise provisoirement le navire.
   See also Du Pontavice, *Le Statut de Navire*, 1976, no. 367; Desdevises and Tassel, "Saisies, ventes des Navires et des Bateaux et Distribution du Prix", Juris Classeur 3, 1988, 1er Cahier, no. 43, p. 9.
   On the need for the deed of sale to be registered in order to prevent an action of the creditors of the seller see Rodière, *Le Navire*, cit. no. 176, p. 216.

27. *Società Liguria* v. *Melchioni*, [1962] Dir. Mar. 20 and, on the effectiveness of the arrest of a ship as security for a claim against the seller after the sale but before its registration in the ships register, Tribunale of Salerno 21 January 1997, *Mario Cirino Pomicino S.p.A.* v. *Liman Company Ltd.—The "Komandor"*, [1998] Dir. Mar. 436. The Tribunale of Salerno held that the requirement of registration of the arrest is not applicable to vessels flying a foreign flag while the requirement of registration of the sale is applicable.

December 1956,[28] be registered in the Registro Mercantil (Mercantile Register).[29]

I.414 Also in Spain, as in other civil law countries, the date of registration is fundamental in order to establish the priority amongst the registrable rights. This is stated by Articles 36(3) and 38 of the law on ships hypothèque of 21 August 1993 (Ley de Hipoteca Naval). Article 36(3) provides that all acts and contracts that are registrable pursuant to the provisions of such law and of the Code of Commerce (Código de Comercio) have no effect vis-à-vis third parties prior to registration. Article 38 in turn provides that in order to establish the priority between two or more registrations of the same date relating to the same ship, regard must be paid to the hour of presentation of the title to the Registrar.[30] Furthermore, the ship must be the property of the debtor at the time the arrest is executed. If title to the ship had already been acquired by a third party, an action is available to such third party in order to prove that at the time of arrest he was the owner of the ship, whereupon the arrest becomes ineffective, save when the claim is secured by a maritime lien.[31] The consequence of these rules is that, as in France and in Italy, the arrest of a ship that has been sold, as security for a claim against the seller, is effective if executed and registered prior to the registration of the sale.

I.415 The above rules apply generally also in respect of the "hypothèque": the credit secured by the hypothèque takes priority over the claim in respect of which the arrest is effected if the "hypothèque" is registered prior to the registration of the arrest.

I.416 This, however, is not the case in all jurisdictions. For example, in England the relevant time is not the time when the arrest is effected, but the time when the action is brought,[32] which is the time when an *in rem* claim form is issued.[33] The *in rem* claim form must be served on the ship within 12 months but the time for serving may be extended.[34] If therefore, when the *in rem* claim form is issued, i.e. when the action is brought, the

---

28. In Spain a double system of registration of ships is in existence. Ships in fact must be registered, in addition to the *Registro Mercantil*, in the *Registro de matrícula de buques* in compliance with article 75(2) of law 27/1992 of 24 November 1992 on Ports and Merchant Marine (*Ley de Puertos del Estado y de la Marina Mercante*). The relevant registration, for private law purpose, is, however that in the *Registro Mercantil*, the registration in the *Registro de Matricula* having only administrative purposes.

29. Article 166(1) of the *Reglamento del Registro Mercantil* provides that the registration in the *Registro Mercantil* shall constitute evidence of title to the ship as well as of the charges on the ship ("Los asientos del Registro Mercantil harán prueba del dominio o propriedad de los buques, así como de los cargas impuestos sobre los mismos").

30. Article 36(3) so provides:

Los actos y contratos relativos a una nave que, según las disposiciones del Código de Comercio y de esta ley, son inscribibles en el Registro mercantil no surtirán efecto en cuanto a tercero, sino desde la fecha de su inscripción.

Article 30 so provides:

Para determinar la preferencia entre dos o más inscripciones de una misma fecha relativas a una misma nave, se atenderá a la hora de presentación en el Registro de los titulos respectivos.

31. The information appearing in the text has been kindly provided by Professor Ignacio Arroyo.

32. S. 21(4) of the Supreme Court Act, 1981 provides that an action *in rem* may be brought in the High Court against the ship in connection with which the claim has arisen if at the time when the action is brought the relevant person is either the beneficial owner of that ship as respects all the shares in it or its demise charterer.

33. Under the new Civil Procedure Rules (CPR) which came into effect on 26 April 1999 the writ is replaced by the claim form. As regards claims *in rem* the writ *in rem* is now called "*in rem* claim form": Practice Direction-Admiralty 2.1(1). The Practice Direction-Admiralty supplements the Civil Procedure Rules and replaces Order 75 of the Rules of the Supreme Court.

34. Practice Direction 2.1(6) states:

The period within which an *in rem* claim form must be served is, subject to CPR rule 7.6, 12 months from the date of issue.

CPR rule 7.6 provides that the claimant may apply for an order extending the period within which the claim

person liable for the claim was either the owner or demise charterer of the ship, she may be arrested whoever owns the ship at the date the arrest is actually effected. This is well illustrated by the leading case on the subject, *The "Monica S"*.[35] In that case a writ *in rem* was issued against that ship by the owners of a cargo that had been carried on board the ship when she was still owned by the carrier, but service of the writ was effected after the ship had been sold to a third party. After having stated that the question to be determined, on which there was no prior decision, was "whether under the law in force before the 1956 Act, a change of ownership of the *res* occurring after the institution of proceedings but before service of process or arrest, defeated a statutory right of action *in rem*", Brandon J. (as he then was) expressed a negative opinion. He then considered the position under the Administration of Justice Act 1956 and stated[36]:

As I said earlier, the jurisdiction which is invoked by an action *in rem*, whether under Sect. 3(2), (3) or (4), is the jurisdiction to hear and determine the questions and claims listed in Sect. 1(1). I see no reason why, once a plaintiff has properly invoked that jurisdiction by bringing an action *in rem*, whether under Sect. 3(2), (3) or (4), he should not, despite a subsequent change of ownership of the *res*, be able to prosecute it through all its stages, up to and including judgment against the *res*, and payment of the amount of the judgment out of the proceeds.

I.417 Now Practice Direction 6.2(4) confirms this solution. It in fact provides that the declaration to be filed by a party making an application for arrest must, in the case of a claim against a ship by virtue of section 21(4) of the Supreme Court Act 1981, shall state, *inter alia*:

(iii) that at the time when the claim form was issued the relevant person was either the beneficial owner of all the shares in the ship in respect of which the warrant is required or (where appropriate) the charterer of it under a charter by demise, as the case may be;

20. ARREST OF OTHER SHIPS OWNED BY THE PERSON LIABLE IN RESPECT OF A MARITIME CLAIM

I.418 As has been mentioned, this was one of the questions in respect of which civil and common law differed. While in civil law all assets of the debtor and thus all ships owned by him could be arrested as security for any debt, whether maritime or not, in common law a ship could be arrested only in respect of a maritime claim and only the ship in respect of which the maritime claim arose could be arrested, but no other ship. It is this difference which laid behind the different purposes of arrest: a means to obtain security in civil law,

---

form must be served (rule 7.6(1)) and that an application must be supported by evidence (rule 7.6(4)). Evidence that it has not been possible to arrest the ship within the jurisdiction will normally justify an extension.

According to Practice Direction 2.2.(a) service of an *in rem* claim must be made, when the action is against a ship:

Upon the property against which the claim *in rem* is brought by fixing the *in rem* claim form, or a copy of it, on the outside of the property proceeded against in a position which may reasonably be expected to be seen.

35. [1967] 2 Lloyd's Rep. 113. For a comment on this judgment see Hill, *Arrest of Ships*, London 1985, p. 31.

36. Subsequently, in *The "Helène Roth"* [1980] 1 Lloyd's Rep. 477, at p. 480, Sheen J. held that if a writ *in rem* is issued before any change of ownership has occurred, a subsequent change of ownership does not prevent the renewal of the writ unless the action has not been pursued with diligence. However in that case the decision may have been influenced by the finding that the change of ownership had taken place within the same group of companies.

a means to found the admiralty jurisdiction in common law. The "compromise" consisted of reducing the unlimited right of arrest of ships only to specified claims and at the same time of extending the right of arrest to other ships in the same ownership.

I.419 The original text prepared by the International Sub-Committee in 1951 and submitted to the Naples Conference was worded as follows[37]:

I. *Tout demandeur, qui se prévaut d'un droit ou d'une créance maritime sur un navire, peut saisir ce navire ou tout autre appartenant aux mêmes armateurs, alors même que le navire serait prêt a faire voile.* (Any claimant who alleges that he has a maritime claim on a ship may arrest that ship or any other ship who is owned by the same operator even though the ship is ready to sail.)

I.420 The reference to "*armateurs*" (operator) in this paragraph was obviously a mistake, for in the following paragraph, which states when two ships must be deemed to be in the same ownership, the word used in "*propriétaire*":

II. *Des navires sont réputés avoir la même propriétaire lorsque toutes les parts de propriété appartiennent a une même ou aux même personnes.* (Ships shall be deemed to be in the same ownership when all shares therein are owned by the same person or persons.)

I.421 During the Conference, the British delegate, explaining further an amendment suggested in the report of the British delegation,[38] pointed out that the wording adopted in the draft could lead to unfair consequences. If, in order to establish which ships were in the same ownership, reference were made to the time of arrest, a shipowner who purchased a ship on which a maritime lien had arisen prior to the passing of title would be subject to the arrest not only of such ship, but also of all other ships owned by him.[39] The proposal was carried and the reference to "sister ships" was worded as follows: "or any other ship which is owned by the person who was, at the time when the maritime claim arose, the owner of the particular ship".[40]

I.422 The moment that is relevant as regards the ownership of the sister ship is, therefore, that of the arrest. The link with the ship in respect of which the maritime claim arose must be established at the time when the claim arose. It is irrelevant when the person

---

37. CMI Bulletin No. 105, p. 19; *Travaux Préparatoires*, p. 314.
38. CMI Bulletin No. 105, p. 49; *Travaux Préparatoires*, p. 316.
39. The following statement was made at the Conference by Mr Miller (CMI Bulletin No. 105, p. 260; *Travaux Préparatoires*, p. 317):

Mr President and gentlemen, this amendment, although it is under the name of Great Britain, is an amendment for which we are indebted to the Netherlands Association, or, rather, to one particular member of it. As subclause (I) of article 3 is at present drafted it reads in this way: "A claimant may arrest the ship herself in respect of which he alleges that a maritime claim arises or any other ship in the same ownership, even if she is ready to sail". It was pointed out that, supposing ship A was subject to a maritime claim through collision and was then sold, as that subclause at present reads the unfortunate buyer of that ship might have another ship in his ownership arrested. That, of course, is not what we wanted to achieve. We must accept the fact that if the ship which is concerned with the casualty or occurrence is sold, the maritime lien passes with her and remains upon her in whose ever hand she may be for two years; but it would be very hard luck on the buyer of a vessel which was susceptible to a maritime claim if, by resale, he rendered all the rest of his fleet liable to arrest.

I must confess that I completely missed this point when we made the final draft of the convention, and Mr Asser missed it, too. We were reminded of it by a member of the Netherlands delegation, and accordingly we redrafted the subclause as follows: "A claimant may arrest the ship in respect of which he alleges that a maritime claim arises or any other ship which at the time of her arrest is owned by the person who was the owner of the particular ship at the time when the maritime claim arose."

40. CMI Bulletin No. 105, p. 89 and *Travaux Préparatoires*, p. 319 where, however, only the French text is reproduced.

liable, who owned the ship in respect of which the claim arose, acquired the ownership of the other ship; what is relevant is that such other ship is owned by him at the time of the arrest. It is also irrelevant whether the ship in respect of which the maritime claim arose is still owned by the original owner or not at the time when the sister ship is arrested.

I.423 The sister ship rule of paragraph (1) of Article 3 is made subject to paragraph (4), wherein an exception is laid down for the case where the ship in respect of which the maritime claim arose is not owned by the person liable for such claim. In such case the sister ship rule does not apply to the owner, but to the person liable (the demise charterer). Only the particular ship may be arrested, but no other ship owned by the "registered" owner of that ship; instead any ship which is owned at the time of arrest by the person liable for the maritime claim may be arrested. The words "subject to the provisions of this Convention", which already existed in the original draft, have merely the purpose of applying all other provisions of the Convention to the arrest of ships owned by the person liable.

I.424 The problem whether the arrest of a "sister ship" is permissible when the claimant is not entitled to arrest the ship in respect of which the claim has arisen does not seem to have been discussed during the *travaux préparatoires*.

I.425 This problem has probably been considered for the first time in *The "Escher-sheim"* [41] in connection with section 1(1)(b) of the UK Administration of Justice Act 1956 which enumerates as one of the "questions and claims" for which Admiralty jurisdiction is recognised "any claim for damage received by a ship". The *Eschersheim* was a sister ship of the *Rotesand*, a tug who had beached a ship, the *Erkowit*, in the attempt to salve her, thereby causing her loss together with the loss of the cargo. In considering whether a right *in rem* could be asserted against the *Eschersheim* on the basis of section 1(1)(d), in a case where the ship in respect of which the claim had arisen was owned by the claimant, Sir Gordon Willmer stated as follows [42]:

It was conceded by Counsel for the defendants that there might be one possible case for asserting a right *in rem* in respect of damage received by a ship. That might arise in the event of the ship receiving the damage being subject to a demise charter. If the damage were caused by the fault of the demise charterers then it could be said that under par. (b) of s. 3(4) of the 1956 Act is might be possible to arrest a sister ship beneficially owned by the demise charterers. But that is not this case.

I.426 He then held that the salvors could not be considered to be in possession or control of the salved ship and that consequently section 3(4) could not apply. There could not, therefore, be jurisdiction *in rem* under paragraph (e) against the *Rotesand* or a sister ship thereof since she was not a sister ship of the *Erkowit*, the ship in respect of which the claim under paragraph (e) would have arisen.

I.427 The theoretical situation envisaged in the passage of the judgment of Sir Gorton Willmer materialised in the case of *The "Permina 108"*. The owners of the ship *Ibnu* enforced their claim against the charterers for unpaid charter hire by arresting the *Permina 108*, a ship owned by the charterers. The Singapore Court of Appeal [43] held that since in

---

41. [1976] 1 Lloyd's Rep. 81.
42. At p. 94.
43. [1978] 1 Lloyd's Rep. 311.

section 4(4)(b) of the High Court (Admiralty Jurisdiction) Act[44] reference is made to situations where the person who would be liable in an action *in personam* is the owner or charterer or person in possession or in control of the ship, the charterers of the *Ibnu* were such person. The word "charterer" in fact could not be limited to charterer by demise.[45]

I.428 Almost at the same time a similar dispute was considered by the Hong Kong Court of Justice. In *The "Ledesco Uno"*[46] that Court differed from the Singapore Court in the construction of the word "charterer" in section 3(4) of the Administration of Justice Act 1956[47] and held that that word meant demise charterer.

I.429 The first case in England in which this issue was expressly considered has been *The "Maritime Trader"*[48] in connection with a claim of the owners of the *Antaios* against the charterers arising out of the breach of the charter party for that ship and of the arrest by the claimants of the *Maritime Trader*, a ship beneficially owned by the charterers. Sheen J., after having stated that Parliament had not yet enacted paragraph 4 of Article 3 of the 1952 Arrest Convention, in the light of *The "Escherscheim"* held that the *Maritime Trader* could not be arrested since she was not a sister ship of the *Antaios*, the ship in respect of which the claim had arisen.

I.430 The arrest of a ship owned by the charterer was subsequently considered in England by the Court of Appeal in the case of *The "Span Terza"*.[49] Sir David Cairns arrived at the same conclusion of the Singapore Court of Appeal. He stated[50]:

The only way of escaping from it is by interpreting the word "charterer" in s. 3(4) to mean "demise charterer". If it is to be supposed that Parliament meant to be included as the "person" mentioned in the sub-section only a person who, like the owner or one of the types of person mentioned after "charterers", was at the time in question a person in possession or control of the ship, then that interpretation would give effect to that contention.

For my part, as a matter of construction I find it impossible to construe the words in that way. If only a demise charterer were meant, one would of course have expected the word "demise" to have been inserted before the word "charterer". Alternatively the word "charterer" could have been omitted altogether, because a demise charterer would be included in the words "the person in possession or control".

I.431 The same conclusion was reached by the Hong Kong Supreme Court in *The "Sextum"*.[51] Penlington J. stated[52]:

44. Section 4(4) of the Singapore High Court (Admiralty Jurisdiction) Act so provides:
(4) In the case of any such claim as is mentioned in paragraphs (d) to (q) of sub-section (1) of Section 3 of this Act, being a claim in connection with a ship, where the person who would have been liable in an action *in personam* was, when the cause of action arose, the owner or charterer or person in possession or in control of, the ship, the admiralty jurisdiction of the Court may (whether the claim gives rise to a maritime lien on the ship or not) be invoked by an action *in rem* against:
(a) that ship, if at the time when the action is brought it is beneficially owned as respects all the shares therein by that person; or
(b) any other ship which, at the time when the action is brought, is beneficially owned as aforesaid.
45. It must be noted that the Court thought that the terms of section 4(4) of the Act were free from any ambiguity and that, therefore, it was unnecessary to look at the 1952 Arrest Convention (to which Singapore was not a party).
46. [1978] 2 Lloyd's Rep. 99.
47. The Administration of Justice Act 1956 was extended to Hong Kong by the Admiralty Jurisdiction (Hong Kong) Order in Council 1962, No. 1547 of 1962.
48. [1981] 2 Lloyd's Rep. 153.
49. [1982] 1 Lloyd's Rep. 225.
50. At p. 227.
51. [1982] 2 Lloyd's Rep. 532.
52. At p. 534 and 535.

I prefer the reasoning behind *The Permina 108* and *The Span Terza*. I consider that I should give the word "charterer" its ordinary meaning and it should not be restricted to demise charterer. I do not think that even if the Convention is worded differently from the Act it is sufficient reason to put such a restrictive meaning on it. Indeed I feel that as the Convention must have been before the House when it was considering the legislation and they apparently declined to use the word "demise" that is an argument for saying that such a decision must be taken to have been deliberate. I think the clause is clear and unambiguous.

I.432 Also in the Netherlands the arrest by the owner of a ship owned by the charterer in respect of unpaid charter hire was held to be permissible under Article 3(4) on the ground that it cannot be assumed that the Convention granted to the charterer a protection that is not also granted, in the opposite situation, to the owner.[53]

I.433 It is worth noting that in none of the cases referred to above the impossibility for the claimant to arrest the ship in respect of which the claim had arisen was expressly considered as a factor that might constitute an obstacle to the arrest of a ship owned by the person liable. This question could have been raised in view of the wording of the relevant Acts, according to which the arrest of the "particular ship" and of a "sister ship" are considered as two alternatives. The problem has on the contrary been considered by the High Court of Australia in *Laemthong International Lines Co. Ltd.* v. *BPS Shipping—The "Laemthong Pride"*.[54] BPS Shipping, disponent owners of the *Nyanza*, chartered the ship to Laemthong International Lines Co. Ltd. for the carriage of a cargo of bagged rice from Bangkok to Nouakchott in Mauritania. BPS alleged that Laemthong, in breach of its contractual obligation, failed to fumigate the cargo and, in consequence, the cargo was infested with beetles. This resulted in the arrest of the *Nyanza* in Nouakchott. BPS claimed damages in the amount of US$ 1,833,285 and commenced proceedings *in rem* against the *Laemthong Pride*, a ship owned by Laemthong, in the Supreme Court of the Northern Territory and obtained the arrest of the ship pursuant to section 19 of the Admiralty Act 1988. The warrant of arrest was discharged and the ship released, but a few days later the Court ordered the re-arrest of the ship pursuant to section 21 of the Act. Laemthong's challenge of the order was dismissed by the Court of Appeal. Special leave to appeal to the High Court of Australia was granted limited to the question whether the *Laemthong Pride* was a "surrogate ship" for the *Nyanza* within the meaning of the Act.[55]

---

53. President of the Arrondissementsrechtbank of Rotterdam 23 January 1984, [1984] Ship en Schade 53, cited by M. H. Claringbould, *Arrest of Ships*, *supra*, note 4, p. 53.

54. (1997) 190 CLR 181. A summary of this judgment is also published in the E&E Review-Transport, Vol. 12, No. 1 at p. 36.

55. Section 19 of the Act so provides:
Right to proceed in rem against surrogate ship.
   19. A proceeding on a general maritime claim concerning a ship may be commenced as an action *in rem* against some other ship if:
   (a) a relevant person in relation to the claim was, when the cause of action arose, the owner or charterer of, or in possession or control of, the first-mentioned ship; and
   (b) that person is, when the proceeding is commenced, the owner of the second-mentioned ship.
The definition of "surrogate ship", which in section 19 appears only in the heading, is given in section 3(6) which so provides:
   For the purposes of this Act, where:
   (a) a proceeding on a maritime claim may be commenced against a ship under a provision of this Act (other than section 19); and
   (b) under section 19, a proceeding on the claim may be commenced against some other ship;
   the other ship is, in relation to the claim, a surrogate ship.

I.434 The High Court unanimously dismissed the appeal. Two issues were considered. The first was whether it is a condition for the arrest of a "surrogate ship" that a proceeding *in rem* could be commenced against the ship in relation to which the claim has arisen. The second issue was whether the charterer, reference to which is made in section 19, must be a charterer by demise or may also be a time or voyage charterer.

I.435 On the first issue, Brennan CJ so held[56]:

The definition of "surrogate ship" in s. 3(6) is thus reserved for use in cases where a general maritime claim can be enforced against one ship under ss 15, 17 or 18 or against a second ship under s. 19. But it is not a condition of the operation of s. 19 that the claim on which proceedings under that section are commenced is a claim *in rem* on which proceedings could be commenced under ss 15, 17 or 18. Section 19 is enacted to give a remedy *in rem* against the "relevant person" who is defined to be a person who would be liable on a maritime claim in an action *in personam*. So construed, s. 19 accords with the policy embraced by the Australian Law Reform Commission as stated in its report *Civil Admiralty Jurisdiction* on which the Act was based:

> "The appropriate rule is one which, as an alternative to allowing an action *in rem* to be commenced against the wrongdoing ship, allows such an action against a ship owned by the relevant person even though this person is not the owner of the wrongdoing ship. This will occasionally allow an action against a surrogate ship even where there could be no action against the wrongdoing ship. The most obvious examples are where the wrongdoing ship has sunk or been sold (where there is no *droit de suite*). *But another case would be where the claim is by an owner against someone using the owner's ship on a time or voyage charter. In such a case the owner has already got possession of his own ship, but he could, under the recommended provision, proceed against any other ship owned by the defendant.*" (Emphasis added).

I.436 A problem that has a certain analogy with that under consideration is that of the right of the charterer to limit his liability in respect of a claim of the owner against him. This question was recently considered by the English Commercial Court in *Aegean Sea Traders Corporation* v. *Repsol Oil International Ltd. and Repsol Petroleo—The "Aegean Sea"*[57] in respect of the right of a voyage charterer to limit his liability for damages claimed by the owner of the chartered ship. Thomas J. so held[58]:

It follows from the development of limitation prior to the 1976 Convention and the way in which the 1976 Convention is structured and its language that, in my view, it does not provide (and is not intended to provide) an entitlement to charterers to limit where the shipowner brings the type of claim I am concerned with against the charterers. Such claims cannot in principle, in my view, be reasonably brought within its language.

The 1976 Convention provides for the aggregation of claims arising from one distinct occasion and the application of the limits of liability and the limitation fund to the claims so aggregated. Although a distinction is drawn between those categorized as shipowners and salvors, no distinction is drawn between owners and charterers. Therefore all claims arising from a distinct occasion where the owners and charterers are responsible are subject to one limit and, if a fund is constituted, to one fund. For example where a vessel is lost and her cargo is carried under owners' and charterers' bills of lading, then there is one limit of liability and one fund in respect of the liabilities under the bills of lading and all the other liabilities in respect of the vessel. It is clear from art. 11.3 that that fund is for the benefit of all claimants and protects equally the owner, charterer, manager and operator in respect of those claims. There is no provision for a separate limit or a separately constituted fund through which the charterers can limit their liability to owners.

56. At p. 184.
57. [1998] Lloyd's Rep. 39.
58. At p. 49.

I.437 Although the arguments on which the decision of the Commercial Court was based are not directly relevant for the solution of the problem under consideration, the criteria adopted can be applied.

I.438 The first question that must be considered in our case is whether a claim of the owner of a ship against the charterer arising out of a charter party is a maritime claim for the purposes of Article 1(1) of the Convention. In *The "Laemthong Pride"* it had been accepted that the disponent owners of the *Nyanza* had a "general maritime claim"[59] within the meaning of section 4(3) of the Australian Act. In all the other cases previously considered no question seems to have ever arisen as to the nature of the claim as one of those enumerated in the provisions of the relevant Acts. Similarly, the description of several maritime claims in Article 1(1) of the Convention is so wide as to encompass both claims against the owner of a ship and claims of the owner arising out of the operation of that ship. Such claims are the following:

(i) salvage (subparagraph (c)): the salvor may have a claim against the owner of the salved ship and the latter may have a claim in damages against the salvor[60];

(ii) agreement relating to the use or hire of a ship (subparagraph (d)): the owner may have a claim against the (demise) charterer and the (demise) charterer may have a claim against the owner;

(iii) agreement relating to the carriage of goods (subparagraph (e)): the situation is the same as that considered by the High Court of Australia;

(iv) general average (subparagraph (g)): the owner of the cargo may claim general average contribution from the owner of the ship and vice versa;

(v) towage (subparagraph (i)): the tug may have a claim against the tow and vice versa;

(vi) pilotage (subparagraph (j)): also in this case, the pilot may have a claim against the owner of the ship and the latter may have a claim against the pilot for damages caused to the ship which may be secured through the arrest of the pilot boat.

I.439 It would appear, therefore, that the conclusion impliedly reached by all Courts whose judgments have been considered holds also in respect of the 1952 Convention: in

---

59. A distinction is made in section (4) of the Australian Admiralty Act 1988 between proprietary claims and general maritime claims. The proprietary maritime claims are enumerated in section (4)(2) and are the following:

    (2) A reference in this Act to a proprietary maritime claim is a reference to:
        (a) a claim relating to:
            (i) possession of a ship;
            (ii) title to, or ownership of, a ship or a share in a ship;
            (iii) a mortgage of a ship or of a share in a ship; or
            (iv) a mortgage of a ship's freight;
        (b) a claim between co-owners of a ship relating to the possession, ownership, operation or earnings of the ship;
        (c) a claim for the satisfaction or enforcement of a judgment given by a court (including a court of a foreign country) against a ship or other property in a proceedings in rem in the nature of a proceeding in Admiralty; or
        (d) a claim for interest in respect of a claim referred to in paragraph (a), (b) or (c).

    The general maritime claims correspond approximately to all other maritime claims enumerated in article 1(1) of the 1952 Arrest Convention, with some additions, such as claims for insurance premiums and mutual insurance call. See para. I.308.

60. See *The "Eschersheim"* [1976] 2 Lloyd's Rep. 1 (H.L.); *N.V. Bureau Wijsmuller* v. *The "Tojo Maru" (Owners)* (H.L.) [1971] 1 Lloyd's Rep. 341.

particular a claim of the owner of a ship against the charterer of that ship is a maritime claim.

I.440 The second question is whether the arrest of a ship which in a wide sense may be described as a "sister ship" is permissible also when the claimant is not entitled to arrest the ship in respect of which the maritime claim has arisen.

I.441 The situations in which the ship in respect of which the claim has arisen cannot be arrested include the following:

(a) that ship has sunk;

(b) that ship has been sold to a *bona fide* purchaser or to a successful bidder in a forced sale;

(c) that ship is owned by the claimant and, therefore, its arrest as security for his claim is not conceivable;

(d) that ship is not owned by the claimant, but the claim is that of the person who has the possession or control of the ship such as the claim of the demise charterer against the time or voyage charterer or the claim of the time charterer against the voyage charterer.

I.442 A distinction must be made between the situations mentioned under (a) and (b) and those mentioned under (c) and (d). In fact in the former two situations the claimant would have been entitled to arrest the particular ship if it had not sunk or it had not been sold and, therefore, he is certainly entitled to arrest another ship owned by the person liable. In the latter two cases, instead, the claimant could not at any time and under any circumstance have arrested the particular ship.

I.443 It is very likely that when drafting paragraphs 1 and 4 of Article 4 the situations that had been envisaged were that of the claimant being entitled to arrest a ship other than that in respect of which the claim has arisen in addition to the particular ship. However, once it is accepted that claims of the owner of a ship against other persons arising out of the operation of the ships, such as those previously mentioned under (i)–(vi) are maritime claims, it follows necessarily that the ship that the claimant may arrest is not the particular ship but another ship. And since the right of arrest is the essential feature of the maritime claims, the conclusion must be that the claimant has the right to arrest "any other ship" owned by the person liable even when he is, for any reason, not entitled to arrest the particular ship.

21. WHEN SHIPS MUST BE DEEMED TO BE IN THE SAME OWNERSHIP

I.444 Paragraph (2) of Article 3 provides that ships shall be deemed to be in the same ownership when all the shares therein are owned by the same person or persons. "Share" in this context means a part of the property in a ship. The words "shares therein" in the English text, and *"parts de propriété"* in the French text, make this abundantly clear. Therefore, the sister ship rule does not apply in case the other ship is not fully owned by the same person or persons owning the ship in respect of which the claim arose. It is, however, sufficient that that ship is fully owned by one or more, albeit not all, of the persons owning the ship in respect of which the claim arose. If ship A, in respect of which the claim arose, is owned for 20 shares by Mr W, for 20 shares by Mr X and for 20 shares by Mr Y, and ship B is owned for 20 shares by Mr W, for 30 shares by Mr X and for 10 shares by Mr Z, ship B may not be arrested. But ship B may be arrested if 50 out of the 60 shares therein are owned by Mr W and 10 by Mr X.

I.445 The right to arrest a sister ship appears to be granted as an alternative. Paragraph (1) states that the claimant may arrest either the particular ship in respect of which the maritime claim arose, or any other ship. In England these words have been construed disjunctively, with respect to section 3(2)(a) and (b) of the Administration of Justice Act 1956, by the Court of Appeal in *The "Banco"*.[61] The opinion was also expressed in that case that the words "any other ship" were to be construed in the singular, so that if more than one ship were liable to arrest, the claimant could select only one of them. The same view was expressed in *The "Elefterio"*,[62] *The "St. Merriel"*[63] and *The "Berny"*.[64] This view appears to be correct also for Article 3(3) and (4) of the Convention, to the extent, however, to which the prohibition to arrest a ship more than once is operative.[65]

I.446 Pursuant to Article 3(1) the sister ship rule does not apply in respect of the following maritime claims enumerated in Article 1(1):

(o) disputes as to the title to or ownership of any ship;
(p) disputes between co-owners of any ship as to the ownership, possession, employment or earnings of that ship;
(q) the mortgage or hypothecation of any ship.

I.447 The exclusion of these maritime claims from the scope of the sister ship rule did not exist in the draft approved by the CMI at Naples.[66] It was first suggested at the Diplomatic Conference by the British delegation on the ground that in the case of a claim arising out of a mortgage only the mortgaged vessel can be arrested and that in cases of disputes between co-owners any person claiming rights on the ship could only arrest such ship and no other.[67] The British proposal was supported by the Spanish and French

---

61. [1971] 1 Lloyd's Rep. 49 (C.A.).
62. [1957] 1 Lloyd's Rep. 283.
63. [1963] 1 Lloyd's Rep. 63.
64. [1977] 2 Lloyd's Rep. 533.
65. See *infra*, para. I.559–565.
66. The text approved by the CMI Naples Conference was the following (CMI Bulletin No. 105, p. 89; *Travaux Préparatoires*, p. 319):
　　1. Without prejudice to the provisions of para. V of this Article, a claimant may arrest either the particular ship in respect of which he alleges that a maritime claim arises or any other ship which is owned by the person who was, at the time when the maritime claim arose, the owner of the particular ship, even though the arrested ship may be ready to sail.
67. The following statement was made by the British delegate (*Procès-verbaux*, p. 59; *Travaux Préparatoires*, p. 320):
　　He indicates that His Majesty's Government would like two points to be modified. The right of arrest of a sister ship should be limited so to exclude the following cases:
　　1. The mortgage
　　2. The cases of co-ownership with respect to claims listed in Art. 1(a) and (f).
In the case of a mortgage, it does not seem possible to arrest a ship other than that which is mortgaged. With respect to paras. (a) and (f), he who alleges to have a right of co-ownership in a ship cannot enforce such claim on another ship.
　　The reference to subpara. (f) is correct, for in the draft submitted to the Diplomatic Conference the claim in respect of mortgage or hypothecation was listed under (f). The reference to subpara. (a) must instead be a printing error since the claims in respect of disputes between co-owners were at that time listed in subparas. (d) and (e).

delegations.[68] The Dutch delegation instead requested that the sister ship rule be applied in respect of claims arising out of mortgages or *hypothèques*, but the request did not meet with the favour of the Conference.[69]

I.448 The real argument in favour of the decision not to apply the sister ship rule in respect of such claims is that their maritime nature does not depend on the nature of the claims, but on the nature of the security: the ship. Quite on the contrary normally the debt secured by the mortgage or by the "*hypothèque*" would not be qualified as "maritime" if it were not so secured: it is in fact a debt for the reimbursement of a loan or for the payment of the purchase price of the ship and sometimes, as in the case of fleet mortgages, it is not even related to the particular ship. Since, however, the restriction of the right of arrest to specified claims of a maritime nature can be explained, on an international basis,[70] by the desire to protect the normal operation of ships and maritime trade, there is no need for such protection when the owner of the ship, in order to obtain financing, voluntarily grants a charge on his ship.[71]

22. ARREST OF "ASSOCIATED SHIPS": IS PIERCING THE CORPORATE VEIL PROHIBITED BY THE CONVENTION?

I.449 In several jurisdictions the corporate form may be disregarded or—as it is commonly said—the corporate veil may be "pierced"[72] or "lifted"[73] in case of fraud or in case two companies are under the full control of the same person or persons.[74]

I.450 It is therefore necessary to consider whether there are in the Convention provisions that do not allow in any circumstance the arrest of a ship which is owned by a company other than that owning the ship in respect of which the maritime claim has arisen. In the Convention there is no definition of "owner".[75] Except in Article 3(4), the word "owner" is never accompanied by any qualification. In Article 3(4), which regulates the arrest of a ship when the charterer by demise is liable in respect of a maritime claim

68. The Spanish delegate (Prof. Garrigues) stated thus (*Procès-verbaux*, p. 62; *Travaux Préparatoires*, p. 320):

> The Spanish Delegation shares the views of the British Delegation on the sister ship. It would not be equitable to permit the arrest of a sister ship in the case of a mortgage. Arrest is in such case rather the commencement of enforcement proceedings on the subject matter of the real right, whilst as regards personal claims, arrest is merely a security measure on a part whatsoever of the assets of the debtor. It would, therefore, be necessary to modify the text of Art. 1 in order to clearly establish a distinction between real and personal rights as the basis of a conservative arrest.

69. *Procès-verbaux*, p. 73; *Travaux Préparatoires*, p. 321.

70. Although in fact the origin of the limitation in common law countries is the establishment of the scope of Admiralty jurisdiction, when the principle of limiting the right of arrest on an international basis was accepted its justification necessarily changed.

71. See *infra*, Book II, para. II.119–123.

72. "Piercing the corporate veil" is the expression commonly used in the United States: see Blumberg, *The Law of Corporate Groups*, Boston & Toronto, 1987 and 1997 Supplement; Thompson, *Piercing the corporate veil: an empirical study*, 76 Cornell Law Review 1036 where over 1500 judgments have been classified. In England this expression has also been used: see for example The *"Aventicum"*, [1978] 1 Lloyd's Rep. 184, at p. 187.

73. This expression has sometimes been used in England: see The *"Maritime Trader"* [1981] 2 Lloyd's Rep. 153, at p. 157.

74. A proposal to regulate the arrest of "associated ships" in the new Arrest Convention had been made by the United Kingdom but did not receive sufficient support. The interesting debate that took place at the Diplomatic Conference is annexed to the *Travaux Préparatoires*. See *infra*, Book II, Appendix III, p. 478–493.

75. A definition of "owner" is given in other conventions.

relating to that ship, reference is made to the case where the charterer by demise "and not the registered owner" is liable. Reference to the "registered owner" is again made in the second sentence of the same paragraph. There is no explanation in the *travaux préparatoires* why in this paragraph reference is made to the registered owner, whilst anywhere else the word used is "owner" and it is difficult to understand such reason in particular considering that the word "owner" is used in paragraph 1 of Article 3, in respect of the "owner of the particular ship" in respect of which the maritime claim has arisen.

I.451 From the *travaux préparatoires*[76] it appears that the original text of paragraph 4 was in French, and did not contain any reference to the owner, nor does the text of the Convention. The words used in French are "lorsque l'affréteur répond, *seul*, d'une créance maritime" which can literally be translated "where the charterer *alone* is liable in respect of a maritime claim". "Seul" (alone) has instead been translated with "and not the registered owner".

I.452 It is very likely that the addition of the word "registered" was not made with the intention to limit the scope of paragraph 4 to the registered owner. In any event, the word "registered" cannot be implied in paragraph 1 and, therefore, its use in paragraph 4 cannot in any way imply a prohibition to consider as owner a company other than that registered as owner. This view has been held, either expressly or impliedly by several judgments in various countries.[77]

I.453 It is thought that the importance of this problem, also in view of the debate that has recently taken place during the Diplomatic Conference held in March 1999 for the adoption of the new Arrest Convention,[78] deserves an investigation on the status of the law in some of the Contracting States.

I.454 The question whether the corporate veil may be pierced in respect of shipowning companies is answered in different manners in the various jurisdictions. A short analysis of the position in a number of States parties to the 1952 Convention follows.[79]

BELGIUM

I.455 In Belgium corporate veil has been pierced several times in connection with the arrest of ships owned by companies other than those owning the ship in respect of which the claim had arisen when it appeared that the creation of separate legal entities was a fiction and the corporate form had been used for fraudulent purposes. In the leading case *King Navigation Ltd.* v. *Bulknedlloyd Holding B.V.—The "Alpha Sun"* decided by the Cour d'Appel of Antwerp on 1 February 1994[80] Bulknedlloyd and Sollac arrested the m/v *Alpha Sun* as security for a claim for the loss of a cargo of iron ore carried on board the m/v *Alfa Star* owned by Lone Eagle Shipping and chartered by Bulknedlloyd for the carriage of iron ore for the account of Sollac. The *Alpha Sun* was owned by King Navigation Ltd. The Cour d'Appel of Antwerp rejected the appeal of King Navigation

---

76. *Travaux Préparatoires*, p. 338.

77. The court decisions in which this problem has been discussed have been analysed by F. Berlingieri, *Sister ships e navi "apparantés"*, [1998] Dir. Mar. 315.

78. See *infra*, Book II, para. II.134–138 and Appendix III, pp. 478–493.

79. The information provided below is mainly based on the replies to the Questionnaire, Appendix II, pp. 250–255.

80. The author is indebted to Mr. Wim Fransen, President of the Belgian Maritime Law Association, for an English translation of this judgment.

against the warrant of arrest stating that the corporate veil can be pierced when it is proved that the separate existence of several legal entities is fictitious and made reference to the legal concepts of simulation, abuse of law and fraud; it then considered in detail all the elements that proved the strict association between the two companies.[81]

CROATIA

I.456 So far piercing the corporate veil has not been permitted. This problem, however, has been recently discussed in respect of shipping companies.[82]

DENMARK

I.457 Danish courts have not yet, and are not expected to, pierce the "corporate veil". Thus Danish law recognises the autonomy of for instance single ship companies and will not permit the arrest of a vessel belonging to another company in the same group.

ENGLAND

I.458 In England the initial approach to the general problem of piercing the corporate veil was negative. In the leading case *Saloman* v. *A. Saloman & Co.*[83] the House of Lords rejected the claims of the creditors against the shareholders of a company in forced liquidation, being a merchant, his wife and their five children. Lord Herschell stated[84]:

How does it concern the creditor whether the capital . . . is owned by seven persons . . . or . . . almost entirely owned . . . by one person?

---

81. The Cour d'Appel so stated (translation provided by Mr. Wim Fransen):
   Considering that from the documents disclosed by parties it appears that Lloyd's Register of Shipping mentions the vessels "Alpha Star", "Alpha Sun", "Alpha Storm", and "Alpha Sky" under 'Le Timon Transport' established at 2 Akti Miaouli and Pavieroustreet in Piraeus (Greece), although for each of these vessels a separate company in Monrovia is mentioned; that these companies are all established at the same address in Monrovia; that also the place of business of Plaintiffs in the appeal is established at the same address with an Agent; that the addresses 97 Akti Miaouli and 2 Pavieroustreet do refer to the same building; that Le Timon Transport is the policy holder for both vessels (cfr. Skuld, List of vessels, 31st December 1993, p. 3); that the registration of the vessel and the deed of sale of the vessel are disclosed; that Defendants in the appeal give proof with regard to two other vessels out of the same group, "Alpha Storm" and "Alpha Sky" that Le Timon Transport is known as the Owner of these two vessels (cfr. report Dinamar "Secondhand Sales"); that from World Shipowning Groups (1993) it appears that Le Timon Transport is known as "Group Fleet: 4 vessels" be it with the mention of various "one ship companies" for the respective vessels; that more specifically the Board of directors of Lone Eagle Shipping and King Navigation Ltd. are in the hands of the same persons; that the Board of directors of Lone Eagle Shipping is managed by P. Skamalou and M. Psalti and the Board of directors of King Navigation by G. Giousepis and M. Psalti and that both companies have the same representative, i.e. P. Skamalou; that the lawyer Harris represents both ms. "Alpha Sun" and ms. "Alpha Star" (telefax of 21st January 1994); that vessels of the same group are "cross collateralised", i.e. one ship is used as collateral for debts of the other ship; that as a matter of fact proof is given that when buying "Alpha Sky", the "Alpha Star" was offered as collateral to the Royal Bank of Scotland, mortgagee; that no proof is given that the various "single ship companies" in reality have a separate life from a financial and administrative viewpoint.
82. See the reply of the Croatian MLA to Question 6 of the Questionnaire, Appendix II, p. 250.
83. 1897 App. Cas. 22 (1896).
84. At p. 44 and 45.

1.459 It seems, however, to be settled now that there may be circumstances in which it is permitted to pierce the corporate veil. In *Woolfson* v. *Strathclyde Regional Council*[85] the House of Lords stated:

The relevant principle is that it is appropriate to pierce the corporate veil only where special circumstances exist indicating that it is a mere facade concealing the true facts.

1.460 In cases relating to the arrest of ships governed by section 3(4) of the Administration of Justice Act 1956[86] the Courts have held that in certain situations it is permitted to "look at the beneficial ownership". This statement was made in *The "Aventicum"*[87] in which this vessel at the time when the claim of Marubeni Corporation and Daiei Papers Ltd. against Navieros Armadora S.A. of Panama was owned by such company and was flying the Panamanian flag. The vessel was then sold to a Singapore company, Longan Shipping Ltd., controlled by the same group which controlled Navieros Armadora, apparently in order to overcome ITF problems, and was registered in Singapore. Subsequently the shares of Longan Shipping were acquired by Anglo-Nurse, which formed a company named Loquat, to which the vessel was sold. Slynn J. considered the contention of Loquat, that it could not be permitted to pierce the corporate veil and stated[88]:

I think that that is wrong and that where damages are claimed by cargo-owners and there is a dispute as to the beneficial ownership of the ship, the Court in all cases can and in some cases should look behind the registered owner to determine the true beneficial ownership. . . . I have no doubt that on a motion of this kind it is right to investigate the true beneficial ownership. I reject any suggestion that it is impossible "to pierce the corporate veil". I of course remember, as Mr. Howard urges, the case of *Saloman* v. *Saloman & Co.* [1897] A.C. 22, but of course it is plain that s. 3(4) of the Act intends that the Court shall not be limited to a consideration of who is the registered owner or who is the person having legal ownership of the shares in the ship; the directions are to look at the beneficial ownership. Certainly in a case where there is a suggestion of a trusteeship or a nominee holding, there is no doubt that the Court can investigate it.

1.461 The claim was then dismissed on the ground that the claimants had not proved that the beneficial ownership[89] had remained the same.

---

85. 1978 S.L.T. 159.
86. Section 4(4) of the Administration of Justice Act, 1956 so provided:
    In the case of any such claim as is mentioned in paragraphs (d) to (r) of subsection (1) of section one of this Act, being a claim arising in connection with a ship, where the person who would be liable on the claim in an action in personam was, when the cause of action arose, the owner or charterer of, or in possession or in control of, the ship, the Admiralty jurisdiction of the High Court . . . may (whether the claim gives rise to a maritime lien on the ship or not) be invoked by an action in rem against:
    (a) that ship, if at the time when the action is brought it is beneficially owned as respects all the shares therein by that person; or
    (b) any other ship which, at the time when the action is brought, is beneficially owned as aforesaid.
87. *The "Aventicum"*, [1978] 1 Lloyd's Rep. 184, at p. 187.
88. At p. 187.
89. The expression "beneficial owner" is used both in s. 3(4) of the Administration of Justice Act, 1956 and in s. 21(4) of the Supreme Court Act, 1981. In this latter Act, however, it is used in respect of the title to the vessel at the time when the arrest is effected whilst in respect of the time when the claim has arisen the word used is "owner". The contrast has been noted by Lord Donaldson, M.R. in *The "Evpo Agnic"* [1982] 2 Lloyd's Rep. 411, at p. 414:
    First, it is a basic rule of construction that where a statute employs different terminology in different provisions, prima facie a different meaning is intended and this is particularly the case if the differing terminology occurs within a single subsection. "Owner" in par. (b) thus falls to be contrasted with "beneficial owner" in pars. (i) and (ii).
Whilst in the *"Andrea Ursula"* [1971] 1 Lloyd's Rep. 145 Brandon J. stated that the demise charterer is the beneficial owner of the vessel, in *The "I Congreso del Partido"* [1977] 1 Lloyd's Rep. 536, at p. 560 and 561 Goff J. stated that the word "beneficially owned as respects all shares therein" refer only to cases of equitable

I.462 In *The "Maritime Trader"*[90] the time charterer of the m/v. *"Antaios"* commenced an action *in rem* by issuing a writ of summons against the m/v. *"Maritime Trader"*, owned by Maritime Trader Ship Holding GmbH (MTS) in respect of a claim against the subcharterers, Maritime Transport Overseas GmbH (MTO). The claimants alleged that the *"Maritime Trader"* was beneficially owned by MTO since MTO owned the entire capital stock of MTS. The Admiralty Judge, Sheen J., stated first that the vessel could not be qualified as a sister ship of the *"Antaios"* and then considered the question relating to the beneficial ownership of the *"Maritime Trader"*. After having stated that it is a "fundamental principle of company law that a shareholder has no property, legal or equitable, in the assets of the company", he said[91]:

> From the starting point there is no way in which it can be said that *"Maritime Trader"* was "beneficially owned as respects all the shares therein" by MTO, unless the corporate veil can be lifted. I would not hesitate to lift that veil if the evidence suggested that it obscured from view a mask of fraud rather than the true face of the corporation.

I.463 Subsequently, in *The "Saudi Prince"*[92] against which a writ *in rem* had been issued (followed by the arrest of the vessel) in connection with a claim for damages suffered by a cargo carried by the m.v. *"Al Dhahran"* owned by a Mr Abdul R. Orri, Sheen J. held that the *"Saudi Prince"* was beneficially owned by Mr Orri. The vessel, originally owned by Mr. Orri, had been sold to Saudi Shipping and Sea Transport Ltd., whose shares were held by Mr Orri and by his sons. Sheen J. held that the transfer had not been perfected and that, in any event, Mr Orri should be considered as the beneficial owner of the vessel on the basis of the criteria set out by Slynn J. in *The "Aventicum"*.[93]

I.464 There followed the case of *The "Evpo Agnic"*,[94] which was arrested by the owners of the cargo laden on the m/v. *"Skipper I"*, which was lost with the vessel. The Court of Appeal rejected the contention that the two vessels were owned by the same persons. The m/v. *"Skipper I"* was owned by Skipper Shipping Co. S.A. of Panama, whose shareholders were a Mr Rodolfo Silva Batista and a Mr José Ignacio de Sedas and whose directors were a Mr Evandelos Pohitos and a Mr Dimitrios Kapsarachis. The m/v. *"Evpo Agnic"* was owned by Agnic Shipping S.A., also of Panama. The claimants alleged that the two vessels were managed, as part of the same fleet, by Pohitos Shipping Co. S.A.

---

ownership, whether or not accompanied by legal ownership and do not apply to the case of a demise charterer. The views of Brandon J. and Goff J. were considered by Sir Thomas Bingham, M.R. in *The "Nazym Khikmet"*, [1996] 2 Lloyd's Rep. 362 (C.A.) who said:

> The amendment was, however, limited to inclusion of a demise charterer; the expression "beneficially owned" was not amended; and Parliament continued to restrict claims against sisterships to ships of which the party liable in an action in personam was at the relevant time the "beneficial owner". In our judgment the effect of the amendment made, and the amendments not made, in the 1981 Act is clear: Parliament accepted the view of Mr. Justice Robert Goff that an amendment was necessary if demise charterers were to be covered by sub-s. (4)(i), and accordingly made that amendment to give effect to the Convention; it did not intend demise charterers to be covered by sub-s. (4)(ii), which indeed the Convention did not require; and it must be taken to have endorsed the ruling of Mr. Justice Robert Goff on the meaning of "beneficial ownership", since otherwise it would have been bound to legislate to reverse his conclusion on that point.

On the notion of beneficial ownership see also Hill, *Arrest of Ships*, London 1985, p. 15.

90. [1981] 2 Lloyd's Rep. 153.
91. At p. 157.
92. [1982] 2 Lloyd's Rep. 255.
93. *Supra*, note 77.
94. [1988] 2 Lloyd's Rep. 411.

and asked the Admiralty Judge to authorise an investigation in respect of the actual ownership of the *"Evpo Agnic"*.

I.465 This decision was appealed by Agnic Shipping and Lord Donaldson, M.R. after having denied that the conditions for a discovery existed, said[95]:

The truth of the matter, as I see it, is that s. 21 does not go, and is not intended to go, nearly far enough to give the plaintiffs a right of arresting a ship which is not "the particular ship" or a sister ship, but the ship of a sister company of the owners of "the particular ship". The purpose of s. 21(4) is to give rights of arrest in respect of "the particular ship", ships in the ownership of the owners of "the particular ship" and those who have been spirited into different legal, i.e. registered, ownership, the owners of "the particular ship" retaining beneficial ownership of the shares in that ship. This was the situation in *The "Saudi Prince"*, [1982] 2 Lloyd's Rep. 255 and was alleged to be the situation in *The "Aventicum"*, [1978] 1 Lloyd's Rep. 184.

I.466 The conclusion seems to be that under section 21(4) of the Supreme Court Act 1981, whose purpose had been, as stated by Lord Diplock in *The "Eschersheim"*,[96] "to bring the right of arrest *in rem* in the English Courts into conformity with the International Convention relating to the Arrest of Sea-going Ships", it is possible to arrest any of the ships owned by the owner of the ship in relation to which the claim has arisen as well as any of the ships that, to use the language of Lord Donaldson, M.R., have been "spirited"—that is conveyed rapidly and secretly—into different legal ownership, the owners of the particular ship retaining beneficial ownership.[97] This situation corresponds to that described by the French Courts as fictitious transfer as it clearly appears from the following statement of Clarke J. in *The "Tjaskemolen"*[98]:

The cases have not worked out what is meant by "piercing the corporate veil". It may not always mean the same thing. But in the present context the cases seem to me to show that, where the alleged transfer is a sham or a façade, it will not have the effect of transferring the beneficial ownership of the transferor in the vessel concerned.

FINLAND

I.467 According to the Maritime Code Chap. 4, § 5, a vessel shall be deemed to be in the same ownership when all the shares therein are owned by the same person or persons. The question of "piercing the corporate veil" is not governed by arrest law. It is an emerging issue relevant especially for corporate law, contract law and tort law.

FRANCE

I.468 In France the arrest of a ship owned by a company other than that liable in respect of the maritime claim has often been granted by the Courts. The basis of such decisions has sometimes been described as the apparent assumption of the debt by the owner of the

---

95. At p. 415.

96. [1976] 2 Lloyd's Rep. 1, at p. 6. See also Hill, *Arrest of Ships*, *supra*, note 89, p. 15 and 16.

97. It is stated in the "Report on Diligence on the Dependance and Admiralty Arrestment" of the Scottish Law Commission (*supra*, note 5) paragraph 8.31, at p. 167 that the approach taken in England likely to be followed in Scotland, is that, while the possibility of piercing the corporate veil does exist, it can be done only if registration of the ship is clearly a sham or amounts to fraud.

98. [1997] 2 Lloyd's Rep. 465 at p. 471.

arrested ship.[99] However in most cases the arrest has been granted on the ground of the close association between the ship in respect of which the claim has arisen (or the person liable in respect of the maritime claim) and the ship the arrest of which is requested or the company owning such ship,[100] or, also, on the ground of the fictitious character of such company which appears as an attempt to give a legal frame to the theory of the "apparentement". For example, in the case of The "Aliakmon Prosperity" the Tribunal de Commerce of Rouen[101] stated that it was apparent that the companies owning the two ships belonged to the same group. In the case of The "Alexander III"[102] the Cour d'Appel of Aix-en-Provence held that there was a presumption that the companies owning that vessel and the "Lides" in respect of which the claim had arisen had a fictitious character; the judgment was quashed by the Cour de Cassation[103] on the ground that the reasons set out by the Cour d'Appel were not sufficient for the purpose of proving the fictitious character of the two companies and the lack by one of them of independent assets, thereby implying that if such evidence had been properly established, the arrest would have been justified. The fictitious nature of the company owning the vessel that had been arrested as security for a claim that had arisen in respect of another vessel owned by a different company has also been the basis of the decisions of the Cour d'Appel of Paris in the case of The "El Jumbo",[104] this time affirmed by the Cour de Cassation,[105] of the Cour d'Appel of Aix-en-Provence in the case of The "Irini M",[106] also affirmed by the Cour de

---

99. This theory, called "théorie de l'apparence", has been adopted by the Cour d'Appel of Bordeaux as the basis of its decision of 2 July 1992 in the case *Constance Navigation and Overseas Reefer Services* v. *Corunesa de Navegacion—The "Osiris I"*, [1992] DMF 510. The Cour d'Appel made reference to the confusion which "permet à quiconque ayant commis, à la suite de cette apparence trompeuse, une erreur légitime, d'invoquer cette apparence comme si elle était réalité" (permits to anybody who has, due to such misleading appearance, made a legitimate mistake, to invoke such appearence as if it were the reality). On this theory see Rohart, *Faut-il se méfier de l'apparence? La saisie conservatoire des navires apparentés*, [1988] DMF 499; Clemens-Jones, *Ship arrest: a study in French confusion*, 1997 Int. Journal of Shipping Law 242; Vialard, "Personnalité morale des sociétés d'armement et apparentement abusif des navires saisis", [1996] DMF 467.

100. Tribunal de Commerce of Rouen 1 April 1980, *Capitaine de l'Aliakmon Prosperity* v. *GIE Uniports—The "Aliakmon Prosperity"*, [1980] DMF 426 affirmed by the Cour d'Appel de Rouen with judgment 27 October 1983, [1984] DMF 238 and by the Cour de Cassation with judgment 11 March 1986, [1987] DMF 363 on which see the comments of Bonassies, "Le droit positif français en 1987", [1988] DMF 81 at paragraph 12; Cour d'Appel of Aix-en-Provence 11 March 1988, *Société Morgul* v. *Eagle Star—The "Hakki-Morgul*, [1989] DMF 367; Cour d'Appel of Rennes 21 June 1989, *Maritime Transports Overseas GmbH* v. *Brave Mother Shipping Ltd.—The "Brave Mother"*, [1989] DMF 649, affirmed by the Cour de Cassation with judgment 12 February 1991, [1991] DMF 315; Cour d'Appel of Bordeaux 13 June 1990, *Constance Navigation* v. *Compania Corunesa de Navegacion—The "Osiris I"*, [1991] DMF 174 with a critical comment of Vialard, "Les sociétés écrans: apparence ou transparence?", affirmed by the Cour de Cassation with judgment 27 November 1991, [1992] DMF 488; the subsequent judgment on the merits of the Cour d'Appel of Bordeaux of 2 July 1992, [1992] DMF 520 based on the "théorie de l'apparence" rather than on the theory of the "communauté d'intérêts" was quashed by the Cour de Cassation with judgment 15 November 1994, [1995] DMF 135 on the ground that no evidence had been provided of the fictitious character of the two companies. Cour d'Appel of Rouen 6 January 1994, *Crighton Navigation* v. *Italmare—The "Trovatore"*, [1994] DMF 559.

101. *Supra*, note 100.

102. Judgment of 18 November 1993, *Lemphy Maritime* v. *Mohamed Zaatari & Bros*, cited by Bonassies, "Le droit positif français en 1996", [1997] DMF, Hors Sèrie n. 1, Février 1997, p. 33 and by Vialard, "Personnalité morale des sociétés d'armement et apparentement abusif des navires saisis", [1996] DMF 467.

103. Judgment of 19 March 1996, [1996] DMF 503.

104. Judgment of 1 June 1987, *La Concorde and Others* v. *Thenamaris Maritime and Vastseas Shipping Ltd.*, [1989] DMF 642.

105. Judgment of 4 July 1989, [1989] DMF 639.

106. Judgment of 19 February 1988, *Mamitank Shipping Enterprises* v. *Shell Française—The "Irini M."*, [1989] DMF 249.

Cassation[107] and of the Cour d'Appel of Rouen in the case of *The "Osiris I"*.[108] In the case of *The "Irini M"* the Cour d'Appel of Aix-en-Provence so held[109]:

Qu'il apparaît à l'évidence, que Surena puis Styga, sont des sociétés de façade liées à la même entité économique réelle Mamitank Shipping Enterprises qui réalise un montage juridique permettant tant des avatanges fiscaux que des obstacles a la poursuite d'éventuels créanciers.

Attendu qu'il y a lieu de relever que l'intimée a ainsi rapporté la preuve de l'absence totale d'autonomie de personnalité morale de la SA Surena Delmare Navigation et de l'existence d'une seule et même entité économique pour la gestion et les capitaux qui doit nécessairement répondre des conséquences de la responsabilité du transporteur.

I.469 The Cour de Cassation affirmed this judgment stating that the Cour d'Appel had found that the operation of the two ships had been separated in order to build up a legal structure advantageous to the owners and that consequently the companies owning the two vessels were only "sociétés de façade".[110] The judgment of the Cour d'Appel of Rouen in the case of *The "Osiris I"* is particularly interesting, since the previous decision on the same case of the Cour d'Appel of Bordeaux[111] had been quashed by the Cour de Cassation[112] on the ground that no acceptable evidence of the fictitious nature of the companies had been established. The Cour d'Appel of Rouen, to which the case had been assigned by the Cour de Cassation, after a careful analysis of the history of the two companies and of their "directing mind" concluded that they were fictitious and were dominated by the same person.[113]

I.470 In several judgments the provisions of Article 3(1) and (2) of the Arrest Convention have been taken into consideration by the French Courts who expressed the view that the arrest of a ship owned by a different company was not, when the two companies were linked by a "communauté d'intérêts" or when their fictitious nature was proved, in conflict with the Convention.

I.471 The Cour de Cassation in its judgment 12 February 1991 in *Brave Mother Shipping Ltd.* v. *Maritime Transports Overseas GmbH—The "Brave Mother"*[114] held:

But whereas, if Art. 3 of the Convention states that, when all parts of the vessel belong to the same person or persons, the ships are deemed to be in the same ownership, this provision does not exclude that evidence be given that a ship belongs to the same person or persons even though the parts do not wholly belong to him or them that having found that the two ships in respect of which the dispute has arisen, even if registered as belonging to distinct legal entities, were owned by companies whose assets were united through the members of the same family and by a *communauté d'intérêts*, the

107. Judgment of 28 November 1989, [1991] DMF 290.

108. Judgment of 30 June 1998, *Constance Navigation S.A. and Overseas Reefer Service S.A.* v. *Compania Corunesa de Navegacion S.A.* [1988] DMF 1035.

109. *Supra*, note 106.

110. Judgment of 28 November 1989, [1991] DMF 290, at p. 12.

111. *Supra*, note 100.

112. *Supra*, note 100.

113. Judgment of 30 June 1998, [1998] DMF 1035. The Cour d'Appel so stated (at p. 1040):
Attendu en définitive qu'Ors et Constance Navigation n'étaient que des sociétés fictives aux seules mains de Monsieur Michael Karayannis, participant exclusivement d'un montage juridique masquant les activités économiques et commerciales de celui-ci.

114. [1991] DMF 315, at p. 316. Previously the same view had been expressed, albeit in a more concise form, by the Cour d'Appel of Rennes in its judgment of 21 June 1989, *Maritime Transport Overseas GmbH* v. *Brave Themis Navigation—The "Brave Mother"*, [1989] DMF 649 at p. 654.

Court of Appeal, without making the finding considered in the appeal, has legally justified its decision and from this follows that the appeal is not founded.

I.472 Practically identical reasons have been given by the Cour d'Appel of Rouen in its judgment of 6 January 1994, in the case *The "Trovatore"*.[115]

GREECE

I.473 The fact that the Greek merchant marine consists mainly of single ship companies has contributed to the admission by jurisprudence and scholars of the process of piercing the corporate veil for imposing personal liability on the individual beneficiaries. For piercing the corporate veil, Greek courts have recourse either to the test of control or the test of the nominee. On a number of cases they have combined both tests. In particular, courts have pierced the corporate veil in the case of shipping companies when one of the shareholders had the absolute control of each company by holding himself or through nominees the whole of the shares therein[116] and exercising himself or through his nominee the powers of the managing director of the company[117] or when the company appeared as "strawman" of the individual hiding behind it.[118] However, as it has been correctly pointed out,[119] recourse to these tests, at least in the manner it is conducted, entails a serious threat to the institution of corporate entity. This is why it is maintained[120] that the corporate veil should be pierced only when the incorporation of a company constitutes an abusive exercise of the faculty granted by the judicial system for the development of business activities through corporate entities. This is especially so when the main shareholder makes use of this faculty for circumventing the law or maliciously causing harm to others or evading the fulfilment of his obligations. On such motive, he usually underfunds the company or uses the company's assets for conducting his personal business, thereby overturning the necessary equilibrium between the assets and the capital of the company.

I.474 As regards Article 3(2) of the Convention, the Piraeus Single-member First Instance Court held[121] that, when two ships are separately owned by two different *sociétés anonymes* whose shares belong to the same individual or individuals, they are not deemed to be part of the same property. The two ships should be deemed to be under the same property only if there was an *in concreto* reason to pierce the corporate veil of the two owning companies.

---

115. *Supra*, note 89.

116. Piraeus Court of Appeals [PCA] 1277/1990, [1990] Maritime Law Review [MLR] 226; Areios Pagos [AP] 1046/1990, [1991] MLR 15; Piraeus Single-member First Instance Court [PSFIC] 1990/1988, [1989] MLR 212; AP 591/1988, [1989] MLR 37; 1058/1987, [1987] MLR 41.

117. AP 1046/1990, *cit.*; 591/1980, *cit.*; Athens Court of Appeals (ACA) 8734/1986, [1986] Commercial Law Review 664; Piraeus Multi-member First Instance Court 2301/1988, [1988] MLR 441; PSFIC 1900/1988, *cit.*; ACA 11452/1986, [1987] MLR 243.

118. Athens Multimember First Instance Court 364/1986, [1986] MLR 664; ACA 11452/1986, [1987] MLR 243; PCA 1514/1988, [1988] Piraiki Nomologia 536; 253/1988, [1988] MLR 106.

119. cf. A. Kiantou-Pabouki, "The protection of maritime creditors in shipping companies by piercing the corporate veil", Records and Introductions of the 1st International Conference of Maritime Law, Piraeus Bar Association (1994) page 44 *et seq.*

120. K. Paboukis, *Commercial Companies Law*, para 44 II page 379; L. Georgakopoulos, *Companies Law* I (1965) pages 551–552; N. Papantoniou, *General principles of civil law* (1983) para 31, page 144; Than. Liakopoulos, *Lifting of the corporate veil in jurisprudence* (1988) page 10.

121. Judgment 2856/1976, MLR 5, 200.

HAITI

I.475 In Haiti a legal person is granted the same position as that of a physical person and, consequently, in no circumstances can the corporate veil be pierced.[122]

ITALY

I.476 In Italy the general problem of the responsibility of a company for the debts of another has been considered in relation to Article 2362 Civil Code which regulates the responsibility of the sole shareholder of a company[123] and to Article 2740 Civil Code which regulates the civil liability (*responsabilità patrimoniale*) of the debtor.[124] Although the operation of Article 2362 is now deemed possible even when the shareholder is a legal entity,[125] Italian Courts have interpreted this provision very strictly by requiring the ownership of 100 per cent of the shares. With judgment 9 January 1987, no. 73, *SIPSA v. Fallimento Ivo Pera*[126] the Corte di Cassazione held that Article 2362 Civil Code could apply in a case in which one shareholder owned 99 per cent of the shares of a company; with judgment 3 September 1992, *S.p.A. Manzoni & C. v. S.r.l. Coedit*[127] the Tribunale of Milano reached the same conclusion in relation to Article 2497 Civil Code, in which the same rule as that of Article 2362 is adopted for the case of voluntary liquidation, in a case when one shareholder held 99.9 per cent of the shares.

I.477 Article 2362 Civil Code has only been held to apply in cases where less than 100 per cent of the shares are owned by one person when the ownership of the balance of the shares by another person is fictitious, whilst the fact that a person or a company fully controls or dominates another company has been held to be relevant only from the economical but not from the legal standpoint.[128]

I.478 In respect of the arrest of ships the legal theory on the basis of which the arrest of a ship owned by a person other than debtor is that of "simulation" whereby a fictitious agreement is not relevant between the parties and, also, vis-à-vis third parties.[129] The Corte d'Appello of Genoa with judgment of 3 August 1971, *Felarugica S.A. v. S.p.A. Italviscosa and Felice Riva*[130] reversed a judgment of the Tribunal di Chiavari which had

---

122. See reply to Question 6 of the Questionnaire, Appendix II, p. 251.
123. Article 2362 Civil Code so provides:
 In case of insolvency of a company in respect of the obligations arisen during the time when all shares are owned by one person only, that person is responsible without any limit.
124. Article 2740 Civil Code so provides:
 The debtor is responsible for the fulfilment of his obligations with all his assets, present and future. Limitations of liability are not permitted unless in the cases statutorily established.
125. Corte di Cassazione—Sezioni Unite 14 December 1981, No. 6594, *S.A. Chocolat Tobler v. Banca Ambrosiana* [1982] 2 Giurisprudenza Commerciale 614.
126. [1988] 2 Giurisprudenza Commerciale 63.
127. [1993] 2 Giurisprudenza Commerciale 659.
128. Corte d'Appello of Palermo 5 November 1980, *Banca Commerciale Italiana v. Raytheon Co. and Machlett Laboratories* [1981] 2 Giurisprudenza Commerciale 615 with a critical comment by Pellizzi, *Unico azionista e controllo totalitario indiretto*.
129. Article 1415 Civil Code provides:
 1415. Effects of simulation on third persons. Simulation cannot be used as a defense by the contracting parties, by their successors in interest, or by the creditors of the simulating transferor, against third parties who, in good faith, have acquired rights from the apparent owner of the right, subject to the effects of transcription of a judicial petition concerning simulation. Third persons can plead simulation against the contracting parties, when it is prejudicial to their rights.
130. [1972] Dir. Mar. 53.

upheld the arrest of the m/y. *"Faella"* owned by Felarugica S.A. of Panama as security for a claim of S.p.A. Italviscosa against Mr Felice Riva on the ground that Mr Riva was the actual owner of the yacht, holding that no evidence of a simulation had been provided. For the same reasons the Tribunale of Chiavari with judgment 15 May 1971, *Robert Butler* v. *John F. Baron and Wanderer Financial Corp.—The "Wanderer"*[131] released the m/y. *"Wanderer"* from the arrest which had been effected as security for a claim against Mr John F. Baron, on the ground that he was the actual owner of the yacht.

I.479 The first judgment based on the Arrest Convention is a judgment of 12 March 1994 delivered by the Tribunale of Ravenna in the case *Secnav Marine Ltd.* v. *Petromin S.A., Breaza Inc. and Tanker Ship Management—The "Breaza"*.[132] The Tribunale of Ravenna affirmed the warrant of arrest of the *"Breaza"*, owned by Breaza Inc. of Monrovia, as security for a claim of Secnav Marine against Petromin S.A. on the ground that Petromin S.A. controlled Breaza Inc. through Petromin Overseas Inc. and that, therefore, the arrest was permissible under Article 3(1) of the Arrest Convention.

I.480 The French "théorie de l'apparence" was instead taken as a basis of the arrest of the m.v. *"Euroshipping One"* by the Tribunale of Livorno,[133] notwithstanding that the vessel had been sold to another company, since the buyer was a company fully owned by the seller and had a branch office located at the registered office of the seller. Rather than the "apparence" of a link between the two companies, this was probably a case in which the fictitious (or simulated) character of the sale could have been the proper basis for the arrest.

NETHERLANDS

I.481 In the Netherlands there does not appear to have been any judgment allowing the arrest of a ship on grounds similar to those that have been considered relevant by the French and Italian Courts.

I.482 The Supreme Court in its judgment of 4 October 1991 in *D.B. Deniz Naklyati T.A.S.* v. *Glorywave Shipping Ltd. (The "Queen Evi")*[134] affirmed a judgment of the Court of Appeal whereby the arrest of a ship on the ground that her owners had a close relationship with the debtor had been annulled. "Close relationship" is a rather vague notion, and it is likely, if not certain, that the same conclusion would have been reached in France and in Italy. The Arrondissementsrechtbank, Rotterdam, in its judgment of 9 July 1993 in *Stichting Rotterdam Trust– en Administratie-Kantoor* v. *Compania Corunesa de Navegacion (The "Yukon")*[135] held that the partial identity of the shareholders of two companies and the fact that both companies shared the same office were not sufficient to justify the arrest of a ship owned by the company which was not indebted to the claimant. Again, the partial identity of the shareholders would not by itself have been considered

---

131. [1972] Dir. Mar. 75.
132. [1994] Dir. Mar. 217.
133. Judgment 18 November 1996, *Enzo Cipriani Shipping S.r.l.* v. *Baltic Shipping Co.—The "Euroshipping One"*, [1998] Dir. Mar. 433.
134. [1994] Dir. Mar. 561, annex to a note of Derogés-van Roosmalen.
135. [1994] Dir. Mar. 559. This judgment is published with a note of Derogée-Van Roosmalen.

relevant in Italy and probably in France. The sharing of the same office could be relevant, but only if accompanied by other elements.

NIGERIA

I.483 Although the legal personality of the company, as distinct from those of the members and the consequences of incorporation, are recognised under Nigerian law, there are certain circumstances in which the corporate entity is disregarded and the veil of incorporation is lifted in accordance with statute or common law, in the interest of justice.[136]

NORWAY

I.484 In principle it is possible to pierce the corporate veil. In practice, however, it is very difficult. There is no legislation directly dealing with the issue. That the possibility to pierce exists has been confirmed by the Supreme Court in a case where such a piercing was denied. The test to be used is the *alter ego* test, much like it is done in e.g. the United States.

SLOVENIA

I.485 Piercing the corporate veil is not permitted.[137]

SPAIN

I.486 In Spain the Tribunal Supremo with its judgment of 28 May 1984[138] held that the doctrine and practice of piercing the corporate veil should be applied in order to avoid that under the protection of such fiction or legal form private or public interests be prejudiced or that the corporate veil be used for fraudulent purposes. It consequently held that Courts can penetrate into such legal entities when this is necessary in order to avoid the abuse of

---

136. The following examples in the Companies and Allied Matters Act, Cap. 59, Laws of the Federation of Nigeria 1990, under the common law have been provided by Louis N. Mbanefo:
   i. When the number of members is below the legal minimum and the company continues to carry on business for a period of six months thereafter: s. 93;
   ii. Where the number of directors of the company falls below two and the company carries on business after sixty days thereafter: s. 246(3);
   iii. Where the company receives money by way of a loan to be applied for certain specified purposes and the loan is not applied for such purposes: s. 290;
   iv. Where the name of the company is not mentioned on business correspondence, cheques, bills of exchange, promissory notes, etc. as required under s. 631(1): s. 631(2);
   v. Where a group of companies is virtually a partnership or where one of the companies is a trustee of the other in respect of some property in issue;
   vi. Where an inspector is appointed under s. 316 of the Act and he thinks it is necessary;
   vii. Where a company is acting for the shareholders or is a sham;
   viii. Generally, where the Courts have found fraud or some improper conduct, they have lifted the veil in the interest of justice.
137. See the reply of the Slovenian MLA to Question 6 of the Questionnaire, Appendix II, p. 253.
138. The judgment of the Tribunal Supremo is analysed by Almudena Jiménez Ruiz-Gálvez and Rocio Merlino-Sánchez-Elvia, "El levantamiento del velo", in Dos Años de Boletin, edited by Ruiz Gálvez Abogados, Madrid and Sanchez y Meya Abogados, Barcelona, 1998.

the corporate independence to the damage of others.[139] The Tribunal Supremo explained that this does not mean that the corporate independence should be eluded or abolished, but that it should be ascertained for the protection of third parties in good faith which is the actual social and economic identity of the company, the actual substratum of its personal and contractual composition.[140]

I.487 The principles laid down by the above judgment, followed by several other judgments of the same Tribunal Supremo,[141] have been applied to maritime cases by the lower Courts. Thus the Juzgado de Prima Instancia No. 4 of Barakaldo held[142] that the arrest of a ship owned by a company other than that who owned the ship in respect of which the claim had arisen is permissible when the two companies had the same address, the same directors and the same management. The Jugzado de Prima Instancia No. 2 of Tarragona held[143] that the corporate veil can be pierced in a case where the various owning companies had the same address, telephone and fax numbers and there was a presumption of all companies having the same management. Both judgments considered that under the 1952 Convention the allegation of a claim which is sufficient to entitle the claimant to arrest a ship applies to all conditions required for the arrest, including ownership.

139. The Tribunal Supremo so held:
" . . . que ya, desde el punto de vista civil y mercantil, la más autorizada doctrina, en el conflicto entre seguridad jurídica y justicia, valores hoy consagrados en la Constitución (arts. 1°.1 y 9°.3), se ha decidido prudencialmente y según los casos y circunstancias, por applicar la vía de equidad, y acogimiento del principio de buena fe (art. 7°.1 del Código Civil), la tesis y práctica de penetrar en el substratum personal de las entidades o sociedades, a las que la Ley confiere personalidad jurídica propria, con el fin de evitar que al socaire de esta ficción o forma legal, (de obligado respeto por supuesto) se puedan perjudicar ya intereses privados o públicos o bien ser utilizada como camino del fraude (art. 6°.4 del Código Civil), admitiéndose la posibiliad de que los jueces puedan penetrar ("levantar el velo jurídico") en el interior de esas personas cuando sea preciso para evitar el abuso de esa independiencia, (art. 7°.2 del Código Civil) en daño ajeno o de "los derechos de los demás" (art. 10° de la constitución) o contra intereses de los socios, es decir, de un mal uso de su personalidad, de un ejercicio antisocial de su derecho, (art. 7°.2 del Código Civil) . . . "
140. The Tribunal Supremo made express reference to the principles laid down by foreign authorities (not identified, but very likely in the United States). It in fact stated that the rule laid down
. . . no significa, (ya en el supuesto del recurso) que haya de soslayarse o dejarse de lado la personalidad del ente gestor constituido en la Sociedad Anónima sujeta al derecho privado, sino solo constatar a los efectos del tercero de buena fe (la actora y recurrida perjudicada), cual sea la auténtica y constitutiva personalidad social y económica de la misma, el sustrato real de su composición personal (o institucional) y negocial (. . .), porque como se ha dicho por la doctrina extanjera "quien maneja internamente de modo unitario y total un organismo no puede invocar frente a sus acreedores que existen exteriormente varias organizaciones independientes" y menos "cuando el control social efectivo está en manos de una sola persona, sea directamente o a través de los testaferros o de otra sociedad según la doctrina patria".
141. Judgment of 2 April 1990 [1990] 4 La Ley 611 with a note by José Miguel Embid Irujo, "En torno al 'levantamiento del velo'"; judgment of 20 June 1991 [1992] 1 La Ley 341, with a note by José Miguel Embid Irujo, "El 'levantamiento del velo' una vez mas"; judgments of 8 April 1996 [1996] La Ley 4764 and of 15 October 1997 [1997] La Ley 10112. In the judgment of 20 June 1991 an interesting analysis is made of the notion of civil fraud, the existence of which appears to be required in order to pierce the corporate veil (levantar el velo). The Tribunal Supremo so stated (at p. 346):
(f) El fraude es sinónimo de daño o perjuicio conseguido mediante un medio o mecanismo utilizado a tal fin, valiendo tanto como subterfugio o ardid, con infracción de deberes jurídicos generales que se imponen a las personas, implicando, en el fondo, un acto *contra legem*, por eludir las reglas del derecho, pero sin un enfrentamiento frontal sino, al revés, buscando unas aparentes normas de cobertura o una cobertura indirecta, respetando la letra de la norma, pero infringiendo su espíritu de forma que el *fraus alterius* o *fraus hominis* implica, con cárcater general, un *fraus legis*. . . .
142. Judgment of 27 May 1997, unreported.
143. Judgment of 22 September 1995, unreported. The author is indebted to Dr. Esther Zarza, of Abogados Marítimos y Asociados of Madrid for the exhaustive information provided on Spanish jurisprudence relating to the "levantamiento del velo".

SWEDEN

I.488 Under Swedish law the corporate form is normally protected. It is in fact felt that the corporate autonomy is an institute that favours development of new business and, therefore, is in the advantage of society in general. However, in certain situations, when the shareholders give the impression that they fully stay behind and take responsibility for the actions of the company or its subsidiaries, as the case may be, piercing the corporate veil may be permitted.

SOUTH AFRICA AND UNITED STATES

I.489 Although the Arrest Convention has not been ratified by South Africa and the United States it is of some interest to glance at the views expressed by South African and American Courts. In fact South Africa is perhaps the only maritime country in which the doctrine of piercing the corporate veil has been given legislative effect in respect of the arrest of ships, while the doctrine of piercing the corporate veil developed in the United States.

(A) SOUTH AFRICA

I.490 In the Admiralty Jurisdiction Regulation Act 105 of 1983 the provision of Article 3(1) of the Convention, according to which the claimant may arrest either the ship in respect of which the claim arose or any other ship which is owned by the owner of that ship, has been replaced by a provision according to which the claimant may arrest an "associated ship" which is so defined in section 3(7)(a) of the Act:

(7)(a) For the purposes of subsection (6) an associated ship means a ship, other than the ship in respect of which the maritime claim arose:

(i) owned, at the time when the action is commenced, by the person who was the owner of the ship concerned at the time when the maritime claim arose; or

(ii) owned, at the time when the action is commenced, by a person who controlled the company which owned the ship concerned when the maritime claim arose; or

(iii) owned, at the time when the action is commenced, by a company which is controlled by a person who owned the ship concerned, or controlled by the company which owned the ship concerned, when the maritime claim arose.

I.491 An "associated ship" is, therefore, either a ship which is owned by the same person or by a person or company who controlled the company or person who owned the ship in respect of which the maritime claim arose.[144]

I.492 "Control" is so defined in section 3(7)(b)(ii):

(ii) a person shall be deemed to control a company if he has power, directly or indirectly, to control the company;

---

144. On the notion of "associated ship" see Hare, *Shipping Law and Admiralty Jurisdiction in South Africa*, Kenwyn 1999, p. 77.

I.493 This definition has been recently considered by the Supreme Court of Appeal of South Africa in *Belfry Marine Limited* v. *Palm Base Maritime SDN BHD—The "Heavy Metal"*.[145] Smalberger JA stated:

The subsection elaborates upon and refines the concept of control by that person. Control is expressed in terms of power. If the person concerned has power, directly or indirectly, to control the company he/she shall be deemed ("geag . . . word") to control the company. "Power" is not circumscribed in the Act. It can be the power to manage the operations of the company or it can be the power to determine its direction and fate. Where these two functions happen to vest in different hands, it is the latter which, in my view, the legislature had in mind when referring to "power" and hence to "control". In South African legal terminology that means (essentially for the reasons given by the court *a quo* at 1998(4) SA 479 (C) at 492 C–F ("the reported judgment"); see also sec 195(1) of the Companies Act 61 of 1973) the person who controls the shareholding in the company. Foreign law is a question of fact. If the appellant wished to make out a case that the law of the Republic of Cyprus differed significantly from the law of South Africa, it should have adduced evidence to that effect. It did not do so. Consequently there is no reason to surmise that the applicable law in Cyprus differs materially from that of South Africa (*cf Caterham Car Sales & Coachworks Ltd v Birkin Cars (Pty) Ltd and Another* 1998(3) SA 938 (A) 954 B—E).

The subsection clearly distinguishes between "direct" and "indirect" power. That distinction must be given a meaning. Indirect power can only refer to the person who *de facto* wields power through, and hence over, someone else. The latter can only be someone who wields direct power *vis-à-vis* the company and the outside world and who therefore, in the eyes of the law (i.e. *de jure*), controls the shareholding and thus determines the direction and the fate of the company. On the facts of the present case Lemonaris is the person in that situation. Of course, the same person may in given circumstances exercise both *de facto* and *de jure* control.

In my view, therefore, direct power refers to *de jure* authority over the company by the person who, according to the register of the company is entitled to control its destiny; and indirect power to the *de facto* position of the person who commands or exerts authority over the person who is recognised to possess *de jure* power (i.e. the beneficial "owner" as opposed to the legal "owner"). This extension of *de jure* power to *de facto* power is in line with the objective of the section: to prevent the true "owner", by presenting a false picture to the outside world, from concealing his assets from attachment and execution by his creditors.

(B) UNITED STATES

I.494 Even if a summary of the views expressed by US Courts is beyond the scope of this book,[146] the basic rule seems to be that the corporate veil may be pierced when the corporate form has been used to achieve fraud.[147] It has, however, also been held that it may be pierced when the corporation has been used as an *alter ego*.[148] The notion of "alter ego" is clarified by the Second Circuit in *Gartner* v. *Snyder*[149]:

145. 1999 (3) SA 1083 (SCA).

146. The cases are very numerous. In a research conducted by Thompson, "Piercing the corporate veil: an empirical study", 76 Cornell Law Review 1036 the cases considered were, until 1985, as many as 1583 of which 1455 from 1960 to 1985. The corporate veil has been pierced in about 40% of the cases (see tables 1 and 2 at pages 1048 and 1049). See also Blumberg, *The Law of Corporate Groups*, Boston and Toronto, 1987 and 1997 Supplement; Wilford, Coghlin and Kimball, *Time Charter*, 4th Ed. London 1995, p. 75.

147. See, amongst the very many decisions, *Itel Containers International Corp.* v. *Atlanttrafik Export Serv. Ltd.*, 909 F.2d 698–2, p. 703 (1990).

148. *Itel Containers International Corp.* v. *Atlanttrafik Export Serv. Ltd.*, *supra*, note 147; *Gartner* v. *Snyder*, (2nd Cir. 1989) 607 F.2d 582, at p. 586.

149. *Supra*, note 148, at p. 586.

Because New York courts disregard corporate form reluctantly, they do so only when the form has been used to achieve fraud, or when the corporation has been so dominated by an individual or another corporation . . . and its separate identity so disregarded, that it primarily transacted the dominator's business rather than its own and can be called the other's alter ego.

I.495 A list of the elements that are relevant in order to establish domination is given by the Second Circuit in *Wm. Passalacqua Builders, Inc.* v. *Resnick Developers South Inc. and Others*.[150] These elements are: (1) the absence of the formalities and paraphernalia that are part and parcel of the corporate existence, i.e. issuance of stock, election of directors, keeping of corporate records and the like, (2) inadequate capitalisation, (3) whether funds are put in and taken out of the corporation for personal rather than corporate purposes, (4) overlap in ownership, officers, directors, and personnel, (5) common office space, address and telephone numbers of corporate entities, (6) the amount of business discretion displayed by the allegedly dominated corporation, (7) whether the related corporations deal with the dominated corporation at arms length, (8) whether the corporations are treated as independent profit centers, (9) the payment of guarantee of debts of the dominated corporation by other corporations in the group, and (10) whether the corporation in question had property that was used by other of the corporations as if it were its own.

I.496 The need to protect the corporate form and the opposite need to protect creditors are summarised as follows by the Second Circuit in the above judgment[151]:

The jury must decide whether—considering the totality of the evidence—the policy behind the presumption of corporate independence and limited shareholder liability—encouragement of business development—is outweighed by the policy justifying disregarding the corporate form—the need to protect those who deal with the corporation.

CONCLUSION

I.497 It appears, therefore, that in the various jurisdictions that have been considered whilst piercing the corporate veil is permitted in case of fraud, the criteria on the basis of which the corporate form may be disregarded differ in quality and quantity. For example, common shareholding is relevant in Italy only if all shares of a company are held by the same person, whilst may be relevant in France and in the United States, together with other elements in order to show respectively a "communauté d'intérêts" or a "domination", even if only partial. However it may become relevant also in Italy in order to prove the fictitious character of the company or, more precisely, that the company has been established for the purpose of using the corporate veil to mask the common operation of several ships. This seems to be the case also in England.[152]

I.498 There is, however, a certain similarity amongst the factors considered in France and Spain and those considered in the United States in order to establish the "communauté d'intérêts" and, respectively, the domination: in both jurisdictions in fact attention has been paid to elements such as common address, telephone and fax numbers, common management, overlap in officers, directors and personnel, amount of business discretion displayed in both companies by the same person or persons, etc.

---

150. (2nd Cir. 1991) 933 F.2d 131, at p. 139; subsequently, however, the Second Circuit in *Morris* v. *New York State Dept. of Taxation and Finance*, 82 N.Y. 2d 135 (1993) held that under the law of the State of New York the corporate veil can be pierced only in case of fraud or wrongdoing.

151. *Supra*, note 150, at p. 139.

152. *The "Saudi Prince"*, [1982] 2 Lloyd's Rep. 255.

STATE OWNED VESSELS

I.499 The arrest of vessels owned by a governmental entity in respect of claims against another entity of the same government has been allowed in France on the basis of a doctrine called *"théorie de l'émanation"* developed in the first part of the 1980s. Such doctrine was based on the assumption that all State-owned shipping companies belonged to the State, so that a claim against one such company could be enforced against ships owned by another State-owned company. The *théorie de l'émanation* was adopted by the Cour d'Appel of Rouen in its judgment of 23 December 1985 in *Navrom Romanian Maritime Navigation* v. *Buenamar Compania Naviera ("The Filaret")*,[153] but was criti-cised by the Cour de Cassation in its judgment of 6 July 1988,[154] which reversed that of the Cour d'Appel.

I.500 This doctrine does not seem to have been considered in other jurisdictions. In the Netherlands it has been held[155] that the corporate identity of different State enterprises must be safeguarded and that, therefore, a State enterprise cannot be held liable for the debts of another and that this conclusion is in accordance with the basic principles of the Arrest Convention. In England and in Italy arrest of ships operated by a Ukrainian governmental agency, Black Sea Shipping Company—BLASCO, in respect of claims against such company has been in most cases allowed on the assumption that the vessels in relation to which the claims had arisen were actually or beneficially owned by BLASCO[156] and has been denied when it was found that the vessel was owned by the Ukrainian State.[157] A different doctrine has, however, been recently expressed in Italy by the Tribunale of Venice in a case involving the Ukrainian Danube Shipping Company,[158] based on the principle of *ordre public* that a debtor is answerable for all his obligations with all his assets. The Tribunale of Venice held that the allocation of title to and operation of a vessel to two different entities violates that principle.

I.501 A different approach has been adopted in England, more closely related to the provisions of the Arrest Convention. In *The "Giuseppe di Vittorio"*[159] Evans, L. J. held in fact that a ship operated by BLASCO could be arrested even if not owned by BLASCO on the basis of section 21(4) of the Supreme Court Act 1981 on the ground that for the purpose of the application of such provision and of Article 3(4) of the Arrest Convention

---

153. [1986] DMF 349.

154. [1988] DMF 595 with a note of Warot.

155. President of the Arrondissementsrechtbank of Rotterdam 30 May 1988, *The "Mehedinti"*, [1989] Schips en Schade 29.

156. In England see *The "Giuseppe di Vittorio"*, [1998] 1 Lloyd's Rep. 136. In Italy see Tribunale of Naples 9 May 1995, *Lloyd Werft Bremerhaven GmbH* v. *Black Sea Shipping Co. and State of Ukraine—The "Odessa"*, [1997] Dir. Mar. 813; Tribunale of Naples 15 July 1998, *Sekavin Replanishment Station for Transport Means Tourist Enterprises* v. *Black Sea Shipping Co.—The "Radomyshil"*, [1999], Dir. Mar. 860. See also, for a critical analysis of this doctrine, Remond Gouilloud, *"Emanation maritime" ou comment faire céder l'écran de la personnalité morale d'un armement* [1992] DMF 451. The doctrine of the "émanation" was rejected by the Tribunale of Latina with judgment of 10 April 1997, *SHIFCO-Somalian High Seas Fish Co.* v. *C.F. Ahrenkiel Ship Management Ltd.—The "21 Oktobaar II"*, [1998] Dir. Mar. 449.

157. *The "Nazym Khikmet"* (C.A.) [1996] 2 Lloyd's Rep. 362. On the conception of ownership in Soviet law see Haslam, *"Soviet property rights in English Courts"* [1999] LMCLQ 491.

158. Judgment of 6 July 1998, *Pied Rich B.V.* v. *Ukrainian Danube Shipping—The "Radomyshil"*, [1999] Dir. Mar. 1237. The Tribunale of Gorizia with judgment 25 March 1998, *Pied Rich B.V.* v. *Ukrainian Danube Shipping—The "Sergey Vasilyev"*, [1999] Dir. Mar. 1226 allowed the arrest of the vessel on the ground that Ukrainian Danube Shipping had her full operational management.

159. [1998] 1 Lloyd's Rep. 136.

it was not necessary that the possession of the vessel and the assumption of her operation be the effect of a contract.[160]

23. ARREST OF A SHIP WHEN A PERSON OTHER THAN THE OWNER IS LIABLE IN RESPECT OF A MARITIME CLAIM RELATING TO THAT SHIP

I.502 The right to arrest a ship in respect of maritime claims for which a person other than the owner of that ship is liable is regulated by Article 3(4) which provides[161]:

When in the case of a charter by demise of a ship the charterer and not the registered owner is liable in respect of a maritime claim relating to that ship, the claimant may arrest such ship or any other ship in the ownership of the charterer by demise, subject to the provisions of this Convention, but no other ship in the ownership of the registered owner shall be liable to arrest in respect of such maritime claim.

The provisions of this paragraph shall apply to any case in which a person other than the registered owner of a ship is liable in respect of a maritime claim relating to that ship.

I.503 The first sentence has the effect of granting the claimant who has a claim against the demise charterer, the right to arrest the ship in respect of which the claim arose. Such right seems to be unrestricted and, therefore, to exist irrespective of the claim being secured by a maritime lien or not.

I.504 The last sentence of Article 3(4) seems to extend the right of arrest when the claim is not against the owner well beyond the case of a claim against the bareboat charterer, viz. to any case in which a person other than the registered owner is liable in respect of a maritime claim relating to the ship. A maritime claim relating to a ship may be against the time charterer and, even if in a more limited number of cases, against a voyage charterer. Examples are those in respect of loss of life or personal injury (Article 1(1)(b)), of agreements relating to the carriage of goods (Article 1(1)(e)) and of loss of or damage to goods (Article 1(1)(f)) when the time charterer is the carrier, in respect of general average (Article 1(1)(g)) if the hire is at risk for the time charterer, in respect of towage (Article 1(1)(i)) and of pilotage (Article 1(1)(j)). The claims mentioned above, except those for towage and pilotage, may also be against a voyage charterer.

---

160. Evans, L. J. so stated (at p. 158):

Must there can be a charter-party, meaning a document which records a consensual agreement between owner and charterer, before the statutory definition can be satisfied? I would hold not, for the following reasons: . . .

(3) I cannot think of any circumstances in which a person could be in possession and control of a ship which he did not own, yet upon terms which were defined as a matter of law, except where the owner is a state and the terms are established by legislation rather than by agreement, express or implied. If therefore Parliament intended that "demise charterer" and "demise charter" should be limited to charters by agreement, it would have done this in order to exclude state-owned ships (operated by a separate legal entity, whether state-owned or independent of it) from the operation of that section. I cannot see any reason why Parliament should have intended to achieve this result.

161. A provision similar to that of art. 3(4) of the Convention may be found in the South African Admiralty Jurisdiction Regulation Act 105 of 1983. Section 3(7)(c) so in fact provides:

(c) If at any time a ship was the subject of a charter-party the charterer or subcharterer, as the case may be, shall for the purposes of subsection (6) and this subsection be deemed to be the owner of the ship concerned in respect of any relevant maritime claim for which the charterer or the subcharterer, and not the owner, is alleged to be liable.

I.505 The *travaux préparatoires* clearly indicate that this provision was adopted without a clear understanding of its possible consequences. It may be objected that resort to them is not possible under the rules laid down by the Vienna Convention of 1969, since the language is clear. It is thought, however, that they may nevertheless be useful in order to establish the object and purpose of this rather unfortunate provision.

I.506 As previously mentioned, when the first draft of a Convention on arrest of ships was prepared in 1932, the right of arrest was expressly granted only in respect of claims against the owner of a ship.[162] The draft prepared in 1951 by the CMI International Sub-Committee had instead in its Article 3, paragraph V, a provision practically identical to that of the first part of Article 3(4) of the Convention.[163] This provision was added, on request of the Associations of the Netherlands and of Norway, to the draft prepared by the CMI International Sub-Committee and submitted to the CMI 1951 Naples Conference. The following statement is made in the Report of the International Sub-Committee[164]:

The rather original provision contained in the fifth paragraph of article 3[165] is justified by the legal regime in force in certain countries, and more specifically the Netherlands and Norway, whereby the actions arising out of maritime claims must, in certain cases, be brought against the manager (armateur gérant) or the demise charterer in the place of the owner, the former being liable in respect of maritime claims in the place of the owner. This situation is considered in the questionnaire discussed at the Amsterdam Conference and is mentioned in the report.

I.507 The Dutch Association in its replies to the Questionnaire stated that a ship operated by a person other than her owner may be arrested in respect of claims for collision and salvage.[166] In a commentary accompanying the replies the Dutch Association explained that when the operator is not the owner the claims against the operator may

---

162. *Supra,* para. I.6, note 21.
163. CMI Bulletin No. 105, p. 19; *travaux préparatoires*, p. 338 and 339.
164. *Travaux Préparatoires*, p. 338. The original text is in French. The *travaux préparatoires* are considered by the Scottish Law Commission in the Report on Diligence on the Dependence and Admiralty Arrestment, *supra*, note 5, p. 165.
165. The text of article 3 submitted to the CMI Naples Conference, available only in the French language, was the following (*Travaux Préparatoires*, p. 463):
I.–Tout demandeur, qui se prévaut d'un droit ou d'une créance maritime sur un navire, peut saisir ce navire ou tout autre appartenant aux mêmes armateurs, alors même que le navire serait prêt à faire voile.
II.–Des navires sont réputés avoir le même propriétaire lorsque toutes les parts de propriété appartiennent à une même ou aux mêmes personnes.
III.–Tout tiers, autre que le demandeur originaire, qui excipe d'une créance maritime par l'effet d'une subrogation, d'une cession ou autrement, sera réputé, pour l'application de la présente Convention, avoir le même domicile ou le même établissement principal que le créancier originaire.
IV.–Un navire ne peut pas être saisi par le même demandeur plus d'une fois pour la même créance, dans le ressort d'un ou de plusieurs Tribunaux d'un quelconque des Etats Contractants.
V.–Dans le cas d'un affrètement d'un navire avec remise de la gestion nautique, lorsque l'affréteur répond, seul, d'une créance maritime relative à ce navire, le demandeur peut saisir ce navire ou tel autre appartenant à l'affréteur en observant les dispositions de la présente convention; mais nul autre navire, appartenant au propriétaire, ne peut être saisi en vertu de cette créance maritime.
166. The second question of the Questionnaire and the Dutch reply (Conférence d'Amsterdam, CMI Bulletin No. 104, p. 74) are reproduced below in their English translation:
2nd Question: Is it possible under your national law to attach assets other than a ship in respect of these claims? (Note: the claims are those for which a ship may be arrested)
Answer: In Dutch law all assets of the owner may be attached in respect of all claims against the owner. When the operator of the ship is not the owner, all assets of such operator may be attached in respect of any claim of any nature whatsoever against such operator.
Moreover, a ship operated by an operator who is not the owner may be arrested in respect of claims for collision and salvage.

be enforced on the ship only if secured by a maritime lien but that, except in respect of claims for collision and salvage, a judgment is first required in order to arrest the ship.[167]

I.508 It would appear, therefore, that the text of the provision suggested by the International Sub-Committee, described as "rather original" (*assez originale*) was probably beyond what was required in order to bring it in line with Dutch law.[168] In any event it is difficult to understand why a peculiar provision existing in the law of one country should entail so radical a change in the legal system of a great number of other countries. The general rule in fact is that the bareboat charterer and not the owner is responsible for the operation of the ship except of course the right of the claimants to proceed against the ship in respect of claims secured by maritime liens.

I.509 The second sentence of Article 3(4) was added during the CMI Naples Conference following a proposal of the Dutch delegate who gave the following explanation[169]:

The same applies to all cases where a person other than the legal owner is liable in respect of a maritime claim. Of course, there are many people who are not owners, and their position must be considered. Therefore the proposal in respect of paragraphs (I) and (IV) of article 3 is to add to paragraph (V) the words "in respect of all cases where a person other than the legal owner is liable in respect of a maritime claim". I do not think that this proposal of ours can do any harm to anybody who is not a legal owner, and therefore no harm will be done by adopting it.

I.510 In view of the previous comments of the Dutch Association it appears that also in this case the condition for the arrest is that the claim is secured by a maritime lien and, in addition, is a claim for collision or salvage.[170]

---

167. Here follows the translation of the comments of the Dutch Association (Conférence d'Amsterdam, *supra*, note 166, p. 73):

2. Under Dutch law the operator and not the actual owner of a ship is generally responsible in respect of what are called in short maritime claims.

When the operator is not the owner of the ship, the maritime claims against the operator may be realized on the ship, but only if they are privileged claims under the Code of Commerce.

Furthermore, all privileged claims except those arising in respect of the ship or resulting from maritime transactions or based on the liability of the operator as defined in article 321 of the Code of Commerce follow the ship in case of change of ownership.

However, it is generally admitted that when the operator is not the owner of the ship, the privileged creditor is not entitled to arrest the ship except for claims resulting from collision or salvage. For all other claims, it is necessary to obtain beforehand a judgment against the operator. Such judgment may then be enforced on the ship by arresting her. In such a case it is advisable to join the owner in the proceeding as a third party.

168. A different explanation has been given by M. H. Claringbould, *Arrest of Ships*, p. 53–57, see *infra*, note 170. At present, under the new Transport Law (Article 360 of Book 8 of the Civil Code) in force since 1 April 1991, the owner of a ship is personally liable in respect of claims against the bareboat charterer. This implies that other ships also in the same ownership may also be arrested. There does not seem to be any conflict between this rule and Art. 3(4) of the Convention, because the prohibition on the arrest of other ships in the ownership of the registered owner is related to the fact that the owner is not personally liable in respect of the claim.

169. CMI Bulletin No. 105, p. 256; *Travaux Préparatoires*, p. 341.

170. For a careful analysis of the *travaux préparatoires* in respect of Article 3(4) and of the influence of the Dutch delegates on its introduction see M. H. Claringbould (*Arrest of Ships*, *supra*, note 5, p. 53–58) who is of the opinion that since the purpose of the whole of this article is to permit the arrest in respect of claims against the operator (*reder*), there was no intention with the last sentence to include claims against the time and voyage charterer (since neither of them becomes the operator of the ship). This can very well be. What is certain is that the explanations provided in support of the proposal were rather obscure.

I.511 However no restriction is made in Article 3(4), which seems to grant an unconditional right of arrest without any reference to the need for the claim to be secured by a maritime lien.

I.512 The amendment was accepted by the Drafting Committee and by the subsequent Plenary Session of the Conference. It was only at the Diplomatic Conference that attention was drawn to the consequences of Article 3(4) by the Norwegian delegate, who stated that it was essential to distinguish between personal claims (*créances personnelles*) and claims against the ship such as *hypothèques* and (maritime) liens.[171] Although the Spanish delegate had supported the observations made by the Norwegian delegate,[172] apparently no agreement was reached on the alternative text suggested by the Norwegian delegation and when further objections were raised at the final reading of the draft, Professor Ripert, on behalf of the French delegation, made the following remarks[173]:

> Mr. Ripert (France) observes that it would be dangerous to discuss again all that has already been discussed in the preceding Conferences which have produced the rules adopted by the Comité Maritime International. We are dealing here only with the conservative arrest effected by a claimant, and it is not necessary to state whether the claim is secured by a mortgage or otherwise this question arises only when the merits are examined and not when the arrest is made. It is necessary to bring back the debate to the essential questions, namely: who are the claimants who may effect the arrest? Which are the ships that may be arrested? Which is the Court having jurisdiction? All the rest is a matter of drafting.

I.513 Professor Ripert was certainly correct when he said that the purpose of the Convention was merely to regulate the right of arrest, as a conservative measure and not the substantive aspect of the (maritime) claims. His statement, however, does not bring any light on the purpose of this provision. On the contrary, it seems to indicate that there was no clear understanding amongst the delegates on the nature and purpose of the provision. In fact the proponents seem to have had in mind the need for the arrest of chartered ships being allowed in respect of certain specific claims (for collision and salvage) secured by a maritime lien, whilst other delegates understood the proposal as if it granted a general right of arrest of demise chartered ships.

---

171. The Norwegian delegate (Mr Alten) stated thus (*Procès-verbaux*, p. 58; *Travaux Préparatoires*, p. 344):

> The right of arrest must be limited to maritime claims listed in Art. 1, but it is necessary to distinguish between the personal claims against the owner of a ship or against the operator and the rights in the ship, such as:
>
> 1. Mortgages and (maritime) liens;
> 2. Right of property, possessory rights and right of operation of the ship as operator.
>
> Such distinction is of essential importance for the interpretation to be given to Art. 3 of this Convention. If the maritime claim alleged by the claimant is a personal claim against the owner of the ship or against the operator not being the owner or against the charterer, arrest may be made of any ship belonging to the debtor, but the debtor must be the owner of such ship and not merely have the right of disposal. If, on the contrary, the claim alleged is a right in the ship, that ship may be arrested, even if after that right has arisen the ship has been sold to a new owner.
>
> Article 3 should thus be modified, in the opinion of the Norwegian Government, in conformity with the text proposed in the observations formulated before the Conference.

172. The Spanish delegate (Mr Garrigues) stated (*Procès-verbaux*, p. 62):

> The list of the cases in which arrest is possible is the first of such questions. Art. 1 is a mixture of claims of very different nature, real rights, personal rights or credits. It is not sufficient to say that in all cases a conservative arrest may take place, for the limits and the conditions of arrest are not the same in all cases. The Spanish Delegation agrees with the observations of Mr. Alten and with the draft amendment of Art. 3, which draws a distinction between personal claims and rights in the ship.

173. *Procès-verbaux*, p. 72.

I.514 Professor Philip has made an attempt to give Article 3(4) a sensible inter-pretation. He expressed the view[174] that since the purpose of the Convention is to limit the cases where arrest may be made, and not to provide in which cases arrest must be made, a vessel can only be lawfully arrested if under the applicable law the claim may be enforced against the ship. In the opinion of Professor Philip, therefore, if the applicable law does not permit the enforcement of a claim against the ship owned by a person who is personally liable, arrest is not permissible.

I.515 In the previous editions of this book,[175] it has been observed that although the solution suggested by Professor Philip is reasonable, it is difficult to accept it in view of the plain language of Article 3(4). If, however, his statement that a chartered ship can be lawfully arrested only if the claim can then be enforced on such ship is interpreted in the sense that the arrest obtained when the claim is not enforceable on the ship is unlawful, Professor Philip's opinion may to some extent be reconciled with the provision of Article 3(4).

I.516 In fact the Convention deals only with arrest as a security measure and does not apply, as clearly appears from the definition in Article 1(2), to the seizure of a ship in execution or satisfaction of a judgment. Consequently, the judicial authority competent for the execution or satisfaction of a judgment cannot, in order to establish whether the ship can be seized and sold in a forced sale in satisfaction of a judgment against a person other than the owner of that ship, apply the provisions of the Arrest Convention.

I.517 Nor was it intended to create new maritime liens with the Arrest Convention.[176] Although the second part of Article 9 was added for the purpose of making clear that the maritime claims do not create any *droit de suite*, this is a feature proper of maritime liens as appears from the English text, where the words used are not *droit de suite* but "maritime liens". Moreover, the intention not to create maritime liens appears clearly in the *travaux préparatoires*.[177]

I.518 No inference therefore can be drawn from Article 3(4) as to the right of the claimant to enforce his claim on the ship through her judicial sale. If he has no such right under any other applicable international convention or national law, he does not acquire it under the Arrest Convention.[178]

I.519 The claimant who arrests a ship which is not owned by the person liable does that at his risk. Where, after the arrest, security is provided by the person liable the claimant will achieve his purpose and will be able to enforce the judgment on the merits against such security. Where, on the other hand, the security is provided by the owner of the ship and under the law of the country where the arrest is made the claim cannot be enforced against the ship, the claimant will not achieve any practical result.

I.520 If, in fact, he would not have been able to enforce his claim against the ship, he cannot be in a better position where the ship is released upon bail or other security

---

174. Philip, "Maritime Jurisdiction in the EEC" [1977] Scandinavia Juris Gentium, 118.
175. F. Berlingieri, *Arrest of Ships*, 2nd Ed., London 1996, p. 80.
176. *Agenzia Marittima Saidelli and Trader S.a.s.* v. *M/v "Dexterity"* (USDC—Eastern District of Louisiana [1994] Dir. Mar. 1195.
177. The Cour d'Appel of Rouen in its judgment of 19 June 1984 in *Master of the "Atlantic Mariner"* v. *Trademar Conasa (The "Atlantic Mariner")* [1985] DMF 167, however, held that Art. 9 is not relevant in the interpretation of Art. 3(4). This view has been criticised by Bonassies [1966] DMF 14 at p. 15.
178. The opposite view is expressed by the Scottish Law Commission in its Report on Diligence on the Dependence and Admiralty Arrestment, *supra*, note 5, paragraphs 8.58–8.62 at pages 173 and 174.

furnished. Nothing is said in the Convention as to what the bail or other security must state with respect to the case where the courts of the country in which the arrest is made have jurisdiction to decide upon the merits. If on the contrary such courts have no jurisdiction to decide on the merits, Article 7(2) requires, as previously stated, that the bail or other security shall "specifically provide that it is given as security for the satisfaction of any judgment which may eventually be pronounced by a court having jurisdiction so to decide". Literally, this provision seems to indicate that the security must be available for the satisfaction of any judgment on the merits, irrespective of the person in whose favour it is given. However, this provision must be interpreted taking into account that it was worded with reference to the general situation and for the purpose of linking the security provided in one country with a judgment delivered in another country. If, therefore, a judgment delivered in the country where the arrest is made against the person liable in respect of the maritime claim could not have been enforced against the ship, neither can a foreign judgment be enforced against the security provided in order to release the ship and that, therefore, replaces the ship for all purposes.

I.521 Moreover, in all cases where the claimant cannot enforce the judgment on the ship, he may be held liable for the damages arising out of the detention of the ship, whenever such damages are not suffered by the person liable for the claim.

I.522 If, for the reasons stated, Article 3(4) goes beyond the intention of its draftsmen, at the same time it does not cover the fundamental case in which arrest is permissible in respect of claims relating to a ship when the person liable is not the owner, viz. the case of claims secured by maritime liens. In reality a proposal had been made by the Italian delegate during the Diplomatic Conference to link the future Arrest Convention with the 1926 MLM Convention,[179] but it had no support.

I.523 It can, however, be stated that an implied acknowledgment that such a link exists is made by Article 9, reference to which is made in Article 3(1).[180] In fact the statement that nothing in the Convention shall be construed as creating any maritime liens which do not exist under the law applied by the Court which has seisin of the case or under the 1926 MLM Convention, if applicable, indicates that the liens recognised by the applicable law or the 1926 MLM Convention are relevant for the purposes of arrest. And since arrest is the ordinary means of enforcement of maritime liens,[181] the consequence is that arrest is permissible under the 1952 Convention of a ship not owned by the person liable when the

---

179. The Italian delegate (Mr G. Berlingieri) stated thus (*Procès-verbaux*, p. 61; *Travaux Préparatoires*, p. 344):

> As he already pointed out at the Antwerp and Paris Conferences, the Arrest Convention should be in line with the Maritime Liens and Mortgages Convention. It has been held by Mr. de Grandmaison that the claims that give rise to arrest are much more numerous than those that give rise to a maritime lien. This is indisputable, but the latter claims are maritime claims. Why then not to bring the two Conventions in line with one another? Why exclude the right of arrest in respect of pilotage fees, of the cost of custody and preservation? The maritime lien entitles one to arrest the ship. He believes that there cannot be any doubt that Art. 9 of the Maritime Liens and Mortgages Convention upholds his view in this respect.

180. For the reason why in article 3(4) reference is erroneously made to Article 10 see *supra*, para. I.402–404.

181. This was already implied in the 1926 MLM Convention, article 9 of which provides that States Parties reserved the right to provide that the extinction periods shall be extended where it has not been possible to arrest the ship. It has then been clearly stated in the 1967 MLM Convention and in the 1993 MLM Convention, articles 8(1) and respectively 9(1) of which provide that the maritime liens shall be extinguished after a period of one year unless the vessel has been arrested (or seized), such arrest (or seizure) leading to a forced sale.

claim relates to that ship and is secured by a maritime lien recognised by the *lex fori*. As it will be seen[182] this rule has now been clearly laid down in the 1999 Convention.

I.524 This provision has given rise to conflicting interpretations in some Contracting States.

I.525 In France, where the Arrest Convention has been given the force of law, it is settled that a demise chartered ship may be arrested in respect of a claim against the demise charterer.[183]

I.526 In Italy, where, similarly to France, the Convention has been given the force of law, the prevailing view is that a ship may be arrested in respect of a claim against the demise charterer and the time charterer.[184] The same conclusion holds in Greece, Haiti and Spain. While, however, in France and in Italy the problem whether the claimant may, after the arrest, enforce his claim on the ship through its forced sale has not been considered, in Greece the view has been expressed that this is only possible if the claimant has obtained a judgment against the owner of the ship:[185] a position very similar to that adopted in the Scandinavian countries. In Spain, instead, the arrest is normally granted, but the forced sale of the arrested vessel cannot take place unless a judgment against the owner is obtained.[186]

I.527 In Croatia Article 3(4) of the Convention has been reproduced in Article 977 of the Maritime Code, which clearly entitles the claimant to arrest a ship in respect of claims against the demise or other charterer.[187]

I.528 In England, where the Convention has not been given the force of law, the prevailing view seems to have been that under section 3(4) of the Administration of Justice Act 1956 the ship in connection with which the claim has arisen may be arrested only if at the time when the action is brought it is beneficially owned by the person who would be liable on the claim in an action *in personam*. In fact, although in *The "Andrea Ursula"*[188] Brandon J. had expressed the view that the expression "beneficially owned" must be given a meaning "related not to title, legal or equitable, but to lawful possession

---

182. See *infra*, Book II, para. I.113–117.
183. Tribunal de Commerce of Nantes 3 September 1991, *United Arab Shipping Co.* v. *Blohm & Voss—The "Trident Beauty"*, [1991] DMF 726; Cour d'Appel of Aix-en-Provence 28 February 1996, *Adriatica S.a.s.* v. *TCA-Trans Container Agency—The "Cordigliera"*, [1997] DMF 594; Cour d'Appel of Rouen 24 May 1995, *Lamyra Marine Co. Ltd.* v. *Cie Sénégalaise de Navigation Maritime—The "Saint Pierre"* [1996] DMF 489.
184. Tribunale of Ravenna 24 January 1987, *Trademar Conasa* v. *Line Island Marine Co.—The "Euro-breeze"* [1988] Dir. Mar. 804; Tribunale of Naples 22 September 1995 and 16 November 1995, *Mamidoil Jetoil Greek Petroleum Co.—The "Carlo R."*, [1997] Dir. Mar. 147 and 152; Tribunale of Bari 26 November 1996, *Les Abeilles Boulogne S.A. and Others* v. *Medimare S.r.l.—The "Sea Road"*, [1998] Dir. Mar. 1218; Tribunale of Naples 20 December 1995, *Alimar Shipping Co.* v. *Mamidoil—The "Carlo R."* [1997] Dir. Mar. 154. The Tribunale of Latina with judgment 9 November 1996, *SHIFCO-Somalian High Seas Fish Co.* v. *Mabutrans S.A.—The "21 Oktobaar II"*, [1998] Dir. Mar. 430 held instead that the arrest of a ship in respect of a claim against a person other than the owner is permissible only when the claim is secured by a maritime lien.
185. For further information see the replies of the Greek MLA to Question 7 of the Questionnaire, Appendix II, p. 255.
186. See the reply of the Spanish MLA to Question 7.2 of the Questionnaire, Appendix II, p. 261.
187. Article 977 of the Croatian Maritime Code so provides in its relevant part (translation of the Croatian MLA: see reply to Question 5 of the Questionnaire, Appendix II, p. 245):
> If the debtor is a charterer by demise of the ship or a charterer, who according to the law applicable to the contractual relation between him and the shipowner or ship operator is alone liable to third persons—this ship may be arrested or any other ship which is owned by the charterer by demise or charterer. The provision of Paragraph 2 of this Article shall also apply in all other cases when the ship operator or charterer who is a personal debtor, and who is not the owner of the ship, is himself liable for the claims for which the arrest of the ship is sought.
188. [1971] 1 Lloyd's Rep. 145.

and control with the use and benefit which are derived from them", thus including the demise charterer,[189] Goff J. subsequently stated in *The "I Congreso del Partido"*[190] that such expression refers only to cases of equitable ownership and this view was upheld by Sir Thomas Bingham, M.R. in *The "Nazym Khikmet"*.[191] The provision of the Administration of Justice Act 1956 has, however, been amended by the Supreme Court Act 1981. Section 21(4) of this Act provides in fact that the ship in connection with which the claim has arisen may be arrested if at the time when the action is brought it is beneficially owned or demise chartered by the person who would be liable on the claim in an action *in personam*.[192]

I.529 The conclusion seems to be, therefore, that in England and Wales paragraph 4 of article 3 of the Convention has been given effect except for its last sentence.

I.530 In Scotland, where sections 47 and 48 of the 1956 Act, which implemented the 1952 Convention, are still in force, the narrow interpretation of section 47(1)(a) corresponding to section 3(4) has been supported.[193]

I.531 In Ireland, where, as in England, the Convention has not been given the force of law, the problem does not seem to arise since the Jurisdiction of Court (Maritime Conventions) Act 1989, with which Ireland has given effect to the Convention, does not include a provision like that of section 21(4) of the British Supreme Court Act 1981.

I.532 In the Netherlands, Article 3(4) of the Convention has been interpreted as allowing the arrest of a ship in respect of a maritime claim against the demise charterer.[194] The leading decision is that of the Supreme Court in the case of *The "Micoperi 7000"* a large semi-submersible platform of Italian flag owned by Micoperi Offshore S.p.A. and demise chartered to Micoperi S.p.A. The platform had been arrested by the owner of tugs chartered by Micoperi S.p.A. for unpaid hire and the Dutch Supreme Court (Hoge Raad) with judgment 12 September 1997[195] held that arrest was permissible under Article 3(4)

---

189. He in fact so stated (at p. 149):
> If sect. 3(4) is to give full effect to Art. 3, including in particular para. (4) of that article and the last three lines following it, the expression "beneficially owned" must be given the second of the two meanings which I suggested earlier that it was capable of having, and not the first. In other words, it must be given a meaning which includes not only a demise charterer, but also any other person with similar complete possession and control who may thereby become liable on a claim within paragraphs (d) to (r) of sect. 1(1) of the Act.

190. [1977] 1 Lloyd's Rep. 536, at p. 560.

191. [1996] 2 Lloyd's Rep. 362, *supra*, note 157.

192. On the Parliamentary background of section 21(4) of the 1981 Act see the Report on Diligence on the Dependence and Admiralty Arrestment of the Scottish Law Commission, *supra*, note 5, paragraphs 8.39 and 8.40, at p. 169 and 170.

193. See the Report on Diligence on the Dependence and Admiralty Arrestment, *supra*, note 5, paragraphs 8.24 and 8.25, at p. 166. In the Report the Scottish Law Commission however recommends (paragraphs 8.53 and 8.54) also on the basis of the comments made in the 2nd edition of this book, that, in order to properly implement the Arrest Convention and bring Scots law in line with English law, that arrestment of a ship in respect of a claim against the demise charterer be permitted.

194. President of the Arrondissementsrechtbank of Rotterdam 23 January 1984—*The "Alcontine"*, [1984] Schip en Schade 53 (claims against the time charterer); Arrondissementsrechtbank of Rotterdam 29 January 1994—*The "Micoperi 7000"*; Hoge Raad 12 September 1997, [1997] Schip en Schade 123 on the same case (claims against the demise charterer). The same view is supported by the Dutch literature: J. T. Asser, "Uniform Zeerecht. De Diplomaticke Zeerecht Conferentie, gehouden te Brussels in Mei 1952", [1953] NJB 757, 768 and 780; M. H. Claringbould, *Arrest of Ships*, *supra*, note 4, p. 53; M. H. Claringbould and C. J. H. van Lynden, "Enige aantekeningen bij het Verdrag Conservatoir Beslag op Zeeschepen", [1986] NJB 837–841.

195. *Supra*, note 194. In such judgment reference is made to a precedent of the same Hoge Raad of 29 June 1979—*The "Odupon"*, [1979] Schip en Schade 82.

of the Convention as well as under the domestic law then in force. On the basis of the *travaux préparatoires* and, in particular, of the fact that the last sentence of Article 3(4) had been added following a proposal of the Dutch delegate who intended to include all claims against the "reder" (operator) of the ship, the opinion has been expressed that arrest is not permissible in respect of claims against the time and voyage charterer.[196]

I.533 In Denmark, Finland, Norway and Sweden a ship chartered by demise cannot be arrested as security for a claim against the demise and other charterer, unless the claim is secured by a maritime lien on the ship. Section 5 of Chapter 4 of the Swedish Maritime Code in fact lays down the rule, now adopted in the Arrest Convention 1999,[197] whereby a vessel may be arrested only if it may be subject to distraint in Sweden.[198] That would require the claimant to obtain a judgment against the owner, while he has no claim against him. On such basis the Svea Court of Appeal in the very recent case of *The "Russ"*[199] rejected the application of arrest of the vessel as security for a claim for the cost of bunker supplied to it on the ground that the owner was not liable for the payment of such bunker, ordered by the charterer, and that the claim was not secured by a maritime lien.

I.534 The law in Germany is halfway between that in the Netherlands and in the Scandinavian States. The general rule according to which only the property of the debtor may be arrested unless the claim is secured by a maritime lien does not prevent the arrest of a ship when the claim is against the bareboat charterer since, pursuant to paragraph 510 HGB, the bareboat charterer, who is the operator (*Ausruster*), is considered the owner of the ship insofar as his relationship with third parties is concerned. A time charterer instead does not qualify as an *Ausruster* and, therefore, the time-chartered ship cannot be arrested in respect of a claim against him.[200]

24. ARREST OF A SHIP READY TO SAIL OR IN THE COURSE OF NAVIGATION

I.535 If a ship is in commercial service, she may be in port for commercial operations, bunkering or temporary repairs or maintenance, she may be ready to sail or she may be sailing. While in the first case there was no doubt, in any country, that a ship was liable to arrest, there was no uniformity of view regarding the second and third cases.

---

196. M. H. Claringbould, *Arrest of Ships, supra*, note 4, p. 53–57. At present article 8:360 of the Civil Code of 1991 provides that if a ship is bareboat chartered, the owner is jointly liable with the bareboat charterer in respect of all contractual obligations of the bareboat charterer relating to the operation of the ship. It would appear, however, that the above provision can apply in respect of a foreign ship arrested in the Netherlands only if a similar provision exists in the law of the State where the ship is registered. This on the assumption that the two-tier system adopted by article 4 of the Netherlands Conflict of Maritime Law Act 1993 in respect of maritime liens (see Tetley, *International Conflict of Laws*, Montreal 1994, p. 941) applies also in respect of the general responsibility of the owner for the bareboat charterer's obligations. The author is greatly indebted to Mr. Taco van der Valk, a partner of Nauta Dutilh, for the very exhaustive explanations provided in respect of Dutch law.

197. See *infra*, para. II.113–117.

198. This information is based on the reply of the Swedish Maritime Law Association to Question 7 of the Questionnaire, Appendix II, p. 257.

199. Information provided by the Swedish Maritime Law Association. See *supra*, note 198.

200. Judgment of the Bundersgerichtshof 56BGHZ 300.

I.536 A ship ready to sail was not subject to arrest in many civil law countries[201] and still is not in some.[202] It was, however, deemed proper to exclude that old-fashioned exemption, even though it still existed in some recent maritime codes[203] and in the 1951 Draft a provision was inserted into Article 3 to the effect that a ship may be arrested *"alors même que le navire serait prêt a faire voile"*.[204] No objection was raised against this provision though the terminology was still that used during the times of sailing ships. These words *"prêt a faire voile"* were translated in English as "ready to sail".

I.537 The Convention does not consider the possibility of arresting a ship in the course of navigation. The fact that specific reference was made to the arrest of ships ready to sail does not seem to imply the prohibition, under the Convention, of arresting a ship in the course of navigation, which is permitted by UNCLOS Article 28(3). This, however, will be possible only within the territorial waters of a State, because the jurisdiction of such State does not extend, at least as respects private law, beyond such waters.[205] The arrest may be applied for, if the domestic rules on jurisdiction and venue permit, even if the vessel at the time of the application is sailing in international waters, but may be enforced only if the vessel subsequently enters the territorial waters of the State in whose jurisdiction the court ordering the arrest is located. The applicability of the *lex fori* seems to also be permitted in such a case pursuant to Article 6 of the Convention, which provides that the rules of procedure relating to the arrest of a ship shall be governed by the law of the Contracting State in which the arrest is made or applied for.[206]

25. SHIPS IMMUNE FROM ARREST

I.538 The Draft Convention approved at Naples provided in its Article 11:

Nothing in this Convention shall modify or affect the laws and principles in force in the respective Contracting States relating to the immunity from arrest of warships and State-owned vessels.

---

201. Such as France (art. 215 Code de Commerce: on this provision, its history and its effects see Ripert, *Droit Maritime* (4th Edn., Vol. I, Paris, 1950), pp. 798 and 811; Rodière, *Droit Maritime—Le Navire* (Paris, 1980) at p. 234; Ripert, *Les Conventions de Bruxelles*, p. 355, *supra*, Chapter IV, note 25. Art. 215, Code de Commerce was, however, abrogated by Law of 3 January 1967.
202. Such as Italy (Art. 645–d CN).
203. For example, in the Italian Codice della Navigazione, although the prohibition does not apply to claims relating to the voyage in course or to be commenced. Art. 645 in fact provides:
The following cannot be subject to expropriation or conservative measures:
(d) ships and craft ready to sail or in the course of navigation, unless in respect of debts relating to the voyage to be commenced or to be continued.
204. At the Diplomatic Conference the French delegate (Mr de Grandmaison) stated (*Procès-verbaux*, p. 60):
2. Ships may be arrested even if ready to sail. It is a practical necessity since it is specially in a port of call that the claimant will be able to enforce his claim.
205. Article 28 of UNCLOS so provides:
Civil jurisdiction in relation to foreign ships
1. The coastal State should not stop or divert a foreign ship passing through the territorial sea for the purpose of exercising civil jurisdiction in relation to a person on board the ship.
2. The coastal State may not levy execution against or arrest the ship for the purpose of any civil proceedings, save only in respect of obligations or liabilities assumed or incurred by the ship itself in the course or for the purpose of its voyage through the waters of the coastal State.
3. Paragraph 2 is without prejudice to the right of the coastal State, in accordance with its laws, to levy execution against or to arrest, for the purpose of any civil proceedings, a foreign ship lying in the territorial sea, or passing through the territorial sea after leaving internal waters.
206. See *infra*, para. I.629–I.631.

I.539 The proposal of the Italian delegation to replace the text approved in Naples with the following: "this Convention shall not apply to warships and to State-owned ships employed in a public non-commercial service", which was based on Article 3 of the 1926 Immunity Convention, was strongly objected to by the British delegation on the ground that such wording would have prevented ratification of the Arrest Convention by the States which had not ratified, and did not intend to ratify, the 1926 Immunity Convention.[207] Such objection was supported by several other delegations[208] and finally the proposal of the British delegation to delete Article 11 altogether was approved without objections.[209] It is interesting to note that the wording suggested by the Italian delegation was then adopted in the 1967 and 1993 Conventions on Maritime Liens and Mortgages (Article 12(2) and Article 13(2) respectively) and in the 1969 Civil Liability Convention (Article 11(1)).

I.540 Whether and to what extent immunity may be invoked is, therefore, left to the law of the *forum arresti*. The immunity, however, must be related to the ownership or the operation of a vessel by a State and not to the nature of the employment. For example, the fact that a privately owned ship is employed on a liner service, which is of public interest, should not justify immunity from arrest.[210]

I.541 This view is supported by the express statement in Article 3(1) that a ship may be arrested even if ready to sail. That indicates that the stage of the operation is not relevant and the type of operation should, by analogy, be subject to the same rule.

26. RIGHT OF REARREST OR OF ARREST OF A SISTER SHIP

I.542 A provision to the effect that a ship may not be arrested more than once in respect of the same maritime claim already existed in the draft prepared by the CMI International Sub-Committee in 1951.[211] In its comments on the draft the French association suggested that an exception could perhaps be made to that rule, in cases where the claimant could not obtain sufficient security after the first arrest.[212] The British association was of the view that as a rule double arrest should be prohibited, but agreed with the French

207. The British delegate (Mr Miller) stated (*Procès-verbaux*, p. 117):

Mr. Miller (United Kingdom) does not want to cause a loss of time to the Conference, but reminds it that his colleagues have already expressed in a manner sufficiently convincing the reasons why it was absolutely impossible for the British Delegation to accept the Italian amendment. The Convention deals with arrest of ships and not with the immunity of State-owned ships. The question has been regulated by another Convention that Great Britain has not ratified. He proposes to replace the present article with the corresponding article dealing with jurisdiction.

The United Kingdom then ratified the 1926 Immunity Convention on 3 July 1979.

208. Finland, France and Brazil (*Procès-verbaux*, p. 118).

209. *Procès-verbaux*, pp. 118 and 119.

210. A similar provision exists, for example, in Italian law. Art. 645 CN provides that a ship employed on a liner service declared to be of national interest cannot be arrested or seized unless with the authorisation of the Minister of Merchant Marine.

211. Art. 3, para. IV of such Draft (*Travaux Préparatoires*, p. 463) provided thus:

IV. A ship may not be arrested by the same claimant more than once for the same claim in the jurisdiction of one or more courts of any Contracting State.

212. The French association stated in its comments (CMI Bulletin No. 105, p. 28; *Travaux Préparatoires*, p. 325):

The text of the Committee on this point is clear. It deals only with the arrest of the same ship, in respect of the same claim. There is, therefore, no doubt that it is possible, if the situation arises, to arrest another vessel for the same claim. The French Association will ask the Conference to express its agreement on this point.

association that there may be situations where a second arrest may be justified and suggested a more elaborate wording of the provision.[213]

I.543 During the Naples Conference the British delegate considered the additional sentence suggested by the French association and, after having given as an example of a situation where the French amendment might apply that of a sudden inflation of the currency in which the security is granted, did not object to such amendment.[214] The French delegate in turn stated that the British text was satisfactory, for it met the point the French association had raised.[215] The matter was then referred to the Drafting Committee,

However, it is possible to consider if the rule laid down in paragraph IV of Art. 3 must be maintained in all its strictness.

In case, for example, the Court who authorizes the first arrest, grants the release against an insufficient security, would it be proper to permit the possibility of a second arrest and should there be added to paragraph IV a second sentence so worded: "If the Court finds that the first arrest does not give the claimant a sufficient security, it may in such case and solely in such case, authorize a new conservative arrest of the same ship or of any other ship belonging to the alleged debtor".

213. The British association stated in its comments (CMI Bulletin No. 105, p. 50; *Travaux Préparatoires*, p. 326):

The Association has noted with great sympathy the comment made on this paragraph by the French Association, who supports "emphatically" this provision, with this temperament, that the Court, before which the request of a second conservative arrest is made, shall be permitted to grant such second arrest solely where it would deem insufficient the bail or other security supplied at the time of the first arrest. The French Association considers cases such as that where, without fault of the claimant, the first security appears insufficient, e.g. in case of a sudden depreciation of the currency in which the security has been given. But, in the desire of giving satisfaction to the praiseworthy wish of the Association, the British Association proposes to amend this paragraph as follows:

A ship may not be arrested nor a bond or other security may be given more than once in one or more jurisdictions of one of the Contracting States, by virtue of the same maritime claim by the same claimant, and where the ship has been arrested in one of such jurisdictions or a bail or other guarantee has been provided in such jurisdiction either in order to obtain the release from arrest or to avoid a threat of arrest, any subsequent arrest of such ship or of another ship in the same ownership by the same claimant for the same maritime claim shall be declared void and the ship shall be released by the court or other competent authority of such State, unless the claimant may prove to the satisfaction of the Court or other competent authority that the bail or other security had been finally released before the second arrest or that there is another good reason for maintaining the second arrest.

It is appreciated that different Courts will interpret in a different manner the term "good reason", but there is no way to avoid it. For example, the Association doubts that the fact that the currency in which the bail or the original guarantee has been given has suffered a depreciation since then, shall be considered by the English Courts as a "good reason" for a second arrest.

214. CMI Bulletin No. 105, p. 263 and 264; *Travaux Préparatoires*, p. 330.

215. The French delegate (Mr de Grandmaison) stated (CMI Bulletin No. 105, p. 265 and 266; *Travaux Préparatoires*, p. 331):

Consequently, our basic position is the following. It should not be possible to arrest several times the same ship for the same claim.

But our attention is drawn to the different points of view. First, it has been said: it is possible that the Court has fixed an insufficient security. I confess that I do not find that relevant. When you want to arrest a ship in a given place, you apply to the competent court and accept, in advance, the decision it will make.

But the Delegation of The Netherlands has then drawn our attention to the fact that it is possible without any fault of the claimant, that the security that has been provided loses a relevant part of its value, by reason of a monetary devaluation.

I confess that in such case it appears reasonable to make an exception to the rule, but it must be an exception. The rule must remain and the exception must be an exception.

This is the reason why we do not see any objection to the proposal made by our friend Miller. When he says that the claimant must prove to the Court the existence of a "good reason", it is extremely difficult to know what the Court will deem to be a "good reason". But all we can do is to show to the Court our intention to have a rule, with an exception in exceptional cases, and to trust the Court that it will draw the conclusions therefrom. Therefore, one arrest only, save exceptions, justified by a "good reason".

on the understanding that the basis should be the text suggested by the British association.[216]

I.544 The text as drafted by the Drafting Committee and then approved by the Conference was that suggested by the British association and was not changed by the Diplomatic Conference.

I.545 Article 3(3) in its English text provides first that "a ship shall not be arrested *nor* bail or other security be given more than once in respect of the same maritime claim. It then provides that "if a ship has been arrested . . . *or* bail or other security has been given" either to release the ship or to avoid a threatened arrest any subsequent arrest of the ship (or of any other ship in the same ownership) for the same maritime claim shall be set aside and the ship released.

I.546 It would appear, therefore, that two alternatives are considered, the arrest or the provision of security and that would mean that a second arrest in respect of the same claim is not allowed irrespective of whether security has been provided in order to release the ship from the first arrest or not.

I.547 The French text is different since arrest and security are connected with the conjunction "et". It says: "un navire ne peut être saisi *et* caution ou autre garantie ne sera donnée"; it then says: "si un navire est saisi . . . *et* une caution ou autre garantie a été donnée". That would mean that a second arrest is not allowed because security has already been provided in order to release the ship from the first arrest.

I.548 That this was the reason why a second arrest is not normally permitted clearly appears from the *travaux préparatoires*. When presenting at the CMI Naples Conference its proposal for what is the present text of Article 3(3) the British Maritime Law Association stated that if a ship has been arrested and released upon a bail being provided a second arrest would be lifted.[217] Also from other statements it clearly appears that the provision of the bail of other security was the reason for which it was considered that a second arrest should not normally be permitted.[218]

I.549 The exception to the general rule provided in the last part of Article 3(3) further confirms that the French text is correct. It in fact permits a second arrest if the bail or other security has been released.

I.550 The prohibition of a second arrest and the consequent release of a ship from a second arrest does not operate, therefore, when the ship has been released without any security having been provided, for example because the arrest was lifted by order of the

---

In these conditions we willingly agree with the proposal of our friend Miller and to the proposal of the Delegation of The Netherlands.

216. The President stated (CMI Bulletin No. 105, p. 268; *Travaux Préparatoires*, p. 333):
Everybody seems to agree that paragraph IV proposed by the British delegation and supported by the French delegation be submitted to a drafting committee? (approved).

217. In its report (*supra*, note 190) the BMLA made express reference to the statement of the French association that the Court, before which the second arrest is applied for, should grant such second arrest only where it would consider the bail supplied at the time of the first arrest to be insufficient.

218. In its comments on the Draft the French Maritime Law Association (*supra*, note 189) made express reference to the situation where the security provided in order to release the ship from arrest is insufficient.

Court[219] or the claimant permitted the ship to sail in order to avoid damages to the owner[220] or because the ship sailed in breach of the order of the Court.

I.551 There are subjective and objective conditions for this provision to apply. The objective conditions relate to the claim, the ship and the bail or other security.

I.552 From the subjective standpoint, Article 4(3) requires that the claimant must be the same. Several situations may be envisaged when the same claim is enforced by a different person: (i) a claim may be assigned by one person to another; (ii) subrogation may occur on a voluntary basis or by operation of law; (iii) succession may occur for a physical person following death or for a legal person following a merger; (iv) a claim may be enforced by different persons who all allege to be entitled to demand payment. In the case mentioned under (i), (ii) and (iii), where there is a succession of one person to another, the second person steps into the position of the first and, therefore, cannot be deemed to be a different person for the purposes of this provision. In the case mentioned under (iv) the claimants may all be entitled to obtain payment *in solidum* or the right to claim is in dispute amongst them. In the former situation they must be treated as one claimant only and, therefore, if one has arrested the ship, the other one cannot do so anymore. In the latter situation one only is the actual claimant and, therefore, if the actual claimant has arrested the ship, the application of the other must be rejected on the ground that he has no claim. In the case of the *M/V "Zanet"* the receivers of a cargo unloaded from the vessel, of Yugoslavian flag, arrested the ship as security for a claim against her owners. Also the time charterers of the *"Zanet"*, fearing an action by the receivers against them, obtained an order of arrest of the ship as security for a possible recourse action against the owners. The arrest was granted and executed, but the Tribunale of Trani,[221] on the application of the owners, held that the second arrest was in violation of Article 3(3) of the Arrest Convention and ordered the release of the ship from the second arrest.

I.553 If, on the contrary, the arrest has been granted to the wrong person, the application of the actual claimant cannot be rejected for such reason, but the first arrest must be vacated.

I.554 From the objective standpoint, it is conceivable that different claims arise out of the same contract or the same occurrence. For example, in the case of the loss of the cargo carried on the ship, where the purchase price of such cargo has been paid only in part by

---

219. In The *"Tjaskemolen"* [1997] 2 Lloyd's Rep. 476, at p. 478 the ship had been arrested in Rotterdam by the charterers in order to obtain security for their claim in an arbitration in London but then the Court in Rotterdam ordered the release of the ship after a summary hearing on the merits. The charterers then issued a writ in England and the vessel was arrested in Liverpool and released after security was provided. The owners made an application to the Admiralty Court that the security be discharged on the ground *inter alia* that article 3(3) of the 1952 Arrest Convention does not permit a second arrest. Clarke J. after having stated that the French text of article 3(3) is to be preferred, so held (at p. 478):

> It appears to me that if art. 3(3) had been intended to prohibit a subsequent arrest in circumstances in which a vessel had been released from her first arrest pursuant to an order of the Court it would have been drafted in very different terms. Mr. Justice Sheen appears to have taken the same view in *The Silver Athens (No. 2)*, [1986] 2 Lloyd's Rep. 583.

> In these circumstances I have reached the conclusion that, even if it is part of English law, art. 3(3) of the Arrest Convention has no application to the facts of this case. I shall however indicate briefly below the conclusion which I would reach on the facts if it were held that that view were wrong.

220. The situations in which re-arrest or arrest of another ship is permissible have been set out in a much more clear way in article 6 of the 1999 Arrest Convention. See *infra*, Book II, para. II.140–148 and, for the *travaux préparatoires*, Appendix III, pp. 511–518.

221. Order of 30 January 1991, *Capt. Ivanov Zdenko* v. *Sadav Lines S.r.l.—The "Zamet"* [1993] Dir. Mar. 416.

the buyer, both the seller, who was the shipper and the buyer, who was the receiver of the cargo, have a cause of action against the carrier and can both arrest the ship as security for their respective claims. Similarly, in case of a collision, the owner of the ship may have a claim for the damage suffered by his ship and the charterer may have a claim for loss of hire. More dubious is the solution in case the amount of the claim has increased or interest has matured. It would appear that in such cases the claim is the same, and only the amount varies, and the claimant may apply for an additional arrest on the ground that there is a "good cause" for such new arrest.

I.555 As regards the ship, the situations expressly covered by this provision are the following:

    (i) arrest of the ship that had been released from a previous arrest after bail or other security has been provided;

    (ii) arrest of a ship after bail or other security has been provided in order to avoid a threatened arrest of such ship; and

    (iii) arrest of another ship in the same ownership in any of the situations envisaged under (i) or (ii).

I.556 The first situation does not call for special comments.

I.557 The second situation occurs frequently. Sometimes the arrestor, before obtaining or after having obtained an order of arrest, informs the owner of the ship or his agent in order to obtain security and, also, to reach an agreement on jurisdiction. Sometimes the court does not issue an order of arrest *ex parte* but fixes a hearing,[222] whereupon the owner of the ship may offer security in order to avoid arrest.

I.558 The third situation differs from the previous two only because the ship that is arrested is a sister ship.

I.559 As previously stated, there are two exceptions to the rule which prohibits a second arrest and provides for the release of the ship from a second arrest. The first is that the bail or other security has been finally released. The reason for which the release has taken place is immaterial. It can be the effect of an order of the Court or of a decision of the claimant. If, for example, the ship has been released after security has been provided in the place of arrest but under local currency regulations money is not freely transferable, the claimant can find it convenient to re-arrest the ship elsewhere and to release the security that had been provided in the place of the first arrest.

I.560 The second exception is described generally with the words "there is other good cause for maintaining the arrest".

I.561 A "good cause" either for maintaining or for granting a second arrest (or for granting an arrest after security has been provided) may be, in addition to that suggested by the Dutch association,[223] the situation where the actual amount of the claim proves to be higher than that originally estimated, for which the arrest was requested and security was obtained.[224] For example, in a collision case the damage suffered by one of the

---

222. This, for example, is the basic procedure in Italian law (art. 669*sexies* CCP), whereby the arrest order is issued at a hearing, but the court may issue an order *ex parte* when prior notice to the other party "may prejudice the execution of the order".

223. See *supra*, note 192. See also Claringbould, *Arrest of Ships, supra*, note 4, p. 52.

224. Reference to this situation has been made by the President of the Arrondissementsrechtbank of Haarlem in his decision in the case of *The "Golfo de Guanahacabibes"* [1995] Schip en Schade 107. In that case the situation was different. In fact the claimant had applied for a second arrest on the ground that the Court who had

colliding vessels may at first sight appear not too great and the other vessel is thus arrested as security for the claim as assessed at that time; subsequently, after the damaged vessel is drydocked, the actual damage is found to be much more serious. There is no reason why, even if the other vessel has been released against bail covering the original amount of the claim, such vessel could not be arrested again to secure the excess of the claim.[225]

I.562 In the case of *The "Despina GK"*[226] the claimants had arrested the ship in Sweden and had released her upon the owners providing security. They then obtained a final judgment in Sweden but the sum liquidated by the Swedish Supreme Court was not fully paid by the owners, probably because the security provided to release the ship from the arrest was insufficient. The claimants then applied for a warrant of arrest in England, where the ship subsequently arrived. The warrant was first refused by the Admiralty Registrar but then was granted by the Admiralty Court and the ship was arrested. In that case, however, the second arrest was not based on the (partial) survival of a maritime claim but on the residual jurisdiction of the Admiralty Court resulting from section 20(1) of the Supreme Court Act 1981 pursuant to which a judgment creditor can bring an action

granted the first arrest had indicated an amount lower than that requested by the claimant and security had been provided for such lower amount. The decision, affirmed by the Gerechtshof of Amsterdam on 6 April 1995, [1995] Schip en Schade 107, appears to be correct since the claimant in that case should have appealed against the first order. This was done by the owner of the *"Bumbesti"* who had claimed US$ 250,000 in damages from Petromin and had arrested in Greece the *"Bumbesti"*, owned by Petromin, whose release had been ordered by the Greek Court against a security of US$ 60,000, then amended, after the ship had sailed, to US$ 250,000: when the *"Bumbesti"* was arrested again in the Netherlands, the President of the Arrondissementsrechtbank of Middelburg with decision of 19 August 1998 [2000] Schip en Schade 29 held that the second arrest was justified. The *"Bumbesti"* was subsequently arrested in Liverpool by the same claimants as security for claims on an award but her release was ordered by the Admiralty Court (Aikens J.) on the ground that sufficient security had been obtained in the form of the detention of other two vessels by the Constantza Court: *The "Bumbesti"* [1999] 2 Lloyd's Rep. 481.

225. This principle has now been adopted by the new English Civil Procedure Rules (CPR). Part 6.7(3) so in fact states:

> Where in relation to a claim *in rem* security has been provided to obtain release of property under arrest or to prevent the arrest of property the Admiralty Court may at any stage:
> (a) order that the amount of security be reduced, and may stay the claim pending compliance with such Order;
> (b) order that the claimant be permitted to arrest or re-arrest the property proceeded against for the purpose of obtaining further security, provided that the total security provided shall not exceed the value of the property at the time of the original arrest or at the time security was originally given if the property was not arrested.

In Sweden the provision of article 3(4) of the Convention has been reproduced almost literally. Section 6 of Chapter 4 of the Swedish Maritime Code so in fact provides:

> A vessel shall not be arrested more than once in respect of the same maritime claim.
> If bail or other security is given to release the vessel from arrest, arrest may not be granted for the same maritime claim. Such arrest may however be granted if the claimant can show that the security has ceased to be effective or that there is otherwise special cause for arrest.

Similar criteria are applied in the Netherlands where Courts normally allow a ship to be arrested a second time where, following the first arrest, the arrestor did not obtain security or where the security obtained was not sufficient to cover the whole claim. Security can be insufficient for the following reasons:

    (i) inflation;
    (ii) if a claim was estimated too low;
    (iii) if after accumulation of legal interest the security is not sufficient to cover the claim;
    (iv) if the guarantee (not the claim period) has expired.

Re-arrest appears to be possible if there is a "good reason" in Denmark, Germany, Greece and Spain but there are no precedents in which the existence of a "good reason" has been assessed.

226. [1982] 2 Lloyd's Rep. 555.

in rem to enforce a judgment.[227] In accordance with the terminology used in the Arrest Convention this has not been an arrest "to secure a maritime claim", but a "seizure of a ship in execution or satisfaction of a judgment" and, therefore, would not have been subject to the Convention.[228] But even if it had been an arrest for example because the foreign judgment could not be immediately recognised, there would have existed, under the Convention, a "good cause" for the re-arrest of the ship.

I.563 It may also occur that security is provided in order to prevent arrest and that the agreement on the jurisdiction on the merits (which would otherwise exist under Article 7(1) of the Convention) is not perfected. This situation has occurred in England in the case of *The "Prinsengracht"*,[229] the arrest of a ship was granted after bail had been provided by the owner of the ship because the defendant had declined expressly to agree to the jurisdiction of the Court. Sheen J. stated[230]:

If the arrest of the ship is necessary to preserve the jurisdiction of this Court, it cannot be wrongful to arrest the ship. Put in another way, if the case on which the defendants rely does show that in order to found jurisdiction in this Court, a plaintiff must arrest a ship and cannot achieve that result by accepting bail, that would show that bail is not the equivalent of the ship except in money terms. Bail can only be the equivalent of a ship if it provides equivalent security without adverse effect upon the plaintiff. If, on the contrary to the view I have expressed, bail can be given without submitting to the jurisdiction and it remains necessary for the plaintiff to arrest the ship that arrest cannot be unlawful.

I.564 Another even better reason is the case of a ship under arrest sailing away and of her re-arrest in another country.[231]

I.565 The granting of a new arrest of the same ship or of a sister ship is also justified in cases where the ship is released from arrest without any bail or other security being provided, for example, in order to avoid the owner suffering relevant damages, as, for example, in the case of the vessel having to meet a close cancelling date.[232]

I.566 The reference to the same claim and the same claimant also covers the case where the claim has been assigned to another person. The identity of the position of the assignee and of the assignor is expressly dealt with in the Convention only as regards the habitual residence and the principal place of business for the purpose of determining the applicability of the exception provided for in Article 8(5) but seems to be of general application.

---

227. Although the reasons given by Sheen J. are not entirely clear, Section 20(1) of the Supreme Court Act, 1981 so provides in its relevant part:
  20(1) The Admiralty jurisdiction of the High Court shall be as follows, that is to say: . . .
  (c) any other Admiralty jurisdiction which it had immediately before the commencement of this Act;
  After an analysis of the previous cases Sheen J. stated (at p. 559):
  A judgment creditor who has obtained a final judgment against a shipowner by proceeding in rem in a foreign Admiralty Court can bring an action in rem in this Court against that ship to enforce the decree of the foreign Court if that is necessary to complete the execution of that judgment, provided that the ship is the property of the judgment debtor at the time when she is arrested.
  On Section 20(1)(c) of the Supreme Court Act 1981 see Jackson, *Enforcement of Maritime Claims*, p. 21, *supra*, Chapter III, note 62.
228. The title of the paragraph in which this judgment is discussed by Hill, *Arrest of Ships*, p. 19 (Is it possible to arrest the same ship twice?) is, therefore, misleading.
229. [1993] 1 Lloyd's Rep. 41.
230. At p. 47.
231. See La China, "Due Novità", *supra*, Chapter IV, note 39.
232. The situations in which rearrest or arrest of a sister ship is permissible are now expressly indicated in article 5 of the 1999 Arrest Convention. See *infra*, para. II.140–148.

I.567 The provisions of Article 3(3) regulate also the subsequent arrest of a sister ship. If, therefore, the ship in respect of which the maritime claim arose has been arrested, no sister ship may be arrested unless there is a "good cause". Conversely, if a sister ship has been arrested, the ship in respect of which the maritime claim arose cannot be arrested unless there is a "good cause". In fact, although paragraph 1 states that a claimant may arrest "either the particular ship in respect of which the maritime claim arose, or any other ship which is owned . . . " and thus seems to involve a choice between two alternatives (with the consequence that if the claimant has arrested the particular ship in respect of which the claim arose, he may not arrest another ship), paragraph 3, when dealing with the right of re-arrest, considers both the case of the subsequent arrest of a ship that has been previously arrested and that of the arrest of another ship. It states, in fact, as follows in the relevant part:

And, if a ship has been arrested . . . any subsequent arrest of the ship or of any ship in the same ownership by the same claimant for the same maritime claim shall be set aside unless the claimant can satisfy the Court . . . that there is other good cause for maintaining that arrest.

I.568 This interpretation is also confirmed by the *travaux préparatoires*. In fact, the British proposal[233] that the arrest of sister ships should be prevented after a ship in the same ownership has been arrested or security has been provided to prevent the arrest, was accepted against the contrary view of the French association.[234] Article 3(3) provides in fact that "any subsequent arrest of the ship or of any ship in the same ownership" must be set aside.

I.569 A "good cause" for the arrest of one or more sister ships, in addition to those previously considered for the ship in respect of which the maritime claim has arisen can consist in the fact that the value of the ship that has first been arrested is not sufficient for the satisfaction of the maritime claim in respect of which the first arrest has been made, or that, in case of forced sale of the arrested ship, the proceeds of sale are distributed amongst several claimants and the claim of the arrestor is not wholly satisfied. In either of these cases, the claimant is entitled to obtain an additional security and, therefore, to arrest another ship, or even more than one, so that his claim is fully secured. Where the value of the arrested ship is insufficient to meet the claim in respect of which the arrest is made, the need for a second arrest appears immediately. Where, instead, the value is sufficient, but no security is provided so that the ship has to be sold, the need for the arrest of another ship will appear only when other claimants participate in the forced sale proceedings. However, it does not seem to be necessary to wait for the distribution of the proceeds of sale in order that the arrest of another ship be justified. When it appears to be reasonably certain that the future sale will not yield a sufficient amount to satisfy all the claimants, the arrest of another ship may be requested.

---

233. When making its proposal, the British Association stated (*Travaux Préparatoires*, p. 327):
> The Association wants also to energically support the proposal, contained in the amendment, that a sister ship may not be arrested by the same claimant for the same maritime claim for which a ship of the same owner has been previously arrested.

234. When making its proposal, the French Association had in fact stated (CMI Bulletin No. 105, p. 29; *Travaux Préparatoires*, p. 325):
> The text of the Commission on this point is clear. It considers only the arrest of the same ship, by the same claimant and for the same claim. There is, therefore, no doubt that it is possible, if need be, to arrest another ship for the same claim. The French Association will request the Conference to express its agreement on this point.

I.570 The problem, however, arises whether Article 3(3) applies in respect of the arrest of a ship owned by the charterer by demise or other charterer when the claimant has previously arrested the ship chartered by the charterer, in respect of a claim relating to such latter ship. The literal formulation of Article 3(3) would exclude such possibility, since reference is made therein to the ship which has been arrested or to any ship in the same ownership. However Article 3(3) also provides that security shall not be given more than once in respect of the same maritime claim. If, therefore, security has been provided after the arrest of the former ship, the arrest of the latter ship should not be allowed. In fact, the purpose of the arrest is to obtain security and, therefore, the second arrest would lead to further security being provided in respect of the same maritime claim. There are, however, situations where the final provision of Article 3(3) can apply. If, for example, the security has been provided by the owner of the first ship and the claimant cannot enforce his claim thereon, a second arrest may be justified, provided, however, the first security is released.[235] The same reasoning applies where the first vessel is still under arrest when the second, owned by the debtor, is arrested.

I.571 The inverse situation may also occur. A claimant may arrest a ship owned by the charterer and then the ship in respect of which the maritime claim arose. In such a case the second arrest may be permitted in the same situations in which it would be permitted if the ships were in the same ownership.

I.572 The prohibition of a second arrest applies when such arrest is made in respect of the same maritime claim by the same claimant. The prohibition does not operate if the claimant is not the same. If such a situation does occur, the courts will exercise their good judgment in order to establish whether the second claimant has a cause of action and, if so, whether the amount of the claim of either the first or the second claimant should be reduced, for the purpose of establishing the amount of the security or, if the security has already been provided, whether the security should be reduced.

I.573 In certain jurisdictions the arrest is endorsed in the ships register or can be replaced by such endorsement. It can be questioned whether such endorsement, for the purposes of Article 3(3) of the Convention, must be deemed equal to the physical arrest when such latter has not taken place. This has been denied by the President of the Arrondissementsrechtbank of Middelburg with decision of 18 March 1992[236] in a case where the arrest of a ship in Greece had been endorsed in the ship's register but the ship could not be arrested because meanwhile she had left Greek waters, whereupon the claimant arrested that ship in the Netherlands.

---

235. The Tribunale of Genoa by order of 9 January 1995, *Fallimento Navalferro Porto S.r.l.* v. *CNAN—Societé Nationale de Transports Maritimes—The "Nemencha"*, unreported, authorised the release of a ship from arrest and the arrest of another ship in the same ownership as security for the same claim in order to enable the first ship to meet a cancelling date. A similar order was issued by the Tribunale of Genoa on 18 April 1995 in *Italiana Contenitori S.r.l.* v. *Black Sea Shipping Co.—The "Lev Tolstoj" and "Pavel Mizikievich"*, unreported, affirmed on 21 April 1995.

236. [1992] Kort Gelding 130. Subsequently the same Court decided again along the same lines in the case of *The "Gozde-B"* on 1 September 1995, [1995] Kort Gelding 395.

CHAPTER 6

Procedure relating to Arrest

27. JURISDICTION FOR THE ARREST

I.574 Article 4 of the Convention provides:

A ship may only be arrested under the authority of a court or of the appropriate judicial authority of the Contracting State in which the arrest is made.

I.575 Three rules are laid down in Article 4: the first is that the arrest must be authorised by a judicial authority; the second is that such judicial authority must be a judicial authority of the Contracting State in which the arrest is made; the third is that the judicial authority of the State which is competent for the arrest is chosen on the basis of the applicable national rules. A fourth rule which is implied in Article 4 is that the jurisdiction of the Court of the State in which the arrest is made exists irrespective of such Court having jurisdiction on the merits or not.

(a) Judicial authority

I.576 The origin of this provision may be traced to Article VI of the Draft Convention on Civil Jurisdiction in Collision Cases discussed by the CMI 1904 Amsterdam Conference,[1] which provided as follows in its relevant part:

La saisie conservatoire d'un navire du chef d'un abordage pourra être opérée dans tout port situé sur le territoire des états contractants.
a) Cette saisie ne pourra être faite qu'avec la permission de l'autorité compétente, désignée par les lois nationales.
(The conservative arrest of a ship by reason of a collision may be made in any port situated in the territory of the Contracting States.
a) Such arrest can only be made with the consent of the competent authority designated by the national laws).[2]

I.577 At the 1937 Paris Conference of the CMI, Article 2 of the Draft Convention on Arrest of Ships provided in its first sentence[3]:

---

1. CMI Amsterdam Conference, 1904, Session of 15 September 1904, p. 363; *Travaux Préparatoires*, p. 350.
2. The English version which appears in the *Procès-verbaux* (*supra*, note 1) is not correct, since the words "saisie conservatoire" have been translated "seizure to preserve rights".
3. CMI Paris Conference, 1937, Bulletin No. 102, p. 341; *Travaux Préparatoires*, p. 350.

La saisie ne pourra être effectuée qu'avec l'autorisation de justice.
Arrest can only be effected under the authority of a Court.

I.578 The purpose of this provision, as it appears from the *travaux préparatoires*,[4] was to make clear that the Convention would apply only to arrest ordered by a judicial authority.

I.579 In the draft submitted by the CMI International Sub-Committee to the CMI Conference held in Naples in 1951, of which only the French version is known,[5] the words "ou de toute autre autorité judiciaire compétente de l'Etat Contractant dans lequel la saisie est pratiquée" (or of any other competent judicial authority of the Contracting State in which the arrest is made) were added.[6]

I.580 When this amended text was discussed and approved by the Conference the English version was worded as follows[7]:

A ship may only be arrested under the authority of a Court or of the appropriate judicial authority of the Contracting State in which the arrest is made.

I.581 This wording differs, however, from the original wording in French in that the words "ou de toute autre autorité judiciaire compétente" were translated "or of the appropriate judicial authority" which seem to imply a distinction between two categories of authorities which may order the arrest: a court and an appropriate judicial authority.

I.582 The correct text is, therefore, the French text and its English equivalent should be: "under the authority of a Court or of any other competent judicial authority". The lack of precision in the translation is confirmed by the fact that in Article 5 the English words corresponding to "Tribunal ou toute autre Autorité Judiciaire" are "Court or other competent judicial authority".

I.583 Although no explanation has been given of the reason of the addition, it seems obvious that the addition was due to the fact that there are judicial authorities which, at least in the French language, are not named "Tribunal" and, therefore, it was deemed advisable to use a wording such as not to preclude the application of the Convention to a conservative arrest ordered by a judicial authority other than a "Tribunal" or a "Court". As it will be seen, also the word "compétente" in the sentence "toute autre autorité judiciaire compétente" was incorrectly translated by the word "appropriate". The substance of this provision, therefore, is that a ship may be arrested only by an order of a judicial authority. This is consistent with the definition of arrest in Article 1(2) whereby arrest "means the detention of a ship by judicial process". The only exception to this rule

---

4. The following statements are recorded in the *Procès-verbaux* (CMI Paris Conference, p. 341; *Travaux Préparatoires*, p. 350):

   M. Skovgaard-Petersen. An arrest effected without the intervention of the judicial authority is not conceivable.

   The President. It could be an arrest authorised by an administrative authority. You are right, it must be following the authority of a Court but it is better to state this.

5. CMI Naples Conference, 1951—CMI Bulletin No. 105, p. 19; *Travaux Préparatoires*, p. 351.

6. The following statement is made in the Report of the CMI International Sub-Committee to the Conference (CMI Naples Conference, 1951, p. 8; *Travaux Préparatoires*, p. 351):

   Cet article reproduit la règle généralement admise que la saisie d'un navire ne peut être pratiquée que moyennant l'autorisation d'un tribunal ou de toute autre autorité judiciaire compétente de l'État Contractant dans lequel la saisie est pratiquée.

7. CMI Naples Conference, 1951, p. 90; *Travaux Préparatoires*, p. 352.

is that stated in Article 2, whereby the existing right or power vested in any governments or their departments, public authorities or dock or harbour authorities is not affected by the Convention.

(b) Authority having jurisdiction

I.584 The wording of Article 4 is clear: the (judicial) authority having jurisdiction for the arrest is that of the State in which the arrest is made.[8] The ship must, therefore, be within the territorial waters of that State at the time of arrest. It does not seem necessary that the ship be within the jurisdiction of the State at the time when the arrest is applied for; the order of arrest, however, may be effectively executed only if the ship enters the territorial waters of that State.[9]

I.585 The possibility of an arrest being made within the jurisdiction of a State, pursuant to an order issued by a court of another State, does not seem to have been considered. Nor can that be implied from the reference in Article 6 to the Contracting State in which the arrest is applied for. The reason for such addition was, in fact, that of covering the situation where the arrest is avoided by the owner of the ship providing security, on the ground that in such a case too the owner may be entitled to claim damages.[10]

I.586 Although the case of the recognition and enforcement of a foreign order of arrest was not taken into consideration, there seems to be nothing in the wording of Article 4 which would prevent the courts of the State in the jurisdiction of which the arrest may be made to recognise and enforce a foreign order of arrest. In fact, in such a case too the ship would be arrested under the authority of that court.

I.587 In practice, the recognition and enforcement of a foreign order of arrest are unlikely to occur, for the reason that it would normally take less time to apply for and obtain an order of arrest than to apply for and obtain the recognition and enforcement of a foreign order.

I.588 In any event, all the provisions of the Convention in which reference is made to the court within the jurisdiction of which the arrest is made would apply to the court authorising the recognition and enforcement of the foreign order of arrest so that there would not be any further link with the original court.

---

8. In France the Cour de Cassation with judgment 5 January 1999, *Jupiter Maritime Corporation* v. *Schiffahrtgesellschaft Detlef Von Appen mbH*, [1999] DMF 130 held that Article 211 of Decree 31 July 1992, pursuant to which the competent Court for the issuance of an order of arrest is that of the domicile of the debtor (in that case a Liberian owner), does not apply in respect of the arrest of ships, for which jurisdiction is established by article 4 of the Convention. See also the comments of the Conseiller Référendaire Rémery (at p. 132) and the note by Vialard (at p. 140).

9. The Tribunale of Genoa with judgments 10 February 1995, *Industria Chimica Subalpina S.p.A.* v. *Navalbuo S.r.l.–The "Bibor"*, [1997] Dir. Mar. 112 and 24 March 1995, *Lockwood & Carlisle and Others* v. *Sicilsud Leasing S.p.A.—The "Depa Giulia"*, [1997] Dir. Mar. 1063 held instead that the ship must be in the Italian territorial waters at the time the arrest is applied.

10. At the CMI 1937 Paris Conference the Norwegian delegate, Mr Alten, stated (CMI Paris Conference, 1937, p. 342; *Travaux Préparatoires*, p. 379):

I take the liberty of asking you if this article should not consider the situation when the owner has avoided the arrest by providing security. It should be stated: "The cost of the security supplied in order to avoid or obtain the release of the arrest".

The President so stated in turn:

There can be the threat of an arrest.

(c) Choice of the judicial authority of the State in the jurisdiction of which the arrest is made

I.589 The use of the indefinite article "a" before "Court" and "un" before "Tribunal" clearly indicates that for the purpose of the application of the Convention it is immaterial which Court of the State in which the arrest is made orders the arrest. The rules on the basis of which the venue is established are, therefore, the domestic rules of procedure of that State.[11]

(d) Jurisdiction for arrest when the Court has not jurisdiction for the merits

I.590 The court of the State in which the arrest is applied for is also competent if proceedings to determine the merits of the dispute are commenced in a different jurisdiction. Although Article 7 expressly considers the case of proceedings on the merits commenced after the arrest of a ship,[12] the possibility of courts in different jurisdictions being competent respectively for the arrest and for the merits is normally admitted.[13] There cannot be, therefore, a denial of the jurisdiction of the court of the country where the ship is to be arrested on the ground of *lis pendens*.[14]

I.591 This conclusion also holds when the court within whose jurisdiction the arrest is made has no jurisdiction to decide on the merits owing to the parties having agreed to submit the dispute to another court or to arbitration. The provision of Article 7(3) is clear

---

11. In its judgment of 5 January 1999, *Jupiter Maritime Corporation* v. *Schiffahrtsgesellschaft Detlef von Appen GmbH—The "Gure Maiden"*, [1999] DMF 130 the French Cour de Cassation has stated, however, that the Tribunal of the place where the vessel lies at the time when the arrest is demanded is competent for the arrest, notwithstanding that pursuant to Article 211 of the French decree 31 July 1992 competent for the arrest is the Tribunal of the place where the debtor is domiciled, on the ground that article 5 of the Convention takes precedence over the provision of domestic law.

12. In this connection Art. 7(2), which requires the court in whose jurisdiction the ship is arrested to fix the time within which the claimant must bring proceedings for the merits, is particularly relevant.

13. In *The "Nordglimt"* [1987] 2 Lloyd's Rep. 470, Hobhouse J. stated (at p. 483):

An additional reason why one should not treat Art. 21 [of the Jurisdiction Convention], even if it applies, as invalidating the arrest is that Art. 7(2) of the 1952 Convention implicitly authorizes the maintenance of the arrest even though the court within whose jurisdiction the ship has been arrested has no jurisdiction to decide upon the merits.

This is a frequent situation in civil law countries, where jurisdiction is not acquired pursuant to an action *in rem*, but exists only, except for the provisions of Art. 7, para. 1, in cases specifically set out in the law.

14. Art. 21 of the Jurisdiction Convention provides:

Where proceedings involving the same cause of action and between the same parties are brought in the courts of different Contracting States, any court other than the court first seised shall of its own motion decline jurisdiction in favour of that court.

A court which would be required to decline jurisdiction may stay its proceedings if the jurisdiction of the other court is contested.

The issue of *lis pendens* was raised in *The "Nordglimt"* [1987] 2 Lloyd's Rep. 470. In English law the issue is perhaps more delicate than in other jurisdictions because in order to obtain a warrant of arrest an action *in rem* must be brought in the High Court against the ship (s.21, Supreme Court Act 1981). Hobhouse J. stated in *The "Nordglimt"* (at p. 481):

In England, since the Judicature Acts, the means by which the judicial arrest of a ship has been obtained is by the commencing of an action *in rem* and the issue, by the court in that action, of a warrant of arrest. Therefore, as a matter of English procedure there has to be an action before there can be an arrest and, subject now to s.26 of the 1982 Act, the arrest has to be in aid of a judgment capable of being obtained in this action.

textual evidence of such rule.[15] The parties may, however, have made some special agreement in this respect. The only precedent known of a similar situation is *Mike Trading and Transport Ltd.* v. *R. Pagnan & Fratelli—The "Lisboa"*[16] in which the bills of lading issued by the carrier contained the following jurisdiction clause:

> Any and all legal proceedings against the carrier shall be brought before the competent court of London, which shall have exclusive jurisdiction subject to appeals, if any, pursuant to English law, unless the carrier declares his option for other jurisdiction or expressly agrees to submit to other jurisdiction.

I.592 Following an engine breakdown, the cargo owners employed and paid for a tug to tow the ship from La Goulette to Chioggia and upon arrival of the ship at Chioggia, the owners having refused to reimburse the towage expenses, the cargo owners arrested the ship. The ship owners brought proceedings in London against the cargo owners and issued a writ claiming that the arrest in Italy was unlawful because there was an exclusive jurisdiction clause in the bill of lading. The ship owners then applied for a mandatory injunction for the vessel to be released. Lord Denning, M.R., having summarised the submission of counsel for the cargo owners, that the jurisdiction clause did not exclude proceedings in a foreign court for the arrest of a ship, stated[17]:

> I think that this is right for two reasons:
> "Any and all legal proceedings" should be construed as relating only to proceedings to establish liability. They do not extend to proceedings to enforce a judgment or award or to obtain security. Test it by taking a case where the cargo owners, in accordance with the clause, bring an action in London and get a judgment for damages against the owners. The ship may be, as here, owned by a one-ship company, which has no other assets. It may be, as here, in a port in Italy. It cannot be supposed that this clause prevents the cargo owners from enforcing the judgment in Italy. If it did, it would be void under r. 3 of the Hague Rules.

I.593 The decision is undoubtedly correct under the Arrest Convention, reference to which was not even made by Lord Denning, M.R., nor by either of the two Lords Justice, perhaps because at that time, though it had been ratified by the United Kingdom, it did not have the force of law in English municipal law.[18]

---

15. In *The "Nordglimt"* [1987] 2 Lloyd's Rep. 470, Hobhouse J. stated (at p. 481):
    Similarly, there is indirect provision for the problem of concurrent proceedings in more than one jurisdiction or tribunal in art. 7(2) of the 1952 Convention which I have already quoted. Article 7 contemplates that an arrest may take place in a country which does not have jurisdiction to decide upon the merits of the dispute between the relevant persons and implicitly recognizes that such arrest shall not be invalid and that, subject to safeguards, the security obtained by the arrest shall remain available to satisfy any judgment that results from a determination of the dispute on the merits by a court having jurisdiction so to decide.
16. [1980] 2 Lloyd's Rep. 546.
17. At p. 548.
18. *The "Nordglimt"* [1987] 2 Lloyd's Rep. 470 at p. 478. However, the Arrest Convention was subsequently incorporated into English municipal law through the 1968 EC Jurisdiction Convention. Hobhouse J. stated in fact (at p. 479):
    Further as a matter of English municipal law, although the 1952 Convention itself has never been made part of English municipal law, international conventions which expressly recognize and preserve the jurisdiction of the United Kingdom under the 1952 Convention have, by the terms of the 1982 Act, been made part of English municipal law. Accordingly there has been an indirect incorporation of the 1952 Convention into English municipal law through the 1968 Convention ("Provisions on jurisdiction contained in special conventions are to be regarded as if they were provisions of the 1968 Convention itself": Schlosser para. 240).

I.594 Article 7(3) refers to proceedings to determine the case upon its merits and, therefore, the use in the clause quoted previously of the qualifying words "any and all (legal proceedings)" cannot extend the notion of proceedings so to include, also, the arrest.

(e) Jurisdiction for arrest when a decision on the merits has already been obtained

I.595 This situation may become distinct from those previously considered when the arrest must be effected in a State other than that whose court has delivered a judgment on the merits of the dispute or that in which an arbitration award has been issued.

I.596 The need for an arrest may arise because the judgment or award is not yet enforceable, or is not likely to be made enforceable before the departure of the ship from the territorial waters of the State where the enforcement is sought.

I.597 Although normally in such a case the courts having jurisdiction for the arrest are those of the State in which the arrest is made, and the arrest is made under the authority of such courts, there is a situation where arrest is permissible without any such (express) authority. Such situation is mentioned in Article 39 of the EEC 1968 Jurisdiction Convention which so provides:

> During the time specified for an appeal pursuant to article 36[19] and until any such appeal has been determined, no measures of enforcement may be taken other than protective measures taken against the property of the party against whom enforcement is sought.
>
> The decision authorising enforcement shall carry with it the power to proceed to any such protective measures.

28. WHETHER AND TO WHAT EXTENT THE CLAIMANT MUST PROVE HIS CLAIM

I.598 The first question that must be considered is whether in the Convention there is any provision which, either expressly or impliedly, regulates the manner in which the claim must be substantiated.

I.599 An express provision existed in the first draft prepared by Léopold Dor in 1933[20] where it was stated (Article 2) that the judge shall authorise the arrest "*sur simple vérification de la vraisemblance de la créance*" (on simple verification of the claim being likely to exist) but it was deleted in the subsequent draft and never reintroduced. The problem, however, arose of finding in the French language an expression equivalent to

---

19. Article 36 so provides:
    If enforcement is authorised, the party against whom enforcement is sought may appeal against the decision within one month of service thereof.
    If that party is domiciled in a Contracting State other than that in which the decision authorising enforcement was given, the time for appealing shall be two months and shall run from the date of service, either on him in person or at his residence. No extension of time may be granted on account of distance.
20. See *supra*, para. I.17, note 21.

"claim". In most circumstances "claim" has been used in the unofficial English translation for *créance* and, subsequently, when Conventions were drawn up in the two languages or in the six United Nations languages, "*créance*" and "claim" were used respectively in the French and English texts ("*créance*" was translated by "claim" in the 1926 Convention on Maritime Liens and Mortgages; "*créance*" and "claim" were then used in the French and English texts of the 1957 Limitation Convention, of the 1967 Maritime Liens and Mortgages Convention, of the 1976 LLMC Convention and of the 1993 Maritime Liens and Mortgages Convention).

I.600 "Claim", however, is a word having a much wider meaning than *créance*. The best evidence of this is the fact that in the maritime law conventions the word "claim" has often been translated with words other than *créance* when the circumstances so required.[21]

I.601 In the context of the Arrest Convention "claim" is not used in the sense of an established right to obtain a certain sum of money or title to or possession of a ship. This is made clear by Article 7 in which the determination of the case upon its merits is dealt with. It follows that when considering a request for the arrest of a ship the court should not determine the merits of the claim or establish whether or not the claim exists, but should merely make a preliminary investigation in order to find out whether the contention that a certain claim exists is reasonable. All this is made clear by the use, in the definition of *créance maritime*, in the French text of the Convention, of the words "*allégation d'un droit ou d'une créance*": "*allégation d'un droit*" means that the claimant must assert that he has a claim, but not prove it. Further evidence of this may be found in the definition of claimant, in Article 1(4). " 'Claimant' means a person who alleges that a maritime claim exists in his favour." This definition is perfectly in line with the French definition of *créance maritime* and confirms that the words "maritime claims" have been used in the sense of "assertion of a right to something".[22]

---

21. For example, in the 1926 Convention on Immunity of State-owned Ships the word "*actions*" in Art. 3 has been translated by "claims"; similarly in the 1961 Passengers Convention (Art. 10) in the French text the word "*action*" and in the English text the word "claim" are used; in the 1962 Nuclear Ships Convention the French equivalent of the words "any person who claims to have suffered nuclear damage" in Art. V(4) is "*toute personne déclarant avoir subi un dommage nucléaire*" and that of the words "may amend his claim" is "*peut modifier sa demande*". In the 1967 Passengers' Luggage Convention the French equivalent of the words "Any claim for damages" in Art. 9 is "*Toute action en responsabilité*". In the 1969 Civil Liability Convention the French equivalent of the words "No claim for compensation" in Art. 3(4) is "*Aucune demande de réparation*", that of the words "no person having a claim for pollution damage" in Art. 6(1)(b) is "*à la suite d'une demande en réparation pour les dommages par pollution*"; still in the same Convention "claim" has been translated by "*demande*" in Art. 7(8). Similarly, "claim" has been translated by "*demande*" in Art. 4 of the 1984 Protocol to the Civil Liability Convention. Then in the title of Art. 12 of the 1974 Athens Convention the French equivalent of the words "Aggregation of claims" is "*Cumul d'actions*" and that of the words "the parties may agree that the claim for damages shall be submitted to any jurisdiction or to arbitration" in Art. 17(2) is "*les parties peuvent convenir de la juridiction ou du Tribunal arbitral auquel le litige sera soumis*". Lastly, the French equivalent of the words "The person against whom a claim is made" in Art. 20(4) of the Hamburg Rules and in Art. 25(3) of the 1980 Multimodal Transport Convention is "*La personne à qui la réclamation a été adressée*".

It appears, therefore, that there is a wide spectrum of meanings in the French language for the English word "claim": *créance, demande, action, droit* and *réclamation*.

In England, in *Mike Trading and Transport Ltd.* v. *R. Pagnan & Fratelli* [1980] 2 Lloyd's Rep. 546 (C.A.), Lord Denning M.R. stated (at p. 549):

> It seems to me that, by the maritime law of the world, the power of arrest should be, and is, available to a creditor—exercising it in good faith in respect of a maritime claim—wherever the ship is found – even though the merits of the dispute have to be decided by a court in another country or by an arbitration in another country.

22. *Shorter Oxford Dictionary*.

I.602 A very clear analysis of the burden of proof which lies on the claimant was made by the French Maritime Law Association in its report prior to the Naples Conference.[23]

I.603 It may be interesting to find out what the requirements are in the various Contracting States.

BELGIUM

I.604 Pursuant to Article 1415 CCP, a conservative arrest may only be granted if the claimant proves that his claim is certain, due and not challengeable. The Cour de Cassation with judgment of 26 March 1982[24] held that the credit must be "due, certain and quantifiable". The lower courts have, however, expressed a different view, holding that the "allegation" of a claim suffices.[25] It would appear, however, that the claimant must prove that the allegations made by him are serious and can resist—both as respects the basis of the claim and its amount—a *prima facie* examination by the Court.[26]

DENMARK

I.605 According to the Danish Administration of Justice Act arrest can be effected (1) if execution for the claim cannot be levied and (2) if it must be assumed that the possibilities of reimbursement at a later stage will otherwise be considerably reduced. It is further provided that arrest cannot be effected if it must be assumed that the claim does not exist.

I.606 The claimant is thus required to produce some limited evidence of his claim, *inter alia*, by way of invoices, charterparties, survey reports or otherwise the claimant is further required to substantiate that it would be detrimental to the recovery of the claim if the arrest were not effected. This latter provision is easily complied with, as in most cases the ship is the only asset available in Denmark, and, therefore, her departure would be detrimental to the recovery.

ENGLAND

I.607 There is no separate definition of claimant, but the claimant is not required to provide *prima facie* evidence of its claim, as such, because there is no formal hearing at

23. In that report, signed by Mr de Grandmaison (CMI Bulletin No. 105, pp. 26 and 27), the following statements are made:

> This article has a great importance, for, following a well-established international custom, the principal terms used in the Convention are herein defined.
> A. It is stated that the term "maritime claim" means the allegation of a right or of a claim arisen out of one or several of the causes subsequently enumerated.
> In fact, contrary to what happens in case of "*saisie-arrêt*" or "*saisie éxécution*", it is not necessary, in respect of conservative arrest, to rely on a judgment already obtained, nor on the certain existence of a right or of a claim in order to request to the competent Court the authorization for a conservative arrest.
> It is sufficient to pretend, i.e. to allege, a right or a claim, and it will be the task of the Court to state if such allegation appears serious and if it is reasonable, to give the arrestor the security that enables him to successfully enforce the future judgment he may obtain.
> Therefore, it is clear that the term "claim" in the Convention does not mean a claim established and justified, but rather an allegation, i.e. the claim made by a person who alleges to have a right or a claim.
> The English word "claimant" does not lend itself to any ambiguity. In French, the word "*créancier*" is employed in the Convention, but with this clarification, that it only means the allegation by the claimant of a right or a claim, the existence of which does not result either from a title or from a judgment.

24. Cited by Verstrepen, "Arrest and Judicial Sale of Ships in Belgium", [1995] L.M.C.L.Q. 131, at p. 138.

25. Verstrepen, "Arrest and Judicial Sale of Ships in Belgium", *supra*, note 24 at p. 137.

26. See the reply of the Belgian MLA to Question 3 of the Questionnaire, Appendix II, p. 235.

which such evidence is considered.[27] There is an "entitlement" to arrest, under paragraph 6.1 of Admiralty Practice Direction 49F, provided however, that the claimant follows a procedure in which its solicitor swears that certain information is believed to be true, i.e. it must swear to its allegations.[28] Under paragraph 6.2(3) of Admiralty Practice Direction 49F, the court has discretion to give permission to issue an arrest warrant even if all the particulars set out below are not provided.

I.608 According to paragraph 6.1 of Admiralty Practice Direction 49F, the claimant in a claim *in rem* is entitled to arrest the property proceeded against by filing the new Form ADM4 which contains an application to arrest and an undertaking. In this Form there is a personal undertaking by the applicant solicitor to pay the fees of the Admiralty Marshal and all his expenses connected with the arrest, including the care and custody of the vessel while under arrest. According to paragraph 6.3 of Admiralty Practice Direction 49F, when filling the application to arrest the claimant must file a declaration. The latter declaration, now in the new Form ADM5, must, according to paragraph 6.2(4)(a), state the nature of the claim, the fact that it has not been satisfied, the name and port of registry of the ship and the amount of security sought. The declaration must be sworn as an "affidavit", which is in effect what was previously required.

I.609 Amongst the information which is required in the declaration is the name of the ship, the amount of the security sought and whether the claim is against the ship in respect of which the claim arose or a sister ship. The declaration must say that the solicitor believes that a particular person would be liable *in personam* and set out the grounds for the belief. It must also state that the person liable had the appropriate connection with the ship, e.g. as shipowner or charterer, and set out the grounds for that belief. Similarly, the grounds for belief in the beneficial ownership of the ship should be set out.

I.610 If the arrest of a "sister ship" is sought then the declaration must state the name of the person who would be liable on the claim if it were commenced *in personam*, and that the latter was when the cause of action arose the owner or charterer of or in possession or in control of the ship in connection with which the claim arose, specifying which, and finally that at the time when the claim form was issued that person was either the beneficial owner of all the shares in the ship in respect of which the warrant is required or the charterer of it under a charter by demise.

FINLAND

I.611 The general provisions of the Code of Judicial Procedure on arrest apply also in respect of arrest of ships governed by the rules of Chapter 4 of the Maritime Code with which the Convention has been enacted into Finnish law.[29] The claimant must, therefore, provide a *prima facie* evidence of his claim[30] and that the owner of the property to be

---

27. It has been said by Professor Jackson (*Enforcement of Maritime Claims, supra,* para. I.197, note 62, p. 341) that arrest is largely an administrative, rather than a judicial, act.

28. Paragraph 6.1 of the Practice Direction so provides:
   Except as provided in this Practice Direction, the Claimant in a claim *in rem* and a judgment creditor in a claim *in rem* is entitled to have the property proceeded against arrested by the Admiralty Court by filing an application to arrest in Admiralty Form No. ADM4 (which shall also contain an undertaking) accompanied by a declaration in Admiralty Form No. ADM5 and an undertaking in Admiralty Form No. ADM6 upon which the Admiralty Court will issue an arrest warrant.

29. *Supra,* para. I.155.

30. The Finnish Supreme Court has placed considerable low demands on the claimant's burden of proof.

arrested hides, destroys or conveys the property or otherwise jeopardises the right of the claimant.[31] In respect of a ship, the fact that it is movable is considered as a *prima facie* evidence of such risk. No evidence, however, is required in respect of claims secured by a maritime lien.

FRANCE

I.612 Article 29 of the Decree of 27 October 1967, as amended by Decree of 24 February 1971, provides that the arrest of a ship may be granted when the claim appears *fondée dans son principe* (grounded in principle).[32] Such requirement, however, has been held not to apply when the arrest is subject to the Convention.[33]

GERMANY

I.613 Pursuant to section 920(2) ZPO, the claimant must prove that the claim probably exists: he need not provide full proof of his claim, but a persuasive evidence (*Glaubhaft-machung*). This requirement is, therefore, similar to that existing in other continental European countries. Pursuant to section 294(1) ZPO any type of evidence is permissible and this includes an affirmation made by the claimant in lieu of an oath.

GREECE

I.614 Under the general rules applicable to arrest of ships the claimant has the burden of providing a *prima facie* evidence of his claim, which clearly is something more than the simple "allegation" of such claim, and the danger that he may not subsequently be able to enforce it, if security is not obtained. It does not appear that so far Greek courts have been asked to decide whether these provisions apply also when the arrest is subject to the Convention. The view has been expressed, however, that some evidence of the claim is required.[34]

HAITI

I.615 It would appear that the claimant has the burden of providing some evidence of his claim. The interpretation of Article 1(4) of the Convention has not been tested.

31. Chapter 7, paragraph 1 of the Code of Judicial Procedure.
32. On the history of this provision see Rodière, *Droit Maritime—Le Navire* (Paris, 1980), p. 246; Poupard, "Note on the judgment of the Tribunal de Commerce of Noumea" [1980] DMF 228; Chauveau, "Retrospectives d'Actualité" [1972] DMF 3.
33. Cour de Cassation 26 May 1987, *Westcott France and Westcott Shipping* v. *Eduard Pommer—The "African Star"*, with a note by A. Vialard [1987] DMF 645; Tribunal Mixte de Commerce of Noumea, 17 November 1979, *Union Maritime du Pacifique Sud* v. *Fenland Ltd.—The "La Bonita")* [1980] DMF 223 with a note by Y. Poupard; Tribunal de Commerce of Bordeaux 28 July 1969, *Captain of the "Barranca Bermeja"* v. *Captain of the "Lady Laura"* [1970] DMF 111 with a note by J. Villeneau; Cour d'Appel of Rouen 2 April 1992, *Uni Europe Compagnie d'Assurance* v. *Sicula Oceanica—The "Repubblica di Amalfi"*, [1993] DMF 235; Cour de Cassation 3 February 1998, *Halic Denizcilik Ticaret Sanayi Turzim A.S.* v. *Banco Exterior Suiza—The "Yildiram"*, [1998] DMF 255; Cour de Cassation 19 March 1996, *Lemphy Maritime Enterprise* v. *Mohamed Zaatari & Bros.—The "Alexander III"*, [1996] DMF 503; Cour d'Appel of Aix-en-Provence 16 October 1996, *S.A. Annico Maritime* v. *Horti International—The "Enarxis"*, [1997] DMF 603; Rodière (*Droit Maritime—Le Navire* (Paris, 1980), p. 248) stated that under the Convention not even a *prima facie* evidence of the claim is required. This view, however, does not seem to be correct. The "*allégation d'un droit*", the fact that the claimant is the person who alleges that a maritime claim exists must, according to the Convention, be submitted to a court, for no arrest is permissible unless authorised by a court (Art. 4). This necessarily implies a control of the court on the claim.
34. See the detailed comments made by Prof. Antapassis in his replies to Question 3 on behalf of the Greek MLA, *infra*, p. 236.

ITALY

I.616 The interpretation of Article 1(4) of the Convention has never been the object of any decision. The general rule is that in order to obtain an order of arrest it is sufficient to provide a *prima facie* evidence of the claim which, with a Latin expression, is described as *"fumus boni juris"*.[35] Italian courts have applied this rule also in respect of arrest of ships governed by the Convention. The *prima facie* evidence relates both to the claims likely to be successful and, perhaps even more, to the amount. Italian courts generally request some evidence as to the amount of the claim in order to establish whether the amount for which the arrest should be granted, as indicated by the claimant, is reasonable or not. For example, in the case of a collision, the court will certainly not investigate the issue of liability, but will consider whether the damage suffered by the ship of the claimant approximately justifies the arrest of the colliding ship for the amount indicated by the claimant. There have, however, been cases in which an assessment has been made in respect of the liability of the defendant. For example, in the case of the *"Karlowicz"*,[36] the Tribunale of Genoa allowed the arrest of that ship as security for damages caused to another ship owing to the former ship having broken her moorings, on the ground that if the moorings are broken, it must be presumed that they are insufficient. Neither the parties nor the court, however, considered the provisions of the Arrest Convention, even though it was applicable.

THE NETHERLANDS

I.617 The claimant is not required to provide full evidence of his claim, but only the nature and amount of his claim. The court has a discretionary power to decide whether or not the information provided is sufficient.[37]

NIGERIA

I.618 There is no reported case in which the definition of "claimant" in Article 1(4) of the Convention has been considered nor is there such a definition in the Administration of

35. Tribunale of Genoa, 11 January 1994, *Rimorchiatori Riuniti Porto di Genova S.r.l.* v. *Morfini Trasporti Marittimi S.r.l.–The "Ninfea"*, unreported. See also Lopez de Gonzalo, "Indicazioni della giurisprudenza francese in relazione alla Convenzione di Bruxelles 1952 sul sequestro di navi" [1981] Dir Mar. 82; Mordiglia, "La Convenzione di Bruxelles 10 Maggio 1952 sul Sequestro Conservativo di Navi e la sua Recente Entrata in Vigore in Italia" [1981] Dir Mar. 133, at p.136.
36. [1996] Dir. Mar. 1059.
37. Article 700(2) of the Dutch Code of Civil Procedure so provides:
The leave shall be requested by means of a petition in which are stated the nature of the attachment to be effected and the grounds relied on by the petitioner and, if it is a monetary claim, the amount or, if the amount is not established, the maximum amount of the claim, without prejudice to the special requirements under the law in respect of the specific type of attachment concerned. The president judges after summary investigation. (. . .)
Article 705(2) of the Code of Civil Procedure provides:
1. The president who granted leave for the attachment may, acting in "kort geding" (référé), lift the attachment at the request of any interested party, without prejudice to the jurisdiction of the regular court.
2. The release shall be ordered i.e. in case of non-compliance with procedural requirements, if the invalidity of the grounds relied on by the attachor or the fact that the attachment was unnecessary is summarily shown, or, if the attachment is effected for a monetary claim, if sufficient security is put up for the claim. (. . .)
The specific statutory provisions relating to the arrest of ships do not provide for any special requirements in this respect.

Justice Act. Pursuant to Order VII, rule 1(2) of the Admiralty Jurisdiction Procedure Rules 1953, applicable to all cases of arrest of ships, the claimant is required, in the affidavit accompanying the application for the arrest of a ship, to disclose a "strong *prima facie* case".

NORWAY

I.619 The claimant is required to establish a *prima facie* case.

POLAND

I.620 The claimant must prove the "credibility" of his claim. He must, therefore, as in Italy, provide some evidence of the claim, but he is not required to satisfy the court that his claim will succeed. The evidence may consist of documents or of a statement of a third party.

PORTUGAL

I.621 As in Italy, the claimant has the burden of providing *prima facie* evidence of his claim (*fumus boni juris*) and such evidence is assessed by the court in its discretion. The evidence may be based on documents and on the depositions of witnesses.

SPAIN

I.622 The Law of 8 April 1967, No. 1 provides that in order to be entitled to the arrest of a ship, the allegation of the claim and of its nature suffices. From the *travaux préparatoires* of this law, it appears that the aforesaid provision was deemed to be in line with the definition of maritime claim in the Convention. Therefore, as in France, the burden of proof resting on the claimant is less onerous when the Convention applies than under the ordinary domestic rules.

SWEDEN

I.623 The definition of "claimant" has not been incorporated in the Swedish Maritime Code, nor have been incorporated in it the definitions of "arrest" and "person". Pursuant to chapter 15, section 1 of the Swedish Code of Civil Procedure, applicable to arrest of ships according to chapter 4, section 2 of the Maritime Code,[38] the claimant in order to arrest assets of his debtor must provide a *prima facie* evidence of his claim and this implies, as regards the arrest of a ship, that he has also to provide *prima facie* evidence of his claim being a maritime claim.[39]

38. Chapter 4, section 2 of the Maritime Code so provides (the text that follows is reproduced from the Swedish Maritime Code):
   What is provided in general for arrest of ships applies also to arrest according to this chapter unless anything to the contrary is provided in this chapter.
39. Chapter 15, section 1 of the Code of Civil Procedure so provides:
   If a person shows probable cause to believe that he has a money claim that is or can be made the basis of a judicial proceeding or determined by another similar procedure, and if it is reasonable to suspect that the opposing party, by absconding, removing property, or other action, will evade payment of the debt, the court may order the provisional attachment of so much of the opponents property that the claim may be assumed to be secured on execution.

29. PERSON ENTITLED TO ARREST

I.624 From Article 3(1) it appears that the person who may apply for the authority to arrest a ship is a claimant as defined in Article 1(4), viz. "a person who alleges that a maritime claim exists in his favour". All questions relating to the identification of the claimant are governed by the *lex fori*. They are in fact part of the "rules of procedure relating . . . to the application for obtaining the authority referred to in Art. 4" (viz. the authority to arrest a ship), which, pursuant to Article 6, are governed by the law of the Contracting State in which the arrest is made or applied for.

30. CONDITIONS FOR OBTAINING THE AUTHORITY

I.625 The question whether the domestic rules setting out the conditions to which the right of arrest is subject apply to arrest under the Convention was considered during the Naples Conference by the Greek Delegate. He enquired of the Conference whether, pursuant to Articles 1 and 3, the right to arrest a ship arises without the competent court assessing the existence of the conditions required for an arrest to be granted under its national law.[40] The Belgian Delegate pointed out that the question was solved by Article 4 according to which a ship could only be arrested under the authority of a court, and that implied that such court had the right to consider the request and to decide thereon.

I.626 Although this statement[41] seems to have met with the approval of the Conference, it is doubtful whether the conclusion may be drawn from Article 4 that all national rules relating to the conditions for the granting of an arrest continue to apply. In fact, as previously pointed out, the purpose of Article 4 seems to be confined only to the

---

40. The Greek delegate (Prof. Spiliopoulos) stated (CMI Bulletin No. 105, pp. 256 and 257):
> My question is the following: is it possible in respect of the claim mentioned under I to obtain the arrest of a ship without the Court appreciating the need for such a measure?
> The Italian Delegation, in fact, states that the code of civil procedure requires, in principle, that in order to obtain a conservative arrest, the claimant must prove that the condition of the debtor gives him the right to believe that he would lose his claim. It adds that, under the Convention legal regime, the claimant will not be required either to allege or to prove the existence of these supplementary conditions.
> I wanted to have an explanation on this point. Can this Convention give in all cases the right of arrest when there is a claim listed in Art. I; or instead, in order that the arrest be granted, is it necessary that the other procedural conditions as applied in most of the Continental States, should exist?
> I suggest to replace the words "may arrest this ship" with the words "may request the arrest of this ship".
> In such a case, there is no misunderstanding any more, and the arrest may only be made when the other conditions exist.

41. The Belgian delegate (Mr Lilar, who was at the time the President of the CMI but was not the President of the Conference) stated (CMI Bulletin No. 105, p. 257):
> The work of our Committee has indicated several times that the Convention could not in any event have as its object that of depriving a court of whatever country ordering a conservative arrest of the possibility of assessing the advisability of the arrest and of the merits of the claim submitted to it.
> These thoughts, that have been expressed very often and that answer the question of Mr. Spiliopoulos, are realized by Art. 4 of the Convention which provides: "A ship may only be arrested with the authority of a Court or other competent judicial authority of the Contracting State where the arrest is made".
> We shall thus be unanimous in stating that when we subordinate the arrest to the authority of a court that means that we give to that court the right to examine the request submitted to it and to decide on it.
> The whole Convention is inspired in this principle and, in such conditions, we think we can ask our colleague not to insist on his amendment since it is well settled that the decision to order the arrest is left to the appreciation of the Court.

requirement that no ship may be arrested unless with the consent of a court or other competent judicial authority. It neither directly nor by implication states that the court to which the arrest is applied for may apply the domestic rules. A distinction must in fact be drawn between the conditions for obtaining the arrest and the procedure relating to the arrest. While the procedure, as stated in the second paragraph of Article 6, is governed by the *lex fori*, the conditions for obtaining the arrest are set out in the Convention itself, and more precisely in Article 1(2), which gives the definition of arrest and in Article 2 which states that a ship flying the flag of a Contracting State may be arrested in respect of any maritime claim (but in respect of no other claim).

I.627 In countries in which a condition for granting the arrest of a ship is the danger of losing the security for the claim (so called "*periculum in mora*") and thus being unable to enforce a further judgment on the ship (or other assets of the debtor),[42] such as Italy, the Netherlands[43] and Portugal, courts have held that when the Convention applies this domestic rule does not operate.[44] This is probably due to the fact that the Convention has been given the force of law in such countries.

I.628 In other countries, where the Convention has not been given the force of law, a different conclusion may hold. For example, in Sweden, where reference is made in the Maritime Code to the Code of Civil Procedure,[45] pursuant to Section 1 of Chapter 15 of that code the claimant must prove that the debtor may evade payment.[46] While in other countries where the Convention has been given the force of law a similar provision[47] has been held to be superseded by the Convention, this is not the case in Sweden.[48]

31. ENFORCEMENT OF THE ARREST

I.629 Pursuant to the provisions of Article 6 the rules of procedure relating to the arrest are governed by the *lex fori*. The reference in that article to the law of the Contracting

---

42. This condition, reference to which is made as "*periculum in mora*" is set out, in Italy, in Article 671 of the Civil Procedure Code which provides as follows:

> The judge, on application of the creditor who has the grounded fear of losing the securities of his credit, can authorize the conservative arrest of movable or immovable assets of the debtor or of the sums or things due to him within the limits in which the law permits the seizure.

43. Although the requisite of the "*periculum in mora*" is generally provided by Article 711 of the Code of Civil Procedure, its existence is presumed in respect of ships. In the legislative history of that provision (for which the author is indebted to Mr. T. van der Valk) the following statement is made:

> The condition of "*periculum in mora*" as referred to in article 711 is not appropriate here as the great mobility of ships must lead to the assumption that such "*periculum in mora*" exists.

44. In Italy see Tribunale of Genoa 10 February 1995, *Industria Chimica Subalpina* v. *Navalbuo and Agenzia Marittima Gastaldi & C.—The "Bibor"*, [1997] Dir. Mar. 112; Tribunale of Naples 22 September 1995, *Mamidoil Jetoil Greek Petroleum Co.—The "Carlo R."*, [1997] Dir. Mar. 147; Tribunale of Genoa 25 January 1997, *North Sea Petroleum GmbH* v. *Duplex Maritime Co. S.r.l.—The "Dumbraveni"*, [1998] Dir. Mar. 1222; Tribunale of Savona 26 April 1999, *Egon Oldendorff* v. *Tor Shipping—The "Ocean Scorpio"* [1999] Dir. Mar. 1266. In Portugal see Supremo Tribunal de Justiça 21 May 1996, *Shell Portuguesa* v. *For Your Eyes Only Shipping Co.—The "Iron Horse"*, [1997] Dir. Mar. 260.

45. *Supra*, note 38.

46. See for the text of this provision *supra*, note 39.

47. For example, Article 671 of the Italian Code of Civil Procedure so provides:

> The Court, on application of the creditor who has a justified concern of losing the securities for his credit, may authorize the conservative arrest of movable or immovable assets of the debtor or of sums due to him within the limits within which seizure is permitted by law.

> An almost identical provision exists in Portuguese law: see Supremo Tribunal de Justiça 21 May 1996, *Shell Portuguesa* v. *For Your Eyes Only Shipping Co.—The "Iron Horse"*, [1997] Dir. Mar. 261.

48. See Swedish reply to Question 3 of the Questionnaire, Appendix II, p. 240.

State in which the arrest "was made or applied for" does not bring in two possible alternative laws. It is only the consequence of the fact that reference was previously made to the arrest and to the application for the arrest but, as previously stated,[49] the ship may only be arrested pursuant to an order of a court in whose jurisdiction the arrest is made.

I.630 Even though the rules of procedure, strictly speaking, are governed by the *lex fori*, the Convention may come into play in connection with the enforcement of an order for arrest if the situation covered by Article 3(3) occurs. The provision whereby a ship shall not be arrested more than once may operate both before the order for arrest is issued, in which event it should prevent it from being issued, or afterwards, before it is executed.

I.631 A claimant may, for example, apply for the arrest of a ship in respect of which a maritime claim has arisen to different courts in the same or in different States. Article 3(3) does not prevent him from doing so, provided he then arrests the ship only once. It follows that when the ship has been arrested pursuant to one of the orders the claimant has obtained, the other orders become ineffective and the competent judicial authority must, if the fact of the previous arrest of the ship for the same maritime claim has been brought to its knowledge, prevent the execution of the arrest.

32. DOMESTIC RULES

I.632 A summary follows of the rules relating to the application for and enforcement of an order for arrest in a number of maritime countries.

BELGIUM

I.633 The *Juge des Saisies* is competent, pursuant to Article 1395 CCP, in respect of the arrest of ships[50] but is not competent in respect of the merits, the decision on which must be referred to the Commercial Court.

I.634 A ship may, therefore, be arrested when it is within the jurisdiction of the *Juge des Saisies* ordering the arrest, even though the order may be issued prior to the arrival of the ship.[51] The general rule whereby conservative arrest is permissible when the claimant has obtained a judgment on the merits, without the need for any special subsequent order, has been deemed not to apply to ships, on the ground that the 1952 Convention expressly provides that arrest is permissible only under the authority of a court.[52]

I.635 The order of arrest is issued in *ex parte* proceedings. The owner of the ship may apply within one month of service of the order of arrest for such order to be set aside or varied and if this application fails, he may appeal against the decision to the Cour d'Appel.[53]

---

49. *Supra*, para. I.584.
50. See, on the procedure for the arrest of ships in Belgium, Verstrepen, "Arrest and Judicial Sale of Ships in Belgium", *supra*, note 24, pp. 133–135.
51. Verstrepen, "Arrest and Judicial Sale of Ships in Belgium", *supra*, note 24, p. 134, citing the decision of the Juge des Saisies of Antwerp, 4 May 1987, *The "Volta Wisdom"*.
52. Verstrepen, "Arrest and Judicial Sale of Ships in Belgium", *supra*, note 24, p. 134.
53. Verstrepen, "Arrest and Judicial Sale of Ships in Belgium", *supra*, note 24, pp. 134 and 141.

DENMARK

I.636 The process of arrest remains what it was before the entry into force of the Convention. The application for arrest must be addressed to the Bailiff's Court, whereupon the bailiff (1) decides whether the conditions for arrest are complied with and (2) determines the amount of the guarantee to be provided by the claimant. This guarantee must be issued to the bailiff by a Danish bank or insurance company as security for any claim for wrongful arrest or detention of the vessel.

I.637 The new Article 288 of the Maritime Code provides that the bailiff shall normally fix the security in an amount not exceeding five days' loss of hire for the ship. However, the bailiff is given discretion to decide that the security shall be increased as a condition for the arrest being maintained.

I.638 Rules additional to the Danish Administration of Justice Act (section 246(a)) have been enacted providing for Danish jurisdiction on the merits not only if the arrest is actually made, but also in cases where it would have been made in Denmark, had it not been prevented by the ship putting up security.

I.639 It should, however, be noted that in cases which do not involve an owner who is a national of a country which is a party to the EC Jurisdiction Convention, Denmark has retained the previous rules that Danish courts have jurisdiction, if a writ is filed with the Danish court at a time when the ship is in a Danish port. In such cases arrest of the ship is not necessary to establish jurisdiction, just as it is not necessary to serve the writ while the ship is in a Danish port. The writ should always be against the owner as defendant, not the ship.

I.640 According to the Administration of Justice Act, the claimant must either institute legal proceedings before the Danish courts within one week after the arrest claiming (1) payment of the amount for which the arrest was made and (2) that the arrest was lawfully made, or if the dispute on the merits has been referred to arbitration or the jurisdiction of a court outside Denmark, institute such arbitration or judicial proceedings within two weeks after the arrest was made. In the latter event, validation proceedings must also be brought in Denmark within two weeks after the arrest. These time limits apply irrespective of whether the arrest was actually made or whether it was prevented by the ship providing security.

I.641 If proceedings for recovery of the amount for which the arrest was made as well as validation proceedings are not brought within the time limits indicated above, the arrest automatically expires, and the ship is released.

ENGLAND

I.642 The procedure for arranging the arrest of a ship is laid down in the Practice Direction-Admiralty, which replaces Order 75 of the Rules of the Supreme Court.

I.643 Paragraph 6.1 of the Practice Direction provides that the claimant in a claim *in rem* is entitled to have the property proceeded against arrested by the Admiralty Court by filing an application to arrest accompanied by a declaration containing the particulars required in paragraph 6.2(4).[54] The arrest warrant is then issued by the Admiralty and Commercial Registry and the arrest is administered by the Admiralty Marshal.

---

54. See *supra*, s. 28, para. I.608.

I.644 Paragraph 6.2(3) provides that any party making an application for arrest must request a search to be made in the caveat book before the warrant is issued in order to ascertain whether there is a caveat in force with respect to the property to be arrested.[55]

I.645 Pursuant to paragraph 6.3(1) of the Practice Direction any person may file in the Admiralty and Commercial Registry a notice requesting a caveat against arrest, undertaking to file an acknowledgment of service and to give sufficient security to satisfy the claim with interest and costs, whereupon a caveat is entered in the caveat book. Although the undertaking to file an acknowledgment of service and to give security, if fulfilled, renders the arrest unnecessary, pursuant to paragraph 6.3(3) of the Practice Direction a ship may be arrested notwithstanding a caveat against arrest has been filed, but the Admiralty Court may, if it considers that it is appropriate to do so, order the arrest to be discharged and that the arrestor pay compensation to the owner of or other persons having an interest in the ship.

I.646 Arrest is effected by service on the ship of an arrest warrant in Admiralty Form No. ADM9 in the manner set out in paragraph 2.2.(a) of the Practice Direction in respect of service of an *in rem* claim[56] or, when it is not reasonably practicable to serve the warrant, by service of a notice of the issue of the warrant in that manner upon the ship or by giving notice to the master.[57]

FRANCE

I.647 The court competent for the arrest is the *Tribunal de Commerce* of the port where the ship lies or, if there is no *Tribunal de Commerce*, the *Juge d'Instance*[58] (Article 29 of the Decree of 27 October 1967, as amended by Decree of 24 February 1971).

I.648 When authorising the arrest, the court must fix the time by which the claimant must commence before the competent court proceedings for the validation of the arrest or for the merits, and failure to do so causes the nullity of the arrest. The order of arrest is notified to the master of the ship and to the port authority to prevent the ship from sailing (Article 26 of Decree 67–967 of 27 October 1967).[59]

GERMANY

I.649 The court in whose district the ship lies at the time of arrest is competent to order the arrest (paragraph 919 ZPO). The arrest is granted upon an application of the claimant wherein particulars of the claim are provided and the identity of the ship is specified. Pursuant to paragraph 917(1) ZPO the claimant has the burden of proving that the arrest is necessary in order to ensure the future enforcement of a judgment. The poor financial

---

55. Pursuant to paragraph 6.3(1) caveats must be entered in the caveat book and the records of all caveats are open for inspection, as provided in the Admiralty Practice Directions.

56. The basic way in which service must be effected is that set out in paragraph 2.2(a):
   Upon the property against which the claim *in rem* is brought by fixing the *in rem* claim form, or a copy of it, on the outside of the property proceeded against in a position which may reasonably be expected to be seen.

57. Paragraph 6.4(2) states that notice must be given "to those in charge of the property". It is assumed that normally the master shall be deemed to be the person in charge of the ship.

58. Rodière, *La Navire* (Paris, 1980), p. 246.

59. See du Pontavice, *Le Statut des Navires* (Paris, 1976), p. 328.

situation of the debtor or even the existence of bankruptcy proceedings is, however, not sufficient to establish this statutory requirement. The arrest is, therefore, a conservative measure and this character has not been altered by the enactment of the Convention.

I.650 In respect of foreign flag ships conclusive evidence that failure to arrest the ship of the debtor may adversely affect the possibility of enforcement of a future judgment is required by paragraph 917(2) ZPO. It is not settled whether or not the application of this provision is conditional on the existence of German jurisdiction on the merits. While the affirmative view has been held by the Court of Appeal of Hamburg,[60] the jurisdiction on the merits of the courts of a State party to the 1968 Jurisdiction Convention has been considered to be sufficient by the Court of Appeal of Dusseldorf.[61] The view has also been expressed that paragraph 917(2) ZPO should apply irrespective of which court has jurisdiction on the merits.[62] This view is correct under the Arrest Convention since Article 7(2) expressly refers to the case where the court which authorises the arrest is not competent for the merits.

I.651 Normally the arrest is granted in *ex parte* proceedings, without a hearing. The order of arrest is enforced by the court bailiff, who takes possession of the ship and adopts appropriate measures for her custody whilst under arrest. The arrest must be executed within one month from the date of the order and service of the order on the owner of the ship must be effected within one week from the execution of the arrest. The failure to observe the time limits entitles the owner of the ship to request that the arrest be set aside. Validation proceedings are not required, but the owner of the ship may, at any time, appeal against the order of arrest before the court which granted the order or, in certain circumstances, may apply for the arrest to be set aside. Furthermore, he may request the court to order the arrestor to commence proceedings for the merits of the claim within a specified time limit, failing which the arrest ceases to have effect.

GREECE

I.652 In order to obtain a court decision for the arrest of the ship, the claimant must satisfy the court on a *prima facie* evidence basis that: (a) he has a good (maritime) claim and (b) there is a need for security and, unless security is granted, the enforcement of an ultimate court decision or arbitration award in favour of the claimant will be impossible or very difficult. Grounds justifying the need for security may be the imminent departure of the ship from the port (coupled with difficulties of relocation), the distinct possibility of sale, sinking or encumbering the ship with mortgages or maritime liens, all of which are relatively easily accepted by the courts in respect of a single-vessel company and companies not based in Greece.

I.653 This evidence is usually produced on two occasions: first, at the time of filing the petition of arrest (when the petitioner seeks a provisional *ex parte* arrest order valid up to the hearing of the arrest petition) and, secondly, at the hearing of the petition (when the defendant has been properly summoned), when the arrest is confirmed or the provisional order lifted.

60. OLG Hamburg, 1 December 1984 [1990] TransportR 112.
61. OLG Dusseldorf, 18 May 1977 [1977] N.J.W. 2034.
62. Grunsky, in Stein-Jonas, *Zivilprozessordnung* (20th ed., 1988), sub-para. 917, Ammerkung 17. For a summary of the various views, see Looks, "Die Arrestierung eines ausländisches Seeschiffes" [1989] Trans-portR 345.

I.654 Pursuant to Article 715 of the Code of Civil Procedure the proceedings on the merits must be initiated within 30 days of the arrest, failing which the arrest is lifted automatically. If the arrest has been replaced by guarantee there is no time limit fixed in law for initiating the proceedings. The court may, however, fix such time limit in accordance with Article 693 of the Code of Civil Procedure. These provisions apply whether the jurisdiction for the merits lies with the same court which ordered the arrest or with any other court or arbitration.

I.655 Both in the case of Articles 715 (time limit fixed in the law) and 693 the law provides for the automatic release of the arrest or the guarantee upon the lapse of the prescribed time limit but in practice a petition is submitted to the court for obtaining an order of release, to be submitted to the port authority for the release of the ship or to the court clerk for the release of the guarantee.

ITALY

I.656 The procedural rules relating to the arrest of a ship are set out in the Code of Navigation, Articles 682–686 and in the Code of Civil Procedure, Articles 669 *bis*–669 *quatuordecies* and 671–687. The court competent for the arrest is the court competent for the decision of the merits of the case, except where the Italian courts have no jurisdiction on the merits or the dispute has to be submitted to arbitration. In such cases, the court competent for the arrest is that of the place where the ship lies (Article 669*ter* CCP). This latter provision has been construed so to make the presence of the ship in the port a condition for the granting of the arrest, with the consequence that the arrest cannot be authorised until the ship has arrived, thus sometimes making the arrest very difficult, given the short period of stay in port of the ships.[63]

I.657 As an ordinary rule, the arrest is granted (or denied) at a hearing. However, it may be granted *ex parte*, if the prior notice to the other party (i.e. the owner of the vessel) may prejudice its enforcement. In such a case, however, a hearing must be fixed by the court within 15 days, when the court will either affirm or revoke the order of arrest (Article 669*novies* CCP).

I.658 The arrest is enforced by means of service on the owner and the master of the ship.[64] If the arrest is granted in respect of a claim secured by a maritime lien against a person other than the owner of the ship, service of the arrest must be made on both the debtor and the owner of the ship (Article 683 CN). Arrest of a ship (of Italian nationality) in the course of navigation is possible, if expressly authorised by the court, by means of a radiogram (Article 683 CN).

I.659 By the warrant of arrest the master is enjoined not to leave the port where the ship lies at the time of arrest or the port where she is destined if at the time of arrest the ship is in the course of navigation (Article 682 CN).

63. Tribunale of Genoa, 20 May 1995, *Übersee-Schiffahrtsagentur Transnautic G.m.b.H. & Co.* v. *Baltic Shipping Co.* [1995] Dir. Mar. 768. The practical difficulties that this requirement may create have been underlined by G. Berlingieri, "Sequestro di Nave: problemi pratici e loro possibili soluzioni" [1995] Dir. Mar. 771. The need for the ship to be in port when the court orders the arrest has been denied by F. Berlingieri, "Considerazioni in margine al problema della competenza per la concessione del sequestro conservativo" [1978] Dir. Mar. 649, who is of the view that the ship must be in port only when the arrest is made. This is in line with Art. 4 of the Convention.

64. The Tribunale of Taranto in its judgment 6 May 1994 in *Bulk Oil International Chartering Ltd.* v. *Baltic Current Inc.* [1995] Dir. Mar. 759 held that the order of arrest, service of which is made only to the master, is a nullity.

I.660 If it is expected that some time will be required before the warrant of arrest is issued or before its service is effected, it is possible to obtain a provisional order of detention of the ship (Article 646 CN).

I.661 The order of arrest must, after service, be endorsed on the ships register where the ship is registered and on the certificate of registry (Article 684 CN). The endorsement has the effect of rendering the arrest valid against any third party acquiring an interest in the ship and endorsing such interest on the ships register after the endorsement of the arrest.

I.662 Service of the arrest must be effected within 30 days from the date of issue of the warrant, failing which the warrant ceases to be effective (Article 675 CCP). After the arrest is made, proceedings on the merits must be commenced within the time limit fixed by the court. Such time limit may not exceed 30 days. If the arrestor fails to bring such proceedings in time, the court shall, upon application of an interested party, declare the arrest ineffective (Article 669*octies* CCP).

I.663 The arrest also becomes ineffective if the claim in respect of which the arrest has been granted is rejected by a judgment not subject to further appeal or if the security for damages in case of wrongful arrest that has been ordered by the court has not been provided within the prescribed time limit (Article 669*novies* CCP).

THE NETHERLANDS

I.664 The arrest is granted by the president of the district court (Arrondissementsrechtsbank) of the place where the ship lies. The arrest is executed by the bailiff by means of service of the petition and of the order of arrest on the master. The bailiff also informs the port authority that the ship, following the arrest, may not leave the port.

I.665 Proceedings for the validation of the arrest must be commenced by the arrestor before the court by which the arrest was granted within eight days from the arrest. If, however, a different court in the Netherlands is competent to decide upon the merits of the case, validation proceedings must also be brought before such court.

I.666 Except where otherwise provided by an international convention, such as the EC Jurisdiction Convention, the court which granted the arrest also has jurisdiction to decide the case upon its merits (Article 767 CCP). In such a case, proceedings on the merits must be brought within eight days from the arrest and are normally brought together with validation proceedings. If a foreign court or an arbitral tribunal has jurisdiction on the merits, proceedings must be brought before such court within a "reasonable time". In view of the uncertainty of what may be deemed a "reasonable time", in the circumstances of each case, proceedings are normally brought within the eight-day period even when a foreign court has jurisdiction on the merits.

I.667 The time limit may be extended by agreement of the parties.[65] When validation proceedings and proceedings on the merits are not brought within the prescribed (or agreed) time limit, the defendant may apply for the release of the ship or of the security, and such application is normally granted by the court. The ship may also be released, or the security returned, following a decision of the president of the district court that granted the arrest, where it is found that the conditions for the arrest did not exist (Articles 298 and 731 CCP).

65. Judgment of the Supreme Court (Hoge Raad), 16 October 1981, [1983] N.J. 778.

PORTUGAL

I.668 The procedural rules relating to the arrest of ships are set out in the Code of Civil Procedure and in the Civil Code. The court competent for the arrest of a ship is that in whose district such ship lies. Pursuant to Law of 4 September 1986, No. 35, which reinstated the maritime courts in Portugal, there will be five maritime courts (Lisbon, Leixoes, Faro, Funchal and Ponta Delgada), but so far only the Lisbon Maritime Court has been reinstated and, therefore, outside its jurisdiction the competent court is that of the port where the ship lies. In addition, pursuant to Article 83, No. 1(a), CCP, the court competent to decide upon the merits of the case is also competent for the arrest of the ship.[66] If the arrest is applied for after proceedings to determine the case upon its merits are commenced, the competent court is that before which such proceedings are pending.

I.669 The petition for arrest must be accompanied by documentary evidence of the conditions required for an arrest. Such conditions are, in addition to *prima facie* evidence of the claim, the danger that, at the time of enforcement of the judgment obtained against the debtor, there may no longer be assets available (*periculum in mora*) or there may be no assets in Portugal of the debtor other than the ship the arrest of which is applied for (Article 691(1) CC and Article 403(5) CCP). The fact that there are no other assets of the debtor in Portugal constitutes conclusive evidence of the danger of being unable to enforce a future judgment. These conditions also apply in the case of arrest as security for a maritime claim under the Convention.

I.670 Portuguese courts are competent in respect of the arrest of any ship lying in Portuguese territorial waters, whether or not they have jurisdiction on the merits. After the arrest, a custodian is appointed by the court.

I.671 Proceedings on the merits of the claim must be brought against the debtor, before the competent court, within 30 days of the arrest. When the court having jurisdiction on the merits is a foreign court, the claimant must provide the Portuguese court that has ordered the arrest with evidence that proceedings before the foreign court have been commenced within the 30–day period (Article 382(1)(a) CCP). When proceedings on the merits are not brought in time, the ship is released from arrest. The ship is also released if proceedings are stayed for over 30 days due to the failure of the claimant, with gross negligence, to take any action that may be required by law.

I.672 The owner of the ship may obtain her release from arrest by offering security. To this effect, he must apply to the court indicating the amount and the type of security he is offering, and notice of the application is given to the arrestor. If no objections are raised by him, the court orders the release of the ship against the security offered by the owner. In case of disagreement, the court decides whether or not the security offered is satisfactory. The usual type of security is a bank guarantee issued by a local bank.

SPAIN

I.673 When the arrest is applied for before proceedings on the merits are commenced, the court competent for the arrest is the *Juez de Primera Instancia* of the place where the ship lies. If the arrest is applied for concurrently with or after proceedings on the merits are

---

66. Judgment of the Supreme Court (Supremo Tribunal de Justica), 22 November 1985, 351 B.M.J. 318.

commenced, the court competent for the arrest is that before which the proceedings are pending, whereupon that court will request the court of the place where the ship lies to execute the arrest. This method is also adopted when the ship does not call at the port where the arrest was applied for and the order for arrest was issued.

I.674 When granting the arrest, the court usually fixes the time (from one to three months) within which proceedings to determine the case upon its merits must be commenced. If no time limit is fixed by the court, proceedings must be commenced within 20 days of the arrest.

I.675 The arrest is granted *ex parte* and the court requires the claimant to put up security, as a condition for the enforcement of the order. The amount of the security for wrongful arrest is left to the discretion of the court.

I.676 The order for arrest is vacated, upon application of the interested party (normally the owner of the ship), if the conditions for arrest do not exist (e.g. the claim is not a maritime claim), if proceedings on the merits are not commenced within the prescribed time limit, if the ship was not arrestable under Article 3 of the Arrest Convention, or if the claim is rejected.

SWEDEN

I.677 In Sweden, the court has full jurisdiction to determine the case upon its merits when the vessel is physically within Swedish territory, unless the dispute arises out of a contract providing for arbitration or a foreign jurisdiction. In such a case, according to Swedish law, the court shall fix a time limit of one month within which the claimant shall bring an action on the merits before the court.

33. RELEASE OF THE SHIP FROM ARREST

I.678 Three situations in which a ship which has been arrested must be released from arrest are considered in Article 3(3) of the Convention: (a) where a ship had already been arrested in respect of the same maritime claim (b) where the owner has furnished security and (c) where the claimant has not brought proceedings within the time limit fixed by the court. A further situation, (d), in which the ship must be released from arrest is considered by the 1957 Limitation Convention, by the 1976 LLMC Convention and by the 1969 Civil Liability Convention when the ship owner has constituted the limitation fund.

(a) Release of a Ship from Subsequent Arrest

I.679 The courts of Contracting States must release the ship if one of the situations mentioned in Article 3(3) occurs.[67] In order to invoke the protection of Article 3(3) the owner of the ship has the burden of proving that, prior to the arrest of the ship, that ship or another ship owned by him (or by the person from whom he has chartered the ship in the situation mentioned in Article 3(4)) had been arrested and security had been provided in respect of the same maritime claim by the same claimant. In order to prevent the release, the claimant has the burden of proving that the security given had been released,

---

67. *Supra*, para. I.545–I.573.

or that there was, to the satisfaction of the court, other good reason for maintaining the arrest.

(b) Release after Provision of Security

I.680 The general rule laid down by Article 5 is that the court or other judicial authority within whose jurisdiction the ship has been arrested must permit the release of the ship "upon sufficient bail or other security being furnished".

I.681 The authority which is required to release the ship is "the court or other appropriate judicial authority within whose jurisdiction the ship has been arrested". Since Article 4 provides that a ship may only be arrested under the authority of a court or of the (which is, as has been seen, equivalent to "other") appropriate judicial authority of the Contracting State in which the arrest is made, the question arises whether the reference in Article 5 to the "Court . . . within whose jurisdiction the ship has been arrested" and not to the court etc. by which the arrest is authorised was made intentionally, in order to differentiate between the two descriptions of the competent court. A difference in fact may exist, because the court (or other appropriate judicial authority) authorising the arrest may not necessarily be the same as that within whose district the ship is then arrested. For example, in Italian law the court competent to authorise the arrest is that which is competent to decide on the merits of the case and the vessel may then be arrested in the district of another Italian court: in such a case the vessel may only be released by an order of the former court. It must be noted that in Article 5 "jurisdiction" is used in order to identify, not the territory of a State, but that over which the jurisdictional power of a specific court is extended. This is made clear by the use in the French text of Article 5 of the word *ressort*.[68]

I.682 It is felt, however, that the obligation laid down in Article 5 on a specific court must apply by analogy to any other court of the same State which is competent for the release of the ship.

I.683 Three questions require consideration as respects the provision of the security: (i) the nature of the security (ii) the amount of the security, and (iii) the conditions upon which the security may be enforced by the claimants.

(i) Nature of the Security

I.684 Article 5 indicates two alternatives, viz. bail or "other security". Bail (the word used in the French text is *caution*) is a payment into court or in the manner directed by the court of a sum of money. Security other than bail may consist of a guarantee by a bank or other guarantor such as a P & I Club. As is known, letters of undertaking of P & I Clubs are often accepted by claimants and by Courts.

(ii) Amount of the Security

I.685 According to Article 5 the bail or other security must be "sufficient". Who can decide this is stated in the subsequent paragraph of this article which provides:

---

68. *Ressort* means the area subject to the cognisance of a specific court in one country.

In default of agreement between the parties as to the sufficiency of the bail or other security, the Court or other appropriate judicial authority shall determine the nature and amount thereof.

I.686 The court therefore has power to determine, in case of disagreement, in addition to the nature, e.g. bail or other type of security, the amount of the security.

(iii) The Conditions for Payment under the Security

I.687 When the security is in the form of a bank guarantee or of a letter of undertaking of a P & I Club, the conditions under which the claimant can obtain payment are usually stated in the document. As a rule, the guarantee or letter of undertaking provides that the guarantor shall pay within a specified maximum limit the sum awarded to the claimant by a judgment or an arbitration award. It also provides that the judgment must be delivered by a court having jurisdiction on the case and that the judgment must be final, or enforceable or, also, not subject to further appeal. In this respect the question may arise whether the owner of the ship is entitled to obtain the release of the ship against a guarantee under which payment may be obtained only against a judgment not subject to further appeal. That would, of course, substantially delay payment. While, in fact, in order to obtain a judgment not subject to further appeal, it may be necessary to wait for a decision of the Supreme Court, or, in civil law countries, even of the Court of Appeal to which the case is referred back by the Supreme Court, an enforceable judgment may be a judgment of a court of first instance. The same problem may arise in respect of an arbitration award, which as a rule is enforceable, but is subject to appeal, even if within certain limits.

I.688 Since the guarantee replaces the ship as a security for the satisfaction of the claim, the correct solution of the problem seems to be that the guarantee must provide payment in the same situation in which the claim could have been enforced on the ship. If, as normally is the case, a claim may be enforced on the basis of an unforceable judgment even if subject to further appeal, the guarantee should contain a corresponding provision. This principle, which has been held in France by the Cour d'Appel of Rouen[69] and by the Cour d'Appel of Saint-Denis de la Réunion,[70] has been approved by the Cour de Cassation.[71]

I.689 If the Court within whose jurisdiction the ship was arrested has no jurisdiction to decide upon the merits, the bail or other security given in accordance with Article 5 to procure the release of the ship shall specifically provide that it is given as security for the satisfaction of any judgment which may eventually be given by a court having jurisdiction so to decide.

I.690 It is not clear from the wording of this rule whether the judgment of the court having jurisdiction on the merits entitles the claimant to payment, without any need for its recognition and enforcement in the jurisdiction of the court where the bail or other security is provided, or whether such recognition and enforcement are required. The fact that it was

---

69. Judgment of 22 June 1994, *Société Soufflet Negoce* v. *Petromin Shipping* [1995] DMF 465, annotated by Tassel.

70. Judgment of 17 October 1995, *Union Réunionnaise des Cooperatives Agricoles* v. *Dancing Shipping Co.—The "Dancing Sister"*, [1996] DMF 494.

71. Judgment of 27 October 1998, affirming the judgment of the Cour d'Appel of Saint-Denis de la Réunion, *supra* note 70, [1999] DMF 51. See also the judgment of the Cour de Cassation of 12 November 1996, *Chapel* v. *Port Autonome de Nantes-Saint Nazaire—The "Sandal"*, [1997] DMF 43.

deemed necessary to insert this rule into the Convention seems to support the first solution, since otherwise a provision in the Convention would not have been necessary. However, Article 7(2) has not been so construed in England, where section 26 of the Civil Jurisdiction and Judgments Act 1982 requires that the foreign judgment or arbitration award be enforceable in England and Wales.[72] This construction is probably the correct one, since the fact that the foreign judgment has been delivered by a court having jurisdiction cannot be established only on the basis of such judgment but, according to ordinary international practice, must be verified by the court within whose jurisdiction the ship has been arrested and security has been provided. Moreover, this is certainly the correct solution where the ship has not been released, and the judgment of the court having jurisdiction on the merits must be enforced against the ship, for it is certain that in such case the ordinary domestic rules on the enforcement of foreign judgments and foreign arbitration awards must apply.

I.691 The rule laid down in Article 7(2) does not directly apply to the situation regulated by paragraph (3) of that article, where the court within whose jurisdiction the arrest is made has no jurisdiction on the merits because the parties have chosen a particular court for the resolution of the dispute or have stipulated an arbitration clause or an arbitration agreement. There seems, however, to be no justification for a different regime governing such case and, therefore, the rule laid down in paragraph (2) should apply. It follows that in all situations where the court within whose jurisdiction the ship is arrested has no jurisdiction on the merits, the bond or other security given to procure the release of the ship must contain the provisions set out in Article 7(2).

National Rules on the Provision of Security

I.692 A summary of the rules regarding the provision of security in a number of maritime countries may be of interest.

---

72. Section 26 of the Civil Jurisdiction and Judgments Act 1982, which came into force on 1 November 1984, as stated by Sheen J. in *The "World Star"* [1986] 2 Lloyd's Rep. 274 at p. 275, provides in its relevant part:

> Where in England and Wales or Northern Ireland a Court stays or dismisses Admiralty proceedings on the ground that the dispute in question should be submitted to arbitration or to the determination of the Court of another part of the United Kingdom or of an overseas country, the Court may, if in those proceedings property has been arrested or bail or other security has been given to prevent or obtain release from arrest:
> (a) order that the property arrested be retained as security for the satisfaction of any award or judgment which—(i) is given in respect of the dispute in the arbitration or legal proceedings in favour of which those proceedings are stayed or dismissed; and (ii) is enforceable in England and Wales or, as the case may be, in Northern Ireland; or
> (b) order that the stay or dismissal of those proceedings be conditional on the provision of equivalent security for the satisfaction of any such award or judgment.

The origin and purpose of this section were so explained by Sheen J. in *The "Sylt"* [1991] 1 Lloyd's Rep. 240 at p. 242:

> Section 26 had its origin in art. 7(2) of the International Convention relating to the Arrest of Seagoing Ships 1952, which deals with the situation which arises when the Court, within whose jurisdiction a ship has been arrested, has no jurisdiction to determine the case upon its merits. Section 26 was intended to make provision and does make provision for the case in which, after a plaintiff has issued a writ *in rem* and arrested the ship, the owners or other persons interested in that ship successfully apply for a stay of proceedings on the ground (a) that the parties have agreed to submit the dispute to arbitration or (b) that the dispute should be submitted to the determination of the Courts of another country.

BELGIUM

I.693 The provisions of the Arrest Convention apply. If the parties do not reach an agreement on the amount of the security, the security is fixed by the *Juge des Saisies* on the basis of the amount of the claim, plus interest and costs. The global amount of interest and costs is normally determined with reference to the capital amount of the claim and varies between 20 and 30 per cent thereof.[73]

I.694 The security may consist in a bank guarantee, in a guarantee of a first-class insurance company, or in a letter of undertaking of a P & I Club,[74] provided such undertaking is accepted by the claimant.[75]

DENMARK

I.695 The arrest must be lifted and the ship released if sufficient bail or security is offered by the owner of the ship or the debtor.

I.696 The security offered must be sufficient to cover the amount claimed, interest already due as well as interest for the expected duration of the proceedings and finally probable costs incurred or to be incurred in respect of the arrest, the validation proceedings and the legal proceedings for the recovery of the amount, for which the arrest was made.

I.697 In default of agreement between the parties as to the sufficiency of the guarantee, the bailiff decides the amount of the guarantee. Foreign guarantees may not be accepted if the claimant insists on a Danish guarantee.

I.698 The Danish courts have jurisdiction on the merits when they have granted the arrest or the arrest has been prevented by the ship putting up security, unless the matter has been referred to arbitration or the jurisdiction of a foreign court, either in the contract or by subsequent agreement between the parties. The validation proceedings must always be brought in Denmark.

I.699 When Danish courts have no jurisdiction to try the merits, they do comply with the provisions of Article 7(2) and (3). In these cases, proceedings brought before the particular court or arbitration must be instituted within two weeks after the arrest was made, and validation proceedings must further be instituted before the court in the jurisdiction of which the arrest was made within the same two-week period.

I.700 The security given in order to secure the release of the ship must further specifically provide that it is given as security for the satisfaction of the judgment or arbitration award as well as interest and the costs of arrest and the validation proceedings.

ENGLAND

I.701 RSC, Order 75, rule 16 laid down detailed rules as to bail bonds, but it appears that the bail bond has been abolished in the Civil Procedure Rules (CPR). A bail bond was a promise to pay which was usually backed by the security of a guarantor. Ultimately, the amount and form of security may now be for the court, see paragraph 6.7(2) of Admiralty

---

73. Verstrepen, "Arrest and Judicial Sale of Ships in Belgium", *supra*, note 24, p. 149.
74. Verstrepen, "Arrest and Judicial Sale of Ships in Belgium", *supra*, note 24, p. 149.
75. See the reply of the Belgian MLA to Question 8 of the Questionnaire, Appendix II, p. 263.

Practice Direction 49F. There seems to be some doubt as to the extent of the court's powers under the CPR as to the type of security, as paragraph 6.7(3) refers expressly only to the power to reduce the amount of security, but it appears to be for the court to be satisfied as to the sufficiency and acceptability of the surety.[76] Under paragraph 12 there is power for agreements between solicitors to become orders of the court. All three types of security have been used in order to obtain release of the ship from arrest, but it will normally be for the claimant in the first instance to agree the form of security.[77]

FINLAND

I.702 The type and amount of security is decided by the bailiff. Normally a cash deposit or a bank guarantee is requested but also a letter of undertaking of a P & I Club may be accepted.

FRANCE

I.703 The President of the *Tribunal de Grande Instance* is competent for the release of the ship if the arrest was granted by the *Juge d'Instance*, or the President of the *Tribunal de Commerce* if the arrest was granted by him.[78] The release may be granted if a sufficient guarantee[79] is provided. As previously stated,[80] the French Cour de Cassation held that the guarantee should state that payment thereunder shall be made upon delivery of an enforceable judgment, albeit not definitive (i.e. subject to further appeal).[81] If the parties do not agree, the type of guarantee is decided discretionally by the Court.

GERMANY

I.704 Pursuant to paragraph 923 ZPO, when ordering an arrest, the court will fix the amount of security to be provided in order to obtain the release of the ship from arrest. As a general rule the amount of the security is equal to the amount of the claim plus costs. It is not clear if this is also so when the value of the ship is less than the amount of the claim, but it is thought that the only way for the owner to avoid putting up a guarantee equal to the claim is to commence limitation proceedings in accordance with the provisions of the 1976 Convention on Limitation of Maritime Claims, which is in force in Germany, and to set up a limitation fund, whereupon the ship is released, pursuant to Article 13(2) of the Convention. When security is provided, the ship is released (paragraph 934 ZPO).

I.705 The choice of the type of security is left to the discretion of the court but, as a rule, a bank guarantee from a first class bank is required.

---

76. Jackson, *Enforcement of Maritime Claims, supra*, note 27, p. 343.
77. This summary is based on the reply of the BMLA to Question 8 of the Questionnaire, Appendix II, p. 266.
78. See du Pontavice, *Le Statut des Navires* (Paris, 1976), p. 346.
79. See du Pontavice, *Le Statut des Navires* (Paris, 1976), p. 346. The Cour d'Appel of Montpellier in its judgment of 9 January 1992 in *Société Mekatrade* v. *Partederiet Borge Moller—The "Vicky"* [1992] DMF 383 held that a letter of undertaking of a P & I Club enforceable within the European Union was sufficient security.
80. *Supra*, para. I.688.
81. A case where the guarantee provided for payment following an enforceable judgment had been considered by the Cour d'Appel of Rouen in its judgment of 11 March 1993 in *ATT and Others* v. *Marmaras Navigation* [1993] DMF 365.

GREECE

I.706 If the nature and amount of the security is not directly agreed by the parties, pursuant to Article 162 of the Code of Civil Procedure the Court has a discretion to determine both the nature and the amount. The security may consist of cash, of government bonds or similar negotiable instruments, of a guarantee issued by a bank or an insurance company, by a letter of undertaking of a P & I Club, provided, in such latter case, there is the agreement of the claimant. In case of a bank guarantee, it is normally required that the bank be an institution operating in Greece. The cash deposit as well as the deposit of bonds, must be made at the Public Deposits and Loans Fund and the deposit receipt must be produced in court in order to obtain the release of the vessel. In case the security consists in a bank or similar personal guarantee, the document must be produced in court.[82]

HAITI

I.707 In order to obtain the release of a ship from arrest either a cash deposit or a bank guarantee is required. A letter of undertaking of a P & I Club is not acceptable.

ITALY

I.708 Pursuant to Article 684 CCP the person liable in respect of the claim for which property has been arrested may obtain from the court the release of the property from arrest by providing suitable security for the amount of the claim and the costs, within the limit of the value of the property arrested. Pursuant to Article 86 of the Implementation Rules (*Norme di Attuazione*), unless otherwise provided by Article 119 CCP security must be provided in cash in the manner prescribed for judicial deposits. Article 119 CCP states that the court, when ordering that security be provided, must indicate what the subject matter of the security must be, the manner in which and the time within which it must be provided.

I.709 Therefore the court has a relevant degree of discretion. In practice payment into court or into a bank and delivery into court of a savings book are not frequent. In most cases, when the parties do not agree among themselves on the manner in which security must be provided, the court prescribes a bank guarantee and sometimes even allows the person liable to provide an undertaking from a P & I Club.

NETHERLANDS

I.710 The ship must be released from arrest if security by way of a guarantee from a first class bank in the Netherlands is provided. The claimant is not required to accept security from a foreign bank, or from a P & I Club, though, in practice, a letter of undertaking from a P & I Club which is a member of the International Group is normally accepted.

NIGERIA

I.711 In addition to a cash deposit or a bank guarantee, a letter of undertaking of a P&I Club is normally accepted.

---

82. This summary is based on the reply of the Greek MLA to Question 8 of the Questionnaire, Appendix II, p. 264.

NORWAY

I.712 Pursuant to the Enforcement Act the release of a ship from arrest is permissible against a cash deposit in a Norwegian bank from which money can be withdrawn only pursuant to an order of the court, or a guarantee of a Norwegian bank. A letter of undertaking of a P & I Club requires to be accepted by the claimant.

POLAND

I.713 A ship may be released from arrest against payment into court of a sum of money sufficient to secure the settlement of the claim of the arrestor or provision of security in the form required by the court, such as a bank guarantee or a letter of undertaking from a P & I Club.

PORTUGAL

I.714 The ship is released from arrest if security by way of a guarantee from a first class bank in Portugal is provided. The claimant is not obliged to accept a guarantee from a foreign bank, or a letter of undertaking from a P & I Club.

SPAIN

I.715 The ship is released from arrest, pursuant to an order of the court by which the arrest was granted, when security for the amount for which the arrest was granted is provided. Security can take the form of a payment into court of the amount required, of a bank guarantee or of a guarantee issued by an insurance company established in Spain. Any other type of security such as a letter of undertaking of a P & I Club needs to be accepted by the arrestor.

SWEDEN

I.716 The ship must immediately be released when sufficient security has been furnished in a satisfactory form.

(c) Failure to bring Proceedings on the Merits within the Time Limit fixed by the Court

I.717 Article 7(2) provides that, if the court within whose jurisdiction the ship was arrested has no jurisdiction to decide upon the merits, such court shall fix the time within which the claimant must bring an action before a court having jurisdiction. A similar provision is made in Article 7(3) for the case where the parties have agreed to submit the dispute to the jurisdiction of a particular court other than that within the jurisdiction of which the arrest was made or to arbitration.

I.718 Paragraph (4) of Article 7 then provides that if the action or proceedings on the merits are not brought within the time so fixed, the defendant may apply for the release of the ship or of the bail or other security.

I.719 In the draft prepared by the International Sub-Committee in 1951, attention was focused on the need to protect the claimant where the court within whose jurisdiction the ship is arrested has no jurisdiction to decide upon the merits of the case. Article 8 of the draft, after having enumerated the situations in which the court within whose jurisdiction the arrest is made has jurisdiction on the merits, considered separately the case where the ship is released against bail or other security, on the one hand, and where the ship remains under arrest, on the other. In the former case the court could not allow the release unless the bail or other security provided that it was established for the amount that might be found to be due by the court having jurisdiction on the merits. In the latter case the judgment on the merits should be directly enforceable against the ship.[83]

I.720 Article 8 then separately covered the situation where the parties agreed to submit the dispute to a jurisdiction of their choice or to arbitration and stated that in such case the arrest would continue to be valid, but the court within whose jurisdiction the ship was arrested should fix the time within which the claimant had to bring an action before the court whose jurisdiction had been agreed or had to commence arbitration proceedings.[84]

I.721 In the report accompanying the draft it was explained that the provision on the enforcement of foreign judgments had been inserted as a consequence of the modification of the rule, originally adopted, whereby the court within whose jurisdiction the ship is arrested always has jurisdiction to decide on the merits of the case. It was added, however, that that provision was perhaps beyond the scope of the Convention and might not be accepted by several countries.[85]

I.722 The French association suggested that in the last paragraph it should be provided that, if the claimant failed to bring an action or to institute proceedings within the time fixed, the court within whose jurisdiction the ship was arrested could release her from the arrest.[86] The Belgian association suggested that the provision in the last paragraph of

---

83. Art. 8 of the 1951 Draft in fact provided thus in its second and third paragraphs (CMI Bulletin No. 105, p. 21; *Travaux Préparatoires*, p. 464):

If the court in whose jurisdiction the ship has been arrested has not, pursuant to the domestic law, jurisdiction to decide on the merits, the release of the ship from arrest cannot be ordered, as provided in Art. 5, unless the bond or other guarantee provides expressly that it is given for the amount (including interest and costs) for which the defendant or the ship may be found liable by a judgment of the Court or of one of the Courts having jurisdiction.

If the Court in whose jurisdiction the ship has been arrested has not, pursuant to the domestic law, jurisdiction to decide on the merits, and if the ship has not been released against a bond or other security, as provided in Art. 5, the judgment that will be rendered by the Court or one of the Courts having jurisdiction to decide on the merits shall be enforceable on the ship under arrest. The Contracting States shall enact in their domestic law the proper rules in order to make such enforcement possible.

84. Art. 8 of the 1951 Draft in fact provided thus in its fourth and last paragraph (CMI Bulletin No. 105, p. 21):

If, however, the parties have agreed to submit the dispute to the jurisdiction of a particular Court or to arbitration, this Convention shall continue to apply and the arrest shall remain in force notwithstanding the preceding provisions. However, the Court or other competent judicial authority in the jurisdiction of which the ship has been arrested shall fix a time limit within which the claimant must commence proceedings before the court chosen or commence arbitration proceedings.

85. The following comments were made in the Report of the Rapporteurs (CMI Bulletin No. 105, pp. 4 and 5):

The system proposed by Dean Ripert may give rise to serious difficulties in England and in the countries the domestic law of which does not necessarily grant jurisdiction to the "forum arresti", or does not authorize the arrest of a ship for a claim in respect of which the national courts have no jurisdiction. For these reasons, the International Committee decided to add in Art. 8 of the draft which deals with this question a provision whereby Contracting States shall enact in their domestic legislation appropriate rules to permit the enforcement of foreign judgments when, either pursuant to domestic law or pursuant to the Convention, their courts have no jurisdiction. It appears, however, doubtful that such latter provision may be acceptable in all interested States and, moreover, that it is advisable to deal in the draft Convention with a number of questions extremely problematic and delicate, which probably are outside the scope. This is the reason why the International Committee recommends that these questions be studied with utmost care by the Naples Conference.

86. CMI Bulletin No. 105, p. 32.

Article 8 should be extended to all situations where the court within whose jurisdiction the ship is arrested is not competent to decide the case on the merits.[87] The British association in turn, having considered the Belgian proposal, suggested that the second paragraph should be amended in order to provide that the court must fix the time within which the action on the merits should be commenced; however, instead of stating that the ship should be released if the action is not brought, the text suggested by the British association stated that the ship should not be released if the action was not brought or if the bail or other security did not provide that it was given for the satisfaction of the judgment.[88] Thus, two entirely different situations were dealt with together, probably in order to avoid any provision on the enforcement of foreign judgments.

I.723 At the Naples Conference the Belgian association, having considered the proposals made by the British and French associations, suggested that the third and the fourth paragraphs of Article 8 should be replaced by one single provision wherein, without any statement as to the enforcement of foreign judgments, the rule should state that a time limit for commencement of the action on the merits should be fixed and that the ship should be released if the action was not so commenced.[89] This proposal met with the approval of the Dutch, French and Italian associations,[90] while the British association reserved its position, again stating the two principles that ought to be laid down by Article 8 in a manner which did not differ in substance from that resulting from the Belgian proposal.[91] It was then decided to request the Drafting Committee to prepare the final text of Article 8.[92]

---

87. CMI Bulletin No. 105, p. 86.

88. The text of Art. 8(2) suggested by the British association was the following (CMI Bulletin No. 105, p. 56):

> When the Court in whose jurisdiction the ship is arrested has not, pursuant to the domestic law, jurisdiction to decide on the merits, the Court shall fix a time limit within which the claimant shall commence proceedings before a Court or other authority having jurisdiction, and the ship shall not be released from arrest as stated in Art. 5 unless no proceedings have been commenced before the expiry of such time limit or the bond or other security supplied for such purpose contains a special stipulation to the effect that it has been supplied to secure the amount (including interest and cost) the defendant or the ship will be found liable to pay pursuant to a judgment of the Court or other authority having jurisdiction to decide.

89. The text suggested by the Belgian Delegation was the following (CMI Bulletin No. 105, p. 305):

> If the Court in whose jurisdiction the ship has been arrested has not, pursuant to the domestic law, jurisdiction to decide on the merits, or if the agreement between the parties contains either a clause conferring jurisdiction to another judicial authority or an arbitration clause, the Court shall fix a time limit within which the arrestor shall commence proceedings on the merits. If such proceedings will not be commenced within the time limit so fixed, the defendant may request the release of the arrest or of the guarantee he has supplied.

90. CMI Bulletin No. 105, pp. 306 and 307; *Travaux Préparatoires*, pp. 428 and 429.

91. Mr Miller, on behalf of the British Delegation, stated (CMI Bulletin No. 105, pp. 305 and 306; *Travaux Préparatoires*, p. 429):

> I understand that the conference is accepting the view which is expressed in the draft convention on two points, one, that, if the arrest of a ship is made in a country in which courts have no jurisdiction over that particular case, the judge has power to maintain the arrest, provided that the claimant pursues his remedy within an appropriate time in a country in which there is jurisdiction to try the claim. I understand that the conference accepts that principle. Secondly, I understand (I hope there is no difficulty about this) that the conference accepts the position that, if an arrest is made and a ship is arrested before the court of a particular jurisdiction and it is subsequently found that the matter in dispute has been agreed to be referred to arbitration by the parties, or, which is the same thing in our law, has been agreed to be referred to a court of another country, the court in which the arrest is made will not release the ship or the bail, but will fix a time within which the arbitration is to proceed or the action before the agreed foreign court is to be brought.

92. CMI Bulletin No. 105, p. 308; *Travaux Préparatoires*, p. 430.

I.724 The text which was finally adopted was as follows[93]:

If the Court within whose jurisdiction the ship has been arrested has not jurisdiction to decide upon the merits, no release of the ship, as provided in article 5 shall be granted unless the bail or other security specifically provides that it is given as security for the amount (including interest and costs) in which the defendant or the ship may be held liable by a judgment of the Court or of one of the Courts having jurisdiction so to decide. But the Court or other appropriate judicial authority of the country in which the arrest is made shall fix the time within which the claimant shall bring an action before a Court having such jurisdiction.

If the parties have agreed to submit the dispute to the jurisdiction of a particular Court other than that within whose jurisdiction the ship has been arrested or to arbitration, the Court or other appropriate judicial authority within whose jurisdiction the ship has been arrested may fix the time within which the claimant shall bring the action or begin proceedings in arbitration, and if the action be not brought or the proceedings in arbitration be not begun within such time, the defendant may apply for the release of the ship or of the bail.

I.725 Although the principle that the action on the merits should be commenced within the time fixed by the court within whose jurisdiction the arrest is made was adopted for all situations, the consequences of the failure to bring a timely action were provided only in respect of the situation where the jurisdiction on the merits of a different court was the result of an agreement between the parties.

I.726 At the Diplomatic Conference, however, this omission was cured and the relevant part of Article 7 (previously numbered 8), as adopted by the Conference, provides (paragraphs (2), (3) and (4)):

(2) If the court within whose jurisdiction the ship was arrested has no jurisdiction to decide upon the merits, the bail or other security given in accordance with article 5 to procure the release of the ship shall specifically provide that it is given as security for the satisfaction of any judgment which may eventually be pronounced by a court having jurisdiction so to decide and the court or other appropriate judicial authority of the country in which the arrest is made shall fix the time within which the claimant shall bring an action before a court having such jurisdiction.

(3) If the parties have agreed to submit the dispute to the jurisdiction of a particular court other than that within whose jurisdiction the arrest was made or to arbitration, the court or other appropriate judicial authority within whose jurisdiction the arrest was made may fix the time within which the claimant shall bring proceedings.

(4) If, in any of the cases mentioned in the two preceding paragraphs, the action or proceedings are not brought within the time so fixed, the defendant may apply for the release of the ship or of the bail or other security.

I.727 The distinction between the situation where the court within whose jurisdiction the ship is arrested has no jurisdiction on the merits and where such jurisdiction is excluded by an agreement between the parties has been maintained, but the consequences of the failure to bring a timely action are the same, viz. the right of the defendant to apply for the release of the ship or of the bail or other security.

I.728 There is, however, a difference between the two provisions, which consists in the fact that while in the first case the court must fix the time within which the action has to be brought, in the second case it may do so and, therefore, the decision whether or not to fix a time limit is left to its discretion. It was probably thought that when the parties choose by agreement the court or the arbitration tribunal to settle the dispute, there was no real need for the protection of the owner of the ship, since he could obtain the undertaking of

---

93. CMI Bulletin No. 105, pp. 91 and 92 for the French text only; *Procès-verbaux*, p. 11 for the French text and p. 21 for the English text; *Travaux Préparatoires*, p. 431 for both texts.

the claimant to commence judicial or arbitration proceedings without delay as one of the terms of the agreement. This, however, would be so only if paragraph (3) applied to agreements made after the arrest. But its wording does not justify such restricted interpretation, particularly if the English text, commencing with the words "If the parties have agreed", is compared with the French text where the sentence commences with the words: "*Si les conventions des parties contiennent . . .* " and, therefore, the conclusion must be that the provision applies to any agreement, irrespective of the time when it is made. If this interpretation is correct, the parties, in the case of an agreement made before a dispute has arisen (where, for example, there is a jurisdiction or arbitration clause in a charterparty or a bill of lading), are unlikely to consider the possibility of a ship being arrested and to agree on a fixed time limit for the commencement of the proceedings in such a case. The different regime is not, therefore, justified.[94]

I.729 The Convention, therefore, in this case sets out specific procedural rules to which the Contracting States, by the ratification or acceptances of the Convention, undertake to give effect. Several questions need to be considered, in connection with the provisions under consideration. Furthermore, it is useful to consider how this provision has been implemented in contracting States.

(i) Which court must fix the time

I.730 Paragraph (a) of Article 7, when considering the situation where there is no jurisdiction on the merits, refers to the "court within whose jurisdiction the ship was arrested" in the English text and to the "*tribunal dans le ressort duquel le navire a été saisi*" in the French text. Subsequently, when providing the time within which the claimant must bring an action on the merits, it refers to "the court or other appropriate judicial authority of the country in which the arrest is made" in the English text and to "*le tribunal ou toute autre autorité judiciaire du lieu de la saisie*", in the French text. The omission, at the beginning of the sentence, of a reference, in addition to the court, to the "other appropriate judicial authority" does not imply that the authority that must fix the time limit differs from that in whose jurisdiction the ship was arrested. The aforesaid reference must in fact be implied, since the type of "authority" considered cannot differ from that considered in Article 4 and Article 5, where reference is made to "other appropriate judicial authority". Nor can the reference in the second part of paragraph (2) to the "court or other appropriate authority of the country in which the arrest is made" imply that it was intended to draw a distinction between the court that has authorised the arrest and the court that must fix the time limit. This is confirmed by the fact that in the French text the words used are "*le tribunal ou toute autre autorité judiciaire du lieu de la saisie*", where the words "*lieu de la saisie*" must have the same meaning as the words "*dans le ressort duquel le navire a été saisi*", except that they are more concise.

I.731 It must be noted that in paragraph (3) reference is no longer made to the "country" in which the arrest is made, but to the "jurisdiction" of the court, while in the French text reference is simply made to the tribunal and no more.

---

94. See also Lopez de Gonzalo, "Sequestro di Nave e Giurisdizione Italiana" [1982] Dir. Mar. 574 at p. 590.

I.732 The conclusion, therefore, is that it is the same court (or other appropriate judicial authority) that authorises the arrest that is competent to fix the time limit.

(ii) When the Time Limit must be Fixed

I.733 The situations envisaged in paragraph (2) and paragraph (3) are different and must be considered separately.

I.734 In paragraph (2) the situation where the ship is not released is not expressly considered. The time limit, however, must be fixed by the court irrespective of whether or not the ship is released. This is confirmed by the rule laid down in paragraph (4), according to which if the action is not brought the defendant may apply for the release of the ship or of the bail or other security as the case may be. The obvious consequence is that the time within which the claimant must bring an action on the merits must be fixed by the court that authorises the arrest concurrently with such authorisation. The court in fact cannot wait for the release of the ship, for such release may never occur and the protection of the interest of the owner of the ship requires that the arrest should last for as short a time as possible and that pressure be made on the claimant to take a timely action in order to prove his claim.

I.735 Nor is this interpretation of paragraph (2) in conflict with the use of the present tense ("the court . . . of the country in which the arrest is made"). In fact, that does not mean that the arrest precedes the fixing of the time limit, as appears from the use of a similar wording in Article 4, where there is no doubt that obtaining the authority of the court must precede the arrest. On the contrary, the use here of the present tense is positively relevant, if compared with the use of the past tense at the beginning of paragraph (2), in respect of the release of the ship from arrest.

I.736 The court that authorises the arrest must, therefore, make a preliminary assessment of whether it has jurisdiction to decide upon the merits or not, since if it has no such jurisdiction it must, when authorising the arrest, immediately fix the time within which the claimant shall bring an action on the merits before the competent court.

(iii) Agreement on the Jurisdiction of a Particular Court or on Arbitration

I.737 As previously stated, the situation is different where the parties have agreed to submit the dispute to the jurisdiction of a particular court or to arbitration, for in such a case the court to which the authorisation of arrest is applied for may ignore, at the time the order of arrest is issued, that it has no jurisdiction to determine the case upon its merits.

I.738 In such a situation the time limit may be fixed by the court upon demand of any of the parties, at any time after the order is issued or the arrest is made.

(iv) Implementation of Article 7(2), (3) and (4) by Contracting States

I.739 Express provisions in respect of the time by which proceedings on the merits must be instituted exist in Croatia, Denmark, Finland, Greece, Italy, the Netherlands, Norway, Slovenia, Spain and Sweden.

I.740 In Croatia and Slovenia proceedings must be instituted, pursuant to Article 981 of the Croatian Maritime Code and to Article 986 of the Slovenian Maritime and Internal Navigation Act, within 15 days from the date of service of the arrest.

I.741 In Denmark proceedings on the merits must, pursuant to section 634 of the Administration of Justice Act, be instituted within one week of the arrest if they can be brought in Denmark or within two weeks of the arrest if the proceedings must be brought abroad.

I.742 In Spain the general domestic rule governing the arrest of assets as a preventive measure (*embargo preventivo*) is that proceedings on the merits must be brought to validate the arrest within 20 days from the arrest (Article 1.411 of the Code of Civil Procedure). However, in cases where the proceedings on the merits are to be commenced in a foreign country the claimant usually asks the court to fix a longer period of time on the basis of Article 7(2) of the Convention. The court usually fixes the time period within which the proceedings on the merits must be commenced when granting the arrest. If no time limit is fixed by the court or there is no particular request on this respect, proceedings must be commenced within 20 days from the date arrest is granted.

I.743 In Finland, Greece, Italy and Sweden the time limit is one month. In Finland proceedings on the merits must be brought within one month of the date when the order of arrest has been finally affirmed. In Greece the period is fixed by statute (Article 715(5) of the Code of Civil Procedure) but in case the ship is released from arrest against the provision of security the period may be fixed by the court, provided it is not less than 30 days. In Italy Article 669 *novies* of the Code of Civil Procedure provides generally that the order (of arrest) loses its effectiveness if proceedings on the merits are not commenced within the time limit fixed by the judge or, if no limit is fixed, within thirty days. This provision applies both where Italian courts have or have not jurisdiction on the merits. Furthermore, Article 669 *novies* provides that when Italian courts have not jurisdiction on the merits, the order (of arrest) loses its effectiveness where the request for the enforcement of the foreign judgment or arbitral award is not made within the time limits set out under penalty of forfeiture by law or by international conventions.

I.744 In Sweden according to Chapter 15, Section 7 of the Swedish Code of Judicial Procedure, if an action has not already been instituted, the claimant must, within one month of the order, either institute a court action on the matter at issue or, if the claim is to be resolved out of court, initiate the appropriate proceedings (e.g. arbitration).

I.745 In Norway proceedings on the merits must be brought within one year of the arrest or the shorter period ordered by the court.

I.746 In France no statutory provision exists. However the Cour de Cassation with judgment 14 October 1997 in *Marine Atlantic Inc.* v. *Interconnection—The "Marine Evangeline"*[95] held that the provision set out for arrest of assets by Article 70 of law no. 91–650 of 9 July 1991 and by Article 215 of decree no. 92–755 of 31 July 1992, pursuant to which proceedings aiming at obtaining an enforceable judgment must be brought within one month, apply also in respect of arrest of ships.

I.747 In Germany pursuant to § 926 ZPO (Code of Civil Procedure) the time within which proceedings on the merits must be brought is fixed by the court competent for the arrest at its discretion and in the Netherlands pursuant to Article 700(3) of the Code of Civil Procedure, proceedings on the merits must be brought within the period fixed by the

---

95. [1998] DMF 24.

court, such period being of at least eight days from the date of the arrest.[96] Similar is, albeit by implication, the situation in Nigeria and in England. In Nigeria the court is empowered to impose on the arrestor any conditions as are just and reasonable. In England according to Civil Jurisdiction and Judgments Act 1982, section 26(1) and (2) where a court stays Admiralty proceedings on the ground that the dispute in question should be submitted to the determination of the courts of an overseas country the court may, if in those proceedings property has been arrested or bail or other security has been given to prevent or obtain release from arrest, order that the property arrested be retained as security for the satisfaction of any award or judgment which is given in respect of the dispute in the arbitration or legal proceedings in favour of which those proceedings are stayed or dismissed, or order that the stay or dismissal of those proceedings be conditional on the provision of equivalent security for the satisfaction of any such award or judgment. Where the court makes such an order it may attach such conditions to the order as it thinks fit, in particular conditions with respect to the institution or prosecution of the relevant legal proceedings. Accordingly, the court may set a time limit within which legal proceedings on the merits of the case ought to commence.

I.748 Finally, it would appear that no time limit is normally fixed in Belgium.

(d) Constitution of the Limitation Fund

(i) Provisions under the 1957 Limitation Convention

I.749 Article 2(4) of the 1957 Convention provides that after the limitation fund has been constituted, no claimant against the fund shall be entitled to exercise any right against any other assets of the shipowner in respect of his claim against the fund, if the limitation fund is actually available for the benefit of the claimant.

I.750 Article 5(1) provides that whenever a shipowner is entitled to limit his liability under the Convention and the ship or another ship in the same ownership has been arrested within the jurisdiction of a Contracting State, or bail or other security has been given to avoid arrest, the court or other competent authority of such State may order the release of the ship or of the security given if it is established that the shipowner has already given satisfactory bail or security for a sum equal to the full amount of his liability under the Convention.

I.751 It is worth noting that the release of the ship or security is not compulsory, but left to the discretion of the court.

---

96. Article 700(3) of the code of Civil Procedure so provides (English translation supplied by Mr. T. van der Valk):

> Unless a claim on the merits has been instituted at the time of the leave for arrest, the leave shall be granted under the condition that the institution thereof shall take place within a period of time to be set by the president of at least eight days after the arrest. The president may extend this period of time if the arrestor so requests before the period of time has expired. Such ruling is not subject to appeal. Expiry of the period of time shall extinguish the attachment.

The Gerechtshof of Gravenhage with judgment of 23 February 1993, [1994] Schip en Schade 38, held that the above provision does not apply in case the ship is voluntarily released from arrest upon provision of security by the owner to the claimant, the applicable period for the commencement of proceedings on the merits being that set out in the guarantee (it would appear that in that case the standard form named "Rotterdam Guarantee Form", which provides also for the time within which proceedings must be instituted, had been used).

(ii) Provisions under the 1969 Civil Liability Convention

I.752 Article 6 of the Civil Liability Convention provides that where the shipowner, after an incident, has constituted a fund in accordance with the provisions of the Convention, no person having a claim for pollution damage shall be entitled to exercise any right against any other assets of the owner in respect of such claim and the court or other competent authority of any Contracting State shall order the release of any ship or other property belonging to the owner which has been arrested in respect of a claim for pollution damage and shall similarly release any bail or other security furnished to avoid the arrest.

I.753 Under the Civil Liability Convention, therefore, the release is not discretionary, but compulsory if the fund has been constituted in accordance with the provisions of the Convention. Pursuant to Article 5(3) the fund must be constituted with the court or other competent authority of any one of the Contracting States in which action is brought under Article 9, pursuant to which action may only be brought in the courts of any of the Contracting States in the territory of which pollution damage has occurred. Therefore a fund may not be constituted prior to an action being brought against any of the persons liable, whereupon, if such action is brought in any of the courts indicated in Article 9, the fund may be constituted with that court and, if several actions are brought in different courts, the fund may be constituted in any of such courts.

I.754 Reference is made to the release of the security, as in the 1957 Limitation Convention, in respect of the security furnished to avoid the arrest, but the rule also applies in case of security furnished to release the ship from arrest.

I.755 The problem arises where arrest of a ship is possible notwithstanding the provisions in Article 6 of the Civil Liability Convention limiting the right of arrest under the Arrest Convention if, as previously stated,[97] claims for pollution damage are covered by the words "or otherwise" in Article 1(1)(a) wherein reference is made to "damage caused by any ship either in collision or otherwise". In view of the special character of the rules of the Civil Liability Convention as compared with those of the Arrest Convention, the correct answer to this problem seems to be that Article 6 of the Civil Liability Convention prevails over Article 2 of the Arrest Convention.

I.756 The Civil Liability Convention as amended by the 1992 Protocol, however, regulates only the liability of the owner of a tanker, and claims may be brought against other persons liable under the ordinary rules (except the servants or agents of the owner: Article 3(4)).

I.757 If, therefore, the charterer is liable in respect of pollution damage, the arrest of the ship seems possible under Article 3(4) of the Arrest Convention subject to the limits within which this provision applies.[98]

(iii) Provisions under the 1976 Convention on Limitation of Liability for Maritime Claims

I.758 The provisions in this Convention are intermediate between those of the 1957 Limitation Convention and those of the Civil Liability Convention. Article 13(2) of the

---

97. See *supra*, para. I.320.
98. See *supra*, para. I.502–I.534.

1976 Limitation Convention, in fact, states that after the limitation fund has been constituted, any ship or other property belonging to a person on behalf of whom the fund has
been constituted which has been arrested or attached within the jurisdiction of a State
party for a claim which may be raised against the fund, or any security given, may be
released by order of the court or other competent authority of such State, but such release
shall always be ordered if the limitation fund has been constituted in one of the places
subsequently specified.[99] There can, therefore, be situations in which the ship is not
released notwithstanding the constitution of the fund. In fact pursuant to Article 11 of the
Convention the fund must be constituted with the court or other competent authority in
any State Party in which legal proceedings are instituted in respect of claims subject to
limitation. Since it is conceivable that proceedings are instituted in the court of a place
other than those indicated in Article 13(2), in such a case the release of the ship is not
compulsory, but only discretional.[100]

(iv) Provisions under the 1996 HNS Convention

I.759 The system realised by the HNS Convention is similar to that of the CLC, but some
of its imperfections have been cured. In fact while Article 5 of the CLC, as Article 11 of
the LLMC Convention, by providing that the fund must be constituted with the court of
a Contracting State in which action is brought, prevents the constitution of the fund prior
to an action being brought, Article 9(3) of the HNS Convention provides also that if no
action is brought the fund shall be constituted with any court in any one of the States
Parties in which an action can be brought under Article 38. The link between Article 9(3)
and Article 38 gives, however, rise to some uncertainty. In fact under Article 38(2) an
action can be brought in the courts of a State Party where the ship is registered, in the
courts of the State Party where the owner has his habitual residence or his principal place

---

99. Article 13(2) of the 1976 Limitation Convention so provides:
   After a limitation fund has been constituted in accordance with article 11, any ship or other property,
   belonging to a person on behalf of whom the fund has been constituted, which has been arrested or attached
   within the jurisdiction of a State Party for a claim which may be raised against the fund, or any security
   given, may be released by order of the Court or other competent authority of such State. However, such
   release shall always be ordered if the limitation fund has been constituted:
   a) at the port where the occurrence took place, or, if it took place out of port, at the first port of call
       thereafter; or
   b) at the port of disembarkation in respect of claims for loss of life or personal injury; or
   c) at the port of discharge in respect of damage to cargo; or
   d) in the State where the arrest is made.
100. The French Cour de Cassation with judgment 5 January 1999, *Jupiter Maritime Corporation* v. *Schiffahrtsgesellschaft Detlef Von Appen mbH*, [1999] DMF 130, so held (at p. 139):
   Mais attendu qu'il résulte des dispositions de l'article 13 de la Convention de Londres du 19 novembre 1976
   sur la limitation de la responsabilité en matière de créances maritimes, applicable en la cause, que c'est
   seulement lorsque le fonds de limitation a été constitué dans l'un des lieux mentionnés par ce texte que le
   juge doit ordonner mainlevée de la saisie de tout navire appartenant à une personne au profit de laquelle
   cette constitution est intervenue; qu'ayant relevé, par un motif adopté, que le fonds de limitation avait été
   constitué, en l'espèce, à Londres, lieu d'arbitrage d'une partie du litige au fond, et non dans l'un des ports
   mentionnés à l'article 13 précité ou en France, Etat où la saisie du navire a eu lieu, c'est dans l'exercice de
   son pouvoir souverain d'appréciation que le cour d'appel a estimé qu'il n'y avait lieu d'ordonner mainlevée
   de la saisie en conséquence de la constitution du fonds; d'où il suit que le moyen n'est fondé en aucune de
   ses branches.

of business or in the courts of the State Party where the fund has been constituted in accordance with Article 9(3). Since this third alternative applies when the action is brought after the fund has been constituted, it is difficult to understand how precisely in the case when no action has been brought yet, the last criterion indicated in Article 38(2) can apply.

34. WHEN THE RELEASE OF A SHIP UNDER ARREST IS NOT PERMITTED

I.760 The rule whereby a ship must be released upon sufficient bail or other security being furnished does not apply when the ship has been arrested in respect of any of the maritime claims enumerated under subparagraphs (o) and (p) covering disputes as to the title to a ship and disputes between co-owners.

I.761 The need for this exclusion had been pointed out by the Italian association, on the ground that disputes regarding ownership or possession could not in Italian law entitle the parties to apply for a "conservative" arrest, but to a judicial arrest whereby the subject matter of the arrest would remain in the custody of the court and could not be released against security.[101] During the Naples Conference the Italian association also suggested that in the case of arrest in respect of any of the claims now enumerated in subparagraphs (o) and (p) of Article 1(1) (disputes as to ownership and disputes between co-owners) the court could permit the ship to continue trading if sufficient bail was furnished.[102] This suggestion was based on an express provision of the Italian Code of Civil Procedure —Article 676. This article states that the court, when ordering a judicial arrest, appoints a custodian and sets out the criteria and limits of the management of the subject matter of the arrest; it further states that the court may appoint as custodian the party who is financially more responsible and is prepared to provide bail.

---

101. In its comments on the Draft Convention prepared in 1951 by the International Sub-Committee the Italian association stated (CMI Bulletin No. 105, pp. 68 and 69; *Travaux Préparatoires*, p. 358 and 359):

The reason behind the distinction made by our law between conservative arrest, which is granted as security for a claim, and judicial arrest, which is granted where a dispute has arisen on the property or possession of a movable or immovable object, cannot be missed by anybody, in view of the substantial difference between the two claims. The former of such actions has the purpose of ensuring the claimant that he may subsequently enforce the judgment of the Court, which will have decided in his favour, on certain assets of the debtor; quite to the contrary, as respects the latter of such actions, it would be unjust for the person that does not claim a generic credit against another person, but a possessory right or a property right on objects at that time in the possession of others, that after he has obtained the arrest of the object in dispute, the person who has it in his possession may continue to dispose of it as if it belonged to him, because he has given a guarantee for an amount equal to the value of the object.

102. The following proposal is recorded in CMI Bulletin No. 105, at p. 273 (see also *Travaux Préparatoires*, p. 360):

The Italian Delegation proposes to add the words:

"except the cases where there is a dispute on the right of ownership, or co-ownership or possession or operation of the ship (Art. 1 letters (d), (e) and (g)); in such cases the release from arrest may not be granted, but the Court shall decide on the operation of the ship against provision of sufficient security".

or

"in such cases the Court may allow the operation of the ship by the person who has possession thereof if he will have provided sufficient security, or dispose of its operation otherwise."

I.762 The Italian proposal was supported by the British association[103] and the second alternative was accepted by the Conference. The following wording was thus added to the original text of the first paragraph of Article 5:

save in cases in which a ship has been arrested in respect of any of the maritime claims enumerated in article 1(1)(o) and (p). In such cases, the court or other appropriate judicial authority may permit the person in possession of the ship to continue trading the ship, upon such person furnishing sufficient bail or other security, or may otherwise deal with the operation of the ship during the period of the arrest.[104]

35. TRADING OF A SHIP UNDER ARREST

I.763 As previously stated,[105] the release of a ship under arrest is not permitted by Article 5 when the arrest has been made in respect of any of the maritime claims enumerated in Article 1(1)(o) and (p). In such a case, however, the court within whose jurisdiction the ship has been arrested may permit the ship to continue trading.

I.764 The decision whether the further trading of the ship should be permitted or not is left to the discretion of the court.

I.765 There appears to be a preference for the person in possession of the ship to continue trading her. In principle this is justified because, as a general rule, where there are conflicting rights, the person who, in good faith, has possession of the ship is to be preferred to others. The court has, according to this provision, a wide discretion. The rule provides in fact that the court "may otherwise deal with the operation of the ship" and other ways to do so include the appointment of the claimant or of a third party as custodian.

I.766 This provision does not apply in respect of the Contracting States which have availed themselves of the right, granted by Article 10, not to apply the Convention to the arrest of a ship for the claims set out in Article 1(1)(o) and (p).[106] In such a case domestic rules only apply in respect of an arrest for such claims.

---

103. The British delegate (Mr Miller) stated (CMI Bulletin No. 105, p. 274; *Travaux Préparatoires*, pp. 362 and 363):

Mr President and gentlemen, in regard to this amendment which has been proposed by the British delegation I am going to speak first simply because the British amendment comes first on the paper, but it was put in by the British Delegation to meet what we thought was a good point made by the Italian Delegation, namely that, when a ship is under arrest in some form of action in which her ownership and the right to possession of her are in issue, the judge ought not to be bound to release the ship, because what the claimant wants is not the value of the ship but the ship herself. The objection made by the Italian Delegation we thought, with respect, was a good one, so we suggested that article 1, paragraphs (d) and (e), which deal with ship possession cases, should be excluded from the ambit of article 5.

We have just seen the Italian proposal, and personally (I am only expressing a personal opinion) I prefer the second Italian version to our amendment, because I think it makes it quite clear that the judge can allow the ship to continue trading provided that it provides a sufficient guarantee, but he is not bound to do so. Obviously, if there is a dispute about the ownership of a vessel in commerce, it should be possible for the judge to allow her to continue trading under sufficient guarantee. Therefore I would support the second of the two Italian amendments in preference to ours. I am, of course, only expressing a personal opinion.

104. On the trading of a ship under arrest see *infra*, para. I.763–I.775.

105. *Supra*, at para. I.760–I.762.

106. Reservations have been made by Egypt, Italy, the Netherlands, Yugoslavia (only in respect of Art. 1(1)(o)) and Cuba.

I.767 There is no doubt that Contracting States may permit a ship to continue trading when she has been arrested in respect of a maritime claim other than those set out in Article 1(1)(o) and (p). In fact, Article 5 requires them to release the ship when sufficient security is provided but does not give any minimum requirement as to the release or the use of a ship under arrest.

I.768 Provisions in respect of the trading of ships under arrest exist in the national laws of some Contracting States as it appears from the analysis which follows.

ENGLAND

I.769 There are no rules in the United Kingdom which allow the person in possession to continue trading the ship after arrest.[107] However now paragraph 6.4(3) of the Practice Direction, by providing that property under arrest may not be moved without an order of the Admiralty Court, seems to leave any decision in this respect to the discretion of the Court.

FRANCE

I.770 A ship under arrest may be authorised by the President of the Tribunal de Grande Instance to perform one or more voyages provided the applicant gives adequate security.[108]

GERMANY

I.771 There are no rules in respect of the trading of the ship while under arrest.

GREECE

I.772 Trading after arrest may be permitted by the court in accordance with Article 720(3) of the Code of Civil Procedure in respect of one or more voyages and on any terms the

---

107. In *Greenmar Navigation Ltd.* v. *The Owner of the Ships "Bazias 3" and "Bazias 4"* [1993] 1 Lloyd's Rep. 101 Saville J. felt justified in allowing the ships to continue trading while remaining technically under arrest in consideration of the fact that the ships were engaged in a cross-channel trade and were in an English port several times a day. Sheen J., however, held that English rules do not allow ships under arrest to leave an English port in these circumstances and his decision was upheld by the Court of Appeal.

108. Art. 27 of the Decree of 22 October 1967, No. 67–957 provides:
Notwithstanding any arrest, the President of the Tribunal de Grande Instance, deciding in the form of *"référé"*, may authorize the sailing of the ship for one or several specified voyages. In order to obtain such authorization, the applicant must provide sufficient security.
Art. 28 provides:
The President fixes a time limit within which the ship must return to the port of arrest. He may subsequently modify such time limit in order to take the circumstances into account and, if deemed proper, authorize the execution of further voyages.
If, at the expiry of the time fixed, the ship has not returned to the port, the sum deposited as security is acquired by the creditors, save the operation of the insurance in case of accident covered by the policy.
The Cour d'Appel of Pau in its judgment of 17 December 1985 in *ENIM* v. *Sarl Teck Ocean—The "Akelare"* [1987] DMF 95 held that the solvency of the owner of the ship could not be considered a *"garantie suffisante"*, since the law referred to the payment into court of a sum of money.
On the trading of a ship under arrest see Rodière, *Droit Maritime* (Paris, 1980), p. 240; du Pontavice, *Le Statut des Navires* (Paris, 1976), p. 366.

court may consider appropriate and in any event on the condition that the ship is insured.

ITALY

I.773 Article 652 CN provides, in respect of the seizure of a ship in satisfaction of a judgment, that the court may, upon request of an interested party, and after having sought the opinion of the holders of *hypothèques*, authorise the ship to perform one or more voyages having prescribed the securities it will deem proper, among which there must be, in any event, adequate insurance cover. The freight earned shall, after deduction of the disbursements incurred, be added to the proceeds of the forced sale. Article 685 CN provides that the rules of Article 652 CN shall apply also in the case of arrest.

THE NETHERLANDS

I.774 Although there are no express rules in respect of the trading of a ship under arrest, it is within the powers of the court to permit the trading of an arrested ship, having set out the rules to be observed, if sufficient security has been provided.

PORTUGAL

I.775 As in Italy, in the case of seizure of a ship in satisfaction of a judgment the court may permit the trading of the ship. Article 852 CCP provides that the custodian may trade the ship provided both the claimant and the owner agree and the trading is authorised by the court. Article 853 CCP then states that the court may also authorise the trading of the ship following an application of any interested party, conditional on the applicant providing satisfactory security in an amount that will cover the claims secured by maritime liens and the costs and arranging of insurance for the ship. These provisions also apply to the arrest of the ship.

36. LIABILITY FOR WRONGFUL ARREST

I.776 As previously mentioned,[109] the question whether the Convention should contain a provision on the right of the owner of the ship to damages in case of wrongful arrest was hotly debated from the outset, the civil law countries generally being in favour of such a provision and the common law countries against.

I.777 The 1951 Draft attempted to solve the problem with a rule of private international law. Its Article 6 provided that all questions relating to the liability of the claimant in respect of damages arising out of the arrest or the provision of security as well as all questions relating to the obligation of the claimant to provide security are decided in

---

109. See *supra*, para. I.8 and I.10.

accordance with the law of the State in whose jurisdiction the ship is arrested.[110] In the report, it was explained that, in view of a compromise between the civil law and the common law systems appearing very unlikely, the suggestion already put forward at the 1937 Paris Conference, to refer to the *lex fori*, was adopted.[111]

I.778 At the Naples Conference, the associations of Finland, Norway and Sweden objected to leaving the matter to the *lex fori* and submitted an alternative article wherein it was provided that, save in exceptional cases, the claimant should, before the arrest, provide security, whose nature and amount should be fixed by the court, and that if the arrest proved to be unjustified, the claimant would be liable in damages.[112]

I.779 This proposal, however, was not supported by any other association. Even the associations of civil law countries, such as France and Italy, were against the proposal, both because they did not favour this rigid provision on the duty to provide security and also, and perhaps more importantly, because it was felt that unless the text suggested by the International Sub-Committee was adopted, an agreement would prove impossible.[113] The text appearing in the 1951 Draft was, therefore, left unaltered.[114]

110. Art. 6 of the 1951 Draft provided (*Travaux Préparatoires*, p. 380):
All disputes relating to the liability of the arrestor in respect of damages caused by the arrest of the ship or for the cost of the bond or security provided in order to release from or prevent the arrest of the ship, or all disputes relating to the obligation of the arrestor to provide security for the payment of damages and costs arising therefrom shall be settled according to the law of the Contracting State in the jurisdiction of which the arrest has been effected or applied for.
111. The following comment is made in the Report (CMI Bulletin No. 105, p. 3; *Travaux Préparatoires*, pp. 380 and 381):
A second problem of about equal importance results from the difference between Anglo-Saxon and continental laws in respect of damages for an unjustified arrest. In English law the settlement of duly proved damages arising out of the immobilization of a ship following an arrest may not be claimed unless the arrestor has acted in bad faith or has been grossly negligent, his negligence being comparable with fraud. Except for such cases, the owner of the arrested ship is only entitled to the payment of the costs of the security. Under the continental laws, on the contrary, the arrestor is responsible for all damages arising out of the arrest of a ship whenever it is proved that the arrest was not justified. It should be recalled that the 1937 Paris Conference solved the difficulty by means of a reference to the law of the State where the arrest is made. It is for this reason that also at present the International Committee is afraid that the opposed views cannot be reconciled and, therefore, has adopted in Art. 6 of the new draft the system of the Paris draft, creating a conflict of law rule instead of a uniform rule.
112. The text of the provision suggested by the delegations of Finland, Norway and Sweden, passionately presented to the Conference by Kaj Pineus, was as follows (CMI Bulletin No. 105, p. 280; *Travaux Préparatoires*, p. 383):
Should an arrest be found unjustified, the claimant shall be liable to pay all costs and damages of whatsoever kind which have arisen on account of the arrest.
Before the arrest of a ship is authorized, the claimant shall ordinarily be bound to furnish a guarantee sufficient to cover the damages and all costs for which the claimant may be liable if it appears that his claim is unjustified.
In exceptional cases, the court or other appropriate authority may permit arrest without such security provided that the claim is considered likely to succeed and if the condition of security will cause undue hardship.
The nature and amount of such security shall be determined by the court or authority who permits the arrest to be made.
113. CMI Bulletin No. 105, p. 284; *Travaux Préparatoires*, pp. 385 and 386.
114. The text approved by The Naples Conference was as follows (*Procès-verbaux*, p. 21; *Travaux Préparatoires*, p. 391):
All questions whether in any case the claimant is liable in damages for the arrest of a ship or for the costs of the bail or other security furnished to release or prevent the arrest of a ship, or whether he shall be required himself to furnish guarantee to secure the payment of such damages or costs, shall be determined by the law of the Contracting State in whose jurisdiction the arrest is made or applied for.

I.780 At the Diplomatic Conference the Drafting Committee appointed by the Plenary Session, in order to meet at least in part the objections of the Scandinavian delegations, amended Article 6 by dividing the text into two paragraphs and by providing in the second paragraph that the court of the place where the ship is arrested may require the claimant to provide security.[115] The previous text, on the contrary, simply stated that all questions relating to liability and security should be determined by the law of the State in whose jurisdiction the ship is arrested. This amended text met, however, with the strong opposition of the British delegation, which stated that the United Kingdom could not accept the Convention if the second paragraph were maintained.[116] The Scandinavian delegations, in turn, requested an amendment of the second paragraph to the effect that the court should, in principle, require security and, in the case of wrongful arrest, grant liquidated damages,[117] repeating, in substance, the proposal made at Naples.[118] The British delegation, after objecting to the Scandinavian proposal, stated that the only possible solution was to delete the second paragraph of the draft Article 6 and keep the first paragraph only. The Scandinavian amendment was rejected and the British amendment was adopted.[119] Thereafter, the Drafting Committee merged Article 6, now reduced to one paragraph only, and Article 7 of the draft, which is now the second paragraph of Article 6.[120]

115. The amended text was as follows (*Procès-verbaux*, p. 111; *Travaux Préparatoires*, p. 392):
All questions whether in any case the claimant is liable in damages for the arrest of a ship or for the costs of the bail or other security furnished to release or prevent the arrest of a ship, shall be determined by the law of the Contracting State in whose jurisdiction the arrest was made or applied for.
The court or other appropriate judicial authority of the country in which the arrest was made or applied for may require the claimant to furnish sufficient bail or other security for such liability as he may ultimately incur under the domestic law.
116. The statement of the British delegate (Mr Miller) was recorded as follows (*Procès-verbaux*, p. 102):
The British Delegation must, however, categorically state that it will not be able to accept the Convention if Art. 6 para. 2 is maintained. The questions of damages and security to be supplied must be governed by the *lex fori*. Her Majesty's Government attributes a great importance to this question. The only countries, the law of which is in conflict with the Draft are the United Kingdom and the United States who, having not had the time to study the Draft and to prepare a Delegation, have only sent an observer. In England, actions for wrongful arrest are very rare, and Mr. Miller has never heard any complaint in this respect. The only effect of paragraph 2 would be to force the United Kingdom and the United States to modify their procedure.
117. The reasons set forth by the Danish delegate (Mr Boeg) are summarised as follows in the *Procès-verbaux*, at p. 111 (see also *Travaux Préparatoires*, pp. 392 and 393):
Mr. Boeg (Denmark) considers Art. 6 of a particular importance. The question has already been discussed at length in the preceding conferences and during the meetings of the Drafting Committee. However, the present text is not considered satisfactory by the Scandinavian countries, Denmark, Finland and Sweden. They have submitted another text, which has been distributed to the members of the Assembly. Such text permits to obtain, in principle, damages for any unjustified arrest that causes damages or costs, and requires the delivery of security for their payment. It is, however, possible that the claimant may be unable to know that the arrest was not justified and the amendment consents that in such cases the claimant may not be responsible.
Similarly, the new text permits that, exceptionally, the provision of security may not be necessary if the arrest is sufficiently justified, or if the claimant has serious difficulties to provide security. But in normal cases, it is considered that the provision of security is a fundamental condition for the arrest, and Denmark could not sign a Convention if the requests of the Scandinavian Countries were not accepted, one way or another.
118. See supra, note 112.
119. The Scandinavian amendment was rejected by 15 votes, with 5 in favour and 1 abstention. The British amendment was adopted with 13 votes in favour, 6 against and 2 abstentions.
120. On this subject see generally Ripert, "Les Conventions de Droit Maritime", p. 357 *supra*, para. 303, note 25; G. Berlingieri, "La Conferenza di Napoli", *supra*, para. I.79, note 24.

I.781 The rejection of the Scandinavian amendment was one of the reasons for which the Scandinavian countries had not ratified the Convention[121] until ratification became necessary for the Scandinavian countries which became members of the European Union.[122] The obligation to ratify the Convention was originally set out in the Accession Convention of 9 October 1978.[123]

I.782 In almost all jurisdictions the claimant may be held liable in damages in case the arrest has proved to be "wrongful". The situations in which such liability arises differ, however, from country to country.

I.783 Normally it is not sufficient that the claim in respect of which the arrest has been applied for is ultimately rejected by the court in order to give rise to a liability of the arrestor. The action of the claimant must, to that effect, be grossly negligent. This is, with certain not insignificant variations, the case for Belgium, England, France, Greece, Haiti, Italy, Nigeria and Spain.

I.784 In some jurisdictions liability arises also if, irrespective of the claim being founded or not, the arrest is not justified,[124] for example because, owing to the financial conditions of the debtor, the claimant had no need for a security. This is the position in Denmark, France, Germany, Haiti, Italy, Norway and Spain. A more detailed analysis of the position in a number of States parties to the 1952 Convention follows.[125]

BELGIUM

I.785 The arrestor is only liable in case of wrongful arrest. The fact that the arrest is not justified does not suffice. The claim for damages is a claim in tort and, therefore, the claimant has the burden of proving the fault of the arrestor, the damages he has suffered and the causal relationship between the arrest and the damages. The arrestor shall be

---

121. For a complete summary of the reasons for which Sweden in particular did not immediately ratify the 1952 Convention see the Swedish reply to Question 1 of the Questionnaire, Appendix II, p. 231.

122. Denmark ratified the Arrest Convention on 2 May 1989 and, therefore, the Convention came into force pursuant to its Art. 14 on 2 November 1989. Sweden ratified the Arrest Convention on 30 April 1993 and the Convention came into force on 30 October 1993. Norway ratified the Convention on 1 November 1994 and the Convention came into force on 1 May 1995; Finland ratified the Convention on 21 December 1995 and the Convention came into force on 21 June 1996.

123. Art. 36 of the Accession Convention of 9 October 1978 provides thus:

For a period of three years from the entry into force of the 1968 Convention for the Kingdom of Denmark and Ireland respectively jurisdiction in maritime matters shall be determined in these States not only in accordance with the provisions of that Convention but also in accordance with the provisions of paragraphs (1) to (6) following. However, upon the entry into force of the International Convention relating to the Arrest of Sea Going Ships signed at Brussels on 10 May 1952 for one of these States these provisions shall cease to have effect for that State.

The first five of the six paragraphs that follow reproduce with some adaptations, the most relevant provisions of the 1952 Arrest Convention: para. 1 reproduces Art. 7, para. 1; para. 2, Art. 3, para. 1; para. 3, Art. 3, para. 2; para. 4, Art. 3, para. 4; para. 5, Art. 1, para. 1.

124. The word "unjustified" has been added to "wrongful" in the 1999 Arrest Convention, article 6(2) of which so provides:

2. The Courts of the State in which an arrest has been effected shall have jurisdiction to determine the extent of the liability, if any, of the claimant for loss or damage caused by the arrest of a ship, including but not restricted to such loss or damage as may be caused in consequence of:

(a) the arrest having been wrongful or unjustified, or

(b) excessive security having been demanded and provided.

See, for the debate that preceded the adoption of this provision, the Travaux Préparatoires of the 1999 Convention, Book II, Appendix III, p. 525–528.

125. For additional information see the replies to Question 9 of the Questionnaire, Appendix II, p. 267.

deemed to be at fault only if he has acted recklessly and knowing that his action would probably cause damages.

DENMARK

I.786 Pursuant to section 639 of the Danish Administration Act the arrestor is liable if the claim will be rejected or, also, if the vessel will subsequently be released because the claim is ungrounded.[126]

ENGLAND

I.787 In the absence of proof of *mala fides* or gross negligence the claimant is not liable in damages for having arrested a vessel: *The Evangelismos*,[127] *The Strathnaver*,[128] and *The Kommunar (No.3)*.[129] *Mala fides* must be taken to exist in those cases where the arresting party has no honest belief in its entitlement to arrest the ship: *The Kommunar (No. 3)*, at p. 30. Gross negligence covers those situations where objectively there is so little basis for the arrest that it may be inferred that the arrestor did not believe in its entitlement to arrest the ship or acted without any serious regard to whether there were adequate grounds for the arrest of the vessel, *ibid*. In general, then, it is very difficult for the shipowner to obtain a remedy unless he can show the narrow category of "wrongful" arrest, described above. There is no question of damages being awarded for "unjustified" arrest, in the sense simply that the claim failed on the merits. It should be noted that the Scottish Law Commission has recently recommended that Scots law should differ from English law by moving closer to a continental system giving a remedy for unjustified arrestments based on a strict liability.[130]

I.788 According to paragraph 6.3(3) of Admiralty Practice Direction 49F, if there is a "caveat against arrest" and an arrest is made, the Admiralty Court may, if it considers that it is appropriate to do so, order the party procuring the arrest to pay compensation to the owner or other party interested in the ship arrested. A "caveat against arrest" provides a system whereby a potential defendant can file a notice in the Admiralty and Commercial Registry, undertaking in advance to file an acknowledgement of service of the claim and to provide security.

---

126. Section 639 of the Administration of Justice Act so provides (translation of the Danish MLA):
A person having obtained an arrest based on a claim which turns out to be non-existent shall pay compensation to the debtor for loss and damages and for tort. The same shall apply in the event that the arrest is lifted or discontinued due to subsequent events if it is assumed that the claim did not exist.
127. (1858) 12 Moo. P.C. 352.
128. (1985) 1 AC 58.
129. [1997] 1 Lloyd's Rep. 22. Colman J. so held (at p. 33):
Even if the plaintiff's claim fails or he is found to have wrongly invoked the jurisdiction he will not have to compensate the shipowner for the expenses and losses arising out of the arrest unless mala fides or crassa negligentia is proved. This is a rule of English law which can bear very harshly on shipowners who for some special reason may be unable to obtain release of their vessel by putting up security. It is not a rule which is found in the civil law systems. The more widely used procedure for obtaining security for a claim in personam in English law is the *Mareva* injunction, but there is an undertaking in damages required and the liability in respect of that undertaking arises upon the basis that, if the underlying claim fails, the plaintiff is liable for all losses caused by the injunction. The absence of a similar facility in Admiralty proceedings in rem may thus leave without remedy an innocent defendant shipowner who has suffered loss by an unjustifiable arrest but who is unable to establish malice or crassa negligentia.
130. Scottish Law Commission – Report on Diligence on the Dependence and Admiralty Arrestments (Scot Law Com. No. 164), section 7.124 at p. 140.

I.789 English Law also recognises a "caveat against release" (much more commonly used than the caveat against arrest) which gives the right to a potential claimant to register his interest in the ship arrested or threatened with arrest, without incurring the cost and formality of an application for arrest.

FINLAND

I.790 Pursuant to section 11 of chapter 7 of the Code of Judicial Procedure the arrestor is strictly liable for loss or damage resulting from the arrest if it is proved that the arrest was unnecessary.

FRANCE

I.791 The arrestor can be held liable for the damages caused by the arrest if it is subsequently established that he has abused his right. An abuse of right can exist when the arrest is unjustified, when it is excessive in respect of the amount of the claim or when the security requested is excessive.[131]

GERMANY

I.792 Pursuant to § 945 HGB the arrestor, irrespective of fault, is liable for damages caused by an unjustified arrest.[132]

GREECE

I.793 As an exception to the general rule laid down in Article 914 of the Civil Code,[133] pursuant to which the arrestor is liable in damages if his claim is rejected, in case of arrest of a ship in order that the liability arises it is necessary that the arrestor knew or ignored by gross negligence that the claim in respect of which the arrest was demanded did not exist. Only damage to property, however, may be claimed. In case the ship is released from arrest against security, the cost of such security can, however, be claimed.

---

131. The Cour de Cassation in its judgment of 19 March 1996, *Lemphy Maritima Enterprise* v. *Mohamed Zaatari and Cie Al Itthad Al Watani—The "Alexander III"* [1996] DMF 503 stated (at p. 506):
  Vu l'article 455 du nouveau Code de procédure civile;
  Attendu qu'en rejetant, à supposer la fictivité de la société Lemphy établie, la demande de dommages-intérêts formée par elle sans répondre par aucun motif à ses conclusions faisant valoir que, la saisie conservatoire du navire *Alexander III* eût-elle été possible pour garantir le recouvrement de la créance litigieuse et celle-ci fût-elle incontestable, la société Zaatari et son assureur n'en auraient pas moins utilisé de manière abusive les voies d'exécution, en pratiquant et maintenant une saisie exagérée par rapport au montant de la créance et en exigeant, pour en donner mainlevée amiable, la fourniture d'une garantie disproportionnée, la Cour d'appel, qui devait, par application de l'article 6 de la Convention précitée du 10 mai 1952, apprécier à cet égard la responsabilité des saisissants sur le fondement du droit français, n'a pas satisfait aux exigences du texte susvisé.
132. § 945 ZPO so provides:
  Erweist sich die Anordnung eines Arrestes oder einer einstweiligen Verfügung als von Anfang an unger-echtfertigt oder wird die angeordnete Maßregel auf Grund des § 926 Abs. 2 oder des § 942 Abs. 3 aufgehoben, so ist die Partei, welche die Anordnung erwirkt hat, verpflichtet, dem Gegner den Schaden zu ersetzen, der ihm aus der Vollziehung der angeordneten Maßregel oder dadurch entsteht, daß er Sicherheit leistet, um die Vollziehung abzuwenden oder die Aufhebung der Maßregel zu erwirken.
133. Article 914 of the Greek Civil Code lays down the general rule on tort liability. It so provides:
  He who, contrary to law, causes by his fault damage to others, is obliged to reparation.

HAITI

I.794 The arrestor is liable in damages if the arrest proves to be illegal, arbitrary or unjustified.

ITALY

I.795 Liability of the claimant for damages resulting from the arrest of the ship can arise under the general rule laid down in Article 96 of the Code of Civil Procedure which so provides:

If the losing party acted or defended himself in the proceeding in bad faith or with gross negligence the judge on request of the other party, will condemn him to pay, in addition to the costs, the damages to be liquidated, also ex officio, with the judgment.

I.796 There are only two known precedents in which the above rule has been applied to the arrest of ships: Tribunale of Genoa 27 December 1989, *Fast Ferries* v. *Giuseppe Meocci—The "Briso II"*,[134] and Tribunale of Genoa 14 June 1955, *Ferrari & Gugenheim* v. *Avigdor & Co.—The "Bracha Fold"*.[135] In the former case the Tribunale of Genoa so held[136]:

Beyond doubt the behaviour of the plaintiffs has proved to be grossly negligent—and thus sanctionable pursuant to article 96 of the Code of Civil Procedure—since they have requested the arrest some of them without being entitled to it and others for a claim considerably higher than the amount owing to them; such behaviour has become more negligent when, after the delivery of the report of the expert appointed by the Court, the disproportion of the arrest effected to secure a claim rather modest could not be ignored.

NETHERLANDS

I.797 The claimant is considered to act at his own risk when he applies for the arrest of a ship and, therefore, is in principle required to make good any loss caused by the arrest, if the arrest was wrongly effected. It would appear that this would be the case when the claim is rejected, even if the claimant reasonably believed that his claim was grounded.

NIGERIA

I.798 The Admiralty Jurisdiction Act 1991, section 13 and the Admiralty Jurisdiction Procedure Rules (AJPR) 1993, Order XI, rule 3(2) provide for a right of action for damages for wrongful arrest. An arrest is wrongful, for example, if made unreasonably and without good cause. Alternatively, there is relief under AJPR, Order XI, rule 2 for a fixed sum compensation for "needless arrest".

NORWAY

I.799 The claimant is strictly liable for all losses that are not too remote.

---

134. [1990] Dir. Mar. 406.
135. [1957] Dir. Mar. 209.
136. At p. 411.

SPAIN

I.800 Pursuant to the general domestic rules on arrest (*embargo preventivo*) the claimant is liable if the arrest proves to be wrongful (Article 1416 of the Code of Civil Procedure). The arrest is wrongful *inter alia* if the conditions for arrest do not exist (the claim is not a maritime claim, the ship is not arrestable under Article 3 of the Convention), if proceedings on the merits are not commenced within the prescribed time limit or if the claim is rejected.

Security for damages

I.801 In some countries security for damages for wrongful arrest is statutorily required, save exceptional cases, as a condition for granting the arrest. This is so, for example, in Denmark,[137] Finland,[138] Germany,[139] Nigeria,[140] Spain,[141] and Sweden.[142]

I.802 In other countries the decision as to the need for security is left to the discretion of the court. This is so, for example, in Belgium,[143] Croatia,[144] France,[145] Greece,[146] Italy,[147] and Norway.[148]

I.803 In still other countries no security seems to be even contemplated. This is so in Haiti[149] and Slovenia.[150]

---

137. In Denmark, as in Sweden, the claimant is normally required to provide security: see the reply of the Danish Association of Maritime Law to Question 10 of the Questionnaire, Appendix II, p. 275.

138. In Finland the arrest is enforced only after the claimant has provided satisfactory security. See the reply of the Finnish MLA to Question 10 of the Questionnaire, Appendix II, p. 270.

139. It would appear that security is normally required by the Court. See the reply of the German MLA to Question 10 of the Questionnaire, Appendix II, p. 270.

140. Pursuant to rule X of the Nigerian Admiralty Jurisdiction Procedure Rules security is required when the claim exceeds Nairas 1 million. See the reply of the Nigerian MLA to Question 10 of the Questionnaire, Appendix II, p. 271.

141. Article 1 of Law 2/1967 of 8 April 1967, enacted in order to provide procedural rules for the implementation of the 1952 Convention, so provides:

Para decretar el embargo preventivo de un buque extranjero por crédito marítimo que se define en al artículo 1.° del Convenio de Bruselas de 10 de mayo de 1952, bastará que se alegue el derecho o créditos reclamados y la causa que los motive.

El Juex exigirá en todo caso fianza en cantidad suficiente para responder de los daños, perjuicios y costas que puedan ocasionarse. Esta fianza podrá ser de cualquiera de las clases que reconce el derecho, incluso el aval bancario.

142. Section 6 of chapter 15 of the Swedish Code of Judicial Procedure so provides:

No measure pursuant to Section 1, 2 or 3 may be granted unless the applicant deposits with the court security for the loss that the opposing party may suffer. If the applicant lacks means to furnish security, however, and if he has shown extraordinary reasons for his claim, the court may waive the security requirement. The state, municipalities, county councils, and local community organizations are not required to deposit security.

See also the Swedish reply to Question 10 of the Questionnaire, Appendix II, p. 272.

143. See the reply of the Belgium MLA to Question 10 of the Questionnaire, Appendix II, p. 270.

144. See the reply of the Croatian MLA to Question 10 of the Questionnaire, Appendix II, p. 270.

145. See the reply of the French MLA to Question 10 of the Questionnaire, Appendix II, p. 270.

146. Pursuant to article 694(1) of the Greek Code of Civil Procedure the Court may at its discretion require the claimant to provide security.

147. Pursuant to article 669 undecies of the Italian Code of Civil Procedure the Court may, with the order of arrest require the claimant, all circumstances having been valued, to provide security for damages, if any.

148. See the reply to Question 10 of the Questionnaire, Appendix II, p. 272.

149. See the reply to Question 10 of the Questionnaire, Appendix II, p. 271.

150. See the reply of the Slovenian MLA to Question 10 of the Questionnaire, Appendix II, p. 272.

I.804 The amount of the security may be left entirely to the discretion of the court[151] even though certain basic criteria are normally followed[152] or may be established by statute.[153]

37. JURISDICTION ON THE MERITS

I.805 The question whether the courts of the country in which the arrest is made should have jurisdiction to determine the case upon its merits had, at the Paris Conference in 1937, been solved by providing that such courts would always have jurisdiction, thereby adopting the common law approach that arrest is a means of obtaining jurisdiction.[154] When the problem was again considered at the Antwerp Conference in 1947, the solution adopted in Paris met with the opposition of the French association, on the ground that in French law the jurisdictional links were expressly stated and the arrest of a ship could not have the effect of attributing jurisdiction to a court that did not have such jurisdiction on the basis of statutory links.[155] The same rules prevailed in many other civil law countries.[156] The International Sub-Committee, therefore, tried to find a compromise solution

151. This is so in Croatia, France, Germany, Italy, Nigeria and Spain.

152. For example, in Denmark it is normally calculated on the basis of the loss of hire for four or five days (section 94(1) of the Merchant Shipping Act) and an identical rule exists in Norway. In Greece the amount is calculated on the basis of the estimated loss that will be suffered by the owner during the time reasonably required for the provision of a guarantee for the release of the ship.

153. This is so in Belgium, where it is quantified in 65 BEF per deadweight ton of the arrested ship.

154. In England the admiralty jurisdiction of the High Court is established with reference to the nature of the claims and may be invoked by an action *in personam* or by an action *in rem* against the ship or property in connection with which the claim or question arises (s. 21 of the Supreme Court Act 1981).

In the United States, pursuant to supplemental rule C of the Federal Rules of Civil Procedure, jurisdiction *in rem* is dependent either on seizure of the vessel by the provision of the Admiralty Court or upon the ability to seize her (see *Benedict on Admiralty* (7th Edn.), Vol. 2A, p. 6–2).

155. In the report of the International Sub-Committee of May 1951 the following comments are made (CMI Bulletin No. 105, pp. 3 and 4; *Travaux Préparatoires*, p. 405):

The third and last of the fundamental problems which has been at length considered by the International Committee is that of jurisdiction; which is the Court which shall judge on the merits of the claim that has given rise to the arrest? It has been deemed necessary to insert a provision in this respect in the Draft, for the reason that the laws of certain countries do not authorize a conservative arrest or its maintenance unless the Court in the jurisdiction of which the arrest is made has jurisdiction on the merits. Such provision did not give rise to any objection at the Paris meeting.

However, at Antwerp serious criticisms were made, mainly by the French Delegates. They and, in particular, Dean Ripert, maintained that the system proposed was such as to bring about very negative consequences by giving jurisdiction to a Court who would not normally have it pursuant to the private international law rules the attention of the Committee was specially drawn to disputes concerning the property in the ship, as well as to other claims without any territorial or chronological link with the arrest or the "forum arresti". The system that had been proposed, it was said, could not be reconciled with the French system and was contrary to the French concepts in the area of private international law. Following a proposal of Dean Ripert the International Committee at its Antwerp meeting resolved to adopt the text which appears in Art. 8 of the present draft.

156. For example, in Italy the jurisdictional links are set out in Art. 4 of the CPC which provides that a foreigner may be sued before an Italian court if he is resident in Italy, if the claim relates to assets located in Italy or to obligations arising or to be performed in Italy, if the claim is connected with another claim in respect of which proceedings are pending in Italy, if it relates to conservative measures to be enforced in Italy and in cases of reciprocity. Similar rules exist in France, Poland, Portugal and Spain. See generally on the Continental European approach Philip, "Maritime Jurisdiction in EEC" [1977] Acta Scandinavia Juris Gentium 113. In Germany, the prevailing view was that pursuant to para. 23 ZPO the court of the place where an asset of a foreign defendant is situated is deemed to be a court of competent jurisdiction. This construction of para. 23 ZPO has, however, been rejected by the Bundesgerichtshof which held ([1991] RIW, 856) that the sole existence of an asset of the debtor is not sufficient to establish jurisdiction, but some other links must be established.

by providing that the courts of the country where the ship is arrested should have jurisdiction to determine the case upon its merits only in a limited number of cases.[157] The criterion on the basis of which these cases were chosen was twofold. First, the Sub-Committee considered whether it was reasonable to state the circumstances in which a jurisdictional link existed between the maritime claim and the courts of the country where the ship was arrested. Apart from the cases where such courts have jurisdiction in accordance with the *lex fori*, it was concluded that such link should exist in the following circumstances:

— when the claimant has his habitual residence or principal place of business in the country where the arrest is made;
— when the claim has arisen in such country;
— when the claim has arisen during the voyage of the ship during which the arrest is made.

I.806 Secondly, it was considered that jurisdiction should be recognised in respect of some particular maritime claims in respect of which the claimants deserved special protection, viz. the following:

— claims arising out of collision;
— claims for salvage.

I.807 At the Naples Conference the British association attempted to revert to the rule adopted in Paris in 1937 and to provide that the courts of the country where the arrest is made should always have jurisdiction to determine the case upon its merits, on the ground that the text that was proposed would cut down the existing English jurisdiction.[158] The French delegate pointed out that the concern of the British delegation was not justified since Article 8, as drafted, provided that the courts of the country where the ship was arrested would have jurisdiction if the *lex fori* gave them jurisdiction and earnestly recommended that the compromise should not be upset.[159]

I.808 After the intervention of the French delegate the British association withdrew its proposal and at the same time supported the Dutch proposal to add another maritime

---

157. Art. 8 of the 1951 Draft provided thus (*Travaux Préparatoires*, p. 464):
   The Courts of that State shall have jurisdiction to decide on the merits of the case, in addition to the cases provided for in the rules of jurisdiction of the domestic law of the state where arrest is made, in the following cases:
   a. if the claimant has his domicile or principal place of business in the State where the arrest was made;
   b. if the maritime claim has arisen in the contracting State in the jurisdiction of which is the place of arrest;
   c. if the maritime claim has arisen in the course of the voyage during which the arrest was made;
   d. if the claim arises out of collision;
   e. if the claim arises out of salvage.
158. CMI Bulletin No. 105, p. 296; *Travaux Préparatoires*, p. 411.
159. Dean Ripert stated (CMI Bulletin No. 105, pp. 298 and 299; *Travaux Préparatoires*, p. 413):
   But the British Amendment has the effect of suppressing, in that article, an attempt of compromise that had been made at Antwerp.
   The problem, in fact, was to reconcile different legal systems. In certain countries, the Court of the place of arrest has jurisdiction; in others, it will never have it. We have then conceived a compromise consisting in granting jurisdiction to the Court of the place of arrest, but only in specified cases. And since we have given serious consideration to the objection of the British Delegate that in such a manner we might, perhaps, restrict the jurisdiction of the English courts, it has been stated, at the beginning of Art. 8, that in addition to the rules of jurisdiction provided by the domestic law of the State where the arrest was made, the Courts of that State shall have jurisdiction on the merits in the cases set out in the Draft. In such a manner, contrary to the statement of the British Delegation, the Draft does not deprive the English Courts of any jurisdiction they have at present, since they can always avail themselves of the domestic jurisdiction rules.

claim, viz. that in respect of mortgages and *hypothèques*.[160] With such addition, Article 8, which then became Article 7, was adopted.[161]

I.809 At the Diplomatic Conference, in addition to a slight change in the wording of the opening sentence, it was agreed to amend subparagraph (d), which referred to claims arising out of a collision, by adding the words "or in circumstances covered by art. 13 of the International Convention for the Unification of Certain Rules of Law with Respect to Collisions between Vessels, signed at Brussels on 23rd September 1910".[162]

I.810 The opposition to the very simple rule, adopted in 1937 at Paris, whereby the courts of the country in which the arrest is made always have jurisdiction to determine the case upon its merits is difficult to understand, otherwise than on the basis of the desire of a number of Contracting States to change their domestic rules on jurisdictional links as little as possible. The so-called "compromise"[163] suggested at the Antwerp Conference in 1947 and thereafter vigorously defended, yielded to the advantage of those Contracting States in which jurisdiction on the merits had always existed, since it did not change their national law.

I.811 In Article 7(1) reference is made to the courts of the country in which the arrest is made and not to the particular court or other appropriate judicial authority within whose jurisdiction the ship has been arrested, as in Article 5. The reason is that it was not intended to affect the domestic rules on the choice of the particular court, within the jurisdiction of the State in which the ship is arrested, that is competent *ratione loci* or for any other reason.

I.812 In order that jurisdiction be acquired under Article 7(1), it is necessary that the ship be actually arrested. If, therefore, security is given to avoid a threatened arrest, Article 7(1) does not apply.[164] Nor can, pursuant to Article 3(3), a ship be arrested after security

---

160. CMI Bulletin No. 105, p. 301; *Travaux Préparatoires*, pp. 414 and 415.

161. The text, as adopted by the Conference, was the first unnumbered para. of art. 8 and provided as follows (*Procès-verbaux*, p. 21; *Travaux Préparatoires*, p. 416):

The courts of the country in which the arrest is made shall have jurisdiction to determine the case upon its merits:

    I. If the domestic law of the country in which the arrest is made gives jurisdiction to such courts.

    II. In the following cases, namely:

       a. if the claimant has his domicile or principal place of business in the country in which the arrest is made;

       b. if the claim arose in the country in which the arrest is made;

       c. if the claim concerns the voyage of the ship during which the arrest is made;

       d. if the claim arose out of a collision;

       e. if the claim is for salvage;

       f. if the claim is upon a mortgage or hypothecation of the ship arrested.

162. *Procès-verbaux*, p. 116.

163. The "compromise" adopted by the Convention is criticised by Chauveau, *Traité de Droit Maritime* (Paris, 1958), No. 246.

164. In *The "Deichland"* [1989] 2 Lloyd's Rep. 113, Neill L.J. stated (at p. 121):

I see the force of the argument that in the light of the 1956 Act the jurisdiction given by art. 7 of the 1952 Convention should not be confined to cases where an arrest has actually been effected.

I have come to the conclusion, however, that the argument must be rejected for the following reasons:

  (1) It is clear, as I have already indicated, that the 1952 Convention was only concluded after long and detailed negotiations had taken place and the final wording represented a compromise. One must be very careful therefore before accepting an argument that the word "arrest" in art. 7 is capable of including a process which falls short of an actual arrest.

  (2) The word "arrest" is defined in art. 2 as meaning the "detention of a ship by judicial process to secure a maritime claim, but does not include the seizure of a ship in execution or satisfaction of a judgment".

  (3) In arts. 3 and 6 respectively reference is made to "bail or other security" given or furnished "to avoid a threatened arrest" or to "prevent the arrest". There are no comparable words in art. 7.

is given.[165]

I.813 The question arises, therefore, whether the claimant may refuse the security offered in order to avoid the arrest and arrest the ship in order that the provisions of Article 7(1) become operative.

I.814 Article 5 of the Convention provides that the court within whose jurisdiction the ship has been arrested shall permit the release of the ship upon sufficient bail or other security being furnished, but does not consider the case where security is offered before the arrest is made. There is, therefore, no express rule in the Convention that prevents the claimant from enforcing an order of arrest if sufficient security is offered. Even though doubts could arise as to the right of the claimant on account of the definition of arrest, in which the continental notion of the arrest as a conservative measure seems to have been adopted, these doubts are overcome by the history of Article 7(1).[166]

I.815 Since it has been deemed proper to link the jurisdiction for the arrest with that on the merits, it appears reasonable that the claimant be entitled to obtain the benefit of Article 7(1).[167]

I.816 The jurisdictional links set out in Article 7(1) are added to those provided by the *lex fori*, which continue to apply. This appears clearly from the French text, where the words "*soit . . . soit*" are used. In the English text instead the two alternatives are preceded by the words "if . . . or" while it would have been better to state "either . . . or" as in Article 14 of the 1910 Salvage Convention.

I.817 The jurisdiction of the courts of the State where the ship is arrested is not exclusive and, therefore, the claimant is free to choose a different court which may, according to the *lex fori*, have jurisdiction in the case.

I.818 In common law countries parties to the 1952 Convention, jurisdiction on the merits is the effect of the existence of Admiralty jurisdiction in respect of maritime claims. This is so in England, where the Supreme Court Act 1981, sections 20(1)(a), 20(2) provide a list of claims to which the Admiralty jurisdiction of the High Court extends. According to section 20(7) of the Supreme Court Act 1981 those provisions apply in relation to all ships whether British or not wherever the residence or domicile of their owners may be, and all claims wherever they arise.[168] It follows that there is generally jurisdiction on the

---

(4) Prof. Schlosser in paras. 122 and 123 of his Report on the Accession Convention commented on the wording of art. 5(7) of the 1968 Convention relating to jurisdiction in connection with the arrest of a salvaged cargo or freight. He explained that art. 5(7)(b) introduced an extension of jurisdiction not expressly modelled on the 1952 Convention. He added:

After salvage operations—whether involving a ship, cargo or freight—arrest is sometimes ordered, but not actually carried into effect, because bail or other security has been provided. This must be sufficient to confer jurisdiction on the arresting court to decide also on the substance of the matter.

It seems to me that this comment or explanation is at least consistent with the view that art. 7 did not confer jurisdiction where bail or other security was given to avoid arrest.
See also Verheul, "The Convention Relating to the Arrest of Seagoing Ships of 1952—Some Questions, [1983] Netherlands International Law Review 383 at p. 384. Contra, Philip, "Maritime Jurisdiction in the EEC", [1979] Nordisk Tidsskrift for Internationale ret 120.

165. See *supra*, at para. I.542–I.547.

166. See *supra*, at para. I.805–I.810.

167. In England it has been held by the Admiralty Court (Sheen J.) in *The "Prinsengracht"* [1993] 1 Lloyd's Rep. 41 that the claimant is entitled to arrest a ship even after bail has been provided when the owner has declined to agree expressly to submit to the jurisdiction of the court. Even if a ship can be protected from arrest by previously filing a caveat in the Admiralty Court Registry (see *The "Anna H."* [1994] 1 Lloyd's Rep. 287), this obliges the owner of the ship to accept English jurisdiction.

168. *The "Anna H"* [1995] 1 Lloyd's Rep. 11.

merits and not simply for those claims listed in Article 7(1)(a)–(f). In the English system there is, therefore, an intimate linking between jurisdiction and arrest. An arrest under the action *in rem* is a basis for jurisdiction on the merits of the case.

I.819 The same rule holds in the Scandinavian countries and in the Netherlands where, prior to the enactment of the new Code of Civil Procedure in 1992, the Hoge Raad (Court of Cassation) held that the proceedings for the validation of the arrest, for which the court granting the arrest has jurisdiction, are so closely connected to the proceedings on the merits that the jurisdiction of that court must be extended also to these latter proceedings. At present the jurisdiction is statutorily established by Article 767 of the new Code of Civil Procedure.[169] This rule holds also in Nigeria, where section 3 of the Admiralty Jurisdiction Act 1991 provides that the Admiralty Jurisdiction of the Federal High Court shall apply to all ships, irrespective of the place of residence or domicile of the owners and to all maritime claims, whenever arising.[170]

38. THE EC CONVENTION ON JURISDICTION AND THE ENFORCEMENT OF CIVIL AND COMMERCIAL JUDGMENTS (THE JURISDICTION CONVENTION)

I.820 Article 7(1) is partly in conflict with the provision on jurisdiction contained in the EC Jurisdiction Convention. The exceptions to the general rule whereby a person domiciled in a Contracting State may only be sued in the courts of that State (Article 2 of the Convention) that are relevant in respect of maritime claims are those according to which any such person may also be sued, in matters relating to a contract, in the courts of the place of performance of the obligation in question (Article 5(1) of the Convention), and in matters relating to tort, delict or quasi-delict, in the courts of the place where the harmful event occurred.[171]

---

169. Article 767 of the Code of Civil Procedure so provides (translation by Mr. T. van der Valk):
> In the absence of any other way of obtaining a title in execution in the Netherlands, the action on the merits, including the action regarding the costs of attachment, may be instituted with the District Court the President of which granted leave for the attachment effected, or prevented or lifted against security.

On the meaning of the phrase "In the absence of any other way of obtaining a title in execution" and on the effects on this provision of the 1968 European Convention on Jurisdiction and the enforcement of Judgments see the reply of the Dutch MLA to Question 11 of the Questionnaire, Appendix II, p. 274.

See also Claringbould, Arrest of Ships(2)—The Netherlands, London 1986, pp. 58 and 59.

170. Section 20 of the Admiralty Jurisdiction Act further provides that the court's jurisdiction is always preserved in the following cases:
   (a) the place of performance, execution, delivery, act or default is or takes place in Nigeria; or
   (b) any of the parties resides or has resided in Nigeria; or
   (c) the payment under the agreement (implied or express) is made or is to be made in Nigeria; or
   (d) in any admiralty action or in the case of a maritime lien, the plaintiff submits to the jurisdiction of the court and makes a declaration to that effect or the *res* is within Nigerian jurisdiction; or
   (e) it is a case in which the Federal Government or a State of the Federation is involved and the Government or State submits to the jurisdiction of the court; or
   (f) there is a financial consideration accruing in, derived from, brought into or received in Nigeria in respect of any matters under the Admiralty jurisdiction of the court; or
   (g) under any convention for the time being in force to which Nigeria is a party the national court of a contracting State is either mandated or has a discretion to assume jurisdiction; or
   (h) in the opinion of the court, the cause, matter or action should be adjudicated upon in Nigeria.

171. See Lopez de Gonzalo, "Sequestro di Nave e Giurisdizione Italiana" [1982] Dir. Mar. 574 at p. 584.

I.821 However, Article 57 of the Jurisdiction Convention contains the following saving provision:

This Convention shall not affect any conventions to which the Contracting States are or will be parties and which, in relation to particular matters, govern jurisdiction and the recognition and enforcement of judgments.[172]

I.822 The meaning and effect of this provision were clarified by Article 25(2) of the Accession Convention, which provides:

With a view to its uniform interpretation, paragraph 1 of article 57 shall be applied in the following manner: (a) the 1968 Convention as amended shall not prevent a court of a Contracting State which is a party to a convention on a particular matter from assuming jurisdiction in accordance with that convention, even where the defendant is domiciled in another Contracting State which is not a party to that convention. The court shall, in any event, apply article 20 of the 1968 Convention as amended.

I.823 The provisions on jurisdiction of the Arrest Convention therefore prevail over those of the Jurisdiction Convention as amended.[173]

172. Jenard ("Report on the Convention on Jurisdiction and the Enforcement of Judgments in Civil and Commercial Matters", in [1973] OJ EC), after having listed among the international agreements to which Member States of the Community are parties the 1952 Arrest Convention (Comment on Art. 57, at p. 59), stated (at p. 60):

The approach adopted by the Committee means that the agreements relating to particular matters prevail over the Convention. It follows that, where those agreements lay down rules of direct or exclusive jurisdiction, the court of the State of origin will have to apply those rules to the exclusion of any others where they contain provisions concerning the conditions governing the recognition and enforcement of judgments given to matters to which the agreements apply, only those conditions need be satisfied, so that the enforcement procedure set up by the EEC Convention will not apply to those judgments.

The Committee adopted this approach in view of the fact that the Member States of the Community, when they entered into these agreements, had for the most part contracted obligations towards non Member States which should not be modified without the consent of those States.

Moreover, the following points must be borne in mind:

1. The rules of jurisdiction laid down in these agreements have been dictated by particular considerations relating to the matters of which they treat, e.g. the flag or port of registration of a vessel; in the maritime conventions the criterion of domicile is not often used to establish jurisdiction in such agreements.

173. *The "Netty"* [1981] 2 Lloyd's Rep. 57; *The "Nordglimt"* [1987] 2 Lloyd's Rep. 470 at p. 480; *The "Deichland"* [1989] 2 Lloyd's Rep. 113 at p. 123; *The "Anna H."* [1994] 1 Lloyd's Rep. 287 at pp. 292–296. Schlosser, "Report on the Convention on the Association of the Kingdom of Denmark, Ireland and the United Kingdom of Great Britain and Northern Ireland to the Convention on Jurisdiction and the Enforcement of Judgments in Civil and Commercial Matters and to the Protocol on its interpretation by the Court of Justice", Official Journal of the European Communities, 5 March 1979, so states (para. 240, at p. 140):

The solution arrived at is based on the following principles. The 1968 Convention contains the rules generally applicable in all Member States. Provisions in special conventions are special rules which every State may make prevail over the 1968 Convention by becoming a party to such convention. Insofar as a special convention does not contain rules covering a particular matter the 1968 Convention applies. This is also the case where the special convention includes rules of jurisdiction which do not altogether fit the interconnecting provisions of the various parts of the 1968 Convention, especially those governing the relationship between jurisdiction and enforcement. The overriding considerations are simplicity and clarity of the legal position.

The most important consequence of this is that provisions on jurisdiction contained in special conventions are to be regarded as if they were provisions of the 1968 Convention itself, even if only one Member State is a Contracting Party to such a special convention. Even Member States which are not Contracting Parties to the special convention must therefore recognize and enforce decisions given by courts which have jurisdiction only under the special convention. Furthermore in the context of two States which are parties to a special Convention, a person who wishes to obtain the recognition or enforcement of a judgment may rely upon the procedural provisions of the 1968 Convention on recognition and enforcement.

See also Philip, "Maritime Jurisdiction in EEC", Acta Scandinavia Juris Gentium, 1977, 121; Hartley, "The Effect of the 1968 Brussels Judgments Convention on Admiralty Actions in Rem" [1989] LQR 640, at p. 649.

I.824 The view has been expressed[174] that since the purpose of Article 57 of the Jurisdiction Convention is not to affect unification realised through conventions on particular matters, only the special jurisdictional links listed in Article 7(1) under (a) to (f) prevail over the provisions of the Jurisdiction Convention, while when jurisdiction is based on the domestic rules of the country in which the arrest is made the provisions of the Jurisdiction Convention remain wholly operative.

I.825 This view is correct. In fact the first sentence of Article 1(1), pursuant to which the courts of the country in which the arrest is made have jurisdiction on the merits if such jurisdiction is granted by the *lex fori*, has the nature of a rule of private international law. The consequence is that if the country where the arrest is made is a party to the Jurisdiction Convention, its provisions shall apply except for the special links set out in Article 7(1).

39. THE EXPRESS LINKS: (a) HABITUAL RESIDENCE; (b) CLAIMS ARISING IN THE COUNTRY IN WHICH THE ARREST IS MADE

I.826 It may now be convenient to analyse each of the six cases enumerated in Article 7(1).[175]

(a) Habitual Residence or Principal Place of Business of the Claimant

I.827 The courts of the country in which the arrest is made[176] have jurisdiction to determine the case upon its merits if the claimant has his habitual residence or principal place of business in such country.

(b) Claims arising in the Country in which the Arrest is made

I.828 The place where the claim arises may be established either by reference to the time when it actually arises or by reference to the time when it may be enforced. The dates established on the basis of those two criteria do not necessarily coincide, for there are situations where a claim may not be enforced immediately upon its coming into existence. For example, the claim in respect of loss of or damage to goods arises when the loss or damage occurs, but the owner of the goods knows that such loss or damage has occurred only at the time of delivery, and for this reason both the Hague-Visby Rules and the Hamburg Rules provide that the time limit begins to run from the delivery of the goods or from the date when they should have been delivered.[177] The claim of the master and

---

174. Philip, "Maritime Jurisdiction in the EEC", [1977] Nordisk Tidss-Krift for internationale ret 121; Verheul, "The Convention Relating to the Arrest of Seagoing Ships of 1952: Some Questions", [1983] Netherlands International Law Review 383, at p. 386.

175. See also Lopez de Gonzalo, "Sequestro di Nave", *supra*, note 171.

176. The Convention is not consistent as regards the tense of the verb. In fact whilst the past tense (the arrest *was* made) is used in the preamble of Art. 7, para. 1 and in subparagraphs (1), (b) and (c), the present tense (the arrest *is* made) is used with reference to the jurisdiction based on the *lex fori*.

For the debate on this provision see International Law Association, Report of the Thirtieth Conference, Vol. II, Proceedings of the Maritime Law Committee, p. 108 *et seq.*; *The Travaux Préparatoires of the Hague-Visby Rules*, edited by F. Berlingieri, Genoa 1997, pp. 299 et seq.

177. *Supra*, para. I.344–348.

crew for wages arises at the time when the wages fall due, but it often cannot immediately be enforced, for example, because the ship is at sea: for this reason, the 1993 MLM Convention provides (Article 9(2)(a)) that the maritime lien securing such claim is extinguished one year after the claimant's discharge from the ship. On the contrary, the time limit begins to run from the date when the claim arises under the 1910 Collision Convention (Article 7) and under the 1910 and 1989 Salvage Conventions (Articles 10 and 23 respectively).

I.829 For the purposes of Article 7(1)(b) of the Arrest Convention, reference must, however, be made to the time when the claim actually arises, for the jurisdictional link is based on the voyage during which the arrest is made. Reference to the time when the claim may be enforceable would not, therefore, be correct in this case.

I.830 In a number of cases, the claim arises when and where the breach which gives rise to the claim is committed. This is true for all tort claims and for some contract claims, such as those in respect of loss of life or of personal injury to passengers and loss of or damage to goods. Different criteria, however, apply in other cases and, therefore, it may be worthwhile to consider the place where each of the maritime claims enumerated in Article 1(1) may be deemed normally to arise. This investigation is unnecessary for claims in respect of which the jurisdiction of the courts of the country where the arrest is made is expressly established, irrespective of the place where the claim has arisen, viz. claims in respect of collision damage, salvage and mortgages or *hypothèques*.

I.831 The loopholes and the uncertainties which will appear from the examination that follows may partly be filled and, respectively, become less relevant on account of the subsequent jurisdictional link set out in subparagraph (c) of Article 7(1), whereby the courts of a country where an arrest is made have jurisdiction upon the merits if the claim concerns the voyage of a ship during which an arrest is made.

Article 1(1)(b): Loss of Life or Personal Injury caused by any Ship or occurring in connection with the Operation of any Ship

I.832 In all situations, whether the claim is in tort or in contract, the time and place where the claim arises must be established in relation to the death or the injury. If, therefore, the death or injury occurred when the victim was outside the territorial waters of the country where the arrest is made, the courts of such country have no jurisdiction on the merits. It is worth noting that in cases of collision the claims in respect of loss of life or personal injury have worse treatment than those in respect of loss of or damage to property including financial damage, for only in respect of such latter category of claims is the jurisdiction of the courts of the country where the arrest is made always affirmed.

Article 1(1)(d): Agreement relating to the Use or Hire of any Ship whether by Charterparty or Otherwise

I.833 As has been seen,[178] this maritime claim refers to bareboat charterparties or other contracts of a similar nature that have the effect of placing the ship at the disposal of the charterer. Claims of the charterer against the owner will normally relate to a breach by the

---

178. See, for example, cl. 11 of "Barecon 'A'", cl. 12 of "Barecon 'B'" and cll. 9 and 12 of "Barecon 89".

owner of his contractual obligations in respect of, for example, the seaworthiness of the ship, the duty to carry out repairs, or the reimbursement of repairs carried out by the charterer. Today, standard forms of bareboat charterparties normally provide that it is the charterer who has a duty to arrange for repairs.[179] However, when the ship is insured by the owner, the charterer, even if he has a duty to carry out repairs, is entitled to obtain reimbursement of all expenses incurred.[180]

I.834 If the claim is in respect of damages suffered by the charterer as a consequence of the breach by the owner of his obligation to repair the ship, the claim arises when and where the damages were suffered. However, to establish this may not be easy. For example, the damages may consist of the liability the charterer has incurred towards third parties as a consequence of the unseaworthiness of the vessel: collision, loss of or damage to cargo, etc. The place where the claim arises may be that where the liability has been incurred, or, alternatively, that where the charterer had to meet his obligations towards third parties who suffered damages.

I.835 If the claim is in respect of reimbursement of monies, the place where the claim arises is either that where the claimant has his habitual residence or his principal place of business or, alternatively, that where he has paid the monies.

Article 1(1)(e): Agreement relating to the Carriage of Goods in any Ship whether by Charterparty or Otherwise

I.836 As previously stated,[181] maritime claims covered by this subparagraph relate to all types of breach by the owner under a contract of affreightment, viz. a time charterparty, a trip charter, a single or consecutive voyage charterparty, a tonnage agreement, a slot charter or a contract of carriage of goods on a liner ship, other than in respect of loss of or damage to goods. These claims include claims in respect of unseaworthiness of the vessel, failures of performance, despatch money, delay in the delivery of the ship at the commencement of the charter, unjustified withdrawal of the ship from the service of the charterer, failure to place the agreed slot space at the disposal of the charterer, etc.

I.837 As regards claims for damages arising out of the unseaworthiness of the ship, the remarks made in respect of subparagraph (d) apply.

I.838 As regards claims for failures of performance, the obvious answer should be that the place is that where the failure occurred. But most such failures are of a continuing nature and, therefore, it is impossible to establish the place where the claim arises. The most sensible solution is to refer to the place where the failure has been or should be established, such as the place where each voyage ends.

---

179. Cl. 12(d) of "Barecon 'A' " provides:
   (d) The Charterers shall, subject to the approval of the Owners or Owners' Underwriters, effect all insured repairs, and the Charterers shall undertake settlement of all miscellaneous expenses in connection with such repairs as well as all insured charges, expenses and liabilities, to the extent of coverage under the insurances provided for under the provisions of sub-clause (a) of this Clause. The Charterers to be secured reimbursement through the Owners' Underwriters for such expenditures upon presentation of accounts.
   Cl. 13(d) of "Barecon 89" is identical to cl. 12(d) of "Barecon 'A' ".
   See *supra*, para. I.332–I.337.
   180. See *Carver's Carriage by Sea* (13th Edn. London, 1982), Vol. 2, paras. 1249–1259.
   181. Jurisdiction of the court of the port where a supply of bunker had been effected has in principle been recognised by the Cour d'Appel of Rennes with judgment 8 July 1998, *CNM Romline Shipping Co. v. The Captain of the m/v "Oscar Jupiter"*, 1999 DMF 436.

I.839 As regards claims for despatch money, these claims clearly arise in the place where the time was saved. As regards claims in respect of delay in the delivery of the ship, probably reference should be made to the place of delivery.

I.840 As regards claims for unjustified withdrawal of the ship, the place should be that where the withdrawal occurred. It must, however, be considered that the withdrawal may take place during a voyage, when the ship is at sea.

I.841 As regards claims for failure to place the agreed slot space, the failure occurs at the port or ports of call where the space would be utilised.

Article 1(1)(f): Loss of or Damage to Goods including Baggage carried in any Ship

I.842 The solution in this case is simpler. Since the obligation of the carrier is to carry and deliver the goods or the baggage safely to destination, the place where the claim arises is that where the goods or the baggage have been or should have been delivered.

Article 1(1)(g): General Average

I.843 The claim for contribution in general average arises at the time and place of the termination of the adventure, where the contributing values are assessed pursuant to Rule XVII of the York-Antwerp Rules 1994.

Article 1(1)(h): Bottomry

I.844 The claim arises at the time and place of safe arrival of the ship at destination, such arrival being a condition precedent to the obligation of reimbursement.[182]

Article 1(1)(i): Towage

I.845 If the claim is in respect of payment of the towage remuneration, the place where the claim arises is that where the towage service is completed. If the claim is for loss of or damage to the tug caused by the tow, the place where the claim arises is that where the loss or damage occurred. If, instead, the claim is for loss of or damage to the tow, in port towage the place is the port where the towage is performed while in deep-sea towage the place is that of destination, since normally the deep-sea towage has the nature of a contract of carriage.

Article 1(1)(j): Pilotage

I.846 The claim is, normally, that by the pilot for his remuneration. The remuneration is earned at the end of the service and, therefore, the place where the claim arises is that where the service is ended.

Article 1(1)(k): Goods or Materials wherever supplied to a Ship for her Operation or Maintenance

I.847 The normal situation will be that of goods or materials supplied on board the ship at the risk and expense of the supplier. In such a case, the claim in respect of the cost of

---

182. *Supra*, para. I.352–I.353.

such goods or materials arises in the place where the ship lies.[183] If, on the contrary, goods or materials are supplied on terms whereby payment must be made at the time when they are delivered to a carrier for transportation from the place of origin to the ship, the place where the claim arises is that agreed upon in the contract or, failing any such agreement, that where delivery to the carrier is made.

Article 1(1)(l): Construction, Repair or Equipment of any Ship or Dock Charges and Dues

I.848 Claims in respect of construction, repair or equipment of a ship arise in the place where the ship is constructed, repaired or equipped. Claims in respect of dock charges or dues arise in the place where the dock is situated.

Article 1(1)(m): Wages of Masters, Officers or Crew

I.849 Claims in respect of wages arise in the place where the ship is when wages fall due.[184] If the ship is on the high seas, claims may be deemed to arise in the country whose flag the ship is flying. An exception to these rules may exist when the owner has agreed to remit a part of the wages to the families of the master, officers and crew; in such a case the claim probably arises at the place where payment should have been made.

Article 1(1)(n): Master's Disbursements, including Disbursements made by Shippers, Charterers or Agents on behalf of a Ship or her Owner

I.850 Unless otherwise provided in the contract, the claim in respect of disbursements arises in the place where the disbursements are incurred.

Article 1(1)(o): Disputes as to the Title or Ownership of any Ship

I.851 The most likely case of a dispute as to the ownership of a ship is that where one person, who is not the registered owner of the ship or is only the registered owner of some shares, claims to be the actual owner of the ship or of other shares in order then to obtain the registration of the ship or shares in his name. It is not easy to establish where such a claim arises. Probably it should be deemed to arise in the place where the claimant alleges that he has acquired title to the ship or shares.

Article 1(1)(p): Disputes between Co-owners of any Ship as to Ownership, Possession, Employment or Earnings of any Ship

I.852 The comments made in respect of subparagraph (o) also apply in respect of disputes between co-owners as to ownership. Disputes as to possession arise when a person who

---

183. *Supra*, para. I.358–I.359.

184. The Cour d'Appel of Rennes in an *obiter dictum* in its judgment of 21 October 1998, *CNM Romline Shipping Co.* v. *The Captain of the m/v "Oscar Jupiter"*, 1999 DMF 438 stated that even if the ship had been arrested the Tribunal de Commerce of Nantes would not have had jurisdiction on the merits of the claims of the crewmembers of a Rumanian ship all of Panamanian nationality, arising out of contracts made in Rumania. See on this judgment the note of Chaumette, 1999 DMF 439.

is not in possession of the ship claims to be entitled to acquire possession and, also, when the person in possession is deprived of such possession. In the first case the claim arises in the place where the right to possession is acquired; in the second case it arises where the possession is lost.

I.853 Claims in respect of the employment of the ship probably arise in the place where the ship lies at the time when the claim has arisen. Claims in respect of the earnings of the ship probably arise where such earnings should have been paid.

40. (c) CLAIMS CONCERNING THE VOYAGE OF THE SHIP DURING WHICH THE ARREST IS MADE

I.854 The English and the French texts differ slightly. While in the English text the words used are "claims concerning the voyage", in the French text the words used are *"créance maritime . . . née au cours du voyage"*.

I.855 The French text indicates a temporal connection between the claim and the voyage, while the English text may indicate a causal connection.[185] The relevant factor, however, is that the claim has arisen in the course of the last voyage and also the word "concerning" must be given a temporal meaning. A relationship between claims and voyages is also established in the 1926 Maritime Liens and Mortgages Convention, for the purpose of ranking maritime liens. Article 5 provides that *"les créances se rapportant a un même voyage"* rank in the order in which they are enumerated in Article 2. These words could indicate a causal connection, but it is certain that they are used to indicate a temporal connection as is confirmed by the provision of Article 6, where it is stated that the maritime liens *"du dernier voyage"* (of the last voyage) are preferred to those of the preceding voyages.

I.856 In order to establish in respect of which claims the courts of the country where the ship is arrested have jurisdiction on the merits it is necessary to identify the notion of voyage.

I.857 For this purpose, it may be relevant to consider the other maritime convention in which the term "voyage" is used, viz. the 1926 Maritime Liens and Mortgages Convention.[186] As already indicated, the term "voyage" is used in Article 5 and in Article 6 for the purpose of ranking the maritime liens that have arisen during different voyages, and, also, in Article 2, no. 5, where reference is made to claims arising out of contracts for the continuation of the voyage, and in Article 4 where among the "accessories" of the ship

---

185. This is confirmed by the fact that the equivalent of the words "concerning the voyage" was used in the report of the CMI International Committee to the 1951 Naples Conference accompanying the draft, when the words *"née au cours du voyage"* (arisen in the course of the voyage) were used. In such report, reference is in fact made to a claim that *"se rapporte au voyage"* (relates to the voyage) (CMI Bulletin No. 105, p. 3; *Travaux Préparatoires*, pp. 405 and 406). In the comments on the Draft of the French association the words used are *"née pendant le voyage"* (arisen in the course of the voyage) (CMI Bulletin No. 105, p. 31; *Travaux Préparatoires*, p. 406), in those of the Italian association, they are *"regarde le voyage"* (CMI Bulletin No. 105, p. 75; *Travaux Préparatoires*, p. 407) and in those of the British association *"se rapporte au voyage"* (CMI Bulletin No. 105, p. 54; *Travaux Préparatoires*, p. 409). It is, therefore, clear that the words "se rapporte au voyage", which correspond to the words "concerning the voyage", have been considered to have the same meaning of *"née au cours du voyage"*.

186. On the possibility of interpreting the provisions of one maritime convention with the aid of those of other maritime conventions, particularly when they deal with a similar subject, see Carbone, *Contratto di Trasporto Marittimo di Cose* (Milano, 1988), p. 114; Ivaldi, *Diritto Uniforme dei Trasporti e Diritto Internazionale Privato* (Milano, 1990), p. 42.

is mentioned the remuneration due to the owner in respect of salvage services rendered at any time before the end of the voyage.[187]

I.858 In this last provision, the voyage clearly relates to the period during which the ship is earning a certain freight, for the salvage remuneration earned by the owner is treated as an accessory of the freight. It is, therefore, an economic notion of the voyage that must be adopted, as appears also from Article 2, which provides that the claims listed thereunder give rise to a maritime lien on the ship, on the freight of the voyage during which the claim arises and on the accessories of the voyage and freight accrued since the commencement of the voyage, and from no. 5 of such article by which, as already indicated, a maritime lien is granted to claims resulting from contracts necessary for the preservation of the ship or the continuation of the voyage.[188] The voyage is, therefore, a well specified period of the commercial operation of the ship.[189]

I.859 If such notion of voyage fits with the provisions of Article 4, no. 3 and of Article 2, no. 5 of the 1926 Convention, it must necessarily fit with those of Article 5 and Article 6.[190]

I.860 The term "voyage" must be deemed to have been used with the same meaning in Article 7(1)(c) of the Arrest Convention, bearing in mind that at that time the 1926 Convention was the only Convention in force in respect of maritime liens and mortgages and that maritime liens were obviously maritime claims.

I.861 If the voyage refers to a specified period of the commercial operation of the ship, its termini may differ according to the type of employment of the ship. If, for example, a ship is employed in the chartering trade on a spot basis, there must be added to the laden voyage the ballast voyage which was performed to take the ship to the loading port. Normally, therefore, the voyage will begin at the time the ballast trip commences and will end upon completion of discharge.[191]

---

187. Art. 4 of the 1926 Convention provides:
The accessories of the vessel and the freight mentioned in article 2 mean:
. . .
3. Remuneration due to the owner for assistance and salvage services rendered at any time before the end of the voyage, any sums allowed to the master or other persons in the service of the vessel being deducted.

188. Art. 2(5) provides:
The following give rise to maritime liens on a vessel, on the freight for the voyage during which the claim giving rise to the lien arises, and on the accessories of the vessel and freight accrued since the commencement of the voyage:
. . .
5. Claims resulting from contracts entered into or acts done by the master, acting within the scope of his authority, away from the vessel's home port, where such contracts or acts are necessary for the preservation of the vessel or the continuation of its voyage, whether the master is or is not at the same time owner of the vessel, and whether the claim is his own or that of shipchandlers, repairers, lenders, or other contractual creditors.

189. F. Berlingieri, *I Diritti di Garanzia sulla Nave, l'Aeromobile e le Cose Caricate* (Padova, 1965), pp. 60–70 and 127. In German law the notion of *Haftungreise* (contributory voyage) had been used in respect of the freight contributing to the limitation fund: Schaps-Abraham, *Das Deutsche Seerecht* (3rd Edn.) (Berlin 1959), Vol. I, p. 359; Wüstendörfer, *Neuzeitliches Seehandelsrecht* (2nd Edn.) (Berlin, 1950), p. 127.

190. F. Berlingieri, *I Diritti di Garanzia, supra*, note 189.

191. F. Berlingieri, *I Diritti di Garanzia, supra*, note 189, p. 65. See also Braekhus, "The Term 'Voyage' in Section 267 No. 5 of the Scandinavian Maritime Codes", in *Liber Amicorum of congratulations to Algot Bagge;* Rygh, *Sjopant efter Norsk Lov* (Oslo, 1934), p. 59 and, for Norwegian case law, Norges Høyesterett, 5 February 1937 [1937] Nordiske Domme i Sjfartsanliggender 1; Norges Høyesterett, 10 February 1951 [1951] Nordiske Domme 136; Norges Høyesterett, 24 September 1954 [1954] Nordiske Domme 298, all cited by Braekhus at p. 34.

I.862 In the case of consecutive voyage charters, each voyage, except the first one, commences with the departure of the ship from the port of discharge and ends with the completion of discharge of the cargo. Of course, there may be variations where the ship can take a return cargo. When a ship is employed on the basis of a time charterparty, the situation does not change: reference must be made to the ballast and laden voyages.

I.863 On the other hand, the position is different in the liner trade where cargo is loaded and unloaded in several ports. It would appear that in such case reference should be made to the termini of the line, where the outward and the inward voyages begin.[192] The Convention on a Code of Conduct refers in Article 2(8) to the national shipping lines "at one end of the trade" and in paragraph (13) of the same article to "groups of national shipping lines of the countries at both ends of the trade". A voyage, therefore, begins at one end of the trade and terminates at the other end, where a new voyage begins.

41. (d) CLAIMS ARISING OUT OF COLLISION; (e) SALVAGE CLAIMS; (f) CLAIMS UPON MORTGAGES OR HYPOTHÈQUES

(d) Claims arising out of a Collision or in Circumstances covered by Article 13 of the 1910 Collision Convention

I.864 The notion of collision, for the purpose of this rule, must be the same as that adopted in Article 1(1)(a) and, therefore, reference is made to the comments made in respect of such provision.[193] In addition to claims arising out of damage caused by the physical contact between two or more ships, the jurisdiction on the merits is recognised in the cases covered by Article 13 of the Collision Convention, which in its English translation provides:

This Convention extends to the making good of damages which a vessel has caused to another vessel, or to goods or persons on board either vessel, either by the execution or non-execution of a manoeuvre or by the non-observance of regulations, even if no collision had actually taken place.[194]

(e) Salvage Claims

I.865 The notion of salvage is necessarily the same as that applicable in respect of Article 1(1)(c) and therefore reference is made to the comments made in respect of such provision.[195]

(f) Claims upon a Mortgage or Hypothecation of the Ship

I.866 The French text differs slightly, for it refers to claims secured by a mortgage or a *hypothèque*.[196]

---

192. F. Berlingieri, *I Diritti di Garanzia*, *supra*, note 189, p. 65; Braekhus, "The Term 'Voyage' ", *supra*, note 191, pp. 25 and 28.
193. *Supra*, para. I.317–I.321.
194. See, for example, the English decision in *The "Umona" and The "Sirius"* (1934) 49 Ll.L.Rep. 461 where due to negligent navigation of one ship a collision occurred between two other ships.
195. *Supra*, at para. I.323–331.
196. The French text is worded as follows: "e) *si la créance est garantie par une hypothèque maritime ou un mortgage sur le navire saisi.*"

I.867 Both because the two texts must be construed with the aid of one another, and because the claims covered by this provision cannot differ from those covered by Article 1(1)(q), there should not be any doubt that the word "upon" in the English text has the same meaning as *"garantie"* (secured by) in the French text. The question whether securities other than mortgages and *hypothèques* are covered by this provision remains in doubt.[197]

197. *Supra*, at para. I.393–397.

APPENDIX I

Text of the 1952 Convention

I.I.1 INTERNATIONAL CONVENTION FOR THE UNIFICATION OF CERTAIN RULES RELATING TO THE ARREST OF SEA-GOING SHIPS, 1952

The High Contracting Parties,

Having recognized the desirability of determining by agreement certain uniform rules of law relating to the arrest of sea-going ships,

Have decided to conclude a convention for this purpose and thereto have agreed as follows:

ARTICLE 1

In this Convention the following words shall have the meanings hereby assigned to them:

(1) "Maritime Claim" means a claim arising out of one or more of the following:

(a) damage caused by any ship either in collision or otherwise;
(b) loss of life or personal injury caused by any ship or occurring in connection with the operation of any ship;
(c) salvage;
(d) agreement relating to the use or hire of any ship whether by charterparty or otherwise;
(e) agreement relating to the carriage of goods in any ship whether by charterparty or otherwise;
(f) loss of or damage to goods including baggage carried in any ship;
(g) general average;
(h) bottomry;
(i) towage;
(j) pilotage;
(k) goods or materials wherever supplied to a ship for her operation or maintenance;
(l) construction, repair or equipment of any ship or dock charges and dues;
(m) wages of masters, officers, or crew;
(n) master's disbursements, including disbursements made by shippers, charterers or agents on behalf of a ship or her owner;
(o) disputes as to the title to or ownership of any ship;
(p) disputes between co-owners of any ship as to the ownership, possession employment or earnings of that ship;
(q) the mortgage or hypothecation of any ship.

(2) "Arrest" means the detention of a ship by judicial process to secure a maritime claim, but does not include the seizure of a ship in execution or satisfaction of a judgment.

(3) "Person" includes individuals, partnerships and bodies corporate, Governments, their Departments, and Public Authorities.

(4) "Claimant" means a person who alleges that a maritime claim exists in his favour.

ARTICLE 2

A ship flying the flag of one of the contracting States may be arrested in the jurisdiction of any of the contracting States in respect of any maritime claim, but in respect of no other claim but nothing in this

Convention shall be deemed to extend or restrict any right or powers vested in any Governments or their Departments, Public Authorities, or Dock or Harbour Authorities under their existing domestic laws or regulations to arrest, detain or otherwise prevent the sailing of vessels within their jurisdiction.

ARTICLE 3

(1) Subject to the provisions of paragraph 4 of this Article and of Article 10, a claimant may arrest either the particular ship in respect of which the maritime claim arose, or any other ship which is owned by the person who was, at the time when the maritime claim arose, the owner of the particular ship, even though the ship arrested be ready to sail but no ship, other than the particular ship in respect of which the claim arose, may be arrested in respect of any of the maritime claims enumerated in Article 1(1)(o), (p) or (q).

(2) Ships shall be deemed to be in the same ownership when all the shares therein are owned by the same person or persons.

(3) A ship shall not be arrested, nor shall bail or other security be given more than once in any one or more of the jurisdictions of any of the Contracting States in respect of the same maritime claim by the same claimant and, if a ship has been arrested in any one of such jurisdictions, or bail or other security has been given in such jurisdiction either to release the ship or to avoid a threatened arrest, any subsequent arrest of the ship or of any ship in the same ownership by the same claimant for the same maritime claim shall be set aside, and the ship released by the Court or other appropriate judicial authority of that State, unless the claimant can satisfy the Court or other appropriate judicial authority that the bail or other security had been finally released before the subsequent arrest or that there is good cause for maintaining that arrest.

(4) When in the case of a charter by demise of a ship the charterer and not the registered owner is liable in respect of a maritime claim relating to that ship, the claimant may arrest such ship or any other ship in the ownership of the charterer by demise, subject to the provisions of this Convention, but no other ship in the ownership of the registered owner shall be liable to arrest in respect of such maritime claims.

The provisions of this paragraph shall apply to any case in which a person other than the registered owner of a ship is liable in respect of a maritime claim relating to that ship.

ARTICLE 4

A ship may only be arrested under the authority of a Court or of the appropriate judicial authority of the Contracting State in which the arrest is made.

ARTICLE 5

The Court or other appropriate judicial authority within whose jurisdiction the ship has been arrested shall permit the release of the ship upon sufficient bail or other security being furnished, save in cases in which a ship has been arrested in respect of any of the maritime claims enumerated in Article 1(1)(o) and (p). In such cases the Court or other appropriate judicial authority may permit the person in possession of the ship to continue trading the ship, upon such person furnishing sufficient bail or other security, or may otherwise deal with the operation of the ship during the period of the arrest.

In default of agreement between the Parties as to the sufficiency of the bail or other security the Court or other appropriate judicial authority shall determine the nature and amount thereof.

The request to release the ship against such security shall not be construed as an acknowledgment of liability or as a waiver of the benefit of the legal limitation of liability of the owner of the ship.

ARTICLE 6

All questions whether in any case the claimant is liable in damages for the arrest of a ship or for the costs of the bail or other security furnished to release or prevent the arrest of a ship, shall be determined by the law of the Contracting State in whose jurisdiction the arrest was made or applied for.

The rules of procedure relating to the arrest of a ship, to the application for obtaining the authority referred to in Article 4, and all matters of procedure which the arrest may entail, shall be governed by the law of the Contracting State in which the arrest was made or applied for.

ARTICLE 7

(1) The Courts of the country in which the arrest was made shall have jurisdiction to determine the case upon its merits:

if the domestic law of the country in which the arrest is made gives jurisdiction to such Courts

or in any of the following cases namely:

(a) if the claimant has his habitual residence or principal place of business in the country in which the arrest was made;

(b) if the claim arose in the country in which the arrest was made;

(c) if the claim concerns the voyage of the ship during which the arrest was made;

(d) if the claim arose out of a collision or in circumstances covered by Article 13 of the International Convention for the unification of certain rules of law with respect to collisions between vessels, signed at Brussels on 23rd September 1910;

(e) if the claim is for salvage;

(f) if the claim is upon a mortgage or hypothecation of the ship arrested.

(2) If the Court within whose jurisdiction the ship was arrested has not jurisdiction to decide upon the merits, the bail or other security given in accordance with Article 5 to procure the release of the ship shall specifically provide that it is given as security for the satisfaction of any judgment which may eventually be pronounced by a Court having jurisdiction so to decide and the Court or other appropriate judicial authority of the country in which the arrest is made shall fix the time within which the claimant shall bring an action before a Court having such jurisdiction.

(3) If the parties have agreed to submit the dispute to the jurisdiction of a particular Court other than that within whose jurisdiction the arrest was made or to arbitration, the Court or other appropriate judicial authority within whose jurisdiction the arrest was made may fix the time within which the claimant shall bring proceedings.

(4) If, in any of the cases mentioned in the two preceding paragraphs, the action or proceedings are not brought within the time so fixed, the defendant may apply for the release of the ship or of the bail or other security.

(5) This Article shall not apply in cases covered by the provisions of the revised Rhine Navigation Convention of 17 October 1868.

ARTICLE 8

(1) The provisions of this Convention shall apply to any vessel flying the flag of a Contracting State in the jurisdiction of any Contracting State.

(2) A ship flying the flag of a non-Contracting State may be arrested in the jurisdiction of any Contracting State in respect of any of the maritime claims enumerated in Article 1 or of any other claim for which the law of the Contracting State permits arrest.

(3) Nevertheless any Contracting State shall be entitled wholly or partly to exclude from the benefits of this Convention any Government of a non-Contracting State or any person who has not, at the time of the arrest, his habitual residence or principal place of business in one of the Contracting States.

(4) Nothing in this Convention shall modify or affect the rules of law in force in the respective Contracting States relating to the arrest of any ship within the jurisdiction of the State or her flag by a person who has his habitual residence or principal place of business in that State.

(5) When a maritime claim is asserted by a third party other than the original claimant, whether by subrogation, assignment or otherwise, such third party shall, for the purpose of this Convention, be deemed to have the same habitual residence or principal place of business as the original claimant.

ARTICLE 9

Nothing in this Convention shall be construed as creating a right of action, which, apart from the provisions of this Convention, would not arise under the law applied by the Court which had seisin of the case, nor as creating any maritime liens which do not exist under such law or under the Convention on Maritime Mortgages and Liens, if the latter is applicable.

ARTICLE 10

The High Contracting Parties may at the time of signature, deposit of ratification or accession, reserve

  (a) the right not to apply this Convention to the arrest of a ship for any of the claims enumerated in paragraphs (o) and (p) of Article 1, but to apply their domestic laws to such claims;

  (b) the right not to apply the first paragraph of Article 3 to the arrest of a ship, within their jurisdiction, for claims set out in Article 1, paragraph (q).

ARTICLE 11

The High Contracting Parties undertake to submit to arbitration any disputes between States arising out of the interpretation or application of this Convention, but this shall be without prejudice to the obligations of those High Contracting Parties who have agreed to submit their disputes to the International Court of Justice.

ARTICLE 12

This Convention shall be open for signature by the States represented at the Ninth Diplomatic Conference on Maritime Law. The protocol of signature shall be drawn up through the good offices of the Belgian Ministry of Foreign Affairs.

ARTICLE 13

This Convention shall be ratified and the instruments of ratification shall be deposited with the Belgium Ministry of Foreign Affairs which shall notify all signatory and acceding States of the deposit of any such instruments.

ARTICLE 14

  (a) This Convention shall come into force between the two States which first ratify it, six months after the date of the deposit of the second instrument of ratification.

  (b) This Convention shall come into force in respect of each signatory State which ratifies it after the deposit of the second instrument of ratification six months after the date of the deposit of the instrument of ratification of that State.

ARTICLE 15

Any State not represented at the Ninth Diplomatic Conference on Maritime Law may accede to this Convention.

The accession of any State shall be notified to the Belgian Ministry of Foreign Affairs which shall inform through diplomatic channels all signatory and acceding States of such notification.

The Convention shall come into force in respect of the acceding State six months after the date of the receipt of such notification but not before the Convention has come into force in accordance with the provisions of Article 14(a).

ARTICLE 16

Any High Contracting Party may three years after the coming into force of this Convention in respect of such High Contracting Party or at any time thereafter request that a conference be convened in order to consider amendments to the Convention.

Any High Contracting Party proposing to avail itself of this right shall notify the Belgian Government which shall convene the conference within six months thereafter.

ARTICLE 17

Any High Contracting Party shall have the right to denounce this Convention at any time after the coming into force thereof in respect of such High Contracting Party. This denunciation shall take effect one year after the date on which notification thereof has been received by the Belgian government which shall inform through diplomatic channels all the other High Contracting Parties of such notification.

ARTICLE 18

(a) Any High Contracting Party may at the time of its ratification of or accession to this Convention or at any time thereafter declare by written notification to the Belgian Ministry of Foreign Affairs that the Convention shall extend to any of the territories for whose international relations it is responsible. The Convention shall six months after the date of the receipt of such notification by the Belgian Ministry of Foreign Affairs extend to the territories named therein, but not before the date of the coming into force of the Convention in respect of such High Contracting Party.

(b) A High Contracting Party which has made a declaration under (a) of this Article extending the Convention to any territory for whose international relations it is responsible may at any time thereafter declare by notification given to the Belgian Ministry of Foreign Affairs that the Convention shall cease to extend to such territory and the Convention shall one year after the receipt of the notification by the Belgian Ministry of Foreign Affairs cease to extend thereto.

(c) The Belgian Ministry of Foreign Affairs shall inform through diplomatic channels all signatory and acceding States of any notification received by it under this Article.

Done at Brussels, on May 10, 1952 in the French and English languages, the two texts being equally authentic.

I.I.2 CONVENTION INTERNATIONALE POUR L'UNIFICATION DE CERTAINES REGLES SUR LA SAISIE CONSERVATOIRE DES NAVIRES DE MER, 1952

Les Hautes Parties Contractantes,

Ayant reconnu l'utilité de fixer de commun accord certaines règles uniformes sur la saisie conservatoire de navires de mer, ont décidé de conclure une convention à cet effet et ont convenu de ce qui suit:

ARTICLE 1

Dans la présente Convention, les expressions suivantes sont employées avec les significations indiquées ci-dessous:

1) "Créance Maritime" signifie allégation d'un droit ou d'une créance ayant l'une des causes suivantes:

    a)   dommages causés par un navire soit par abordage, soit autrement;

    b)   pertes de vies humaines ou dommages corporels causés par un navire ou provenant de l'exploitation d'un navire;

    c)   assistance et sauvetage;

    d)   contrats relatifs à l'utilisation ou la location d'un navire par charte-partie ou autrement;

    e)   contrats relatifs au transport des marchandises par un navire en vertu d'une charte-partie, d'un connaissement ou autrement;

    f)   pertes ou dommages aux marchandises et bagages transportées par un navire;

    g)   avarie commune;

    h)   prêt à la grosse;

    i)   remorquage;

    j)   pilotage;

    k)   fournitures, quel qu'en soit le lieu, de produits ou de matériel faites à un navire en vue de son exploitation ou de son entretien;

    l)   construction, réparations, équipement d'un navire ou frais de cale;

    m)   salaires des capitaine, officiers ou hommes d'équipage;

    n)   débours du capitaine et ceux effectués par les chargeurs, les affréteurs ou les agents pour le compte du navire ou de son propriétaire;

    o)   la propriété contestée d'un navire;

    p)   la copropriété contestée d'un navire ou sa possession ou son exploitation, ou les droits aux produits d'exploitation d'un navire en copropriété;

    q)   toute hypothèque maritime et tout mortgage.

2) "Saisie" signifie l'immobilisation d'un navire avec l'autorisation de l'autorité judiciaire compétente pour garantie d'une créance maritime, mais ne comprend pas la saisie d'un navire pour l'exécution d'un titre.

3) "Personne" comprend toute personne physique ou morale, société de personnes ou de capitaux ainsi que les Etats, les Administrations et Etablissements publics.

4) "Demandeur" signifie une personne, invoquant à son profit, l'existence d'une créance maritime.

ARTICLE 2

Un navire battant pavillon d'un des Etats Contractants ne pourra être saisi dans le ressort d'un Etat Contractant qu'en vertu d'une créance maritime, mais rien dans les dispositions de la présente Convention ne pourra être considéré comme une extension ou une restriction des droits et pouvoirs que les Etats, Autorités publiques ou Autorités portuaires tiennent de leur loi interne ou de leurs règlements, de saisir, détenir ou autrement empêcher un navire de prendre la mer dans leur ressort.

ARTICLE 3

1) Sans préjudice des dispositions du paragraphe 4) et de l'article 10, tout demandeur peut saisir soit le navire auquel la créance se rapporte, soit tout autre navire appartenant à celui qui était, au moment où est née la créance maritime, propriétaire du navire auquel cette créance se rapporte, alors même que le navire saisi est prêt à faire voile, mais aucun navire ne pourra être saisi pour une créance prévue aux alinéas o), p) ou q) de l'article premier à l'exception du navire même que concerne la réclamation.

2) Des navires sont réputés avoir le même propriétaire lorsque toutes les parts de propriété appartiendront à une même ou aux mêmes personnes.

3) Un navire ne peut être saisi et caution ou garantie ne sera donnée, plus d'une fois dans la juridiction d'un ou plusieurs des Etats Contractants, pour la même créance et par le même demandeur; et si un navire est saisi dans une des dites juridictions et une caution ou une garantie a été donnée, soit pour obtenir la mainlevée de la saisie, soit pour éviter celle-ci, toute saisie ultérieure de ce navire, ou de n'importe quel autre navire, appartenant au même propriétaire, par le demandeur et pour la même créance maritime, sera levée et le navire sera libéré par le Tribunal ou toute autre juridiction compétente du dit Etat, à moins que le demandeur ne prouve, à la satisfaction du Tribunal ou de toute autre Autorité Judiciaire compétente, que la garantie ou la caution a été définitivement libérée avant que la saisie subséquente n'ait été pratiquée ou qu'il n'y ait une autre raison valable pour la maintenir.

4) Dans le cas d'un affrètement d'un navire avec remise de la gestion nautique, lorsque l'affréteur répond, seul, d'une créance maritime relative à ce navire, le demandeur peut saisir ce navire ou tel autre appartenant à l'affréteur, en observant les dispositions de la présente Convention, mais nul autre navire appartenant au propriétaire ne peut être saisi en vertu de cette créance maritime.

L'alinéa qui précède s'applique également à tous les cas où une personne autre que le propriétaire est tenue d'une créance maritime.

ARTICLE 4

Un navire ne peut être saisi qu'avec l'autorisation d'un Tribunal ou de toute autre Autorité Judiciaire compétente de l'Etat Contractant dans lequel la saisie est pratiquée.

ARTICLE 5

Le Tribunal ou toute autre Autorité Judiciaire compétente dans le ressort duquel le navire a été saisi, accordera la mainlevée de la saisie lorsqu'une caution ou une garantie suffisantes auront été fournies, sauf dans le cas où la saisie est pratiquée en raison des créances maritimes énumérées à l'art. premier ci-dessous, sous les lettres o) et p); en ce cas, le juge peut permettre l'exploitation du navire par le possesseur, lorsque celui-ci aura fourni des garanties suffisantes, ou régler la gestion du navire pendant la durée de la saisie.

Faute d'accord entre les parties sur l'importance de la caution ou de la garantie, le Tribunal ou l'Autorité Judiciaire en fixera la nature et le montant.

La demande de mainlevée de la saisie moyennant une telle garantie, ne pourra être interprétée ni comme une reconnaissance de responsabilité, ni comme une renonciation au bénéfice de la limitation légale de la responsabilité du propriétaire du navire.

ARTICLE 6

Toutes contestations relatives à la responsabilité du demandeur, pour dommages causés à la suite de la saisie du navire ou pour frais de caution ou de garantie fournies en vue de le libérer ou d'en empêcher la saisie, seront réglées par la loi de l'Etat Contractant dans le ressort duquel la saisie a été pratiquée ou demandée.

Les règles de procédure relatives à la saisie d'un navire, à l'obtention de l'autorisation visée à l'article 4 et à tous autres incidents de procédure qu'une saisie peut soulever sont régies par la loi de l'Etat Contractant dans lequel la saisie a été pratiquée ou demandée.

ARTICLE 7

1) Les Tribunaux de l'Etat dans lequel la saisie a été opérée, seront compétents pour statuer sur le fond du procès:

— soit si ces Tribunaux sont compétents en vertu de la loi interne de l'Etat dans lequel la saisie est pratiquée;

221

— soit dans les cas suivants, nommément définis:

a) si le demandeur a sa résidence habituelle ou son principal établissement dans l'Etat où la saisie a été pratiquée;

b) si la créance maritime est elle-même née dans l'Etat Contractant dont dépend le lieu de la saisie;

c) si la créance maritime est née au cours d'un voyage pendant lequel la saisie a été faite;

d) si la créance provient d'un abordage ou de circonstances visées par l'article 13 de la Convention Internationale pour l'unification de certaines règles en matière d'abordage, signée à Bruxelles, le 23 septembre 1910;

e) si la créance est née d'une assistance ou d'un sauvetage;

f) si la créance est garantie par une hypothèque maritime ou un mortgage sur le navire saisi.

2) Si le Tribunal, dans le ressort duquel le navire a été saisi n'a pas compétence pour statuer sur le fond, la caution ou la garantie à fournir conformément à l'article 5 pour obtenir la mainlevée de la saisie devra garantir l'exécution de toutes les condamnations qui seraient prononcées par le Tribunal compétent de statuer sur le fond, et le Tribunal ou toute autre Autorité Judiciaire du lieu de la saisie, fixera le délai endéans lequel le demandeur devra introduire une action devant le Tribunal compétent.

3) Si les conventions des parties contiennent soit une clause attributive de compétence à une autre juridiction, soit une clause arbitrale le Tribunal pourra fixer un délai dans lequel le saisissant devra engager son action au fond.

4) Dans les cas prévus aux deux alinéas précédents, si l'action n'est pas introduite dans le délai imparti, le défendeur pourra demander la mainlevée de la saisie ou la libération de la caution fournie.

5) Cet article ne s'appliquera pas aux cas visés par les dispositions de la Convention révisée sur la navigation du Rhin du 17 octobre 1868.

ARTICLE 8

1) Les dispositions de la présente Convention sont applicables dans tout Etat Contractant à tout navire battant pavillon d'un Etat Contractant.

2) Un navire battant pavillon d'un Etat non Contractant peut être saisi dans l'un des Etats Contractants, en vertu d'une des créances énumérées à l'art. 1er, ou de toute autre créance permettant la saisie d'après la loi de cet Etat.

3) Toutefois, chaque Etat Contractant peut refuser tout ou partie des avantages de la présente Convention à tout Etat non Contractant et à toute personne qui n'a pas, au jour de la saisie, sa résidence habituelle ou son principal établissement dans un Etat contractant.

4) Aucune disposition de la présente Convention ne modifiera ou n'affectera la loi interne des Etats Contractants en ce qui concerne la saisie d'un navire dans le ressort de l'Etat dont il bat pavillon par une personne ayant sa résidence habituelle ou son principal établissement dans cet Etat.

5) Tout tiers, autre que le demandeur originaire qui excipe d'une créance maritime par l'effet d'une subrogation, d'une cession ou autrement, sera réputé, pour l'application de la présente Convention, avoir la même résidence habituelle ou le même établissement principal que le créancier originaire.

ARTICLE 9

Rien dans cette Convention ne doit être considéré comme créant un droit à une action qui, en dehors des stipulations de cette Convention, n'existerait pas d'après la loi à appliquer par le Tribunal saisi du litige.

La présente Convention ne confère aux demandeurs aucun droit de suite, autre que celui accordé par cette dernière loi ou par la Convention Internationale sur les privilèges et hypothèques maritimes, si celle-ci est applicable.

ARTICLE 10

Les Hautes Parties Contractantes peuvent au moment de la signature du dépôt des ratifications ou lors de leur adhésion à la Convention, se réserver:

a) le droit de ne pas appliquer les dispositions de la présente Convention à la saisie d'un navire pratiquée en raison d'une des créances maritimes visées aux o) et p) de l'article premier et d'appliquer à cette saisie leur loi nationale;

b) le droit de ne pas appliquer les dispositions du premier paragraphe de l'article 3 à la saisie pratiquée sur leur territoire en raison des créances prévues à l'alinéa q) de l'article premier.

ARTICLE 11

Les Hautes Parties Contractantes s'engagent à soumettre à arbitrage tous différends entre Etats pouvant résulter de l'interprétation ou l'application de la présente Convention, sans préjudice toutefois des obligations des Hautes Parties Contractantes qui ont convenu de soumettre leurs différends à la Cour Internationale de Justice.

ARTICLE 12

La présente Convention est ouverte à la signature des Etats représentés à la neuvième Conférence diplomatique de Droit Maritime. Le procès-verbal de signature sera dressé par les soins du Ministère des Affaires étrangères de Belgique.

ARTICLE 13

La présente Convention sera ratifiée et les instruments de ratification seront déposés auprès du Ministère des Affaires étrangères de Belgique qui en notifiera le dépôt à tous les Etats signataires et adhérents.

ARTICLE 14

a) La présente Convention entrera en vigueur entre les deux premiers Etats qui l'auront ratifiée, six mois après la date du dépôt du deuxième instrument de ratification.
b) Pour chaque Etat signataire ratifiant la Convention après le deuxième dépôt, celle-ci entrera en vigueur six mois après la date du dépôt de son instrument de ratification.

ARTICLE 15

Tout Etat non représenté à la neuvième Conférence diplomatique de Droit Maritime pourra adhérer à la présente Convention.

Les adhésions seront notifiées au Ministère des Affaires étrangères de Belgique qui en avisera par la voie diplomatique tous les Etats signataires et adhérents.

La Convention entrera en vigueur pour l'Etat adhérent six mois après la date de réception de cette notification, mais pas avant la date de son entrée en vigueur telle qu'elle est fixée à l'article 14 a).

ARTICLE 16

Toute Haute Partie Contractante pourra à l'expiration du délai de trois ans qui suivra l'entrée en vigueur à son égard de la présente Convention, demander la réunion d'une conférence chargée de statuer sur toutes les propositions tendant à la révision de la Convention.

Toute Haute Partie Contractante qui désirerait faire usage de cette faculté en avisera le Gouvernement belge qui se chargera de convoquer la conférence dans les six mois.

ARTICLE 17

Chacune des Hautes Parties Contractantes aura le droit de dénoncer la présente Convention à tout moment après son entrée en vigueur à son égard. Toutefois, cette dénonciation ne prendra effet qu'un an après la date de réception de la notification de dénonciation au Gouvernement belge qui en avisera les autres Parties Contractantes par la voie diplomatique.

ARTICLE 18

a) Toute Haute Partie Contractante peut, au moment de la ratification, de l'adhésion, ou à tout moment ultérieur, notifier par écrit au Gouvernement belge que la présente Convention s'applique aux territoires ou à certains des territoires dont elle assure les relations internationales. La Convention sera applicable aux dits territoires six mois après la date de réception de cette notification par le Ministère des Affaires étrangères de Belgique, mais pas avant la date d'entrée en vigueur de la présente Convention à l'égard de cette Haute Partie Contractante.

b) Toute Haute Partie Contractante qui a souscrit une déclaration au titre du paragraphe a) de cet article pourra à tout moment aviser le Ministère des Affaires étrangères de Belgique que la Convention cesse de s'appliquer au Territoire en question. Cette dénonciation prendra effet dans le délai d'un an prévu à l'article 17.

c) Le Ministère des Affaires étrangères de Belgique avisera par la voie diplomatique tous les Etats signataires et adhérents de toute notification reçue par lui au titre du présent article.

Fait à Bruxelles, le 10 mai 1952, en langues française et anglaise, les deux textes faisant également foi.

APPENDIX II

Questionnaire and Replies

I.II.1 QUESTIONNAIRE ON THE IMPLEMENTATION OF THE 1952 ARREST CONVENTION

I.II.2 REPLIES FROM THE MARITIME LAW ASSOCIATIONS OF BELGIUM, CROATIA, DENMARK, FINLAND, FRANCE, GERMANY, GREECE, ITALY, NETHERLANDS, NIGERIA, NORWAY, POLAND, SLOVENIA, SPAIN, SWEDEN, UNITED KINGDOM AND THE GOVERNMENT OF HAITI ARRANGED UNDER EACH QUESTION

1. HOW HAS THE CONVENTION BEEN IMPLEMENTED BY YOUR COUNTRY?

Belgium

The ratification of the Convention was approved by law on 24 March 1961. This law was published in the official journal on 19 July 1961. The Convention acquired force of law in Belgium as from 10 October 1961. In order to avoid conflict between the newly adopted provisions of the 1952 Convention and the at that time prevailing provisions of Belgian law on arrest of vessels (law of 4 September 1908) a new law was adopted on 4 December 1961. This law incorporated the provisions of the Arrest Convention 1952 in our internal law (Article 1467 and following of the Belgian Judicial Code) and replaced the former legislation.

Denmark

The Arrest Convention has been implemented into Danish law by incorporation of some of the provisions of the Convention.

Finland

The 1952 Arrest Convention entered into force in Finland on 21 June 1996. The main provisions of this Convention were incorporated into the Finnish Maritime Code (FMC) chapter 4 by an Act of 1995 (234/95). Vessels not covered under chapter 4 are arrested under the rules of chapter 7 of the Finnish Code of Judicial Procedure (CJP). Enforcement issues in connection with the arrest of a vessel are governed by chapters 3, 4 and 7, of the Enforcement Act of 1895. Consequently, the Convention in its original text has not been given force of law. But as Finland has ratified the Convention, courts and other authorities have an obligation to take into consideration the rules and principles of the Convention.

France

Comme il en est de toutes les Conventions internationales de droit privé, et notamment des conventions de droit maritime, la Convention de 1952 a été intégrée au droit français par sa ratification et sa publication au Journal Officiel, ce en exécution d'un décret du 4 janvier 1958 (J.O. du 14 janvier).

Germany

Yes. The Convention entered into force for Germany on 6 April 1973.

Greece

Greece has signed the Convention and then proceeded to its ratification by a specific law, law 4570/1966, which ratified the Greek translation of the text of the Convention. The Convention has come into force in Greece since 27 February 1967. The Greek Code of Civil Procedure (CCP) which came into force posteriorly—i.e. on 16 September 1968, notwithstanding that it contains provisions on the arrest of ships, did not affect the Convention since it was stipulated in its Introductory Law (Article 2) that its provisions do not prejudice the validity of procedural provisions based upon international conventions. Following the adoption of the new 1975 Constitution, there is no further question of abolition or alteration of an international convention by a posterior law since Article 28, paragraph 1(a) of the new Constitution expressly provides that international conventions shall supersede national laws.

The CCP regulates the arrest of ships on a national level. Its provisions diverge to a large extent from those of the Convention. For example, under the provisions of CCP the arrest of a ship is not conditional upon the maritime nature of the relevant claim. This is the reason why setting the borders of field of application of the Convention bears great practical importance. It was initially maintained that the Convention applies only when the arrest of a ship under the flag of *another* Contracting State is requested. It was subsequently admitted that the Convention applies also in the case of the arrest of Greek ships in Greece whenever the claim is not purely national but bears also international elements as is the case where the creditor has its residence or principal place of business in another Contracting State. This view prevailed in jurisprudence. The view has been recently expressed that the provisions of the Convention (save for that of Article 2) also apply to ships flying the flag of non-Contracting States (see A. Antapassis, *The Convention of 1952 relating to the arrest of ships* [in Greek], 1998, p. 72 et seq.).

Haiti

Le contenu matériel de la Convention de 1952 sur la saisie conservatoire des navires a été intégré dans le droit interne haïtien par un décret de l'Assemblée Nationale d'Haïti en date du 29 août 1953, publié au journal officiel "Le Moniteur" No. 107 du 9 novembre 1953.

Italy

The Convention has been implemented by giving it the force of law. The mechanism used is that of the so-called "law of execution", which simply enacts a convention into the Italian legal system. One of the original texts of the Convention is annexed, together with an Italian unofficial translation.

Netherlands

The 1952 Convention was ratified by the Kingdom of the Netherlands on 20 January 1983 with entry into force on 20 July 1983, on the basis of Article 14(b) of the Convention ("six months after the date of the deposit of the instrument of ratification of that State"). The ratification of the 1952 Convention extends to the entire realm, being the Kingdom in Europe and its dependencies, i.e. the Netherlands Antilles and Aruba. The 1952 Convention was ratified subject to both reservations permitted under Article 10 of the Convention. Article 93 of the Dutch constitution provides that provisions of international conventions of a "self-executing" nature shall have the force of law after they have been promulgated (in the official treaty series "Tractatenblad"). Article 94 of the Constitution further states that statute law which is not in conformity with such provisions shall not be applied. The relevant provisions of the Convention are considered to be of a "self-executing" nature. The legislative history (Kamerstukken 17110) also clearly states that the adoption of the Convention does not require any changes or additions to Dutch statute law.

Nigeria

The Convention has not been directly implemented in Nigeria although Nigeria acceded to the Convention on 7 November 1963.

Norway

The Convention has been incorporated into our Maritime Code and the Act on Enforcement of Claims.

Poland

The Convention is strictly a convention of civil procedure. Its provisions have been binding for Poland by operation of law from the moment of signing and ratification.

The normal procedure in such cases is as follows:

1.1. Testing of the text of the Convention and its signing or initialling by a representative not possessing the authority to sign the Convention.

1.2. However by amending the Maritime Code on 1 January 1991 (entry into force on 28 March 1991). Article 1, §1a states that the Code is not implemented if international convention regulates otherwise (general rule).

The Polish Republic accepted, ratified and attested the said Convention on 16 July 1976.

Apart from the binding force period is the factor of coming into force in relation to the State. Usually it does not take place immediately, but after a certain period (*vacatio legis*), which as a matter of fact is mentioned in the Convention.

Sweden

Yes. The Convention has been implemented by Sweden.

1.1. HAS THE CONVENTION IN ITS ORIGINAL TEXT BEEN GIVEN FORCE OF LAW?

Croatia

Notification of the succession as from 8 October 1991 to the 1952 Arrest Convention has been published in the Official Gazette of Republic of Croatia (NN-MU 1/92 dated 14 November 1992).

France

La ratification de la Convention et sa publication au Journal Officiel ont emporté d'elles-mêmes force de loi pour la Convention, cette force l'emportant même sur les lois internes (article 55 de la Constitution de 1958).

Germany

The Convention has been given force of law by ratification law from 1972.

Haiti

La promulgation de la loi de ratification fait inclure la Convention dans le droit positif haïtien.

Italy

Yes. The Convention is part of the Italian legal system in its original French and English texts.

Netherlands

Yes.

Nigeria

The Convention in its original text has not been given force of law. However, some of its provisions were incorporated into the UK Administration of Justice Act 1956 ("AJA '56") which the Supreme Court of Nigeria in the case of *American International Insurance Co.* v. *Ceekay Traders Ltd* (1981) 2 N.S.C. 65, held was applicable in admiralty actions in Nigeria. Therefore, to the extent that some of the provisions of the Convention were applicable in England by virtue of the AJA '56 to that extent did some of the provisions of the Convention apply in Nigeria. That was the position until 30 December 1991 when the Admiralty Jurisdiction Decree No. 59 of 1991 ("AJD") came into force. The AJD contains some provisions which are similar to AJA '56.

Slovenia

The Republic of Slovenia is a Contracting State of the 1952 Arrest Convention. According to Article 8 of the Constitution of the Republic of Slovenia, international conventions which have been proclaimed and to which Slovenia adheres shall take immediate effect, in the wording which has been ratified and published.

Consequently, the Convention is used whenever the vessel to be arrested is flying the flag of a Contracting State, in its original text.

Spain

Yes. The Convention was ratified by Spain in December 1953 and immediately afterwards, in January 1954, the text was published in the Spanish Official Gazette so becoming part of the Spanish legislation with force of law, it came into force upon the expiry of six months from the date the instrument of ratification was deposited.

Sweden

No. The original text has not been given force of law.

United Kingdom

The UK is a party to the 1952 Arrest Convention but the original text of the latter has not been specifically reproduced by the UK Parliament, or given the force of law—as is now customary for other international maritime conventions, such as the 1989 Salvage Convention.

1.2. HAVE ITS PROVISIONS BEEN INCORPORATED IN WHOLE OR IN PART IN YOUR DOMESTIC LEGISLATION?

Croatia

The provisions of the Convention have been incorporated in great part in our domestic legislation, i.e. in the Maritime Code published in Official Gazette (NN 17/94 dated 7 March 1994) and in force as from 22 March 1994. Arrest of ships is regulated in the Part 10, chapter IV.3.—Provisional Measures in Articles 974 up to 989.

France

La réponse est négative.

Haiti

Il n'y a pas d'autre manière d'intégrer une Convention dans le droit interne haïtien dans son état actuel.

Germany

Only one provision of the Convention has been transformed into the German Commercial Code: § 482 HGB which excludes the enforcement of an arrest in respect of ships "sailing and not lying in a port". The provision complies with Article 3(1) of the Convention.

Italy

See 1.1 above.

Netherlands

No.

Nigeria

The provisions of the Convention have not been incorporated in whole or in part in domestic legislation. However, some provisions of the AJD, especially in section 2 on the delimitation of maritime claims and section 5 on the modes of enforcing a maritime claim, are similar to provisions of the Convention.

Slovenia

Slovenia has temporarily adopted some laws of the former Yugoslavia, which are still in force in Slovenia. One of the aforementioned laws is the Maritime and Internal Navigation Act (MINA), which entered into force on 1 January 1978. However, in the near future the new Slovenian Maritime Code will be enacted, which is based on the aforementioned Act but updated in accordance with the new development of maritime law.

MINA has almost entirely adopted the provisions of the Arrest Convention. However, there are some differences.

Spain

In 1967, as a consequence of the work and promotion of the Spanish Maritime Law Association, a special law was enacted introducing some procedural specialities in development of the 1952 Arrest Convention. The Act 2/1967 was passed to achieve a specific goal, i.e. the adjustment of the relevant Spanish rules of procedure—to which Article 6 of the Convention refers—relating to attachment of assets (the preventive embargo as a precautionary measure to secure the results of an eventual condemning judgment) in a manner appropriate so as to facilitate the application and use of the 1952 Arrest Convention. The provisions of the Act 2/1967, expressly referring to the arrest of foreign vessels being inclusive of vessels from non-Contracting States, were mainly addressed to give effect to the Convention by accommodating the relevant procedural rules of the Spanish Civil Procedural Code of 1881 to the arrest of foreign vessels, so that the general rule providing that the claim must be proven by submitting documentary evidence before the arresting court (Article 1400 of the CPC), is not a requirement to apply in cases of arrest of vessels under the Convention.

Sweden

The Convention's provisions have been incorporated in part by the Law (1993:103) on Arrest of Ships in international legal relations (Lag 1993:103 om kvarstad på fartyg i internationella rättsförhållanden). The law has subsequently been incorporated in chapter 4 of the Swedish Maritime Code (Sjölagen 1994:1009).

The following historical background in respect of Sweden's attitude to the 1952 Arrest Convention should be noted.

Sweden was critical of the contents of the Convention and, therefore, did not become a signatory State.

When the Convention was sent out for consideration by the Government in 1955 a majority of the instances were negative to accepting the Convention. The criticism concerned not only structural deficiencies in the Convention, but also that too much room was left for national regulations, that the rules on double arrest were unclear and, in particular, the peculiarity that the Convention seemed to make it possible to obtain arrest—even if the claim was not a maritime lien claim—for a claim against somebody other than the owner of the ship, whether a charterer by demise or not.

The need for a revision of the 1952 Arrest Convention was that great that, at CMI's Conference in Lisbon 1985, a full new draft Convention was worked out and agreed. Although great efforts had been made to present to the conference a draft aiming at solving problems of the kind, which had made Sweden stay outside the Convention in 1952, the draft agreed by the majority still contained a number of compromises, *inter alia*, in respect of the question whether it would be possible to arrest a ship for a claim against somebody other than the owner in cases where there is no maritime lien, and without at least there being clear rules in respect of piercing the corporate veil. Therefore, Sweden abstained from voting.

The question whether Sweden should be a signatory to the 1952 Arrest Convention became actual again in connection with Sweden becoming a member of the Lugano Convention. In fact, it now became necessary for Sweden to accede to the Arrest Convention.

For the reasons mentioned above, the Swedish Government found itself facing, in certain respects, the same dilemma as in 1952 with regard to the structure and ambiguity of the Convention. However, these problems have been solved to a great extent by the implementation of the Convention, which, hopefully, the following answers to the Questionnaire will make clear.

United Kingdom

The Administration of Justice Act 1956 and subsequently the Supreme Court Act 1981 were enacted with the purpose (amongst others) of giving effect to the 1952 Arrest Convention in English law, although the latter is not mentioned anywhere in them. However, English courts are ready to consider the provisions of the 1952 Arrest Convention in order to construe the wording of the statutes, *The Eschersheim* [1976] 2 Lloyd's Rep. 1, *The Banco* [1971] 1 Lloyd's Rep. 49, *The Kommunar (No.2)* [1997] 1 Lloyd's Rep. 8.

The result of such incorporation in domestic law has been that there have arguably been differences between English law and the text of the 1952 Arrest Convention. In England, arrest of ships is available only in the context of an action *in rem*, see the answers to Questions 4 and 11, below. Scottish law has a system of Admiralty "arrestments" which has some conceptual and terminological differences from arrest in English law and has features which are consistent with a continental civil law approach. Scottish law arrestments in admiralty are still governed by provisions of the Administration of Justice Act 1956, but this area of law is currently under revision as a result of the "Report on Diligence on the Dependence and Admiralty Arrestments", produced by the Scottish Law Commission (Scot. Law Com. No. 164, 1998). The responses to the questions are therefore generally based upon the position in English law, although there are great similarities between the two systems. Scottish law appears to differ more in terms of remedies and procedure (and see the answer to Question 9, below).

2. IF THE MECHANISM UNDER 1(2) ABOVE HAS BEEN ADOPTED, HAVE ADDITIONAL RULES BEEN ENACTED IN ORDER TO IMPLEMENT FULLY THE PROVISIONS OF THE CONVENTION?

Belgium

No additional rules have been adopted in order to implement the provisions of the Convention.

Croatia

In addition to the articles of the Maritime Code, provisions of the general Enforcement Proceedings Act related to Provisional Measures will apply where appropriate.

Denmark

Some of the provisions in chapter 4 are not found in the Convention, but were found necessary under Danish law. Furthermore a few sections were enacted in the Administration of Justice Act (AJA).

Finland

See under 1, *supra*.

France

La question est sans objet (voir réponse à Question 1.2).

Germany

No. The German national provisions on arrest apply. A conflict with the Convention cannot arise because most of the German conditions of arrest of ships are either stricter than those laid down in the Convention or let rules of the Convention appear superfluous.

Greece

See the answer to Question 1 above.

Haiti

Not applicable.

Italy

No.

Netherlands

Not applicable.

Nigeria

Apart from such provisions of the AJA '56 as are repeated in the AJD, additional rules have not been enacted with a view to implementing the provisions of the Convention.

Norway

The basic approach of the Norwegian legislator has been to apply the general rules on arrest also to arrest of ships but with some modifications, particularly modifications that follow from the Convention.

Poland

In general the Republic of Poland has accepted the International Convention on the Arrest of Ships without the provision of any supplementary executory regulations. This does not of course mean that the provisions of the Convention are not set firmly within the legal structure of the State.

In Poland many legal acts are in force, among which a key position is held by the Code of Civil Procedure (1974) which regulates the procedure of securing claims, among others, securing claims by the arrest of ships. Please note that on 1 March 1996 the Code was amended and now Article 732, § 2 says that the ship arrest's motion (*inter alia*) must be reviewed immediately, but not later than within seven days. The following legal acts are relevant:

— The Code of Civil Procedure—CPC of 1964.
— The Polish Maritime Code as amended in 1977, 86, 91, 96.
— The Act on Private International Law of 1965.
— The International Convention for the Unification of Certain Rules Concerning the Immunity of State-owned Ships of 1926.

— The International Convention for the Unification of Certain Rules of Law Relating to Maritime Liens and Mortgages of 1926.
— The Protocol on Arbitration Clauses of 1923.
— The European Convention on International Commercial Arbitration of 1961.
— The Convention Concerning Civil Procedure of 1954.
— Law on the Structure of Common Law Courts.
— Regulation as to Legal Costs in Civil Procedure.

Slovenia

If the vessel is flying the flag of a Contracting State the 1952 Arrest Convention is directly applied by the Slovene Court. So, only the maritime claims specified in Article 1 of the Convention may be the basis for the arrest of a vessel flying the flag of a Contracting State. Otherwise, when the Convention is not applicable, MINA applies.

MINA has specific rules regarding arrest of ships (Articles 979–993). As complementary law is used the Forced Execution and Security Act (ZIZ) and through this also the Civil Procedure Act (ZPP).

MINA applies, when the vessel to be arrested is flying the Slovene flag or a flag of a non-Contracting State, provided that the State applies reciprocity to vessels flying the flag of the Republic of Slovenia.

Otherwise, MINA applies but without being limited to certain specified maritime claims, in this case, the vessel could be arrested for practically any claim.

The maritime claims enacted in Article 877 of MINA are very similar to those enumerated in the Convention.

Article 877 of MINA defines "maritime claims" as follows:

1. damage caused by collisions between vessels, whether directly or otherwise;
2. injury or loss of life caused by the vessel or arising from the use of the vessel;
3. salvage;
4. agreements relating to the use of the vessel;
5. general average;
6. pilotage;
7. goods or materials supplied to a vessel for her maintenance or operation;
8. construction, repair or equipment of a vessel;
9. wages of the crew;
10. expenses incurred by a master, shipper, contracting party, operator or owner in connection with a vessel.

In the proposal of the new Slovene Maritime Act the maritime claims listed in Article 840 are still the same as in Article 877 of MINA. But there is no longer the condition of reciprocity.

According to the proposal of the new Slovene Maritime Act, the vessel flying the flag of a non-Contracting State may be arrested only in respect of claims for maritime liens and mortgages (including hypothecs), and for the claims listed in Article 840 of the aforementioned proposal.

Spain

The only additional legislation enacted for the implementation of the provisions of the Convention is the above referred Act 2/1967.

Sweden

Yes. Additional rules have been enacted. It is probably not correct to say that this has been done to implement fully the provisions of the Convention. The additional rules have, rather, been inserted to clarify the Swedish interpretation in some respects of the Convention, where it—in the Swedish view—seems unclear and ambiguous. This is the case, *inter alia*, in respect of the risk of creating maritime liens which do not exist under national law or the Convention on Maritime Mortgages and Liens.

Sweden has used the possibility, in accordance with Article 8(4), of excluding from the scope of the Convention arrest of Swedish ships, if the claimant has his habitual residence or principal place of business in Sweden (chapter 4, section 1). (Please observe the incomplete translation of the Swedish text in the edition referred to above, which should read "the provisions in this chapter apply to arrest of vessels for civil claims which are, or may be, adjudicated in Sweden *or in another country* in the prescribed . . . ".)

United Kingdom

There have been additional, mainly procedural, rules like the Rules of the Supreme Court (RSC) Order 75 or the new Civil Procedure Rules (CPR) which have replaced Order 75 as from 26 April 1999. There is a new Admiralty Practice Direction 49F, paragraph 6 of which now sets out the appropriate procedure in maritime arrest cases. Those Rules, however, are not specifically designed to implement the 1952 Arrest Convention, as such, but reform the whole of the English Rules of civil procedure. Nevertheless, they are directly relevant to arrest actions. The text of the Rules and the Practice Directions can be found on the Web at http://www.open.gov.uk/lcd/civil/procrules_fin. It should be noted that there have already been changes to the Rules and Practice Directions, even since their introduction.

3. HOW HAS THE DEFINITION OF "CLAIMANT" BEEN INTERPRETED AND, IN PARTICULAR, THE WORDS "A PERSON WHO *ALLEGES* THAT A MARITIME CLAIM EXISTS"? IS THE MERE ALLEGATION BY THE CLAIMANT SUFFICIENT OR IS THE CLAIMANT REQUIRED TO PROVIDE PRIMA FACIE EVIDENCE OF HIS CLAIM?

Belgium

"Claimant" is to be construed as a person alleging a maritime claim. Allegation means that the claimant will not have to provide evidence—as it is the rule for any other arrest—that the claim is in all respects certain, quantified/quantifiable and due. The claimant will nevertheless have to prove that the allegations are serious and can resist—both in respect of the merits and its *quantum*—a *prima facie* examination by the judge.

Croatia

The claimant has to provide *prima facie* evidence of the valid claim which falls within the claims listed in Article 878 of the Maritime Code which relates to Article 1(1) of the Convention and the danger that without the arrest enforcement of the claim will not be possible once the claimant obtains an enforceable judgment. Article 878 so provides:

The provisions of general proceedings on the restrictions of enforcement shall not apply if enforcement is undertaken for the purpose of settlement of claims secured by the right of pledge on ships.

The provisions of general proceedings on the restrictions of enforcement shall neither apply to enforcement through sale of a ship nor to enforcement whereby settlement is demanded of the following claims:

1) damages arising from a collision of a ship on which enforcement is being conducted or damages otherwise caused by the aforementioned ship;

2) loss of life or personal injury caused by any ship on which enforcement is being conducted or damages occurring in relation to the operation of the same ship;

3) salvage operations;

4) contract for the employment of the ship subject to enforcement;

5) general average;

6) pilotage;

7) supplying of a ship subject to enforcement, for the purpose of maintenance or employment of such a ship;

8) construction, conversion, repair, outfitting or docking of the ship subject to enforcement;

9) labour-related rights of the ship's crew;

10) disbursements related to the ship made by the master, shipper, charterer or agent on behalf of the ship, shipowner or ship operator."

Denmark

Under Danish law anyone who can provide *prima facie* evidence of a maritime claim is considered to have fulfilled the requirements under chapter 4 to effect an arrest of a vessel, if all the other requirements of chapter 4 are met.

Finland

What is provided in general concerning arrest of vessels applies also to arrest under the FMC chapter 4. Consequently, the applicant must show both probable reasons for his maritime claim (the Finnish Supreme Court has placed considerably low demands on the applicant's burden to show probable reasons for his claim) and that there is a risk that the opposing party hides, destroys or conveys the vessel or otherwise jeopardises the right of the applicant (CJP chapter 7, § 1). The movability of vessels usually constitutes such a risk. If the applicant's claim is secured by a maritime lien on the vessel in accordance with the FMC chapter 3, § 2, the vessel may be arrested without any proof of the opposing party jeopardising the right of the applicant (chapter 4, § 3).

France

Dans le principe la simple allégation d'une créance "maritime" suffit à fonder une demande de saisie conservatoire. Les cas où la demande de saisie est rejetée sont extrêmement rares (voir, cependant, Court d'Appel de Rouen, 2 avril 1992, *DMF* 1993, 245, arrêt qui a d'ailleurs été critiqué). La situation est très différente pour ce qui est des saisies fondées sur le droit interne (loi du 3 janvier 1967), où le demandeur doit faire la preuve d'une "créance paraissant fondée en son principe".

Germany

According to § 920 ZPO (Code of Civil Procedure) a claimant has to produce *prima facie* evidence that the claim exists and he is the holder of the claim. The same is required in respect of the reason why the ship should be arrested. Pure allegations do not suffice.

Greece

Under the CCP, in order for the judge to grant permission for the arrest of a ship, it is required that he finds probable both the existence of the relevant claim (Article 690, paragraph 1) and the concurrence of an emergency situation or an imminent risk of frustration of the satisfaction thereof (Article 682).

Greek courts examine whether the same conditions (i.e. probability of the existence of the claim, emergency or imminent risk) are met when they are asked to order the arrest of a ship pursuant to the provisions of the Convention. However, having not dealt so far with the issue, they seem not to take account of the question arising from Article 1, paragraph 4, and Articles 2 and 3, paragraph 1 of the Convention. In theory, the view that the claimant needs only allege a maritime claim for arresting a ship in respect of which the claim arose or any other ship of the respondent has been rebutted as this view is based upon a formalistic adherence to the letter of the provision which entails intolerable consequences—such as the arrest of the ship as security of a claim that has evidently been time barred, excessively favourable to the claimant. The Convention has submitted the arrest of a ship to prior specific court permission in order to prevent abuses and restrict the number of wrongful arrests. Nevertheless, this purpose would have been in fact impossible to achieve if courts were assigned with a strictly administrative task to grant the arrest permission without having power to proceed to an, even limited, examination of the merits of the allegation of the claimant that a maritime claim exists in his favour. This serious disadvantage may not be countervailed by the fact that the claimant is personally liable for wrongful arrest. The mechanism instituted by the above rebutted view could only balance the conflicting interests if it were combined in practice with the provision of counter security by the claimant which would be sufficient to cover the damages caused by unlawful or unjustified arrest. However, as is the case with courts of other countries, Greek courts have not followed this direction. It is beyond doubt that, since the purpose of the arrest is to secure satisfaction of a maritime claim whose merits are to be subsequently assessed authentically, it is not necessary for ordering the arrest that such claim is fully evidenced and verified. But this should not lead to the conclusion that one can merely allege the existence of a maritime claim in his favour. The fact that the Convention (Article 4) submits the granting or not of the permission to arrest to a court judgment implies necessarily that the court will have to proceed to an examination, albeit limited, of such allegation and rule whether such allegation is materially justified to some extent. Within the frame of the Greek judicial system, the court may proceed to such examination even *ex officio* by gathering the necessary evidence for reaching its decision (Article 691, paragraph 1 CCP). Moreover, this approach of the court definitely constitutes a procedural matter (Article 6, paragraph 2 of the Convention).

Regardless of this, whoever alleges the existence of a claim in his favour bears the onus of satisfying the court to some extent that it is founded and *needs* to be secured. Admitting the view that, since the Convention does not require the existence of an emergency or an imminent risk of frustration of satisfaction of the claim, it allows the claimant to seek the arrest of a ship without "lawful interest"—i.e. without the existence of a need for granting the particular judicial remedy, would entail unacceptable consequences. In such case, the claimant could easily arrest more than one ship of the same respondent even if the arrest of just one of them would suffice or levy an arrest on a ship although he possesses an enforceable title whereby he could have seized the ship being thus able to obtain a more effective judicial remedy. The existence of a lawful interest constitutes a fundamental condition for granting any form of judicial remedy which has not been dealt with—nor could it have been—within the frame of a specialised regulation such as that of the Convention. Thus, whenever the claimant is in possession of an enforceable title he is not precluded from levying an arrest on the ship by the mere fact that seizure of ships falls out of the scope of the Convention if there is lawful interest to this effect as is the case of a foreign enforceable title (foreign court judgment or foreign arbitration award) which has not yet been declared enforceable in Greece since the completion of the relevant procedure implies a considerable period of time or a domestic enforceable title against a foreign ship which is ready to sail since her seizure requires the lapse of the time prescribed by law before execution may take place (Article 211, paragraph 1 CPML).

Haiti

Le mot "demandeur" en droit haïtien est équivalent de "petitioner". Il s'agit de la personne qui produit une demande par devant le tribunal haïtien "invoquant à son profit l'existence d'une créance maritime". Ce terme signifie donc que le demandeur estimant qu'il est créancier d'une créance maritime, se présente par devant le tribunal pour faire consacrer son droit. Il ne suffit pas que le demandeur allège d'une créance. Il faut qu'il en prouve l'existence. La matière étant commerciale, tous les moyens de preuve sont permis.

Italy

The interpretation of Article 1(4) of the Convention has never been the object of any decision. The general rule is that in order to obtain an order of arrest it is sufficient to provide a *prima facie* evidence of the claim which, with a Latin expression, is described as *"fumus boni juris"*. Italian courts have applied this rule also in respect of arrest of ships governed by the Convention. The *prima facie* evidence relates both to the likelihood of the claim being successful and, perhaps even more, to the amount. Italian courts generally request some evidence as to the amount of the claim in order to establish whether the amount for which the arrest should be granted, as indicated by the claimant, is reasonable or not. For example, in the case of a collision, the court will certainly not investigate the issue of liability, but will consider whether the damage suffered by the ship of the claimant approximately justifies the arrest of the colliding ship for the amount indicated by the claimant. There have, however, been cases in which an assessment has been made in respect of the liability of the defendant. For example, in the case of the *"Karlowicz"* [1996] Diritto Marittimo 1059, the Tribunale of Genoa allowed the arrest of that ship as security for damages caused to another ship owing to the former ship having broken her moorings, on the ground that if the moorings are broken, it must be presumed that they are insufficient. Neither the parties nor the court, however, considered the provisions of the Arrest Convention, even though it was applicable.

Netherlands

As far as I am aware no particular attention has been given, in the Dutch legislative history, literature or case law, to the interpretation of "claimant" or "a person who alleges that a maritime claim exists" mentioned in Article 1(4) of the Convention. The reason may be that:

— Dutch statute law with regard to the extent to which the claimant had to prove his claim was procedural in nature, so that Article 1(4) of the Convention might have been seen in the light of Article 6 of the Convention;

— Dutch statute law with regard to the extent in which the claimant had to prove his claim was very lenient towards the claimant. The claimant was only required to show summarily the validity of his claim, while in cases of arrest of assets of debtors which were not resident in the Netherlands (*"saisie foraine"*) the law specifically mentioned that no written evidence was required;

— Dutch statute law provided for a quick procedure to obtain permission for an arrest (petition *ex parte*) and a similarly quick procedure (kort geding = référé) to obtain an order for the release from arrest. A release order would generally be granted if the debtor was able to summarily show that the claim was invalid;

— some courts in the Netherlands (including the Rotterdam Court) allowed the advocate of a party expecting an arrest to request the court to be heard upon the filing of the petition for arrest (so-called "blacklisting" of an arrest). Any arguments about the insufficiency of the evidence may be put forward at this stage.

The position under current Dutch statute law (in force since 1 January 1992) is not very different. Article 700 sub 2 of the Dutch Code of Civil Procedure gives the general provision (for all types of arrest):

The leave shall be requested by means of a petition in which are stated the nature of the arrest to be effected and the grounds relied on by the petitioner and, if it is a monetary claim, the amount or, if the amount is not established, the maximum amount of the claim, without prejudice to the special requirements under the law in respect of the specific type of arrest concerned. The president judges after summary investigation.

Article 705 sub 2 of the Dutch Code of Civil Procedure provides:

1. The president who granted leave for the arrest may, acting in "kort geding" (= référé), lift the arrest at the request of any interested party, without prejudice to the jurisdiction of the regular court.

2. The release shall be ordered, i.e. in case of non-compliance with procedural requirements, if the invalidity of the grounds relied on by the arrestor or the unnecessariness of the arrest is summarily shown, or, if the arrest is effected for a monetary claim, if sufficient security is put up for this claim. (. . .)

The specific articles of Dutch statute law relating to the arrest of ships do not provide for any special requirements in this respect. The practice of "blacklisting" is also still in existence.

Nigeria

The AJD neither includes a definition of "claimant" nor the words "a person who alleges that a maritime claim exists". Also, reported authorities do not disclose that Nigerian courts have had occasion to define the term "claimant" or the phrase "a person who alleges that a maritime claim exists". A mere allegation by the claimant is not sufficient since the Admiralty Jurisdiction Procedure Rules 1993 ("AJPR"), made pursuant to the AJD (specifically Order VII, rule 1(2)), requires that the claimant disclose a "strong *prima facie* case" in the affidavit accompanying an application for the arrest of a ship.

Norway

We generally use the term "creditor" and in relation to arrest, "arrestseeker", who will have to establish a *prima facie* claim.

Poland

Polish law allowing the security for claims demands compliance with two conditions:

1. the claim must be credible (substantiated),
2. the lack of protection would prevent the creditor to satisfy his claim. So the claimant must, at least:

   1. make probable the claim, which in case of absence of code definition of making probable, means substitution remedy not providing reliability but only credibility. In consequence it means that the claimant must not necessarily present all documents and in favourable conditions, a written declaration of a third party would be sufficient, in which case the court would not need to recognise the facts as made probable, and in extreme situations could demand security for damages in favour of the owners of the arrested ship;
   2. show that the lack of security would prevent the creditor to satisfy his claim;
   3. prove a connection (ownership) between the defendant and the ship.

One of the basic elements of the institution of preventive measures is the fact that the arrest is justified because absence of that safeguard could deprive the creditor of satisfaction. The financial condition of the debtor as shown by his bank account does not belong to *"essentialia negotii"*, however it is connected with the arrest of the ship quite firmly. The bad financial condition in the absence of other guarantees exposes the creditor to the danger that in case he wins the litigation, he will not be able to obtain satisfaction of his claim, and therefore it is a sufficient substantiation for the arrest of a ship.

On the other hand, in the case of good financial conditions of the debtor, the arrest would not be justified.

However it must be mentioned here, that in some situations, although good financial conditions are obvious, the arrest is admissible, due to the fact that the absence of security could deprive the creditor of satisfaction. This, among others, is the case when the debtor's bank is of doubtful credibility.

So in all cases it is important to test if the absence of security could deprive the creditor of satisfaction. The other elements of the facts of the case, for example the financial condition, can constitute substantiation of one or other solutions.

Slovenia

In accordance with Article 16 of the Forced Execution and Security Act (ZIZ) the claimant is "a person who is seeking an arrest order".

The mere allegation of the claimant is not enough to provide an evidence of his claim. MINA in Article 979 requires that a claimant seeking an arrest order must establish firstly that he has a "probable claim", and secondly that there is a danger that the opposite party may try to avoid payment or that there is a risk that the claim may not be recovered.

The burden of proof is on the claimant, who has to convince the judge that the arrest order is necessary. The claimant has to demonstrate the existence of a probable "claim" and to show that on the facts of the case (the attitude of the opposite party) there exists a reasonable possibility that the opposite party (debtor) may try to avoid payment or that there is a risk that the claim may not be recovered.

The claimant can adduce evidence in any form permitted by the Civil Procedure Act (ZPP), such as documents, witnesses, etc.

All documents submitted as exhibits must be translated by a court interpreter into the Slovenian language.

Spain

The definition of "claimant" is that provided by Article 1 of the Convention; in accordance with Article 1 of the 1967 Act, the mere allegation of the claim is sufficient without the need of providing *prima facie* evidence or any other documentary proof of the claim. (So the Convention provides for a less onerous requirement to the claimant, as respects the burden of proof, than the ordinary domestic rules governing the preventive "embargo" (Article 1400 and subsequent articles of the Civil Procedural Code).)

Sweden

Sweden has not incorporated the part of the Convention, which defines "arrest", "person" and "claimant". Instead there is in chapter 4, section 2 a reference to the Swedish ordinary rules on arrest as a supporting set of rules, which apply unless anything to the contrary is provided for in chapter 4 of the Maritime Code. The reference made is to chapter 15 of the Swedish Code on Judicial Procedure (which does not contain any general rules specifically in respect of ships as the wording of this section seems to indicate).

As can be found from chapter 15, section 1 of the Code of Judicial Procedure, the claimant is not obliged to prove his claim. But it is not sufficient merely to allege that there exists a right to claim. It is necessary that the claimant—as the translation reads—" . . . shows probable cause to believe that he has a money claim that is or can be made the basis of a judicial proceeding or determined by another similar procedure . . . ". This is meant to include, in respect of the special chapter in the Maritime Code on Arrest of Ships in international legal relations, that the claimant has to make likely that it is also a matter of a maritime claim.

As regards the authority to which the application should be made, reference is made to chapter 21 of the Swedish Maritime Code. It follows that the application for an arrest has to be made with the maritime courts only.

To obtain an arrest decision the requirements of the Swedish Code of Judicial Procedure also have to be complied with, which means that, with a certain exception (see the answer to Question 4) the claimant has to make it likely that the other party tries actively to avoid paying the debt. It should be noted, though, that in respect of a ship, which only once or occasionally enters a Swedish port, there is an implied risk of the owners or other liable subjects trying to avoid paying by leaving the port. The courts will normally accept this as meeting the requirements in the Code. The claimant has to seek enforcement of the decision by filing a request with the local bailiff within the relevant area (the port) where the ship is.

United Kingdom

There is no separate definition of claimant, but the claimant is not required to provide *prima facie* evidence of its claim, as such, because there is no formal hearing at which such evidence is considered. It has been said by Professor Jackson (*Enforcement of Maritime Claims*, 2nd ed., 1996, p. 341) that arrest is largely an administrative, rather than a judicial, act. There is an "entitlement" to arrest, under paragraph 6.1 of Admiralty Practice Direction 49F provided, however, that the claimant follows a procedure in which its solicitor swears that certain information is believed to be true, i.e. it must swear to its allegations. Under paragraph 6.2(3) of Admiralty Practice Direction 49F, the court has discretion to give permission to issue an arrest warrant even if all the particulars set out below are not provided.

According to paragraph 6.1 of Admiralty Practice Direction 49F, the claimant in a claim *in rem* is entitled to arrest the property proceeded against by filing the new Form ADM4 which contains an application to arrest and an undertaking. In this Form there is a personal undertaking by the applicant solicitor to pay the fees of the Admiralty Marshal and all his expenses connected with the arrest, including the care and custody of the vessel while under arrest. According to paragraph 6.3 of Admiralty Practice Direction 49F, when filing the application to arrest the claimant must file a declaration. The latter declaration, now in the new Form ADM5, must, according to paragraph 6.2(4)(a), state the nature of the claim, the fact that it has not been satisfied, the name and port of registry of the ship and the amount of security sought. The declaration must be sworn as an "affidavit", which is in effect what was previously required.

Amongst the information which is required in the declaration is the name of the ship, the amount of the security sought and whether the claim is against the ship in respect of which the claim arose or a sister ship. The declaration must say that the solicitor believes that a particular person would be liable *in personam* and set out the grounds for the belief. It must also state that the person liable had the appropriate connection with the ship, e.g. as shipowner or charterer, and set out the grounds for that belief. Similarly, the grounds for belief in the beneficial ownership of the ship should be set out.

If the arrest of a "sister ship" is sought then the declaration must state the name of the person who would be liable on the claim if it were commenced *in personam,* and that the latter was when the cause of action arose the owner or charterer of or in possession or in control of the ship in connection with which the claim arose, specifying which, and finally that at the time when the claim form was issued that person was either the beneficial owner of all the shares in the ship in respect of which the warrant is required or the charterer of it under a charter by demise.

4. DOES THE PROHIBITION TO ARREST A SHIP IN RESPECT OF A CLAIM WHICH IS NOT LISTED IN ARTICLE 1(1) MEAN THAT NATIONAL MARITIME LIENS SECURING CLAIMS OTHER THAN THOSE LISTED IN ARTICLE 1(1) CANNOT BE ENFORCED BY MEANS OF THE ARREST OF THE SHIP?

Belgium

Belgium adopted the 1926 Convention on liens and mortgages. As for the Arrest Convention its provisions were incorporated in our internal law (Article 23 and following of the Maritime Code). According to Article 37 of the Maritime Code (Article 9, Convention 1926) the liens listed in Article 23 of the Maritime Code (Article 2 of the Convention 1926) cease to exist at the expiration of one year. The only way to preserve the lien from becoming time-barred is to arrest the vessel to which the lien attaches. In as far as the claim, secured by a lien, cannot be construed as a maritime claim according to Article 2 of the 1952 Brussels Convention an arrest will indeed be authorised beyond the limit/prohibition of that Convention.

Croatia

Article 976 of the Maritime Code so provides in its relevant part:

"Temporary arrest of a ship may be ordered only for the claims referred to in article 878, paragraphs 1 and 2, of this law."

Denmark

Danish law will not permit an arrest of a vessel for claims other than those mentioned in the closed list of maritime claims in MSA section 91 (1–17), corresponding to Article 1(1) of the Arrest Convention. Thus, even if a claim has the status of maritime lien under some other national law, the claimant for such a claim cannot arrest a vessel in Denmark.

Finland

Vessels covered by the FMC chapter 4 (see *infra,* under 13) may be arrested only for a maritime claim mentioned in § 4 (corresponding to Article 1(1) of the Convention). For other vessels, i.e. vessels which may be arrested in accordance with the CJP chapter 7, there is not a demand for the claim to be in any way connected with the vessel or its use, although this is usually the case.

Germany

In Germany some claims are secured by maritime liens but not covered by the list of Article 1(1) of the Convention (§ 754, section 1, no. 2; no. 5: public fees, except pilot fees; social security contributions due to the owner). The enforcement of claims listed in Article 1(1) may cause problems if the debtor of the claim and the owner of the vessel are different persons. (As to particulars see Looks, *Maritime Law Handbook*, Federal Republic of Germany, Arrest, Section 5.)

241

Greece

Greek courts have not so far dealt with the matter. The reason is that most of the claims giving rise to maritime liens under Greek law (Article 205, paragraph 1 CPML) also rank among the maritime claims listed in Article 1 of the Convention. In my view, there might be a question in three particular cases. The first case concerns taxes in connection with navigation of the ship. Under Greek law, these taxes are secured by a maritime lien but they do not rank among the claims listed in Article 1(1) of the Convention. Nevertheless, in practice there is no question of arrest of the ship since the State may easily impose a seizure. The second case relates to claims of the master and crew other than those for wages such as claims for damages caused by labour accident. This is because Greek law (Article 205, paragraph 1 CPML) does secure with a maritime lien all claims of the master and crew arising out of the contract of employment but Article 1(1) of the Convention refers only to the wages of the master, officers and crew. The third case has to do with the rights of the Greek Seamen's Pension Fund (NAT) since they give rise to a lien under Greek law but they are not listed in Article 1(1) of the Convention. In practice, however, there is again no question of arresting the ship since the NAT may easily seize the ship.

Italy

In all the cases in which Italian courts have applied the Convention, consideration has been given to the nature of the claim as one of the claims listed in Article 1(1) of the Convention. It is likely, therefore, that the arrest would not be granted in respect of a claim which is not listed therein. This could give rise to a conflict between the Arrest Convention and the 1926 MLM Convention to which Italy is a party. In fact, some of the claims mentioned in Article 2(1) of the 1926 MLM Convention are not listed in Article 1(1) of the Arrest Convention. It is thought that the Arrest Convention, as later in time, should prevail.

Netherlands

Although not entirely certain, I presume you are not referring to the application of Article 8 of the Convention as a way of avoiding the application of the list of Article 1(1). I will therefore limit myself to circumstances in which the list applies and the claimant wishes to attach a ship for a claim which is not a maritime claim as referred to in Article 1(1). The list itself is (of course) considered to be a closed list by the Dutch courts. The prohibition to arrest a ship in respect of a claim which is not listed in Article 1(1) does not in itself mean that national maritime liens securing claims other than those listed in Article 1(1) cannot be enforced by means of the arrest of the ship. The use of the phrase "national maritime liens" in the question is complicating in so far as it is difficult to compare this legal concept of common law jurisdictions to the concepts of civil law jurisdictions as in the Netherlands. I will therefore try to summarise briefly the relevant concepts of Dutch arrest law. This summary is based on a larger document which I wrote earlier. This summary is also relevant when answering other parts of the Questionnaire. Under Dutch law in general an arrest on property may be effected if the arrestor/creditor has a so-called right of recourse on the property concerned, meaning that the creditor has a right of execution of that property in order to recover his claim from the net proceeds of the judicial sale of the property in question. As a general rule the creditor has a general right of recourse on all property of his debtor. There are, however, circumstances where Dutch law confers on the creditor a right of recourse on certain property of a third party who is not debtor of the particular claim. Examples are to be found in the area of maritime law. These exceptional rights of recourse are, as a matter of principle, only granted in respect of (maritime) claims which Dutch law has designated as privileges. A privilege is synonymous to a preferential claim, that is to say a claim in respect of which the law grants preference to the creditor when exercising his right of recourse. In order to benefit from the preference it is therefore a condition that the creditor (still) has a right of recourse on the property concerned. The rights in the Netherlands of a creditor of a claim which is not listed in Article 1(1) (a non-maritime claim) are therefore determined by the question whether the creditor (still) has a right of recourse on the particular ship (to be) attached. It is irrelevant whether or not this right of recourse is of a national origin. It may also be based on a foreign right of recourse recognised under the rules of Dutch private international law. Furthermore it is not relevant whether the right of recourse is derived from a "maritime source" or not. On that basis I may come back to answering the specific question. With regard to exercising a right of recourse Dutch law distinguishes between a conservatory phase (conservatory arrest) and an execution phase (arrest in execution). As the 1952 Convention is limited to matters of conservatory arrest, a creditor—whether Dutch or foreign—of a non-maritime claim may still effect an arrest in execution, provided he has a right of recourse on the particular ship. As said above, this right of recourse may be a Dutch right or a foreign right recognised in the Netherlands under rules of Dutch private international law. Such an arrest in execution may be effected on the basis of a deed of hypothec, an arbitration award or a regular court judgment. Such a court judgment may be obtained through regular (and more time consuming) proceedings, but also by means of "kort geding" proceedings (= référé). An example of the last mentioned strategy is Pres. Rb. Middelburg 30 January 1992 (*Kananga*).

Nigeria

The AJD in section 5(3) lists the maritime liens recognised under Nigerian law. These are in respect of salvage, damage done by a ship, wages of the master or of a member of a crew and master's disbursements. Also, there are other maritime claims under AJD section 2 described as proprietary maritime claims and general maritime claims, which are neither within the section 5(3) definition of a maritime lien nor listed in Article 1(1), and which are enforceable by the arrest of a ship by virtue of AJD, sections 5(2) and 5(4).

In summary, under Nigerian law, to effect the arrest of a ship, the action has to be commenced as an action *in rem* (AJPR, Order VII, rule 1(1)), and the cause of action must be enforceable *in rem* within the meaning of AJD, sections 5(2)–5(4).

Norway

There are no maritime liens provided for in the Norwegian Maritime Code, which are not "maritime claims". A Norwegian court, by virtue of section 75 of the Maritime Code, applies *lex fori* to maritime liens and rights of retention. It follows from the second paragraph of the same section, that foreign "national liens" may be recognised if they rank in priority after registered mortgages. Any claim secured by such a foreign national lien cannot, however, be enforced in Norway by means of an arrest of the ship in question unless the claim is a maritime claim.

Slovenia

According to MINA the vessel may be arrested only in respect of claims listed in Article 877 of the aforementioned Act (if there is reciprocity) and in the case if the vessel is under hypothecation. All claims listed in Article 877 of MINA are also listed in Article 1 of the Convention.

Only in case that the State, whose flag the vessel to be arrested is flying, is not applying reciprocity to vessels flying the Slovenian flag, that vessel can be arrested for practically any claim.

Poland

Between non-Contracting States Polish civil law can be applied apart from the Arrest Convention.

Spain

The closed list of maritime claims in Article 1 of the Convention does not affect the arrest of a ship outside the scope of the Convention. Therefore the provision of paragraph 1 of Article 2 stating that a ship can only be arrested as a security for a maritime claim, does not affect the possibility of arresting a ship under domestic rules in respect of any other claim for which the *lex fori* may permit the arrest (it is so provided in the second paragraph of said Article 2 with respect to the domestic powers vested in the government and public authorities, and also, *contrario sensu*, inferred from Article 8.1 and 8.2).

For instance, in Spain a ship can be arrested by order of an authority other than a judicial authority in cases of tax debts or other public debts for the purposes of enforcing public law (as provided by the Revenue Act); preventive measures inclusive of detention and arrest of a ship can be ordered by Marine Authorities in cases of non-fulfilment of safety requirements, guilty collision in cases where national interest is involved or for the assessment of salvage remuneration (Salvage Act 1962).

In a similar way, Article 584 of the Spanish Commercial Code allows the arrest of a ship, and its immediate public sale, in cases of credits due to the tax revenue, port dues, judicial costs, deposit and/or storage costs, master and crew salaries and wages arising from the last voyage, etc.

On the other hand it is to be noted that the arrest being a conservative measure which may be executed against "any" asset of the debtor as security for "any claim", a ship, as any other debtor's asset, may be arrested in respect of any claim against the owner as security for the enforcement of an eventual condemning judgment subject to and under the general domestic rules and conditions regulating the "embargo preventivo" contained in our Civil Procedural Code (Articles 1.397 *et seq.* CPC). It follows that a vessel could be arrested, according to our domestic ordinary rules dealing with arrest in general, even though the claim is not within the list of Article 1 of the Convention, such an arrest being so granted outside the scope of the Convention, though subject to the more onerous rules of the Civil Procedural Code. It is, however, doubtful that these rules can apply in respect of the arrest of ships flying the flag of a Contracting State since it would be contrary to and expressly prohibited by Article 2, paragraph 1 of the Convention.

Furthermore, Spain is party to the 1968 European Convention on Jurisdiction and enforcement of civil and commercial judgments. Though according to Article 57 of said Convention the provisions of the 1952 Arrest Convention shall prevail, it is alleged, in some cases successfully, that Article 27 of the 1968 Convention applies to the arrest of a vessel as a preventive measure, while the main proceedings are pending before the courts of any other Contracting State, irrespective of the nature of the claim involved.

Sweden

Yes. There are claims, which under the Maritime Liens Convention and the corresponding part of chapter 3 of the Swedish Maritime Code are secured by a maritime lien, but which are not covered by the list of maritime claims in the Arrest Convention. An example is port, canal and waterway dues. An arrest in respect of a claim for such dues is possible, though, under the ordinary rules for arrest in chapter 15 of the Swedish Code of Judicial Procedure, provided that the claim concerns dues to the government or a Swedish municipality. In respect of private harbour dues, however, it is not possible to obtain arrest. The problem is aggravated by the fact that it is only by obtaining an arrest decision by a court that the claimant is able to interrupt time-barring (see chapter 3, section 40 of the Swedish Maritime Code). (In the Arrest Convention this problem has been solved.)

United Kingdom

Because of the way the 1952 Arrest Convention has been incorporated into English law, arrest is available whenever an action *in rem* against a ship is available. It so happens that all claims secured by a maritime lien under English law are found in the list set out in section 20(2) of the Supreme Court Act 1981 (and in Article 1 of the Arrest Convention 1952). There is a maritime lien recognised in English law for the obsolescent action for respondentia, but this type of claim is listed neither in the Arrest Convention 1952, nor in the Supreme Court Act 1981. Section 21(3) of the Supreme Court Act 1981 provides that an Admiralty action *in rem* may be brought in any case where there is a maritime lien, which thus confers the jurisdiction to arrest the ship or aircraft to which that maritime lien is attached. This section therefore theoretically grants jurisdiction to arrest for a claim secured by a national maritime lien not listed in Article 1(1) of the Arrest Convention 1952, but in reality there is no such claim in English law. According to section 21(4), an action *in rem* is available for a list of claims, contained in section 20(2) which is largely the same as the list of maritime claims contained in Article 1(1) of the 1952 Arrest Convention. The wording is, however, not identical. Thus, the Supreme Court Act 1981 has already been amended to allow for arrest for any claim under the 1989 Salvage Convention, which is wider than the mere reference to "salvage" in Article 1(c).

5. HAS ARTICLE 3(1) BEEN INTERPRETED TO THE EFFECT THAT, EXCEPT WHEN THE CLAIM IS SECURED BY A MARITIME LIEN, THE SHIP IN RESPECT OF WHICH THE CLAIM HAS ARISEN MAY BE ARRESTED PROVIDED IT IS STILL OWNED BY THE DEBTOR AT THE TIME OF ARREST?

Belgium

Article 3(1) has been interpreted to the effect that a conservative arrest can be made:

(a) *either of the vessel(s) in respect of which the maritime claim arose irrespective of whether the person liable for the claim is the owner of the ship or not*

Therefore even if the person liable for the maritime claim is not the owner but a distinct person such as a demise charterer, voyage or time charterer, subcharterer, manager, etc., the 1952 Brussels Convention allows an arrest on condition that the arrested vessel is the one to which the maritime claim relates. The only restriction is that such arrest is no longer possible if the vessel changed ownership in between the time the maritime claim arose and the time of the (intended) arrest.

(b) *or of the vessel(s) owned by the person liable for the claim*

If the owner is liable for the claim not only the ship to which the claim relates will have to secure that claim but also all other ships in the same ownership.

Croatia

Article 977 of the Maritime Code so provides:

Any ship may be arrested on which there exists the right of ownership, or which is owned by the same personal debtor, or which, for the claim for which arrest is sought, is encumbered by a maritime lien or a hypothec or another right of pledge based on a foreign law and for other claims as referred to in article 878, paragraph 2, of this law which relates to the ship.

If the debtor is a charterer by demise of the ship or a charterer, who according to the law applicable to the contractual relation between him and the shipowner or ship operator is alone liable to third persons—this ship may be arrested or any other ship which is owned by the charterer by demise or charterer.

The provision of paragraph 2 of this article shall also apply in all other cases when the ship operator or charterer who is a personal debtor, and who is not the owner of the ship, is himself liable for the claims for which the arrest of the ship is sought.

At a request which relates to the right of ownership, co-ownership and the right of pledge on the ship, only the ship to which this request relates may be arrested.

Denmark

Yes.

Finland

Arrest under the FMC chapter 4 may be laid upon the vessel to which the maritime claim relates. If a maritime claim is based on any circumstances mentioned in § 4, items 1–14, or item 17, arrest may be also be laid on any other vessel belonging to the person who, at the time when the maritime claim arose, was the owner of the vessel to which the maritime claim refers. Furthermore, if any other person than the vessel's owner is liable for such a maritime claim, arrest may be laid either on the vessel to which the maritime claim relates or on any other vessel belonging to the debtor. Finally, arrest can be imposed on a vessel only if the vessel may be subject to execution measures for maritime claims in Finland (§ 5). For vessels covered under the CJP chapter 7, an arrest may be imposed only for claims against the owner. However, if the claim is secured by a maritime lien, an arrest may be laid upon the vessel even if the debtor is an operator or a charterer or other person who manages the vessel for her owner (*cf.* the FMC chapter 3, § 2).

France

La question posée ici a soulevé des difficultés en droit français. Dans un arrêt du 31 mars 1992, la Cour de Cassation avait admis la possibilité de saisir un navire après sa vente sans exiger que le juge constate l'existence d'un privilège au bénéfice du saisissant (*DMF* 1992, 435). Mais devant les critiques suscitées par cet arrêt (voir Bonassies, *DMF* 1993, 78), la jurisprudence a évolué. La jurisprudence la plus récente n'autorise la saisie du navire vendu qu'aux créanciers titulaires d'un privilège maritime: Cour d'Appel de Montpellier 31 juillet 1996, *DMF* 1997, 31 et Aix en Provence 15 mai 1996, *DMF* 1997, 598.

Germany

Yes. The result can be derived from the normal principles of German law regarding the enforcement of claims which makes it possible to arrest any ship owned by the debtor at the time of the arrest.

Greece

The provision of Article 3, paragraphs 1, 2 and 3 of the Convention makes the granting of an arrest order conditional to whether the claim sought to be secured relates to the particular ship. The beneficiary of such claim is entitled to arrest the ship in respect of which the claim arose if she is still owned by the debtor—i.e. the person liable in respect of the claim, as well as any other ship owned by such person at the time of the arrest (Article 3, paragraph 1). However, the liability of the owner who operates his own ship against the creditors of the ship may not be based on this provision nor may the owner be deemed thereunder to be the debtor of claims arising from the ship since "Nothing in this Convention shall be construed as creating a right of action, which, apart from the provision of this Convention, would not arise under the law applied by the Court which had seisin of the case" (Article 9, paragraph 1). The provision of Article 3, paragraph 1 of the Convention departs from the consideration that most maritime laws worldwide treat the owner who operates his own ship as a debtor of the claims arising therefrom whilst they hold liable against such creditors not only the ship in respect of which such claim arose, provided that the same remains in his property, but also any other ship owned by him at the time of the arrest. The Convention provides for two exceptions from this rule. The first concerns the arrest of a ship as security of claims which arise in respect thereof whose debtor, however, is a third party operating the ship (Article 3, paragraph 4). The other exception consists in the right granted to the creditors arising out of the operation of the ship to arrest her in the hands of the transferee if, under either the material law applicable by the court having seisin of the case or the Maritime Liens and Mortgages Convention, if applicable, they are granted maritime liens or similar *droits de suite* on the ship in the hands of the transferee (Article 9, paragraph 2). Thus, each time Greek material law applies, creditors originating from the employment of the ship by her owner may arrest her in the hands of the transferee if their claim is secured by a maritime lien on the ship (Article 207 CPML[1] = 559 para 5 *Codice della navigazione*) or the conditions of Article 479 of the Greek Civil Code (CC)[2] are met. Such creditors may not arrest any other ship of the transferee. Nevertheless, the Piraeus Multi-member First Instance Court held in its judgment No. 325/1990 (Maritime Law Review 18, 408)—erroneously in my opinion, that—"the Brussels International Convention which applies in the case in question, allows the arrest of a ship only in respect of maritime claims among which do rank those arising out of salvage but not those arising out of cumulative assumption of debt under article 479 CC even if such debt arose out of a maritime claim."

---

1. Article 207 CPML reads as follows: "If a ship is alienated by contract, a lien shall continue to exist provided it is recognised in a judgment given against the transferee of the ship, but it shall be extinguished if the relevant action is not brought within three months from the contract of alienation being registered in the register of ships. In the case of claims secured by liens arising out of the contract of employment of the master and crew as well as the rights of Seamen's Pension Fund arising out of the employment thereof, such liens are extinguished in one year."

2. Article 479 CC reads as follows: "If a patrimonium or enterprise has been contractually transferred in its entirety, the transferee shall be liable towards a creditor for the debts burdening the patrimonium or the enterprise to the extent of the value of the assets transferred. The responsibility of the transferor shall be maintained. Any agreement to the contrary between the contracting parties to the detriment of the creditors shall be void."

Haiti

Si le navire est vendu par son propriétaire, la créance existe contre ce propriétaire et non contre l'acquéreur qui, en définitive, n'a pas d'obligation personnelle envers les créanciers. En droit maritime haïtien, le droit de suite n'existe qu'en cas d'hypothèque sur le navire en litige.

Italy

The general rule under Italian law is that, except when the claim is secured by a maritime lien or by a hypothec on the ship, the ship in respect of which the claim has arisen cannot be arrested if she is not owned any more by the person liable. As regards the moment when the sale becomes effective and prevents an arrest, the controlling factor is registration: if the arrest is registered prior to the registration of the sale, it is effective *vis-à-vis* the buyer; if the sale is registered first, the arrest (whether registered or not) is not effective. Article 250 Code of Navigation (CN) in fact provides that for the purposes provided for in the Civil Code (CC) all acts creating, transferring or extinguishing title to or other real rights on ships are made public by means of registration in the ships register. Article 2644 CC in turn provides that the acts listed in the preceding article (which include contracts of sale) have no effect *vis-à-vis* third parties who have acquired a right on the property. Article 684 CN then provides that the warrant of arrest after service shall be registered in the ships register.

Netherlands

As far as I am aware Article 3, sub 1 of the Convention has never been an issue in Dutch case law. I refer to M.H. Claringbould, "The Netherlands", in: J. Theunis e.a., *Arrest of Ships 2. Belgium, The Netherlands, India, Yugoslavia*, London: Lloyd's of London Press 1986, pp. 51 and 52 for the only relevant discussion in Dutch legal literature. Professor Claringbould's argumentation on p. 51 is consistent with the outline of Dutch arrest law in the reply to Question 4. The relevant question to be answered is whether the arrestor/creditor (still) has a right of recourse on the ship concerned. In the absence of an exceptional right of recourse (i.e. recourse on the property of a non-debtor), which is only granted in connection with privileges, the creditor will indeed only be able to attach a ship which is the property of the debtor.

Nigeria

No. In the equivalent provision of the AJD, section 5(4)(a), where the claimant is proceeding against the ship in respect of which the claim has arisen, the debtor must be the beneficial owner of all the shares in the ship at the time the action is brought and not at the time of arrest.

With particular reference to a maritime lien, current ownership (or change of ownership) of the vessel is irrelevant, provided that the claim is secured by a maritime lien by reference to AJD, section 5(3).

Norway

Yes.

Poland

The problem is connected with the principle of legal succession. In all cases where the new owner—therefore not the same person—is a successor in right of the previous owner, under general or specific title (in the sense of succession of obligations), the action of arresting the ship, against this new owner is possible. Such actions may take place, among others, in cases where the owners transform into a company with limited liability, by amalgamation or merging with another company, as also in cases of inheritance.

There can be also certain variations as to the object of security, and so in accordance with Article 1030 of the CC the inheritor until the moment of taking over the inheritance is responsible only for objects constituting the inheritance so the arrest of another ship of the inheritor would not be possible.

In cases of original acquisition of ownership, for example, by sales agreement without taking over the burdens of the former owner, the arrest of such ship would not be possible. In this situation the principle is correct and the creditors can defend their interests by invoking the ineffectiveness of the debtor's deeds made to the detriment of his creditors.

Of course apart from personal responsibility there exists the principle of liability for debts secured on real or personal property in respect of the ships (lien, mortgage, privileges, encumbrances) which however are not the subject of this elaboration.

Slovenia

The vessel to be arrested must be still owned by the debtor at the time of arrest. Otherwise, an arrest order cannot be issued, mainly because the maritime claims listed in Article 877 of MINA do not create maritime liens and they do not follow the vessel after her change of ownership.

Sweden

No. As indicated above, Article 3(1) refers to 3(4) and Article 10. Seen separately, these rules clearly say the arrest is possible also for claims against somebody else, other than the owner. However, Sweden has focused on Article 9, second part (see further below).

Spain

Spain is party to the 1926 Convention on maritime liens and mortgages and, therefore, a ship may be arrested even after her purchase by a bona fide buyer when the claim is secured by a maritime lien under the 1926 Convention.

United Kingdom

The relevant provision of the Supreme Court Act 1981 is section 21(4), which resembles Article 3(1) of the 1952 Arrest Convention. Section 21(4) states "in the case of any such claim as is mentioned in section 20(2)(e) to (r) where (a) the claim arose in connection with a ship and (b) the person who would be liable on the claim in an action *in personam* ("the relevant person") was, when the cause of action arose, the owner or charterer of, or in possession or in control of the ship, an action *in rem* may . . . be brought in the High Court against: (a) that ship, if at the time when the action is brought the relevant person is either the beneficial owner of that ship as respects all the shares in it or the charterer of it under a charter by demise; or (b) any other ship of which, at the time when the action is brought, the relevant person is the beneficial owner as respects all the shares in it." Thus, the effect of that provision is that when the action is *brought*, an *in rem* claim form is issued (CPR Practice Direction 49F, paragraph 2.1(1)), and the person liable *in personam* for the claim is the owner or demise charterer of the ship, the latter can be arrested.

Moreover, it seems that the ship may be arrested, even if ownership has changed hands after the time when the action is brought, e.g. the issuing of the claim form (formerly the writ) and the arrest being actually effected, *The Monica S* [1967] 2 Lloyd's Rep. 113, *The Helene Roth* [1980] 1 Lloyd's Rep. 477. Although note that CPR Practice Direction 49F, paragraph 6.2(6) states that a warrant of arrest may not be *issued* as of right, and therefore an arrest may not be effected, in the case of property in respect of which the beneficial ownership, as a result of a sale or disposal by any court exercising Admiralty jurisdiction, has changed since the claim form (the old writ) was issued.

5.1 IF SO, IN CASE THE VESSEL IS SOLD TO A BONA FIDE BUYER, IS IT NECESSARY, IN ORDER THAT THE VESSEL MAY NOT BE ARRESTED ANY MORE BY THE PERSON WHO HAS A CLAIM AGAINST THE SELLER, THAT THE SALE BE ENDORSED IN THE SHIPS REGISTER?

Croatia

Under Croatian law the time of the endorsement of the sale in the ship's register is also relevant, but there is no endorsement of arrest in ships register. Therefore, in order that the sale be effective *vis-à-vis* the claimant, it is necessary that the sale be endorsed in the ships register before the time when the arrest is effected.

Denmark

MSA section 28 stipulates that the passing of title only has effect against third party claims if it is registered in the ships register. Therefore if an arrest is made in good faith and is registered before or simultaneously with the registration of the new title, the arrest will have effect against the vessel to the detriment of the buyer. Thus it is the timing of the registration in the ships register which is the determining factor.

France

Si on limite le droit de saisie aux seuls créanciers privilégiés, la saisie n'est possible que pendant un délai de deux mois après la vente et la publication de celle-ci au fichier des navires, ce délai éteignant le privilège (article 40.3° de la loi du 3 janvier 1967 sur le navire). Si on accorde le droit de saisir aux créanciers non privilégiés, aucun texte ne peut être invoqué qui fixerait une limite à ce droit (. . . ce qui démontre que la solution est déraisonnable).

Greece

1. As a rule, the claimant may arrest the ship if she is still owned by the debtor at the time of the arrest. Hence, it is critical whether at the time of the arrest the transfer of ownership to a third party has been concluded. According to Article 6 CPML, in order for the property in a ship to pass, there shall be an agreement. This agreement must be made in writing and entered in the Ships Registry whereupon property passes. Consequently, if the agreement of transfer of ownership of a Greek ship has been made (whether this is an agreement to sell, donate, exchange, etc.) but has not been entered in the Ships Registry, the transferor still remains proprietor of the ship *erga omnes*. His creditors may, therefore, still arrest her. It should be noted that, if the registration of an arrest and the registration of a transfer of ownership concur on the same day, the arrest has priority (Article 214, paragraph 3 CPML).

2. However, it is arguable whether it is possible to register the arrest of the ship made by virtue of the Convention. This is because the arrest levied by virtue of the Convention can only entail the immobilisation of the ship without having any effect on her legal status nor preventing the transfer of ownership. Nevertheless, in practice all arrests are entered in the Ships Registry whether they rely on the Convention or the CCP.

Italy

Article 250 CN provides that for the purposes provided for in the Civil Code all acts creating, transferring or extinguishing title to or other real rights on ships are made public by means of registration in the ships register. Article 2644 Civil Code in turn provides that the acts listed in the preceding article (which include contracts of sale) have no effect *vis-à-vis* third parties who have acquired a right on the property. Article 684 CN in turn provides that the warrant of arrest after service shall be registered in the ships register. The controlling factor is, therefore, registration: if the arrest is registered prior to the registration of the sale, it is effective *vis-à-vis* the buyer; if the sale is registered first, the arrest (whether registered or not) is not effective.

Norway

The answer to this question is that it is probably sufficient that title passes from the seller to the buyer in order that the sale be effective *vis-à-vis* a claimant who has a claim against the seller. It would therefore not be necessary for the sale to be endorsed in the ships register.

Sweden

Swedish law does not deal, to the best of the Swedish MLA's knowledge, with the question whether a sale has to be endorsed in the ships register.

6. IS IT PERMITTED BY YOUR LAW TO PIERCE THE CORPORATE VEIL AND, IF SO, IN WHICH CIRCUMSTANCES?

Belgium

Belgian jurisprudence has indeed on several occasions accepted that within the frame of conservative arrest proceedings the corporate veil of the shipowning company is pierced. There have been different cases in which the courts uphold the arrest of a ship owned by one person as security for the debts of another (shipowning) company. In all these cases the court lifted the corporate veil and treated as if they were in the same ownership ships owned by different companies once evidence was provided that there was a blending and commingling of the said companies to such an extent that—although they were formally separate legal entities—they were to be considered as "one". In legal terms such piercing is construed on the basis of abuse of corporate veil, *fraus omnia corrumpit* and/or the *actio pauliana*.

Croatia

Piercing the corporate veil is not allowed, although, recently there was discussion in this respect within the maritime community.

There is no provision in the Maritime Code corresponding to Article 9 of the Convention. However, Article 984 provides that the arrest of the ship shall not be prejudicial to the rights and duties of the parties and Article 980 provides that the giving of the security shall not imply recognition of liability.

Denmark

Danish courts have not yet, and are not expected to, pierce the "corporate veil". Thus Danish law recognises the autonomy of, for instance, single ship companies and will not permit the arrest of a vessel belonging to another company in the same group.

Finland

According to the FMC chapter 4, § 5, a vessel shall be deemed to be in the same ownership when all the shares therein are owned by the same person or persons. The question of "piercing the corporate veil" is not governed by arrest law. It is an emerging issue relevant especially for corporate law, contract law and tort law.

France

La possibilité de "percer le voile" d'une personne morale est admise par le droit français. A une certaine époque elle a été largement utilisée, dès lors que le juge constatait une simple "communauté d'intérêts" entre deux sociétés d'armateurs. Mais la Cour de Cassation, dans plusieurs décisions récentes, a brisé cette jurisprudence. Dans un arrêt du 19 mars 1996, la Cour a posé la règle que le juge ne pouvait "percer le voile" de la personnalité morale qu'en caractérisant la fictivité de l'une des sociétés impliquées dans le litige (*DMF* 1996, 503 et, dans le même sens, 21 janvier 1997, *DMF* 1997, 612).

Germany

Piercing the corporate veil is possible in Germany if the legal form (GmbH) has being abused. This depends on the circumstances of the single case.

Greece

The fact that Greek merchant marine consists mainly of single ship companies has contributed to the admission by jurisprudence and scholars of the process of piercing the corporate veil for imposing personal liability on the individual beneficiaries. For piercing the corporate veil, Greek courts have recourse either to the test of control or the test of the nominee. On a number of cases they have combined both tests. In particular, courts have pierced the corporate veil in the case of shipping companies when one of the shareholders had the absolute control of each company by holding himself or through nominees the whole of the shares therein (Piraeus Court of Appeals [PCA] 1277/1990 Maritime Law Review [MLR] 1277/1990, 226; Areios Pagos [AP] 1046/1990 MLR 1991, 15; Piraeus Single-member First Instance Court [PSFIC] 1990/1988 MLR 1989, 212; AP 591/1988 MLR 1989, 37; 1058/1987 MLR 1987, 41) and exercising himself or through his confidant the powers of the managing director of the company (AP 1046/1990 op. cit.; 591/1980 op. cit.; Athens Court of Appeals [ACA] 8734/1986 Commercial Law Review 1986, 664; Piraeus Multi-member First Instance Court 2301/1988 MLR 1988, 441; PSFIC 1900/1988 op. cit.; ACA 11452/1986 MLR 1987, 243) or the company appeared as "strawman" of the individual hiding behind it (Athens Multi-member First Instance Court 364/1986 MLR 1986, 664; ACA 11452/1986 MLR 1987, 243; PCA 1514/1988 Piraiki Nomologia 1988, 536; 253/1988 MLR 1988, 106). However, as it has been correctly pointed out [*cf.* A. Kiantou-Pabouki, *The protection of maritime creditors in shipping companies by piercing the corporate veil*, Records and Introductions of the 1st International Conference of Maritime Law, Piraeus Bar Association (1994) pp. 44 *et seq.*] recourse to these tests, at least in the manner it is conducted, entails a serious threat to the institution of corporate entity. This is why in the literature [K. Paboukis, *Commercial Companies Law*, paragraph 44 II p. 379; L. Georgakopoulos, *Companies Law* I (1965) pp. 551–552; N. Papantoniou, *General principles of civil law* (1983) paragraph 31, p. 144; Than. Liakopoulos, *Lifting of the corporate veil in jurisprudence* (1988) p. 10] it is maintained that the corporate veil should be pierced only when the incorporation of a company constitutes an abusive exercise of the faculty prescribed by the judicial system for the development of business activities through corporate entities. This is especially so when the main shareholder makes use of this faculty for circumventing the law or maliciously causing harm to others or evading the fulfilment of his obligations. On such motive, he usually underfunds the company or uses the company's assets for conducting his personal business which overturns the necessary equilibrium between the assets and the capital of the company.

As regards Article 3(2) of the Convention, the Piraeus Single-member First Instance Court held (judgment 2856/1976, MLR 5,200) that, when two ships are separately owned by two different sociétés anonymes whose shares belong to the same individual or individuals, they are not deemed to make part of the same property. The two ships should be deemed to be under the same property only if there was an *in concreto* reason to pierce the corporate veil of the two owning companies.

Haiti

Non, on ne peut pas percer le voile de la personnalité morale. En droit haïtien, une personne morale a exactement les mêmes droits et les mêmes attributions qu'une personne physique.

Italy

In Italy the general problem of the responsibility of a company for the debts of another has been considered in relation to Article 2362 CC which regulates the responsibility of the sole shareholder of a company (Article 2362 CC so provides: "In case of insolvency of a company in respect of the obligations arisen during the time when all shares are owned by one person only, that person is responsible without any limit") and to Article 2740 CC which regulates the civil liability ("respon-sabilità patrimoniale") of the debtor (Article 2740 CC so provides: "The debtor is responsible for the fulfilment of his obligations with all his assets, present and future. Limitations of liability are not permitted unless in the cases statutorily established"). Although the operation of Article 2362 is now deemed possible even when the shareholder is a legal entity (Corte di Cassazione—Sezioni Unite 14 December 1981, No. 6594, *S.A. Chocolat Tobler* v. *Banca Ambrosiana* [1982] 2 Giurisprudenza Commerciale 614), Italian courts have interpreted this provision very strictly by requiring the ownership of 100 per cent of the shares. With judgment 9 January 1987, No. 73, *SIPSA* v. *Fallimento Ivo Pera*, [1988] 2 Giurisprudenza Commerciale 63, the Corte di Cassazione held that Article 2362 CC could apply in a case in which one shareholder owned 99 per cent of the shares of a company; with judgment 3 September 1992, *S.p.A. Manzoni & C.* v. *S.r.l. Coedit*, [1993] 2 Giurisprudenza Commerciale 659, the Tribunale of Milano reached the same conclusion in relation to Article 2497

CC, in which the same rule as that of Article 2362 is adopted for the case of voluntary liquidation, in a case when one shareholder held 99.9 per cent of the shares.

Article 2362 CC has been held to apply in cases where less than 100 per cent of the shares are owned by one person only when the ownership of the balance of the shares by another person is fictitious, whilst the fact that a person or a company fully controls or dominates another company has been held to be relevant only from the economical but not from the legal standpoint (Corte d'Appello of Palermo 5 November 1980, *Banca Commerciale Italiana* v. *Raytheon Co. and Machlett Laboratories* [1981] 2 Giurisprudenza Commerciale 615 with a critical comment by Pellizzi, *Unico azionista e controllo totalitario indiretto*).

In respect of the arrest of ships the legal theory on the basis of which the arrest of a ship owned by a person other than debtor is that of "simulation" whereby a fictitious agreement is not relevant between the parties and, also, *vis-à-vis* third parties (Article 1415 CC provides: "Effects of simulation on third persons. Simulation cannot be used as a defence by the contracting parties, by their successors in interest, or by the creditors of the simulating transferor, against third parties who, in good faith, have acquired rights from the apparent owner of the right, subject to the effects of transcription of a judicial petition concerning simulation. Third persons can plead simulation against the contracting parties, when it is prejudicial to their rights). The Corte d'Appello of Genoa with judgment of 3 August 1971, *Felarugica S.A.* v. *S.p.A. Italviscosa and Felice Riva*, [1972] Dir. Mar. 53, reversed a judgment of the Tribunale of Chiavari which had upheld the arrest of the m.y. *"Faella"* owned by Felarugica S.A. of Panama as security for a claim of S.p.A. Italviscosa against Mr. Felice Riva on the ground that Mr. Riva was the actual owner of the yacht, holding that no evidence of a simulation had been provided.

For the same reasons the Tribunale of Chiavari with judgment 15 May 1971, *Robert Butler* v. *John F. Baron and Wanderer Financial Corp.—The "Wanderer"* [1972] Dir. Mar. 75, released the m.y. *"Wanderer"* from the arrest which had been effected as security for a claim against Mr. John F. Baron, on the ground that he was the actual owner of the yacht.

The first judgment based on the Arrest Convention is a judgment of 12 March 1994 delivered by the Tribunale of Ravenna in the case *Secnav Marine Ltd* v. *Petromin S.A., Breaza Inc. and Tanker Ship Management—The "Breaza"* [1994] Dir. Mar. 217. The Tribunale of Ravenna affirmed the warrant of arrest of the *"Breaza"*, owned by Breaza Inc. of Monrovia, as security for a claim of Secnav Marine against Petromin S.A. on the ground that Petromin S.A. controlled Breaza Inc. through Petromin Overseas Inc. and that, therefore, the arrest was permissible under Article 3(1) of the Arrest Convention.

The French "théorie de l'apparence" was instead taken as a basis of the arrest of the m.v. *"Euroshipping One"* by the Tribunale of Livorno (judgment 18 November 1996, *Enzo Cipriani Shipping S.r.l.* v. *Baltic Shipping Co.—The "Euroshipping One"* [1998] Dir. Mar. 433), notwithstanding that the vessel had been sold to another company, since the buyer was a company fully owned by the seller and had a branch office located at the registered office of the seller. Rather than the "apparence" of a link between the two companies, this was probably a case in which the fictitious (or simulated) character of the sale could have been the proper basis for the arrest.

Nigeria

Yes. Although the legal personality of the company, as distinct from those of the members and the consequences of incorporation, are recognised under Nigerian law, there are certain circumstances in which the corporate entity is disregarded and the veil of incorporation is lifted in accordance with statute or common law, in the interest of justice.

Examples in the Companies and Allied Matters Act, Cap. 59, Laws of the Federation of Nigeria 1990, under the common law are as follows:

   i. When the number of members is below the legal minimum and the company continues to carry on business for a period of six months thereafter: section 93;
   ii. Where the number of directors of the company falls below two and the company carries on business after sixty days thereafter: section 246(3);
   iii. Where the company receives money by way of a loan to be applied for certain specified purposes and the loan is not applied for such purposes: section 290;

iv. Where the name of the company is not mentioned on business correspondence, cheques, bills of exchange, promissory notes, etc. as required under section 631(1): section 631(2);

v. Where a group of companies is virtually a partnership or where one of the companies is a trustee of the other in respect of some property in issue;

vi. Where an inspector is appointed under section 316 of the Act and he thinks it is necessary;

vii. Where a company is acting for the shareholders or is a sham;

viii. Generally, where the courts have found fraud or some improper conduct, they have lifted the veil in the interest of justice.

Norway

In principle yes. In practice, however, it is very difficult to pierce the corporate veil. There is no legislation directly dealing with the issue. That the possibility to pierce exists has been confirmed by the Supreme Court in a case where such a piercing was denied. The test to be used is the *alter ego* test, much like it is done in, e.g. the United States.

Poland

No, it is not possible.

Slovenia

According to Slovenian law the court cannot pierce the corporate veil.

Spain

Yes. Spanish courts are increasingly applying the doctrine of the piercing of the corporate veil by imposing liability upon the interests (individuals and/or companies) hidden behind a company. The piercing of the corporate veil doctrine has been also used in cases of companies which, hiding the same interests, are established just as "instruments" to disperse liability. This jurisprudencial trend is based on a liability in tort arising from what is deemed to be an unlawful act done with the purpose of escaping from creditors.

In view of the numerous decisions of our Tribunals in the matter, in the literature the following circumstances have been deemed relevant in order to allow the piercing of the corporate veil: (1) there should be enough evidence to infer that there is a coincidence of interests and action between the companies, the piercing of the corporate veil tries to avoid that under legal entities, apparently separated, it is hidden a unity of activity, organisation, patrimony, management and assets; (2) the structure should have been created to avoid the application of the law, there must be evidence of a fraudulent act done with the intention of damaging creditors, and (3) the piercing of the corporate veil should be applied as a subsidiary criteria (*ultima ratio*). The effective concurrence of these elements is applied in a flexible way by our courts attending to the particular circumstances of each case.

Sweden

The issue of piercing the corporate veil is very comprehensive and could, in fact, give rise to a doctoral thesis. It is, therefore, not easy to answer the Questionnaire in this respect in a few lines. Generally, however, it could be said that under Swedish law the corporate veil is normally upheld, whilst in many other countries it would be possible to pierce it. In other words, we are rather reluctant here to change what has been created by the establishing of a separate company with limited liability. One reason is that it has been found favourable to society in general that new business is created by the help of a possibility of limiting the liability to the assets of a company.

However, in certain situations, such as that when the shareholders have expressed themselves or otherwise behaved in a way which gives their opponent the impression that they are fully standing behind and taking responsibility for the actions of their company or subsidiary, as the case may be, there might be a possibility of piercing the corporate veil, although the term has then been used extensively.

United Kingdom

Piercing the corporate veil is allowed in England in exceptional circumstances. See the answer to Question 6.1.

6.1 HOW HAS ARTICLE 3(2) BEEN INTERPRETED IN THIS RESPECT?

Belgium

We have never come across a situation where Article 3(2) has been invoked in cases where the corporate veil was pierced. This article only applies to cases of ships in co-ownership and such provision is not helpful to treat as in a same ownership ships owned by different companies but fraudulently controlled by the same group of person(s).

France

Pour la jurisprudence française, il faut certainement interpréter l'article 3-2 comme visant non seulement les parts des copropriétaires d'un navire, mais aussi les actions et sociétés commerciales. Mais, en pratique, le problème de l'interprétation de l'article 3-2 n'est pas abordé par les juges, qui, pour décider que deux navires ont le même propriétaire, se réfèrent seulement à la notion de fictivité.

Haiti

Le paragraphe 2 de l'article 3 est d'application stricte.

Nigeria

Article 3(2) is not repeated in the AJD. In view of the fact that the AJD does not include specific provisions on lifting the corporate veil, general principles of company law referred to in paragraph 6 *supra*, will ordinarily apply.

Norway

Article 3(2) has not been the subject of litigation in relation to piercing the corporate veil. I assume that Article 3(2) would at the outset simply be construed to mean that the sister ship should be owned by the same legal person as the ship in relation to which the maritime claim arose.

Spain

We are aware of some cases in which the "piercing of the corporate veil doctrine" has been invoked by the claimant and applied by the courts in respect of arrest of ships in connection with Article 3(2) of the Convention. As far as we could search from said decisions, there are some courts which have understood that a *prima facie* evidence of being in presence of the same ownership (i.e. an "apparent" unity of activity, organisation or patrimony) suffices to grant the arrest since the full proof of said coincidence of ownership, by effectively piercing the corporate veil, is something to be determined in the course of the main proceedings, due to the special nature of the arrest just as a "preventive" and cautelar measure, without need of full proof whilst other courts have lifted the arrest in cases where the arrest has been contested by showing documentary evidence (i.e. a registration certificate) proving that the registered owner appears to be a person other than that liable for the claim in respect of which the arrest was brought.

Sweden

The only comment in respect of Article 3(2), which is found in the Preparatory Works of the chapter on Arrest in the Swedish Maritime Code is that the article is unclear and that no corresponding rule should be included in the Swedish Code. Reference is made here to the general legal situation in respect of piercing the corporate veil under Swedish law, which roughly corresponds to what was explained above.

Article 3(2) has to be seen together with Article 3(4) and the answers under the next Questions will, therefore, cover partly also Article 3(2).

United Kingdom

The relevant provision resembling Article 3(2) of the 1952 Arrest Convention is section 21(4) of the Supreme Court Act 1981, mentioned in the answer to Question 5, above.

Courts will allow the piercing of the corporate veil in cases where either the company form has been created and used as a way to avoid existing liabilities or duties imposed by law, *The Evpo Agnic* [1988] 1 W.L.R. 1090, *The Maritime Trader* [1981] 2 Lloyd's Rep. 153, *The Saudi Prince* [1982] 2 Lloyd's Rep. 255, or when a sham transaction has taken place and ownership of the ship has changed hands after the liabilities arose so that the ship cannot be used to satisfy the claimants, *The Tjaskemolen* [1997] 2 Lloyd's Rep. 465. In both cases, the courts will examine the motive behind the use of the corporate form, *Adams* v. *Cape Industries* [1991] 1 All E.R. 929 and *Ord* v. *Belhaven Pubs Ltd* [1998] 2 B.C.L.C. 447. It appears that Scottish law would follow the approach taken in England (see the 1998 Report referred to in the answer to Question 1, at p. 167).

7. HOW HAS ARTICLE 3(4) BEEN INTERPRETED?

Denmark

The Danish legislature has interpreted Article 3(4) restrictively. Despite Article 3(4) Danish law maintains the fundamental condition for arrest of a vessel that the claim may be enforced against the vessel through for instance a forced sale. So even if Article 3(4) permits arrest even when the claim cannot be enforced against the vessel, the Danish legislature has chosen not to allow such arrest, referring to Article 9 of the Arrest Convention.

Finland

See under 5, *supra*. As was said, an arrest can be imposed on a vessel only if the vessel may be subject to execution measures for maritime claims in Finland. This means, *de facto*, that the claims have to be against the owner of the vessel—with the exception of claims secured by a maritime lien.

France

Bien que la jurisprudence soit ici très rare, il est admis que l'article 4-3 autorise un créancier, même non privilégié, à saisir le navire affrété coque-nue par son débiteur. En revanche, dans le cas d'affrètement à temps, il est généralement admis qu'un créancier de l'affréteur ne peut saisir le navire affrété que s'il bénéficie d'un privilège maritime. En l'absence de privilège, la saisie n'est pas possible (en ce sens, Rouen 3 décembre 1992, *Juris Classeur Périodique* 1993.4. 1986).

Greece

Greek law (Article 106, paragraph 2 CPML) draws the distinction between ownership and operation of a ship. When the shipping and trading management of the ship is carried out by a person other than her owner (bareboat charterer, demise charterer), then such person is called operator. The operator is liable in respect of claims arising out of the employment of the ship by himself. Nevertheless, the holders of such claims may satisfy themselves by turning against the ship in respect of which they arose if they obtain an enforceable title against her owner and levy execution against the ship. Such creditors, however, are not entitled to levy execution against any other ship or asset of the shipowner.

This regulation of Greek law is similar to that of Article 3(4) of the Convention. This is the reason why the implementation of the above provision of the Convention has not given rise to particular problems. It has been maintained (A. Antapassis, *The Convention of 1952 for the Arrest of Ships* [in Greek] pp. 180 *et seq.*) that this provision does not impose liability on the part of the shipowner but merely grants the right to creditors originating from her employment to arrest her. The court may not, relying upon the provision of Article 3(4), hold the shipowner liable in respect of obligations arising from the operation of the ship by another party and submit the ship to forced sale in satisfaction thereof. This matter is governed by the relevant *lex causae*.

As regards the final sentence of Article 3(4), it has been maintained (A. Antapassis, *op. cit.*, p. 188), that any holder of a maritime claim relating to a chartered ship in respect of which her charterer (whether time or voyage charterer) is liable, may arrest such ship or any other ship owned by the debtor, time or voyage charterer.

Article 9 of the Convention serves to enforce the above interpretation of Article 3(4).

Haiti

La réponse fournie ci-dessus concernant la Question 6.1 s'applique au paragraphe 4 de l'article 3.

Netherlands

For the interpretation of Article 3(4) I refer to the following literature:

— J. T. Asser, "Uniform Zeerecht. De Diplomatieke Zeerecht Conferentie, gehouden te Brussel in Mei 1952", *NJB* 1953, pp. 757, 768 and 780 *et seq.*;

— M. H. Claringbould, "The Netherlands", in J. Theunis e.a., *Arrest of Ships 2. Belgium, The Netherlands, India, Yugoslavia*, London: Lloyd's of London Press 1986, pp. 53 *et seq.* (this article, or perhaps its Dutch spin-off M. H. Claringbould en C. J. H. van Lynden, "Enige aantekeningen bij het Verdrag Conservatoir Beslag op Zeeschepen", *NJB* 1986, pp. 837–841, seems to have been very influential in the Dutch courts);

For the relevant case law I refer to the following cases: Pres. Rb. Rotterdam 23 January 1984, Rb. Rotterdam 13 March 1987, Rb. Middelburg 7 September 1988, Hof's-Gravenhage 5 December 1989 Rb. Rotterdam 28 January 1994, Rb. Rotterdam 4 February 1994, HR 12 September 1997.

Nigeria

AJD, section 5(4) which also deals with enforcement of claims against a demise charterer, includes terms which are similar to Article 3(4).

Poland

In all situations where the agreement between the registered owner and the charterer transfers the management of the ship the problem of arrest/stopping of the ship becomes complicated.

Bare-boat Charter In case of charter by demise on basis of which the possession of the ship and navigational management has been transferred on to the charterer, and if the charterer and not the registered owner is liable for maritime claims connected with the ship, the creditor can arrest such ship, or any other ship belonging to the charterer by demise. But no other ship of the registered owner can be arrested in connection with the same maritime claims.

Time Charter In the time charter agreement for some obligations of the charterer *vis-à-vis* third parties—that is parties not involved in the charter agreement—also the owner of the ship is responsible. This is the generally known and recognised principle, resulting mainly from the stability and certainty of the conduct of legal transactions. If for the obligations of the charterer the owner is not responsible, then the security of the claim by arrest/seizure is not possible. This is the effect of the purpose of security, which lies in the fact that in case of winning the litigation the creditor was not deprived of satisfaction, which in absence of liability on the part of the owner, could never be realised by the arrest. In other instances the arrest or the ship would be permissible.

Voyage Charter The voyage charter is apart from the booking agreement one of the forms of contract of carriage, where the carrier is usually the registered owner. Most of the claims which could result would be claims between the parties to the contract of voyage charter. Other incidental claims of third parties against the voyage charterer could not be secured by the arrest of ship belonging to a registered owner unless he would be accessorily liable.

Sweden

Chapter 4, section 4 of the Swedish Maritime Code, in fact, corresponds essentially to Article 3(1), (2) and (4). This was probably necessary in order for Sweden to be able to accede to the Convention at all. As is clear from the wording, the section is not limited to cover situations where a demise charterer is responsible for the claim.

However, in cases where there is no maritime lien securing the claim, the effect of Article 4, section 4 of the Swedish Maritime Code will be very limited. The reason is that in chapter 4, section 5 it is expressly stated that arrest may be imposed on a vessel only "if the vessel is subject to distraint for maritime claims in Sweden", in other words, only if a judgment by a Swedish or foreign court on the merits is *enforceable* in Sweden. The answer to Question 7 of the Questionnaire is, consequently, that Article 3(4) has been interpreted to be in harmony with Article 9 of the Convention, i.e. that the Convention is not meant to create maritime liens, which do not already exist according to the applicable rules.

Chapter 4, section 5 was relied on by the Svea Court of Appeal in Stockholm in a very recent case, 1 October 1999 *"The Russ"*, where arrest was denied on the ground that the owner of the vessel, who appeared in the court as an intervenient, was not responsible for bunker deliveries to the charterers, since the claim was not secured by a maritime lien.

In the view of the Swedish MLA, which is shared by the Swedish Government, Article 3(4) of the Convention is misleading in its present text, since it clearly leaves open the possibility of creating maritime liens.

United Kingdom

Article 3(4) has been described as "controversial and difficult to interpret" (see 1998 Report of the Scottish Law Commission, referred to in the answer to Question 1, at p. 164) and its drafting was criticised in *The Span Terza* [1982] 1 Lloyd's Rep. 225.

7.1 CAN A SHIP BE ARRESTED IN RESPECT OF A CLAIM AGAINST THE DEMISE CHARTERER? IF SO, CAN THE CLAIM BE ENFORCED THROUGH THE FORCED SALE OF THE SHIP?

Belgium

See our reply to Question 7.2.

Denmark

See our reply to Question 7.2.

France

Comme indiqué *supra* au n° 8, la saisie est possible en cas d'affrètement coque nue. La question de savoir si la créance peut être exécutée même si la créance n'est pas privilégiée n'a jamais été abordée par la jurisprudence. Et la doctrine est elle aussi muette sur cette question précise. Personnellement, je pencherais pour une réponse négative. L'exercice d'une voie de droit sur un bien n'appartenant pas au débiteur est chose tout à fait exceptionnelle. On ne peut, ici, aller au delà des textes.

Germany

If the debtor is the owner of the ship and the claim has arisen in connection with the operation of any other ship arrest would be permitted. If the debtor is not the owner of the ship but only bare-boat charterer arrest would not be admitted. But if the maritime claim against the bare-boat charterer arose from the operation of the ship this particular ship may be arrested (§ 510, section 2 HGB) as well as other ships owned by the bare-boat charterer.

Haiti

Oui, le navire peut être saisi même s'il appartient à un affréteur. Il revient à ce dernier d'établir que le navire est sa propriété. S'il ne fait pas, le navire sera réputé comme appartenant au débiteur.

Italy

See our reply to Question 7.2.

Netherlands

A ship can be attached in respect of a claim against the demise charterer if the applicable law grants a right of recourse on the ship for a claim against a demise charterer. If Dutch national law is to be applied, the relevant article is Article 8:361 of the Dutch Civil Code:
The shipowner is solidarily liable with the bare-boat charterer for a juridical act which binds the latter and which is directly intended to put the ship into operation or to keep it in operation.
This article is special as it does not create an exceptional right of recourse on the ship (owned by a non-debtor/shipowner) for a claim against the debtor/demise charterer, but in fact simply states that shipowner and demise charterer are joint debtors for the particular kind of claims stated. As a consequence the ship may be attached even if, for instance, the demise charter has come to an end. In the case of international aspects (ship flying a foreign flag, or claim governed by foreign law), rules of Dutch private international determine whether a right of recourse on the ship is recognised. As the right of recourse is a *condicio sine qua non* for arrest, it naturally follows that the conservatory arrest lead up to execution and therefore forced sale of the ship.

Nigeria

Yes, under AJD, section 5(4), a ship can be arrested in respect of a claim against a demise charterer and under AJPR, Order XIV, rule 1(1), the court may, upon the application by a party either before or after final judgment, order that a ship which is under arrest be valued and sold, or be sold without valuation.

Norway

No. We apply "lex Allan Philip", see p. 217 in Professor Falkanger's article.

Slovenia

According to Article 982, paragraph 2 of MINA, if the debtor is the charterer by demise of the ship or the employer—who according to the law applicable to the contractual relation between him and the owner of the ship or the operator, is alone liable to third persons—this ship may be arrested or any other ship which is owned by the charterer by demise or employer.

If the ship is not owned by the charterer by demise, it cannot be sold. Therefore, that claim cannot be enforced through the forced sale of the ship.

Spain

See our reply to Question 7.2.

Sweden

As could already be understood from the main answer, a ship could, on the face of it, be arrested in respect of a claim against the demise charterer (Article 3(4)). However, in practice it will not be possible in Sweden because of the ruling in chapter 4, section 5 of the Swedish Maritime Code, unless the claim is secured by a maritime lien or it is possible to pierce the corporate veil.

United Kingdom

A ship can be arrested in respect of a claim against the demise charterer, see Supreme Court Act 1981, section 21(4), Question 5, above. The claim can be enforced through the forced sale of the ship.

7.2 HAS THE FINAL SENTENCE OF ARTICLE 3(4) READING "THE PROVISIONS OF THIS PARAGRAPH SHALL APPLY TO ANY CASE IN WHICH A PERSON OTHER THAN THE REGISTERED OWNER OF A SHIP IS LIABLE IN RESPECT OF A MARITIME CLAIM RELATING TO THAT SHIP" BEEN INTERPRETED SO TO PERMIT THE ARREST OF A SHIP ALSO IN RESPECT OF CLAIMS AGAINST PERSONS OTHER THAN THE DEMISE CHARTERER, SUCH AS THE TIME CHARTERER, THE VOYAGE CHARTERER, THE SLOT CHARTERER, THE AGENT OR MANAGER OF THE SHIP?

Belgium

There is no conflict between Article 3(4) and the interpretation of Article 3(1) as set out above. The answers to Questions 7.1 and 7.2 are affirmative in view of the interpretation of Article 3(1) (see answer to Question 5).

Article 9 has been considered relevant for the interpretation of Article 3(1) and also 3(4).

Some earlier jurisprudence accepted that the provision authorising arrest of the particular ship in respect of which the maritime claim arose in cases where persons other than the owner were liable/indebted was unlimited and therefore regardless of a change of ownership in between the time the claim arose and the arrest. Such an extensive interpretation, could, however, be construed as creating a lien on the vessel for claims not existing under the applicable Convention and/or laws and therefore prohibited by Article 9 of the 1952 Convention.

It is now unanimous jurisprudence that the ship to which the claim relates can no longer be arrested if it changed ownership between the time the claim arose and the time of arrest.

Denmark

Arrest for a claim against a demise or other charterer can only be made for claims which are secured by maritime liens, see section 93(4).

France

La question n'a guère été traitée en droit français. Il n'existe aucune autorité pour ce qui est du gérant ou de l'agent (au cas où, par exception, un gérant ou un agent serait reconnu comme *personnellement* tenu d'une dette concernant le navire). S'agissant de l'affréteur à temps, voir *supra*, réponse à la Question 7.

Germany

No. Claims against time charterers, voyage charterers, slot charterers, agents of ship managers would not permit an arrest of the ship itself.

Haiti

La phrase finale du paragraphe 4 de l'article 3 est interprétée de manière stricte en Haïti. Même dans le cas d'un affrètement à temps ou au voyage, le navire affrété peut être saisi pour une créance maritime quelconque. Le droit de saisir un navire en garantie d'une créance existe que la créance soit privilégiée ou maritime.

Italy

Italian courts have considered in several cases the right of arrest of a ship in respect of a claim against the time charterer and have held that under Article 3(4) of the Convention the claimant is entitled to arrest the ship: Tribunale of Ravenna 24 January 1987, *Trademar Conasa* v. *Line Island Marine Co.—The "Eurobreeze"* [1988] Dir. Mar. 804; Tribunale of Naples 22 September and 16 November 1995, *Mamidoil Jetoil Greek Petroleum Co.—The "Carlo R"* [1997] Dir. Mar. 147 and 152; Tribunale of Naples 20 December 1995, *Alimar Shipping Co.* v. *Mamidoil—The "Carlo R"* [1997] Dir. Mar. 154; Tribunale of Bari 26 November 1996, *Les Abeilles Boulogne S.A.* v. *Medimare—The "Sea Road"* [1998] Dir. Mar. 1218. This last order is worthy of particular consideration, since the court drew a clear distinction between arrest and seizure in execution of a judgment and held that the claimant may under Article 3(4) of the Convention arrest the ship but in order to seize her and cause her forced sale he needs an enforceable judgment. In two relatively recent decisions, however, the right of arrest of a ship in respect of a claim against a person other than the owner has been denied, except the case where the claim is secured by a maritime lien: Tribunale of Latina 9 November 1996, *Shifco-Somalian High Seas Fish Co.* v. *Mabutrans S.A.—The "21 Oktubaar II"* [1998] Dir. Mar. 430; Tribunale of Venezia 5 June 1998, *Exnor Craggs Ltd* v. *Companie de Navigatie Petromin S.A.—The "Tirgu Neamt"* [1999] Dir. Mar. 438.

Netherlands

I now particularly refer to the legal literature and case law mentioned above (general part of 7). Particularly the article of Professor Claringbould sheds light on the point of view of the Dutch delegate Loeff who introduced the text of the final sentence of Article 3(4). My colleague Professor Claringbould informed me that, when writing the articles referred to above, he was able to share his thoughts with Mr Loeff. I understand that Loeff agreed to the view set out in Professor Claringbould's articles. The standing interpretation in the Netherlands is therefore that the provisions of Article 3(4) shall apply in any case in which a person other than the legal owner of the ship is liable in respect of a maritime claim relating to that ship, if the person in question is responsible for the general operation of the ship (more exactly if the person in question has appointed the master). There are other legal concepts which in this respect may have a similar result as a demise charter. Asser particularly mentions the usufructuary. Where a shipowner does not grant a demise charter but a right of usufruct on the ship the usufructuary in principle has the general responsibility for the operation for the ship. It should be noted, however, that the final sentence of Article 3(4) is also used by the Dutch courts to overcome the "Algerian problem". I may refer you to the case law with regard to Article 3(4) which is mentioned above.

Nigeria

No. Under AJD, section 5(4), if the defendant was at the date the cause of action arose the charterer or some other person in possession or control of the ship, then if the ship to be arrested is the ship in respect of which the claim has arisen, it must be shown that at the time the action is brought, the debtor is the beneficial owner of all the shares in the ship *or its demise charterer*. In respect of any other ship, it must be shown that at the time action is brought, the debtor is the beneficial owner of all the shares in that ship.

Norway

Not to my knowledge. In principle, however, I believe that a maritime claim against a time charterer of the ship in relation to which the claim arose could be enforced by means of arresting a vessel owned by the time charterer.

Slovenia

The arrest of a specific vessel is permitted by MINA also in cases that the claim arises against a person who is not the owner of the vessel or demise charterer (time charterer, voyage charterer, the agent, manager of the ship, master, also a crew member).

Article 982 (pargraph 3) of MINA provides that the provisions of Article 2 of this article shall also apply in all other cases where an operator or employer who is personal debtor, and who is not the owner of the ship, is himself liable for the claims for which the arrest of the ship is sought.

According to Article 992 of MINA, it is also possible to arrest assets belonging to a charterer.

Spain

In view of the wide wording of Article 3(4), allowing the arrest of the particular ship from which the maritime claim arose in all those cases in which a person other than the owner of the ship is liable in respect of that maritime claim relating to that particular ship, our courts have interpreted said article so to permit the arrest of a ship in respect of claims, relating to that ship, against persons other than demise charterers such as the time charterer, the voyage charterer or the manager.

In such cases, the enforcement of the claim through the forced sale of the arrested vessel, or the bail given to replace it, will depend on whether the judgment obtained in the main proceedings on the merits can be enforced against the vessel. It should be noted that in Spain, as well as in other civil law countries, technically speaking only "actions *in personam*" are contemplated, therefore the eventual judgment on the merits could be only enforced against the arrested vessel as far as the claim is of that nature that the claimant has the guarantee of the vessel as security for his credit—in other words whether the claim is secured by a maritime lien on the vessel irrespective of its ownership, giving the claimant the guarantee of the vessel itself—or whether otherwise the claimant is successful in obtaining a judgment upon the merits condemning the vessel itself or the owner of the arrested vessel as the person liable for the claim. At the end of the day, the result of said proceedings on the merits, as well as the wording of the guarantee given in replacement of the vessel in case such a bail was given to permit its release, would determine the enforceability of the arrest.

Sweden

Yes. In fact, chapter 4, section 4 of the Swedish Maritime Code, according to its wording is not limited to demise charter situations as a result of the wording of the Article 3(4) second paragraph of the Convention. However, as mentioned, because of chapter 4, section 5, this seems irrelevant in practice in Sweden, unless there is a maritime lien.

United Kingdom

It has been held that section 3(4) of the Administration of Justice Act 1956 (which is now largely re-enacted in section 21(4) of the Supreme Court Act 1981) applies in cases involving time charterers, *The Span Terza* [1982] 1 Lloyd's Rep. 225, although the dissenting judge, Donaldson L.J., considered that the reference to "charterer" was confined to demise charterers. In a recent case it was also held that section 21(4) of the Supreme Court Act 1981 applied in cases involving slot charterers, as they are a species of voyage charter, *The Tichy* [1999] 2 Lloyd's Rep. 11.

7.3 HAS ARTICLE 9 BEEN CONSIDERED RELEVANT FOR THE PURPOSE OF INTERPRETING ARTICLE 3(4)?

Denmark

Yes, see 7.

France

Le problème de l'article 9 a longtemps été ignoré par le droit français. Je pense avoir été le premier à l'avoir évoqué, dans une note au *DMF* 1993, 78, où je m'inspire fortement des observations du Prof. Berlingieri, *Arrest of Ships*, 1ère éd., pp. 81–82. Cette note n'est pas restée sans effet: dans un arrêt du 31 juillet 1996 la Cour de Montpellier, écartant du débat les dispositions de l'article 10, s'est fondée sur l'article 9 pour refuser à un créancier non titulaire d'un privilège le droit de saisir le navire auquel la créance se rapportait dans les mains d'un nouveau propriétaire (*DMF* 1997, 31).

Germany

No.

Haiti

L'article 9 est également interprété de manière stricte. D'après les tribunaux haïtiens, l'article 9 est considéré important pour l'interprétation du paragraphe 4 de l'article 3.

Italy

Reference to Article 9 of the Convention has been made by the Tribunale of Bari in The *"Sea Road"* case (*supra*, under reply to Questions 7.1 and 7.2), where the court held that the right of arrest under the Convention did not entail a right of action other than that granted under the Convention and in particular does not grant the claimant the right of a lienor. This statement must be related to that previously referred to, whereby the enforcement of the claim on the ship by her forced sale requires a judgment which is enforceable on that ship. Under Italian law this is the case only if the judgment is against the owner of the ship or the claim in respect of which it is delivered is secured by a maritime lien. Reference to Article 9 of the Convention has been more directly made in the *"Tirgo Neamt"* case (*supra*, under reply to Questions 7.1 and 7.2), where Article 3(4) has been interpreted in the light of Article 9.

Netherlands

Yes. Again I refer you to the literature and case law referred to above (general part of 7).

Nigeria

There is no corresponding provision under the AJD. Therefore, the need for the provision to be used or considered in interpreting AJD, section 5(4) does not arise.

Norway

Article 9 is used in support of "lex Allan Philip".

Sweden

Yes. As mentioned, reference has been made to Article 9 as a ground for inserting the special rule in chapter 4, section 5.

United Kingdom

There is nothing in the Supreme Court Act 1981 to suggest that Article 9 of the 1952 Arrest Convention is considered relevant for the purpose of interpreting section 21(4). This is mainly because there is no express reference to Article 9 in English law. The Scottish Law Commission in its 1998 Report (referred to in the answer to Question 1) noted that there were problems if time and voyage charterers were covered and stated, at p.165, that there is "the further difficulty that if art. 9 can be invoked so as to preclude the creation by the final sentence in art. 3(4) of maritime liens and hypothecs, it is difficult to see what that final sentence does in fact mean."

8. WHICH TYPE OF SECURITY IS REQUIRED IN ORDER TO OBTAIN THE RELEASE OF THE SHIP?

   8.1 A cash deposit?
   8.2 A bank guarantee?
   8.3 A letter of undertaking of a P&I Club?

Belgium

Only a cash deposit and/or a bank guarantee are accepted to obtain the release of the ship. Strictly speaking also a letter of undertaking by a first class underwriter, such as a P&I Club, would be acceptable but only in as far as they have their seat of incorporation within the jurisdiction where the ship is arrested, which is never the case. In practice however a guarantee of a first class P&I Club (London Club) is mostly accepted. At law claimants can refuse such undertaking and request for a bank guarantee and/or cash deposit.

Croatia

Article 987 does not specify the type of security required and it is up to the court to determine the quantum and whether the security offered by debtor is "available and transferable in favour of the creditor". Article 978 so provides:

If provisional measures are ordered to secure monetary claims, the Court will release the ship from arrest or watching if securities and other property values are sufficient to cover the total amount of the claims for which the arrest is sought, on condition that these securities or other property values are available and transferable in favour of the creditor.

If claims are involved for which the debtor may limit his liability, the amount of the securities or other property values referred to in paragraph 1 of this article need not be higher than the amount of limited liability.

When one of the Courts in the territory of the Republic of Croatia releases a ship from arrest, on the basis of the provision of paragraph 1 of this article, no other Court on the territory of the Republic of Croatia may order arrest either of this ship or of any other ship for the same claim and for the same creditor, provided that the securities or other property values given are still available and transferable in favour of the creditor.

Denmark

Danish law does not stipulate any particular type of security. In practice claimants and courts will accept any of the types mentioned in 8.1–8.3.

Finland

According to the FMC chapter 4, § 6, if guarantee or other security is given to release a vessel from arrest, arrest may not be granted for the same maritime claim. The executory officer decides which type of security is required in order to obtain the release of the vessel. A cash deposit or a bank guarantee is usually approved as security. *In casu* also a letter of undertaking of a P&I Club may be approved.

France

En droit français la caution peut prendre l'une des trois formes évoquées par la question, le juge du fond appréciant souverainement la caractère approprié de la garantie fournie.

Germany

According to § 923 ZPO the order of arrest has to state the amount of security to be provided in order to obtain the release of the ship. There is no statutory form of security. In practice an irrevocable and unconditional reputed bank guarantee is accepted by the court.

Greece

The Convention provides that the court which ordered the arrest *shall* permit the release of the ship upon sufficient bail or other security. It does not clarify, however, who is entitled to submit the relevant petition. Since, in default of any provision in the Convention, the rules of procedure relating to the arrest are governed by the *lex fori*, whenever the *forum* is Greece any party having a lawful interest may apply—i.e. not only the shipowner but also a third party, e.g. the purchaser of the arrested ship.

Under the formulation of the relevant provision of the Convention, the court permits the lifting of the arrest upon bail only if the arrest has taken place. However, this would be extremely unfavourable to the shipowner. This is why it should be sufficient for the arresting order to be issued. The interests of shipowner and claimant would be better protected that way since, on the one hand, the shipowner would not be submitted to or would be discharged from the onerous consequences of the arrest as soon as possible whilst, on the other hand, the creditor would not suffer any harm as he could still be able to proceed to the arrest in case the shipowner should fail to lodge the bail.

Nevertheless, since the lodging of the bail depends on the will of the shipowner or the third party that was ordered to provide the bail, the lifting of the arrest and, consequently, the release of the ship is concluded once the bail has been actually provided.

The security may consist either in bail or other form of security (Article 5, paragraph 1). In default of agreement between the parties as to the sufficiency of the bail or other security, the court determines the nature and amount thereof (Article 5, paragraph 2). Hence, in the event of disagreement between the parties the court has the faculty to determine the object of security, the *quantum* and the time within which it should be lodged (Article 162 CCP).

In particular, the court may determine that the security should be in the form of cash deposit. In such case, the deposit is made at the Public Deposits and Loans Fund evidenced by the issue of the deposit receipt. The deposit receipt must be lodged, within the time prescribed, with the clerk of the court that ordered the replacement of the arrest with the bail (Article 163 CCP). Upon the lodging of the deposit receipt with the clerk of the court, the arrestor acquires a pledge on the deposit (Article 166 CCP). Nevertheless, the court, in determining that bail should be lodged in the form of cash deposit, may not go beyond the limits of its discretionary power (Article 25, paragraph 3 of the Constitution; Article 116 CCP; Article 281 CC). This could be the case if the court would decline the request of the owner of the arrested ship to provide alternative security—such request not being unusual since the shipowner may not wish to deposit the money in cash given the financial benefit from its use, without the existence of good cause for ordering the cash deposit.

The court may order, instead of cash deposit, the deposit of titles such as negotiable shares or bonds.

In order, however, for the court to determine the amount of the security—on which its sufficiency depends, it will have to appraise the value of each such title. The decisive value is not the nominal value or the stock market value but the actual market value thereof.

The deposit of the titles is made at the Public Deposits and Loans Fund evidenced by the issue of the deposit receipt (Article 165, paragraph 1 CCP). The deposit receipt will have to be lodged, within the time prescribed, with the clerk of the court that ordered the replacement of the arrest with the lodging of the security (Article 165, paragraph 2 CCP) whereupon the claimant acquires a pledge on the titles (Article 166 CCP).

Nevertheless, the court usually determines as security the provision of a letter of guarantee from a solvent bank operating in Greece. As a rule, the bank will require to obtain its own security prior to issuing the letter of guarantee which usually consists of either a pledge of an equivalent cash deposit of the shipowner or a third party or a mortgage or pledge of other assets in its favour or an assignment of claims of the shipowner.

It is not required under the Convention (Article 5, paragraph 2) unlike Article 164 CCP that the third party granting the security should be a bank. If the security is validly granted by such third party pursuant to the Greek rules of private international law (in its strict sense), the court may not, whenever the Convention applies, decline such security by the sole reason that such third party is not a bank. As a result, when the Convention applies, the court may order as security the provision of a letter of guarantee by the ship's insurer or a letter of undertaking by the shipowner's protection and indemnity club which, in any event, is usually acceptable by the arrestor. As a rule, the letter of undertaking of a P&I Club suffices to lift the arrest if there is consent of the claimant.

The bank letter of guarantee is lodged with the clerk of the court that ordered the lodging of the security (Article 165, paragraph 2 CCP). This should also be the case when the court orders provision of security, by virtue of the Convention, by a third party which is not a banking corporation.

As already mentioned, the Convention grants discretion to the court to determine the object of security. However, the security so ordered will have to be valid in accordance with the applicable law. In view of this, the court may not order the registration of a mortgage on real estate within the Greek territory as security in the form of a conservative measure mainly because the CCP (Article 706) introduces the prenotation of mortgage as a special conservative measure.

Haiti

Une caution en argent permet d'obtenir la main levée de saisie.
Une garantie bancaire produit le même effet.
Quant à la garantie P&I Club on ne la connaît pas en Haïti.

Italy

Article 684 of the Italian Code of Civil Procedure (CCP) provides that the debtor may obtain from the court the revocation of the arrest by providing suitable bail ("cauzione") for the amount of the claim and for costs, in relation to the value of the things that have been arrested. Article 119 CCP provides that the court must indicate in the order in which he requires a "cauzione" to be provided, the object of it, the manner in which and the time by which it must be provided. In turn Article 86 of the rules for the implementation of the Code provides that, unless otherwise decided by the court, the "cauzione" must be provided in cash or public debentures. Courts nowadays never require a cash deposit in order to release a ship from arrest. They instead accept guarantees of first class Italian banks and, with the agreement of the claimant, of foreign banks or letters of undertaking of P&I Clubs. But if there is no agreement, they will require a guarantee of a first class Italian bank.

Netherlands

The relevant provision is Article 705, sub 2 of the Dutch Code of Civil Procedure:

The release shall be ordered i.e. in case of non-compliance with procedural requirements, if the invalidity of the grounds relied on by the arrestor or the unnecessariness of the arrest is summarily shown, or, if the arrest is effected for a monetary claim, if sufficient security is put up for this claim.

This article does not provide any requirement regarding the security except that the security must be sufficient. Apart from the amount, of course, it is generally thought that for the security to be sufficient the security must be enforceable in the Netherlands just as easily as an arrest on a ship in the Netherlands. Arrestors therefore usually demand security to be put up by a first class Dutch bank. However, arrestors may accept guarantees put up by (foreign) P&I Clubs of cash deposits in escrow accounts with Dutch banks. In general the security is a guarantee issued on the basis of the Rotterdam Guarantee Form (current issue 1992).

Nigeria

In addition to the types of security listed in 8.1, 8.2 and 8.3, the court may order the release of a ship upon the provision of a bail bond.

Norway

Unless the creditor agrees to some other form of security, such as a P&I Club letter of undertaking, it follows from the Act of Enforcement that security can only be provided as a deposit in a Norwegian bank, which confirms the deposit and the bank's instruction that the deposit cannot be disposed of other than by consent of the competent enforcement authority. A bank guarantee "as for our own debt" by a Norwegian bank will also be acceptable according to the Enforcement Act.

Poland

All types of security can be required by the claimant. 8.2 and 8.3 is mostly demanded. 8.1 is very seldom.

Slovenia

To obtain the release of the ship the opposite party (debtor) is required to provide a cash deposit or any other properties in the amount of the claims (Article 983 of MINA). A bank guarantee or a letter of undertaking from a P&I Club is acceptable to the court only if the claimant agrees to it.

Spain

The ship is released from arrest upon the lodging of a security in the amount for which the arrest is granted. The security can, in principle, take any form allowed by the law, such as a payment into court or a bank guarantee. Any other type of security, such as a P&I Club letter of undertaking will need the acceptance of the arrested party. The bank guarantee is the most common form of security nowadays.

Sweden

The court will decide the kind of security, unless the parties are able to agree on it, and will normally accept any of these kinds of securities, if found appropriate to its value (normally as a maximum corresponding to the ship's value).

United Kingdom

RSC, Order 75, rule 16 laid down detailed rules as to bail bonds, but it appears that the bail bond has been abolished in the CPR. A bail bond was a promise to pay which was usually backed by the security of a guarantor. Ultimately, the amount and form of security may now be for the court, see paragraph 6.7(2) of Admiralty Practice Direction 49F. There seems to be some doubt as to the extent of the court's powers under the CPR as to the type of security, as paragraph 6.7(3) refers expressly only to the power to reduce the amount of security, but it appears to be for the court to be satisfied as to the sufficiency and acceptability of the surety (Jackson, *op. cit.*, p. 343). Under paragraph 12 there is power for agreements between solicitors to become orders of the court. All three types of security have been used in order to obtain release of the ship from arrest, but it will normally be for the claimant in the first instance to agree the form of security.

9. IS THE CLAIMANT LIABLE IN CASE OF WRONGFUL OR UNJUSTIFIED ARREST?

Belgium

A claimant will only be liable in case of wrongful arrest. An unjustified arrest is not sufficient. A claim for wrongful arrest is based on an action in tort. It means that the shipowner will have to prove the fault of the claimant by arresting the vessel, the damages it caused and the causal relationship between fault and damages. A claimant will only be considered as having acted at fault by arresting the vessel if he obtained and put the arrest in a thoughtless and reckless way knowing that by doing so he would cause damages. Our courts are extremely reluctant to grant such claim for wrongful arrest. Such claim for wrongful arrest must not necessarily be brought before our courts. It can also be filed as a counter claim in the proceedings on the merit or even as a separate principal claim before the jurisdiction where the claimant/arrestor can be summoned.

Croatia

Yes, but it has to be claimed in the same proceeding within 30 days or if not in this time limit, then in separate proceedings for damages. This is not regulated by the Maritime Code but by general Enforcement Proceeding Act.

Denmark

Yes, the claimant is liable for wrongful arrest under AJA, section 639.

Finland

The applicant is strictly liable for the loss or damage if it is later proved that the arrest was unnecessary (CJP chapter 7, § 11).

France

Le demandeur peut certainement, en droit français, être déclaré responsable du dommage financier subi par le saisi, s'il a agi abusivement. Et l'abus du droit de saisir peut résulter soit du manque total de fondement de la saisie, soit du caractère exagéré de la saisie par rapport au montant de la créance, soit de l'exigence d'une garantie excessive (voir, en ce sens, Cassation 19 mars 1996, *DMF* 1997, 503).

En revanche, dans un important arrêt du 3 mars 1998, la Cour de Cassation affirme que le saisissant n'est pas responsable d'un défaut d'entretien pendant la durée de la saisie (*DMF* 1998, 6999). Et la doctrine considère que la solution doit être étendue au dommage subi par le navire du fait d'un tiers (abordage à quai ou autre): voir en ce sens le rapport du Conseiller Rémery et la note Y. Tassel, sous l'arrêt ici cité; *adde* nos propres observations, *DMF* 1999, hors série n° 3. n° 61.

Germany

Yes. § 945 HGB stipulates that the claimant, irrespective of fault, would be liable for damages caused by an unjustified arrest. Any loss including lost profit would be covered.

Greece

If the arrest of the ship is levied in Greece, the liability of the arrestor constitutes the consequence of a civil offence which is regulated in a special manner. Article 703 CCP imposes on the party that asserted the order of conservative measures, in the event that the action brought on the merits of the case would be finally rejected as not founded, to pay compensation for the damages caused by reason of the execution of the judgment ordering such measures or the provision of the security if he knew or ignored by gross negligence that he had no such right.

Consequently, the issue of a judgment ordering the arrest of a ship is not enough for the petitioner to be found liable for compensation. It is also necessary that the judgment has been executed—i.e. that the arrest has been levied.

Furthermore, the levy of the arrest will need to have caused a damage to property whether actual or future. There is no question of liability for damage other than damage to property since such other damages may be compensated only in the circumstances prescribed by law (Article 299 CC). The damages are normally suffered by the owner of the arrested ship. Yet it is not excluded that the arrest may cause damages only to the demise charterer or the time charterer.

In order for the legal consequence of liability for indemnity to arise, the damage will also have to be unlawful. The law specifically stipulates that this is the case when a final court judgment rejects the action as not founded in law or in fact.

It is obvious that, in order for the damage to property in question to be compensated, the unlawful act—i.e. the levy of the arrest as security of a non-existing maritime claim, will have to be a proximate cause.

Moreover, in order for the above legal consequence to arise, it is required, as an exception to the general rule of Article 914 CC, that the arrestor knew or ignored by gross negligence that the maritime claim secured by the arrest did not exist, was not founded. This divergence from the rule of Article 914 CC serves two purposes: on the one hand, to preclude the arrestor from raising the defence of contributory negligence—i.e. that the plaintiff did not properly oppose the relevant petition; on the other hand, to prevent the assertion of the arrest without good cause.

What precedes goes also for the case where the arrest of the ship was avoided or lifted by provision of security by the shipowner. Hence, whoever alleged a certain maritime claim, asserted the arrest of a ship and had such claim secured by security lodged either before or after the levy of the arrest is liable for restitution of the damage caused by the provision of such security if he knew or ignored by gross negligence that no maritime claim existed. As a rule, the damage sustained consists in the costs of lodging the security—i.e. the pecuniary costs, the care, efforts and other services consecrated to this effect as well as the obligations undertaken against third parties for lodging the security.

Haiti

Le demandeur peut être tenu pour responsable pour les dommages causés par la saisie du navire si la saisie se révèle illégale, arbitraire et inopportune et que cette saisie a causé des dommages soit à l'affréteur ou au débiteur. Il est donc nécessaire pour le créancier de s'assurer que non seulement la créance qu'il évoque est une créance maritime mais aussi que la procédure suivie pour pratiquer la saisie est celle tracée par la Convention de 1952.

Italy

Yes. Liability arises under the general rule set out in Article 96 CPC which so provides:

If the losing party acted or defended himself in the proceeding in bad faith or with gross negligence the judge on request of the other party, will condemn him to pay, in addition to the costs, the damages to be liquidated, also *ex officio*, with the judgment.

There are only two known precedents in which the above rule has been applied to the arrest of ships: Tribunale of Genoa 27 December 1989, *Fast Ferries* v. *Giuseppe Meocci—The "Briso II"* [1990] Dir. Mar. 406 and Tribunale of Genoa 14 June 1955, *Ferrari & Gugenheim* v. *Avigdor & Co.—The "Bracha Fold"* [1957] Dir. Mar. 209.

Netherlands

The arrestor is considered to act at his own risk and is in principle required to make good any loss caused by the arrest, if the arrest was wrongly effected. This rule applies even when the arrestor had reasonable grounds to consider he had a right of claim and did not act rashly. In the absence of special circumstances the wrongly effected arrest will be considered to be an unlawful act (= tort).

Nigeria

The AJD, section 13 and AJPR, Order XI, rule 3(2), provide for a right of action for damages for a wrongful arrest (i.e. made unreasonably and without good cause). Alternatively, there is relief under AJPR, Order XI, rule 2 for a fixed sum compensation for "needless arrest". Also, a caveator against arrest, by virtue of AJPR, Order VI, rule 8, is entitled to recover damages for an arrest made without "a good and sufficient reason".

Norway

Yes, the claimant is strictly liable for all losses that are not "too remote".

Poland

The claimant is liable in case of wrongful arrest.

Slovenia

Article 279 of the Forced Execution and Security Act (ZIZ) provides that an arresting party is liable to pay damages to the opposite party if the arrest subsequently turns out not to have been justified.

Spain

Yes. According to general domestic rules dealing with arrest as a precautionary measure (preventive embargo) the claimant is liable for damages in case of the arrest proving to be wrongful (Article 1.416 of the CPC). It is to be noted that once the arrest (embargo) becomes effective the debtor may oppose it on the grounds that it is contrary to the law, because the conditions for the arrest do not exist. The opposition, upon application of the party at interest, is dealt with by the arresting court as an incident from the arrest proceedings.

As set forth by Article 1 of the Act 2/1967, the claimant is required to provide a security high enough to cover any damages and costs that may be caused thereby to the other party. This requirement comes from the domestic rules governing the arrest (preventive embargo) of debtors' assets in general, which also provide for such a requirement (Article 1.402 of the CPC though it is applicable to the cases where the claimant is not solvent, in practice the security is required by the court in all or most of the cases). This security will serve to satisfy the damages to which the arresting claimant might be condemned in case of wrongful arrest, i.e. if the conditions for the arrest do not exist (the claim is not a maritime claim or the ship is not arrestable under Article 3 of the Convention), if proceedings on the merits are not commenced within the prescribed time limit (Article 7.4 of the Convention in relation to Article 1.411 of the CPC) or if the claim is rejected.

Sweden

Yes. See chapter 15 of the Swedish Code of Judicial Procedure.

United Kingdom

In the absence of proof of *mala fides* or gross negligence the claimant is not liable in damages for having arrested a vessel, *The Evangelismos* (1858) 12 Moo. P.C. 352, *The Strathnaver* [1875] 1 A.C. 58, and *The Kommunar (No.3)* [1997] 1 Lloyd's Rep. 22. *Mala fides* must be taken to exist in those cases where the arresting party has no honest belief in its entitlement to arrest the ship, *The Kommunar (No.3)*, at p. 30. Gross negligence covers those situations where objectively there is so little basis for the arrest that it may be inferred that the arrestor did not believe in its entitlement to arrest the ship or acted without any serious regard to whether there were adequate grounds for the arrest of the vessel, *ibid*. In general, then, it is very difficult for the shipowner to obtain a remedy unless it can show the narrow category of "wrongful" arrest, described above. There is no question of damages being awarded for "unjustified" arrest, in the sense simply that the claim failed on the merits. It should be noted that the Scottish Law Commission has recently recommended that Scots law should differ from English law by moving closer to a continental system giving a remedy for unjustified arrestments based on a strict liability (see 1998 Report referred to in the answer to Question 1, at p.140).

According to paragraph 6.3(3) of Admiralty Practice Direction 49F, if there is a "caveat against arrest" and an arrest is made, the Admiralty Court may, if it considers that it is appropriate to do so, order the party procuring the arrest to pay compensation to the owner or other party interested in the ship arrested. A "caveat against arrest" provides a system whereby a potential defendant can file a notice in the Admiralty and Commercial Registry, undertaking in advance to file an acknowledgement of service of the claim and to provide security.

Note that English law also recognises a "caveat against release" (much more commonly used than the caveat against arrest) which gives the right to a potential claimant to register his interest in the ship arrested or threatened with arrest, without incurring the cost and formality of an application for arrest.

10. IS THE CLAIMANT NORMALLY REQUIRED TO PROVIDE SECURITY FOR DAMAGES IN CASE OF WRONGFUL ARREST? IF SO, HOW IS THE AMOUNT OF THE SECURITY DETERMINED?

Belgium

Our law provides that the judge, issuing the injunction granting leave for arrest, can impose a counter security as a condition for the arrest. Such counter security must guarantee the damages suffered by the shipowner in case the arrest would ultimately be considered as wrongful. The amount of the counter security is quantified as: 65 BEF × dwt of the arrested ship.

Croatia

Security for damages could be ordered by the court on the request of the debtor and the court will determine the quantum.

Denmark

The claimant is normally required to provide security for damages in case of wrongful arrest and the amount is usually calculated at five days' loss of hire, see MSA, section 94(1).

Finland

When the applicant has delivered the arrest decision together with satisfactory financial security to the executory officer, he enforces the arrest upon the vessel. The security, usually a bank guarantee, should cover all the costs and economic losses caused to the opposing party if it is later proved that the arrest was unnecessary. The executory officer decides the amount of the guarantee, which is usually considerable. Furthermore, in addition to the bank guarantee, he usually demands a supplemental guarantee from one or two persons. The State and its institutions are free from the obligation to deliver security.

France

Dans la très grande majorité des cas, les tribunaux français autorisent la saisie conservatoire sans exiger du saisissant une garantie.

Germany

The determination of the security is in the court's discretion. The court normally takes into account possible damages and costs of the proceedings. It is therefore a high risk to commence arrest proceedings in Germany.

Greece

The court has the discretion when ordering the conservative measure of the arrest of a ship to impose provision of security by the petitioner even if the defendant shipowner has not submitted such demand, and fix the time within which such security should be provided (Article 694, paragraph 1 CCP). Failure to provide the security within the time fixed by court, entails the lifting of the conservative measure *ipso jure* (Article 694, paragraph 2 CCP). The defendant shipowner may also submit the demand for provision of security by the petitioner verbally at the hearing of the petition for the arrest. After the issue of the order of arrest, the shipowner may file a petition for modification thereof in case of actual change of circumstances (Article 696, paragraph 3).

The court is free to evaluate the extent to which the claim sought to be secured is founded, the solvency of the petitioner and the eventual loss of the shipowner in case the claimant would lose the case on the merits in order to decide whether the claimant should provide security to the shipowner. The amount of the security, the form and method of provision thereof is determined by the court pursuant to the provisions of Article 162 *et seq.* CCP. As a rule, the amount of the security is not determined on the basis of the loss sustained by the shipowner by reason of the immobilisation of the ship throughout the period of the litigation on the merits. It takes into account the loss anticipated to be suffered by the shipowner during the period required for lifting the arrest by furnishing the security. Further to such loss the court also assesses the costs required for the shipowner to lodge the security as well as the expenses and, generally, the losses sustained by reason of the litigation on the merits.

As regards the form of security, what has been stated in respect of the security provided by the owner for releasing the ship shall also apply here *mutatis mutandis*.

Nevertheless, it should be mentioned that Greek courts have rarely imposed provision of security on the petitioner.

Haiti

Le demandeur n'a aucune garantie à fournir. Il suffit qu'il établisse l'existence de sa créance et que cette dernière ait un caractère maritime tel que cela est prévu par la Convention de 1952.

Italy

No. But this may be the case, particularly if the owner of the ship so requests. Article 669 *undecies* CCP so provides:

With the order with which the request is granted, confirmed or modified the judge may order the applicant, all circumstances having been assessed, to provide a "cauzione" [bail] for the payment of damages, if any.

Courts in assessing the amount of the "cauzione" have normally considered the daily cost of the ship.

Netherlands

The relevant provision is Article 701 of the Dutch Code of Civil Procedure:

1. The president may grant leave under the condition that security must be put up to an amount to be determined by him, for loss which may be caused by the arrest.
2. The security must be offered to the attached debtor before or upon the service of the writ of arrest. (...)

In practice this provision is used very little. The last published cases which contain any information relating to the security for wrongful arrest (counter security) in a maritime setting date back to 1987. In both cases the amount of counter security was set at the expected cost of the security to be put up by the attached debtor for the release of the ship from arrest.

Nigeria

Order X of the AJPR expressly stipulates that the claimant must provide security for damages where the claim exceeds Nairas 1 million. In practice, the claimant files, or is ordered by the court to file an undertaking as to damages in respect of the application for the arrest of a ship. Such a requirement is within the terms of AJPR, Order XI, rule 1 which empowers the court, upon making an order for arrest, to impose such terms and conditions as the court deems fit.

Also Order X, rule 1(b) provides that in assessing security, the court shall have regard to the interest rate if any, payable by the defendant on a bank loan.

Norway

Practice would seem to vary between different Norwegian courts and it is my impression—which is entirely unscientific and not backed by any statistical data—that it is not common to ask for security. Likewise there are no firm rules as to how such a security should be determined. My impression, *cfr.* above, is that where the parties are in a position to argue about such security, courts would be sensitive to the argument that security to have the vessel released may normally be arranged within three to four days, wherefore security from the claimant should not exceed, say, five days' time charter hire at the current market rate for the vessel in question. Of course, if the vessel is actually employed under a contract which gives the owner more or less than the current market rate, the actual earnings would probably be used as a basis.

Poland

If the decision, including an interim order concerning preventive arrest, was passed before commencement of proceedings on the merits and the claimant failed to conform with the assigned time limit for the institution of such proceedings, the debtor may, within two weeks of the lapse of such period, lodge a motion to the court requesting payment of costs. If the claimant does not institute proceedings in the assigned time or withdraws the statement of claim concerning the institution of proceedings, or also when his demand is dismissed, the debtor is entitled to claim against the claimant the recovery of the damages caused by the execution of the preventive arrest. This claim loses its validity if the claimant does not bring it to court within a year from its being lodged.

Claimants who jointly executed preventive arrest are jointly and severally liable for the damage caused thereby. If within one month of the establishment of the claim for indemnity following the execution of an interim order concerning the arrest of a ship the debtor does not institute an action (by issuing/serving a writ of summons) then the court will return to the claimant, on its motion, the bail deposited to secure the claim.

Slovenia

According to MINA and the Forced Execution and Security Act (ZIZ), there is no need for the claimant to provide security for damages in case of wrongful arrest. However, if the claimant's claim fails, the claimant will be liable for damages according to Article 279 of the Forced Execution and Security Act (ZIZ).

Spain

The claimant is always required to put up security, as a condition for the arrest order being effective (Article 1 of Act 2/1967). The amount of said security for wrongful arrest is left to the discretion of the particular court.

Sweden

Yes. See chapter 15 of the Swedish Code of Judicial Procedure. The aim is to secure the claim for damages in respect of the time during which the ship will be arrested. However, this period of time is not easy to foresee. Some consideration should be given to the ship's daily costs, which would now be useless and the likely income which is lost. However, a lump sum amount presented to the court in respect of an interim arrest (i.e. where there is no communication with the owners before the arrest is decided), which does not seem too low, will normally be accepted by the court. Afterwards, there may be a discussion between the owners and the claimant, which will set out the gap between the opinions of the parties, and the court will rule on the matter based on those positions.

United Kingdom

The claimant is not normally required to provide security for damages in case of wrongful arrest, as defined in the answer to Question 9, above. The Scottish Law Commission has recently recommended that Scots law should differ from English law by empowering the court to demand counter-security to cover damages for wrongful or unjustified arrestment (see 1998 Report referred to in the answer to Question 1, at p.140).

Note that under the Civil Jurisdiction and Judgments Act 1982, section 26(2), where a court stays Admiralty proceedings, e.g. on the basis that the dispute should be referred elsewhere because of an arbitration or jurisdiction clause, it may attach such conditions to the order as it thinks fit. In theory, this might allow for a cross undertaking in damages to be given by the person effecting the arrest. It appears that there has been a reluctance to exercise this power (see *The Bazias 3 and 4* [1993] 1 Lloyd's Rep. 101), but there may be cases where it could be ordered (see Jackson, *op. cit.*, p. 331).

11. HAVE YOUR COURTS JURISDICTION ON THE MERITS IN RESPECT OF ANY CLAIM FOR WHICH A VESSEL HAS BEEN ARRESTED OR ONLY IN RESPECT OF THOSE LISTED IN ARTICLE 7(1)(A)–(F)?

Belgium

Our courts do not have jurisdiction with respect to the merits of the claim for which the vessel was arrested. The provisions of Article 7 will only apply in cases where no other jurisdiction is competent either contractually either by virtue of a compulsory applicable law and/or Convention. Exception must be made when the arrest has been made to secure a claim arising out of a collision.

Croatia

Exclusive jurisdiction of our courts is regulated by Article 1009 of the Maritime Code and for the other claims the court could have jurisdiction in accordance with the law regulating jurisdiction in case of international elements.

Denmark

Denmark has jurisdiction on the merits of any claims for which a vessel has been arrested, pursuant to AJA section 246a, unless the parties have entered into a binding agreement on foreign jurisdiction.

Finland

The FMC chapter 4 contains a reference to the general rules on maritime jurisdiction in chapter 21 (§ 8).

France

Depuis un arrêt du 17 janvier 1995 (*Juris-Classeur* 1996, II, 22430) qui a renversé la jurisprudence antérieure établie en 1979 (laquelle modifiait elle-même une jurisprudence plus ancienne), les tribunaux français ne se reconnaissent compétents que dans les cas énoncés à l'article 7-1 de la Convention. Mais la solution actuelle est vivement critiquée en doctrine.

Germany

A Federal High Court decision from 1991 has led to a restricted practice as regards the jurisdiction of German courts for the arrest of ships. The mere presence of the ship as an asset being in German waters would not be sufficient. (As to the particular see Looks, as mentioned above, section 3.) But according to § 23 ZPO the deposition of a security would create jurisdiction on the merits.

Greece

Under Greek law, the jurisdiction of Greek courts to examine a case on the merits is not based on the fact that the ship in respect of which the relevant claim arose, was arrested in Greece. As an exception to the rule, in the event of collision between ships Greek courts have jurisdiction even if the arrest of the ship has been lifted before the relevant action is brought (Article 242 CPML).

However, in view of the amplitude of the provisions of the CCP on the jurisdiction of Greek courts *ratione loci* it is not excluded that they may also have jurisdiction in cases other than those provided under Article 7(1) a–f of the Convention. This is mainly so because Article 40 CCP provides for the jurisdiction of a Greek court when proceedings are instituted against non-residents having assets located in its district. Thus, proceedings in respect of property may be instituted against shipowners who are not domiciled in Greece when the asset in question or any other property of the defendant is situated within the geographical limits of the court—i.e. when the ship lies within the limits of a Greek court. Nevertheless, it should be pointed out that, if the determination of the dispute on the merits falls within the ambit of the 1968 Brussels Convention on the Jurisdiction and the Enforcement of Judgments on Civil and Commercial Matters, it is not possible, in view of Article 3 of this Convention, to rely upon the provision of Article 40 CCP in respect of jurisdiction relating to property.

Haiti

Les tribunaux haïtiens saisis d'une demande en validité de saisie d'un navire statuent sur la forme et sur le fond. En d'autres termes, l'article 7 ne pose aucune restriction à la saisie des tribunaux haïtiens. La condition sine qua non pour qu'ils statuent sur une demande est l'existence d'une créance maritime telle que définie par la Convention de 1952.

Italy

Except in the cases listed in Article 7(1)(a)–(f) of the Convention, jurisdiction on the merits does not exist on the basis of the arrest, but may exist on the basis of the general rules of the Code of Civil Procedure or of the 1968 EC Convention on Jurisdiction and the Enforcement of Judgments in Civil and Commercial Matters.

Netherlands

The concept of arrest *ad fundandem iurisdictionem* or *forum arresti* was first accepted in the Netherlands by the Court of Cassation on 12 May 1916, NJ 1916, 728 (*Colette* v. *Pastoors*) on the basis of the argument that the action regarding validation of the arrest (an action for which the former text of Article 767 of the Dutch Code of Civil Procedure contained a *forum arresti* rule) was so much connected to the action on the merits that the rule of Article 767 was also applied to the action on the merits. For the interpretation of Article 7 of the Convention in connection with Article 767 of the Dutch Code of Civil Procedure I may refer to the following literature:

— J.T. Asser, "Uniform Zeerecht. De Diplomatieke Zeerecht Conferentie, gehouden te Brussel in Mei 1952", *NJB* 1953, pp. 778–780;
— J.P. Verheul, "The Convention relating to the arrest of seagoing ships of 1952. Some questions", NILR 1983, pp. 383–386;
— M.H. Claringbould, "The Netherlands", in: J. Theunis e.a., *Arrest of Ships 2. Belgium, The Netherlands, India, Yugoslavia*, London: Lloyd's of London Press 1986, pp. 58–60;
— J.P. Verheul, "The *forum non conveniens* in English and Dutch Law and under some international conventions" *ICLQ* 1986, pp. 413–423.

For the application of (Article 7 of) the 1952 Convention and Article 57 of the 1968 Brussels Convention see Hof's-Gravenhage 21 February 1989, HR 9 February 1990, ECJ 6 December 1994, Rb. Middelburg 11 December 1996, HR 12 September 1997. The current provision relating to arrest *ad fundandem iurisdictionem* is Article 767 of the Dutch Code of Civil Procedure (in force since 1 January 1992) which states:

In the absence of any other way of obtaining a title in execution in the Netherlands, the action on the merits, including the action regarding the costs of arrest, may be instituted with the District Court the President of which granted leave for the arrest effected, or prevented or lifted against security.

The phrase "In the absence of any other way of obtaining a title in execution in the Netherlands" has been clarified in the legislative history and in three important cases of the Hoge Raad, the Dutch Court of Cassation. The legislative history states that Article 767 does not apply in cases where jurisdiction of a(nother) Dutch court with regard to the claim on the merits can be based on other Dutch statutory provisions. Furthermore, Article 767 does not apply in cases where the parties in the dispute have chosen a particular forum (arbitration or otherwise), provided an "exequatur" can be obtained in the Netherlands in respect of the arbitration award or the judgment obtained on the basis of the choice of forum. For a long time the common view was that jurisdiction (still) could be based on an arrest and Article 767 in cases where the parties in the dispute had chosen a forum in a country which was not a party to an "enforcement convention" similar to:

— the 1968 Brussels Convention on Jurisdiction and the Enforcement of Judgments in Civil and Commercial Matters, as amended;
— the 1989 Lugano Convention on Jurisdiction and the Enforcement of Judgments in Civil and Commercial Matters;
— the 1958 New York Convention on the recognition and enforcement of foreign arbitration awards.

However the Dutch Court of Cassation has recently ruled that any choice of forum should be honoured. In view of Article 7(3) of the Convention this is of limited importance. Nevertheless it seems that the introduction of "enforcement conventions" as mentioned above and the introduction of the current text of Article 767 of the Dutch Code of Civil Procedure have downgraded the former extensive *forum arresti* jurisdiction in the Netherlands as described by Asser on pp. 778–760 to a level where Article 7(1)(a)–(f) indeed have become relevant. In situations where the "enforcement conventions" do not apply, jurisdiction can of course be based on Article 767 of the Dutch Code of Civil Procedure in respect of any claim, provided the parties in the dispute have not chosen a particular forum.

Nigeria

Under AJD, section 3, the admiralty jurisdiction of the Federal High Court extends to all ships irrespective of the places of residence or domicile of their owners and all maritime claims, wherever arising. Section 20 of AJD further provides that the court's jurisdiction is always preserved in the following cases:

(a) the place of performance, execution, delivery, act or default is or takes place in Nigeria; or
(b) any of the parties resides or has resided in Nigeria; or
(c) the payment under the agreement (implied or express) is made or is to be made in Nigeria; or
(d) in any Admiralty action or in the case of a maritime lien, the plaintiff submits to the jurisdiction of the court and makes a declaration to that effect or the *res* is within Nigerian jurisdiction; or
(e) it is a case in which the Federal Government or a State of the Federation is involved and the Government or State submits to the jurisdiction of the court; or
(f) there is a financial consideration accruing in, derived from, brought into or received in Nigeria in respect of any matters under the Admiralty jurisdiction of the court; or
(g) under any convention for the time being in force to which Nigeria is a party to the national court of a Contracting State is either mandated or has a discretion to assume jurisdiction; or
(h) in the opinion of the court, the cause, matter or action should be adjudicated upon in Nigeria.

Norway

Norwegian courts have jurisdiction on the merits in respect of any claim for which a vessel has been arrested in Norway, subject to any contractual jurisdiction or arbitration clauses only.

Poland

Polish jurisdiction, that is the possibility of examining and deciding a case of a civil nature, results from conventions as well as rules of the Polish Civil Code. According to Article 1103 of the Polish Civil Code the jurisdiction of Polish courts exists in the following situations:

— where the defendant possesses assets in Poland;
— where the case relates to a subject matter in Poland.

The arrest of a ship executed by Polish courts for the purpose of securing a claim, can take place only within the territorial boundaries of the Polish Republic. Therefore, it is impossible to arrest a ship without fulfilling one of the two conditions mentioned in Article 1103 of the Polish Civil Code, because a ship that is an asset of the debtor/subject matter of the claim, for the purpose of arrest, must be in Poland.

Polish courts executing the arrest of a ship have jurisdiction as to the merits, but this does not flow from the fact of arrest itself, but from the rules of the Code of Civil Procedure.

There is then the situation where the parties have agreed to exclude the jurisdiction of Polish courts for the benefit of:

1. foreign court or arbitration; or
2. law and courts of foreign State.

In the first case Polish courts would be entitled to arrest the ship for the purpose of securing the claim without the jurisdiction as to the merits. This results from the written arbitration agreement, which does not encompass the right to decide in respect of the security for the claims, belonging to such court which would be competent in case no written arbitration agreement were in existence.

In respect of the second case, I should like to begin by recalling the definition of the internal (domestic) jurisdiction. Domestic jurisdiction rules regulate who and in what cases can seek legal protection in civil cases before the domestic courts, and who and in what cases can be affected by the consequences of civil litigation in the domestic courts.

The decision to secure a claim by the arrest of a ship would in this situation not be valid, as the lack of domestic jurisdiction would cause that the parties would not come under the effects of this accessory proceedings (civil proceedings)—this being shown also by practice. The courts assume an attitude as to the objection of no domestic jurisdiction, not overlooking it as of no consequence.

Also in the last case before the court, refuting the charge of no jurisdiction (domestic) the court alluded that no valid agreement had been presented which excluded the jurisdiction of Polish courts for the benefit of a foreign court.

Slovenia

Orders of arrest (called decision for temporary measure) may be issued in Slovenia only by the District Court of Koper. That court can issue arrest orders irrespective of whether a contract contains an arbitration clause and even if a contract contains an exclusive foreign jurisdiction clause. This is because the arrest order is issued in a special kind of proceedings, named non-litigious proceedings, which is not directly connected with the merits of the claim.

If the vessel is flying the flag of a Contracting State, jurisdiction is established pursuant to the Arrest Convention. Otherwise, if there is no contractual jurisdiction clause, the Slovenian law is applied, especially the Conflict of Law Act.

Spain

In general, Spanish courts would have jurisdiction on the merits when it so results by virtue of the relevant jurisdiction rules (namely, under Articles 21–25 of the Judicial Power Act) or when there is a jurisdiction clause by means of which the parties have agreed to submit the particular dispute to the jurisdiction of Spanish courts, otherwise Spanish courts shall only have jurisdiction in the cases listed in Article 7(1)(a)–(f).

Sweden

Yes. The court granting an arrest acquires jurisdiction on the merits of the case. At least, this is the position taken by the Swedish Government, which is expressly reflected in chapter 21, section 2, paragraph 5 of the Maritime Code in dealing with the relation to the Lugano Convention. (This text has been amended in 1998 to read "the Brussels Convention".)

Consequently, there is an exception, in respect of arrest under the Arrest Convention from the main rule that the Brussels Convention takes over as concerns so-called *exorbitant fori*. Our answer could therefore end here.

However, it should be noted that the European Court in *The Tatry* case [1995] I E.C.R. 5439, held that a specialised convention, such as the Arrest Convention (1952), excludes the application of the provisions of the Brussels Convention only in matters which are expressly governed by the specialised convention. It was found that the Arrest Convention does not contain any specific provisions (in that case) as regards *lis pendens* and consequently the Brussels Convention should be applied. This meant that the English Admiralty Court in London had to stay its proceedings. Also when not a matter of *lis pendens*, i.e. there is no case already pending in another court, the result of the *The Tatry* case should be that it is not open to a State under the Brussels Convention to use Article 7 in the Arrest Convention as a basis for making national law to the effect that the arrest creates jurisdiction. The other grounds for jurisdiction, Article 7 (a–f) of the Arrest Convention should take over, though, if applicable, in the individual case.

This problem has been encountered in Sweden and the Swedish Government is aware of it. However, the problem seems to disappear under the 1999 Arrest Convention, which expressly says that the court acquires jurisdiction.

Arrest may be granted also when the court has no jurisdiction on the merits.

Consequently, the rules of chapter 4 apply, as mentioned, also in situations where other countries have jurisdiction through valid prorogation by the parties, provided, though, that the foreign court judgment or arbitration award is enforceable in Sweden. There is no conflict with Article 7 of the Convention.

United Kingdom

Arrest is available only in the context of the action *in rem*. The action *in rem*, along with the action *in personam*, are the two modes of exercise of Admiralty jurisdiction. The Supreme Court Act 1981, sections 20(1)(a), 20(2) provide a list of claims to which the Admiralty jurisdiction of the High Court extends. According to section 20(7) of the Supreme Court Act 1981 those provisions apply in relation to all ships whether British or not wherever the residence or domicile of their owners may be, and all claims wherever they arise. See *The Anna H* [1995] 1 Lloyd's Rep. 11. It follows that there is generally jurisdiction on the merits and not simply for those claims listed in Article 7(1)(a)–(f). In the English system there is, therefore, an intimate linking between jurisdiction and arrest. An arrest under the action *in rem* is a basis for jurisdiction on the merits of the case.

12. IS THERE ANY STATUTORY PROVISION ON THE TIME LIMIT WITHIN WHICH PROCEEDINGS ON THE MERITS MUST BE COMMENCED BEFORE THE COURT HAVING JURISDICTION OR IS THE TIME FIXED BY THE COURT IN WHOSE JURISDICTION THE ARREST IS MADE, AS PROVIDED BY ARTICLE 7(2)?

Belgium

There is no statutory provision on the time limit within which proceedings on the merits must be commenced before the competent court. Nor is such time fixed by the court ordering leave for arrest.

Croatia

Yes, there is a time limit in Article 981 of 15 days which could be extended by the court.

Denmark

Proceedings on the merits must be brought within one week of the arrest if such proceedings can be brought in Denmark, or if proceedings must be brought abroad within two weeks of the arrest, see AJA section 634. If these limits are not followed, the arrest will be lifted.

Finland

According to the CJP chapter 7, § 6, the applicant has an obligation to start proceedings regarding his claim within one month from the day on which the final decision approving his application for the arrest was made. Failing this, the enforcement of the arrest will be cancelled.

France

Il n'existe aucune dispositions dans les textes sur la saisie conservatoire (loi du 3 janvier 1967 et décret du 27 octobre 1967) imposant au saisissant un délai pour agir au fond devant le tribunal compétent. Mais, dans un arrêt du 14 Octobre 1997 (*DMF* 1998, 24), la Cour de Cassation a décidé que le délai de un mois institué, pour les saisies de droit terrestre (saisies "de droit commun"), par l'article 215 du décret du 31 juillet 1992 sur les voies d'exécution, s'appliquait à la saisie conservatoire (solution qui, quant à moi, me paraît dangereuse par son automaticité).

Germany

According to § 926 ZPO the determination of a time limit for the merits is in the discretion of the court competent for the arrest.

Greece

CCP (Article 715, paragraph 5) diverges from the Convention since it always imposes on the claimant the onus of bringing action on the merits of the dispute within a period of 30 days from service of the arresting order on the debtor. But if the arrest has been lifted against provision of security, the claimant is so obliged only if the court had fixed a period for bringing the relevant action in accordance with Article 693, paragraph 1 CCP which may not be shorter than 30 days.

Haiti

Il n'y a pas à proprement parler dans le droit haïtien une disposition qui fixe un délai pendant lequel le demandeur peut introduire une action par devant le tribunal compétent. Si sa créance est valide, l'action pourra être introduite dans un délai de 20 ans.

Italy

Article 669 *novies* CCP provides generally that the order (of arrest) loses its effectiveness if proceedings on the merits are not commenced within the time limit fixed by the judge or, if no limit is fixed, within 30 days. This provision applies both where Italian courts have or have not jurisdiction on the merits. Furthermore, Article 669 *novies* provides that when Italian courts have not jurisdiction on the merits, the order (of arrest) loses its effectiveness where the request for the enforcement of the foreign judgment or arbitral award is not made within the time limits set out under penalty of forfeiture by the law or by international conventions.

Netherlands

The relevant statutory provision is Article 700(3) of the Dutch Code of Civil Procedure:

Unless a claim on the merits has been instituted at the time of the leave for arrest, the leave shall be granted under the condition that the institution thereof shall take place within a period of time to be set by the president of at least eight days after the arrest. The president may extend this period of time if the arrestor so requests before the period of time has expired. Such ruling is not subject to appeal. Expiry of the period of time shall extinguish the arrest.

There is a practice in Rotterdam whereby the court may grant a period of time within which the claim on the merits must be instituted, which period may be extended between the parties to the dispute up to a certain extent. It may also be relevant to mention that the Hof's-Gravenhage (Court of Appeal of the Hague) 23 February 1993, S&S 1994, 38 (Fen) ruled that the provision of Article 700(3) of the Dutch Code of Civil Procedure does not apply in cases where the arrest has been voluntarily lifted against security. In this case the period of time of Article 700(3) was ruled to have been replaced by the period of time the parties had agreed to in the text of the Rotterdam Guarantee Form.

Nigeria

Our procedure is similar to Article 7(2).

Section 10 of AJD gives the court power to stay proceedings and refer the parties to foreign arbitration or litigation. No time limit is prescribed for the commencement of such proceedings, but the court is empowered to impose any conditions as are just and reasonable in the circumstances.

Norway

An arrest will be automatically removed if proceedings on the merits have not been commenced within one year or within any shorter period decided by the arresting court.

Poland

Yes. It depends on the nature of the claim and is ruled by the Civil Code, the Maritime Code and other statutory acts.

Slovenia

Article 986 of MINA provides that the claimant must commence proceedings on the merits and give formal notice to the court, all within 15 days from the date of notification of arrest. Otherwise, the vessel may be released upon application by the opposite party.

Spain

The general domestic rule governing the arrest of assets as a preventive measure (*embargo preventivo*) is that proceedings on the merits must be brought to validate the arrest within the 20 days from the arrest (Article 1.411 CPC). However, in cases where the main proceedings are to be commenced in a foreign country the claimant usually asks the court to fix a longer period of time making use of the prerogative at Article 7.2 of the Convention. The court usually fixes the time period within which main proceedings on the merits must be commenced when granting the arrest (by stating the period in the same arrest order), if no time limit is fixed by the court or there is not a particular request on this respect, proceedings must be commenced within 20 days from the date arrest is granted.

Sweden

Yes. According to chapter 15, section 7 of the Swedish Code of Judicial Procedure, if an action has not already been instituted, the applicant shall, within a month of the order, either institute a court action on the matter at issue or, if the claim is to be resolved out of court, initiate the appropriate proceedings (e.g. arbitration).

United Kingdom

According to the Civil Jurisdiction and Judgments Act 1982, section 26(1) and (2) where a court stays Admiralty proceedings on the ground that the dispute in question should be submitted to the determination of the courts of an overseas country the court may, if in those proceedings property has been arrested or bail or other security has been given to prevent or obtain release from arrest, order that the property in respect of the dispute in the legal proceedings in favour of which those proceedings are stayed or dismissed, or order that the stay or dismissal of those proceedings be conditional on the provision of equivalent security for the satisfaction of any such award or judgment. Where the court makes such an order it may attach such conditions to the order as it thinks fit, in particular conditions with respect to the institution or prosecution of the relevant legal proceedings. Accordingly, the court may set a time limit in which legal proceedings on the merits of the case ought to commence.

13. ARE THE PROVISIONS OF THE CONVENTION APPLIED ALSO IN RESPECT OF SHIPS FLYING THE FLAG OF NON-CONTRACTING STATES?

Belgium

Since the provisions of the Convention have been incorporated in our internal law they also apply in respect of ships flying the flag of non-Contracting States.

Denmark

Yes.

Croatia

The same provisions are applicable to foreign ships, and limitation that the foreign ship can be arrested only for the claims listed in Article 878, paragraphs 1 and 2 is applicable "if there is reciprocity between the State whose flag the ship flies and the Republic of Croatia" (see Article 976, paragraph 2).

Finland

The FMC chapter 4 covers arrest of vessels for maritime claims which are or may be adjudicated in Finland or in another country. The provisions apply to vessels entered in the Finnish Ship Register or a corresponding foreign ship register. The provisions do not, however, apply to Finnish vessels if the applicant has his habitual residence or principal place of business in Finland. Furthermore, vessels owned or exclusively used by States for non-commercial purposes fall outside the scope of application. Finally, the provisions of chapter 4 are not applicable to public charges such as port, canal and other waterway dues and pilotage dues (§ 1).

France

Les tribunaux français appliquent ici sans hésiter les dispositions de l'article 8 de la Convention. Ils décident que le créancier maritime titulaire d'une créance se rapportant à un navire qui bat pavillon d'un Etat non signataire peut, à son choix, saisir ce navire soit sur le fondement de la loi interne du 3 janvier 1967, soit sur le fondement de la Convention.

Germany

Yes.

Greece

As regards the application of the provisions of the Convention also to ships flying the flag of non-Contracting States, there have been formulated two views in jurisprudence. The first view favours the application of the provisions of the Convention only to ships of Contracting States (Corinthe Single-member First Instance Court 23/1977, Commercial Law Review [CLR] 1977, 95; Thessaloniki Single-member First Instance Court 3456/1980, CLR 1980, 651). The more particular aspect that the provisions of the Convention apply to ships flying the flag of a Contracting State *other* than that where the arrest is pursued (PSFIC 2511/1977 MLR 6, 42; 849/1989 MLR 18, 130) does not seem to have prevailed (PSFIC 1057/1985 MLR 14, 209). The provisions of the Convention apply also to ships flying the flag of the Contracting State where the arrest is pursued if the relation between the parties implies also international aspects. Nevertheless, there have been a number of Greek court judgments which did not apply the provisions of the Convention in the arrest of ships registered in non-Contracting States without assigning any reason thereto (Crete Court of Appeals 56/1970 CLR 1970, 485; PSFIC 1556/1973 CLR 1973, 387; Patras SFIC 1042/1976 CLR 1976, 409; PSFIC 2668/1976 MLR 5, 242; 139/1983 (unreported); 769/1983 MLR 11, 181; 1873/1983 MLR 11, 452; Thessaloniki SFIC 4156/1983 MLR 12, 18; PSFIC 1056/1983 Piraiki Nomologia 1983, 173; 2384/1985 MLR 14, 211; 869/1987 CLR 1987, 466; 2075/1987 MLR 16, 42; 2155/1990 CLR 1991, 315). The second view asserts that the provisions of the Convention apply also on ships flying the flag of non-Contracting States (Nauples Court of Appeals 196/1972 Hellenic Jurists Journal 39, 730; PSFIC 595/1974 CLR 1974, 225; 864/1979 MLR 1981, 6).

Haiti

Oui, les dispositions de la Convention sont applicables aux navires battant le pavillon d'un Etat non-contractant. Haïti, signataire de la Convention, est liée par les dispositions de cette dernière. Que le navire provienne d'un pays non-signataire, cela ne produit aucune différence.

Italy

This question is not settled, but the prevailing view is that the Convention as a whole applies also in respect of ships flying the flag of non-Contracting States: Tribunale of Salerno 21 January 1997, *Mario Cirino Pomicino S.p.A.* v. *Liman Company Ltd—The "Komandor"* [1998] Dir. Mar. 436; Tribunale of Livorno 18 November 1996, *Enzo Cipriani Shipping* v. *Baltic Shipping Co.—The "Euroshipping One"* [1998] Dir. Mar. 433; Tribunale of Genoa 20 May 1995, *Uberseeschiffsahrtsagentur Transnautic GmbH & Co. K.G.* v. *Baltic Shipping Co.—The "Akademic Gorbunov"* [1995] Dir. Mar. 768. Contra: Tribunale of Ravenna 19 February 1996, *Atlas Factoring Hizmetleri A.S.* v. *Turkai Denizcilik Ve Tikaret-The "Recai B"* [1998] Dir. Mar. 1165; Corte di Cassazione 25 May 1993, *Equinox Shipping Co. Ltd* v. *Ryszard Lysko—The "Al Taif"* [1994] Dir. Mar. 157.

Netherlands

I may refer to the following literature:

— J.T. Asser, "Uniform Zeerecht. De Diplomatieke Zeerecht Conferentie, gehouden te Brussel in Mei 1952", *NJB* 1953, pp. 758–759;
— J.P. Verheul, "The Convention relating to the arrest of seagoing ships of 1952. Some questions", NILR 1983, p. 384;
— M.H. Claringbould, "The Netherlands", in: J. Theunis e.a., *Arrest of Ships 2. Belgium, The Netherlands, India, Yugoslavia*, London: Lloyd's of London Press 1986, p. 48 and pp. 60–61.

For the relevant case law and annotations I refer to HR 29 June 1979, Pres. Rb. Rotterdam 4 March 1983, Hof's-Gravenhage 5 June 1987, Pres. Rb. Middelburg 28 April 1989, Pres. Rb. Middelburg 30 January 1992, Pres. Rb. Rotterdam 9 July 1992, HR 2 April 1993, HR 28 May 1993, Pres. Rb. Amsterdam 9 March 1994, ECJ 6 December 1994, Pres. Rb. Middelburg 1 September 1995.

Notwithstanding arguments to the contrary, Dutch case law supports the view that the 1952 Convention should not be applied in respect of ships flying the flag of non-Contracting States.

Nigeria

Not applicable. As expressed in paragraph 1, *supra*, the provisions of the Convention do not apply in Nigeria in their capacity or status as provisions of the Convention but only to the extent that they have been incorporated in the AJD. In accordance with AJD, section 3, the admiralty jurisdiction of the Federal High Court extends to all ships irrespective of the places of residence and domicile of their owners. In accordance with AJD, section 5, a ship can be arrested in an action commenced as an action *in rem* in respect of any claim under AJD, section 2.

Norway

Yes.

Poland

Yes.

Slovenia

For vessels flying the flag of a non-Contracting State, MINA applies.
MINA has almost entirely adopted the provisions of the Arrest Convention.

Spain

Yes. As provided by Article 8.2 of the Convention the right of arrest in respect of maritime claims extends to ships flying the flag of a non-Contracting State. Furthermore, as indicated in the reply to Question 1 above, the 2/1967 Act expressly extends its scope of application to vessels from non-Contracting States.

Sweden

Yes. Chapter 4 of the Swedish Maritime Code applies also in respect of ships flying the flag of non-Contracting States. Although arguments were raised during the work of implementing the Convention, to the effect that the chapter on arrest should be limited to covering ships from Contracting States, the Government found that the benefit of making the law clear and uncompli-cated was outweighing the negative effects referred to. The difficulty sometimes in establishing the nationality of a ship, e.g. in cases of double registration, was also referred to. (As mentioned above, Swedish ships are excluded from the scope of the Convention in respect of claims by Swedish subjects.)

United Kingdom

As noted in the answer to Question 1, above, the 1952 Arrest Convention was not given the force of law by Parliament, nor was reference made to Convention parties. The Supreme Court Act 1981, section 20(7) states that the provisions regarding the Admiralty jurisdiction of the High Court apply to all ships whether British or not and all claims wherever arising. Paragraph 6.2(7) of the Admiralty Practice Direction 49F provides that there shall be no arrest of certain State-owned ships, where the UK has an international obligation to minimise the possibility of arrest of ships of that State, unless certain procedural notices have been served on consular officers: see also the answer to Question 15, below.

14. CAN SUCH VESSELS BE ARRESTED ALSO IN RESPECT OF CLAIMS OTHER THAN THE MARITIME CLAIMS ENUMERATED IN ARTICLE 1(1)?

Belgium

Since the same provisions apply such vessels can only be arrested for a maritime claim as listed in Article 1(1).

Croatia

See reply to Question 13.

Denmark

No, only for such claims enumerated in MSA section 91(1–17), corresponding to Article 1(1) of the Arrest Convention.

Finland

See reply to Question 4.

France

La réponse est affirmative. Le créancier qui a choisi de saisir un navire étranger battant pavillon d'un Etat non contractant peut, conformément d'ailleurs aux dispositions mêmes de l'article 8-2, saisir ce navire, non seulement en invoquant une créance maritime selon la Convention, mais aussi en invoquant n'importe quelle créance (même non maritime), dès lors que cette créance paraît "fondée en son principe".

Germany

Yes.

Greece

The judgments submitting to the provisions of the Convention ships flying the flag of non-Contracting States have not dealt with the question of not applying Article 2 of the Convention—i.e. permitting the arrest in respect of non-maritime claims.

Haiti

Les navires quel que soit leur pavillon d'appartenance tombent sous le coup de la Convention de 1952, laquelle a été ratifiée par l'Assemblée Nationale comme mentionné plus haut. Mais au-delà de cette Convention, et cela est du ressort du droit interne haïtien, le patrimoine du débiteur constituant le gage du créancier, un navire peut être saisi même en dehors du cadre de la Convention.

Italy

Yes.

Netherlands

I refer to the same literature and case law as mentioned under 13. Yes, provided of course a valid right of recourse on the ship exists.

Nigeria

See reply to Question 13.

Norway

No.

Poland

According to my knowledge there are no precedents till now.

Slovenia

A vessel may be arrested in respect of claims deriving from mortgages (hypothec) indifferently from the flag of the vessel. If any State does not apply reciprocity to vessels flying the flag of the

Republic of Slovenia, the vessel flying the flag of that State may be arrested for practically any claim.

Spain

See answer to Question 4 above.

Sweden

Yes. Vessels could be arrested also for maritime lien claims, which are not enumerated in Article 1(1) of the Convention. An example is harbour dues etc., which are not listed as maritime claims in the 1952 Convention. (They are now listed in the 1999 International Convention on Arrest of Ships.)

United Kingdom

As noted in the answer to Question 4, above, arrest is available only in the context of the action *in rem*. Whenever such an action is brought against a ship then arrest of that ship is possible. The Supreme Court Act 1981, section 21 states the cases when the Admiralty jurisdiction of the High Court can be exercised through an action *in rem*. An action *in rem* can generally be brought against a ship for most of the claims listed in Supreme Court Act 1981, section 20(2) which is broadly similar to the one in Article 1(1) of the 1952 Arrest Convention.

15. HAS THE PROVISION OF ARTICLE 8(3) BEEN APPLIED IN YOUR COUNTRY?

Belgium

The provision of Article 8(3) has not been applied in our country.

Denmark

No.

Finland

No.

France

L'article 3-8 n'est pas appliqué aux saisies faites en France, la France n'ayant jamais fait usage de la réserve (ou du refus) prévu par ce texte.

Germany

Yes.

Greece

If my research has been accurate, there is no court precedent concerning specifically the application of Article 8(3) of the Convention.

Haïti

Oui, la disposition du paragraphe 3 de l'article 8 est appliquée en Haïti, car le décret de ratification de l'Assemblée Nationale n'avait posé aucune réserve. La Convention dans toutes ses dispositions est applicable intégralement.

Italy

Not to our knowledge.

Netherlands

No. I refer to M.H. Claringbould, "The Netherlands", in: J. Theunis e.a., *Arrest of Ships 2. Belgium, The Netherlands, India, Yugoslavia*, London: Lloyd's of London Press 1986, p. 61 and the following cases Hof's-Gravenhage 28 June 1985, Hof's-Gravenhage 5 June 1987, Pres. Rb. Rotterdam 9 July 1992, HR 2 April 1993, ECJ 6 December 1994.

Nigeria

No.

Norway

Not to my knowledge.

Poland

As far as I know Article 8 has not been applied.
In Poland whether or not the vessel is registered in the ships register the claimant may not arrest such ship already transferred under MOA/Bill of Sale to bond file purchaser (new owner).

Spain

As indicated above (reply to Question 1) Spain gave the force of law to the Convention in its original text at the time of ratification of the Convention (December 1954) by its publication in the Official Gazette without implementing any specific legislation. Therefore there was not a particular instrument by means of which Spain could avail itself of the right granted by this paragraph to exclude non-Contracting States from the benefits of the Convention.

On the contrary, Act 2/1967 (adapting our procedural rules for the purposes of making clear that the right to arrest ships exists, as respects maritime claims, on the basis of a mere allegation of a claim without the need of providing evidence of the claim) expressly extends its application to vessels from non-Contracting States. Clearly the purpose of such express reference in the 2/1967 Act, was not to exclude from "the benefits" of the Convention persons or vessels from a non-Contracting State but to make clear that "the right of arrest", on said basis, is extended to vessels flying a flag of a non-Contracting State.

Sweden

No. See the answer to Question 13 above.

United Kingdom

According to Admiralty Practice Direction 49F, paragraph 6.2(7) no warrant of arrest will be issued against a ship owned by a State where, by any convention or treaty, the United Kingdom has undertaken to minimise the possibility of arrest of ships of that State until notice has been served on a consular officer at the consular office of that State in London or the port at which it is intended to cause the ship to be arrested and a copy of the notice is exhibited to the declaration filed: see the answers to Questions 13 and 3, above.

The UK and the Soviet Union entered into such an undertaking as respects such ships and cargo on board them, see Articles 2 and 3 of the 1977 Protocol to the 1968 Treaty on Merchant Navigation between the UK and the Union of Soviet Socialist Republics, the relevant provisions of which were brought into force in English law by the State Immunity (Merchant Shipping) (Union of Soviet Socialist Republics) Order 1978 (S.I. 1978 No. 1524). The provisions of the Order took precedence

285

over the provisions of the State Immunity Act 1978, section 13(4) whereby arrest will lie in respect of commercial activities. There were doubts about the extent of the Order after the break up of the Soviet Union (see *The Giuseppe di Vittorio* [1998] 1 Lloyd's Rep. 136), but the Merchant Shipping (Sovereign Immunity) Order 1997 (S.I. 1997 No. 2591) extended protections to Georgia and the Republic of Ukraine, in addition to the Russian Federation. However, the State Immunity (Merchant Shipping) (Revocation) Order 1999 (S.I. 1999 No. 668) revoked the 1997 Order and came into force on 29 April 1999, the date on which the UK's termination of the Protocol took effect.

BOOK II

The International Convention on Arrest of Ships, 1999

CHAPTER 1

History of the Convention[1]

1. THE WORK OF THE CMI

II.1 The decision to consider the revision of the 1952 Arrest Convention was taken by the CMI following a resolution of IMO[2] and UNCTAD[3] to place on their working programme the revision of the 1926 and 1967 Maritime Liens and Mortgages Conventions and of the 1952 Arrest Convention. The CMI International Sub-Committee appointed by the CMI Executive Council in respect of this latter Convention, under the chairmanship of Professor Allan Philip, considered, *inter alia*, the additions that should be made to the list of maritime claims, the problems of whether a ship can be arrested in respect of claims against persons other than the owner of the ship, and whether the arrest should in all circumstances give rise to jurisdiction. In view of the quality and quantity of changes that were being discussed, the International Sub-Committee decided that it would have been difficult to carry out the revision by means of a protocol and, therefore, prepared the draft of a new Convention for consideration by the forthcoming CMI Lisbon Conference in 1985.[4] The draft was considered by the Conference and, as amended by it, was approved with 23 votes in favour, three against and seven abstentions.[5]

II.2 The draft,[6] reference to which will be made as the Lisbon Draft, was then submitted by the President of the CMI to IMO and UNCTAD, together with the draft of the revised 1967 Maritime Liens and Mortgages Convention.

---

1. The history of the 1999 Convention is written in a concise form since in Appendix III the *travaux préparatoires* of the Convention are reproduced on an article by article basis.
2. Res. A. 405 (x) of the Assembly of IMO at its 10th session. A more detailed account of IMO's involvement with maritime liens and mortgages and related subjects was given in the report entitled "Consideration of Work in respect of Maritime Liens and Mortgages and related Subjects: Preliminary report by the Secretariat" (Doc. LEG 52/5/Add. 1, 8 August 1984), which was submitted to the Legal Committee of IMO at its 52nd session in September 1984.
3. Pursuant to Res. 49 (x) of the Committee on Shipping at its 10th session, the following three subjects were included in the work programme of the Working Group on International Shipping Legislation, namely:
    (i) maritime liens and mortgages;
    (ii) registration of rights in respect of vessels under construction; and
    (iii) arrest of vessels or other sanctions, as appropriate.
A more detailed account on the background to the UNCTAD's involvement with maritime liens and mortgages and related subjects was given in the report entitled "Preliminary Analysis of possible reforms in the existing international regime of maritime liens and mortgages" (Doc. TD/B/C.4/ISL/48, 24 July 1984), which was submitted to the Working Group at its 10th session in September 1984.
4. Report of the CMI on the Draft Revision of the International Convention for the Unification of Certain Rules Relating to the Arrest of Sea-Going Ships, 1952, in Lisboa II, p.126.
5. Report of the CMI, *supra*, note 4, p. 126.
6. Draft Revision of the International Convention for the Unification of Certain Rules Relating to the Arrest of Sea-Going Ships, 1952, Lisboa II, p. 42.

2. THE WORK OF THE JIGE

II.3 A Joint Intergovernmental Group of Experts on Maritime Liens and Mortgages and Related Subjects (JIGE) was established with the following terms of reference pursuant to a recommendation of the Legal Committee of IMO, endorsed by the Council of IMO at its 56th session[7] and pursuant to resolution 6(XI) of the Working Group on International Shipping Legislation of UNCTAD, endorsed by the Trade and Development Board of UNCTAD at its 32nd session:

To examine the subject of maritime liens and mortgages, including the possible consideration of:

(a) The review of the maritime liens and mortgages conventions and related enforcement procedures, such as arrest;
(b) The preparation of model laws or guidelines on maritime liens, mortgages and related enforcement procedures, such as arrest.
(c) The feasibility of an international registry of maritime liens and mortgages.

II.4 After the approval, at its sixth session held in London from 25 to 29 September 1989, of the Draft Articles for a Convention on Maritime Liens and Mortgages,[8] the IMO-UNCTAD Joint Intergovernmental Group of Experts, on the basis of a note prepared by the Secretariats of UNCTAD and IMO[9] adopted the following recommendation[10]:

With regard to arrest, the Joint Group recommends that consideration of any further work be postponed until after the adoption of the final text of the Convention on Maritime Liens and Mortgages by a diplomatic conference.

II.5 In May 1993 the United Nations/IMO Conference, having adopted the new Convention on Maritime Liens and Mortgages on the basis of the draft prepared by the JIGE, approved a resolution in which it recommended that "the relevant bodies of UNCTAD and IMO, in the light of the outcome of the Conference, reconvene the Joint Intergovernmental Group with a view to examining the possible review of the International Convention for the Unification of Certain Rules Relating to the Arrest of Sea-Going Ships, 1952".

---

7. See Final Report of the Joint Intergovernmental Group of Experts on Maritime Liens and Mortgages and Related Subjects, adopted by the JIGE at its 6th session, held from 25 to 29 September 1989, UNCTAD Doc. TD/B/C.4/AC.8/27, 20 December 1989 and IMO Doc. LEG/MLM/27.

8. Report of the Joint UNCTAD/IMO Intergovernmental Group of Experts on Maritime Liens and Mortgages and Related Subjects on its Sixth Session (IMO Doc. LEG/MLM/26 and UNCTAD Doc. TD/B/C.4/AC.8/26).

9. "Consideration of Future Work on Other Aspects of the Terms of Reference of the Joint Intergovernmental Group of Experts-Note by the Secretariats of UNCTAD and IMO" (UNCTAD Doc. TD/B/C.4/AC.8/13 and IMO Doc. LEG/MLM/13). At para. 4 the following statement is made:

With regard to the question of enforcement procedure, most representatives were of the view that the 1952 Convention Relating to Arrest of Sea-Going Ships was successful, considering that it had been ratified by over 60 States. It was suggested that any decision to align the terminology of this Convention with that of any new convention on maritime liens and mortgages should only be made after determining the course of action concerning the latter convention. Note was taken of the concern expressed regarding the possibility of extending the provisions of arrest to State-owned vessels engaged in commercial service. It was also suggested that arrest of sea-going ships should be covered by a separate convention. It was pointed out, in this context, that arrest was not merely confined to maritime rights and it should, therefore, not be dealt with merely as an annex to another subject. One representative emphasized the importance of arrest as an enforcement mechanism and stated that this tool should not be restricted to maritime liens above the mortgage.

10. Doc. TD/B/C.4/AC.8/27–LEG/MLM/27.

II.6 Following such resolution, a note was prepared by the UNCTAD and IMO Secretariats in consultation with the CMI,[11] wherein some of the changes to the Convention on Maritime Liens and Mortgages were highlighted. It was stated in the note that the JIGE should take a decision on the scope of the revision of the 1952 Convention, which might be confined to drafting amendments consequential upon the adoption of the 1993 MLM Convention, or consist of a thorough revision of the Arrest Convention.

II.7 The seventh session of JIGE (the first to deal with the arrest of ships) was held in Geneva, from 5 to 9 December 1994 under the chairmanship of Mr George Ivanov. JIGE decided to take as a basis of its work the draft of a new Arrest Convention approved by the Lisbon Conference of the CMI and discussed most of the Articles of the draft, among which particular attention was paid to Article 1—Definitions, Article 3—Exercise of right of arrest, and Article 5—Right of rearrest and multiple arrest. On the basis of the outcome of such discussion, "Draft articles for a convention on arrest of ships" (hereafter referred to as "First Draft Articles") were prepared by the IMO and UNCTAD Secretariats[12] for consideration at the eighth session, which was agreed would take place in London on 7 and 8 October 1995.

II.8 Immediately after the session started, the German delegation questioned the need for a new convention and the adoption of an open-ended list of maritime claims. A debate followed, during which some delegations supported the German position, expressing the view that no decision had been taken at the previous session[13] and, in particular, no consensus had been reached on the adoption of the Lisbon Draft as a basis of future work. After some discussion, the Joint Group decided to use the First Draft Articles as a basis for its deliberations; it further decided that the outcome of the work would be embodied in a new convention, rather than a protocol.

II.9 The discussion then focused, in particular, on Article 3, which was intended to replace Article 3(4) of the 1952 Convention and the proposal was made by the delegation of the United States to permit the arrest in respect of claims secured by maritime liens recognised by the *lex fori*.

II.10 The ninth and last session was held in Geneva from 2 to 6 December 1996 under the chairmanship of Mr. Karl-Johan Gombrii. The most important matters that were discussed and settled were the following:

(a) definition of arrest in Article 1(2)[14];
(b) the power of arrest except the arrest of ships ready to sail or sailing[15];

11. UNCTAD Doc. TD/B/CN.4/GE/2/2, 9 August 1994.
12. IMO Doc. LEG/MLM/32, 15 June 1995, and UNCTAD Doc. TD/B/CN.4/GE/2/5. Consideration of the Possible Review of the International Convention for the Unification of Certain Rules Relating to the Arrest of Sea-Going Ships, 1952.
13. Report on the Work of the Sessional Group of the Joint UNCTAD/IMO Intergovernmental Group of Experts on Maritime Liens and Mortgages and Related Subjects at its Eighth Session, Annex I to the Report of the Joint Intergovernmental Group of Experts, Doc. JIGE (VIII) 7, 8 November 1995, IMO Doc. LEG/MLM/37–UNCTAD Doc. TD/B/CN.4/GE.2/10, para. 2–4. A report on the 7th session was also published in issue No. 4/1994 of the CMI *News Letter* at p. 12.
14. Report on the Work of the Sessional Group of the Whole of the Joint UNCTAD/IMO Intergovernmental Group of Experts on Maritime Liens and Mortgages and Related Subjects at its Ninth Session, Annex II to the Report of the Joint UNCTAD/IMO Intergovernmental Group of Experts, Doc. JIGE(IX/4), IMO Doc. LEG/MLM/41–UNCTAD Doc. TD/B/44/3–TD/B/IGE.1/4, paragraphs 19 and 20.
15. Report, *supra* note 14, paragraphs 32–38.

  (c) the release of the ship from arrest (Article 4) except for the maximum amount of the security[16];
  (d) rearrest and multiple arrest (Article 5);
  (e) the protection of owners and demise charterers of arrested ships (Article 6) except the reference to security for damages in case the arrest is unjustified;
  (f) the jurisdiction on the merits (Article 7);
  (g) the scope of application of the convention (Article 8);

The most important matters that could not be settled were the following:

  (a) whether the list of maritime claims should be a closed list or an open list[17];
  (b) whether mention should be made of the power of arrest of ships ready to sail or which are sailing[18];
  (c) whether the maritime liens securing claims for which arrest is permissible irrespective of the ship being owned by the person liable should only be the "international" maritime liens or, also, the maritime liens recognised by the *lex fori*[19];
  (d) whether and to which extent arrest should be permissible in respect of claims against the demise charterer[20];
  (e) whether the security to be provided for the release of the ship from arrest should not exceed the value of the ship[21];
  (f) whether in the provision on the security for damages that may be imposed on the claimant reference should be made, in addition to the arrest being wrongful, to the arrest being unjustified.[22]

II.11 At the end of the ninth session, the following recommendation was adopted by the JIGE[23]:

> The Joint UNCTAD/IMO Intergovernmental Group of Experts on Maritime Liens and Mortgages and Related Subjects recommends to the International Maritime Organization (IMO) Council and to the Trade and Development Board of UNCTAD that they consider favourably, on the basis of the useful work done so far, proposing to the General Assembly of the United Nations the convening of a diplomatic conference to consider and adopt a convention on certain rules relating to the arrest of sea-going ships on the basis of the draft articles prepared by the Group of Experts.

II.12 A new set of Draft Articles was subsequently prepared, at the request of the JIGE, by the IMO and UNCTAD Secretariats,[24] and constituted the basis of discussions at the Diplomatic Conference, which was convened at Geneva from 1 to 12 March 1999, following the endorsement of the recommendation of the JIGE by the IMO Council at its seventy-eighth session and by the UNCTAD's Trade and Development Board at its fifteenth executive session.

---

16. Report, *supra* note 14, paragraphs 68–71.
17. Report, *supra* note 14, paragraphs 2–3.
18. Report, *supra* note 14, paragraphs 32–38.
19. Report, *supra* note 14, paragraphs 50–56 and 60.
20. Report, *supra* note 14, paragraphs 54.
21. Report, *supra* note 14, paragraphs 68–71.
22. Report, *supra* note 14, paragraphs 85–87.
23. Report, *supra* note 14, Annex I.
24. Draft Articles for a Convention on Arrest of Ships, IMO document LEG/MLM 42, UNCTAD document TD/B/IGE.1/5 of 14 April 1997. On the Draft Articles generally see Barroilhet Acevedo, *El Arraigo de Naves y Especialmente el Arraigo de Nave Hermana*, Santiago 1999, p. 170–177.

II.13 The Draft Articles were considered by the Main Committee established by the Conference, under the chairmanship of Mr. Karl-Johan Gombrii and the debate that took place during the first and second reading of the Draft Articles is reported in Appendix III.

II.14 The text of the Convention was adopted by the Conference on 12 March 1999[25] and the Convention is now open for signature since 1 September 1999 until 31 August 2000.

II.15 In order to make a comparison between the 1952 Convention and the new Convention easier, the provisions of the new Convention will be considered following the same scheme adopted for the 1952 Convention.

25. Appendix I.

CHAPTER 2

Scope of Application of the Convention

3. THE GENERAL RULE

II.16 The two distinct provisions of the 1952 Convention governing the application of the Convention to ships flying the flag of Contracting States and to ships flying the flag of non-Contracting States (Article 8(1) and (2)), which have given rise to conflicting inter-pretation,[1] have been replaced in the 1999 Convention by a provision according to which the Convention shall apply to any ship, whether or not flying the flag of a State Party. Thus all ships flying the flag of non-party States will be subject to the new Convention and, otherwise than under the 1952 Convention, may be arrested only in respect of a maritime claim. The provision of Article 8(2) of the 1952 Convention has not in fact been reproduced in Article 8 of the 1999 Convention, but instead it has been provided in Article 10(1)(b) that States may reserve the right to exclude the application of the Convention to ships not flying the flag of a State Party. The effect of these provisions is that either all the provisions of the Convention apply in respect of ships not flying the flag of a State Party, including that whereby a ship may only be arrested in respect of a maritime claim, or none applies if a State has availed itself of the reservation.[2]

II.17 The Convention applies to all ships, whether seagoing or not. The word "sea-going", which in Article 8(1) of the Draft Articles qualified the word "ship", was in fact deleted following the proposal of the delegate from the United Kingdom[3] and, similarly to what was done in the 1976 Convention on the Limitation of Liability for Maritime Claims,[4] States Parties are permitted to reserve the right to exclude the application of the Convention to ships which are not seagoing. The technique used in the two Conventions is, however, different. In fact, while in the LLMC Convention States Parties are permitted to regulate the system of limitation to be applied to such ships by provisions other than those set out in the Convention, in the Arrest Convention States may reserve the right not to apply the provisions of the new Convention to such ships. The former provision is not, strictly speaking, a reservation and in fact States are not required to avail themselves of the right granted to them at the time of ratification, acceptance or approval or of accession

---

1. *Supra*, Book I, section 10 p. 23.
2. Appendix III, p. 551.
3. Appendix III, p. 550.
4. Article 15(2) of the LLMC Convention so provides:
   A State Party may regulate by specific provisions of national law the system of limitation of liability to be applied to vessels which are:
   a) according to the law of that State, ships intended for navigation on inland waterways; . . .

but they may do so at any time thereafter, their only obligation being that of informing the depositary.

II.18 Also the words used in the two Conventions differ: while in the LLMC Convention reference is made to ships "intended for navigation on inland waterways", in the Arrest Convention reference is made to ships which are not seagoing. The first definition is positive and is qualified by a purposive element; the second definition is negative and is qualified by an objective element. It should be established which ships are excluded from the scope of application of the Convention if a State Party avails itself of the reservation. The qualification of a ship as seagoing or not seagoing can be related to the capability of the ship to navigate the sea or to the intended employment of the ship. Since it seems reasonable to assume that the distinction between the two categories of ships is the same in the various maritime conventions, the wording adopted in the LLMC Convention—"ships intended for navigation on inland waterways"—should be relevant for the interpretation of the provision of the Arrest Convention. It should follow that the ships which are not seagoing are the ships intended for navigation on inland waterways, irrespective of their capability to navigate the sea or not. Conversely, ships that are intended for navigation on the sea, do not lose their characteristic of seagoing ships if they navigate on inland waterways.

4. EXCEPTIONS TO THE GENERAL RULE

(a) Arrest of a ship within the jurisdiction of the flag State by a person having his habitual residence or principal place of business in that State

II.19 The provision of Article 8(4) of the 1952 Convention has been reproduced in the 1999 Convention and the subsequent paragraph (5) whereby the person who has acquired a claim by subrogation or assignment is deemed to have the same habitual residence or principal place of business of the original claimant has been merged into the previous one, so that the new rule contained in paragraph (6) of Article 8, so states:

6. Nothing in this Convention shall modify or affect the rules of law in force in the States Parties relating to the arrest of any ship physically within the jurisdiction of the State of its flag procured by a person whose habitual residence or principal place of business is in that State, or by any other person who has acquired a claim from such person by subrogation, assignment or otherwise.

II.20 This provision is obsolete since, contrary to other recent conventions (e.g. the 1976 LLMC and the 1993 MLM Conventions), it limits the global character of the new Arrest Convention).

(b) State-owned ships

II.21 When, during the CMI 1951 Naples Conference, the proposal was made to include in the Convention a rule excluding from the scope of the Convention State-owned ships used on Government non-commercial service, strong opposition thereto was encountered from some delegations.[5] The reason for such opposition was that at that time the 1926 Brussels Convention on Immunity of State-owned Ships had not yet been ratified by

---

5. *Supra*, Book I, para. I.538–I.541.

several maritime countries, including the United Kingdom. Subsequently, the principle that private maritime law conventions should not apply to State-owned ships used on Government non-commercial service was generally accepted, while all proposals for a wider exemption in respect of State-owned ships were rejected.

II.22 A provision on immunity of State-owned ships has thus been inserted in Article 8(2) of the 1999 Convention as follows:

2. This Convention shall not apply to any warship, naval auxiliary or other ships owned or operated by a State and used, for the time being, only on government non-commercial service.

II.23 While the text of the Draft Articles was based on the provision of the 1993 MLM Convention, the text adopted by the Conference is based on Article 3 of the 1926 Immunity Convention, even if not all the types of ships reference to which is made in that article are mentioned in Article 8(2) of the 1999 Convention.[6]

(c) Ships detained or prevented from sailing by Public Authorities

II.24 While the provision on the scope of application was removed from Article 2 of the draft 1952 Convention, that relating to the power of public authorities to prevent or detain a ship was left in Article 2, as it was thought that it constituted an exception to the rule whereby ships could only be arrested in respect of maritime claims. At the Lisbon CMI Conference it was, however, deemed more appropriate to move that provision to the article—Article 8—wherein the scope of application of the Convention was regulated.

II.25 In fact, as pointed out when commenting on Article 2 of the 1952 Convention,[7] the provision contained in that article is also a provision on the scope of application of the Convention. The effect of such provision is not only that of permitting public authorities to arrest or detain a ship in situations where no maritime claim is involved, but also to exclude in respect of any such action the application of all other provisions of the Convention.

II.26 The decision made at Lisbon was, therefore, correct and was adopted by the JIGE and then by the Diplomatic Conference.

II.27 The provision under consideration is now placed in paragraph (3) of Article 8 and reference is made therein, in addition to domestic laws or regulations, also to international conventions. The power to detain a ship, in particular for safety reasons, arises in fact out of several conventions, such as the SOLAS Convention, the Load Line Convention and the 1969 CLC.[8]

II.28 Article 8(3) is worded as follows:

3. This Convention does not affect any rights or powers vested in any Government or its departments, or in any public authority, or in any dock or harbour authority, under any international convention or under any domestic law or regulation, to detain or otherwise prevent from sailing any ship within their jurisdiction.

---

6. Article 3(1) of the 1926 Brussels Convention for the Unification of Certain Rules Concerning the Immunity of State-Owned Ships so provides in its original French text:

1. Les dispositions des deux articles précédents ne sont pas applicables aux navires de guerre, aux yachts d'Etat, navires de surveillance, bateaux-hôpitaux, navires auxiliaires, navires de ravitaillement et autres bâtiments appartenant à un Etat ou exploités par lui et affectés exclusivement au moments de la naissance de la créance, à un service gouvernemental et non commercial . . .

7. *Supra*, Book I, para. I.275.

8. *Supra,* Book I, para. I.278–I.285.

(d) Ships under arrest adversely affecting the use of the port installations

II.29 Although no provision is made in the Convention in order to take care of the problems that a ship under arrest may cause to the port authority, it is worth mentioning that the existence of this problem had been repeatedly affirmed by the International Association of Ports and Harbours and that some attempts have been made to find a solution to them in the Convention.[9]

II.30 France suggested to impose on States Parties the obligation to enact in their legislation rules limiting the financial implications of the arrest for ports.[10]

II.31 Egypt suggested to tackle the problem by providing in Article 6(1) that the security that may be ordered by the court should cover also port dues and costs arising out of the arrest.[11]

II.32 Romania instead suggested to provide in Article 8(4) that port authorities may request that the ship be ordered to leave the port.[12]

II.33 All such proposals were rejected by a strong majority of the delegates on the ground that the consequences for a port of ships under arrest occupying a berth for a long time or even causing a danger to other ships are all matters to be regulated by domestic laws or regulations.[13]

II.34 It would appear, therefore, that even if nothing is said in this respect in Article 8(3), it has been recognised that the provisions of the Convention do not affect any right or power vested in any Government or public authority or harbour authority, to give orders in respect of the location of an arrested ship.

(e) Ships in respect of which the limitation of liability is invoked

II.35 The arrest of a ship in respect of which limitation of liability is invoked is the subject of specific rules in the CLC 1969 and in the 1976 LLMC Convention. Article 6 of the CLC 1969 provides that after the constitution of the limitation fund and provided the owner is entitled to limit his liability, no person having a claim for pollution damage shall be entitled to exercise any right against any other assets of the owner in respect of such claim. It provides further that the court of any Contracting State shall order the release of any ship belonging to the owner which has been arrested in respect of a claim for pollution damage arising out of the incident as a consequence of which the fund was constituted, and shall similarly release any bail or other security furnished to avoid the arrest. Article 13 of the LLMC Convention differs from Article 6 of the CLC 1969 only in that the court has a discretionary power to order the release of the ship from arrest or the release of the security, save when the limitation fund was constituted in one of the places listed in such article.

II.36 There could, therefore, be a conflict between those conventions and the Arrest Convention, according to which a ship can not be arrested only if sufficient security in

---

9. The discussion which took place during the Eighth Session of the JIGE is summarised in Annex I to the Report. See Appendix III, p. 443.
10. See Appendix III, p. 444.
11. Conference document A/CONF.188/CRP.9 of 4 March 1999, Appendix III, p. 525.
12. Conference document A/CONF.188/CRP.13 of 5 March 1999, Appendix III, p. 552.
13. The French proposal was considered at the Ninth Session of the JIGE. See for the summary of the debate Appendix III, p. 445.

respect of the particular claim has been given, the limit of the security being the value of the ship, and the ship must be released from arrest against security the nature and amount of which are determined by the court, always not exceeding the value of the ship.

II.37 A provision aiming at avoiding a conflict between conventions was, therefore, advisable. Paragraph (5) of Article 8 states:

5. Nothing in this Convention shall affect the application of international conventions providing for limitation of liability, or domestic law giving effect thereto, in the State where the arrest is effected.

II.38 Quite logically this rule applies only in respect of international conventions on limitation and national laws implementing them: domestic rules on limitation in fact cannot prevail over uniform rules on arrest.

(f) Ships owned by a person subject to bankruptcy or similar proceedings

II.39 A conflict similar to that between conventions providing for limitation of liability and the Arrest Convention may arise where the owner is adjudicated bankrupt or put into forced liquidation or made subject to similar proceedings. In fact, in such cases, individual actions against the assets of the owner are normally prohibited.

II.40 A provision in this respect has been included in Article 8 of the Lisbon Draft and then in the Draft Articles and in the Convention. Paragraph (5) of Article 8 states:

4. This Convention shall not affect the power of any State or Court to make orders affecting the totality of a debtor's assets.

II.41 The words used in the Lisbon Draft, and now adopted by the Diplomatic Conference, are such as to cover any type of liquidation proceedings.

II.42 Although reference is made generally to the powers of any State or court, such State must be that in whose jurisdiction the ship is arrested and such court must be a court of that State. In fact, this provision cannot imply the recognition in a State Party of orders issued in other States Parties.

CHAPTER 3

The Notion of Arrest and Claims in Respect of which a Ship may be Arrested

5. THE NOTION OF ARREST

II.43 The definition of arrest in Article 1(2) is the following:

2. "Arrest" means any detention or restriction on removal of a ship by order of a Court to secure a maritime claim but does not include the seizure of a ship in execution or satisfaction of a judgment or other enforceable instrument.

II.44 In the Lisbon Draft the definition of arrest was much more articulated. Article 1(2) of such Draft provided, in fact, as follows:

2. "Arrest" means any detention, or restriction on removal, of a ship by order of a Court to secure a maritime claim when at the time of such detention or restriction that ship is physically within the jurisdiction of the State where the order has been made.
   "Arrest" includes "attachment" or other conservatory measures, but does not include measures taken in execution or satisfaction of an enforceable judgment or arbitral award.[1]

II.45 Objections, however, were raised by several delegations against such definition, that had been incorporated in the 1994 JIGE Draft Articles[2] in the course of the Eighth and Ninth Sessions of the JIGE, in particular against the requirement that the ship should be, at the time of arrest, physically within the jurisdiction of the State in which the order of arrest is made[3] and it was suggested that the definition given in the 1952 Convention should be reinstated.[4]

II.46 It was also pointed out that the presence of the ship within the jurisdiction should be mentioned elsewhere, preferably in Article 8.

II.47 The following draft was then submitted by the Chairman in the course of the Ninth Session and was adopted[5]:

"Arrest" means any detention or restriction on removal of a ship as a conservatory measure by order of a Court to secure a maritime claim, but does not include the seizure of a ship in execution or satisfaction of a judgment, arbitral award or other enforceable instrument.

II.48 The requirement that the ship should be physically within the jurisdiction of the State in which the (order of) arrest is made was in reality not part of the definition of arrest

1. See the Report of the CMI on this provision in Appendix III, p. 426.
2. Appendix III, pp. 426 and 427.
3. Appendix III, pp. 427 and 428.
4. Appendix III, p. 427, para. 8.
5. Appendix III, p. 428, para. 19.

and the objection which was raised was correct. It is questionable, however, whether the proper place for such a provision was Article 8, rather than Article 2.[6]

II.49 There is a difference between the wording of the Lisbon Draft and that added to Article 8(1). While, in fact, in the Lisbon Draft reference is made to the State where the order is made, in Article 8(1) it is provided that the Convention applies to any ship within the jurisdiction of any State Party and Article 2(1) provides that a ship may be arrested only under the authority of a court of the State Party in which the arrest is effected.[7] The combined wording of Article 8(1) and of Article 2(1), as that of Article 4 of the 1952 Convention, is such as to permit the recognition and enforcement of a foreign order of arrest, because such recognition and enforcement comes under the description of "authority of a Court" reference to which is made in Article 2(1).

II.50 The words "restriction on removal" were added in the Lisbon Draft in order to cover situations where there is no physical detention.[8] It is not clear, however, why the word "removal" was used while in the French text of the Lisbon Draft the more appropriate word "départ" was used and is still used now in the Convention.[9]

II.51 The words "as a conservatory measure", which appeared both in the Lisbon Draft and in all JIGE Drafts, have been deleted for the reason that the word "conservatory" has not, in English, the meaning of the word "conservatoire" in French.[10] Those words, which do not exist in the 1952 Convention, had been added in order to make clear that the notion of arrest does not include actions taken in order to enforce a judgment.[11] They, however, were superfluous, for the notion of arrest is made clear both by its purpose—to secure a maritime claim—and by the express statement that it does not include seizure.

II.52 The reference to the execution of an arbitral award has been deleted because it has been considered to be superfluous, in view of the general reference, after "judgment", to "other enforceable instrument" which includes in addition to awards, instruments such as promissory notes and acknowledgements of debts that in certain jurisdictions are enforceable in the same manner as a judgment.[12]

6. CLAIMS IN RESPECT OF WHICH A SHIP MAY BE ARRESTED

(a) The closed list of maritime claims

II.53 When the problem of enumerating the maritime claims in respect of which a ship may be arrested was discussed by the CMI International Sub-Committee, prior to the

---

6. See the comments in the II Edition, at p. 163.

7. During the 8th session of JIGE it was suggested that the words "where the order has been made" could be replaced by "where the arrest is effected". The reasons for the change are summarised thus in para. 24 of the Report on the Work of the Sessional Group (Appendix III, p. 427):

> In this way, if the ship was not physically under the jurisdiction of a Court issuing an arrest order, it would nevertheless be clear that the arrest would be enforced only under the authority of the Court in the jurisdiction where the ship is physically present.

8. Appendix III, p. 426.

9. The suggestion had been made by the CMI (Appendix III, p. 428) to replace "removal" by "departure" but it was not taken into consideration.

10. The first meaning of "conservatory" is, in fact, "greenhouse for tender plants" (Oxford dictionary).

11. CMI Report, Appendix III, p. 429.

12. Proceedings of the Main Committee, Appendix III, p. 429.

Lisbon Conference, three alternative solutions were considered. The first was to maintain the solution of the 1952 Convention of a closed list, revising the existing list as far as necessary. The second was to replace the closed list with a general definition of maritime claims. The third was that of adopting a mixed approach: a general clause followed by a non-exhaustive list.[13]

II.54 The Lisbon Conference adopted the third solution. It was, in fact, considered that a closed list would not be exhaustive, as certain maritime claims could, even unintentionally, be omitted and those listed could be described in such a manner as to leave some uncertainty as to the precise nature of the claim in question. Furthermore, technical and commercial developments might give rise to new claims of a maritime nature. It was also considered that a non-exhaustive list could be useful first because the traditional maritime claims would be expressly mentioned, thus avoiding in respect of such claims any problem of interpretation of the general definition and, secondly, because it would assist the interpreter in the identification of maritime claims not expressly mentioned. For this purpose the words "including but not restricted to", which originally ended the general clause, were replaced by the Lisbon Conference with "such as".[14] The consequence of this approach would have been that any claim falling within the general definition would be deemed to be a maritime claim, whether included in the list or not. The words "such as", which precede the list, introduce an element of *ejusdem generis*. The effect of these words should have been that in case of doubt as to whether a claim falls within the definition, the claims specifically listed should serve as a guidance.

II.55 The view expressed by Lord Brandon in *Samick Lines Co. Ltd.* v. *Owners of the Ship "Antonis P. Lemos"*[15] was taken into consideration and the word "concerning" was added in preference to "arising out of". The general clause in Article 1(1) of the Lisbon Draft was worded as follows:

1. "Maritime claim" means any claim concerning or arising out of the ownership, construction, possession, management, operation or trading of any ship, or out of a mortgage or a "hypothèque" or a charge of the same nature on any ship, or out of salvage operations relating to any ship, such as any claim in respect of:

II.56 The solution adopted by the CMI at Lisbon was approved during the seventh session of JIGE by a large majority of the delegations. The only amendment which was made to the general clause (or "*chapeau*") was the addition of the word "registrable" prior to "charge of the same nature".[16]

II.57 Some delegations objected to the replacement of the closed list by an open-ended list, but the large majority of the delegations confirmed their preference for the open list and the retention of the words "such as" at the end of the "*chapeau*".[17]

II.58 At the Diplomatic Conference the position surprisingly appeared to be the opposite: the majority in fact supported the closed list approach, mainly on the ground that an open list would have defeated the purpose of uniformity since it would have granted to the courts of the States Parties too great a discretion in establishing which claims not

13. Report of the Chairman of the International Sub-Committee, Appendix III, p. 389.
14. Report of the CMI, Appendix III, p. 389.
15. [1985] 1 Lloyd's Rep. 283.
16. Appendix III, p. 390.
17. Report on the Work of the Sessional Group, paras. 11 and 12, Appendix III, p. 390.

specifically listed are maritime claims.[18] It was appreciated that new technological developments could in the future give rise to new types of maritime claims and it was suggested to take care of this problem by providing a mechanism for the amendment of the list.

II.59 An attempt was made to find a compromise between the majority in favour of the closed list and the minority in favour of the open list by suggesting to add at the end of the list the general description of maritime claims contained in the chapeau[19] or a reference to other claims of a similar nature of those previously listed, but it failed. At the end, however, the idea behind such proposal was accepted, but only in respect of environmental claims, by adding at the end of subparagraph (d) the words "and damage, costs, or loss of a similar nature to those identified in this subparagraph (d)".[20]

(b) The individual maritime claims

(a) Loss or damage caused by the operation of the ship

II.60 In the Lisbon Draft the description of this maritime claim appearing in the 1952 Convention had been left unaltered. When the JIGE decided to make all changes necessary in order to bring the draft in line with the 1993 MLM, the following wording was suggested[21]:

(a) physical loss or damage caused by the operation of the vessel other than loss of or damage to cargo, containers and passengers' effects carried on the vessel; (1993 MLM Convention, article 4(1)(e)).

II.61 This wording was subsequently amended by deleting the word "physical" before "loss" and the words "other than loss of or damage to cargo, containers and passengers effects carried on the ship" because the loss in respect of which a maritime claim should exist is not only physical[22] and claims in respect of loss of or damage to cargo and passengers effects are specifically mentioned amongst the maritime claims. Although probably the claims covered by this subparagraph are only tort claims, the definition is certainly very wide; much wider than the corresponding definition under the 1952 Convention.

(b) Loss of life or personal injury occurring, whether on land or on water, in direct connection with the operation of the ship

II.62 The suggestion was made at the Conference to delete this subparagraph on the ground that it was superfluous in view of the very wide wording of subparagraph (a) but it was pointed out that it was required, for the sake of clarity, since a maritime lien is granted in respect of the claims listed thereunder by the 1993 Convention (Article 4(1)(b)).[23] The word "direct" did not appear in the corresponding provision of the 1952 Convention. However, since then a closer connection between the event and the operation of the ship was considered necessary in the 1976 LLMC Convention (Article 2(1)(a))

18. See Appendix III, pp. 393 and 394.
19. Appendix III, p. 394.
20. See the summary of the debates during the second reading, Appendix III, p. 394.
21. Appendix III, pp. 396 and 397.
22. See the summary of the proceedings of the Main Committee, Appendix III, p. 398.
23. Appendix III, p. 398.

and then in the 1993 MLM Convention and co-ordination with such Conventions in this respect was advisable.

(c) Salvage operations or any salvage agreement including, if applicable, special compensation relating to salvage operations in respect of a ship which by itself or its cargo threatened damage to the environment

II.63 Reference to "salvage operations" instead of "salvage" as in the 1952 Convention is due to the fact that this is the terminology used in the 1989 Salvage Convention. Reference to "salvage agreements" is due to the fact that salvage agreements may give rise to claims which are not based on salvage operations actually performed.[24] The words "including, if applicable, special compensation relating to salvage operations in respect of a ship which by itself or its cargo threatened damage to the environment" have been added during the Diplomatic Conference. It was in fact pointed out[25] that the expenses recoverable under Article 14 of the 1989 Salvage Convention may include expenses simply related to the salvage operations and could fall in a gap between salvage operations and salvage agreement and that, therefore, an express reference to the special compensation was required. The reference to Article 14 of the 1989 Salvage Convention was replaced by a description of the principle underlying Article 14, in view of the principle that reference to other conventions should be avoided.[26]

(d) Damage or threat of damage caused by the ship to the environment, coastline or related interests; measures taken to prevent, minimise, or remove such damage; compensation for such damage; costs of reasonable measures of reinstatement of the environment actually undertaken or to be undertaken; loss incurred or likely to be incurred by third parties in connection with such damage; and damage, costs, or loss of a similar nature to those identified in this subparagraph (d)

II.64 This subparagraph did not exist in the 1952 Convention. It was added into the Lisbon Draft in order to cover claims in respect of preventive measures to avoid pollution damage.

II.65 The description of environmental claims, which in the CMI Lisbon Draft was limited to the removal or attempted removal of a threat of damage and to preventive measures,[27] had been expanded by the JIGE so to include also losses incurred, or likely to be incurred, by third parties.[28] Proposals were made during the Diplomatic Conference with a view to expanding further the description of environmental damage and finally a consensus was reached on the text proposed by the United States delegation,[29] consisting

---

24. *The "Hassel"* [1959] 2 Lloyd's Rep. 82. See also *The "Unique Mariner"* [1978] 1 Lloyd's Rep. 438.
25. This was a proposal of the United Kingdom delegation. See Appendix III, p. 400.
26. This was a proposal of the United States delegation. See Appendix III, pp. 400 and 401.
27. The text of this maritime claim in the Lisbon Draft and in the 1994 JIGE Draft (Appendix III, p. 401) was the following:
    (d) liability to pay compensation or other remuneration in respect of the removal or attempted removal of a threat of damage, or of preventive measures or similar operations, whether or not arising under any international convention, or any enactment or agreement.
28. See Appendix III, p. 401.
29. Appendix III, p. 404.

in the addition to the JIGE draft of the specific reference to occurrences described in other conventions as follows:

(i) *"damage or threat of damage caused by the ship to the environment,*[30] *coastline or related interest"*: that text is derived from UNCLOS Article 211(1) except that in UNCLOS reference is made to the "marine environment" but the word "marine", existing in the US proposal, was deleted on the ground that, even though reference to marine environment was made in UNCLOS, no similar reference existed in other private law conventions, such as the CLC 1969.[31] The suggestion to delete the words "coastline and related interest"[32] on the ground that the word "environment" covers also the coastline was not supported because, it was said,[33] there are damages, such as those to fisheries or hotel interest, that are different from simply environmental damages.[34]

(ii) *"measures taken to prevent, minimize or remove such damage"*: this wording is based on the definition of "preventive measures" in Article 1(7) of the CLC 1969;

(iii) *"compensation for such damage"*: "such damage" is that referred to in the previous two sentences;

(iv) *"costs of reasonable measures of reinstatement of the environment actually undertaken or to be undertaken"*: this wording is taken from the definition of pollution damage as amended by Article 2(1) of the 1992 Protocol to the CLC;

(v) *"losses incurred or likely to be incurred by third parties in connection with such damage"*: this wording existed in the JIGE text; the reference to third parties was questioned by the CMI[35] but the US delegate stated that such reference should be retained since it refers to other interests which are damaged, such as fisheries, shellfish, shoreline.[36]

(vi) *"damage, costs, or loss of a similar nature to those identified in this subparagraph (d)"*: as previously indicated, the concept of "opening" the list in order to cover possible future new types of claim was accepted by the Conference only in relation to claims for environmental damage.

II.66 The wording adopted is not very clear. Although the claims listed in (ii)–(vi) are intended to be specific categories of the claims listed under (i), and, therefore, must be related to a "damage or threat of damage caused by the ship to the environment", such link does not always appear and, when it appears, is not stated in full. This is the case for the claims listed under (ii), (iii) and (v), in respect of which reference is made to "such damage", while under (i) reference is made to "damage or threat of damage". The question arises, therefore, whether a threat of damage is relevant in respect of the

---

30. While in sub-paragraph (c) the word used in the French text for "environment" is "environnement" the word used in sub-paragraph (d) is "milieu".

31. Proposal of the delegation from Japan, supported by the delegation from the United Kingdom, and Canada, as well as other delegations: Appendix III, pp. 404 and 405.

32. The suggestion was made by the delegate from the Russian Federation, supported by the delegates from Latvia and Tunisia: Appendix III, pp. 406 and 407.

33. Comments of the US delegate, Appendix III, p. 408.

34. Comments of the UK delegate, Appendix III, p. 408.

35. Appendix III, pp. 403 and 404.

36. Appendix III, p. 407.

occurrences described under (ii), (iii) and (v). As respect those under (ii)—measures taken to prevent, minimise or remove such damage—it is certain that such measures may also be taken to prevent, minimise or remove a threat of damage and that also the cost of such measures is a maritime claim. Doubts may instead arise as to whether a threat of damage is relevant in respect of the claims under (iii)—"compensation for such damage": can a compensation be envisaged for a threat of damage? A threat of damage can cause a loss, but probably such situation would come under (v)—"losses incurred or likely to be incurred by third parties". In fact such losses can be incurred also in case where there is not an actual damage: for example, a threat of environmental damage can discourage customers to visit a sea resort. Also under (vi), which "opens" the list of this type of maritime claims, reference is only made to "damage": was it intended to exclude "threat of damage"? It is thought that the omission was not intentional.

II.67 A different category of omissions, is that relating to the link of the damage or threat of damage with the ship. Such link, which is clearly set out under (i), appears also under (ii), (iii) and (v) where the words "such damage" are used; in fact "such damage" is a damage described under (i), viz. a damage caused by the ship. It does not appear under (iv) and (vi). There is no doubt, however, that the reinstatement of the environment must be the consequence of a damage caused to it by the ship and that the damage, costs, or loss of a similar nature must all be caused by the ship.

(e) Costs or expenses relating to the raising, removal, recovery, destruction or the rendering harmless of a ship which is sunk, wrecked, stranded or abandoned, including anything that is or has been on board such ship, and costs or expenses relating to the preservation of an abandoned ship and maintenance of its crew

II.68 This subparagraph, too, was added at Lisbon in consideration of the fact that in the Draft Revision of the Maritime Liens and Mortgages Convention a maritime lien was provided (Article 4(1)(v)) in respect of wreck removal. It was felt advisable to refer expressly to the cargo laden in a sunken ship, for cargo may be removed irrespective of the removal of the ship and whether or not it is still inside the ship. In the 1993 MLM Convention wreck removal is no longer included in the list of maritime liens but, to the extent that the removal is effected by a public authority in the interest of safe navigation or the protection of the marine environment, the costs of such removal are paid out of the proceeds of sale before all other claims secured by a maritime lien on the vessel (Article 12(4)). Within the above limits, therefore, the costs of the removal had to be qualified as a maritime claim. It appeared, however, reasonable to qualify all costs of removal as a maritime claim, irrespective of their priority in the distribution of the proceeds of sale.

II.69 The suggestion made by the CMI to use the same wording of Article 2(1)(d) of the 1976 LLMC Convention was accepted by the Conference except that the word "recovery" was added. It must be noted, however, that now in this subparagraph mention of an "abandoned ship" is made twice: first in connection with costs or expenses relating to the raising, removal, destruction or the rendering harmless of an abandoned ship and, secondly, in connection with a quite opposite action, that of the preservation of such ship. The concept of abandonment is not the same in all cases: in the first case the "abandoned ship" is the ship abandoned by the crew which, therefore, may become a danger to other ships; in the second case the same conclusion cannot hold, since reference is also made to the maintenance of the crew of the abandoned ship. It follows that this time the intention is to refer to a ship abandoned by its owners. In fact, in connection with subparagraph (d) it had been suggested by some delegations that mention ought also to be made of the claims relating to costs incurred for the preservation of a ship abandoned by its owners[37] and the addition at the Diplomatic Conference by the Working Group on Articles 1 and 3 of the last phrase reading "and costs or expenses relating to the preservation of an abandoned ship and maintenance of its crew" was made in order to implement such suggestion.

(f) Any agreement relating to the use or hire of the ship, whether contained in a charterparty or otherwise

II.70 This subparagraph corresponds to subparagraph (d) of the 1952 Convention. The only change, which originates from the Lisbon Draft, is that the charter party is not referred to as the type of contract, but as the document of the contract. The words "agreement . . . whether by charterparty or otherwise" have in fact been replaced by "agreement . . . whether contained in a charterparty or otherwise".

II.71 In the comment on the provision of the 1952 Convention[38] the view was expressed that the word "hire" in the context of this subparagraph probably covered only bareboat charters, for time charters were covered by the subsequent subparagraph (e). This view seems also to be correct with respect to the present wording. The purpose of subparagraph (f) is to cover any agreement relating to the use of a ship the purpose of which is not the carriage of goods, for any agreement relating to the carriage of goods is covered by the subsequent subparagraph (g).

(g) Any agreement relating to the carriage of goods or passengers on board the ship, whether contained in a charterparty or otherwise

II.72 The same change as in the preceding subparagraph was made in the subparagraph now under consideration. Moreover, the reference to the agreements relating to the carriage of passengers has been added. The words "or otherwise" include, for the carriage of goods, bills of lading and sea waybills and, for the carriage of passengers, tickets or similar documents issued to the individual passenger.

II.73 The claims covered by this subparagraph are claims in respect of breach of contract, but probably do not include claims for loss of or damage to cargo or luggage, which are covered by the following subparagraph (h), nor loss of life of or personal injury to passengers, which are covered by subparagraph (b).

(h) Loss of or damage to or in connection with goods (including luggage) carried on board the ship

II.74 The wording of this subparagraph differs slightly from that of the corresponding provision (subparagraph (f)) of the 1952 Convention. The words "loss or damage to goods" have been replaced by "loss of or damage to or in connection with goods". The loss in connection with goods may consist, for example, in economic loss and damage for

---

37. Appendix III, p. 411.
38. *Supra*, Book I, para. I.332–I.337.

delay. The word "baggage" has been replaced by "luggage" and, therefore, the question raised in connection with the meaning of "baggage"[39] is overcome.

(i) General average

II.75 In the 1952 Convention this subparagraph (lettered (i)), which has been left unaltered, was preceded by a subparagraph (h) in which reference was made to claims in respect of bottomry, which has been deleted, for bottomry has not been used for a long time.

(j) Towage

II.76 No change has been made as respects the 1952 Convention, in which this maritime claim is listed in Article 1(1)(i).[40]

(k) Pilotage

II.77 Pilotage was already mentioned in the 1952 Convention under subparagraph (j).[41]

(l) Goods, materials, provisions, bunkers, equipment (including containers) supplied or services rendered to the ship for its operation, management, preservation or maintenance

II.78 In the comment on the corresponding provision of the 1952 Convention[42] it was stated that the word "supplied" does not necessarily refer to a sale, but may also include supply by way of hire and, therefore, may include the lease of containers. The new wording of this maritime claim now expressly refers to containers and, therefore, all problems of interpretation are overcome. It was, however, pointed out that the containers should be intended for a particular ship as was held by Lord Brandon in *The "River Rima"*.[43] The fact that in the new text the words "supplied . . . to the ship for its operation and maintenance" have not been changed supports that view.

II.79 The addition of the words "provisions, bunkers, equipment (including containers) supplied or services rendered" to the words "goods or materials" considerably expands the scope of this subparagraph so as to include not only all kinds of supplies but, also, services which differ from those expressly mentioned in other subparagraphs of Article 1(1),[44] such as mooring, fireguard, surveys by classification societies and other surveyors, etc. Also the purpose of the supplies and of the services has been widened by the reference to the preservation and management of the ship, in addition to the operation and maintenance. The addition of the word "preservation" has been suggested because in

---

39. *Supra*, Book I, para. I.350.
40. *Supra*, Book I, para. I.354.
41. *Supra*, Book I, para. I.355.
42. *Supra*, Book I, para. I.358.
43. [1988] 2 Lloyd's Rep. 193 at p. 197.
44. Salvage operations (subparagraph (c)); raising, removal, recovery, destruction or the rendering harmless of a ship etc. (subparagraph (e)); towage (subparagraph (j)); pilotage (subparagraph (k)); construction, reconstruction, repair, converting or equipping of the ship (subparagraph (m)).

the 1926 MLM Convention (Article 2 no. 5), which is still in force in several maritime States, a maritime lien is granted in respect of claims resulting from contracts entered into or acts done by the master for the preservation of the ship.

(m) Construction, reconstruction, repair, converting or equipping of the ship

II.80 The changes as respects the corresponding provision of the 1952 Convention (subparagraph (l)) consist in the addition of the reference to the reconstruction and converting of a ship and the deletion of the reference to "dock charges and dues".

II.81 In the Lisbon Draft the word "converting" had been added while in the Draft MLM Convention a right of retention was permitted to secure claims for repair, including reconstruction.

II.82 The reason why the word "converting" was mentioned in the Draft Arrest Convention while the word "reconstruction" was mentioned in the draft MLM Convention is not clear. These different words, however, continued to be used in the JIGE Draft and in the 1993 MLM Convention respectively. The CMI drew the attention of the Conference on this difference, suggesting the use of both words since "converting" and "reconstruction", are not the same thing and this suggestion was adopted.[45]

II.83 The words "dock charges and dues" have been moved from this subparagraph to the new subparagraph (n), in which reference is also made to port, canal and other waterways dues.

(n) Port, canal, dock, harbour and other waterway dues and charges

II.84 This subparagraph was added at Lisbon in consequence of a maritime lien having been recognised in respect of port, canal and other waterway dues in Article 4(1)(ii) of the Draft Revision of the MLM Convention.[46] As previously indicated, claims in respect of dock charges and dues are not new maritime claims since they were previously mentioned in subparagraph (l) of the 1952 Convention. To dock charges and dues there have been added harbour charges and dues for the reason that they are claims of the same nature and the omission of a reference to port could have been considered to be intentional.[47]

(o) Wages and other sums due to the master, officers and other members of the ship's complement in respect of their employment on the ship, including costs of repatriation and social insurance contributions payable on their behalf

II.85 The wording of the corresponding subparagraph of the 1952 Convention (subparagraph (m)) was amended at Lisbon in order to bring it into line (although not completely) with the wording of the Draft Revision of the MLM Convention (Article 4(1)(i)). At the seventh session of the JIGE the text adopted at Lisbon was amended so as to reproduce verbatim the provision of the 1993 MLM Convention.[48]

---

45. Appendix III, p. 415.
46. The provision has been left unaltered in the 1993 MLM Convention and is now set out in Art. 4(1)(d).
47. Ninth Session of JIGE and Diplomatic Conference—Proceedings of the Main Committee, Appendix III, p. 417.
48. Appendix III, p. 418.

II.86 The wording adopted in the Lisbon Draft of the MLM Convention and in the 1993 MLM Convention with respect to social insurance contributions was the effect of the decision to exclude a maritime lien for claims of the insurers.[49] The proposal of the CMI to qualify generally claims for social insurance contributions as maritime claims, thus including also claims of the social insurance institutions,[50] was not accepted by the Conference. It is thought, however, that such claims come under subparagraph (q) where reference is made to insurance premiums in respect of the ship.

(p) Disbursements incurred on behalf of the ship or its owners

II.87 The substance of the corresponding subparagraph (subparagraph (n)) of the 1952 Convention has not changed, but the rather loose language of the Convention has been corrected, following the suggestion of the CMI,[51] by replacing the words "master's disbursements, including disbursements made by shippers, charterers or agents etc." with the words "disbursements incurred on behalf of the ship or its owner". In fact, the wording of the 1952 Convention is at the same time too wide and too narrow. It is too wide because disbursements made by shippers may not relate to the operation of the ship and if they do not, they are not maritime claims. It is too narrow because there are disbursements incurred on behalf of the ship that are not incurred by charterers or agents and because the disbursements incurred by charterers and agents are not "included" in those incurred by the master.

(q) Insurance premiums (including mutual insurance calls) in respect of the ship, payable by or on behalf of the shipowner or demise charterer

II.88 This subparagraph was added at Lisbon and fills a gap in the 1952 Convention, since claims for insurance premiums (and mutual insurance calls) are clearly maritime claims.[52] The text adopted at Lisbon was left unaltered by JIGE and by the Conference.

II.89 Two questions arise in respect of this head of claim: firstly, which kinds of insurance may give rise to claims for premiums covered by this subparagraph; secondly, against whom the claim must arise.

II.90 The notion of premium is very wide, since it includes also mutual insurance calls and, therefore, the manner in which the premium is calculated is irrelevant. The premium must, however, be related to the ship the arrest of which is requested.

II.91 Such relationship, which is expressed by the words "insurance premiums ... in respect of the ship" does not need to be physical, in the sense that the insurance must

49. The following statement was made in the CMI Report, Lisboa II, 80 at p. 96:
    The question whether a maritime lien should be granted to secure claims for social insurance contributions, which had already been discussed within the International Sub-Committee without a clear majority emerging from the discussion, was the object of a further debate. The issue was whether a maritime lien should be granted to all claims for social insurance contributions, whether the claimants were members of the crew or the insurers, or only to claims of the master and crew. The proposal to restrict the maritime lien to claims of the master and crew made by the UK Delegation was adopted with a large majority (26 votes in favour, 4 against and 1 abstention).
50. See Appendix III, p. 418.
51. See Appendix III, pp. 419 and 420.
52. See *supra*, Book I, para. I.308.

cover loss of or damage to the ship, but includes any insurance connected with the operation of the ship. If this were not the case, all types of mutual insurance, which basically cover third party liability, would not be included, while express reference is made in subparagraph (q) to mutual insurance calls. Such interpretation of the words "in respect of the ship" is supported by the fact that these words are also used in subparagraph (r) in respect of commissions, brokerages and agency fees which obviously relate to the operation of the ship. Therefore, all kinds of protection and indemnity cover are included, such as liabilities in respect of passengers, seamen and third parties, damage to property, liability for pollution, wreck liabilities, etc.

II.92 There are then other types of insurances that are related to the operation of the ship, even though they do not cover loss of or damage to the ship or liabilities arising out of the operation of the ship, such as the loss of hire insurance, the defence and all forms of social insurance of the crew, all of which come under this subparagraph (q).

II.93 The premiums (or mutual insurance calls) must be "payable by or on behalf of the shipowner or the demise charterer". The claim must, therefore, be against the person who operates the ship, be he the owner of the ship or the charterer by demise. Therefore, premiums paid by brokers or mortgagees on behalf of the shipowner are included, while premiums paid by mortgagees in respect of the mortgagee's interest insurance are not included. Nor are premiums payable by or on behalf of other charterers.[53]

II.94 The arrest of a ship in respect of such claims for premiums payable by or on behalf of the demise charterer is permitted only when the condition imposed by Article 3(3) is met, namely when under the law of the State where the arrest is sought a judgment in respect of that claim can be enforced against the ship by judicial or forced sale of that ship.

(r) Any commissions, brokerages or agency fees payable in respect of the ship by or on behalf of the shipowner or demise charterer

II.95 This subparagraph was also added at Lisbon, for, as with insurance premiums, claims for commissions, brokerages and agency fees are clearly maritime claims. The questions considered in respect of subparagraph (q) arise also in respect of sub-paragraph (r): the words "in respect of the ship" must clearly be interpreted as referring to the operation of the ship generally. Therefore, commissions and brokerages may be due in relation to insurance contracts, contracts for the use or hire of a ship, contracts of carriage of cargo or passengers, towage contracts, salvage contracts, shipbuilding and ship repair contracts, contracts for the supply of materials, provisions, bunkers, equipment or services and this list is almost certainly not exhaustive.

II.96 Agency fees may be due in respect of the call of the ship at any port, for services rendered in connection with the arrival and departure of the ship, such as requesting a berth to the port authority, entering into contracts for the towage, pilotage and mooring of the ship, filing documents with the custom authority, entering into contracts for the supply of bunker and provisions or for repairs, etc. As for insurance premiums, when commissions, brokerages or agency fees are due by the charterer by demise, arrest is permissible only when the condition set out in Article 3(3) is met.

---

53. See the request for clarification of the delegate from Australia and the reply of the observer from the CMI, Appendix III, p. 421.

(s) Any dispute as to ownership or possession of the ship

II.97 The unsatisfactory wording of subparagraph (o) of the 1952 Convention, in which reference is made to disputes as to the title or ownership of the ship, thus repeating twice the same concept, while reference to disputes as to possession is only made in the subsequent subparagraph, has been cured by deleting the reference to disputes as to title and adding those as to possession.

(t) Any dispute between co-owners of the ship as to the employment or earnings of the ship

II.98 The reference to disputes about possession, which existed in the corresponding provision of the 1952 Convention (subparagraph (p)), was correctly deleted. However, the description of the disputes between co-owners of a ship is not complete, for there may also be other disputes, such as those relating to the sale or the mortgage of the ship which are probably more likely to justify the arrest[54] than disputes as to the employment or earnings.

(u) A mortgage or a "hypothèque" or a charge of the same nature on the ship

II.99 Mortgages and hypothèques (and now charges) are included in the list not as much in consideration of the nature of the claim secured thereby (which may not necessarily be maritime), but rather in consideration of the nature of the security. The holder of the security, though he normally may enforce it by means of the seizure and forced sale of the ship, needs sometimes to make recourse to a provisional measure such as the arrest in order to prevent the sailing of the ship and gain time for the subsequent seizure. In the Draft Convention submitted by the JIGE to the Diplomatic Conference reference was made to registered mortgage and registered "hypothèque"[55] and, as in Article 1(1), to registrable charges. The CMI in its Position Paper had pointed out that it was not correct to refer to *registered* mortgages and "hypothèques" and to *registrable* charges, thereby indicating that only claims related to registered mortgages and "hypothèques" are maritime claims whilst for other charges it is sufficient that they may be registrable but do not need actually to be registered. The CMI therefore suggested to replace the word "registrable" in respect of charges with "registered". The Conference agreed that the difference was not justified, but decided to delete any reference to registration in order to extend this maritime claim so to include also equitable mortgages.[56] The effect of the deletion is clearly wider, since now also claims arising out of a "hypothèque" prior to its registration are included, as well as all claims arising out of a charge of the same nature.

---

54. The co-owners may not agree on the right of one of them to mortgage his share in the ship or on the mortgage of the whole of the ship. These matters are specifically regulated in certain jurisdictions. For example, in Italy Art. 263 CN provides that a co-owner may not hypothecate his share in the ship without the consent of the majority of the co-owners and Art. 262 CN provides that the resolution to hypothecate the whole ship must be approved by a majority holding 16 shares (*carati*) out of 24, i.e. by a two thirds majority. In France each co-owner may hypothecate his share (Art. 24 of Décret 68–845 of 24 September 1968), but the whole ship may be hypothecated by the manager with the consent of the co-owners who represent 75% of the value of the ship (Art. 25 of Décret 68–845). In Argentina a ship in co-ownership may be hypothecated as security for debts incurred in the common interest by a resolution of a two-thirds majority (Art. 500 of Ley de Navegacion).
55. The CMI Draft instead made no reference to registration.
56. See Appendix III, pp. 423 and 424.

II.100 The word "registrable" (charge) had been used in order to adopt the same language of the 1993 MLM Convention, in which it had the purpose to include charges of a nature similar to the mortgage and the "hypothèque" which, however, are named differently in certain legal systems; provided they are registrable as mortgages and "hypothèques" are. The deletion of the word "registrable", however, does not entail any change of substance in the type of charges in respect of which arrest of a ship is permissible, since such charges must have the "same nature" of mortgages and "hypothèques".

(v) Any dispute arising out of a contract for the sale of the ship

II.101 This subparagraph was added at Lisbon because it was agreed that claims arising out of the sale of a ship are maritime claims. The claimant may be the seller, if after possession of the ship has been transferred to the buyer (even if title has not passed yet to the buyer) the buyer is in breach of his obligations, which will mainly consist in the payment of the purchase price. The claimant may also be the buyer, if the seller has failed to transfer possession of or title to the ship to the buyer or defects have appeared for which the seller is responsible. The claim must arise out of a contract of sale and, therefore, claims in respect of pre-contractual damages are not maritime claims.

CHAPTER 4

Ships that may be Arrested

7. THE SHIP IN RESPECT OF WHICH THE MARITIME CLAIM IS ASSERTED

II.102 In all previous drafts, commencing from the CMI Lisbon Draft, it was first provided that a ship may be arrested (a) in respect of a claim secured by a maritime lien, (b) in respect of a claim based upon a mortgage or a hypothèque or a charge of the same nature, and (c) in respect of a claim related to ownership or possession of the ship and then that a ship may be arrested in respect of (maritime) claims other than those listed under (a), (b) and (c) above if the owner or the bareboat charterer of the ship is personally liable.

II.103 Prior to the Diplomatic Conference the CMI in its Position Paper had pointed out that it would have been more logical to set out first (a) the basic rule, according to which a ship may be arrested if the claim is against the person who owned the ship when the claim arose and is still the owner when the arrest is effected, and then the exceptions arranged in the following order:

    (b) arrest of a ship when the claim is against the demise charterer;

    (c) arrest of a ship when the claim is based upon a mortgage or a hypothèque or a charge of the same nature;

    (d) arrest of a ship when the claim is related to ownership or possession;

    (e) arrest of a ship when the claim is secured by a maritime lien.

II.104 The proposal of the CMI has been accepted by the Diplomatic Conference[1] and paragraph 1 of Article 3 has been arranged as suggested by the CMI. Each of the situations covered therein will be examined below.

(a) Claim against the owner of the ship

II.105 Article 3(1) of the 1952 Convention provides that a claimant may arrest the particular ship in respect of which the maritime claim arose, but does not expressly state that the owner of the ship must be personally liable in respect of that claim and must still be the owner of the ship when the arrest is effected. This omission[2] has been remedied by

---

1. See the proposal of the CMI in Appendix III, p. 459 and its introduction by the observer from the CMI at the Diplomatic Conference. See also the ensuing debate in Appendix III, pp. 460–472.
2. See the comments made in respect of Art. 3(1) of the 1952 Convention *supra*, Book I, section 19, para. I.382–I.406.

Article 3(1) of the 1999 Convention. Article 3(1)(a) provides in fact that arrest is permissible of any ship in respect of which a maritime claim is asserted if the person who owned the ship at the time when the maritime claim arose is liable for the claim and is owner of the ship when the arrest is effected.

II.106 The proposal had been made by Canada to replace the words "when the arrest is effected" by "when action is commenced" in order to prevent a last minute change in the ownership between the time when action is commenced and that when arrest is effected. It was however pointed out by the observer from the CMI that such change could adversely affect the interest of a *bona fide* buyer who is unaware of the commencement of an action by a claimant.[3] The view of the observer from the CMI was supported by the majority of the delegations, and the Canadian proposal was not adopted.[4]

II.107 This provision, however, does not clarify the problems discussed in respect of the 1952 Convention regarding the manner in which priority between the sale of the ship and the arrest must be established. The comments made in respect of the 1952 Convention and the analysis of the rules applicable in some States parties to the 1952 Convention apply also in respect of the 1999 Convention, both as regards the need for the registration of the sale and the need for the registration of the arrest.[5]

(b) Claim against the charterer by demise

II.108 After it had been decided at the Lisbon Conference that only claims against the demise charterer, the manager or operator of the ship,[6] are secured by a maritime lien, the question of the arrest of a ship in respect of claims not secured by a maritime lien was automatically confined to the claims against the demise charterer. The view then prevailed that it would not be reasonable to permit the arrest of a demise chartered ship in respect of such claims if the judgment that the claimant would obtain could not be enforced against the ship or against the security given in order to release the ship from arrest. It was, therefore, agreed that arrest should be permissible only if, under the law of the State where the arrest is sought, a judgment in respect of the claim against the demise charterer could be enforced against the chartered ship. It was also agreed that arrest should be permissible only when the demise charterer is still the demise charterer or the owner of the ship when the arrest was effected.

II.109 These provisions were adopted by the JIGE and then by the Diplomatic Conference and, as in the previous draft, are contained in two separate paragraphs. The rule whereby arrest is permissible of a ship in respect of a claim against the charterer by demise is set out in paragraph 1(b) of Article 3 and, as in the Lisbon Draft, it provides that the demise charterer at the time when the maritime claim arose who is liable for the claim, must still be the demise charterer of the ship when the arrest is affected, the only exception being that of the demise charterer having become the owner of the ship. In the CMI Report on the Lisbon Draft the following statement is made in respect of this provision, which

---

3. See for the introduction of the Canadian proposal and the remarks of the observer from the CMI, Appendix III, p. 460.
4. See for the ensuing debate Appendix III, p. 461.
5. *Supra*, Book I, para. I.412–I.417.
6. See the comments on Art. 3(4) of the 1952 Convention in the Report of the Chairman of the CMI International Sub-Committee to the Lisbon Conference, Appendix III, p. 450.

was at that time contained in paragraph 1(d) of Article 3, jointly with the provision relating to the arrest of a ship in respect of a claim against the owner:[7]

Paragraph (1)(d) of article 3 provides for the permissibility of arrest if either the owner or the bareboat charterer is liable for the claim. However, a *droit de suite* is not permitted. Arrest is only possible if the owner is still owner when arrest is effected or if the bareboat charterer is still bareboat charterer or has become owner when the arrest is effected.

II.110 The reason why arrest is permissible only if the demise charterer is still the demise charterer at the time of arrest appears, therefore, to be the same for which arrest in respect of a claim against the owner is only permissible if the owner is still the owner at the time of arrest and such reason is the denial of a *droit de suite* in cases where the claim is not secured by a maritime lien.

II.111 The explanation which was given, which is correct in respect of claims against the owner, does not seem to be equally correct in respect of claims against the demise charterer, because in that case a *droit de suite* is not conceivable. If, for example, a claim against the demise charterer is secured by a maritime lien, the *droit de suite* would materialise in the right to follow the ship into the hands of a new owner, and the fact whether the ship is still chartered by the same charterer or not would be immaterial.

II.112 It is thought, therefore, that it would probably have been preferable to require that, as for claims against the owner, arrest in respect of claims against the demise charterer had been made conditional to the ship being still owned at the time of arrest by the person who owned the ship when the claim arose. The practical difference between this hypothetical provision and that existing in Article 3(1)(b) is, however, minimal, since normally if the demise charterer is still the same, the owner is, except in the rare case of the transfer of the contract in case of sale, always the same.

II.113 The exceptional (though limited) character of this provision is evidenced by the maintenance in the 1999 Convention of the rule, set out in Article 9 of the 1952 Convention,[8] according to which nothing in the Convention shall be construed as creating a maritime lien. In the 1952 Convention the English text of this provision differed significantly from the French text,[9] but now the two texts are identical, and the wording is simpler and clearer.

II.114 The proposal was made during the Diplomatic Conference to delete the word "demise", thereby extending the right of arrest to claims against any charterer, and thus also to claims against the time and voyage charterer.[10] The observer from the CMI pointed out, however, that arrest of a ship in respect of claims against the charterer by demise is an exception to the general rule according to which, unless the claim is secured by a maritime lien, a ship may only be arrested in respect of claims against its owner and that it would have been dangerous to widen that exception.[11] Following these observations, supported by the delegate from the United Kingdom,[12] the proposal was not adopted.

II.115 Since in the CMI draft the word "personally" (liable) which appeared in the Draft Articles had been omitted, the proposal was made to reinstate that word, whereupon, on request of the delegate from Denmark, the observer from the CMI stated that the

7. Appendix III, p. 451.
8. *Supra,* Book I, para. I.523.
9. *Supra,* Book I, para. I.517.
10. Appendix III, p. 462.
11. Appendix III, pp. 462 and 463.
12. Appendix III, p. 463.

deletion of the word "personally" did not imply any change of substance.[13] That word had in fact been inserted to mark a difference between *in rem* liability and personal liability but it was felt that it was not necessary, because if liability of a person is not qualified, it is impliedly personal liability. On the other hand the reference to personal liability could have been wrongly interpreted as excluding liability for acts or neglects of servants and agents.[14]

II.116 During the proceedings of the Main Committee the suggestion had been made to insert the word "allegedly" before "liable" in order to make clear that there is no need for the liability to be established. While initially that suggestion had been accepted, it was then decided by the Drafting Committee to delete that word, since it is clear from the definition of "claimant" in Article 1(4) that the issue of liability is not yet decided at the time of arrest.[15]

II.117 The rule whereby the arrest of a ship in respect of a claim against the demise charterer is permissible only when a judgment in respect of such claim can be enforced on such ship is contained in paragraph (3) of Article 3, but, as in the Lisbon Draft, is set out in a general way. Paragraph (3), in fact, refers generally to the arrest of a ship which is not owned by the person liable for the claim and is formulated as an exception to the provisions of paragraphs (1) and (2). The general reference to paragraph (1), therefore, makes the exception applicable not only in respect of claims against the demise charterer, but also in respect of claims secured by a maritime lien, by a mortgage, "hypothèque" or charge as well as in respect of claims relating to the ownership or possession of the ship.

II.118 The State under whose law the judgment can be enforced against the ship must necessarily be a State Party, since the Convention applies, pursuant to its Article 8(1) to the arrest of any ship within the jurisdiction of a State Party.

(c) Claim based upon a mortgage, "hypothèque" or charge

II.119 The requisite that the ship be owned by the person liable for the claim both at the time when the claim arose and at the time when the arrest is effected does not apply when the claim is based upon a mortgage, "hypothèque" or charge since any of such securities may be granted by a person who is not the debtor and all follow the ship in case of voluntary sale.

II.120 Pursuant to Article 1 of the 1993 MLM Convention registration of mortgages, "hypothèques" and charges is a condition for their recognition and enforcement in States Parties. The provision of the 1999 Arrest Convention whereby a ship may be arrested in respect of a claim arising out of any of the above securities irrespective of their registration is not in conflict with Article 1 of the 1993 MLM Convention. In fact this provision does not forbid States Parties to recognise and enforce unregistered securities, but only requires them to do so when the securities are registered.

II.121 The abolition of the requisite of registration for all the types of securities mentioned in this subparagraph will be practically ineffective in the jurisdictions where

---

13. Appendix III, p. 463.

14. See the closing remarks of the Chairman of the Main Committee, Appendix III, p. 464. See also the comments previously made by Thailand in Document 188/3, Appendix III, p. 457.

15. See the summary of the report from the Chairman of the Drafting Committee in Appendix III, p. 463.

the registration of the "hypothèque" is a condition for the very existence of the security.[16] If, in fact, the unregistered security has not yet come into existence, there is no claim based upon a "hypothèque" yet and, consequently, the arrest is not possible under the Convention.

II.122 The extended application to mortgages, "hypothèques" or charges of the provision of Article 3(3), according to which arrest is permissible only if, under the law of the State where the arrest is applied for, a judgment in respect of the claim can be enforced against the ship, does not entail that, contrary to the generally accepted rule that mortgages, "hypothèques" and charges are governed by the law of the State where the ship is registered, for the purpose of arrest they are governed by the law of the State where the arrest is made. In fact Article 3(3) only provides that the claim must be enforceable against the ship by judicial sale. As a consequence, if the court of the State of arrest applies the generally recognised rule referred to above, it will permit the enforcement of the claim if the security is valid under the law of the State where the ship is registered. The only exception to validity of that conclusion is where the mortgage is not registered. In fact, although that mortgage may be valid in the State of registration, it does not necessarily follow that it will be recognised in the State where the ship is arrested since in all international conventions on maritime liens and mortgages the obligation of contracting States to recognise foreign mortgages and "hypothèques" is limited to registered mortgages and hypothèques.[17]

II.123 It follows that if in the State where the arrest is requested an unregistered mortgage or "hypothèque" on a ship flying a foreign flag is not recognised in case it secures a claim against a person other than the owner of the ship, pursuant to Article 3(3) the ship can not be arrested.

(d) Claim relating to the ownership or possession of the ship

II.124 As respects claims relating to the ownership or possession of the ship the basic rule that the person liable for the claim must be the owner of the ship cannot apply, since in a strict sense there is no person liable, the subject matter of the claim being the ship itself and not a sum of money. It is even doubtful whether the definition of arrest (Article 1(2)) as "any detention . . . to secure a maritime claim" applies in respect of claims relating to ownership or possession, for the purpose of the arrest is not, strictly speaking, that of securing a claim, but rather of preventing the continued use of the ship by a person who allegedly is not the owner or the person entitled to the possession of the ship.

II.125 The special character of these claims, and of the arrest of the ship in respect of them, is evidenced by the fact that the right to exclude the application of the Convention in respect of claims relating to ownership or possession is granted to States Parties by

---

16. This is so, for example, in Italy and in Spain.

17. Article 1 of the 1926 MLM Convention provides that mortgages, "hypothèques" and other similar charges upon vessels duly effected in accordance with the law of the Contracting State to which the vessel belongs and registered in a public register shall be regarded as valid in all other Contracting States.

A similar, albeit more detailed, provision is contained in Article 1 of the 1967 MLM Convention, whose article 2 then provides that the ranking of registered mortgages and "hypothèques" and their effect in regard to third parties shall be determined by the law of the State of registration.

Almost identical rules are set out in Articles 1 and 2 of the 1993 MLM Convention.

Article 10(1)(c), similarly to what is provided in the 1952 Convention under Article 10.[18]

II.126 In respect of claims relating to ownership or possession the application of Article 3(3) is difficult to conceive. Firstly, there is no person liable for the claim in a strict sense. Secondly, a judgment on a claim relating to ownership or possession is not enforced by the judicial or forced sale of the ship, but by the registration of the ship in the name of the actual owner or by the transfer of possession respectively.

(e) Claim secured by a maritime lien

II.127 This has been the most controversial provision. In fact at Lisbon it had been agreed that the right to arrest a ship, irrespective of the claim being against the owner (or the bareboat charterer), should be limited to the claims secured by one of the maritime liens at that time listed in the draft of the new Convention on Maritime Liens and Mortgages, in the course of preparation and, consequently, such maritime liens were also listed in the draft Arrest Convention. The reproduction of the maritime liens was due to the desire to comply with the general principle, now adopted in all conventions, that no express reference should be made in one convention to other conventions in order to avoid that ratification of one convention be adversely affected by the reference to another convention which a State is not willing to become a party to. However it was not considered that this obstacle was not avoided by the reproduction of the maritime liens enumerated in the MLM Convention.

II.128 In fact States in which maritime liens other than the MLM Convention liens are recognised would not favourably consider the limitation of the right to arrest a ship as security for a claim against a person other than the owners of the ship to the MLM Convention liens. The restriction of the maritime liens to those enumerated in Article 4(1) of the 1993 MLM Convention had already given rise to a hot debate during the 1993 Diplomatic Conference, at which a compromise was reached on the basis of the recognition of the right of States Parties to grant other maritime liens against the owner, demise charterer, manager or operator (but against no other persons[19]) under the conditions set out in Article 6.[20] It was probably in view of this provision that the terms "international maritime liens" and "national maritime liens" came into use.

II.129 The same problem was raised during the sessions of the JIGE in which the draft Arrest Convention was considered. In fact the delegations of the States that had fought for

---

18. In respect of the 1952 Convention such reservation has been made by Costa Rica, Croatia, Italy and the Netherlands. See CMI Yearbook 1998, p. 226.

19. The 1926 MLM Convention makes reference (Article 13) to claims against the "affréteur principal" ("principal charterer"): a term of an unclear meaning. The 1967 MLM Convention provides (article 7) that the maritime liens arise whether the claims secured by such liens are against the owner or against the demise or *other* charterer, manager or operator of the ship, thereby including also claims against the time and voyage charterers.

20. Article 6 requires that "national" maritime liens shall be subject to the provisions of Articles 8, 10 and 12 of the Convention and shall be extinguished after a period of 6 months instead of 12 months and, in case of voluntary sale to a *bona fide* purchaser, at the end of a period of 60 days following the registration of the sale in accordance with the law of the State where the ship is registered. In so far as the priority aspect is concerned, such liens would rank after the registered mortgages, "hypothèques" and charges.

the permission to create "national" maritime liens in 1993 requested that reference also be made in the Arrest Convention to maritime liens recognised under the law of the State where the arrest is requested.[21]

II.130 The CMI supported this proposal and pointed out that, if it were accepted, there would be no need to list the maritime liens set out in the 1993 MLM Convention, since if the Convention has been ratified by the State where the arrest is requested and has come into force, its provisions would become part of the law of that State. The CMI therefore suggested the adoption of a very simple provision, wherein reference is only made to the maritime liens recognised by the law of the State where the arrest is requested, provided, however, the claim arises against the owner, demise charterer, manager or operator of the ship.[22] One additional reason for the deletion of the maritime liens enumerated in the 1993 MLM Convention was that the reference to such liens actually created a link with that Convention and therefore could in the future adversely affect the prospects of acceptance of the new Arrest Convention.[23] This is not inconsistent with the need for a co-ordination between the two Conventions, the purpose of which is only to ensure that all claims normally secured by maritime liens—and thus, first of all, those secured by the 1993 MLM Convention maritime liens—are included in the list of the Convention maritime claims in respect of which arrest is permitted.[24]

II.131 The proposal of the CMI was accepted, but it was requested by a large majority to replace the word "recognised" with the word "granted" since the reference to the maritime liens "recognised" under the *lex fori* would have entailed also the application of the private international law rules of the *lex fori* and thus the possible reference to maritime liens granted in other jurisdictions. Two objections were raised against the use of the word "granted". The first was that by preventing the application of the national rules of private international law the Convention would entail the obligation of States Parties to change such rules. The second was that in common law countries maritime liens are not "granted", in that they are not created by statute. In the attempt to find a compromise on the first issue the suggestion was made to add a provision to the effect that States Parties would be permitted to apply their domestic private international law rules[25] but such suggestion was not adopted. The second issue was instead solved by adding the words "or arises under" after "granted".[26]

---

21. See the proposal of the US delegation during the eighth session of the JIGE, Report – Annex I, paragraphs 45–47, Appendix III, p. 466.

22. See the CMI Position Paper, in Appendix III, p. 456 and the statement of the observer from the CMI, in Appendix III, p. 459.

23. See the statement of the observer from the CMI, Appendix III, p. 464.

24. The statement made at the Diplomatic Conference by the observer from ICS (Appendix III, p. 470) that one of the objectives of the new Arrest Convention was to align its provisions with those of the MLM Convention is, therefore, an undue extension of a much more restricted purpose.

25. The following proposal was made by the delegation of the United States (Conference document A/CONF.188/CRP.16 of 5 March 1999):

The United States offers as a compromise the following revised version of the present text of Art. 3(1)(v):

    (v) the claim is against the owner, demise charterer, manager or operator of the ship and is secured by a maritime lien which is granted or arises under the law of the State where the arrest is applied for. However, nothing in this Convention prevents any court of a State party from arresting a ship for a claim secured by a maritime lien granted or arising under foreign law.

26. This was a proposal submitted by the delegation of Norway (Conference document A/CONF.188/CRP.14 of 5 March 1999), Appendix III, p. 458. For the subsequent statement of the Norwegian delegation see Appendix III, p. 465.

II.132 Although in this case the application of the provision of Article 3(3) may be justified, it must be noted that under the 1993 MLM Convention, such claims may be enforced against a ship which is not owned by the person liable both where that person is the demise charterer, manager or operator of the ship and where the person liable was the owner of the ship when the claim arose, but is no longer the owner when the arrest is demanded. The arrest of a ship, therefore, would not be permissible in a State Party to the Arrest Convention who, however, is not a State Party to the 1993 MLM Convention and whose law does not permit the enforcement of a claim secured by the particular maritime lien the enforcement of which is sought or, in any event, does not permit the enforcement of a maritime lien on a ship which is not owned, or is no longer owned, by the person liable for the claim.

8. OTHER SHIPS OWNED BY THE PERSON LIABLE FOR THE CLAIM

II.133 Paragraph (2) regulates the arrest of what may be called sister ships in a wide sense. Two situations are covered: first, the arrest of a sister ship in a strict sense, which in the 1952 Convention is regulated by Article 3(1); secondly, the arrest of a ship owned by the person liable for the maritime claim, who, when the claim arose, was the demise charterer, time charterer or voyage charterer of the ship in respect of which the claim arose. This is an extension of the rule laid down in Article 3(4) of the 1952 Convention, in which reference was made only to ships owned by the demise charterer. The purpose of this provision is to extend the sister ship rule to cases where the person liable for the maritime claim is not the owner of the ship in respect of which the claim arose but is the owner of another ship.

9. ASSOCIATED SHIPS

II.134 In view of the evolution in several countries of the jurisprudence relating to the situations in which it is permitted to pierce the corporate veil, the CMI had deemed it convenient to recommend, in its Position Paper,[27] that is should be made clear that the Convention does not prevent the courts of States Parties to pierce the corporate veil when this is permitted by the *lex fori*.[28] The UK delegation at the Conference made a more far reaching proposal, suggesting that express provisions be included in the Convention in this respect, and that arrest be permissible of a ship not owned by the person against whom

---

27. Document No. 188/3, paragraph 142, Appendix III, p. 477.

28. The Lisbon Draft, and thus the Draft Articles, do not reproduce the provision of Article 3(2) of the 1952 Convention, according to which ships are deemed to be in the same ownership when all the shares therein are owned by the same person or persons. This provision was in fact deemed to be unnecessary while the problem of lifting the corporate veil was left to national law. The following statement is made in this respect in the CMI Report on the Lisbon Draft (Lisboa II, p. 142 and Appendix III, p. 474):

> The International Sub-Committee made an attempt to draft a rule in relation to the sistership rule permitting the lifting of the veil between several companies owning ships when those companies are owned or controlled by the same persons. The 1952 Convention contained a not very clear provision of this nature in article 3 paragraph (2). The Conference found that this problem is of a more general nature and that a solution should not be attempted with specific application in arrest situations but that the problem would have to be left to national law.

the claim has arisen when it is "controlled" by such person suggesting a number of factors relevant in order to establish the existence of such control.[29]

II.135 This proposal gave rise to a lengthy debate during the sessions of the Main Committee, both at the time of the first reading and at the time of the second reading. A relatively small number of delegations supported in principle the UK proposal[30] while the large majority of the delegations opposed to it on different grounds. Such grounds were mainly the following: (a) the question whether and in which circumstances the corporate veil can be pierced, is a question that involves general principles of corporate law and cannot be regulated in a particular maritime convention regulating a very specialised area;[31] (b) attempts to give a legislative solution to this problem at a national level had very often failed;[32] (c) piercing the corporate veil would adversely affect maritime trade and only protect the interests of certain groups;[33] (d) the growth of single ship companies is well justified and is not at all due to the intention to circumvent the sistership arrest;[34] (e) the notion of control, on which the UK proposal is based, is unclear and its application would give an unacceptable discretion to the courts;[35] (f) the adoption of the suggested rules would adversely affect crews and ship management companies.[36]

29. The delegation from the United Kingdom had suggested to replace paragraph (2) of Article 3 with the following text (Appendix III, p. 485); this text was submitted to the Main Committee at its second reading. A slightly different text had been originally proposed in Document 188/3/Add.2, paragraphs 9–17, in Appendix III, p. 475:

3(2) (a) Arrest is also permissible of any other ship which, when the arrest is effected, is:

   (i) owned by the same person who, when the maritime claim arose, was liable for the claim as owner of the ship in respect of which the claim arose,
   (ii) owned by the same person who, when the maritime claim arose, was liable for that claim as the demise charterer, time charterer or voyage charterer of the ship in respect of which the claim arose, or
   (iii) effectively controlled by a person as if that person owned the arrested ship, provided that at the time the maritime claim arose such person controlled the person who is liable for that claim.

(b) In determining whether a ship is effectively controlled by a person, a Court may take into account all relevant factors including, but not restricted to, whether that person is able to:

   (i) make decisions in respect of that ship,
   (ii) influence the implementation of those decisions, and
   (iii) direct the distribution of profits from the operations of that ship.

(c) If the ship is not owned by the person who is liable for the maritime claim, the question whether there is a connection between the person owning the ship and the person liable for the maritime claim such as to justify the arrest shall be decided in accordance with the law of the State in which the arrest is applied for.

(d) This paragraph (2) shall not apply to claims in respect of ownership or possession of a ship.

A proposal leading in the same direction had also been made by Canada who had suggested the following provision (Conference document A/CONF.188/CRP.1 of 1 March 1999—Appendix III, p. 478):

Notwithstanding the provisions of paragraphs (1) and (2) of this article, the arrest of a ship which is not owned *or beneficially owned* by the person allegedly liable for the claim shall be permissible only if, under the law of the State where the arrest is demanded, a judgment in respect of that claim can be enforced against that ship by judicial or forced sale of that ship.

30. Malta, Denmark, Finland, Norway, Sweden, Rep. of Korea.

31. Canada (who had submitted a proposal along the same lines), the Netherlands, Japan, France, Sri Lanka, Belgium, Australia, Thailand, Ghana, Philippines and, amongst the observers, CISL. Many of the delegations of the above countries, however, indicated that they had doubts about the notion of "control" stating that the problem deserved further investigation. Then some at the second reading did not support the proposal anymore.

32. Denmark, Finland, Norway, Sweden, Croatia.

33. Greece, Hong Kong, Thailand, Panama.

34. ICS, Malta.

35. ICS, Malta, Hong Kong, Mexico.

36. China, Malta, ICS.

II.136 It was probably correct that the proposal had been made at too late a stage for it to be considered and for a clear and acceptable solution to be found. However no attempt was made in that direction, and the suggestion to investigate the possibility of defining in a satisfactory manner the notion of "control"[37] was ignored. It was also correct that the problem of the corporate identity and of the situations in which it can be set aside and the corporate veil can be pierced is not a maritime problem only but is a general problem of corporate law. However, this would not have been—and would not be in the future—the first time in which shipping law has been the forerunner of new legislative concepts: suffice it to mention general average and limitation of liability.

II.137 The problem exists and is serious. The attempts that have been made by several delegations to justify the proliferation of single ship companies are not persuasive and sometimes are clearly misconceived. Even if there can be cases in which single ship companies are created for justifiable reasons, it is a fact, as the analysis of the present status of the law and of the jurisprudence has shown,[38] that quite often they are created in order to build up an additional and illegitimate shield to the owner's responsibility. This is not tolerable and although it has to be regretted that it has not proved possible to find an internationally agreed solution to this problem in the Arrest Convention, the problem should not be forgotten, and attempts ought to be made to solve it in the not too distant future.

II.138 The result of the rejection of the UK proposal is that no uniformity has been achieved on the question whether and in which circumstances the corporate veil can be pierced and, consequently, whether ships owned by companies having a different corporate identity from that of the company liable for the claim may be arrested. It follows that the *lex fori* will apply. The rejection of the UK proposal, and the failure by the Main Committee to adopt, at its second reading, the CMI proposal to provide expressly for the application of the *lex fori*, which had been favourably received at the first reading,[39] cannot in fact be interpreted as an implied decision to prohibit the piercing of the corporate veil. The great majority of the delegations who opposed the UK proposal recognised that the problem existed and many of them expressly stated that its solution should be left to national law[40] or perhaps to an *ad hoc* convention. In addition, the fact that the new Convention has not a provision similar to that in Article 3(2) of the 1952 Convention, according to which ships are deemed to be in the same ownership when all the shares therein are owned by the same person or persons, indicates that it was intended to leave to national law the decision of this question.

10. SHIPS READY TO SAIL

II.139 When the provision of the 1952 Convention whereby a ship may be arrested even if ready to sail[41] was discussed by the JIGE it was stated that the reference to the arrest

---

37. That suggestion had been made by the delegate of the CMI: see Appendix III, pp. 487 and 488.
38. *Supra*, Book I, para. I.449–I.497.
39. The only delegation who spoke against it was that of Denmark (Appendix III, p. 489).
40. The suggestion to leave the matter to the *lex fori* was made by Italy (Appendix III, p. 483), Greece (Appendix III, p. 483), Turkey (Appendix III, p. 484), Republic of Korea (Appendix III, p. 498). Other delegations, such as those of Norway (Appendix III, p. 484), Sweden (Appendix III, p. 485), Finland (Appendix III, p. 486), Malta (Appendix III, p. 487), Croatia (Appendix III, p. 496) hinted impliedly at the same solution.
41. *Supra*, Book I, para. I.535.

of a ship ready to sail did not seem to imply the prohibition, under the Convention, of arresting a ship in the course of navigation.[42] The words used in the Lisbon Draft, and left unaltered in the Draft Articles, were, however, "or is sailing". These words offered some problems of interpretation. They could in fact refer to the time when the ship is leaving her berth, but has not yet left the port, or to the time when the ship is actually in the course of navigation. Objections were raised during the eighth session of JIGE to the recognition of the right to arrest a ship in the course of navigation and the request was made to delete the words "or is sailing".[43] But this request was rightly opposed by the majority of the delegations on the ground that the denial of the right of arrest of ships within the limits of the territorial waters of any one State would be in violation of the rules laid down in the 1958 Geneva Convention on the Territorial Sea and the Contiguous Zone and now by the UN Convention on the Law of the Sea.[44] In the draft submitted by the JIGE to the Diplomatic Conference this provision was placed in square brackets and the CMI in its Position Paper suggested that it should be deleted, so that the question whether a ship ready to sail or which is sailing may be arrested be left to national law.[45] This proposal was supported by several delegations[46] and the Main Committee decided to delete the provision, on the understanding that it is left to national law to regulate this issue.[47]

11. RIGHT OF REARREST AND MULTIPLE ARREST

II.140 The exceptions to the general rule whereby the rearrest of a ship in respect of the same maritime claim is not permitted, which in Article 3(3) of the 1952 Convention consisted in the bail or other security that had been given to release the ship or to avoid the arrest having been released or in the existence of "other good cause for maintaining the arrest",[48] were considered inadequate by the CMI International Sub-Committee and

---

42. *Supra*, section 22, para. I.537 and Appendix III, p. 439.
43. Appendix III, p. 439.
44. Art. 20 of the 1958 Geneva Convention in fact provides:
    1. The coastal State should not stop or divert a foreign ship passing through the territorial sea for the purpose of exercising civil jurisdiction in relation to a person on board the ship.
    2. The coastal State may not levy execution against or arrest the ship for the purpose of any civil proceedings, save only in respect of obligations or liabilities assumed or incurred by the ship itself in the course or for the purpose of its voyage through the waters of the coastal State.
    3. The provisions of the previous paragraph are without prejudice to the right of the coastal State, in accordance with its laws, to levy execution against or to arrest, for the purpose of any civil proceedings, a foreign ship lying in the territorial sea, or passing through the territorial sea after leaving internal waters.

    Art. 28 of UNCLOS provides:
    Civil jurisdiction in relation to foreign ships.
    1. The coastal State should not stop or divert a foreign ship passing through the territorial sea for the purpose of exercising civil jurisdiction in relation to a person on board the ship.
    2. The coastal State may not levy execution against or arrest the ship for the purpose of any civil proceedings, save only in respect of obligations or liabilities assumed or incurred by the ship itself in the course or for the purpose of its voyage through the waters of the coastal State.
    3. Paragraph 2 is without prejudice to the right of the coastal State, in accordance with its laws, to levy execution against or to arrest, for the purpose of any civil proceedings, a foreign ship lying in the territorial sea, or passing through the territorial sea after leaving internal waters.
45. Appendix III, p. 441.
46. Appendix III, pp. 440 and 443.
47. See the summing up of the Chairman during the second reading in Appendix III.
48. *Supra*, Book I, para. I.561.

then by the CMI Lisbon Conference.[49] It was, in fact, deemed convenient to set out specifically in which cases a ship may be rearrested or another ship may be arrested for the same maritime claim. Furthermore, it was deemed convenient expressly to refer the exceptions also to the case of a second arrest being sought, but not yet granted.

II.141 The provision of the Lisbon Draft was adopted by the JIGE and then by the Diplomatic Conference almost without any change.[50] Article 5, containing these provisions, is divided into two parts, the first dealing with the rearrest of a ship after its release from arrest and with the arrest of a ship in respect of which security was given to avoid the arrest and the second dealing with the arrest of other ships, called "multiple arrest".

(a) Rearrest

II.142 The first part, contained in paragraph (1), sets out the following three exceptions to the general rule prohibiting rearrest or arrest:

(i) Inadequacy of the nature or amount of the security already obtained

II.143 The amount of the security is inadequate where it is less than the amount of the claim. It is not necessary for the amount of the claim to have increased after the arrest, for example because the injury suffered by the claimant has proved to be higher than originally expected. This exception applies even if the amount has not increased since the first arrest or the time when security was given to avoid the arrest and the security was knowingly accepted as being less than the amount of the claim. This provision operates to the extent that the security given is for an amount lower than the value of the ship, since it is a general principle of the 1999 Convention that the security cannot exceed the value of the ship.[51]

II.144 The nature of the security is inadequate, for example, when the period of its validity is not long enough to permit the enforcement of a judgment or award or when the security provides that payment shall be made pursuant to the judgment of a court which is not the court with jurisdiction to decide upon the merits of the case.

(ii) Inability of the person who has given the security to fulfil his obligations

II.145 It is sufficient that that person is unlikely to be able to meet his obligations. The inability may consist, for example, in the lack of financial means or in foreign currency restrictions.

---

49. Appendix III, p. 517.

50. When at the seventh session of the JIGE it was decided that the Lisbon Draft should be taken as a basis of the review by the JIGE of the 1952 Convention, Article 5 of the Lisbon Draft on rearrest and multiple arrest was accepted by the majority of the delegations. An alternative provision was, however, proposed by the delegations of the United States, Liberia and the Republic of Korea (Appendix III, para. 517). Such alternative provision differed from that of the Lisbon Draft in that the rearrest of a ship was permitted only if there had been fraud or material misrepresentation in connection with the release or the posting of the security. At the ninth session, however, it was decided to retain only the text of the Lisbon Draft (Appendix III, para. 518).

51. *Infra*, para. II.182.

(iii) Release of the arrested ship or of the security previously given

II.146 Two different situations are considered. The first is that the release occurs upon the application or with the consent of the claimant. In this case, however, a further condition is required, namely that the claimant has acted on reasonable grounds, and the burden of proof rests on him. Such condition is satisfied if, for example, the owner is unable immediately to provide security and a delay in the sailing of the ship may cause relevant damages to the owner, such as the loss of a cancelling date, or if the owner or a third party has undertaken to provide security and the claimant acting on reasonable grounds has released the ship in the expectation that the security will actually be provided. The assessment of the existence of reasonable grounds may probably differ according to whether the release occurred upon the application of the claimant or upon the application of the owner and with the consent of the claimant. The second situation considered in subparagraph (c) is that of the claimant being unable to prevent the release by taking reasonable steps. This would, for example, be the case if the ship is ordered to be released because it constitutes a danger for the safety of the port or if the berth at which the ship is moored is required for commercial reasons and no other berth is available. This would, however, not be the case if the claimant did not commence proceedings on the merits within the prescribed time limit, if he did not provide security for damages as ordered by the court, or if he did not pay the cost of custody of the vessel as ordered by the court.

II.147 During the first and the second reading clarifications were requested to the observer from the CMI by several delegates and, after such clarifications were given and examples similar to those previously mentioned were made, the Main Committee decided to adopt this subparagraph.[52]

(b) Multiple arrest

II.148 The general prohibition of arresting one or more other ships after security has been provided applies both when the ship that has been arrested and released or the ship in respect of which security has been provided to prevent the arrest is the ship in respect of which a maritime claim is asserted or a "sistership". The exceptions are identical, except for the amount of the security. While, in fact, the first ship may be rearrested or arrested only if the amount of the security already obtained is both inadequate and lower than the amount of the claim, that condition does not apply in respect of the arrest of other ships.[53] If, in fact, the claimant has been unable to obtain a security for the full amount of his claim because the value of the ship he has arrested is lower, he may arrest one or more[54] other ships in order to obtain an additional security such as to cover the balance of his claim, The rule whereby the aggregate amount of security may not exceed the value of the ship in fact is not repeated in paragraph 2(a).

---

52. Appendix III, p. 520.
53. See the explanations given by the observer from the CMI in Appendix III, p. 520.
54. During the first reading the question was asked whether two other ships may be arrested at the same time in case the value of one appears to be insufficient to cover the outstanding amount of the claim. The Chairman replied that this is the case, on the assumption, of course, that the value of one ship is lower than the amount of the claim. This statement was not challenged by anyone (Appendix III, p. 522).

CHAPTER 5

Procedure relating to Arrest

12. JURISDICTION FOR THE ARREST

II.149 The relevant provision of the 1952 Convention is Article 2, whereby a ship may only be arrested under the authority of a court of the Contracting State in which the arrest is made. Pursuant to Article 5, the same court is also competent to order the ship to be released.

II.150 In the Lisbon Draft, and thus in the first Draft Articles, there were two provisions on jurisdiction: Article 1(2) giving the definition of arrest, stated that the ship must be physically within the jurisdiction of the State where the order of arrest has been made;[1] then Article 2(1) stated that a ship may be arrested or released from arrest only by or under the authority of a court of the State in which the arrest is demanded or has been effected.[2]

II.151 The reference in the definition of arrest to the need for the ship to be within the jurisdiction of the State where the order of arrest is made was quite rightly deemed to be superfluous and misleading[3] and was consequently deleted and did not appear any more in the Draft Articles submitted to the Diplomatic Conference.

II.152 Originally the provision in Article 2(1) contained a reference to the courts of the State in which the arrest has been demanded or effected. The reference to the State in which the arrest is demanded was opposed by the delegation of the United Kingdom on the ground that it was superfluous[4] and was consequently deleted, the majority of the delegates being in favour of the text in Article 4 of the 1952 Convention in which reference is only made to the courts of the State in which the arrest is effected.

II.153 A ship, therefore, may not be arrested under the authority of the courts of a State other than that in which the arrest is effected.

II.154 The jurisdiction of the courts of the State where the ship is at the time the order is made exists irrespective of whether such courts have jurisdiction to decide on the merits of the case. This rule, which in the 1952 Convention is implied in paragraph (2) of Article 7, has now been moved to paragraph (3) of Article 2, which regulates the powers of arrest and is worded as follows:

A ship may be arrested for the purpose of obtaining security notwithstanding that, by virtue of a jurisdiction clause or arbitration clause in any relevant contract, or otherwise, the maritime claim in respect of which the arrest is effected is to be adjudicated in a State other than the State where the

1. Appendix III, p. 426.
2. Appendix III, p. 426.
3. *Supra*, para. II.48.
4. Appendix III, p. 428.

arrest is effected, or is to be arbitrated, or is to be adjudicated subject to the law of another State.

II.155 The words "or otherwise" after the words "by virtue of a jurisdiction clause or arbitration clause in any relevant contract" were added on the request of the UK delegation at the eighth session of the JIGE on the ground that there are circumstances other than a jurisdiction clause or an arbitration clause that could result in the merits of the case being considered by a court or by an arbitrator in a State other than that in which the arrest was made.[5]

II.156 The question arises whether in this provision the State, reference to which is made three times in the above paragraph, must be a State Party.[6] This is certainly so the second time, because the State where the arrest is effected is that where the arrest is permitted under this provision. On the contrary the State, other than the State where the arrest is effected, in which the claim is to be adjudicated or the State the law of which applies may either be another State Party or a non-party State. It would not in fact make sense that the right of arrest of a ship in cases where the courts of the State in which the arrest is to be effected have not jurisdiction on the merits be limited to the case where the courts of another State Party has jurisdiction on the merits or to the case where the applicable law is the law of another State Party.

II.157 The delegation of Sweden raised the question whether, notwithstanding the provision of Article 2(3), the courts of a State Party would be entitled to refuse granting the arrest in a case where the foreign judgment on the merits would not be enforceable: a situation that could occur if the judgment is delivered in a non Party State. In order to make this clear the delegation of Sweden suggested adding the following paragraph at the end of Article 2[7]:

Notwithstanding this provision the arrest of a ship shall be permissible only if, pursuant to article 7(5), a judgement or a arbitral award in respect of that claim can be enforced against that ship by judicial or forced sale of that ship in the State where the arrest is made or applied for.

II.158 This proposal was not adopted on the ground, it is believed, that the purpose of Article 2(3) is that of making clear that the lack of jurisdiction on the merits does not deprive the courts of the State where the ship may be arrested of jurisdiction to order the arrest, but does not imply that an arrest must be ordered in any event.

13. AUTHORITY COMPETENT TO ORDER ARREST

II.159 Article 4 of the 1952 Convention provides that a ship may only be arrested "under the authority of a Court or of the appropriate judicial authority". In the commentary on this provision[8] it was pointed out that the words "or of the appropriate judicial authority", following the words "under the authority of a Court" did not contribute to the clarity of the provision.

---

5. Appendix III, p. 444.
6. In the Convention reference is made sometimes to a "State" (Articles 1(5), 2(3) and (4), 3(1)(e) and (3), 6(2), (3) and (4), 7(1), (2), (3), (5) and (6), 10(2), 12(2), 13(1) and 14(1) and (2)); sometimes to a "State Party" (Articles 2(1), 4(4) and (5), 8(1) and (6), 10(1)(b) and (2), 13(3), 15(1) and 16(1)); sometimes to "any State" (Articles 5(1), 10(1) and 12(1)); and in one occasion (Article 4(4) and (5)) to a "non-party State".
7. Appendix III, p. 445.
8. *Supra*, Book I, section 27, para. I.581–I.583.

II.160 The reference to another "appropriate judicial authority" was omitted in the Lisbon Draft and does not appear in the Convention. Article 2(1) in fact provides that a ship may be arrested only "under the authority of a court". The word "Court" is in fact sufficiently wide, considering the definition given in Article 1(5) according to which "Court" means any judicial authority of a State.

II.161 While Article 4 of the 1952 Convention provides that a ship may be arrested only under the authority of a court (or of the appropriate judicial authority), Article 2(1) of the 1999 Convention provides that a ship may be arrested (or released) only *by* or *under the authority of* a court.

II.162 The words "or under" were added because while in certain jurisdictions the order of arrest is made by a court,[9] in others it is not directly made by a court, even if it is effected under the authority of a court.[10] It must be noted that the French text differs from the English, inasmuch as it provides that a ship may only be arrested (or released) "*par décision*" (i.e. by the authority) of a court.

II.163 As in the 1952 Convention, the court having jurisdiction for the arrest is a court of the State where the arrest is made.

14. WHETHER AND TO WHAT EXTENT THE CLAIMANT MUST PROVE HIS CLAIM

II.164 It has always been considered that the definition of claimant in Article 1(4) of the 1952 Convention as the person who alleges that a maritime claim exists in his favour is relevant for the purpose of establishing whether and to what extent the claimant must prove his claim. However, as it has been seen,[11] there is no uniformity in the interpretation of this provision, since in some countries it has been decided that the claimant is wholly dispensed from any burden of proof, while in other countries he must at least provide *prima facie* evidence that he has a claim.

II.165 While the words used in the 1952 Convention are "a person who *alleges* that a maritime claim exists in his favour", those used in the Lisbon Draft and in the Draft Rules, that have been adopted by the Conference, are "any person *asserting* a maritime claim". There has been no intention of making any change in the substance of the definition.[12] The change in the English text was made in order to bring it closer to the new French text which in turn had been changed in order to ensure that it corresponded more closely to the 1952 English text. In fact while the words used in the 1952 English text are "a person who alleges that a maritime claim exists in his favour", those used in the 1952 French text are "invoquant à son profit l'existence d'une créance maritime". It was thought that the heart of the definition was the verb "to allege" and that, therefore, it was preferable to use in French the verb "alléguer" rather than that "invoquer", the English equivalent of which

---

9. This is so in most civil law countries.

10. The following statement appears in Annex I to the Report on the Eighth Session of the JIGE (Appendix III, p. 435):

> It was noted that the expression "by or under" the authority of a Court had been introduced to cover arrest effected by Court Officers as well as by other authorities in charge of executing a Court order of arrest.

11. *Supra*, Book I, para. I.598–624.

12. See Appendix III, p. 431.

is "to invoke" and not "to allege". Once this change had been made in the French text of the definition, it became necessary, in order that the wordings could match, to replace in English the verb "to allege" with that "to assert" which has the same meaning but allowed the replacement of the words "(alleging) that a maritime claim exists in his favour" with the words "(asserting) a maritime claim".

II.166 This is an improvement as respects the 1952 text because the sentence both in English and French is shorter and clearer and because the verbs "alléguer" and "to assert" mean both to affirm something without proof.

II.167 Moreover, the word "allegation", used in the 1952 Convention for the definition of "créance maritime" in the *chapeau* of Article 1(1), was used also in the Lisbon Draft and, therefore, it had appeared at that time proper to use the same verb in the definition of "créancier". The use of the words "allégation d'un droit ou d'une créance" in order to convey the meaning of the English word "claim" was due to the fact that "claim" and "créance" have not the same meaning, "claim" being a demand for something and "créance" being a thing (sum of money) one is entitled to. This attempt to find an equivalent in French to the English word "claim" has now been dropped, since in the 1999 Convention "créance maritime" is defined as a "créance" *tout court* which is not correct. But on account of this it was even more desirable to define "créancier", for the purposes of the Convention, as a person "alléguant une créance maritime".

II.168 The question whether the definition of "claimant" had the effect to dispense, wholly or partly, the claimant from the burden of proving his claim has not been discussed by the CMI, nor has it been discussed during the sessions of the JIGE and during the Diplomatic Conference. In view of the fact that the change in the wording was not intended to modify the substance of the provision, it appears that the same lack of uniformity now existing in respect of the interpretation of Article 1(4) of the 1952 Convention will continue to exist also in respect of the interpretation of Article 1(4) of the 1999 Convention.

II.169 Irrespective of whether or not the claimant must prove his claim, it is thought that, in any event, he must prove that he has a maritime claim and must identify a ship that may be arrested in respect of such claim in accordance with Article 3 of the 1999 Convention. That ship may be that in respect of which the maritime claim is asserted or any other ship which is owned by the person liable. This is made clear by Article 3, pursuant to which arrest is permissible of any ship in respect of which a maritime claim is asserted under certain specified conditions and, therefore, in so far as such conditions are concerned, the normal rules on the allocation of the burden of proof apply. It is, therefore, the claimant that must prove the existence between the maritime claim and the ship the arrest of which is requested of one of the links set out in Article 3(1) and (2).

15. PERSON ENTITLED TO ARREST

II.170 Pursuant to Article 3(1) arrest is permissible of any ship in respect of which a maritime claim is asserted if one of the conditions set out therein or in the subsequent paragraph are met. In view of the definition of claimant in Article 1(4) as the person asserting a maritime claim, the person entitled to arrest is that person, provided one of the conditions set out in Article 3(1) and (2) is met.

16. CONDITIONS FOR OBTAINING THE AUTHORITY

II.171 Article 2(4) reproduces, albeit with certain changes, the second paragraph of Article 6 of the 1952 Convention. The changes consist first in the express statement that the reference to the *lex fori* is subject to the provisions of the Convention (a fact that, however, was already implied) and, secondly in a more concise description of what is subject to the *lex fori*. While in the 1952 Convention mention was made of the procedure relating to the arrest, to the application for obtaining the authority to effect the arrest and to all matters of procedure that the arrest may entail, in the 1999 Convention mention is simply made of the procedure relating to the arrest of a ship or its release. The meaning of the provision, however, is the same. At first sight it might appear important to distinguish procedure from substance, because reference is made in Article 2(4) only to procedure. But since the provisions of the Convention, whether substantive or procedural, prevail over those of the *lex fori*, any matter not governed by the Convention is governed by the *lex fori* or by the law applicable pursuant to the private international law rules of the *lex fori* except for the purposes of Article 3(1)(e).[13]

II.172 The relevant test for the application of the *lex fori* is, consequently, whether or not any particular matter is governed by the Convention itself. One relevant question is that relating to the relevance of the financial conditions of the debtor.

II.173 An attempt had been made by the CMI to clarify this issue by proposing the addition in Article 2(4) of words to the effect that the *lex fori* applies in respect of the circumstances in which arrest or release from arrest may be obtained.[14]

II.174 This proposal was supported by some delegations, but the Chairman found that such support was not sufficient, in particular because it was based on the consideration that the CMI text was not in conflict with the JIGE text but clarified its meaning.[15] The reasons given by those who opposed it do not bring any particular light on the question whether the text of the Draft Articles should be interpreted as to leave the States Parties the freedom to decide whether the arrest should be made conditional to the existence of a risk of the claimant being subsequently unable to enforce his claim.[16] On the contrary the Chairman acknowledged that this was the present situation[17] and since his statement was not challenged, the conclusion that must be drawn from the debate is that the rejection of the CMI proposal does not imply a denial of the freedom of States Parties to regulate the conditions for the arrest.

17. ENFORCEMENT OF THE ARREST

II.175 The provision of Article 2(4) is in this respect directly in point. The procedure relating to the enforcement of the arrest is clearly governed by the law of the State in

---

13. See *supra*, section 7(e), para. II.131.

14. See Appendix III, p. 448.

15. Appendix III, p. 450.

16. The delegate from Hong Kong feared that the CMI proposal could introduce something which goes beyond questions of procedure and permit States to require substantive prerequisites (Appendix III, p. 449). The delegate from the United States was concerned that the text proposed by the CMI could create uncertainty as to whether the claimant may arrest even for one of the maritime claims (Appendix III, p. 450).

17. Appendix III, p. 450.

which the arrest is effected, nor are there any provisions in this respect in the Convention.

II.176 Matters pertaining to the enforcement of the arrest are the manner in which the order of arrest is notified to the owner or demise charterer as well as to the master of the ship, the court official in charge of the procedure, the appointment and powers of a custodian, etc.

18. RELEASE OF THE SHIP FROM ARREST

II.177 In the 1952 Convention provisions on the release of the ship from arrest are made in three situations: (a) when security is provided; (b) when the ship or a sistership has been previously arrested in respect of the same maritime claim; (c) when proceedings for the merits have not been commenced within the time fixed by the court. The first and the third situations are also regulated in the 1999 Convention, while the second is not, but release of the ship in such case is implied.

II.178 The above three situations will therefore be considered below.

(a) Release after the provision of security

II.179 While in Article 5 of the 1952 Convention, the obligation to release the arrested ship upon sufficient security being furnished is imposed on the court or other appropriate judicial authority within whose jurisdiction the ship was arrested, in the 1999 Convention the authority who must release the ship is not identified. Paragraph (1) of Article 4, in fact, provides that a ship which has been arrested shall be released when sufficient security has been furnished in a satisfactory form.

II.180 The reason for this change is that the obligation lies not only on the competent court, but also, and in the first place, on the claimant who applied for the arrest. In certain jurisdictions an order of the court is not necessary: the ship may be released if the arrestor gives his consent. Pursuant to the rule laid down in Article 4(1), the arrestor must consent to the release, and take any necessary action to this effect, "when sufficient security has been provided in a satisfactory form".

II.181 The obligation to release the arrested ship therefore arises when two conditions are met: (a) the security must be sufficient in its amount and (b) the security must be in a satisfactory form.

II.182 The first condition is expressed in identical terms as under the 1952 Convention. Article 4 of the 1999 Convention, however, provides an indication with respect to the maximum amount of the security. Pursuant to paragraph (2), in fact, the security, if determined by the court, cannot exceed the value of the ship. It follows that, as regards the amount, security for an amount equal to the value of the ship is always sufficient, even if the amount of the claim is higher. The security, in fact, is provided in place of the ship and, therefore, the claimant cannot refuse to consent to the release of the ship if security for an amount equal to the value of the ship is provided. Had he enforced his claim on the ship and obtained payment of the proceeds of its sale, he would not have received more. Of course, if the amount of the claim is less than the value of the ship, the security must be deemed to be sufficient if it covers the capital amount of the claim, plus interest and costs.[18]

II.183 The second condition refers to the form of the security. In the 1952 Convention, one type of security is specifically mentioned—bail—and there follows a general indication of other types, not identified or described otherwise than by the words "other security". If the *ejusdem generis* rule could be applied, it would follow that such other security should be similar to bail. In Article 4(4) of the 1999 Convention, any specific reference to the type of security has been omitted and has been replaced by the provision that the form of the security must be satisfactory.[19]

II.184 It may be questioned whether this criterion is subjective or objective, namely whether the security must satisfy the personal requirement of the claimant or be in a form normally accepted. It is believed that this latter alternative is the correct one and this is confirmed by the fact that the objective criterion would certainly be adopted by the court, which in the last resort has to decide when there is no agreement between the parties. The judicial authority must intervene, obviously upon request of one of the parties (normally of the owner of the ship or of the person who has offered the security), only if an agreement on the amount and form of security has not been reached. Article 4(2) provides:

2. In the absence of an agreement between the parties as to the sufficiency and form of the security, the Court shall determine its nature and the amount thereof, not exceeding the value of the ship.

II.185 In this provision, probably because its wording follows that of the corresponding provision of the 1952 Convention, reference is made[20] to the "nature" of the security instead of to its "form", as in the previous paragraph. The two terms clearly have the same meaning, since the agreement between the parties the absence of which triggers the intervention of the court would have related to the amount and the form of the security and the court should decide what the parties have failed to agree. Reference to the "nature" of the security rather than to its form is made in other provisions, and more precisely in Article 5(1)(a) and (2)(a).

II.186 Reference is made in this paragraph to the "court" generally, as in the second paragraph of Article 5 of the 1952 Convention. But while in the 1952 Convention the court is identified in the first paragraph as that "within whose jurisdiction the ship has been arrested", no such identification is made in Article 4 of the 1999 Convention. The competent court, however, is that of the State in which the arrest was effected.

II.187 Nothing is said in the 1952 Convention as regards the possibility of modifying the security once it has been provided and the ship has been released. A specific provision, instead, exists in this respect in the 1999 Convention. Paragraph (6) of Article 4 so in fact provides:

18. During the sessions of the JIGE the rule that the security cannot exceed the value of the ship was criticised and further criticisms were made at the Diplomatic Conference in the comments (Appendix III, pp. 507 and 508) but after the explanations given by the observer from the CMI the maintenance of the rule was supported by a large majority (Appendix III, p. 514).

19. A proposal was made at the Diplomatic Conference by the delegation of Greece (Conference document A/CONF.188/CRP.17 of 5 March 1999) to add after "satisfactory form" the words "such as bail, bank guarantee or security provided by a financial institution, P & I Club or any similar institution" but it was deemed preferable to leave to the competent court discretion as to the acceptable form of the security. See Appendix III, p. 503.

20. The wording of Article 4(2) was the same in the Lisbon Draft and in the JIGE Drafts.

5. Where pursuant to paragraph 1 of this article security has been provided, the person providing such security may at any time apply to the Court to have that security reduced, modified or cancelled.

II.188 In this paragraph, too, reference is made to the "court" without any further specification but, again, the competent court is that of the State where the arrest was effected.

II.189 The right to apply to the court belongs to the person providing the security, irrespective of whether such person is the owner or not. It follows that if the security is provided by a person other than the owner of the ship, the owner is not entitled to apply for its reduction, modification or cancellation. Such right also exists if the security has been agreed between the parties. The reference to paragraph (1) confirms this. Perhaps reference could also have been made to paragraph (2).

II.190 The reduction refers to the amount. The owner may, in order to release the ship as quickly as possible, avoid lengthy negotiations on the amount of the security and provide or cause to be provided security in the amount requested by the claimant.

II.191 Similarly, the form required by the claimant and initially accepted by the owner may imply an excessive cost and can, therefore, be changed. For example, a payment into court may be replaced by a bank guarantee or by a letter of undertaking of the P & I Club.

II.192 Security may also be cancelled. Cancellation may be ordered by the court where the court is satisfied that the claim does not exist. In this case, as in paragraph (2), the court reference to which is made must be the court of the State where the arrest was effected. The possibility, therefore, is envisaged that the court ordering the arrest may, after reviewing the allegations of the claimant also in the light of the defences raised by the owner of the ship or by the demise charterer, where the ship is arrested as security for a claim against the demise charterer,[21] order that the security be cancelled prior to a decision on the merits of the case. The cancellation of the security contemplated in Article 4(5) differs, therefore, from the release of security regulated in the preceding paragraph (4), which will be examined below, and in Article 7 in the case of failure by the claimant timely to commence proceedings on the merits.[22]

II.193 Paragraph (5) applies both when the security has been agreed between the parties and when it has been determined by the court. In fact paragraph (1), reference to which is made in paragraph (5), regulates generally the release of the ship from arrest in case security is provided, irrespective of whether its nature and amount has been agreed by the parties or determined by the court.

II.194 Paragraph (2) is in fact supplementary to paragraph (1) and merely indicates how the nature and amount may be determined and, therefore, there was no need to refer to paragraph (2) in paragraph (5).

II.195 Finally, Article 4(3) repeats the provision of the last paragraph of Article 5 of the 1952 Convention by stating that the request for the ship to be released upon security being provided shall not be construed as an acknowledgement of liability nor as a waiver of any defence or of any right to limit liability.

---

21. Defences may be raised also by other parties at interest, when the claim is secured by a maritime lien, such as the time charterer or the voyage charterer.
22. See *infra*, para. II.240.

(b) Release from subsequent arrest

II.196 Article 3(3) of the 1952 Convention provides that if a ship has been arrested in breach of the prohibition on rearresting a ship or arresting another ship in respect of the same maritime claim, that ship must be released save in the cases specifically mentioned in that paragraph. This provision was not reproduced in the Lisbon Draft nor in the JIGE Draft and in the 1999 Convention since it would have been superfluous. It is obvious in fact that if a ship has been rearrested or arrested in breach of Article 5 such arrest must be set aside and the ship must be released.

(c) Failure to bring proceedings on the merits within the time fixed by the court

II.197 Article 7(4) provides, similarly to Article 7(4) of the 1952 Convention,[23] that if proceedings are not brought within the period ordered by the court in accordance with the preceding paragraph (3),[24] the ship arrested or the security given shall, upon request, be ordered to be released. While, therefore, the period of time within which the claimant must bring proceedings is left to the discretion of the court or may be fixed by national law,[25] the consequence of the failure to bring proceedings within such period of time is stated by the Convention itself. The wording of paragraph (4) is such as not to allow any discretion to the court in respect of a possible extension of the period of time fixed by the court itself (or by statute). The manner in which the time is calculated may be indicated by the court or, failing any such indication, may be regulated by the *lex fori*. For example, the running of the time may be suspended, under the *lex fori*, during the recess of the court, or when service of proceedings is prevented by causes of *force majeure*.

19. RELEASE OF THE SECURITY

II.198 Express provisions are made in the 1999 Convention in respect of the release of the security. The situations considered in the Convention are three. Two are related to the arrest of a ship in a non Party State and the provision of security in (or also in) a State Party; one is related to the failure to bring proceedings on the merits within the time ordered by the court.

(a) Provision of security in a State Party

II.199 The situation considered is that of a ship arrested in a non Party State which is not released after the provision of security in a State Party. Article 4(4) provides that in such a case the security must be released.

II.200 This rule was subject to an exception in the Lisbon Draft expressed with the words "save in exceptional cases where it would be unjust to do so". Objections were raised during the sessions of the JIGE against this exception, on the ground that the term

---

23. On which see *supra*, Book I, section 33, para. I.717–I.738.
24. *Infra*, para. II.239.
25. The suggestion to indicate in the Convention a maximum period of time for commencement of proceedings on the merits was not adopted. See Appendix III, p. 539.

"unjust" was too vague[26] and, therefore, in the JIGE Draft the sentence was placed in square brackets. At the Diplomatic Conference no effort was made to find a better term and a strong majority was in favour of the deletion of the exception.[27] The decision of the Conference has, therefore, the effect of making the rule applicable in all circumstances and of excluding any discretion of the court of the State Party in which security has been provided. Although the wording of the provision is not very precise, since reference is made to the court of *the* State Party rather than to the court of *that* State Party,[28] there cannot be any doubt that the courts of competent jurisdiction are those of the State Party in which security has been provided.

II.201 The nationality of the ship reference to which is made in this provision and in that of paragraph 5 may be that of a State Party or that of a non Party State. Even if this view cannot be based on Article 8(1) in which, for the purpose of establishing the scope of application of the Convention, reference is made to "any ship within the jurisdiction of a State Party", the general reference to "a ship" in Article 4 seems to indicate that its nationality is irrelevant. In a sense, paragraphs 4 and 5 of Article 4 deal with situations that are external to the scope of application set out in Article 8(1), since they consider cases where there is no ship within the jurisdiction of a State Party. However they consider the case where a security has been provided in a State Party and, to this extent, competent for the decision as to whether such security may be maintained or must be ordered to be released is a court of a State Party.

II.202 The view that such jurisdiction must be exercised irrespective of the nationality of the ship is supported by what may be called a principle of reciprocity: as ships flying the flag of a non Party State are subject to the Convention when they are in the jurisdiction of a State Party, they should be granted the same protection of ships flying the flag of a State Party when they are arrested in a non Party State but security is—or is also—provided in a State Party.

II.203 It is not clear, however, why in paragraph 4 reference is made to "a ship" and in paragraph 5 to "the ship". The use of the indefinite Article in the first case and of the definite Article in the second case was perhaps justified when the two provisions were part of the same paragraph but it is not justified now, when such provisions are placed in two separate paragraphs.

(b) Provision of security in a non-Party State and in a State Party

II.204 The situation considered is that of a ship arrested in a non Party State which is released after security has been provided both in that non Party State and in a State Party. Article 4(5) provides that in such a case the security provided in a State Party must be ordered to be released when the total amount of the security provided in the non Party State in which the ship has been arrested and in a State Party exceeds the amount of the

---

26. The expression in Article 5(1)(c)(i) "reasonable grounds", which leaves a similar discretion, was instead accepted by the Conference.

27. Appendix III, p. 512.

28. In the same provision, instead, the first time reference is made to the ship the indefinite Article "a" is used, but when reference is made to the security provided in respect of such ship, the pronoun "that" is used.

claim for which the ship has been arrested or the value of the ship, if such value is lower than the amount of the claim.

II.205 The purpose of this provision is to treat, to the extent possible, the arrest in a non Party State and the provision of security for the release of the ship in the same manner as in the case of arrest in a State Party.[29]

II.206 The reason why the security that must be released or reduced is that provided in a State Party is that the Convention does not apply in the jurisdiction of a non Party State and cannot therefore provide what courts in such State must or must not do. As in other conventions, however, the release or reduction of the security provided in the non Party State in which the ship has been arrested is conditional to the security provided in such State being actually available to the claimant and freely transferable.

II.207 The most likely reason for which security is provided in a State Party when a ship is arrested in a non Party State is that the claimant and the person liable for the claim have agreed to submit the dispute to the jurisdiction of the courts of or to arbitration in that State. Therefore, the availability and free transferability of the security provided in the non Party State in which the ship is arrested must be established with respect to the State Party in which the additional security has been provided, rather than to the domicile of the claimant. The reference to the value of the ship was accepted by the Conference after it had been decided that it was correct in the preceding paragraph 2 of this Article 4.

(c) Failure to bring proceedings on the merits within the time fixed by the court

II.208 As previously stated, pursuant to Article 7(4) if proceedings are not brought within the period ordered by the court the security given in order to release the ship from arrest must be ordered to be released.[30]

20. WHEN THE RELEASE OF A SHIP UNDER ARREST IS NOT PERMITTED AND TRADING OF THE SHIP UNDER ARREST

II.209 Article 4(1) reinstates[31] the exception already existing in Article 5 of the 1952 Convention to the rule whereby a ship must be released when sufficient security is provided in a satisfactory form: such rule in fact does not apply when a ship has been arrested in respect of claims arising out of any dispute as to ownership or possession of the ship (Article 1(1)(s)) and of any dispute between co-owners of the ship as to the employment or earnings of the ship (Article 1(1)(t). The reason why in such cases the provision of security does not entail the release of the ship is that the ship is not arrested for the purpose of obtaining security, but for the purpose of preventing its future employment by the person in possession of the ship. The contradiction between the rule whereby the ship must be released when sufficient security is provided in a satisfactory form, and the rule whereby when the ship is arrested in respect of any of the claims enumerated in Article 1(1)(s) and (t) the court may permit the person in possession of the ship to continue trading the ship upon

29. The deletion of this paragraph was proposed by the delegate from Canada, but his proposal was not adopted after the observer from the CMI had explained the reasons for which this paragraph had been included in Article 4. See Appendix III, p. 530.

30. *Supra*, para. II.197.

31. The provision of Article 5 of the 1952 Convention had not been reproduced in the Lisbon Draft nor was it reproduced in the 1994 JIGE Draft. At the eighth Session of the JIGE the proposal to reinstate such provision was made by Japan and such proposal was accepted by the JIGE at the ninth Session (See Appendix III, p. 503.

such person providing sufficient security is apparent but not real. In fact in this latter case the purpose of the security is not to guarantee the satisfaction of a claim, but to guarantee that the continued operation of the ship by the person in possession will not adversely affect the interest of the claimant in the ship, for example as a consequence of liabilities incurred during such operation or of the loss of or damage to the ship itself.

II.210 The philosophy underlying this provision is that when a ship is arrested in respect of any of the claims enumerated in Article 1(1)(s) and (t) it should not remain idle in a port until the dispute is settled but should continue trading.

II.211 Discretion is left to the court as to the choice of the person who should continue operating the ship: in fact Article 4(1) provides that the court may either permit the person in possession of the ship to continue trading the ship or otherwise deal with its operation during the period of arrest.[32]

II.212 It must be noted, however, that not all the claims enumerated in Article 1(1)(s) and (t) belong to the same category. This does not seem to be the case for the disputes between co-owners as to the earnings of the ship, which appear to be disputes as to the manner in which the earnings must be allocated between the co-owners.

21. LIABILITY FOR WRONGFUL OR UNJUSTIFIED ARREST

II.213 The question whether uniform rules should be provided in respect of the obligation of the arrestor to provide security and of his liability in the event of wrongful arrest was again debated by the CMI International Sub-Committee and by the Lisbon Conference.

II.214 It was found, however, that the reasons that previously prevented the incorporation into the 1952 Convention of any rule to that effect still existed. It was, therefore, decided not to regulate the substantive aspects of the matter, but specifically to give the court power to impose security and jurisdiction in respect of the assessment of liability for wrongful or unjustified arrest.[33] The first aspect is regulated in paragraph (1) of Article 6, which provides:

1. The Court may as a condition of the arrest of a ship, or of permitting an arrest already effected to be maintained, impose upon the claimant who seeks to arrest or who has procured the arrest of the ship the obligation to provide security of a kind and of an amount, and upon such terms, as may be determined by that Court for any loss which may be incurred by the defendant as a result of the arrest, and for which the claimant may be found liable, including but not restricted to such loss or damage as may be incurred by the defendant in consequence of:
   (a) the arrest having been wrongful or unjustified; or
   (b) excessive security having been demanded and obtained.

II.215 The deletion of the words "or unjustified" was requested by several delegations on the ground that the term "unjustified" is ambiguous. A very lively debate took place during the first and the second reading of the JIGE Draft and three proposals emerged: (a) to delete the words "or unjustified"; (b) to delete the word "wrongful"; (c) to keep both

---

32. Operation of the ship while under arrest is, for example, regulated in Italian law (Article 685 CN) which applies to arrest a provision existing in this respect of the seizure in satisfaction of a judgment. Article 652 CN provides that the court may, upon the request of any interested party and after having heard the holders of "hypothèques", authorise the execution by the ship of one or more voyages prescribing the securities and other measures deemed to be advisable, including in any event adequate insurance. The net proceeds of the voyage(s) are added to the proceeds of the sale.

33. The proposal of the delegation of Canada to delete this provision (Conference document A/CONF.188/CRP.1 of 1 March 1999) on the ground that courts possess the power to impose countersecurity in any event was not adopted.

words.[34] The explanations given by the CMI on the reasons why the term "unjustified" had been used in addition to the term "wrongful"[35] were supported by many delegations and finally the JIGE Draft, in which both terms were used[36] was adopted.[37]

II.216 The court, reference to which is made in this paragraph, is that in which arrest is sought. The person in favour of whom the security may be imposed is in this provision called the "defendant". It is in fact obvious that if the security may be imposed for any loss that may be incurred by the "defendant", that is the person in favour of whom the security must be provided. The term "defendant" presupposes the existence — or the future commencement — before that court of proceedings on the merits of the case between the arrestor and the person liable for the maritime claim in respect of which arrest is sought. However, this may not always be the case. In fact under Article 7 jurisdiction on the merits is granted, alternatively, to the court of the State in which the ship has been arrested and to the courts of the State in which security has been provided to obtain the release of the ship, which may be a State different from that in which the arrest has been effected. Furthermore, such courts may refuse to exercise jurisdiction or the parties may have validly agreed to submit the dispute to a Court of another State or to arbitration.

II.217 In any event, at the time when the arrest is sought normally there is not yet a defendant, because proceedings on the merits have not yet been commenced by the claimant.

II.218 The only logical explanation for the use of the term "defendant" is that the loss arising out of the arrest is normally incurred by the person liable in respect of the maritime claim. This is the case where the claim is against the owner or against the demise charterer even though in such latter case damages may be incurred also by the owner. This instead is not the case when the claim is secured by a maritime lien and is against the manager and may not be the case when the claim is against the operator, or when the mortgage, "hypothèque" or charge is granted by the owner as security for the debt of another person.[38]

II.219 The fact that the loss is normally incurred by the owner or by the demise charterer explains the rubric of Article 6. In view of the rather vague language of this provision, the identification of the person who is likely to incur losses as a consequence of the arrest and, thus, of the person in whose favour the security must be provided, is certainly within the power and discretion of the court.

II.220 In the first two paragraphs of Article 6 there are two parallel provisions. Paragraph (1) sets out the purpose of the security and states that such purpose is to cover any loss for which the claimant may be found liable and then specifies the two types of such loss previously considered. Paragraph (2) states that the courts of the State in which an arrest has been effected shall have jurisdiction to determine the extent of the liability, if any, of the claimant for any such loss and repeats word for word the language used in the previous paragraph.

---

34. Appendix III, p. 530.
35. Conference document 188/3 paragraph 150–152. Appendix III, p. 528.
36. The words "or unjustified" had been placed in square brackets owing to the opposition of some delegations.
37. Appendix III, p. 533.
38. This problem was raised at the Conference, but nothing was done in order to find a better term. See Appendix III, p. 533.

II.221 Paragraph 1, therefore, does not impose on the court of the State in which the arrest is applied for any obligation to request as a condition for the arrest the provision of security, but leaves any decision in that respect to the discretion of the court itself[39] who can, as for the security provided in order to release the ship from arrest, on application of the claimant reduce, modify or cancel the security (paragraph 5).

II.222 Article 6(1) does not set out binding rules regarding the kind, the amount and the terms of the security. But if the court decides to impose a security, such security must cover the types of loss specified therein. In this respect there is no discretion any more: the security must cover any loss that may be incurred by the "defendant".

II.223 Correspondingly paragraph (2) grants jurisdiction to the same court to determine the existence and amount of the liability of the claimant for any such loss, on the basis of the *lex fori* (paragraph 3).

II.224 The parallelism between the two provisions is not perfect, since while in paragraph (1) reference is made to "any loss which may be incurred by the defendant", in paragraph (2) reference is made to "loss or damage caused by the arrest of a ship". The difference in the wording of the two paragraphs is, therefore, twofold: "any loss" in the first case and "loss or damage" in the second case; loss incurred by the "defendant" in the first case, no identification of the person who may suffer the loss or damage in the second case.

II.225 Such difference, that existed already in the Lisbon Draft and for which there is no explanation, is inconsequential. In fact the purpose of paragraph (1) is to allow the provision of security and that of paragraph (2) is that of establishing jurisdiction in respect of the assessment of the liability, if any, in relation to which security is provided. It would, therefore, make no sense that jurisdiction be granted in respect of liabilities for which no security is envisaged. Nor can the fact that the person claiming damages is not indicated in paragraph (2) imply that such person is different from the "defendant" mentioned in paragraph (1), in whose favour security may be provided.

II.226 The reference in the Lisbon Draft to loss (or damage) caused in consequence of the arrest having been unjustified, in addition to the case of the arrest having been wrongful was the subject of opposition during the sessions of the JIGE and consequently the words "or unjustified" were placed in square brackets. At the Diplomatic Conference the suggestion was made to delete such words, on the ground that it was difficult to conceive situations where the arrest could be unjustified without being wrongful. The observer for the CMI mentioned as an example the situation where the need for a security does not exist, in view of the sound financial conditions of the owner of the ship. Finally the words "or unjustified" were retained.

II.227 The loss that may be suffered when excessive security was demanded and obtained normally will consist in the cost of the increased security. Loss may, however, be suffered when excessive security was demanded but was not obtained, and, consequently, the ship has remained under arrest. In such case, the loss may be much greater. Such

---

39. A discussion had taken place in respect of the question whether the provision of countersecurity by the claimant should be made compulsory, rather than left to the discretion of the court. The proposal was made to replace in paragraph 1 the words "The Court may ... impose upon the claimant ... the obligation to provide security ... " with the words "The Court shall ... impose upon the claimant ... ". The proposal was also made by the delegation of Denmark (Appendix III, p. 529) to restrict the power of the Court by adding the words "(The Court shall) save in cases where it would be unreasonable to do so ... ". Neither of these proposals was adopted and the text of paragraph 1 was left unchanged.

situation may perhaps be qualified as wrongful arrest, because even if the arrest was justified, the amount in respect of which the arrest was sought was excessive. A loss may also be suffered when excessive security was demanded but a proper security was then obtained, for example, because prior to a decision of the court in respect of the proper amount, the ship has remained under arrest.

II.228 When, pursuant to Article 7(1), the courts of the State in which the arrest has been effected or security has been provided to obtain the release of the ship have jurisdiction to determine the case upon its merits, the issue of the liability, if any, of the claimant will be determined in the course of the proceedings brought for the decision on the merits and such decision may exert an influence on the decision of liability of the claimant in respect of damages suffered by the defendant. If, however, such courts have no jurisdiction on the merits, pursuant to Article 6(1) the proceedings may be stayed pending a decision on the merits in order to enable the court that must determine the issue of liability to take such decision into account.

II.229 The State reference to which is made in paragraphs (2), (3) and (4) must be a State Party. This is so in respect of paragraphs (2) and (3), because such State is that in which the arrest is effected and the Convention, as already stated, applies to the arrest of ships within the jurisdiction of States Parties. This is also so in respect of paragraph (4), since the other State the court of which is competent for the merits in accordance with Article 7, must be a State Party inasmuch as the provision on recognition of judgments is obviously limited to judgments issued in States Parties.

22. JURISDICTION ON THE MERITS

II.230 As was previously mentioned,[40] the rule that had been adopted in 1937 at Paris, whereby the courts of the State in which the arrest is made always have jurisdiction on the merits, was subsequently opposed by the French association and such opposition generated the hybrid compromise embodied in Article 7(1) of the 1952 Convention. At the CMI Lisbon Conference it was agreed to revert to the formula adopted in Paris and to establish, as a general rule, that the courts of the State in which an arrest is effected or security given shall have jurisdiction to determine the case upon its merits.[41]

II.231 In the Lisbon Draft and in the JIGE Draft jurisdiction on the merits was provided in three situations: when arrest is effected, when security is given to prevent arrest and when security is given to obtain the release of the ship. In all such situations jurisdiction was granted to the courts of the State in which the arrest has been effected or security given. At the Diplomatic Conference strong objections were raised against the second situation, on the ground that if jurisdiction is granted to the courts of the State in which security is given to prevent the arrest the choice of the forum would be left to the

---

40. *Supra*, Book I, section 37, para. I.805.

41. This provision, as that of Article 7(1) of the 1952 Convention, would be in conflict with Article 21 of the Hamburg Rules when the claim in respect of which jurisdiction of the courts of the State where the arrest is effected is a claim arising out of loss of or damage to or in connection with goods carried on board the ship, if the State whose courts would have jurisdiction is a State Party to both the Hamburg Rules and the 1999 Arrest Convention. Attention to the possibility of a conflict has been drawn in the CMI Report on Uniformity of the Law of the Carriage of Goods by Sea (CMI News Letter No. 2–1999) where (at p. 15) it has been stated that in case Article 21 of the Hamburg Rules were taken as a basis of a provision on jurisdiction in a future convention, the second sentence of its paragraph (2)(a) should be deleted.

owner of the ship.[42] The reference to the security given to prevent arrest was therefore deleted. Although the remark that has been made has merits, the practical consequence will be that the claimant who wants to ensure that the courts of the State in which the arrest may be effected have jurisdiction on the merits, cannot accept an offer of security prior to the arrest. The ensuing issue would be whether the claimant who has been offered a sufficient security in a satisfactory form may be held liable for damages on the ground that the arrest, after the offer of a security, was wrongful or unjustified.

II.232 It is thought that this should not be the case, since the fact that the Convention grants jurisdiction on the merits to the courts of the State where the arrest is made cannot entitle the owner to avoid such jurisdiction by offering security in order to prevent the arrest. It is also thought that in such a situation the claimant would be entitled to make his acceptance of the security conditional to the agreement by the owner on the jurisdiction of the courts of the State in which the arrest would have been effected.

II.233 There are two exceptions to the general rule that the courts of the State where the arrest is made or security given have jurisdiction on the merits.

II.234 The first is where the parties have agreed or agree to submit the dispute to a court of another State or to arbitration provided, however, that the agreement is valid and that the court chosen by the parties accepts jurisdiction.

II.235 The condition of the validity of the agreement applies both to the choice of another court and to arbitration.

II.236 Doubts were also raised on the formulation of the exception to the general rule on jurisdiction, since reference was made in the JIGE Draft (as well as in the Lisbon Draft) to the parties validly agreeing or having agreed to submit the dispute to a court of another State or to arbitration on the ground that it was not clear what the conditions were for a previous jurisdiction or arbitration agreement. The question was settled by adding the word "validly" also before the reference to a prior agreement so that the sentence now reads: "unless the parties validly agree or have validly agreed to submit the dispute to a Court of another State which accepts jurisdiction, or to arbitration".

II.237 The condition of the acceptance (of jurisdiction) applies only in the first case, while no parallel condition is mentioned in respect of arbitration. It is theoretically possible that the arbitrators do not accept the appointment, and, in this event, unless the parties agree to replace them, the condition of acceptance of jurisdiction should, by analogy, apply.

II.238 The second exception, which does not exist in the 1952 Convention, is where the courts of the State in which the arrest is made or security given refuse to exercise jurisdiction. This exception, however, operates under two conditions: that the refusal is permitted by the law of the State, e.g. for reasons of *forum non conveniens* where such doctrine prevails, and that a court of another State accepts jurisdiction.

II.239 The provisions relating to the fixing of a period of time within which the parties have to bring proceedings on the merits before a court having jurisdiction or before an arbitral tribunal have been maintained, but have been assembled in one paragraph (paragraph (3) of Article 7). The only material difference as respects the 1952 Convention is that now all cases in which a court of the State in which the arrest is made does not have jurisdiction on the merits or refuses to exercise such jurisdiction are covered by the same

---

42. Appendix III, p. 540.

provision, whilst in the 1952 Convention when the court does not have statutory jurisdiction, the order of a period within which proceedings on the merits must be brought is obligatory, and when the lack of jurisdiction is due to the parties having agreed to submit the dispute to the courts of another State or to arbitration such order is discretional. The difference is due to the fact that now the courts of the State where the arrest has been made have always statutory jurisdiction on the merits save that the parties have agreed otherwise or such courts refuse to exercise jurisdiction. The court may fix the time limit on its own initiative, but must do so if one of the parties so requests.[43]

II.240 Paragraph 4 then provides, similarly to paragraph 3 of Article 7 of the 1952 Convention, that if proceedings are not brought within the time so ordered, the ship arrested or the security given must be released.

23. RECOGNITION AND ENFORCEMENT OF JUDGMENTS

II.241 The 1952 Convention, in order to ensure the enforcement of a foreign judgment in the cases where the courts of the State where arrest is made have no jurisdiction on the merits, provides that the security given in order to release the ship must require that it is given as security for the satisfaction of any judgment that may eventually be pronounced by a court having jurisdiction. Apart from the lack of any reference to arbitration awards, this provision does not cover the case where no guarantee is given and the judgment must be enforced on the ship itself. For this reason the CMI Lisbon Draft provided that if proceedings are brought within the specified time limit, a final judgment issued by a competent court or a final award shall be recognised and given effect with respect to the arrested ship or to the security.[44]

II.242 At the Diplomatic Conference objections were raised against this provision on the ground that it bypassed the national rules on the exequatur of foreign judgments and the proposal was made to replace the words "shall be recognized" with "may be recognized".[45] It was objected, however, that the purpose of the provision was precisely to ensure the rapid recognition and enforcement of judgments, without which the enforcement of claims on the arrested ship when the court of the place of arrest has no jurisdiction on the merits would require an unpredictable amount of time.[46] The principle underlying this provision was then accepted.

II.243 The recognition and enforcement of the foreign judgment or of the arbitral award in the State in which the ship was arrested or the security given is subject to a special and a general condition.

II.244 The special condition is that the proceedings must have been brought within the period ordered by the court of the State in which the arrest was made or the security given. This condition applies when the period of time has been ordered. But this may not be the case since the court of the State where the arrest has been effected is required to do so only if a request is made, in all likelihood by the owner of the arrested ship, while if no such request is made the issuance of such order is left to the discretion of the court. The

43. *Supra*, Book I, section 33, para. I.717–I.738.
44. See the statement made by the CMI on its Report on the Lisbon Draft, Appendix III, p. 536.
45. See, in particular, the Belgian proposal during the first reading (Appendix III, p. 547 and 548) and the French proposal during the second reading (Appendix III, p. 548 and 549).
46. See the comments of the observer from the CMI during the first reading (Appendix III, pp. 547 and 548).

situation where no period of time is ordered is considered in paragraph (5) by the addition to the sentence "If proceedings are brought within the period of time ordered in accordance with paragraph 3 of this Article" of the sentence "or if proceedings before a competent Court are brought in the absence of such order". The meaning of such rather cumbersome formulation is that if no period is ordered, proceedings may be brought at any time, subject always to the statutory time bar applicable. The fact that the reference to "a competent Court or arbitral tribunal" is made only in connection with the situation where no period of time is ordered is probably due to such requirement being mentioned in paragraph (3).

II.245 The general condition is that the proceedings brought before another court (or an arbitral tribunal) must satisfy certain public law requirements. In the Lisbon Draft as well as in the JIGE Draft the exception to the recognition of the judgment or award on the merits issued by the court or arbitration tribunal of a State other than that in which the arrest is effected was the failure of the proceedings to satisfy general requirements of due process of law. The CMI in its Position Paper stated that the words "due process of law" would not have a clear meaning in certain jurisdictions and suggested a language similar to that adopted in Article 10(1) of CLC 1969 where the words "reasonable notice and a fair opportunity to present his case" are used.[47] This proposal was adopted and the further condition of the recognition not being against public policy (*ordre public*) was added.[48]

II.246 As previously stated, both the State reference to which is made in Article 7(1), (2), (3) and (6) and the other State reference to which is made in Article 7(1) and (5) must be States Parties. In the first case because it is the State where the arrest is effected and in the second case because it is the State the courts of which may issue judgments recognisable in the State where the arrest is effected.

II.247 With a view to avoiding the problem that this provision may impliedly restrict the effects of the recognition and enforcement of a judgment or an arbitral award to its enforcement on the arrested ship or on the security, the following final paragraph—paragraph 6—was added:

Nothing contained in the provisions of paragraph 5 of this article shall restrict any further effect given to a foreign judgment or arbitral award under the law of the State where the arrest of the ship was made or security given to prevent its arrest or obtain its release.

24. RESERVATIONS AND DECLARATIONS

II.248 Article 10(1) allows States Parties to exclude the application of the Convention to:

(a) ships which are not seagoing:

As previously indicated,[49] word "seagoing" has been deleted in Article 8(1) and, therefore, similarly to the 1976 LLMC Convention, States Parties are granted the right to exclude the application of uniform rules in respect of ships which are not seagoing[50];

47. Appendix III, p. 538.
48. Appendix III, p. 549.
49. *Supra*, para. II.17.
50. Appendix III, p. 562.

(b) ships not flying the flag of a State Party:

Article 8(3) of the 1952 Convention permits to States Parties to provide that a ship flying the flag of a non Party State may be arrested both in respect of a maritime claim and in respect of any other claim for which the national law permits arrest. The CMI in its Position Paper had suggested to reinstate such provision but the Conference has deemed more convenient to allow States Parties to exclude wholly such ships from the scope of application of the Convention[51];

(c) claims in respect of disputes as to ownership or possession of the ship:

These are claims of a special character, since their object is not payment of a sum of money and in some jurisdictions may be secured by a different kind of arrest; their exclusion from the scope of application of the uniform rules is also permitted under the 1952 Convention and several States have availed themselves of such option.

II.249 Paragraph 2 of Article 10 allows States Parties, who are also parties to a treaty on navigation on inland waterways, to declare that the rules on jurisdiction, recognition and execution of court decisions provided for in such treaties shall prevail over the rules contained in Article 7 of the 1999 Arrest Convention. This provision was inserted following a request of the Swiss delegation in order to allow States Parties to the revised Rhine Navigation Convention of 1868 to apply the provisions of such Convention.[52]

II.250 The Rhine Convention was signed at Mannheim on 17 October 1868 and was then amended by an additional Protocol of 18 September 1895, by the Convention of 20 November 1963 and by the additional Protocols of 25 October 1975, 17 October 1979 and 25 April 1989. It is presently in force between Belgium, France, Germany, the Netherlands, Switzerland and the United Kingdom.

II.251 The rules on jurisdiction are set out in Articles 34–35*ter*. Pursuant to Article 34 the Tribunals for the Rhine navigation are competent, in civil matters, in respect of disputes relating to pilotage, crane and similar dues, to obstructions placed on the haulage ways, to damage caused by boatsmen and to claims in respect of damage caused by horses. As it may be seen, the possibility of conflicts between the Arrest Convention and the Rhine Convention is, to say the least, rather remote.

25. STATES WITH MORE THAN ONE SYSTEM OF LAW

II.252 Article 13 provides that if a State has two or more territorial units in which different systems of law are applicable in relation to matters dealt with in the Convention, it may at the time of signature, ratification, acceptance, approval or accession declare that the Convention shall extend to all its territorial units or only to one or more of them and may modify this declaration by submitting another declaration at any time. This provision was added to the text of the Convention following a proposal of the delegation of Hong Kong China.[53]

---

51. Appendix III, p. 557.
52. Appendix III, p. 562.
53. Appendix III, p. 564.

APPENDIX I

Text of the 1999 Convention

II.I.1 INTERNATIONAL CONVENTION ON ARREST OF SHIPS, 1999

The States Parties to this Convention,
Recognizing the desirability of facilitating the harmonious and orderly development of world seaborne trade,
Convinced of the necessity for a legal instrument establishing international uniformity in the field of arrest of ships which takes account of recent developments in related fields,
Have agreed as follows:

ARTICLE 1: DEFINITIONS

For the purposes of this Convention:
1. "Maritime Claim" means a claim arising out of one or more of the following:

    (a) loss or damage caused by the operation of the ship;
    (b) loss of life or personal injury occurring, whether on land or on water, in direct connection with the operation of the ship;
    (c) salvage operations or any salvage agreement, including, if applicable, special compensation relating to salvage operations in respect of a ship which by itself or its cargo threatened damage to the environment;
    (d) damage or threat of damage caused by the ship to the environment, coastline or related interests; measures taken to prevent, minimize, or remove such damage; compensation for such damage; costs of reasonable measures of reinstatement of the environment actually undertaken or to be undertaken; loss incurred or likely to be incurred by third parties in connection with such damage; and damage, costs, or loss of a similar nature to those identified in this subparagraph (d);
    (e) costs or expenses relating to the raising, removal, recovery, destruction or the rendering harmless of a ship which is sunk, wrecked, stranded or abandoned, including anything that is or has been on board such ship, and costs or expenses relating to the preservation of an abandoned ship and maintenance of its crew;
    (f) any agreement relating to the use or hire of the ship, whether contained in a charter party or otherwise;
    (g) any agreement relating to the carriage of goods or passengers on board the ship, whether contained in a charter party or otherwise;
    (h) loss of or damage to or in connection with goods (including luggage) carried on board the ship;
    (i) general average;
    (j) towage;
    (k) pilotage;
    (l) goods, materials, provisions, bunkers, equipment (including containers) supplied or services rendered to the ship for its operation, management, preservation or maintenance;
    (m) construction, reconstruction, repair, converting or equipping of the ship;

349

    (n) port, canal, dock, harbour and other waterway dues and charges;
    (o) wages and other sums due to the master, officers and other members of the ship's complement in respect of their employment on the ship, including costs of repatriation and social insurance contributions payable on their behalf;
    (p) disbursements incurred on behalf of the ship or its owners;
    (q) insurance premiums (including mutual insurance calls) in respect of the ship, payable by or on behalf of the shipowner or demise charterer;
    (r) any commissions, brokerages or agency fees payable in respect of the ship by or on behalf of the shipowner or demise charterer;
    (s) any dispute as to ownership or possession of the ship;
    (t) any dispute between co-owners of the ship as to the employment or earnings of the ship;
    (u) a mortgage or a "hypothèque" or a charge of the same nature on the ship;
    (v) any dispute arising out of a contract for the sale of the ship.

2. "Arrest" means any detention or restriction on removal of a ship by order of a Court to secure a maritime claim, but does not include the seizure of a ship in execution or satisfaction of a judgment or other enforceable instrument.
3. "Person" means any individual or partnership or any public or private body, whether corporate or not, including a State or any of its constituent subdivisions.
4. "Claimant" means any person asserting a maritime claim.
5. "Court" means any competent judicial authority of a State.

ARTICLE 2: POWERS OF ARREST

1. A ship may be arrested or released from arrest only under the authority of a Court of the State Party in which the arrest is effected.
2. A ship may only be arrested in respect of a maritime claim but in respect of no other claim.
3. A ship may be arrested for the purpose of obtaining security notwithstanding that, by virtue of a jurisdiction clause or arbitration clause in any relevant contract, or otherwise, the maritime claim in respect of which the arrest is effected is to be adjudicated in a State other than the State where the arrest is effected, or is to be arbitrated, or is to be adjudicated subject to the law of another State.
4. Subject to the provisions of this Convention, the procedure relating to the arrest of a ship or its release shall be governed by the law of the State in which the arrest was effected or applied for.

ARTICLE 3: EXERCISE OF RIGHT OF ARREST

1. Arrest is permissible of any ship in respect of which a maritime claim is asserted if:
    (a) the person who owned the ship at the time when the maritime claim arose is liable for the claim and is owner of the ship when the arrest is effected; or
    (b) the demise charterer of the ship at the time when the maritime claim arose is liable for the claim and is demise charterer or owner of the ship when the arrest is effected; or
    (c) the claim is based upon a mortgage or a "hypothèque" or a charge of the same nature on the ship; or
    (d) the claim relates to the ownership or possession of the ship; or
    (e) the claim is against the owner, demise charterer, manager or operator of the ship and is secured by a maritime lien which is granted or arises under the law of the State where the arrest is applied for.

2. Arrest is also permissible of any other ship or ships which, when the arrest is effected, is or are owned by the person who is liable for the maritime claim and who was, when the claim arose:
    (a) owner of the ship in respect of which the maritime claim arose; or
    (b) demise charterer, time charterer or voyage charterer of that ship.

This provision does not apply to claims in respect of ownership or possession of a ship.
3. Notwithstanding the provisions of paragraphs 1 and 2 of this article, the arrest of a ship which is not owned by the person liable for the claim shall be permissible only if, under the law of the State where the arrest is applied for, a judgment in respect of that claim can be enforced against that ship by judicial or forced sale of that ship.

ARTICLE 4: RELEASE FROM ARREST

1. A ship which has been arrested shall be released when sufficient security has been provided in a satisfactory form, save in cases in which a ship has been arrested in respect of any of the maritime claims enumerated in article 1, paragraphs 1 (s) and (t). In such cases, the Court may permit the person in possession of the ship to continue trading the ship, upon such person providing sufficient security, or may otherwise deal with the operation of the ship during the period of the arrest.
2. In the absence of agreement between the parties as to the sufficiency and form of the security, the Court shall determine its nature and the amount thereof, not exceeding the value of the arrested ship.
3. Any request for the ship to be released upon security being provided shall not be construed as an acknowledgement of liability nor as a waiver of any defence or any right to limit liability.
4. If a ship has been arrested in a non-party State and is not released although security in respect of that ship has been provided in a State Party in respect of the same claim, that security shall be ordered to be released on application to the Court in the State Party.
5. If in a non-party State the ship is released upon satisfactory security in respect of that ship being provided, any security provided in a State Party in respect of the same claim shall be ordered to be released to the extent that the total amount of security provided in the two States exceeds:

(a) the claim for which the ship has been arrested, or
(b) the value of the ship,

whichever is the lower. Such release shall, however, not be ordered unless the security provided in the non-party State will actually be available to the claimant and will be freely transferable.
6. Where, pursuant to paragraph 1 of this article, security has been provided, the person providing such security may at any time apply to the Court to have that security reduced, modified, or cancelled.

ARTICLE 5: RIGHT OF REARREST AND MULTIPLE ARREST

1. Where in any State a ship has already been arrested and released or security in respect of that ship has already been provided to secure a maritime claim, that ship shall not thereafter be rearrested or arrested in respect of the same maritime claim unless:

(a) the nature or amount of the security in respect of that ship already provided in respect of the same claim is inadequate, on condition that the aggregate amount of security may not exceed the value of the ship; or
(b) the person who has already provided the security is not, or is unlikely to be, able to fulfil some or all of that person's obligations; or
(c) the ship arrested or the security previously provided was released either:
  (i) upon the application or with the consent of the claimant acting on reasonable grounds, or
  (ii) because the claimant could not by taking reasonable steps prevent the release.

2. Any other ship which would otherwise be subject to arrest in respect of the same maritime claim shall not be arrested unless:

(a) the nature or amount of the security already provided in respect of the same claim is inadequate; or
(b) the provisions of paragraph 1 (b) or (c) of this article are applicable.

3. "Release" for the purpose of this article shall not include any unlawful release or escape from arrest.

ARTICLE 6: PROTECTION OF OWNERS AND DEMISE CHARTERERS OF ARRESTED SHIPS

1. The Court may as a condition of the arrest of a ship, or of permitting an arrest already effected to be maintained, impose upon the claimant who seeks to arrest or who has procured the arrest of the ship the obligation to provide security of a kind and for an amount, and upon such terms, as may be determined by that Court for any loss which may be incurred by the defendant as a result of the arrest, and for which the claimant may be found liable, including but not restricted to such loss or damage as may be incurred by that defendant in consequence of:

  (a) the arrest having been wrongful or unjustified; or
  (b) excessive security having been demanded and provided.

2. The Courts of the State in which an arrest has been effected shall have jurisdiction to determine the extent of the liability, if any, of the claimant for loss or damage caused by the arrest of a ship, including but not restricted to such loss or damage as may be caused in consequence of:

  (a) the arrest having been wrongful or unjustified, or
  (b) excessive security having been demanded and provided.

3. The liability, if any, of the claimant in accordance with paragraph 2 of this article shall be determined by application of the law of the State where the arrest was effected.
4. If a Court in another State or an arbitral tribunal is to determine the merits of the case in accordance with the provisions of article 7, then proceedings relating to the liability of the claimant in accordance with paragraph 2 of this article may be stayed pending that decision.
5. Where pursuant to paragraph 1 of this article security has been provided, the person providing such security may at any time apply to the Court to have that security reduced, modified or cancelled.

ARTICLE 7: JURISDICTION ON THE MERITS OF THE CASE

1. The Courts of the State in which an arrest has been effected or security provided to obtain the release of the ship shall have jurisdiction to determine the case upon its merits, unless the parties validly agree or have validly agreed to submit the dispute to a Court of another State which accepts jurisdiction, or to arbitration.
2. Notwithstanding the provisions of paragraph 1 of this article, the Courts of the State in which an arrest has been effected, or security provided to obtain the release of the ship, may refuse to exercise that jurisdiction where that refusal is permitted by the law of that State and a Court of another State accepts jurisdiction.
3. In cases where a Court of the State where an arrest has been effected or security provided to obtain the release of the ship:

  (a) does not have jurisdiction to determine the case upon its merits; or
  (b) has refused to exercise jurisdiction in accordance with the provisions of paragraph 2 of this article,

such Court may, and upon request shall, order a period of time within which the claimant shall bring proceedings before a competent Court or arbitral tribunal.
4. If proceedings are not brought within the period of time ordered in accordance with paragraph 3 of this article then the ship arrested or the security provided shall, upon request, be ordered to be released.
5. If proceedings are brought within the period of time ordered in accordance with paragraph 3 of this article, or if proceedings before a competent Court or arbitral tribunal in another State are brought in the absence of such order, any final decision resulting therefrom shall be recognized and

given effect with respect to the arrested ship or to the security provided in order to obtain its release, on condition that:

    (a) the defendant has been given reasonable notice of such proceedings and a reasonable opportunity to present the case for the defence; and

    (b) such recognition is not against public policy (*ordre public*).

6. Nothing contained in the provisions of paragraph 5 of this article shall restrict any further effect given to a foreign judgment or arbitral award under the law of the State where the arrest of the ship was effected or security provided to obtain its release.

ARTICLE 8: APPLICATION

1. This Convention shall apply to any ship within the jurisdiction of any State Party, whether or not that ship is flying the flag of a State Party.

2. This Convention shall not apply to any warship, naval auxiliary or other ships owned or operated by a State and used, for the time being, only on government non-commercial service.

3. This Convention does not affect any rights or powers vested in any Government or its departments, or in any public authority, or in any dock or harbour authority, under any international convention or under any domestic law or regulation, to detain or otherwise prevent from sailing any ship within their jurisdiction.

4. This Convention shall not affect the power of any State or Court to make orders affecting the totality of a debtor's assets.

5. Nothing in this Convention shall affect the application of international conventions providing for limitation of liability, or domestic law giving effect thereto, in the State where an arrest is effected.

6. Nothing in this Convention shall modify or affect the rules of law in force in the States Parties relating to the arrest of any ship physically within the jurisdiction of the State of its flag procured by a person whose habitual residence or principal place of business is in that State, or by any other person who has acquired a claim from such person by subrogation, assignment or otherwise.

ARTICLE 9: NON-CREATION OF MARITIME LIENS

Nothing in this Convention shall be construed as creating a maritime lien.

ARTICLE 10: RESERVATIONS

1. Any State may, at the time of signature, ratification, acceptance, approval, or accession, or at any time thereafter, reserve the right to exclude the application of this Convention to any or all of the following :

    (a) ships which are not seagoing;

    (b) ships not flying the flag of a State Party;

    (c) claims under article 1, paragraph 1 (s).

2. A State may, when it is also a State Party to a specified treaty on navigation on inland waterways, declare when signing, ratifying, accepting, approving or acceding to this Convention, that rules on jurisdiction, recognition and execution of court decisions provided for in such treaties shall prevail over the rules contained in article 7 of this Convention.

ARTICLE 11: DEPOSITARY

This Convention shall be deposited with the Secretary-General of the United Nations.

ARTICLE 12: SIGNATURE, RATIFICATION, ACCEPTANCE, APPROVAL AND ACCESSION

1. This Convention shall be open for signature by any State at the Headquarters of the United Nations, New York, from 1 September 1999 to 31 August 2000 and shall thereafter remain open for accession.

2. States may express their consent to be bound by this Convention by:

    (a)   signature without reservation as to ratification, acceptance or approval; or

    (b)   signature subject to ratification, acceptance or approval, followed by ratification, acceptance or approval; or

    (c)   accession.

3. Ratification, acceptance, approval or accession shall be effected by the deposit of an instrument to that effect with the depositary.

ARTICLE 13: STATES WITH MORE THAN ONE SYSTEM OF LAW

1. If a State has two or more territorial units in which different systems of law are applicable in relation to matters dealt with in this Convention, it may at the time of signature, ratification, acceptance, approval or accession declare that this Convention shall extend to all its territorial units or only to one or more of them and may modify this declaration by submitting another declaration at any time.

2. Any such declaration shall be notified to the depositary and shall state expressly the territorial units to which the Convention applies.

3. In relation to a State Party which has two or more systems of law with regard to arrest of ships applicable in different territorial units, references in this Convention to the Court of a State and the law of a State shall be respectively construed as referring to the Court of the relevant territorial unit within that State and the law of the relevant territorial unit of that State.

ARTICLE 14: ENTRY INTO FORCE

1. This Convention shall enter into force six months following the date on which 10 States have expressed their consent to be bound by it.

2. For a State which expresses its consent to be bound by this Convention after the conditions for entry into force thereof have been met, such consent shall take effect three months after the date of expression of such consent.

ARTICLE 15: REVISION AND AMENDMENT

1. A conference of States Parties for the purpose of revising or amending this Convention shall be convened by the Secretary-General of the United Nations at the request of one-third of the States Parties.

2. Any consent to be bound by this Convention, expressed after the date of entry into force of an amendment to this Convention, shall be deemed to apply to the Convention, as amended.

ARTICLE 16: DENUNCIATION

1. This Convention may be denounced by any State Party at any time after the date on which this Convention enters into force for that State.

2. Denunciation shall be effected by deposit of an instrument of denunciation with the depositary.

3. A denunciation shall take effect one year, or such longer period as may be specified in the instrument of denunciation, after the receipt of the instrument of denunciation by the depositary.

ARTICLE 17: LANGUAGES

This Convention is established in a single original in the Arabic, Chinese, English, French, Russian and Spanish languages, each text being equally authentic.

DONE AT Geneva this twelfth day of March, one thousand nine hundred and ninety-nine.

IN WITNESS WHEREOF the undersigned being duly authorized by their respective Governments for that purpose have signed this Convention.

II.I.2 CONVENTION INTERNATIONALE DE 1999 SUR LA SAISIE CONSERVATOIRE DES NAVIRES

Les États parties à la présente Convention,
    Considérant qu'il est souhaitable de faciliter le développement harmonieux et ordonné du commerce maritime mondial,
    Convaincus de la nécessité d'un instrument juridique établissant une uniformité internationale dans le domaine de la saisie conservatoire des navires, qui tienne compte de l'évolution récente dans les domaines connexes,
    Sont convenus de ce qui suit:

ARTICLE PREMIER: DÉFINITIONS

Aux fins de la présente Convention:
1. Par "créance maritime", il faut entendre une créance découlant d'une ou plusieurs des causes suivantes:

a)   pertes ou dommages causés par l'exploitation du navire;

b)   mort ou lésions corporelles survenant, sur terre ou sur eau, en relation directe avec l'exploitation du navire;

c)   opérations de sauvetage ou d'assistance ainsi que tout contrat de sauvetage ou d'assistance, y compris, le cas échéant, une indemnité spéciale concernant des opérations de sauvetage ou d'assistance à l'égard d'un navire qui par lui-même ou par sa cargaison menaçait de causer des dommages à l'environnement;

d)   dommages causés ou risquant d'être causés par le navire au milieu, au littoral ou à des intérêts connexes; mesures prises pour prévenir, réduire ou éliminer ces dommages; indemnisation de ces dommages; coût des mesures raisonnables de remise en état du milieu qui ont été effectivement prises ou qui le seront; pertes subies ou risquant d'être subies par des tiers en rapport avec ces dommages; et dommages, coûts ou pertes de nature similaire à ceux qui sont indiqués dans le présent alinéa d);

e)   frais et dépenses relatifs au relèvement, à l'enlèvement, à la récupération, à la destruction ou à la neutralisation d'un navire coulé, naufragé, échoué ou abandonné, y compris tout ce qui se trouve ou se trouvait à bord de ce navire, et frais et dépenses relatifs à la conservation d'un navire abandonné et à l'entretien de son équipage;

f)   tout contrat relatif à l'utilisation ou à la location du navire par affrètement ou autrement;

g)   tout contrat relatif au transport de marchandises ou de passagers par le navire, par affrètement ou autrement;

h)   pertes ou dommages subis par, ou en relation avec, les biens (y compris les bagages) transportés par le navire;

i)   avarie commune;

j)   remorquage;

k)   pilotage;

l)   marchandises, matériels, approvisionnement, soutes, équipements (y compris conteneurs) fournis ou services rendus au navire pour son exploitation, sa gestion, sa conservation ou son entretien;

m) construction, reconstruction, réparation, transformation ou équipement du navire;
n) droits et redevances de port, de canal, de bassin, de mouillage et d'autres voies navigables;
o) gages et autres sommes dus au capitaine, aux officiers et autres membres du personnel de bord, en vertu de leur engagement à bord du navire, y compris les frais de rapatriement et les cotisations d'assurance sociale payables pour leur compte;
p) paiements effectués pour le compte du navire ou de ses propriétaires;
q) primes d'assurance (y compris cotisations d'assurance mutuelle) en relation avec le navire, payables par le propriétaire du navire ou par l'affréteur en dévolution ou pour leur compte;
r) frais d'agence ou commissions de courtage ou autres en relation avec le navire, payables par le propriétaire du navire ou par l'affréteur en dévolution ou pour leur compte;
s) tout litige quant à la propriété ou à la possession du navire;
t) tout litige entre les copropriétaires du navire au sujet de l'exploitation ou des droits aux produits d'exploitation de ce navire;
u) hypothèque, "mortgage" ou droit de même nature sur le navire;
v) tout litige découlant d'un contrat de vente du navire.

2. Par "saisie", il faut entendre toute immobilisation ou restriction au départ d'un navire en vertu d'une décision judiciaire pour garantir une créance maritime, mais non la saisie d'un navire pour l'exécution d'un jugement ou d'un autre instrument exécutoire.
3. Par "personne", il faut entendre toute personne physique ou morale ou toute société de personnes, de droit public ou de droit privé, y compris un État et ses subdivisions politiques.
4. Par "créancier", il faut entendre toute personne alléguant une créance maritime.
5. Par "tribunal", il faut entendre toute autorité judiciaire compétente d'un État.

ARTICLE 2: POUVOIRS DE SAISIE

1. Un navire ne peut être saisi, ou libéré de cette saisie, que par décision d'un tribunal de l'État partie dans lequel la saisie est pratiquée.
2. Un navire ne peut être saisi qu'en vertu d'une créance maritime, à l'exclusion de toute autre créance.
3. Un navire peut être saisi aux fins d'obtenir une sûreté, malgré l'existence, dans tout contrat considéré, d'une clause attributive de compétence judiciaire ou arbitrale, ou de toute autre disposition, prévoyant de soumettre la créance maritime à l'origine de la saisie à l'examen au fond du tribunal d'un État autre que celui dans lequel la saisie est pratiquée, ou d'un tribunal arbitral, ou d'une clause prévoyant l'application de la loi d'un autre État à ce contrat.
4. Sous réserve des dispositions de la présente Convention, la procédure relative à la saisie d'un navire ou à sa mainlevée est régie par la loi de l'État dans lequel la saisie a été pratiquée ou demandée.

ARTICLE 3: EXERCICE DU DROIT DE SAISIE

1. La saisie de tout navire au sujet duquel une créance maritime est alléguée peut être pratiquée si

a) la personne qui était propriétaire du navire au moment où la créance maritime est née est obligée à raison de cette créance et est propriétaire du navire au moment où la saisie est pratiquée; ou
b) l'affréteur en dévolution du navire au moment où la créance maritime est née est obligé à raison de cette créance et est affréteur en dévolution ou propriétaire du navire au moment où la saisie est pratiquée; ou
c) la créance repose sur une hypothèque, un "mortgage" ou un droit de même nature sur le navire; ou
d) la créance est relative à la propriété ou à la possession du navire; ou

e)   il s'agit d'une créance sur le propriétaire, l'affréteur en dévolution, l'armateur gérant ou l'exploitant du navire, garantie par un privilège maritime qui est accordé ou applicable en vertu de la législation de l'État dans lequel la saisie est demandée.

2. Peut également être pratiquée la saisie de tout autre navire ou de tous autres navires qui, au moment où la saisie est pratiquée, est ou sont propriété de la personne qui est obligée à raison de la créance maritime et qui, au moment où la créance est née, était:

a)   propriétaire du navire auquel la créance maritime se rapporte; ou
b)   affréteur en dévolution, affréteur à temps ou affréteur au voyage de ce navire.

Cette disposition ne s'applique pas aux créances relatives à la propriété ou à la possession d'un navire.

3. Nonobstant les dispositions des paragraphes 1 et 2 du présent article, la saisie d'un navire qui n'est pas propriété d'une personne prétendument obligée à raison de la créance ne peut être autorisée que si, selon la loi de l'État où la saisie est demandée, un jugement rendu en vertu de cette créance peut être exécuté contre ce navire par une vente judiciaire ou forcée de ce navire.

ARTICLE 4: MAINLEVÉE DE LA SAISIE

1. Un navire qui a été saisi doit être libéré lorsqu'une sûreté d'un montant suffisant et sous une forme satisfaisante a été constituée, sauf dans le cas où la saisie est pratiquée en raison des créances maritimes énumérées aux alinéas s) et t) du paragraphe 1 de l'article premier. En ce cas, le tribunal peut permettre l'exploitation du navire par la personne qui en a la possession, lorsque celle-ci aura constitué une sûreté d'un montant suffisant, ou régler de toute autre façon la question de la gestion du navire pendant la durée de la saisie.

2. Si les parties intéressées ne parviennent pas à un accord sur l'importance et la forme de la sûreté, le tribunal en détermine la nature et le montant, qui ne peut excéder la valeur du navire saisi.

3. Aucune demande tendant à la libération du navire contre la constitution d'une sûreté ne peut être interprétée comme une reconnaissance de responsabilité ni comme une renonciation à toute défense ou tout droit de limiter la responsabilité.

4. Si un navire a été saisi dans un État non partie et n'est pas libéré malgré la constitution d'une sûreté concernant ce navire dans un État partie relativement à la même créance, la mainlevée de cette sûreté est autorisée par le tribunal de l'État partie, par ordonnance rendue sur requête.

5. Si, dans un État non partie, le navire est libéré contre la constitution d'une sûreté suffisante concernant ce navire, la mainlevée de toute sûreté constituée dans un État partie relativement à la même créance est autorisée par ordonnance si le montant total de la sûreté constituée dans les deux États dépasse:

a)   soit le montant de la créance au titre de laquelle la saisie a été pratiquée;
b)   soit la valeur du navire;

la moins élevée des deux devant prévaloir. Cette mainlevée n'est toutefois autorisée par ordonnance que si la sûreté constituée est effectivement disponible dans l'État non partie et librement transférable au profit du créancier.

6. Toute personne qui a constitué une sûreté en vertu des dispositions du paragraphe 1 du présent article peut, à tout moment, demander au tribunal de réduire, modifier ou annuler cette sûreté.

ARTICLE 5: DROIT DE NOUVELLE SAISIE ET SAISIES MULTIPLES

1. Lorsque, dans un État, un navire a déjà été saisi et libéré ou qu'une sûreté a déjà été constituée pour garantir une créance maritime, ce navire ne peut ensuite faire l'objet d'aucune saisie fondée sur la même créance maritime, à moins que:

a)   la nature ou le montant de la sûreté concernant ce navire déjà constituée en vertu de la même créance ne soit pas suffisant, à condition que le montant total des sûretés ne dépasse pas la valeur du navire; ou

b) la personne qui a déjà constitué la sûreté ne soit ou ne paraisse pas capable d'exécuter tout ou partie de ses obligations; ou

c) la mainlevée de la saisie ou la libération de la sûreté ne soit intervenue:

    i) soit à la demande ou avec le consentement du créancier agissant pour des motifs raisonnables,

    ii) soit parce que le créancier n'a pu par des mesures raisonnables empêcher cette mainlevée ou cette libération.

2. Tout autre navire qui serait autrement susceptible d'être saisi en vertu de la même créance maritime ne peut être saisi à moins que:

a) la nature ou le montant de la sûreté déjà constituée en vertu de la même créance ne soit pas suffisant; ou

b) les dispositions du paragraphe 1 b) ou c) du présent article ne soient applicables.

3. La "mainlevée" aux fins du présent article exclut tout départ ou toute libération du navire de nature illégale.

ARTICLE 6: PROTECTION DES PROPRIÉTAIRES ET AFFRÉTEURS EN DÉVOLUTION DE NAVIRES SAISIS

1. Le tribunal peut, comme condition à l'autorisation de saisir un navire ou de maintenir une saisie déjà pratiquée, imposer au créancier saisissant ou ayant fait saisir le navire l'obligation de constituer une sûreté sous une forme, pour un montant et selon des conditions fixées par ce tribunal, à raison de toute perte causée par la saisie susceptible d'être subie par le défendeur et dans laquelle la responsabilité du créancier peut être prouvée, notamment mais non exclusivement, à raison de la perte ou du dommage éventuels subis par le défendeur par suite:

a) d'une saisie abusive ou injustifiée; ou

b) d'une sûreté excessive demandée et constituée.

2. Les tribunaux de l'État dans lequel une saisie a été pratiquée sont compétents pour déterminer l'étendue de la responsabilité éventuelle du créancier à raison de pertes ou dommages causés par la saisie d'un navire, notamment mais non exclusivement, de ceux qui seraient subis par suite:

a) d'une saisie abusive ou injustifiée; ou

b) d'une sûreté excessive demandée et constituée.

3. La responsabilité éventuelle du créancier, visée au paragraphe 2 du présent article, est déterminée par application de la loi de l'État où la saisie a été pratiquée.

4. Au cas où le litige est, conformément aux dispositions de l'article 7, soumis à l'examen au fond d'un tribunal d'un autre État ou d'un tribunal arbitral, la procédure relative à la responsabilité du créancier prévue au paragraphe 2 du présent article peut être suspendue dans l'attente de la décision au fond.

5. Toute personne qui a constitué une sûreté en vertu des dispositions du paragraphe 1 du présent article peut à tout moment demander au tribunal de réduire, modifier ou annuler cette sûreté.

ARTICLE 7: COMPÉTENCE SUR LE FOND DU LITIGE

1. Les tribunaux de l'État dans lequel une saisie a été pratiquée ou une sûreté constituée pour obtenir la libération du navire sont compétents pour juger le litige au fond, à moins que les parties, de façon valable, ne conviennent ou ne soient convenues de soumettre le litige au tribunal d'un autre État se déclarant compétent, ou à l'arbitrage.

2. Nonobstant les dispositions du paragraphe 1 du présent article, les tribunaux de l'État dans lequel une saisie a été pratiquée, ou une sûreté constituée pour obtenir la libération du navire, peuvent décliner leur compétence si le droit de cet État le leur permet et si le tribunal d'un autre État se reconnaît compétent.

3. Lorsqu'un tribunal de l'État dans lequel une saisie a été pratiquée ou une sûreté constituée pour obtenir la libération du navire:

    a)   n'est pas compétent pour statuer au fond sur le litige; ou

    b)   a décliné sa compétence en vertu des dispositions du paragraphe 2 du présent article,

ce tribunal peut et, sur requête, doit fixer au créancier un délai pour engager la procédure au fond devant un tribunal compétent ou une juridiction arbitrale.

4. Si, au terme du délai fixé conformément au paragraphe 3 du présent article, la procédure au fond n'a pas été engagée, la mainlevée de la saisie ou de la sûreté constituée est, sur requête, autorisée par ordonnance.

5. Si la procédure est engagée avant le terme du délai fixé conformément au paragraphe 3 du présent article, ou si la procédure devant un tribunal compétent ou un tribunal arbitral d'un autre État est engagée en l'absence de fixation d'un délai, toute décision définitive prononcée à l'issue de cette procédure est reconnue et prend effet à l'égard du navire saisi ou de la sûreté constituée pour prévenir la saisie du navire ou obtenir sa libération, à condition que:

    a)   le défendeur ait été averti de cette procédure dans des délais raisonnables et mis en mesure de présenter sa défense;

    b)   cette reconnaissance ne soit pas contraire à l'ordre public.

6. Aucune des dispositions du paragraphe 5 du présent article ne limite la portée d'un jugement ou d'une sentence arbitrale étrangers rendus selon la loi de l'État où la saisie du navire a été pratiquée ou une sûreté constituée pour en obtenir la libération.

ARTICLE 8: APPLICATION

1. La présente Convention est applicable à tout navire relevant de la juridiction d'un État partie, quel qu'il soit, et battant ou non pavillon d'un État partie.

2. La présente Convention n'est pas applicable aux navires de guerre, navires de guerre auxiliaires et autres navires appartenant à un État ou exploités par lui et exclusivement affectés, jusqu'à nouvel ordre, à un service public non commercial.

3. La présente Convention ne porte atteinte à aucun des droits ou pouvoirs, dévolus par une convention internationale, une loi ou réglementation interne à un État ou à ses administrations, à un établissement public ou à une autorité portuaire, de retenir un navire ou d'en interdire le départ dans le ressort de leur juridiction.

4. La présente Convention ne porte pas atteinte au pouvoir d'un État ou tribunal de rendre des ordonnances applicables à la totalité du patrimoine d'un débiteur.

5. Aucune disposition de la présente Convention ne porte atteinte à l'application de conventions internationales ni d'aucune loi interne leur donnant effet, autorisant la limitation de responsabilité dans l'État où une saisie est pratiquée.

6. Aucune disposition de la présente Convention ne modifie ou ne concerne les textes de loi en vigueur dans les États parties relativement à la saisie d'un navire dans la juridiction de l'État dont il bat pavillon, obtenue par une personne ayant sa résidence habituelle ou son principal établissement dans cet État, ou par toute autre personne qui a acquis une créance de ladite personne par voie de subrogation, de cession, ou par tout autre moyen.

ARTICLE 9: NON-CRÉATION DE PRIVILÈGES MARITIMES

Aucune disposition de la présente Convention ne peut être interprétée comme créant un privilège maritime.

ARTICLE 10: RÉSERVES

1. Un État peut, au moment de la signature, de la ratification, de l'acceptation, de l'approbation ou de l'adhésion, ou à tout moment par la suite, se réserver le droit d'exclure du champ d'application de la présente Convention:

a)   les bâtiments autres que les navires de mer;
b)   les navires ne battant pas le pavillon d'un État partie;
c)   les créances visées à l'alinéa s) du paragraphe 1 de l'article premier.

2. Un État qui est aussi partie à un traité sur la navigation intérieure, peut déclarer, au moment de la signature, de la ratification, de l'acceptation ou de l'approbation de la présente Convention ou de l'adhésion à celle-ci, que les dispositions de ce traité concernant la compétence des tribunaux et la reconnaissance et l'exécution de leurs décisions prévalent sur les dispositions de l'article 7 de la présente Convention.

ARTICLE 11: DÉPOSITAIRE

La présente Convention est déposée auprès du Secrétaire général de l'Organisation des Nations Unies.

ARTICLE 12: SIGNATURE, RATIFICATION, ACCEPTATION, APPROBATION ET ADHÉSION

1. La présente Convention est ouverte à la signature des États au Siège de l'Organisation des Nations Unies, à New York, du 1er septembre 1999 au 31 août 2000. Elle reste ensuite ouverte à l'adhésion.
2. Les États peuvent exprimer leur consentement à être liés par la présente Convention par:

a)   signature sans réserve quant à la ratification, l'acceptation ou l'approbation; ou
b)   signature sous réserve de ratification, d'acceptation ou d'approbation, suivie de ratification, d'acceptation ou d'approbation; ou
c)   adhésion.

3. La ratification, l'acceptation, l'approbation ou l'adhésion s'effectuent par le dépôt d'un instrument à cet effet auprès du dépositaire.

ARTICLE 13: ÉTATS AYANT PLUS D'UN RÉGIME JURIDIQUE

1. S'il possède deux ou plusieurs unités territoriales dans lesquelles des régimes juridiques différents sont applicables pour ce qui est des matières traitées dans la présente Convention, un État peut, au moment de la signature, de la ratification, de l'acceptation, de l'approbation ou de l'adhésion, déclarer que la présente Convention s'applique à l'ensemble de ses unités territoriales ou seulement à une ou plusieurs d'entre elles, et il peut modifier cette déclaration en présentant une autre déclaration à tout moment.
2. La déclaration est notifiée au dépositaire et précise expressément les unités territoriales auxquelles s'applique la Convention.
3. Dans le cas d'un État partie qui possède deux ou plusieurs régimes juridiques concernant la saisie conservatoire des navires applicables dans différentes unités territoriales, les références dans la présente Convention au tribunal d'un État et à la loi ou au droit d'un État sont considérées comme renvoyant, respectivement, au tribunal et à la loi ou au droit de l'unité territoriale pertinente de cet État.

ARTICLE 14: ENTRÉE EN VIGUEUR

1. La présente Convention entre en vigueur six mois après la date à laquelle 10 États ont exprimé leur consentement à être liés par elle.
2. Pour un État qui exprime son consentement à être lié par la présente Convention après que les conditions de son entrée en vigueur ont été remplies, ce consentement prend effet trois mois après la date à laquelle il a été exprimé.

ARTICLE 15: RÉVISION ET AMENDEMENT

1. Le Secrétaire général de l'Organisation des Nations Unies convoque une conférence des États parties pour réviser ou modifier la présente Convention, à la demande d'un tiers des États parties.

2. Tout consentement à être lié par la présente Convention exprimé après la date d'entrée en vigueur d'un amendement à la présente Convention est réputé s'appliquer à la Convention telle que modifiée.

ARTICLE 16: DÈNONCIATION

1. La présente Convention peut être dénoncée par l'un quelconque des États parties à tout moment à compter de la date à laquelle elle entre en vigueur à l'égard de cet État.

2. La dénonciation s'effectue au moyen du dépôt d'un instrument de dénonciation auprès du dépositaire.

3. La dénonciation prend effet un an après la date à laquelle le dépositaire a reçu l'instrument de dénonciation ou à l'expiration de tout délai plus long énoncé dans cet instrument.

ARTICLE 17: LANGUES

La présente Convention est établie en un seul exemplaire original en langues anglaise, arabe, chinoise, espagnole, française et russe, chaque texte faisant également foi.

FAIT À Genève, le douze mars mil neuf cent quatre-vingt-dix-neuf.

EN FOI DE QUOI, les soussignés, dûment autorisés à cet effet par leurs gouvernements respectifs, ont apposé leur signature à la présente Convention.

II.I.3 CONVENIO INTERNACIONAL SOBRE EL EMBARGO PREVENTIVO DE BUQUES, 1999

Los Estados Partes en el presente Convenio,

Reconociendo la conveniencia de facilitar el desarrollo armonioso y ordenado del comercio maritimo mundial,

Convencidos de la necesidad de un instrumento juridico que establezca una uniformidad internacional en la esfera del embargo preventivo de buques y que tenga en cuenta la evolución reciente en esferas conexas,

Han convenido en lo siguiente:

ARTÍCULO 1: DEFINICIONES

A los efectos del presente Convenio:

1. Por "credito marítimo" se entiende un credito que tenga una o varias de las siguientes causas:

   a) pérdidas o daños causados por la explotación del buque;

   b) muerte o lesiones corporales sobrevenidas, en tierra o en el agua, en relación directa con la explotación del buque;

   c) operaciones de asistencia o salvamento o todo contrato de salvamento, incluida, si corresponde, la compensación especial relativa a operaciones de asistencia o salvamento respecto de un buque que, por sí mismo o por su carga, amenace causar daño al medio ambiente;

   d) daño o amenaza de daño causados por el buque al medio ambiente, el litoral o intereses conexos; medidas adoptadas para prevenir, minimizar o eliminar ese daño; indemnización por ese daño; los costos de las medidas razonables de restauracion del medio ambiente efectivamente tomadas o que vayan a tomarse; pérdidas en que hayan incurrido o puedan incurrir terceros en relación con ese daño; y el daño, costos o pérdidas de carácter similar a los indicados en este apartado d);

   e) gastos y desembolsos relativos a la puesta a flote, la remoción, la recuperación, la destrucción o la eliminación de la peligrosidad que presente un buque hundido, naufragado, embarrancado o abandonado, incluido todo lo que esté o haya estado a bordo de un buque, y los costos y desembolsos relacionados con la conservación de un buque abandonado y el mantenimiento de su tripulación;

   f) todo contrato relativo a la utilización o al arrendamiento del buque formalizado en póliza de fletamento o de otro modo;

   g) todo contrato relativo al transporte de mercancías o de pasajeros en el buque formalizado en póliza de fletamento o de otro modo;

   h) las pérdidas o los daños causados a las mercancías (incluidos los equipajes) transportadas a bordo del buque;

   i) la avería gruesa;

   j) el remolque;

   k) el practicaje;

   l) las mercancías, materiales, provisiones, combustibles, equipo (incluidos los contenedores) suministrados o servicios prestados al buque para su explotación, gestión, conservación o mantenimiento;

m) la construcción, reconstrucción, reparación, transformación o equipamiento del buque;
n) los derechos y gravámenes de puertos, canales, muelles, radas y otras vías navegables;
o) los sueldos y otras cantidades debidas al capitán, los oficiales y demás miembros de la dotación en virtud de su enrolamiento a bordo del buque, incluidos los gastos de repatriación y las cuotas de la seguridad social pagaderas en su nombre;
p) los desembolsos hechos por cuenta del buque o de sus propietarios;
q) las primas de seguro (incluidas las cotizaciones de seguro mutuo), pagaderas por el propietario del buque o el arrendatario a casco desnudo, o por su cuenta, en relación con el buque;
r) las comisiones, corretajes u honorarios de agencias pagaderos por el propietario del buque o el arrendatario a casco desnudo, o por su cuenta, en relación con el buque;
s) toda controversia relativa a la propiedad o a la posesión del buque;
t) toda controversia entre los copropietarios del buque acerca de su utilización o del producto de su explotación;
u) una hipoteca, "mortgage" o gravamen de la misma naturaleza sobre el buque;
v) toda controversia resultante de un contrato de compraventa del buque.

2. Por "embargo" se entiende toda inmovilización o restricción a la salida de un buque impuesta por resolución de un tribunal en garantía de un crédito marítimo, pero no comprende la retención de un buque para la ejecución de una sentencia u otro instrumento ejecutorio.
3. Por "persona" se entiende toda persona física o jurídica o toda entidad de derecho público o privado, esté o no constituida en sociedad, inclusive un Estado o cualquiera de sus subdivisiones políticas.
4. Por "acreedor" se entiende toda persona que alegue un crédito marítimo.
5. Por "tribunal" se entiende toda autoridad judicial competente de un Estado.

ARTÍCULO 2: POTESTAD PARA EMBARGAR

1. Sólo se podrá embargar un buque o levantar su embargo por resolucián de un tribunal del Estado Parte en el que se haya practicado el embargo.
2. Sólo se podrá embargar un buque en virtud de un crédito marítimo, pero no en virtud de otro crédito.
3. Un buque podrá ser embargado a los efectos de obtener una garantia aunque, en virtud de una cláusula de jurisdicción o una cláusula de arbitraje contenida en cualquier contrato aplicable o de otra forma, el crédito marítimo por el que se haga el embargo deba someterse a la jurisdicción de los tribunales de un Estado distinto de aquel en que se practique el embargo o a arbitraje o deba regirse por la ley de otro Estado.
4. Con sujeción a lo dispuesto en el presente Convenio, el procedimiento relativo al embargo de un buque o al levantamiento de ese embargo se regirá por la ley del Estado en que se haya solicitado o practicado el embargo.

ARTÍCULO 3: EJERCICIO DEL DERECHO DE EMBARGO

1. El embargo de todo buque con respecto al cual se alegue un crédito marítimo procederá:

a) si la persona que era propietaria del buque en el momento en que nació el crédito marítimo está obligada en virtud de ese crédito y es propietaria del buque al practicarse el embargo; o
b) si el arrendatario a casco desnudo del buque en el momento en que nació el crédito marítimo está obligado en virtud de ese crédito y es arrendatario a casco desnudo o propietario del buque al practicarse el embargo; o
c) si el crédito se basa en una hipoteca, "mortgage" o gravamen de la misma naturaleza sobre el buque; o
d) si el crédito se refiere a la propiedad o la posesión del buque; o

e) si el crédito es contra el propietario, el arrendatario a casco desnudo, el gestor o el naviero del buque y está garantizado por un privilegio marítimo concedido por la legislación del Estado en que se solicita el embargo o en virtud de esa legislación.

2. Procederá también el embargo de cualquier otro buque o buques que, al practicarse el embargo, fueren propiedad de la persona que esté obligada en virtud del crédito marítimo y que, en el momento en que nació el crédito, era:

a) propietaria del buque con respecto al cual haya nacido el crédito marítimo; o
b) arrendataria a casco desnudo, fletador por tiempo o fletador por viaje de ese buque.

La presente disposición no se aplica a los créditos relativos a la propiedad o la posesión de un buque.

3. No obstante lo dispuesto en los párrafos 1 y 2 del presente artículo, el embargo de un buque que no sea propiedad de la persona obligada en virtud del crédito sólo será admisible si, conforme a la ley del Estado en que se solicita el embargo, se puede ejecutar contra ese buque una sentencia dictada en relación con ese crédito, mediante su venta judicial o forzosa.

ARTÍCULO 4: LEVANTAMIENTO DEL EMBARGO

1. Un buque que haya sido embargado será liberado cuando se haya prestado garantía bastante en forma satisfactoria, salvo que haya sido embargado para responder de cualquiera de los créditos marítimos enumerados en los apartados s) y t) del párrafo 1 del artículo 1. En estos casos, el tribunal podrá autorizar a la persona en posesión del buque a seguir explotándolo, una vez que esta persona haya prestado garantía suficiente, o resolver de otro modo la cuestión de la operación del buque durante el periodo del embargo.

2. A falta de acuerdo entre las partes sobre la suficiencia y la forma de la garantía, el tribunal determinará su naturaleza y su cuantía, que no podrá exceder del valor del buque embargado.

3. La solicitud de levantamiento del embargo del buque previa constitución de garantía no se interpretará como reconocimiento de responsabilidad ni como renuncia a cualquier defensa o al derecho a limitar la responsabilidad.

4. Si un buque hubiera sido embargado en un Estado que no sea parte no hubiera sido liberado pese a la garantía prestada en relación con ese buque en un Estado Parte respecto del mismo crédito, se ordenará la cancelación de la garantía previa solicitud ante el tribunal del Estado Parte.

5. Si un buque hubiera sido liberado en un Estado que no sea parte por haberse prestado garantía suficiente, toda garantía prestada en un Estado Parte en relación con el mismo crédito se mandará cancelar en la medida en que la cuantía total de la garantía prestada en los dos Estados exceda:

a) del valor del crédito por el que se hubiera embargado el buque; o
b) del valor del buque;

de ambos el que sea menor. Sin embargo, no se ordenará dicha liberación a menos que la garantía prestada en el Estado que no sea parte esté efectivamente a disposición del acreedor y le sea libremente transferible.

6. La persona que haya prestado una garantía en virtud de las disposiciones del párrafo 1 del presente artículo podrá en cualquier momento solicitar al tribunal su reducción, modificación o cancelación.

ARTÍCULO 5: DERECHO DE REEMBARGO Y PLURALIDAD DE EMBARGOS

1. Cuando en un Estado un buque ya hubiera sido embargado y liberado, o ya se hubiera prestado garantía respecto de ese buque en relación con un crédito maritimo, el buque no podrá ser reembargado o embargado por el mismo crédito, a menos que:

a) la naturaleza o la cuantía de la garantía respecto de ese buque ya prestada en relación con ese crédito sea inadecuada, a condición de que la cuantía total de la garantia no exceda del valor del buque; o

b) la persona que haya prestado ya la garantía no pueda, o no sea probable que pueda, cumplir total o parcialmente sus obligaciones; o

c) se haya liberado el buque embargado o se haya cancelado la garantía prestada anteriormente, ya sea:

　　i) a instancias o con el consentimiento del acreedor, cuando actúe por motivos razonables, o

　　ii) porque el acreedor no haya podido, mediante la adopción de medidas razonables, impedir tal liberación o cancelación.

2. Cualquier otro buque que de otro modo estaría sujeto a embargo por el mismo crédito marítimo no será embargado a menos que:

a) la naturaleza o la cuantía de la garantía ya prestada en relación con el mismo crédito sean inadecuadas; o

b) sean aplicables las disposiciones de los apartados b) o c) del párrafo 1 del presente artículo.

3. A los efectos del presente artículo, la expresión "liberación" excluye toda salida o liberación ilegal del buque.

ARTÍCULO 6: PROTECCIÓN DE LOS PROPIETARIOS Y ARRENDATARIOS A CASCO DESNUDO DE BUQUES EMBARGADOS

1. El tribunal podrá, como condición para decretar el embargo de un buque o, hecho éste, para autorizar su mantenimiento, imponer al acreedor que solicite o que haya obtenido el embargo del buque la obligación de prestar garantía de la clase, por la cuantía y en las condiciones que determine el tribunal para responder de los perjuicios que puedan irrogarse al demandado como consecuencia del embargo, y de los que se pueda tener como responsable al acreedor, en particular, pero no exclusivamente, la pérdida o el daño que puedan ocasionarse al demandado:

a) por ser ilícito o no estar justificado el embargo; o

b) por haberse pedido y prestado una garantía excesiva.

2. Los tribunales del Estado en que se haya practicado un embargo serán competentes para determinar el alcance de la responsabilidad del acreedor, cuando hubiere incurrido en ella, por la pérdida o el daño causados por el embargo de un buque, en particular, pero no esclusivamente, los que se hubieren causado:

a) por ser ilícito o no estar justificado el embargo; o

b) por haberse pedido y prestado una garantía excesiva.

3. La responsabilidad en que, en su caso, hubiere incurrido el acreedor a tenor de lo dispuesto en el párrafo 2 del presente artículo se determinará por aplicación de la ley del Estado en que se haya practicado el embargo.

4. Si un tribunal de otro Estado o un tribunal arbitral tuviere que resolver sobre el fondo del litigio de conformidad con el artículo 7, la sustanciación del procedimiento relativo a la responsabilidad del acreedor a tenor de lo dispuesto en el párrafo 2 del presente artículo podrá suspenderse hasta que recaiga decisión sobre el fondo.

5. La persona que haya prestado una garantía en virtud de las disposiciones del párrafo 1 del presente artículo podrá en cualquier momento solicitar al tribunal su reducción, modificación o cancelación.

ARTÍCULO 7: COMPETENCIA PARA CONOCER DEL FONDO DEL LITIGIO

1. Los tribunales del Estado en que se haya practicado un embargo o se haya prestado garantía para obtener la liberación del buque serán competentes para resolver sobre el fondo del litigio, a menos

que válidamente las Partes acuerden o hayan acordado someter el litigio a un tribunal de otro Estado que se declare competente o a arbitraje.

2. No obstante lo dispuesto en el párrafo 1 del presente artículo, los tribunales del Estado en que se haya practicado un embargo o se haya prestado garantía para obtener la liberación del buque podrán declinar su competencia si la ley nacional les autoriza a ello y el tribunal de otro Estado se declara competente.

3. Cuando un tribunal del Estado en que se haya practicado un embargo o se haya prestado garantía para obtener la liberación del buque:

    a)   no tenga competencia para resolver sobre el fondo del litigio; o

    b)   haya declinado su competencia de conformidad con el párrafo 2 del presente artículo,

ese tribunal podrá de oficio, y deberá a instancia de parte, fijar un plazo para que el acreedor entable la demanda ante un tribunal de justicia competente o ante un tribunal arbitral.

4. Si no se entabla la demanda dentro del plazo fijado de conformidad con el párrafo 3 del presente artículo, se decretará a instancia de parte la liberación del buque embargado o la cancelación de la garantía prestada.

5. Si se entabla la demanda dentro del plazo fijado de conformidad con el párrafo 3 del presente artículo o, de no haberse fijado ese plazo, si se entabla la demanda ante un tribunal competente o un tribunal arbitral de otro Estado, toda resolución definitiva dictada en ese procedimiento será reconocida y surtirá efecto con respecto al buque embargado o a la garantía prestada para obtener la liberación del buque, a condición de que:

    a)   se haya comunicado la demanda al demandado con suficiente antelación y se le ofrezcan oportunidades razonables para defenderse; y

    b)   ese reconocimiento no sea contrario al orden público.

6. Ninguna de las disposiciones del párrafo 5 del presente artículo limitará otros posibles efectos que la ley del Estado en que se haya practicado el embargo del buque o se haya prestado garantía para obtener su liberación, reconozca una sentencia o un laudo arbitral extranjeros.

ARTÍCULO 8: APLICACIÓN

1. El presente Convenio se aplicará a todo buque que navegue dentro de la jurisdicción de un Estado Parte, enarbole o no el pabellón de un Estado Parte.

2. El presente Convenio no se aplicará a los buques de guerra, a las unidades navales auxiliares y a otros buques pertenecientes a un Estado o explotados por él y destinados esclusivamente, en ese momento, a un uso público no comercial.

3. El presente Convenio no afectará a los derechos o facultades que, con arreglo a un convenio internacional o en virtud de una ley o reglamento internos, correspondan a la Administración del Estado o a alguno de sus órganos, los poderes públicos o a la administración portuaria para retener un buque o impedir de otro modo que se haga a la mar dentro de su jurisdicción.

4. El presente Convenio no menoscabará la facultad de un Estado o tribunal para decretar medidas que afecten a la totalidad del patrimonio de un deudor.

5. Las disposiciones del presente Convenio no afectarán a la aplicación en el Estado en que se practique un embargo de los convenios internacionales que establezcan una limitación de responsabilidad o de la ley interna dictada para darles efectividad.

6. Las disposiciones del presente Convenio no modificarán las normas jurídicas en vigor en los Estados Partes, ni afectarán a su aplicación, relativas al embargo de un buque que se encuentre dentro de la jurisdicción del Estado cuyo pabellán enarbole, practicado a instancias de una persona que tenga su residencia habitual o su establecimiento principal en ese Estado o de cualquier otra persona que haya adquirido un crédito de ésta por subrogación, cesión o cualquier otro medio.

ARTÍCULO 9: NO CREACIÓN DE UN PRIVILEGIO MARÍTIMO

Las disposiciones del presente Convenio no se interpretarán en el sentido de que crean un privilegio marítimo.

ARTÍCULO 10: RESERVAS

1. En el momento de la firma, ratificación, aprobación o aceptación del presente Convenio o de la adhesión a él, o en cualquier momento posterior, todo Estado podrá reservarse el derecho de excluir de su aplicación a algunas o todas las categorías siguientes:

a) los buques que no sean de navegación marítima;
b) los buques que no enarbolen el pabellón de un Estado Parte;
c) los créditos a que hace referencia el apartado s) del párrafo 1 del artículo 1.

2. En el momento de la firma, ratificación, aprobación o aceptación del presente Convenio o de la adhesión a él, todo Estado que sea también Parte en un determinado tratado sobre vías de navegación interior podrá declarar que las normas sobre competencia, reconocimiento y ejecución de sentencias judiciales de ese tratado prevalecen sobre las disposiciones del artículo 7 del presente Convenio.

ARTÍCULO 11: DEPOSITARIO

El presente Convenio quedará depositado en poder del Secretario General de las Naciones Unidas.

ARTÍCULO 12: FIRMA, RATIFICACIÓN, ACEPTACIÓN, APROBACIÓN Y ADHESIÓN

1. El presente Convenio estará abierto a la firma en la Sede de las Naciones Unidas, en Nueva York, desde el 1° de septiembre de 1999 hasta el 31 de agosto del año 2000 y después quedará abierto a la adhesión.
2. Los Estados podrán manifestar su consentimiento en obligarse por el presente Convenio mediante:

a) firma, sin reserva de ratificación, aceptación o aprobación; o
b) firma, con reserva de ratificación, aceptación o aprobación, seguida de ratificación, aceptación o aprobación; o
c) adhesión.

3. La ratificación, aceptación, aprobación o adhesión se efectuarán mediante el deposito de un instrumento a tal efecto en poder del depositario.

ARTÍCULO 13: ESTADOS CON MÁS DE UN RÉGIMEN JURÍDICO

1. Todo Estado integrado por dos o más unidades territoriales en las que sea aplicable un régimen jurídico distinto en relación con las materias objeto del presente Convenio podrá declarar en el momento de dar su firma, ratificación, aceptación, aprobación o adhesión al mismo que el presente Convenio será aplicable a todas sus unidades territoriales, o sólo a una o varias de ellas, y podrá en cualquier momento sustituir por otra su declaración original.
2. Esa declaración se notificará al depositario y en ella se hará constar expresamente a qué unidades territoriales será aplicable el Convenio.
3. En relación con un Estado Parte que tenga dos o más regimenes juridicos en lo que respecta al embargo preventivo de buques, aplicables en diferentes unidades territoriales, las referencias en el presente Convenio al tribunal de un Estado o a la legislación de un Estado se entenderán respectivamente como relativas al tribunal de la unidad territorial pertinente dentro de ese Estado y a la legislación de la unidad territorial pertinente de ese Estado.

ARTÍCULO 14: ENTRADA EN VIGOR

1. El presente Convenio entrará en vigor seis meses después de la fecha en que diez Estados hayan manifestado su consentimiento en obligarse por él.

2. Respecto de un Estado que manifeste su consentimiento en obligarse por el presente Convenio después de que se hayan cumplido los requisitos para su entrada en vigor, ese consentimiento surtirá efecto tres meses después de la fecha en que haya sido manifestado.

ARTÍCULO 15: REVISIÓN Y ENMIENDA

1. El Secretario General de las Naciones Unidas convocará una conferencia de los Estados Partes para revisar o enmendar el presente Convenio, si lo solicita un tercio de los Estados Partes.
2. Todo consentimiento en obligarse por el presente Convenio manifestado después de la fecha de la entrada en vigor de una enmienda al presente Convenio se entenderá que se aplica al Convenio en su forma enmendada.

ARTÍCULO 16: DENUNCIA

1. El presente Convenio podrá ser denunciado por cualquier Estado Parte en cualquier momento después de la fecha en que haya entrado en vigor respecto de ese Estado.
2. La denuncia se efectuará mediante el deposito de un instrumento de denuncia en poder del depositario.
3. La denuncia surtirá efecto un año después de la fecha en que el depositario haya recibido el instrumento de denuncia, o a la expiración de cualquier plazo más largo que se señale en ese instrumento.

ARTÍCULO 17: IDIOMAS

El presente Convenio se consigna en un solo original, cuyos textos en árabe, chino, español, francés, inglés y ruso son igualmente auténticos.

HECHO en Ginebra el día doce de marzo de mil novecientos noventa y nueve.
EN TESTIMONIO DE LO CUAL los infrascritos, debidamente autorizados al efecto por sus respectivos gobiernos, han firmado el presente Convenio.

APPENDIX II

Report of the United Nations/International Maritime Organization Diplomatic Conference on Arrest of Ships*

II.II.1 CHAPTER I: FINAL ACT OF THE UNITED NATIONS/ INTERNATIONAL MARITIME ORGANIZATION DIPLOMATIC CONFERENCE ON ARREST OF SHIPS

1. The General Assembly of the United Nations, by resolution 52/182 of 18 December 1997, endorsed the convening of a Diplomatic Conference in order to consider and adopt a convention on arrest of ships.
2. The United Nations/International Maritime Organization Diplomatic Conference on Arrest of Ships was convened at Geneva from 1 to 12 March 1999.
3. Representatives from the following States participated in the Conference: Algeria, Angola, Argentina, Australia, Belarus, Belgium, Benin, Brazil, Bulgaria, Burundi, Cameroon, Canada, Chile, China, Colombia, Côte d'Ivoire, Croatia, Cuba, Cyprus, Denmark, Dominican Republic, Ecuador, Egypt, El Salvador, Estonia, Ethiopia, Finland, France, Gabon, Gambia, Georgia, Germany, Ghana, Greece, Guinea, Haiti, Honduras, Hungary, India, Indonesia, Iran (Islamic Republic of), Iraq, Israel, Italy, Japan, Kenya, Latvia, Lebanon, Liberia, Lithuania, Madagascar, Malta, Marshall Islands, Mauritania, Mexico, Monaco, Morocco, Mozambique, Netherlands, Nigeria, Norway, Pakistan, Panama, Peru, Philippines, Poland, Portugal, Republic of Korea, Romania, Russian Federation, Senegal, Singapore, Slovakia, Slovenia, South Africa, Spain, Sri Lanka, Sudan, Sweden, Switzerland, Syrian Arab Republic, Thailand, Trinidad and Tobago, Tunisia, Turkey, Ukraine, United Arab Emirates, United Kingdom of Great Britain and Northern Ireland, United Republic of Tanzania, United States of America, Uruguay, Viet Nam, and Yemen.
4. Hong Kong Special Administrative Region of China and Macao, associate members of the International Maritime Organization, were represented by observers.
5. The following intergovernmental organizations were represented by an observer: Arab Labour Organization, Organization of African Unity, Organization of American States, Organization of the Islamic Conference, Intergovernmental Organization for International Carriage by Rail.
6. The following non-governmental organizations were represented by an observer: *general category*: International Chamber of Commerce, International Confederation of Free Trade Unions, World Federation of United Nations Associations; *special category*: International Ship Suppliers Association, International Association of Ports and Harbours, Latin American Association of Navigational Law and Law of the Sea, International Chamber of Shipping, Comité Maritime International, Institute of International Container Lessors, Ibero-American Institute of Maritime Law, International Group of P & I Clubs, International Union for Conservation of Nature and Natural Resources.
7. The Conference elected the following officers:

President:	Mr. Zhu Zengjie	(China)
Vice-Presidents:	Mrs. Ida Barinova	(Russian Federation)
	Mr. Marc Gauthier	(Canada)
	Mr. Mykola Maimeskul	(Ukraine)
	Mr. Mahmoud BaHey Eldin Ibrahim Nasrah	(Egypt)

---

* Held at the Palais des Nations, Geneva, from 1 to 12 March 1999

Mr. Eladio Peñaloza	(Panama)
Mr. Luigi Rovelli	(Italy)
Mr. Lalchand K. Sheri	(Singapore)
Rapporteur-General: Mr. Walter de Sa'Leitao	(Brazil)

8. The Conference established a Main Committee, a Drafting Committee and a Credentials · Committee.

MAIN COMMITTEE

Chairman:	Mr. K.J. Gombrii	(Norway)
Members:	open-ended	

DRAFTING COMMITTEE

Chairman:	Mr. Malcolm J. Williams, Jr.	(United States of America)
Core members:	Algeria, Argentina, Belgium, China, Côte d'Ivoire, Croatia, Denmark, Egypt, France, Gambia, Germany, Ghana, Lithuania, Mexico, Russian Federation, Spain, Sri Lanka, Tunisia, Turkey, United Kingdom of Great Britain and Northern Ireland, and United States of America.	

CREDENTIALS COMMITTEE

Chairman:	Ms. Sama Payman	(Australia)
Members:	Australia, Benin, Brazil, China, Haiti, Mozambique, Philippines, Russian Federation, United States of America.	

9. The secretariat of the Conference included the following officers: Secretary-General of UNCTAD, Mr. Rubens Ricupero; Executive Secretary, Mr. Jean Gurunlian, Director, Division for Services Infrastructure for Development and Trade Efficiency, UNCTAD; Deputy Executive Secretary, Mrs. Rosalie Balkin, Director, Legal Affairs and External Relations Division, IMO; Mrs. Monica N. Mbanefo, Senior Deputy Director, IMO; Mr. Agustín Bianco-Bazán, Senior Legal Officer, IMO; Ms. Mahin Faghfouri, Head, Legal Unit, SITE, UNCTAD; Mr. Carlos Moreno, Legal Officer, SITE, UNCTAD; Mr. Erik Chrispeels, Senior Legal Officer, UNCTAD; Mr. Awni Behnam, Secretary of the Conference, UNCTAD; Mr. Karma Tenzing, Deputy Secretary of the Conference, UNCTAD.

10. The Conference had before it, as a basis for its work, the draft articles for a convention on arrest of ships,[1] prepared by the Joint UNCTAD/IMO Intergovernmental Group of Experts on Maritime Liens and Mortgages and Related Subjects, and the compilation of comments and proposals by Governments, and by intergovernmental and non-governmental organizations, on the draft convention on arrest of ships.[2] The Conference adopted its rules of procedure[3] and its agenda.[4]

11. On the basis of its deliberations as recorded in its report,[5] the Conference established the text of the INTERNATIONAL CONVENTION ON ARREST OF SHIPS, 1999.

12. The text of the Convention was adopted by the Conference on 12 March 1999. The Convention will be open for signature at United Nations Headquarters, New York, from 1 September 1999 to and including 31 August 2000.

Done in Geneva, on this twelfth day of March one thousand nine hundred and ninety-nine, in one original in the Arabic, Chinese, English, French, Russian and Spanish languages, all texts being

---

1. TD/B/IGE.1/5.
2. A/CONF.188/3 and Add. 1–3.
3. A/CONF.188/2.
4. A/CONF.188/1.
5. A/CONF.188/5.

equally authentic. The original of the Final Act shall be deposited in the archives of the United Nations Secretariat.

Zhu Zenjie
President of the Conference

R. Ricupero
Secretary-General of UNCTAD

J. Gurunlian
Executive Secretary of the Conference

R. Balkin
Deputy Executive Secretary of the Conference

M. Faghfouri
Head, Legal Unit, SITE

E. Chrispeels
Senior Legal Officer

A. Behnam
Secretary of the Conference

IN WITNESS WHEREOF the undersigned representatives have signed this Final Act.

The States whose representatives signed the Final Act are: Algeria, Argentina, Australia, Belgium, Benin, Brazil, Cameroon, Canada, China, Colombia, Côte d'Ivoire, Croatia, Cuba, Denmark, Ecuador, Egypt, El Salvador, Estonia, Finland, France, Gabon, Gambia, Germany, Ghana, Greece, Guinea, Haiti, Honduras, Indonesia, Iran (Islamic Republic of), Italy, Japan, Latvia, Liberia, Lithuania, Madagascar, Malta, Marshall Islands, Mexico, Monaco, Mozambique, Netherlands, Nigeria, Norway, Pakistan, Panama, Peru, Philippines, Portugal, Republic of Korea, Romania, Russian Federation, Singapore, Slovenia, Spain, Sri Lanka, Sudan, Syrian Arab Republic, Sweden, Switzerland, Thailand, Tunisia, Turkey, Ukraine, United Kingdom of Great Britain and Northern Ireland, United Republic of Tanzania, United States of America, and Viet Nam.

(the text of the Convention follows)

II.II.2 CHAPTER II: PREPARATION AND ADOPTION OF A CONVENTION ON ARREST OF SHIPS (AGENDA ITEM 8)[6]

1. For its consideration of this item, the Conference had before it the following documentation:

"Draft articles for a convention on arrest of ships" (TD/B/IGE.1/5);
"Compilation of comments and proposals by Governments and by intergovernmental and non-governmental organizations on the draft articles for a convention on arrest of ships" (A/CONF.188/3 and Add. 1–3);
"Report of the Joint UNCTAD/IMO Intergovernmental Group of Experts on Maritime Liens and Mortgages and Related Subjects on its ninth session" (TD/B/IGE.1/4).

OPENING STATEMENTS

2. The **Deputy Secretary-General of UNCTAD** stressed the importance of the cooperation between UNCTAD and IMO in achieving international uniformity in respect of arrest of ships. The work of the Conference was undoubtedly of paramount importance to the international shipping and trading community, since the establishment of up-to-date rules and regulations governing the arrest of ships would clearly play an important role in facilitating maritime transport and world trade. It was essential that any new instrument should succeed in striking a balance between the interests of owners of cargo and owners of ships in securing the free movement of ships and the light of claimants to obtain security for their claims. This might not be an easy task bearing in mind the differences in approach adopted by common law, which allowed arrest of a ship only in respect of certain maritime claims raised against it, and civil law systems, permitting the claimant to arrest any ship for claims against the owner regardless of the nature of such claims. This goal could only be achieved if a spirit of cooperation and compromise prevailed among delegations. He was confident that the Conference would be able to adopt the final text of a Convention on arrest of ships.

3. The **Director, Legal and External Relations Division, International Maritime Organization (IMO)**, speaking on behalf of the Secretary-General of IMO, referred to the importance of adopting a new Arrest Convention aimed at providing certainty of law and justice for the benefit of administrations, shipowners, owners of cargo and all those involved in the process of maritime claims. Differences between civil and common law should be overcome in order to ensure, through global international rules, the effectiveness of free trade through shipping. The mandate contained in the General Assembly resolution 52/182 was a clear expression of the will to do just that.

4. The **President of the Conference** stressed the importance of the subject of arrest of ships to the international shipping and trading community. The draft Convention was the result of the hard work and cooperation of the delegations and observers who had taken part in the three sessions of the Joint UNCTAD/IMO Intergovernmental Group of Experts on Maritime Liens and Mortgages and Related Subjects, which had prepared the draft. The preparation of any international legal instrument necessarily required compromise on the part of delegations representing different legal systems. This was particularly true in relation to subjects such as arrest of ships, which received divergent legal treatment in different jurisdictions following the civil law and common law systems.

6. Document A/CONF.188/5.

CONSIDERATION OF A DRAFT CONVENTION

5. Consideration of a draft convention proceeded in informal meetings of the Main Committee and the Drafting Committee.

PROCEEDINGS OF THE CLOSING PLENARY

6. The **Chairman of the Main Committee**, reporting on the substantive work carried out by the Main Committee on the draft convention on arrest of ships, highlighted some of the decisions taken by the Committee concerning issues which had been the subject of considerable debate within the Committee. One of the major points on which opinions had been divided was article 1 on the definition of a "maritime claim"; the main issue had related to whether the Convention should adopt an approach similar to that of the 1952 Convention and provide for a closed list of claims giving rise to a right of arrest or whether it should adopt a flexible approach providing for an open-ended list of claims and avoiding the exclusion of genuine maritime claims from giving rise to right of arrest. After an extensive discussion and an examination of various proposals, the Committee had succeeded in reaching a delicate compromise solution which involved keeping a closed list of claims giving rise to right of arrest, while allowing some flexibility in certain categories of maritime claims. For example, in subparagraph 1(d) of the draft convention, covering environmental claims, a reference had been included to damage, costs, or loss of a similar nature to those identified in the subparagraph, and in subparagraph (u) the requirement for registration of a "mortgage" or "hypothèque" or a charge of the same nature had been deleted.

7. Another important issue which had given rise to a lengthy debate was article 3, dealing with the exercise of the right of arrest. With regard to paragraph 1 concerning arrest of a ship in respect of which a maritime claim was asserted, the Committee had agreed to rearrange the order of the subparagraphs by first stating the general rule requiring the liability of the owner for the purpose of arrest and then cases where the demise charterer was liable for claim, followed by exceptions where liability of the owner was not required for the purpose of arrest. The arrest of a ship irrespective of the liability of the owner was permitted if the claim was based on a mortgage or hypothèque or concerned ownership or possession of the ship, or if the claim was against the demise charterer, manager or operator of the ship and was secured by a maritime lien which was granted or arose under the law of the State where the arrest was applied for. In that way, all maritime liens granted or arising under the law of the forum arresti would be covered. Hence, if the State concerned was also a Party to the 1993 International Convention on Maritime Liens and Mortgages, both liens afforded under articles 4 and 6 of that Convention would be covered.

8. Paragraph 2 of article 3 dealing with so-called sister ship arrest had also been debated at length. It had been pointed out by some delegations that the proliferation of single-ship companies since 1952 had often in effect excluded the possibility of sister ship arrest and had meant that the only option available to many claimants was to arrest the particular ship in respect of which a maritime claim arose. It had therefore been proposed to adopt provisions specifically providing for the arrest of "associated" ships using the concept of control as the criterion for establishing an association. A further proposal to the same effect had been put forward using the concept of "beneficial owner-ship". Most delegations considered that although the problem did exist, it was more of a general nature, with implications for other areas of law such as corporate law and contract law, and it could not be solved in the context of the Convention. Other delegations felt that the issue was of particular importance in relation to shipping and should not be left to national law. Although the proposal had been further considered and developed in an informal group, it had not received wide support in the Committee. The Committee had therefore decided to maintain the existing text of article 3, paragraph 2, of the draft convention, subject to drafting amendments.

9. Article 7 dealing with jurisdiction on the merits of the case had been amended so that, as a general rule, jurisdiction to determine a case upon its merits would be granted only to the Courts of the State in which an arrest was effected or security provided to obtain the release of the ship. The reference to jurisdiction of States in which security was given to prevent arrest had been deleted. Article 7, paragraph 5, dealing with the recognition and enforcement of foreign judgments, had been debated extensively. Proposals had been made to leave the matter to the relevant laws in the country

where the ship was arrested. It had further been pointed out that reference to "due process of law" was ambiguous and needed clarification. The Committee had agreed to amend the paragraph by stating that such final decisions would be recognized and given effect provided that the defendant had been given reasonable notice of such proceedings and reasonable opportunity to present his case and that such recognition was not against public policy (*ordre public*).

10. In article 8, dealing with scope of application, the reference to seagoing ships had been deleted. As a result, the Convention would apply to all ships whether or not flying the flag of a State Party. This would promote wider application of the Convention. On the other hand, article 10 permitted States, when becoming Parties to the Convention, to reserve the right to exclude its application to ships which were not seagoing or which did not fly the flag of a State Party.

Adoption of the Convention by the Conference

11. At its third plenary meeting, on 12 March 1999, the **UN/IMO Diplomatic Conference** adopted the International Convention on Arrest of Ships 1999 (A/CONF.188/L.2). (For the text of the Convention, see chapter I above.)

Statements made subsequent to the adoption of the Convention

12. The representative of the **United Kingdom**, referring to the proposal of his delegation on the arrest of ships under the control of effectively one owner, said that his delegation was disappointed that the Conference had been unable to address this issue in the Convention. However, the United Kingdom was heartened to learn that the Conference was not indifferent to the issue and that a number of delegations had acknowledged that there was indeed a significant problem that needed to be addressed. He expressed the hope that other Governments with an interest in furthering the best interests of the maritime community and of claimants in coastal States would continue to discuss appropriate means of dealing with those who would seek to use the corporate veil to avoid their obligations under international agreements.

13. The representative of the **Marshall Islands** said that, during the first session of the Joint Intergovernmental Group of Experts on Maritime Liens and Mortgages and Related Subjects, the point had been made that the draft text of what was now the 1999 Convention on Arrest of Ships did not fully take into account the powers granted to the holder of a mortgage, under the laws of many nations, to obtain the interlocutory sale of a ship. These powers were available under national law and by virtue of the provisions of the mortgage. In the view of his delegation, a ship mortgage as described in the 1993 Convention on Maritime Liens and Mortgages did not require the detention of a ship in order to obtain security. The mortgage itself provided security, at least under the law of many States. In his view, the present Convention did not preclude the commencement of proceedings to directly enforce those mortgage rights, and he would have preferred this to have been so stated in the Convention. Such legal rights and powers derived from the mortgage, and might not come within the definition of a maritime claim under Article 1 of the Convention.

14. He called upon intergovernmental organizations, including IMO, UNCTAD, UNIDROIT and UNCITRAL, to continue work on the development and harmonization of laws relating to recognition of security interests in movable property and their enforcement internationally. His delegation would have preferred it if the Convention had given recognition to arrest as a concept in the broader context because it believed that the Convention should include the methods of enforcement which were contemplated in articles 11 and 12, among others, of the 1993 Convention on Maritime Liens and Mortgages and under which a mortgage foreclosure action could be initiated without any need for the restrictive and often lengthy process of a "saisie conservatoire". His delegation would continue to work for recognition of the rights of secured parties under mortgages and other enforceable instruments, and it strongly supported the continued work of international bodies in this direction.

15. The representative of **Malta** expressed the satisfaction of his delegation with the work accomplished by the Conference and called upon IMO and UNCTAD to do everything in their power to ensure the early implementation of the Convention, which constituted a milestone in the history of international shipping. Follow-up activities should include the provision of technical assistance to ensure the implementation of the Convention in national legislation.

16. The representative of **Denmark** said that the objective of the Convention was to facilitate international seaborne trade. To reach agreement on the text, difficult compromises had been necessary to take account of the interests of all parties involved. As provided under the Convention, arrest for damage could take place in many situations, including instances of environmental damage and claims of a similar nature. She highlighted the spirit of cooperation which had prevailed among participants at the Conference.

17. The representative of the **International Ship Suppliers Association** expressed dissatisfaction with article 3 of the Convention, which limited the protection of its members as compared with the existing regime under the 1952 Convention on Arrest of Seagoing Ships. Under the provisions of the new Convention, ship owners and managers might find suppliers unwilling to supply vessels on open credit terms if any doubt existed as to payment being properly protected by international law. This could interfere significantly with the smooth operating of a vessel.

Adoption of the Final Act

18. At its third plenary meeting, on 12 March 1999, the **UN/IMO Diplomatic Conference** adopted the Final Act of the Conference (A/CONF.188/L.3). The Final Act was then signed by the representatives of 68 States. (For the text of the Final Act, including a list of the 68 signatories, see chapter I above.)

Closing statements

19. The **Secretary-General of UNCTAD** highlighted the importance of the new Convention in terms of contributing to the harmonization of international maritime legislation. The Convention, by taking account of recent developments, represented an improvement over the 1952 Convention. He expressed his satisfaction with the work achieved by the Conference on an issue which had traditionally been the subject of divergent approaches in various legal systems. Having underlined some of the changes introduced by the Convention, he expressed the hope that the new international legal instrument would receive wide international acceptance and achieve its objectives of facilitating international trade and transport and promoting global development. He noted, however, that adopting a new international instrument by itself was not sufficient to achieve this. It was the ratification and implementation of its provisions which were essential for its success. He therefore invited States which had participated in the Conference to consider early ratification of the new treaty. Finally, he emphasized that the preparation and successful conclusion of the new legal instrument by UNCTAD and IMO was another example of the way in which UNCTAD could work in harmony with other international agencies for the furtherance of common objectives.

20. The **Director, Legal and External Relations Division, International Maritime Organization** (IMO), speaking on behalf of the Secretary-General of IMO, said that, despite the wide degree of acceptance enjoyed by the 1952 Convention on Arrest of Seagoing Ships, nearly half a century had passed since the treaty had been adopted, and during that time decisive changes had occurred in the field of international navigation. These changes had given rise to the need for the new treaty which, within a framework of legal certainty, reflected a modern approach to language and took account of new features of maritime claims. She noted that the 1999 International Convention on Arrest of Ships, while clearly a compromise text, was nevertheless sufficiently flexible to accommodate the main requirements and interests of all those involved in global sea trade. This, she underlined, was reason enough to consider its early ratification and consequent entry into force.

21. The **President of the Conference** said that the adoption of the new Convention constituted an important expression of political will to update international rules of law. The text adopted provided a good compromise between different legal systems and did not depart from the main thrust of the 1952 Convention as regards protecting the interests of both shipowners and claimants. The new Convention clarified a number of legal concepts and succeeded not only in aligning its provisions with the 1993 International Convention on Maritime Liens and Mortgages but also in taking account of recent developments in the field of maritime law. He applauded the excellent cooperation between UNCTAD and IMO as a good example of the vitality and capacity of the United Nations system.

APPENDIX III

The Travaux Préparatoires of the International Convention on Arrest of Ships

CONTENTS

II.III.1 LIST OF DOCUMENTS

DRAFT ARTICLES

Draft of the CMI International Sub-Committee: Draft Revision of the International Convention for the Unification of Certain Rules Relating to the Arrest of Sea-Going Ships, Document Arrest 32/II–1985, Lisboa I, p. 168.

CMI Draft: Draft Revision of the International Convention for the Unification of Certain Rules Relating to the Arrest of Sea-Going Ships, Document LIS-Arrest 30, Lisboa II, p. 42.

Draft Articles 1994: Joint UNCTAD/IMO Intergovernmental Group of Experts on Maritime Liens and Mortgages and Related Subjects, Seventh Session—Draft Articles for a Convention on Arrest of Ships, Doc. TD/B/CN.4/GE.2/CRP.1, 6 December 1994.

Draft Articles 1997: Draft Articles for a Convention on Arrest of Ships, Doc. JIGE(IX)5 of 14 April 1997, annexed to Doc. TD/B/IGE.1/5, 14 April 1997.

REPORTS

Report of the Chairman of the CMI International Sub-Committee: Revision of the International Convention for the Unification of Certain Rules Relating to the Arrest of Sea-Going Ships —Report of the Chairman of the International Sub-Committee, Document Arrest 31/II–1985, Lisboa I, p. 146.

CMI Report: Report of the CMI on the Draft Revision of the International Convention for the Unification of Certain Rules Relating to the Arrest of Sea-Going Ships, Lisboa II, p. 118.

Seventh Session, Report—Annex I: Draft Report on the Work of the Sessional Group of the Joint UNCTAD/IMO Intergovernmental Group of Experts on Maritime Liens and Mortgages and Related Subjects at its Seventh Session, Doc. TD/B/CN.4/GE.2/3, 21 December 1994.

Eighth Session, Report: Report of the Joint Intergovernmental Group of Experts on Maritime Liens and Mortgages and Related Subjects on its Eighth Session, Doc. TD/B/CN.4/GE.2/10, 8 November 1995.

Eighth Session, Report—Annex I: Report on the Work of the Sessional Group of the Joint UNCTAD/IMO Intergovernmental Group of Experts on Maritime Liens and Mortgages and Related Subjects at its Eighth Session, Doc. JIGE(VIII)7, Annex I to the Report.

Ninth Session, Report—Annex II: Report on the Work of the Sessional Group of the Whole on the Joint UNCTAD/IMO Intergovernmental Group of Experts on Maritime Liens and Mortgages and Related Subjects at its Ninth Session, Annex II to the Report of the Joint UNCTAD/IMO Intergovernmental Group of Experts on Maritime Liens and Mortgages and Related Subjects on its Ninth Session, Doc. TD/B/44/3 – TD/B/IGE.1/4, 6 February 1997.

Ninth Session, Report—Annex III: Report on the Work of the Sessional Group of the Whole – Paper of the Informal Working Group on Article 1.

SUBMISSIONS—COMMENTS AND PROPOSALS

Submission by the International Chamber of Shipping: Submission for consideration by the Joint Intergovernmental Group of Experts at its eighth session, Doc. TD/B/CN.4/GE.2/7.

Comments and Proposals by Japan: Consideration of the review of the International Convention for the Unification of Certain Rules relating to the Arrest of Sea-going Ships, 1952—Compilation of comments and proposals by Governments on the draft articles for a convention on arrest of ships, Doc. TD/B/IGE.1/3, 23 October 1996.

Comments and Proposals by the United Kingdom: Consideration of the review of the International Convention for the Unification of Certain Rules relating to the Arrest of Sea-going Ships, 1952—Compilation of comments and proposals by Governments on the draft articles for a convention on arrest of ships, Doc. TD/B/IGE.1/3, 23 October 1996.

Proposal by the United States: Proposal submitted by the United States of America to the Joint Intergovernmental Group of Experts at its ninth session, Doc. TD/B/IGE.1/CRP.2, 3 December 1996.

Proposal by France: Proposal submitted by France to the Joint Intergovernmental Group of Experts at its ninth session, Doc. TD/B/IGE.1/CRP.1, 3 December 1996.

Document 188/3: Preparation and Adoption of a Convention on Arrest of Ships—Compilation of comments and proposals by Governments and by intergovernmental and non-governmental organizations on the draft articles for a convention on arrest of ships, Document A/CONF.188/3 of 25 November 1998.

Document 188/3/Add.1: Preparation and Adoption of a Convention on Arrest of Ships—Compilation of comments and proposals by Governments and by intergovernmental and non-governmental organizations on the draft articles for a convention on arrest of ships, Document A/CONF.188/3/Add.1 of 11 January 1999.

Document 188/3/Add.2: Preparation and Adoption of a Convention on Arrest of Ships—Compilation of comments and proposals by Governments and by intergovernmental and non-governmental organizations on the draft articles for a convention on arrest of ships, Document A/CONF.188/3/Add.2 of 23 February 1999.

Document 188/3/Add.3: Preparation and Adoption of a Convention on Arrest of Ships—Compilation of comments and proposals by Governments and by intergovernmental and non-governmental organizations on the draft articles for a convention on arrest of ships, Document A/CONF.188/3/Add.3 of 23 February 1999.

PROCEEDINGS OF THE MAIN COMMITTEE

Document CRP.1: Document A/CONF.188/CRP.1—Proposals by Canada, Articles 3, 6 and 7.

Document CRP.2: Document A/CONF.188/CRP.2—Proposal by the United Kingdom, Article 1.

Document CRP.3: Document A/CONF.188/CRP.3—Proposal by Norway, Article 3.

Document CRP.4: Document A/CONF.188/CRP.4—Proposal by Namibia, Article 1.

Document CRP.5: Document A/CONF.188/CRP.5—Proposal by Denmark, Article 6.

Document CRP.6: Document A/CONF.188/CRP.6—Proposal by the Netherlands, Article 9.

Document CRP.8: Document A/CONF.188/CRP.8—Draft articles referred by the Main Committee to the Drafting Committee.

Document CRP.9: Document A/CONF.188/CRP.9—Proposal by Egypt, Article 6.

Document CRP.10: Document A/CONF.188/CRP.10—Proposal by Sweden, Article 2.

Document CRP.11: Document A/CONF.188/CRP.11—Proposal by Ukraine, Articles 1, 2, 3, 4, 5, 6.

Document CRP.12: Document A/CONF.188/CRP.12—Proposal by Turkey, Article 7.

Document CRP.13: Document A/CONF.188/CRP.13—Proposal by Romania, Article 8.

Document CRP.14: Document A/CONF.188/CRP.14—Proposal by Norway, Article 3.

Document CRP.15: Document A/CONF.188/CRP.15—Proposal by Hong Kong, China, Article E bis.

Document CRP.16: Document A/CONF.188/CRP.15—Proposals by the United States, Articles 1, 3.

Document CRP.17: Document A/CONF.188/CRP.17—Proposal by Greece, Article 4.

Informal Papers

Document A/CONF.188/3/Add.1/Corr.1—Proposal by Morocco

Paper by France: Informal paper by France on article 7 of 5 March 1999

II.III.2 INTRODUCTION

The travaux préparatoires of the 1999 Convention are based on the documents of the CMI, of the Joint UNCTAD/IMO Intergovernmental Group of Experts (JIGE) and of the Diplomatic Conference.

Two drafts were prepared by the CMI. The first (to which reference will be made as the "Draft of the CMI International Sub-Committee") was prepared by the International Sub-Committee appointed by the CMI Executive Council under the chairmanship of Professor Allan Philip and was then submitted to the CMI Conference held in Lisbon in September 1985. The second draft (to which reference will be made as the "CMI Draft") was approved by the Lisbon Conference and submitted to IMO and UNCTAD.

Two further drafts were then prepared by the JIGE during its seventh, eighth and ninth sessions. The first (to which reference will be made as the "Draft Articles 1994") reproduced almost literally the CMI Draft. The second draft (to which reference will be made as the "Draft Articles 1997" or simply "Draft Articles" or "JIGE Draft") was prepared by the IMO and UNCTAD Secretariats on the basis of the deliberations of the JIGE and was submitted to the Diplomatic Conference.

Since in the Report of the Diplomatic Conference[1] only the proceedings of the Closing Plenary are contained, while no official records are available of the proceedings of the Main Committee, before which the Draft Articles were considered, the author has obtained from the courtesy of the UNCTAD Secretariat, to which he is greatly indebted, the 80 tapes containing the complete records of such proceedings.

After having listened at all the tapes the author has made a complete transcript of the debates in respect of issues of particular importance and a summary of the other most significant parts of the debates that took place when the Draft Articles were considered for the first time (First Reading) and when, for the provisions on which a consensus had not been reached, they were considered for the second time (Second Reading). All summaries are in italics in order to distinguish them easily from the portions that have been transcribed. The number of the tapes from which summaries and transcripts are taken are shown in the footnotes. The author is responsible for the English translation of the statements in the French and Spanish languages. He is indebted to Prof. Zhu Zengjie and to Mr Oleg V. Boznikov respectively for the transcription and translation of the relevant statements made by the delegates from the Peoples Republic of China and from the Russian Federation.

In order to make consultation easier, the travaux préparatoires are arranged under each individual article of the Convention and, in certain cases, under each paragraph of each article except for the comments and statements of a general nature, that precede those relating to individual articles and paragraphs.

---

1. Document A/CONF.188/5 of 19 July 1999, Chapter II, paragraphs 6–21, Appendix II, p. 374.

II.III.3 GENERAL COMMENTS

Report of the Chairman of the CMI International Sub-Committee to the Lisbon Conference

I. Introduction

1. Following the decision of IMO and UNCTAD to place on their work programme the revision of the 1926 and of the 1967 Brussels Conventions on Maritime Liens and Mortgages, and of the 1952 Brussels Convention on Arrest of Ships, the CMI decided to offer its co-operation to both those Intergovernmental Organizations, and two International Sub-Committees were appointed by the Assembly under the chairmanship respectively of Professor Francesco Berlingieri and of Prof. Allan Philip.

The Assembly of the CMI held in Venice on 2nd June 1983 resolved to place both subjects on the Agenda of the next CMI Conference, to be held in Lisbon in May of this year.

II. Summary of the work of the International Sub-Committee

2. The study on the revision of the 1952 Convention on arrest of seagoing ships started with the distribution to National Associations of a questionnaire drawn up by a working group and supplemented by a paper by Professor Francesco Berlingieri containing an analysis of the 1952 Convention and a paper by the chairman of the sub-committee on Maritime Jurisdiction in the EEC.

The questionnaire raised especially the following questions:

1. Should the list of maritime claims be expanded?
2. To which extent should arrest be possible when the claim for which arrest is requested is against someone other than the owner of the ship?
3. What should be the future of the sister ship rule?
4. Should the Convention be concerned with the consequences of wrongful arrest?
5. Should the Convention regulate jurisdiction of courts in respect of cases concerning the underlying claim for which arrest is made and regulate recognition of judgments?

Replies to the questionnaire have been received from the following National Associations:

Belgium, Italy, German Democratic Republic, Canada, Japan, Portugal, Argentina, the Soviet Union, Sweden, United Kingdom, Yugoslavia, Spain, Korea, United States, Czechoslovakia, Australia and New Zealand, and France.

3. Most National Associations thought that certain additions ought to be made to the list of maritime claims in the 1952 Convention. Views were divided as to the permissibility of arresting a ship for claims against persons other than the owner. Practically all Associations agreed that the sister ship rule should be continued. Many Associations believed that the Convention should contain rules about wrongful arrest. A majority thought that arrest should create jurisdiction and a considerable number thought that the Convention should provide for recognition and enforcement of judgments. The question of arrest of foreign government owned ships was raised by Italy and the Soviet Union.

4. On the 4th and 5th of April 1984 a meeting of the sub-committee was held in Brussels. Due to the illness of Prof. Philip, Professor J.C. Schultsz took the chair. At that meeting the possibility

was mentioned of replacing the list of maritime claims in art. 1 by a general clause. It was agreed that arrest should be possible also for claims against bareboat charterers. It was also agreed to include a provision permitting bilateral agreements on guarantees issued by a State to be deemed sufficient security to avoid arrest.

During the meeting in Brussels a joint meeting with the International Sub-committee on maritime liens and mortgages was held in the afternoon of the 5th April, when matters of common interest were discussed, especially whether there should be one or two Conventions and, if there were to be two, whether a better co-ordination should be ensured between them.

In the joint meeting it was by a very large majority decided that it was preferable to keep the two conventions separate, but that they should be better co-ordinated.

5. On the basis of the replies to the questionnaires and Mr. C. W. H. Goldie's report of the Brussels meeting the chairman prepared a first report and draft convention which were discussed at a meeting in Copenhagen on the 24th August 1984. Based upon the discussions and with the invaluable assistance of Mr. Goldie, the chairman prepared a new report and draft (hereinafter draft 2) which were distributed to National Associations for comments. Comments were received from the National Associations of Japan, Federal Republic of Germany, France, Sweden, United Kingdom, Czechoslovakia, Spain, Canada and Italy. A meeting of the international sub-committee was then held in Copenhagen on the 11th January, 1985, to discuss the draft. In the light of these discussions the present report and draft (hereinafter draft 3) has been prepared by the chairman in conjunction with Mr. Goldie for submission to the Lisbon conference.

6. In the work of the international sub-committee delegates of the following National Associations have taken part : Belgium (L. Delwaide), Danemark (J. Erlund), France (J. S. Rohart), Federal Republic of Germany (V. Looks), Italy (E. Vincenzini), Japan (S. Ochiai), Netherlands (K.E. Japikse), Nigeria (F. Sasegbon), Norway (K.J. Gombrii), Poland (S. Suchorzewski), Portugal (J.T. Batista da Silva), Spain (E. Albors and J.L. Goñi), United Kingdom (C.W.H. Goldie), United States (Th. A. Le Gros), U.S.S.R. (I. Barinova and A. Kolodkin), Yugoslavia (Mr. Kapetanovic). In addition, Dr. R. Vigil of UNCTAD participated in the first meeting of the International Sub-Committee.

III. The Arrest Convention, 1952

In most countries not parties to the 1952 Convention ships are subject to arrest regardless of the character of the claim for which arrest is made. The primary purpose of the 1952 Convention was to protect the interests of both ship and cargo in avoiding interruption of the voyage by arrest for claims without any relationship to the operation of the ship.

Art. 1 of the 1952 Convention lists a number of so-called maritime claims and art. 2 provides that arrest may be made in respect of such claims but for no other claims. This is the principal rule of the Convention.

According to art. 3 arrest may be made in most cases either of the ship in respect of which the maritime claim arose or other ships in the same ownership. In the case of ships under bare-boat charter and other cases where the owner is not liable for the claim, other ships in the same ownership may not be arrested but instead ships in the ownership of the bareboat charterer or other person liable may be arrested.

Art. 3 also prevents arrest from being made twice. Art. 4 provides that ships may only be arrested under judicial authority and art. 5 contains rules on the release of a ship against security.

According to art. 6 procedural problems and all questions concerning liability for wrongful arrest are referred to the law of the *forum arresti*.

Art. 7 contains rules on jurisdiction in respect of the merits of the case and the recognition of foreign judgments with respect to any security given to obtain the release of the ship.

Art. 8 regulates the scope of the Convention based upon the principle of reciprocity and makes it possible for States to exclude certain cases from the Convention. And art. 9 provides that the Convention must not be construed as creating rights of action or maritime liens which do not exist under the law of the forum arresti.

The Convention has been ratified or acceded to by 63 countries.

IV. The proposed draft for revision of the 1952 Convention

The revised draft takes its point of departure in the 1952 Convention. However, it has not been found possible to limit the revision to a protocol containing certain additions or modifications. Both from the point of view of presentation, language, and substance it has been found that the Convention is in need of a thorough revision. A new Convention has been drafted using such parts of the old Convention as have been found acceptable. A conversion table between the articles of the old Convention and the draft is attached.

JIGE Seventh Session
5–9 December 1994

Report Annex I

2. The Sessional Group considered document JIGE (VII)/2, issued by UNCTAD under cover of TD/B/CN.4/GE.2/2 and by IMO under cover of LEG/MLM 29, prepared by the secretariats of UNCTAD and IMO, which outlined possible modifications to the 1952 Arrest Convention that might be required in the light of the adoption of the 1993 MLM Convention. The Group also had before it document JIGE(VI)/3 (TD/B/C.4/AC.8/22–LEG/MLM/22), which included the draft revision of the 1952 Convention prepared by the CMI at its 1985 Lisbon conference (hereinafter "the CMI Draft"). The Group started a preliminary reading of the articles of the Convention, bearing in mind the comments and observations contained in document JIGE(VII)/2 prepared by the secretariats of UNCTAD and IMO.

33. The Sessional Group, having completed preliminary consideration of the subject, instructed the secretariats to prepare a new set of articles on the basis of the CMI Draft, together with amendments made necessary as a result of the adoption of the 1993 MLM Convention and observations made by delegations during the session. The text prepared by the secretariats, entitled "Draft articles for a Convention on Arrest of Ships" (TD/B/CN.4/GE.2/CRP.1), was put before the Sessional Group for consideration. The Group held a brief exchange of views and the following is an account of the discussion.

Eighth Session
9–10 October 1995

Report Annex I

1. The Sessional Group discussed extensively whether the 1952 Convention or the draft articles for a new convention for arrest of ships prepared by the Secretariat should be considered as the basic text for its deliberations.

2. Some delegations favoured using the 1952 Arrest Convention as the basic text. In their opinion it provided legal certainty regarding the conditions for arrest of ships. This was particularly important in connection with the definition of maritime claims to be secured by arrest. In their view the closed list system regulated in the 1952 Convention ensured that procedures of arrest were limited to claims properly defined. The alternative of an open list, such as the one established by the draft articles prepared by the Secretariat on the basis of the CMI Lisbon text, would introduce uncertainty and could become the source of disputes as to whether a specific maritime claim could be subject to arrest. Moreover, it was stated that the reference to national law in article 3, paragraph 3, and article 6 of the draft, would not contribute to any further unification. The view was also expressed that in establishing a list of claims giving right to arrest, an equitable balance between the interest of the major and the small creditors should be maintained.

3. These delegations were of the view that in principle, the scope of revision of the 1952 Convention should be restricted to the introduction of amendments consequential upon the adoption of the 1993 International Convention on Maritime Liens and Mortgages and minor adjustments to take account of other developments since the adoption of the 1952 Convention. The view was expressed that, in the light of the 1993 MLM Convention, no changes to the 1952 Arrest Convention were necessary. If, however, other changes were to be considered necessary, they should be kept to a minimum. Bearing in mind the wide international acceptance of the 1952 Convention, it was

essential not to go too far in its revision so as to avoid undermining the unification achieved through the Convention.

4. The vast majority of delegations, however, were in favour of using the draft articles prepared by the Secretariat at the request by the Group at its VIIth session as the basis for its further deliberations. In their opinion, the considerations in connection with the possible up-dating of the 1952 Arrest Convention in the light of the 1993 Convention on Maritime Liens and Mortgages provided an excellent opportunity to undertake a general review of the 1952 Convention. This had been the background for the request by the 1993 Diplomatic Conference to reconvene the JIGE. A general review would enable the Group to take stock of many years of international experience of application of the 1952 Convention to repair some deficiencies in the present system and to consider some further amendments which had prevented certain countries from becoming parties to the Convention. This could be done without deviating from the basic principles established by the 1952 Convention.

5. In response to those advocating a closed list it was suggested that an open list was to be preferred; it allowed claims to be secured which, while not specifically addressed in the open list, were beyond doubt of a maritime nature such as claims for unpaid insurance premiums, agency fees and stevedoring charges. An open list would furthermore provide flexibility for future developments in this regard.

6. In the view of one delegation an open list would provide uncertainty rather than flexibility for future developments.

7. After further discussions the Group decided to use the draft articles prepared by the Secretariat as the basis for its deliberations.

8. Several comments were made in connection with the format of the instrument to be finally agreed upon by the Group. The alternative for a new convention rather than a protocol amending the present 1952 Convention was considered advisable, bearing in mind the comprehensive character of the review and the procedures to be accomplished for adoption of the new treaty by a Conference convened by the United Nations and IMO. The draft articles prepared by the Secretariat would provide the substantive contents of the new treaty and the Preamble and Final Clauses would be prepared as appropriate, bearing in mind the usual procedures involved in treaty-making preparatory work.

9. Several delegations made reference to discrepancies between the English text of the draft articles and texts in other languages. These delegations were invited to submit their comments or proposals in writing to the Secretariat, in order to ensure that the texts in all languages reflected the same substantive meaning.

10. Bearing in mind its preliminary discussions and the decisions adopted at its last session, the Group started to consider the revised set of draft articles contained in document JIGE(VIII)/2.

II.III.4 ARTICLE 1: DEFINITIONS

PARAGRAPH 1: OPEN/CLOSED LIST

Draft of the CMI International Sub-Committee

(1) "MARITIME CLAIM" MEANS ANY CLAIM ARISING OUT OF THE OWNERSHIP, CONSTRUCTION, POSSES-SION, MORTGAGE OR HYPOTHECATION, MANAGEMENT, OPERATION OR TRADING OF ANY SHIP, OR OUT OF SALVAGE OPERATIONS RELATING TO ANY SHIP, INCLUDING BUT NOT RESTRICTED TO:

Report of the Chairman

Para 1 corresponds to art. 1, para 1 of the 1952 Convention.

Draft 2 contained several alternative drafts. The choice is between a clause defining in general terms what a maritime claim is and a clause containing a detailed list of maritime claims.

The argument for a general clause is that such a clause makes it possible, without having to revoke the Convention, to take into consideration new developments in shipping when in future new types of claims, not foreseen at present arise. The argument against such a clause is that it may lead to different interpretations of the Convention in different countries, while a list to a larger extent ensures uniformity of interpretation.

The international sub-committee has come to the conclusion that it is desirable to have a rule which permits adaptability to future developments, i.e. a general clause. However, in order to ensure uniformity to as large an extent as possible the suggestion is to supplement the general clause with a non-exhaustive list of claims which according to the Convention are deemed to be maritime claims. The list found in the 1952 Convention has, therefore, been supplemented by additional categories of claim which have been proposed by National Associations, as well as some others.

In draft 2, the third alternative draft of para 1 contained an attempt at a more systematic and logical drafting of the list. However, in order not to create too many uncertainties in relation to existing case law the list contained in the present draft is based upon the list in the 1952 Convention with only minor changes.

CMI Draft

(1) "MARITIME CLAIM" MEANS ANY CLAIM CONCERNING OR ARISING OUT OF THE OWNERSHIP, CON-STRUCTION, POSSESSION, MANAGEMENT, OPERATION OR TRADING OF ANY SHIP, OR OUT OF A MORTGAGE OR AN "HYPOTHÈQUE" OR A CHARGE OF THE SAME NATURE ON ANY SHIP, OR OUT OF SALVAGE OPERATIONS RELATING TO ANY SHIP, SUCH AS ANY CLAIM IN RESPECT OF:

Report of the CMI

12. Article 1 was adopted by 32 votes to 2 with 3 abstentions. It contains a number of definitions. Many of the important problems to which the Convention gives rise are problems which arise in connection with these definitions.

13. Article 1 paragraph (1) corresponds to the same paragraph in the 1952 Convention.

In the same way as in the 1952 Convention, in the new Convention the concept of maritime claim is decisive in describing the situation in which arrest of a ship may be made. The 1952 Convention contained an exhaustive list of maritime claims. The National Associations desired an extension of this list to include a number of claims such as claims for insurance premiums, stevedoring services, brokerage fees, etc.

14. Some associations proposed the replacement of the list by a general clause covering all claims in connection with the ownership, operation and management of a ship. The principal argument was the risk that new developments might cause an exhaustive list to become out of date in the same way as had happened to the 1952 Convention. It is difficult to revise Conventions.

Others argued that a general clause would give rise to different interpretations and, therefore, not ensure uniformity of interpretation. It was also argued by some delegations that the opportunities for arrest should not be extensive. A general clause would extend too much the area where arrest could be made.

15. Various possibilities were discussed: 1. The retention of an exhaustive list as in the 1952 Convention. 2. A general clause only. 3. A general clause followed by a non-exhaustive list.

16. The possibility mentioned as n. 3 was proposed in order to ensure a maximum degree of uniformity of interpretation and was thought of as a compromise between the two other possibilities.

17. The Lisbon Conference adopted the compromise solution. Originally, the general clause contained at the end the words: "including but not restricted to:" as an introduction to the list. This was thought to make the definition very open-ended and, on the suggestion of the British Association, these words were replaced by the words: "such as", which were thought to be somewhat more restrictive in that they would limit maritime claims to those within the categories exemplified in the list of claims.

18. In drafting the Convention the policy has been followed of using language as closely as possible similar to that used in the Convention on Maritime Liens and Mortgages also drafted at the Lisbon Conference. This appears for the first time in the general clause in the words: "a mortgage or an "hypothèque" or a charge of the same nature".

19. The list in many respects corresponds to the list in the 1952 Convention. It has been revised in order to resolve any doubts of interpretation that have arisen. In view of the purpose of the list no attempt has been made to avoid duplication between different subparagraphs and such duplication undoubtedly exists.

JIGE
Seventh Session, 5 December 1994

Report – Annex I

3. Some delegations considered that the list of maritime claims set out in article 1 of the 1952 Convention was incomplete and out of date. They preferred the approach adopted by the CMI Draft, providing for an open-ended list of maritime claims. In the opinion of these delegations, the inclusion of general wording in the "chapeau", enabling an open-ended list of claims reflected a compromise solution for different legal systems. This was considered appropriate, bearing in mind that article 6 of the 1993 MLM Convention allowed States Parties to grant under their law national maritime liens other than those mentioned in article 4, paragraph 1. Unless the list of claims in article 1 of the Arrest Convention became open-ended, there was a risk that a maritime lien granted in accordance with article 6 of the MLM Convention would not be secured by arrest if it was not included in the list in article 1 of the Arrest Convention.

4. Some delegations opposed this. In their view, the list should remain a closed one, in order to ensure that arrest remained an exceptional measure to be used only as a last resort to secure maritime claims. An open list could lead to abusive exercise of the right of arrest in respect of claims of only relative importance. Claims given national maritime lien status under article 6 of the MLM Convention should not necessarily be included in the list, bearing in mind that the matter should be regulated by national law.

Draft Articles 1994

(1) "MARITIME CLAIM" MEANS ANY CLAIM CONCERNING OR ARISING OUT OF THE OWNERSHIP, CON-STRUCTION, POSSESSION, MANAGEMENT, OPERATION OR TRADING OF ANY SHIP, OR OUT OF A MORTGAGE

OR AN "HYPOTHÈQUE" OR A CHARGE OF THE SAME NATURE ON ANY SHIP, OR OUT OF SALVAGE OPERATIONS RELATING TO ANY SHIP, SUCH AS ANY CLAIM IN RESPECT OF:

37. One delegation suggested placing the term "such as any claim" in the chapeau of article 1 in brackets to avoid creating an open-ended list of maritime claims.

Eighth Session, 9–10 October 1995

Submission by the International Chamber of Shipping

ICS proposes deletion of the words "such as" in the "chapeau" of this Article to avoid creating an open-ended list of maritime claims.

We share the view expressed by some delegations at the last session that the list should remain a closed one in order to ensure that arrest remains an exceptional measure to be used only as a last resort to secure maritime claims. An open-ended list could lead to unreasonable exercise of the right of arrest in respect of claims of only minor importance which would be contrary to the object of the Convention.

Report – Annex I

2. Some delegations favoured using the 1952 Arrest Convention as the basic text. In their opinion it provided legal certainty regarding the conditions for arrest of ships. This was particularly important in connection with the definition of maritime claims to be secured by arrest. In their view the closed list system regulated in the 1952 Convention ensured that procedures of arrest were limited to claims properly defined. The alternative of an open list, such as the one established by the draft articles prepared by the Secretariat on the basis of the CMI Lisbon text, would introduce uncertainty and could become the source of disputes as to whether a specific maritime claim could be subject to arrest.

5. In response to those advocating a closed list it was suggested that an open list was to be preferred; it allowed claims to be secured which, while not specifically addressed in the open list, were beyond doubt of a maritime nature such as claims for unpaid insurance premiums, agency fees and stevedoring charges. An open list would furthermore provide flexibility for future developments in this regard.

6. In the view of one delegation an open list would provide uncertainty rather than flexibility for future developments.

11. The Sessional Group considered the proposal put forward by the International Chamber of Shipping (ICS) to delete the words "*such as*" in the chapeau of article 1 in order to avoid creating an open-ended list of maritime claim. Some delegations which favoured the approach adopted by the 1952 Convention supported this proposal. It was argued that having a closed list of maritime claims provided certainty as to the exercise of right of arrest. In that connection concern was expressed that the words "*such as*" would be interpreted differently in various jurisdictions. Most delegations, however, preferred an open-ended list of maritime claims so as to retain flexibility and avoid excluding genuine maritime claims from having right of arrest. It was at the same time noted that the present draft text, although open-ended, restricted the power of arrest to types of claims similar to those listed within article 1(1). In response, the observer for the ICS pointed out that although in common law countries the principle of *ejusdem generis* would probably apply, this would possibly not be the case in all civil law countries.

12. The observer for the International Union for Conservation of Nature and Natural Resources (IUCN) drew attention to the fact that environmental claims, such as costs for the restoration of the environment, did not fit in the categories of listed maritime claims. His delegation would therefore prefer to retain the open-ended approach in the present draft.

13. In view of the above, the Sessional Committee decided to retain the words "*such as*" in the chapeau.

14. One delegation questioned the purpose of using the words "*concerning or arising out of*" and "*out of*" in the chapeau. The observer for the CMI explained that the wording was mistakenly abbreviated and the intention was to express the same thing in the second and third lines of the chapeau by repeating "*concerning or arising out of*". The question was considered to be a matter of drafting. Some delegations questioned whether the use of the words "*salvage operations*" in the

chapeau and "*salvage operations and any salvage agreement*" in sub-paragraph (c) was repetitive.

Ninth Session, 2–6 December 1996

Report – Annex II

2. The Sessional Group discussed the question as to whether Article 1 (1) should adopt a similar approach to that of the 1952 Convention and provide an exhaustive list of maritime claims, or whether it should adopt a more flexible approach by retaining a non-exhaustive list. Opinions were divided on the subject; while many delegations preferred flexibility and a non-exhaustive list, others favoured having a closed list of maritime claims. One delegation proposed adopting a closed list provided that each maritime claim was described in general terms and that Article 3 (1) permitted arrest irrespective of whether the claim was secured by a maritime lien and whether the shipowner was personally liable for the claim.

3. The Sessional Group agreed that the question was decisive and could not be agreed at this stage. It was, therefore, decided to place the relevant words in the chapeau of Article 1 (1) in brackets and leave the matter to be decided at a later stage, possibly by a diplomatic conference.

Diplomatic Conference
Comments and Proposals

Hong Kong, China

DOCUMENT 188/3

2. The definition of "maritime claims" should be a well defined and closed list.

Italy

DOCUMENT 188/3/ADD.3

2. In view of the stance already taken by the Italian delegation at the eighth session of the UNCTAD/IMO Joint Intergovernmental Group of Experts on Maritime Liens and Mortgages and Related Subjects (London, 9–10 October 1995), we reaffirm that it is appropriate to establish a *non-exhaustive* list of maritime claims. This would leave some flexibility in the wording of the article so that the Convention could be continually adjusted to suit any legal changes that occurred in this area in future.

Japan

DOCUMENT 188/3

25. Opinions were divided within the Joint Group as to whether this article should adopt a similar approach to that of the 1952 Convention and provide an exhaustive list of maritime claims, or whether it should adopt a more flexible approach of retaining an open-ended list. The government of Japan support the position that this article should adopt an open-ended list, as we expressed ourselves at the ninth session of JIGE.

Mexico

DOCUMENT 188/3

34. The Government of Mexico is of the view that an approach admitting of both proposals should be adopted in the definitions. A definition and an open-ended list giving examples should be included, together with a list of possible claims likely to give rise to arrest of the ship; the article should end with a sentence permitting inclusion in the future of grounds for arrest not originally envisaged.

35. The proposed text for paragraph 1 of article 1 would read as follows:

"1. 'Maritime claim' means any claim in respect of: [repeat the list of subparagraphs (a) to (v), replacing the English term 'mortgage'] . . .

The foregoing shall be without prejudice to the possibility of entertaining any other claims concerning or arising out of the ownership, construction, possession, management, operation or trading of any ship, or concerning or arising out of a mortgage or maritime claim, or a registrable charge of the same nature, on any ship, other than those mentioned."

Slovakia

DOCUMENT 188/3

61. In the interest of uniformity of international law and elimination of different explanations in individual jurisdictions we agree with the draft Article 1–Definitions, stating the term of "maritime claim" and list of maritime claims that gives right to a claimant to arrest a ship. In the light of future development in the shipping we support wording "such as" used therein, that allows flexibility in enforcement of claims which are not enumerated in the list but may arise out of the operation of a ship in the future and are of maritime nature.

Thailand

DOCUMENT 188/3

80. As regards the meaning of "maritime claim" in paragraph 1, the mixed approach combining a general definition clause with a non-exhaustive list of claims for introducing the examples of the categories of claims is more preferable. The square bracket should therefore be removed. Sub-paragraph (p) should be reverted to "disbursements made in respect of ship, by or on behalf of the master, owner, demise or other charterer or agent".

United Kingdom

DOCUMENT 188/3/ADD.2

2. The current draft text for the definition of "maritime claim" in article 1(1) provides for two alternatives, either:

    (a) An exhaustive list (the current text of article 1(1) with the square brackets, and the text between them, deleted from the chapeau); or

    (b) A general description, followed by a list of examples (the current text of article 1(1) with the square brackets deleted, but the text between them retained).

3. The decision on the definition of "maritime claim" is linked to decisions on other key issues, in particular, the circumstances in which a claimant may obtain the arrest of a ship, and what the consequences of doing so will be for the claimant. Together with other key elements, the form of definition will determine the balance that the new convention strikes between shipping interests and claimants.

4. The preference of the Government of the United Kingdom would be to have an expanded, exhaustive list for the definition of "maritime claim" (alternative (a)). However, once such a claim exists, we believe that it ought not to be unduly onerous for the claimant to obtain an arrest.

5. The negotiations within the Joint Intergovernmental Group of Experts on Liens and Mortgages and Related Subjects suggest that, while there will be support for both of the current alternatives for article 1(1), neither might obtain sufficient support to permit its adoption according to the rules of procedure. The Conference may therefore wish to consider a compromise option.

6. The Government of Mexico has already proposed such an option (document A/CONF.188/3, para. 35). While the Government of the United Kingdom would prefer an exhaustive list, we may be able to accept such a compromise option if the Conference decides most of the other key issues in favour of claimants.

7. Should the Conference decide to consider a compromise option, it may wish to consider a simpler formulation than the one proposed by the Government of Mexico. For example the Conference could delete the square brackets and the text between them from the chapeau, and add a new subparagraph at the end of article 1(1) as follows:

" 'Maritime claim' means any claim in respect of:
  [(a) – (v)]; and
  (w) any other claim of a similar nature to those referred to under (a) to (v) above."

8. The advantage of this approach is that it would provide an element of *ejusdem generis*, like current alternative (a). However, the flexibility provided would be more restricted than under current alternative (b).

CMI

DOCUMENT 188/3

130. It is suggested that the adoption of an open-ended list is the best solution. The closed list originates from section 22 of the UK Supreme Court of Judicature (Consolidation) Act, 1925 pursuant to which admiralty jurisdiction was granted only in respect of the claims listed therein. Even though there is, according to the Draft Rules, a link between the right of arrest and jurisdiction, because the Courts of the State in which the arrest is made have jurisdiction on the merits of the claim (Article 7), the main purpose of the uniform rules is to regulate the right of the claimant to obtain security for his claim. The compromise reached between the common law approach which restricts the right of arrest and the civil law approach, according to which arrest is permissible of any asset of the debtor as security for any claim, consisted, and must consist even in the future, in limiting the right of arrest of a ship to claims of a maritime nature but not to certain maritime claims only. A closed list, however carefully prepared, may not be or remain complete. The additions that have already been made to the list contained in Article 1(1) of the 1952 Convention illustrate this point.

ICS

DOCUMENT 188/3

117. The ICS preference is for a clearly defined and closed list of maritime claims in the interests of certainty and to ensure that arrest remains an exceptional measure. A closed list of clearly defined maritime claims would ensure consistency in interpretation in different jurisdictions and thereby promote greater international uniformity. The compromise reflected in the 1952 Convention between the common law and civil law approaches whereby arrest is only permitted in respect of claims of a maritime nature must be maintained. An open-ended list could lead to the exercise of the right of arrest in respect of claims which are not of a maritime nature and/or are of only minor importance thereby causing needless detentions and consequential disruptions to international trade. ICS would be even more strenuously opposed to an open-ended list should the proposal to allow a right of arrest in respect of claims secured by non-internationally recognised maritime liens be accepted (see Article 3 paragraph 2 (b)).

Proceedings of the Main Committee

First reading—1 March 1999[2]

The delegate from the CMI explained the origin of the chapeau. He said the following:
In 1985, when the question of the revision of the 1952 Convention was discussed by the CMI in Lisbon, the prevailing view was that the closed list of the 1952 Convention should be replaced by a general statement that a ship can be arrested in respect of maritime claims of which a general definition only should be given. The alternatives which we have discussed were only two: a closed list or a general description of the maritime claims with no specific list of the claims at all. The origin of this latter alternative was that in a quite relevant number of civil law countries arrest was permissible as a general security in respect of any assets of the debtor. Therefore a ship could be arrested also in respect of claims of any nature whatsoever. When the 1952 Convention was adopted a number of civil law countries was not happy of the solution adopted, and this was the reason why in 1985 at Lisbon the other solution was proposed and at the beginning prevailed. Then a compromise solution was suggested, namely that there should still be a list of maritime claims as in the 1952 Convention but a chapeau should be included in art. 1 § 1 to the effect that a general statement

2. Text and summary from tapes Nos. 1 and 2.

should be made that arrest is permissible for any claim of a maritime nature, followed by a list of specific maritime claims which was linked to the chapeau by the words "such as".

The delegate from Hong Kong China stated that he favoured a closed list. He stated that if the list were left open, there would emerge widely different interpretations in respect of the nature of the other items that might be added, while for the purpose of ensuring uniformity certainty was essential. He then added that if in the future new maritime claims would emerge, agreement could be reached on their addition to the list. Similar views were expressed by many other delegations, the main reason for the adoption of a closed list being the need for certainty and the danger of lack of uniformity if the decision as to whether a particular claim had a maritime nature or not were left to the national Courts. Some delegations suggested, however, that a mechanism should be envisaged in order to facilitate the addition of new maritime claims to the list.

Although several delegations supported the open list approach, there appeared to be a swing of the majority in favour of the closed list. The Chairman noted this but since views were still divided, suggested that the possibility of compromise should be explored.

It is worth noting that the views were not divided on the basis of the common law versus civil law system, as one might have expected. In fact the closed list approach was favoured, amongst others, together with UK and Hong Kong, by France, Russian Federation, China, Germany and Greece, while the open list approach was supported, together with Italy, the Netherlands, Norway and Japan, by Canada and the United States.

Second reading—8 March 1999[3]

With reference to Doc. CRP.16 the U.S. delegate stated that the required flexibility could be obtained by moving the chapeau down to the end of the list but deleting the words "such as" and inserting the words "of a similar nature". The new head of claim (w) that had been suggested would provide flexibility for future developments in technology, ships financing arrangements, etc. At the same time it would provide very important restrictions: claims in order to be granted the status of maritime claims must first meet two requirements: (1) they must concern or arise out of the few items listed, and (2) they must be similar in nature to those listed in sub-paragraphs (a) to (v). Although the substantial majority of the delegations who spoke after the presentation of the U.S. proposal supported it, after it had been noted that a difference in substance existed between the English text of the proposal (in which the words "of a similar nature" were used) and the French text (in which the words "de la même nature" were used) any decision was postponed. When the problem was again discussed, several delegations opposed to the concept of flexibility that of certainty, stating that only a closed list could ensure certainty in the description of maritime claims. Other delegations observed that flexibility could be ensured by providing a mechanism for the revision of the list through a revision conference. Still some other delegations stated that the problem of an open or closed list was strictly connected with that of the requirement of registration for mortgages, "hypothèques" and charges, such requirement in fact preventing any flexibility. Since at the end of the debate it had appeared that the U.S. proposal had not received a sufficient support, a decision was adjourned in the hope that a compromise could be reached, both in respect of the "chapeau" and in respect of sub-paragraph (u) wherein claims arising out of mortgages, "hypothèques" and charges are listed.

The following day the Canadian delegate reported that a compromise had been reached on the basis of the amendment of three individual maritime claims:

— *sub-paragraph (d) was "opened-up" by adding at the end the words "and damage, costs, or loss of a similar nature to those identified in this sub-paragraph (d)";*
— *sub-paragraph (l) was amended by adding the word "management";*
— *sub-paragraph (u) was amended by deleting the word "registered" and a consequential corresponding amendment was made in article 3(1)(c).*

Article 1(1) as amended was accepted by a very large majority.

---

3. Summary from tapes Nos. 58–60.

1999 Convention

For the purpose of this Convention:
1. "Maritime Claim" means a claim arising out of one or more of the following:

THE INDIVIDUAL MARITIME CLAIMS
GENERAL COMMENTS AND DISCUSSION

Report of the CMI

22. Some discussion took place as to whether the list of maritime claims was wide enough to cover any claims secured by maritime liens under existing conventions. This was found to be the case. There was, therefore, no need for a catch-all clause in this respect. It was also discussed whether the list of maritime claims should start with an enumeration of the claims secured by maritime liens according to the Convention on Maritime Liens and Mortgages drafted at Lisbon, and then go on to enumerate such other claims as were to be recognized as maritime claims. This, however, was not found to be practical.

JIGE
Seventh Session, 5 December 1994

Report—Annex I

5. The Group had a preliminary discussion on several aspects of the list of claims contained in article 1 of the 1952 Arrest Convention and of the CMI Draft in order to introduce amendments needed as a result of the adoption of the 1993 MLM Convention.
6. It was agreed that terminology used in the Arrest Convention in respect of claims with maritime lien status should be closely aligned with that of the 1993 MLM Convention.

Report—Addendum

1. The Group noted that the text of sub-paragraphs (a), (b), (n) and (o) of article 1(1) had been changed to reflect the terminology used in the 1993 MLM Convention.

Eighth Session, 9–10 October 1995

Report—Annex I

8. ... A small working group was set up with the task of ensuring that all claims with maritime liens status under the 1993 MLM Convention are included in the list of maritime claims.

Ninth Session, 2–6 December 1996

Report—Annex II

4. The Chairman of the Informal Working Group on Article 1 (1), reporting on the work of the Informal Group, said that the paper submitted to the Sessional Group (see annex III below) was the result of discussions by 12 delegations. It identified which changes had been agreed in London and Geneva respectively. In addition, a number of endnotes were attached to the paper in order to provide a more accurate account of the different views expressed by delegations.
5. With respect to the relationship between "maritime claims" and "maritime liens", the observer for the International Maritime Committee (CMI) noted that, in ensuring that maritime liens recognized by the 1993 International Convention on Maritime Liens and Mortgages (MLM Convention) were covered by the definition of "maritime claim", there was no need strictly to use the same wording, since "maritime liens" were by nature more restrictive than "maritime claims".
6. One delegation referred to the task of the Working Group of ensuring that the list of maritime claims in Article 1 should include all claims with maritime lien status under the 1993 MLM Convention but should not necessarily be restricted to claims with maritime lien status.

Note of the Editor. The following note is appended to the chapeau of article 1(1) in the Draft Articles:

Article 1(1) was amended by the Informal Working Group set out during the 8th session of the Joint Group to ensure that all claims granted maritime lien status under the 1993 International Convention on Maritime Liens and Mortgages are included without creating duplication or inconsistency within various sub-paragraphs. Sub-paragraphs (d) and (p) have been redrafted. The word "construction" in original sub-paragraph (m) has been replaced by "building" and the term "charges" has been used in sub-paragraph (n) in place of "pilotage dues". Sub-paragraphs (s) and (v) had been merged by the Informal Working Group. They are, however, kept separate because of the cross-reference made in article 4(1) to article 1(1)(s) as pointed out at the Sessional Group. The word "registered" has been added before "mortgage" and "hypothèque". For discussions on article 1(1), see the report of the Informal Working Group (annex III of the report of the Joint Group) and the report on the work of the Sessional Group (annex II, paragraphs 2–14).

Diplomatic Conference
Comments and Proposals

Republic of Korea

DOCUMENT 188/3

56. Article 1 lists twenty-two different types of claims by which ships can be arrested. The 1993 Convention on Maritime Liens and Mortgages also lists in Article 4 paragraph 1 grounds related to liens and mortgages on which claims can be made. As there are two lists that deal with very similar issues, it seems appropriate to ensure that any conflict between the two conventions is avoided.

Ukraine

DOCUMENT CRP.11

1. The list of maritime liens that can serve as grounds for arrest of a ship must be clearly defined. This would be consistent with the requirement to standardize international maritime law in this respect. The list of maritime liens should also be enlarged to include liens relating to dock and harbour fees.

PARAGRAPH 1(a)

Draft of the CMI International Sub-Committee

(a) DAMAGE CAUSED BY ANY SHIP (WHETHER IN COLLISION OR OTHERWISE);

CMI Draft

(a) DAMAGE CUASED BY ANY SHIP, WHETHER IN COLLISION OR OTHERWISE;

J1GE
Draft Articles 1994

(a) PHYSICAL LOSS OR DAMAGE CAUSED BY THE OPERATION OF THE VESSEL OTHER THAN LOSS OR DAMAGE TO CARGO, CONTAINERS AND PASSENGERS' EFFECTS CARRIED ON THE VESSEL (1993 MLM CONVENTION, ARTICLE 4(1)(e));

Eighth Session, 9–10 October 1995

Report – Annex I

15. The majority of delegations agreed that the claims giving rise to a maritime lien under the 1993 Convention on Maritime Liens and Mortgages should be included among the claims listed in article 1(1). It was, however, pointed out that merely aligning terminology with the 1993 MLM Convention could result in creating contradictions between various sub-paragraphs of article 1(1), as was the case with sub-paragraphs (a) and (h). It was therefore suggested that the words "*other than loss of or damage to cargo*" in sub-paragraph (a) be deleted. Other delegations proposed the deletion of the word "*physical*" at the beginning of sub-paragraph (a) so as to include also economic

and consequential loss. Some delegations, however, preferred to retain the word "*physical*". One delegation doubted whether it was necessary to have any link at all between the MLM and Arrest Conventions. In response it was explained that linkage between the two Conventions was necessary to the extent that all maritime liens covered in the MLM Convention needed to be included in the list of maritime claims in the Arrest Convention. In other words, linkage referred to the wording and not to the Conventions. The two Conventions should remain entirely independent.

Report—Annex II

Pursuant to the direction of the Joint Intergovernmental Group of Experts, an informal Working Group convened to consider issues relating to the definition of "maritime claim" under article 1, definitions of the revised draft articles for a Convention on Arrest of Ships (LEG/MLM/32). The Committee directed the Group to consider the draft of paragraph 1 of article 1 and to take into account the necessity of being compatible with the provisions of the 1993 MLM Convention, bearing in mind that repetitions should be avoided.

The Working Group met from 9 to 10 October 1995. Mr. P. Calmon Filho (Brazil) was unanimously elected as Chairman. Delegations from Brazil, Canada, China, France, Germany, Greece, Italy, Liberia, Mexico, Netherlands, Norway, Poland, the Russian Federation and Spain were represented.

1. The Group considered whether to add a sub-paragraph or paragraph under article 1, containing a precise reference to the Maritime Liens and Mortgages Convention 1993, in order to make it clear that maritime claims secured by a lien under the 1993 MLM Convention would fall within the scope of article 1.

2. The Group did not reach a decision and concluded that the matter should be further discussed particularly in connection with article 3.

3. As to the wording of clause 1, the Group took into consideration the various proposals presented in the plenary and agreed, in principle, with the following:

....

5. Item (a): Delete "physical" from the beginning of the sentence, and what comes after "operation of the ship" in the first line, so the text reads as follows:
"loss or damage caused by the operation of the ship;"

The question had been raised as to whether it would be sufficient to follow the 1952 Arrest Convention text, and to delete the word "*loss or*". It was felt that this has to be decided by the plenary.

Ninth Session, 2–6 December 1996

Report—Annex II

TEXT SUGGESTED BY THE INFORMAL WORKING GROUP

(a) LOSS OR DAMAGE CAUSED BY THE OPERATION OF THE SHIP;

8. One delegation . . . expressed concern as to the suggestion to include the word "physical" in subparagraph (a), as suggested in the endnotes by two other delegations, since such inclusion would prevent "economic losses" from being covered by subparagraph (a).

11. One delegation noted that subparagraphs (a) and (h) were kept because the second part of subparagraph (a) was deleted. The suggestion to retain the word "physical" in subparagraph (a) was made so that consequential losses would not be included.

Draft Articles 1997

(a) LOSS OR DAMAGE CAUSED BY THE OPERATION OF THE SHIP;

Note of the Editor. For convenience, the relevant part of the note appended to article 1(1) of the Draft Articles 1997 is reproduced below:
Sub-paragraph (a) has been amended to avoid inconsistency with sub-paragraph (h).

Diplomatic Conference: Proceedings of the Main Committee

First reading—1 March 1999[4]

The delegate from Spain asked why the word "physical", that preceded the words "loss or damage" in the Draft Articles 1994, had been deleted. On request of the Chairman the delegate from the CMI explained that the deletion was due to the decision to include also economic and consequential loss. The delegate from the Russian Federation so stated:

Professor Berlingieri has already thrown light on this issue. The position of the group of experts was defined very clearly in paragraph 11 of the JIGE's report at the 9th session: it was unanimous that the wording of the claim secured by a maritime lien, which is contained in subparagraph "e" of article 4.1. of the International Convention on Maritime Liens and Mortgages, 1993, should not be repeated in subparagraph "a" of article 1.1 of the Convention on Arrest of Ships. The term "physical" in the claim secured by a maritime lien has been correctly used before the words "loss or damage". This claim is narrower in comparison with the maritime claim provided for by the Convention on Arrest of Ships. Claims based on pure economic loss are not secured by the maritime lien. On the contrary, under the Convention on Arrest of Ships there must be provided for a possibility of arresting a ship under the claims arising out of the "physical loss or damage" and economic loss connected with it. For example, claims arising out of the collision of ships. For that purpose the Convention on Arrest of Ships must use the words "loss or damage" without adding the word "physical" before them. Based on that, we think that the proposed wording of subparagraph "a" of article 1.1 is quite correct and must be kept unchanged in the text of the Convention. Thank you for your attention.

Following that explanation sub-paragraph (a) was adopted.

1999 Convention

(a) LOSS OR DAMAGE CAUSED BY THE OPERATION OF THE SHIP;

PARAGRAPH 1(b)

Draft of the CMI International Sub-Committee

(b) LOSS OF LIFE OR PERSONAL INJURY CAUSED BY ANY SHIP OR OCCURRING IN CONNECTION WITH THE OPERATION OR MANAGEMENT OF ANY SHIP;

JIGE
Draft Articles 1994

(b) LOSS OF LIFE OR PERSONAL INJURY OCCURRING, WHETHER ON LAND OR ON WATER, IN DIRECT CONNECTION WITH THE OPERATION OF THE VESSEL;

Note of the Editor. This sub-paragraph has remained unchanged except for the addition of the word "direct" before "connection" made by the Secretariats in order to bring the text in line with that of article 4(1)(b) of the 1993 MLM Convention.

Seventh Session, 5 December 1994

Report—Annex I

34. The Group noted that the text of sub-paragraphs (a), (b), (n) and (o) of article 1(1) had been changed to reflect the terminology used in the 1993 MLM Convention.

37. . . . Another delegation proposed deleting the word "direct" in sub-paragraph (b) so as to avoid creating a limitation which did not exist in the chapeau of article 1(1).

---

4. Summary from tapes Nos. 3 and 4.

Ninth Session, 2–6 December 1996

Report—Annex II

11. . . . This delegation suggested that the word *"direct"* in subparagraph (b) should be kept in brackets, since the Group was divided as to whether it should be retained or deleted.

Diplomatic Conference
Proceedings of the Main Committee

First reading—1 March 1999[5]

The suggestion was made to delete this sub-paragraph on the ground that it was superfluous, in view of the wide wording of sub-paragraph (a). The observer from the CMI explained that (b) had been inserted in order to ensure uniformity of language between the Arrest Convention and the 1993 MLM Convention, where a corresponding maritime lien was granted under article 4(1)(b) and the Committee then decided to retain this maritime claim. The retention of sub-paragraph (b) was supported, amongst others by the UK and the Russian delegations. The delegate from the Russian Federation so stated:

We support the opinion expressed by the United Kingdom delegation on the desirability of retaining subparagraph "b" of article 1.1 of the Convention. Professor Berlingieri is right, that the claim arising out of loss of life or personal injury caused by the operation of a ship, is an independent claim, which is confirmed, in particular, by the 1993 Convention. In this connection it should be noted that maritime conventions traditionally single this claim out of others. Besides the 1993 Convention, we can also mention the Convention on Limitation of Liability for Maritime Claims, 1976, where the claims in respect of loss of life or personal injury caused by the operation of a ship exist alongside with other claims connected with the operation of a ship. That is why we are of the opinion that sub-paragraph "b" of article 1.1 must be present in the draft Convention irrespective of the presence of sub-paragraph "a" of article 1.1.

1999 Convention

(b) LOSS OF LIFE OR PERSONAL INJURY OCCURRING, WHETHER ON LAND OR ON WATER, IN DIRECT CONNECTION WITH THE OPERATION OF THE SHIP;

PARAGRAPH 1(c)

Draft of the CMI International Sub-Committee

(c) SALVAGE OPERATIONS OR ANY SALVAGE AGREEMENT;

J1GE
Seventh Session, 5 December 1994

Report—Annex I

8. Some delegations expressed views in favour of including in the list claims related to the special compensation provided for in article 14 of the 1989 Salvage Convention. Those delegations accordingly considered that the present text in the CMI Draft (article 1(1) (c)) should be maintained.

9. Other delegations stated they were in favour of excluding such special compensation. In their opinion, the right to arrest should be granted only in respect of liens securing claims for reward for salvage of the vessel.

Draft Articles 1997

(c) SALVAGE OPERATIONS OR ANY SALVAGE AGREEMENT;

5. Summary from tape No. 4.

Diplomatic Conference
Comments and Proposals

Proposal by Ukraine

DOCUMENT CRP.11

2. We propose the wording: "Payment for salvage operations or fulfilment of the terms of a salvage agreement".

Proposal by the United Kingdom

DOCUMENT CRP.2

In article 1(1)(c), add the following wording:

"including, if applicable, any claim for special compensation under article 14 of the International Convention on Salvage 1989".

Proceedings of the Main Committee

First reading—1 March 1999[6]

The delegate from the United Kingdom so stated:

Our reading of paragraph (c) is that it covers traditional salvage claims. It would be our view that this paragraph should cover any claim under a salvage contract, for example the Lloyd's Open Form or what is presently being discussed and described as the "Skopic" agreement, that it would be useful perhaps to clarify that point and also to cover special compensation under an article 14 award.

The observer from the International Group of P&I Clubs pointed out that the purpose of the "Skopic" agreement was to reflect in practice the provisions of article 14 of the 1989 Salvage Convention and that the P&I Clubs never had any doubt at all that the provisions of the "Skopic" agreement were covered by the words "any salvage agreement".

On request of the Chairman to clarify whether he agreed that the special compensation of article 14 was already covered by the present wording of (c) the United Kingdom delegate stated:

The problem is simply that under the 1989 Salvage Convention there is created a right of recovery by salvors of special compensation which is expenses incurred in the course of salvage operations when the vessel or her cargo threatens damage to the environment. Now the expenses which are recoverable under article 14 as special compensation may include expenses which are simply related to the salvage operation and not to the removal of the threat to the environment; so strictly speaking these expenses could fall in a gap between (c) which is "salvage operations" pure and simple or "salvage agreement" because salvage may be a claim which is not covered by an agreement and removal of the threat or preventive measures because they are simply the reimbursement of salvage expenses. It is simply to clarify that that this delegation would suggest wording which would be similar to that included in the 1996 Protocol on Limitation of Liability, to specify that special compensation payable under article 14 of the 1989 Salvage Convention is also covered by (c). We would be prepared to submit a written proposal.

The Chairman then noted that the United Kingdom delegation would have reverted with a specific proposal.

The delegate from the Russian Federation so stated:

I have already dropped the card, because you said that one should wait for the text which the United Kingdom delegation would submit. We suppose that the wording of sub-paragraph (c) of article 1.1 is sufficiently broad, and that the notion "salvage operations" also covers salvage operations in respect of a ship which by itself or its cargo threatened damage to the environment. It seems to us unnecessary to specify this claim in respect of remuneration for salvage or special compensation, as has been done in the 1996 Protocol on Amending the 1976 Convention. It is possible that we shall change our opinion depending on what the wording proposed by the United Kingdom delegation will be, but in principle the present wording of sub-paragraph (c) suits us.

---

6. Text and summary from tape No. 3.

Second reading—8 March 1999[7]

Two proposals were made in respect of the reference in this sub-paragraph to special compensation. One from the United Kingdom wherein an express reference was made to the 1989 Salvage Convention and one from the United States, wherein the special nature of the services was described without, however, any reference to the 1989 Convention.

The United Kingdom delegate introduced his proposal and so stated:

The JIGE draft contained the words "salvage operations or any salvage agreement", while the 1952 Convention mentions salvage only. (. . .) The reason for the addition by the CMI of the words "salvage agreement" has been to add obligations which may arise which are not pure salvage agreement itself. A problem has however arisen in the past as to whether the special compensation which is payable in accordance with article 14 of the 1989 Salvage Convention may not strictly speaking be salvage in the traditional sense of the word and may not arise under a salvage agreement if no agreement has been signed and for that reason when the 1996 Protocol to the 1976 LLMC Convention was drafted a clause was inserted to make it clear that it was not possible for a shipowner to limit his liability for special compensation payable under the 1989 Salvage Convention and the wording of the addition to clause (c) put forward in Conference Paper CRP.2 is in fact lifted verbatim from the 1996 Protocol to LLMC 1976. Having thought a little further since this particular paper was put in we noted in fact in LLMC 1976 the words "as amended" have been added at the end after International Convention on Salvage 1989 and this delegation would suggest to the Conference that it may be prudent to add to the words in quote in CRP.2 the words "as amended" at the end since that would allow for any subsequent modification of the 1989 Salvage Convention at a future date. This delegation is aware that certain delegations in the room do have an objection in principle to any reference in our Convention, the Arrest Convention, to any other convention at all. Our first answer to that is that the claim for special compensation is absolutely unique. It does not arise under a salvage agreement, it is not a claim in contract, it is not a claim in tort, it is not a claim in debt, it is absolutely a unique right to compensate a salvor and encourage (his action) and that was the reason why with the 1996 Protocol a reference was made to the 1989 Salvage Convention despite reservations expressed by certain delegations at the 1996 Diplomatic Conference. Another wording drafted by the United States has been circulated which could meet that objection if delegates to this Conference feel that a reference to the 1989 Salvage Convention is objectionable.

The Chairman invited the delegation from the United States to comment on its alternative proposal and the U.S. delegate so stated:

What we did was to put the language from the Salvage Convention and place it in (c) and in that way avoiding specific reference to another convention. It is just another alternative for consideration by this Committee. It is a three lines of text which I could read if that could be helpful. So our version of (c) would read as follows:

> Salvage operations or any salvage agreement, including any claim for special compensation relating to salvage operations in respect of a ship which by itself or its cargo threatened damage to the environment.

That language comes right out of the article referred to in the UK proposal.

The US proposal was deemed to be preferable in that it avoided a reference to another convention and was adopted except that the words "if applicable" were added before the reference to special compensation.

1999 Convention

(c) SALVAGE OPERATIONS OR ANY SALVAGE AGREEMENT, INCLUDING, IF APPLICABLE, SPECIAL COMPENSATION RELATING TO SALVAGE OPERATIONS IN RESPECT OF A SHIP WHICH BY ITSELF OR ITS CARGO THREATENED DAMAGE TO THE ENVIRONMENT;

---

7. Text and summary from tape No. 50.

PARAGRAPH 1(d)

Draft of the CMI International Sub-Committee

(d) LIABILITY TO PAY COMPENSATION OR OTHER REMUNERATION IN RESPECT OF THE REMOVAL OR ATTEMPTED REMOVAL OF A THREAT OF DAMAGE, OR OF PREVENTIVE MEASURES OR SIMILAR OPERATIONS, WHETHER OR NOT ARISING UNDER ANY INTERNATIONAL CONVENTION, ENACTMENT OR AGREEMENT;

Note of the Editor. This text was adopted by the Lisbon Conference, with the addition of the words "or any" before "enactment or agreement" and reproduced without change in the Draft Articles 1994.

CMI Report

20. Subparagraph (d) is new and is designed in particular to cover claims in respect of preventive measures to avoid pollution damage.

JIGE
Eighth Session: 9–10 October 1995

Report—Annex I

16. One delegation proposed the inclusion of a reference to "in direct connection with the operation of the ship" in sub-paragraph (d) in the same way as in sub-paragraph (b), so as to exclude claims not related to the operation of the vessel.

Report—Annex II

7. Item (d): There was no time to conclude the discussions. At the time the meeting was adjourned it was agreed in principle (except for the final phrase) that the following wording replace the present (d) on the draft:
"Preventive measures, the removal or attempted removal of a threat of damage or similar operations if the aim was to mitigate a maritime claim".
As to the last words (underlined) there was no agreement. One delegation proposed to replace "to mitigate a maritime claim", with "similar operations in connection with the operation of the ship".

Ninth Session: 2–6 December 1996

Report—Annex III

(d) THE REMOVAL OR ATTEMPTED REMOVAL OF A THREAT OF DAMAGE INCLUDING DAMAGE TO THE ENVIRONMENT OR OF PREVENTIVE MEASURES OR SIMILAR OPERATIONS, WHETHER OR NOT ARISING UNDER ANY INTERNATIONAL CONVENTION, OR ANY ENACTMENT OR AGREEMENT, OR LOSSES INCURRED, OR LIKELY TO BE INCURRED, BY THIRD PARTIES.

Comments by the Greek delegation on Article 1 (d): In negotiating the Maritime Liens and Mortgages Convention of 1993, a compromise was reached, which was reflected in Article 4 (2) of the above-mentioned Convention, where no maritime lien shall be attached to a vessel to secure claims which arise out of or result from the cases mentioned there.

The same compromise should be reflected in the new draft articles for new rules on the arrest of sea-going ships.

Therefore, a vessel should not be arrested for claims which arise out of: (a) damage in connection with the carriage of oil or other hazardous or noxious substances by sea for which compensation is payable to the claimants pursuant to international conventions or national law providing for strict liability and compulsory insurance or other means of securing the claims; (b) the radioactive properties or a combination of radioactive properties of nuclear fuel or of radioactive products or waste.

Report—Annex II

11. One delegation . . . Concerning subparagraph (d), this delegation felt that, in keeping with the compromise in relation to the MLM convention, a vessel should not be arrested for claims which

arose out of the damage in connection with the carriage of oil or other hazardous or noxious substances for which compensation was payable to the claimants pursuant to international conventions or national law providing for strict liability and compulsory insurance.

Draft Articles 1997

(d) LIABILITY TO PAY COMPENSATION OR OTHER REMUNERATION IN RESPECT OF THE REMOVAL OR ATTEMPTED REMOVAL OF A THREAT OF DAMAGE, OR OF PREVENTIVE MEASURES OR SIMILAR OPERATIONS, WHETHER OR NOT ARISING UNDER ANY INTERNATIONAL CONVENTION, OR ANY ENACTMENT OR AGREEMENT;

Note of the Editor. For convenience, the relevant part of the note appended to article 1(1) of the Draft Articles 1997 is reproduced below:
Sub-paragraphs (d) and (p) have been redrafted.

Diplomatic Conference
Comments and Proposals

CMI

DOCUMENT 188/3
133. The words "removal or attempted removal" and "preventive measures or similar operations" seem to repeat twice the same concept. In both the CLC 1969 and the 1996 HNS Convention "preventive measures" are defined as "reasonable measures taken to prevent or minimize" damage. It is suggested that perhaps this definition may be used here and that the reference to "similar operations" is unnecessary.

The words "or losses incurred, or likely to be incurred by third parties" give the impression that the losses referred to are a new category of maritime claim, not connected with the "removal or attempted removal of [a threat of] damage" etc. Furthermore, it is not clear why the expression "third parties" has been used.

Perhaps the Conference might consider the following text:
"the cost of measures taken by any person to prevent or minimize damage including environmental damage, [whether] [when] such claim arises under any international convention [,] any enactment or agreement, including losses incurred [,] or likely to be incurred in connection with such measures".

The use of the word "whether" instead of "whether or not" has the effect that only a claim which arises under an international convention or under an enactment or under an agreement would be within the scope of this category of claim. If that is so, there seems to be no reason to use the word "whether". "When" might in such case be a better word.

The comma after "international convention" and the comma after "losses incurred" may be deleted.

ICS

DOCUMENT 188/3
118. Claims falling under the CLC and HNSC should be exempted as in Article 4, paragraph 2(a) of the MLM Convention.

Ukraine

DOCUMENT CRP.11
3. We propose the wording:
"Compensation for the removal or attempted removal of a threat of damage, including damage to the environment, or for preventive measures or similar operations, whether or not arising under an international agreement or enactment, or for losses incurred."

United States

DOCUMENT CRP.16:

   (d) damage or threat of damage to the marine environment, coastline or related interests; measures taken to prevent, minimize, or remove such damage; compensation for such damage; costs of reasonable measures of reinstatement of the environment actually undertaken or to be undertaken; and losses incurred or likely to be incurred by third parties in connection with such damage;

Proceedings of the Main Committee

First reading—1 March 1999[8]

   The observer from ICS stated that since it had been decided to align the Arrest Convention to the MLM Convention, this head of claim should be deleted because pollution claims under the CLC had been excluded from the scope of the MLM Convention.

   The observer from the CMI in turn so stated:

   It is true that all claims secured by maritime liens should be included in the arrest convention. But that does not mean that the opposite is true also. In other words there may be maritime claims which are not secured by maritime liens but still are maritime claims. Therefore the fact that all claims secured by maritime liens in the 1993 Convention must be included in the Arrest Convention does not mean that some claims in respect of which there is no maritime lien under the 1993 MLM should not be granted the status of maritime claims. Therefore with great respect to my friend Dr. Kröger I think that I cannot agree with what he said. So the reason that there is no maritime lien does not mean by itself that there should not be a right of arrest in respect of this type of claims which should still be considered claims of a maritime nature.

   The delegate from the Russian Federation so stated:

   We think that sub-paragraph (d) of article 1.1 must be retained in the Convention, and the bright explanation made by Professor Berlingieri strengthens us in this opinion. To our great regret Professor Berlingieri has not said that the CMI proposes to make the wording of that sub-paragraph more precise. It seems to us that the text proposed by CMI is good, and deserves attention. We are inclined towards the wording proposed by the CMI.

   Following the invitation of the Chairman the delegate from the CMI introduced the CMI proposal as follows:

   Mr. Chairman I am grateful to the distinguished delegate of the Russian Federation to have referred to the CMI proposal. In actual fact I doubt whether it is a proposal of substance or a drafting point. Since now I have been asked to put forward the CMI proposal I will do that very quickly. It seems to the CMI that the words used in the draft "removal or attempted removal of a threat of damage" and then "preventive measures or similar operations" repeat twice the same concept contained in both the CLC 1969 and in 1996 HNS Convention. Preventive measures are defined as "reasonable measures to prevent or minimize damage". It is suggested that perhaps this definition may be used here and that the reference to similar operation is unnecessary. Then the words "or losses incurred or likely to be incurred by third parties" give the impression that the losses referred to are a new category of maritime claims not connected with removal or attempted removal of the threat of damage etc. Furthermore it is not clear why the expression "third parties" has been used. The text suggested by the CMI which I can read but is already included in the documents which are in front of you is the following: "the cost of measures taken by any person to prevent or minimize damage including environmental damage when such claims arise under an international convention any enactment or agreement including losses incurred or likely to be incurred in connection with such measures". This wording is printed in one of the documents in front of you, I shall give you the reference any moment.

   The delegate from the United States made then the following comments:

   The United States is not married to the particular wording in subsection (d). We do believe that certain points set out in that subsection may need to be retained in any revised draft and which are not retained in the CMI proposal. First from my prospective there is a difference between preventive measures on one hand and removal or removal actions on the other. The preventive measures will

---

8. Text and summary from tapes Nos. 3 and 4.

be those taken prior to the oil or the substances resulting from the pollution incident entering the water such as measures to remove the ship from a reef prior to a breach of her tanks, whereas removal would refer to claims arising after the oil has entered the water. So we believe it important to leave both of those concepts in the draft. Second the deletion of the words "whether or not" in the CMI draft appears to limit claims to those arising strictly under a convention, an enactment or an agreement and therefore appear to eliminate the possibility of a claim arising under a traditional tort action. Thirdly we think it is important that the provisions allow for third parties losses. For that reason if there is a change we would like it to reflect those three points.

The Chairman concluded as follows:

It seems to me that since there is a majority in favour of keeping (d) but there is disagreement on its drafting I think that we should revert when dealing with the UK proposal on (c) and see whether we can combine the CMI proposal and the comments and suggestions of the US delegation.

Second reading—8 March 1999[9]

United States The United States working with other delegations has developed a proposal on sub-paragraph (d) concerning claims arising from incidents affecting the marine environment. The paragraph seeks to combine the concepts contained in the JIGE text with concepts already used in other international regimes to enumerate the categories of claims that may arise in the context of a marine environmental incident. The reference to the "marine environment coastline or related interest" is derived from article 211 paragraphs (1) and (7) in part XII of the 1982 Law of the Sea Convention, the part entitled "Protection and preservation of the marine environment". The reference to "measures taken to prevent, minimize and remove such damage" draws upon the JIGE text by referring to removal and preventive measures and adds measures to minimize damage which may in some cases be viewed as differing from either removal or prevention efforts. The reference to "costs of reasonable measures of reinstatement of the environment actually undertaken or to be undertaken" comes from article 1(6) of the CLC as amended by the 1992 Protocol to the CLC. That phrase also appears in article 6(c) of the Convention on Liability and Compensation for Damage in Connection with the Carriage of Hazardous and Noxious Substances by Sea, the 1996 HNS Convention. The purpose of those articles is to ensure that compensation for the impairment of the environment as a result of an oil or hazardous substances spill is limited to reasonable costs of reinstatement. Finally, the reference to third party losses is based on the existing JIGE text. The overall purpose of sub-paragraph (d) is to encompass the type of claims that may arise from a marine environmental incident, while still ensuring that such claims are appropriately limited by reference to existing international regimes.

Japan We basically support the idea just presented by the delegation from the United States. However we wish to have slight more discussion on two points of the proposal in CRP 16. The first point is just for clarification, to make clear that this maritime claim arises in respect of a ship. It depends to some degree on what phrase is adopted in the chapeau. However at this stage we wish to make this clear in (d), i.e. adding at the very end of (d) a phrase like this: "arising out of the operation of the ship". That would make it more clear that the claim based on environmental damage is deemed to be a maritime claim, provided it arises out of the operation of the ship. That is the first point. The second is—some delegations may take it as a drafting matter—however that is the case of the term "marine" environment, of course we understand that it is a phrase taken from the Convention on the Law of the Sea, however this is a public law convention. In our understanding the usual term used in private law convention—for example CLC—is just "environmental damage" or "impairment to the environment" and does not include the term "marine". So we prefer that version: just say "environment".

Norway We support fully what was very eloquently expressed by the Japanese delegation.

Germany We fully support what was said by the Japanese delegation.

Finland We have a question concerning the suggestion put forward by the US delegation. The expression "threat of damage to the marine environment, coastline or related interest" does it also cover threat to human life, for instance when a gas tanker has an explosion or an accident and there

9. Text from tapes Nos. 58–60. In view of the importance of this head of claim and of the interest of the debate, the full transcript of the proceedings is reproduced.

will be a threat to human life, for instance a lot of cost, evacuating cost for instance, and other costs. Does this text also take care of this kind of situation?

United States   We believe that both types of damages, loss of life etc. are addressed in sub-paragraph (b) of the list and could also be included in the last phrase of (d) "losses incurred or likely to be incurred by third parties in connection with such damage".

United Kingdom   We certainly support the principle that is explained by the US We also can support the proposal by Japan, that we should delete the word "marine". I think that seems to be consistent with other conventions. I am just looking at the words that we were given for the addition at the end of the paragraph, "arising out of the operation of the ship" and I am almost drafting as I talk, but I think we might like something, instead of that phrase from the Japanese delegation, to say simply such damage "caused by the ship", so the ship may not actually be moving, but something is come off the ship or has arisen from the ship. If that concept is accepted, I think that this just a drafting point, for the drafting Committee, Mr. Chairman.

IUCN   As an environmental organization, naturally we are concerned by any provision such as this. I would give it cautions support but I have to say I am a little concerned with the explanation by United States that one has to phrase the definition and limit it by reference to the existing regimes. One of the problems with the Arrest Convention of 1952 is that some of the provisions become dated and we would prefer that the references to the damage to the environment were more general so that if there are developments in the future, which go beyond existing law, then the provisions of the Arrest Convention would be up to meet them, so we would be a little concerned about some of the references here which are restricted and limited by existing regimes: but otherwise we do not oppose this proposal.

Canada   The Canadian delegation was one of the delegations who during the JIGE and the early stages of this Diplomatic Conference that was not pleased with the current drafting of sub-paragraph (d). We thought that there were some internal cohesion drafting problems to begin with and we have also pointed out on several occasions that it did not really mirror the state of the essential elements of the subject. We find that the proposal submitted by the United States is a tremendous improvement in that direction. We are certainly a delegation who favours as much uniformity in this area as possible. We recognize these words from the major international pollution treaties and certainly from that point of view support the initiative. We heard our Japanese colleague suggest a few improvements. We also heard the UK and having heard these delegations we find that deleting the word "marine" in line 1 would be consistent first of all with the HNS Convention which does not have that word "marine" in article 1 paragraph (6)(c) and we find that is an improvement we can accept. As to the words suggested to be added at the end of the paragraph, of course they are helpful to situate the context and this Convention would stand alone and clearly we are speaking of the arrest of ships and some language to that effect is probably a welcome improvement. I think the UK version is definitely the one that we would support. I think to restrict in some manner to the operation of the ship it might not be appropriate in this case but the more generic language suggested by the UK is that we would approve.

Sri Lanka   Sri Lanka support the US proposal contained in CRP 16. We support also the Japanese amendment in respect of the deletion of the word "marine". With regard to the second proposal of the delegation of Japan we would prefer the UK proposal to have in the words "caused by the ship".

Brazil   The Brazilian delegation supports the proposal of the United States with the amendment proposed by Japan in respect of the word "marine" and at the end the addition suggested by UK.

Turkey   I also wish to add my voice to that of the delegations who have thanked the delegation of the United States for improving the text of sub-paragraph (d). We support the original proposal, but we could also go along with the amendment proposed by Japan particularly as regards the deletion of the word "marine" and the UK proposal as to the last part of this proposal. We again thank the US delegation for their efforts.

Russian Fed.   First of all we thank the delegation of the United States for the efforts to overcome the difficulties that emerged in connection with this paragraph. There are two remarks which we still have as regards this paragraph: they concern the first line and the last phrase of the paragraph. We share the opinion of those delegations which raise a question of replacing the term "marine environment" by the term "environment", which would exclude the necessity of the words "coastline or related interests". The term "marine environment" is taken from the 1982 UN Convention on the Law of the Sea and is less acceptable for regulating civil law relations. We share the CMI's position, which has been pronounced orally and in the written remarks, that the notion "loss incurred or likely to be incurred by third parties", contained in the last phrase of the text, really creates an impression that it concerns loss that represents a new category of maritime claims, not connected with the removal or attempted removal of a threat of damage. Therefore we support the CMI's wording: "loss incurred in connection with such measures" or "loss likely to be incurred in connection with such measures". This wording also excludes the erroneous reference to third parties.

xxx My delegation like many other speakers would like to support the proposal made by the United States to improve the existing language, to make it much broader than it was drafted in the JIGE text. We also would like to support the amendments made by Japan and UK I am wondering after the last intervention by the delegate from Russia whether the text needs to be improved regarding the comments made by the CMI. It is my understanding that the text now is broader that it was proposed by the CMI submission, but I am open for further comments on that.

Singapore Like the distinguished delegate from Canada we too find the US proposal a much improved text as respects the JIGE text. We agree with the Japanese delegation that the word "marine" appearing in the first line should be deleted. Again we agree with the UK delegation that the words "caused by the ship" should be added at the end of that paragraph and arising from the comments made by the Russian Federation we wonder whether the phrase "such damage" in the last line should be modified so to take into account the comments made by the Russian Federation. We wonder whether the phrase should be "such measures" instead of "such damage". This may be a drafting point.

. . .

Greece The Greek delegation believes that we should retain the word "marine". We can see from the US paper that the reference to the marine environment is derived from the UNCLOS Convention and if am not mistaken there is a reference also included in the CLC and Fund Convention, so we find it consistent. Apart from that the reference to "coast line and related interest" covers satisfactorily the whole issue so I think to broaden it more with just the word "environment" is not advisable. As to the words "likely to be incurred by third parties", we cannot find them in the relevant international conventions. It is a new concept which should be avoided for the time being.

Italy The Italian delegation is in favour of the proposal of the United States. As regards the Japanese proposal we might go along with it.[10] In any case we could accept also to leave the words "marine environment" because after this comes the word "coastline" and so it is clear that also the coast will be included. But we think that may be we might give some more attention to the problem whether to include in this paragraph the mention to any international convention. Do we want to leave it very broad so that it can cover any damage not considered by international texts or do we want to be more precise and in this case to adopt the JIGE formula "whether or not arising under an international convention" or the CMI formula "when arising from an international convention'? I think this is a point worthy of attention.

Philippines As party to various conventions relating to the environment the Philippines welcomes this inclusion of small letter (d) to article 1 of the draft convention. As to the text we support the US proposal as it aligns the small letter (d) to various conventions cited therein including the CLC and the HNS and may I add also the IOPC one. As to further amendments Mr. Chairman we support the deletion of the word "marine" but we urge the retention of the words "coastline or related interests". These words reflect the very important basic language at issue so we wish to retain this particular phrase. As to the changes or to the addition of the last words "caused by the ship" we would support the proposal of the UK for a generic reference to the ship.

Denmark We like to add our voice to all the other voices of the whole orchestra before us and thank the US delegation for taking up this task and we are truly grateful for that. As to the amendments which have been presented we support the Japanese amendment, the first amendment under "marine" and I haven't heard anyone to disagree anyway. As to the second Japanese amendment I think the UK proposal was more in line because it was covered by other conventions and even the Japanese delegation agreed that it was a better proposal. And then of course my Russian friend suggested some interesting words to the text as well. Of course we have not really

10. Text from tape No. 59.

focused on this ourselves but I think the Russian delegation pointed to the fact that there might be some wording in this text which should be expanded further and these are the words "likely to be incurred by third parties". It is so that it has something futuristic about it which was pointed to by my Russian colleague and of course that gave us some thoughts, and we had some doubts about the text anyway. So I think it will be nice before we continue if I through you Mr. Chairman could ask the American delegation whether or not they could explain which situation particularly they are thinking of because surely it will be so that at least when you arrest the ship you would also have some notion of which claim you want to present because it will be difficult to put up a security if you do not have a precise text. I am sorry to put the US delegation on this task but they only I think are repeating the wording of the CMI in this respect and perhaps could give us some clarification because I am sure that it is a point worth discussing.

United States   Yes, initially it was in part simply to reflect the existing JIGE text; however "likely to be incurred by third parties" would also refer to other interests which are damaged whether it be fisheries, shellfish, shoreline, interests in which the full extent of the damage may not be known at the time of the arrest of the ship because the full assessment of the damage to those interests will not be known. And so the security then would be in a context not only of known damages but damages likely to be incurred.

Latvia   This delegation also like to support the US proposal as amended by the Japanese delegation in respect of the deletion of the word "marine". At the same time we consider in the same line of the Russian delegation that the word "environment" covers also coastline, so the words "coastline" should also be deleted if the word "marine" is deleted. As respect to the amendments proposed by the UK delegation we would like to support the insertion of the words "caused by the ship" at the end of this paragraph.

Cyprus   The Cyprus delegation welcomes and supports the proposal submitted by the US with the amendment suggested by the UK about damages caused by the ship. As regard the question of the deletion of the word "marine" we believe that it should be maintained as drafted by the US for the reasons stated by the Greek delegation and other delegations.

Tunisia   My delegation associates itself to the previous delegations in thanking the United States and the delegations who have worked together in order to make this proposal. I have however three comments. The first concerns the proposal itself, that it seems to us to be acceptable and thus we support it with the amendments proposed by the United Kingdom delegation, viz. adding at the end of (d) the words "damages caused by the ship". As regards the amendment proposed by the Japanese delegation, at least in so far as the French text is concerned, when the word "marin" is deleted and the word that remains is "milieu", its meaning significantly decreases. We shall talk about "milieu": which "milieu"? In our opinion if the word "marin" is deleted, in the French text it can be replaced by "environnement" and the word "littoral" can be deleted. The second comment relates to the fact that this proposal in our view only takes into consideration damages caused to the environment. This represents a limitation of the scope of sub-paragraph (d) as compared with the CMI proposal. Also we think useful to take that proposal and widen its scope by adding the word "including" between the word "damages" and the word "marine environment". I read the text: "damage or threat of damage including damage to the marine environment".

Finland   We support the proposal to delete the word "marine" from the environment and just leave "environment" and also to delete "coastline or related interest" because logically the word "environment" takes care of this other interest. May I remind you that both the CLC Convention and the HNS Convention use the word "environment" without any specifications, "environment" is a very very large concept as we know.

Thailand   We also support the US proposal as modified by Japan and UK. We also prefer the deletion of the words "marine coastline and related interest" in order to have the words simply "damage to the environment". Another point, we think the proper place to put the words "caused by" is at the beginning. I think the wording will be much more clear if we use the words "damage or threat of damage to the environment caused by the ship". This amendment can accommodate the suggestion made by the Russian Federation.

Rep. of Korea   My delegation supports the US proposal and the amendment suggested by the distinguished delegation of Russia because I suggest two points: the first point is that the word "marine environment" should be retained and the second point is that in view of the CMI comment the last phrase of the proposal of US, that is "losses incurred or likely to be incurred by third parties in connection with such damage" is not related to this type of damage to the marine environment so I think that that phrase should be deleted. The concept of losses incurred by third parties is not clear.

Ukraine In general we favour the proposal made by the US delegation with the modifications as to deletion in the first line of the words "marine and coastline related interest". At the same time we think that the proposal made by the Russian Federation also makes sense and in our view the last sentence of this paragraph should read as follows: "and losses incurred in connection with such measures" so to delete the words "or likely to be incurred by third parties".

Mexico As Denmark, we should like to obtain a clarification from the United States, in particular in respect of the practical cases of how the threat of damage can give rise to a maritime claim. While it is easy to understand that when damage has occurred a claim has arisen, this is not so when there is a mere threat of damage: how can it give rise to a claim?

United States A whole series of measures may have to be taken in order to prevent damage to the environment that is when a threat has arisen but a pollution or the incident has not yet occurred and this is intended to capture claims that would arise in response to a threat of damage even though the damage itself did not occur. As to the suggestions about deleting the phrase "related interest", that phrase in other contexts has referred to damages suffered by those in the fisheries or those who have property which have been damaged in a pollution incident ashore and at least in the United States that may be viewed as damages which are different from simply environmental damages and so in the view of our delegation the phrase "related interest" has a specific meaning separate from the meaning contained in the word "environment" alone.

Cameroon The delegation of Cameroon congratulates the United States for the improvement made to the drafting of article 1(1)(d) and supports the amendments aiming at replacing the words "milieu marin et littoral" with the word "environnement". It also supports the addition suggested by the United Kingdom.

Malta Malta would like to support the proposal of the United States here in front of us. However we would like to agree with those delegations who have suggested the deletion of the word "marine" and the other word "coastline". We also support the amendments suggested by the delegation of the United Kingdom.

United Kingdom I apologize taking the floor again but an issue has arisen since we spoke early in the debate. And that is the question about a couple of points: "coastline and related interests". I would strongly support those who wish to keep this text. We see "coastline" and "related interests" as being tied together. They could be interests that those of us who are in the IOPC Fund are well aware of: hotel interest, fishing interest and so on and the US touched on that; so coastline and related interests we see as tied together and essential. Coming then down to the bottom of the paragraph as drafted by the US the words "or likely to be incurred by third parties" again we see this tying back to the related interests referred to in the first line and it is crucial in the view of this delegation that we keep these words.

CMI As you would have seen from the comments made by the CMI in the text before the Conference we were puzzled originally by the use of the words "third parties" in the JIGE text. I am still puzzled by the use of the words here and the reference to third parties seems to be inappropriate in this context.

Philippines I am sorry for coming back on this issue again but it seems that, as pointed out by the UK, the issue of "coastline and other related interests" is an important point for this delegation. In our earlier intervention we requested and urged the retention of these words because not only do they represent property interests or fisheries as pointed out by the US, and this is an issue for IOPC Fund, as noted by the UK, but it would involve basic issues and so we would urge that this phrase "coastline or other related interests" be retained.

Netherlands Also my delegation apologizes for intervening on this issue for the second time but like to previous interventions my delegation shares the concern raised that coastline or related interests should be read as one concept which you cannot split.

Turkey Sorry for having asked for the floor again. We also concur with the view of the UK that the coastline and related interests should be maintained in this paragraph for exactly the same reasons they have explained and we feel that the damages or the losses likely to be incurred is closely related first to the damage and to the related interests because changes in the ecosystem due to an accident or a damage caused by a ship is not immediately detectable and here the potential losses that could be incurred due to damage to the ecosystem or the marine environment could give right to potential economic losses particularly for tourism and fisheries, sea transport and property interest and in order to be able to cover such potential economic losses I think we should maintain the last part of the American delegation suggestion.

Spain   As the other distinguished delegations who have taken the floor before me my delegation is of the view that this question of pollution or foreseeable pollution is very important, and it is important to maintain the expression "coastline and related interests". Therefore we join the previous delegations in the request to maintain these words.

Belgium   Merci Monsieur le Président. La délégation Belge pense qu'il faut un peu s'éclaircir les idées. Si on limite dans la première frase le mot "milieu marin" par "environnement" qui est un mot beaucoup plus large, nous n'avons pas de problèmes avec le mots "le littoral". Par contre si on limite au texte original américain le "milieu marin" nous avons des réelles problèmes avec le mots "le littoral" et nous pensons tout simplement aux pays qui ont des rivières très profondes et qui peuvent souffrir dans les rivière—je pense par exemple au Brésil à Manaos—des pollutions importantes mais qui ne sont pas liées au concept de littoral: l'on peut difficilement soutenir que Manaos qui est à 2000/3000 Km à l'intérieur de terre fasse encore partie du mot littoral. Alors pour nous c'est une alternative: ou bien l'on tient le texte général "environnement" au lieu de "milieu marin" mais si l'on retiens "milieu marin" il nous semble que qu'il faut laisser tomber le mot "littoral" parce qu'il est limitatif.

Liberia   Mr. President certainly this delegation welcomes the paper on the table being discussed. We can agree with the deletion of "marine" and the retention of "coastline or other related interests". We have not heard any arguments put forward today that would cause us to believe that the inclusion of the phrase "coastline or other related interests" is something that is not acceptable. The arguments have been all encompassing the word "environment". I think they have been redundant and repetitive, may be necessary to satisfy everyone, and retaining those words in our view should not cause any significant problem to any of the delegations that have spoken so far. We do have some concern as to the inclusion of the words "third parties". When you speak of "losses incurred or likely to be incurred" that in itself is not specific and I think the Courts will interpret that with respect to the proximity of the event. However, to specifically include the words "third parties" in this Convention would *de facto* make the Courts to accept claims that are perhaps far remote from the incident than they would otherwise have been inclined to do, so perhaps we could do without the words "third parties" and "losses incurred or likely to be incurred" could be interpreted within the context of the causation and the proximity of the event.

Chairman   Well, on the basis of this debate I think that the following can be accepted by most in relation to art. 1, § 1, (d): The base is the US proposal as tabled in CRP 16 with the deletion of the word "marine" in the first line. Then we have the problem in relation to "coastline or other related interests". During the first part of the debate the issue of related interests was not focused down and a number of people felt that if we refer to environment as such, it would be unnecessary or illogical to also refer to coastline and then somebody focused down on the related interests and I think that a couple of delegates said that "coastline or related interests" is a concept; but perhaps you also can say that you can refer in principle to the marine environment or related interests but those who spoke after the issue was identified seem to prefer to keep "coastline or related interests" as a concept, so that the reference would be to "the environment, coastline or related interests" and it is my feeling that that would meet with the approval of most in this room. I think that there is also acceptance of the UK proposal to add "caused by the ship" towards the end of this paragraph. Then reference was made to "losses incurred or likely to be incurred by third parties" and a number of delegations have problems with that. I think however that they are in a minority. Most delegations would not seem to have a problem with that expression or with the different concerns in relation to that expression. But I think that the majority does not seem to have a problem with that expression. So it is my feeling therefore (d) can be adopted on the basis of the US proposal with the deletion of the word "marine" in the first line and with the addition of the words "caused by the ship". Is that acceptable?

Thailand   If you put the words "caused by" just at the end of the sentence that would mean that the word "caused by" would be applicable only to "loss incurred or likely to be incurred by third parties in connection with such damage" only in that particular phrase, or are you going to apply the words "caused by . . . " to every item of this sub-section (d).

Chairman I think your proposal was a very good one. It was not addressed by anybody else.
United Kingdom We come to the same conclusion. The words should be placed in the first line after "damage or threat of damage".
Chairman Agreed.

1999 Convention

(d) DAMAGE OR THREAT OF DAMAGE CAUSED BY THE SHIP TO THE ENVIRONMENT, COASTLINE OR RELATED INTERESTS; MEASURES TAKEN TO PREVENT, MINIMIZE, OR REMOVE SUCH DAMAGE; COMPENSATION FOR SUCH DAMAGE; COSTS OF REASONABLE MEASURES OF REINSTATEMENT OF THE ENVIRONMENT ACTUALLY UNDERTAKEN OR TO BE UNDERTAKEN; LOSS INCURRED OR LIKELY TO BE INCURRED BY THIRD PARTIES IN CONNECTION WITH SUCH DAMAGE; AND DAMAGE, COSTS, OR LOSS OF A SIMILAR NATURE TO THOSE IDENTIFIED IN THIS SUBPARAGRAPH (D);

PARAGRAPH 1(e)

Draft of the CMI International Sub-Committee

(e) COSTS OR EXPENSES RELATING TO THE RAISING, REMOVAL OR DESTRUCTION OF THE WRECK OF ANY SHIP;

CMI Draft

(e) COSTS OR EXPENSES RELATING TO THE RAISING, REMOVAL, RECOVERY OR DESTRUCTION OF THE WRECK OF THE SHIP OR HER CARGO;

CMI Report

21. Subparagraph (e) is also new. It covers the cargo whether it is still in the ship or not.

JIGE
Draft Articles 1994

Note of the Editor. The text of the CMI Draft has been reproduced in the Draft Articles 1994 and 1997.

Ninth Session: 2–6 December 1996

Report—Annex II

11. ... Concerning subparagraph (e), this delegation felt that ships in distress should not be arrested due to the inherent risks involved.

Report—Annex III

Comments of the Greek delegation on Article 1, paragraph 1 (e): "In discussing this definition, Greece would like to make clear to everybody that a ship in distress cannot be the subject of arrest due to the tremendous risks involved for the safety of passengers, crew and cargo of the vessel, for the vessel itself and for the environment."

Diplomatic Conference

Proceedings of the Main Committee

First reading—1 March 1999[11]

The delegate from Malta so stated:
I should like to ask a clarification. May I ask whether either (d) or (e) would cover a vessel which has been abandoned by its owners, a vessel which is not serviced by its owners, whether a claim or

11. Text and summary from tapes Nos. 4 and 5.

an arrest can be made under (d) if it is retained or (c) although I don't see it very much. But it is a point which I think is worth considering because ports are sometimes occupied by ships which are not serviced by their owners either because owners have disappeared or they are bankrupt or because the vessels have been abandoned in some way and I think we have to treat this matter. I would be grateful if we could know whether this could be covered under (d).

The suggestion to include in this sub-paragraph a reference to abandoned ships was supported by other delegates.

Second reading—8 March 1999[12]

The suggestion made by the delegation of the Netherlands to replace the text of the JIGE Draft by that of article 2(1)(d) of the 1976 LLMC Convention was supported, but the Maltese delegation stated again that reference should also be made to the situation of ships abandoned by their owners and of the crews on board such ship. This proposal was supported by a great number of delegations and the further addition to the text of article 2(1)(d) of the LLMC Convention of the word "recovery", which appeared in the JIGE Draft was similarly supported.

1999 Convention

(e) COSTS OR EXPENSES RELATING TO THE RAISING, REMOVAL, RECOVERY, DESTRUCTION OR THE RENDERING HARMLESS OF A SHIP WHICH IS SUNK, WRECKED, STRANDED OR ABANDONED, INCLUDING ANYTHING THAT IS OR HAS BEEN ON BOARD SUCH SHIP, AND COSTS OR EXPENSES RELATING TO THE PRESERVATION OF AN ABANDONED SHIP AND MAINTENANCE OF ITS CREW;

PARAGRAPH 1(f)

Draft of the CMI International Sub-Committee

(f) ANY AGREEMENT RELATING TO THE USE OR HIRE OF ANY SHIP (WHETHER BY CHARTERPARTY OR OTHERWISE);

CMI Draft

(f) ANY AGREEMENT RELATING TO THE USE OR HIRE OF THE SHIP, WHETHER CONTAINED IN A CHARTER-PARTY OR OTHERWISE;

Note of the Editor. After the drafting change made at Lisbon this sub-paragraph remained unaltered and was never the subject of any discussion.

Draft Articles 1997

(f) ANY AGREEMENT RELATING TO THE USE OR HIRE OF THE SHIP, WHETHER CONTAINED IN A CHARTER PARTY OR OTHERWISE;

Diplomatic Conference
Proceedings of the Main Committee

First reading—1 March 1999[13]

This sub-paragraph was adopted without discussion.

1999 Convention

(f) ANY AGREEMENT RELATING TO THE USE OR HIRE OF THE SHIP, WHETHER CONTAINED IN A CHARTER PARTY OR OTHERWISE;

12. Summary from tapes Nos. 66 and 67.
13. Summary from tape No. 5.

PARAGRAPH 1(g)

Draft of the CMI International Sub-Committee

(g) ANY AGREEMENT RELATING TO THE CARRIAGE OF GOODS OR PASSENGERS IN ANY SHIP (WHETHER BY CHARTERPARTY OR OTHERWISE);

CMI Draft

(g) ANY AGREEMENT RELATING TO THE CARRIAGE OF GOODS OR PASSENGERS IN THE SHIP, WHETHER CONTAINED IN A CHARTERPARTY OR OTHERWISE;

Note of the Editor. This sub-paragraph was the subject of two drafting changes, the first by the Lisbon Conference and the second by the Diplomatic Conference.

Diplomatic Conference
Comments and Proposals

Hong Kong, China

DOCUMENT 188/3

The words "or passengers in the ship" should be deleted from the text as it may encourage litigations for numerous trivial claims (e.g. for disappointing holidays) which could lead to numerous unjustified arrests.

Proceedings of the Main Committee

First reading—1 March 1999[14]

The delegate from Hong Kong China suggested to delete from this sub-paragraph the word "passenger" since claims in respect of passengers were already covered under (b). The delegate from the United States objected that reference to passengers should be retained since claims under (b) arise in tort, while claims under (g) arise in contract and this comment was widely supported.

Sub-paragraph (g) was thus adopted without any change.

1999 Convention

(g) ANY AGREEMENT RELATING TO THE CARRIAGE OF GOODS OR PASSENGERS ON BOARD THE SHIP, WHETHER CONTAINED IN A CHARTER PARTY OR OTHERWISE;

PARAGRAPH 1(h)

Draft of the CMI International Sub-Committee

(h) LOSS OF OR DAMAGE TO GOODS (INCLUDING BAGGAGE) CARRIED IN ANY SHIP;

CMI Draft

(h) LOSS OF OR DAMAGE TO OR IN CONNECTION WITH GOODS (INCLUDING LUGGAGE) CARRIED IN THE SHIP;

Note of the Editor. After the addition at the Lisbon Conference of the words "or in connection with" this sub-paragraph was left unaltered and was not the subject of any discussion.

14. Summary from tape No. 5.

**Diplomatic Conference
Comments and Proposals**

Hong Kong, China

DOCUMENT 188/3

4. The words "(including luggage)" should be deleted as this could lead to a serious risk of frivolous claims.

Mexico

DOCUMENT 188/3

36. Subparagraph (h) in this paragraph duplicates with subparagraph (a) and should therefore be deleted. The transport of goods and passengers' luggage is covered by the contracts under which ships are used, sometimes known as "ship operation" contracts.

Proceedings of the Main Committee

First reading—1 March 1999[15]

Following a comment of the delegate from Iran the words "carried in the ship" were replaced by the words "carried on board the ship".

1999 Convention

(h) LOSS OF OR DAMAGE TO OR IN CONNECTION WITH GOODS (INCLUDING LUGGAGE) CARRIED ON BOARD THE SHIP;

PARAGRAPH 1(i)

Draft of the CMI International Sub-Committee

(i) GENERAL AVERAGE;

Note of the Editor. No comment or discussion has ever been made in respect of this sub-paragraph during the sessions of the JIGE

**Diplomatic Conference
Proceedings of the Main Committee**

First reading—1 March 1999[16]

This sub-paragraph was adopted without discussion.

1999 Convention

(i) GENERAL AVERAGE;

PARAGRAPH 1(j)

Draft of the CMI International Sub-Committee

(j) TOWAGE;

Note of the Editor. No comment or discussion has ever been made in respect of this sub-paragraph during the session of the JIGE.

15. Summary from tape No. 5.
16. Summary from tape No. 5.

Diplomatic Conference
Proceedings of the Main Committee

First reading—1 March 1999[17]

This sub-paragraph was adopted without discussion.

1999 Convention

(j) TOWAGE;

PARAGRAPH 1(k)

Draft of the CMI International Sub-Committee

(k) PILOTAGE;

Note of the Editor. No comment or discussion has ever been made in respect of this sub-paragraph during the sessions of the JIGE.

Diplomatic Conference
Proceedings of the Main Committee

First reading—1 March 1999[18]

This sub-paragraph was adopted without discussion.

1999 Convention

(k) PILOTAGE;

PARAGRAPH 1(l)

Draft of the CMI International Sub-Committee

(l) GOODS, MATERIALS, PROVISIONS, BUNKERS, EQUIPMENT (INCLUDING CONTAINERS) OR SERVICES SUPPLIED TO ANY SHIP FOR HER OPERATION OR MAINTENANCE;

CMI Draft

(l) GOODS, MATERIALS, PROVISIONS, BUNKERS, EQUIPMENT (INCLUDING CONTAINERS) OR SERVICES SUPPLIED TO THE SHIP FOR HER OPERATION OR MAINTENANCE;

JIGE
Seventh Session, 5 December 1994

Report—Annex I

10. The observer for the Institute of International Container Lessors supported article 1(l) of the CMI Draft, provided it was not taken to mean that containers had to be supplied to a particular ship.

Draft Articles 1997

(l) GOODS, MATERIALS, PROVISIONS, BUNKERS, EQUIPMENT (INCLUDING CONTAINERS) OR SERVICES SUPPLIED TO THE SHIP FOR ITS OPERATION OR MAINTENANCE;

17. Summary from tape No. 5.
18. Summary from tape No. 5.

Note of the Editor. No comment has been made by any delegate on the statement of the observer for the Institute of International Container Lessors.

Diplomatic Conference
Proceedings of the Main Committee

First reading—1 March 1999[19]

    The proposal of the Maltese delegate to add the word "preservation" in view of the possible intervention of the port authority in connection with a ship abandoned by its owners was adopted.

1999 Convention

    (l) GOODS, MATERIALS, PROVISIONS, BUNKERS, EQUIPMENT (INCLUDING CONTAINERS) SUPPLIED OR SERVICES RENDERED TO THE SHIP FOR ITS OPERATION, MANAGEMENT, PRESERVATION OR MAINTENANCE;

PARAGRAPH 1(m)

Draft of the CMI International Sub-Committee

    (m) CONSTRUCTION, REPAIR, CONVERTING OR EQUIPPING OF ANY SHIP;

JIGE
Ninth Session, 2–6 December 1996

Report—Annex III

    (m) BUILDING, REPAIRING, CONVERTING OR EQUIPPING OF THE SHIP;

Report—Annex II

    8. One delegation questioned the changes in subparagraph (m), where the word "construction" was replaced by "building".

Draft Articles 1997

    (m) BUILDING, REPAIRING, CONVERTING OR EQUIPPING OF THE SHIP;

Note of the Editor. The word "construction" had been replaced by "building" because this is the word used in the 1993 MLM Convention (article 7(1)(a)) although the word "reconstruction" is subsequently used. For convenience the relevant part of the note appended to article 1(1) of the Draft Articles 1997 is reproduced below:
The word "construction" in original sub-paragraph (m) has been replaced by "building".

Diplomatic Conference
Comments and Proposals

CMI

DOCUMENT 188/3
    133. In the 1993 MLM Convention reference is made (Article 7, para. 1) to claims of the shiprepairer for repair "including reconstruction" of the vessel. Since converting and reconstructing is not the same thing, it is suggested that it would be appropriate to use both terms.

---

19. Summary from tapes Nos. 5 and 7.

This sub-paragraph could, therefore, be amended as follows:
(m) building, repairing, converting, reconstructing or equipping of the ship;

Proceedings of the Main Committee

First reading—1 March 1999[20]

The observer from the CMI drew the attention of the Committee to the fact that the wording of this sub-paragraph differed from that of article 7(1)(b) of the 1993 MLM Convention since no reference is made in this sub-paragraph to the reconstruction of a ship. It was agreed that the Drafting Committee would take care of that.

1999 Convention

(m) CONSTRUCTION, RECONSTRUCTION, REPAIR, CONVERTING OR EQUIPPING OF THE SHIP;

PARAGRAPH 1(n)

Draft of the CMI International Sub-Committee

(n) PORT AND DOCK CHARGES AND DUES;

CMI Draft

(n) PORT, CANAL AND OTHER WATERWAY DUES AND DOCK CHARGES;

JIGE
Draft Articles 1994

(n) PORT, CANAL, AND OTHER WATERWAY DUES AND PILOTAGE DUES; (1993 MLM CONVENTION, ARTICLE 4 (1) (D))

Ninth Session: 2–6 December 1996

Report—Annex II

10. Another delegation suggested that to refer only to *"port dues and charges"* in subparagraph (n) might be interpreted in a restrictive manner, since it might not include all the charges originating in the port, such as mooring and wharfage charges. It asked for subparagraph (n) to be redrafted to ensure that all port fees and charges were included.

12. Another delegation stressed that the word *"charges"* in subparagraph (n) was satisfactory as drafted and would cover all charges incurred by a ship in a port.

Report—Annex III

(n) PORT, CANAL, AND OTHER WATERWAY DUES <u>AND CHARGES</u> ~~AND PILOTAGE DUES~~;

Draft Articles 1997

(n) PORT, CANAL, AND OTHER WATERWAY DUES AND CHARGES;

Note of the Editor. For convenience the relevant part of the note appended to article 1(1) of the Draft Articles 1997 is reproduced below:
    ... the term "charges" has been used in sub-paragraph (n) in place of "pilotage dues".

20. Summary from tape No. 6.

Diplomatic Conference
Comments and Proposals

Hong Kong, China

DOCUMENT 188/3

5. To include the words "docks and harbours" as many countries have dues for using the docks and harbours.

CMI

DOCUMENT 188/3

133. It is not clear why there is no longer any reference to "dock charges". Dock charges are probably included in (l) under "services", but if there is any doubt about this, it would be advisable to insert the words "including dock charges".

Proceedings of the Main Committee

First reading—1 March 1999[21]

The delegate from Hong Kong China introduced the proposal of his delegation and stated that it was desirable to refer to any possible kind of charge that might need to be covered. The proposal to add the words "dock and harbour" (charges) was supported by other delegations.

The delegate from the Netherlands suggested to reinstate the reference to pilotage since this sub-paragraph reflected article 4(1)(d) of the 1993 MLM Convention. The Chairman pointed out that pilotage was already covered under (k) and that although it had been agreed that the new Convention should be in line with the MLM Convention it was not required to follow every word of it as long as the substance was covered.

1999 Convention

(n) PORT, CANAL, DOCK, HARBOUR AND OTHER WATERWAY DUES AND CHARGES;

PARAGRAPH 1(o)

Draft of the CMI International Sub-Committee

(o) WAGES OR OTHER SUMS RELATING TO THEIR EMPLOYMENT PAYABLE TO OR ON BEHALF OF OR FOR THE BENEFIT OF THE MASTER, OFFICERS, OR CREW;

CMI Draft

(o) WAGES AND OTHER SUMS (INCLUDING SOCIAL INSURANCE CONTRIBUTIONS) PAYABLE TO OR ON BEHALF OR FOR THE BENEFIT OF THE MASTER, OFFICERS OR OTHER MEMBERS OF THE SHIP'S COMPLEMENT IN RESPECT OF THEIR EMPLOYMENT;

Note of the Editor. This was the wording adopted by the Lisbon Conference in the Draft Convention on Maritime Liens and Mortgages.

JIGE
Seventh Session, 5 December 1994

Report—Annex I

6. . . . Bearing in mind article 4, paragraph 1(a) of the MLM Convention, the Group agreed that costs of repatriation should be included in the list of maritime claims in article 1.

---

21. Summary from tape No. 6.

Draft Articles 1994

(O) WAGES AND OTHER SUMS DUE TO THE MASTER, OFFICERS AND OTHER MEMBERS OF THE VESSEL'S COMPLEMENT IN RESPECT OF THEIR EMPLOYMENT ON THE VESSEL, INCLUDING COSTS OF REPATRIATION AND SOCIAL INSURANCE CONTRIBUTIONS PAYABLE ON THEIR BEHALF;

Diplomatic Conference
Comments and Proposals

Hong Kong, China

DOCUMENT 188/3

6. "Social insurance" should be deleted since it is the responsibility of the individual crew member to pay the amount.

CMI

DOCUMENT 188/3

133. There does not seem to be any reason to categorise as a maritime claim only the social insurance contributions payable on behalf of the master, officers and other members of the ship's complement when all claims for insurance premiums in respect of a ship are within the categories of maritime claims. If this remark is accepted the following text may be considered:

> Wages and other sums due to or payable in respect of the Master, officers and other members of the ship's complement in respect of their employment on the ship, including but not restricted to costs of repatriation and social insurance contributions.

Proceedings of the Main Committee

First reading—2 March 1999[22]

The delegate from the CMI introduced the proposal of the CMI and stated:
Mr Chairman, the language of subparagraph (o) is taken from the 1993 MLM Convention. In that Convention it had been decided that the part of social insurance contributions to be secured by a maritime lien was only that part payable on behalf of the crew. It had been decided that generally speaking insurance premiums and also social insurance contributions should not be the subject of a special protection such as that granted by a maritime lien but the CMI is wondering whether in this Convention there is any justification in restricting the maritime claim only to that part of social insurance contribution payable on behalf of the crew when in subparagraph (q) insurance premiums generally are qualified as maritime claims. The suggestion of the CMI is therefore to delete the words "payable on their behalf" in subparagraph (o).

The delegate from Hong Kong China stated that he was not in favour of that proposal and said:
The reason for this is that the one effect of that would presumably be that a vessel could be arrested in respect of a failure by an individual member of the crew to pay a social security contribution, whereas it was our understanding when the draft as currently before us is confined to bringing about the possibility of arrest where the social insurance contributions are payable on their behalf that is principally perhaps by the shipowner.

The majority of the delegates agreed with the comments made by the delegate from Hong Kong China and the text was adopted without change.

1999 Convention

(O) WAGES AND OTHER SUMS DUE TO THE MASTER, OFFICERS AND OTHER MEMBERS OF THE SHIP'S COMPLEMENT IN RESPECT OF THEIR EMPLOYMENT ON THE SHIP, INCLUDING COSTS OF REPATRIATION AND SOCIAL INSURANCE CONTRIBUTIONS PAYABLE ON THEIR BEHALF;

22. Text and summary from tape No. 7.

PARAGRAPH 1(p)

Draft of the CMI International Sub-Committee

(p) DISBURSEMENTS MADE ON BEHALF OF ANY SHIP, HER OWNER, BARE BOAT OR OTHER CHARTERER OR AGENT;

CMI Draft

(p) DISBURSEMENTS MADE IN RESPECT OF THE SHIP, BY OR ON BEHALF OF THE MASTER, OWNER, BAREBOAT OR OTHER CHARTERER OR AGENT;

JIGE
Draft Articles 1994

(p) DISBURSEMENTS MADE IN RESPECT OF THE SHIP, BY OR ON BEHALF OF THE MASTER, OWNER, BAREBOAT OR OTHER CHARTERER OR AGENT;

Ninth Session, 2–6 December 1996

Report—Annex III

(p) MASTER'S DISBURSEMENTS AND DISBURSEMENTS MADE BY SHIPPER, DEMISE CHARTERERS, OTHER CHARTERERS OR AGENTS ON BEHALF OF THE SHIP OR ITS OWNERS;

Report—Annex II

9. Another delegation requested some clarification as to the reasons for including "shippers" in subparagraph (p). It was hard to imagine a concrete situation in which shippers made disbursements on behalf of the ship. The delegation proposed the deletion of the word "shipper" and reversion to the JIGE draft if the change was not intentional.

11. One delegation . . . The word "shipper" in subparagraph (p) was introduced following the 1952 text of the Convention. One delegation pointed out that the specific issue of inserting the word "shipper" had not been discussed in the Working Group.

Draft Articles 1997

(p) MASTER'S DISBURSEMENTS AND DISBURSEMENTS MADE BY SHIPPERS, DEMISE CHARTERERS, OTHER CHARTERERS OR AGENTS ON BEHALF OF THE SHIP OR ITS OWNERS;

Diplomatic Conference
Comments and Proposals

CMI

DOCUMENT 188/3

133. It is suggested that the existing text be deleted and replaced by: "Disbursements made in respect of the ship". It does not in fact seem necessary to indicate by which persons the disbursement are made.

Proceedings of the Main Committee

First reading—2 March 1999[23]

The delegate from the CMI introduced the proposal of the CMI and stated:
The language of (p) seems to be rather cumbersome and old fashioned. Nowadays disbursements are rather seldom incurred by the master personally but are incurred by the agents of the ship whilst

23. Text and summary from tapes Nos. 7 and 8.

it does not seem to happen very frequently that disbursements on behalf of the ship are incurred by shippers. The CMI wonders whether the language of (p) could not be significantly simplified by referring generally to disbursements made in respect of the ship without indicating the persons who may effect such disbursements on behalf of the ship.

The delegate from the United Kingdom stated:

We would support the principle of the text proposed by Prof. Berlingieri, namely that the notion of a ship being personified as a party to litigation is an outdated notion in modern era and therefore disbursements are not made or incurred on behalf of a ship. They are really made on behalf of the owner or the charterer or whoever it is. So we certainly support the idea of disbursements incurred in respect of the ship. This delegation would prefer the word "incur" rather than "make". We think that disbursements are incurred on behalf of somebody.

After a request of clarification of the delegate from Denmark, the Chairman so stated:

I think it is clear to everybody that the wording proposed by the CMI covers the substance of the present (p) but in a more modern language. Your concern is whether by adopting that modern language you include other claims or other persons who may incur disbursements in respect of a ship.

The delegate from the Marshall Islands stated that in his view the principal purpose of the suggested new draft was to avoid any reference to the shipper and that he agreed on such proposal.

The Chairman concluded that further consultations appeared to be necessary, so that this sub-paragraph should be considered at the second reading.

Second reading—8 March 1999[24]

The delegate from Denmark supported the CMI proposal, stating that it was not wider than the text in the Draft Articles, but was clearer. She suggested, however, to replace the words "in respect of the ship" with "on behalf of the ship or its owner" and such proposal was supported by a very large majority.

1999 Convention

(p) DISBURSEMENTS INCURRED ON BEHALF OF THE SHIP OR ITS OWNERS;

PARAGRAPH 1(q)

Draft of the CMI International Sub-Committee

(q) INSURANCE PREMIUMS PAYABLE BY OR ON BEHALF OF THE SHIPOWNER OR BARE BOAT CHARTERER IN RESPECT OF ANY SHIP;

CMI Draft

(q) INSURANCE PREMIUMS (INCLUDING MUTUAL INSURANCE CALLS) IN RESPECT OF THE SHIP, PAYABLE BY OR ON BEHALF OF THE SHIPOWNER OR BAREBOAT CHARTERER;

JIGE
Draft Articles 1994

Note of the Editor. The text of the CMI Draft has been reproduced in the Draft Articles 1994 and 1997.

Seventh Session, 5 December 1994

Report—Annex I

36. The observer for the CMI noted that, as the 1993 MLM Convention used the term "demise charterer", consideration should be given to the use of the same term in place of "bareboat

24. Summary from tape No. 50.

charterer" in sub-paragraphs (q) and (r) of article 1(1), and indeed elsewhere in the draft convention.

Diplomatic Conference
Proceedings of the Main Committee

First reading—2 March 1999[25]

The delegate from Australia sought clarifications on use of the words "payable on behalf of the shipowner or demise charterer" stating that in Australian law the words used are "insurance premiums in respect of the ship" and asked whether there were some categories of premiums that were excluded.

The Chairman asked if anybody wished to answer that question and the delegate from the CMI stated:

Mr. Chairman I would confirm what you just said. The reference to the demise charterers was inserted, if my recollection is right, precisely in order to exclude other charterers such as the time charterers. If this was right or wrong is another matter, but the intention was that one.

The Chairman then stated that (q) was acceptable subject to further consideration by some delegations.

1999 Convention

(q) INSURANCE PREMIUMS (INCLUDING MUTUAL INSURANCE CALLS) IN RESPECT OF THE SHIP, PAYABLE BY OR ON BEHALF OF THE SHIPOWNER OR DEMISE CHARTERER;

PARAGRAPH 1(r)

Draft of the CMI International Sub-Committee

(r) AGENCY FEES OR COMMISSIONS PAYABLE BY OR ON BEHALF OF THE SHIPOWNER OR BARE BOAT CHARTERER IN RESPECT OF ANY SHIP;

CMI Draft

(r) ANY COMMISSIONS, BROKERAGES OR AGENCY FEES PAYABLE IN RESPECT OF THE SHIP BY OR ON BEHALF OF THE SHIPOWNER OR BAREBOAT CHARTERER;

JIGE
Draft Articles 1994

Note of the Editor. The text of the CMI Draft has been reproduced in the Draft Articles 1994 and 1997.

(r) ANY COMMISSIONS, BROKERAGES OR AGENCY FEES PAYABLE IN RESPECT OF THE SHIP BY OR ON BEHALF OF THE SHIPOWNER OR BAREBOAT CHARTERER;

Diplomatic Conference
Proceedings of the Main Committee

First reading—2 March 1999[26]

This sub-paragraph was adopted without discussion.

1999 Convention

(r) ANY COMMISSIONS, BROKERAGES OR AGENCY FEES PAYABLE IN RESPECT OF THE SHIP BY OR ON BEHALF OF THE SHIPOWNER OR DEMISE CHARTERER;

25. Text and summary from tape No. 8.
26. Summary from tape No. 8.

PARAGRAPH 1(s)

Draft of the CMI International Sub-Committee

(s) ANY DISPUTE AS TO THE OWNERSHIP OR POSSESSION OF ANY SHIP;

Note of the Editor. The text of this sub-paragraph has remained unaltered, save for the proposal, which was not adopted, to merge into it the text of sub-paragraph (v).

Diplomatic Conference
Proceedings of the Main Committee

First reading—2 March 1999[27]

This sub-paragraph was adopted without discussion.

1999 Convention

(s) ANY DISPUTE AS TO OWNERSHIP OR POSSESSION OF THE SHIP;

PARAGRAPH 1(t)

Draft of the CMI International Sub-Committee

(t) ANY DISPUTE BETWEEN THE CO-OWNERS OF ANY SHIP AS TO THE EMPLOYMENT OR EARNINGS OF THAT SHIP;

Note of the Editor. No comment or discussion has ever been made in respect of this sub-paragraph.

Diplomatic Conference
Proceedings of the Main Committee

First reading—2 March 1999[28]

This sub-paragraph was adopted without discussion.

1999 Convention

(t) ANY DISPUTE BETWEEN CO-OWNERS OF THE SHIP AS TO THE EMPLOYMENT OR EARNINGS OF THE SHIP;

PARAGRAPH 1(u)

Draft of the CMI International Sub-Committee

(u) THE MORTGAGE OR HYPOTHECATION OF ANY SHIP;

CMI Draft

(u) A MORTGAGE OR A "HYPOTHÈQUE" OR A CHARGE OF THE SAME NATURE ON THE SHIP;

JIGE
Draft Articles 1994

(u) A MORTGAGE OR AN "HYPOTHÈQUE" OR A CHARGE OF THE SAME NATURE ON THE SHIP;

27. Summary from tape No. 8.
28. Summary from tape No. 8.

Seventh Session, 5 December 1994

Report—Annex I

35. One delegation suggested that in sub-paragraph (u) , the term "registrable charges" of the same nature as a mortgage or "hypothèque" should be used so as to conform to the wording used in the MLM Convention. This delegation also proposed avoiding the use of "she" in reference to a vessel in the text of the Convention.

Draft Articles 1997

(u) A REGISTERED MORTGAGE OR A REGISTERED "HYPOTHÈQUE" OR A REGISTRABLE CHARGE OF THE SAME NATURE ON THE SHIP;

Note of the Editor. For convenience the relevant part of the note appended to article 1(1) of the Draft Articles 1997 is reproduced below:
The word "registered" has been added before "mortgage" and "hypothèque".

Diplomatic Conference
Comments and Proposals

Hong Kong, China

DOCUMENT 188/3

7. The words "registrable" should be changed to "registered" as "registrable" is undefined.

CMI

DOCUMENT 188/3

133. For the reasons stated with respect to the Preamble the word "registrable" before "charges" should be deleted and sub-paragraph (u) should read:
a <u>registered</u> mortgage, a <u>registered</u> "hypothèque" or a <u>registered</u> charge of the same nature on the ship.

ICS

DOCUMENT 188/3

118. Registration is a precondition for the recognition and enforcement of mortgages, "hypothèques" and charges under the MLM Convention. In the interest of aligning the Arrest Convention with the MLM Convention, ICS suggests that sub-paragraph (u) should read:
"a registered mortgage, a registered "hypothèque" or a <u>registered</u> charge of the same nature on the ship".

Ukraine

DOCUMENT CRP.11

4. Here and hereafter we propose replacing "registrable charge" by "registered charge".

Proceedings of the Main Committee

First reading—2 March 1999[29]

The delegate from the Marshall Islands proposed to use the word "registered" throughout, as suggested by ICS. The delegate from Canada instead was of the view that the word "registrable" before "charges" should be deleted and that the word "registered" should not be inserted.

The statement made by Canada is reproduced below, together with the statements of the Russian Federation, the CMI and Germany.

Canada In the view of our delegation this paragraph (u) refers to, as it clearly indicates, registered mortgages and registered hypothèques and were put in ostensibly to align the arrest

29. Text and summary from tape Nos. 8 and 9.

convention with the MLM Convention. The purpose of the MLM Convention however is to create an international system of registration of mortgages against ships. The MLM Convention does not in itself address the rights of lender in situations where for example a mortgage or a similar charge may be defective or unregistrable for whatever reason. In such case in our view a lender will continue to be in the need to be able to arrest the ship in order to secure his rights. My delegation therefore is strongly of the view that we should delete the word "registered" as it appears in this particular provision and equally the word "registrable" so that the provision would in fact relate to mortgages whether or not they are registered and similar charges whether or not they are registrable or registered as the object here is just as indicated to protect the rights of lenders and not in any way to refer or have a reference back to the particular status of a registered mortgage under the MLM Convention, viz. to priorities. This is an entirely different story. If this change were accepted of course Mr. Chairman there would be a need for the Drafting Committee to be concerned with the domino effect as of course "registered" and "registrable" and so on appear here and there throughout the Convention beginning of course with the chapeau where remarkably the word "registered" does not appear in front of the word mortgage.

Russian Fed. We support the proposal by the Marshall Islands. As to Canada's proposal concerning the deletion of the word "registered" before the word "mortgage" and "registrable" before the word "charge", we think that their deletion is undesirable, since in the law of many countries, including the law of our country, legal effects are connected with the registered mortgage or registered charge of the same nature.

CMI Mr Chairman, in so far as the word "registrable" is concerned, I may perhaps explain that this word was inserted merely by error because in the MLM 1993 Convention the word "registrable" was used in the chapeau of art. 1 in order to restrict the similarity of charges other than mortgages and hypothèques to such securities. It was deemed it convenient to admit other charges to the same regime of the mortgages and hypothèques provided however they were registrable. It is accepted by everybody that mortgages and hypothèques are registrable and are then registered. So the word "registrable" was included only to try to limit the application of the convention to charges other than mortgages and hypothèques to those charges that under the applicable law were registrable. So the word "registrable" then was transferred in the Lisbon Draft and then in the JIGE draft merely because the language was used in the 1993 Convention but I think that there is no doubt that in this connection, if it is accepted that the right of arrest should be confined to registered mortgages and hypothèques also charges must be registered because it will be rather odd that the requisite of registration is admitted for mortgages and hypothèques and not for other charges. In so far as the requisite of registration is concerned, Mr Chairman, I share the views expressed by ICS and wish to add another argument, that is that the arrest may lead to forced sale. Now in many countries, whether or not the 1993 Convention has been ratified or adopted, there exists a principle that recognition of foreign mortgages and hypothèques is limited to the registered mortgages and hypothèques.

Germany After having heard the very convincing statement of CMI and ICS we strongly support the proposal that we should delete the word "registrable" and replace it with the words "registered charge". We must be aware that the question of mortgages in one country and in another differs very much and if we just decide to except "registrable" whatever this charge will lead to nowhere and cause some legal uncertainty in this field. So once again only registered mortgages, registered hypothèques and registered charge of the same nature should be covered by this text.

The Chairman concluded the debate as follows:

We have to come back to this provision. The majority was in favour of using the word "registered" in particular in order to delete reference to "registrable". But perhaps some of such delegations would accept the Canadian proposal as a compromise.

Second reading—10 March 1999[30]

Canada We achieved a compromise, absent one delegation . . . Next is sub-paragraph (u). A number of delegations had some difficulty with the JIGE text for the use of the word "registered". It was agreed to insert flexibility by deleting such word.

---

30. Text from tape No. 72.

1999 Convention

(u) A MORTGAGE OR A "HYPOTHÈQUE" OR A CHARGE OF THE SAME NATURE ON THE SHIP;

PARAGRAPH 1(v)

Draft of the CMI International Sub-Committee

(v) ANY DISPUTE ARISING OUT OF A CONTRACT FOR THE SALE OF ANY SHIP;

Note of the Editor. Except for the suggestion of the Working Group to merge this sub-paragraph into sub-paragraph (s), no other comment or suggestion has been made in respect of this sub-paragraph, which has been left unaltered.

Diplomatic Conference
Proceedings of the Main Committee

First reading—2 March 1999

This sub-paragraph was adopted without discussion.

1999 Convention

(v) ANY DISPUTE ARISING OUT OF A CONTRACT FOR THE SALE OF THE SHIP.

PROPOSED ADDITIONAL MARITIME CLAIMS
NOT ADOPTED

Diplomatic Conference

Namibia

DOCUMENT CRP.4

It appears that the definition of "maritime claim" as defined therein does not seem to be exhaustive. It is therefore proposed that the following addition be made to the definition:

"(w) damages or loss to or in connection with freight and cargo;
(y) any other matter which by law falls within the jurisdiction of the Admiralty Court or which by virtue of its nature or subject matter is a maritime claim."
"(z) Any claim relating to the pollution of the sea or the seashore by oil or any other similar substance, . . . "

United States

DOCUMENT CRP.16

(w) the ownership, construction, repair, maintenance, preservation, possession, management, operation, or trading of a ship, or arising out of a mortgage or hypothèque or charge on a ship, provided such claim is of a similar nature to the claims described in subparagraphs (a) through (v);

PARAGRAPH 2

Draft of the CMI International Sub-Committee

(2) "ARREST" FOR THE PURPOSE OF THIS CONVENTION MEANS THE DETENTION OF A SHIP BY JUDICIAL PROCESS TO SECURE A MARITIME CLAIM. IT DOES NOT INCLUDE THE SEIZURE OF A SHIP IN EXECUTION OR SATISFACTION OF AN ENFORCEABLE JUDGEMENT OR OF AN ARBITRAL AWARD.

CMI Draft

(2) "ARREST" MEANS ANY DETENTION, OR RESTRICTION ON REMOVAL, OF A SHIP BY ORDER OF A COURT TO SECURE A MARITIME CLAIM WHEN AT THE TIME OF SUCH DETENTION OR RESTRICTION THAT SHIP IS PHYSICALLY WITHIN THE JURISDICTION OF THE STATE WHERE THE ORDER HAS BEEN MADE.

"ARREST" INCLUDES "ATTACHMENT" OR OTHER CONSERVATORY MEASURES, BUT DOES NOT INCLUDE MEASURES TAKEN IN EXECUTION OR SATISFACTION OF AN ENFORCEABLE JUDGEMENT OR ARBITRAL AWARD.

Report of the CMI

23. Article 1 paragraph (2) corresponds to the same paragraph in the 1952 Convention.

24. The 1952 Convention only spoke of detention of a ship. The new draft also mentions restriction on removal. It had been argued that such restriction if not combined with physical detention was not covered by the concept of arrest in the 1952 Convention. Reference was made to the Mareva injunction in English law and similar injunctions in the law of other countries.

25. A majority of the delegations participating in the Conference found that for the purpose of the Convention no distinction should be made between cases where a ship was detained by physical possession and where the ship was simply prevented from sailing by order of a court. It was, however, felt that there might be a need to point out that where an order is not especially directed to a ship but affects the totality of a debtor's assets and only incidentally a ship amongst them, then the Convention shall not apply. (cf. Article 8 paragraph 5).

26. The definition makes it clear that arrest for the purpose of the Convention only comprises cases where the ship is physically within the jurisdiction of the State of arrest. This means that rules of law of a State providing for measures to be taken against a ship flying the flag of the State, regardless where the ship is, by entering an order on the file of the ship in the ship's register of that State, do not come within the concept of arrest in the draft.

27. The definition in its second part makes it clear that it is not important what terminology is used in national law, e.g. the word attachment instead of the word arrest, as long as the measure in question is a conservatory measure as defined in the definition. On the other hand, measures taken in execution of an enforceable judgment or arbitral award are not arrest in the sense of the draft.

28. Where a judgment is not yet enforceable in a country any measure taken to enable its enforcement when it becomes enforceable is a conservatory measure and, therefore, covered by the draft.

29. In some countries an arrest not only prevents the physical removal of the ship but also results in a prohibition against disposal of the ship by sale or otherwise. The Conference did not find it reasonable to include such a requirement in the definition of arrest.

JIGE
Draft Articles 1994

(2) "ARREST" MEANS ANY DETENTION, OR RESTRICTION ON REMOVAL, OF A SHIP BY ORDER OF A COURT TO SECURE A MARITIME CLAIM WHEN AT THE TIME OF SUCH DETENTION OR RESTRICTION THAT SHIP IS PHYSICALLY WITHIN THE JURISDICTION OF THE STATE WHERE THE ORDER HAS BEEN MADE.

"ARREST" INCLUDES "ATTACHMENT" OR OTHER CONSERVATORY MEASURES, BUT DOES NOT INCLUDE MEASURES TAKEN IN EXECUTION OR SATISFACTION OF AN ENFORCEABLE JUDGEMENT OR ARBITRAL AWARD.

Eighth Session, 9–10 October 1995

Report—Annex I

21. Several comments and proposals were made in connection with the definition of arrest. It was noted that the definition in the basic text substantially differed from the one contained in the 1952 Convention in that the latter did not include the requirement that the ship is physically within the jurisdiction of the State where the order of arrest has been made. In this regard, it was explained that the purpose of the inclusion of this requirement was to distinguish physical arrest from the so-called

documentary arrest, which refers to the registration of arrest in the ships' registry. Some delegations were of the opinion that this restriction should be considered in connection with the recognition of judicial orders; other delegations suggested that this provision should be placed in article 8; otherwise the requirement of the physical presence of the ship in the definition of arrest would affect the implementation of several articles of the Convention. These delegations favoured the inclusion of the definition of the 1952 Convention instead of the one in the basic text.

22. One delegation suggested that if the definition in the 1952 Convention were to attract the preference of the Sessional Group, the second part contained in the present text should be retained. This delegation proposed that new language should be added securing that arrest can be ordered in cases where there is a real risk for the alleged claim not to be satisfied.

23. Other delegations were of the view that the physical presence of the ship in the jurisdiction of the State where the arrest order has been made should be considered as an enforcement requirement inherent in the concept of arrest. Accordingly, it should be included within the definition.

24. It was suggested that the expression "where the order has been made" could be replaced by "where the arrest is effected". In this way, if the ship was not physically under the jurisdiction of a Court issuing an arrest order, it would nevertheless be clear that the arrest would be enforced only under the authority of the Court in the jurisdiction where the ship is physically present.

25. One delegation suggested that the term "judgement" be preferred to that of "order", so as to make clear that the defendant would have the benefit of appearing in Court to contest the request for arrest. This view was opposed by several delegations on the grounds that circumstances of arrest frequently do not permit the delay caused by the procedures leading to a judgement. It was stated that judicial guarantees were implied by the fact that the order should be issued by a Court. Some delegations favoured the use of the expression "judicial process" as used in the 1952 Convention.

26. In response to comments by several delegations it was noted that the preventative character of arrest, as opposed to the seizure for the execution of a judgement, was clearly reflected in the definition of arrest. It was also noted that any reference to this preventative character specifically attached to the expression of "arrest" in languages other than English was a question of terminology only to be considered in connection with the texts in those languages.

27. The Group decided to revert to the definition of arrest contained in article 1, paragraph 2 of the 1952 Convention.

Ninth Session: 2–6 December 1996

Comments and proposals by Japan

2. Add the following phrase at the end of paragraph 2: "or other documents which are enforceable under the law of the State where such measures have been taken".

3. So, para 2, amended by the above addition, will read as follows:
   "Arrest" means the detention of a ship by judicial process to secure maritime claim, but does not include the seizure of a ship in execution or satisfaction of a judgement or other documents which are enforceable under the law of the State where such measures have been taken.

3. Reason for the above amendment: We believe that this Convention aims at restriction of the detention of a ship as provisional measure prior to obtaining enforceable judgement. Its article 4, which regulates release from arrest by sufficient security, and the article 7, which sets forth a tribunal to determine the merits of the case, can be understood only in that context. Therefore, the seizure of a ship based on the documents which are enforceable in the same way as judgements under the law of the State should be excluded from the definition of "Arrest". In Japan, such documents include:

— conciliation protocol;
— officially authenticated instruments which are agreements of the parties, written before a judge or a notary public;
— copy of register that certifies the right of hypothecation, and so forth.

Comments and proposals by the United Kingdom

7. Following the discussion on this provision at the eighth session of the JIGE, it was concluded that the definition of "arrest" in the JIGE text should be identical to that in the 1952 Convention (document JIGE(VIII)/7, Annex I, paragraph 27).

8. The United Kingdom delegation entirely agrees that the JIGE definition should be modelled more closely on that of the 1952 Convention and, in particular, that the phrase "when at the time of such detention or restriction the ship is physically within the jurisdiction of the State where the order has been made" in the first sentence of the JIGE text should be deleted. There is no equivalent of this phrase in the 1952 Convention. Its inclusion would add unnecessary ambiguity to the definition. Article 2(1) of the JIGE text contains rules on which courts are able to order the arrest of a ship. Article 7 contains rules on which courts have jurisdiction to consider the case upon its merits.

9. Discussions are under-way in the United Kingdom on whether it would be desirable for the Mareva injunction to be covered by the definition of "*arrest*".

Report—Annex II

16. The Group noted that, at its last session, it had decided to revert to the definition of arrest contained in Article 1, paragraph 2, of the 1952 Convention. Most delegations supported in principle the proposal made by Japan (document JIGE(IX)/3, paras. 2 and 3) to specifically exclude in arrest procedures consideration of any document which could be enforced in a way similar to a judgement. In the opinion of several of these delegations, the expression "other documents" contained in this proposal was too imprecise, and adequate wording would have to be found. The Group also considered the proposal by the United Kingdom (JIGE(IX)3, paras. 7–9) that the definition of "arrest" should be modelled more closely on that of the 1952 Convention and, in particular, the words "when at the time of such detention or restriction the ship is physically within the jurisdiction of the State where the order has been made" in the first sentence should be deleted.

17. It was suggested that, if the definition included in Article 1 (2) of the 1952 Convention with the inclusion of the proposal made by Japan was going to be retained, the second part of this definition, as contained in Article 1, paragraph 2, which had been prepared by the JIGE, could be retained.

18. A suggestion that the definition of arrest should include not only reference to physical measures but also the regulation of legal effects was not supported on the grounds that legal effects would be very difficult to enforce worldwide on account of the operation of national law.

19. Following consultations with several delegations, the Chairman made a proposal for a new text for this paragraph contained in document TD/B/IGE.1/CRP.3. Bearing in mind several amendments made in connection with this proposal, the Group adopted the following text:

"Arrest" means any detention or restriction on removal of a ship as a conservatory measure by order of a Court to secure a maritime claim, but does not include the seizure of a ship in execution or satisfaction of a judgement, arbitral award or other enforceable instrument.

20. Views were expressed on the possible inclusion of reference to the physical presence of the ship within the jurisdiction of the State where the arrest was made. This issue was settled, however, in Article 8 (1).

21. The Group noted that, in view of its paramount importance, this definition might require further consideration.

22. A discussion was also held on whether reference should be made to the legal constraints which might be the result of an arrest, such as a ban on mortgaging or selling the ship under arrest. The Group did not agree to the inclusion of any text in this regard, since it was felt that the effects of an arrest ought not to be regulated in any definition of the Convention but left to national law.

Draft Articles 1997

(2) "ARREST" MEANS ANY DETENTION, OR RESTRICTION ON REMOVAL OF A SHIP AS A CONSERVATORY MEASURE BY ORDER OF A COURT TO SECURE A MARITIME CLAIM, BUT DOES NOT INCLUDE THE SEIZURE

OF A SHIP IN EXECUTION OR SATISFACTION OF A JUDGEMENT, ARBITRAL AWARD OR OTHER ENFORCEABLE INSTRUMENT.

Diplomatic Conference
Comments and Proposals

CMI

DOCUMENT 188/3

134. Whilst in the English text the words "removal of a ship" are used, in the French text the words used are "depart d'un navire". The word "depart" seems preferable and, if this is agreed, "removal" could be replaced by "departure".

Ukraine

DOCUMENT CRP.11

5. Ukraine favours the wording of paragraph 2 given in the draft Convention itself:

> "Arrest means any detention or restriction on removal of a ship as a conservatory measure by order of a Court to secure a maritime claim, but does not include the seizure of a ship in execution or satisfaction of a judgment, arbitral award or other enforceable instrument."

Proceedings of the Main Committee

First reading—2 March 1999[31]

The delegate from Mexico stated that the reference to arbitration award was inappropriate since arbitration awards as such are not enforceable and, when made enforceable, are in any event covered by the reference in the definition to other enforceable instrument. The suggestion to delete the reference to arbitration award was supported by other delegations.

The delegate from Hong Kong expressed some concern about the meaning of the words "as a conservatory measure". This view was supported by other delegations of common law countries while the delegates of civil law countries stated that the words "as a conservatory measure" were useful since they distinguished the arrest regulated by the Convention from the seizure in satisfaction of a judgment. It was however pointed out that the qualification of the nature and purpose of the arrest were already made clear by the words "to secure a maritime claim".

The delegate from the Russian Federation so stated:

The definition of arrest given in paragraph 2 is, in our opinion, rather precise. The deletion of the second part of this definition may break its precision. The definition of arrest given in paragraph 2 is based on the definition of arrest in the 1952 Convention. The long-term practice of operation of the 1952 Convention does not give the grounds to doubt the appropriateness of this definition. To a certain extent we share the doubt expressed by the delegate from Hong Kong concerning expediency of retaining the characteristic of the arrest "as a conservatory measure" in the definition. In case these words are deleted, the definition itself will not suffer. However, their retention will make the definition more precise. Therefore we are inclined to support in general the definition of the arrest in paragraph 2.

The delegate from Thailand asked clarifications about the meaning of the words "other enforceable instrument". He wondered what types of instruments would be covered by that expression.

The observer from the CMI stated that in certain jurisdictions promissory notes and notarial deeds embodying an acknowledgment of debt are enforceable as a judgment and that the intention was to cover such types of instruments.

---

31. Summary from tape No. 10.

1999 Convention

2. "Arrest" means any detention or restriction on removal of a ship by order of a Court to secure a maritime claim, but does not include the seizure of a ship in execution or satisfaction of a judgment or other enforceable instrument.

PARAGRAPH 3

Draft of the CMI International Sub-Committee

(3) "Person" include individuals, partnerships, unincorporated associations and bodies corporate, governments, their departments and public authorities.

Note of the Editor. The text of this sub-paragraph has been adopted by the Lisbon Conference and has been reproduced in the Draft Articles 1994.

Report of the CMI

30. Article 1 paragraphs (3) and (4) correspond to the same paragraphs in the 1952 Convention. Some drafting changes have been made.

JIGE
Eighth Session, 9–10 October 1995

Report—Annex I

28. In response to a question from one delegation, it was indicated that the expression "unincorporated associations" intended to cover cases of companies which, although not incorporated, were considered legal entities in accordance with the national law in some countries.

Ninth Session, 2–6 December 1996

Comments and proposals by the United Kingdom

10. There is a clear definition of "person" in Article 1(2) of the 1969 Civil Liability Convention. The 1992 Protocol did not change the definition. The same definition has now also been adopted in Article 1(2) of the 1996 HNS Convention. The United Kingdom delegation therefore proposes that the JIGE should not adopt a revised wording for the sake of it but should adopt this tried and tested definition:

"Person" means any individual or partnership or any public or private body, whether corporate or not, including a State or any of its constituent subdivisions.

11. The United Kingdom delegation submits that the intended meaning of the definition contained in Article 1(3) of the JIGE text is the same as that of the CLC precedent. However, while the meaning of the JIGE text has been queried, that of the text used in CLC is well understood.

Report—Annex II

23. The Group accepted the proposal made by the United Kingdom in document JIGE(IX)/3, paragraphs 10 and 11, to replace the definition of "*person*", by the one contained in the 1969 Civil Liability Convention and the 1996 Hazardous and Noxious Substances (HNS) Convention.

Draft Articles 1997

(3) "Person" means any individual or partnership or any public or private body, whether corporate or not, including a State or any of its constituent subdivisions.

Diplomatic Conference
Proceedings of the Main Committee

First reading—2 March 1999[32]

This paragraph was adopted without discussion.

1999 Convention

3. "Person" means any individual or partnership or any public or private body, whether corporate or not, including a State or any of its constituent subdivisions.

PARAGRAPH 4

Draft of the CMI International Sub-Committee

(4) "Claimant" means any person making a maritime claim.

CMI Draft

(4) "Claimant" means any person asserting a maritime claim.

Report of the CMI

30. Article 1 paragraphs (3) and (4) correspond to the same paragraphs in the 1952 Convention. Some drafting changes have been made.

Note of the Editor. The text of this sub-paragraph has remained unaltered.

JIGE
Ninth Session, 2–6 December 1996

Report—Annex II

24. One delegation was of the opinion that arrest should be permitted only if there was a risk that the alleged claim might not be satisfied. This was not accepted by the Sessional Group. It was pointed out in that context that definitions should not be unnecessarily burdened with substantive requirements, which should be dealt with in other articles of the Convention.

Diplomatic Conference
Proceedings of the Main Committee

First reading—2 March 1999[33]

This paragraph was adopted without discussion.

1999 Convention

4. "Claimant" means any person asserting a maritime claim.

PARAGRAPH 5

Draft of the CMI International Sub-Committee

(5) "Court" means any Court or other appropriate judicial authority of a State.

32. Summary from tape No. 10.
33. Summary from tape No. 10.

432

CMI Draft

(5) "COURT" MEANS ANY COMPETENT JUDICIAL AUTHORITY OF A STATE.

Report of the CMI

31. Paragraph (5) is new but has only drafting significance.

Note of the Editor. The text of the CMI Draft has not been changed.

JIGE
Eighth Session, 9–10 October 1995

Report—Annex I

29. It was noted that the main purpose of the introduction of the definition of "Court" was to indicate that arrest could only be ordered by a competent judicial authority.

30. The Group decided to revert to the consideration of this article at a later stage of its discussions.

Ninth Session, 2–6 December 1996

Report—Annex II

25. No comments were made in respect of this paragraph. The Sessional Group accepted the text of this subparagraph as presently drafted.

26. Some delegations suggested that the text in Spanish of this Article be rephrased so as to reflect the meaning of this provision in a positive rather than a negative way, as in the English text.

Diplomatic Conference, Proceedings of the Main Committee

First reading—2 March 1999[34]

This paragraph was adopted without discussion.

1999 Convention

5. "COURT" MEANS ANY COMPETENT JUDICIAL AUTHORITY OF A STATE.

DEFINITIONS NOT INSERTED

"Ship"

CMI Report

32. It has not been found necessary to include a definition of ship in the Convention. It is left to the law of the forum to determine what is understood by that term.

Diplomatic Conference
Comments and Proposals

United Nations Economic Commission for Europe (ECE)

DOCUMENT 188/3

180. In 1965 ECE Governments adopted a Convention on the Registration of Inland Navigation Vessels, with two protocols annexed to it: Protocol No. 1 concerning Rights in rem in Inland

34. Summary from tape No. 10.

Navigation Vessels; and protocol No. 2 concerning Attachment and Forced Sale of Inland Naviga-tion Vessels (E/ECE/579-E/ECE-TRANS/540, copy attached). These Protocols, which are currently in force, deal with the same questions as the Convention on Maritime Liens and Mortgages of 1993 and the new draft Convention on Arrest of Ships, although exclusively with regard to inland navigation vessels.

181. We understand that the future UN/IMO instrument is expected to be applied to sea ships. Article 2(2) of the draft says, for example, that " ... a ship may only be arrested in respect of maritime claim but in respect of no other claim".

182. In this respect, I believe the use of the term "inland navigation vessel" in the UN/ECE Protocol No. 2 and the term "ship" in the draft Convention on Arrest of Ships may lead to confusion, especially as far as so-called vessels of mixed sea-river navigation are concerned.

183. I therefore suggest that, in order to avoid any possible overlapping between the two instruments, the text of the draft Convention be adapted so that it is clear which of the two regimes is applicable in each particular case. I think this could be of help to Governments in implementing the future instrument.

Proceedings of the Main Committee

First reading—2 March 1999[35]

The Chairman stated that the observer from ICS had suggested to include a definition of ship but that since no delegation had made a proposal in that respect, the suggestion could not be con-sidered.

35. Summary from tape No. 11.

II.III.5 ARTICLE 2: POWERS OF ARREST

PARAGRAPH 1

Draft of the CMI International Sub-Committee

(1) A SHIP MAY BE ARRESTED OR RELEASED FROM ARREST ONLY BY OR UNDER THE AUTHORITY OF A COURT OF THE STATE IN WHICH THE ARREST IS MADE OR APPLIED FOR.

CMI Draft

(1) A SHIP MAY BE ARRESTED OR RELEASED FROM ARREST ONLY BY OR UNDER THE AUTHORITY OF A COURT OF THE STATE IN WHICH THE ARREST IS DEMANDED OR HAS BEEN EFFECTED.

CMI Report

33. Paragraph (1) corresponds to Article 4 of the 1952 Convention.

JIGE
Draft Articles 1994

Note of the Editor. The text is the same as that of the CMI Draft.

Eighth Session, 9–10 October 1995

Report—Annex I

31. It was noted that the expression "by or under" the authority of a Court had been introduced to cover arrest effected by Court Officers as well as by other authorities in charge of executing a Court order of arrest. The opinion was also expressed that an arrested vessel should be released following an agreement of the parties involved to that effect.

32. Some delegations were in favour of the formulation contained in article 4 of the 1952 Convention, which avoided the expression "is demanded" contained in this paragraph. It was noted that this expression reappeared in article 2 paragraph 5 but was omitted in article 6, paragraph 2 and article 7, paragraphs 1, 2, and 3 of the basic draft. It was suggested that this expression might have been used to refer to situations where an application for arrest was made but not granted because security was deposited before the arrest took place.

Ninth Session, 2–6 December 1996

Comments and proposals by the United Kingdom

12. The United Kingdom delegation believes that the reference in Article 2(1) of the JIGE text, to the State in which the arrest is *demanded* is unnecessary and misleading. The provision should, as in Article 4 of the 1952 Convention, refer only to the State in which the arrest is made:

> A ship may be arrested or released from arrest only by or under the authority of a Court of the State in which the arrest is *made*.

Report—Annex II

27. There was wide support for the proposal made by the United Kingdom in document JIGE(IX)/3, paragraph 12, to delete reference to arrest "demanded" and replace the expression "effected" by "made". Some delegations also proposed the inclusion of the reference to "Contracting State" as in Article 4 of the 1952 Convention. A proposal to include a reference to the fact that the vessel should be within the jurisdiction of a contracting State did not find support on the grounds that several delegations considered this circumstance to be self-evident.

28. The Group discussed whether a decision by a court was necessary in all cases to release a ship from arrest. Some delegations were of the opinion that agreement between the claimant and the defendant duly communicated to port authorities could be accepted as providing sufficient title for a release without the intervention of the court which had authorized the arrest. Such a procedure could be helpful in cases where the parties had reached an agreement during public holidays when courts were not operating.

29. Most delegations opposed this view. In their opinion the intervention of a court for the release of a ship was required on grounds of the need for legal certainty and on a basis for the protection of eventual interests of third parties. Reference was also made to cases where court authorities were in fact available at all times during public holidays in order to ensure prompt release of a vessel.

30. The Sessional Group accepted the proposal made by the United Kingdom concerning the inclusion of the reference to "Contracting State", as in Article 4 of the 1952 Convention.

Draft Articles 1997

(1) A SHIP MAY BE ARRESTED OR RELEASED FROM ARREST ONLY BY OR UNDER THE AUTHORITY OF A COURT OF THE CONTRACTING STATE IN WHICH THE ARREST IS MADE.

Diplomatic Conference
Proceedings of the Main Committee

First reading—2 March 1999[36]

The delegate from Spain suggested to replace the words "Contracting State" with "State Party". It was agreed that that was a drafting point.

1999 Convention

1. A SHIP MAY BE ARRESTED OR RELEASED FROM ARREST ONLY UNDER THE AUTHORITY OF A COURT OF THE STATE PARTY IN WHICH THE ARREST IS EFFECTED.

PARAGRAPH 2

Draft of the CMI International Sub-Committee[37]

(3) A SHIP MAY BE ARRESTED AS PROVIDED IN THIS CONVENTION IN RESPECT OF A MARITIME CLAIM BUT IN RESPECT OF NO OTHER CLAIM.

CMI Draft

(2) A SHIP MAY BE ARRESTED IN RESPECT OF A MARITIME CLAIM BUT IN RESPECT OF NO OTHER CLAIM.

---

36. Summary from tape No. 12.

37. In the draft of CMI International Sub-Committee this paragraph was numbered (3) because it was preceded by the following paragraph, which was deleted by the Lisbon Conference:

(2) A ship may only be arrested when at the time of arrest is within the territorial jurisdiction of the State in which arrest is applied for.

CMI Report

34. Paragraph (2) corresponds to the first sentence of Article 2 of the 1952 Convention. It contains the principal rule of the draft, viz. that a ship may be arrested in respect of a maritime claim but in respect of no other claim. The provision permits arrest for maritime claims; it does not impose an obligation to arrest whenever a maritime claim is asserted. Whether arrest is made when a maritime claim is asserted depends upon the *forum arresti*. It should be noted that even where a maritime claim is asserted arrest may only be made of ships fulfilling the conditions in article 3.

JIGE
Draft Articles 1994

Note of the Editor. The text is the same as that of the CMI Draft.

Eighth Session, 9–10 October 1995

Report—Annex I

33. A proposal was made to include the expression "only" after the word "may" (as in article 4 of the 1952 Convention). It was also suggested that the expression "but in respect of no other claim" could be deleted. The latter proposal was objected to by several delegations. In this connection, reference was made to the English version of article 2 of the 1952 Convention that contained the same words.

Ninth Session, 2–6 December 1996

Report—Annex II

31. The Sessional Group decided to insert the word "only" after "A ship may", so that the paragraph would read "A ship may only be arrested in respect of . . . ".

Draft Articles 1997

(2) A SHIP MAY ONLY BE ARRESTED IN RESPECT OF A MARITIME CLAIM BUT IN RESPECT OF NO OTHER CLAIM.

Diplomatic Conference
Proceedings of the Main Committee

First reading—2 March 1999[38]

The delegate from Greece requested that provision should be made in this paragraph in respect of the conditions in which arrest of a ship should be permissible, and made reference to the situation where the risk of satisfaction of the claim does not exist.

The delegate from the Russian Federation so stated:

As regards the proposal by Greece, we object to the way the question is put in connection with paragraph 2. Paragraph 2 is aimed at providing that the arrest of a ship is possible only under a maritime claim, and pursues no other aim. The delegation of Greece proposes to connect paragraph 2 with the procedural issue and introduce unified procedural norms into the international convention. We presume that the procedural issues are normally a prerogative of national law, and international unification must not affect them. This issue may be considered in the light of paragraph 5, in respect of which we shall state our position at a later stage. We see neither necessity, nor expediency to connect the procedural issue raised by the delegation of Greece, with paragraph 2 that clearly and precisely fulfils its purpose in the wording included in the draft Convention.

The Chairman indicated that this problem should be discussed under paragraph 5, whereupon paragraph 2 was approved without any change.

38. Summary from tape No. 12.

1999 Convention

2. A SHIP MAY ONLY BE ARRESTED IN RESPECT OF A MARITIME CLAIM BUT IN RESPECT OF NO OTHER CLAIM.

PARAGRAPH 3[39]

Draft of the CMI International Sub-Committee

(4) A SHIP MAY BE ARRESTED EVEN THOUGH IT IS READY TO SAIL.

CMI Draft

(3) A SHIP MAY BE ARRESTED EVEN THOUGH SHE IS READY TO SAIL OR IS SAILING.

CMI Report

35. A provision corresponding to paragraph (3) may be found in Article 3 paragraph (1) of the 1952 Convention. It has been found useful to retain it in respect of the law of some countries where the opposite rule applies.

JIGE
Draft Articles 1994

Note of the Editor. The text is the same as that of the CMI Draft.

Eighth Session, 9–10 October 1995

Submission by the International Chamber of Shipping

With respect to Article 2(3): "A ship may be arrested even though it is ready to sail or is sailing", ICS is of the view that it might be dangerous and impractical to arrest a ship which "is sailing". We therefore propose the deletion of this phrase.

Report—Annex I

34. The Observer delegation of ICS introduced its submission that it might be impractical or dangerous to arrest a ship which "is sailing" and accordingly this expression should be deleted.

35. This proposal was supported by some delegations. The majority of delegations, however, were against this proposal on grounds that their national legislation as well as International Law, specifically the United Nations Convention on the Law of the Sea, enabled States to arrest a ship in connection with civil law cases as long as the ship was in their territorial jurisdiction, including the right of hot pursuit, and a valid order for the arrest could be produced.

36. One delegation cautioned against mixing private law issues such as arrest with situations clearly under the scope of public law. In this regard it was stated that the limits to the power of a Court to arrest ships were clearly established in paragraph 2 and related to the nature of the claims rather than the situation of the ship. The view was also expressed that claimants should not be encouraged to apply for an arrest at the last moment, thus creating extreme difficulties and unnecessary expense.

37. A number of comments were made regarding the proper meaning of the expression "is sailing". It could be seen as offering a rather wide scope of application in that it could cover situations as different as that of a ship already unmoored and ready to sail or taken in tow inside the harbour or a ship already sailing.

---

39. This paragraph, which was placed in square brackets by the JIGE at its ninth session, was deleted by the Diplomatic Conference.

Ninth Session, 2–6 December 1996

Report—Annex II

32. The Sessional Group considered the proposal of the Observer for the International Chamber of Shipping (ICS) to delete the words "or is sailing" from this paragraph.

33. Some delegations suggested that the arrest of a ship already sailing would be difficult to implement and could also pose safety problems. In response, other delegations mentioned cases where the return of a ship already sailing could be secured, especially in the case of ships which were still within large port areas.

34. A discussion was held on the implications, if any, of this paragraph, bearing in mind provisions of the 1982 United Nations Convention on the Law of the Sea (the LOS Convention). In this regard, reference was made to Article 28, paragraph 3, of this Convention, which recognized the right of the coastal State, in accordance with its law, to arrest, for the purpose of any civil proceedings, a foreign ship lying in the territorial sea or passing through the territorial sea after leaving internal waters.

35. In this context a reference was made to the right of hot pursuit by the coastal State. It was noted that Article 111 of the LOS Convention allowed the exercise of this right when the coastal State had good reason to believe that a foreign ship had violated the laws and regulations of that State. It was submitted that this matter of public law did not relate to the scope of implementation of a prospective arrest convention.

36. Bearing in mind the reasons for the inclusion of the possibility to arrest a ship even if it was already sailing, consideration was given to the effect of the possible suppression of the words "or is sailing" from the draft. In the opinion of some delegations, the coastal State would in any case retain the possibility of arresting a ship which was leaving or had left port as long as it was within its jurisdiction. It was suggested that clear terms be included in the convention indicating that arrest could be effected only in respect of ships within the jurisdiction of the coastal State. While some delegations preferred to keep the text of Article 2 (3) as presently drafted, other delegations favoured either deleting or placing the paragraph in brackets.

37. In the view of other delegations, deletion could be interpreted as imposing a limitation on the power of the State to arrest a foreign ship. Such a restriction could in fact result in the impossibility of making arrests in many cases where the claim had not been properly substantiated due to lack of time but was nevertheless legitimate. Reference was also made to the difference between the physical intervention and the legal effects of an arrest, which in many cases was the source of confusion regarding the extent to which a State could enforce jurisdiction in this regard.

38. The Group decided that the text of this paragraph should be placed within brackets.

Draft Articles 1997

[(3) A SHIP MAY BE ARRESTED EVEN THOUGH IT IS READY TO SAIL OR IS SAILING.]

Diplomatic Conference
Comments and Proposals

Hong Kong, China

DOCUMENT 188/3

9. The square bracket may be removed but the words "or is sailing" should be deleted as it may endanger the safety of the ship and persons on board and persons involved in the arrest of a ship.

Italy

DOCUMENT 188/3/ADD.3

3. This is an addition to the provision of the 1952 Convention, and causes confusion mainly on practical grounds, since arresting a ship that is already sailing would appear to be difficult to accomplish.

Japan

DOCUMENT 188/3

26. This paragraph should not contradict the 1982 United Nations Convention on the Law of the sea. Therefore, this paragraph can be admitted on condition that it does not affect the rules of other international conventions relating to arrest of a ship in the course of navigation.

Republic of Korea

DOCUMENT 188/3

57. Paragraph 3 of this article stipulates that a ship may be arrested even though it is ready to sail or is sailing. However, it is the view of the Republic of Korea that arrest of a ship which is ready to sail or is sailing is not desirable because it may destabilize normal practice of commerce by affecting customers not involved in the claim. Therefore, this paragraph should be deleted.

Netherlands

DOCUMENT 188/3

54. This provision is between square bracket and now reads:

[(3) A ship may be arrested even though it is ready to sail or is sailing.]

In particular the insertion of the last three words: "or is sailing" is of concern for the Netherlands. One might recall that during the preparation by the Joint Group this subject was considered to a certain extent. In particular reference was given to the corresponding article 3, paragraph 1, of the 1952 Convention and it was suggested to retain the original text.

55. Apart from the difficulties that might arise from implementing the arrest of a ship already sailing and the safety implications that it might have, it is also very questionable whether such an arrest is the most efficient form of safeguarding maritime claims with a private interest. Therefore the Netherlands would like to support, at least, the deletion of the words "or is sailing" from the paragraph.

Slovakia

DOCUMENT 188/3

62. In Article 2, paragraph 3 the wording " . . . or is sailing" is to be deemed additional although is placed in the brackets. Because the Convention does not consider arresting of ships in the course of navigation, leaving apart the possibility to do it under the national law in accordance with Article 6 of the Convention, we would support the notion not to include this wording in text of Article 2.

Sudan

DOCUMENT 188/3

70. When a ship is "ready to sail or is sailing": we believe that this is unfair towards the owners of the goods, particularly if the goods are perishable, such as fruit and vegetables, or form the subject of contracts or in the case of ships transporting livestock or passengers. In our view, security should be an alternative to arrest.

Thailand

DOCUMENT 188/3

83. The terms "or is sailing" in paragraph 3 should be deleted. The matter may be left to be decided by the law of the court where arrest is made.

Aldenave

DOCUMENT 188/3/ADD.3

Article 2.3: No ship which at the time of its arrest is loaded and has permission to sail from the maritime authority may be arrested.

15. The arrest of a ship "ready to put to sea" must be rejected, it being an incontrovertible principle that navigation must always be facilitated, especially when the ship is "ready to sail" or has permission to do so from the Maritime Authority. The stipulation that the ship must be loaded has been added to prevent it from sailing empty solely in order to evade arrest. Argentine law (art. 541), the Italian Code (art. 645), the Netherlands (Code of Civil Procedure, art. 582), and the Swedish (art. 345), Finnish (art. 278) and German (art. 482) Codes rule out arrest of a ship that is "ready to sail". Before then the ship may be ordered arrested as a conservatory measure, but the prohibition on sailing may not be enforced.

CMI

DOCUMENT 188/3

136. In view of the comments made during the sessions of the JIGE it is suggested that this paragraph be deleted and that the question whether a ship ready to sail or which is sailing may be arrested, should be left to the *lex fori* to decide.

ICS

DOCUMENT 188/3

119. Arrest of ships while sailing may be dangerous from a safety perspective. Thus ICS cannot support departure from the text of Article 3(1) of the 1952 Convention and accordingly we are of the view that the phrase "or is sailing" should be deleted. Deletion of the phrase would not affect any rights under international public law conventions or national law.

Proceedings of the Main Committee

First reading—2 March 1999[40]

Three different proposals were made: the first was to keep the text as drafted; the second to delete the words "or is sailing"; the third to delete the entire paragraph. The speeches of the delegates and observers that are reproduced below give a clear picture of the reasons behind the various proposals.

ICS   Arrest of ships when sailing may give rise to difficulties. Such right may be exercisable only when the ship is in territorial waters and requires claimant to know exactly when ship is sailing in or leaving territorial sea and the Court has to decide in order not to miss the time frame when the ship is passing within the territorial waters. Then the Court has to notify the captain and instruct him when to go. If arrest is formalised during navigation somebody on behalf of the Court should attend on board. All this would be very expensive. In practice the words "or is sailing" would be of very little practical importance.

Russian Fed.   Many participants remember that paragraph 3 was much discussed at the JIGE sessions. The rule providing for the arrest of a ship also in the case when it is sailing found its adherents and opponents. There were arguments both for and against. Taking into account an endless discussion concerning the conformity of this provision to the principles of international public law, it would be expedient, in our view, at least, to return to the text of the 1952 Convention, deleting the words "or is sailing" in paragraph 3 and putting a full stop after the words "it is ready to sail".

United Kingdom   We had already a very long debate on this before. The 1952 Convention was deficient in this respect because it did not touch on the question "or is sailing". This delegation prefer the text as drafted. There is a more radical option open to us and it was proposed in the CMI paper, to take out all the text and let the Convention remain silent. Notwithstanding what has been said before about the purpose of this particular Convention we think it is important that we do reflect on what UNCLOS said. States may sometimes be involved in arrest of ship. We touched this matter this morning as well. But I think that the Japanese colleague refers to art. 28(3) of UNCLOS which confirms the right of coastal States to arrest ships in territorial sea in certain circumstances. Therefore we believe that there is no need for the purpose of the arrest convention to necessarily

40. Text and summary from tapes Nos. 12–15.

address this issue. So we could support what the CMI has proposed deletion in entirety but on two conditions: first that the Conference must add no new words to the convention to restrict coastal State right to arrest ships which are sailing and secondly I suggest that the record of decisions should make clear that in deleting this provision the Conference did not intend to restrict coastal States right.

After having explained the purpose of article 28 of UNCLOS the delegate from the UN Legal Office stated:

In our opinion there should be a clear understanding that if the words "or is sailing" are retained this is to be in line with art. 28 of the Law of the Sea Convention. Of course if this paragraph is removed the problem is removed and there will be clear understanding that the limits are set by the Law of the Sea Convention. The other option would be to take over the language of the 1982 Convention.

CMI   For the reason stated by the distinguished delegate from the United Kingdom the CMI would strongly recommend to entirely delete this paragraph. This is in line also with the comments which have just been made by the Legal Officer. The original wording which was adopted in the 1952 Convention related back to the time of sailing ships and the wording in French of the 1952 Convention makes that very clear. The wording is "alors même que le navire saisi est prêt a faire voile". This is an expression which goes back to the last century and the reason for the addition of this provision in the 1952 Convention was that in certain jurisdictions, and I think at that time still in France—the position I understand now is changed—a vessel ready to sail could not be arrested. This was and still is the position in Italy. Therefore it was deemed convenient to make this provision in order to make clear that a vessel "prêt a faire voile" or ready to sail could be arrested. It seems to the CMI that nowadays this has become obsolete and therefore the reason for this provision does not exist any more. Therefore it is by far better to delete entirely the provision and leave the matter to be dealt with by national law.

United States   United States supports the position of the UK and associates itself to the remarks of the UN representative and of CMI. An implication that a coastal State does not have the right to arrest a ship that is sailing from port would be in direct conflict with customary international law as reflected in the Law of the Sea Convention. The Law of the Sea Convention recognizes certain coastal States rights including under art. 28(3) "the right of the coastal State in accordance with its laws, to levy execution against or to arrest, for the purpose of any civil proceedings, a foreign ship lying in the territorial sea, or passing through the territorial sea after leaving internal waters". Reference to arrest for any civil proceedings is an indication that the coastal State right extends to matters of private law contrary to assertions that have been made previously. Also under art. 1 of this draft convention it is made clear that this convention applies to any seagoing ship within the jurisdiction of a State party so although an arrest can be made for a ship that is sailing, it is within context that it will be limited to being within the jurisdiction of the State party. As to the issue of safety we recognize that even where the words of *lex fori* provide for such procedures in relation to arrest when the ship is sailing the arresting authority may in good faith decline to carry out an arrest where the sea conditions prohibit the arrest from being carried out safely. We initially preferred that the language be retained and the brackets removed; however we also think that a reasonable alternative would be to delete the section in its entirety, again subject to the provision that no words would be placed in this Convention to restrict rights granted to coastal States under the Law of the Sea Convention, and that any report in Plenary or otherwise indicates that this Convention is not intended to detract in any way from rights guaranteed under the Law of the Sea Convention

Canada   This delegation believes that the Arrest Convention should provide every reasonable possibility for a claimant to assert his maritime claim by means of arrest, of course within the confines and the restrictions of existing international law. We know from experience that often the last clear chance a claimant will have to exercise his right is to arrest the vessel that has indeed left port and is sailing and this is, again from experience, known to be quite feasible with the assistance of pilotage and other means. All of which of course was discussed very extensively in the JIGE and there is no need to repeat here to-day. We also heard that very much the law of the sea is both a sword and a shield in this respect in so far as it clearly provides in unequivocal language the right to arrest a vessel that has sailed but of course places restrictions that this must be done within the territory of the State and we repeat that in our very own article 8 paragraph 1. So we sense that the language that we have in the text in subparagraph 3 of article 2 is completely legal and is also from the point of view of the claimants of good assistance in securing maritime claims and our clear preference is to keep the language and delete the brackets. Now we heard many interventions here on this subject and we detect that a number of delegations, very substantial indeed, have a problem with this approach. We have also heard the UK put up a proposition that it might be feasible to delete the entire paragraph and we would like to go on record as supporting that approach as a fall back to retain the language.

Second reading—8 March 1999[41]

The Chairman Although the provision is short, it created a lot of debate in the first reading. I reviewed my own notes and I have seen that as the debate developed there were in fact a number of delegations which felt that perhaps the whole paragraph could be deleted. That was perhaps the best solution, which would mean that it would be left to national law to decide the extent to which vessels can be arrested when they are ready to sail or indeed when they are sailing within the territorial waters of a State, subject always to the obligations that may follow from the UNCLOS or other Conventions. The CMI said that perhaps we could delete the whole provision and leave to national law to decide these issues. The United Kingdom agreed; Turkey agreed but perhaps something would have to be said in the Plenary to record why it was deleted or rather record that it was felt that when it was deleted that means that it was left to national law to regulate these issues. Belgium concurred; Thailand, Singapore, Australia, Norway could live with the deletion; Pakistan could live with the deletion; Argentina, Sri Lanka, Indonesia and a couple of others. So it would seem to me that unless there has been a group working which has been able to create consensus on a solution on the drafting of this paragraph (c); unless there has been such a group and such a result, it would be the best thing to delete this paragraph; On the understanding that it would then be left to national law to regulate this issue. Any objection? If there is no objection I assume that paragraph (3) can be deleted.

PARAGRAPH 3[42]

Draft of the CMI International Sub-Committee

(4) A SHIP MAY BE ARRESTED IN ACCORDANCE WITH THIS CONVENTION FOR THE PURPOSE OF OBTAINING SECURITY NOTWITHSTANDING THAT BY VIRTUE OF A JURISDICTION CLAUSE, ARBITRATION CLAUSE OR CHOICE OF LAW CLAUSE IN ANY RELEVANT CONTRACT THE MARITIME CLAIM IN RESPECT OF WHICH THE ARREST IS MADE IS TO BE ADJUDICATED UPON IN A COURT IN A STATE OTHER THAN THE STATE WHERE THE ARREST IS MADE OR IN ARBITRATION OR IS TO BE ADJUDICATED UPON SUBJECT TO THE LAW OF ANOTHER STATE.

CMI Draft

(4) A SHIP MAY BE ARRESTED FOR THE PURPOSE OF OBTAINING SECURITY NOTWITHSTANDING THAT BY VIRTUE OF A JURISDICTION CLAUSE, ARBITRATION CLAUSE OR CHOICE OF LAW CLAUSE IN ANY RELEVANT CONTRACT THE MARITIME CLAIM IN RESPECT OF WHICH THE ARREST IS EFFECTED IS TO BE ADJUDICATED IN A STATE OTHER THAN THE STATE WHERE THE ARREST IS EFFECTED, OR IS TO BE ARBITRATED, OR IS TO BE ADJUDICATED SUBJECT TO THE LAW OF ANOTHER STATE.

---

41. Summary from tape No. 52.
42. This paragraph, originally numbered (5) in the Draft of the CMI International Sub-Committee and then (4), was renumbered (3) after the deletion by the Diplomatic Conference of paragraph (3) dealing with arrest of ships ready to sail.

Report of the CMI

37. Paragraph (5) corresponds to Article 6 paragraph 2 of the 1952 Convention.

JIGE
Draft Articles 1994

Note of the Editor. The text is the same as that of the CMI Draft.

Eighth Session, 9–10 October 1995

Report—Annex I

38 Although the Group found that this provision was in principle acceptable, proposals were made to clarify the meaning of the expression "for the purpose of obtaining security" or to delete those words, since that expression was already used in article 1, paragraph 2.

Comments and proposals by the United Kingdom

13. The United Kingdom delegation agrees that it is helpful to clarify that a ship may be arrested for the purpose of obtaining security under the authority of a court other than that with jurisdiction to examine the case on its merits. As currently drafted, however, Article 2(4) of the JIGE text suggests that an arrest in such circumstances is only possible in two specific cases: namely, where there is a jurisdiction clause or arbitration clause in any relevant contract.

14. There are other circumstances which could result in the merits of the case being considered by a court or arbitrator in a State other than that in which the arrest was made. For example, the Brussels Convention on Jurisdiction and the Enforcement of Judgements may prevent the court under the authority of which the ship has been arrested from assuming jurisdiction over the merits (*The Tatry*); the application of the doctrine of *forum non conveniens* or rules on *lis alibi pendens* may also prevent the court under the authority of which the ship has been arrested from exercising jurisdiction over the merits. It is therefore necessary to amend Article 2(4) so as to separate more clearly the ability of a court: (a) to hear a claim on the merits, and (b) to award provisional security by way of arrest.

15. The UK delegation proposes that clarification be added to Article 2(4) of the JIGE text by amending the provision as follows:

> A ship may be arrested for the purpose of obtaining security notwithstanding that, by virtue of a jurisdiction clause or arbitration clause in any relevant contract, *or otherwise*, the maritime claim in respect of which the arrest is *made* is to be adjudicated in a State other than the State where the arrest is made, or is to be arbitrated, or is to be adjudicated subject to the law of another State.

Ninth Session, 2–6 December 1996

Report—Annex II

38. Although the Group found that this provision was in principle acceptable, proposals were made to clarify the meaning of the expression "for the purpose of obtaining security" or to delete those words, since that expression was already used in article 1, paragraph 2.

Draft Articles 1997

(4) A SHIP MAY BE ARRESTED FOR THE PURPOSE OF OBTAINING SECURITY NOTWITHSTANDING THAT, BY VIRTUE OF A JURISDICTION CLAUSE OR ARBITRATION CLAUSE IN ANY RELEVANT CONTRACT, OR OTHER-WISE, THE MARITIME CLAIM IN RESPECT OF WHICH THE ARREST IS MADE IS TO BE ADJUDICATED IN A STATE OTHER THAN THE STATE WHERE THE ARREST IS MADE, OR IS TO BE ARBITRATED, OR IS TO BE ADJUDICATED SUBJECT TO THE LAW OF ANOTHER STATE.

Diplomatic Conference
Comments and Proposals

Sweden

DOCUMENT CRP.10

In article 2(4), add a new paragraph with the following wording:

"Notwithstanding this provision, the arrest of a ship shall be permissible only if, pursuant to article 7(5), a judgement or an arbitral award in respect of that claim can be enforced against that ship by judicial or forced sale of that ship in the State where the arrest is made or applied for."

Proceedings of the Main Committee

First reading—2 March 1999[43]

This paragraph was adopted after the Swedish proposal in document CRP.10 had been rejected.

1999 Convention

3. A SHIP MAY BE ARRESTED FOR THE PURPOSE OF OBTAINING SECURITY NOTWITHSTANDING THAT, BY VIRTUE OF A JURISDICTION CLAUSE OR ARBITRATION CLAUSE IN ANY RELEVANT CONTRACT, OR OTHERWISE, THE MARITIME CLAIM IN RESPECT OF WHICH THE ARREST IS EFFECTED IS TO BE ADJUDICATED IN A STATE OTHER THAN THE STATE WHERE THE ARREST IS EFFECTED, OR IS TO BE ARBITRATED, OR IS TO BE ADJUDICATED SUBJECT TO THE LAW OF ANOTHER STATE.

PARAGRAPH 4[44]

Draft of the CMI International Sub-Committee

(6) SUBJECT TO THE PROVISIONS OF THIS CONVENTION, THE PROCEDURE RELATING TO THE ARREST OF A SHIP OR ITS RELEASE SHALL BE GOVERNED BY THE LAW OF THE STATE IN WHICH THE ARREST IS MADE OR APPLIED FOR.

CMI Draft

(5) SUBJECT TO THE PROVISIONS OF THIS CONVENTION, THE PROCEDURE RELATING TO THE ARREST OF A SHIP OR HER RELEASE SHALL BE GOVERNED BY THE LAW OF THE STATE IN WHICH THE ARREST IS DEMANDED OR HAS BEEN EFFECTED.

JIGE
Seventh Session, 5 December 1994

Report—Annex I

12. In the context of article 2(5) of the CMI Draft, one delegation favoured the complete standardization of procedures relating to arrest. This delegation proposed inclusion in the Arrest Convention of a provision for the interlocutory sale of an arrested vessel in appropriate circumstances, such as failure of the owner to post security within a reasonable period of time, or where the costs of maintaining the vessel under arrest were excessive etc. This proposal was opposed by another delegation which felt that the issue was outside the scope of the Arrest Convention, since the term "arrest", being confined to "conservatory" measures, did not include measures for

---

43. Summary from tape No. 15.
44. This paragraph, originally numbered (6) in the Draft of the CMI International Sub-Committee and then (5) was renumbered (4) after the deletion by the Diplomatic Conference of paragraph (3) of the Draft Articles 1997.

satisfaction of judgement. The matter, therefore, was governed by the applicable law, and could not be covered under the Arrest convention.

Draft Articles 1994

Note of the Editor. The text is the same as that of the CMI Draft.

Eighth Session, 9–10 October 1995

Report—Annex I

39. One delegation suggested that although procedures leading to arrest should be regulated by national law, it was important that a new convention established an obligation for the claimant to notify the shipowner of the nature and amount of the claim. This proposal was not supported.

40. The observer delegation of IAPH referred to the observations made in its submission. The delegation stated that since the effective arrest of a ship could only take place in a port, the implications for ports of the arrest should be clearly addressed. Port authorities could be unable to exploit for months the space of berth in which the arrested ship is moored. They were also compelled to take measures to ensure safety and the protection of the marine environment. In order to ensure that port interests were adequately protected, a new paragraph under article 2 could be included, which would stipulate that port authorities should be involved in the proceedings leading to arrest. The new provision could also provide that the claimant would have to deposit a financial guarantee to cover for port costs.

41. Several delegations expressed their support to the need of protecting legitimate interests of ports vis-à-vis the enforcement of arrest procedures. In this regard, it was suggested that the interests of port authorities be safeguarded, particularly when the period between the arrest and judgement phases is long. It was also proposed that suitable provisions be included in article 2(5) on the procedures to be effected during the period of arrest.

42. However, most delegations stated their opposition to the proposed new paragraph. In their view reasons of expediency in the pursuance of maritime claims made unpractical the involvement of port authorities in arrest procedures. The deposit of a guarantee with the port authorities to cover for costs incurred by port authorities would mean a financial burden for the claimant in addition to any eventual advance payment required in some jurisdictions as a precondition for the enforcement of the arrest.

43. The Group decided to revert to the consideration of this article at a later stage of its discussions.

Comments and proposals by the United Kingdom

16. As in Article 2(1) (see paragraph 12), the United Kingdom delegation believes that the reference to the State in which the arrest is *demanded* is unnecessary and misleading. The provision should instead, as in Article 6 of the 1952 Convention, refer to the State in which the arrest is made:

> Subject to the provisions of this convention, the procedure relating to the arrest of a ship or its release shall be governed by the law of the State in which the arrest is *made*.

Proposal by France

The French delegation wishes to take account of the interests of ports in which arrests take place, as the immobilization of a ship, especially if prolonged, can be injurious to a port. Port authorities are often forced to spend substantial amounts on having the arrested ship moved so as to be able to continue making full use of their facilities and accommodate other vessels. They are also compelled to stand in for defaulting arrested persons and defray the costs of ensuring the security and maintaining the arrested ship.

The French delegation believes that an amendment is needed whereby Contracting States would undertake to pass legislation limiting the costs incurred by port authorities in the event of an arrest.

This amendment would involve adding a new subparagraph to paragraph 5, to read:
"Contracting States undertake to include in their domestic legislation rules, applicable to the arrest of ships, in accordance with the provisions of this Convention, limiting the financial implications of such arrest for ports."

Ninth Session, 2–6 December 1996

Report—Annex II

40. The Sessional Group discussed the proposal submitted by the United Kingdom (JIGE(IX)/3, para. 16) to refer only to the law of the State in which the arrest was made, thus deleting reference to the law of the State where the arrest was demanded.

41. Some delegations noted that, while a similar proposal had been adopted by the Group in paragraph 1, a distinction should be made in relation to paragraph 5, which covered a different situation. Reference to an application for arrest was in this case important, since it was related to the procedural aspects of the *lex fori*, and cases where arrest was applied for and not granted must also be borne in mind.

42. The Group considered that the language used in the 1952 Convention should be preferred. Accordingly, the Group agreed to replace the words "is demanded or has been effected" by "was made or applied for".

43. One delegation proposed including in the text of this paragraph a requirement according to which, before an arrest was made, notice of the claim should be given to the shipowner or the master of the ship concerned. The proposal contained the proviso that this notice should not be a condition to enable arrest. The delegation explained that this should be considered as the sole procedural requirement to be included in the Convention. It would then be left to national law to decide who should comply with it and whether sanctions for non-compliance should be applied, as well as what the consequences would be of such non-compliance. The inclusion of this proposal in the arrest convention was regarded as preventing the remedy of arrest being used to blackmail shipowners into payment of claims.

44. Most delegations opposed this proposal on the grounds that procedural matters should be considered entirely within the scope of national law. It was also noted that, since the proposal was not a precondition upon which the granting of arrest would depend, it would not achieve its main purpose, namely avoiding a situation where a ship was prevented from sailing by the authorities of the State in which arrest was applied for.

45. The Group was unable to adopt the proposal.

46. The Sessional Group considered a proposal made by France (contained in document TD/B/IGE.1/CRP.2) that Contracting States undertake to include in their domestic legislation rules limiting the financial implications for ports of the arrest of ship. This proposal was in line with several interventions of the International Association of Ports and Harbours (IAPH) on the need to address the implications of arrest of ships for ports.

47. There was general acknowledgment that there was a need to regulate the question of financial implications for ports arising from arrest of ships. While some delegations indicated their readiness to support this proposal, other delegations conditioned their support on the amendment of the proposal to the effect that the enactment of legislation by contracting States would be optional rather than compulsory. One delegation suggested that, as an alternative, a requirement could be introduced in Article 6 that the claimant offer financial security to cover port expenses.

48. Most delegations, however, were of the opinion that, notwithstanding the need for appropriate national legislation, the opportunity and circumstances for the accomplishment of this task should be left entirely to the decision of States. Accordingly, no provision in this regard should be included in a prospective arrest convention.

49. The Group was unable to adopt the proposal made by France.

Draft Articles 1997

(5) SUBJECT TO THE PROVISIONS OF THIS CONVENTION, THE PROCEDURE RELATING TO THE ARREST OF A SHIP OR ITS RELEASE SHALL BE GOVERNED BY THE LAW OF THE STATE IN WHICH THE ARREST WAS MADE OR APPLIED FOR.

**Diplomatic Conference
Comments and Proposals**

CMI

DOCUMENT 188/3

135. It is not clear from the present wording of this Article whether it has been intended that a mere assertion of a claim should be sufficient in order to obtain an order of arrest. Nor is it clear whether the claimant must prove that he needs security, for example because the financial conditions of the debtor are such as to create uncertainty in respect of the future enforcement of a judgment. The provisions of the 1952 Convention have been differently interpreted in different jurisdictions in these respects. It is suggested that all these matters should be left to the *lex fori* and that, in order to make that clear, reference should be made to the circumstances in which the arrest may be obtained. Paragraph 5 could be re-worded as follows:

> Subject to the provisions of this Convention, *the law of the State in which the arrest of a ship or its release is applied for shall determine the circumstances in which arrest or release from arrest may be obtained and the procedure relating thereto.*

Ukraine

DOCUMENT CRP.11

7. Here we propose deleting "or applied for" to avoid a conflict in legal provisions.

Proceedings of the Main Committee

First reading—2 March 1999[45]

Introducing the CMI proposal the observer from the CMI stated:

Mr Chairman, I do not think it is a drafting point this one. The basis of the suggestion which has been made by the CMI is that the CMI has found that the interpretation of the 1952 Convention in respect of the conditions under which an arrest may be granted varies from State to State. There are Contracting States of the 1952 Convention in which in order to grant an arrest the Court will look into the situation of the debtor generally speaking and consider whether there are sufficient reasons to grant an arrest even if the nature of the claim is that of a maritime claim. In other countries the fact that a maritime claim exists is sufficient in order to entitle the claimant to obtain an arrest. In view of this difference, which exists in different countries at present and which is not solved by the 1952 Convention, the CMI thought that it would be advisable to leave the matter to national law because it is impossible, I believe, although the CMI of course will be delighted to reach as wide a uniformity as possible, because this is the object of the CMI, however if it is impossible to reach uniformity on these matters it is by far preferable to make it clear that certain matters are left to national law. This is the basis of the suggestion which has been made by the CMI when in the redraft of this provision it is stated that the law of the State in which the arrest is made shall determine the circumstances in which the arrest may be granted. This is not only a matter of procedure but refers also to the basic conditions according to which an arrest may be granted. For example the general law in my country, Italy, is that a claimant cannot arrest properties of his debtor if there is no reasonable danger that in the future he will lose the possibility of enforcing his claim. If the debtor, for example, owns very many ships and is very well off, why grant an arrest? An Italian judge would probably refuse the arrest in these circumstances. This I understand is the case in other countries and I may ask for example the distinguished delegate from Denmark to state what the position is in his country, because I understand that it is rather similar. I wonder also what is the position in Germany. Therefore, instead of leaving this matter in the air as it is left by the 1952 Convention it is felt, also considering certain comments made this morning, that it is by far preferable to make clear that the conditions under which arrest should be granted or may be granted should be left to the *lex fori*.

The speeches of the delegates reproduced below and the conclusions of the Chairman provide some useful information on the reasons why the proposal was not adopted.

---

45. Text and summary from tapes Nos. 15 and 16.

Chairman I think that the situation in Italy is similar to the situation in many countries I believe Denmark, I believe Germany and certainly Norway and the other Nordic countries and this of course touches upon the question that the delegate of Greece raised before the coffee break. He wanted to have the requirement for an arrest that the claim should be at risk as he put it, whereas the CMI proposal is to leave that to national law which as Prof. Berlingieri indicated has led to the requirement being introduced in national law in many countries although it is not a requirement of the Convention. So what do you think? Do you think that the CMI proposal is a good proposal that we should adopt or do you like the JIGE text or do you prefer any other alternative?

Denmark We support CMI text. It is very difficult to add something more to the words of Prof. Berlingieri.

Marshall Isl. We also can support the position of the CMI.

United Kingdom This delegation too can support the proposal of the CMI for the reasons given by Prof. Berlingieri. The UK supports the CMI proposal.

Hong Kong The position of my delegation is that we find the present draft text to be clear and to be correct. In our view it is correct to confine this paragraph to questions of procedure. When we look at the proposal by the CMI we are concerned that it is introducing into this paragraph something which goes way beyond the questions of procedure and seems to be dealing with the prerequisites that may be prescribed nationally before an arrest can be carried out and these could be substantive prerequisites and it seems to us to open up a possibility of great disparity in the substantive prerequisites of what should be an exceptional measure of carrying out an arrest. In particular looking at the rationale in the written comments for this proposed change to the draft text we note that it is intended that one effect of the redraft is that a mere assertion of a claim should be sufficient to obtain an order of arrest. It strikes this delegation as rather worrying and a matter of concern if there is the possibility of no requirement whatsoever of any evidence even preliminary evidence in support of the claim before the ship can be arrested and that the mere assertion of a claim should lead to the arrest of the vessel. So my delegation Mr. Chairman prefers the draft text as tabled.

Chairman The text which you prefer is I believe the text of the 1952 Convention which has given rise to the uncertainties referred to by the CMI.

Japan We basically support the proposal made by Prof. Berlingieri on behalf of the CMI, subject to drafting.

United States The United States prefers the text in the current draft. We are concerned about particularly the words in the CMI proposal relating to the circumstances in which arrest may be obtained. By granting the Courts of the States the power to determine "circumstances in which arrest may be obtained" ambiguity and uncertainty are created as to whether the claimant may arrest even for one of the mentioned claims described in article 1(1). Having accepted those claims as forming a basis for the right of arrest undefined circumstances should not be invoked to prohibit the arrest. This matter should not be left to be decided on a case by case basis and therefore in an unpredictable manner by individual judges. Therefore we are in favour of retain the present text.

Russian Fed. Our delegation shares the attitude of Hong Kong and the United States. We believe that paragraph 5 does not need any amendments. It is enough that it refers to the law of the State, in which the arrest of a ship is effected, for the establishment of the procedure for the arrest of a ship or its release from arrest. The proposal of the CMI to determine the circumstances, under which the arrest of a ship may be effected or a ship may be released from arrest, by the law of the State in which the arrest is effected, is fraught with the possibility of a conflict with the basic provisions of the Convention, that is why we categorically object to amending paragraph 5 in such a way. We think that paragraph 5 corresponds to its purpose.

Norway We can support the text proposed by the CMI. In our national law we have some requirements in addition to the requirements of the Convention. In order to obtain an arrest the claimant must make probable that he has a claim and that the claim must be at risk and also the Courts require securities from the claimants. We understand this to be in line with paragraph 5 as it stands but we believe that the CMI suggestion further clarifies these matters, so it has a high level of precision. We prefer the CMI text even if we believe the same issue is covered by the present text.

Greece We can suggest to add wording we have suggested in art. 2 and leave text of this paragraph unaltered.

Chairman I am not certain whether there is support for that in the room here. I think that quite many delegations have spoken in favour of the JIGE text as it stands and that text came before us without any square brackets and had been agreed in the JIGE. Some or quite a few delegations supported the CMI proposal as being a clarification as it was put by the delegate from Norway but I don't think that the ones supporting the CMI proposal would feel that there is a conflict between the CMI wording and the wording of the JIGE text, the text before us. They would only support the CMI because they think it could be even better than the 1952 wording. So I do feel that the majority would support the JIGE text as we have it before us but I am not certain that there is support for your proposal[46] that the Convention should actually regulate and decide in which circumstances an arrest can be made. You referred to paragraph 2 of article 2 where the requirement is that the claim should be a maritime claim and that there can be an arrest in respect of no other claim but you want to qualify that the claim should be at risk. I see your point that quite a number of countries have in their national legislation provisions to that effect but the question is whether there is support here for introducing such requirement in the Convention. That is not my feeling but I leave to the delegates to decide whether they want such a requirement, such a qualification. And if there is no support for the Greek proposal, and I stick to my conclusion that I feel that there is no such support, that the delegates really want to keep both paragraph 2 and paragraph 5 as they stand before us. If I see no objections I conclude on that basis. So we adopt paragraph 5 as it stands in the text before us.

1999 Convention

4. Subject to the provisions of this Convention, the procedure relating to the arrest of a ship or its release shall be governed by the law of the State in which the arrest was effected or applied for.

---

46. The Chairman referred to a proposal of the Greek delegation.

II.III.6 ARTICLE 3: EXERCISE OF THE RIGHT OF ARREST

PARAGRAPH 1

Draft of the CMI International Sub-Committee

(1) ARREST MAY BE MADE OF ANY SHIP IN RESPECT OF WHICH A MARITIME CLAIM HAS ARISEN IF:

    (A)   (I)   THE PERSON WHO OWNED THE SHIP AT THE TIME WHEN THE MARITIME CLAIM AROSE IS PERSONALLY LIABLE FOR THE CLAIM, AND

           (II)   THE PERSON STILL OWNS THE SHIP AT THE TIME WHEN ARREST PROCEEDINGS ARE COMMENCED, OR

[ALTERNATIVE TEXT FOR ART. 3(1)(A):

    (A)   THE PERSON WHO OWNED THE SHIP AT THE TIME WHEN THE MARITIME CLAIM AROSE IS STILL THE OWNER OF THE SHIP AT THE TIME WHEN ARREST PROCEEDINGS ARE COMMENCED, OR]

    (B)   THE CLAIM GIVES RISE TO A MARITIME LIEN AGAINST THE SHIP ACCORDING TO [THE LISBON CONVENTION 1985 ON MARITIME LIENS AND MORTGAGES], OR

    (C)   THE CLAIM IS BASED UPON A [REGISTERED] MORTGAGE OR HYPOTHECATION OF THE SHIP, OR

    (D)   THE CLAIM RELATES TO THE OWNERSHIP OR POSSESSION OF THE SHIP, OR

    (E)   THE CLAIM IS AGAINST A PERSON WHO

           (I)   WAS BARE BOAT CHARTERER OF THE SHIP AT THE TIME WHEN THE CLAIM AROSE, AND

           (II)   STILL IS BARE BOAT CHARTERER OF THE SHIP AT THE TIME WHEN ARREST PROCEEDINGS ARE COMMENCED.

Report of the Chairman of the CMI International Sub-Committee

Art. 3 corresponds to para 1, 2 and 4 of the 1952 Convention.

According to the 1952 Convention it seems that arrest may always be made of the ship in respect of which the maritime claim arose, regardless whether the owner is liable for the claim for which arrest is made, and regardless whether the ownership has changed since the claim arose.

The significance of the rule as contained in the 1952 Convention is uncertain. Is it merely a rule permitting arrest in these cases or are national courts bound to arrest a ship even where the owner is not personally liable? Must the ship be arrested even if the claim cannot be enforced against the ship by its forced sale because the law of the forum does not permit enforcement of claims against one person by action against the property of another person? Or does the right of arrest under the Convention imply a right of enforcement if the arrest is justified?

The last question, at least, must be answered in the negative. Art. 9 of the 1952 Convention makes it clear that the Convention does not create any new rights of action or any new maritime liens. If arrest of a ship were to mean that the claim could also be enforced against the ship even if the owner of the ship were not liable for the claim and even if the claim was not protected by a maritime lien in the ship under the applicable law, it would, in fact, mean that a new maritime lien had been created.

If arrest may be made even in cases where the claim cannot be enforced against the arrested ship, it means that the owner of the ship who is not liable for the claim for which arrest is made will have to put up security to obtain the release of his ship. The result is that the claimant by means of the arrest is able to obtain a security, a kind of maritime lien, which otherwise he has no right to get.

Some of the National Associations represented in the International Sub-Committee were of the opinion that arrest should always be possible even if it means that the ship thereby, directly or indirectly, will serve as security for a claim for which the owner is not liable and even if a maritime lien or mortgage does not exist. That was true, especially, of representatives of countries having predominant cargo interests. Other representatives were of the opinion that it should only be possible to arrest a ship if the claim can be enforced against the ship when a final judgment has been obtained, i.e. either because the owner is personally liable for the claim or because the claim is protected by a maritime lien in the ship.

The discussion reflects not only the different interests of cargo owners and ship owners but also the conflict between those who want to extend maritime liens as much as possible and those who want to limit the number of maritime liens. An unlimited right of arrest brings the maritime lien in by the back door.

The above discussion is reflected in the proposed text of art. 3 in the two alternative texts of para (1) (a) and in para (3).

Para 1 regulates the case in which arrest may be made of the ship in respect of which the maritime claim arose. Para 2 contains the so-called sister ship rule. Para 3 provides that arrest may only be made if the claim can also be enforced against the arrested ship.

The principal text of para 1 permits arrest when the person liable for the claim was owner when the claim arose and still is owner (a), or there is a maritime lien (b), or mortgage (c) against the ship. A lien or mortgage may be connected with a personal claim against the owner but may also exist as security for the debt of a third party, thus without a personal claim against the owner.

The alternative text of para (1) (a) goes further.

It permits arrest of the ship even if the owner is not personally liable for the claim and even if no lien or mortgage exists, provided the owner at the time of arrest is the same as at the time when the maritime claim arose. The rule is intended to meet the wishes of those who think arrest should always be possible but is somewhat restrictive as it prohibits arrest if there has been a change of ownership since the claim arose.

It is not all maritime liens that should give rise to arrest, cf. (b). It seems natural in this respect to connect the Convention to the Convention on maritime liens and mortgages. However, it might be possible also to refer to such maritime liens as are recognized by the *forum arresti*.

Para 1 also permits arrest when the claim relates to the ownership or possession of the ship (d) or when the claim is against bareboat charterer (e).

CMI Draft

(1) ARREST IS PERMISSIBLE OF ANY SHIP IN RESPECT OF WHICH A MARITIME CLAIM IS ASSERTED IF:

(A) THE CLAIM IS SECURED BY A MARITIME LIEN AND IS WITHIN ANY OF THE FOLLOWING CATEGORIES:

    (I) WAGES AND OTHER SUMS, INCLUDING SOCIAL INSURANCE CONTRIBUTIONS, DUE TO THE MASTER, OFFICERS AND OTHER MEMBERS OF THE SHIP'S COMPLEMENT IN RESPECT OF THEIR EMPLOYMENT ON THE SHIP,

    (II) PORT, CANAL, AND OTHER WATERWAY DUES AND PILOTAGE DUES,

    (III) LOSS OF LIFE OR PERSONAL INJURY OCCURRING, WHETHER ON LAND OR ON WATER, IN DIRECT CONNECTION WITH THE OPERATION OF THE SHIP,

    (IV) LIABILITY IN TORT ARISING OUT OF PHYSICAL LOSS OR DAMAGE CAUSED BY THE OPERATION OF THE SHIP OTHER THAN LOSS OF OR DAMAGE TO CARGO, CONTAINERS AND PASSENGERS EFFECTS CARRIED ON THE SHIP,

    (V) SALVAGE, WRECK REMOVAL AND CONTRIBUTION IN GENERAL AVARAGE; OR

(B) THE CLAIM IS BASED UPON A REGISTERED MORTGAGE OR A REGISTERED "HYPOTHÈQUE" OR A REGISTERED CHARGE OF THE SAME NATURE; OR

(C) THE CLAIM IS RELATED TO OWNERSHIP OR POSSESSION OF THE SHIP; OR

(D) THE CLAIM IS NOT COVERED BY (A), (B), OR (C) ABOVE AND IF:

    (I) THE PERSON WHO OWNED THE SHIP AT THE TIME WHEN THE MARITIME CLAIM AROSE IS PERSONALLY LIABLE FOR THE CLAIM AND IS OWNER OF THE SHIP WHEN THE ARREST IS EFFECTED, OR

(II) THE BAREBOAT CHARTERER OF THE SHIP IS PERSONALLY LIABLE FOR THE CLAIM AND IS BARE-
BOAT CHARTERER OR OWNER OF THE SHIP WHEN THE ARREST IS EFFECTED.

Report of the CMI

38. Article 3 corresponds to article 3 paragraph (1), (2) and (4) of the 1952 Convention. It was adopted by 18 votes to 6 with 9 abstentions.

39. Article 3 is the article of the Convention which has given rise to most discussion and controversy during the preparatory discussions in the International Sub-Committee, in the comments of the National Associations and at the Conference in Lisbon. This is principally due to the existence of two points of view which are opposed to each other.

40. One opinion is that the ship is the focal point of all transactions and acts which give rise to maritime claims. According to this view, therefore, it should always be possible to arrest a ship in respect of which a maritime claim is asserted, regardless who is the owner of the ship and whether the owner is liable for the claim or not. This view is based partly on practical, partly on legal considerations.

41. On the basis of practical considerations the interests of third parties lead to this view. Third parties who have a claim or at least assert that a claim has arisen in connection with the operation of a ship, be it in contract or in tort, find it natural to be able to pursue this claim against the ship, regardless who the owner is. On a legal basis this approach could be said to derive from the doctrine of the "fortune de mer". In Anglo-American law the existence of the *in rem* procedure leads in this same direction.

42. The contrary opinion is that arrest of a ship for a maritime claim should only be possible if the claim is secured by a maritime lien or by a mortgage in the ship, or if the owner is personally liable for the claim. The argument is that if arrest is possible in cases where these conditions are not fulfilled that would amount to putting undue pressure on the owner of a ship to put up security for a claim for which he is not personally liable in order to obtain the release of his ship. Indirectly, the arrest would create a security, a maritime lien, to which the claimant would not otherwise have any right. This becomes especially clear considering that, in most jurisdictions, if the owner were not to put up security, the arrest of a ship for a claim which is not secured by a maritime lien or mortgage in the ship and for which the owner is not personally liable cannot lead to a forced sale. Thus, the only purpose of the arrest is to put pressure on the owner to provide security for the debts of a third party.

43. During the discussions in the International Sub-Committee, and even during the discussions at committee level in the Conference in Lisbon, it was not possible to find a majority for either of these views.

Alternative solutions were, therefore, proposed. One solution—which was finally adopted by the plenary session of the Conference—was to require the personal liability of the owner (or of the bareboat charterer) as a condition for arrest. The other solution was not to put such a condition and to permit arrest regardless of the personal liability of the owner (or bareboat charterer) provided that the person who owned the ship at the time when the maritime claim arose is still the owner of the ship when the arrest is effected. This solution would, therefore, exclude a droit de suite, a right to pursue the ship even into the hands of a new owner. Although the outcome was uncertain until the last moment, at the plenary session the solution which was adopted was passed by 23 votes against 6 votes for the other alternative and with 4 abstentions.

44. Another point which was the subject of considerable controversy related to the question of which maritime liens may be invoked as a basis for arrest. The solution adopted which was mentioned above provides that arrest is always permissible if a maritime claim is asserted and the owner (or the bareboat charterer) of the ship is personally liable. If he is not personally liable arrest is only permissible if there is a maritime lien or a mortgage and, therefore, it becomes of great importance which maritime liens are accepted as a basis for arrest.

45. Several possibilities were discussed. Only the more important are mentioned here.

46. The International Sub-Committee in its draft has proposed to limit the liens which as such may make arrest permissible to those recognized in the draft for the revision of the Convention on Maritime Liens and Mortgages. The reason for proposing this more restrictive rule was that a rule

accepting a greater number of maritime liens would so to speak bring these in through the back door, cf. the argument above in paragraph 42.

47. The Belgian delegation in Doc. Arrest–23 proposed to accept as a basis for arrest maritime liens recognized by either of the Conventions on Maritime Liens and Mortgages of 1926 and 1967 and in addition those to be recognized in a future Convention based upon the Lisbon draft. This proposal was rejected by 30 votes to 11 with 2 abstentions.

48. Other proposals, even more far reaching than that of Belgium, were for acceptance of any maritime lien recognized in the *forum arresti*. The argument for the Belgian and these other proposals was that without a possibility of arrest it would not be possible to enforce these liens in cases where neither the owner nor the bareboat charterer was personally liable for the claim underlying the lien.

49. The Conference adopted the original proposal of the International Sub-Committee.

50. Following the above report on the main points of controversy with respect to Article 3 comments are set out below on certain of the provisions of that Article.

51. Both paragraphs (1) and (2) of Article 3 provide that "arrest is permissible" in certain cases. The purpose of this phraseology is to make it clear that in these cases the Convention does not impose an obligation to arrest but rather makes arrest permissible in these cases provided arrest is possible under national law, and prohibits arrest in any other cases, cf. also Article 2 paragraph (2).

52. Paragraph (1) (a) of Article 3 imposes the requirement, as a condition for making arrest permissible, that the maritime claim for which arrest is demanded must fall within one of the categories listed in the text and, in addition, that according to the applicable law the claim is secured by a maritime lien. Although the categories of claims listed correspond to the list of maritime claims recognized by the draft for the revision of the Convention on Maritime Liens and Mortgages as claims secured by a maritime lien, there is no necessary link between the two Conventions. A State having ratified the Arrest Convention but not the Lien Convention may arrest a ship under Article 3 (1) (a) if according to its law, including its rules of conflict of law, the claim is secured by a maritime lien.

53. The enumeration of maritime liens in Article 3 paragraph (1) (a) corresponds to the list of maritime liens recognized by the draft for the revision of the Convention on Maritime Liens and Mortgages. Any later changes in that draft should, therefore, be followed by corresponding changes in the present draft Convention. The national liens accepted by Article 6 of the draft for revision of the 1967 Convention with priority after mortgages are not accepted as liens which may give rise to arrest according to the Arrest Convention.

54. Paragraph (1) (d) of Article 3 provides for the permissibility of arrest if either the owner or the bareboat charterer is liable for the claim. However, a *droit de suite* is not permitted. Arrest is only possible if the owner is still owner when arrest is effected or if the bareboat charterer is still bareboat charterer or has become owner when the arrest is effected.

55. It was generally accepted by the Conference that arrest should be permissible with respect to claims against the bareboat charterer even where the owner is not personally liable for the claim. However, paragraph (3) should be taken into consideration in this connection.

56. With respect to the time element this was subject to some discussion. The term used, "when the arrest is effected", connotes the moment when the arrest is actually made effective by the seizure of the ship or by other means according to national law, e.g. notification to the master, the port authorities or the owner. Thus, it does not refer to the decision to arrest which in some countries may be taken prior to arrival of the ship, in other countries at a stage subsequent to the seizure.

JIGE
Seventh Session, 5 December 1994

Report—Annex I

15. Some delegations preferred the approach adopted by the CMI Draft regarding the requirement of personal liability of the owner for the purpose of arrest under the Convention. The text of the 1952 Arrest Convention was considered inadequate, as it did not clearly link arrest with personal liability of the owner. Some delegations, however, considered that national maritime liens granted under article 6 of the 1993 MLM Convention should be given right of arrest under the Arrest

Convention, irrespective of personal liability of the owner. Personal liability of the owner should only be required when the claim was not secured by a maritime lien.

Some delegations, on the other hand, considered that the approach adopted by the 1952 Arrest Convention was satisfactory.

16. Some delegations, however, considered that national maritime liens granted under article 6 of the 1993 MLM Convention should be given right of arrest under the Arrest Convention, irrespective of personal liability of the owner. In their view, the compromise reached in article 6 of the 1993 Maritime Liens and Mortgages Convention required Contracting States to recognize the national maritime liens of other Contracting States. Personal liability of the owner should only be required when the claim was not secured by a maritime lien. With regard to claims secured by a "maritime lien", a number of delegations felt that the right of arrest under the Convention should only be given to those claims covered under article 4 of the 1993 MLM Convention and not under article 6. In their view, it was not the intention of article 6 to impose an obligation on other States Parties to recognize and enforce national maritime liens granted in a State Party. It was, however, recognized that some reference could be made to such national liens in the Arrest Convention. One delegation referred to paragraph 27 of document JIGE(VII)/2 (TD/B/CN.4/GE.2/2–LEG/MLM/29) concerning avoidance of a situation when a vessel can be arrested in a State Party but the underlying claim cannot be enforced against that vessel.

17. One delegation proposed amending the first sentence of article 3(2) of the CMI Draft to read "(2) Arrest is *also* permissible of any *other* ship or ships . . . ".

18. The representative of the Institute of International Container Lessors (IICL) stated that article 3(1)(d) of the CMI Draft appeared to deal with cases where claims were not secured by "maritime liens" but did not include the case of time charterers. He considered that specific provisions were required to secure suppliers with the right of arrest in such circumstances.

Draft Articles 1994

(1) ARREST IS PERMISSIBLE OF ANY SHIP IN RESPECT OF WHICH A MARITIME CLAIM IS ASSERTED IF:

(A) THE CLAIM IS SECURED BY A MARITIME LIEN AND IS WITHIN ANY OF THE FOLLOWING CATEGORIES:

    (I) WAGES AND OTHER SUMS DUE TO THE MASTER, OFFICERS AND OTHER MEMBERS OF THE VESSEL'S COMPLEMENT IN RESPECT OF THEIR EMPLOYMENT ON THE VESSEL, INCLUDING COSTS OF REPATRIATION AND SOCIAL INSURANCE CONTRIBUTIONS PAYABLE ON THEIR BEHALF,

    (II) LOSS OF LIFE OR PERSONAL INJURY OCCURRING, WHETHER ON LAND OR ON WATER, IN DIRECT CONNECTION WITH THE OPERATION OF THE VESSEL,

    (III) REWARD FOR THE SALVAGE OF THE VESSEL,

    (IV) PORT, CANAL, AND OTHER WATERWAY DUES AND PILOTAGE DUES,

    (V) PHYSICAL LOSS OR DAMAGE CAUSED BY THE OPERATION OF THE VESSEL OTHER THAN LOSS OF OR DAMAGE TO CARGO, CONTAINERS AND PASSENGERS' EFFECTS CARRIED ON THE VESSEL; OR

(B) THE CLAIM IS BASED UPON A REGISTERED MORTGAGE OR A REGISTERED "HYPOTHÈQUE" OR A REGISTERED CHARGE OF THE SAME NATURE; OR

(C) THE CLAIM IS RELATED TO OWNERSHIP OR POSSESSION OF THE SHIP; OR

(D) THE CLAIM IS NOT COVERED BY (A), (B) OR (C) ABOVE AND IF:

    (I) THE PERSON WHO OWNED THE SHIP AT THE TIME WHEN THE MARITIME CLAIM AROSE IS PERSONALLY LIABLE FOR THE CLAIM AND IS OWNER OF THE SHIP WHEN THE ARREST IS EFFECTED, OR

    (II) THE BAREBOAT CHARTERER OF THE SHIP IS PERSONALLY LIABLE FOR THE CLAIM AND IS BAREBOAT CHARTERER OR OWNER OF THE SHIP WHEN THE ARREST IS EFFECTED.

Report—Annex I

41. The Sessional Group noted that in article 3(1)(a), the list of maritime liens contained in (i) to (v) had been changed to reflect the terminology used in article 4(1) of the MLM Convention.

42. The Sessional Group heard the report of the Chairman of the Informal Group which it had set up to examine the question of aligning the provisions of article 6 of the MLM Convention dealing with national maritime liens with those of the Arrest Convention. It appeared that there were

differing views as to the intention of article 6. While the majority of delegations believed that article 6 did not impose an obligation on other States Parties to recognize and enforce national maritime liens, some delegations held the opposite view. No unified solution could therefore be found. The following proposals thus emerged: (a) to retain the text of article 3(1) as contained in CRP.1 as it was; (b) to delete the text after "maritime lien" in article 3(1)(a) including (i) to (v), which would have the effect of making national maritime liens enforceable in all States; (c) to insert in article 3(1) a new sub-paragraph (b) which would read: "the claim is secured by a maritime lien granted by the law of the State where the arrest is requested pursuant to the provisions of article 6 of the International Convention on Maritime Liens and Mortgages, 1993;". The latter proposal had been put forward by the Chairman of the Informal Group in an attempt to provide a compromise so as to clarify that a vessel might be arrested for claims secured by national maritime lien even if it were sold, but with effect only in the enacting State and without any obligation on other States.

In concluding, the Chairman of the Informal Group expressed the view that the question of aligning the Arrest Convention with article 6 of the MLM Convention in a satisfactory manner was crucial for the future of both the MLM Convention and the Arrest Convention.

Eighth Session, 9–10 October 1995

Submission by the International Chamber of Shipping

ICS believes that Alternative 1, the CMI text, is to be preferred. We are of the view that it should only be possible to arrest in respect of maritime claims which are secured by internationally recognized maritime liens.

Report—Annex I

44. The Sessional Group had before it three alternative texts related to the exercise of the right of arrest irrespective of the personal liability of the owner. Alternative one permitted such an arrest for claims secured by maritime liens listed in article 4 of the MLM Convention. Alternative 2, which had been proposed by the delegation of the United States of America, also covered national liens granted under article 6 of the MLM Convention. Alternative 3, which had been proposed by the Chairman of the Informal Group on consideration of national maritime liens set up during the VIIth session, in addition to maritime liens set out in article 4 of the MLM Convention, also permitted arrest in respect of a claim secured by a maritime lien granted by the law of the state where the arrest is requested in accordance with article 6 of the MLM Convention.

45. The delegation of the United States of America emphasized that the success of both the MLM Convention and the Revised Arrest Convention depended to a large extent on resolution of this matter. In its view the difficulty arose because the MLM Convention did not specifically address the choice of law rule to be applied in deciding the effect to be given to national maritime liens. In the view of this delegation alternative 2 was the only alternative which fully implemented the compromise adopted regarding article 6 of the MLM Convention which provided shorter life spans for national maritime liens especially following the sale of a vessel. If such liens were not recognised internationally by State Parties to the Arrest Convention, then article 6 of the MLM Convention would be rendered meaningless.

46. Its delegation offered as a possible compromise another alternative based on alternative 3 to read as follows:

    "Article 3(1)(a)

    (a)   . . . (no change from Alternative 1);

    (b)   the claim is secured by a maritime lien recognized by the law of the State where the arrest is requested;

    (b)–(d) . . . (reordered as (c)–(e) with no change)".

47. It was stated that the proposal did not impose any obligation on States to recognize maritime liens beyond what was permitted by their domestic law. It was left to the applicable law in the jurisdiction where the arrest is requested to determine if a maritime lien existed. Furthermore, reference to article 6 of the MLM Convention had been removed, because it was felt that the prospective arrest convention should stand on its own.

48. Some delegations considered that the proposal contained positive elements but needed further examination at the next session. Some other delegations felt that alternative 2 as referred to by the delegation of the United States of America was contrary to the compromise adopted by article 6 of the MLM Convention. As compared to alternative 2, the proposal now introduced by the United States of America was considered to be a step in the right direction. In keeping with the said compromise, the proposal did not imply an obligation on a State Party to the MLM Convention to recognise national maritime liens and would not place an obligation to do so on a State Party to the Revised Arrest Convention. However, a choice of law rule in the proposed form would lead to forum shopping and thus defy the object of the MLM Convention.

49. Many delegations favoured the text of alternative 1, but expressed their readiness to consider the other alternatives to see if they could form the basis for a compromise. One delegation which felt that the problem was caused by having an open-ended list of maritime claims in article 1 preferred to have a closed list of maritime claims in article 1 and keep flexibility in article 3. In the view of this delegation there were problems also with regard to the structure of article 3, and noted, for instance, that the key provision was given only in paragraph (1)(d)(i).

50. One delegation stated that the sole purpose of article 3 should be to supplement other provisions by allowing arrest of any ship for claims secured by a maritime lien if it was not owned by the person liable. This delegation proposed the following text for article 3:

"Arrest is also permissible of any ship for the purpose of enforcing a lien securing a maritime claim indicated in article 1(1)."

51. The observer for the International Ship Suppliers Association (ISSA) expressed a view that the present text of article 3, even if accepted on the basis of any of the three alternatives in the present draft, may deprive a ship supplier of the right to arrest a ship which has not paid for supplies. Where there was no maritime lien and the supply was not to the shipowner or to the demise charterer but, for example, to a time charterer who did not own a ship, the ship supplier could not effect an arrest under article 3 of either the ship to which the supply was furnished or a sister ship. Nor did this article assist a ship supplier when the owner at the time of the supply was not the same as at the time of the arrest. This was considered a lacunae and a radical departure from the 1952 Convention.

52. The observer for the Federation of National Associations of Ship Brokers and Agents (FONASBA) stated that it would support the proposal of the ISSA if the proposal of the United States of America is not adopted.

53. The Sessional Group agreed to continue its examination of article 3 at the next session.

Ninth Session, 2–6 December 1996

Proposal by the United States

(1) Arrest is permissible of any ship in respect of which a maritime claim is asserted if:

(a) the claim is secured by a maritime lien and is within the following categories:
    (i)–(v) [as in alternative 1, JIGE(IX)/2]; or
(b) the claim is secured by a maritime lien, other than those referred to in subparagraph (a), recognized under the law of the State where the arrest is requested; or
(c) the claim is based on a registered mortgage or "hypothèque" or a charge of the same nature; or
(d) [as (c) in alternative 3 in JIGE(IX)/2, page 13]; or
(e) [as (d) in alternative 3 in JIGE(IX)/2, page 13].

Article 3 paragraphs 2 and 3 would remain unchanged (JIGE(IX)/2, pages 13–14).

Comments and proposals by the United Kingdom

17. While there are differing interpretations of Article 3(1) of the 1952 Convention, it can be argued that that Convention provides an unfettered right for a claimant to arrest the particular ship in respect of which a maritime claim arose, irrespective of whether the claim is secured by a maritime lien or whether the shipowner is personally liable for the claim. It is generally agreed,

however, that—even if the 1952 Convention does not provide such an unfettered right—there is nothing in the Convention to prevent a State from providing such a right under national law.

18. The United Kingdom delegation is not convinced that there is any need to depart from the general approach of the 1952 Convention, particularly if it is agreed that the list of maritime claims in Article 1(1) should be exhaustive. However, if there is to be a link between the right to arrest a ship and the existence of a maritime lien, the drafting of Article 3(1) could be made considerably simpler by referring only to maritime liens recognized by the law of the State in which the arrest was made.

19. The United Kingdom delegation also proposes that the reference to mortgages, "hypothèques" and registrable charges of a similar nature in Article 3(1)(b) should follow the wording used in the chapeau, and subparagraph (u), of Article 1(1).

20. In order to implement the two changes proposed above, Article 3(1) of the JIGE text should be amended as follows:

Arrest is permissible of any ship in respect of which a maritime claim is asserted if:

  (a) the claim is secured by a maritime lien recognized under the law of the State where the arrest is made;
  (b) the claim is based upon a mortgage, an "hypothèque" or registrable charge of a similar nature;
  (c) [...]; or
  (d) [...].

Comments and proposals by Japan

4. According to the Law of Civil Provisional Remedies of Japan, provisional detention measures against a ship can be granted if the ship, regardless of whether the claim arose in respect of that ship or not, is owned by the debtor at the time when the detention measure is effected. From this standpoint, with respect to paragraph 1(d)(i) and paragraph 2, it is not necessary to require that the debtor who owns the ship at the time of arrest also possess or charter the ship when the claim arose.

Draft Articles 1997

(1) ARREST IS PERMISSIBLE OF ANY SHIP IN RESPECT OF WHICH A MARITIME CLAIM IS ASSERTED IF:[47]

(A) THE CLAIM AGAINST THE OWNER, DEMISE CHARTERER, MANAGER OR OPERATOR OF THE SHIP IS SECURED BY A MARITIME LIEN AND IS WITHIN ANY OF THE FOLLOWING CATEGORIES:

  (I) WAGES AND OTHER SUMS DUE TO THE MASTER, OFFICERS AND OTHER MEMBERS OF THE SHIP'S COMPLEMENT IN RESPECT OF THEIR EMPLOYMENT ON THE SHIP, INCLUDING COSTS OF REPATRIATION AND SOCIAL INSURANCE CONTRIBUTIONS PAYABLE ON THEIR BEHALF,

  (II) LOSS OF LIFE OR PERSONAL INJURY OCCURRING, WHETHER ON LAND OR ON WATER, IN DIRECT CONNECTION WITH THE OPERATION OF THE SHIP,

  (III) REWARD FOR THE SALVAGE OF THE SHIP,

  (IV) PORT, CANAL, AND OTHER WATERWAY DUES AND PILOTAGE DUES,

---

47. Article 3 has been subject to extensive discussions within the Joint Group. The text of the article has been amended at the 9th session on the basis of the proposal put forward by the delegation of the United States of America and proposals of other delegations. The words "claims against the owner, demise charterer, manager or operator of the ship" have been included in Paragraphs 1(a) and (b); sub-paragraph (b) dealing with the right of arrest in respect of national maritime liens is placed in bracket. The words "a mortgage, or an 'hypotheque' or registrable charge of the same nature" are used in paragraph 1(c). It was however felt that the use of the term "registrable" in this context should be further considered. Paragraphs 1(e)(ii) and 2(b), dealing with the right of arrest for claims not secured by a maritime lien for which demise charterer and time charterer were personally liable, are placed in brackets. The concept of claims based on tort is introduced in paragraph 1(a)(v) in the same way as article 4 of the 1993 MLM Convention. For discussions on article 3, see the report of the Joint Group at its 9th session, ibid., paras. 50–65.

(V) PHYSICAL LOSS OR DAMAGE (BASED ON TORT) CAUSED BY THE OPERATION OF THE SHIP OTHER THAN LOSS OF OR DAMAGE TO CARGO, CONTAINERS AND PASSENGERS' EFFECTS CARRIED ON THE SHIP; OR

(B) [THE CLAIM AGAINST THE OWNER, DEMISE CHARTERER, MANAGER OR OPERATOR OF THE SHIP IS SECURED BY A MARITIME LIEN, OTHER THAN THOSE REFERRED TO IN PARAGRAPH (A), RECOGNIZED UNDER THE LAW OF THE STATE WHERE THE ARREST IS REQUESTED; OR]

(C) THE CLAIM IS BASED UPON A MORTGAGE OR AN "HYPOTHÈQUE" OR A REGISTRABLE CHARGE OF THE SAME NATURE; OR

(D) THE CLAIM IS RELATED TO OWNERSHIP OR POSSESSION OF THE SHIP; OR

(E) THE CLAIM IS NOT COVERED BY (A), (B) , (C) or (D) ABOVE AND IF:

    (I) THE PERSON WHO OWNED THE SHIP AT THE TIME WHEN THE MARITIME CLAIM AROSE IS PERSON-ALLY LIABLE FOR THE CLAIM AND IS OWNER OF THE SHIP WHEN THE ARREST IS EFFECTED [, OR

    (II) THE DEMISE CHARTERER OF THE SHIP IS PERSONALLY LIABLE FOR THE CLAIM AND IS DEMISE CHARTERER OR OWNER OF THE SHIP WHEN THE ARREST IS EFFECTED].

Diplomatic Conference
Comments and Proposals

CMI

DOCUMENT 188/3

137. It is submitted that the order in which the provisions contained in Article 3 have been set out in the Lisbon Draft and now in the Draft Articles should be reconsidered. In fact, the general rule on the conditions for the arrest of a ship is that set out in the present paragraph 1 (e) (i). It is thought that it would be clearer if the general rule were set out first, followed by the rules presently contained in sub-paragraphs (e) (ii), (c), (d) and by the special provisions in respect of claims secured by maritime liens.

138. The incorporation of the 1993 MLM Convention maritime liens in sub-paragraph (a) had been done in order to avoid a reference to such Convention. Subsequently, during the sessions of the JIGE it was proposed to add a reference also to the maritime liens recognized under the law of the State where the arrest is requested. It is thought that this proposal is sound, for the reference to such liens would significantly facilitate ratification of the Convention by States that do not intend to become parties to the 1993 MLM Convention.

139. If the proposal mentioned above were to be accepted by the Conference, the reproduction in sub-paragraph (a) of the 1993 MLM Convention maritime liens would become superfluous, because such liens would obviously be recognized by the law of the State where the arrest is applied for if such State is a party to the Convention.

140. Paragraph (1) of Article 3 would thus become less heavy and could read as follows:

(1) Arrest is permissible of any ship in respect of which a maritime claim is asserted if:

    (i) the person who owned the ship at the time when the maritime claim arose is liable for the claim and is owner of the ship when the arrest is effected; or

    (ii) the demise charterer of the ship at the time when the maritime claim arose is liable for the claim and is demise charterer or owner of the ship when the arrest is effected; or

    (iii) the claim is based upon a registered mortgage or a registered "hypothèque" or a registered charge of the same nature on the ship; or

    (iv) the claim relates to the ownership or possession of the ship; or

    (v) the claim is against the owner, demise charterer, manager or operator of the ship and is secured by a maritime lien which is recognized under the law of the State where the arrest is applied for.

141. The following comments are necessary:

(1) Paragraph 1(ii) (presently paragraph 1(e) (ii)) has been amended by including, as in paragraph 1(i), the words "at the time when the maritime claim arose".

(2) Since in Article 1(i)(u) reference is made to registered mortgages, "hypothèques" or charges, such reference is even more necessary in this Article 3(2)(a) where the fact that the claim is secured

by a mortgage, "hypothèque" or charge enables the holder of the security to arrest the ship even if it is not owned by the debtor.

(3) It has been clearly stated during the Sessions of the JIGE that the reference to the law of the State where the arrest is applied for includes the conflict of law rules in force in such State.

Hong Kong, China

DOCUMENT 188/3

13. The square brackets (in sub-paragraph (b) of the Draft Articles) may be removed but the word "operator" should be deleted as it is too broad and the term is undefined.

14. The word "registrable" (in sub-paragraph (c) of the Draft Articles) should be reworded as "registered" as stated in paragraph 7.

15. "When the arrest is effected" (in sub-paragraph (e) of the Draft Articles) should be changed to "when proceedings in which the arrest is effected are commenced" as this should quite comfortably fit civil law and common law jurisdictions". "When the arrest is effected" will give rise to uncertainty and dispute and it should be avoided as should claims for unjustified arrest which may be generated by the transfer of ownership of a ship between commencement of proceedings and the date when an arrest is effected, whether in a common law or civil law jurisdiction. It may be impossible to ascertain whether there has been any such change of ownership between these two dates.

16. "The demise charterer of the ship is personally liable" should be changed to "The demise charterer of the ship at the time when the maritime claim arose is personally liable".

Mexico

DOCUMENT 188/3

40. The Government of Mexico considers the drafting of (sub-paragraph (b) of the Draft Article) this article confused. In its view the Spanish term "gestor" ("manager" in English) should be replaced by the word "operador" and that the term "naviero" ("operator" in English) should be placed immediately after the word "owner" in sub-paragraph (b). The text would then read as follows:

"[If] the claim against the owner, operator or demise charterer of the ship is secured by a maritime lien other than those mentioned in paragraph (a) and recognized under the law of the State where the arrest is requested; or"

41. The proposal made by the United Kingdom would be acceptable as regards sub-paragraphs (a) and (c) of paragraph 1 of this article, but sub-paragraph (b) would be superfluous.

Slovakia

DOCUMENT 188/3

63. In our opinion Article 3(1) should include sub-paragraph b) as it is drafted i.e. to include the claim against the owner, demise charterer, manager or operator of the ship and to not include claims against time and voyage charterers as proposed by the delegation of the United States of America (JIGE (IX)/4).

Thailand

DOCUMENT 188/3

84. The square bracket in paragraph 1(b) should be removed to allow the enforcement of national maritime liens through arrest. Without it, the right of national maritime lien holder can be affected by the limit caused by paragraph 1(e).

85. The square bracket in paragraph 1(e)(ii) should also be removed. The right to arrest within this paragraph depends on personal liability. Personal liability includes liability through employment and delegation. For example, the shipowner is normally liable for the acts of the master and crew. Where a claim arises when the ship is under voyage charter or time charter whereby the master and crew remain the servants of the owner, though being put under the disposal of the charterers, the personal liability is on the owner, not the charterers. However, in case of demise charter where the

master and crew are the servants of the charterers, the owner will not be personally liable for the acts of the servants of the charterers. Arrest may be made against the ship in respect of which the claim is asserted if, at the time when arrest is made, the charterers are still the demise charterers or have become the owner of the ship. Paragraph 1(d)(i) and (ii) pose a clear position about personal liability. The claimant of the demise charterer needs to effect an arrest within the currency of the charter. The right to arrest may come to an end when the charter is expired, unless the charterers become the owner of the ship.

ICS

DOCUMENT 188/3

120. ICS is of the view that it should only be possible to arrest in respect of maritime claims which are secured by internationally recognised maritime liens. To allow arrest in respect of claims secured by national maritime liens would lead to considerably increased rights of arrest. However if there is a wish to seek a compromise, ICS would be prepared to accept a right of arrest in respect of maritime claims secured by MLM Article 6 "other maritime liens". We would therefore propose that text should be added to the draft sub-paragraph to make it clear that the national maritime liens in question are those which meet the basic requirements of MLM Article 6. In addition, with reference to the second line of the draft sub-paragraph, if MLM Article 6 maritime liens are accepted, ICS would deem it essential that "recognised" be deleted and replaced with "granted". "Granted" is consistent with MLM Article 6 which provides that "Each State Party may, under its law, *grant* other maritime liens . . . ". As was noted at the ninth session of the JIGE, the use of the word "recognised" could lead to increased forum shopping and would not promote harmonisation of law.

121. To be consistent with Article 1, paragraph 1(u) the word "registrable" should be changed to "registered".

122. ICS is of the view that Article 3 paragraph 1(e)(ii) should be deleted because it would allow, in jurisdictions where it is permissible, the judicial or forced sale of a ship which is owned by someone other than the person personally liable for the claim.

Norway

DOCUMENT CRP.3

It may well follow the general conflict of law rules of a State that national liens of another State shall be recognized (and therefore be given a right of arrest under the JIGE-wording), although the first state does not wish to provide for such national liens in its own maritime legislation. For that reason the word "recognized" should be replaced by "granted".

Article 3, paragraph 1(v), would then read:

(v) the claim is against the owner, demise charterer, manager or operator of the ship and is secured by a maritime lien which is *granted or arises* under the law of the State where the arrest is applied for.

Ukraine

DOCUMENT CRP.11

8. We suggest replacing the words "requested" and "demanded" by "made".

United States

DOCUMENT CRP.16

The United States offers as a compromise the following revised version of the present text of Art. 3(1)(v):

(v) the claim is against the owner, demise charterer, manager or operator of the ship and is secured by a maritime lien which is granted or arises under the law of the State where the arrest is applied for. However, nothing in this Convention prevents any court of a State party from arresting a ship for a claim secured by a maritime lien granted or arising under foreign law.

Proceedings of the Main Committee

The debate that has taken place during the First reading and the Second reading has been arranged by reproducing first the debate on the structure of paragraph (1) and subsequently the debate on the individual sub-paragraphs according to the new structure of paragraph (1), suggested by the CMI and adopted by the Conference.

The structure of Paragraph 1

First reading—3 March 1999[48]

Chairman   I suggest that the CMI introduces its proposed revision of art. 3. To a large extent it is a drafting proposal. In the view of the CMI its presentation is more logical. I invite the representative of CMI Prof. Berlingieri to introduce his proposal.

CMI   The CMI is of the view that the fundamental situation in which an arrest may be granted is that where the claimant has a claim against the owner of the ship. In other words that where the claim has arisen in connection with a ship which is owned by the debtor. In the present draft this, which in the view of the CMI is the basic rule, is confined to subparagraph (e)(i) whilst the first situation which is dealt with in the present draft of article 3(1) is so to say an exception to the basic rule, the exception being that where a claim is secured by a maritime lien the claimant may arrest the ship in respect of which the claim has arisen even if it is not owned by the debtor. The suggestion of the CMI is therefore to start with the basic rule, that is to say that the claimant is always entitled to arrest the ship which is owned by the debtor, and then continue with possible exceptions. In so far as the exceptions are concerned of course the basic one is that of the claim secured by a maritime lien. I put the words "maritime lien" in inverted commas, Mr. Chairman, because there have been different views in the JIGE on how the maritime lien should be identified. The present philosophy is that there is a list of maritime liens which corresponds to the maritime liens of the 1993 Convention; although the Convention is not expressly referred to, the liens are exactly those set out in art. 4(1) of the MLM Convention. However during the JIGE sessions different suggestions have been made. A proposal was made by the delegation of the United States that reference should be made, in addition, to the liens recognized by the *lex fori*. If my recollection is correct, also the United Kingdom made a similar proposal. It is therefore, the CMI submits, a problem for consideration by this meeting to decide which are the liens in respect of which an arrest is permissible, even if the ship is not owned by the debtor. In case the proposal put forward by the United States is accepted, that reference should be made to the *lex fori* and that therefore the arrest should be permissible as security for claims in respect of which the *lex fori* admits a maritime lien, in that case it would become unnecessary to set out the so called international maritime liens because if the State where arrest is demanded has ratified the Convention or enacted the international liens, it would admit those international liens without any need for such liens to be set out expressly in this Convention. Once it is accepted that the basic rule is that the claimant is entitled to arrest the ship owned by his debtor, then the problem which are the maritime liens to be accepted in this Convention is a problem which must be considered by this meeting. In case it were accepted that the maritime liens are those recognized by the *lex fori*, in such a case probably the reference which is made presently in the draft that the claim should be against the bareboat charterer, the manager or operator of the ship would become superfluous because if it is the *lex fori* which governs then it will be the *lex fori* which will state whether or not the claim must be against some specified persons. For the time being I think that I should not go on any further.

Chairman   You have correctly pointed out that it is the task of this conference to decide whether the vessel may be arrested when the claim is not against the owner and I think this must be agreed before we must take into account the Liens and Mortgages Convention, so there should be no contradiction between the MLM Convention of 1993 and this Convention. This can be achieved in many ways and one way is the way which the JIGE has approached by actually listing the maritime liens in the 1993 Convention. Another way is the way indicated by the CMI, by Prof. Berlingieri, that we have a much more general approach and say that any lien recognized by the *lex fori* should be the basis of whether or not the claim is against the owner or the manager or whoever. A lien

---

48. Text and summary from tapes Nos. 16–21.

recognized by the *lex fori* should be a possibility for an arrest. Of course we can adopt a more general approach, that is a specific link to the 1993 MLM Convention if that is acceptable to the delegates of course. Those that would like that we impose the restrictions of the 1993 Convention also to the States that ratified the arrest Convention would prefer the JIGE approach and others may favour the more general CMI approach. I leave the floor open. I would like to know whether you think that we should face a deliberation on the CMI proposal. I look upon the CMI as a drafting change, merely the way of rearranging the substance of art. 3 of the JIGE text or whether you prefer to work on the JIGE text. I think we have to take a decision on that. There is no contradiction between the JIGE text and the CMI proposal. Even if we work on the JIGE text it may be considered later that it should be redrafted in a more comprehensive way perhaps in the way the CMI has done it. Even if you decide that at this stage you want to work on the basis of the JIGE text that does not exclude the possibility of later redrafting the language into a more easily comprehensive way. What are your views? On what basis you wish to proceed?

Italy I believe that the CMI text is much simpler, because we have first the general rule and then the exceptions.

Chairman Yes I agree the substance is the same.

Canada We see it very much in the same way. I think that allowing Prof. Berlingieri to introduce his proposition is a step forward in our work. We detect that it would be a great advantage to base our work essentially on this text as opposed to, if I can use a sort of an expression we have in Canada – spinning our wheels – as it were on the original text which has caused to JIGE a considerable difficulty. I think that if we would concentrate our work initially on the CMI text we would have a far greater chance to resolve most of our problems. I fully endorse it Mr. Chairman.

United Kingdom The UK could live with the text as drafted. But in answer to your question would we prepared to accept the CMI draft as perhaps getting some consensus the answer would be yes, we would be interested in doing this. If we had to fall back to my initial statement we can accept this draft and we are more than happy to work on the text that the CMI has proposed subject that we could not accept any other proposal which would include a reference to the MLM Convention, because we want this to be a free standing proposal and a free standing instrument. Subject to that we are more than happy to work with the CMI text.

China After intensive study of the proposals and the thoughts behind the proposals made by Prof. Berlingieri, the Chinese Delegation is of the opinion that the text in the proposals is more explicit and simple than that in the JIGE provisions. So if we take CMI's proposals as the basis of discussion and deliberation, it would give us a greater chance to achieve uniformity or clarification in this area for the differences existing in different national laws or regulations and practices. The Chinese Delegation agree that the CMI proposals should be taken as a basis of discussion.

Thailand We are also in favour of the CMI text as a working document.

Chairman I take it that you agree to work on CMI text.

SUB-PARAGRAPH (a)

First reading—3 March 1999[49]

Canada We have made a proposal couched with reference to the JIGE draft. (...)

Chairman I think we have to deal with it. I understand your proposal is to replace in sub-paragraph (a) the words "arrest is effected" by "action is commenced".

Canada That is exactly correct. If I can summarize in a nutshell what has been said in the paper, what we are trying to attempt here is to block a loophole when by fixing the time as the time of the arrest, knowing well enough that very often litigation is commenced prior to the actual arrest, in effect some considerable time prior in certain cases, it provides an opportunity, a chance for – I shall be frank – an unscrupulous ship operator to avoid or to frustrate the ability of a claimant to exercise his right of arrest whereas by fixing the time at the time the action is commenced then it prevents that result. So it is an attempt really to close a loophole.

Chairman For further clarification may I ask a couple of questions: "action is commenced": that is the filing of the writ. OK. So I get your point. Would you be concerned of the risk of a hidden

49. Text from tapes nos. 16 and 17.

charge with the vessel? I mean if a writ had been filed somewhere and then the vessel was sold subsequently to a bona fide buyer. Could under your wording the claimant then come to the new owner and say, sorry I had instituted a claim somewhere in respect of this, and I now wish to secure that claim and you have to pay for it or put up security for it or sell your vessel.

Canada   Well, yes indeed, on a question and answer basis I am pleased to tell you that in my view the answer is yes to your question and this would require some more diligence undoubtedly on the part of the ship purchaser that happens to be considered a possibility. It would require a search of the court dockets in the country where the ship is owned to make sure that no suit is lodged. But this is done fairly customarily by engaging lawyers to do this in any event.

Hong Kong China   I just want to say we had exactly the same concern that was expressed in our written comments sometime ago. We had a slightly different form of wording which is set out in our submission. Our alternative wording was "when proceedings in which the arrest is effected are commenced". That had the same purpose of Canada.

Russian Fed.   We categorically object to the use of the word "personally" before the word "liable" in article 3.1, and share in this connection the position taken by Canada, United Kingdom, and Belgium.

CMI   Mr Chairman, this proposal is causing to me some concern because from the time when action is commenced to the time when arrest is effected there may be a change in the ownership of the vessel and such a change may not be known to third parties in good faith. There may be a buyer in good faith who buys the vessel between the time action is commenced and arrest is effected. What would be the position in that case if arrest is effected after the passing of title? Would the arrest be still permissible notwithstanding the fact that title has passed to an innocent buyer? It seems to me that it would be dangerous to replace a moment which is known to everybody, the moment of the arrest, with the moment which is unknown to third parties, the commencement of an action. Therefore, notwithstanding the reasons that may be behind the Canadian proposal the suggestion of the CMI is that the reference to the time of arrest is preferable.

Norway   We agree fully with remarks just made by Prof. Berlingieri.

Australia   We support Canada. The wording is reflected in our domestic legislation.

Denmark   We support Prof. Berlingieri, and I think that this draft Convention has been prepared over the years by the CMI and if we try to make adjustments at the very last moment you might lose something.

Netherlands   We support the comments of Prof. Berlingieri. There is a need for legal certainty.

Germany   We share the position made by Norway and by the CMI. In case there is a change of ownership during the procedure of arrest, this must be left to national legislation to handle the case. There has been no problem with the 1952 Convention which did not deal with this problem either. In our country we have special rules to solve the problem that someone in the meantime during the proceedings changes ownership and the other one is in good faith in respect of the ownership of the seller. So we can handle the problem and I don't think it would be wise to change the draft.

United Kingdom   This is a particular problem for English law and common law jurisdictions where an arrest necessitates the commencement of proceedings on the merits but those proceedings can be commenced substantially before an arrest is effected. The unjustice to which Prof. Berlingieri has referred, with great respect is in fact not faced by our system because once the proceedings are commenced the writ is a public document, there is a register which can be searched by the purchaser of a ship between the commencement of the action and the arrest so that that registration is deemed to be noticed to the world for all purposes. It certainly is a practice which is followed by the UK and other English law jurisdictions such as Australia and we would certainly support the Australian position.

Italy   We agree with the observations of Prof. Berlingieri.

Sweden   We support the views expressed by CMI.

Greece   We support the comments made by the CMI although we understand the concern expressed by the UK, but they can be solved as suggested by Germany.

Japan   We share the views of Germany. We can understand what the common law system is on this point. However in our country the Court order, a kind of a writ in common law countries is valid only after it is served to the shipowner or master on behalf of the shipowner.

China   The Chinese delegation wishes to make the following comments. We think we should retain the term "arrest is effected" in the JIGE text and it should not be changed to "action is commenced", because under Chinese law, there are two types of arrest of ships, one is arrest of ships before commencement of legal proceedings, and another is after the commencement. The Chinese legal practice shows that the majority falls under the first type, that is arrest of ships before the commencement of legal proceedings. It means that in China, arrest of ships before the commencement of legal proceedings does not necessarily lead to legal proceedings on the merits of the case, therefore, we support the retention of the term in the JIGE original text.

Brazil   We support the original CMI text.

Chairman   It would seem that there is a problem for common law countries. My conclusion is that the Canadian and Hong Kong proposals are not carried. I consider that (i) is adopted.

SUB-PARAGRAPH (b)

First reading—3 March 1999[50]

Three proposals were made in respect of this sub-paragraph: to delete the sub-paragraph altogether; to delete the word "demise"; to reinstate the word "personally" before "liable". The purpose of the first and of the second proposals was opposite: the purpose of the first was to exclude the possibility of arresting a ship in respect of claims against persons other than the owner and that of the second to extend it, without limitations to claims against all types of charterers. The statements of the observer from ICS and of the delegates from Belgium and France illustrate this.

ICS   We refer to our paper at p. 19. We propose that (ii) be struck out because it would allow in jurisdictions where it is permissible the judicial or forced sale of the ship which is owned by someone other than person who is personally liable for the claim.

France   We think we can work with other delegations who have the same concern. It may perhaps suffice to complete the text by widening the term charterer. The charterer of the ship when the claim has arisen is personally liable and is the charterer or owner of the ship when the arrest is effected.

Belgium   We support the French proposal and to delete word "demise".

When the observer from the CMI objected to the deletion of the word "demise" (see below), the delegate from Belgium so stated:

Belgium   Some reflections of my Government on the views of CMI. The very concept expressed by CMI is overtaken by to-day's economical situation. It has been intentionally that I have suggested to drop the word "demise". To-day's circumstances are no more those of 1952 or of 1985. We are in the world of international commerce confronted with two problems. First, maritime carriage is now performed in great part by one ship companies under flags of convenience under the responsibility of the carrier by sea. The owner becomes untouchable. Second change: many owners build up legal systems to create a barrier between them and their responsibility. There are owners who cause all contracts to be executed by fictitious companies. 75% of ships work under responsibility of persons other than their owner.

Here follow the statements made in support of the maintenance of the word "demise".

CMI   Two entirely different issues are being discussed at the same time. The first is whether or not the word "personally" should be included in the text and the second, which is by far a more general question, is whether or not the word "demise" should be deleted. It seems to me that we should consider generally the problem of when a claimant may arrest a ship which is not owned by its debtor and I wonder, Mr. Chairman, if it is the right time now to make a general introduction of this problem or you prefer that this be done at a later stage.

Chairman   I think, Prof. Berlingieri, that the deliberations would be assisted if you make a statement now, please.

CMI   There are two different situations in which a claimant may arrest a ship which is not owned by its debtor. The first, which existed already in a rather uncertain manner in the 1952 Convention, is that of claims against persons who operate the ship, the demise charterer and, under the 1952 Convention, other charterers. There was a very unfortunate provision in the 1952 Convention—at least I think it was very unfortunate, maybe others do not share my views—and that is the last

---

50. Text and summary from tapes nos. 17 and 18.

paragraph of article 3(4). Paragraph 4 states generally that a ship may be arrested as security for a claim against the demise charterer. Then there was an additional paragraph, the history of which is very complicated—but I do not want now that you lose your time with this—which says: "The provisions of this paragraph shall apply to any case in which a person other than the registered owner of the ship is liable in respect of a maritime claim relating to that ship". When in Lisbon the CMI discussed that provision, it was agreed that it was already exceptional that a claim might justify the arrest of the ship in case such claim was against the demise charterer and this should not be extended any further. Not only that, but even a claim against the demise charterer could give rise to the arrest of the ship provided always that under the *lex fori* the claimant could then enforce his claim against the ship. In other words cause the sale of the ship at a later stage. This is still in the JIGE text in article 3(3). This is one category of situations which is regulated in the JIGE text and which the CMI did not intend to change in its proposal. The claim may be only against the demise charterer, but conditionally to this claim being then enforceable under the *lex fori*. The second big category is that of claims secured by maritime liens, which is an entirely different category. I don't want now to go into details but I just want, if I am allowed to do so, to draw the attention of all the distinguished delegates to the importance of the proposal to delete the word "demise" in this context.

United Kingdom   We just want to make it clear that in the context of this particular paragraph we are more than happy to keep the notion of demise charterer for the reasons that Prof. Berlingieri has explained.

In reply to the comments made by the delegate from Belgium the observer from the CMI so stated:

Mr. Chairman, I listened with great attention the explanations given by the distinguished delegate from Belgium and it seems to me that the problem he has raised is a real problem indeed, but has nothing to do with the contract of affreightment. This is a problem which is connected with the possibility of piercing the corporate veil. This is an issue which has been raised by the CMI – perhaps the distinguished delegate of Belgium has not read the report of the CMI – and it has been raised also by the United Kingdom. The United Kingdom suggested to inject in the Convention the theory of control which is something which exists in several jurisdictions with different terminology. It seems to me, Mr. Chairman and distinguished delegates, that the problem which has now been raised is a real problem indeed, but should be discussed when the UK proposal of inserting in this Convention the concept of control of the ship will be considered.

Second reading—10 March 1999[51]

As regards the suggestion to reinstate the word "personally", the following statements were made by the delegate from Denmark and by the observer from the CMI:

Denmark   We have a problem with the text which I don't know whether or not it is a drafting matter. It is so that looking at the CMI text where it says "is liable" and the word "personally" is missing; I think that it is the same thing which in fact has been with the text that we have already been discussing and I guess that the CMI when they went through this I hope that they did not intend to change it because it is in the JIGE text. I think we should have a discussion whether this word should be taken out.

CMI   The word "personally" has been omitted without any intention to make any change of substance with respect to the JIGE Draft.

The debate on the three issues was closed by the Chairman as follows:

Several questions need to be answered. The first one is whether we should have this sub-paragraph or it should be deleted. I think that the majority is in favour of keeping it in one form or another. A number of delegates have suggested that the word "demise" should be deleted which would indeed change the substance of the paragraph and of the Convention. My sense is that a substantive majority would like to keep the word "demise" and I think that some of the ones that want to delete "demise" in this context would be content to address the problem in another context, i.e. the context of sister ships or associated ships as was suggested by the CMI. My conclusion is, therefore, that the word "demise" should be kept. As to the word "personally" I think that there is

---

51. Text and summary from tape No. 74.

really agreement on substance; I think that as pointed out by Norway the critical thing to note is that we are talking about *in rem* liability on the one hand and liability for one's own fault or fault or act of one's agents and employees on the other hand. I really consider it to be a drafting matter. I think that there is agreement in the room and perhaps when we come into plenary and this provision is dealt with perhaps it will be appropriate for someone to put on records the background for the change. On that basis I think that there is broad agreement to the effect of keeping the text as it is before us.

The Chairman of the Drafting Committee reported that there had been a debate in the Committee in connection with the word "allegedly" that had been added in sub-paragraphs (a) and (b) of article 1(1) and that the decision had been taken to delete that word. It had in fact been accepted that the definition of "claimant" as any person asserting a maritime claim clearly indicates that the issue of liability is not yet decided at the time of arrest. The CMI text of these sub-paragraphs was therefore left unaltered.

SUB-PARAGRAPH (c)[52]

First reading—3 March 1999

There were divided views as to whether the word "registered" should be kept or deleted. The Chairman concluded the exchange of views so stating:

There is a link between this sub-paragraph and sub-paragraph (u) in article 1(1) and we kept that open. I understand that contacts are in progress in order to find a solution in respect of sub-paragraph (u) and if there is a solution that solution should logically be reflected in this sub-paragraph. I propose to adopt (iii) provisionally but to reopen it if agreement on (u) should logically require it.

SUB-PARAGRAPH (d)[53]

First reading—3 March 1999

This sub-paragraph was adopted without discussion.

SUB-PARAGRAPH (e)[54]

First reading—3 March 1999

Three questions were discussed in respect of this paragraph. Firstly, the structure: the proposal of the CMI to refer generally to the maritime liens recognized under the lex fori *rather than list the "international" maritime liens and then to refer separately to the national maritime liens met with the support of some delegations and with the opposition of others. Secondly, different views were expressed in respect of the use in the CMI text of the word "recognized" and its replacement by the word "granted" was suggested by some delegations. Thirdly, a clarification was requested in respect of the term "operator". Since the discussion of the first two questions was conducted globally, it is impossible to separate the comments made in respect of each of them.[55]*

Norway The sub-paragraph in the CMI text covers both maritime liens under art. 4 and 6 of the MLM Convention. Prof. Berlingieri explained this yesterday and I understood that he meant that this was merely a drafting point to deal with both types of liens in the same paragraph. In our view we are not sure that this is only a drafting point and would like a debate on this whether we should have the system in the JIGE text or in the CMI text. Our preference would be in favour of the JIGE text, i.e. to deal with article 4 liens in one paragraph and with article 6 liens in another paragraph.

52. Text and summary from tape No. 19.
53. Summary from tape No. 19.
54. Text and summary from tapes No. 19–21
55. The statements in favour of one of the proposals without specific comments are not reproduced.

CMI   Mr. Chairman, if you allow me to do so I should like to explain further the philosophy of this simplified text which is suggested by the CMI. Many of the delegates present here attended the JIGE sessions and they will remember that originally the draft contained only the international maritime liens, if I may call them so, the list of the liens adopted in the 1993 MLM Convention. During the debates in the JIGE the suggestion was then put forward by several delegates that also national maritime liens should be recognised or more precisely the liens existing in the place where the arrest is effected. Therefore an additional provision was inserted which appears in square brackets in the last JIGE text of the draft articles. The problem of whether or not the liens recognized by the *lex fori* should be admitted has been debated and I understand is still open to day. The CMI, after having given to this problem careful thoughts, has come to the conclusion that in order to ensure a wider acceptance of the new Arrest Convention the maritime liens recognized by the *lex fori* should be accepted because it is the feeling of the CMI that this is the best way to ensure a wider acceptance of the new Convention. The second thought which came to the CMI is that if the liens recognized by the *lex fori* are accepted, there is no real reason to list in the Convention specific maritime liens. These specific maritime liens which are listed are those of the 1993 Convention but any link with the 1993 Convention has been avoided. Therefore since these are not international liens in a strict sense, but are just copied from the 1993 Convention, if it is accepted, and of course this is the main question, Mr Chairman, I would submit this should be discussed first. If the liens of the *lex fori* are recognized, the opinion of the CMI is that it is entirely useless to specify certain maritime liens any further. So my suggestion is, but of course you are free to decide in any other way, that the problem of the admission of the liens of the *lex fori* is a first problem to be discussed. That would perhaps open the avenue for further decisions whether in case the liens of the *lex fori* are accepted there is a need for specifying certain maritime liens or not.

Chairman   Yes I think that rather to deal with the structure of this provision we should deal with the substance. I think that that was what the Norwegian delegation suggested.

Norway   We have a paper in A/CONF.CRP.3. Our proposal is that the word "recognized" should be replaced by the word "granted" and this is a quite substantial point because the reference to the recognition of such lien includes the conflict rules in force in that State, whereas the word "granted" deals only with the *lex fori* liens. That is the substantial difference. The reason we believe "recognized" should be replaced by "granted" is that it may very well follow from the general conflict of law rules of a State that national liens of another State shall be recognized and therefore be given the right of arrest, although the first State does not wish to provide for such national liens in its own maritime legislation. For that reason the word "recognized" should be replaced by "granted". We may also have the situation where a State may wish to recognize foreign national liens which are alien to the national laws of the State but without wishing to give the right of arrest on the basis of such liens. This may be so especially since the national liens will rank after all other maritime liens and all registered mortgages, hypothèques or charges according to art. 6 of the 1993 MLM Convention. A State may therefore not wish to give the right to arrest a ship on the basis of a foreign lien of this lower rank but may still wish to recognize such a national lien if the ship is sold by a forced sale instigated by an arrest made by another claimant. Also for that reason the word "recognized" should be replaced by the word "granted". There are States that do not wish to give the right of arrest on the basis of national liens but would wish to recognize the liens in other respects or would not to recognize such national liens at all in order to avoid the consequences with regard to an arrest, because there was no obligation under MLM Convention 1993 to recognize for a national lien.

China   In general, the Chinese delegation can go along with item 5 of the CMI proposals. We think it is reasonable to provide in that item that the establishment of maritime liens should be left to the provisions of national law. This is obviously to give a special protection to the claimant, and such protection should be based on the rules of the national law of the country where the arrest of the ship is effected. As to the term "recognised", according to our knowledge about the English word, the use of the term "recognised" gives too much power to the court where the arrest is effected. We think the term "granted" is much more proper, because by using "granted" to replace "recognised" it means that maritime liens are only to be determined by national law. This is a sort of restriction to the establishment of maritime liens, and thus having a better chance to arrive at a proper balance among the shipowner and other parties concerned. Following the above observations the Chinese delegation suggest that the term "recognised" in article 3 paragraph (b) of the JIGE text should also be replaced by the term "granted".

Denmark   We support Norway and China. We fully appreciate the words which have been proposed by the CMI trying to give us an easier text that I think was the explanation yesterday. But in doing so I think we are missing some point as pointed out by our Norwegian Colleague i.e. the fact that there are two sorts of liens, the art. 4 liens, i.e. the international recognized maritime liens system and then the national liens and of course in the MLM Convention there was a compromise in this respect when it was decided to have article 4 and article 6, article 4 dealing with the international liens and article 6 dealing with the national liens. And the JIGE text in fact tries in its own to federate these issues and this is of course the difficulty with the CMI text because it does not take a different view on the two different sorts of liens. On the international liens we would support the issue that they should be recognized or accepted regardless as to whether or not such liens are recognized in a member State which is not a Contracting State. For the national liens we would take a different view as explained by Norway and China. If the country concerned is Denmark we would take such national liens if it is a system that we have in our own national substantive law. And this is why we prefer the word "granted" so that we do not have to accept a system which we don't have in our national law and that I think is the basic difference between "recognized" and "granted". And I think it is essential that if we work on the CMI text we might note the difference between the article 4 and the article 6 liens of the MLM system.

Netherlands   We welcome the proposal of the CMI in this respect, that is a much more simpler approach than that in the JIGE Draft since in the Netherlands there exist only national liens. Netherlands is not a party to any international convention in which there is a more international framework of liens to be established. We like to support the addition of the phrase that has to do with liens which are recognized under the law of the State where the arrest is requested. Any Contracting State could thus decide itself which foreign liens would be recognized. Therefore we are supporting the text as it now stands.

United States   We prefer the CMI text as is. The structure of article 3(1) of the CMI text is premised entirely on the concept that States recognize maritime liens claim. This concept applies whether the liens are MLM 1993 art. 4 or art. 6 liens. Without this concept under the present draft even art. 4 liens under the MLM Convention may not be enforceable if the arresting State does not in its domestic law "grant" such liens. Or perhaps has different variations or different limitations on them. Similarly the same concept applies to the recognition and enforcement of art. 6 liens. The proposed language does not interfere with the power and authority of Contracting States to adopt their own choice of law rules to recognize or to refuse to recognize liens granted by other States. The wording of (v) states maritime liens which are recognized under the law of the State where the arrest is applied for and not under the law of the State where the lien was created. Therefore it is up to every individual State where the arrest is applied for to decide whether or not they would recognize that lien under their own law and no State would be forced to recognize a lien they would care not to recognize. As pointed out by CMI recognition of article 6 liens is designed to give the Convention broader potential acceptance. It is important to note that art. 6 of the MLM was in itself a compromise. Under that compromise national maritime liens are recognized as a valid basis to secure a claim. However these national liens are severely restricted in that they are extinguished after a short period of time and given a low priority. To now refuse to allow these liens to be recognized by other nations if they chose to would effectively render these liens unenforceable in an international context and render art. 6 and the MLM compromise meaningless in an international context. Accordingly the United States supports retention of the word "recognized" in the present text.

Canada   In our view the CMI Draft is a vast improvement on the JIGE text we had before us. You will recall that the reason why we came up with the JIGE text was an attempt to ensure to have concordance between the MLM Convention and the Arrest Convention in this particular area. However the MLM Convention is all above creating liens, a system of liens, that Countries might wish to support and create a system among themselves for the recognition of particular claims elevated to the lien status, is all about priorities, is all about the relationship between mortgages and liens whereas the Arrest Convention is all about something entirely different. All about allowing a claimant to arrest a ship in order to secure a claim. In our view there is no need for the specificity that we have in the JIGE text in making an attempt on one hand to reproduce the liens that we find and we chose in the 1993 MLM Convention and then of course if you go down that road you must inevitably come up with the problem that was just recently highlighted by our US colleague, as to what you do with those other liens that were referred to in the Convention, namely the so called national liens of art. 6. The elegance of the CMI proposal is that it focuses on the arrest of ship for maritime claims by merely saying that there is another circumstance for the arrest of a ship of course and that is if there is a maritime lien at play and by saying indeed as our American colleague has pointed out that all this is going to arise in the port in the jurisdiction of the arresting State and surely it is up to that State and its courts to determine whether there is a maritime lien that would give rise to an arrest. A lien that a Court in that State must in its judicial system recognize. It seems to inevitably follow that the word "recognized" is the word that we need here and if I may just inject my view, perhaps contrary to what we heard earlier this morning, recognition in my sense does not imply that the Court of an arresting State is somehow obliged to recognize foreign lien. It has the jurisdiction to do so if it so wishes, but of course if is not within his system to recognize a particular lien that it itself does not have in its own domestic legislation of course is free to do so but this issue will arise in the State where the ship is being arrested, whether or not there is ground for a claimant to demand the arrest of the ship. It has nothing to do in particular what lien or what charge. Therefore we are quite content with the text we now are calling "the text on the screen" and we will support it entirely.

United Kingdom   This delegation welcomes the CMI approach. We think that this is a big improvement on what we had before. We have to say to delegations that have difficulty with the proposal of using the word "granted" instead of the word "recognized", that some liens rise rather than come about because they are "granted" in any formal sense; they are not granted in a formal manner by a court or such. In UK liens are a creation of common law rather than a statute. So, for these reasons we would prefer to stick with the text that is before us on the screen. We sense that the numbers can cause some difficulty. If this committee were to move towards the replacement of "recognized" with "granted" I think we would hope that something else can be added. I am not entirely confident yet that we got the right words but I would suggest something like after "granted" to add in addition "or arising" and may be that we help those of us who prefer to stick with "recognized" but at this stage I am not offering a compromise but to keep the CMI text.

Italy   In principle we are in favour of the text as proposed by the CMI. However if we should replace the word "recognized" with "granted", it would be necessary to well clarify that maritime lien "granted" is also the maritime lien which is "recognized" by the law applicable pursuant to the private international law rules in force in the State where the arrest is made, even if that lien is not granted by the domestic law.

Germany   I think those delegates who think that the text proposed by the CMI is very elegant they are completely right, it is an elegant text. But in my view it seems to mix up two problems, that of the international liens and of the national liens, both problems are mixed under one provision. That causes problems. I think we must distinguish between national liens and international liens. As far as international liens we prefer the text of the JIGE, for the national liens we wish to replace "recognized" with "granted".

Ghana   We support the CMI text. It gives a broader basis for recognition. We favour the word "recognized". Some maritime liens are not granted, but arise.

Marshall Isl.   We support the CMI text in general and suggest to replace "recognized" by "granted" or "arise under".

Norway   We suggested "granted" in order to refer to *lex fori*; "arising under" is OK.

Chairman   If I may look at the debate "granted" versus "recognized", it is a very close poll according to my notes, but as I said the ones in favour of "recognized" have perhaps different motives, different problems dictating their preferences and indeed it was indicated by some in the "recognized" group that they could perhaps accept "granted" if some additional words were added like "or arising under" and Norway which made the initial proposal to replace "recognized" by "granted" confirmed afterwards that "granted or arising under" would be in line with its thinking. That I suppose would not help the United States or Ghana or the ones that have that motivation for preferring "recognized". I think therefore it is difficult to make a ruling. If there is a majority it is not clear, it was not made clear during the debate. Of course there were different motives for preferring "recognized". We also had the issue of drafting. Some have strongly indicated that although they appreciated that the CMI's solution or approach may be elegant, it does have an effect of substance in not distinguishing clearly between what they referred to as internationally recognized liens, that is the liens which are listed in article 4 of the MLM Convention on the one hand and national liens on the other hand. It is my feeling that those who would be in favour of such a distinction as we have in the JIGE text, that they could perhaps accept the CMI text if "recognized" were replaced by "granted". I don't know whether that is correct. I get a nod from Norway.

CMI Mr Chairman I was trying to put myself in the position of a judge who in a number of years to come will have to interpret this provision and the reason why the word "granted" or the word "recognized" has been adopted and to be quite frank, from this debate I wouldn't be able to draw any conclusion at all because many delegates have just said that they prefer one word and not the other but I have not heard the reason for which they do prefer one word or the other one. Some delegation have been very clear: they said that they want the word "granted" because they don't want that the Court of the place of arrest be able to refer to liens other than the national liens of that country. On the other hand the US delegate for example, who expressed his opinion in favour of the word "recognized", clearly stated that it is necessary to permit also the adoption of liens recognized in other countries if the local law permits to do so. I think that we should look at the substance of this problem. It seems to me that if the decision is not to permit the Court of the place of arrest to apply liens other than the national liens you would infringe upon the private international law of that country and I wonder whether we have an interest or we have the power to do so. I give you an example which is based on my own country law. Under Italian law the liens are governed by the law of the flag of the ship; so if a Tunisian ship comes to Italy, an Italian judge would apply the maritime liens existing in Tunisian law. If the word "granted" means that the Italian judge cannot do so, what on earth should he do? Would you modify private international law in Italy or in any other countries? I have doubt that this can be done but in any event, Mr Chairman, what I think is more important of all is when a decision is reached, to make clear what is the effect of that decision.

The statements relating to the term operator are reproduced below.

Denmark We have a question for the CMI in respect of the word "operator".

Chairman We can leave this last point. We inherited that word from the MLM Convention.

Chairman Are there comments as to the word "operator'?

Hong Kong Query about meaning and effect of word "operator". It has an unclear meaning. It has been suggested that it may include the "agent". Suggest deletion.

CMI I hope I can be of assistance. The term "operator" is used in several international conventions and I should like to refer specifically to the 1976 Limitation of Liability Convention where the term is used. The corresponding term used in the French version of the 1976 Convention is "armateur". It is clear therefore that the operator is the person who undertakes to operate the ship and he may be either the owner of the ship or the bareboat charterer, he is a person who employs the crew, that is the person who operates the ship. This is clear in very many jurisdictions and may not be clear in others but I wonder whether since a convention is drawn up in a number of different languages and all the texts have the same value, the fact that the corresponding term in the French text is "armateur" would help everybody.

Denmark We are grateful for CMI explanation. Very helpful.

The Chairman summarized the debates on all the above issues as follows:

Chairman We were considering paragraph (1) of article 3, on the basis of the CMI draft thereof. You will recall that there was a number of different things that were addressed and discussed. One question is the structure of paragraph 1. The question is whether we should place ourselves on the CMI draft as we tentatively decided yesterday or on some other basis as indicated by some delegations. I think that the majority were in favour of the CMI structure for paragraph (1). When it comes to sub-paragraph (v) of this paragraph which reads "the claim is against the owner, demise charterer, manager or operator of the ship and is secured by a maritime lien which is recognized under the law of the place where the arrest is applied for". A couple of things were addressed in that connection. One was the word "operator" and a couple of delegations indicated that the word was not clear and might need clarification such as in a definition. It was pointed out by the representative from the CMI that the term "operator" is one that is used in other international conventions such as in the 1976 LLMC Convention and it is also used of course in the 1993 MLM Convention and it was specifically pointed out that if it is felt that the English word "operator" in this context is unclear, guidance might be found in the other languages of the Conventions, that is the 1976 LLMC Convention and the 1993 MLM Convention and particularly the French version could be of guidance as I understood it. I assume therefore that we can retain the word "operator". When it comes to the word "recognized", you will recall that there was a very much divided view as to whether we should have the word "recognized" or the word "granted". I think that the views were evenly divided, according to my count at least. We did not explore in detail the reasons why particular delegations favoured one or the other word and it would seem to me as if some of them who prefer "recognized" could perhaps live with the word "granted" if that word was supplemented by other words such as "or arising under". I don't think I have the basis to say that that is or could be a compromise that is accepted by a majority in this room. I think that it is too early to say that. I therefore feel we must keep that issue open.

Second reading—9 March 1999[56]

Chairman   We have two sub-paragraphs outstanding in paragraph (1) of article 3 and I hope that you have the text as proposed by the CMI before you because we agreed to work on the basis of that version of paragraph (1). The first one, the first open issue is (iii) which reads: "the claim is based upon a registered mortgage, or a registered "hypothèque" or a registered charge of the same nature on the ship". That of course is also tied to sub-paragraph (n) of article 1(1) and indeed to (w) of the same paragraph or the chapeau of paragraph (1). So we will have to keep that also in abeyance for the time being. Sub-paragraph (v) of paragraph (1) of article 3 is also outstanding and is my proposal that we deal with the word "recognized" in the CMI text "recognized under the law of the State where the arrest is applied for". You will recall that this created a relatively intensive debate and it also resulted in consultations being carried out afterwards and I understand that quite a bit of work has been done and there are two CRPs which have been issued, CRP.14 which is a proposal by Norway and CRP.16 by the United States. So I suggest that we begin with CRP.14. May I invite the Norwegian delegate please?

Norway   Last week Norway presented a paper CRP.3 with a proposal that the word "recognized" in article 3(1)(b) of the JIGE text which now is paragraph (1)(v) in the text should be replaced by the word "granted". In view of the debate on this the UK delegation suggested that the text as amended according to the Norwegian proposal should read "granted or arising under" because in common law systems a lien may arise without being actually granted. On this basis Norway has amended its proposal accordingly so that it now reads "the claim is against the owner etc. and is secured by a maritime lien which is granted or arises under the law of the State when the arrest is applied for". The amended proposal is submitted in CRP.14. In the debate last week as perceived by our delegation there was a majority in favour of the Norwegian proposal, but there was also a number of delegations who stated that their preference was to keep the word "recognized". It was not entirely clear from the debate, however, how many of these who did not support the Norwegian proposal disagreed on a matter of substance and for how many of these delegations it was the actual wording of the proposal and not in fact the substance of it that was not found satisfactory. On this background we carried out informal consultations with most of the delegations whose preference last week was to keep the word "recognized". Most of the delegations that we have had the time to consult with have indicated to us that the text "granted or arising under" is acceptable for them. However there are also some delegations that we have consulted with who did not support the substantive idea of the Norwegian proposal and this, Mr Chairman, is when the United States proposal comes into the picture. In that proposal a second sentence is added which has the effect that the United States proposal represents the opposite view on the substance than the Norwegian proposal. In order that I do not speak twice on this subject I might give some comments on the US proposal, if that is OK. This delegation appreciates the United States delegation's efforts in this matter but I am afraid that we do not perceive the United States proposal as a compromise. I will come back to that. The question we considered is whether the reference to the law of the State where the arrest is applied for in (v) shall include also the conflict of law rules of that State, in which case the word "recognized" should be kept. If the rules should include only the substantive law of that State, which is our position, in that case the wording should be "granted or arises". I would like to elaborate a little further on the Norwegian point of view, Mr Chairman. There are three points I

---

56. Text and summary from tapes Nos. 61–63. The most relevant statements are reproduced in whole or in part.

would like to make. Firstly I would like to point out – and this is quite important – the fact that our concern relates only to the national liens and not to the international liens. That is why it was our preference last week that these two different kind of maritime liens should be dealt with in two different paragraphs as it was done in the JIGE text and not in one and the same paragraph which is done in the CMI text of sub-paragraph (v). So our concern really relates only to national liens. As for the international liens we think the rule should be as it is in the JIGE text. The second point I would like to make is that the effect of the Norwegian proposal is not that one may not arrest the ship to secure a claim for which there is a foreign national lien. The effect is only that for such an arrest to be made the requirement of the main rule of article 3(1)(i) and (ii) as drafted or the sister ship rule must be complied with, unless such lien is granted or arises under the substantive law of the arresting State. As we understand it, the effect of the United States proposal would be the opposite. In fact to this delegation it seems that the United States proposal goes even further in the other direction than the JIGE text, as in the United States proposal it is not even a requirement that the lien shall be recognized by the arresting State in order to be a basis for arrest. As I understand it in the American proposal the existence of a national lien is only a requirement for arrest to be made and this is clearly not acceptable by this delegation. This leads me to the third point which is in this delegation's view the basic question to be considered that is the following. Do we want an article 3 which is effectively binding for States parties regarding which ships may be arrested, which is the objective of this delegation or we want article 3 to be in fact only a minimum rule allowing States parties to arrest any ship on the basis only that in the claimant's State there is a national lien for the claim? This is the effect of the United States proposal, if we understand it correctly. This is a question that we think goes to the core of this Convention and the matter is one of deep concern to this delegation. In our view it is absolutely essential that article 3 is in effect binding with regard to what ship may be arrested. If this Convention shall effectively strike the necessary balance with regard to the free movement of trade, this is not a question which should be left to national law to the creation and recognition of national maritime liens and therefore it is this delegation's view that unless the lien is granted or arises under the substantive law of the State where the arrest is made the general requirement of article 3 must be complied with for the arrest to be made. And this is why we propose that in paragraph 1(v) the word "recognized" shall be replaced with "granted or arises" and without the second sentence proposed in CRP.16 of the United States.

United States The written proposal submitted by the United States[57] leaves to the domestic law of the State where the arrest is sought the issue of whether to allow an arrest for a lien such as those granted under article 6 of the 1993 MLM Convention. The proposed change to delete the word "recognized" and substitute for it the phrase "granted or arising under" in article 3(1)(5) has the effect of prohibiting a country from arresting for any claim not reflected in a local law. The addition of the second sentence provides necessary flexibility. It does not impose any obligation on any State to enforce article 6 liens, but it does permit countries whose choice of law rules allow the application of foreign law to apply it. This is consistent with the approach taken in other parts of this Convention and the discussions reflecting that the *lex fori* applies in a number of circumstances including article 2(5) with respect to procedures, article 3(2) with respect to ownership, article 6 with respect to securities to be posted by arresting parties and issues of wrongful or unjustified arrest, article 7 with respect to the timing of initiation of suits on the merits. The provisions of the Arrest Convention should not prohibit countries from choosing to enforce article 6 liens if such enforcement is permitted under the local law. Accordingly the United States proposes the revision of article 3(5) set forth in our written proposal.

ICS We fully agree with the statement made by the Norwegian delegation. Our preference would also be to retain the JIGE text of article 3(1)(a) and 3(1)(b) replacing "recognized" with "granted" in article 3(1)(b) of the JIGE text. This was partly because we preferred that structure which drew a distinction between international maritime liens on the one hand and national liens on the other and also because we had understood that one of the objectives of this Conference was to align this Arrest Convention with the MLM Convention, that of course without specifically referring to the MLM Convention, so that the Arrest Convention would stand alone. We can however support the Norwegian proposal to amend the CMI text but we cannot accept the United States proposal. Article 1 contains a long list of claims and the individual categories of claims are very broad. We haven't yet

57. The proposal is in document CRP.16, *supra*, p. 458.

decided whether that list is going to be open or closed. The fact is that some States may grant maritime lien status to all the claims in article 1 and I think that it would be going against the spirit of the Arrest Convention if we allow those national maritime liens to travel with the ship to other jurisdictions. We have the general rule in article 3 that permits arrest of a ship owned by the person personally liable for the maritime claim and then we have the exception to the general rule, one of which is claims secured by maritime liens. But if we allow that claims which are secured by national maritime liens which as I said earlier could mean all of the claims in article 1, then the exceptional case in fact becomes the rule and there would be no need for the claimant to establish personal liability on the part of the debtor. He will simply be allowed to say my claim is secured by a maritime lien and this to us seems to undermine the whole structure of the Arrest Convention and is going to lead to great uncertainty on the part of shipowners and other debtors.

Sweden   We would like to thank the Norwegian delegation for their excellent introduction of their proposal. In short we are in favour of their proposal, so therefore we support the Norwegian proposal.

Italy   We are in principle in agreement with the Norwegian proposal. But we think we may have a suggestion in order to simplify the wording. We could substitute for the word "granted" the word "applicable", i.e. "secured by a maritime lien applicable in accordance with the law of the State in which arrest is demanded". Then the applicable law, viz. the law of the State where the arrest is demanded would also include conflict of law rules and this would include also the last part of the proposal: it would include both the national maritime liens and the national maritime liens applicable pursuant to the conflict of law rules.

Netherlands   When the question first arose under the proposal made by CMI we were quite happy so to say with the word "recognized" and during the debate the words "granted or arises" came up and our understanding at that time was that it also did not create very much problems. But the problem was created when, as it was explained just in the statement by Norway that this kind of drafting would exclude what we could refer to as rules of private international law by which other law systems would be applicable that is granting liens for claims being recognized under national law. And in that sense my delegation has problems with that because the way the Courts in Holland apply the rules of private international law is such that liens are being recognized that are established under the law where the ships are registered, so to say we have a specific ruling to the effect that foreign national liens are being recognized as such in the Netherlands law. When Italy in its intervention came up with the suggestion that the word "recognized" could be replaced by "acceptable" that would have addressed our concerns in this respect. We need something in addition to what has been proposed by Norway and the way in which the United States has drafted an additional sentence comes in that respect in that direction. In order perhaps to find some common field to reach a further compromise my delegation would like to offer a further restricted approach, not to just refer to the law system under which maritime liens are granted by the applicable foreign law but just more specifically in the last sentence to refer to the law of the State in which the ship is registered. So in that sense the interest of the shipowner would also be safeguarded in the sense that it could rely on his own national law, but then claims that are granted a lien under the law of the flag State would be also enforceable within the jurisdiction of another State.

Denmark   We support the Norwegian proposal. When we decided last week to speak on this issue we in fact went from the JIGE text to the CMI text and the difference between those two texts was as explained by our Norwegian colleague that in the JIGE text there is a separation between different sorts of maritime liens. Maritime liens according to article 4 in the MLM Convention were dealt in one point, in fact we could go along in accepting all those maritime liens, the international ones, in article 4 of the MLM Convention. But the second part of course is the difficult part, the one about the national liens, which was of course, I think—I wasn't present in 1993 when the Conference adopted the MLM Convention—but that was the discussion point there as well and this was why the national maritime liens were placed in article 6 and of course that was a discussion point there and still is a discussion point to-day. . . . To come back to the two proposals, they might look very similar, but as pointed the speakers before me, the Norwegian colleague and ICS, it is so that the sheer existence of a maritime lien, and that is of course a national maritime lien, would be enough for the arrest issue. That is I think the concept of the American proposal, whereas it is not the concept of the Norwegian proposal and would be so that the exceptional case would be the general rule. . . . Just a few comments on the other issues which were raised by other delegates. I would say

I don't think the Dutch proposal would solve the question, because is still much wide, but we would thank the Dutch colleague for his imagination and to try to help us along the way. As for the Italian proposal, one must realize that what we are discussing is whether or not we will accept that the international private law should establish a basis for recognition or acceptance of maritime liens or whether or not it should be up to the substantive law. I think that is the whole problem we are discussing, and it has been referred to in all the interventions, those at least in fact supporting the Norwegian proposal. In order to clarify this I would suggest that in the text of the Norwegian proposal after the word "the" and before the word "law" we could add the word "substantive", because then there would be no confusion at least about what we are discussing.

Malta   We support wholeheartedly the Norwegian proposal. This is the more attractive one because it ensures certainty. I would like to comment on the Italian proposal in respect of the word "applicable". In our view that word is too vague and therefore detracts from the certainty and clarity of the position as expounded by Norway.

United States   In the discussions this morning some delegations pointed out that an important goal of this Diplomatic Conference is to align the Arrest Convention with the 1993 MLM Convention. That is the intent of CRP.16, our proposal. Another delegation suggested that article 6 liens do not follow the ship and that that was agreed to at the 1993 MLM, but under the 1993 MLM Convention is was expressly provided in article 6(a) that article 6 liens "shall be subject to the provisions of article 8, 10 and 12". Article 8 of the MLM Convention states: "Maritime liens follow the vessel notwithstanding any change of ownership or registration or of flag". Article 10 provides that such liens are assignable. Article 12 provides that all claims, article 4 liens, article 6 liens and mortgages are extinguished on a judicial sale. These essential clauses of the liens are the same whether they arise under article 4 or article 6. The compromise reached in 1993 was that these liens would have the same characteristics than article 4 liens but would have a lower priority and a shorter duration. According to the agreement reached in 1993 the priority of a lien is irrelevant to the decision to allow an arrest for that lien. That agreement is now being ignored and the status of article 6 liens is effectively erased. The United States proposal simply allows a State Party to apply its own law including its choice of law rules in determining whether to arrest for a maritime lien claim. If the choice of law rules do not permit application of foreign law then you do not have to arrest the ship, we reiterate that there are two elements which must be met before a ship can be arrested: 1) the claim must give rise to a maritime lien under the relevant foreign law and, 2) the *lex fori* must provide the application of that foreign law. Without these two elements no arrest can be allowed. Under the Norwegian proposal some States Parties would be compelled to ignore their own choice of law rules. This infringement on the Coastal States rights should not be allowed.

Chairman   When you say that the characteristic of a lien, be it an article 4 or an article 6 lien under the MLM Convention is that they travel with the vessel, that is correct, I think. But that does not really connote the geographical movement, it does not really connote that the lien would have survived the passing of the frontier, that it will survive from one country to another. What it basically means is that if the vessel is sold the lien will attach to the vessel, so I think that the question of recognition is a different issue from the concept "travels with the vessel". I think you agree and on that basis I don't think with respect that either of the proposals would be in conflict with the MLM Convention.

United States   With respect Mr Chairman I believe that if an arrest is not allowed for an article 6 lien it essentially becomes useless. The MLM 1993 did not address the question of when, where or how a ship would be arrested. That was expressly left for this Group in the JIGE 7, 8 and 9 and in the Diplomatic Conference that has been called for the attempt to implement a new Arrest Convention to address the questions of when, where and how an arrest would be made. The choice of law rules of a country are their own creation. The proposal put forward by Norway would require some States to ignore their choice of law rules in applying MLM 1993, should it be adopted.

Chairman   That does not mean that it is in conflict with the MLM Convention, because this Convention can impose obligations on States to restrict whatever national rules they have.

Chairman   It seems that there is an overwhelming majority in favour of the Norwegian proposal as contained in CRP.14. Denmark has suggested that it should be further clarified adding the words "under the substantive law". Nobody has referred to it. I think that is a drafting point.

Peru   We do not share the view that it is a drafting point in that we would deal with the capability of a court to apply its own rules. If we talk about conflict of law rules, these are not included in the substantive law, since they are conflict rules. Consequently it would not be proper to add an adjective to the law of the State. In our country when we talk about substantive law we exclude procedural law which determines the form of the arrest.

United Kingdom   We are against the addition.

1999 Convention

1. ARREST IS PERMISSIBLE OF ANY SHIP IN RESPECT OF WHICH A MARITIME CLAIM IS ASSERTED IF:

    (A)   THE PERSON WHO OWNED THE SHIP AT THE TIME WHEN THE MARITIME CLAIM AROSE IS LIABLE FOR THE CLAIM AND IS OWNER OF THE SHIP WHEN THE ARREST IS EFFECTED; OR

    (B)   THE DEMISE CHARTERER OF THE SHIP AT THE TIME WHEN THE MARITIME CLAIM AROSE IS LIABLE FOR THE CLAIM AND IS DEMISE CHARTERER OR OWNER OF THE SHIP WHEN THE ARREST IS EFFECTED; OR

    (C)   THE CLAIM IS BASED UPON A MORTGAGE OR A "HYPOTHÈQUE" OR A CHARGE OF THE SAME NATURE ON THE SHIP; OR

    (D)   THE CLAIM RELATES TO THE OWNERSHIP OR POSSESSION OF THE SHIP; OR

    (E)   THE CLAIM IS AGAINST THE OWNER, DEMISE CHARTERER, MANAGER OR OPERATOR OF THE SHIP AND IS SECURED BY A MARITIME LIEN WHICH IS GRANTED OR ARISES UNDER THE LAW OF THE STATE WHERE THE ARREST IS APPLIED FOR.

PARAGRAPH 2

Draft of the CMI International Sub-Committee

(2) ARREST MAY BE MADE OF ANY SHIP WHICH AT THE TIME WHEN ARREST PROCEEDINGS ARE COMMENCED IS OWNED [OR CONTROLLED] BY [OR IN THE POSSESSION OF] THE PERSON WHO, AT THE TIME WHEN THE MARITIME CLAIM AROSE WAS:

    (I)   OWNER OF [OR IN CONTROL OR POSSESSION OF] THE SHIP IN RESPECT OF WHICH THE MARITIME CLAIM AROSE, OR

    (II)   BARE BOAT CHARTERER, TIME CHARTERER OR VOYAGE CHARTERER OF THAT SHIP

AND IS PERSONALLY LIABLE FOR THAT CLAIM.

Report of the Chairman of the CMI International Sub-Committee

The sister ship rule in para 2 makes it possible to arrest the debtor's other ships. The rule is the same as in the 1952 Convention. However, between square brackets an extension of the rule is suggested. The text within square brackets would make it possible to arrest a ship owned by a subsidiary of the debtor or, if the debtor is a person, by a company owned by him. It would also make it possible to arrest a ship in his possession, i.e. by virtue of a charter party. At least the latter extension may be thought to go too far.

In draft 2 an attempt was made to formulate a rule on the lifting of the veil. In the present draft this attempt has been limited to the text in square brackets.

CMI Draft

(2) ARREST IS PERMISSIBLE OF ANY OTHER SHIP OR SHIPS WHICH, WHEN THE ARREST IS EFFECTED, IS OR ARE OWNED BY THE PERSON WHO IS PERSONALLY LIABLE FOR THE MARITIME CLAIM AND WHO WAS, WHEN THE CLAIM AROSE:

    (A)   OWNER OF THE SHIP IN RESPECT OF WHICH THE MARITIME CLAIM AROSE; OR

    (B)   BAREBOAT CHARTERER, TIME CHARTERER OR VOYAGE CHARTERER OF THAT SHIP.

THIS PROVISION DOES NOT APPLY TO CLAIMS IN RESPECT OF OWNERSHIP OR POSSESSION OF A SHIP.

CMI Report

The "sistership" rule

57. Under the 1952 Convention it is always possible to arrest the particular ship in respect of which the maritime claim has arisen regardless against whom the claim is made. Only when it comes to other ships than the ship in respect of which the maritime claim has arisen does the 1952 Convention take the personal liability into consideration. Ships other than the particular ship in respect of which the maritime claim has arisen which are owned by the owner of that ship may be arrested only if the owner is personally liable for the claim. On the other hand, if somebody else, be it the bareboat or other charterer or any other party, is personally liable for the claim, any ships owned by such charterer or other party may be arrested for the claim.

58. Paragraph (2) of Article 3 provides for a rule practically identical to the situation under the 1952 Convention. Sisterships belonging to the owner may be arrested if the owner is liable for the claim. Any ships belonging to the bareboat, time or voyage charterer may be arrested if that charterer is liable for the claim. However, such ships may not be arrested if the claim is for the ownership or possession of a ship. Then only that ship may be arrested. This is also in conformity with the 1952 Convention. A proposal was made that this restriction should be deleted, but it was upheld by the Conference.

59. The relevant time with respect to ownership of the sistership is the time when the arrest is effected.

60. There is no limitation on the number of ships that may be arrested other than that when sufficient security has been obtained to cover the whole of the claim no more ships may be arrested.

61. The International Sub-Committee made an attempt to draft a rule in relation to the sistership rule permitting the lifting of the veil between several companies owning ships when those companies are owned or controlled by the same persons. The 1952 Convention contained a not very clear provision of this nature in Article 3 paragraph (2). The Conference found that this problem is of a more general nature and that a solution should not be attempted with specific application in arrest situations but that the problem would have to be left to national law.

JIGE
Seventh Session, 5–9 December 1994

Report—Annex I

17. One delegation proposed amending the first sentence of article 3(2) of the CMI Draft to read "(2) Arrest is <u>also</u> permissible of any <u>other</u> ship or ships . . . ".

Draft Articles 1994

(2) ARREST IS [ALSO] PERMISSIBLE OF ANY [OTHER] SHIP OR SHIPS WHICH, WHEN THE ARREST IS EFFECTED, IS OR ARE OWNED BY THE PERSON WHO IS PERSONALLY LIABLE FOR THE MARITIME CLAIM AND WHO WAS, WHEN THE CLAIM AROSE:

   (A)   OWNER OF THE SHIP IN RESPECT OF WHICH THE MARITIME CLAIM AROSE; OR

   (B)   BAREBOAT CHARTERER, TIME CHARTERER OR VOYAGE CHARTERER OF THAT SHIP.

THIS PROVISION DOES NOT APPLY TO CLAIMS IN RESPECT OF OWNERSHIP OR POSSESSION OF A SHIP.

Report—Annex I

43. The Sessional Group agreed to place the three proposals in brackets for further discussion. It was also agreed to remove the brackets around the words "also" and "other" in paragraph (2) of article 3.

Draft Articles 1997

(2) ARREST IS ALSO PERMISSIBLE OF ANY OTHER SHIP OR SHIPS WHICH, WHEN THE ARREST IS EFFECTED, IS OR ARE OWNED BY THE PERSON WHO IS PERSONALLY LIABLE FOR THE MARITIME CLAIM AND WHO WAS, WHEN THE CLAIM AROSE:

    (A)   OWNER OF THE SHIP IN RESPECT OF WHICH THE MARITIME CLAIM AROSE[; OR

    (B)   DEMISE CHARTERER, TIME CHARTERER OR VOYAGE CHARTERER OF THAT SHIP].

THIS PROVISION DOES NOT APPLY TO CLAIMS IN RESPECT OF OWNERSHIP OR POSSESSION OF A SHIP.

Diplomatic Conference
Comments and Proposals

Hong Kong, China

DOCUMENT 188/3

15. "When the arrest is effected" should be changed to "when proceedings in which the arrest is effected are commenced" as this should quite comfortably fit civil law and common law jurisdictions. "When the arrest is effected" will give rise to uncertainty and dispute and it should be avoided as should claims for unjustified arrest which may be generated by the transfer of ownership of a ship between commencement of proceedings and the date when an arrest is effected, whether in a common law or civil law jurisdiction. It may be impossible to ascertain whether there has been any such change of ownership between these two dates.

17. Delete the words "or ships" and "or are" in the first line in order to avoid multiple arrests.

Thailand

DOCUMENT 188/3

86. The square bracket in paragraph 2(b) should also be removed. As a general principle, all assets of the debtor are available for execution. It is therefore logical to allow the arrest of any ship belonging to the party personally liable to a maritime claim in alternative to the ship in respect of which the claim arose. For example, the owner of the ship in respect of which the claim arose should be allowed to arrest a vessel belonging to the charterers for disputes on charter party. Paragraph 2 follows the concept of the 1952 Convention but the wording is amended to clarify that any ship belonging to the owner of the ship in respect of which the claim arose is arrestable only where the owner is personally liable for the claim, and any ship belonging to the demise, time or voyage charterer is arrestable where that charterer is personally liable to the claim.

United Kingdom

DOCUMENT 188/3/ADD.2

Introduction

9. The Government of the United Kingdom proposes an amendment to article 3 of the draft convention on the arrest of ships. Like the proposal made by the International Maritime Committee (CMI), the proposed amendment would clarify that national law would determine whether a claimant may arrest a ship other than the particular ship in respect of which the maritime claim arises. It goes further than the CMI proposal, however, by providing explicitly for the arrest of "associated" ships (associated ships are ships that are in common control). We also discuss the definition of control, and whether the convention ought to contain any guidance.

Background

10. The 1952 Convention on Arrest of Ships seeks to strike an equitable balance between the interests of shipowners and those of claimants. Article 3(1) of the 1952 Convention provides for the

arrest of "sister" ships. A claimant may arrest either the particular ship in respect of which a maritime claim arises, or any other ship owned by the person who is, at the time when the maritime claim arises, the owner of the particular ship. Article 3(2) of the 1952 Convention provides that ships shall be deemed to be in the same ownership when all the shares therein are owned by the same person or persons.

11. Since 1952, the stratagem of the single-ship company has proliferated. As a result, few ships have "sisters" within the meaning of the 1952 Convention. The only option available to many claimants, therefore, is to arrest the particular ship in respect of which the maritime claim arises. The balance that the 1952 Convention sought to strike has tilted in favour of the shipowner.

12. The Government of the United Kingdom understands that article 3(2) of the draft convention addresses this problem by implicitly allowing States to specify which ships are in common owner-ship under national law. We agree with the CMI that it would be better to make this explicit. Our preference, however, would be to go further. We believe that article 3(2) should provide explicitly for the arrest of associated ships.

Proposal

13. As currently drafted, the new convention would provide for the arrest both of the particular ship in respect of which the claim arises, and of other ships owned by the person liable for the claim. We wonder, however, whether this approach would provide sufficient flexibility.

14. The use of the concept of ownership might limit the scope of the provision. In the same way that the single-ship company proliferated after 1952, future developments in the shipping industry might reduce the usefulness of the concept of common ownership.

15. We therefore propose that the provision provide explicitly for the arrest of "associated" ships. We propose further that it use the concept of control as the criterion for establishing an association. We believe that this would provide greater scope for national law to keep pace with developments that might otherwise prevent attempts to pierce the corporate veil.

16. The following amendments to article 3 would give effect to these proposals:

    (1) [No change.]

    (2) Arrest is also permissible of any ship or ships controlled by the person who:

        (a) is allegedly liable for the maritime claim; or

        (b) controls the company that is allegedly liable for the maritime claim,

      and who was, when the claim arose:

        (i) the person who controlled the ship in respect of which the maritime claim arose[; or

        (ii) the demise charterer, time charterer or voyage charterer of that ship[, or any part of it]].

    (3) For the purposes of this article, a person controls a ship if that person owns the ship or controls the company that owns it. The national law of the State in which the arrest is applied for shall determine whether, for these purposes, a person owns a ship or controls a company that owns a ship.

    (4) Paragraph (2) shall not apply to claims in respect of ownership or possession of a ship.

    (5) Notwithstanding the provisions of paragraph (1), the arrest of a ship which is not controlled by the person allegedly liable for the claim shall be permissible only if, under the law of the State where the arrest is applied for, a judgment in respect of that claim can be enforced against that ship by judicial or forced sale of that ship.

17. The changes of substance are those that we have made to paragraphs (2) and (3). The new paragraph (4) is the tail-piece to the current article 3(2). The new article 3(5) is the current article 3(3), to which we have some consequential amendments.

18. As under the current wording of article 3(2), a claimant would not be able to arrest an associated ship which happened to be demise-, voyage- or time-chartered to the person liable for a maritime claim. However, if a person became liable for a maritime claim while chartering a ship, a claimant would be able to arrest any ship which that person controlled (either by owning it or

controlling the company that owns it). We do not intend that a demise charterer would be a person having "control" of a ship simply by virtue of being a demise charterer.

19. We have added the words "or any part of it" to the new article 3(2)(b) to cover slot charterers. We believe that the drafting of article 1(1), particularly subparagraph (f), is sufficiently wide for claims for which a slot charterer might be liable to fall within the definition of "maritime claim".

Definition of control

20. In the interests of the uniformity of international maritime law, the Diplomatic Conference might wish to provide States with some guidance on how national law might define the concept of "control". Should the Conference decide that this is desirable, we suggest that the guidance should consist of a list of criteria, as in article 13 of the 1989 International Convention on Salvage.

21. The Conference may wish to include such criteria in the convention itself. Alternatively, it may prefer to offer them as a model for national law, perhaps by means of a conference resolution. The Conference may wish to consider the following text as a basis for either of these approaches:

> The State in which the arrest is applied for may set criteria in its national law, or provide for a case-by-case examination, for the purpose of determining whether a person owns a ship or controls a company that owns a ship. All relevant factors should be taken into account, including whether the following criteria (without regard to their order) apply in respect of the ships concerned:
> (a) Common or similar names;
> (b) Common shareholding of the companies owning the ships;
> (c) Common management of the shipowning companies;
> (d) Common financing arrangements;
> (e) Cross-guarantees or other security between the shipowning companies; and
> (f) Insurance on a fleet basis.

Evidence

22. Another important issue that national law would need to consider is the burden of proof. For example, national law could place the burden of proof on the claimant, or on the person that the claimant has alleged controls two associated ships. However, there is no need to make this explicit in the convention. The rule contained in article 2(5) suffices: procedural issues are a matter for national law.

Action requested of the Diplomatic Conference

23. The delegation of the United Kingdom requests that the Diplomatic Conference:

(a) Adopt the amendment to article 3 set out in paragraph 16 above;
(b) Consider the need for guidance as suggested in paragraph 20 above.

CMI

DOCUMENT 188/3

142. Two problems arise in respect of this paragraph: (a) whether the right to arrest other ships may be granted also when the person liable is the demise charterer, time charterer or voyage charterer of the ship in respect of which the maritime claim arose, and (b) whether the owner of such other ship(s) is only the registered owner or whether piercing the corporate veil is permitted.

(a) The right of arrest of ships owned by the demise charterer, time charterer or voyage charterer as security for claims that have arisen in respect of the chartered ship is the only means available to the claimant to obtain security, since he may not – except for the demise charterer but only within the limits set out in the subsequent paragraph 3 – arrest the ship in respect of which the claim has arisen.

It is thought, therefore, that the provision in sub-paragraph (b) should be maintained and the square brackets should be deleted.

(b) Article 3(2) of the 1952 Convention provides that ships are deemed to be in the same ownership when all shares therein are owned by the same person or persons. This provision has sometimes been considered not to permit piercing the corporate veil. In particular, the French decisions upholding the arrest of a ship owned by a different company, when the same person or persons control and operate that company and the company owning the ship in respect of which the maritime claim arose have been considered to be in breach of Article 3(2).

This provision has not been reproduced in the Lisbon Draft nor in the Draft Articles. However, Art. 3(2) of the Draft Articles could be interpreted in such a way as to limit the right of arrest and to prohibit piercing of the corporate veil.

If the Conference agrees that this problem should be left to national law and will consider that Article 3(2) could be interpreted as suggested above, an amendment for the purpose of excluding the possibility of such interpretation would be advisable.

In such a case the following sentence, to be added after sub-paragraphs (a) and (b), could be considered:

> The question whether a ship is owned by the person who is liable for the maritime claim shall be decided in accordance with the national law of the State in which the arrest is applied for.

Canada

DOCUMENT CRP.1

2.3 Articles 3(1)(e)(i) and 3(2) provide that the power of arrest described therein can be exercised respectively if the person who owned the ship owned it at the time when the "arrest is effected" or if the demise charterer was the demise charterer at the time the "arrest is effected".

2.4 The problem created by using the time of arrest rather than the time of commencement of an action is that a defendant shipowner might avoid arrest by concealing the ship or possibly by selling it in order to defeat a claim that is already the subject matter of litigation.

2.5 Canada therefore proposes that the words "arrest is effected" where they appear in these provisions be replaced with "action is commenced".

2.6 Article 3(2) addresses the issue of the arrest of "sister" ships. One problem experienced with existing legislation in this area is that a very narrow range of ships is included because of the requirement that the owner of the ship, as the subject of the action, must be identical to the "beneficial owner" of the target ship. With one-ship companies in a large fleet, each of the ship-owning companies usually owns only one ship, and is not the "beneficial owner" of any others.

2.7 Therefore Canada proposes to remedy this problem by amending the text of this provision as follows:

> "3(2) Arrest is also permissible of any other ship or ships which, when the arrest is effected, is or are owned or beneficially owned by the person who was, when the claim arose:
> (a) owner or beneficial owner of the ship in respect of which the maritime claim arose; or
> (b) demise charterer, time charterer or voyage charterer of that ship.
> This provision does not apply to claims in respect of ownership or possession of a ship.
> 3(3) Notwithstanding the provisions of paragraphs (1) and (2) of this article, the arrest of a ship which is not owned or beneficially owned by the person allegedly liable for the claim shall be permissible only if, under the law of the State where the arrest is demanded, a judgment in respect of that claim can be enforced against that ship by judicial or forced sale of that ship."

Proceedings of the Main Committee

The Main Committee considered the proposals of the delegations of Canada and of the United Kingdom as well as the proposal of the CMI. Although none of these proposals was accepted, the problem raised by them is of so great an interest that it is convenient to reproduce here the full transcript of the debate which took place during the first reading and then during the second reading.

First reading—3 March 1999[58]

United Kingdom   Doc. A/Conf.188/3/Add.2. The UK is aware that the proposal we have made is a significant one. This proposal has been made after very interesting consultations with all interested sectors in the UK. We have been encouraged by the positive responses we have received. Naturally there have been some concerns in certain quarters but tried to keep the proposal we have made within reasonable limits and consistent with the broad principles set out in this draft convention. We heard earlier from the distinguished delegate from Belgium and others that there are good reasons to deal with those who try to take advantage of one ship company to avoid the effect of the sister ship provision in the 1952 Convention. We believe our proposal is essential to meet the changed circumstances that have come about since the 1952 Convention. As currently drafted the new Arrest Convention would provide for the arrest both of the particular ship in respect of which the claim arose and other ships owned by the person liable for the claim. The UK's proposal to amend art. 3 is similar in one respect at least to the proposal made by the CMI. These proposals would we believe clarify that national law determining whether a claimant may arrest a ship other than the particular ship in respect of which the maritime claim arose. But our proposal goes further than the CMI. It provides explicitly for the arrest of associated ships. Associated ships are those that are in common control and I emphasize "control". The absence of a definition of ownership should enable States to define the concept under national law. This would provide States with some scope to re-establish a fair balance between the interest of shipowners and the interest of claimants. I wonder however whether that approach would provide sufficient flexibility. The use of the concept of ownership might limit the scope of the provision. After 1952 the single ship companies proliferated severely limiting the scope for arrest of sister ships and further developments of the shipping industry might similarly reduce the usefulness of the new Arrest Convention unless we build some flexibility from the outset. We therefore propose a provision to provide for the arrest of associated ships. We propose further that we use the concept of control and I emphasize "control" as the criterium for establishing an association and by establishing an association we mean association by virtue of in the UK what we would call ownership but with effective control. In other words we do not intend to catch professional ships management companies nor agents simply acting on behalf of shipowners; neither do we intend to catch banks or other investors with minority share ownership but no element of effective control. This approach would provide greater scope for national law to keep pace with developments that otherwise might prevent attempts to pierce the so called corporate veil. We believe some further drafting may be appropriate to take account of decisions already taken in this Committee and discussions with other delegations who have expressed interest in our proposal. Turning to the definition of control if the Conference adopts the approach of associated ships arrest it might wish to provide States with some guidance on how national law should define the concept of control. This would help to promote the uniformity of international maritime law that we are here to seek. Delegations may wish to refer to paragraph 1 of our paper as a possible way forward, not the only one necessarily, but a possible way. The Conference may wish to introduce such criteria in the Convention itself. Alternatively it may prefer to offer them as a model for national law perhaps by means of a Conference resolution. The UK proposal includes some texts the Conference may wish to consider as a basis for either of these approaches.

Canada   Canada in A/CONF.188/CRP.1[59] paragraphs 2.6 and 2.7 in effect made a proposal somewhat similar to the proposal put forward by the UK, based on the concept of "beneficial ownership". We do not insist that our proposal be given independent consideration and can perhaps work on the basis of the UK proposal.

58. Text from tapes Nos. 22–25.
59. *Supra*, at p. 481.

Netherlands We associate ourselves with the UK and Canada proposals. We are ready to work on the basis of either the concept of "control" or that of "beneficial ownership". It would be necessary to make clear in the Convention what is meant by "control" or by "beneficial ownership". It should be made clear that this is meant to restore the balance that existed in 1952 that has been distorted since there. My delegation would be happy to explain these concepts further.

Italy The problem raised by Belgium must find a solution in the concept of control but it is a difficult task since it implies piercing the corporate veil of the legal person. The notion given by UK is that is deemed owner the person who controls the owner. This is probably insufficient since it is not sufficient the majority shareholding but an actual control is required. I believe that the second part of the proposal, viz. to refer to the *lex fori* is the best solution.

Denmark We are not in favour of piercing the corporate veil. We have a very negative view on this system. The word "control" is not very precise and I think that to this the UK would say we would like to make it more precise so to open a discussion on that or have a resolution or whatever but I think it does not satisfy our concern. As to the words "beneficial owner" it is not a system that we recognize in our own national legislation and it would be difficult for us to have it here. What we have here is a preliminary measure that must be decided in a very short period of time and within that limited period of time the claimant would have to prove something that in my country has been difficult even in criminal cases that go on for many years to establish this sort of economic link. Our Court would decide that it is beyond their powers to pierce the corporate veil. You can put something in your national law. But that would go against uniformity.

Greece We are against. The proposal protects the interests UK has in the whole shipping industry. It protects the interests of the banking institutions, the interests of ship management companies. Greece as traditional maritime country has other interests, it is interested in shipping per se and because I like frank talking our shipping is against it. Is against it not only for economic reasons, because we believe that this proposal is going really to create a mess in international transportation by sea. That is why, Mr. Chairman, we strongly voice our disagreement to this proposal. But because we are here in order to reach a compromise we have a fall back position. Our fall back position is the position taken by CMI, that is if other countries think that this is important, to put something in the text suggesting that this matter should be left to national law, that national law decides on it, especially if a sovereign State wants to lift the corporate veil across the board, but in this Convention on Arrest of Ships we cannot agree with the UK proposal.

Japan We basically support the idea that is present in the UK and Canada proposals. We have an established rule, not a statutory rule, an established case law of piercing the corporate veil and recently for example the Tokyo District Court lifted the corporate veil of a shipping company. But we are not glad if the Convention goes into the details of the conditions when the corporate veil is pierced because according to our case law the Court is to take account of relevant factors and no specific factors are named to be taken into consideration.

Russian Fed. We object to the United Kingdom proposal stated in document 183/3/Add. 2, although we highly appreciate the efforts of the United Kingdom delegation in the preparation of the rules relating to the arrest of associated ships on the basis of using the concept of common control. We share the opinion of other delegations concerning the grounds of unacceptability of this concept for the unification of the rules relating to the arrest of ships. We remain adherents to the concept of common ownership, which is used in the 1952 Convention and in the draft of the new Convention. We are not going to dwell on the details of this proposal, but we note the indefiniteness of the concept of common control. The list of criteria for the determination of control, proposed by the United Kingdom delegation for inclusion into the Convention itself, or alternatively as a model of the national law, gives rise to a whole number of objections, and can hardly correspond to the aims of the unification. An attempt to find a way out of the existing situation is made in the proposal by the Canadian delegation, however the Conference is invited to use the notions which are inherent only to the system of common law (such as "beneficial owner", and therefore such proposal can hardly be acceptable. The CMI soberly evaluates the existing situation and does not see ways of resolving this issue at the Conference. In our opinion, the CMI's reasonable proposal should be heard, taking into account ineffectiveness of the conducted discussion and hopelessness of its continuation.

Turkey Our difficulty is with the issue of personal liability, which we failed to solve this morning. Our legislative system restricts the liability to the ship, so personal liability of the owner is a difficult issue for us to start with and therefore we have some difficulty with the UK proposal. Our preference is to keep to the original JIGE text, which may be perhaps combined with the CMI text which is in A/CONF.188/3, paragraph 142. Our proposal is to take the JIGE text but try to combine it with the CMI proposal to strengthen the emphasis to use national law in this respect.

France   We are in favour of the two proposals made by UK and Canada. We think that they raise the right question, since, as it has been pointed out after the 1952 Convention a deplorable practice developed and we are at present actually at a crossing point. However, if in principle we are in favour, we think we have also to adhere to a more limited position. We would follow the Dutch position. We are ready to work on the basis of these proposals, but it is true that as it is now presented the notion of "control" is still a bit fluid and we would have some difficulties, in consideration of our domestic law, to give effect to it. I think that it is a concern that will remain in existence and we should work on that notion because there is the key of a fair maritime trade that cannot bear for example that certain ports are victims of ships whose owners disappear, while there are other ships that actually belong to the same person established in the same place, in the same road, in the same country. We think that this is something that will remain in existence. We should like to underline a translation difficulty since in the English text of the Canadian proposal reference is made to the "beneficial owner" and in the French translation the words used are "propriétaire effectif". I think that in the Canadian text there is something more precise, i.e. the ship held for the account of a third party, it is also the ship from which a third party draws benefit. It is a notion badly reflected in the French version of the document.

CISL   Wishes to associate itself strongly with the UK proposal, both in their written submission to the Conference and in the comments made today, to provide in this Convention for the concept of the arrest of associated ships. We represent an often forgotten constituency, and that is the vast number of seafarers working on the world shipping fleet. On their behalf we would especially like to lend our support to the notion that the 1952 Convention sought to strike an equitable balance between the interest of shipowners and those of claimants. We are particularly concerned about the welfare of this international work force which already finds itself in a weak position vis-à-vis its employers. The distinguished delegates of this Conference will be well aware of the not insignificant number of vessels lost at sea invariably with the loss of all or most of the lives on board. It is a long experience that such losses are most common on vessels that, whether by coincidence or not, belong to the one ship companies referred to by the distinguished delegate of the United Kingdom and which proliferated so rapidly since the 1952 Convention was drafted. We would particularly draw the Conference's attention to the grave consequences that ensue from such total losses for the families of officers and crew lost on these ships. For instance families of crew members are frequently located in different jurisdictions from each other and frequently in different jurisdictions from the person who owns or controls the vessel. Moreover in our experience the seafarers' income is the only source of income for the affected family and is almost never the case that an owner who has lost the ship provides an interim relief for the families who suddenly find themselves without income. Meanwhile the owner of the vessel continues to operate the other vessels in his fleet secured by the knowledge that these and his other assets are beyond the reach of his dependants. In short then the associated ship is the only asset against which such families can obtain at least security for their claims. It is therefore the view of this delegation that the equitable balance referred to in the submission of the United Kingdom can only be restored if the amendment proposed by that distinguished delegation is adopted by this Conference. Further we would note for the record that in the vast majority of countries which have implemented the 1952 Convention the burden of proof in establishing ownership of a vessel or alleged associated ship rests on the maritime claimant. Therefore in order to give effect to the principle of permitting the arrest of associated vessels or of other vessels in the same effective ownership of the offending vessel recognition should be given to the difficulty a maritime claimant faces in establishing ownership in the light of the corporate structure which is most commonly used in the shipping industry to-day. We consider therefore that it is also important to place the burden of disproving an allegation of common control of two or more vessels on the shipowner denying the allegation, because it is the shipowner who is in possession of the relevant information.

Norway   We want to say we appreciate the efforts of the States who have taken the initiative to address this important question and we sympathise with the good intention of these suggestions but we are afraid that we are amongst those that are sceptical about the proposal. The proposal goes to the core of the private law system. Piercing the corporate veil has important implications with regard to the way the shipping world would operate as was pointed out by Greece. In our country we have just devised general company law and in that context the rules on piercing the corporate veil were discussed thoroughly and it was decided not to have provisions on that. We have discussed the proposal with our shipping industry and their point of departure is criticism to the proposal. On this basis rules on piercing the corporate veil would be quite difficult to accept for us. We agree that they address an important problem and this is not only with regard to this question. It is also a problem with regard to civil liability, insurance, criminal law and other public law issues. So our point of departure is that it would be quite exceptional to have rules on piercing the corporate veil. Still we think it is very worthwhile a discussion but we believe that if this issue shall be addressed in an international convention it will be necessary with a high degree of uniformity with regard to the requirements necessary to pierce the corporate veil. A general concept such as "control" with some guidelines would not be sufficient as this leaves the door open and creates legal uncertainty with regard to when the sister ship rule would apply. So in our view it would be necessary to have clear cut detailed provisions regarding what is control or when we may pierce the corporate veil. But we believe it may be worthwhile discussing if we can accomplish such certainty.

Sri Lanka The one ship company attempts to undermine the sister ship concept that is one of our main ideas. But the UK control concept and the Canadian beneficial ownership concept need a definition. It is extremely difficult to define these words. If this were left to national law, then of course there would not be any uniformity. Further, it would not be very practical for the person arresting to find the person in control in a few hours when the ship is in your port. But anyway we think that this is something which should be explored but we are doubtful whether we could succeed here.

Germany Like other delegations before us we also appreciate the proposals made by the UK and Canada. I think they draw attention to a very important problem but nevertheless in the end we are sceptical about the language of the proposal. We think that the concept of "control" needs to be precisely defined and it is not a good idea to leave the definition of those terms to the national legislation or to the national Courts because the purpose of this Convention is unification of law and this is in contradiction with that to hand over the interpretation of those terms to national legal systems, but if it would be possible to work out a precise, clear and strict list of criteria, for example specific pressure on shareholding to define the term of control. This might be a solution that perhaps could find a majority here and which we could support.

Belgium I would like to take notice at the outset of two things. Nobody in this room has contested that at present there is a problem with these more or less fictitious companies. Secondly, we are in a Conference that does not concern the shipowners or does not intend to protect shipowners but intends to promote international trade. For that reason it is necessary to find a balance between the two. I don't like at all the idea that has been put forward to leave that choice of the balance to the States themselves, since we can very easily expect what the result would be. States that take advantage of one ships companies on one side and the States who have as principal object trade on the other side will have disagreement on the principles. I think that would not be a good solution. It is necessary to treat this problem internationally and arrive at a result in an international convention. At the outset my Government liked very much the UK proposal. It is not the case to define "control" as a juridical control with reference to shares and participation and holding companies. This is not the problem. What is needed is an approach to the real control, of fact, that precisely in an international convention permits on the basis of established rules to pierce in all countries the corporate veil. Obviously since the problem has come on the table only today or more precisely this afternoon it is certain that it will be necessary to still refine the words employed and eventually the guidelines, as indicated by the UK delegation. But this is another point. I have here intended to consider only the principles.

Australia There is no doubt Mr. Chairman that there are conflicting interests here. As a nation of ships users we are strongly in favour of the UK proposal. The avoidance of action *in rem* by some restructuring of ownership is a big problem in Australia. Therefore, although the proposal by the UK may need to be refined, it certainly represent the direction in which we wish to go.

Sweden We would like to express our sympathy for the goal of the UK and Canadian proposals. However this problem is not at least in Sweden a typical maritime law problem. The problem exists in many other fields of business. Therefore we think that we cannot solve this problem within the frame of this Convention.

Thailand   In the view of this delegation the proposal to address the problem of piercing the corporate veil, to shut the back door that is left open by the second paragraph of this article, would do more good than harm. We fully support the approach proposed by the UK and are keen to introduce this principle into our domestic law. However we feel that this approach will find difficulties in getting approval and to become part of this new Convention. We therefore believe that the CMI proposal should represent a good compromise for this issue.

China   The Chinese delegation has made a careful study of the proposals presented by the delegations of UK and Canada. We have not only realised their good intentions but also the existing real problems as stated in their proposals. In shipping practices, there are ships "controlled or partially controlled or beneficially owned" by another company; such situations are really in existence. However we have to consider other situations as well. Usually, maritime claims rise in very urgent circumstances; when the claimant asks the court to effect the arrest of a ship, the defendant will usually plead that he is not the owner of the ship. Under such circumstances, the only way for the claimant is to prove that the ship at issue is controlled or beneficially owned by the defendant, and it is hardly possible for the claimant to meet his burden of proof in such a short period of time. So this practice will be detrimental to the legal rights and interest of the claimant. Moreover, the term "beneficially" or "controlled" will probably have different interpretations in different countries or legal systems and thus result in distortion or disputes, and this is contradictory to the aim or object of the international convention. The Chinese delegation strongly supports the text in the JIGE provisions, for its clearness and explicitness, and thus for ensuring a better chance of reaching international uniformity of law in this area. Meanwhile we suggest that we might also consider acceptance of the supplementary provisions presented by CMI.

Finland   We oppose the proposal made by the UK and Canada and associate ourselves with the views and concerns presented especially by Norway and several other delegations.

Ghana   I think that it is important for us to bear in mind that this may occur in other business fields but ships are different and we need to be very careful because the nemesis of 1952 is likely to confront us again if we leave her without being able to solve something that all of us acknowledge is indeed a problem and I think it becomes very pertinent that though we recognize the difficulty we do not need to run away because of the fact that this difficulty exists. We therefore share very much the concern expressed by the UK and Canada and we believe that we need to explore much further this question of control and beneficial ownership as was pointed out by the distinguished delegates of Germany and Australia. I think it is important that we give ourselves some little more time to reflect about those issues because they strike at the very core of our acceptance of a Convention like this.

ICS   I have been listening with interest to the debate and have to say that I share the views of those delegations who have spoken against the proposal. I just like to make some practical points, if I may. Some of the delegations that have spoken have given the impression that the sole purpose of single ship companies is to circumvent the sistership arrest provision and we feel that this is really not the case. The main reason for the growth in single ship companies is an economic one; it is really to reduce the shipowner operating costs. Shipowners who trade to countries who have unlimited regimes for example where insurance coverage is not available, they want to restrict their liability in those jurisdictions and therefore they use the mechanism of single ship companies. Another reason is finance. Shipowners wanting to attract equity capital. Some countries encourage investment in shipping by offering tax incentives and these are best obtained through the mechanism of the single ship company. Also some delegations have spoken about restoring the balance of 1952 Convention. Just a point I would like to make here is we don't think the balance has changed in respect of some claims both relating to the finance, ownership and possession of ships. We think the balance here is probably the same as it was in the 1952 Convention. We are worried about this concept of control. We think that if we were to introduce something like that in the Convention it would have to be very clearly defined and we are really very strongly against the suggestion of leaving that to the Court to decide, because that obviously would lead to different national interpretations and we just want to end up with forum shipping if we go down that route. Turning to the guidelines that have been suggested by the UK in their paper I don't want to go into that in detail, but I just want to make some practical observations. We don't think that these guidelines would solve the problem because the guidelines in themselves contain a lot of uncertain terms and if I just go through a couple of the guidelines very briefly:

- common financing is one of the guidelines which I think has been suggested. Some shipyard offer financing arrangements to all customers, but that does not necessarily mean that there is any connection between the customers;
- the same can be said about common names: liner companies chartering in ships often change the names of the ships, so that they have common names; this fact does not mean that that company is really controlling the operation of the ships;
- insurance on a fleet basis: it is not an uncommon practice for ship managers to arrange insurance on a fleet basis to wholly unrelated shipowners.

That is what I wanted to say about the guidelines. I think that in themselves they could give rise to uncertainty. Another point, which has been touched upon by some delegations, I think the Chinese and Danish in particular, that the proposal may in fact be false to claimant. The cost associated with finding out whether the ship is controlled by the same person may be great and considerable research might be necessary to determine that and although the proposal looks attractive to claimants and looks like it is going to be to their advantage, but in practice these claimants, for example the seafarers which were mentioned earlier and their dependants, they could actually face a very difficult and expensive task when trying to determine whether there is common control. Finally I want to touch upon the burden of proof also mentioned by the CISL. In the UK paper it has been suggested that the burden of proof could be placed on the person who alleged control of the ship. In that case the claimant would only have to make a prima facie case that there is common control and it would be up to the shipowner to prove that he had no connection with the ship giving rise to the claim. But we think that this would be highly unfair for that shipowner to have the burden of proof because it would be stopping his source of income by arresting his ship and then asking him to prove that he is not connected with some other person and some other ship. So we find that to be unfair. Just leave it at that Mr Chairman.

Hong Kong My delegation has listened to this debate and followed it closely. I would like on behalf of my delegation to just intervene on one point arising out of the reference to the balance of conflicting interests which seems to be clearly recognized in various contributions to this discussion. In particular to the interest of seafarers. We have heard reference to their interest; we have heard in particular of the problems that may be faced by the families of those who serve on ships owned by one ship companies when there is a total loss. However Hong Kong China has consulted the interests of seafarers and would like to make the point that it doesn't seem to this delegation that the interests of those who serve on ships are necessarily going to be served by the proposal which has been so forcefully put together by the UK delegation. After all the interest of crew will be adversely affected in proportion to the increase in the number of vessels that may be subject to arrest because the interest of those who serve on vessels will be immediately impacted upon by arrest.

Malta I have to say that our delegation doesn't agree with the proposals both put forward by the UK or Canada although we do sympathize with the reasons why they have put forward these proposals. There is very little I have to add to what ICS have just said. In fact the case they have put forward is so good that adding anything to it is rather superfluous. I have to make one small comment however on what the distinguished delegate of Sweden has said, because it also merits attention that the problem that is being addressed here is not only related to shipping, not only related to maritime law, but is related to other aspects of the industry that we live in or that serves us and that trying to deal with them in this Convention we would do something which is definitely beyond our grasp. We therefore cannot agree with the proposal.

CMI The CMI is very likely responsible for this debate which has been indeed very interesting. The CMI has the feeling that from the JIGE draft the conclusion could be drawn that the new Convention would prohibit, and I stress prohibit, piercing the corporate veil and that would indeed have been a very bad conclusion. The CMI felt that it probably would have been very difficult to regulate in this international Convention the conditions in which corporate veil could be pierced and therefore suggested that it should be made clear in the Convention that the provisions of the Convention itself would not prohibit Contracting States to pierce the corporate veil in situations in which under the national law corporate veil could be pierced: a very modest and a very limited suggestion Mr Chairman. The UK delegation went further than that. I don't want now to consider the details of the UK proposal, I just want to say that it would appear from the debate that there are some delegations in favour, a sizeable number of delegations against and then a third group: delegations which think that the definition of control should not be left to national law but attempt should be made to try to find an international agreement by this Committee on the notion of control. Mr Chairman my conclusion is whether it would be worthwhile to devote some time to make an attempt to define "control", a working group could be established for this purpose, it might fail, but it might even succeed. It might be possible, without delaying the work of this Committee, to make such attempt and since with some very limited exceptions, the general view of all the delegates is that this is indeed the real problem and that something at some level sometime ought to be made to solve it, it seems to me that it would be worthwhile to make such attempt.

United Kingdom   If I may take the floor again since a lot has been said since I last spoke. I suspected that there might be a debate and we are grateful to the CMI. I think they have put their finger on the issue here and I just like to pick out from one or two comments that have been made. This is perhaps the time for an essential difference between this and the 1952 Convention and I think as the distinguished delegate from Ghana said ships are different and I think that is why essentially we put in this proposal. So I think that the idea that has been put forward by Prof. Berlingieri deserves considerable consideration.

Chairman   I was going to say that it is always dangerous to be met with so much sympathy as you have in this debate because people tend to add on a qualification afterwards and indeed many have done so. Almost everybody has been in favour of the general idea, but a lot have also qualified that with a statement that your proposal is not clear enough and that it would be difficult to do it in an international Convention and that it should be left to national law. I think provisionally therefore I would say that there is not enough support at this stage to adopt the proposal along the lines of your proposal or that of Canada. As was indicated by Prof. Berlingieri I think we have to go on but this does not exclude the possibility of an informal working group to be set up and I think really it is for the proponents of the UK and Canadian proposals to convince those who were in favour in principle but not in reality when it comes to the proposal itself, to the wording. I think that there is work to be done and I suggest it should be done on an informal basis and I would assume that the UK and Canadian delegations should take responsibility for it. I should like to know when we leave an issue open that somebody or preferably more than one feel a particular responsibility for a development, for further work to be carried out. So on that basis I think that we have to say that we can only adopt paragraph 2 provisionally subject to any development as a result of the work of an informal group. If that would result in substantive developments, then we would be able to come back to this paragraph; but for the time being it is adopted. I am a bit uncertain as to whether we should on the same provisional basis add on the proposal by the CMI which was referred to by a great number of delegates who either said that it was a fall back position for them or that was something that could beneficially be included. You have that proposal on the top of page 26 of document A.CONF.188/3 and the idea would be to add at the end of paragraph 2 the following: "the question whether a ship is owned by the person who is liable for the maritime claim shall be decided in accordance with the national law of the State in which the arrest is applied for". Is it the feeling of this Group in this room that it should be added unless the work of the UK and Canada on the other result in a positive result? Should we have that? I see nodding heads.

Norway   I have to admit that the CMI text is not absolutely clear to me because the question of who is liable for the claim shall be decided in accordance with the national law. I mean the question of ownership in itself is what this text deals with and as I understand the question of ownership it is always decided by national law. If we are dealing with the question of the corporate veil I think the text should say so in one way or another and then we could discuss it. Now it is not quite clear what we do if we adopt the CMI text. So I would like to have a clarification.

CMI   Mr Chairman the reasons for which the suggestion was made to add that sentence is clearly set out before the text and the purpose was to make clear that the question whether or not the corporate veil can be pierced must be left to the law of the State where the arrest is effected. The wording is, I agree with the distinguished Norwegian delegate, not very clear but the concept of the purpose is clear. Therefore I think Mr Chairman that on the basis of the concept, subject to drafting, a decision may be arrived at as to whether or not this clarification should be added and the purpose is simply to make clear that the Convention does not prevent the piercing of the corporate veil under national law.

Chairman   Yes. I think that also the Norwegian delegate would agree to that. There should be agreement in substance. So, subject to drafting, there can be an addition along the lines of the proposal. Members of the Drafting Committee will be happy to receive also that task. They would also, I suppose, when they consider paragraph 2 have to deal the concept "personally liable" in the second line of paragraph 2 but they will do that at the same time as they solve that problem in the previous articles that have been referred to them. I understood during the break that there may be some uncertainty as to what the position is with respect to paragraph 2 of article 3. The decision was that paragraph 2 is provisionally adopted as in the JIGE text and it should be referred to the Drafting Committee and the Drafting Committee should specifically consider whether words to the effect of the CMI proposal in A/CONF.188/3 are necessary. There is agreement in substance that there is nothing in this Convention, in the JIGE text which would prevent a Contracting State to pierce the corporate veil in accordance with its own national legislation. There is agreement to say that in the Convention, one way or the other, such as has been proposed by the CMI. I also said that the Drafting Committee would have to consider an expression like "personally liable" which appears in the second line of paragraph 2. We have touched upon the same concept earlier on, in earlier provisions and we decided then that it would be the Drafting Committee to decide whether "personally" is necessary or whether it could be expressed in any other way. You will recall that a number of delegates were not keen on keeping the word "personally" which caused problems for them and I think that there was agreement again on substance. It is only a matter of finding a language to reflect the agreement on substance. One final thing I would like to mention in relation to paragraph 2 and that is the fact that there is a set of square brackets. The deletion of the square brackets or of the language in the square brackets were not addressed really by anybody so when I said that paragraph 2 was adopted it was my intention to say that it was adopted without the square brackets. Since that was not addressed I just wanted to raise it now to avoid any misunderstanding. Do you agree that if for example a person as a time charterer or as a voyage charterer of a vessel becomes personally liable, becomes liable, to use words more neutral, for a maritime claim and actually owns a vessel, can that vessel be arrested to secure a maritime claim, that is really what is dealt with in (b) here. So unless somebody raises his card I will assume then that you accept that this paragraph is provisionally adopted, without the square brackets but with the language which was previously within the brackets.

Denmark   Just before the coffee break I raised my flag because I wanted in fact the clarification which you gave and I thank you for that. As to the CMI text I personally feel we should leave it out. I think that if we are sticking to the 1952 system I think we have the 1952 and must live with that, not adding anything which could in fact disturb the interpretation afterwards and I do not continue Mr Chairman because I am interfering with your conduct of the meeting.

United Kingdom

Proposal for amendment of Article 3(2)—draft 9.3.99 9.30am

3(1)   [As per modified CMI draft].
3(2)   (a)   Arrest is also permissible of any other ship which, when the arrest is effected, is:
　　　　　(i)   owned by the same person who, when the maritime claim arose, was liable for the claim as owner of the ship in respect of which the claim arose,
　　　　　(ii) owned by the same person who, when the maritime claim arose, was liable for that claim as the demise charterer, time charterer or voyage charterer of the ship in respect of which the claim arose, or
　　　　　(iii) effectively controlled by a person as if that person owned the arrested ship, provided that at the time the maritime claim arose such person controlled the person who is liable for that claim.
　　　　(b)   In determining whether a ship is effectively controlled by a person, a Court may take into account all relevant factors including, but not restricted to, whether that person is able to:
　　　　　(i)   make decisions in respect of that ship,
　　　　　(ii) influence the implementation of those decisions, and
　　　　　(iii) direct the distribution of profits from the operations of that ship.

    (c) If the ship is not owned by the person who is liable for the maritime claim, the question whether there is a connection between the person owning the ship and the person liable for the maritime claim such as to justify the arrest shall be decided in accordance with the law of the State in which the arrest is applied for.

    (d) This paragraph (2) shall not apply to claims in respect of ownership or possession of a ship.

  (3) Notwithstanding the provisions of paragraphs (1) and (2) of this article, the arrest of a ship which is neither owned by the person liable for the claim nor within paragraph (2)(a)(iii) shall be permissible only if, under the law of the State where the arrest is applied for, a judgment in respect of that claim can be enforced against that ship by judicial or forced sale of that ship.

Second reading—10 March 1999[60]

United Kingdom   Last evening you referred to the fact that consultations were continuing on the further proposal which has been offered on the basis of the text which was circulated last evening by the Secretariat. Indeed discussions have continued in the margins of the Committee right up to the start of this session and as a result some further suggestions have been made as to how best to present the option. I'll cover this shortly. However at the outset I should have to emphasise that three formal and open meetings were held. These meetings were chaired by Canada and were attended by a good number of delegates including some that were not inclined towards the original UK proposal. In addition UK and others have sought to discuss all the concerns which were raised in the initial debate last week by a number of other delegations. The text circulated yesterday is more tightly drawn than the original proposal and introduces the test which the Court may apply or can apply. Before going into the details of the revised proposal Mr Chairman I should like to say a few words of introduction. The first discussion showed that there were a good number of delegations that recognise that there are presently problems in trying to arrest sister ships. Some, like the UK, Canada and others were firmly of the view that it would be wrong to come to this conference and simply ignore the problem just because drafting a solution is difficult. Delegations such as those of Greece, Hong Kong, Sri Lanka, Thailand and a number of others were inclined to go towards the CMI proposal in the last discussion while some other delegations were reluctant to seek to cover the issue in this convention. Mr Chairman, while there was no agreement at the first session last week I venture to suggest that the number of delegations wanting associated ships arrest to be covered or at least to deal with the problem through the CMI proposal were in fact significant. In the discussion in the Working Group comparison was made to the parable of the Good Samaritan who seeing a difficulty refuses to walk away from it. If this Conference is seriously to address the question of the arrest of ships in 1999 and beyond, there has to be some recognition that there has been a significant change since the original Convention was drafted. As the distinguished delegate from Belgium so eloquently explained last week, there are some shipowners who blatantly use the device of artificial barriers through their corporate structures simply to ensure that if certain circumstances arise they can evade the provisions of internationally agreed remedies—such as the Hague Rules—and they do this in order to avoid paying those who have suffered losses. Mr Chairman, to ignore that fact is likely to weaken the proposed Convention and to risk the likelihood of further legal inconsistency around the world as States adopt artificial constructions to try to deal with the problem. We (and other sponsors of the proposal which I will go into in a moment) have no intention undermining the perfectly acceptable option opened to conference lines and pooling arrangements or to professional ship management organizations nor are we preventing the use of one ship companies for legitimate financial purposes. However we do need to provide some protection from those who would deliberately circumvent the Convention for their own protection at the expense of legitimate claimants. Naturally there have been concerns from certain quarters but we have tried to keep the proposal within reasonable limits and consistent with the broad principles of this draft Convention. As currently drafted the new Arrest Convention would provide for the arrest of both the particular ship in respect of which a claim arose and of other ships owned by the person liable for the claim. The Working Group has included similar provisions in paragraph (2)(a) (i) and (ii) of the new

60. Text from tapes Nos. 68–71.

proposal as circulated. The new proposal to amend article 3 seeks to build on the proposal originally made by the CMI. The absence of a definition of "ownership" should enable States to define the concept under national law. This would provide States with some scope to re-establish a fair balance between the interest of the shipowners and the interest of the claimants. We considered, however, that reliance of the concept of ownership alone would not provide sufficient flexibility. We therefore propose that provision be made for the arrest of "associated" ships which are effectively controlled by a person we can call for the purposes of this debate "Mr Big", who also controls the person (or corporate body) who is liable for the claim. In other words we want to catch those cases where there is a less direct relationship between this mastermind figure who I called "Mr Big" and the ship which *de facto* he operates. As stated last week we do not intend to catch professional ship management companies nor agents simply acting on behalf of shipowners. Neither do we intend to catch banks and other investors with minority share ownership but no element of effective control. This approach will provide greatest scope for national law to keep pace with developments that might otherwise prevent attempts to pierce the so called "corporate veil". Mr Chairman, I would like to go through the provisions of the new proposal if you feel that that would help. However, before doing so I should like to make one general remark. Last evening the Committee agreed that article 1(1)(e) should be amended to deal with the issue of abandoned ships and their crews. By definition the vast majority of such ships are likely to have little or no value and if they are owned—as is likely—by one ship companies, claimants will have no effective recourse unless the proposal, or something very close to it, is adopted by this Conference. Mr Chairman if you are agreeable I shall go through the details and I think we shall use the screen. Is that acceptable? If I could ask the Secretary to show on the screen the first of our illustrations. I guess the shape of this more important than perhaps the details. I'll go through it in some details for delegations. First I should like to refer delegations to paragraph 3(2)(a)(iii) of the document circulated yesterday morning by the Secretariat. In the last line of this subparagraph it is now proposed to add the following text after the words "such person". The additional words are "is liable for that claim or". This is an addition offered as a clarification following further discussions last evening. Also in the first line of paragraph 3(2)(c) after the initial words "if the ship" should be inserted the words "to be arrested". Now Mr Chairman I can go through the proposal and refer perhaps from time to time to the shape of what is on the screen. In each of the examples to be shown we have presumed that it is ship "B" that is to be arrested. If I could ask the Secretariat to scroll up a little bit and there should be three examples on the screen. In each of these examples we would presume that it is ship "B" that is to be arrested. Both of these examples now on the screen are covered by both the 1952 Convention and the JIGE text. Referring to the document the whole of paragraph 3(2)(a) covers three situations in which it is permissible to arrest another ship (that will be ship "B" in each example), that is a ship other than ship "A" in respect of which the claim arose. Paragraph 3(2)(a)(i) is covered by the first example on the screen. This is the classic and simple sister ship concept. The owner clearly owns both ships "A" and "B" which are therefore sisterships. In the second example on the screen we deal with the sister ship scenario where the owner is more remote. This is also dealt with by both the 1952 Convention and the JIGE text. The owner who is shown now as "X" and that we were calling "Mr Big" owns vessel "B" (the one to be arrested) and charters ship "A". Ship "B" can therefore be arrested by the owner of ship "A" in respect of Mr Big's liabilities under the charter of ship "A". I would now ask if the third example could be put up on the screen. Thank you. Paragraph 3(2)(a)(iii) of the document shows the new situation which we are trying to deal with and there will be two illustrations of this. The first example on the screen now: here we have Mr Big who effectively controls ship "B" which is the one to be arrested but this ship is owned by a company or a corporate body which we can call "Z". Ship "A" is controlled by company "Y" who is liable for this ship. Mr Big in fact controls both company "Y" and "Z". Therefore in fact both ships are associated ships. Now the next example if I could ask that to be put up, the final one. In the second scenario covered by paragraph 3(2)(a)(iii) we show a slightly different arrangement in respect of ship "A". Here the circumstances are such that Mr Big (X at the top of the tree as it were) is directly liable for the claim relating to ship "A" and he effectively controls company "Z" which owns the ship to be arrested. So this diagram illustrates the various scenarios as we see them. I will now turn back to the paper and go through a couple of other paragraphs. Paragraph 3(2)(b) of the document develops paragraph (a)(iii) and deals with the relationship between Mr Big (that is "X") and ship "B" the one to be arrested. The court of the State in which the arrest is to be applied for has discretion to take into account all relevant factors including the factors we have given as example on the screen. The text does not provide a definition of the control by Mr Big, that is "X", of company "Y" which will in practice probably be a corporate body. That matter is to be left to the court to determine. Turning to paragraph 3(2)(c) of the document this also deals with paragraph 3(2)(a)(iii) and deals with the relationship between companies "Y" and "Z". It leaves it to the national law of the State in which arrest is applied for to decide if there is a connection between "Y" and "Z" such as to justify the arrest. Mr Chairman, this is the revised CMI text. Paragraph (d) is just a reiteration of the existing JIGE text and this prevents paragraph (2) from applying to claims in respect of ownership or possession relating to ship "A". Paragraph 3(3) of the document slightly amends the JIGE text. The JIGE text imposes an overriding restriction on the powers of arrest in paragraphs (1) and (2). The amendment here is that if a ship is not owned by a person who is liable for the claim and is not effectively controlled by Mr Big (or "X") as in paragraph 3(2)(a)(iii), then arrest of that ship is only permissible if it could be sold to enforce the judgment in respect of the maritime claim. So for example if a ship is chartered by demise to a person who is liable for the claim arrest is only permissible if a judgment could be enforced against that ship by the judicial of forced sale. Mr Chairman, I hope these examples (and what I appreciate is a very detailed explanation of them) will show more clearly how the proposal can and will work without damaging legitimate sister ship arrangements which were a concern of a number of delegates. Mr Chairman may I thank you for your attention and of course for the attention of the Committee.

The debate that followed is reported below.

Chairman   I think that the presentation was indeed extremely clear and I think that your proposal is understood. Are there any comments please?

Cuba   The exposition has been actually very clear. In my view it is a Pandora's box with the notion of "control". We are definitely not in agreement with such notion.

Hong Kong China   May I through you express thanks to the UK delegation for their hard work and clear explanation that has gone into this proposal. As was explained by the UK the 1952 Convention does already permit the arrest of sisterships and I mention that because I would like to make clear at the outset that that Convention—the 1952 Convention—is binding on Hong Kong at the moment so I would like delegates to be aware of that when I made my remarks on this proposal. This subject is important of course to shipowners and cargo interest but it is also important to those who serve on ships, to seafarers world-wide. In the limited time available to us Hong Kong China has tried to take account of all these interests in formulating its views. The purpose of an arrest convention and of this draft convention is to promote harmony and stability and certainty in the application of the law of the arrest of ships around the world and we are in Hong Kong China very concerned at the implication of the proposal by the UK. We have several grounds upon which we would not be able to support this proposal. First the proposal amounts to a fundamental change in the legal approach that would be adopted towards the concept of separate corporate ownership in many jurisdictions. Secondly and not unrelated to that first point the introduction of the concept of effective control will in our view lead to a great variety of different interpretations and judicial decisions in different jurisdictions. Thirdly and again partly as result of the first point it will lead to undue anxiety and potential confusion to the international shipping community. Fourthly it would have implications perhaps profound for other areas of law including and not limited to commercial and corporate law for many jurisdictions represented at this Conference including Hong Kong China. In these circumstances the position of Hong Kong China is that we would as between the JIGE text and this proposal much prefer and commend the JIGE text.

CISL   CISL would like to give its strong support to the proposal made by the distinguished delegation of UK and for the wording which the Committee has before it which has been explained so clearly by the delegation of the UK. During the discussions last week a substantial number of delegates acknowledged the problems posed by the proliferation of the one ship companies. In its intervention last week this delegation expressed the serious concern about the diminution in the equitable balance between the interests of shipowners and those of claimants as a result of the one ship companies. We spoke specifically about the position of seafarers and the circumstances where an entire crew is lost at sea along with the only asset against which their families could currently enforce the claim for the loss of the breadwinner. I refer of course to the ship which was lost and invariably owned by a one ship company and we have been heartened by the comments of support we received from a substantial number of delegates both in this room and outside for the position of the seafarer. It is the view of this delegation that the proposed text has substantial merits for two reasons: firstly the concept of control is introduced and it gives a guidance to the national court. The proposed article 3(2)(b) strikes to the heart of the genuinely associated ship while leaving parties such as managers and pooling arrangements and other legitimate interests outside the scope of the provision as explained by the distinguished delegate of the UK. Secondly the text that the Committee has before it leaves any issue to be determined under article 3(2)(a) to existing national law and future national legislation. So for these reasons we believe that the Working Group on article 3(2) and the UK delegation have managed to achieve a wording which goes some way to restoring the balance where a serious unbalance has developed. And also I believe that the Working Group has dealt with the concerns and objections raised by this Committee. Two points Mr Chairman, I am going to be brief. Ships are different, as the UK said last week, and a number of other delegations has acknowledged. Secondly many delegations here come from countries where corporate legislation prevents piercing the corporate veil so by giving national legislatures and courts a discretion to allow associated ships arrest a balance can be restored where claimants such as crewmembers or the family of those who died on ships at sea can at least secure their claims and achieve a hope of enforcement which has then be absent. So for these reasons Mr Chairman we would urge the Conference to adopt the wording submitted by the UK.

Greece   Greece would like to be consistent. As you can imagine Greece is against the UK proposal and we prefer to keep the JIGE text as it stands and as it was provisionally adopted. UK made a very powerful and very nice presentation but as it was mentioned in the previous week by the German delegation we are not here for a beauty contest. We are here to try to find and formulate a convention which will provide for uniformity of law. The Hong Kong delegation had previously explained quite clearly what kind of mess—may I use this word—is going to be created in the international seaborne trade if the approach proposed by the UK is going to be accepted. We had mentioned in our presentation the previous week that this proposal is bad for shipping per se. Is bad especially for those countries which do not have financial institutions who do not generate cargo and who rely only on their operators in order to have a shipping. It might be even more detrimental to the shipping companies of those States who are now in a transition from an economic system to another and who try hard to stick to their own maritime traditions. We have also said that this whole notion of corporate veil is something which should be dealt in another framework, in the framework of company law, and in another form and should not be restricted solely to shipping and especially in this convention. The only thing that we would like to add to this argument is our admiration for British tenacity. It is not a joke, it is not an irony, it is true admiration. That is why we believe the term "Thin red line", which is a title of a movie now here in Geneva, was originally attributed to the British and not to the US marines in Guadalcanal. But our British friends in their fighting spirit tend to forget that when you are in an international forum and when you propose an option you must take other considerations seriously not only your own interest but also the interest, the need and the concern of your friends and partners and because at least according to our own interpretation the British have failed to do so and in this concrete case Greece is against this proposal.

ICS   Mr Chairman I have listened presentation this morning from the UK but I am not sure that I actually managed to take in all the details of the proposal. But I think that what we have before us is a very radical proposal. As the Hong Kong China delegate said earlier it goes against the basic principles of company law that to form a separate company is a legitimate way of limiting liability. A company is the basis of many businesses and I really don't see why the use of this medium by shipowners should be penalized. As I stated the other day there are legitimate commercial reasons for single ship companies. Many of these companies haven't in fact been set up with the specific intention of circumventing the sistership arrest provision and perhaps I have missed something this morning; one problem that I see with this proposal is that it doesn't distinguish between those shipowners who may have deliberately set up to avoid sistership arrest and those who haven't. The way that I see it the proposal would allow piercing the corporate veil in all cases. We are not just going to catch Mr Big, we are going to be catching all legitimate shipowners who also are going to be affected. Although again I have perhaps missed something because it has been a bit much for me to take in all these things for the first time on the screen this morning but despite what the UK and CISL have said, I think that the concept of the effective control and the criteria in (b) are just as likely to catch the professional ship managers or those shipowners with pooling arrangements and that completely unrelated ships are going to be subject to associated ship arrest. The confusion and the unfairness of arresting and impeding a totally unrelated ship and the consequent effect that this would have on that innocent shipowner's charterparty and finance arrangements is I would hope self evident. So for those reasons we simply cannot support the UK proposal. While I say so Mr Chairman can I just say that ICS cannot support the CMI proposal on the subject either because we think that it will promote forum shopping once the approach of different national courts becomes known. Since we are having this discussion, since all things are coming up again, can I just say that our preference would in fact be to retain the language of the 1952 Convention. We can live with the JIGE text but if we are looking for certainty our preference will be to adopt the language of the 1952 Convention which has been ratified by some 75 States.

Finland The principle of piercing the corporate veil we don't see that it is a specific maritime law problem. It is more a general problem that is emerging and also at some extent approved in some countries. However the conceptual issues rules and principles are quite differing in different jurisdictions. We do not see it appropriate to deal with these complicated issues of corporate law, contract law, tort law in this Arrest Convention without primarily dealing with security for claims not liability for claims. So our conclusion is that again we have to spill some cold water on our English friends, sorry about that.

China Now allow me on behalf of the Chinese delegation to say something about the proposals made by the UK delegation. We have seriously considered the UK proposals which are purposely designed to amend article 3 paragraph 2 of the JIGE text. We appreciate with deep understanding the efforts exerted by the distinguished UK delegation. Nevertheless, we with much regret, are not to give a favorable response to these proposals, we are just unable to accept their proposals. We agree with the comments made by the distinguished delegations from Greece, Cuba and Hong Kong China. Mr Chairman, may I add to the above mentioned comments my following supplements: (1) We are of the opinion that the UK proposals are not in line with the internationally generally accepted legal persons system or the limited liability corporate system. Under modern corporate law, one of the legal persons system is limited liability system, under which the limited liability corporation shall pay all its civil liabilities or company debts only with its properties or assets, and for shipping companies, with mainly their owned ships. No other persons shall be liable for the civil liabilities or company debts of the limited liability company. Even the shareholders of the company are only liable with the shares or the capital amount invested as shares in the company. In line with the comments stated by the delegation of Finland, the Chinese delegation holds that the corporate system is an important system prevailing in the modern market economy. As the developments of the market economy are not balanced, we have developed market economy countries, and also we have countries in transitional period to market economy. Notwithstanding different legal systems of the above-mentioned countries, they have basically the same principles of the corporate system. Therefore it clearly shows that the UK proposals are in conflict with the internationally generally accepted corporate legal persons system. In fact, we have paid much attention to article 3 paragraph 2(a)(iii) and (b) in the UK proposals and the criteria listed, we presume that the main object of the proposals is to break through the legal boundaries between limited liability companies so as to create associated ships, associated companies . . . a sort of associated system. This means a fundamental shaking of the foundation of a modern internationally generally accepted legal person system. (2) As regards the piercing of the corporate veil, the Chinese delegation is aware that some shipowners for the purpose of evading certain legal obligations, have done what they ought not to do, but this phenomenon not only exists in shipping circles, but also in international trading or other business circles as well. Hence we believe that piercing the corporate veil is a problem of general nature and therefore should be handled, settled and treated as a specific issue of general nature. So it is neither proper nor suitable to embody it in a purely and simply international shipping convention dealing only with arrest of ships. (3) In judicial practices, the UK proposals will bring about many difficulties in practical handling. Article 3 paragraphs 2(a)(iii), (b) and (c) are too vague. In particular, in judicial practices, arrest of ships is a judicial measure to secure a maritime claim, done in a very urgent situation. In such a very short period of time, the court is unable to decide, on the basis of the criteria contained in the proposals, whether there exists a so-called effective control or a so-called connection in sub-paragraph (c), and "connection" is also a very difficult criterion. The decision even ultimately made will probably be disputable or not stable and thus possibly resulting in further difficulties. Moreover, the term "control" is a very dangerous conception, and with "connection" added, it means that you may consider to arrest any ship belonging to any other company! We believe the aim or object of the international convention on arrest of ships is to regulate and unify the judicial practices in arrest of ships, and in no sense to encourage abuses in arrest of ships. We are afraid that if the UK proposals were adopted and enforced, they would certainly create such orderless practices in arrest of ships that not only the Chinese delegation but also other distinguished delegations as well are most reluctant to hear. Mr Chairman, please allow me to refer to another point. Now we are on Wednesday, we do not have much time left for us. Since the opening of the conference, we have conducted our business in accordance with the statement of the President that the conference should proceed in a spirit of cooperation and compromise. We have witnessed success and also we have witnessed compromises. The Chinese delegation have made quite a few compromises. Even yesterday, notwithstanding we strongly support the closed form of the definition of the maritime claim, we accepted the US compromise proposals. And as to article 6 paragraph (1), whether we use "shall" or "may" after "court", we also made a concession and reluctantly accepted "may". Therefore, the Chinese delegation suggests that the conference in a spirit of cooperation and compromise, adopts the JIGE text. At the same time, for the purpose of compromise, the Chinese delegation can also consider to add the CMI proposal contained in A/C/188/3 page 26 or page 29 for the Chinese text, which is designed to settle this problem.

Chairman We have heard very elegant interventions that were for the UK proposal and against it in view of the fact that this is in reference to a paragraph which has been provisionally adopted already I think that the tendency is quite clear. Since however this seems to go to the rules of the legal training of the distinguished delegates and creates emotions and of course the topic is very interesting, for that reason I would like you to indicate your position but I urge you to be brief. I cannot imagine that there are other arguments either for or against. So on that basis I continue with my list of speakers.

Mexico Mr President for us the proposal of the United Kingdom is absolutely unacceptable, basically for the words "effectively controlled" since they are words very ambiguous, lacking of any precision, if we consider that our Courts have not reached an agreement on the theory of delegation and whether and when the corporate veil can be pierced, we think that by accepting one interpretation, in whatever Court of the world, that would give rise to chaos.

Canada You will recall that the Canadian delegation in CRP/1 put forward a proposal in relation to sister ship arrest indicating very clearly that we were unsatisfied with the JIGE text and we continue to be of that view. You will also recall that we then agreed to participate actively in the Working Group on the strength of the UK proposal which we did with great interest and great enthusiasm. We believe that the text the UK has prepared tackles the phoney subject head on and we believe that it does strike a balance between providing a certain level of necessary details within the text and yet leaving an amount of discretion for the courts to amplify the regime if I can put it that way, in where the ship was arrested. In our view the proposal overcomes the rigidity of the current sister ship arrest regime and remedies a serious shortcoming in our view, that precludes claimants from fully advancing their claims when faced with the one ship company which of course now proliferate. We believe that the UK proposal will very much improve our regime on sister ship arrest and for those reasons we strongly support it.

Russian Fed. We continue to hold a negative attitude to the United Kingdom proposal. We associate negative rather than positive consequences with the adoption of this proposal. The representative of Hong Kong outlined very clearly those negative consequences, which the adoption of this proposal may lead to. We share this opinion and object to the United Kingdom proposal.

Norway We would prefer the JIGE text but I would like to add few comments if I may. The problems which this proposal is directed at are of deep concern for Norway. In the IMO the Legal Committee are working from another angle in order to secure the victims accessibility to assets, through establishing rules of strict liability combined with rules on mandatory assurance and a reduction. This is not the way of securing that their assets are available to cover claims and Norway is participating very actively in that working of IMO which for the time being is related to passengers, pollution and wreck removal. The proposal to pierce the corporate veil presented by the UK delegation here is a very different approach from the liability of the insurance on which work is done in IMO however, and I believe that the problem for us making the UK proposal more difficult to consider for us is that the remedy proposed, if I may use that word, involves State corporate law. Mr Chairman I would stop myself here and I will not go into that as other delegations have spoken on that.

495

Netherlands   Last week my delegation like many others shared sympathy with the approach which was taken by the UK and by Canada to make this Convention more in line with the balance as was obtained up in 1952. As pointed out last week my delegation was prepared further to explore the possibility to refine the balance of 1952 without exposing the interest of shipowners in that sense that we would go beyond the balance which was being established in the 1952. In that respect my delegation was doing this exploration taking into account the considerations made by many delegations as regards the consequences. For these reasons within the informal work that was been carried out my delegation took a more restricted approach and what we find now, it seems in my opinion that we have a more moderate proposal than we had last week and it is restricting the original thought in that sense that it might be a good thing to look upon. And as pointed out, to succeed in finding the balance again we have to rely on a very precise and concrete definition and in that sense the work carried out during this week produced a text which comes a long way to achieve that. But whether this way is long enough depends on the outcome of this debate of course. Further Mr Chairman I have one particular point that relates to how concrete the definition is we rely upon. Therefore I would like to focus very briefly on paragraph 2(c) of the proposal, in which there is reference to the national law of the State where the arrest is applied for. This paragraph is only acceptable to my delegation if it is a matter of the so called jurisdiction provision but we can't agree if it is just being made as a substantial provision to be added to the definition. In that sense such a provision might not be invoked to institute a forum shopping as was pointed out by the distinguished delegate from ICS.

Croatia   When I asked for the floor it was quite a time ago, so most of the arguments are on the table and I don't want to repeat them. We admire very much the proposal of UK and I shall use this nice graphica in my seminars but a friend of mine who is a practising lawyer tried nearly 20 years to find, it is a problem of injured seafarers, it just needed nearly 20 years to find this Mr Big because it is not one corporate veil, it is more than that, more than seven corporate veils so it is quite impossible to find who is this mister standing behind and this is really a problem, I think, of company law and we can't solve it here. So we are for the JIGE proposal.

Cyprus   The Cyprus delegation even though they understand the position of the UK, cannot possibly support it and for the reasons very strongly and eloquently presented by those delegations who are opposed to this proposal we believe that the JIGE text, which has already been adopted, should be maintained.

Thailand   Apart from the reasons presented by other members that have spoken before me I think that one effect or one result that the British proposal will have on the shipping business is that it will shift away Mr Small who will be investing in shipping companies owned by Mr Big. It will be difficult to attract shipping business especially in developing countries like mine. So for these reasons I cannot accept the British proposal.

Panama   For the reasons clearly and eloquently indicated by the delegations of Hong Kong, Cuba, Greece and Norway we cannot support the UK proposal.

Japan   This delegation has been listening to the debate very closely and since this delegation has been involved in the preparation of this draft we felt some need for clarification. First we would like to emphasise that the draft is devised very carefully. I wish you Mr President and all the distinguished delegates in this hall to examine thoroughly the factors listed in (b). These factors are devised to concentrate strictly to the reality of business activity of the shipping company not looking at the apparent factors easily observable from outside but may be irrelevant. We believe that this system effectively excludes the case where bona fide consortia, pooling agreements or bona fide shipowners are involved. And still we invite you to take a notice that this (b) is not made decisive but rather gives the Court authority to look to the reality. In short Mr President this delegation fully supports the proposal made by the UK and we believe this is not a radical change but rather a modest step forward. Nevertheless we believe that this is a significant step forward.

Iran   This delegation thanks the distinguished delegation of UK for the good presentation but we prefer the JIGE text as it is.

Denmark   As you said we will try to be brief. We would like to thank the UK delegation and also all the countries who participated in the working group because I think that there was more than one country who contributed to this. But I still would maintain my position along with the other speakers before me that I would be against the proposal and I would like to refer to the reasons (already indicated) because as yourself said Mr Chairman I think it is very difficult to add to the list of reasons why we could not accept this. I would refer to the very elegant speech by Hong Kong China and by my Chinese colleague as well as others. I think this is essential. Just a minor remark before I leave the floor Mr Chairman: I think it is essential, I would like to say, that to us it is not the protection against any seafarers claims whatsoever which was pointed to. I think it is so as our Norwegian colleague said that we have to take that into consideration even in IMO regulations; we are presently discussing this issue in IMO on the issue of compulsory insurance for third party claims. Regardless of this fact, my country has other systems which provide for sufficient satisfaction in the situation which was spoken of. I can only encourage other countries to do so. I think that it is fair enough to say that, Mr Chairman, I am on the negative side and I have the benefit of speaking as one of the last speakers and I still like to give a personal remark to the UK delegation, I like to say they have my highest regards for their competence and spirit.

Chairman I think the rest has to be brief and not to repeat some of the arguments.

Liberia Mr Chairman, as a very large offshore corporate registry I think one that caters for the maritime industries it is important that we go on record on this particular issue. Before I left last week I handed a note to my distinguished friend from the UK delegation after the discussion on his initial proposal and that note read as follows: nice try, good luck! Mr Chairman I think everyone had given good reasons for why we will oppose this proposal. We will also just for the benefit of the Committee indicate that in this room we have perhaps two or more learned lawyers. Outside of this room you have close to a million! The word from New York is that there is a way around the UK text and you have the same result as in the 1952 Convention did on single company shipowners. So perhaps it is not so great a problem as the UK think we have. For those reasons Mr Chairman we don't think we can support it and we prefer the JIGE text.

Brazil We have a text provisionally approved by this Committee and a proposal. Brazil wholeheartedly favours the maintenance of the JIGE text and is against the UK proposal.

Chairman My list of speakers seems to grow on time. I know that you have strong feelings about this issue but I must urge you to be briefer than some previous speakers otherwise we have to draw a line.

Spain We deeply regret not to be able to accept the UK proposal.

Australia Australia fully supports the UK proposal.

Sri Lanka Sri Lanka cannot support the UK proposal. We support the JIGE text.

Belgium I will try to explain my thoughts on another level than accepting or refusing the UK proposal. When we try to come to a useful international convention the point in my opinion is not to obtain a majority of votes in this Plenum. The point is to have a text that can be ratified by enough countries to become efficient and to avoid forum hunting and other things like that. Now having listened to the speakers here my clear feeling is that there are clearly two tendencies in this Forum and that the more we progress the more two blocks are created. A first block, sorry for the expression, I would say is trying to draft a convention how to avoid arrest of ships and another block is trying to face the problems which everybody agrees that they exist. So it is my deep concern personally that the way we are working a gap between the parties becomes bigger and bigger and that there is no real attempt from one side or from the other to find a solution and in such circumstances I think that we all are doing bad work because voting a convention knowing that such convention shall not be ratified in important ports of the world is not a good work. So, Chairman, I will not say that I am in favour of the UK proposal or against the UK proposal. That is not for the time being the point.

Malta Mr Chairman I would first of all like to start by sharing your view on the excellent presentation by the UK and also to congratulate them for their considerable efforts in working to the text. We understand that there are problems, however, Mr Chairman. To be brief, for the following reasons my delegation, I am afraid, is not in a position to support the UK proposal and must go along with the JIGE text. The reasons why we cannot support the UK proposal are very briefly the following: first of all, for the same reasons explained by a number of other delegations but particularly at the beginning by the Hong Kong China delegation, this amendment may affect negatively crews and managing companies. Secondly Mr Chairman, and this is a very important point in our view, we have here a real issue of corporate law and we are now discussing issues which are basic in a number of jurisdictions adhering to the notion of individual personality of each company. Consequently Mr Chairman we feel that such corporate matter should be deliberated in an alternative forum.

Philippines   First of all we would like to thank other delegations in expressing appreciation to the presentation of the UK. We wonder if the UK has any and intellectual property right over this illustration because it is a very ideal example for presentation especially on lectures. Mr Chairman it seems that the crew claim is used as a basis to raise concern over the associated ship arrest. Evidently this issue on arrest of associated ships is not solely about crew or crew claims. Perhaps there have been a broad or different focus of the presentation by the UK, some delegations may have looked differently on the proposal. But despite the trend in the floor this delegation joins the minority in support of the UK proposal but as it may be noted by some delegations the matter of claims by crew of abandoned ships would be addressed by the IMO in the nature of a strict liability and compulsory insurance for seafarers.

El Salvador   Our position is that we do not accept the UK proposal and support the JIGE text.

Rep. of Korea   My delegation prefers the JIGE text because my delegation thinks also that the concept of effective control is a matter of company law as the distinguished delegation of Hong Kong China said. That concept is too broad to provide in this Convention. So it is better for a new Convention to leave that matter to the national law.

Ghana   I will endeavour to be brief. Mr Chairman we wish to thank the UK delegation for that very intelligent exposition. Mr Chairman we have said earlier and we still go by what we said that we identified that there is a problem and that to the extent that the UK delegation has made so much effort for coming to solve this problem with what has been proposed, Mr Chairman we fully support the UK proposal.

Chairman   Now we have run through the list of speakers. In view of the interest I think it was right to let everybody indicate its position.

United Kingdom   We are grateful to the Committee for many of the comments which were made. At the moment the book is not published so we cannot read it. This Conference has recognized that there is a difficulty. A number of delegations said that and it is our belief that this will become even more apparent if this Convention does come into force when we will see the operation of article 1(1)(e) in particular. That has been by way of an example and not the central point of our presentation. Mr Chairman, this issue of associated ships arrest was obviously, in view of what we have been doing at the Conference, an issue of considerable importance and concern for my Government. Obviously, I have to report back and I'll take instructions and reflect on what has gone on here. But I think the reason why I have taken the floor again is to reflect on comments by China and particularly Belgium. I think those delegations made some very important points. Regardless of the issue immediately before us I think this delegation is considerably concerned in case we cannot produce a document that will work. And I think Belgium in particular put their finger on the fact that we seem to be becoming more entrenched as the week progresses. This delegation does not want that to happen. We came here to produce an instrument which would work and which would have checks and balances and that is certainly what we have been seeking to do. Obviously we have lost the issue so we need not to prolong that. But I think that there are other issues which are still open and I strongly urge that this Committee thinks hard.

Chairman   Yes as he indicates this proposal is obviously not carried. It seems to be the destiny of the United Kingdom in relation to this particular topic to draw admiration and appreciation but not enough support.

1999 Convention

2. ARREST IS ALSO PERMISSIBLE OF ANY OTHER SHIP OR SHIPS WHICH, WHEN THE ARREST IS EFFECTED, IS OR ARE OWNED BY THE PERSON WHO IS LIABLE FOR THE MARITIME CLAIM AND WHO WAS, WHEN THE CLAIM AROSE:

(A) OWNER OF THE SHIP IN RESPECT OF WHICH THE MARITIME CLAIM AROSE; OR

(B) DEMISE CHARTERER, TIME CHARTERER OR VOYAGE CHARTERER OF THAT SHIP.

THIS PROVISION DOES NOT APPLY TO CLAIMS IN RESPECT OF OWNERSHIP OR POSSESSION OF A SHIP.

PARAGRAPH 3

Draft of the CMI International Sub-Committee

(3) NOTWITHSTANDING THE PROVISIONS OF PARAGRAPHS (1) AND (2) OF THIS ARTICLE, THE ARREST OF A SHIP WHICH IS NOT OWNED BY THE PERSON LIABLE FOR THE CLAIM SHALL BE PERMISSIBLE ONLY IF UNDER THE LAW OF THE STATE WHERE THE ARREST IS DEMANDED THE CLAIM CAN BE ENFORCED AGAINST THAT SHIP OR BY THE FORCED SALE OF THAT SHIP.

Report of the Chairman of the CMI International Sub-Committee

The provision in para 3 is intended to ensure that arrest is not made as a means of putting pressure on the owner in cases where the ship itself is not released against security and would not be the subject of enforcement when the case has been determined as its merits.

CMI Draft

(3) NOTWITHSTANDING THE PROVISIONS OF PARAGRAPHS (1) AND (2) OF THIS ARTICLE, THE ARREST OF A SHIP WHICH IS NOT OWNED BY THE PERSON ALLEGEDLY LIABLE FOR THE CLAIM SHALL BE PERMISSIBLE ONLY IF, UNDER THE LAW OF THE STATE WHERE THE ARREST IS DEMANDED A JUDGEMENT IN RESPECT OF THAT CLAIM CAN BE ENFORCED AGAINST THAT SHIP BY JUDICIAL OR FORCED SALE OF THAT SHIP.

CMI Report

62. Paragraph (3) of Article 3 relates to those cases, first of all in respect of ships under bareboat charter, where a ship may be arrested even though the owner is not personally liable for the claim. It provides that such arrest may only be made if under the law of the *forum arresti* a judgment may be enforced by the sale of the ship. This is to ensure that the arrest is not used only as means of putting pressure on the owner to obtain security.

JIGE
Draft Articles 1994

Note of the Editor. The text of the CMI Draft has been reproduced without any change in the Draft Articles 1994 and 1997.

Diplomatic Conference
Proceedings of the Main Committee

First reading—3 March 1999[61]

Chairman   We then deal with paragraph 3 of article 3 of the JIGE text.
United Kingdom   We certainly want this paragraph in. Without this we have considerable problems, in fact it would be problems which would be disastrous and I suspect for others. However there is the word in the third line, the person "allegedly" liable. We do have some difficulty with the word "allegedly". If we would delete it, it would be the best option.
CMI   Mr Chairman, an arrest is granted under the Convention on the basis of the allegation of a claim. Therefore the creditor who applies for the arrest when he is the holder of a maritime claim does not have to provide any proof of this claim. Therefore the words "the person liable" which appear in various provisions of the Convention do not imply that a proof of liability or a definitive

---

61. Text from tape No. 25.

proof of liability is required because under the Convention it suffices that an allegation of the claim is made by the claimant. The fact that in this particular provision the word "allegedly" is inserted is in contrast with the rest of the Convention and it seems to me it is not necessary each time to say that there must not be a definitive proof of liability. The words "person liable" mean the person against whom a claim has been made and it is only an allegation of liability. I don't think it is necessary at all to state that the person is "allegedly liable" but it is clear from the global interpretation of the Convention what is meant by the words "liable" and it would be bad for the interpretation of the global Convention that in one individual provision the word "allegedly" is inserted. So, if you allow me to do so, I would suggest and recommend that the word "allegedly" here be deleted.

Sweden We think this a very important article. It contains the rule that an arrest is permissible only if a final judgment can be enforced against the ship. So in practice if the Court from the beginning finds it clear that a final judgment cannot be enforced the Court then will not grant the application at all. However this article 3(3) is written in a too narrow way in our opinion. Its present wording concerns only the situation where the person allegedly liable for the claim is not the owner of the ship. Sweden will therefore propose that the words "which is not owned by the person allegedly liable for the claim" should be deleted. In our opinion the rule should be applicable to all situations when a final judgment cannot be enforced against the ship by the forced sale of it. We think this is a basic principle.

Chairman The first proposal was to delete the word "allegedly" and I take it this is accepted. What about the Swedish proposal?

Spain We have doubts about this proposal and want to postpone a decision.

Ghana We support Spain. We want to have some time to think about it.

Italy We should like to ask Sweden which may be the situation when the claimant cannot enforce his claim on the ship otherwise than when the ship is not owned by the debtor.

Russian Fed.   We must approach very carefully the proposal regarding the deletion of the words which constitute the meaning of this item. Their deletion will deprive the paragraph of all sense. The presence of these words is an indispensable precondition of this paragraph's viability.

United Kingdom   I stressed how important this article is for us and as the Russian Fed. has said there is a very real danger we actually undo what this part of the article is intended to achieve. We therefore are extremely cautious about this proposal.

Japan   We also would like to be very cautious. If we delete this phrase a ship owned by the person allegedly liable for the claim comes within the scope of this provision. For example consider this case. There is agreement about jurisdiction or arbitration and the claimant cannot enforce his claim in that Court (when the arrest is applied for): in that case is the arrest of a ship not permissible?

CMI   Mr Chairman, I should like only to mention that the origin of this provision was strictly related to the recognition of the right of arrest as security for a claim against the demise charterer and it was agreed in Lisbon and then was agreed also during the JIGE sessions that a condition for admitting the arrest of a ship as security for a claim against the demise charterer was the possibility for the claimant to enforce a judgment against that ship. This was the origin of the provision. Then it was slightly expanded by eliminating an express reference in paragraph 3 to the demise charterer by replacing it with the words "a ship which is not owned by the person allegedly liable for that claim". That was the origin. There is a strict relationship that would now entirely disappear if the words "which is not owned by the person allegedly liable etc." are deleted. This is a matter which deserves very serious consideration.

Singapore   We cannot agree with the Swedish proposal because it changes the meaning of the provision.

Belgium   We share the views of the majority. But we have a problem with the words "under the law of the State where the arrest is demanded" and I think we should consider the bearing of that phrase. The observation has been made that a dispute may very well be submitted to arbitration or to the jurisdiction of another State which would recognize the validity of the arrest, while the text we have could be in conflict with the law competent to decide the dispute which recognizes such right while the court of the State where the arrest is applied for does not. I believe that this also should be discussed. My suggestion is to delete such words.

Chairman There is agreement on deletion of "allegedly" while I don't think there is agreement on the Swedish proposal. We therefore adopt provisionally this paragraph with deletion of "allegedly" subject to Sweden being able to obtain support for its proposal. So decided.

Second reading—11 March 1999[62]

The Chairman of the Drafting Committee reported as follows:
There was a debate in the Drafting Committee in respect of the word "allegedly" in connection with the word "liable". It was discussed and the decision was taken to delete that word. The substance is clear: the words "any person asserting a maritime claim" in article 1(4) indicate that the liability has not been decided upon the Court. It is clear that when we talk about "person liable" in article 3(3) we intend an alleged liability. The deletion of the word "allegedly" was approved and paragraph (3) was adopted.

1999 Convention

3. NOTWITHSTANDING THE PROVISIONS OF PARAGRAPHS 1 AND 2 OF THIS ARTICLE, THE ARREST OF A SHIP WHICH IS NOT OWNED BY THE PERSON LIABLE FOR THE CLAIM SHALL BE PERMISSIBLE ONLY IF, UNDER THE LAW OF THE STATE WHERE THE ARREST IS APPLIED FOR, A JUDGMENT IN RESPECT OF THAT CLAIM CAN BE ENFORCED AGAINST THAT SHIP BY JUDICIAL OR FORCED SALE OF THAT SHIP.

62. Text from tape No. 75.

II.III.7 ARTICLE 4: RELEASE FROM ARREST

PARAGRAPH 1

Draft of the CMI International Sub-Committee

(1) THE COURT WITHIN WHOSE JURISDICTION THE SHIP HAS BEEN ARRESTED SHALL ORDER THE RELEASE OF THE SHIP WHEN SUFFICIENT SECURITY HAS BEEN FURNISHED IN A SATISFACTORY FORM.

Report of the Chairman of the CMI International Sub-Committee

Art. 4 corresponds to the present art. 5.

It has not been found necessary to distinguish, as in the present art. 5, between arrest in ownership disputes and in other cases. Security in the sense used in art. 4 includes a limitation fund according to one of the Conventions on global limitation of liability.

CMI Draft

(1) A SHIP WHICH HAS BEEN ARRESTED SHALL BE RELEASED WHEN SUFFICIENT SECURITY HAS BEEN FURNISHED IN A SATISFACTORY FORM.

CMI Report

63. Article 4 corresponds to art. 5 of the 1952 Convention. It has not been found necessary to uphold the distinction in that article between ownership disputes and other disputes. Article 4 was adopted by 27 votes with 7 abstentions.

JIGE
Draft Articles 1994

(1) A SHIP WHICH HAS BEEN ARRESTED SHALL BE RELEASED WHEN SUFFICIENT SECURITY HAS BEEN FURNISHED IN A SATISFACTORY FORM.

Eighth Session: 9–10 October 1995

Report—Annex I

54. A proposal was made to include, in paragraph 1 of article 4, other cases where the vessel can be released as in case of extinction of claim for lapse of time for commencing substantive proceeding, etc. While the proposal received some support, most delegations were cautious in establishing an exhaustive list to that effect. It was pointed out that paragraph (1) was not restrictive and covered other cases of possible release. Furthermore it would be difficult to provide an exhaustive list of cases where the vessel can be released. However, one delegation favoured adopting language which would permit release only upon payment also of custody costs.

55. The observer for the International Chamber of Shipping (ICS) expressed concern regarding the use of the term "satisfactory form" which did not exist in the 1952 Arrest Convention. It was

explained that the words had been added so as to permit the court which decides on release to decide also on the satisfactory form of security.

56. In view of the above the Sessional Group agreed to retain the text of article 4(1) as presently drafted.

Comments and proposals by Japan

5. Article 4, which concerns mandatory release from arrest by security, should not apply to the arrest relating to the disputes as to ownership or possession of the ship, because such disputes can not be always solved by preliminary compensation. In this connection, paragraph 1 of article 5 of the 1952 Arrest Convention clearly excludes the arrest in respect of such disputes from the application of release by security. Therefore, we propose that paragraph 1 of Article 4 of the revised draft should be reverted to the text of 1952 Arrest Convention.

Ninth Session, 2–6 December 1996

Report—Annex II

66. The Sessional Group considered the proposal of Japan (document JIGE(IX)/3) that the Group should revert to the text of the 1952 Convention in so far as it excluded mandatory release by provision of security in the case of arrest relating to disputes as to ownership or possession of a ship. This proviso should be added to the present paragraph 1. A second sentence would incorporate the second sentence of the first paragraph of Article 5 of the 1952 Convention, with the following two language corrections of a consequential kind: the expressions "or other appropriate judicial authority" and "bail or other" should be deleted.

67. The Group accepted this proposal.

Draft Articles 1997

(1) A SHIP WHICH HAS BEEN ARRESTED SHALL BE RELEASED WHEN SUFFICIENT SECURITY HAS BEEN FURNISHED IN A SATISFACTORY FORM, SAVE IN CASES IN WHICH A SHIP HAS BEEN ARRESTED IN RESPECT OF ANY OF THE MARITIME CLAIMS ENUMERATED IN ARTICLE 1(1)(S) AND (T). IN SUCH CASES, THE COURT MAY PERMIT THE PERSON IN POSSESSION OF THE SHIP TO CONTINUE TRADING THE SHIP, UPON SUCH PERSON FURNISHING SUFFICIENT SECURITY, OR MAY OTHERWISE DEAL WITH THE OPERATION OF THE SHIP DURING THE PERIOD OF THE ARREST.

Diplomatic Conference

Proposal by Greece

DOCUMENT CRP.17

In article 4, paragraph (1), after the words "satisfactory form" add the following wording: "such as bail, bank guarantee or security provided by a financial institution, P&I club or any similar institution."

Proceedings of the Main Committee

First reading—3 and 4 March 1999[63]

Australia We have problems in respect of the mandatory release of the ship upon sufficient security being furnished in a satisfactory manner. Under Australian legislation the Court must also be satisfied that the fees of the Marshal have been paid in connection with the custody of the ship while under arrest, and consideration must also be given to a caveat that may have been lodged against release, so that the words "sufficient security" are not adequate in our case.

Chairman I think that a lot of delegates share your concern. This has been discussed before and I think that the understanding has been that there is nothing in article 4(1) which prevents a State

63. Text from tapes Nos. 25–29.

from adding further claims or that there are further requirements of a procedural nature for the release. But that is my own understanding and recollection.

United Kingdom   Our understanding as how this article would work is very much as you have suggested. But I have to say that we liked what we have heard from the Australian delegation. We would be more than happy to see that in writing if that is acceptable by this Committee.

Chairman   I suppose that there may be others who would like to see the Australian proposal in writing. We shall come back as soon as the Australian proposal is available. We revert to the Australian proposal to the effect of replacing the text with the following:

"A ship which has been arrested shall be released when the Court is satisfied that:

(a) sufficient security has been furnished;

(b) any payment relevant to the maintenance of the ship under arrest has been paid, and

(c) the legal requirements of the State of arrest which protect the interest of third parties have been met."

Hong Kong   The text suggested should replace the whole paragraph 1? *Yes*. There is no reference to art. 1(s) and (t). Was it intentional?

Australia   We felt that there was no need for the exception.

CMI   Mr Chairman, it seems to me that the requirements which are set out are too specific and that the effect would be to impose upon Contracting States possible changes in their provisions relating to the consequences of arrest of a ship and the obligations of the arrestor following the arrest of ship. This is a matter which must be left to national law and on the other hand I think that the rest of paragraph 1 of article 4 must be maintained because it is important for example to make clear that this provision does not apply in the cases mentioned in art. 1(1) sub-paragraphs (s) and (t). I wonder whether it would not satisfy the Australian delegation to add after the words in the text "sufficient security has been furnished in a satisfactory form" the following words or similar words "and that the other conditions which are required by the law of the Court are complied with". In other words to refer to the *lex fori* in respect of possible other conditions rather than to impose to all Contracting States to accept conditions which may be in order in some national jurisdictions but may not be acceptable in other jurisdictions.

Chairman   Please repeat what you said.

CMI   Mr Chairman I have read this proposal just now, I could not have any specific wording in writing yet Mr Chairman but the words I have suggested are related to the existing text, if I may read it: "a ship which has been arrested shall be released when sufficient security has been furnished in a satisfactory form". After the words "satisfactory form" I would suggest, in order to meet the Australian problem, words such as "and the other conditions required by the law of the Court where the arrest is made are complied with" and then continue "save in cases in which a ship has been arrested in respect of any of the maritime claims enumerated in art. 1(1)(s) and (t)" and then follows the existing second sentence of paragraph 1. So it is a mere insertion in the JIGE text of the words I have indicated Mr. Chairman. Of course I can put them in writing but I can't do that right now.

United Kingdom   Like Australia we felt the text is convoluted. I think we can go along with the suggestion made by Prof. Berlingieri. As regards the second sentence, we could live without that but also with that.

Russian Fed.   We are practically completing the discussion of the issue. Evaluating various approaches in respect of paragraph 1 of article 4 we come to the conclusion that this paragraph suits us completely. We do not see an alternative to paragraph 1 in the Australian proposal. The provisions contained in sub-paragraphs "b" and "c" of the Australian proposal, in essence, have nothing to do with paragraph 1. The Argentine delegation is, evidently, right in their opinion that sub-paragraphs "b" and "c" relate to executory process, which must not be regulated by the Convention. Therefore we are firmly convinced that paragraph 1 of article 4 of the draft Convention corresponds to its purpose.

Chairman   There is a very strong majority in favour of the JIGE text. I shall come back to the proposal of CMI. The possible addition indicated by Prof. Berlingieri was made on the spot. My conclusion is that we adopt the JIGE text which will be given to the Drafting Group which will consider if from the drafting standpoint it is clear.

Second reading—9 March 1999[64]

The Greek delegate introduced CRP.17 stating that the indication of the types of guarantee that may be provided for the release of the ship from arrest would facilitate the task of the Courts. The proposal was supported by some delegations who stated that failing any such indication a Court might decide that the only satisfactory security is cash which may be difficult to provide quickly, specially on a weekend. Other delegations objected, stating that Courts should be absolutely free to decide the type of security stating, in particular, that they could not accept a reference to the P&I Club. The Chairman asked the Greek delegation to clarify whether Courts would be bound by the parameters of the provision as suggested or they would be free to decide, for example, that a cash deposit is required. The Greek delegate replied stating that the Courts would be free to decide as they wished, whereupon some delegations observed that if the purpose was only to give some non-binding suggestions, the provision had no purpose at all.

The Chairman then stated that there was not enough support for the Greek proposal and that consequently article 4(1) should stay as it was presently worded.

1999 Convention

1. A SHIP WHICH HAS BEEN ARRESTED SHALL BE RELEASED WHEN SUFFICIENT SECURITY HAS BEEN PROVIDED IN A SATISFACTORY FORM, SAVE IN CASES IN WHICH A SHIP HAS BEEN ARRESTED IN RESPECT OF ANY OF THE MARITIME CLAIMS ENUMERATED IN ARTICLE 1, PARAGRAPHS 1 (S) AND (T). IN SUCH CASES, THE COURT MAY PERMIT THE PERSON IN POSSESSION OF THE SHIP TO CONTINUE TRADING THE SHIP, UPON SUCH PERSON PROVIDING SUFFICIENT SECURITY, OR MAY OTHERWISE DEAL WITH THE OPERATION OF THE SHIP DURING THE PERIOD OF THE ARREST.

PARAGRAPH 2

Draft of the CMI International Sub-Committee

(2) IN THE ABSENCE OF AGREEMENT BETWEEN THE INTERESTED PARTIES AS TO THE SUFFICIENCY AND FORM OF THE SECURITY, THE COURT SHALL DETERMINE THE NATURE AND AMOUNT THEREOF.

CMI Draft

(2) IN THE ABSENCE OF AGREEMENT BETWEEN THE PARTIES AS TO THE SUFFICIENCY AND FORM OF THE SECURITY, THE COURT SHALL DETERMINE ITS NATURE AND THE AMOUNT THEREOF, NOT EXCEEDING THE VALUE OF THE SHIP.

CMI Report

64. There are no mandatory requirements relating to an agreement between the parties with respect to security, whether or not that agreement affects the form of the security or its amount or the place where it is deposited. Unless the parties agree otherwise, the security cannot exceed the value of the ship. Similarly, unless the parties agree otherwise, the security must be given in the country of arrest.

Security in the sense of art. 4 includes a limitation fund according to one of the Conventions on global limitation of liability.

JIGE
Draft Articles 1994

(2) IN THE ABSENCE OF AGREEMENT BETWEEN THE PARTIES AS TO THE SUFFICIENCY AND FORM OF THE SECURITY, THE COURT SHALL DETERMINE ITS NATURE AND THE AMOUNT THEREOF, NOT EXCEEDING THE VALUE OF THE SHIP.

64. Summary from tape No. 65.

Eighth Session, 9–10 October 1995

Report—Annex I

12. One delegation suggested that the phrase "not exceeding the value of the ship" be deleted from paragraph 2, bearing in mind that the total amount of the claim to be secured by the arrest could exceed this value.

13. This proposal was opposed by the majority of delegations. In this regard, it was explained that the action of arrest, being by nature "*in rem*", was necessarily restricted to the provision of a security which could not exceed the value of the ship.

57. One delegation proposed to delete the words "not exceeding the value of the ship" from paragraph (2). It was argued that as the security was fixed on the basis of the amount of the claim, arrest could not be limited to the value of the ship. Furthermore, the words did not exist in the 1952 Convention. Alternatively, this delegation proposed to add after "thereof" a semicolon and to replace the words in question by the words "if the arrest is limited to the ship, the security shall not exceed the value of the ship".

58. The proposal received some support, but the majority of delegations were in favour of retaining the text as drafted. It was pointed out that since the security was a substitute for the ship, it could not exceed the value of the ship. It was further explained that the arrest under the Convention was for a maritime claim on the ship, therefore security had to be limited to the value of the ship.

59. The Sessional Group, therefore, agreed to keep the present text of article 4(2).

Comments and proposals by the United Kingdom

21. Unlike Article 5 of the 1952 Convention, Article 4(2) of the JIGE text provides that the amount of security should not exceed the value of the ship. Article 8(6) of the JIGE text, however, provides that international Conventions on limitation of liability would take precedence over the new Arrest Convention.

22. The reference to the value of the ship in Article 4(2) is confusing, therefore, since the applicable limitation amount will very often exceed the value of the ship. The recent entry into force of the 1992 Protocol to the 1969 Civil Liability Convention and the adoption of the HNS Convention and the 1996 Protocol to the Convention on the Limitation of Liability for Maritime Claims 1976 make this even more likely than in the past.

23. The United Kingdom delegation believes that it is poor drafting to suggest, in Article 4(2), that the amount of security is restricted to the value of the ship when, by virtue of Article 8(6), the relevant restriction in most cases will be the applicable limit on the shipowner's liability, which will generally be a greater amount. Article 4(2) should therefore provide, as Article 5 of the 1952 Convention does, that:

> In the absence of agreement between the parties as to the sufficiency and form of the security, the Court shall determine its nature and the amount thereof.

24. Consequential amendments will be needed to Articles 4(4)(b) and 5(1)(a).

Ninth Session, 2–6 December 1996

Report—Annex II

68. The Group considered the proposal made by the United Kingdom (document JIGE(IX)/3) to delete reference to the value of the ship.

69. This proposal was supported by several delegations on the grounds that the limitation amount applicable in determining the security would, very often, exceed the value of the ship.

70. Other delegations opposed this proposal. In their view the security provided to obtain release should necessarily be related to the value of the ship which would, in the end, be the only value which could be obtained in the case of forced sale. Some of these delegations pointed out that Article 8(5) made it clear that the Arrest Convention would not affect the application of international conventions providing for limitation of liability.

71. The Group decided that the expression "*not exceeding the value of the ship*" should be included within square brackets.

Draft Articles 1997

(2) IN THE ABSENCE OF AGREEMENT BETWEEN THE PARTIES AS TO THE SUFFICIENCY AND FORM OF THE SECURITY, THE COURT SHALL DETERMINE ITS NATURE AND THE AMOUNT THEREOF [, NOT EXCEEDING THE VALUE OF THE SHIP].[65]

Diplomatic Conference
Comments and Proposals

Hong Kong, China

DCOUMENT 188/3

20. Remove the square bracket and keep the words within the bracket as the amount of security should not exceed the value of the ship.

Italy

DOCUMENT 188/3/ADD.3

4. Following the comments made at UNCTAD by certain delegations on limiting the amount of security to be provided, the phrase "not exceeding the value of the ship" in paragraphs 2 and 4(b)(ii) will be the subject of discussion at the forthcoming Diplomatic Conference.

5. Italy is in favour of retaining the phrase, given the provisions of its Code of Civil Procedure, governing distraint which, according to article 463 of the Shipping Code, apply by extension to the Shipping Code.

6. Article 468 of the Code of Civil Procedure explicitly states that in order to secure a release from distraint from the courts, the debtor must furnish sufficient security, due regard being had to the "amount owed which gave rise to the distraint" and the expenses incurred "by reason of the value of the items distrained".

7. Limiting the security that must be furnished under the Convention in order to secure a release from arrest thus seems perfectly consistent with current national legislation on the matter.

Mexico

DOCUMENT 188/3

42. As regards release from arrest, and with reference to paragraph 2 of this article and subparagraph (b) of paragraph 4, the Government of Mexico considers that the brackets around the phrase "not exceeding the value of the ship" should be deleted, provided that, in the light of the 1969 protocols to the (Convention) concerning oil pollution damage and the 1971 protocol [sic] on the establishment of the international compensation fund, the owner of the ship is able to limit his liability if he becomes a party in any event giving rise to the necessity of paying compensation in respect of damage caused in the territory of the State in which that event occurred.

43. In addition, the 1971 Convention establishing the fund (now known as the 1992 Convention) sets certain ceilings on the amounts of compensation payable in respect of accidents; those ceilings are fixed on the basis of various hypotheses (damage due to natural causes, to negligence, etc.). Finally, none of the above-mentioned conventions establishes a possibility that the liability of the owner of the ship may exceed the value of the latter in the event of an incident or an accident.

44. In the light of the foregoing, Mexico cannot agree to guarantees of payment of compensation for damage caused by its merchant shipping exceeding the ceilings laid down in those conventions.

Tanzania

DOCUMENT 188/3

97. The phrase "not exceeding the value of the ship", appearing in paragraphs 2 and 4(b)(ii) be retained.

---

65. Following comments made by some delegations concerning limiting the amount of the security to the value of the ship the phrase "not exceeding the value of the ship" in paragraphs 2 and 4(b)(ii) is placed in brackets. See the report of the Joint Group at its 9th session, ibid., paras. 68–77.

Thailand

DOCUMENT 188/3

87. The expressions "not exceeding the value of the ship" in paragraph 2 should be deleted. Reference to value of the ship could eventually force the court to pay more attention to the value of the ship than the amount of the claim. Moreover, in cases where it is clear that the amount of claim is considerably higher than the value of an arrestable ship, it is unlikely that the claimant will arrest that ship for securing the claim because it is foreseeable that the recovery from the enforcement against the arrested ship will not be adequate. On the other hand, where the amount of claim is not much higher than the current ship value, the claimant may be willing to effect an arrest, despite knowing that the ultimate recovery (from forced sale) may be less than the amount of claim, in order to pressurise the shipowner to lodge alternative security. Reference to value of the ship also seems to disturb "interim measure" and "urgency" nature of arrest. The matter should entirely be on the court's discretion.

CMI

DOCUMENT 188/3

143. The provision, added in the Lisbon Draft, whereby the amount of the security may not exceed the value of the ship was criticised by the UK Delegation, who pointed out that it may be in conflict with the applicable limitation convention (which, pursuant to Article 8(6) takes precedence over the new Arrest Convention), since the limitation may often exceed the value of the ship. This comment is very likely based on the provision of Article 13(2) of the 1976 Convention, whereby after the limitation fund has been constituted any ship belonging to a person on behalf of whom the fund has been constituted which has been arrested for a claim which may be raised against the fund may (or shall, in certain cases) be released. Following the comment from the UK the words "not exceeding the value of the ship" have been placed in square brackets.

144. The reason given for the deletion of these words seems, however, to be misconceived. In fact, there is no connection at all between the reason why a ship should be released from arrest when security is given for an amount equal to the value of the ship and the reason why the ship may not be arrested after the limitation fund has been established.

145. In the former case, the ship is arrested as security for the claim of the arrestor and in case the security is enforced, the amount the arrestor may obtain cannot exceed the value of the ship. It follows that the owner of the ship should be entitled to replace the ship with other security of equal value.

146. In the case of the establishment of the limitation fund, the release of the ship is not the consequence of the provision of security for the claim of the arrestor, but rather the consequence of the claimants being prevented from enforcing their claims on assets of their debtor other than the limitation fund. If the owner of the ship has obtained the release of the ship by providing security, whatever its amount, he may still be subject to the actions of other claimants in respect of claims arising out of the same accident or occurrence and, in order to prevent individual actions against his ships and his other assets, he must commence limitation proceedings and constitute a limitation fund. Only after the fund has been constituted the security may be released in the circumstances set out in Article 11 of the Limitation Convention.

147. The security for the release of the ship from arrest and the limitation fund are, therefore, entirely separate and relate to different interests.

ICS

DOCUMENT 188/3

123. ICS is of the view that the phrase "not exceeding the value of the ship" should be retained. However, we are concerned that it could be interpreted to mean that security up to the value of the ship must be provided in all cases in order to obtain release of the ship. The maximum security required should be the lowest of the limitation amount/global limitation of the ship or the value of the ship, and of course not more than the size of the claim. The square brackets in Article 4, paragraphs (2) and (4)(b)(ii) should be deleted and the words therein retained. Article 5, paragraph (1)(a) should remain as drafted.

Ukraine

DOCUMENT CRP.11

9. Remove the square brackets and incorporate the wording inside the text.

Proceedings of the Main Committee

First reading—4 March 1999[66]

The proposal of the CMI to keep the words "not exceeding the value of the ship" was supported by a strong majority. The observer from the CMI so stated:

Mr Chairman, it has been pointed out by several delegates that the ship is a security for the claimant and that if the ship is not released from arrest she will be sold in a forced sale and the claimant will obtain, if his claim is at least equal to the value of the ship, the proceeds of sale and no more. The claimant will not obtain the insurance value of the ship because the insurance value of the ship is not the proceeds of sale. The insurance value of the ship does not change in time or for quite some time, while the market value of the ship may change continuously. There are many cases in which the insurance value is below the market value and in other cases the insurance value is significantly above the market value. So I submit, Mr Chairman, that it would be a great mistake to include in this Convention a reference to the insurance value.

The text of this paragraph was subsequently adopted and the brackets deleted.

1999 Convention

2. IN THE ABSENCE OF AGREEMENT BETWEEN THE PARTIES AS TO THE SUFFICIENCY AND FORM OF THE SECURITY, THE COURT SHALL DETERMINE ITS NATURE AND THE AMOUNT THEREOF, NOT EXCEEDING THE VALUE OF THE ARRESTED SHIP.

PARAGRAPH 3

Draft of the CMI International Sub-Committee

(3) ANY REQUEST FOR THE SHIP TO BE RELEASED UPON SECURITY BEING PROVIDED SHALL NOT BE CONSTRUED AS AN ACKNOWLEDGEMENT OF LIABILITY NOR AS A WAIVER OF ANY DEFENCE OR ANY RIGHT TO LIMIT LIABILITY.

Note of the Editor. This sub-paragraph has been left unchanged throughout the travaux préparatoires and has been adopted by the Diplomatic Conference.

JIGE
Eighth Session, 9–10 October 1995

Report—Annex I

61. Two delegations questioned whether the text of this paragraph could not be misinterpreted as implying acknowledgement of the shipowner's liability. In response, it was noted that the deposit of a security was clearly related to the characterisation of arrest as a conservatory measure. This conservatory character meant that the deposit of a security to obtain release from arrest could not be interpreted as an acknowledgement of liability or as prejudicing any consideration related to the shipowner's liability in connection with the claim which led to the arrest of the ship.

Ninth Session, 2–6 December 1996

Report—Annex II

72. No comments were made in respect of this paragraph.

---

66. Text and summary from tape No. 28.

Diplomatic Conference
Proceedings of the Main Committee

First reading—4 March 1999

This paragraph was adopted without discussion.

1999 Convention

3. ANY REQUEST FOR THE SHIP TO BE RELEASED UPON SECURITY BEING PROVIDED SHALL NOT BE CONSTRUED AS AN ACKNOWLEDGEMENT OF LIABILITY NOR AS A WAIVER OF ANY DEFENCE OR ANY RIGHT TO LIMIT LIABILITY.

PARAGRAPHS 4 AND 5[67]

Draft of the CMI International Sub-Committee

(4) (A) IF A SHIP HAS BEEN ARRESTED IN A NON-CONTRACTING STATE AND IS NOT RELEASED ALTHOUGH SECURITY HAS BEEN GIVEN IN A CONTRACTING STATE, THAT SECURITY SHALL BE ORDERED TO BE RELEASED ON APPLICATION TO THE COURT IN THE CONTRACTING STATE.

(B) IF IN A NON-CONTRACTING STATE THE SHIP IS RELEASED UPON SATISFACTORY SECURITY BEING PROVIDED, ANY SECURITY GIVEN IN A CONTRACTING STATE SHALL BE ORDERED TO BE RELEASED TO THE EXTENT THAT THE TOTAL AMOUNT OF SECURITY GIVEN IN THE TWO STATES EXCEEDS:

(I) THE CLAIM FOR WHICH THE ARREST HAS BEEN MADE, OR

(II) THE VALUE OF THE SHIP,

WHICHEVER IS THE LOWER.

Report of the Chairman of the CMI International Sub-Committee

When a ship has been arrested in a State, art. 5 prevents its re-arrest in a Contracting State. No such assurance exists against re-arrest in a non-Contracting State. Para 4, therefore, provides for the release of security already given in a Contracting State if the ship is arrested in a non-Contracting State or released there only after giving security.

CMI Draft

(4) (A) IF A SHIP HAS BEEN ARRESTED IN A NON-PARTY STATE AND IS NOT RELEASED ALTHOUGH SECURITY HAS BEEN GIVEN IN A STATE PARTY, THAT SECURITY SHALL BE ORDERED RELEASED ON APPLICATION TO THE COURT IN THE STATE PARTY SAVE IN EXCEPTIONAL CASES WHERE IT WOULD BE UNJUST TO DO SO.

(B) IF IN A NON-PARTY STATE THE SHIP IS RELEASED UPON SATISFACTORY SECURITY BEING PROVIDED, ANY SECURITY GIVEN IN A STATE PARTY SHALL BE ORDERED RELEASED TO THE EXTENT THAT THE TOTAL AMOUNT OF SECURITY GIVEN IN THE TWO STATES EXCEEDS:

(I) THE CLAIM FOR WHICH THE SHIP HAS BEEN ARRESTED, OR

(II) THE VALUE OF THE SHIP,

WHICHEVER IS THE LOWER.

SUCH RELEASE SHALL, HOWEVER, NOT BE ORDERED UNLESS THE SECURITY GIVEN IN THE NON-PARTY STATE WILL ACTUALLY BE AVAILABLE TO THE CLAIMANT AND WILL BE FREELY TRANSFERABLE.

CMI Report

65. When a ship has been arrested, Article 5 prevents its re-arrest in a Contacting State. No such assurance exists against re-arrest in a non-Contracting State. Paragraph (4), therefore, provides for the release of security already given in a Contracting State if the ship is arrested in a non-Contracting

---

67. Prior to the Diplomatic Conference the provisions now in paragraphs (4) and (5) were part of the same paragraph, numbered (4).

State or released there only after security has been given. An exception is made where it would be unjust to release the security, such as when the security in the non-Contracting State is not available to the claimant. The provisions on exceptions are based upon similar provisions in the Conventions on global limitation. However, the need in individual cases to protect the claimant may not always be the same in the Arrest Convention since the claimant can avoid release in the Contracting State by himself releasing the security in the non-Contracting State.

66. There may be a need for further co-ordination between this article and the Conventions on global limitation, cf. also Article 8, paragraph (6).

JIGE
Draft Articles 1994

Note of the Editor. The text is the same as that in the CMI Draft.

Eighth Session, 9–10 October 1995

Report—Annex I

62. It was noted that the expression "unjust" in sub-paragraph (a) was not appropriate treaty language due to its imprecise meaning. It was also suggested that the whole reference to "exceptional cases" in which it would be unjust to release the security should be deleted.

63. One delegation suggested that an additional provision should be added to the effect of relating the upper limits of the limitation fund established to cover for the liability of the shipowner to the limits of the security to be requested to release the ship.

Ninth Session, 2–6 December 1996

Report—Annex II

73. The Group noted the views of two delegations according to which the expressions "in respect of the same claim" should be incorporated in subparagraphs (a) and (b) after the first reference to the security given in a State party.

74. The Group considered whether the phrase "save in exceptional circumstances where it would be unjust to do so" should be deleted from subparagraph (a). Some delegations favoured this deletion, bearing in mind the imprecise meaning of the word "unjust" and the unlikelihood of application of this proviso.

75. Other delegations, while accepting that the wording was defective, were of the opinion that the proviso was needed in order to address any possible case where decisions taken within the jurisdiction of a non-party could affect the implementation by a State party of the basic provisions of the convention regarding the release of security.

76. The Group decided that the phrase should be kept within square brackets.

77. Bearing in mind the decision taken on paragraph 2 of Article 4, the Group decided to keep within square brackets the reference to the value of the ship in subparagraph 4 (b).

Draft Articles 1997

(4) (A) IF A SHIP HAS BEEN ARRESTED IN A NON-PARTY STATE AND IS NOT RELEASED ALTHOUGH SECURITY HAS BEEN GIVEN IN A STATE PARTY, THAT SECURITY SHALL BE ORDERED RELEASED ON APPLICATION TO THE COURT IN THE STATE PARTY [SAVE IN EXCEPTIONAL CASES WHERE IT WOULD BE UNJUST TO DO SO].

(B) IF IN A NON-PARTY STATE THE SHIP IS RELEASED UPON SATISFACTORY SECURITY BEING PROVIDED, ANY SECURITY GIVEN IN A STATE PARTY SHALL BE ORDERED RELEASED TO THE EXTENT THAT THE TOTAL AMOUNT OF SECURITY GIVEN IN THE TWO STATES EXCEEDS:

    (I) THE CLAIM FOR WHICH THE SHIP HAS BEEN ARRESTED[, OR
    (II) THE VALUE OF THE SHIP,
  WHICHEVER IS THE LOWER].

SUCH RELEASE SHALL, HOWEVER, NOT BE ORDERED UNLESS THE SECURITY GIVEN IN THE NON-PARTY STATE WILL ACTUALLY BE AVAILABLE TO THE CLAIMANT AND WILL BE FREELY TRANSFERABLE.

Diplomatic Conference

PARAGRAPH 4

Comments and Proposals

Hong Kong, China

DOCUMENT 188/3

19. Delete the words within the square bracket as the "exceptional cases" and "unjust to do so" is too vague.

Mexico

DOCUMENT 188/3

45. As regards the phrase between brackets in sub-paragraphs (a) and (b) of paragraph 4, Mexico considers that it would be desirable to include the words "in respect of the same claim", as suggested in footnote 7. It also recommends deletion of the phrase "save in exceptional cases where it would be unjust to do so"; the phrase contains terms of a subjective nature, and the Government of Mexico therefore recommends a more precise legal drafting.

Tanzania

DOCUMENT 188/3

98. With regard to Article 4(4)(a) the proposed phrase "in respect of the same claim", after the words "a State party" in paragraphs 4(a) and 4(b) of this Article be inserted.

Thailand

DOCUMENT 188/3

88. The terms "save in exceptional cases where it would be unjust to do so" in paragraph 4(a) should be retained to give the court more flexibility in dealing with the matter.

Proceedings of the Main Committee

First reading—4 March 1999[68]

The addition of the words "in respect of that ship" was proposed by the delegate from Canada who so stated:

The use of word "security" without qualifier is unclear. The words "in respect of that ship" should be added. A reference to security in this instance is not necessarily a reference to security for the entire claim thereby obviously allowing the possibility as we see further in our text for further arrest if the amount of security were considered insufficient, and we think that this would be the necessary qualifier. Again, as I was saying yesterday, we are dealing with a provision where a ship has been arrested and it is quite different from a provision that deals with an anticipated arrest. My second point deals with the bracketed text. We would support the retention of the text and the removal of the square brackets. We think that this decision is needed in order to deal with any possible case where decisions taken within the jurisdiction of a non-Contracting State could affect the implementation by a Contracting State of the basic provisions of this Convention regarding the release of security.

The retention of the words in brackets in the text which was originally paragraph 4(a), supported by the delegate from Canada in the statement quoted above, was also supported by the delegate from the CMI who so stated:

Mr Chairman the question that has been asked is which may be the cases covered by the sentence in brackets. We are considering a situation where a vessel is arrested in a non-party State and a security is given in a State party. In such a situation it is possible that notwithstanding the intention

---

68. Summary and text from tape No. 32.

in good faith of the arrestor to cause the ship to be released, for some reason the judicial or other authority in the non-party State does not consent to the release and does not consider to be relevant that the security is given in a party State which is a different country from the State where the ship has been arrested. There are situations in which without any cooperation, if I may say so, or against the intention of the arrestor, the ship cannot be released and if in that case the consequence would be that the guarantee is released, I think that this would be against justice and fairness. There may therefore be situations in which the sentence in the square brackets may apply.

The addition proposed by Canada was adopted, while the words in brackets "save in exceptional cases where it would be unjust to do so" were deleted.

PARAGRAPH 5

Comments and proposal

Hong Kong, China

DOCUMENT 188/3

20. Remove the square bracket and keep the words within the bracket as the amount of security required should not be excessive.

Mexico

Note of the Editor. See paragraph (4) above.

Sudan

DOCUMENT 188/3

72. We believe that the phrase "whichever is the lower" should be amended to read "whichever covers or meets the maritime claim".

Tanzania

DOCUMENT 188/3

97. The phrases "not exceeding the value of the ship", appearing in paragraphs 2 and 4(b)(ii) be retained.

98. With regard to Article 4(a) the proposed phrase "in respect of the same claim", after the words "a State party" in paragraphs 4(a) and 4(b) of this Article be inserted.

Thailand

DOCUMENT 188/3

89. Paragraph 4(b)(ii) should be adjusted in accordance with the comment made in regard to paragraph 2.

Ukraine

DOCUMENT CRP.11

Article 4, para. 4(a)

10. Before "has been given in a State party", add "for the claim concerned".

Article 4, para. 4(b)

11. We suggest deleting "satisfactory", and removing the square brackets.

513

Proceedings of the Main Committee

First reading—4 March 1999[69]

The deletion of what in the JIGE Draft was paragraph 4(b) was proposed by the delegate from Canada who so stated:

We believe that different considerations apply to this paragraph in respect of the reference to the value of the ship. This for the following reason: at a point in time in which paragraph (b) (now § 5) applies the ship has been released and we are only dealing now with the issue of security. It strikes us why there would be a need to refer to the value of the ship that has been released. That value is no longer in issue. The ship has been released and it is only a question of the security. In fact it strikes us that if those words were retained, the words that appear now in (ii), the result might well be that if the claim exceeds the value of the security the provision may well deprive the opportunity of the claimant to seek additional security by means of a further arrest which is dealt with of course in article 5. So the real text here is really only what we see in the language of (i). (ii) is not of any relevance. In fact it can actually be detrimental to a claimant subsequently seeking to top up, if I can put it that way, the security because it is found to be inadequate. The conclusion would be that we recommend the deletion of the words in square brackets.

The observer of the CMI instead supported the adoption of the text of the JIGE Draft including the reference to the value of the ship. He so stated:

The situation covered in (b) is that of a security being provided in the State where the ship is arrested which is a non-Contracting State and a security is also provided in a Contracting State. I think it is a rather exceptional situation which is covered by this provision as well as that which is covered in sub-paragraph (a). In any event the purpose of this provision is that it is possible that in the non-Contracting State the vessel is released against a security which is insufficient and that therefore for some reason there is another security provided in the Contacting State, for the parties may have agreed to provide a security in a Contracting State. The order to release or the principle that the security provided in the Contracting State should be released is made conditional to the global amount of the two securities being in excess of either the amount of the claim or the value of the ship, whichever is the lower. If the global amount of the two securities is below or not in excess of either the amount of the claim or the value of the ship there does not seem to be any reason which justifies the release of the security granted in a Contracting State. The value of the ship is relevant here, it seems to me, because I don't think that it may be the intention of the two parties to agree to a security in excess of the amount of the value of the ship. Circumstances may have been such to cause securities to be granted in a specified amount but it doesn't seem to me that there is an implied agreement of the parties to grant securities in excess of the value of the ship. It seems to me that the comment made by the distinguished delegate of Canada implies, since the vessel is released, an agreement as to the global amount of the securities but I wonder if such an implied agreement may be deemed to exist.

The Chairman then so concluded:

It seems that the majority is in favour of keeping this paragraph and of keeping it without square brackets with the same addition of the previous paragraph.

1999 Convention

4. IF A SHIP HAS BEEN ARRESTED IN A NON-PARTY STATE AND IS NOT RELEASED ALTHOUGH SECURITY IN RESPECT OF THAT SHIP HAS BEEN PROVIDED IN A STATE PARTY IN RESPECT OF THE SAME CLAIM, THAT SECURITY SHALL BE ORDERED TO BE RELEASED ON APPLICATION TO THE COURT IN THE STATE PARTY.

5. IF IN A NON-PARTY STATE THE SHIP IS RELEASED UPON SATISFACTORY SECURITY IN RESPECT OF THAT SHIP BEING PROVIDED, ANY SECURITY PROVIDED IN A STATE PARTY IN RESPECT OF THE SAME CLAIM SHALL BE ORDERED TO BE RELEASED TO THE EXTENT THAT THE TOTAL AMOUNT OF SECURITY PROVIDED IN THE TWO STATES EXCEEDS:

(A) THE CLAIM FOR WHICH THE SHIP HAS BEEN ARRESTED, OR

(B) THE VALUE OF THE SHIP,

---

69. Text and summary from tape No. 32.

WHICHEVER IS THE LOWER. SUCH RELEASE SHALL, HOWEVER, NOT BE ORDERED UNLESS THE SECU-
RITY PROVIDED IN THE NON-PARTY STATE WILL ACTUALLY BE AVAILABLE TO THE CLAIMANT AND
WILL BE FREELY TRANSFERABLE.

PARAGRAPH 6[70]

Draft of the CMI International Sub-Committee

(5) WHERE PURSUANT TO PARAGRAPH (1) OF THIS ARTICLE SECURITY HAS BEEN PROVIDED, THE PARTY
PROVIDING SUCH SECURITY MAY AT ANY TIME APPLY TO THE COURT TO HAVE THAT SECURITY REDUCED,
VARIED OR DISPENSED WITH.

CMI Draft

(5) WHERE PURSUANT TO PARAGRAPH (1) OF THIS ARTICLE SECURITY HAS BEEN PROVIDED, THE PERSON
PROVIDING SUCH SECURITY MAY AT ANY TIME APPLY TO THE COURT TO HAVE THAT SECURITY REDUCED,
MODIFIED OR CANCELLED.

Note of the Editor. This text has been reproduced without changes in the Draft Articles 1994 and in the Draft
   Articles 1997.

JIGE
Eighth Session, 9–10 October 1995

Report—Annex I

64. No comments were made in connection with this paragraph.
65. The Group decided to revert to this article at a later stage.

Ninth Session, 2–6 December 1996

Report—Annex II

78. No comments were made in respect of this paragraph.

Diplomatic Conference
Comments and Proposals

Madagascar

DOCUMENT 188/3/ADD.1

4. The right of the person who has furnished security should be limited to the possibility of
requesting that such security should be reduced. It would be pointless to ask him to provide security
if, under the provisions of article 4, paragraph (5), he may apply to the court to have that security
cancelled.

Proceedings of the Main Committee

First reading—4 March 1999

This paragraph was adopted without discussion.

1999 Convention

6. WHERE, PURSUANT TO PARAGRAPH 1 OF THIS ARTICLE, SECURITY HAS BEEN PROVIDED, THE
PERSON PROVIDING SUCH SECURITY MAY AT ANY TIME APPLY TO THE COURT TO HAVE THAT SECU-
RITY REDUCED, MODIFIED, OR CANCELLED.

70. This paragraph was numbered 5 in all the drafts.

II.III.8 ARTICLE 5: RIGHT OF RE-ARREST AND MULTIPLE ARREST

Draft of the CMI International Sub-Committee

(1) WHERE IN ANY STATE A SHIP HAS ALREADY BEEN ARRESTED AND RELEASED OR BAIL OR OTHER SECURITY HAS ALREADY BEEN GIVEN TO A CLAIMANT IN RESPECT OF A MARITIME CLAIM, NEITHER THE SAME SHIP NOR A SHIP WHICH WOULD OTHERWISE BE SUBJECT TO ARREST PURSUANT TO PARAGRAPH (2) OF ARTICLE 3 SHALL THEREAFTER BE ARRESTED NOR THREATENED WITH ARREST IN THAT OR ANY OTHER STATE, NOR SHALL SECURITY BE DEMANDED IN ANY SUCH STATE, BY THE SAME CLAIMANT IN RESPECT OF THE SAME MARITIME CLAIM UNLESS:

    (A) THE AMOUNT OF THE SECURITY ALREADY OBTAINED IS INADEQUATE; OR

    (B) THE PERSON WHO HAS ALREADY GIVEN THE SECURITY IS OR IS REASONABLY BELIEVED BY THE CLAIMANT TO BE, UNABLE TO FULFIL SOME OR ALL OF THE OBLIGATIONS UNDERTAKEN BY SUCH PERSON IN RESPECT OF SUCH SECURITY; OR

    (C) THE SHIP ARRESTED OR THE SECURITY PREVIOUSLY GIVEN WAS RELEASED EITHER:

        (I) UPON THE APPLICATION OR WITH THE CONSENT OF THE CLAIMANT ACTING ON REASONABLE GROUNDS, OR

        (II) BECAUSE THE CLAIMANT COULD NOT BY TAKING REASONABLE STEPS PREVENT THE RELEASE.

(2) "RELEASE" FOR THE PURPOSE OF PARAGRAPH (1) ABOVE SHALL NOT INCLUDE ANY UNLAWFUL ESCAPE OR RELEASE FROM ARREST.

CMI Draft

(1) WHERE IN ANY STATE A SHIP HAS ALREADY BEEN ARRESTED AND RELEASED OR SECURITY IN RESPECT OF THAT SHIP HAS ALREADY BEEN GIVEN TO SECURE A MARITIME CLAIM, THAT SHIP SHALL NOT THEREAFTER BE RE-ARRESTED OR ARRESTED IN RESPECT OF THE SAME MARITIME CLAIM UNLESS:

    (A) THE NATURE OR AMOUNT OF THE SECURITY ALREADY OBTAINED IN RESPECT OF THE SAME CLAIM IS INADEQUATE, PROVIDED THAT THE AGGREGATE AMOUNT OF SECURITY MAY NOT EXCEED THE VALUE OF THE SHIP; OR

    (B) THE PERSON WHO HAS ALREADY GIVEN THE SECURITY IS NOT, OR IS UNLIKELY TO BE, ABLE TO FULFIL SOME OR ALL OF HIS OBLIGATIONS; OR

    (C) THE SHIP ARRESTED OR THE SECURITY PREVIOUSLY GIVEN WAS RELEASED EITHER:

        (I) UPON THE APPLICATION OR WITH THE CONSENT OF THE CLAIMANT ACTING ON REASONABLE GROUNDS, OR

        (II) BECAUSE THE CLAIMANT COULD NOT BY TAKING REASONABLE STEPS PREVENT THE RELEASE.

(2) ANY OTHER SHIP WHICH WOULD OTHERWISE BE SUBJECT TO ARREST IN RESPECT OF THE SAME MARITIME CLAIM SHALL NOT BE ARRESTED UNLESS:

    (A) THE NATURE OR AMOUNT OF THE SECURITY ALREADY OBTAINED IN RESPECT OF THE SAME CLAIM IS INADEQUATE; OR

    (B) THE PROVISIONS OF PARAGRAPH (1) (B) OR (C) OF THIS ARTICLE ARE APPLICABLE.

(3) "RELEASE" FOR THE PURPOSE OF THIS ARTICLE SHALL NOT INCLUDE ANY UNLAWFUL RELEASE OR ESCAPE FROM ARREST.

CMI Report

67. Article 5 corresponds to Article 3, paragraph (3) of the 1952 Convention. It was adopted by 25 votes to 1 with 7 abstentions.

68. Article 5 seeks to strike a balance between, on the one hand, the interest of the owner to avoid a situation in which the same ship or his other ships are arrested continuously for the same claim and, on the other hand, the creditor's reasonable interest in getting security for the whole of his claim. The Article distinguishes between re-arrest of the same ship (paragraph (1)) and arrest of other ships (paragraph (2)).

JIGE
Seventh Session, 5–9 December 1994

Report—Annex I

19. Some delegations preferred the approach adopted by the 1952 Convention whereby a second arrest of a vessel was not permitted. They could not, therefore, support article 5 of the CMI Draft in permitting re-arrest and multiple arrest in certain cases. In the view of these delegations, the right of re-arrest and multiple arrest should be restricted to exceptional circumstances, such as fraud or misrepresentation, in order to protect the legitimate interests of shipowners as well as the cargo interests. Paragraph 1(c) of the CMI Draft was criticised in this regard.

20. Other delegations favoured a more flexible approach to cases other than fraud or misrepresentation which would justify a re-arrest in respect of the same maritime claim. In this regard mention was made of cases such as collisions where a proper assessment of the claim could only be effected at a later stage, or if the amount of the claim exceeded the value of the arrested vessel, which should give right to the arrest of a sister ship.

21. The Group agreed that this article should be put in brackets for consideration at a later stage, together with alternative proposals which might be submitted by delegations.

Draft Articles 1994

Note of the Editor. The text in the Draft Articles 1994 is the same as that in the CMI Draft but has been placed in square brackets.

Report—Annex I

46. The delegations of the United States of America, Liberia and the Republic of Korea introduced a proposal to amend article 5, as contained in TD/B/CN.4/GE.2/CRP.2.[71] In their opinion the proposal would ensure that re-arrest remained in principle an exceptional measure.

47. The proposal was considered by the majority of delegations as too restrictive and therefore could not be supported. In this regard reference was made to cases previously mentioned during the session which justified not only re-arrest of the same vessel but also of a sister ship. To limit the possibility of a new arrest to fraud or material misrepresentation could have a negative impact on the shipowner, because the arrestor would have to request the highest possible security to protect his interest. These delegations were of the opinion that the text of the present article offered a fair compromise and equitable solutions to any conflict.

71. Draft proposal submitted by the representatives of the United States of America, Liberia and the Republic of Korea (UNCTAD Doc. TD/B/CN.4/GE.2/CRP.2 of 6.12.1994).
Article 5 of the CMI draft should be amended, to read as follows:
(1) Where in any State a ship has already been arrested and released or security in respect of that ship has already been given to secure a maritime claim, that ship shall not thereafter be re-arrested or arrested in respect of the same maritime claim, unless there has been fraud or material misrepresentation in connection with the release or the posting of the security.
(2) Any other ship which would otherwise be subject to arrest in respect of the same maritime claim shall not be arrested unless the nature or the amount of the security already obtained in respect of the same claim is inadequate.
(3) "Release" for the purpose of this article shall not include any unlawful release or escape from arrest.

48. The observer for the CMI explained that paragraph 1(c) envisaged cases where, on reasonable or justifiable grounds, release of a ship was decided without requesting any guarantee to secure claims. This could be the case of any agreement between the arrestor and the shipowner in which the first one would agree to release a vessel in order to prevent losses which would result out of non-compliance of terms of a charter-party. Release could also take place at the request of a port authority on grounds of safety considerations or any other circumstance which could lead to the need to vacate the area in which the ship was arrested.

49. Several delegations nevertheless maintained their reservations regarding the wording and purpose of this paragraph.

50. The observer delegation of the International Association of Ports and Harbours (IAPH) referred to the need to ensure that the full value of claims regarding damages to port installations was also protected by the possibility of re-arrest. Very frequently port authorities could only assess the real magnitude of these damages after a ship had been released. The possibility of re-arrest would facilitate the release of ships amicably and promptly.

51. The Sessional Group agreed to retain the present text of the article and also to include as an alternative the proposal put forward by the delegations of the United States of America, the Republic of Korea and Liberia.

Submission by the International Chamber of Shipping

ICS believes it is essential that any rights of re-arrest and multiple arrest should only exist in specific and clearly defined circumstances. ICS supports the approach adopted by Alternative 2 in preference to Alternative 1.

Ninth Session, 2–6 December 1996

Report—Annex II

79. The Sessional Group considered the two alternative texts of the draft articles. The majority of delegations favoured the text of alternative 1, since it was considered to provide a clear and balanced basis for the question of re-arrest and multiple arrest. These delegations felt that alternative 2 was too restrictive. Some doubts however, were expressed concerning subparagraph (c) of alternative 1. It was considered to be ambiguous, for example in its use of terms such as "taking reasonable steps", which could give rise to varying interpretations. A few delegations preferred alternative 2 in order to restrict the right of re-arrest so as to make seaborne trade more efficient.

80. In the view of one delegation, alternative 1 did not serve the object of the Convention. It was also pointed out that questions of sufficiency of security for the purpose of release of the ships was covered by the provisions of Article 4. This delegation questioned the point of time and the authority to decide on the sufficiency of security for the purpose of Article 5 (1) (a). In its view, Article 5 (1) (a) would only be relevant if the circumstances of the case had been changed. It was pointed out that such a situation could only arise at a later stage after a vessel had been released through the provision of security, the nature and amount of which had been determined by the court. If the nature and the amount of the security were agreed by the parties involved, such an agreement should be respected and could not be cancelled unilaterally. One delegation proposed that consequential amendments should be made in Article 5 (1) (a) if suggestions to amend Article 4 (2) to include reference to "global limitation of liability of the ship" or "the size of the claim" were accepted.

81. The observer for the International Chamber of Shipping (ICS) recalled that comments submitted by its delegation during the eighth session of the Joint Group (contained in document JIGE(IX)/4) were still valid. Its delegation supported the text of alternative 2 so as to limit any right of re-arrest to specific and clearly defined circumstances.

82. The observer for the International Maritime Committee (CMI) expressed doubts as to whether Article 5 (2) covered the situation where the arrested vessel was sold in a forced sale but the proceeds of sale were not sufficient to satisfy the claim.

83. The Sessional Group agreed to retain the text of alternative 1, keeping subparagraph (c) in brackets, and to delete alternative 2.

Draft Articles 1997

Note of the Editor. The text in the Draft Articles 1997 is the same as that in the CMI Draft, except that paragraph 1(c) has been placed in square brackets.

Diplomatic Conference
Comments and Proposals

Hong Kong, China

DOCUMENT 188/3

21. Not supported as the present legislation in Hong Kong, China, states that in relation to certain categories of claim, where a ship has been served with a writ or arrested in an action *in rem* brought to enforce the claim, no other ship may be served with a writ or arrested in that or any other action *in rem* brought to enforce that claim. We wish to maintain this and are not in favour of re-arrest and multiple arrest.

Mexico

DOCUMENT 188/3

46. The Government of Mexico considers that there should be no room for ambiguity in a legal instrument of the kind in course of preparation. Consequently the use of the terms "reasonable grounds" and "reasonable steps" in subparagraph (c) of paragraph 1 are not acceptable.

Tanzania

DOCUMENT 188/3

100. With regard to Article (5)(1)(c), it is our view that the circumstances of the release of a security be clearly spelt out to avoid unnecessary abuses.

Thailand

DOCUMENT 188/3

90. Reference to the value of ship in paragraph 1(a) should be deleted.

CMI

DOCUMENT 188/3

Paragraph 1

148. The situation where security is given to prevent the arrest should be mentioned in the preamble of this paragraph, as it is mentioned in Article 7(1). The preamble could consequently be amended as follows:

(1) Where in any State a ship has been arrested *to secure a maritime claim or security has been given to prevent arrest or obtain the release of the ship*, that ship shall not thereafter be re-arrested or arrested in respect of the same maritime claim unless:

Paragraph 2

149. In order to make clear that this paragraph regulates the case of multiple arrest, the present text should be preceded by a preamble similar to that of paragraph (1). Furthermore, the case should be mentioned where a ship has been arrested and is still under arrest at the time when the arrest of another ship is requested. To this effect this paragraph could be reworded as follows:

(2) *Where in any State a ship has been arrested to secure a maritime claim or security has been given to prevent arrest or obtain the release of the ship, any other ship which would otherwise be subject to arrest in respect of the same maritime claim shall not be arrested unless:*
   (a) *no security has been given to obtain the release of the first ship from arrest, or the value of that ship is less than the amount of the claim; or*

(b)　the nature or amount of the security already obtained in respect of the same claim is inadequate; or

(c)　the provisions of paragraph (1)(b) or (c) of this article are applicable.

Proceedings of the Main Committee

First reading—4 March 1999[72]

PARAGRAPH 1

Doubts were expressed and clarifications were asked in respect of sub-paragraphs (b) and (c). The debate which took place is reproduced below.

Greece　Our position was in favour of a more restrictive approach. However we would suggest to approach more carefully the wording of (1)(c)(i). It should be more clear.

Netherlands　We wonder if (b) and (c) are really necessary. They cover very specific cases.

Chairman　I would like to make clear that the decision was taken to remove the brackets.

Netherlands　It is matter of drafting. It is odd to set out the general principle and then set out specific cases.

Chairman　I apologise if I have rushed you. There appear to be some delegations that have problems with (c). Can I ask you to give an indicative vote on whether (c) should be kept or deleted? *Equal.*

CMI　Mr. Chairman I wonder whether it may assist all delegates if I try to explain the reason behind (c) because it has been stated that (c) is ambiguous and this seems the reason why several delegations have voted against (c). The purpose of (c) is to cover situations which can materialise from time to time. I can give perhaps some examples of such situations. If you consider (c)(i)—upon application with the consent of the claimant acting on reasonable grounds—there are situations in which the owner of the arrested ship asks the arrestor to release the ship even without providing a guarantee because he has no possibility of providing a guarantee, because the ship must meet a cancelling date and it would be very damaging for the owner of the arrested ship to lose a cancelling date because he would have no other employment for the ship. The claimant may cooperate in those situations under the condition that the next ship which will come to a port in the same country or another country may be arrestable. This is a situation which in practice may take place. In my own experience as a lawyer I did authorise twice the release of a ship because she had to meet a cancelling date, because I thought that this was a fair behaviour by the claimant to cooperate with the owner of the arrested ship. In that case I think it would be unfair to punish the claimant because he has consented to the release of the ship without obtaining any guarantee. This is an example. As regards the second alternative in (ii) there are situations where the vessel may be or is released without the consent of the claimant, for example a ship may be arrested in a port where there is no place where the ship may stay under arrest and in this case, and this has happened, the port authority may apply to the Court for an order for the release of the ship because the ship remaining under arrest may cause danger to other ships in the port or a ship may be laying at anchor in a road and she may become a danger in case of heavy weather. In those cases the port authority and the competent Court may order the release of the ship notwithstanding the fact that the claimant does not agree to such release. In such a case it would be again unfair to prevent the claimant to arrest the same ship in another port or to arrest another ship in the same ownership.

Tanzania　After the explanations from the CMI we support the maintenance of this paragraph (c).

Chairman　In view of what has happened, since I cannot ask again for an indicative vote, I suggest that we still keep (c) in square brackets.

---

72. Text and summary from tape Nos. 32 and 33.

Second reading—8 March 1999[73]

> The Chairman stated that a decision should be made as to whether sub-paragraph (c) should be kept or deleted.

United Kingdom   Our position would be that we would not wish to make things more difficult for claimants. If people can assure us that we would not make it more difficult as quickly as possible, we would have no problem with the deletion. That is our prime concern with this particular part of this article. We would just like some reassurance on that, that by deletion we would not make more difficult a multiple arrest. This is part of the balance of not having a claim exceeding the value of the ship. This is the other side of the coin, as far as we are concerned.

Cyprus   This delegation believes that this sub-paragraph should be maintained because certainly the position of claimants would be prejudiced by the deletion, because there may be cases where the ship may be released on some formal procedural grounds, which may be very trivial, and it would be unjust for a claimant not to be able to arrest because of a release for some trivial formal grounds. So we believe that it is important that the sub-paragraph should be maintained. I agree with the UK on that point.

Chairman   We remember that Prof. Berlingieri gave a couple of examples in which it would have been useful to have a provision of this type.

Russian Fed.   We support the maintenance of this provision for the reasons stated by Prof. Berlingieri.

Netherlands   During the first reading my delegation made some comments on this specific article 5(1) on the issues being dealt in (1), (b) and (c). We pointed out, and this perhaps may be a clarification for the UK, that this kind of exception from the general rule that re-arrest is not possible is allowed in cases in which the position of the claimant is indeed at stake, the circumstances in which there might be a concern for the claimant is when there are deficiencies as regards the security being given and therefore we are of the opinion that there should be a very short ruling on article 5(1) such as re-arrest is not possible except when security might give rise to problems. In that respect (b) and (c) in our understanding would operate in case the security or the way it was given would not be adequate and in that respect my delegation interprets (c) in such a sense that it can only be applicable in case there are some doubts about the security being given. For that reason we could live with the deletion of (b) and (c).

Japan   We share the concern expressed by the UK delegation and the Russian Federation. The deletion of (c) might in some cases—they may be exceptional cases—cause prejudice to the claimant.

Australia   We support maintaining article 5(1) as it appears in the JIGE text taking into account the comments that were made by Mr Berlingieri some time ago and also the support of some delegations today in that regard.

Greece   We support the Dutch proposal to delete (c).

Canada   We would like to join those delegations who would wish to retain (c). We appreciate that it is a provision that would be used probably in extraordinary circumstances, nevertheless we see some, we see an obvious one in (ii) for example, if a ship is released beyond the control of the claimant and we think that is a circumstance that may indeed arise from time to time and for that reason we would prefer to retain (c).

Tanzania   We prefer to maintain (c).

Chairman   Of the delegates that have spoken the majority would seem to wish to keep (c). So unless a number of people would now object.

Philippines   We recall the discussions and particularly the explanations of Prof. Berlingieri last week regarding two specific circumstances that would justify (c)(i) and (ii) and following his explanations this delegation fully supports the retention of this paragraph because there are clear circumstances where this would be applicable.

Chairman   It is so decided.

---

73. Text from tape No. 52.

PARAGRAPH 2

First reading—4 March 1999[74]

Thailand I am seeking some clarifications on this paragraph. When the claimant knows that the security received from the arrest will not exceed the claim is it possible to apply for an arrest of more than one ship at the same time? If the answer is yes, I think we have some problems about the compatibility in paragraph 2(a). If the answer is no, that would mean that you have to arrest the ships one by one.

Chairman Prof. Berlingieri, have you given any thoughts to this?

CMI Mr Chairman, paragraphs 1 and 2 of this article deal respectively with the re-arrest of the same ship – paragraph 1 – and with the arrest of another ship in respect of the same maritime claim and the possibility of re-arresting the same ship or arresting another ship is made conditional to the situations listed respectively under (a), (b) and (c) of paragraph 1 and under (a) and (b) of paragraph 2. If the security obtained for the release of the arrest of the first ship is insufficient to cover the claim, and this will be the case if the value of the ship is below the amount of the claim, then I think it is fair and this was the thought which was expressed by JIGE, to authorise the claimant to proceed to a further arrest in order to be able to cover the balance of his claim. It would be unfair to prevent the claimant, who could not do anything else than arrest a ship the value of which was below the amount of his claim to seek additional security in order to obtain the full cover of his claim. This is the purpose of this provision. It seems to me, I may be mistaken, that the purpose is made clear by the language which has been adopted respectively in paragraphs 1 and 2.

Thailand If the claimant knows that the value of the ship in respect of which the claim has arisen is insufficient to secure his claim, can he arrest a second ship at the same time? From the wording it would appear that you must first arrest one ship and obtain security and then if such security is insufficient, you may arrest another ship.

Chairman I wonder whether you have a system similar to that in England and Hong Kong, whereby you can serve a writ before the vessel is in the vicinity and you may then have a problem whether you can serve a writ to more vessels for the same claim. In most other jurisdictions the vessel must be in port in order to be able to arrest her. The problem will not arise in practical terms. I would guess that if you are lucky enough to have two ships at the same time in a port and one is not sufficient to cover the claim you may arrest both of them in order to get enough security. I wonder whether the problem arises only in some jurisdictions.

Chairman We revert now to paragraph (2). Is it accepted as it stands? That is the case.

PARAGRAPH 3

First reading—4 March 1999[75]

This paragraph was adopted without discussion.

1999 Convention

1. WHERE IN ANY STATE A SHIP HAS ALREADY BEEN ARRESTED AND RELEASED OR SECURITY IN RESPECT OF THAT SHIP HAS ALREADY BEEN PROVIDED TO SECURE A MARITIME CLAIM, THAT SHIP SHALL NOT THEREAFTER BE RE-ARRESTED OR ARRESTED IN RESPECT OF THE SAME MARITIME CLAIM UNLESS:

   (A) THE NATURE OR AMOUNT OF THE SECURITY IN RESPECT OF THAT SHIP ALREADY PROVIDED IN RESPECT OF THE SAME CLAIM IS INADEQUATE, ON CONDITION THAT THE AGGREGATE AMOUNT OF SECURITY MAY NOT EXCEED THE VALUE OF THE SHIP; OR

   (B) THE PERSON WHO HAS ALREADY PROVIDED THE SECURITY IS NOT, OR IS UNLIKELY TO BE, ABLE TO FULFIL SOME OR ALL OF THAT PERSON'S OBLIGATIONS; OR

   (C) THE SHIP ARRESTED OR THE SECURITY PREVIOUSLY PROVIDED WAS RELEASED EITHER:

---

74. Text from tape No. 33.
75. Summary from tape No. 33.

    (I) UPON THE APPLICATION OR WITH THE CONSENT OF THE CLAIMANT ACTING ON REASONABLE GROUNDS, OR

    (II) BECAUSE THE CLAIMANT COULD NOT BY TAKING REASONABLE STEPS PREVENT THE RELEASE.

2. ANY OTHER SHIP WHICH WOULD OTHERWISE BE SUBJECT TO ARREST IN RESPECT OF THE SAME MARITIME CLAIM SHALL NOT BE ARRESTED UNLESS:

    (A) THE NATURE OR AMOUNT OF THE SECURITY ALREADY PROVIDED IN RESPECT OF THE SAME CLAIM IS INADEQUATE; OR

    (B) THE PROVISIONS OF PARAGRAPH 1 (B) OR (C) OF THIS ARTICLE ARE APPLICABLE.

3. "RELEASE" FOR THE PURPOSE OF THIS ARTICLE SHALL NOT INCLUDE ANY UNLAWFUL RELEASE OR ESCAPE FROM ARREST.

II.III.9 ARTICLE 6: PROTECTION OF OWNERS AND DEMISE CHARTERERS OF ARRESTED SHIPS

Draft of the CMI International Sub-Committee

(1) THE COURT MAY AS A CONDITION OF THE ARREST OF A SHIP, OR OF PERMITTING AN ARREST ALREADY MADE TO BE CONTINUED, IMPOSE UPON THE CLAIMANT WHO SEEKS TO ARREST OR WHO HAS ARRESTED THE SHIP THE OBLIGATION TO PROVIDE SECURITY OF A KIND AND FOR AN AMOUNT, AND UPON SUCH TERMS, AS MAY BE DETERMINED BY THAT COURT FOR ANY LOSS WHICH MAY BE INCURRED BY THE DEFENDANT, AND FOR WHICH THE CLAIMANT MAY BE FOUND LIABLE, AS A RESULT OF THE ARREST, INCLUDING BUT NOT RESTRICTED TO SUCH LOSS OR DAMAGE AS MAY BE INCURRED BY THAT DEFENDANT IN CONSEQUENCE OF:

    (I) THE ARREST HAVING BEEN WRONGFUL OR UNJUSTIFIED, OR

    (II) EXCESSIVE SECURITY HAVING BEEN DEMANDED AND OBTAINED.

[Alternative text for Article 6(1)

(1) UNLESS THE COURT DETERMINES OTHERWISE IN EXCEPTIONAL CASES, ARREST SHALL ONLY BE MADE IF THE CLAIMANT

    [(A) SHOWS A GOOD ARGUABLE CASE, OR]

    (B) PROVIDES SECURITY OF A KIND AND FOR AN AMOUNT, AND UPON SUCH TERMS, AS MAY BE DETERMINED BY THE DEFENDANT, AND FOR WHICH THE CLAIMANT MAY BE FOUND LIABLE, AS A RESULT OF THE ARREST, INCLUDING BUT NOT RESTRICTED TO SUCH LOSS OR DAMAGE AS MAY BE INCURRED BY THAT DEFENDANT IN CONSEQUENCE OF:

        (I) THE ARREST HAVING BEEN WRONGFUL OR UNJUSTIFIED, OR

        (II) EXCESSIVE SECURITY HAVING BEEN DEMANDED AND OBTAINED.]

(2) THE COURT OF THE STATE IN WHICH AN ARREST HAS BEEN MADE SHALL HAVE JURISDICTION TO DETERMINE THE EXTENT OF THE LIABILITY, IF ANY, OF THE CLAIMANT FOR LOSS OR DAMAGE CAUSED BY THE ARREST OF A SHIP, INCLUDING BUT NOT RESTRICTED TO SUCH LOSS OR DAMAGE AS MAY BE CAUSED IN CONSEQUENCE OF

    (A) THE ARREST HAVING BEEN WRONGFUL OR UNJUSTIFIED, OR

    (B) EXCSSSIVE SECURITY HAVING BEEN DEMANDED AND OBTAINED.

(3) THE LIABILITY, IF ANY, OF THE DEFENDANT IN ACCORDANCE WITH PARAGRAPH (2) OF ARTICLE 6 SHALL BE DETERMINED BY APPLICATION OF THE LAW OF THE STATE WHERE THE ARREST WAS MADE.

(4) IF A COURT IN ANOTHER STATE OR AN ARBITRAL TRIBUNAL IS TO DETERMINE THE MERITS OF THE CASE IN ACCORDANCE WITH THE PROVISIONS OF ARTICLE 7 OF THIS CONVENTION THEN PROCEEDINGS RELATING TO THE LIABILITY OF THE CLAIMANT IN ACCORDANCE WITH PARAGRAPH (2) OF THIS ARTICLE 6 MAY BE STAYED PENDING THAT DECISION.

(5) WHERE PURSUANT TO PARAGRAPH (1) OF THIS ARTICLE SECURITY HAS BEEN PROVIDED, THE PARTY PROVIDING SUCH SECURITY MAY AT ANY TIME APPLY TO THE COURT TO HAVE THAT SECURITY REDUCED, VARIED OR DISPENSED WITH.

Report of the Chairman of the CMI International Sub-Committee

Art. 6 provides rules with respect to wrongful arrest.

The problem of security for wrongful arrest was also discussed before the adoption of the 1952 Convention. In the end, art. 6, para. 1 of that Convention left the problem to be determined by the State of arrest.

Some countries automatically require security for wrongful arrest as a condition for arrest. In other countries the question is left to the discretion of the courts.

The draft contains alternative texts in this respect. The first draft gives the court complete discretion while the alternative draft only gives the courts a very limited discretion.

In para. (2) and (3) questions of jurisdiction and choice of law are regulated. Para. (4) permits staying of the proceedings while awaiting a decision by another court as to the merits of the case.

CMI Draft

(1) THE COURT MAY AS A CONDITION OF THE ARREST OF A SHIP, OR OF PERMITTING AN ARREST ALREADY EFFECTED TO BE MAINTAINED, IMPOSE UPON THE CLAIMANT WHO SEEKS TO ARREST OR WHO HAS PROCURED THE ARREST OF THE SHIP THE OBLIGATION TO PROVIDE SECURITY OF A KIND AND FOR AN AMOUNT, AND UPON SUCH TERMS, AS MAY BE DETERMINED BY THAT COURT FOR ANY LOSS WHICH MAY BE INCURRED BY THE DEFENDANT AS A RESULT OF THE ARREST, AND FOR WHICH THE CLAIMANT MAY BE FOUND LIABLE, INCLUDING BUT NOT RESTRICTED TO SUCH LOSS OR DAMAGE AS MAY BE INCURRED BY THAT DEFENDANT IN CONSEQUENCE OF:

(A) THE ARREST HAVING BEEN WRONGFUL OR UNJUSTIFIED; OR

(B) EXCESSIVE SECURITY HAVING BEEN DEMANDED AND OBTAINED.

(2) THE COURTS OF THE STATE IN WHICH AN ARREST HAS BEEN EFFECTED SHALL HAVE JURISDICTION TO DETERMINE THE EXTENT OF THE LIABILITY, IF ANY, OF THE CLAIMANT FOR LOSS OR DAMAGE CAUSED BY THE ARREST OF A SHIP, INCLUDING BUT NOT RESTRICTED TO SUCH LOSS OR DAMAGE AS MAY BE CAUSED IN CONSEQUENCE OF:

(A) THE ARREST HAVING BEEN WRONGFUL OR UNJUSTIFIED, OR

(B) EXCESSIVE SECURITY HAVING BEEN DEMANDED AND OBTAINED.

(3) THE LIABILITY, IF ANY, OF THE CLAIMANT IN ACCORDANCE WITH PARAGRAPH (2) OF THIS ARTICLE SHALL BE DETERMINED BY APPLICATION OF THE LAW OF THE STATE WHERE THE ARREST WAS EFFECTED.

(4) IF A COURT IN ANOTHER STATE OR AN ARBITRAL TRIBUNAL IS TO DETERMINE THE MERITS OF THE CASE IN ACCORDANCE WITH THE PROVISIONS OF ARTICLE 7, THEN PROCEEDINGS RELATING TO THE LIABILITY OF THE CLAIMANT IN ACCORDANCE WITH PARAGRAPH (2) OF THIS ARTICLE MAY BE STAYED PENDING THAT DECISION.

(5) WHERE PURSUANT TO PARAGRAPH (1) OF THIS ARTICLE SECURITY HAS BEEN PROVIDED, THE PERSON PROVIDING SUCH SECURITY MAY AT ANY TIME APPLY TO THE COURT TO HAVE THAT SECURITY REDUCED, MODIFIED OR CANCELLED.

CMI Report

69. Article 6 corresponds to Article 6, paragraph (1) of the 1952 Convention. It provides rules with respect to wrongful arrest. It was adopted with 25 votes to 1 with 7 abstentions.

70. The draft submitted to the Lisbon Conference contained alternative proposals on this point. One proposal was to leave the decision on whether security should be provided for wrongful arrest to the complete discretion of the judge. Another proposal was to make it the principal rule that security for wrongful arrest should be given and give the judge a possibility in exceptional cases to dispense with the security. The Conference chose the former alternative. Even a proposal that security should be obligatory in cases other than those where the claim is secured by a maritime lien was rejected.

71. The provisions of paragraphs (2) to (4) do not prevent the parties from agreeing to submit the question of compensation for wrongful arrest to the court or arbitral tribunal to which they have agreed to submit the merits of their case for decision, cf. Article 7.

JIGE
Seventh Session, 5–9 December 1994

Report—Annex I

22. One delegation believed that the Convention should not, even as a matter of discretion, permit courts to make arrest conditional upon the provision of security by the claimant. In the

opinion of some other delegations, the Convention should include guidelines as to whether courts should make the arrest conditional upon the provision of security by the claimant, as well as provisions on liability for loss or damage in case of wrongful arrest.

23. Some delegations opposed this view on the grounds that it would limit the discretion of the courts to rule on cases of wrongful arrest in accordance with the law of the *forum arresti*. The article contained in the CMI draft was accordingly considered a suitable one. Some delegations, however, considered this provision unsatisfactory and preferred to retain the original provision contained in the 1952 Convention.

24. Some delegations referred to the need to include appropriate text to ensure that seamen would be exempted from the obligation to provide guarantees against wrongful arrest in respect of claims secured by maritime liens mentioned in article 4(1)(a) of the 1993 MLM Convention.

25. The majority of delegations, however, agree that the text of the CMI Draft should be used as a basis for future work.

Draft Articles 1994

Note of the Editor. The text of this article in the Draft Articles 1994 is the same as that in the CMI Draft.

Report—Annex I

52. The observer for IAPH said that the liability of the claimant in a case of wrongful arrest was not regulated by the provisions of the draft Convention. This was the case not only *vis-à-vis* the owner or bareboat charterer but also the Port Authority, who could well suffer considerable economic loss arising out of immobilisation of an arrested ship when the owner, bareboat charterer or arrestor went into liquidation. This situation could also seriously affect other port users. He stressed the importance for the Convention to address these issues and said that port authorities should be associated with the competent judicial authority ordering the arrest of a ship in order to examine the consequences and modalities of the arrest, such as the need for unloading dangerous cargo, transferring the ship to a waiting safe berth, etc. The Convention should provide for appropriate security to be requested from the claimant who sought arrest in order to cover ordinary port dues and expenses.

Submission by the International Chamber of Shipping

ICS believes that there should be an obligation on the part of the claimant to provide security for any loss incurred by the defendant for which the claimant may be found liable. This obligation should be mandatory rather than discretionary. ICS therefore proposes that the opening words of Article 6(1) be amended to read:
"*The court shall as a condition of the arrest of a ship . . . *".

Comments and proposals by the United Kingdom

25. The United Kingdom delegation is not convinced that there is any valid reason to change the simple provision contained in Article 6 of the 1952 Convention. If, however, the majority view is that the additional detail contained in Article 6 of the JIGE text is desirable, the United Kingdom delegation would suggest that the references to "unjustified" arrest should be deleted from paragraphs 1(a) and 2(a).

26. Without the deletion of the references to "unjustified" arrest, the provision might conflict with United Kingdom law, which is based on the premise that, with the exception of wrongful arrest, a claimant should not be penalised for having arrested a ship, even it the action fails on the merits. The concept of an "unjustified" arrest is also ambiguous: an arrest might be perfectly justified based on the facts available to the claimant at the time the arrest is demanded, but could turn out not to be justified when the true facts of the case become clear. Paragraphs 1(a) and 2(b) should therefore be amended to refer only to:
the arrest having been wrongful.

Paragraph (1)

84. Some delegations supported the view expressed by the observer for the ICS that there should be an obligation on the part of the claimant to provide security for any loss incurred by the defendant for which the claimant might be found liable. Thus, it was suggested that paragraph 1 should contain a mandatory rule for the court to impose the obligation to provide security upon a claimant seeking arrest. The expression "may" should accordingly be replaced by "shall". The majority of delegations were unable to accept this proposal. In their view, courts should be given discretion to decide as to if, when and in what nature and amount security should be required from an arrestor. In this regard mention was made of the right of crew members to request the arrest of a ship to secure payment of wages; their right to obtain arrest should be recognised even if they were unable to provide security. In the view of the delegations supporting the replacement of "may" by "shall", these situations were, however, properly addressed in the remaining paragraphs of the article. These delegations were also of the view that this matter had been correctly categorised by the Chairman as a matter of principle which required consideration by the diplomatic conference. To that effect, these delegations suggested that the word "may" be placed in brackets.

85. The Group considered a proposal made by the United Kingdom (document JIGE(IX)/3, paras. 25 and 26) to delete reference to "unjustified" arrest from paragraphs 1 (a) and 2 (a). It was suggested that, with the exception of wrongful arrest, a claimant should not be penalised for having arrested a ship, even if the action failed on its merits. This proposal was opposed by several delegations. In their view, the deletions suggested would result in narrowing the possibilities of defence of the defendant, who would be compelled to prove the existence of bad faith on the part of the claimant to obtain compensation for loss resulting from the arrest. In connection with the argument that reference to unjustified arrest might conflict with national law, it was noted that such conflicts could be avoided by the operation of paragraph 3 of this article, according to which the liability of the claimant would be determined by the application of the law of the State where the arrest was effected.

86. It was noted that, while in Article 7 (1) reference was made to the jurisdiction on the merits of the case in connection not only with effected arrests but also with security given to prevent arrest, reference to this last case had not been included in Article 6, paragraph (2). In this regard, it was suggested that reference in this paragraph to "security given to prevent arrest" and "obtain the release of the ship" could be included.

87. The Sessional Group agreed to retain the text of Article 6 as presently drafted, but leave the word "unjustified" in paragraph 1 (a) and 2 (a) in brackets.

Paragraph (2)

88. The observer for the CMI said that paragraph (2) did not expressly provide which State should have jurisdiction if security was provided before an arrest.

Paragraphs (3), (4) and (5)

89. No specific comments were made in connection with these paragraphs.

Draft Articles 1997

Note of the Editor. The text of this article in the Draft Articles 1997 is the same as that in the CMI Draft, except that the words "or unjustified" in paragraphs 1(a) and 2(a) have been placed in square brackets following a proposal from the delegation of the United Kingdom which was supported by some other delegations.

Diplomatic Conference
Comments and Proposals

Hong Kong, China

DOCUMENT 188/3

22. This article introduces the right of a court to set counter security for wrongful or unjustified arrest as condition for the arrest of a ship. This right exists in some jurisdictions. It can be beneficial in making a claimant reconsider arrest in doubtful circumstances or where arrest may be contemplated as means of applying unreasonable pressure. Certain interests, particularly cargo claimants may, therefore, object if this right extends beyond wrongful arrest claims to "unjustified" arrest claim. This article is supported as it deters wrongful arrests.

Mexico

DOCUMENT 188/3

47. As in article 5, the words in brackets "or unjustified" in subparagraph (a) of paragraph 1 are considered to be a subjective criterion which should not appear in this text. The Government of Mexico therefore proposes that it be deleted and that the phrase should simply read: "the arrest having been wrongful".

Tanzania

DOCUMENT 188/3

101. Article 6(1) and 2(a), it is our opinion that the word "unjustified" be well defined.

Thailand

DOCUMENT 188/3

91. The principles of the Article are acceptable. However, the word "unjustified" in paragraph 1(a) and 2(a) should be deleted. "Unjustified" should be inherent in the general meaning of "wrongful". Having the new word which has never been internationally tried or tested can lead to the increase in disputes or problem in interpretation.

Madagascar

DOCUMENT 188/3/ADD.1

5. Paragraph (1) of this article should be amended so that the authorisation to arrest a ship or maintain an arrest already effected is not systematically subject to the provision of security by the arresting claimant. It may happen that the claimant does not have the means to furnish security. This is the case of a crew member whose wages have not been paid.

6. Moreover, if the prior provision of security is necessary, the amount should not exceed that of the claim asserted.

7. The comments made on article 4 also apply to paragraph (5) of article 6.

CMI

DOCUMENT 188/3

150. In the heading of Article 6 reference is made to the owner and to the demise charterer. It would appear therefore that the intention was to consider the owner and the demise charterer as the persons in whose favour security can be provided even though no reference is made to the demise charterer in the text of this article. It is thought however that in certain jurisdictions persons other than the demise charterer may be entitled to obtain protection such as, for example, time charterers. It is suggested, therefore, that the present heading be replaced by a more general one, such as: "*Liability for wrongful arrest*" or "Liability for wrongful or unjustified arrest" if the words "or unjustified" are retained in paragraphs 1(a) and 2(a).

151. The words "or unjustified" in paragraph (1)(a) as well as in paragraph 2(a) have been placed in square brackets since it was objected that under (a) they would have enabled courts to impose

security upon the claimant and under 2(a) to determine his liability in situations the nature of which is not clearly defined.

152. It is thought that there are situations which do not come within the concept of wrongful arrest but nevertheless justify the imposition of security and the assessment of liquidated damages. This is the case, for example, when there is no possible doubt about the solvency of the owner or when the arrest is not required in order to prevent the extinction of a maritime lien.

153. Attention must be drawn to the fact that there would in any event be complete freedom of the courts in respect of the imposition of security and the liquidation of damages since the situations mentioned in (a) and (b) are preceded by the words "including but not restricted to such loss or damage as may be incurred . . . in consequence of".

154. The remark made during the ninth session of JIGE that in paragraph 2 of Article 6 reference should also be made to the case in which security is given to prevent arrest is correct. In fact a loss may also occur in such a case if the amount of the security is excessive.

155. This paragraph could, therefore, be amended as follows:

(2) The Courts of the State in which an arrest has been effected *or security given to prevent arrest* shall have jurisdiction to determine the extent of the liability, if any, of the claimant for loss or damage caused *thereby*, including but not restricted to such loss or damage as may be caused in consequence of:
(a) the arrest having been wrongful or unjustified; or
(b) excessive security having been demanded and obtained.

ICS

DOCUMENT 188/3

124. ICS is of the view that the square brackets in Article 6, paragraphs 1(a) and 2(a) should be deleted and the words "or unjustified" should remain.

125. ICS believes that at present the draft Convention is unbalanced because a defendant has to furnish security in order to obtain the release of the vessel whereas claimants are not compelled to provide any security for losses incurred by the defendant for which the claimant may be found liable. ICS therefore strongly believes that the word "may" in the first line of Article 6, paragraph 1 should be deleted and replaced with "shall". Concern has been expressed about the ability of certain claimants to provide security (e.g. crew members). However, that concern is addressed in the remainder of the paragraph which provides flexibility to deal with such situations. If the claimant's obligation to provide security was mandatory rather than discretionary, the court would remain responsible for determining the kind, amount and the terms of the security. In the situations which aroused concern, such security could in fact be nominal.

Denmark

DOCUMENT CRP.5

Article 6, paragraph 1

"The Court *shall save in cases where it would be unreasonable to do so* as a condition of the arrest of a ship, or of permitting an arrest already effected to be maintained, impose upon the claimant who seeks to arrest or who had procured the arrest of the ship the obligation to provide security of a kind and for an amount, and upon such terms, as may be determined by that Court for any loss which may be incurred by the defendant as a result of the arrest, and for which the claimant may be found liable, including but not restricted to such loss or damage as may be incurred by that defendant in consequence of"

Canada

DOCUMENT CRP.1

3.1 In effect this provision vests courts with the discretion to impose counter-security in certain circumstances. Canada is of the view that such a provision would have the effect of slowing down and complicating the arrest process, thereby making it ineffective in many cases. A routing requirement for counter-security would greatly discourage the arrest of ships.

3.2 Canada notes that national courts possess the power to impose counter-security in any event.

3.3 Canada therefore proposes the entire deletion of this article.

Egypt

DOCUMENT CRP.9

Article 6, paragraph 1

We propose that not only the defendant but also the ports should benefit from the security that the court might impose on the claimant to cover any loss which might be incurred as a result of wrongful arrest.

Accordingly, we believe that the text should be amended to read as follows:

"The court may, as a condition of the arrest of a ship, or of permitting an arrest already effected to be maintained, impose upon the claimant who seeks to arrest or who has procured the arrest of the ship the obligation to provide security of a kind and for an amount, and upon such terms, as may be determined by that court for any loss which may be incurred by the defendant or to cover the normal port dues and costs as a result of the arrest, and for which the claimant may be found liable, . . . etc."

Ukraine

DOCUMENT CRP.11

14. After "for an amount" add ", not to exceed the value of the ship,". In subparagraphs (a) of this and the following paragraphs, Ukraine prefers the expression "unjustified" arrest.

Proceedings of the Main Committee
Report of the Chairman of the Drafting Committee

11 March 1999[76]

TITLE

The Chairman of the Drafting Committee reported as follows:
There was some discussion. First the question of title. We did not discuss headings at all. We did not have the time. We have to live with the present heading.

PARAGRAPH 1

First reading—4 March 1999[77]

Two issues have been debated. Firstly, whether the provision of counter security should be compulsory or decided discretionally by the Court. Secondly, whether the words "or unjustified" in sub-paragraph (a) should be maintained. It was also suggested that security should be provided also in favour of third parties such as port authorities. Some delegations made also the radical proposal to delete the entire article 6. The most significant part of the debate is reproduced below.
Canada We have made a proposal in CRP.1 at § 3. In our view this provision vests courts with discretion to impose counter-security in certain circumstances. We believe that there are real practical difficulties to vest courts with such a power specifically in this Convention. We fear that

76. Text from tape No. 75.
77. Text and summary from tapes Nos. 33 and 34.

those representing the interest of ships may well try to persuade courts that counter-security must be imposed or on the contrary to impose counter-security in all cases. This favours forum shipping. Suggests deletion of article 6 as a whole.

Spain   As respects (1) we request replace "may" with "shall". We have doubts about word "unjustified" in (1)(a).

Denmark   We have made a proposal in CRP.5. Our amendment is to change "may" to "shall". Our purpose is to avoid forum shipping but our solution is opposite to the Canadian one. There may be, however, some special cases in which it would be unreasonable to demand counter-security as in case of crew members. We prefer to have the word "unjustified" in. The reason for this is that the system in our country is that if someone causes a lawsuit and he doesn't win, he would have to pay for whatever costs opponents will have. It has nothing to do with preventive arrest.

CMI   If this is not too boring for the delegates present here I may try to summarise in two words the background of this provision. As far back as 1952 the issue which we are discussing today was raised by the Scandinavian delegations. The Scandinavian delegations at that time asked for a provision in the draft 1952 Convention to the effect that a security should be provided in any event by the arrestor. There was no agreement on that and therefore in the 1952 Convention a rather vague provision was inserted which is art. 6 of the 1952 Convention. When the new draft Convention was discussed at Lisbon by the CMI the same issue was raised again and it was deemed proper to rephrase art. 6 of the 1952 Convention in a much more detailed manner, indicating that the competent court could request the claimant to provide security and the details are now provided in art. 6. So this was a sort of compromise which was arrived at first before 1952 and then in the course of the debates which have now brought this draft Convention in front of you. This is the situation if this may be of interest to the delegates.

Egypt   We suggest that security be provided not only for shipowner, for also for possible losses of third parties, such as a port authority.

IIDM   Security should be obligatory.

United States   Supports deletion of entire article. In any event delete "unjustified".

United Kingdom   JIGE did at least an attempt to achieve a balance. I feel more than happy with the explanation of Prof. Berlingieri. We certainly could not accept the Spanish proposal. If we must keep something I would propose deletion of word "unjustified". The notion is novel and ambiguous. Keep text with deletion of that word.

Germany   To restore a fair balance it is necessary to have counter-security. As to term "unjustified", it should be retained, because this term is regulated and widely accepted because the defendant is entitled to damages if the claim fails. As to harbour fees, we think this belongs to article 1(5) since it refers to the cost of proceedings. It is not necessary to regulate this in article 6. We prefer the JIGE text but can live with Danish proposal.

Chairman   1) There is a strong opposition to the Danish proposal.

2) With respect to the words in square brackets, the division is more even. We have to keep this as an open issue. First agreement on the substance is necessary.

3) As to the Egyptian proposal, there has been some support. There is equal agreement on the substance. It is up to the State concerned to see that protection be granted to ports. This can be ensured in article 2(5) or in article 8(4). There is a risk that if we introduce this concept here, there may be implied that States have no right otherwise to take action in order to protect port.

At this stage we cannot decide if something must be introduced in this article.

Second reading—8 March 1999[78]

Three different views were expressed. Firstly that the words "or unjustified" should be deleted; secondly that the word "wrongful" should be deleted and, thirdly that both words should be maintained. Here follows the transcript of the most significant statements made during the debate.

Chairman   We have also article 6(1) and (2). In both of these provisions reference is made to wrongful or unjustified arrest. The words "or unjustified" are in square brackets in both paragraphs.

---

78. Text from tapes Nos. 52 and 53.

There was an inconclusive debate in this respect. Some delegations promised to look into this further and the Belgian delegate I think is able to report on what has been done.

Belgium   We have indeed had a meeting. We were only three delegations. We worked on a very simple example: a collision between two or three vessels, dense fog, followed by the arrest of the wrong ship. The arrest is unjustified, but is it wrongful? It all depends on what "wrongful" and "unjustified" mean. The Hong Kong delegate proposed that everything that is wrongful is in some way unjustified, but the reverse is not true. "Wrongful" is what is not in accordance with the law, "unjustified" covers a lot more. And the Danish law, however, and may be other national laws, from the moment the arrest appears not to be justified, it gives automatic right to damages, apparently on tort. Therefore "unlawful" or "unjustified" give the same result: liability and damages for arrest by mistake. The Belgian delegation believes that there should be no problem. Article 6(2) gives a wide power of appreciation to the Court of the State in which the arrest has been effected and this should satisfy the Danish delegation, at least for all arrests effected in their country. The question whether there is a difference under the terms of the Convention between "wrongful" and "unjustified" could arise in England, when an arrest could be wrongful, i.e. against the law, and decide that "unjustified", for instance is as respects an owner who has sufficient solvency. Reference is made to the CMI document A/Conf.188/3 p. 28. "Wrongful" must be translated, this is important, in usual French, as "unjuste" and in more legal language as "illegale", "injustifié". Therefore the difficulty arises when one adds the word "abusive", that refers more to the abuse of law, *abus de droit*, but it is not necessary since under civil law the abusive use of right is illegal in any case and I quote a famous Author who said "la formule 'usage abusif de droit' est une logomachie, car si j'use de mon droit mon acte est licite et quant il est illicite, ce que je dépasse mon droit et s'agis sans droit selon la loi aquilienne". After considering the comments of the Danish delegate and the interpretation of the wording by the Hong Kong delegation the Belgian delegation suggests in English to delete "wrongful" and to keep "unjustified" and in French to delete "abusif" and to keep "unjustifié". I must say that the Hong Kong delegation disagrees with this proposal.

Hong Kong China   I should make it quite clear that the Hong Kong suggestion is to delete the words "or unjustified" because in our view they purport to expand the scope of liability beyond what is merely wrongful, to some ill-defined notion of what is unjustified. In fact we had a meeting and the first report was I think that the conclusion reached was that the words "or unjustified" should be deleted. Unfortunately there was a second revised version prepared saying that they should be retained. Our position has been consistent throughout and we would like seeing those words deleted.

Mexico   We support the views of the Belgian delegation.

Cyprus   We support the Hong Kong delegation. We consider that the word "unjustified" would entail unnecessary lengthy and cumbersome litigation in order to consider what is unjustified. "Wrongful" we believe is sufficient to discourage any arrest which is not in accordance with the law. And this is what we are concerned with, that the arrest should be in accordance with the law.

Benin   We prefer the term "unjustified" in as much as an arrest that is unjustified is not necessarily wrongful and we think that in all cases where an arrest is unjustified it should give right to a claim for damages. But in order to reach a compromise we would accept the Belgian proposal to keep both "unjustified" and "wrongful".

Chairman   That is different from the Belgian position, but we noted your views.

United Kingdom   When we spoke on this issue before, we said that we would wish the words in brackets to be deleted; that is still our preference. In making our point before we made the point that we didn't want article 6 to become mandatory and as I understand the debate at the moment that doesn't seem likely. If article 6(1) allows the Court, because the Court may as a condition of the arrest etc. etc. the Court has some discretion, and if the Court retains its discretion under 6(2) the Court shall have jurisdiction that is the Court of the State concerned is allowed to determine the issue. As long as things stay like that, in the interest of progress we could live with the removal of the brackets and the retention of the JIGE text. That is to say our overwhelming preference would be to delete the words "or unjustified" but I am trying to help you finding your middle way, Mr Chairman.

Norway   Because the principle of security is important in our national law we prefer to keep "wrongful or unjustified". However, as it was explained by the UK the law of the State may still require security in more cases than in (a) anyway. Therefore we could accept deletion of "or unjustified".

Denmark   I noted that the Belgian delegation already presented what are our views. I have listened carefully to the interventions and as explained by the UK there is already flexibility built in the text. I think that since some delegations wanted both "wrongful" and "unjustified" in the text and although we think that what is unjustified is also wrongful in a spirit of compromise we could live with having both in the text.

Canada   We would like to associate ourselves with the comments that were made and the position taken by Hong Kong China and supported by Cyprus and others, to delete the words "or unjustified". We believe that they may give rise to unfairly penalising the claimant simply on the ground that he would fail in his action on the merits and we think that is entirely inappropriate and unduly restrictive of the right of arrest.

Italy   We are in favour of keeping both terms. We think it is possible that there is an arrest that is not wrongful and can be unjustified, for example if there was no doubt on the solvency of the debtor. But in a spirit of compromise we could accept the proposal of Belgium, to maintain the word "unjustified" and delete "wrongful".

Argentina   We think that there may be an arrest not justified that may give rise to liability and therefore we wish to delete the square brackets and keep both terms.

Chairman   There hasn't been much development since last time. The views are still divided. I am not in a position to make a ruling on what is a consensus view or a view that can be adopted by the Committee. I think we have to consider it further. I think that the remark made by the United Kingdom may be worth recalling, that the wording is such that it does not impose any obligations on the Contracting States or on the Courts of a Contracting State. The provision indicates what Contracting States or the Courts may do, but it doesn't really tell them what to do and I think that it is worth bearing in mind when we revert to this article later on. You may also wish to consider the possibility of putting a full stop earlier on in the text. For example if you look at paragraph (1) you may put a full stop after the words "and for which the claimant may be found liable".

Turkey   We think that the inclusion of (a) and (b) doesn't add too much because in any case in paragraph (3) it is left to the law of the State, to the Court's discretion to establish the liability and the extent of damages. Therefore it may be a good idea to stop where you have suggested in paragraphs (1) and (2).

Iran   Putting a full stop as you suggested I think doesn't add much to the Convention. It seems to me that when we are drafting the Convention we should clarify and should go more in the detail of the debate. If everything is left to the discretion of the Court we do not reach uniformity. I think we should keep sub-paragraphs (a) and (b). May be we can have some informal consultation in order to keep the words "or unjustified".

Chairman   This would be most welcome.

When article 6(1) and (2) was again discussed, the UK delegation, who had originally objected to the word "unjustified", stated that they could accept it, whereupon it was agreed to keep the word and delete the square brackets.

The Chairman of the Drafting Committee reported that there had been some discussion on the word "defendant" in paragraph (1), which it was stated not to be a proper word in the context of this paragraph and that the suggestion was made to delete it. But since this would have implied a change of substance, it was decided to keep it.

PARAGRAPH 2

First reading—4 March 1999

This paragraph was adopted without any relevant discussion.

PARAGRAPH 3

First reading—4 March 1999

This paragraph was adopted without discussion.

PARAGRAPH 4

First reading—5 March 1999

This paragraph was adopted without discussion.

PARAGRAPH 5

First reading—5 March 1999

This paragraph was adopted without discussion.

1999 Convention

1. THE COURT MAY AS A CONDITION OF THE ARREST OF A SHIP, OR OF PERMITTING AN ARREST ALREADY EFFECTED TO BE MAINTAINED, IMPOSE UPON THE CLAIMANT WHO SEEKS TO ARREST OR WHO HAS PROCURED THE ARREST OF THE SHIP THE OBLIGATION TO PROVIDE SECURITY OF A KIND AND FOR AN AMOUNT, AND UPON SUCH TERMS, AS MAY BE DETERMINED BY THAT COURT FOR ANY LOSS WHICH MAY BE INCURRED BY THE DEFENDANT AS A RESULT OF THE ARREST, AND FOR WHICH THE CLAIMANT MAY BE FOUND LIABLE, INCLUDING BUT NOT RESTRICTED TO SUCH LOSS OR DAMAGE AS MAY BE INCURRED BY THAT DEFENDANT IN CONSEQUENCE OF:

   (A) THE ARREST HAVING BEEN WRONGFUL OR UNJUSTIFIED; OR

   (B) EXCESSIVE SECURITY HAVING BEEN DEMANDED AND PROVIDED.

2. THE COURTS OF THE STATE IN WHICH AN ARREST HAS BEEN EFFECTED SHALL HAVE JURISDICTION TO DETERMINE THE EXTENT OF THE LIABILITY, IF ANY, OF THE CLAIMANT FOR LOSS OR DAMAGE CAUSED BY THE ARREST OF A SHIP, INCLUDING BUT NOT RESTRICTED TO SUCH LOSS OR DAMAGE AS MAY BE CAUSED IN CONSEQUENCE OF:

   (A) THE ARREST HAVING BEEN WRONGFUL OR UNJUSTIFIED, OR

   (B) EXCSSSIVE SECURITY HAVING BEEN DEMANDED AND PROVIDED.

3. THE LIABILITY, IF ANY, OF THE CLAIMANT IN ACCORDANCE WITH PARAGRAPH 2 OF THIS ARTICLE SHALL BE DETERMINED BY APPLICATION OF THE LAW OF THE STATE WHERE THE ARREST WAS EFFECTED.

4. IF A COURT IN ANOTHER STATE OR AN ARBITRAL TRIBUNAL IS TO DETERMINE THE MERITS OF THE CASE IN ACCORDANCE WITH THE PROVISIONS OF ARTICLE 7, THEN PROCEEDINGS RELATING TO THE LIABILITY OF THE CLAIMANT IN ACCORDANCE WITH PARAGRAPH 2 OF THIS ARTICLE MAY BE STAYED PENDING THAT DECISION.

5. WHERE PURSUANT TO PARAGRAPH 1 OF THIS ARTICLE SECURITY HAS BEEN PROVIDED, THE PERSON PROVIDING SUCH SECURITY MAY AT ANY TIME APPLY TO THE COURT TO HAVE THAT SECURITY REDUCED, MODIFIED OR CANCELLED.

II.III.10 ARTICLE 7: JURISDICTION ON THE MERITS OF THE CASE

Draft of the CMI International Sub-Committee

(1) THE COURTS OF THE STATE IN WHICH AN ARREST HAS BEEN MADE OR SECURITY GIVEN TO AVOID ARREST OR OBTAIN THE RELEASE OF THE SHIP SHALL HAVE JURISDICTION TO DETERMINE THE CASE UPON ITS MERITS, UNLESS THE INTERESTED PARTIES VALIDLY AGREE OR HAVE AGREED TO SUBMIT THE DISPUTE TO THE COURTS OF ANOTHER STATE OR TO ARBITRATION.

[(2) NOTWITHSTANDING THE PROVISIONS OF PARAGRAPH (1) OF THIS ARTICLE, THE COURTS OF THE STATE IN WHICH AN ARREST HAS BEEN MADE OR SECURITY GIVEN TO AVOID ARREST OR OBTAIN THE RELEASE OF THE SHIP MAY REFUSE TO EXERCISE THAT JURISDICTION WHERE THAT REFUSAL IS PERMITTED BY THEIR OWN LAW.]

(3) IN CASES WHERE THE COURTS OF THE STATE WHERE AN ARREST HAS BEEN MADE OR SECURITY GIVEN TO AVOID ARREST OR OBTAIN THE RELEASE OF THE SHIP DO NOT HAVE JURISDICTION TO DETERMINE THE CASE UPON ITS MERITS, THE COURT TO WHICH THE APPLICATION FOR ARREST WAS MADE SHALL UPON REQUEST ORDER A PERIOD OF TIME WITHIN WHICH THE CLAIMANT SHALL BRING PROCEEDINGS BEFORE AN APPROPRIATE COURT OR TRIBUNAL.

[Alternative text for article 7(3), to be used if paragraph (2) of this article is adopted:

(3) IN CASES WHERE THE COURTS OF THE STATE WHERE AN ARREST HAS BEEN MADE OR SECURITY GIVEN TO AVOID ARREST OR OBTAIN THE RELEASE OF THE SHIP

    (A) DO NOT HAVE JURISDICTION TO DETERMINE THE CASE UPON ITS MERITS, OR

    (B) HAVE REFUSED TO EXERCISE JURISDICTION IN ACCORDANCE WITH THE PROVISIONS OF PARA-GRAPH (2) OF THIS ARTICLE,

THE COURT TO WHICH THE APPLICATION FOR ARREST WAS MADE SHALL UPON REQUEST ORDER A PERIOD OF TIME WITHIN WHICH THE CLAIMANT SHALL BRING PROCEEDINGS BEFORE AN APPROPRIATE COURT OR TRIBUNAL.]

(4) IF PROCEEDINGS ARE NOT BROUGHT WITHIN THE PERIOD OF TIME ORDERED IN ACCORDANCE WITH PARAGRAPH (3) OF THIS ARTICLE THEN THE SHIP ARRESTED OR THE SECURITY GIVEN SHALL UPON REQUEST BE ORDERED TO BE RELEASED.

(5) IF PROCEEDINGS ARE BROUGHT WITHIN THE PERIOD OF TIME ORDERED IN ACCORDANCE WITH PARAGRAPH (3) OF THIS ARTICLE, AND IF SUCH PROCEEDINGS SATISFY GENERAL REQUIREMENTS IN RESPECT OF DUE PROCESS OF LAW, THEN ANY FINAL DECISION RESULTING THEREFROM SHALL BE RECOGNISED AND GIVEN EFFECT WITH RESPECT TO THE ARRESTED SHIP OR TO SECURITY GIVEN IN ORDER TO AVOID ITS ARREST OR OBTAIN ITS RELEASE.

(6) NOTHING CONTAINED IN THE PROVISIONS OF PARAGRAPH (4) OF THIS ARTICLE SHALL RESTRICT ANY WIDER EFFECT GIVEN TO A FOREIGN JUDGMENT OR ARBITRATION AWARD UNDER THE LAW OF THE STATE WHERE THE ARREST WAS MADE OR SECURITY GIVEN TO AVOID OR PREVENT ARREST.

Report of the Chairman of the CMI International Sub-Committee

This article corresponds to art. 7 of the present Convention. It gives the courts of the *forum arresti* jurisdiction to determine the merits of the case but permits them to refuse jurisdiction if that may be done under the law of the forum. The latter rule is within square brackets because such discretion in the courts is unusual in many countries.

Para. (3) and (4) protect the shipowner by ensuring that the case on the merits will not be unreasonably delayed. Corresponding provisions are found in the present Convention art. 7, para. 3 and 4.

Para. 5 provides that where the decision as to the merits of the case must be taken by the courts of a country other than that where the ship was arrested or security given, then that decision shall be enforceable with respect to the ship or security. This rule corresponds to art. 7, para. 2 of the present Convention. It follows that the decision will, thus, not by virtue of the Arrest Convention be enforceable against other property of the defendant. However, other rules may lead to such more far reaching recognition of the foreign judgment; cf. para. (6).

CMI Draft

(1) THE COURTS OF THE STATE IN WHICH AN ARREST HAS BEEN EFFECTED OR SECURITY GIVEN TO PREVENT ARREST OR OBTAIN THE RELEASE OF THE SHIP SHALL HAVE JURISDICTION TO DETERMINE THE CASE UPON ITS MERITS, UNLESS THE PARTIES VALIDLY AGREE OR HAVE AGREED TO SUBMIT THE DISPUTE TO A COURT OF ANOTHER STATE WHICH ACCEPTS JURISDICTION, OR TO ARBITRATION.

(2) NOTWITHSTANDING THE PROVISIONS OF PARAGRAPH (1) OF THIS ARTICLE, THE COURTS OF THE STATE IN WHICH AN ARREST HAS BEEN EFFECTED, OR SECURITY GIVEN TO PREVENT ARREST OR OBTAIN THE RELEASE OF THE SHIP, MAY REFUSE TO EXERCISE THAT JURISDICTION WHERE THAT REFUSAL IS PERMITTED BY THE LAW OF THAT STATE AND A COURT OF ANOTHER STATE ACCEPTS JURISDICTION.

(3) IN CASES WHERE A COURT OF THE STATE WHERE AN ARREST HAS BEEN EFFECTED OR SECURITY GIVEN TO PREVENT ARREST OR OBTAIN THE RELEASE OF THE SHIP:

   (A) DOES NOT HAVE JURISDICTION TO DETERMINE THE CASE UPON ITS MERITS; OR
   (B) HAS REFUSED TO EXERCISE JURISDICTION IN ACCORDANCE WITH THE PROVISIONS OF PARAGRAPH (2) OF THIS ARTICLE,

SUCH COURT MAY, AND UPON REQUEST SHALL, ORDER A PERIOD OF TIME WITHIN WHICH THE CLAIMANT SHALL BRING PROCEEDINGS BEFORE A COMPETENT COURT OR ARBITRAL TRIBUNAL.

(4) IF PROCEEDINGS ARE NOT BROUGHT WITHIN THE PERIOD OF TIME ORDERED IN ACCORDANCE WITH PARAGRAPH (3) OF THIS ARTICLE THEN THE SHIP ARRESTED OR THE SECURITY GIVEN SHALL, UPON REQUEST, BE ORDERED RELEASED.

(5) IF PROCEEDINGS ARE BROUGHT WITHIN THE PERIOD OF TIME ORDERED IN ACCORDANCE WITH PARAGRAPH (3) OF THIS ARTICLE, OR IF PROCEEDINGS BEFORE A COMPETENT COURT IN ANOTHER STATE ARE BROUGHT IN THE ABSENCE OF ANY SUCH ORDER, THEN UNLESS SUCH PROCEEDINGS DO NOT SATISFY GENERAL REQUIREMENTS IN RESPECT OF DUE PROCESS OF LAW, ANY FINAL DECISION RESULTING THEREFROM SHALL BE RECOGNISED AND GIVEN EFFECT WITH RESPECT TO THE ARRESTED SHIP OR TO THE SECURITY GIVEN IN ORDER TO PREVENT HER ARREST OR OBTAIN HER RELEASE.

(6) NOTHING CONTAINED IN THE PROVISIONS OF PARAGRAPH (5) OF THIS ARTICLE SHALL RESTRICT ANY FURTHER EFFECT GIVEN TO A FOREIGN JUDGMENT OR ARBITRAL AWARD UNDER THE LAW OF THE STATE WHERE THE ARREST OF THE SHIP WAS MADE OR SECURITY GIVEN TO PREVENT HER ARREST OR OBTAIN HER RELEASE.

CMI Report

72. Article 7 corresponds to Article 7 of the 1952 Convention. It was adopted by 21 votes to 1 with 10 abstentions.

73. Paragraph (1) confers jurisdiction upon the courts of the *forum arresti* to determine the case upon its merits unless the parties agree otherwise. This jurisdiction is not exclusive and the ordinary rules on jurisdiction of the countries concerned continue to apply. In this connection it may be noted that where several ships have been arrested in different countries for the same claim because the claim exceeds the value of the ship first arrested there will be jurisdiction in each of these countries under Article 7.

74. Paragraph (2) permits the courts which have jurisdiction under paragraph (1) to refuse to exercise that jurisdiction if such refusal is permitted under the law of the forum and the courts of another country accept jurisdiction. The refusal may be made e.g. for reasons of *forum non conveniens*. Countries which do not know or do not wish to introduce this rule are free not to apply it.

75. Paragraphs (3) and (4) have the purpose of ensuring that proceedings to determine the merits of the case are undertaken so that a decision may be obtained within a reasonable time and the ship or security may either be used for fulfilling the claim or be released. In some countries the case must be brought before the court within a time limit fixed by law and, then, the rule is superfluous. Where such a rule does not exist the list in paragraph (3) of cases where an order should be made may be too short. The need to have a decision within a reasonable time seems to exist regardless of where it should be made. Consideration may be given to deleting subparagraphs (a) and (b) and making the rule one of general application.

76. In countries where foreign judgments are not recognised, or recognised only under certain conditions, there is a need for a rule on recognition and enforcement of foreign judgments in cases where arrest has been made or security given but the case is determined on its merits in another country. Without a provision of this nature arrest seems meaningless. Enforcement under the provision of paragraph (5) is, however, limited to the ship or security. The judgment may, of course, be enforced on other assets of the debtor if other rules of the *forum arresti* so provide, cf. paragraph (6).

JIGE
Seventh Session, 5–9 December 1994

Report—Annex I

26. In reply to a question by one delegation, the observer for the Comité Maritime International (CMI) explained that article 7(1) of the 1952 Convention was a compromise between the view held by common law countries, which considered arrest as a means of obtaining jurisdiction, and the opposing view held by civil law countries which required the application of general principles in this respect. The approach adopted by article 7(1) in giving jurisdiction on the merits only in certain cases not being considered satisfactory, the CMI Draft granted general jurisdiction to the courts of the country where the ship was arrested in respect of all claims.

27. One delegation preferred the approach adopted by the 1952 Convention. In its view, the provisions of the 1952 Convention were more consistent with general principles of international maritime law and maritime Conventions such as the Convention on Limitation of Liability. It was further pointed out that granting general jurisdiction to the courts of the country where the ship was arrested would not be equitable.

28. Many delegations expressed support for retaining article 7 of the CMI Draft, whereby jurisdiction was granted to the courts of the *forum arresti* to determine the case upon its merits unless the parties agreed otherwise, or where the court refused to exercise its jurisdiction and that refusal was permitted by the *lex fori* and a court of another country accepted jurisdiction.

Draft Articles 1994

Note of the Editor. The text of this article in the Draft Articles 1994 is the same as that in the CMI Draft.

Ninth Session, 2–6 December 1996

Report—Annex II

90. In reply to a question as to the reason for providing broader scope in the draft Article 7 for jurisdiction on the merits of the case, the observer for the CMI explained that Article 7 (1) of the 1952 Convention was not in effect a compromise between civil law and common law systems as it is purported to be. As a result, common law countries retained their system under which arrest for maritime claims provided a ground for acquiring jurisdiction, while in civil law countries jurisdiction was only afforded by the Convention in respect of certain claims with no specific reason. To achieve uniformity, it had been felt necessary by the drafters of the CMI text in 1985 to grant jurisdiction in all cases and not in respect of certain maritime claims. The observer for the CMI also proposed including a reference to "arbitral tribunal" in Article 7 (5) after the words "competent court", so that it read " . . . or if proceedings before a competent court or arbitral Tribunal in another State are brought . . . ".

537

91. One delegation questioned which law would be applied to decide whether agreements to submit disputes to a Court of another State under Article 7 (1) were validly concluded. The view was expressed that this question was left to national law to decide. That view was commonly shared. Some other delegations proposed to delete the word "validly" in Article 7 (1), since it was not sufficiently clear and could give rise to dispute. One delegation pointed out that the translation of the terms "claim", "claimant" and "maritime claim" into Arabic should be reviewed.

92. The Sessional Group decided to retain Article 7 of the JIGE text, with the addition of "arbitral Tribunal" in paragraph (5).

Draft Articles 1997

Note of the Editor. The text of this article in the Draft Articles 1997 is the same as that in the CMI Draft except that in paragraph (1) the words "an arrest has been effected" have been replaced by "an arrest has been made".

Diplomatic Conference
Comments and Proposals

Aldenave

DOCUMENT 188/3/ADD.3

Article 7.3: insert: " . . . order a period of time not to exceed 30 days, after which the claimant . . . "

17. Stipulating that the court should order a period of no more than 30 days prevents the claimant from being allowed time *ad libitum* and prevents such time from being construed as a procedural delay.

CMI

DOCUMENT 188/3

156. The meaning of the words "due process of law" in paragraph (5) may not be clearly understood in some jurisdictions and it is, therefore, suggested to use the same expression adopted in article 10(1) of the CLC 1969: "reasonable notice and a fair opportunity to present his case". Paragraph 5 should consequently be amended as follows:

If proceedings are brought within the period of time ordered in accordance with paragraph (3) of this Article, or if proceedings before a competent Court or arbitral tribunal in another State are brought in the absence of such order, then *unless the defendant has not been given a reasonable notice of such proceedings and a reasonable opportunity to present his case*, any final decision resulting therefrom shall be recognised and given effect with respect to the arrested ship or to the security given in order to prevent its arrest or obtain its release.

Canada

DOCUMENT CRP.1

4. *Proposal for Article 7—Jurisdiction on the merits of the case*

4.1 Articles 7(1) and (2), read together, confer a very broad discretion on the court of the State in which the arrest is made to reject jurisdiction as long as a court of another State accepts jurisdiction. That other State may be a very inconvenient or impractical place for an action to proceed. In such cases, a choice of forum clause in a contract for the carriage of goods effectively excludes the carrier's liability.

4.2 Articles 7(1) and (2) will conflict with the Hamburg Rules, in particular Article 21 thereof. This result will not only prejudice claimants, as stated above, but will also contribute to a lack of uniformity of law.

4.3 To avoid this result, Canada proposes a new text for Article 7 as follows:

"Article 7

Jurisdiction on the Merits of the Case

(1) In cases where a Court of the State where an arrest has been made or security given to prevent arrest or obtain the release of the ship:

    (a) does not have the jurisdiction to determine the case on the merits; or

    (b) has refused to exercise jurisdiction,

such Court may, and upon request shall, order a period of time within which the claimant shall bring proceedings before a competent Court or arbitral tribunal.

(2) If proceedings are not brought within the period (of) time ordered in accordance with paragraph (1) of this Article, then the ship arrested or the security given shall, upon request, be ordered released.

(3) If proceedings are brought within the period of time ordered in accordance with paragraph (1) of this Article or if proceedings before a competent Court or tribunal in another State are brought in the absence of such order, then unless such proceedings do not satisfy general requirements in respect of due process of law, any final decision resulting therefrom shall be recognised and given effect with respect to the arrested ship or to the security given in order to prevent its arrest or in order to obtain its release.

(4) Nothing contained in the provision of paragraph (3) of this Article shall restrict any further effect given to a foreign judgment or arbitral award under a law of the State where the arrest of the ship was made or security given to prevent its arrest or obtain its release."

France

Article 7, paragraph 5

"If proceedings are brought within the period of time ordered in accordance with paragraph (3) of this article, or if proceedings before a competent Court or arbitral tribunal in another State are brought in the absence of any such order, then unless such proceedings do not satisfy general requirements in respect of due process of law, any final decision resulting therefrom shall take effect provided that the rules on the recognition of foreign decisions, with respect to the arrested ships or the security given to obtain its release, under the law of the State where the arrest was made are respected."

Note of the Editor. The proposal by France was circulated on 8 March 1999 without having been formally registered as a Conference document.

Turkey

DOCUMENT CRP.12

    New paragraph 1(bis)

The Courts of the State in which an arrest has been made or security given to prevent arrest or obtain the release of the ship may order a period of up to 10 days within which the claimant shall lodge the main case before such courts.

New paragraph 4

If proceedings are not brought within the period of time ordered in accordance with paragraph 1*bis* and 3 of this article, the ship arrested or the security given shall, upon request, be ordered released.

Working Group

Article 7, para. (5)

"If proceedings are brought within the period of time ordered in accordance with paragraph (3) of this article, or if proceedings before a competent Court or arbitral tribunal in another State are brought in the absence of such order, any final decision resulting therefrom shall be recognised and given effect with respect to the arrested ship or to the security given in order to prevent its arrest or obtain its release, provided that:

    (a) the defendant has been given a reasonable notice of such proceedings and a reasonable opportunity to present his case; and

    (b) such recognition is not against public policy (ordre public)

[*para. (7)*]

This article shall not apply in cases covered by the provisions of the revised Rhine Navigation Convention of October 17, 1868]

Proceedings of the Main Committee

PARAGRAPH 1

First reading—5 March 1999[79]

This paragraph has been the subject of a careful consideration by the Main Committee and in view of the importance of the provision contained therein, it is felt appropriate to reproduce the debate in full.

Canada CRP.1 in § 4.1–4.3 contains a Canadian proposal. Article 7(1) and (2) when read together confer a very broad jurisdiction on the Court of the State in which the arrest is made to reject jurisdiction just as long as the Court of another State accepts jurisdiction. That other State may be a very inconvenient or impractical place for an action to proceed. In such a case a choice of forum clause in a contract of carriage of goods, for example, could effectively exclude the carrier's liability. Article 7(1) and (2), again read together in our view conflict with known international law, in particular the Hamburg Rules which in article 21 strive with the difficulty to overcome forum choice clauses, assuring that pursuant to a contract of carriage a Court would not lose jurisdiction, very readily by the simple agreement on an arbitration for example. We sense that if article 7(1) and (2) were to be retained as they are in the text we would be heading in the same direction, in a direction contrary to the accepted principles of international law as embodied in the Hamburg Rules. To overcome this problem, Mr Chairman, we have proposed a text for article 7 which you will see in paragraph 4.3 of CRP.1 which in effect does away with paragraphs (1) and (2) of this article and basically commences with what in our JIGE text is paragraph (3) and continues to the end. That draft contains all the elements that are necessary in this area of jurisdiction on the merits of the case, in our view, without encountering the pitfalls, if I may so describe them, of proceeding in accordance with the JIGE draft which has a straight statement about jurisdiction being vested in the Court *ab initio*. We would only make one more comment with respect to the redraft of article 7 and that to correct a typographical error, at the bottom of page 3 of CRP.1 in paragraph 1(a) which now reads "does not have the justification to determine" it should read "jurisdiction".

Spain We do not support the Canadian proposal. It does not solve the problem created by the present text, which for us is a big problem. We have two proposals in respect of the JIGE text. The first one consists in deleting the words in paragraph (1) "or security provided to obtain the release of the ship". We consider that the fact of providing security in a State Party should not be a reason to grant jurisdiction on the merits. We would in fact create with this paragraph a conflict of jurisdiction. We believe it is not proper that the mere delivery of security in a voluntary manner by the shipowner may give rise to jurisdiction on the merits, since this has the effect of attracting jurisdiction. This attraction of jurisdiction is, we think, a serious matter, since a shipowner may have delivered in advance security before a Court of a State Party to cover any future claim and thereby preventing any arrest in another State Party that may not be party to the Convention. In a few words we would establish with a quasi definitive character the *forum arresti* as in the 1952 Convention, which, however, in that Convention was moderated by a series of exceptions, as those of collision etc. Here those exceptions disappear, and we are introducing the security forum, I do not know how to call it. This freedom of choice does not exist in the LLMC Convention of 1976, since in that Convention the limitation fund must be constituted in the Court before which proceedings are commenced. Here we have absolute freedom, since the shipowner may deliver security when he likes. We also have problems over the effects of the presentation of a voluntary security and would like Professor Berlingieri to answer the following questions: with this text we are permitting to leave to the arbitrary decision of the shipowner the choice of the jurisdiction where to commence proceedings on the merits? In other words the debtor will be able to make a forum shipping in advance of the arrest since this is a case when arrest is prevented. We are not considering the case where the arrest has been effected but that of preventing the arrest. Our proposal would be, as previously stated, to delete the words "or security has been provided to prevent arrest or obtain the release of the ship". Our second proposal in respect of paragraph 1 is a problem we think arises with

---

79. Text from tapes Nos. 38, 39 and 40.

the present text, in which we are changing the jurisdiction rules on the merits that may be established in other international conventions. We have doubts that conventions such as the International Convention on Civil Jurisdiction in the matter of Collision of 1952 may have interfered with the present drafting of this Convention. Therefore we think it would be advisable to insert in this paragraph words to the effect that this Convention does not affect other International Conventions on jurisdiction on the merits. We therefore ask for the deletion in paragraph (1) of the words "or security given to prevent arrest or obtain the release of the ship" with the consequential amendments to paragraphs (2) and (3).

Sri Lanka We have made a proposal in document 65 of document 188/3 in respect to paragraph (2). We think that there should be a connection between the Court accepting jurisdiction and the dispute for which the ship has been arrested, such as the place where the claim arose or the place of registration of the ship.

IIDM We prefer to wait for the explanations of Prof. Berlingieri before presenting our point of view.

CMI Mr Chairman, I think that in order to clarify this provision the history of this provision may be useful. In 1952 when the Convention was prepared the situation was that in common law countries and more particularly in the United Kingdom there was always jurisdiction on the merits for all maritime claims because the maritime claims gave and give rise to Admiralty jurisdiction. On the contrary in civil law countries the fact that the ship is arrested in a certain place does not give rise to jurisdiction on the merits or at least this was at that time the basic solution on the basic principles of civil law countries. A compromise was arrived at—so to say a compromise, I don't think it was at all, though it was described like that—according to which the common law countries preserved their position since art. 7 of the 1952 Convention provides that the Courts where the arrest is made have jurisdiction on the merits if the domestic law of the country in which arrest is made gives such jurisdiction: common law countries were thus protected. Then in order to grant something or to change to some extent the law in civil law countries, jurisdiction on the merits was recognised in a number of specified cases. I am not listing the cases, but there are five cases if I remember well, or six, in which jurisdiction on the merits was granted. In 1985 it was deemed convenient to try to reach uniformity in common and civil law countries and therefore to grant jurisdiction on the merits in all cases in which a ship is arrested as security for a maritime claim. This was the background of the present article 7(1) and (2). The purpose was to have the same system both in common and civil law countries. Now the proposal of Canada would destroy entirely this system. As regards the comments made by the distinguished delegate from Spain, I think he has today, as yesterday, if I remember well, touched upon a point which has merit in this sense: when reference is made in paragraph 1 of article 7 to the place where security is given to prevent the arrest, the idea was that the security is normally given in the place where the arrest has been or would be applied for. The normal situation when security is given to prevent arrest is that the claimant informs the owner that he is going to arrest the ship and suggests the owner to provide security in order to avoid the arrest, so what is not expressly stated in this provision—and this perhaps has not been properly done—is that the security is given or should be given in the place where the arrest would be made. In other words, a ship arrives in a certain port, there is a threat of arrest and the owner in order to prevent the arrest provides security in agreement with the claimant, and the security would normally be given in that port. It was not at all thought that it would be possible for the owner to provide security in an entirely different place. Amongst other things, very likely if the owner were to provide security in a place other than that where the ship lies, probably the claimant would not accept such security and would execute the arrest in order to obtain jurisdiction in that place. In any event, what it is not expressly stated in paragraph 1, Mr Chairman, is that the assumption is that the security is provided in the place where the ship lies at that time, not anywhere else, and if security is limited to such a situation then the problem which has been quite correctly raised by the distinguished delegate from Spain in my submission does not arise. May I also draw your attention and the attention of all the distinguished delegates, Mr Chairman, to the fact that the part the deletion of which is suggested, in actual fact deals with two different situations: the first is that the security is given to prevent the arrest, and the second is that the security is given to release the ship from the arrest which has already been made; and in the second case it is obvious that the security would be given in the place where the arrest was made. I hope I have been able to clarify a bit the situation

Mr Chairman. In any event I am at the disposal of all the delegates if some further information is required.

IIDM   From the explanation of Prof. Berlingieri it would appear that this provision is dangerous, since it can give rise to forum shipping. We support the Spanish proposal in the part relating to the deletion of the words "to prevent the arrest" while we have doubt as to whether also the words "obtain the release of the ship" should be deleted.

Thailand   We have the same concern as expressed by Spain. It may happen that arrest is made in one State and security is given in another State. In that case it is not clear which Court would have jurisdiction on the merits.

Cyprus   We believe that when the ship is arrested, there is the jurisdiction to deal with the merits of the case. The way paragraph (1) is drafted makes Canadian comments valid. We think the words "or have agreed" should be deleted and only the words "validly agree" should stay, since this implies an agreement after the arrest. Otherwise we agree with the JIGE text.

CMI   Only two words Mr Chairman. I wonder whether the problem would be solved by referring the word "validly" both to "agree" or "have agreed" because in this case what is implied is that the existing or future agreement must be a valid agreement. If it is not valid under another international convention, such as the Hamburg Rules, then this provision will not apply.

Cyprus   I don't think the suggestion solves the problem. What I am trying to avoid is that the Court of the place of arrest is deprived of jurisdiction on the merits.

Italy   I have the impression that the Spanish proposal does not adversely affect the compromise between civil law and common law countries even though the danger of forum shipping may be minimum. It is necessary to draw a distinction between the two situations of the sentence the deletion of which has been requested. The first situation is that of security given to prevent arrest; in such case it is difficult that security is given in a Court other than that where the arrest is going to be applied for. But if that is the case, it would be a private agreement that should not have any effect on jurisdiction, unless it is precisely an agreement on jurisdiction. If the situation is that of obtaining the release of the ship from arrest, as Prof. Berlingieri has said, it is rather difficult that the claimant accepts that the security be provided in a State other than that of arrest. If this takes place it is only on the basis of an agreement between the parties. In conclusion we suggest to delete only the first part, relating to security given to prevent arrest, but keeping the second part.

United Kingdom   We think the Canadian proposal does raise an important issue here. Broadly we have been quite content with the JIGE text. There have of course been a number of cases in the UK where the issue of determining jurisdiction has arisen and we are fairly comfortable with that. Perhaps our interpretation of this article in its entirety is not dealt with in the draft articles and I would put it this way: we see it being for the law of the place in which the ship was arrested to decide the question of jurisdiction and perhaps if that helps people we might usefully record that sort of sentence in our report and in terms of proposals made by Cyprus and Spain I am afraid we can't support those. The CMI proposal to add the word "validly" seems to have considerable merits and we feel might help people.

Peru   It is evident that the Spanish delegation has touched a sensitive point in article 7, even if the Italian counterproposal is based on the actual situation that ordinarily occurs in the majority of the ports of the world in that it would admit the possibility that both parties as indicated by article 4 of the Convention agree to release the ship from arrest. It is evident that the declaration of Prof. Berlingieri is a valid interpretation in respect of the power to exercise what is known as forum shopping; it is a door that now is kept open with the text of the draft Convention and that should be closed. The alternative might be to add at the beginning or at the end of this article the following: "in no case the provision of security in a unilateral manner in a jurisdiction other than that in which the ship has been arrested". By this the door to exercise the choice of jurisdiction more convenient for the interest of the debtor would be shut.

Mexico   We have a serious problem with the whole of this article. The jurisdiction on the merits should pertain to the courts that have normally jurisdiction. It is not convenient to grant jurisdiction on the merits to the Court that has granted arrest. This is a matter of "ordre public" in Mexico.

Greece   Paragraph (1) strikes a good balance between common law and civil law. We wish to retain the text.

Denmark   The proposal of Canada has some merits. Then we listened very carefully to the explanations and the amendments from CMI which I think could solve all the problems. We didn't realise ourselves, I must say, not being English speaking as some others in this room, the real extent of the word "valid" or "validity" which was put in the text and I think it has solved a lot of problems for us. Of course we could have wished for a further explanation in the text but at this stage it would imply going over and over again. I would like to thank Prof. Berlingieri trying to solve the problem for us. We can go along with the JIGE text with the amendment prepared by him.

China The Chinese delegation thinks that in general, the text in article 7 paragraph 1 is reasonable, we can support this text. We can also agree, if my memory does not fail me, with the suggestion presented by the Spanish delegation pursuant to which the phrase "security given to prevent arrest" should be deleted. The arrest of ships has become a common judicial practice in modern times, especially since the coming into force of the 1952 Convention. The maritime claimant generally has two objects for the arrest of a ship, one is to obtain a security, another is to obtain jurisdiction on the merits of the case. Article 7 paragraph 1 has provisions to satisfy the above mentioned objects. Hence, it is also logically reasonable. It also provides that arbitration or jurisdiction agreements concluded before or after the arrest, for instance, the arbitration clause or the choice of jurisdiction clause in a charter party, shall prevail over the jurisdiction obtained from the arrest of ships, and the jurisdiction from arrest must be conditional to the actual arrest of a ship. We therefore suggest that the phrase "security given to prevent arrest" be deleted so as to avoid that the shipowner may unreasonably obtain the jurisdiction. We think it is necessary to delete the above mentioned phrase.

France We agree with statement made by Peru. The object of this Convention is arrest and not to regulate disputes. And we think that with the Spanish proposal we have a much clearer text. We thus support the deletion of the words "to prevent arrest". On the other side we have a text which provides that the Courts of the State where arrest is effected or security provided to release the ship, have jurisdiction on the merits. This is something wanted by the parties, viz. to have a full jurisdiction, while we have reservations on the term "validly" which has very little meaning in civil law countries. I think we would delete this term and if it is decided to keep it it would be necessary to find something having a juridical content for civil law countries such as a reference to a legitimate jurisdiction clause.

Netherlands We support the compromise established. In that respect the JIGE text is very clear. Much clearer than that of the 1952 Convention. We are quite happy with it. But since some concern has been expressed, we would like to support the suggestion of CMI.

Canada In an effort to move the work forward it strikes us that the problem we have raised, which of course was hinged to carriage of goods situations, not obviously tort matters, where you cannot agree on jurisdiction before the tort arises, would be solved in my view, first of all if we accept the language prepared by the CMI. We certainly have an understanding of the term "validly" in our common law. We also appreciate what our French colleagues said about the lack of understanding of that term in civil law system that could be remedied. But in any event assuming "validly" would remain in English we would support that. But we would add after the word "agreed" the words "after the arrest has been made or security given to prevent arrest". That clearly, you will appreciate, situates in time, i.e. the agreement between the parties and again I am referring particularly to the carriage of goods situation, where agreement has arisen after the arrest and therefore would not be subject to pre-existing jurisdiction clauses which, as I said in my earlier intervention, are contrary to the correct status of international law in these matters as particularly exemplified in article 20 of the Hamburg Rules.

Argentina We have listened to the previous speakers and have seen that the major concern that exists amongst delegations is an anticipated obtention of jurisdiction that in some way may be favourable to one of the parties. We believe that in order to avoid this problem, since apparently it is not the objective of this article, we can add after the word "arrest", i.e. "the Court that has effected the arrest, or where with the agreement of the parties security has been provided to prevent arrest" would solve in any way the problem.

Norway We agree with everything Denmark said and therefore we want to keep the JIGE text with the amendment proposed by the CMI. We don't agree with the last proposal of Canada.

Philippines We appreciate the background provided by various delegations, especially Prof. Berlingieri explaining to us the significance of this article in relation to common law and civil law countries but this delegation has come to this forum with a specific view on this issue of jurisdiction and we believe that the interests represented by this delegation would be better represented in this Convention by associating itself with the views expressed by Spain and by Peru.

Finland   We are in favour of the CMI and coming to the Canadian latest proposal we don't support it.

Spain   In principle we can agree with the proposal of Peru and Italy which amends our initial proposal of deleting only the first part viz. "to prevent arrest". Our initial proposal, Mr. Chairman, was much wider and consisted in deleting all the words "has provided security to prevent arrest or obtain the release of the ship". The reason was no other than to avoid the redundancy that in our opinion exists with the words "or has provided security in order to obtain the release of the ship". After the explanations of Prof. Berlingieri, that normally the provision of security for release of the ship is effected in agreement and before the Court that has granted the arrest, and this seems to be the usual practice, notwithstanding that we may have in principle some doubts, we may in principle accept them. Our doubts are due to the fact that if the Courts of the State in which the arrest is effected are already competent, it would appear sufficient, and would not be necessary to repeat that they are competent because security is provided in order to release the ship. If these words are kept it appears that we create a new jurisdiction. This is the doubt we have. However, as previously stated we accept the proposal made by Peru and Italy.

Sweden   We prefer the JIGE text with the CMI amendment.

Marshall Isl.   We are of the same view. We think that the observation made by Canada deserves to be noted. This particular article will come into play, we believe, in the majority of cases in cargo damage situations in which there is often a degree of cooperation between the lawyers for the plaintiff and the lawyer for the vessel's owner. We like article 7 as it exists in the present text with the improvement proposed by the CMI because it does provide several alternatives and we feel that to try to find an exclusive channel for jurisdiction may in fact frustrate the commercial interests of the parties who although they may be fighting one another, nevertheless have some interest in common, namely the commercial interest to keep in business the ship's sailing, to keep trade moving. To the extent that this article encourages a degree of cooperation in not forum shopping, but a choice of forum by the parties, this delegation would suggest that the existing text is quite helpful and satisfactory commercially.

Chairman   It seems that there is one delegation which has a fundamental problem with the basic concept of paragraph 1, the concept of the jurisdiction on the basis of arrest and that is the Mexican delegation. And I understand that for the same reason they have not ratified the 1952 Convention. I have not heard of any other delegation having the same basic fundamental problem. I think that the Canadian problem and that referred to by others is not of that fundamental nature; as I understand it, they have a problem in what they see as a potential conflict of conventions, which is another type of a problem. So I think that I can say that it is clear that the majority, the strong majority, wishes to have a text along the lines of paragraph (1). It is also clear to me that the proposal made by Spain as subsequently defined by Peru and Italy which was accepted by Spain has met with the approval of the Group. So I think that as I understood the Spanish delegate he now wants the text with the opening of paragraph 1 to read as follows:

> The Courts of the State in which an arrest has been made or security given to obtain the release of the ship shall have jurisdiction etc.

So, subject to drafting refinements in the Drafting Committee, I consider that the opening of this paragraph is adopted as I just read it out. Then we have the words "validly agree or have agreed" to which a number of proposals were made. The CMI suggested the word "validly" should be repeated so it would read: *unless the parties validly agree or have validly agreed.* A number of delegations supported that and felt that that was a clarification. Others had philosophical problems with that word, at least as translated in, for example, French. I think the French problem is a drafting problem, it doesn't transfer well into French. The concept of validity does not make sense if you transfer it directly into French. But I don't think that it is basically a problem of substance. I think the delegations agree that an agreement which is in conflict with a convention which the Court is bound by, that agreement would not be honoured by that Court. And then we have the Canadian proposal, which I think was in line with the intervention by Cyprus, to add the words that the agreement should be after the arrest has been made or security given to prevent arrest and I assume the delegation of Cyprus would be able to support that and some others would be able to support it. Others again spoke clearly against it; could not accept it. I think that is geared to the same problem, namely the potential conflict of conventions and it was mentioned by the delegation of the Marshall Islands that perhaps this problem is mostly related to carriage of goods and I think if you talk in terms of conflict of conventions, I think that is right. But I also feel that we must not forget that there are a number of contracts of affreightment which do not involve either the Hamburg Rules or Hague Visby or any convention, but when for example arbitration agreements are included as a matter of routine, most standard charter parties have standard arbitration clauses and perhaps it would be drastic to suggest that all those arbitration clauses be invalid when there is an arrest. I feel that there is not enough support for me to make any conclusion in respect to these words "validly agree or have validly agreed". But I can say there is support for adding the word "validly" as suggested by the CMI. But other than that I don't feel that I can rule on any amendment. So my position is to adopt article 7(1) with the Spanish-Peruvian-Italian amendments and with the CMI amendment. Provisionally. Provisional adoption, and if the Canadian delegation and the Cyprus delegation can find support for a means of dealing with what they consider to be a conflict of conventions then we can revert to it. Is that acceptable?

Spain Mr Chairman, we should like through your intermediary to solicit the French delegation. I think that by this solution we may have bypassed the problem and may arrive at the definitive approval of the article, if the concept of validity, as I understand it in my legal system is directly tied to the validity of the juridical act, that is that the juridical act by means of which the parties have decided to agree on something is not subject to any cause of nullity or voidability. I think that if we consider that the juridical meaning of the word "validly" is this one, the problem would be solved. Otherwise we would ask to find in the Spanish and French text a more appropriate word.

France Actually in your summing up, or at least in its French translation you said that this was a philosophical question. I think that it goes beyond philosophy, and is actually a question which touches upon the basis of the law. There are certain clauses between the parties which will be acceptable and others which will be referred to the Courts. This is the reason why this notion of "validity" in English requires a very refined translation. I think that actually we can find an agreement if we clearly reserve, I would say, the licit character of these clauses. These are, as I said a while ago, licit jurisdiction clauses. That means that in certain cases the agreement of the parties will not be recognised by the Court.

United Kingdom We listened with great attention the submission of the Spanish delegation but had some difficulty in understanding precisely what was the amendment. Clearly you, Mr Chairman, understood it better than we did. Could we possibly ask you to read out the text incorporating the Spanish amendment as understood by you? One other very small point was that the Canadian delegation indicated that public international law is represented by the Hamburg Rules and this delegation would wish to record the view of this delegation that the Hamburg Rules have received enough ratification to enter into force but a substantial number of those ratifications are land-locked States in which the arrest of ships is an entirely irrelevant consideration and that is not simply defending the UK corner on jurisdiction, but a matter of fact that the question whether the Hamburg Rules represent generally accepted principles of international law is a matter that should be discussed in another place.

Chairman As to the first part of your intervention I read out what I believe to be the text as amended by the Spanish proposal:

> The Courts of the State in which the arrest has been made or security given to obtain the release of the ship shall have jurisdiction etc.

So in the English text just delete three words "prevent the arrest or".

PARAGRAPH 2

First reading—5 March 1999[80]

This paragraph was adopted without discussion, with the deletion of the words "to prevent the arrest or".

80. Summary from tape No. 40.

PARAGRAPH 3

First reading—5 March 1999[81]

   The suggestion to indicate a maximum period of time for the commencement of proceedings on the merits was not accepted and this paragraph was adopted, with the deletion of the words "to prevent arrest or" as in paragraph (1).

PARAGRAPH 4

First reading—5 March 1999[82]

   This paragraph was adopted without discussion.

PARAGRAPH 5

First reading—5 March 1999[83]

   The issues of recognition and enforcement of foreign judgments and of the conditions for such recognition and enforcement gave rise to a hot debate. It is felt appropriate to reproduce it.

Spain   We have difficulty with the final part of this paragraph when reference is made to "due process of law". It is not specified to which State reference must be made, whether it is the State in which proceedings on the merits are conducted or the State in which the judgment must be enforced. We consider that it should be the State where the merits are decided, but it is not clear.

CMI   Mr Chairman, in order first to reply to the question which has been raised by the distinguished delegate from Spain I should have assumed that from the text it was very clear that the question whether the due process of law has been complied with must be decided by the Court where the judgment should be recognised. The CMI had one minor suggestion then Mr Chairman regarding this provision. The words "due process of law" may not be easily understood in certain jurisdictions and the CMI wonders whether language such as that which has been adopted in other Conventions, such as the CLC 1969, could be adopted here. In the CLC 1969 the words used instead of "due process of law" are "reasonable notice and fair opportunity to present his case" which seems to the CMI to be words which can be more easily understood all the world over, in all jurisdictions. So in the CMI proposal the change which is suggested is underlined. If you wish me to read the entire provision as amended by the CMI I would of course do it. Mr Chairman the paragraph would read: "if proceedings are brought in the period of time ordered in accordance with paragraph 3 of this article or if proceedings before a competent Court or arbitral Tribunal in another State are brought in absence of such order then unless (*and here the new words follow*) the defendant has not been given a reasonable notice of such proceedings and the reasonable opportunity to present his case any final decision resulting therefrom etc.".

Italy   We support the CMI proposal.

Netherlands   We suggest deletion of this paragraph.

Peru   We refer to the New York Convention of 1958. Reference should be made to the law of the forum of execution.

Sweden   We have a proposal in CRP 10. Our proposal for an additional provision to article 2(4) may be placed somewhere else. If a foreign judgment cannot be enforced, the arrest should not be granted. Article 2(4) seems to compel a Court in a Contracting State to grant an application for arrest if the circumstances mentioned in the article are fulfilled. Therefore there is a need for an additional rule in article 2(4) saying that notwithstanding this provision arrest of a ship shall be permissible only if pursuant to article 7(5) the judgment or arbitral award in respect of the claim can be enforced against the ship in the State where arrest is made or applied for. We have had a short discussion with the delegate from the CMI Prof. Berlingieri if the rule in article 2(5) of the Convention takes care

---

81. Summary from tape No. 41.
82. Summary from tape No. 41.
83. Text from tapes Nos. 41, 42 and 43.

of this specific problem. As the text now stands in that article we are not sure. Therefore we propose the additional rule in article 2(4) as contained in CRP 10. If, however, the Conference will make it clear that article 2(5) takes care of this problem, there will be no need for an additional rule as we now have proposed. The CMI proposal on article 2(5) contained in document 188/C/§135 would be very clarifying on this matter.

Chairman I understand that your proposal is not incompatible with article 7(5) and I propose that we deal with article 7 first. Then I shall invite comments on your proposal.

Norway We support CMI proposal on paragraph (5).

Belgium Enforcement of a foreign judgment requires in many States a special procedure of *exequatur*. Therefore this provision would be impossible to comply with in such States.

Philippines In many civil jurisdictions the element of due notice, reference to which is made in the CMI proposal, is only one of the elements that are required for the recognition of a foreign judgment. We suggest retention of the words "due process".

Cyprus There are conventions for international recognition of both foreign awards and foreign judgments. By adopting the suggestion of the CMI we in effect eliminate several defences which the defendant would have to stop the application of a foreign award in the jurisdiction where originally the arrest was made because there are for example defences like if the judgment was against public policy. They are not referred to here and by simply accepting what the CMI is proposing we are in effect eliminating those defences.

Russian Fed. We, as well as a number of other delegations, are inclined to consider the CMI's proposal as appropriate, removing a whole number of complicated issues connected with this paragraph. We support it.

Thailand We are in favour of JIGE text.

Argentina We would accept this paragraph with the deletion suggested by Belgium. We suggest we should provide that the judgment is not in conflict with "ordre public" of the State where enforcement is sought.

Chairman Your proposal that the judgment should not be in conflict with "ordre public" would solve the Belgian problem as well? The Belgian problem being that the text now says that the judgment or award shall be recognised. I thought that was his problem because that would seem to indicate that would rule out the *exequatur* requirement that they have in that country. Do you feel that your proposal would solve his problem as well? Is it enough to say that there shall be compliance with "ordre public" requirement?

Argentina We think so, for if the State where enforcement is sought will control compliance with the provisions of the State where proceedings have been conducted.

Switzerland We are against CMI proposal. The notion of "due process" goes much further than the CMI proposal. Our delegation as well is not very much in favour of the JIGE draft using "due process" but we would support the delegation of Argentina.

Denmark We support the JIGE text with the CMI amendment which in fact defines the due process of law and while I am speaking I would like to thank the CMI for telling us about the competent Court being the Court where the arrest takes place that was a very helpful explanation for us and I hope it was for the other colleagues as well.

Canada We support the JIGE text for the reasons given by the Philippines.

France We are in favour of the proposal made by Argentina. We think it would be proper to refer here to the *exequatur* procedures.

Belgium We suggest to replace the words "shall be recognised" with "may be recognised". This would give more flexibility.

Iran We support the JIGE text as amended by Belgium.

Sri Lanka We support the JIGE text.

Mexico We agree with Belgium and Argentina.

Netherlands We agree with Argentina and Belgium to overcome difficulty.

Philippines We have difficulty with the mandatory nature of the provision because we do not have an automatic recognition of foreign judgments. Agree with replacement of "shall" with "may".

United Kingdom We favour the retention of the JIGE text with the CMI proposed amendment.

United States We also favour the retention of the JIGE text with the CMI proposed amendment.

Chairman   May I ask Argentina if the Belgian proposal to replace "shall" with "may" reflects his proposal or has he any other proposal.

Argentina   We think that it could be added that the judgment is enforceable unless it does not meet the conditions required in order to obtain the *exequatur* in the State where the judgment must be enforced.

Chairman   This is a different issue. I think we have to leave it open. One side is the Belgian proposal, to replace "shall" by "may". I know that Argentina puts it differently but they think along the same lines they want to achieve the same thing. The JIGE text represents the other position, that is "shall" and the views have been divided. Further agreement will have to be achieved.

Peru   I propose that to the proposal of Argentina there should be added the words: "meets with the conditions required for its enforcement".

Chairman   The question still remains, do we wish to make recognition compulsory or not? I think that is the basic question.

CMI   Mr Chairman, the purpose of this paragraph was to ensure the enforcement of the judgments in the country where the ship is arrested in order to expedite the realisation of the security. If reference is made to the *exequatur* procedure the paragraph becomes entirely pointless. It is better to delete it entirely. If the word "may" is used instead of "shall" this provision is reversed because it would limit the possibility of States to enforce the judgments because the provision would read: "the proceedings are brought etc.". It would make the enforcement conditional to certain specific elements which are included in this paragraph; so it would infringe upon the right of Contracting States to recognise foreign judgments. So the purpose would be reversed. This, with all respect, does not make sense Mr Chairman.

Russian Fed.   Our delegation is in favour of adopting the text of article 6 prepared by the JIGE, deleting the square brackets and retaining the text contained in them. Our attitude towards the proposal to replace the verb "may" by the verb "shall" is negative. Those who propose this change, do not consider the fact that it may whittle away the arrest as it is. The Court may make the arrest dependent on the provision of security, but it is impermissible to bind the Court to do so. The Court may, proceeding from the character of a claim, such as the demand of a ship's crew concerning payment of their wages, arrest a ship without the provision of security by the crew. This is the right of the Court. The proposal by the Danish delegation that the Court may make the arrest of a ship dependent on the provision of security, proceeding from reasonable circumstances should not be introduced into the article. It is unnecessary to do it. In conformity with the national rules of civil procedure, Courts, using their own discretion, are obliged to follow the principles of rationality and justice. Due to that we are in favour of retaining article 6 in its presented version.

France   I have listened to the comments of Prof. Berlingieri. As I said before we have some difficulties. There are rules that must be complied with for the recognition of foreign judgments in our country. If the Committee is in agreement with the idea that has been previously suggested, I would have a drafting proposal that could meet with the interests of the two groups. In the JIGE text we should read "all final judgments issued at the completion of these proceedings shall have effect subject to the rules relating to recognition of foreign judgment in the State of the place of arrest". This would meet the requirement of due process of law whilst reserving to civil law countries their own procedure.

Chairman   Perhaps that can serve a basis for further discussion. For the time being we have to conclude. Further work has to be done by you in relation to this provision.

France   Also in § 6 the words "to prevent arrest" should be deleted.

Chairman   Yes.

Second reading—8 March 1999[84]

   The following is the summary of the debate.

   The French delegation submitted a proposal to replace the last part of paragraph (5) reading "any final decision resulting therefrom shall be recognised and given effect with respect to the arrested ship or to the security given in order to prevent its arrest or obtain its release" with the following text:

---

84. Summary from tapes Nos. 54, 55 and 71.

" . . . any final decision resulting therefrom shall take effect provided that the rules on the recognition of foreign decisions, with respect to the arrested ship or the security given to obtain its release, under the law of the State where the arrest was made are respected."

The delegations who supported the French proposal stated that their support was conditional to the provision not implying the revision of the merits of the case. Other delegations suggested to adopt the CMI suggestion.

The Chairman stated that no overwhelming majority had developed in favour of the French proposal and that further efforts should be made in order to reach a consensus on the text of the provision.

The UK delegate stated that the purpose of article 7(5) is to make the enforcement simple and quick and referred to the comment of the CMI observer, who had stated that if reference were made to all rules of the State where the arrest is made, the provision of article 7(5) would be useless.

The Chairman indicated that two issues, exequatur and notion of due process, had to be further investigated and requested a working group to consider them.

The delegate from Hong Kong China, who acted as Chairman of the Working Group, submitted to the Committee the following text:

"5. If proceedings are brought within the period of time ordered in accordance with paragraph 3 of this article, or if proceedings before a competent Court or arbitral tribunal in another State are brought in the absence of such order, any final decision resulting therefrom shall be recognised and given effect with respect to the arrested ship or to the security provided in order to obtain its release, on condition that:

(a) the defendant has been given reasonable notice of such proceedings and a reasonable opportunity to present the case for the defence; and

(b) such recognition is not against public policy (ordre public)."

He stated that it had proved to be difficult to define the exceptions to the obligations to recognise foreign judgments and that what was suggested was to repeat in the chapeau the text of the JIGE draft and then to insert under (a) the text of the CMI proposal, and under (b) a reference to public policy, which may be found in other international conventions, such as the 1958 New York Convention on the Recognition and Enforcement of Foreign Arbitral Awards (article V(2)(b)) and the Brussels and Lugano Conventions on Jurisdiction and the Recognition of Judgments in Civil and Commercial Matters (article 27).

He added that it had been deemed convenient, following the practice adopted in some other conventions, to use in the same text both the English and French wording, in order to make the meaning of the expression more clear.

A new paragraph had then been added in order to exclude any possible conflict between the new Arrest Convention and the 1868 Rhine Convention.[85]

The Chairman noted that nobody appeared to have problems with the text submitted by the Working Group.

PARAGRAPH 6

First reading—5 March 1999[86]

This paragraph was adopted without any relevant discussion.

1999 Convention

1. THE COURTS OF THE STATE IN WHICH AN ARREST HAS BEEN EFFECTED OR SECURITY PROVIDED TO OBTAIN THE RELEASE OF THE SHIP SHALL HAVE JURISDICTION TO DETERMINE THE CASE UPON ITS MERITS, UNLESS THE PARTIES VALIDLY AGREE OR HAVE VALIDLY AGREED TO SUBMIT THE DISPUTE TO A COURT OF ANOTHER STATE WHICH ACCEPTS JURISDICTION, OR TO ARBITRATION.

2. NOTWITHSTANDING THE PROVISIONS OF PARAGRAPH 1 OF THIS ARTICLE, THE COURTS OF THE STATE IN WHICH AN ARREST HAS BEEN EFFECTED, OR SECURITY PROVIDED TO OBTAIN THE RELEASE

85. See *infra*, p. 556.
86. Summary from tape No. 48.

OF THE SHIP, MAY REFUSE TO EXERCISE THAT JURISDICTION WHERE THAT REFUSAL IS PERMITTED BY THE LAW OF THAT STATE AND A COURT OF ANOTHER STATE ACCEPTS JURISDICTION.

3. IN CASES WHERE A COURT OF THE STATE WHERE AN ARREST HAS BEEN EFFECTED OR SECURITY PROVIDED TO OBTAIN THE RELEASE OF THE SHIP:

(A) DOES NOT HAVE JURISDICTION TO DETERMINE THE CASE UPON ITS MERITS; OR

(B) HAS REFUSED TO EXERCISE JURISDICTION IN ACCORDANCE WITH THE PROVISIONS OF PARAGRAPH 2 OF THIS ARTICLE,

SUCH COURT MAY, AND UPON REQUEST SHALL, ORDER A PERIOD OF TIME WITHIN WHICH THE CLAIMANT SHALL BRING PROCEEDINGS BEFORE A COMPETENT COURT OR ARBITRAL TRIBUNAL.

4. IF PROCEEDINGS ARE NOT BROUGHT WITHIN THE PERIOD OF TIME ORDERED IN ACCORDANCE WITH PARAGRAPH 3 OF THIS ARTICLE THEN THE SHIP ARRESTED OR THE SECURITY PROVIDED SHALL, UPON REQUEST, BE ORDERED TO BE RELEASED.

5. IF PROCEEDINGS ARE BROUGHT WITHIN THE PERIOD OF TIME ORDERED IN ACCORDANCE WITH PARAGRAPH 3 OF THIS ARTICLE, OR IF PROCEEDINGS BEFORE A COMPETENT COURT OR ARBITRAL TRIBUNAL IN ANOTHER STATE ARE BROUGHT IN THE ABSENCE OF SUCH ORDER, ANY FINAL DECISION RESULTING THEREFROM SHALL BE RECOGNISED AND GIVEN EFFECT WITH RESPECT TO THE ARRESTED SHIP OR TO THE SECURITY PROVIDED IN ORDER TO OBTAIN ITS RELEASE, ON CONDITION THAT:

(A) THE DEFENDANT HAS BEEN GIVEN REASONABLE NOTICE OF SUCH PROCEEDINGS AND A REASONABLE OPPORTUNITY TO PRESENT THE CASE FOR THE DEFENCE; AND

(B) SUCH RECOGNITION IS NOT AGAINST PUBLIC POLICY (ORDRE PUBLIC).

6. NOTHING CONTAINED IN THE PROVISIONS OF PARAGRAPH 5 OF THIS ARTICLE SHALL RESTRICT ANY FURTHER EFFECT GIVEN TO A FOREIGN JUDGMENT OR ARBITRAL AWARD UNDER THE LAW OF THE STATE WHERE THE ARREST OF THE SHIP WAS EFFECTED OR SECURITY PROVIDED TO OBTAIN ITS RELEASE.

THE TRAVAUX PRÉPARATOIRES

II.III.11 ARTICLE 8: APPLICATION

Draft of the CMI International Sub-Committee[87]

(1) THIS CONVENTION SHALL APPLY TO ANY SEA-GOING SHIP, WHETHER OR NOT THAT SHIP IS FLYING THE FLAG OF A CONTRACTING STATE.

(2) THIS CONVENTION SHALL NOT APPLY TO STATE-OWNED SHIPS EXCLUSIVELY USED FOR GOVERNMENTAL NON-COMMERCIAL SERVICE.

(3) NOTHING IN THIS CONVENTION SHALL BE CONSTRUED AS CREATING A RIGHT OF ACTION OR AS CREATING A MARITIME LIEN.

(4) THIS CONVENTION DOES NOT AFFECT ANY RIGHTS OR POWERS VESTED OTHERWISE THAN UNDER THIS CONVENTION, OR ANY LAW ENACTING THE SAME, IN ANY GOVERNMENT OR ITS DEPARTMENTS, OR IN ANY PUBLIC AUTHORITY, OR IN ANY DOCK OR HARBOUR AUTHORITY, UNDER ANY DOMESTIC LAW OR REGULATION OR INTERNATIONAL CONVENTION, TO DETAIN OR OTHERWISE PREVENT FROM SAILING ANY SHIP WITHIN THEIR JURISDICTION.

Report of the Chairman of the CMI International Sub-Committee

It is proposed that the application of the rules of the Convention should not be dependent upon reciprocity or subject to other restriction, cf. para. (1).

It is thought prudent in para. (3) to retain a provision corresponding to art. 9 of the present Convention.

CMI Draft

(1) THIS CONVENTION SHALL APPLY TO ANY SEA-GOING SHIP, WHETHER OR NOT THAT SHIP IS FLYING THE FLAG OF A STATE PARTY.

87. In the draft of the CMI International Sub-Committee this article was numbered (9) because it was preceded by the following article, which was then deleted by the Lisbon Conference:

[Article 8
Inter State agreements
(1) Notwithstanding the preceding articles, any State may enter into agreement with one or more other States providing that a guarantee issued by the Government of a State, its departments or other institutions in respect of ships owned by that State shall be sufficient security for claims in respect of such ships.

(2) Where a guarantee is issued in accordance with the provisions of paragraph (1) of this article, such ships may not be arrested within the jurisdiction of the State which has entered into the agreement with the State issuing the guarantee.

(3) Notwithstanding paragraphs (1) and (2) of this article, the provisions of this Convention shall otherwise apply as if the ship had been released upon the giving of security.]

The following comment was made in the Report of the Chairman:

This rule is included as a result of an initiative by the Soviet Association. The Soviet Union has already concluded 21 conventions of this type.

The Soviet Association has proposed a rule making state guarantees sufficient security by virtue of the terms of the Convention itself, subject only to allowing the possibility that States may make a reservation against the automatic acceptance of such state guarantees. The international sub-committee has found it more prudent to suggest that the acceptance of a State guarantee should always be left to bilateral agreement.

(2) THIS CONVENTION SHALL NOT APPLY TO STATE-OWNED SHIPS EXCLUSIVELY USED FOR GOVERN-MENTAL NON-COMMERCIAL SERVICE.

(3) NOTHING IN THIS CONVENTION SHALL BE CONSTRUED AS CREATING A MARITIME LIEN.

(4) THIS CONVENTION DOES NOT AFFECT ANY RIGHTS OR POWERS VESTED IN ANY GOVERNMENT OR ITS DEPARTMENTS, OR IN ANY PUBLIC AUTHORITY, OR IN ANY DOCK OR HARBOUR AUTHORITY, UNDER ANY INTERNATIONAL CONVENTION OR UNDER ANY DOMESTIC LAW OR REGULATION, TO DETAIN OR OTHERWISE PREVENT FROM SAILING ANY SHIP WITHIN THEIR JURISDICTION.

(5) THIS CONVENTION SHALL NOT AFFECT THE POWER OF ANY STATE OR COURT TO MAKE ORDERS AFFECTING THE TOTALITY OF A DEBTOR'S ASSETS.

(6) NOTHING IN THIS CONVENTION SHALL AFFECT THE APPLICATION OF INTERNATIONAL CONVENTIONS PROVIDING FOR LIMITATION OF LIABILITY, OR DOMESTIC LAW GIVING EFFECT THERETO, IN THE STATE WHERE AN ARREST IS EFFECTED.

(7) NOTHING IN THIS CONVENTION SHALL MODIFY OR AFFECT THE RULES OF LAW IN FORCE IN THE STATES PARTIES RELATING TO THE ARREST OF ANY SHIP PHYSICALLY WITHIN THE JURISDICTION OF THE STATE OF HER FLAG PROCURED BY A PERSON WHO HAS HIS HABITUAL RESIDENCE OR PRINCIPAL PLACE OF BUSINESS IN THAT STATE, OR BY ANY OTHER PERSON WHO HAS ACQUIRED A CLAIM FROM SUCH PERSON BY SUBROGATION, ASSIGNMENT OR OTHERWISE.

CMI Report

77. Article 8 corresponds to Articles 2, 8 and 9 of the 1952 Convention. It was adopted by 29 votes to 1 with 3 abstentions.

Reciprocity

78. In accordance with the general trend in modern Conventions on uniform law, but contrary to the rule in the 1952 Convention, it follows from paragraph (1) that the Convention is of general application and that its application does not depend upon reciprocity. However, upon the proposal of the delegation of The Netherlands Article 9 was added by 13 votes against 11 and with 9 abstentions. This provides that States may reserve the right not to apply the Convention to ships from non-contracting States.

State-owned ships

79. It follows from paragraph (2) that the Convention also applies to ships which are State-owned except if they are exclusively used for non-commercial service.

80. The International Sub-Committee has proposed a rule permitting States to enter into bilateral agreements to provide that a guarantee issued by a State for ships owned by that State should be sufficient security for claims in respect of such ships. Arrest should then not be possible but all other provisions of the Convention should apply.

81. The Soviet delegation had proposed to the International Sub-Committee deletion of the requirement for a bilateral agreement, so that the rule described in paragraph 80 above would apply directly as a rule of the Convention. The International Sub-Committee had drafted the more restrictive rule requiring a bilateral agreement because it assumed that governments might well be willing to enter into bilateral agreements with foreign governments of their own choice but that they would not undertake a general obligation to accept government guarantees. There are already several bilateral agreements of this kind in force.

82. The Conference rejected both the Soviet proposal and the proposal by the International Sub-Committee.

Other provisions

83. The purpose of paragraph (6) is to avoid any conflicts between Conventions.

JIGE
Seventh Session, 5–9 December 1994

Report—Annex I

29. It was noted that article 8(2) of the 1952 Convention had given rise to problems of inter-pretation in various jurisdictions. The wording of article 8(2) did not make it clear whether the whole of the provisions of the Convention were to apply to ships of non-Contracting States, or only article 8(1) providing for right of arrest in respect of maritime claims. Most delegations preferred

the approach adopted by the CMI Draft providing for application of the whole Convention to ships of non-Contracting States.

30. The Group also agreed that the sovereign immunity provision in article 8 of the CMI Draft did not go far enough, in that it did not exclude State-operated ships from the scope of the Convention. Accordingly, the Group agreed that the text of paragraph 2 of article 8 of the CMI Draft should be amended to correspond with article 13, paragraph 2 of the 1993 MLM Convention.

Draft Articles 1994

Note of the Editor. The text of this article in the Draft Articles 1994 is the same as that in the CMI Draft except that in paragraph (2) the words "State-owned ships exclusively used for governmental non-commercial service" have been replaced by the words "ships owned or operated by a State used only on Governmental non-commercial service" in conformity with the 1993 MLM Convention.

Report—Annex I

54. In the view of one delegation, paragraph 3 of this article should be either an independent article or form part of article 3.

Ninth Session: 2–6 December 1996

Report—Annex II

Paragraph (1)

93. The observer for the Latin American Association of Navigational Law and Law of the Sea (ALDENAVE) drew attention to the fact that this paragraph would make the provisions of the Convention applicable to every sea-going ship, irrespective of its flag. He suggested following the approach adopted in Article 13 (1) of the MLM Convention, adding at the end of the paragraph the following sentence "provided the ship of a non-Contracting State under arrest is subject to the jurisdiction of the State party at the time of the arrest".

94. One delegation supported this proposal, subject to drafting changes. Another delegation favoured the narrow approach provided by the 1952 Convention. While Article 8 of the new draft widened the scope of application of the Convention, Article 8 had the opposite effect. In the view of this delegation, if the 1952 approach was adopted there would be no need for further provision or reservation. This proposal, however, was only supported by one other delegation.

95. The observer for the CMI said that Article 8, paragraph 2, of the 1952 Convention extended the right of arrest in respect of maritime claims also to ships flying the flag of a non-Contracting State but did not extend to these ships the benefit granted by Article 2. There was a problem due to the difference in wording of paragraphs 1 and 2 of Article 8. The new text as drafted in Lisbon was more precise and in line with the approach adopted by new conventions such as the 1993 MLM Convention.

96. Most delegations favoured the JIGE text and could not initially accept the introduction into Article 8 of the concept of Article 13 (1) or the MLM Convention, which provided that the vessel be subject to the jurisdiction of the State Party. This was considered unnecessary, since it was evident that the Court could not proceed with arrest unless it had jurisdiction. The majority of delegations, therefore, preferred to keep the present text of Article 8 (1).

97. Subsequently, one delegation proposed the following addition to Article 8 (1): "subject to the condition that the ship of a non-Contracting State under arrest is within the jurisdiction of the Contracting State at the time that the arrest is made". Another delegation proposed a second alternative more in line with the 1952 Convention: "This convention shall apply to any sea-going ship within the jurisdiction of any State Party".

98. Another delegation proposed a third alternative, consisting of the addition of the following phrase to Article 8 (1): "provided the ship is within the jurisdiction of the State Party".

99. Most delegations supported the second alternative as being simple and concise.

100. One delegation said that the convention should apply to any sea-going ship within the jurisdiction of a State Party where an order has been made. This delegation requested that the proposal be included as a footnote in the draft text. Other delegations supported this proposal.

101. Several delegations suggested the convenience of adding to the second alternative the following wording: "whether or not that ship is flying the flag of a State Party". It was finally agreed that the text would read as follows:

> "This Convention shall apply to any sea-going ship within the jurisdiction of any State Party, whether or not that ship is flying the flag of a State Party."

102. It was furthermore agreed to include a footnote reflecting the view of four delegations to the effect of adding: "where the order has been made" after " . . . jurisdiction of any State Party".

Paragraph (2)

103. The observer for ALDENAVE suggested that the paragraph should be aligned with Article 3 (1) of the International Convention for the Unification of Certain Rules concerning the immunity of State-owned Ships, 1926, and that immunity should be granted to the ship at the time when the cause of action arises.

104. The Sessional Group agreed to retain the paragraph as presently drafted, subject to the consideration of any written proposal from ALDENAVE.

Paragraph (3)

105. In the view of one delegation, the paragraph should either be an independent article or form part of Article 3. The Group accepted the content of the paragraph and decided to postpone the decision as to the place of the paragraph.

106. The observer for the International Association of Ports and Harbours (IAPH) said that his organisation was currently carrying out a survey in order to ascertain the undesirable effects of arrest of ships in ports. The replies received so far made it very clear that, although large ports enjoyed in general a good level of legal protection, that was not, unfortunately, the case with respect to ports in developing countries, where ships under arrest often disturbed the commercial life of ports and, by occupying in certain cases up to 20 per cent of their capacity, could seriously affect other port users. It was suggested that the provisions of the new Convention should reflect the interests of ports, which should be considered as a third party directly affected by the arrest. One delegation sympathised with the IAPH remarks and said that it would submit a written proposal in relation to Article 2 (5).

107. One delegation expressed concern as to the many powers vested in harbour authorities, that were protected by a lien and often by domestic law that permitted the arrest of ships.

108. The observer for the CMI said the purpose of the provision was to provide freedom to maritime authorities wishing to detain or prevent ships from sailing within their jurisdiction for safety reasons.

109. Some delegations supported the retention of the paragraph as presently drafted.

110. The Sessional Group decided to maintain the present text but agreed to consider any written proposal in relation to Article 2 (5).

Paragraph (5)

111. The Sessional Group agreed to keep the present text of Article 8 (5).

Paragraph (6)

112. The Sessional Group agreed to keep the present text of Article 8 (6).

Paragraph (7)

113. The Sessional Group agreed to keep the present text of Article 8 (7).

Draft Articles 1997

Note of the Editor. The text of this article in the Draft Articles 1997 is the same as that in the Draft Articles 1994 except that in paragraph (1) the words "within the jurisdiction of a State Party" have been added.

Diplomatic Conference
Comments and Proposals

Mexico

DOCUMENT 188/3

49. The Government of Mexico considers that the third paragraph of this article should be a separate article, since it refers not to the application of the Convention, as does the rest of the article, but to the question of maritime liens as mentioned in article 3 of the instrument. It is therefore proposed that a new article (8 *bis*) be introduced.

Tanzania

DOCUMENT 188/3

102. With regard to Article 8(1), we agree that the words "where the order has been made" be added after the phrase "jurisdiction of any State party".

103. With regard to Article 8(3), we wish to agree with the proposal that the paragraph either be an independent Article or form part of Article 3, depending on the reasons given by the delegation which has offered the proposal.

Thailand

DOCUMENT 188/3

93. Paragraph 3 should be an independent article as in the 1952 Convention.

Aldenave

DOCUMENT 188/3/ADD.3
Article 8.2
Insert: " . . . to ships operating in the service of the public authorities when the claim in respect of which arrest is sought arose."

18. This is proposed in response to paragraph 99 of document TD/B/IGE.1/L.2. The intention is to establish that a ship not being subject to arrest is not a matter of its being owned or operated by a State but of its being used in the "public service" (as a hospital, isolation hospital etc.), even if owned by a third party, *at the moment when the claim arises.*

CMI

DOCUMENT 188/3

157. A question to be considered is whether it would be advisable to reinstate the principle that ships flying the flag of a non-Party State may also be arrested for any claim, whether maritime or not, for which the law of the State Party permits arrest.

158. Art. 8(2) of the 1952 Arrest Convention provides that a ship flying the flag of a non-Contracting State may be arrested in the jurisdiction of any Contracting State in respect of any of the maritime claims enumerated in Article 1 or of any other claim for which the law of the Contracting State permits the arrest. Since it was not clear whether that meant that the Convention as a whole applied to ships flying the flag of non-Contracting States, subject to such ships being liable to arrest also in respect of claims for which the *lex fori* permits arrest, Article 8(1) of the Lisbon Draft provided generally that the Convention applies to any seagoing ship whether or not that ship is flying the flag of a State Party and this provision was adopted by the JIGE.

159. If the Conference will decide that total equality of treatment for ships flying the flag of States Parties and ships flying the flag of non-Party States is not the right solution, because it may eliminate an incentive to ratification, the provision of Article 8(2) of the Arrest Convention could be reinstated and Art. 8(1) of the Draft Articles amended as follows:

(1) This Convention shall apply:

 (a) to any seagoing ship within the jurisdiction of a State Party flying the flag of a State Party; and

 (b) to any seagoing ship within the jurisdiction of a State Party flying the flag of a State non-Party except that notwithstanding Article 2 paragraph 2 any such ship may be arrested in respect of any claim, in addition to those listed in Article 1(1), for which the law of such State Party permits arrest.

If this amendment is adopted, Article 9 become superfluous.

160. The provision in this paragraph has no relation with the application of the Convention, and it is suggested that it should be moved to a separate article.

Romania

DOCUMENT CRP.13

 Proposal to supplement the text of article 8, paragraph 4—Application

4. This Convention does not affect any rights or powers vested in any Government or its departments, or in any public authority, or in any dock or harbour authority, under any international convention or under any domestic law or regulation, to detain or otherwise prevent from sailing any ship within their jurisdiction. "Nor shall it prevent the manager of a port, for a serious reason, from obtaining permission from a competent court to let the arrested ship leave the port."

Proceedings of the Main Committee

PARAGRAPH 1

First reading—5 March 1999[88]

 Two issues were debated by the Main Committee: the application of the Convention to all ships, whether seagoing or not and the application of the Convention to ships flying the flag of States non-Parties.

 The proposal to delete the word "seagoing" was made by the delegate from the United Kingdom who so stated:

We suggest to delete word "seagoing". In article 8(1) there is a reference to "seagoing ship". Our reading of the Convention suggests that that is the only place where we define "ship" with "seagoing". It is our impression perhaps that what we have got here is a hang over from the old days. But in 1952 when the Arrest of Ships Convention was negotiated it was appropriate. In 1957 the description "seagoing ship" was also applicable to the 1957 Limitation Convention. But in 1976 the description "seagoing" had been dropped for reasons that people are very well aware of and certainly that is carried forward into the 1996 Protocol to LLMC. Mr Chairman I think that if people feel that there is a need for a distinction, it might be more appropriate that we make some provisions for a reservation for inland navigable craft if that is the case, but the description of our Convention is the Arrest of Ships and I think it is better to keep the general definition in that way, just the same as we did in the LLMC Convention.

 The proposal was supported by an overwhelming majority. As regards the application of the Convention to ships of non-Party States, the CMI had suggested to provide, as in the 1952 Convention, that States Parties should be permitted to arrest such ships in respect of maritime claims and of other claims in respect of which arrest is permitted under the lex fori. *Even though the proposal was not adopted, it is felt useful to reproduce the debate that took place in that respect.*

Russian Fed. We would like to support the CMI's proposal in respect of this article relating to the Convention's scope of application. The adoption of this proposal would render the reservations which are provided for by article 9 unnecessary. We share the CMI's opinion that the establishment (in article 8) of the same regime in respect of ships flying the flag of a State Party, and ships flying

---

 88. Summary and text from tape No. 44.

the flag of a non-party State, does not stimulate the ratification of the Convention. We deem it desirable that the new Convention resolves this issue in the same way as it is resolved in the 1952 Convention, i.e. so that the Convention establishes the limits of applying the rules of the Convention for ships flying the flag of a non-party State. This is the essence of our statement in favour of the CMI's proposal.

Switzerland   We are of the opinion that the Convention should apply only to ships flying the flag of States Parties. We support the CMI proposal.

Netherlands   We also would support the proposal of CMI that in principle the Convention would be applicable to ships flying the flag of States Parties. As to ships flying the flag of non-Party States we should refer to the system of the 1952 Convention. If so article 9 would become superfluous.

Chairman   There are two issues which we have to address. One is the extent to which the Convention shall apply to ships flying the flag of non-Contracting States. The other issue is that raised by the United Kingdom, as to whether the Convention should apply to ships in general, or to seagoing ships. However we should limit the scope of application. I have some feedback with respect to the first question: three delegations speaking in favour of it and I heard none against so perhaps there is the feeling that the CMI proposal is a good one. But I need your guidance with respect the issue raised by the UK.

CMI   Mr Chairman I heard that the CMI proposal has been very kindly supported without any need for me to introduce it but I think that for the sake of clarity I should like to explain what is the precise purpose of this revised text which the CMI has suggested. The purpose is, as the distinguished delegate from Russia has indicated, to exert pressure on non-Contracting States to ratify the Convention. The text suggested by the CMI does not mean that the Convention as a whole does not apply to ships flying the flag of non-Party States, it means that States Party have the possibility not to apply art. 2(2) to ships flying the flag of non-Party States and the consequence of this would be that ships flying the flag of non-Party States may be arrested both for maritime claims and for any other claims for which the *lex fori* permits arrest to be made. So there is in this case *vis-à-vis* ships flying the flag of non-Party States a position which is worse than that applicable to ships flying a flag of Contracting or Party States because the ships flying the flag of non-Party States may be arrested also as security for claims other than the specific maritime claims listed in art. 1(1) of this draft Convention.

Denmark   We are very thankful for the explanations of the CMI because it helps us at least to form our position on their proposal. I think that of course it is always nice to have as many parties to a convention as possible, but to treat people outside the Convention differently, to punish them for not being party to it, I think is very difficult. That is the second part of the CMI proposal and I think that is very difficult; of course that would encourage people to adopt such measures. I think that was explained by Prof. Berlingieri. The benefit you get from the Convention should be the encouragement and not a discrimination clause. As for the seagoing, we have very few ships which are not seagoing. It is not a problem.

Peru   We think we cannot impose the application of the Convention in non-Contracting States. We believe that the JIGE draft is made more harmless for the interest of claimants as respects the CMI proposal. We should like to have a clarification in this respect.

CMI   Mr Chairman I should like to mention first of all that the proposal of the CMI is no novelty. The principle suggested by the CMI already exists in the 1952 Convention art. 8(2). The CMI has only suggested that the provision of art. 8(2) of the 1952 Convention be incorporated also in the new Convention and there is no novelty at all. The only difference is that in the new Convention it is made clear that except for this possibility of States Parties to apply also the national criteria for arrest of ships flying the flag of non-Contracting States, the Convention applies to all ships. This is a basic principle which now is accepted in all modern conventions and the *lex fori* applies in all cases. As regards the request for clarification that the distinguished delegate of Peru has made, I think I can say that there is no intention to impose on non-Contracting States the application of the provisions of this Convention. The text provided for by the CMI, which I repeat reconfirms the principle of the 1952 Convention, only provides that in States Parties certain principles will apply. This has no effect at all on non-Contracting States except that their ships will be subject in States Parties to certain rules but this is within the limit of States Parties.

Norway   We thank Prof. Berlingieri for the clarification, but still we tend to agree with Denmark. I believe that the rationale behind the Arrest Convention is to make less constraints on the ships as possible because this is in the interest of trade in general. On the other hand we have the interest of the claimants and our objective is to strike a fair balance between them and in my opinion this balance should apply to all ships.

Japan   The result behind the CMI proposal can be achieved through Article 9, i.e. to reserve not to apply the Convention to ships flying the flag of non-Contracting States, but to apply its national legislation to such States. The difference between this reservation system and the CMI proposal is that reservations are known to all States Parties through the depositary, while national laws are not. If CMI proposal is adopted we suggest that a system to make national laws known should be envisaged.

Second reading—8 March 1999[89]

The UK delegation proposed to delete the word "seagoing", with the understanding that a reservation should be permitted to exclude from the scope of application of the Convention ships that are not seagoing. This proposal was accepted.

PARAGRAPH 2

First reading—5 March 1999[90]

The debate that led to the change in the wording of this paragraph is reproduced below.
United States   We would like to suggest two modifications to clarify this provision and to align it with the sovereign immunity provision in the UNCLOS. The two changes are as follows: *First*: insert at line 1 after "not apply to": "any warship, naval auxiliary, or other"; *Second*: following the word "used" add "for the time being".
UN Legal Office   Attention is drawn to language used in UNCLOS. Art. 28, regulating innocent passage and covering civil jurisdiction in sub-section (c), mentions "rules applicable to warships and other government ships operated for non-commercial purposes".
Philippines   We agree with the US proposal and the proposal of UN Legal Office. Then we suggest to replace "and" in line two with "and/or".
United Kingdom   We support the US proposal. In English law "and" equals "and/or" and it seems to work pretty well.

PARAGRAPH 3

First reading—5 March 1999[91]

The Rumanian proposal, to insert an express reference to the power of port authorities to permit the movement of arrested ships gave rise to the debate reproduced below.
Rumania   We suggest to add to para. 4 the words "it does not affect either the power of a port authority for serious reasons to obtain from a competent court the authority to permit the arrested ship to leave the port".
Cameroon   We support the Rumanian proposal. A ship arrested may be abandoned by its owner and may be lacking of maintenance, thereby causing problems and risks to the port authority. For safety reasons the port authority should be able to obtain the authority of the Court to move the ship outside the port.
Côte d'Ivoire   We support the Rumanian proposal for safety reasons. Also cargo on board may cause risks to other ships and the environment.
Peru   We have doubts. We think that this article does not bring any positive element to the Convention because we are intervening in the administrative power of the States. We don't think it to be necessary nor useful. We think that a port authority may adopt administrative action in respect

89. Summary from tape No. 55.
90. Text and summary from tape No. 45.
91. Text and summary from tapes Nos. 46 and 47.

of an arrested ship but if it intends to cause its departure, it must apply to the Courts. This provision could not apply in our country.

Chairman   Perhaps article 8(3) is sufficient. But the proposal was made to create clarity.

Netherlands   This problem arises in Rotterdam. We have sympathy with the Rumanian proposal, provided the power is restricted to the area of the port. The concerns of interests of third parties should be considered so to provide security to them.

Argentina   We support the JIGE text. The power granted to a port authority pertains to administrative matters and if it is required to move a ship for safety reasons, an application should be made to the Court.

Cyprus   The scope of paragraph 4 is to preserve the right under domestic law conferred upon governmental authorities and therefore we support the JIGE text. We do not agree with the Rumanian proposal because it takes a step further and tries to give powers to the port authority which we believe should be given to them by domestic law and not by an international convention.

France   We support the Rumanian proposal and perhaps our Rumanian colleague could explain what he intends for "serious reasons" and that the reasons relates to security problems.

Rumania   In certain cases it happens that an arrested ship for commercial debts, gives rise to serious problems of navigation safety as well as social problems and sanitary problems. In such cases the port as a third party in the relationship claimant/owner finds itself in a delicate position, the berth been occupied sometimes for months, that which entails also a commercial loss for the port, since the loading/unloading installations cannot operate. Experience has shown that sometimes some Courts refuse to let the ship leave the port in order to be shifted to another port where a berth is available in the same country entailing thereby a loss to the generality of port users. In such cases we believe that the interests of the generality of port users should prevail over those of the claimants.

United Kingdom   We are all well aware of the problem. However we have some fears about the proposal from Rumania. The text as we have in the JIGE Draft sought to take the 1952 Convention and to build in a little more latitude. I think, however, as I understood it, the notion of port interest being greater than the interest involved in the arrest of the ship is an extremely awkward addition to this text and I think that it could have substantial impact to frustrate what could be a proper arrest. It is for the Court to look at all of the issues when it determines whether the arrest shall or shall not be permitted. For what it is worth in the UK we have the Admiralty Marshal who would determine where the ship under arrest shall be positioned and have regard to safety, conservancy and that sort of thing. On that basis we wish to stick wholeheartedly to the JIGE text.

China   The Chinese delegation are of the opinion that Article 8 paragraph 4 in JIGE text (*Now paragraph (3) of the Convention*) is a very important article. We should consider the rights and interests of the port while arrest of ships is effected. The provisions in article 8 paragraph 4 are both necessary and to the point. However, they should not go too far. We believe no conditions of arrest of ship or release of ship may be established in addition to the provisions in the International Convention on Arrest of Ships, otherwise there will be no protection for the safe navigation of the ships in the world. We have also noticed the problem raised by the Rumanian delegation and the laws and regulations referred to, we believe that the provisions in article 8 paragraph 4 have satisfactorily answered the above questions, and we think it is quite enough. Therefore we hope the present provisions in the JIGE text will be adopted.

Malta   We seek clarification from the Rumanian delegation as to what they want to get with their proposal. Are we considering the right of the Port Authority to ask the Court to permit a movement of the ship within the port or to other ports within the same country or to completely release the vessel? In the first case, then we should consider whether we should leave this to national law or to make reference to the problem in the Convention.

Rumania   Our proposal considers possible movement of the ship from one to another port of the same country.

Sweden   In our opinion it is difficult to decide upon the Rumanian proposal. Therefore we prefer the JIGE text.

Brazil   We prefer the JIGE text. The problem raised by Rumania may be solved by national law.

Thailand   We believe this matter does not require to be addressed by the Convention but should be left to national law. We therefore support the JIGE text.

Benin   Suggests to postpone the decision. The problem is very important.

Chairman   We are on day five of the Conference. This proposal has been submitted today. Although there is a considerable measure of support to the proposal, there is also a strong opposition. A very strong support would be required to move away from the JIGE text. This paragraph should be provisionally adopted in my view.

Cameroon   I would suggest an amendment to this paragraph, by replacing the words "to detain or otherwise prevent from sailing" with "to detain or otherwise shift the ship to another port in the same jurisdiction".

Chairman   There is a difference between "prevent from sailing" and "authorise the departure": this is not a drafting amendment. It is accepted that we adopt this paragraph as in the JIGE text? *Agreed.*

PARAGRAPH 4

First reading—5 March 1999[92]

This paragraph was adopted without discussion.

PARAGRAPH 5

First reading—5 March 1999[93]

This paragraph was adopted without any significant discussion.

PARAGRAPH 6

First reading—5 March 1999[94]

This paragraph was adopted without discussion.

1999 Convention

1. THIS CONVENTION SHALL APPLY TO ANY SHIP WITHIN THE JURISDICTION OF ANY STATE PARTY, WHETHER OR NOT THAT SHIP IS FLYING THE FLAG OF A STATE PARTY.

2. THIS CONVENTION SHALL NOT APPLY TO ANY WARSHIP, NAVAL AUXILIARY OR OTHER SHIPS OWNED OR OPERATED BY A STATE AND USED, FOR THE TIME BEING, ONLY ON GOVERNMENT NON-COMMERCIAL SERVICE.

3. THIS CONVENTION DOES NOT AFFECT ANY RIGHTS OR POWERS VESTED IN ANY GOVERNMENT OR ITS DEPARTMENTS, OR IN ANY PUBLIC AUTHORITY, OR IN ANY DOCK OR HARBOUR AUTHORITY, UNDER ANY INTERNATIONAL CONVENTION OR UNDER ANY DOMESTIC LAW OR REGULATION, TO DETAIN OR OTHERWISE PREVENT FROM SAILING ANY SHIP WITHIN THEIR JURISDICTION.

4. THIS CONVENTION SHALL NOT AFFECT THE POWER OF ANY STATE OR COURT TO MAKE ORDERS AFFECTING THE TOTALITY OF A DEBTOR'S ASSETS.

5. NOTHING IN THIS CONVENTION SHALL AFFECT THE APPLICATION OF INTERNATIONAL CONVENTIONS PROVIDING FOR LIMITATION OF LIABILITY, OR DOMESTIC LAW GIVING EFFECT THERETO, IN THE STATE WHERE AN ARREST IS EFFECTED.

6. NOTHING IN THIS CONVENTION SHALL MODIFY OR AFFECT THE RULES OF LAW IN FORCE IN THE STATES PARTIES RELATING TO THE ARREST OF ANY SHIP PHYSICALLY WITHIN THE JURISDICTION OF THE STATE OF ITS FLAG PROCURED BY A PERSON WHOSE HABITUAL RESIDENCE OR PRINCIPAL PLACE OF BUSINESS IS IN THAT STATE, OR BY ANY OTHER PERSON WHO HAS ACQUIRED A CLAIM FROM SUCH PERSON BY SUBROGATION, ASSIGNMENT OR OTHERWISE.

92. Summary from tape No. 48.
93. Summary from tape No. 48.
94. Summary from tape No. 49.

II.III.12 ARTICLE 9: NON-CREATION OF MARITIME LIENS

Diplomatic Conference: Proceedings of the Main Committee

First reading—5 March 1999[95]

This article, which in the Draft Articles was paragraph 3 of Article 8, was adopted without discussion.

1999 Convention

NOTHING IN THIS CONVENTION SHALL BE CONSTRUED AS CREATING A MARITIME LIEN.

95. Summary from tape No. 46.

II.III.13 ARTICLE 10: RESERVATIONS

**Diplomatic Conference
Comments and Proposals**

Netherlands

DOCUMENT CRP.6

Proposal to add the following sentence to Article 9—Reservations

"A State may, when signing, ratifying, accepting or acceding to this Convention, reserve the right to refrain from applying the Convention to the arrest of a ship for any claim under (s) of paragraph 1, of Article 1, but to apply its national law to such claim."

Proceedings of the Main Committee

PARAGRAPH 1

First reading—5 March 1999[96]

The UK delegation stated it would submit a proposal regarding the addition of the right not to apply the provisions of the Convention to ships which are not seagoing.

Second reading—8 March 1999[97]

The UK delegation proposed to delete from article 8(1) the word "seagoing" with the understanding that States Parties should be permitted to exclude from the scope of application of the Convention ships that are not seagoing. This proposal was accepted. The delegation of the Netherlands proposed to permit a reservation in respect of the maritime claim listed in article 1(1)(s). Also this proposal was accepted.

PARAGRAPH 2

Second reading—11 March 1999[98]

The delegate from Switzerland pointed out that a provision aiming at avoiding any possible conflict between the new Arrest Convention and the 1868 Rhine Convention existed in the 1950 Arrest Convention but, when it was suggested that it would have been preferable to regulate the matter of a possible conflict in the article on reservations, declared that in principle he would not object.

---

96. Summary from tape No. 44.
97. Summary from tape No. 55.
98. Text and summary from tapes Nos. 75 and 76.

The Chairman asked if the reservation could be formulated in such a way as to avoid expressly mentioning the Rhine Convention, since it had been agreed to avoid any express reference to other conventions. Other delegates supported this solution, pointing out that the Rhine Convention is a regional convention, and that other similar conventions may exist in other regions of the world.

The Chairman of the Working Group appointed with the task to formulate an appropriate reservation reported as follows:

We have reached consensus on a text which is generic and neutral. This text we feel should go in article 10(2). We felt we should be explicit. It can apply to any group of countries that have conventions similar to the Rhine Convention. The text is the following:

A State may, when it is also a State Party to a specified international convention on navigation on inland waterway, declare when signing, ratifying, accepting, approving or acceding to this Convention, that rules on jurisdiction, recognition and execution of court decisions provided for in such treaties shall prevail over the rules contained in article 7 of this Convention.

Croatia   We are against reservations in general, but think that this particular reservation will help unification.

Brazil   We support it.

Turkey   We support it, but suggest to replace "conventions" with "treaties", which is more general, and to delete "international".

Chairman   (Reads provision as amended). Adopted.

1999 Convention

1. Any State may, at the time of signature, ratification, acceptance, approval, or accession, or at any time thereafter, reserve the right to exclude the application of this Convention to any or all of the following :
   (a) ships which are not seagoing;
   (b) ships not flying the flag of a State Party;
   (c) claims under article 1, paragraph 1 (s).

2. A State may, when it is also a State Party to a specified treaty on navigation on inland waterways, declare when signing, ratifying, accepting, approving or acceding to this Convention, that rules on jurisdiction, recognition and execution of court decisions provided for in such treaties shall prevail over the rules contained in article 7 of this Convention.

II.III.14 ARTICLE 13: STATES WITH MORE THAN ONE SYSTEM OF LAW

Diplomatic Conference
Proceedings of the Main Committee

Second reading—9 March 1999[99]

The delegate from Hong Kong China presented his proposed new article (in document CRP.15) and stated that it was helpful to include in the Convention a provision that takes account of the fact that sometimes different systems of law apply in different parts of the same State. Provisions of this kind have been included in conventions drawn up by the Hague Conference on Private International Law. He explained that the reason of the interest of his delegation was due to the fact that although Hong Kong is a part of China, it retains its common law system which is different from the law in the rest of China. National laws of China do not generally apply to Hong Kong China, which has its own ships register, different from that of China.

The article was drafted generally, without any specific reference to Hong Kong China.

The proposal, supported by China, was adopted.

1999 Convention

1. IF A STATE HAS TWO OR MORE TERRITORIAL UNITS IN WHICH DIFFERENT SYSTEMS OF LAW ARE APPLICABLE IN RELATION TO MATTERS DEALT WITH IN THIS CONVENTION, IT MAY AT THE TIME OF SIGNATURE, RATIFICATION, ACCEPTANCE, APPROVAL OR ACCESSION DECLARE THAT THIS CONVENTION SHALL EXTEND TO ALL ITS TERRITORIAL UNITS OR ONLY TO ONE OR MORE OF THEM AND MAY MODIFY THIS DECLARATION BY SUBMITTING ANOTHER DECLARATION AT ANY TIME.

2. ANY SUCH DECLARATION SHALL BE NOTIFIED TO THE DEPOSITARY AND SHALL STATE EXPRESSLY THE TERRITORIAL UNITS TO WHICH THE CONVENTION APPLIES.

3. IN RELATION TO A STATE PARTY WHICH HAS TWO OR MORE SYSTEMS OF LAW WITH REGARD TO ARREST OF SHIPS APPLICABLE IN DIFFERENT TERRITORIAL UNITS, REFERENCES IN THIS CONVENTION TO THE COURT OF A STATE AND THE LAW OF A STATE SHALL BE RESPECTIVELY CONSTRUED AS REFERRING TO THE COURT OF THE RELEVANT TERRITORIAL UNIT WITHIN THAT STATE AND THE LAW OF THE RELEVANT TERRITORIAL UNIT OF THAT STATE.

99. Summary from tape No. 64.

Index

*This index does not cover the footnotes. References to the main text are to book and paragraph numbers, eg I.218 refers to paragraph 218 in Book I. References to Appendices are given as page numbers in **bold type**.*

Agency fee, 1999 Convention
  payable by or on behalf of shipowner or demise
    charterer, II.95–II.96
Agreement
  1952 Convention
    carriage of goods, I.218, I.338–I.343,
      I.836–I.841
    international, arrest by government and public
      authority, I.278–I.285
    jurisdiction of particular court or arbitration,
      I.737–I.738
    use or hire of ship, I.218, I.332–I.337,
      I.833–I.835
  1999 Convention
    carriage of goods, II.72–II.73
    use or hire of ship, II.70–II.71
Arbitration, 1952 Convention
  agreement on, I.737–I.738
Arrest. *See also* Jurisdiction, for the arrest; Notion
    of arrest; Rearrest and multiple arrest; Release
    from arrest; Trading of ship under arrest;
    Wrongful arrest
  1952 Convention
    associated ship, I.449–I.502, **250–255**
    claim for which permitted, I.208–I.210
    claim other than closed list claim, for, **282–284**
    conditions for obtaining authority, I.625–I.628
    enforcement, I.629–I.631
    government or public authority, by, I.273–I.277
      international Conventions and Agreements,
        I.278–I.285
      national law, I.286–I.302
    immunity from, I.538–I.541
    order for, application and enforcement,
      I.632–I.677
    owner liable for claim, I.392–I.417, **245–248**
    person entitled to, I.624
    person having habitual residence or principal
      place of business in flag state, exclusion of
      arrest of ship by, I.65–I.73
    person other than owner liable for claim,
      I.502–I.534
    purpose, I.264–I.272
    ship deemed to be in same ownership,
      I.444–I.448
    ship ready to sail or in course of navigation,
      I.535–I.537

Arrest—*cont.*
  1952 Convention—*cont.*
    ship which may be placed under
      Article 3 rules summarised, I.388–I.391
      Denmark, I.147–I.148
      Nigeria, I.161–I.164
      Norway, I.181
      Sweden, I.192
      United Kingdom, I.232–I.241
  1999 Convention
    associated ship, II.134–II.138
    claim asserted, for, II.102–II.132
    conditions for obtaining authority, II.171–II.174
    enforcement, II.175–II.176
    immunity from, II.21–II.23
    person entitled to, II.170
    person having habitual residence or principal
      place of business in flag state, exclusion of
      arrest of ship by, II.19–II.20
    powers, **435–450**
    public authority, by, II.24–II.28
    recognition and enforcement of judgments,
      II.241–II.248
    right of, **451–501**
    right of rearrest and multiple arrest,
      II.140–II.148
    ship adversely affecting use of port
      installations, II.29–II.34
    ship for which limitation of liability invoked,
      II.35–II.38
    ship for which maritime claim asserted,
      II.102–II.132
    ship owned by person subject to bankruptcy or
      similar proceedings, II.39–II.42
    ship ready to sail, II.139
Arrest Convention 1952. *See* International
  Convention for the Unification of Certain Rules
  Relating to the Arrest of Sea-Going Ships 1952
Arrest Convention 1999. *See* International
  Convention on Arrest of Ships 1999
Asser, Jan, I.16–I.17
Associated ship
  1952 Convention, I.449–I.502, **250–255**
  1999 Convention, II.134–II.138
Australia, 1952 Convention
  arrest of other ship owned by person liable for
    claim, I.433–I.435

565

Index—Travaux Préparatoires

Travaux préparatoires, 1999 Convention, App. II.III

Diplomatic Conference—Statements of delegates
and observers—*cont.*
  United Kingdom, 399, 400, 405, 408, 410, 420,
    441, 449, 463, 464, 466, 479, 482, 487, 489,
    490, 491, 492, 498, 499, 500, 504, 521, 531,
    532, 542, 545, 547, 549, 556, 557, 558, 559,
    562
  United States, 394, 400, 404, 405, 407, 408, 412,
    442, 449, 469, 473, 474, 531, 547, 558
Droit de suite, 453, 454
Due process of law, 538, 546

Enforcement of judgments, 546–549

Hamburg Rules, 538
HNS Convention 1996, 404, 405, 406

Inland navigation vessels, 432, 556, 557

Jurisdiction for arrest, 444
Jurisdiction on the merits, 444, 538

Law governing arrest, 446, 447
LLMC Convention 1976, 400, 411

Manager, 459
Marine environment, 404, 409
MLM Convention 1993, 397, 403, 417, 418, 455,
    459, 462, 463, 468
Maritime claims, Article 1, paragraph 1
  (a), 396
  (b), 398
  (c), 399
  (d), 401
  (e), 410
  (f), 411
  (g), 412
  (h), 412
  (i), 413
  (j), 414
  (k), 414
  (l), 414
  (m), 415
  (n), 416
  (o), 417
  (p), 419
  (q), 420
  (r), 421

Maritime claims, Article 1, paragraph 1—*cont.*
  (s), 422
  (t), 422
  (u), 422
  (v), 425
Maritime liens, 395, 452, 454, 455, 456, 457, 462
Multiple arrest, 512

National maritime liens, 455, 456, 457, 461, 462,
    467–476

Operator, 459
Ordre public. *See* Public policy
Ownership, when relevant, 463, 464

Person (allegedly) liable, 499
Physical loss, 396, 397
Ports, interest of, 447, 448, 558, 559
Procedure relating to arrest, 446
Public policy, 539, 547
Purpose of arrest, 444, 445

Rearrest, 516, 520, 521
Registration of mortgages and hypothèques, 423,
    424, 467, 472
Related interest, 408
Release of arrested ship, 502–514
Removal of wreck, 410
Rhine Convention 1868, 562

Salvage agreement, 400
Salvage Convention 1989, 400
Scope of revision, 386
Seagoing ships, 556
Security
  nature, 504
  value of ships, 505–509
Ship arrested in a non-Party State, 510–515
Ship ready to sail or sailing, 435–442
Ships that may be arrested, 451
Sisterships, 476
Skopic Agreement, 399
Social insurance contributions, 418

UNCLOS, 405, 436
Unjustified arrest. *See* Wrongful arrest

Wrongful arrest, 524–533

OWL

INTERNAL MIGRATION IN CONTEMPORARY CHINA

Also by Delia Davin

WOMAN-WORK: Women and the Party in Revolutionary China

CHINA'S ONE-CHILD FAMILY POLICY (*editor with E. Croll and P. Kane*)

CHINESE LIVES: an Oral History of Contemporary China (*by Zhang Xinxin and Sang Ye, editor and translator with W. J. F. Jenner*)

MAO ZEDONG

Internal Migration in Contemporary China

Delia Davin

Head of Department and
Reader in Chinese Social Studies
University of Leeds

Published by PALGRAVE MACMILLAN
Houndmills, Basingstoke, Hampshire RG21 6XS and
175 Fifth Avenue, New York, N.Y. 10010
Companies and representatives throughout the world

PALGRAVE MACMILLAN is the global academic imprint of the Palgrave
Macmillan division of St. Martin's Press, LLC and of Palgrave Macmillan Ltd.
Macmillan® is a registered trademark in the United States, United Kingdom
and other countries. Palgrave is a registered trademark in the European
Union and other countries.

Outside North America
ISBN 0–333–71731–7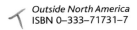

In North America
ISBN 0–312–21718–7

This book is printed on paper suitable for recycling and
made from fully managed and sustained forest sources.

A catalogue record for this book is available from the British Library.

Library of Congress Catalog Card Number: 98–28378

Transferred to digital printing 2002

Printed and bound in Great Britain by
Antony Rowe Ltd, Chippenham and Eastbourne

Contents

List of Tables

List of Figures

Graphics based on copy supplied by the Graphics Unit, School of Geography, University of Leeds.

Chinese-language Newspapers and Magazines Cited in English in the Text

Beijing Youth News (*Beijing Qingnianbao*)
Chinese Business Times (*Huasheng Shibao*)
Chinese Rural Economy (*Zhongguo Nongcun Jingji*)
Chinese Youth (*Zhongguo Qingnian*)
Consumer Times (*Xiaofei Shibao*)
Democracy and Law (*Minzhu yu Fazhi*)
Guangming Daily (*Guangming Daily*)
Labour News (*Laodong Bao*)
Legal Daily (*Fazhi Ribao*)
Peasant Daily (*Nongmin Ribao*)
Outlook (*Liaowang*)
Population and Economics (*Renkou yu Jingji*)
Tianjin Evening News (*Jinwanbao*)
Wenhui News (*Wenhuibao, Shanghai*)
Yangcheng (*Guangzhou*) *Evening News* (*Yangcheng Wanbao*).

Money and Measures

Yuan – Chinese unit of currency also known as renminbi, RMB. There were approximately 13 yuan to the £ sterling and 8 yuan to the US$ in 1998.

Mu – Chinese measurement of area. There are 6.6 mu to an acre and 15 mu to a hectare.

Acknowledgements

I am grateful to the Nuffield Foundation and to the University of Leeds for grants to me and a colleague, Dr Mahmood Messkoub of the Leeds Business School, which enabled us to make a research trip to Beijing and Sichuan in September 1994. I also wish to record my gratitude to the British Academy for funding to attend a migration conference in Beijing in December 1994. Like many other researchers on Chinese population mobility, I am indebted to the Beijing Office of the Ford Foundation whose programme of support for research on China's rural–urban mobility not only made possible much work by Chinese scholars, but also enabled them to come together both with each other and with foreign scholars to share ideas and findings. I would particularly like to thank Mr Steve McGurk, the Economics Programme Officer at the Foundation's Beijing Office, for his vision in promoting this programme and his generosity to me with time, information and contacts on many occasions.

In Beijing I received help and advice from colleagues at the China Population Information and Research Centre, the Institutes of Sociology and of Rural Development of the Chinese Academy of Social Sciences, the Research Centre for the Rural Economy of the Ministry of Agriculture, Horizon Market Research and Policy Analysis Inc., and at Beijing University and the People's University. In Chengdu, in 1994, members of the Institute of Rural Development of the Sichuan Academy of Social Sciences were generous with extended briefings on the research they were carrying out and with assistance for fieldwork. I am grateful for their time and patience. I also received much help and hospitality from friends in China, among them, Mary Ann Burris, David and Isabel Crook, Michael Crook, Jørgen Delman, David Jacobsen, Liu Bohong, Tan Shen, Wan Shanping, Gladys Yang and Yang Xianyi, Yang Zhi and Zhang Kaining.

I was often surprised by the tolerance of migrant informants in China who gave up time to talk to me – often the first foreigner to whom they had even spoken – to help with a project whose purposes remained unclear to them. They helped me greatly by sharing their experiences and perceptions and I would like to acknowledge their kindness.

I learnt much from papers presented by Chinese and western colleagues at three international conferences on Chinese population mobility held in 1996: at Cologne in May, Beijing in June, and Oxford in July. Many friends have shared their ideas and their work with me or given me help with mine. I cannot name them all, but would especially like to mention Haleh Afshar, Judith Banister, Jean Philippe Béja, Greg Benton, Michel Bonnin, Ray Bush, Flemming Christiansen, Kam Wing Chan, Elisabeth Croll, Jutta Hebel, Caroline Hoy, the late Frank Leeming, Hein Mallée, Ma Xiaodong, Mahmood Messkoub,Thomas Scharping, Christopher Smith, Dorothy Solinger, Lina Song, Emma Stone, Owen Wells, Loraine West, Xiang Biao and Marilyn Young.

I want to thank my colleagues in the Department of East Asian Studies at the University of Leeds, my friends and, above all, my family, for their patience with the extra burdens that my preoccupation with this book has inevitably imposed on them. Finally, I wish to record my debt to my parents. From my earliest childhood, stories of the migration of their parents and grandparents from the west of Ireland to New Zealand gave me an interest in the forces that drive people to leave their homes and families in search of a living elsewhere, and a sympathy with the struggles and sufferings of migrants everywhere.

Delia Davin
Leeds 1998

Introduction

This book attempts to take an overview of internal migration in contemporary China. Since the economic reforms took effect in the early 1980s, migration has become a highly visible phenomenon as millions of rural people seek a better life and greater economic opportunity in the urban areas. China has enjoyed extraordinary rates of economic growth in the last two decades, but this growth has been concentrated in certain areas. The areas of rapid growth have acted as magnets, drawing labour migrants from all over the country, but especially from the rural hinterland.

China's economic reforms have resulted in the development of a labour market. People from all over China crowd into her booming coastal regions to seek work that is much better paid than they could hope to find at home. The cities attract migrants to work in services, on construction sites and as petty traders. Other migrants seize new opportunities in underdeveloped frontier areas such as Xinjiang where there are opportunities in construction or business. Traders and craftsmen are prepared to travel hundreds or even thousands of miles if they think a new place will offer a better living than they already have. Women from the countryside seek jobs as maids in the families of the newly prosperous urban middle classes. Some peasants in poor or overcrowded villages in the hinterland even travel to other provinces to subcontract the land of peasants who have already managed to move into non-agricultural employment.

There are many different types of migration. Although the main direction of migration is from the countryside to the urban areas, there is also rural–rural migration and even, on a very small scale, urban–rural migration. Some migrants leave their homes to travel only a short distance to the nearest urban area. Others travel further, but only on a seasonal basis, returning for the busy times of the agricultural year or for the major festivals. A minority stay away for years, perhaps even for life.

The impact of migration is equally varied and has to be considered separately for the origin and the destination areas. Migrants provide cheap labour and are thus contributing to China's economic miracle. Migration has given some people the chance to lift themselves out of poverty and to acquire new skills. However the influx of rural population

1

to the urban areas has put the urban infrastructure under considerable strain. Many migrants live difficult lives in overcrowded and insanitary conditions. Migrant remittances have brought a new wealth to the countryside, but the fear is sometimes expressed that the departure of so many of the youngest and best educated of the rural population will be to the detriment of rural society.

There are gender issues in migration too. As migration streams are rarely equally balanced between men and women, they create imbalances between the sexes in both the origin and the destination areas. Women from poor regions may use marriage migration to acquire prosperous husbands in the hope of a better standard of living and a happier life. Trafficking in women, an especially unpleasant form of population movement, bringing great suffering to the women involved, appears to be on the increase despite efforts to suppress it. Like marriage migration it occurs largely, but not exclusively, between poor and prosperous regions.

Migration has attracted an enormous amount of attention in China. It appears as a new phenomenon in a society where for many years there was very little population mobility. It concerns and alarms officials, who believe that the influx of people into the cities threatens law and order and perhaps even the survival of the urban infrastructure. Many urban residents are hostile to migrants whom they see as newcomers threatening their established and comparatively privileged way of life. There is a sense of alarm in much of what is written about migrants, and, as in other reactions to social change, a sense of nostalgia for a more ordered past. Official policy promotes the idea of the free labour market, but many measures have been implemented to control and regulate the entry, sojourn and life of migrants in the urban areas. The migrants' right to be in an urban area is treated as highly provisional and there are sometimes sweeps in which all unregistered migrants are simply expelled from the areas where they are living.

Chinese migrants have been the subject of a considerable amount of academic study by both Chinese and non-Chinese scholars. One bibliography lists over 1,000 Chinese articles and monographs on population mobility published between 1984 and 1995 (Ji and Shao 1995). In the West, and in Japan, social science journals and journals concerned with China have also recently carried many articles on particular aspects of migration in China. Large numbers of local surveys and studies have been reviewed in this literature. There have been several major international conferences on migration in China, three taking place in the space of only four months in Cologne, Beijing and Oxford in the summer of 1996.

The present study is an attempt to take an overview of migration in China. It is offered with considerable trepidation. Conditions in China vary enormously not only from province to province, but even within each province. Population mobility in this vast country takes diverse forms, has varied impacts, different meanings and different outcomes in different economic, social and spatial contexts. Inevitably any attempt to generalise is fraught with difficulty and may mask important local specificities. But national studies are necessary for the specialist and non-specialist alike. The non-specialist needs an introduction to the subject and cannot be expected to absorb the detail of large numbers of small local studies. Specialists need something with which they can compare and contrast their own data, even if only to say, 'it is different in my area'.

Population mobility in China is a subject of such great significance, I have no doubt that it will be studied ever more closely in decades to come. I hope this book will help to spark more interest in migration and more understanding of those who migrate.

1 Migration in China after 1949

During the famine after the Great Leap Forward the first people who starved to death were put in thin coffins, then bodies were put in a couple of vats joined rim to rim. Later on, when everyone was so weak with hunger they couldn't move, whole families died and were just left where they lay. That's when I stopped being a cadre: I really wanted out. I wanted to go down a big pit near here as a miner. I wasn't bothered about getting killed in a cave-in as long as I could get the money for off-ration grain, and that cost plenty. But they wouldn't take me. They wouldn't let anyone with a rural registration become a worker. I was a farmer so I was stuck scraping a living out of the soil.

(Interview with a peasant, 1983, Zhang and Sang, 1987, pp. 120–1)

RESTRICTIONS ON POPULATION MOVEMENT

The great increase in migration in China in recent years is not in itself extraordinary. Population movement and increased urbanisation have accompanied economic growth and industrialisation everywhere in the world and it was to be expected that this process would occur in China too. However, political and economic factors unique to China make the Chinese case especially dramatic and worthy of study. First, there is the sheer size of China's internal migration since the economic reforms. Estimates of the numbers on the move in recent years vary greatly but are of magnitudes of 40 million, 80 million or even 100 million. Second, large-scale voluntary migration was a new phenomenon in the 1980s. The Chinese state in the Maoist period played a highly directive and interventionist role in relation to population movement. From the early 1950s to late 1978, there was little population mobility in China and, in effect, no labour market. The great majority of jobs were allocated by the state and migration was highly restricted by a system of population registration, with the result that by the time of the 1982 Census, China still had a very low level of urbanisation for a country at its level of development (Kirkby 1985; Chan 1994).

4

Although China's citizens now have far greater freedom of movement than they had in the past, considerable restrictions continue to hamper movement. Freedom of movement was not recognised as a right in the 1982 Constitution, and the idea that people should be free to move as they wish within their own country is still widely contested, or condemned as impractical. Few voices advocate the lifting of all controls on movement within the country and there is little consensus among policy-makers or academics over how strict the restrictions should be.

Barriers to migration in China go back to the 1950s. Through a series of regulations culminating in the 'Regulations of Household Registration in the People's Republic of China' issued in 1958, the Chinese government developed perhaps the strictest set of controls over the movement of population of any state in the modern world (Cheng and Selden 1994). The basis of control was the *hukou*, or household registration system (Christiansen 1990). This derived from the registration system of imperial China which functioned to maintain social control; it also incorporated elements of the labour registration system of the USSR (Dutton 1992: 207). Under the system each household possessed a registration book in which its members were listed. The first page of the book categorised the household and its members as 'agricultural' or 'non-agricultural'. The division between the agricultural and non-agricultural population has become a fundamental social divide in China. It is crucial to the control of migration and contributes to the restrictions and difficulties experienced by migrants in the places to which they migrate.

In the past, people were supposed to reside and work only where they had their *hukou*. Transfer of *hukou* was normally granted only in certain well-defined circumstances, which included assignment to a job in another area, marriage across administrative boundaries and moves to join family members established elsewhere. The administration of the *hukou* system was complex and involved different government offices. A transfer needed the permission of the authorities in the area where the *hukou* had been held and the authorities in the area to which it was being transferred. Even when individuals fitted the official criteria and the move was not opposed by either side, a *hukou* transfer could take months or even years to come through. Where there was a conflict of interest, it could be even slower.

The *hukou* system confirmed and reinforced a spatial hierarchy in China. Beijing, Shanghai and the other great cities, considered the most desirable places to live, became the most difficult to move to.

After them came in order the medium sized cities, large towns, county towns and small country towns. At the bottom of the hierarchy were the villages. Movement down this hierarchy met with few obstructions, movement between two places at the same level was possible, but movement up the hierarchy was severely controlled. The most difficult move was for a person with an agricultural *hukou* to enter the city. According to the 1958 regulations, 'To move from a rural area to a city, one must hold an employment certificate from an urban employment department, or be enrolled in a university, or have been granted permission by the authorities of urban household registration in the place of destination, and must then apply to migrate by going through the out-migration formalities in the place of origin' (Ma Xia 1994: 4).

Thus the *hukou* came to be both a marker and a source of social status. The registration hierarchy was quite elaborate. The most prized *hukou* was one for a large city, and at the bottom of the urban hierarchy, that for small towns. There were subdivisions even among those with agricultural registration. Peasants with a *hukou* for a suburban area of a city where good incomes could be obtained by cultivating vegetables for the urban market had higher status than the mass of peasants living far from urban areas depending on grain production for their income (Mallée 1996: 4).

Children born to mothers with a rural *hukou* had rural status regardless of their fathers' registration. Even a child born in a town or city to an urban father could not acquire urban status if the mother had a rural *hukou*. Such a child had no right to rations or schooling in the urban areas. This regulation demands further consideration. China's patrilineal and patriarchal traditions mean that a child is normally seen as belonging to the father's family. Why then did the state insist that the child inherit the mother's status? The explanation lies in the state's determination to limit the numbers of the urban population. It is socially acceptable for men to 'marry down' in Chinese society but much less so for women. Accordingly, 'mixed marriages' between high status (urban *hukou*) men and low status (rural *hukou*) women occur more often than between urban women and rural men. Men are also more occupationally 'mobile' than women, being more likely to move up the spatial hierarchy through the state employment system, conscription into the army or higher education. Therefore, among the few who succeeded in transferring from rural to urban registration, the majority would be men. By insisting that *hukou* registration should follow the female line, the state ensured that these men could not confer their new status on their children. The ruling also kept the dependency ratio in the urban areas to a minimum by ensuring that these children were brought up in the countryside.

ENFORCEMENT OF THE *HUKOU* SYSTEM

Not only was it extremely difficult to obtain permanent residential status in urban areas, even temporary sojourns in the cities were strictly controlled. Visitors had to register at the local branch of the Public Security Bureau for any stay of longer than three days. The enforcement of the *hukou* system was possible because the power of the state extended into almost every area of Chinese life. A system of mutual surveillance in the cities was sustained through residence committees. Strangers were noticed in the crowded but stable populations of city neighbourhoods and were quite likely to be reported. Even the protection of urban relatives could not help an incomer who had not completed the necessary formalities.

Prior to the reforms, the state had near-monopoly power over employment and housing in the urban areas, and over the supply and distribution of the necessities of life. Without proper papers, incomers could not find employment or independent accommodation. Above all, however, the enforcement of the *hukou* system depended on the rationing system. Grain, oil, cloth, fuel and many other products were rationed from the 1950s to the early 1980s. Peasants, being expected to produce their own food, were not entitled to a grain ration. They received grain in their villages, through their membership of a commune. Grain coupons were issued to the urban population by local authorities and could be used only in the locality. These coupons not only had to be produced in order to obtain the month's supply of uncooked grain, they were usually necessary even for the purchase of a bowl of rice in a restaurant, or of bread or noodles. The rationing system severely restricted movement into the cities from the countryside and affected the ease of movement between urban areas. Cadres travelling on official business were given national grain coupons valid throughout the country, but the issue of these was strictly controlled. Other people had to rely on friends or relatives to feed them if they went away from home. Rationing was at its most severe in the years of shortage at the beginning of the 1960s, but even in the 1970s while most urban residents had enough spare coupons to feed a visitor for a few days, a long stay caused problems. For peasants it was thus literally hard to survive in the urban areas.

THE ECONOMICS OF THE URBAN/RURAL DIVIDE

The rigid distinction maintained from 1958 between the agricultural and non-agricultural population produced what has been called 'a caste-like system of social stratification' (Potter and Potter 1990), designed to keep the peasants on the land and minimise the urban population. The barrier to rural–urban migration was raised quite deliberately. In the early 1950s, rural migrants moved to the cities in large numbers. Although new enterprises and construction work provided employment for many of them, other migrants failed to gain employment. Pressure on housing, transport and education and health facilities grew, and it seemed to policy-makers that the cities were reaching saturation point. Planners expressed great concern about the costs of urbanisation. A system designed to monitor urban population movement had been introduced in 1951 based on the Ministry of Public Security's 'Regulations Governing the Urban Population' (Cheng and Selden 1994). Between 1953 and 1956 there were various measures and directives intended to limit what was already then being referred to as the 'blind flow' of migrants from the rural to the urban areas. Finally, the 1958 Regulations extended the *hukou* system to whole population and greatly increased the difficulty of rural–urban movement. New migrants without a certificate of employment or of school admission had now to obtain a moving-in certificate (*zhun qian zhen*) from the police in the city to which they intended to move (*Hukou* Regulations, 1958, article 10). Without this approval they were unable to obtain a moving-out certificate (*qian yi zhen*), which they needed to leave their home area. The effect was that after 1958 rural people could no longer seek employment in the cities at will. Urban enterprises were still permitted to recruit labour from the countryside when they required it, but increasingly sought short-term contract workers who were not given the job security or social benefits of permanent workers, and had to return to their place of origin at the end of their contracts.

The power that the state thus acquired to regulate the supply of labour and the size of the urban population was particularly important at this time because widening gaps were opening up between the city and the countryside. Non-agricultural residence conferred great privileges on the urban population. Urban residents enjoyed a guaranteed entitlement to a ration of grain and other foodstuffs at subsidised prices. Peasants, by contrast, were not allowed to buy grain. The size of the allocation of grain and other foodstuffs they received from their commune depended on the size of the harvest and on their labour contribution to the collective. Peasants could only receive help from the state in the form of relief grain at times of natural disaster or famine. Such relief was provided at subsistence levels and recipients were stigmatised. City people were not only advantaged in their entitlements to food, they also enjoyed housing at nominal rents, superior education, health and welfare, and, compared to rural people, had better water supplies, drainage systems and other urban amenities. State employees had particularly favourable access to free healthcare, welfare and pensions. The cost of extending similar provision to the countryside would have been prohibitive. Instead, the state attempted to minimise the size of the urban population that was so expensive to maintain. As far as possible, new entrants were barred, and new demand for labour in the cities was met by increasing the female participation rate or by recruiting peasants as temporary contract workers. In the course of the 1960s and 1970s the gap between urban and rural incomes and entitlements grew.

The gap between rural and urban living standards was always a sensitive topic in China. After all, it had been a peasant revolution which brought the Communist Party to power. As early as 1953, Liang Shuming, a writer who had been involved in rural development projects in the 1920s, became concerned that peasants were not getting a fair deal under the new regime. He expressed his misgivings frankly at a meeting of the National Committee of the People's Consultative Conference, observing that the life of peasants was very hard and that in comparison with factory workers they were badly paid. He went on to say that where remuneration was concerned, factory workers were in the ninth level of heaven and peasants on the ninth level of hell (Rice 1974: 137). Unfortunately for Liang, Mao Zedong was present at the meeting. Infuriated by the writer's remarks, Mao seized the microphone and launched into a stream of personal invective. Liang was never forgiven. Yet Mao himself showed an increasing consciousness of the inequitable gap between city and countryside. He made visionary attempts in both the Great Leap Forward and in the Cultural Revolution to bring city and countryside closer through human engineering on a grand and ultimately disastrous scale. What Maoist China lacked were budgetary or development policies capable of reducing the gap in a more orthodox fashion.

During the Cultural Revolution, the cause of the contract workers was taken up by leftists. Mao's wife Jiang Qing used the issue of discriminatory treatment of peasant migrants as a stick with which to beat the official trade union movement and her enemies within the government (Rice 1974: 281–2). But her championship of the contract workers appears to have been purely opportunistic; there was no sustained attempt to change the contract system.

The barriers to population movement trapped a rapidly growing rural population on the land. The number of agricultural labourers in China grew from 165 million in 1949 to 313 million in 1980 and 380 million in 1986 (Taylor 1988: 746). Not only was this population denied the right to seek an alternative means of making a living in the urban areas, the possibility of non-agricultural work in the countryside was severely constrained by increasing official hostility to anything that could be construed as private enterprise. It is true that rural industries and sidelines run as collective enterprises were officially promoted, but peasants were denied the right to engage in such activities as individuals or to run them as family businesses. Rural households became trapped in poverty because they were forced to rely on the cultivation of a shrinking per capita supply of land for a living. Rural living standards were further depressed by a price structure deliberately biased against agriculture. The state as the monopolistic purchaser of agricultural products paid the peasants very low prices for their crops, while charging them high prices for industrial goods. This made it possible both to supply the urban population with cheap grain and to squeeze funds for the industrialisation effort out of agriculture. Elsewhere in the world, some peasants would have sought relief in migration to the towns. In China where this was difficult except when directed by the state, the pressure of population on the land led to stagnating or even falling living standards. It is hardly surprising that when the valve was eased open in the 1980s there was such a rush to the towns.

RURAL TO URBAN MIGRATION, 1950s TO THE 1970s

Despite the severe restrictions before the 1980s, rural to urban migration was not negligible in the first three decades of the People's Republic of China (Lary 1997). Unfortunately it is difficult to quantify this with any precision. Officially sanctioned migration involving *hukou* transfer was recorded at local level through the household registration system from the 1950s, but little of these data has been collated or published. According to official estimates, between 25 and 30 million people obtained *hukou* transfers in moves from one province to another between 1949 and 1978 (Lary 1996: 57). This figure does not include *hukou* migration within provinces, which would have been of a greater magnitude, or unsanctioned, non-*hukou* migration, for which estimates are still harder to obtain.

Another important source of data for the Chinese population is the National Census. Censuses were carried out in China in 1953, 1964, 1982 and 1990. However, the Census schedules did not contain a direct migration question until 1990. A large-scale retrospective survey of migration covering 74 towns and cities was carried out by the Population Research Institute of the Chinese Academy of Social Sciences in 1986 in recognition of the need for more information about contemporary and past migratory movements in China (CASS 1988). This survey and publications which derive from it (Day and Ma 1994; Goldstein and Goldstein 1994; and Cheng 1991) are valuable sources for the study of Chinese migration before the reforms and in the early reform period.

Extrapolations from the survey reveal that there were in the region of 50–60 million surviving rural–urban migrants in China's urban areas by 1986 (Wang 1994: 27; Ma 1994: 204). This figure does not reflect the full extent of rural–urban migration in the period because it omits those who died as well as those who returned to the villages (Wang 1994: 27). The magnitude of this migration does not indicate that attempts to control population movement failed to have any effect. In fact, the impact of such attempts is clearly visible in the fluctuations of migration over time, and in the characteristics and destinations of the migrants. The rate of rural to urban migration in most developing countries has increased continuously, and if short-term fluctuations are discounted, steadily. By contrast, in China since 1949, migration to the urban areas has undergone sharp peaks and troughs. Of the total number of migrants to cities and towns from 1949 to 1986, the Survey found that 21 per cent came during the 1950s, 17 per cent during the 1960s, 33 per cent during the 1970s and 29 per cent in the six years 1981–6 (Wang 1994: 25). Although the exact effect of mortality and return to the rural areas is impossible to gauge, the earlier migration figures will obviously have suffered more such attrition than later ones. As we are looking here only at figures for survivors, and one would expect fewer of these from the earlier period, the decline indicated in migration from the 1950s to the 1960s is doubtless understated. Both this decline and the upturn experienced in the 1970s and 1980s have to be understood against the background of political and economic change.

At the time of the establishment of the People's Republic in 1949, urbanisation was seen as a necessary and desirable corollary to recovery and industrialisation. There was official recruitment of the peasants to supply labour for expanding industries while rural people were drawn to the cities by the hope of economic betterment. Estimates suggest that the urban population grew by 20 million from 1949 to 1953, of which 70 per cent was attributable to migration rather than natural growth (Sit 1985: 13). The share of migration in urban growth fell to 42 per cent during the first five year plan (1953–7), probably due in part to attempts to control the migration into the cities. However, the urban bias of the plan and its emphasis on industry ensured that some rural–urban migration continued. Over half of all state investment went into industry compared with 8 per cent to agriculture, the sector which still employed 80 per cent of the labour force (Lardy 1987: 158). This was also a period in which urban privilege was becoming institutionalised and the cities seemed increasingly attractive to peasants. The urban authorities became ever more concerned about the numbers of rural migrants, the growing problem of urban unemployment and the strain on housing, health, education and welfare. As we have seen, these pressures led the Standing Committee of the National People's Congress to adopt the 'Regulations on Household Registration' in 1958.

Ironically, the Regulations had little immediate effect because 1958 was the year in which China was overtaken by the chaos of the Great Leap Forward. The major expansion of industry attempted in this movement at first stimulated higher rural–urban migration; indeed in their optimism about the pace of economic growth the authorities themselves promoted migration and ignored the regulations. Even when it became apparent that the Great Leap had been a disastrous failure and industry began to lay off workers, the movement into the urban areas was for a time sustained as peasants sought refuge in the cities from the terrible famine that had begun to grip many rural areas in the aftermath of the Great Leap. The functioning of the central bureaucracy was so adversely affected by the Great Leap that it was for some time impossible to implement the Household Registration Regulations. When order was restored, however, the Regulations were used to expel millions of recent migrants from the cities. Economic crisis was dealt with by a severe retrenchment programme, and even citizens formerly registered as urban dwellers were relocated to the villages in an attempt to reduce the urban unemployment that had resulted from the closure of many enterprises. The first half of

the 1960s produced a decline in China's urban population, an extraordinary phenomenon in a developing country (Chan 1994: 37–40).
The results of this retrenchment can be seen clearly in figures from
Ningxia Province, where urbanisation had proceeded swiftly during
the Great Leap and where the economic crisis that followed was correspondingly severe. The number of people with non-agricultural registration, and thus the right to receive the urban grain ration, in
Ningxia fell by over 40 per cent from 463,000 in 1960 to 286,000 by
1962 (Brookes 1994: 110).

The Cultural Revolution period is now usually held to cover the ten
years 1966–76, a historiography that has been adopted in post-Mao
China because it allows the whole period to be condemned for leftist
excesses. For most purposes it is more useful to divide the decade into
the three years of chaos and anarchy, 1966–9, when order more or less
broke down, and 1970–6, years of authoritarian and arbitrary government, by comparison with which the 1950s seem almost liberal. The
period has a complex migration history. The breakdown of central
authority probably made it easier to enter the urban areas until 1969,
but disorder and the closure of some enterprises at times reduced
their attractions. All this changed in the 1970s as millions of urban
people were sent to live in the countryside, the Household
Registration Regulations were again enforced with great severity and
surveillance of daily life in the cities reached unprecedented levels.

The politics of the Cultural Revolution directly affected population movement. An anti-urban ideology was promoted and peasants
were lauded for their political purity, their simple way of life and
their hard work. Over 20 million urban people, Red Guards,
intellectuals and politically disgraced officials were sent to the countryside to settle (Bernstein 1977). Millions of other cadres, teachers
and students were required to spend periods of months or years in
the rural areas on a rotating basis. Ironically, however, this movement
coincided with a continued flow of peasants into the cities. At first
these were illegal migrants taking advantage of the chaos, but millions were also taken on by urban enterprises on temporary contracts
and issued with temporary permits. Like contract workers in earlier
times they had to return to the villages when their jobs came to an
end. Any assessment of net flow in this period is also complicated by
the fact that some of the rusticated urbanites retained their urban
registration while living in the villages and many peasant migrants to
the cities continued to be registered as agricultural population
(Scharping 1987: 101–4).

TYPES OF MIGRATION IN PRE-REFORM CHINA

It has already been made clear that there were different types of migration in China before the reform period of the 1980s. Perhaps the clearest division was between organised migration where people moved because they were directed to do so by the state, and individual migration where motivation was personal. The latter group can be further subdivided into those who obtained authorisation (*hukou* migrants) and those who did not (non-*hukou* migrants).

There have been many organised migrations in the period of the People's Republic. In the 1950s the state took control of the economy and investment. The assumption of greater control over the labour force and its location increasingly came to be seen as a natural corollary of planned development The direction of labour was applied most fully to the trained and educated workforce: many engineers, doctors, intellectuals and skilled workers were redeployed in the 1950s, and graduates from higher education were subject to a national work allocation system, that is they could be assigned work anywhere in the country on graduation. This allowed the government to transfer qualified people and workers with particular skills from the comparatively advanced coastal region to the inland cities and other areas where they were needed to support the drive for development and industrialisation. Tens of thousands of skilled workers were sent from Shanghai to work on sites all over China every year in the Maoist period (Howe 1981: 182). In the 1950s, as we have seen, peasants were officially recruited into the urban labour force and given non-agricultural status. In the 1960s and 1970s this type of migration gave way to the recruitment of contract workers for the urban labour force and for labour gangs engaged in railway and other construction both in the urban areas and outside them. The contract system contributed to the reduction of permanent migration as contract workers had no right to remain in the urban areas when their contracts ended.

Since the establishment of the People's Republic in 1949, large-scale development projects such as dams and reservoirs have sometimes necessitated the evacuation or migration of significant numbers of people. By the mid-1980s, 5.04 million people had been moved to make way for reservoir construction (Yan Hao 1991: 226). Most were given land to farm in less densely populated regions, which could mean moving great distances to places that were difficult to cultivate. In 1958, for example, the *Ningxia Daily* announced that 140,000 people were to be moved to this impoverished province from the site of the Sanmen Xia reservoir in the provinces of Shaanxi and Henan (Brookes 1994: 104). This type of large-scale compulsory population movement has continued up to the present. The construction of the Three Gorges Dam on the Yangzi will cause the largest such displacement of people for a single project yet seen in China. Evacuation has already started and it is estimated that between 1 million and 1.6 million people will eventually be moved (Dai 1994: 225). Farmland has also been lost to urban and industrial expansion. Where this occurred, peasants might also be evacuated but could alternatively be compensated by a change of status that allowed them to seek a non-agricultural living in the expanding urban area. This practice continued in the reform era, for example, when all the arable land of Beixincun in Changping county north of Beijing was taken over for the construction of a golf course, the villagers were given non-agricultural status and jobs (Zhao 1992: 123).

Students in higher education away from their place of origin were granted 'collective household registration' in the city where they were studying. On graduation in the past, except during the period of the Cultural Revolution, the employment assigned to them by the state was normally in urban areas. At this stage they acquired urban household registration in their own right, even if they originally had an agricultural *hukou*. However, such educational migration had a limited impact. The percentage of each cohort in higher education was small and only a minority of students originated from the countryside. Higher education did not therefore contribute much to movement into the urban areas. Education and the graduate job assignment did, however, account for significant numbers of movements between urban areas and into and out of 'education capitals' such as Beijing and Shanghai. Graduates from the major universities might be assigned jobs anywhere in China. An interesting, unintended result of this system was the reinforcement of networks of ex-classmates, friends and relatives across China. This has been an important factor in shaping the culture of the educated elite.

The types of official migration we have looked at so far have been economic in nature. Some other types would perhaps be better classified as political, although the distinction is not always sharp. Migration to both the cities and the countryside of the frontier areas of Xinjiang, Ningxia, Qinghai, Inner Mongolia, Heilongjiang, Hainan and Yunnan was officially promoted for most of the Maoist period. The primary motive for promoting this migration was geopolitical – the wish to increase the population and the level of development in frontier areas. Some of the participants, such as technicians and skilled workers, were selected because they were needed in the destination areas, but this sort of migration also included people not wanted in their origin areas, peasants from heavily populated provinces, demobilised soldiers, the urban unemployed, urban secondary school graduates for whom no work was available and those in political trouble. The numbers were involved in such movements were large even before the Cultural Revolution. For example, between 1955 and 1960, over 1 million people were moved from heavily populated areas of Shandong Province to open up sparsely populated areas elsewhere (Lary 1996: 61), while in January 1959, it was announced that Zhejiang Province was to send 300,000 young people to 'help with the development of Ningxia Province' (Brookes 1994: 104). This type of officially sponsored population movement involved *hukou* transfer, making it hard for those who had been moved to return to their places of origin.

Conscription provided another official way for young people to leave their places of origin. The vast majority of those involved were young male peasants. Usually they returned to their villages after two or three years' service, having acquired the skills and status necessary for them to advance within the collective structure. Some, however, gained the chance to settle elsewhere, in the urban areas if they were lucky, on state farms or oilfields in remote areas if they were not.

The urban–rural movement produced by punishment or political exile was substantial. Urban intellectuals or cadres in political disgrace were sent to live in the countryside from the 1950s. A particularly large number was forced to leave in 1957 when it is estimated that between 400,000 and 700,000 rightists were exiled to the rural areas, where some were to stay for over 20 years (Goldman 1987: 257). The fortunate ones went to villages with which they had family connections, the least fortunate to labour reform camps in poor remote areas where conditions were grim. In such exiles the penal system was actually making use of the *hukou* system, and the loss of an urban *hukou* became part of the punishment of urban offenders.

The numbers exiled from the urban areas in the earlier period were dwarfed by the exodus to the countryside during the Cultural Revolution. The net loss to the urban areas through migration in this period was almost 5 million. Individuals who had been politically disgraced were sent for particularly long periods, but ordinary intellectuals and cadres also had to go to the countryside in rotation to undertake months or even years of labour reform. The greatest of all these movements was that of the Red Guards who were directed to go to the villages for re-education in 1970. About 20 million urban people in their teens and twenties were involved in this flow. As it was envisaged that their exile would be permanent, most were deprived of their urban household registration. Their struggles to return to the urban areas in the years after Mao's death centred on the difficulties of transferring household registration and illustrate how difficult it had become to cross the bureaucratic barriers which separated the urban and rural worlds in China.

The rigid control of migration hampered 'spontaneous' migration – the migration of individuals who made their own decisions – for most of the first three decades of the People's Republic. We have seen how difficult labour migration was made by the restrictions of the 1950s. None the less it has been estimated that from 1949 to the mid-1980s there were at least 10 million spontaneous permanent migrations in China, and a study of Shandong has shown that many people did succeed in moving without government approval (Lary 1996: 66–7). Most such migrants were peasants continuing migration patterns already established before restrictions were imposed. They could go to live with relatives or friends while they established themselves in a new area. The knowledge that they would be helped at the end of their journey gave peasants from areas with a tradition of migration a confidence that peasants elsewhere would not have had. Spontaneous migration was tolerated by the authorities when it involved a shift of population from densely populated areas like Shandong to more sparsely populated areas such as Manchuria. Unofficial migrants to the cities were more likely to be returned to their places of origin.

Another cause of spontaneous migration was natural disaster. When food was in very short supply, people ignored the regulations and sought survival by moving to more fortunate areas. The largest movements took place in the early 1960s as a result of the great famine which followed the Great Leap Forward. Millions of people tried to avoid starvation by seeking work or charity elsewhere. Many went to beg in the less afflicted areas. Again, those who lived in areas with a tradition of migration were the most fortunate as they could seek help from friends and relatives who had left in earlier years.

Not all spontaneous or non-state migration was labour or economic migration. People also migrated for family considerations. The most common of these types, marriage migration, will be discussed in detail in chapter 7. But it is relevant to note here that of all forms of population movement, marriage migration was the least affected by the restrictions. Most marriages involved a move for the bride to her husband's village, normally within a short distance of her own. The change of household registration was usually simple because it did not involve movement up the spatial hierarchy, peasants tended to marry peasants and urbanites were likely to choose their partners from their own town or city.

Restrictions on migration caused much hardship and suffering to individuals in the Maoist era. There were many instances of tragic family separations. Matches between people with different types of *hukou* or inhabitants of different towns or cities caused some of these. Marriage did not confer the right for one spouse to acquire the *hukou* of the other and it appears that the authorities were resolute that this would not become a way to move up the spatial hierarchy. Urban men who married women with rural registration usually had to accept permanent separation. Separations could also come about when a man or woman was assigned a new job in some far-off place. There was no automatic right to be joined by a spouse, and even when this right was granted to individuals, they sometimes waited years for the necessary *hukou* and job transfers to be arranged. Some indication of the scale of this problem can be gained from the estimate that 11.4 million couples in stable marriages were geographically separated at the time of the 1982 Census (Ma, et al. 1996: 877).[1]

Migration to achieve other types of family reunion could also be difficult. Many families separated by the events of the Cultural Revolution spent years waiting for applications to move back together to be processed. The easiest form of family reunion was that involving individuals moving down the hierarchy of *hukou* registration as when a wife in a city moved to join her husband in a small town, or someone agreed to leave an urban area to join family in the countryside. Not surprisingly, most individuals sought reunions that involved movement in the other direction. Applications from aged parents to join adult children in the towns appear to have been treated with some sympathy, perhaps partly in deference to traditions of filiality, but also no doubt because the urban authorities worried less about incomers whose reproductive years were over and who were not expected to make demands for employment or housing.

SUMMARY

The roots of China's present migration problems lie in the policies of the first decades of the People's Republic. In this period the growing inequality between rural and urban areas set up conditions that would have been conducive to high levels of rural–urban migration had free movement been permitted. To prevent this, the state set up institutional barriers to migration which, by the 1970s, had made spontaneous movement from a village to an urban area as difficult as movement across national frontiers elsewhere in the world. Although various forms of population movement did persist, migration to the towns was not an option for most peasants before the economic reforms of the late 1970s. After the death of Mao in 1976 and the end of the Cultural Revolution policies, a new leadership took power and introduced economic reforms that transformed the social and economic context against which migration took place. At the same time strict birth control policies affected the natural growth rate of population in the urban areas. Eighty per cent of urban population growth in 1978–81 is attributable to migration (Goldstein and Goldstein 1990: 66). This new period in China's migration history will be the subject of the remaining chapters of this book.

2 An Overview of Migration in China since 1978

No, I'm not a migrant, I've just come to Chengdu to see my sister. She is working here. I came last year twice too. Looked at the shops, walked about a lot, saw the city and then went home. Of course, if I found a job, I might stay, but I'm not one of those floating population. I'm not a migrant, no.
(interview with young rural woman, Chengdu Railway Station 1994)

INVESTIGATING MIGRATION IN THE POST-REFORM ERA

All authorities agree that the scale of internal migration in China increased enormously with the advent of the economic reforms. Migration and the problems to which it gives rise have been invest-igated and discussed exhaustively since the mid-1980s by policy-makers, academics and the popular press. Yet much remains uncertain. Even the number of migrants is disputed, as we have seen: figures commonly given for the migrant population vary from 40 to 80 million, but can go as high as 100 million.[1] There are obvious reasons for this difficulty. The first problem is that of definition. Who is a migrant? How long do migrants have to stay away from home to be so classified? How far do they have to have moved and what boundaries must they have crossed? When do they cease to be migrants and count as settled population? Do all those who move count as migrants no matter what their motivation? The woman quoted at the beginning of the chapter illustrates the difficulty. She did not identify herself as a migrant, yet as she was about to start her third lengthy stay in Chengdu, her travels, if recorded, would have increased the count of population movements within the province by three. She saw herself only as a visitor to the city, but might well have become a labour migrant if the opportunity had been offered.

Different agencies in China work with different definitions of migrants and migrations and this contributes to the differences in esti-mated figures. Some methods of collecting data count only the migrants, while others count migrations. This difference is important because when much migration is short-term or seasonal, one person may be involved in many migrations. Some agencies are interested in all population movements, while others focus exclusively on the floating population, rural to urban migration or labour migration. When counts are taken at a particular point in time, the point chosen biases the result because much migration is seasonal and short-term.

The absolute size of the Chinese population makes investigating it on a national scale both complex and expensive. Only agencies of the state are in a position to do it. The national-level data thus collected reflect the big picture, but are inevitably of limited use for understanding trends at the provincial level or for gaining insight into individual motivation. Smaller-scale studies have been made by both Chinese and western scholars in specific localities in order to obtain detailed information about particular aspects of migration. These yield interesting information but give rise to the usual problems of sample size, representativeness and comparability. Chinese researchers do not always provide explicit methodological information about their surveys and this can make their data even harder to evaluate. Moreover, migrants can be particularly hard to survey. They are often suspicious of investigators and may have good reason not to co-operate with being counted. Migrants' status in the cities is still something of a grey area. Unofficial migrants fear that any contact with officials may end in expulsion or the need to pay fines, levies or bribes. They are therefore fearful of outsiders, especially those who ask questions.

CATEGORIES AND TERMINOLOGY IN CHINESE MIGRATION STUDIES

The system of household registration has not only served to inhibit and shape migration in modern China, it profoundly affects the way migrants are viewed, and thus the terminology used to discuss them. Migrants are commonly categorised according to their registration status. Some discussions use the word 'migrant' (*qianyi renkou*) only to refer to those who have crossed an administrative border with permission, transferring their *hukou* with them. These migrants may also be referred to as formal, legal or official migrants. Unofficial migrants who move without permission are referred to as the floating population (*liudong renkou*) (Hoy 1996: 8–9).

The two groups are also distinguished as 'permanent' and 'temporary'. In this usage those whose *hukou* has been transferred are expected to stay at the destination and are therefore quite logically called 'permanent migrants'; the rest are called temporary. The distinction being made here is one of legal status. Migrants are designated temporary without reference to the actual duration of the stay, nor to their aspirations as to length of stay. In 1985 new regulations made it possible for migrants whose *hukou* remained in their area of origin to obtain temporary registration in a destination area (Mallée 1995: 13). This has made divisions more complex. Registration confers some legal status on temporary migrants although they are not entitled to the privileges enjoyed by those with an urban *hukou*. Many temporary migrants do not choose to register as the process is expensive and may entail paying a monthly fee to the local Public Security Bureau.

The distinctions made between migrants are generally inexact and inconsistent. The terms often convey the speaker's attitude towards the group discussed rather than the characteristics of the migrants. In official usage, the term 'floating population' covers all those absent from the place where they are officially registered for a night or more but less than a year, for whatever reason, and whether or not they have notified the Public Security Bureau of their presence. It thus includes tourists, traders, people on business trips and those visiting relatives or seeking medical treatment, as well as labour migrants. After sojourners have been resident in a destination area for more than one year, they are classified as *de facto* migrants (*shishi qianyi*) (Hoy 1996: 9–10). The concept of the floating population held by ordinary people in urban areas appears a little different. It is used of migrants who are actually on the move, as well as those searching for work, hawking goods or in short-term employment in the urban areas. Urban residents probably would not see a well-established migrant, even one without registration, as a 'floater', nor would they identify their own friends and relatives on visits from other parts of the country as floaters, although these people would be so identified under the Public Security Bureau definition. In popular usage, the term tends to be applied to those who are easily identifiable as incomers and it usually has negative connotations. A still more derogatory or condescending term, 'blind migrant' (*mangliu*), is used of those considered to have taken an impulsive decision to migrate and who are perceived as vagrants wandering around aimlessly in search of employment. Doubtless there are 'floaters' in small towns and cities, but discussion of the floating population is almost exclusively concentrated on the big cities such as Beijing, Shanghai, Guangzhou and

Wuhan where this population is estimated to form between one fifth and one third of the total (Solinger 1995: 114).

Discussion of migrants and migration in the first years after large-scale migration began reflected the alarm felt by many urbanites at the phenomenon. Migration was described as a 'wave' or 'tide', and migrants were said to be 'flooding' the cities. Rural labour migrants were referred to as *'mingong'* (labourer) or *'dagongzi'* and *'dagongmei'* (brother labourers and sister labourers). Both terms have slightly folksy connotations and set the migrants apart from the category of *'gongren'* – workers in the formal sector. *'Mingong'* also has connotations of 'not run by the government'. In recent years a new scholarly discourse much more sympathetic to migrants and migration has grown up in which terms such as *'mangliu'* (blind migrant) have been dropped, *'mangmu'* (blind) and *'luan'* (chaotic) have been replaced with *'wuxu'* (disorderly), and *'laodongli zhuanyi'* (the transfer of labour) is used in preference to terms such as *'mingongchao'* (the migrant labour wave).

In this study I refer to all those who leave their areas of origin to live elsewhere, for whatever reason, as migrants. I call those who do so with permission and with the expectation of transferring their *hukou*, 'official' migrants and the rest 'unofficial' ones. Following Chinese sources my use of 'permanent' and 'temporary' refers to legal status rather than temporal factors. I employ the term 'floating population' sparingly only to describe the least settled of migrants.

SOURCES FOR MIGRATION DATA

We have seen that much information about population in China is drawn from the household registration records. However, although it became much easier to move from one area to another, and even from the countryside into the city after 1978, household registration has remained extremely difficult to change without official backing. The result is that household registers are still a poor source for migration data. They can yield information about formalised moves and marriage migration because they show registration transfers. In some cases they also record that a household member has gained temporary registration elsewhere. However, the primary concern of the household register is with *de jure* residence, that is where people *should* be living rather than where they actually live.

The 1986 Survey of Migrants in 74 Cities and Towns (CASS 1988) discussed in Chapter 1 covered in-migrants to urban areas who had arrived between 1949 and 1986 and who were still alive and living in an urban area at the time of the survey. The Survey and the studies based on it (Day and Ma 1994; Cheng 1991; and Goldstein and Goldstein 1997) provide much useful information on migration to urban areas in the first decades of the People's Republic. However, as the Survey was carried out just as large-scale migration was getting underway in China, it could not capture the full scale of post-reform migration.

The growing importance of migration in the course of the 1980s made clear the gravity of the omission of questions on migration in the first three national Censuses. Migration was investigated in the 1987 One in One Thousand National Population Survey (hereafter National Population Survey) and migration questions were included in the 1990 Census. Both yielded valuable information about numbers of migrants, their origins, destinations, sex ratios, marital status, educational levels, occupations and reasons for moving, but failed to provide a comprehensive picture because their definitions resulted in the omission of most short-term migrants.

The National Population Survey and the Census operated with definitions of migration that were similar but not identical. The Survey defined migrations as movements from other cities, towns or rural counties during 1982 to 1987 that resulted in (1) a change of household registration, or (2) absence from the official place of registration for at least six months. The exclusion of those absent for less than six months was intended to cut out very temporary movements that were due simply to people making short business or shopping trips, or visits to friends and family. According to two studies of temporary migration, a very large proportion of movements to urban areas are for such purposes (Goldstein and Goldstein 1991; Goldstein, Goldstein and Guo 1991). Work done on a sample of the micro-data of the National Population Survey for the three years 1984–7 has found that it implies a migration rate of 7 per 1,000 or about 21 million population movements for the three-year period covered (Ma, Liaw and Zeng 1997: part 4).

The general principle of the 1990 Census was to reflect residence on a *de facto* basis, but its procedures meant that a *de jure* element remained. Enumerators in a given place were told to count (1) persons who lived and had their registration in that place; (2) persons who had lived in that place for more than one year although their household registration was for a different place; (3) persons who, although they had lived in that place for less than a year, had been away from the place of their household registration for more than one year; (4) persons living in that place awaiting permanent household registration; (5) persons now working or studying abroad who were therefore temporarily without household registration, but whose registration had been in that place (SSB 1991a: 696). With these definitions it recorded a total of 34 million people for the period covered living in a place different from that of their place of residence in July 1985.

Both the Survey and the Census could be expected to understate temporary migration in various ways. In the case of the Census, for example, temporary migrants who had spent less than a year away from their places of origin, or who had returned to their place of origin for a visit in between migrations to take up contract or seasonal work, will have been registered in their places of origin even if absent from them at the time of enumeration. Also, as much migration is still seasonal or very short-term, this ruling must have meant that large numbers of short-term migrants were not captured as migrant population in the Census. Both the National Population Survey and the Census derived information on migration from questions about current residence and residence five years earlier. They could not therefore reflect the fact that in a five-year period many individuals would have been involved in multiple population movements. For these reasons the Survey and Census data must understate the number of individuals involved in migration, and, to an even greater degree, the number of migratory movements.

Many surveys of the migrant population in particular cities have been made by agencies of the local government and by the Public Security Bureau. These tend to be concerned with law and order and with the stresses and strains put on the urban infrastructure (Solinger 1993). They indicate that the transient population of China's large cities averages between one sixth and one quarter of the total city population (Gaubatz 1995: 42). Such 'counts' are usually produced by a census of guests in hotels and lodging houses, a sampling of residents' houses to estimate the number of lodgers and relatives from outside staying in private homes, and a count of people arriving at train and bus stations on a particular day (SASS 1994; Gaubatz 1995). Their figures are therefore inflated by short-term visitors, but they are likely to miss some others, for example, migrant workers who rent accommodation just outside the city and come into work daily by bicycle.

Recently there have been a number of surveys which focus more on the sending areas and on the connections between rural problems and rural mobility.[2] Their purpose has been to provide a better basis for discussion and policy formation and their perspective is very much more sympathetic to the migrants. These surveys also came up with rather varied findings due no doubt to differences of definition, timing, methodology and focus. The proportion of the rural workforce thought to be on the move was between 10 and 15 per cent and there was agreement that rural out-migrants numbered somewhere between 50 and 60 million. If we remember that this figure excludes migrants originating in the urban areas, then an estimate of 70–80 million migrants or members of the mobile population in total seems quite plausible.

The lack of agreement on a definition of a migrant, the varied objectives of investigations into migration and problems of methodology, sampling and timing make it impossible to produce a meaningful figure for China's migrant population. However, rough as the overall picture of the numbers involved undoubtedly is, it is enough to indicate the importance of population movement in recent years. The often used but perhaps rather high estimate of 80 million recent migrants, for example, would imply over 1 in 15 of the population or about 1 in 8 of the labour force.

That 7 per cent of the total population has moved across an administrative boundary at some time in the past few years does not indicate the Chinese population, even in the 1990s, has been highly mobile by international standards. None the less, internal migration in China has had a considerable impact, and merits the attention it has received. First, as a new phenomenon it is challenging many of the established systems and institutions in China, such as household registration, educational and health provision and access to housing and employment. It has therefore become the site of struggle and negotiations between the state and individuals who are seeking to control the direction of their own lives. Second, the absolute numbers involved are enormous and the flow is concentrated on comparatively few favourite destination areas. The numbers entering large cities such as Beijing and Shanghai or flourishing regions such as Jiangsu and southern Guangdong Province are very large in proportion to the resident population.

SEX AND AGE DISTRIBUTION OF MIGRANTS

Sex Ratios

In most third world countries migration has been predominantly male, although there is evidence that this pattern is changing in some areas, for example in the industrialising countries of South America (Parnwell 1993: 81). In China, it is generally agreed that the majority of labour migrants are men. However, there are considerable differences in the sex ratios reported in the various studies of migration probably because of differences in the group studied. Sources such as the 1986 Survey and the Census recorded all population movement for whatever reason, and therefore included marriage and other family-related migration, in which females outnumbered men. Surveys of labour migrants or the floating population focus on rural to urban migration or labour migration in which men predominate.

The 1986 Survey of Migrants in 74 Cities and Towns which covered in-migrants to urban areas who had arrived between 1949 and 1986, found that male migrants outnumbered female migrants generally, especially in the larger urban settlements. For example, in extra-large cities males were 54 per cent of all migrants and in large cities 58 per cent (Xiong and Day 1994: 109). The micro-data of the 1987 Population Survey surprisingly came up with a different picture. It indicated that of the 21 million people who migrated to another city, town or rural county during 1984–7, females accounted for 55.7 per cent and males for 44.3 per cent (Ma, et al. 1997: section 4). The 1990 Census reversed these proportions. Of the total 34 million people it recorded as having moved in the five years prior to 1990, 57 per cent were male and 43 per cent female (Messkoub and Davin 1998). The 1986 Migration Survey reflected only migration to urban areas and covered the years 1949–86 – a long historical period. Its data show surviving in-migrants after the attrition of death or return to the countryside. No comparability should be expected between its sex ratios and those of the 1987 National Population Survey or the Census, for these included all population movement and covered a shorter time period.

The different sex ratios produced by the 1987 National Population Survey and the 1990 Census are very interesting. They may partly be the result of sampling problems. The Survey was itself based on a 1 per cent sample, and the migrant sex ratio cited here is taken from a sub-sample used by Ma, Liaw and Zeng, of just over 500,000 people. The difference may also reflect the changing distribution of reasons for migration. The Population Survey and the Census used the same set of nine possible reasons for migration.[3] The time period covered by the two data sets, however, is different. The sex ratio for the Survey is for movements in 1985, 1986 and 1987. The Census reflects movements between 1985 and 1990. Although the two overlap, the Census is weighted towards the later years compared with the Survey.

The distribution of reasons shows a sharp increase in migrations attributed to work and trade from 10.8 per cent in the Survey to 23 per cent in the Census. For education, the shift was from 9.9 per cent to 14 per cent. By contrast 26.5 per cent of inter-provincial migrations were attributed to marriage in the Survey, against only 14 per cent in the Census (Ma et al. 1997: Table 3; Messkoub and Davin 1998: Tables 4 and 5). As we shall see in chapter 4, men outnumber women in migrations for work-related migration, while women make up the great majority of marriage migrants. Thus the change in the migrant sex ratio between the Survey and the Census can probably be explained by trends in the causes of migration in the 1980s. As the importance of labour migration in which males were dominant grew, there was a relative reduction in the importance of marriage migration, which is largely female. Another factor in the change in sex ratio was that migration over greater distances was becoming commoner, and migration to larger urban settlements easier. As long-distance migration and migration to the big cities predominantly involve men, while female migration tends to be over shorter distances and to smaller urban settlements, this could also have produced some decline in the female share of migration.

The Census data allow us to look more closely at sex ratios of different types of migrants It can be seen from Table 2.1 that women were rather more strongly represented in migration within the same province – 45 per cent of the total – than in-migration between provinces – 39 per cent of the total. They were also strongly represented in all migration from rural areas to other rural areas; indeed, they actually outnumbered men in both intra- and inter-provincial migration of this type. They were close to equality in numbers with men for in-migration from the rural areas to all towns (48 per cent) and to cities within the same province (44 per cent). However, their share fell to 37 per cent in the case of migration from the rural areas to cities in other provinces. This pattern is affected by the importance of marriage as a cause of female migration rather than as a cause of male migration. Of all female migration, about 30 per cent was due to marriage, against only 2 per cent of male migration (see chapter 8, Tables 8.1 and 8.2). Of all marriage migrants over 90 per cent were female. (Marriage migration is the subject of chapter 8.)

Studies of the floating population in the big cities confirm the supposition that more men than women migrate to large urban centres. The Ministry of Construction reported that 87 per cent of transients in Beijing were male, as were 74 per cent in the great industrial city of

Table 2.1 Female migration as a percentage of internal migration by origin (residence in 1985) and destination (residence 1990)

Destination 1990		Total	Female	Origin 1985 Urban: City No. (000s)	Female	Town No. (000s)	Female	Rural: County No. (000s)	Female
Other Provinces									
Total		11,085	4,274	2,812	881	1,549	510	6,724	2,883
	%		39		31		33		43
City		6,500	2,255	2,046	684	911	271	3,543	1,300
	%		35		33		30		37
Town		2,401	977	493	144	455	169	1,453	664
	%		41		29		37		46
County		2,184	1,042	273	53	183	70	1,728	919
	%		48		19		38		53
Same Province									
Total		23,014	10,461	3,576	1,279	4,852	2,179	14,586	7,003
	%		45		36		45		48
City		14,746	6,461	2,376	952	3248	1,486	9,122	4,023
	%		44		40		46		44
Town		4,553	2,017	764	228	1180	523	2,609	1,266
	%		44		30		44		49
County		3,715	1,983	436	99	424	170	2,855	1,714
	%		53		23		40		60

Table 2.1 Continued

Destination 1990		Total	Female	Origin 1985 Urban: City No. (000s)	Female	Town No. (000s)	Female	Rural: County No. (000s)	Female
National									
Total		34,109	14,735	6,388	2,160	6,401	2,689	21,310	9,886
	%		43		34		42		46
City		21,246	8,716	4,422	1,636	4,159	1,757	12,,665	5,,323
	%		41		37		42		42
Town		6,954	2,994	1,257	372	1635	692	4,062	1,930
	%		43		30		42		48
County		5,899	3,025	709	152	607	240	4,583	2,633
	%		51		21		40		57

Source: Calculations by Mahmood Messkoub and Delia Davin, based on the 1990 Census, vol. IV, table 11.1.

Wuhan in Central China (Solinger 1995: 119). Studies of rural out-migration focusing on labour migration have found high proportions of males among the migrants. Findings from recent surveys of rural out-migration discussed by Mallée reported proportions of women varying from 16 to 30 per cent (Mallée 1995–6: 114–15). In China, as in other developing countries, social constraints have traditionally restricted women's mobility. These will be discussed at greater length in chapter 7. Such constraints are gradually being broken down by social and economic change. However, the rate of change in China's vast countryside is very variable. Pronounced local variations in the sex ratios of out-migrants are found. For example, a study of Wuwei county in Anhui, the county from which large numbers of women go to be housemaids in Beijing and other large cities, found that women comprised 46 per cent of out-migrants (Mallée 1995–6: 115). By contrast, a study of three villages in Gansu, Anhui and Zhejiang provinces made in 1990 found that fewer than 10 per cent of all migrants were female in each of the villages selected (Qian 1996).

Age

Just as migrant streams throughout the world are predominantly male, so they are also predominantly young. Young people are less likely to be tied down by family responsibilities and can be more easily spared from their homes. They are more adaptable, and, in many countries at least, are better educated than their elders, know more about the outside world and are better equipped to function in it. All these observations seem to hold true for China.

The 1986 Survey of 74 Cities and Towns showed that in the period since 1949, the peak age for migration had been 20–4, with about a quarter of all migrants having moved at these ages. The next most mobile age groups were 15–19 years and 25–9 years, although the percentages moving at these ages were considerably lower. The three young adult age groupings taken together accounted for more than half of all migrations.

It is generally agreed that young adults continued to dominate migration, in the post-reform period. The 1990 Census did not provide tabulated data relating to the age of migrants (Census 1990). However, migration schedules have been constructed from a sampling of the 1987 National Population Survey to show the rates of male and female migration at different ages (Ma et al. 1997: figure 1). These schedules show that between 1985 and 1987, migration was highest for young males between the late teens and early twenties, peaking at nearly 14.4 per 1,000 in the 20–3 age group. Female migration and male migration were both under 5 per 1,000 until the mid-teens. Male migration then grew faster than female migration until the late teens, when female migration took a dramatic lead, peaking at 30 per 1,000 for the 20–3 age group. However, if marriage migration is excluded from this peak, female migration falls to just 7 per 1,000, showing that men were still much more heavily involved in labour migration than women. Other significant features of these migration schedules are the rather low migration propensities at most ages, and the near-absence of change from infancy to the mid-teens. Normally a steep decline would be expected, with small children showing much greater mobility than those in their mid-teens. The low migration propensities indicate that restrictions constrained migration in all age groups and were especially effective in restricting the movement of parents with their infant children.

Evidence from recent surveys of rural migrants in the reform period also indicates that the majority are young, with 70 or 80 per cent of the total being under 30 (Mallée 1995–6: 117). Like the 1987 Population National Survey, these surveys show differences in age for male and female migrants. Female migration is concentrated across a narrower age range and falls off rapidly after the mid-twenties. Thus in data from a Ministry of Agriculture Survey about 83 per cent of female migrants were under 30 against only 55 per cent of male migrants (Mallée 1995–6: 117). Marriage affects the likelihood of migration differently for men and women. While marriage tends to confine women to their villages, it has little effect on the male propensity to migrate. These differences will be discussed in greater detail in chapters 7 and 8.

EDUCATIONAL LEVEL

Education to high levels leads to greater specialisation in work and often to greater mobility. Even the most basic education tends to impart transferable skills, extends horizons and increases aspirations. It is hardly surprising, therefore, that migrants everywhere tends to be more highly educated than the average population of their place of origin.

A strong positive association between education and the propensity to migrate emerges from the data of the 1986 Survey. In the 37-year period covered by the Survey, university graduates were 6 per cent of all graduates to towns and 13 per cent of migrants to extra-large cities, although they formed less than 1 per cent of the total population of China. A senior or even a junior middle school education was also, though to a lesser extent, associated with an increased propensity to migrate. People with less education were less likely to migrate. According to the Survey, illiterates and those with only a primary school education were under-represented. They made up only 11–13 per cent and 20–8 per cent of all migrants respectively, but 32 and 36 per cent respectively of the total population (Xiong and Day 1994: 11–12).

In post-reform China there is evidence that the majority of rural migrants have had at least junior middle school education (Mallée 1996: 118). The proportion of migrants who had completed this level of education was higher than the proportion in their communities of origin. Permanent migrants are much better educated than seasonal migrants, indicating perhaps that they are better able to secure the most desirable jobs in China's highly competitive labour market.

There are many factors that make us expect a positive association between educational level and migration, and such an association is commonly found in studies of migration elsewhere in the world. However, as Mallée points out, we should beware in the case of the Chinese data of accepting that what we are seeing is educational selectivity in migration. The young are the best educated age group in the Chinese countryside, and males of all ages tend to be better educated than females. The 1990 Census showed that about 50 per cent of the population aged 15–29 years had a junior high school education, a figure that declined to 14 per cent for the over-fifties. Illiteracy among males was concentrated in the older age brackets, but surprising numbers of young women were illiterate (Census 1990: Vol. 2, Tables 5.8 and 5.12). As migrants tend to be young men, we would therefore expect them to have a better education than an average uncontrolled for age or sex for their home communities.

DIRECTION AND DESTINATION OF MIGRATION

The majority of migrations in China are within the same province. According to the 1990 Census there were over 23 million movements within the same province in 1985–90 compared to over 11 million between provinces. Available data indicate a split which was approximately two-thirds intra- and one third inter-provincial in 1990, representing rapid change from 1988 when less than one fifth of

Table 2.2 Percentages of intra-county, intra-provincial and inter-provincial migrants among migrants nationally and in each of the three regions

Year	Region of origin	Destination		
		Same county	Same province	Other provinces
1988	National	43.6	36.5	19.9
1990	National	30.7	33.1	36.2
	Eastern	47.7	31.1	21.2
	Central	26.3	35	38.7
	Western	30.9	29.2	39.9

Source: Data from a Ministry of Agriculture Survey reported in 'Rural Labour Mobility in Economic Development', *Chinese Rural Economy*, no. 1, 1995, 48–9.

migration had been inter-provincial (see Table 2.2). If we use destination as a marker of distance, assuming that the distance travelled will be least for migrants who stay within the same county and most for inter-provincial migrants, we can draw some interesting conclusions. Long-haul migration as a proportion of all migration increased remarkably between 1988 and 1990. As Table 2.2 shows, migrants from the more developed Eastern Region tend to stay closer to their origin areas, whereas migrants from the less developed Central and Western Regions are more heavily involved in long-haul migration.[4] The most common direction of longer-haul migration is therefore from west to east; from the inland provinces of west and central China to the seaboard provinces; especially those of southeast China. There are other streams, for example of construction workers, engineers, technicians and traders to the developing border provinces, but the numbers involved are smaller.

Big cities everywhere have attracted very large numbers of migrants, and the peasant in the big city has caught the attention of the press, becoming the stereotype of the migrant in media coverage. Other migrants also go to still rural but rapidly industrialising areas such as the Pearl River Delta in Guangdong Province and the countryside of southern Jiangsu. Some small towns also experience considerable influxes. There is a hierarchy of migratory flows in China between the rural areas and the different categories of urban areas. Discussion of these, like all discussion of urbanisation in China, is bedevilled by methodological problems. First, Chinese definitions of urban and non-urban populations vary. Counts of urban population sometimes include the peasant population living in agricultural areas within the administrative boundaries of urban areas, but do not do so consistently. Second, the definitions of the various ranks of urban places have changed several times. Third, with the growth of urbanisation, urban places are sometimes promoted, for example, from 'town' to 'city' as they achieve the population threshold set for a new status. Fourth, as we have seen, household registration status is not necessarily the same as residential reality. People may retain their rural registration despite many years' residence in urban areas while a minority of those who live in the rural areas such as engineers, technicians or officials retain their urban registration.[5]

The 1986 Migration Survey used five categories of urban settlement for its analysis (extra-large cities, large cities, medium-sized cities, small towns and towns). The Census uses only three geographical divisions: cities, towns and counties. These categories are also commonly used in China in popular discourse, in media reports and in scholarly discussion. As administrative units, prior to 1982, they could be fairly precisely defined. Cities were designated by the state on the basis of population size (usually over 100,000 residents). Towns obtained their designation on the basis of both the size and *hukou* status of their population. Thus a settlement of 3,000 or more was a town if over 70 per cent of its population had non-agricultural registration. With a population of 2,500–3,000, 85 per cent of the population had to have non-agricultural registration for the settlement to be designated as a town. The 'county' category is usually treated as being synonymous with 'the rural areas'. Small rural towns which have not been given urban status are included in this category. 'County' in Chinese demographic terminology should therefore be understood as meaning 'country' or 'rural'. In the 1980s there was an enormous increase in the number of settlements designated as cities and towns, with the result that newly designated urban areas contained much agricultural land and many people with agricultural household registration. It was recognised that these changes, though perhaps useful in promoting the development of smaller urban settlements, had destroyed the statistical consistency of figures for the urban populations and had inflated the urban population unrealistically. In response to this difficulty, the designers of the 1990 Census drew up complex rules which in effect set up a new system for defining the urban population. One set of totals for the urban population was still based on the population of administrative units designated urban. This yields a total urban population of nearly 53 per cent, clearly a gross exaggeration in terms of people's occupations and lifestyles. Another, much deflated set was obtained by abandoning the administrative principle and subtracting the population of non-urban areas now included within the administrative boundaries of a larger urban area. The data produced by this statistical manoeuvring are generally regarded as plausible. They yielded an urban population of just over 26 per cent of total population recorded by the 1990 Census, up from 21 per cent in the 1982 Census.

In popular consciousness, the hierarchy of size coincides with a hierarchy of desirability: most people would like to go to the big cities. However, entry to larger settlements has tended to be much more strictly controlled than access to smaller ones, so in the past many had to settle for a town. The differential effect of control is clear in evidence from the 1986 Survey of 74 Cities and Towns which showed the proportion of permanent in-migrants in the urban population was in inverse relation to the size of the settlement. Migrants were 7.3 per cent of the population of towns compared with 3.5 per cent in medium cities and only 2.7 per cent in extra large cities in the period 1985–6 (Wang 1994: 29; Goldstein and Goldstein 1991: 5). There were policy changes in the mid-1980s, with a new regulation which enlarged the area of some existing cities and promoted the development of new towns in the rural areas.

In 1985, the Ministry of Public Security issued a new regulation on temporary residence certificates for the urban areas. Migrant workers who obtained these were in future to be allowed to live in the urban areas but without enjoying the social benefits to which permanent urban residents were entitled. Together with the evolution of a private market in food, this measure made it possible for rural migrants to survive in the cities for significant periods. Migration was thereafter characterised by upward flows, especially by rural to city and rural to town flows (Ma et al. 1997: 13).

Evidence from the 1992 Census shows the same trends. Of the 34 million migrants recorded by the Census, 62 per cent originated in the rural areas. Of these, 43 per cent went to cities within the same province and 17 per cent to cities in other provinces. Twelve per cent went to towns within the province and 7 per cent went to towns in other provinces. Thus 79 per cent of all rural migrants went to the urban areas. Of the 19 per cent of all migrants who originated in the towns, 65 per cent went to the cities, 26 per cent to other towns and only 9 per cent to rural counties. The remaining 19 per cent of all migrants originated in the cities, and of these 69 per cent went to other cities, 20 per cent to the towns and 11 per cent to the rural areas (See Table 2.3).

Table 2.3 Internal migration in China by origin (residence in 1985) and destination (residence in 1990)

Destination 1990		Total	Origin 1985 Urban: City No. (000s)	%	Town No. (000s)	%	Rural: County No. (000s)	%
Other Provinces								
Total		11,085	2,812	44	1,549	24	6,724	32
	%	100	25		14		61	
City		6,500	2,046	32	911	14	3,543	17
	%	100	31		14		55	
Town		2,401	493	8	455	7	1,453	7
	%	100	21		19		60	
County		2,184	273	4	183	3	1,728	8
	%	100	13		8		79	
Same Province								
Total		23,014	3,576	56	4,852	76	14,586	68
	%	100	16		21		63	
City		14,746	2,376	37	3,248	51	9,122	43
	%	100	16		22		62	
Town		4,553	764	12	1,180	18	2,609	12
	%	100	17		26		57	
County		3,715	436	7	424	7	2,855	13
	%	100	12		11		77	
National								
Total		34,109	6,388	100	6,401	100	21,310	100
	%	100	19		19		62	
City		21,246	4,422	69	4,159	65	12,665	59
	%	100	21		20		59	
Town		6,954	1,257	20	1,635	26	4,062	19
	%	100	18		24		58	
County		5,899	709	11	607	9	4,583	22
	%	100	12		10		78	

Source: Calculations by Mahmood Messkoub and Delia Davin based on the 1990 Census, vol. IV, table 11.1.

The forms and patterns of migration change and develop constantly. Migration now takes place over much greater distances than it did in the early 1980s. Seasonal migration is still dominant but the importance of longer-term migration is growing. In the early period, most migration was from comparatively well-developed areas to growth points nearby. In recent years there has been a rapid growth in migration from poorer areas.

SUMMARY

It is very difficult to estimate the number of internal migrants in China, but the proportion of the population on the move is certainly significant and has caused great concern in a country where mobility rates have, until recently, been extraordinarily low, owing to the dominance of the traditional small peasant economy and exceptionally effective policies to discourage migration. Although it is not easy to be exact about the sex ratios, it is clear that migrants are predominantly male. If marriage migration is excluded, male migrants appear still more dominant, reflecting the fact that most labour migrants are men. Most migrants are in their late teens or early twenties, but the age concentration is more marked for women than for men. Migrants are well educated by the standards of the community from which they come, most having attended junior middle school.

The relaxation on population movement and the rapid economic growth which China has experienced in recent years has created a great variety of population flows. Not only peasants, but urban people too are migrating in much greater numbers than in the past. But rural to urban population flows have grown fastest and the typical migrant in China is a young male peasant from west or central China seeking employment in an urban area either within his own province or in the rapidly developing areas of coastal China.

It is very difficult to estimate the number of internal migrants in China, but the usual guestimates of around 60 or 70 million do not imply a particularly mobile population by international standards. A high percentage of the country's population is still involved in small-scale peasant agriculture in which, until very recently, the expectation is that one will be born, live and die in the same small area. In addition, a rigid system of movement control and an employment system which discouraged mobility has until recently prevented free movement of peasants or even urban people. The subject of the next chapter will be the modifications made to this system in the 1980s.

3 Reform Era Policies on Population Movement

> Massive, disorderly movement of the population has been one of China's most serious social problems since the 1980s. Due to the rapid development of the urban economy, peasant migration to urban areas now numbers in the hundreds of millions and has become a social trend. ... The cities have limited capacity; they have their own weight to carry and they require the mobile population to have qualities that are compatible with the cities' own development. Therefore, reducing the 'swelling' by limiting entry to the cities has once again become a hot issue in the cities this year.
>
> (Zhang Wenyi, *The Mobile Population should not have Free Reign of the Cities*, 1995)

The impact of the economic reforms since 1978 has undermined the state's ability to suppress rural–urban migration and has created pressure for the reform of the household registration system. The response of the state has been cautious. It has reversed Maoist policies designed to limit urbanisation and has recognised that urbanisation is a necessary and desirable development for China, but at the same time it tries to keep control of the type of urbanisation that occurs. It has allowed criticism of the household registration system and discussion of how it might be reformed. Experimental modifications of the system have been tried at local level, and, when these have been successful they have been introduced at national level. It has further introduced a national identity card. Finally, by allowing very large numbers of people to live in urban places despite their lack of a non-agricultural registration, it has reduced the impact that registration once had on an individual's choices and chances.

Despite the calls for further reform, the complete abolition of the household registration system does not seem to be on the horizon. The system is embedded in and supports the functioning of China's whole economic and social system. It is a means of social control for the state, but also underpins much social stratification and allows a particular form of labour market segmentation. It is frequently argued in Chinese debates about the system that thorough-going reform would lead to chaos and disorder, especially in the cities and that only a gradual approach is possible.[1]

THE SMALL TOWN POLICY

The urbanisation policy promoted after the economic reforms was summed up in the rather unwieldy slogan: 'Strictly control the development of the large cities, rationally develop the medium sized cities and vigorously promote the development of small cities and towns' (Cheng 1991: 63). It was hoped that migrants could be kept away from large cities of 500,000 and more. This would be achieved in part by allowing medium cities of 200,000–500,000 to grow if they had the potential to do so, and by actively encouraging the development of small cities and towns with fewer than 200,000 inhabitants. The main focus of this policy has been on *xian* (county towns) and on the *zhen* (rural towns) and *xiang* (townships) which come below them in the urban hierarchy and might average around 15,000 inhabitants.

The focus on small towns fitted very well with the promotion of non-farm employment and of rural industry, already an important growth sector in 1970s and one of the great successes of the 1980s. Traditional China had a well-developed system of rural market towns that functioned as centres of distribution and exchange for the wider countryside (Skinner 1964–5). After 1949, as the state took control of the distribution of goods, markets were discouraged and suppressed, and as peasant sideline production was obstructed, these market towns went into decline. In the collective period, the main importance of rural towns was as administrative and educational centres.

In the 1970s, the growth of rural industrialisation transformed the function of small rural towns. Most rural industries, especially those concerned with processing and manufacturing, are based in small towns. When collective farming was abandoned, non-farm and sideline production that had been within the commune structure fell into private hands or came under the control of village committees (Byrd and Lin 1990). The privatisation of farming under the household responsibility system and the increases in the prices paid for agricultural goods provided new sources of capital for rural industry. The government recognised the potential of this sector as an alternative to rural–urban migration for reducing the surplus agricultural labour force in the slogan 'leave the soil but not the countryside' (*'litu bu lixiang'*). The promotion of small towns and rural industry was undertaken in a deliberate attempt to limit rural urban migration (Goldstein and Goldstein 1990; Middelhoek 1992: 241). Support for these alternative foci of growth in the form of tax concessions and special incentives was made available. Rural industry enjoys other advantages over its competitors. It pays lower wages and offers very limited benefits compared with urban-based state industry. From 1984 the restriction of private operations in rural industry ceased completely. The results were phenomenal. The number of rural enterprises grew from 1.5 million in 1978 to 18.5 million in 1990 and 23 million by 1996. The percentage of the rural workforce employed by rural industry increased about 10 per cent in 1978 to over 22 per cent in 1990 and almost 30 per cent in 1996. (SSB 1991b and 1997). By 1995, 120 million rural surplus labourers were said to have found work in rural industry (FBIS, 30 May 1996).

Entry into the 60,000 small market towns (*zhen*) below county level was eased in 1984 by the introduction of a new registration category, small town household, self-supplying in grain (*zili kouliang chengzhen hukou*). The measure was thought important enough to be announced as an experiment in a Central Committee Circular (Document No. 1 1984) and was extended to the whole country later in the year. It allowed peasants who wished to settle in small towns to obtain a non-agricultural registration for themselves and for family members (Davis 1995: 108). The conditions were that they had to find employment and housing in the towns themselves, and that they should either obtain grain for themselves from their villages or buy it from a grain-shop at a non-subsidised rate. A further condition was that they should give up their contract land in the village.

This new measure allowed many peasants already living in small towns to regularise their position. They could obtain urban registration not only for themselves, but also for family members. This was a significant concession: the right to be accompanied by family members is not automatically conceded even to official migrants who move as a result of a state job assignment. On the other hand, this new urban *hukou* for small towns was inferior to normal urban registration in that it did not carry with it the right to housing, subsidised healthcare and a guaranteed food supply. In the long run the influence of this new category may be limited. By 1988 about 4.6 million peasants had transferred their registration to small towns, but thereafter there have been fewer reports of peasants taking up this new *hukou* (Mallée 1995: 14–15).

THE INTRODUCTION OF TEMPORARY REGISTRATION

Despite the impressive growth of rural industry, the small town strategy was not enough to solve the problem of the surplus rural labour force. More and more labour became surplus. At the same time, the 1980s saw an increased demand for labour in the cities, in construction, the service trades and even manufacture. This demand could not always be satisfied from within the urban population, partly because natural growth rates had been extremely low since the 1970s, and also because urban people were increasingly unwilling to take on heavy, dirty or menial work. By the mid-1980s, millions of peasants had been drawn into the urban labour force and were living and working in the urban areas, although their household registration remained in the villages. Free markets, the easy availability of grain and the fact that employers welcomed migrant labour made it more difficult to exclude them. Many of these workers were brought into the cities under contract to state enterprises and state construction companies. Under the 1958 *hukou* regulations, incomers were obliged to register with the Public Security Bureau if they stayed more than three days, and to apply for permission to stay more than three months, but these rules were increasingly ignored.

The situation had some real advantages for the state. The fast-growing economy had access to a cheap but highly flexible labour force. Not only could extra labour be recruited at short notice, the uncertain legal status of unofficial migrants meant that they could be rounded up and returned to their villages when there was a downturn in economic activity. As the incomers had no rights to health services and education or housing, the costs to the state of their presence in the urban areas were minimal. On the other hand, complaints about the migrant presence were growing. It was claimed that migrants were responsible for overcrowding, births outside the plan, disruption to the traffic, crime and other social ills. There was intense debate about what should be done. The *hukou* regulations were being so widely ignored that they were in danger of falling into disrepute, and the state lacked the machinery to monitor and supervise the migrant population. Moreover the state's claim that it should control the movement of labour looked increasingly anachronistic when in most spheres the market was being pronounced sovereign.

The solution was to introduce new regulations for temporary residence. The city of Wuhan had experimented with such measures in local regulations in the early 1980s (Solinger 1997) and they were introduced on a national scale in regulations issued by the Ministry of Public Security in 1985. Applicants for temporary registration had to be 16 years or over, and had to supply proof of identity and a photograph. Married women of child-bearing age also had to show their birth planning card which recorded their fertility history and the contraception they were using (see chapter 7). Temporary registration cards (*jizhuzheng* for labour migrants and *zanzhuzheng* for the rest) were issued for six months or for a year, and were renewable (Hoy 1996: 22–3). Holders were required to show their cards on request, to agree to abide by local and state regulations and not to engage in criminal activity. A fee was charged when the card was issued, and migrants were sometimes required to return to the Public Security Bureau at monthly intervals to pay another fee supposed to compensate for their use of urban amenities (fieldwork interviews, Chengdu and Beijing, 1994). The 1985 regulations allowed migrants with temporary registration to rent housing in the urban areas, thus legitimising an already widespread practice.

It was hoped that the system of temporary registration would restore some control of the migrant population to the local authorities, assist with the maintenance of social order and help urban planners. The fertility of migrants was a matter of particular concern to officials, hence the special rules for the registration of married women of child-bearing age. The system also enabled local administrations to raise revenue from the migrant population in the form of registration fees. The existence of a temporary registration system allows local governments to reduce migrant populations selectively when they so wish by expelling all unregistered outsiders. This also gives them a rough-and-ready way of distinguishing between the more successful and stable migrants who are more likely to register, and unemployed or underemployed transients. Migrants have to pay fees for temporary registration. Nonregistered migrants can be rounded up, fined and even sent back to their native places. Registration drives are held to try to increase the numbers registering but it seems that success remains variable, and the energy devoted to implementing the system varies widely from one location to another. Unless they feel there is a real danger that they will be caught, migrants have little incentive to register. It was estimated in Shanghai in 1993 that only about 20 per cent of the transient population had escaped registration (Mallée 1995: 13), but elsewhere registration rates are believed to be much lower. In 1995, the *People's Daily* carried a report that of 80 million migrants, 36 million (45 per cent) had not registered (Hoy 1996: 23). The success of the temporary registration system has been limited, but it has introduced enough flexibility to allow the *hukou* system to survive, albeit in a modified form. Since 1985, the authorities have been able to keep official migration with *hukou* transfers to a very low level indeed.

HUKOU TRANSFERS AND SALES

The limits on formal transfer of registration were less severe in the 1980s and 1990s than they had been in the 1960s and 1970s (Mallée 1995: 11–12) and this is reflected in the percentage of the population holding non-agricultural registration in the 1980s (see Table 3.1). At first the growth only made up lost ground. In 1988 the proportion of the population holding non-agricultural *hukous* once more attained the level it had been at the Great Leap Forward period (1959–60). The government appears to be determined to retain control over transfers from agricultural to non-agricultural registration. In the late 1980s, perhaps influenced by an economic downturn, new control measures were introduced for *hukou* transfer. The impact is reflected in the lack of growth in the proportion of the total population holding non-agricultural registration from 1989 to 1990 (see Table 3.1). Of course, the growth of the urban population has been quite rapid, but a

Table 3.1 Non-agricultural population, selected years, 1956–95

Year	Non-agricultural population (1000s)	% of total population	Year	Non-agricultural population (1000s)	% of total population
1956	100,020	15.9	1985	210,540	20.1
1957	106,180	16.4	1986	209,020	19.8
1959	135,670	20.2	1987	215,920	20.1
1960	137,310	20.7	1988	225,510	20.7
1962	112,710	16.7	1989	233,710	21.1
1975	142,780	15.4	1990	238,870	21.1
1979	161,860	16.6	1991	244,180	21.3
1980	168,000	17.0	1992	252,980	21.9
1981	174,130	17.4	1993	260,680	22.4
1982	179,100	17.6	1994	276,380	23.5
1983	183,780	17.9	1995	282,430	23.8
1984	196,860	19.0			

Source: SSB, *China Population Statistics Yearbook*, 1996, 351.

high proportion of the growth is due to the presence of temporary migrants whose entitlements are minimal compared to those of the non-agricultural population. Urban population growth is thus being achieved at a low cost to the state.

As explained in chapter 1, a *hukou* transfer can be obtained when a person is transferred or assigned to a job in another place, or when they move for education. *Hukou* transfer was sometimes also granted for the purposes of family reunion, but such applications had low priority and were often refused. State enterprises often have difficulty in arranging even lateral *hukou* transfers between one urban area and another for their employees or their family members.[2] This was considered one of the most troublesome of managerial tasks in government offices in the 1960s and 1970s (fieldwork, 1975–6). One problem was that a large number of agencies tended to be involved in transfers. This is demonstrated by the fact that when Shanghai decided to set up a Population Control Office to co-ordinate *hukou* transfer in 1987, five organisations had to be represented: the Public Security Bureau, the Labour Bureau, the Personnel Bureau, the Higher Education Bureau and the Demobilisation Bureau (Mallée 1995: 11). Chinese researchers have estimated that the national rate of *hukou* transfer is 2:10,000. In an article that appeared in 1989 pleading for greater flexibility, it was claimed that at the rate then prevailing it would take the steel town of Anshan seven years to clear the accumulated backlog of *hukou* transfer applications.

A new form of *hukou* transfer has been the sale of non-agricultural *hukou*. The smaller cities began to sell permanent registration certificates in the late 1980s and the practice was introduced in the big cities in the early 1990s. The price seems to depend very much on what the market would bear. In Haian, Jiangsu Province a permit cost 3,500–6,000 yuan in 1993. In the Pearl River Delta the price could be as high as 20,000–30,000 yuan (Li 1995: 41). A Beijing *hukou* in 1994 cost 30,000 for suburban residence but as much as 50,000 yuan for a city permit, or 100,000 if it was paid by the employer (*Jingji Wanbao*, 22 June 1994). In 1994 Shanghai introduced a 'Blue Seal' card, which gave the carrier rights equal to those of a permanent resident but required the investment of 1 million yuan over a two-year period (Hoy 1995: 25). The government of Shenzhen charged 40,000–60,000 for a *hukou* for the Special Economic Zone (Zhou 1996: 140). Similar systems exist in Liaoning Province and elsewhere (Cao 1993). A purchased non-agricultural *hukou* is valid only in the area for which it is purchased. Peasants also have to pay for a certificate confirming that they have permission to leave their villages because this must be presented when they buy an urban *hukou*. The sum of money involved, however, is usually quite small. There are reports of ordinary peasant migrants purchasing urban registration for towns and small cities, but it seems likely that most purchasers of urban registration for the largest cities are the new rich, successful entrepreneurs of rural origin. The sale of *hukous* does not take place on a scale sufficient to affect the numbers of the non-agricultural population significantly, but the trade gives urban areas a new way to raise revenue and allows them to attract rich permanent residents selectively. On the negative side the practice seems to have increased cynicism and resentment about the stratification imposed by the *hukou* system. It has also opened up considerable scope for corruption and the development of a black market in household registrations. Enterprises have sometimes been required to pay charges for each floater they employ, but again it seems likely that this would be difficult to enforce (Chan 1992: 12–16).

IDENTITY CARDS

Regulations to establish a system of identity cards were introduced in 1986. They were not intended to replace household registration; on the contrary they were to be issued by the offices that supervised registration. They should probably be seen as a refinement of the registration system. The card was supposed to allow carriers to establish their identity. They were to be produced when applications were made for loans and business licences. Householders letting rooms to migrants were supposed to check their tenants' cards (Hoy 1995: 32).

The system is not yet well established. Cards were issued first in the large cities and it was thought that it would take some years before the system could be extended to the countryside. This caused indignation among city residents who regarded cards as an instrument of social control and argued that it was rural migrants, not residents, who needed such control (fieldwork interviews, 1994). There have been reports of cards being forged, and a market for stolen cards has developed. However, identity cards are still of rather marginal importance in Chinese life. For the moment at least the household registration system is much more important in social control and in the management of migration.

FACILITATING MIGRATION

In addition to the many policies developed to control migrants, some official effort has been made to design policies that will facilitate migration and help migrants find employment. In co-operation with local governments in the destination areas the Ministry of Personnel has established regional 'talent markets' at which professionals can register in order to seek work in the coastal cities (*China Daily*, 8 September 1994). In a more humble way some ordinary employment bureaux have been established in the destination areas to bring employers and migrant labourers together. The Women's Federation, an official body that promotes the interests of women, helps female migrants find jobs and has been especially active in introducing maids to would-be employers in the big cities.

Unsurprisingly, destination area governments tend to be most concerned with the problems of migrant control, while the governments of the sending areas try to ensure that migrants are as well prepared as possible and sometimes assist them in reaching their destinations. Imitating the private labour contractors, some county governments in provinces such as Sichuan actively recruit migrant labour and seek contracts for the workers in the industrialising coastal areas. They may organise transport for the workers either simply for the initial journey, or, if strong contacts are established, for return journeys at the Chinese New Year. Two of the richer counties in the Chengdu area have even established schools for would-be migrants at which teenagers from local villages improve their literacy, book-keeping and other skills in the hope of obtaining a better job than is usually open to the unskilled migrants (fieldwork, 1994). County government offices in Sichuan display recruitment advertisements for migrant labour, including calls for skilled Sichuanese cooks to join Chinese restaurants in New York.

Governments in the sending areas clearly recognise a self-interest when they engage in activities to promote migration and assist migrants. Officials are quite aware of the importance of remittances not only to the villages but even to the provincial economy. Interestingly they also recognise some conflict of interest with the destination areas. Officials in Sichuan sometimes voice the opinion that migrants to Guangdong and other areas of the country should be allowed to settle there if they so wish. Already concerned about a situation that they feel forces their province to act as a 'nursery' producing labourers for richer areas, they resent discussions that appear to label Sichuanese migrants as a 'problem'. However, some also argue that out-migration and settlement elsewhere may be the only solution to Sichuan's population problems (fieldwork interviews, 1994).

SUMMARY AND PROSPECTS

In the early 1980s the urbanisation policy of the Chinese government was based on the promotion of small town development. Thanks to the remarkable growth of rural industry, small towns did provide employment for many millions of rural labourers but this was not sufficient to stem the tide of rural to urban migration. The growth and dynamism of the Chinese economy in 1980s created a need for much greater labour mobility than the operation of the household registration system in past decades had allowed. The advent of a free market in grain made it possible for migrants to work in the cities while retaining agricultural registration.

The authorities have introduced various modifications to the household responsibility system in order to give it more flexibility. Most notably they set up a system of temporary registration in order to legalise the migrant presence in the city without a concomitant increase in the non-agricultural population. There have also been some very limited measures to streamline *hukou* transfer. Urban household registration is now offered for sale to those few who can afford exorbitant prices. The introduction of identity cards may have been envisaged as a step to reforming the *hukou* system but has so far been taken no further.

There is much debate on the *hukou* system but little agreement. Radicals argue that it is a breach of the human right to freedom of movement, that it impedes normal economic growth and that it causes much human misery through the separation of families (Ren 1996). Conservatives prophesy chaos and disorder as migrants flood into the cities if the system is abolished (Zhang 1995). It is certainly true that the reform of the *hukou* system raises many complex problems because the system is so deeply enmeshed in the social fabric and economic structures. It is the basis of important forms of social stratification, and inevitably those interest groups which benefit from its existence, notably most urban residents, will not welcome its demise. It seems probable that the Chinese state will for some time be too fearful of the consequences to attempt the abolition of household registration. It will therefore be forced to continue to modify and adapt the system, attempting to reconcile it with the needs of a modern economy.

4 Why People Migrate

The very first year we farmed our contract land the crops failed. The grain we got was next to nothing – never mind paying our taxes, it wasn't even enough to keep belly from backbone. That's why there's so many of us trying to make a living in the city this year. Some of the men pop corn and some of them are in construction teams putting up buildings for the government. The women have gone to the cities as maids. None of us are beggars, at least none from our village. ... We leave the village to work and make money. ... We started working when we got to Hefei. We worked there for a week and then made enough for our fares to Beijing. Making money in the big cities is easy.

(Child migrant from Anhui interviewed in Beijing in 1984. Zhang and Sang 1986: 3–7)

Individuals migrate because they think that they can improve their own lives or those of their families by doing so. Economic migration is triggered by the knowledge (or belief) that better economic opportunities exist in some other place. It follows that where regional and local economic inequality is considerable, people are likely to migrate if it is possible for them to do so. Factors such as poverty, lack of economic opportunity, land shortage and low living standards at home function as push factors, while prosperity, opportunity, available employment and higher living standards in the place of destination are pull factors. The individual's decision to migrate involves a process of weighing up potential costs and benefits.[1] Migrants have to consider general factors such as the cost of travel and accommodation, the chances of finding work and the prevailing wage rates in the destination area compared with those in the home area. They will also be swayed by individual factors such as contacts with relatives or friends in the destination areas, or the potential effect of their absence on the household left behind. Knowledge of conditions elsewhere is important in migration decisions and therefore modern communications play a significant role. Potential migrants may learn of opportunities from the media, from television images or from returnees. Naturally, the migrant will tend to have a more accurate knowledge of conditions at home than of those prevailing in the place of destination, but the

49

belief that a better life is to be had elsewhere can suffice as a pull factor, even if it turns out to be mistaken.

This chapter will look at the determinants of migration first at the macro level, exploring national and regional developments in China that have induced so many millions of people to move, and then at the micro or local level, examining the sort of factors which explain why, even within the same area, some individuals take the decision to seek for work elsewhere, while others stay where they are.

MACRO PERSPECTIVES

Regional Inequalities in China: Origins and Present Realities

[I]nequalities in the pattern and process of development provide the backdrop against which a great deal of migration involving the Third World can be viewed.

(Parnwell 1993: 73)

Mainland China is governed as a single political entity. Useful generalisations can be made about the history, society and economics of China as a country, or as a distinct cultural area. Yet cultural and political unity should not be allowed to obscure the fact that China, like the USA and the former USSR, has a geographical, climatic and agricultural diversity more usually associated with a continent. It is hardly surprising that there are also great contrasts in the country's regional levels of economic development and thus in income levels and standards of living. Differences in resource endowments, in climate and in accessibility and patterns of trade and foreign impact have all played a part in the historical development of these disparities. Despite a political commitment to bring about greater equality, economic development in the past four decades has not succeeded in eliminating regional inequalities. Indeed there are now striking contrasts in levels of development because of the rapid economic progress made in some regions in recent years. In terms of national income per capita, still a useful if somewhat crude criterion of development, China qualifies as one of the world's poorest countries, yet it contains foci of development such as parts of the provinces of Guangdong, Jiangsu and Liaoning, where per capita income, living standards and measures of welfare approach those of a middle income country. Figure 4.1 shows the wide spectrum of per capita gross domestic product by province.

51

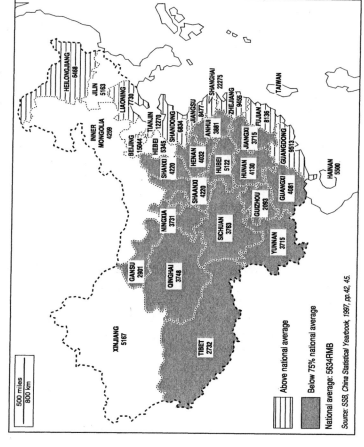

Figure 4.1 Per capita gross domestic product by province, 1996 (RMB)

Source: SSB, *China Statistical Yearbook*, 1997, pp. 42, 45.

The government in the Maoist period wanted to promote greater spatial equality in economic development for ideological and security reasons. It was committed to improving the lot of the poorest people, many of whom lived in the underdeveloped provinces of the hinterland. The concentration of industrialisation in the coastal region was widely attributed by patriotic intellectuals to the impact of foreign imperialism. Skewed industrial development symbolised China's past humiliations. Establishing a better balance could thus also be presented as righting these wrongs. Specifically, this meant encouraging economic and industrial development in the hinterland, especially in the western provinces. This policy had the added advantage that industry constructed far from the coast would be less vulnerable from attack by China's enemies.

The industrial development of the interior involved great problems. Chief among these was the high cost. It is true that the location of industry in China prior to 1949 was to some extent the result of the involvement of foreign capital. Much industry had grown up in and around the treaty ports and was associated with foreign trade. There were docks and shipyards, textile factories, plants which processed agricultural goods for export and others which produced utilities and goods for the consumption by the treaty port population. The most advanced heavy industry was in the northeast China, much of it developed under Japanese colonial rule. A small amount of industry was evacuated into the interior during the Second World War when the coastal regions were occupied by the Japanese, but the costs of this enterprise were very high. At the end of the war most companies shifted their operations back to the coast. The location of industry in the first half of the twentieth century in China was not merely the consequence of its close connection with foreign trade, it also reflected the general comparative advantage of the areas where it had been set up. The interior had originally offered less favourable prospects for development. By the mid-twentieth century it was at a further disadvantage to the coastal provinces being far from existing industrial centres, lacking industrial and urban infrastructure and having no pool of skilled or experienced labour. Inevitably the policy of creating new industries in the interior after 1949 was extremely expensive. Growth rates and returns to investment there were low compared with those which resulted from expanding existing industrial centres. It is hardly surprising that the rhetoric of promoting industry in the interior was not always reflected in the reality of the distribution of investment in the Maoist period.

Figure 4.2 Provinces and economic regions in China

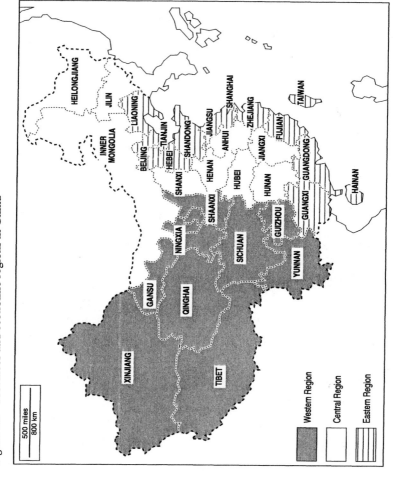

Economists of China have for some years argued that contrary to official claims, Maoist economic policy tolerated and even promoted regional disparities in economic development (Paine 1981). Recent analyses have given a better understanding of how and why these disparities continued under Mao, and of the effects that Deng Xiaoping's policies have had on them.[2] China's size makes detailed discussion of regional disparity difficult. The comparison of large units such as regions or even provinces involves much generalisation. This discussion will employ the division of China into the Eastern Region, the Central Region and the Western Region (shown in Figure 4.2) devised in China to facilitate the analysis of development. In terms of development, the Eastern or coastal region is the most developed, with comparatively high productivity and incomes, a skilled workforce, advanced technology, foreign connections and access to foreign investment. The Western Region is the least developed, lacks infrastructure, is overwhelmingly agricultural and is as a whole sparsely populated. The Central Region occupies an intermediate position. It is very mixed in development terms, containing densely populated provinces such as Hunan and Hubei whose economies are comparatively sophisticated and, at the other extreme, the sparsely populated underdeveloped territory of Inner Mongolia (Nei Menggu).

These regional divisions are not, of course, completely satisfactory as units of analysis. The pattern of regional disparity in China is too complicated to be captured in such a simple scheme. Chengdu and the Chengdu plain area in the Western Region are more developed than some areas of the coastal provinces. Moreover although the majority of counties officially designated 'poverty counties' lie in the Western Region, poverty counties are also to be found in the Central Region and the Eastern Region (Küchler 1990: 129). Even the most prosperous provinces like Guangdong and Shandong contain such pockets of poverty. Nearly all the areas of extreme difficulty suffer from harsh environments and inaccessibility. Although the regional division of China obscures some of the detail of diversity within regions, the contrasts it allows us to make at the macro level are useful to the study of inter-regional migration.

Table 4.1 shows the comparative population and area of the three regions and Figure 4.3 records the regional shares in total investment in capital construction between 1953 and 1992 (Zhao 1996: 135). It will be seen that the Eastern Region has received the largest share of investment capital for most of the four decades of the People's Republic. Only in 1966–70, when policy was determined by politics

Table 4.1   Population and area by region (1995)

Region	Population (millions)	Total population (%)	Area (10,000 sq. km)	Total area (%)
East	495.99	41.24	129.4	14.3
Central	429.94	35.75	273.0	29.4
West	276.70	23.01	527.6	56.3
Total	1202.63	100	903	100

Source: Calculated from SSB, *China Population Statistics Yearbook*, 1996.

Figure 4.3   Regional shares of total investment in capital construction (Index %)

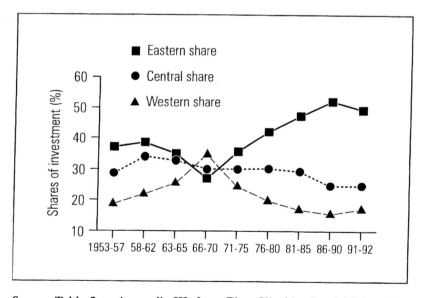

Source: Table 2 or Appendix III, from Zhao Xiaobin, Spatial Disparities and Economic development in China' *Development and Change* 27: 1, 1996.
© Blackwell Ltd, 1996. Reproduced by permission of the publisher.

rather than economics and the external threat loomed very large in the eyes of the Maoist leadership, did the Eastern Region lose its leading position in investment share. However, the Central and Western Regions' shares were not negligible – together they received more than 60 per cent of national investment (a little more than their share of population) for most of the Maoist years. In the Cultural Revolution years of 1966–70 this climbed to over 70 per cent. Moreover, looked at in per capita terms, the Eastern Region's advantage in investment in the earlier period disappears. It contains just over 40 per cent of China's population, yet, as Figure 4.3 shows, it did not gain a commensurate share of investment in capital construction until the mid-1970s.

Investment in the interior produced rapid industrial growth rates as these regions were starting from a very low base, but the impact of investment on economic growth as a whole was much less significant and it did little to eliminate regional disparities. Indeed, in no period did the effort to reduce regional inequality have any striking success, and regional inequality actually worsened over the four decades of the People's Republic (Zhao 1996; Leeming 1993: 65–7). More surprisingly, there is evidence that inequality grew fastest in the years of the late Maoist period when investment policy was most favourable to the interior (Zhao 1996: 137). A part of the explanation for this apparent contradiction may lie in a time lag between an investment being made and its return being realised. The time lag factor is not considered by Zhao, but it would also help to account both for the slight upturn he notes in the fortunes of the two poorer regions in the second half of the 1970s when their share of construction investment was falling. Doubtless, however, Zhao is right in his suggestion that the level of return on economic investment, low everywhere in the Maoist years, and especially disappointing in the less developed regions, contributed to the failure of investment in the interior to produce a narrowing of the gap. Even in the years when areas such as east Sichuan were exceptionally favoured by investment policy, they failed to shine (Zhao 1996: 142–3). Another factor in the poor performance of the interior regions was the so-called 'price scissors'. As in other socialist economies, in China in the Maoist period, agriculture was forced to finance industrialisation. To achieve this, agricultural goods, primary products and raw materials were underpriced, and industrial and manufactured goods overpriced. This pricing policy, designed to subsidise industry at the expense of agriculture, had unintended regional implications as well as its intended sectoral ones. Because the poor areas of the interior were largely agricultural whereas industry was concentrated in the coastal regions, the 'price scissors' inevitably transferred profit from the interior regions to the coastal provinces, thereby reducing the potential of Maoist investment policy for regional economic equalisation.

The 1980s and 1990s were marked by sharp change. Economic policy under Deng Xiaoping overtly favoured the Eastern Region in accordance with the slogan that 'some must get rich first'. The Eastern Region's share in construction investment rose sharply and there was a corresponding decrease in the shares of the Western and the Central Regions (see Figure 4.3). Moreover, the Eastern Region has been advantaged in other ways. Favourable and preferential policies in the treatment of foreign currency earnings, foreign trade, finance and investment were first established for the Special Economic Zones on the south China coast, and were later extended to the coastal cities and areas in the Eastern Region. This region has received almost all the foreign investment which has poured into the country under the Open Door policy. The coastal provinces share in total foreign investment has been much higher than the national average and the share of Guangdong province alone 25–30 per cent of total foreign direct investment in China in recent years (SSB 1996 and 1997).

It seems that this pronounced eastern bias did not immediately accelerate the growth of regional inequality (Zhao 1996: 149–55). The effect of the prioritisation of the coastal region took time to show through. Moreover some of Deng's policies may have worked to the advantage of the interior. The most spectacular reforms in the early 1980s were in agriculture. The increases achieved in agricultural productivity with the introduction of responsibility systems, the consequent increase in efficiencies and the hike in prices paid to the producer worked to the benefit of the primarily agricultural economy of the interior. The hike in agricultural prices also advantaged the agricultural regions by reducing the effect of the price scissors, although by the late 1980s the trend was once more against agriculture with an increase in agricultural production costs.

Increased disparities did become visible by the end of the 1980s. The whole of China under Deng benefited from greater efficiency of investment and significantly higher growth rates. However, most measures of economic progress in the years since the introduction of the economic reforms reflect the advantaged position of the Eastern Region. Its national income grew by 8.55 per cent per annum between 1981 and 1992 by comparison with 8.23 per cent growth in the Western Region and 7.7 per cent growth in the Central Region. Moreover, from the early 1990s, the evidence of both growth rates and investments indicates a pronounced trend to growing spacial disparity (Zhao 1996: 155).

If we put attempts to measure trends to one side and look at point-in-time measures, there is much evidence of uneven economic development and its consequences for wages and living standards. Per capita gross domestic product for 1996 was displayed in Figure 4.1. Figures 4.4–4.8 show the provincial variations in other indicators of economic development for 1995 – per capita industrial output, per capita rural household net income, per capita output of town and village enterprises, per capita foreign direct investment and per capita total construction output value. The data on which the tables are based are given in Table 4.2. Together these indicators illustrate the pre-eminence of the coastal region. The disparities of wealth, development, industrialisation and employment implied by these variations have obvious implications for migration. If labour is free to move, there will be migration from poorer areas to wealthier ones where earnings are higher. The regional pattern of past and present development would clearly lead us to expect movement into the coastal region.

The record of township and village enterprises and foreign-owned or joint Sino-foreign enterprises, the two types of industry where growth of employment has been most rapid, provides another explanation of the pulling power of the coastal region. The fastest and most successful development of town and village enterprises has been in Shandong, Jiangsu, Zhejiang, Fujian and Guangdong, while foreign investment has been concentrated in Guangdong Province (see Figures 4.4 and 4.5).

The case of construction is perhaps different. Construction, while reinforcing the existing pull towards the coast, also gives rise to migrations to other destinations. Figure 4.8 shows per capita gross output value of construction by province. It shows the expected concentration of construction in the coastal provinces and the capital, but also that there is considerable construction activity in the border provinces of Xinjiang and Heilongjiang, while Inner Mongolia falls into a middle category. Construction is relevant to a study of migration. It generates a temporary demand for labourers to do heavy, dirty and unpleasant work which local people, especially in the more developed or urbanised areas, may not be willing to perform. It also creates jobs for skilled workers for which, in the less developed areas, local people may lack the training. In both cases a high level of construction activity will tend to induce in-migration.

Figure 4.4 Per capita industrial output by province, 1995

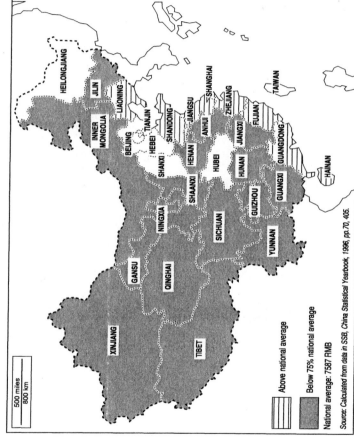

Source: Calculated from data in SSB, *China Statistical Yearbook*, 1996, pp. 70, 405.

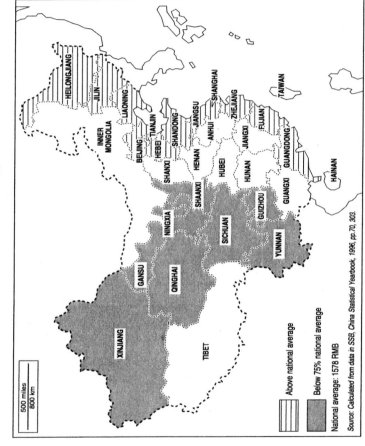

Figure 4.5 Per capita rural household net income by province

Source: Calculated from data in SSB, *China Statistical Yearbook*, 1996, pp. 70, 303.

Figure 4.6 Per capita output of town and village enterprises by province, 1995

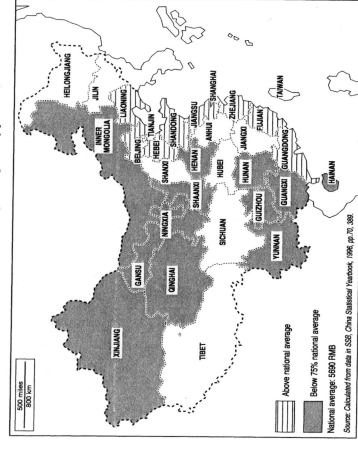

Source: Calculated from data in SSB, *China Statistical Yearbook*, 1996, pp.70, 389.

62

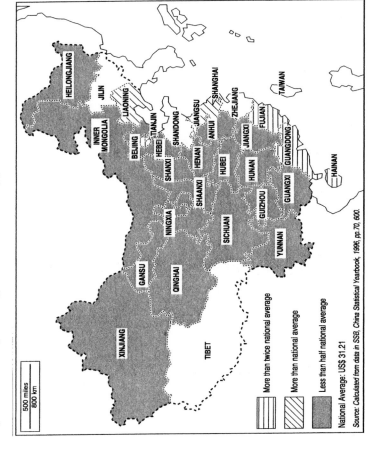

Figure 4.7 Per capita foreign direct investment by province

500 miles
800 km

More than twice national average

More than national average

Less than half national average

National Average: US$ 31.21

Source: Calculated from data in SSB, China Statistical Yearbook, 1996, pp.70, 600.

Source: Calculated from data in SSB, *China Statistical Yearbook*, 1996, pp. 70 and 600.

63

Figure 4.8 Per capita total construction output value by province

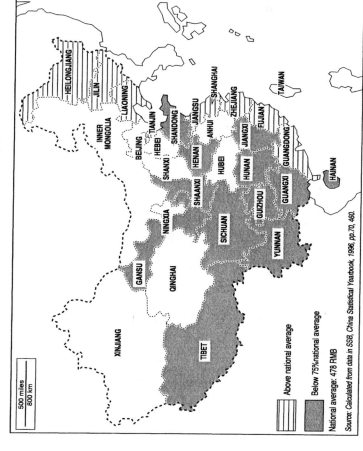

Source: Calculated from data in SSB, *China Statistical Yearbook*, 1996, pp. 70, 460.

64

Table 4.2   Data for Figures 4.1 and 4.4–4.8

Province	Fig.4.1 Per capita GDP by province	Fig.4.4 Per capita industrial output by province (at current prices, RMB), 1995	Fig.4.5 Per capita rural household net income by province (RMB), 1995	Fig.4.6 Per capita output of TVEs by province (RMB), 1995 (1996)	Fig.4.7 Per capita direct foreign investment, ($US)	Fig.4.8 Per capita of total construction output value by province (RMB)
National Average	5,634	7,586.94	1,577.74	5,689.78	31.21	478.34
Beijing	15,044	15,256.75	3,223.65	4,495.60	86.33	2,962.91
Tianjin	12,270	22,229.41	2,406.38	11,561.57	161.46	1,680.95
Hebei	5,345	6,207.43	1,668.73	5,794.31	8.49	405.92
Shanxi	4,220	5,698.99	1,208.3	4,556.71	2.07	477.23
Neimenggu	4,259	3,422.64	1,208.38	2,781.52	2.53	361.85
Liaoning	7,730	12,157.62	17,56.5	8,107.28	34.81	995.34
Jilin	5,163	5,512.96	1,609.6	2,476.47	15.74	493.81
Heilongjiang	6,468	5,954.55	1,766.27	2,539.58	13.97	555.45
Shanghai	22,275	36,247.14	4,245.61	10,743.46	204.42	2,766.20
Jiangsu	8,447	16,717.89	2,456.86	12,581.38	73.46	760.28
Zhejiang	9,455	18,725.98	2,966.19	17,314.66	29.13	818.85
Anhui	3,881	5,248.43	1,302.82	5,009.81	8.03	232.99
Fujian	8,136	8,652.09	2,048.59	7,964.16	124.93	513.35
Jiangxi	3,715	3,178.37	1,537.36	5,154.81	7.11	187.01
Shandong	6,834	9,714.33	1,715.09	10,553.82	30.89	296.32

Table 4.2 Continued

Province	Fig.4.1 Per capita GDP by province	Fig.4.4 Per capita industrial output by province (at current prices, RMB), 1995	Fig.4.5 Per capita rural household net income by province (RMB), 1995	Fig.4.6 Per capita output of TVEs by province (RMB), 1995 (1996)	Fig.4.7 Per capita direct foreign investment, ($US)	Fig.4.8 Per capita of total construction output value by province (RMB)
Henan	4,032	5,181.44	1,231.97	3,707.25	5.26	200.07
Hubei	5,122	7,107.73	1,511.12	5,256.24	10.83	393.98
Hunan	4,130	3,835.22	1,425.16	3,719.34	7.94	232.78
Guangdong	9,513	13,883.84	2,699.24	7,043.83	149.39	925.79
Guangxi	4,081	3,667.40	1,446.14	2,176.10	14.81	204.42
Hainan	5,500	2,669.34	1,519.71	1,567.68	146.69	242.99
Sichuan	3,763	3,908.49	1,158.29	4,546.49	4.78	316.34
Guizhou	2,093	1,588.20	1,086.62	492.02	1.63	153.61
Yunnan	3,715	3,023.93	1,010.97	1,227.32	2.45	237.32
Tibet	2,732	374.58	1,200.31	no data	no data	149.36
Shaanxi	3,313	3,365.74	962.89	2,047.52	9.22	303.25
Gansu	2,901	3,382.81	880.34	1,728.88	2.62	249.41
Qinghai	3,748	3,090.23	1,029.77	3,40.96	0.34	425.91
Ningxia	3,731	3,849.90	998.75	608.19	0.76	394.08
Xinjiang	5,167	4,828.54	1,136.45	678.51	3.31	527.23

Urban-Rural Inequalities

We have already seen in chapter 2 that there were important differences in entitlements between the urban population and the rural population in the Maoist era. The greatest advantage of the urban population lay in its access to subsidised food. A high proportion of urban employees had guaranteed lifetime employment with associated benefits such as sick pay, free medical care, pensions and low subsidised rent for housing. By contrast peasant life was full of risk and uncertainty (Davis 1989). Peasant incomes fluctuated with the success of crops. There was some minimal state aid after natural disasters, but the emphasis was still on self-help. Crop failures always brought great difficulty and in the wake of the Great Leap Forward the countryside experienced widespread starvation.

Social security and medical care in the countryside were locally financed. Systems were adopted and financed on a local basis and levels of provision were therefore very much more variable than in the towns, but were everywhere at a lower level. In some communes a healthcare insurance system eased the difficulty of meeting medical expenses and in most the 'five guarantee' system existed for people unable to work with no relatives on whom to call. This provided minimal amounts of food, clothing, fuel, medical care and the guarantee of a burial after death. It was a last resort system and dependence on it was regarded as a humiliation. The rural household was by far the most significant provider of welfare and security in the Chinese countryside (Davin 1994). It was responsible for the care, education and training of children and for looking after the sick, the elderly and the disabled. Rural people also had to house themselves. Peasants owned their own houses and were responsible for maintaining them. The family normally built or refurbished a new room for each son when he got married, bearing all the costs themselves.

These striking disparities between urban and rural life continued with only limited changes after the economic reforms. The income gap appears to be widening. In 1990 average per capita rural income was 45 per cent of average per capita urban income. By 1993 this had fallen to 39 per cent (Davis 1996: 113; Sun 1997: 203). This is not to argue that rural poverty has increased under the economic reforms. On the contrary, the general rise in standard of living has lifted many peasants above the poverty line and others have been helped by effective anti-poverty campaigns involving the sponsorship of sideline production and even of out-migration from the poorest areas. As a result,

the number of rural residents living at or below subsistence declined
from 125 million in 1985 to 80 million in 1992 (Davis 1996: 117).
However the existence of large income differentials between the
urban and the rural areas, and the fact that almost a tenth of the rural
population still live in absolute poverty, doubtless contribute to the
rural–urban migratory flow.

Although the poorer people in the towns have suffered from
inflation, from reductions of the level of subsidy on food, and from
movement to commoditise social services and housing, change has
been slow. Urban residents are still advantaged in welfare, medical services and education. They have access to higher quality schools and
better healthcare and hospitals for which they pay a lower percentage
of the costs than rural residents. Retired workers in the urban areas
benefit from generous pension provision (Davis-Friedmann 1991).
State employees retain many of their former privileges, while positions
in commerce and private industry often carry wages which compensate
for the lack of other benefits. In the countryside, decollectivisation
severely weakened the already minimal level of social services. The
'five guarantee system' continues, but it is estimated that of those
designated 'five guarantee households', only 75 per cent receive the
guarantees (Davis 1996: 113). Most peasants now have to pay for their
own medical care, and as always most rely on the family in old age.
The household must plan not only to meet the needs of present consumption but also to finance the great life events such as marriages and
funerals for its members, and to cover against serious illnesses, the loss
of ability to work and disasters affecting crop yields.

Life in the urban areas continues to be easier in mundane ways
which deeply affect the quality of life. Most urban households have
electricity and access to running water. These utilities are low-priced.
Central heating, washing machines and flush toilets are not uncommon. In the countryside this is not so. In most households water must
still be fetched from some distance away, fuel has to be gathered and
human waste dug out from latrines for use as fertiliser. The ordinary
business of life, keeping clean and warm, cooking food and washing
clothes is thus much harder work. Urban life also offers amusements
and diversions which are unobtainable in the countryside. There are
cinemas, parks and karaoke bars. Many households own a colour television. A greater variety of food and clothing is on sale in the urban
areas. Window shopping is available even to those who cannot afford
to buy and there is entertainment to be had walking through any urban
market. Street lighting allows the streets to be used for conviviality or

even reading after dark. The paved streets of the towns provide a cleaner environment and the urban housewife has an easier fight against dirt does than her rural counterpart. Flies, lice and other parasites also tend to pose less of a problem in the cities.

Migrants to the urban areas do not, as we have seen, acquire urban residential status simply by the process of migration. Without this status, they are excluded from many of the benefits enjoyed by urban residents such as access to cheap food and housing, subsidised medical care, education and social security. On the other hand, the very fact that unlike urban residents they have to finance welfare, education and housing for themselves probably makes rural people more ready to endure the rigours of migration in order to obtain the higher wages it brings. Other attractions of urban life, consumer goods, access to fashions and the excitement of the streets are undoubtedly a draw for young migrants. Rural–urban inequalities thus clearly contribute to rural–urban migration in China.

Rural Surplus Labour

The existence of a huge pool of surplus labour in the Chinese countryside has been another factor in economic migration in recent years. We know from Buck's two great surveys of Chinese farms that there was already a labour surplus in the Chinese countryside in the 1920s and 1930s (Buck 1930 and 1937). The concentration of the demand for labour in certain months of the year might mask this surplus, and the peak planting and harvesting periods, some of which overlapped, even brought temporary labour shortages in some areas, yet Buck noted that under-utilisation of rural labour was one of the great problems of Chinese agriculture, and that many able-bodied peasants were idle for significant periods every year (Buck 1930: 49). On the basis of data collected for the 1929–33 survey Buck concluded that only 35 per cent of male peasants were fully employed throughout the year (Buck 1937: 294–7). When the unemployment or underemployment of the rest was taken into account, Buck concluded that on average able-bodied men in the countryside were idle for two months every year.[3] With inadequate investment, a lack of credit and a deteriorating land:labour ratio, it is likely that the position was even worse by 1949.

The new communist government was very well aware of the problem of surplus labour when it took power in 1949. It was anxious to improve labour utilisation in the countryside for both economic and political reasons. Labour-intensive development strategies were introduced in the rural areas. Multiple cropping, inter-cropping, intensive husbandry, extended irrigation and land reclamation were all encouraged in an effort to use labour more intensively and to generate agricultural surpluses. The average number of days spent cultivating a hectare per year rose for all major crops (Taylor 1988: 740). The construction of dams, dykes, terraces and retaining walls mopped up underemployment in the slack seasons of the agricultural year. Rural small-scale industries, labour-intensive because they used traditional techniques or intermediate technology, were encouraged from the time of the Great Leap Forward in 1958 and despite some early failures and closures they employed around 10 million people by 1980 (Taylor 1988: 755). An additional 10 million were employed in other non-agricultural activities in the rural areas.

Despite all these development strategies designed to absorb the maximum possible amount of labour, the problem of rural underemployment was not solved and surplus labour continued to exist throughout the Maoist period (Taylor 1988). This is hardly surprising. Demographic trends alone were enough to undermine the limited successes achieved. The population almost doubled in the first three decades of the People's Republic, resulting in a further deterioration of the land:population ratio. The rural labour force was also swelled by the addition of female labour. Women were encouraged to work on the land in areas where it had not been customary for them to do so. Yet, as we have seen, rural to urban migration at this time, which was acting as a safety valve in many other parts of the developing world with similarly high rates of population growth, was severely restricted in China. The proportion of the population living in rural areas in 1949 was 89 per cent, by 1980 it was still 81 per cent, reflecting the low rate of urbanisation. Meanwhile the size of the rural labour force increased from 165 million in 1949 to 380 million in 1986 (Taylor 1988: 745). At the same time there was an alarming drop in the per capita area of cultivated land, which is estimated to have fallen from 10 mu per agricultural worker in 1956 to 4 mu in 1985.[4]

Given this background, the fact that, with the notable and tragic exception of the post-Great Leap Forward famine, Chinese agricultural production kept up with the population increase for most of the first decades of the People's Republic is quite impressive. The record of labour productivity, however, was poor. Rural cadres, who were in effect farm managers in the collective period, had little incentive to use labour efficiently. The commune was obliged to provide a living to everyone born within its borders. Few peasant men left the villages of their birth. Women who married out of the collective unit were replaced by other women marrying in. Steady population growth meant that rural cadres had somehow to find ways to employ an ever-increasing labour force and this was difficult. Too sudden a decline in the marginal return to labour (the value of each extra day worked) could cause problems because it would produce a decline in the value of the work-point and thus a decline in what the labourer was paid for a day's work. In the medium term, however, given the worsening land:labour ratio, the trend in many places was inevitably a rise in the number of days worked without a commensurate rise in production or in remuneration. This was the only way in which the commune could keep its growing labour force even partially occupied.

The superficial camouflage given to surplus rural labour by the organisational structure of collective agriculture was removed by the rural reforms after 1978. The commune system was replaced by production contracts with individual peasant households, procurement prices were increased and peasants were allowed to sell surplus produce on the free market. Higher incentives produced remarkable increases in agricultural output while the use of labour in agriculture fell sharply (Taylor 1988: 749). Shifts in cropping patterns produced a further decline in the per mu use of labour as the area planted to crops with low labour requirement such as sugar beet, millet and gaoliang rose. Surplus rural labour became a recognised problem. The growth of sideline production and rural industry has provided some new jobs. Non-agricultural employment rose from 6 per cent of total rural employment in 1978 to over 25 per cent in 1993. None the less estimates of the surplus rural labour force in the press put it at between 30 per cent and 40 per cent, while more scholarly calculations also put it at around 30 per cent with big regional variations (Taylor 1988: 750). Despite very high levels of migration, many estimates imply that rural surplus labour is still a significant problem. For example, in 1996 the Guangdong provincial government reported that from 1979 to 1995, 12 million of the province's rural population moved into the urban areas, yet of the remaining 25 million rural labour force, 4 million were considered to be surplus (FBIS, 10 April 1997).

In fact surplus labour in the countryside is such a vague concept that it is impossible to expect a true measure of its extent. If we remember Buck's average male labourer who was idle for two months a year, we might argue that this meant that one sixth of the male labour force was surplus to requirements. However, if by custom the rural labour force expected two months of leisure, or if each man had his own holding that he wished to retain and to cultivate himself, such a surplus could be difficult to utilise in other ways. On the other hand, if sufficiently tempting opportunities became available elsewhere to provide an incentive, agricultural work could be reorganised to free some labourers to leave the land. This is indeed what is happening in China today. When migrants leave, the people left behind may work harder, contract land may be farmed by friends or relatives and the proceeds shared, or cropping patterns and farming practices modified so as to economise on the use of labour. The full extent of surplus labour in the Chinese countryside became visible only when worthwhile economic opportunities arose elsewhere and peasants had an incentive to use labour more economically.

DEMOGRAPHIC FACTORS

Another influence on migration is the present age structure of the Chinese population. High rates of population growth in the past, followed by a drop in fertility, produced a population in which there is a disproportionate number of young adults. The phenomenon is especially marked in the countryside because fertility fell earlier in the urban areas. This age structure is conducive to high levels of migration. Migrants in most societies are predominantly young adults and, as we have seen in chapter 2, that this is true for China. Table 4.3 shows that in 1982 at the onset of mass migration the 15–19 year olds were the second largest age group, with the 10–14 age group a little larger. By 1990 the largest groups were the 15–19 year olds and the 20–4 year olds. The total percentage of the population aged between 15 and 24, the peak age for migration, was 19.9 in 1982, and 21.75 in 1990. By 1995 it had fallen to 16.12 per cent. If we add the 25–9 year olds, still a group likely to have a high propensity to migrate once the migration habit has been established, we find 29.12 per cent of the population between the ages of 15 and 29 in 1982. In 1990 this figure was 30.77. The skewing of the population towards this age group affects migration in two ways. First, migration is likely to be higher because there are more people in the age group with the greatest propensity to migrate; and second, young people who belong to large cohorts are more likely to be able to migrate because there are other people to take their places in the villages and they can more easily be spared.

Table 4.3   Age distribution of Chinese population: changing percentages of total population in different age groups, selected years, 1964–95

	1964 (Census)	1982 (Census)	1990 (Census)	1995 (1% population survey)
0–4	14.42	9.43	10.30	7.29
5–9	13.56	11.03	8.79	10.68
10–14	12.43	13.13	8.60	8.77
15–19	8.94	12.49	10.63	7.38
20–24	7.32	7.41	11.12	8.74
25–29	7.26	9.22	9.22	10.17
30–34	6.72	7.27	7.42	8.82
35–39	5.93	5.40	7.64	6.95
40–44	5.13	4.82	5.64	7.41
45–49	4.44	4.72	4.34	5.54
50–54	3.82	4.07	4.04	4.24
55–59	3.25	3.38	3.69	3.85
60–64	2.54	2.73	3.01	3.47
65–69	1.68	2.12	2.33	

Source: China Population Statistics Yearbook, 1996, 76–7.

Summary

Rapid economic growth in China has taken place in recent years through the establishment and growth of modern industry, the commercialisation of agriculture and the more intensive use of resources above all of China's abundant labour. The spatial development of industry in China has been very uneven and the same is true, though to a lesser extent, of the commercialisation of agriculture. This uneven development has been reflected in an uneven growth in the demand for labour and in opportunities for small entrepreneurs, triggering large-scale movements of labour all over China. The macro-level determinants of migration examined in this section – the existence of great regional inequalities, of rural/urban inequalities, of unequal rates of growth and a large surplus labour force in the countryside – provide the general setting for an understanding of why these large movements of labour are occurring. To move from this general structural understanding to an appreciation of why people migrate from some villages and not from others in apparently similar circumstances, or why some people move from a particular village while others do not, we have to consider lower-level or more specific determinants, the sorts of factors which influence behaviour at the individual or household level.

MICRO DETERMINANTS OF MIGRATION AND MIGRATORY BEHAVIOUR

The Local Socio-economic Setting

Chinese agriculture is generally characterised by labour-intensive cultivation, low labour productivity and a poor ratio of land to labour. Obviously local conditions vary considerably, and it is to be expected that areas where the land cannot be made to yield more will be those that send out most migrants. Statistics from Sichuan, the province with the highest rate of migration, would seem to confirm this. Nationally in China there is 1.2 mu of cultivated land per peasant, in Sichuan only 0.87 mu is available.[5] However, the relationship between population density, land shortage and migration is not necessarily a simple one. In some densely populated areas of Jiangsu Province and the Pearl River Delta, rural industry provides sufficient non-agricultural employment not only to absorb local surplus labour but also to attract migrants from elsewhere (Christiansen 1992). But such areas may simultaneously experience out-migration. Potter and Potter (1990) found that as Zengbu, the community which they studied in the Pearl River Delta, had developed economically and industrially, even better opportunities had tempted local people to move on to more urbanised areas, leaving the least desirable work in Zengbu to be done by outsiders from poorer more remote areas of Guangdong.

Knowledge and Communication

One of the most important obstacles to migration is a lack of knowledge. Obviously no one will migrate if nothing is known of opportunities elsewhere. Even when there is widespread awareness, a fear of the unknown may still inhibit migration. Life in the urban areas is very difficult for rural migrants who have no one to help them find work and accommodation, especially as they may also have to face major changes of climate, dialect, food and lifestyle. Once a few migrants have left a village and are established elsewhere, they send or bring information back and help fellow villagers to find work and accommodation elsewhere. In China, as elsewhere, once such migration chains are set up they may continue for years or even decades. The existence of such chains helps to explain why a steady flow of migrants leaves some villages while there are others, with apparently very similar socio-economic characteristics, from which nobody migrates.

Linked to knowledge and communication is transport. Where there is good natural transport as on the rivers, or a long-established rail link, there are migration chains with a long history of which new migrants can make use. Proximity to urban areas obviously makes migration easier. Of the 217 counties in Sichuan Province, only 84 send out migrants on a big scale.[6] Some counties from which migration is heaviest are quite prosperous but happen to be close enough to Chengdu to ensure ease of travel and communication. Some of the counties from which there is little or no migration are particularly poor and remote, so much so that the flow of information is inhibited and it is hard for peasants to raise fares. Remote villages are also less likely to receive information about the outside world through television or even newspapers.

The authorities are aware that migrants may lack the information they need. As we have seen in chapter 2, where they wish to encourage migration, local governments may try to provide migrants with the information they need. Sichuan has been especially active in this respect with officially sponsored employment centres, migrant training schools, buses arranged by the county and county government offices that contract with labour supply companies in the destination areas. Official sponsorship of migration in these various forms stimulates migration from the areas where it operates.

The Household Economy and the Decision to Migrate

The household is the basic building brick of Chinese rural society. As in most other societies it is a social unit within which children are brought up and the sick and elderly are cared for. Although it may sometimes contain outsiders such as servants, labourers or apprentices, it is normally made up of close relatives. The household provides food and accommodation to its members. Its activities are financed through pooled resources. Originally, most of the household budget in peasant families was raised by working the family land and might come in cash or kind. It was controlled by senior members of the household who made the decisions as to how it should be used. Collective agriculture brought considerable change to the household economy. Production was no longer organised at the household level, the land was farmed in much larger units and its produce had to be divided among peasant households. The collective paid taxes and retained funds for reinvestment, administration, welfare and other purposes. The remainder of the harvest was distributed on the basis of the amount of work performed by each member of the collective, but was usually paid over to the head of household. The head of household thus retained control over a reduced household budget which consisted mainly of funds for consumption within the household.

The economic reforms allowed households to farm land which they contracted from the state for their own profit. This has greatly increased the size and importance of the household budget. It now includes subsistence grain, cash to buy consumption goods and funds for the purchase of seeds, fertiliser, pesticides and other reinvestments in agriculture. An increasing number of households are involved in non-agricultural sideline enterprises, which have also increased the size and complexity of household budgets. Finally, the expansion of rural industry and small private enterprises in the countryside, as well as the employment of agricultural labour by the more successful farmers, has increased the number of rural residents who now receive some sort of wage payment, whether full-time or part-time. Wages paid to individuals challenge the traditional economic organisation of peasant societies. They raise the possibility that the individuals may retain at least a part of what they earn for their own use, rather than contributing it to the pooled household budget. Fieldwork accounts, however, seem to indicate that the household economy remains strong, despite the development of a wage economy in rural China (Potter and Potter 1990: 136–7; Judd 1994).

The household is the setting within which most migration decisions in China are taken. We have already seen that the household controls a complex budget. It also deploys its own labour force. Decisions about who will work where, which members of the family will work on the land and which at waged labour, and how much time will be spent on various types of work are made within the household according to the opportunities available and the relative costs and benefits involved. Migration may be one of a range of options considered by household members in deciding how to deploy its labour.

Obviously the land:labour ratio is likely to be a factor when migration is considered. Households that are land-short and cannot keep all their available labour busy might be expected to send out more migrants than household that farm more land. But other factors play a role. Land-short households may be too poor to afford the costs of migration. Moreover, if opportunities for migrants are good enough even households with plenty of land may be tempted it to send out a member. Even well-to-do villagers may be able to earn more as labour migrants than they can make from the land. They are likely to have the resources to meet the costs and the risks of migration. In Laifeng village, Quxian county, Sichuan, for example, eight out of 20 households had a member who had migrated in 1994. The village head had sent two sons and a daughter-in-law to Guangdong. The villagers were agreed that he could do this because his was a wealthy household producing poultry for the market. The poorest households would have had difficulty in raising even one fare and had less access to information and to the necessary contacts (fieldwork notes, 1994).

We have seen that there is an overall surplus of labour in the Chinese countryside. Many families can spare an adult member for migration simply by redistributing work between others in the household. If remittances are good, everyone may then live better. Where this is not possible and the family is too short of labour to farm its land, the land may be leased or subcontracted to another household or even farmed less intensively if the potential return to migration makes this worthwhile.

Migration may also be a way for families to rid themselves of the burden of feeding members whose labour they cannot utilise. Wan (1992) reports that one reason that young women in Wuwei county, Anhui province leave to work as maids in the big cities is that there is hardly enough land to keep even male peasants busy and it is not customary for women to work in agriculture there.

Family responsibilities play a role in the decision to migrate. All over the developing world, young single adults are the most likely people to be involved in migration. The expenses of migration are lower for single people: they only have one fare to find and can sleep in dormitory-style accommodation. However, married men may also migrate, especially if they face economic difficulties. Men who have many dependants may see migration as the best was to support them and their migration may gain them social esteem.[7] In China as elsewhere, men are free to take this way out because they can expect their wives to cope with their children in the villages where they can call on the help of other relatives. Their migration may be quite short-term or seasonal, marked by frequent returns to help with the land in the busiest seasons. Married women are much less likely to migrate especially if they are the mothers of young children (see chapter 8).

The special difficulties of Chinese rural migrants in the cities no doubt affect the interplay between family responsibilities and Chinese migratory behaviour. Elsewhere in the world internal rural migrants may leave for the city with the hope that they will be able to bring their families to join them when they have saved enough to pay their fares and set up a home. This has also been a common pattern in international migration when restrictions on movement across national frontiers have allowed. As we have seen, China's *hukou* restrictions make permanent family settlement in the cities extremely difficult for rural migrants; indeed, the barriers bear comparison with the barriers to trans-national migration elsewhere in the world. A minority of migrants succeed in bringing their families to join them. These are likely to be 'official migrants' who have been assigned or transferred to a new job, or traders who have prospered and are able to raise considerable funds. By contrast most ordinary migrants do not at present expect to set up a long-term home in the city. Rural migrants have a further tie to their places of origin in the form of the land tenure system. As rural residents they retain a right to an allocation of responsibility land in their village. Rural to urban migration in China therefore often takes the form of circulation. Migrants leave the village for a few years most often in their late teens or early twenties and return to establish their families. For individuals migration is thus a stage in the life cycle rather than a permanent transformation of life. The implications of the dominance of circulation in Chinese migration are considered in chapter 5.

5 The Impact of Migration in the Sending Areas

That's our new house. It's got two storeys and a concrete floor. We had nothing like that before. But my son, my daughter-in-law and my daughter are all working outside. We used their money to do it.

(peasant woman age 50, Sichuan province 1994)

Migration is only one factor in the economic and social transformation of the Chinese countryside that has been underway since the early 1980s. Decollectivisation, the introduction of the market, administrative reform and the development of small towns have all contributed to the transformation, and it is not always possible to isolate the effects of the various processes. Migration is certainly very important among them. It impacts on the sending areas in various different ways. First, the absence of the migrants affects those who are left behind. Then, remittances and presents produce other changes. Finally, the migrants bring many outside influences into the rural areas by their continued contact with their villages. This comes through letters, visits home and finally, in many cases, permanent return.

The circulation type of migration maximises the effect of migration on the sending area. Each year a number of young migrants depart, while others who have already spent time away come back. Some of the migrants who go to work in small local towns may settle, but a great number of those who go to larger towns and cities will return because the bureaucratic difficulties of permanent settlement, poor living and working conditions and the difficulty of establishing a family in the destination area leave them with little choice. Moreover, migrants have something to return to. They retain a right to land in their villages of origin so long as they have permanent registration there. Circulation and the expectation of return gives them a strong incentive to maintain close links with their families by sending remittances, making visits home where possible, bringing back gifts and investing in small enterprises. Circulatory migration also creates a situation where migration can be an episode in life rather than a choice for life. It thus maximises the numbers who may be involved in migration over time. Obviously the effects of circulation are likely to be different in important ways from long-term or permanent migration.

Notably, circulation produces greater and more continuous flows to the villages of information, skills, capital, innovation and influences on lifestyle. In time, circulation may become less prevalent. If, in future, reform of the household registration system or other changes made it easier for migrants to settle in the urban areas, or if they lost their rights to land in the villages, it is likely that fewer of them would return. This might in turn change the impact of migration on the sending areas.

WORK, LAND AND HOUSEHOLD

As migration is a highly selective process, the gap left by the departure of migrants tends to be greater than might be expected from migrant numbers. If we take a village with a population of 700 people from which 20 migrants have left, this would represent a loss of under 3 per cent from which no great impact would be expected. Suppose, however, that all the migrants were young males aged 20–4. Typically, given the age population of the population of China, this age group would make up about 11 per cent of the villagers, or 77 young people. If 38 of these were male, the 20 migrants would make up over half the males in their age group, a significant loss. At household level the effects of migration can be still more dramatic. Many households have only one or two young adults in their labour force and the departure of a single migrant may halve the household labour force, or leave it without a young man or a young woman, or indeed without a young person of either sex. It is because migration is so selective in terms of age and sex that it has the power to change the existing allocation of labour.

The most significant labour shift since the reforms has been the movement of young men out of agriculture. We have seen that the majority of those who leave the villages are men. Migration has not been the sole cause of this labour shift; the growth of demand for labour in non-agricultural pursuits locally has also had an effect in some places where men 'leave the soil without leaving the country-side'. In Xindu county, Sichuan Province, in the early 1990s a man could earn 2 yuan a day in agriculture, 4 yuan in rural industry and 6 yuan in commerce (SASS 1994). Obviously, such differentials will draw workers out of agriculture when opportunities are available. Generally in rural China, many more men have withdrawn from agriculture than have women. Many rural industries such as machine repair shops, cement works and local mines create jobs for men rather than women. Men also dominate other non-agricultural employment in the rural areas such as construction, transport and the administration. Other rural enterprises such as those producing garments, toys and electronic goods tend to prefer women on the production line. However, such industries usually draw only *young* women out of agriculture. In many places in rural China the agricultural labour force is losing everyone who can obtain non-agricultural employment, whether locally or by migration. Fieldwork is being left to those who lack the initiative, skills, strength or mobility to get other work.

There are various possible household responses to departure of labour from the land. If the household remains involved in farming, members of the family not formerly involved in the agricultural labour force may begin to do fieldwork, help can be sought from relatives or from hired labour, or cropping patterns and cultivation practices can be changed to reduce the demand for labour. Other alternatives are to rent the land to tenants or to allow it to go out of cultivation. This whole repertoire of response has been employed in rural China, but is too early to estimate the scale of any of these trends or to assess their impact. None the less it is worth looking at each strategy to consider whether its widespread use is likely and what the implications might be.

Changes in the Cultivated Area

Economic analyses of Chinese agriculture from the 1920s onwards have shown that there is a surplus of agricultural labour, that labour productivity in the countryside is too low and that Chinese farmers need to be helped to diversify their economic activities and to commercialise their production (Tawney 1932; Buck 1930 and 1937; Myers 1970). As we have seen, the problem of surplus labour became even worse under collectivisation.

The related problem of land shortage has also become more serious over time, with population increase and a steady reduction in the area of arable land. The area of arable land fell by 0.2 per cent per annum in 1970–8, and by 0.4 per cent per annum in 1978–86 (Walker 1988: 593). It has continued to fall, although at a slower rate, since 1986 (SSB 1996: 355). This loss of arable land is due to the growth of industry and urbanisation, transport, water conservation, forestry and grassland.

There is widespread consciousness of the land shortage in China. It was once fostered by the emphasis on opening new land (often with little consideration as to its suitability), which was a feature of Maoist development policy. Now the concern about the area under cultivation is more nuanced, and the ecological costs of bringing marginal land under cultivation are better recognised. However, the possibility that the shortage of labour might produce the abandonment of arable land still causes considerable concern. Is such concern really justified? Despite the growth of non-agricultural employment nationally, the numbers of those engaged primarily in agriculture continued to grow until 1991. Numbers declined only very slowly thereafter and are still significantly higher than the levels of the late 1980s (SSB 1996: 354). This reflects the steady growth in the working population in China, but also the continuing importance of agriculture. Moreover, it is widely agreed that there are surpluses of labour in the countryside. In this situation it is difficult to believe that there can be many areas where absolute shortages of labour have caused tracts of good land to go out of cultivation. In parts of the developing world such as the northwest Malayan state of Kedah, the Dominican Republic or the Yemen Arab Republic, the volume of male out-migration has had this result (Parnwell 1983: 104). In land-short China, however, where peasants can call on the help of kin or get in tenants to get their land farmed, it is unlikely that land on which a worthwhile return is possible will be left untilled. It is probably usually the most marginal, least productive plots that are allowed to return to the wild. Where this occurs it may be a positive outcome of the flow of labour from the rural areas. In the past, population pressure has forced both the over-cultivation of good land and the cultivation of marginal land, leading to problems of declining soil fertility and increasing erosion (Smil 1993; Edmonds 1994). Recognition of these ecological problems has even led the Chinese authorities to impose a planned contraction of the arable acreage in some areas of the northwest where priority was given to the need to restore and extend grassland and forest areas (Walker 1988: 594). In areas such as the poor counties of Sichuan, environmental protection rules including the prohibition on cultivating hillsides above the tree-line are frequently broken by peasants desperate to increase their cultivated land (SASS 1994). Thus the authorities themselves recognise that the abandonment of arable land is not always undesirable.

The abandonment of marginal land should, of course, be distinguished from the loss of cultivated land to urban, commercial and industrial development. Such losses are a much more serious trend because they tend to involve fertile, well-husbanded, high-yielding soils close to urban areas (Kirkby 1985: 180–1). This loss of arable land has nothing to do with labour shortages but is, like migration, a result of economic development and urbanisation.

Changes in Cropping Patterns

Another strategy the peasant household may employ when its labour force shrinks is to change its farming practices. This may involve growing less labour-intensive crops or farming the land less intensively. It can be shown from national statistics that shifts to less labour-intensive crops took place early in the reform era (Taylor 1989), presumably as a result of the household's desire to maximise its profits and to deploy its labour force in the most effective way. Such shifts should have the effect of raising the productivity of labour and could thus be a positive development, provided that the labour released from agriculture can be more profitably employed elsewhere in the economy.

A common way of farming less intensively is to reduce the sown area. The sown area is the area sown to crops each year. In China, especially in the south where it is quite usual to raise two or even three crops a year on the same land, there is an important difference between the area of arable land and the sown area. For many years, even when the area under cultivation was declining, increases in the sown area were achieved by the increased use of multi-cropping. However multi-cropping is very labour-intensive. The land must be prepared, planted, weeded and harvested twice or even three times a year. Moreover, overlaps of crops on the land necessitate great care. For example, when winter wheat is interplanted with maize it must be harvested by hand to avoid damage to the young corn plants.

The multi-cropping index and the total sown area fell between 1978 and 1986 as peasants made decisions about their cropping practices based on profitability. There was a remarkable fall in the total area sown to grain, whereas the area sown to cash crops showed a dramatic rise. This clear evidence that the area sown to different crops is price-sensitive was reinforced by the experience of 1984–5. The good harvest of 1984 resulted in grain surpluses and problems in selling grain (Walker 1988). The peasants resisted by sharply reducing the area sown to grain in 1985. In alarm, the government took measures to reward grain production, resulting in an upturn in the grain area in 1986. The total area sown to grain has fluctuated around 110 million hectares in subsequent years compared with over 112 million in 1978

(SSB 1997: 380). However, despite this slight decline in the areas sown to grain, steady increases in the output of grain and of other major agricultural products were registered in both the 1980s and in the first half of the 1990s, demonstrating that, at a national level at least, migration and associated changes in farming regimes have not had too adverse an effect (SSB 1997: 336).

The Chinese authorities are understandably very sensitive to any developments which might threaten China's ability to feed her population and concern is often expressed that the flight of labour from the land poses this danger. However, official statistics seem to indicate that food and grain production have held up well, despite a contraction in arable land, in the sown area and very recently, in the agricultural labour force. It is probable that factors other than migration were mainly responsible for the contraction in the cultivated and the sown areas. The contraction was fastest in the early years of the reform period when migration had only just started and has slowed from the mid-1980s as the volume of migration increased. Both the sown area and the area of cultivated land appeared to stabilise with small fluctuations in the 1990s (SSB 1997: 369 and 383).

The Deployment of Labour

Many observers have commented on the shift in the composition of the agricultural labour force towards more female and more elderly workers. The shift is often attributed to migration, although it is obviously also connected with the availability of better paid non-farm income locally for young males. The changing composition of the labour force concerns Chinese analysts, who worry that the land will be less intensively cultivated and thus less productive. As we have seen, rising agricultural output in the early 1990s seems to indicate that whatever the situation in particular localities, nationally, this concern is not justified.

More investigation of the extent of the labour shift is needed. It is likely that there are enormous regional variations. Overall it is sometimes claimed that women now form 60–70 per cent of the agricultural work force (Meng 1994: 113). This is not supported by 1990 Census figures (Census of 1990: Vol. 11, 276–7) which showed 246 million males with agriculture as their main activity as opposed to 221 million females. Discussion of this subject is fraught with problems of definition. A major difficulty is that so many peasants have more than one occupation and the division of their time between occupations will vary with the time of year. Mallée's survey of 2,835 households in seven provinces found that of the 28.8 per cent villagers who engaged in agriculture as their sole pursuit, 56 per cent were women (Mallée, in Christiansen and Zhang eds. 1998). Eighteen per cent of men surveyed were full-time cultivators as opposed to 24 per cent of women. Another 10 per cent of women engaged in both cultivation and domestic work. A small-scale Japanese survey in 1986 showed both feminisation and greying of the agricultural labour force in Wuxi county, Jiangsu Province, where the importance of agriculture is clearly declining. Only 12 of the 27 village families surveyed still engaged in agriculture (Oshima 1990: 210). Their total agricultural labour force consisted of nine women and four men. Between them the 27 families included 30 adult children. None of this generation worked on the land. Although the trend for women and older men to become more important in the agricultural labour force is probably fairly general, its extent clearly varies from one area to another, reflecting differences in the alternative economic opportunities available. This survey, carried out in an area of rapid industrial growth, reflects an extreme. Mallée's survey, indicating that women are now a majority among full-time cultivators, but that men still play a substantial role in agriculture, is probably a better indication of the situation in China as a whole.

Although the extent of the shift in the agricultural labour force towards women and older men is sometimes exaggerated, it is certainly a trend where young men are being drawn away by good non-farm opportunities and women are not. In most places, given the rural labour surplus, the remaining labour force should still be adequate for the needs of agriculture. Where it is not, it still seems unlikely that peasants will neglect crops if proper cultivation is capable of bringing worthwhile returns. More research on peasant strategies is needed, but there are indications that seasonal migration is used to ensure that extra labour will be available on the land in the busy periods. Research in Thailand has shown that migrants time their outward and return movements in relation to the agricultural cycle, so that visits home coincide with peak periods of farming activity (Parnwell 1993: 105). Similar patterns appear in China. Male migrants return to Sichuan at the time of the winter wheat harvest which coincides with rice transplanting, and again at the time when the rice, maize and sorghum are being harvested (SASS 1994). Data from the 100 Village Survey on Labour of 1987 showed that long-term out-migrants accounted only for 20.7 per cent of the total out-migrants. The others were seasonal migrants who kept their farmland and their homes in the village and sought work outside the village only when their marginal economic contributions at home fell below a certain level (Ma Xia 1997: 15; Yu Dechang 1989).

Migrant Cultivators

In certain areas in the most developed regions, especially around the big cities, *local* people have ceased to farm because they can earn more in other occupations, either locally or as migrants elsewhere, but they lease their land to migrants from poorer regions. Many peasants close to the city of Beijing now work in non-agricultural employment and their fields are tilled by migrant cultivators from other provinces. The same is true in the Pearl River Delta where land is leased to migrant cultivators from Guangxi and even from Sichuan. A survey of two villages in Zhejiang Province found that a strong worker could earn about 800 yuan a year from the land locally, compared with about 3,000–4,000 yuan in construction work or mining in Shanxi or Hubei (Qian 1996). In some cases everyone in the family capable of work had migrated out, but there had been no loss to agricultural production because they simply rented their land to fellow villagers or to poorer outsiders.

Replacing Female Labour

Although migration is predominantly male, there is a considerable outflow of young women from some sending areas. The effects of their departure will depend on the sexual division of labour, and on the age, marital status and household responsibilities of the migrating women. Most female migrants are young and unmarried. Married women are less likely to move because their household responsibilities are so heavy and also because they are seen as a reserve army of labour for agriculture. It may be impossible for the couple to leave together because one of them is needed to look after the land, to supervise the household and to care for dependants. Male migrants are likely to earn more than female migrants and the household therefore maximises its benefits if the husband leaves and the wife stays at home to care for the land and the family. Where married women do migrate they often accompany or join their husbands.[1]

The situation is different for young unmarried women. They are not indispensable in the household. Some come from areas where there they cannot earn their keep in the villages. As we have seen, young women leave Wuwei county, Anhui, the home county of large numbers of the domestic servants, to go to Beijing and other big cities, because there is no work in agriculture for women in their land-short county (Wan 1992: 89–90). Female hotel workers in Chengdu told the same story in interviews (fieldwork interviews, 1994). Their labour was not needed on the small plots their families farmed. But if the female pull factors are sufficient, migration may occur even where female labour is valued. The boom areas of Guangdong Province draw female labour from areas of the south where women have traditionally performed a significant share of the agricultural work. In areas where women customarily work on the land, both men and women of the household have to work harder if a woman migrates. Otherwise the effect of a woman's departure on the distribution of labour is probably felt mainly by older women. It is the mothers and mothers-in-law who take up the burden. If there is no older woman present within the household, men may take on new roles, as in Anhui where it has been reported that men cook, clean and even sew when female members of their families have gone to work in the cities (Wan 1992: 101). The work in the house and in the courtyard economy previously performed by a woman migrant has to be taken on by someone within the household, but childcare can be supplied by close relatives in other households. From observations made during my fieldwork in Sichuan it seemed that the children of female migrants were usually cared for by the paternal grandmother, but the maternal grandmother might also help.

Issues of women and migration will be further discussed in chapter 7.

Prospects

As labour migration is predominantly male, it follows that the majority of villages from which migration takes place have to adjust to having a labour force that is older and is short of young men. Where there is rural industry its recruitment often shows the same selectivity and exacerbates the problem. As we have seen, the household may use various strategies to deal with the situation. Given the existence of surplus labour and the shortage of cultivable land in the Chinese countryside it is not to be expected that these developments will automatically lead to good land being left uncultivated or to catastrophic falls in the productivity of the land.

On a national scale there has not yet been a sustained fall in the output of agriculture. The Chinese authorities are understandably very sensitive to the possibility of such a fall, since the feeding of their population is seen as a major business of state. Developments in China have implications for the rest of the world too. If China's harvest falls by even a few per cent, and the shortfall is made good by purchases from abroad, the impact on world grain markets is considerable (Lu Feng 1994). However, recent history in China and the development experience of the rest of the world would indicate that a reduction of the relative size of the agricultural labour force is necessary to development and growth, and that the output of agriculture is best maintained and increased by proper attention to price incentives in this sector.

REMITTANCES AND PRESENTS

Migrant remittances are important to the economies of the sending areas and to the incomes of the households that receive them. In 1993, 6 million migrants left Sichuan Province and the province received an estimated 6–10 billion yuan in remittances through bank and post offices (SASS 1994). By 1994 remittances to Sichuan had risen to 15 billion yuan (Xinhua news agency, quoted in SWB, 12 March 1997: 62). This compares with a gross domestic product for the province of 278 billion yuan in 1994 (SSB 1997: 44). More is brought home by the migrants themselves in the form of cash and goods, although it is not possible to quantify the amounts.

At the village and household level, regular receipt of remittances can transform the lives of families. Although in poor areas some of the money may be used for subsistence, much of it seems to be set aside for house construction, wedding finance and investment in setting up small enterprises. Wan reports that in Wuwei, Anhui, families whose daughters work as maids occupy conspicuously better houses than those without migrants. In 1988 a brick and cement house in Anhui cost 5,000–7,000 yuan, far more than could be saved from the income from the land (Wan 1992: 95–6). In the sending areas of Sichuan also, new homes mark out the villages and indeed the households from which migrants have left. Often made conspicuous with the use of whitewash or white tiles, they are usually larger and more elaborate than the dwellings they replace, and typically have two storeys with big balconies. Their proud owners are very ready to detail the way in which their building was financed with the remittances of absent sons and daughters.

The earnings of migrants are also used to cover the increasing expenses of rural marriages. Marriage costs are a major expense for peasants in contemporary China. They were the second most important use of remittances after housebuilding in Anhui where at the beginning of the 1990s the brideprice cost 3,000–4,000 yuan and a dowry ranged from a few hundred to 2,000 yuan (Wan 1992: 97). The man's family bears the greater share of the costs of marriage. Unmarried male migrants may save for their own weddings, but if other members of the family have emigrated, their remittances could also be put towards the marriages of the young men of the household. The earnings of an unmarried woman will often go to help with a brother's marriage costs or to building a house for her parents. In China, as in Hong Kong and Taiwan, young women feel an obligation to give what they can to their families to repay them for the expense of their upbringing (Salaff 1981; Kung 1983). Conscious that on marriage they will belong to another household, they wish to contribute to their natal families' budgets while they can. Young women may also accumulate the cost of their own dowries, thus saving their families an expense (Wan 1982; and fieldnotes, 1994). Some older women migrants in the cities save to make their retirement to the countryside more comfortable.

When the young couple sets up a new household in the rural areas, much of the brideprice and the dowry go to finance the purchase of household goods. The earnings of migrants make it possible to increase both dowry and brideprice. Remittances sent back by migrants are also spent directly on consumer durables. The families of migrants are therefore more likely than other villagers to own bicycles, sewing machines, cassette recorders, televisions and even videos.

Many businesses in the sending areas are owned by returned migrants or by the families of migrant workers. Migrants sometimes acquire new skills or new ideas which they are able to use to their advantage when they return to the villages. Some returned women workers in Sichuan have set up small dressmaking concerns catering to local demand. Exceptionally, returned migrants may even be able to mobilise contacts in the destination area to set up more ambitious enterprises supplying or processing for plants there (Wan 1992). Capital, entrepreneurial know-how and contacts outside the immediate area are all in short supply in the rural areas. Clearly migrants are likely to be at an advantage in obtaining such resources.

LIFESTYLE AND ATTITUDINAL CHANGE

The movement of population backwards and forwards between the sending areas and the destination areas has an important impact on the sending areas. As Caldwell has written, 'Circular forms of movement, far more than permanent migration, have the potential of spreading new ideas, attitudes and knowledge to rural areas and contributing greatly to processes of social change' (Caldwell 1969: 45). Migrants to the urban areas are influenced by urban lifestyles and customs and they take some of these influences back to the villages with them. The influences received and the degree to which they are absorbed differ because individual experiences of migration are so different. At one end of the scale are male construction workers. In their shanty accommodation in the cities they may live without electricity, sanitation or a convenient source of running water. Their accommodation is often more crowded and offers less comfort than they would have in the countryside. Among their deprivations is the absence of women to service their domestic needs. They learn to do tasks which in the countryside are seen as women's work. They fetch water, prepare simple meals and wash and mend their clothes. As they undertake all this from unpleasant necessity, they are unlikely to wish to continue doing it when they return home. Of all migrants, construction workers probably interact least with urban people. If they are influenced by urban lifestyles at all, it is likely to be through television, films or simply what they see on the street.

At the other extreme, the strongest urban influences are absorbed by the young rural women who work as maids. Living within an urban family they become aware of even the most intimate details of their employers' lives. Their work is focused on care of the home, and often of children, so that domestic arrangements, home furnishings and consumer durables are all things of importance in their lives. They see a different model of marriage and family interaction, and a family setting in which very low fertility is accepted as desirable. They become used to running water, flush lavatories, mains drainage, fridges and even washing machines. Obviously when they return to their villages they have to accept life without these amenities, but they may aspire to have them for themselves one day.

Factory workers who live in dormitories are less close to urban residents, but they also have the chance to get used to living with electricity, running water and sanitation. They observe urban life from the streets and from the magazines, television and films with which they fill their few leisure hours.

The urban popular culture to which migrants are exposed through films and popular magazines tends to cater to fantasies and to promote consumerism. It features people who are well-dressed and live in homes of far higher quality than ordinary Chinese, even in the urban areas, could realistically hope for. Magazines for men tend to be concerned with stories and films about violence, martial arts, sports, great men and beautiful women. Sex is often associated with violence. Fashion is dominant in magazines for women, which also contain features on grooming, make-up and hairstyles. Articles on films focus on appearance and romance. Where allusions are made to sex it is the context of moral codes, happy marriages or romance (Honig and Hershatter 1988; Evans 1997).

When young migrants return to the rural areas they have to readjust to life in a very different environment. The urban influences they have received may make the process difficult. They re-enter a household whose age-based hierarchy will mean for most of them the loss of the autonomy and independence that they had when they were away from home. If they were successful as migrants their earnings fall on their return. But the reintegration of these more fortunate migrants may be eased by the esteem accorded to them for the contributions they have made to family income and their knowledge of the outside world. Migrants who return and set up successful businesses are similarly privileged. Others, whose life away from home was hard and who did not succeed in earning much, may be relieved to come home but have to endure a sense of failure.

For many, the most difficult adjustments are connected with the urban influences they have absorbed. The ideas they take back from the cities whether about love, or more companionate marriage, or about home comforts, consumer goods and luxuries, will sometimes involve them in conflict and perhaps disappointment when they return to their rural lives.

One of the most likely areas for conflict is marriage. In a peasant society where marriage is a family affair and marriage finance is supplied by the family, a bride is seen as a new daughter-in-law and a new member of the family, just as much as she is a wife. Her health, character and abilities, the contacts she will give her husband's kin, the brideprice her family require and the dowry she will bring, all are matters of concern to her husband's family. Where young migrants have been influenced by an urban popular culture that promotes ideals of courtship, mutual attraction and love matches there may be conflicts over the arrangement of marriages.

The older generation may also disapprove of the extravagance of the young when returnees seek to furnish and equip their houses or dress themselves and their children according to their new tastes. Many returnees experience considerable difficulty in resettling in the countryside and deep frustration at the things they cannot change. Returned migrants speak of their unhappiness at being criticised for their clothes and showed a nostalgic longing for news about the cities. In rural Anhui Province Wan Shanping noted the dislike felt by young women who had lived in the cities for rural latrines (Wan 1992: 106). They found it hard to reaccustom themselves to these and other features of rural life which in their childhood they had taken for granted.

Young people who have worked in the city can often be distinguished from other villagers by their appearance. This is especially the case with the young women who wear brightly coloured, more fashionable clothes, more expensive and less practical shoes and sport modern hairstyles. Their appearance often seems to deny their current environment. In defiance of Chinese tradition, they sacrifice warmth and comfort for appearance. I recall seeing a young returned migrant in a village outside Chengdu. She was sitting in her doorway knitting. It had been raining heavily and none of the roads in the village were made up. All around her was a sea of mud, yet she was wearing white high-heeled shoes made of thin leather. The distinctive appearance of the returnees makes them attractive as models for other young women. In Anhui the desire to buy clothes was found to be an important motive for female migration (Wan 1992: 58). The return of one cohort to the village reinforces the desire of the next to experience urban life and the movement of population may thus be self-perpetuating.[2]

The experience of being left behind may also change individuals. A study in Kerala showed that the migration of male relatives to the Gulf had profound effects on the development and capabilities of the women they left behind (Gulati 1993). When a married man migrates, his wife takes on new responsibilities. This is especially clear if the couple have already established an independent household. The wife then becomes head of household and takes on her husband's role of representing it in the public arena. She also makes all the day-to-day decisions about the land, the home and the children that formerly they would probably have shared. If the couple still live with the husband's parents the change will be less marked because the wife will remain subordinate to her in-laws but she will try to protect her interests and those of her children within the greater household. Male migrants may be anxious about leaving so many decisions about farming to their wives and may seek seasonal work in order to return to the village in the busy times not only to help in the fields but also to make the key decisions about the crops to be grown (Wang 1997).

Migration gives a new relevance to reading and writing in the rural areas when migrants stay in touch through letters. The illiterate become conscious of their disadvantage as they must find someone they trust to read and write letters for them. Those who attended school for long enough to acquire literacy have an incentive to renew and maintain their skills. When remittances start to arrive family members have to go to banks or post offices, possibly for the first time, and learn to use bank accounts. An improvement in functional literacy is thus to be expected in the sending areas when migration becomes part of the way of life.

Migration has a profound influence on life in the sending areas by reducing their isolation. Migrants bring back new ideas, new attitudes and capital. Migration also creates new links between the villages and the outside world and thus accelerates the pace of change in many aspects of life in the sending areas.

MIGRATION AND ECONOMIC INEQUALITY

A final impact on the sending areas is on equality and stratification. We have seen that there is much spatial inequality in China and that migration tends generally to be from the poorer to the richer areas. We might expect therefore that migration would tend to reduce income inequality. In fact its impact is probably more complicated. Migrants are not always from the poorest families or the poorest areas. Successful migration requires contacts, know-how and some capital or at least the ability to borrow. In many villages, the poorest families lack these resources; indeed, only a few elite families may command them. Moreover, because there is a close association between the household's labour power and its income per capita, better-off families are also those most likely to be able to spare somebody for migration.

Some of the poorest counties and villages also miss out on the potential gains from migration. Families in these areas lack contacts and cash. Their expenses are likely to be particularly high because the poorest areas are also almost always remote and inaccessible. Without traditions of migration the difficulties of migration are also compounded by a lack of information.

Thus even in labour migration a distinctive hierarchy emerges. The best-off areas and families can send migrants further. Their choice is likely to be better informed and made from a larger range of options. Being on the whole better educated, or more skilled, they will have the pick of jobs. The poorest, when they can afford migration at all, are more likely to send their migrants to the nearest place because costs will be lower. They are less likely to be able to provide the contacts needed to secure work. The migration of the poorest will therefore tend to yield less in income and remittances and to include the greatest number of failures where no employment is found.

Migration is seen as one of a number of ways in which official poverty areas in China can be helped, but the difficulties of independent migration are recognised and migration or 'labour export' has been officially sponsored from these areas. Official agencies provide links with employers in the destination areas. In 1987, 150,000 labourers from six counties of the Yimeng Shan Poverty area in Shandong Province were working outside the district boundaries. This amounted to between 5 and 10 per cent of the labour force of the area. At a time when the criterion for recognition as a poverty area was an average per capita income of 150 yuan these migrant labourers earned an average annual income of 960 yuan each, enough to support a household (Küchler 1990: 135). There has been extensive official sponsorship of migration from Gansu, a poor province with a population of 22 million which exported 1 million labourers in 1987. In Sichuan, too, migration is officially aided by local governments which have set up employment and information centres and training schools for would-be migrants.

Migration has created flows of money from the more developed to the less developed regions of China. Moreover, because economic status influences access to migration and determines the destination of migrants, migration is some cases will reinforce and even increase existing inequalities. Migrants from better-off families are likely to be able to earn and remit more. Their remittances are also more likely to be invested in income-generating activities than those of the poorest families who use remittances to survive. Migrants from poor areas may only be able to reach a nearby town where economic activity is modest and wages are low. Migration brings great benefits to the areas around the great cities that tend in any case to be the best-off rural areas in China. Migrants from these areas have the contacts and know-how to obtain jobs in the city. Suburban peasants can gain other benefits from migration by letting house space to migrants from further away and even, when they themselves have ceased to cultivate, by subcontracting their land to migrants from more remote and impoverished areas. Migration does raise the income of some poor areas and some poor families, but its effects are uneven and like many forms of economic growth it tends to benefit those who already have some advantages over other members of their community.

COSTS AND BENEFITS OF MIGRATION FOR THE SENDING AREAS

It is difficult to draw up a balance sheet for migration. Large-scale migration has only been underway for a decade in China and many of the consequences have yet to work themselves out. The problems of measuring even the *economic* costs or benefits are considerable. Many of the gains and losses from migration are still less tangible, being connected with emotion, culture and community. It is not possible to put a value on these.

For the individual household, the migration of one of its members usually brings economic gains for the family although the amount is very variable. When things go wrong there may even be a loss. Rural migrants who lack the information and contacts to find work may spend very significant sums without finding employment. In 1987 I interviewed a couple at Chengdu railway station who had spent 300 yuan travelling in Yunnan and Sichuan hunting unsuccessfully for work. In addition to the risks of unemployment, there are those of sickness, injury and even death. Male migrants are concentrated in dangerous occupations such as mining and construction where accident rates are high. There are frequent fires and accidents also in manufacturing because health and safety regulations tend to be ignored in the sweatshops of the new industries (Knox 1997). The deaths of migrants so frequently reported in the destination areas mean that bereaved families in the sending areas have lost a major earner. Migrants too badly injured or sick to continue to work will return home to be supported by their families.

The personal costs of migration can also be considerable. There may be prolonged family separations. When a couple are separated or children grow up far from their parents their subsequent relationships may be difficult. Family members who are left behind must take on work and responsibilities to which they are not accustomed, and must worry about the migrant who has gone to live alone in a strange new environment.

There is uncertainty about the balance of costs and benefits of migration for the sending area. Many development experts are sceptical of the benefits of migration. They point out that migration tends to remove the youngest, most enterprising and best educated of the labour force (Harris 1995; Todaro 1997: 279). The young adults who remain behind are the least educated and least likely to engage in new initiatives. The population of the sending areas becomes unbalanced with disproportionate numbers of females, elderly people and children. Not only is there a lack of impetus for new developments locally, the area becomes less and less attractive to outside investors. Economic development and enterprise within the sending areas is thus inhibited and the economy stagnates.

This pessimistic model fits the historical experience of areas of Europe such as the west of Ireland, or the Massif Central in France, as well as some developing countries in the contemporary world. It may be less appropriate for China, or at least for many of the sending areas in China. In most cases of Chinese migration the impact on the sending areas is mitigated by various specific factors. For the present, most migrants seem to be preserving strong links with their home areas. Their retention of land rights in the village contributes to a sense of belonging. The circulatory nature of migration ensures a high level of remittances and brings many migrants back to the villages after comparatively short periods. The level and continuity of remittances is kept up by the strength of Chinese family links and also by the possibility of contact through letters and regular visits home. Modern transport, banking and postal services, and more general literacy, enable the migrants of late twentieth-century China to maintain links with their families far more easily than would have been possible in China in the past, or indeed even in Europe in the period of the great migrations to the New World.

Remittances can raise local standards of living in the short term when they are used for consumption. This carries the danger that local people simply become dependent on remittances to the detriment of the local economy. It creates a vulnerability in the sending areas to events and developments outside as clearly illustrated in the financial crisis in southeast Asia in 1998 in the course of which millions of migrant workers were deported from Korea and Thailand. Sending areas in China suffered in 1989 when the political crisis interrupted migration to the urban areas (Küchler 1990: 135).

If remittances can be invested instead of going to consumption, the establishment of new enterprises creates local employment and raises incomes and production, thus providing a sounder base for higher consumption in the sending areas in the long term. There is some evidence from field studies and from anecdotes that this is occurring in China but it is impossible to determine the scale.

There is official concern about the negative effects of migration in the sending areas in China. The trend for competent people such as medical staff, teachers and mechanics to leave the villages and even the small towns is causing anxiety, as they are perhaps the least likely to return. Chinese employers, in common with employers elsewhere (Todaro 1996: 285), use educational attainment as a criterion for selection in labour recruitment. Educated migrants thus find jobs more easily in the destination areas and are more likely to retain them. Furthermore, *hukou* transfer is often made easier for the educated. Thus the selectivity of the receiving areas reinforces the brain drain effect of migration. The most educated are both more likely to leave the rural areas and to settle elsewhere. Sichuan government officials complain that their province is becoming 'a nursery, a school and an old people's home', bearing the cost of the reproduction and education of the labour force for the new industrial areas, and of caring for people in the dependent stage of their life cycle, without benefiting from their labour when they are in the productive stage (fieldwork notes, 1994). Such complaints exaggerate the scale of migration and ignore the compensatory role of remittances, but they are understandable.

However, the position taken by the Sichuan provincial government on the *hukou* system appears to recognise the value of migration to the province. The provincial government believes that the problem of surplus labour cannot be solved by the development of industry and small towns within the province which has been disappointingly slow. Migration to other provinces is therefore necessary. Although the provincial government does not call for the abolition of the *hukou* system, it would like migrants to be able to obtain permanent residence and employment in the receiving areas. In the early 1990s it was calculated that the result of such a policy in Guangdong Province alone could be that 2 million Sichuanese migrants already there might settle, bringing perhaps another 6 million family members to join them. The Guangdong provincial government has refused to agree to this (SASS 1994).

Another effect of migration has been the spotlight that it has directed onto the sending areas. The concern of the Chinese government at the level of rural to urban migration and the social problems to which it is giving rise, especially in the big cities, has forced it to recognise the rural poverty and regional inequality that act as push factors. If the government wished to reduce the levels of rural migration it could follow the Todaro prescription for doing so through a well-designed programme of integrated rural development (Todaro 1997: 287). In the Chinese case this should involve closing the price scissors by offering fairer prices for agricultural goods, continuing to expand non-agricultural employment in the villages, and improving the quality of life in rural areas through the development of education and health services and amenities such as water, electricity and roads. There would be obvious benefits for the sending areas if the Chinese government were to adopt this approach to reducing excessive rural–urban migration. However the costs would be high. There is no indication that the Chinese government will take up this policy option.

This discussion has explored the impact of migration on the sending areas. It is clear that its costs and benefits are difficult to measure. For the moment we have too little information to reach any certain conclusion on their balance. The more general question of the impact of internal migration on China as a whole will be taken up in the concluding section.

6 Migrants' Lives and Impacts in the Destination Areas

People here don't like us because we come from outside. But we work hard here and they need us.

(interview with migrant from Guizhou Province, street labour market, fieldwork Beijing 1994)

The destination areas for internal migrants in China are as varied as the occupations they take up and the lives they live. Migrants go to great cities like Beijing and Shanghai and the new urban areas of the Special Economic Zones, but also to lesser urban settlements and to small towns and even villages. Some construction workers employed on dams, railways or roads do not live in permanent settlements at all. Their homes are shacks on the construction site and their long-term legacy is not a new community or one transformed by their presence, but simply the structure on which they were working. In other types of destination area, migrants have had a very significant impact on life. These include the big cities themselves, the small towns where the government would like urban growth to be concentrated, the Special Economic Zones and the agricultural belt around the great cities where migrant peasants have taken over much of the cultivation.

The lives of migrants vary greatly according to the type of destination area and the occupation taken up. The labour market of Chinese cities is highly segmented. People with urban *hukous* monopolise jobs in state industry, government administration, education and the rest of the formal sector. Those with only a rural *hukou*, which includes most migrants, are formally excluded from these high-status jobs. Most migrants to the cities therefore work in trade, the service sector, construction or small privately run sweatshops. A few have achieved prosperity or even wealth through their hard work and entrepreneurial ability. The majority are restricted to jobs that local people would not want because the pay is too low or the work too hard or dirty. In the great cities at least, the informal sector, the catering trade and construction offer most employment to migrants and therefore merit attention. Domestic service, important as an employer of female

98

migrants, will also be discussed. Despite the barriers, migrants are beginning to break into industrial employment in some areas. In Beijing, industry provides employment to only 5 per cent of migrants, but in Shanghai textile factories almost all the workers on the assembly-lines are 'girls from outside' (*wailaimei*). Many state-owned enterprises employ migrants on temporary contracts even when they are laying off regular workers. Migrants are preferred for labouring jobs not only because their wages are low but also because they are not entitled to the welfare benefits that impoverished state enterprises find increasingly difficult to pay. Moreover, migrants on short-term contracts are easy to get rid of when the demand for labour falls. In other words, these migrants have become a classic 'reserve army of labour'. A different migrant labour force has grown up in the areas of new industrial growth, mainly in south China where there has been very considerable foreign investment and many foreign companies and multinationals have set up plants. These developments have led to the establishment of important migratory chains of young workers who take up jobs in electronics and garment manufacture. The last section of this chapter will look at their experiences.

MIGRANTS IN THE CHANGING CITIES

The migrant presence has contributed the transformation of Chinese cities since the early 1980s. Prior to the economic reforms Chinese cities were, by comparison with today at least, quiet, drab and orderly. Bicycles, pedestrians and carts drawn by horses, mules or donkeys filled the streets in daylight hours and there was little motor traffic. Chinese cities were quite unlike other densely populated urban areas in Asia. Although crowded, they lacked the bustle of the market. Commercial activity was restricted and controlled. Almost the only street traders were the women who belonged to co-operatives through which ice-lollies were sold. They sat beside white painted handcarts that were insulated like their own jackets and trousers with thick cotton wadding, calling out the set price of their standardised wares. Each handcart had a trading number. There were no regular vendors outside the co-operatives. Very occasionally, one might see a peasant peddling produce surreptitiously by the roadside, ready to flee at any sign of official attention.

Retail trade was a monopoly of the state, there were few open air markets and shopping mostly took place hidden from the street in state stores and markets, usually rather gaunt, comfortless structures built since 1949. Prices were predictable and fixed. Even in the big commercial areas shops closed early. The streets were empty by 7 pm in winter and 10 pm in summer. Queues, and the need to shop daily for fresh food, made routine shopping a time-consuming chore. The purchase of items other than daily necessities was inhibited by poverty, shortages, rationing and a strong emphasis on frugality. Although people took pleasure in such shopping, it had yet to develop as the leisure activity it has become today.

Eating out needed good timing. There were no private restaurants and state establishments kept very strict hours. In Beijing, for example, they usually opened for lunch between 11.30 am and 1.30 pm and for the evening meal from 5.30 to 7.30 or 8 pm. Eating places were very crowded during opening hours and it was frequently necessary to queue for a table in even the most ordinary eating places. There were many hours of the day when it was impossible to buy a meal. These timetables of shopping and eating varied a little with climate and region – the cities of the south were more lively than those of the north, while those of the northeast were duller still – but all were characterised by quietness and drabness.

The suppression of private enterprise made it extraordinarily difficult for the private citizen to get small jobs done. Some government departments had their own maintenance sections to look after their buildings, others had to buy in services from inefficient service companies. Simple plumbing, glazing or decorating jobs were a major bureaucratic task to arrange, even in state-owned housing. Things were even more difficult for owner-occupiers unless they could do the job themselves. There was a serious shortage of people to undertake work such as roof repairs, painting or joinery. Self-employed craftsmen could be accused of 'capitalist activity' and found the materials they needed hard to come by. From the 1960s, workshops and service companies organised by the street committees filled some of these gaps, but building maintenance remained a major problem for urban dwellers as the neglected almost derelict appearance of many urban structures attested.

These peculiarities of Chinese urban life in the 1960s and 1970s were the result of government policies designed to wipe out private enterprise and to support industry, above all heavy industry, at the expense of other sectors of the economy. The government starved the service sector of investment and almost completely suppressed private economic activity. Chinese cities lacked an informal sector. In most developing countries the informal sector provides a living to many of the unskilled and semi-skilled, provides opportunities in the urban areas to rural migrants, and allows small savings to used in ways that contribute to economic growth. It is an extremely important supplier of goods and services to the urban population. In China prior to the economic reforms of the 1980s the absence of a well-developed informal sector adversely affected the quality of life in the cities and was also a brake on economic development. In particular, without an informal sector it was difficult to maintain full employment or to supply all the goods and services the urban population wanted. The development of the informal sector in the 1980s and 1990s transformed both the appearance of urban areas and the lives of urban people and provided an important new channel by which rural migrants could enter the urban areas.

The Development of the Informal Sector

The beginning of the revival of the informal sector in Chinese cities was linked to a very particular migration stream: the return to the towns of the urban young people who had been exiled to the countryside during the Cultural Revolution decade. About 20 million of them returned to the cities in the years after Mao's death, creating real problems of unemployment. It was impossible to expand the state sector fast enough to provide jobs simultaneously for these young adults and for the younger cohort just finishing school. As the political climate liberalised, it was decided that people 'awaiting employment', as those for whom no job had yet been found were called, should be allowed to run small individual enterprises and to offer goods and services for sale on the streets. Many such young people had learnt to be self-reliant and to seize any opportunity that presented itself during their years in the countryside, some had even acquired useful skills. They set up roadside stalls selling cooked food, or offering haircuts, bicycle repairs and made-to-measure furniture. Soon there was a more general relaxation of the restriction of private commercial activity and all sorts of people began to set up as 'individual households' (*'getihu'*) as the new small enterprises were known. At first these were very much family concerns as the use of the word household implies, but once they were allowed to employ labour, some of the most successful small enterprises began to grow. The majority remained small and became the foundation of China's flourishing informal sector.

The most visible part of the informal sector are the free markets that began to open up all over urban China in the early 1980s. At first most stalls sold foodstuffs produced by peasants from nearby villages who came into town to sell their produce. They might stay a few nights in town but they soon returned to their homes in the villages. By the mid-1980s private stalls in street markets were selling a huge variety of goods, including clothes and manufactured items brought from all over China. The stalls were more substantial and their goods more valuable. 'Native place' loyalties and associations were important in the lives of the new residents. People from the same areas of China helped each other settle and saw each other through the inevitable crises of migrant life. In the Ganjiakou market of northwest Beijing in the early 1980s, local peasants had already begun to sell vegetables and fruit. At night they slept on their stalls. The market attracted crowds and other people plying many different trades came to it. By the mid-1980s it was possible to have watches, bicycles and shoes mended in the market, to have hair cut and clothes made, and to print business cards. Uyghur migrants from the urban areas of Xinjiang in Chinese Central Asia set up stalls and later small restaurants and shops selling kebabs, special local breads, *halaal* meat and dried fruit. Migrant traders lived in hostels and privately rented accommodation. By the late 1980s, garment traders from Zhejiang were also well established and the market had expanded greatly. Small stalls were replaced by more permanent structures and the variety of produce expanded continuously.

A great range of occupations has grown and flourished within the informal sector giving employment both to the urban poor and, increasingly, to the migrant population. Catering is perhaps the most important of these. Eating places ranging from mobile pancake and noodle stalls run from the back of pedi-carts to well-built private restaurants now flourish in China's cities and towns. The variety of cooked food on offer is extraordinary and the competition for custom is fierce. In sharp contrast to the practice of state restaurants in earlier years, these establishments are open for very long hours. Working conditions in catering are poor and eating places tend to be staffed by migrant workers. In cities like Beijing, where local people are reluctant to do such work, migrants predominate to such an extent that there are complaints when many enterprises close at Chinese New Year in order to allow their workers to return home for the holiday. In addition to catering, migrants are engaged in many other minor service trades. In bustling street markets they offer made-to-measure tailoring and alterations, mend clothes, wash and cut hair, fix watches and kitchen pans, shine shoes, give massages and tell fortunes.

The collection, sorting and recycling of domestic waste provides other migrants with a way of making a living. In the urban areas garbage is collected daily from households, hotels, offices, factories and other premises and ferried out by pedi-cart to collection points in the suburbs. There it is sorted so that metals, textiles, glass and other recyclable materials may be recovered. The money to be made from recycling can be considerable by migrant standards and the right to collect, especially the right to collect from 'good premises' likely to dispose of profitable waste, is jealously guarded by particular groups of migrants. In Beijing, waste collection is usually the preserve of families from Henan Province, who make up 66.6 per cent of all collectors. Of the rest, 12.2 per cent are from Hebei, 8.5 per cent from Anhui and only 12.7 per cent from other provinces (Zou 1996: 362). Waste collection tends to be monopolised by migrants from a particular locality in other cities too, illustrating the tendency of migrants to help relatives, friends and others from the same locality to enter a trade in which they are already established while, if possible, excluding others.

The Migrant Labour Market

When the influx from the countryside first began, the term 'blind migrants' (*mangliu*) was frequently used of the incomers. In fact, in China as elsewhere in the world, most migrations are carefully planned. Migration is expensive. The migrant has to raise both the fare and sufficient money to live on until a job can be found in the destination area. Migrants must therefore start work as soon as possible and most have a clear idea before they leave the sending areas of how they will go about finding it. There is much movement backwards and forwards and exchange of information between the sending areas and the destination areas. Most migrants know something of the area to which they migrate, and some will be making a second or third trip. Few travel alone, most make the trip in small groups of two or three, often in company with someone who has done it before. Many migrants already have a job when they arrive. Labour recruitment companies and construction enterprises contract with county governments in the sending areas and bring large groups into the cities or to the major construction sites together. Some migrants are recruited directly by particular enterprises or by labour contractors. Some rely on a relative or a fellow villager who has found them employment or is willing to do so. Others at least have the names and addresses of relatives or friends from whom to seek help or temporary accommodation. The media stereotype of the 'blind migrants' who arrive full of hopes but with little idea of how to fulfil them is misleading. The thousands of young peasants who sit on the forecourts of the railway stations of major cities huddled in coats and quilts waiting to be hired lend support to this idea of the migrant, but most are far more purposeful.

For those who can find their way around even a little, the stations are not the only places to look for work. Every town or city of any size has 'labour markets' (*laodong shichang*), as the places where migrants gather and wait to be hired are known. These tend to be pieces of waste ground near busy intersections where there will be plenty of passers-by. In cities such as Chengdu, which have retained something of their traditional layout, the labour markets are near gates or bridges which mark the old entry points to the city. Often, also, they are situated near railway stations or drop-off points for long-distance buses. Some are for general labourers and are full of young men looking tired and anxious or full of hope according to what their prospects seem to be. Others are more specialised. The hiring point for maids in Beijing is a lively place full of young women dressed in their best clothes. In other places one can find house painters waiting for hire with their brushes and paint rollers, or carpenters with the tools of their trade.

In the highly segmented urban labour market migrants are employed in jobs that city people would shun because they are heavy, dirty and insecure or are seen as demeaning. Equally, migrants are excluded from more desirable work. State-owned enterprises normally recruit permanent workers only from the urban population. Taxi licences are granted only to those with a local urban *hukou* in cities such as Beijing, Shanghai, Tianjin, Chengdu and Kunming. Possession of a local urban *hukou* is a condition of employment also for jobs in many offices, hotels and shops. There are other ways of discriminating. Job advertisements often contain specifications about the education and appearance of the applicants. When I enquired in a shop in Chengdu why it had been thought necessary to state a minimum height for would-be assistants I was told that short people were often from the country and would not be suitable as they were not polite or cultured (fieldnotes, 1994).

Migrant Accommodation and Family Life

Accommodation is a major problem for migrants. Chinese cities are desperately overcrowded. Most housing is state-owned. The employees of state enterprises are given apartments at heavily sub-sidised rents. Apartments in some recently constructed blocks are now offered for sale, but at prices that can only be afforded by very affluent families or those who receive help from relatives overseas. An urban *hukou* may also be required for such a purchase. Migrants are thus doubly excluded from this market. According to survey evi-dence, 40 per cent migrants live in the homes of residents (Solinger 1995: 133). This would include both those given shelter by friends and relatives and those who rented space in a house in the urban area or the villages around. Another 20 per cent live in collective accommo-dation such as factory dormitories and construction site shacks. Hotels and hostels accommodate a further 20 per cent, while the remaining 20 per cent sleep in 'other places'. This presumably includes those who build shacks in squatter settlements, the market traders who sleep on their stalls, those who camp out under bridges and at railway stations and in all the other places where the homeless seek shelter in cities.

The unsatisfactory nature of much accommodation for migrants encourages them to make their stay temporary. Such conditions can be endured for a short time by those whose hopes for the future are focused elsewhere. Survey evidence from various large cities in the late 1980s indicates that while 61.5 per cent of migrants had stayed more than a month, only 28.7 per cent of those interviewed had been at destination for more than a year (Li and Hu 1991: 9). A Beijing survey of 1994 found that 59.2 per cent of migrants had been in the city for less than one year and only 18.4 per cent for more than three years (Zou 1996: 113). Migrants who come to the city intending to save as much as they can in a few years, and then return to their vil-lages to make a better life, will accept very poor accommodation as long as it is cheap. If they rent from local residents they usually live in very overcrowded conditions. The best shacks in migrant shanty towns are of rough brick, but other are constructed from corrugated iron, plastic sheeting and straw mats. Migrants who stay longer, especially those who acquire their own shacks or bring members of their families to live with them, may be willing to invest more in their housing. However, insecurity still discourages them from doing so. If migrants lack the right to stay in the city and fear that their shack may be razed to the ground in the next drive to clear out illegal residents, they are not likely to want to pay to install electricity or water in their homes.

Most migrants live and socialise with other migrants in single-sex communities. Only a minority have a family life. The State Commission for Education recently estimated that there are 2–3 million children with migrant parents in the destination areas (FBIS, 6 June 1996) – a modest number in relation to the usual estimates of migrant numbers, which seems to confirm the assertion that the majority of migrants are young and childless or that they leave their children at home. For those who bring their children (usually long-established settlers), poor accommodation makes family life difficult. If no affordable childcare is available, the mother will find it difficult to work unless she is involved in trading where it is easier to keep the child with her. Temporary residents have very inferior access to education and medical services. The children of migrants are likely to spend less time in school and to have less healthcare than the children of urban residents, or possibly than children in their areas of origin. Data from Beijing indicate that only 40 per cent of migrant children in the 5–14 age group are enrolled in school compared with 100 per cent residents' children. In the 0–4 age group 80.2 per cent of the migrant children have been vaccinated against polio compared to 95 per cent of the children of residents (Yuan et al. 1996). It is interesting that in the most prosperous of Beijing's migrant communities, Zhejiang Village discussed below, migrant businessmen early began to solve these problems for themselves by setting up kindergartens, schools and clinics. Poorer migrant communities do not have the resources, either financial or organisational, to do this. Their members tend to spend shorter periods in the city and are less likely to bring their families to the destination areas.

The Visibility of Rural Migrants in the Cities

There is a high consciousness of the presence of migrants in China's big cities. There are various reasons for this. Peasant migrants tend to look different. They wear older, less stylish clothes than city people and often have darker skins having worked outside for much of their lives. They tend to concentrate in certain areas of the city where they work or can enjoy the company of others from their own part of the country. Their poor accommodation means that they may spend much time milling around in public places and their occupations in markets and on construction sites also make them highly visible. Migrants who are searching for work naturally hang around in places where they will be seen by potential employers. Most important of all, although the mobility rate of the Chinese population as a whole is not high, a limited number of big cities exert a powerful pull on migrants and in these places migrant numbers are considerable. Temporary migrants made up a quarter of the population of Beijing city in 1994, while in 1990 they made up 37.8 per cent of Hangzhou's population and 12.4 per cent of that of Tianjin (Li 1996). In Shanghai the proportion of transients to permanent residents is thought to be about one fifth (Sun 1987: 205). The ratio of transients to registered population in Guangzhou is reported as 1:3 (Li 1994: 2). The concentration of migrants in the big cities has changed city life in many ways. It has also produced the negative reactions that are examined in chapter 9.

Migrant Settlements

Migrants who do well in the city tend to bring in friends and relatives from their home area. Such chain migration may take several forms. Settled migrants may be able to employ newcomers, to recommend them to their own bosses or to give them accommodation. At very least they should be able to advise on how to find jobs and accommodation. This mutual aid based on geographical origin leads fellow provincials and indeed fellow villagers to concentrate in the same urban areas. The process has gone so far in Beijing that certain parts of the municipality have been dubbed 'Zhejiang Village', 'Anhui Village', 'Xinjiang Village' and 'Henan Village'. These names can be misleading. They are not true villages but rather peri-urban areas where there is very little agriculture left and where the informal economy and small businesses run by established migrants offer enough employment to attract migrants in large numbers. Moreover, with the exception of the well-established Zhejiang Village, these villages contain only a minority of migrants from the province after which they are named. For example, local people vastly outnumber Xinjiang migrants in Beijing's 'Xinjiang Village'. It is not the numbers of migrants in this area that make people so conscious of their presence, it is rather that *halaal* restaurants and kebab stalls give the area a special atmosphere, and the distinctive physical appearance and dress of Xinjiang people make them particularly conspicuous. The most established of these migrant settlements, 'Zhejiang Village', is rather different. Elsewhere in China migrants are usually in the lowest status groups. In Zhejiang Village there are migrants among both the best-off households and among the poorest. A well-off trader may still be disadvantaged by the lack of an urban *hukou*, but is much better able to find a way round the problems that arise from migrant status than a migrant labourer would be. The community leaders in Zhejiang Village are themselves migrants. The village has developed as a complete community with its own social stratification and a distinctive social and economic system.

Zhejiang Village

Zhejiang Village is worth a closer look, not because it is typical of migrant settlements, but rather because as one of the largest and most successful migrant communities in China it has some interesting characteristics.[1] It is not simply an urban area in which a lot of migrants have settled, but rather a formerly agricultural area that has been urbanised by migrants and by the new economic activities they have introduced. The urbanisation process is incomplete. Although the streets of Zhejiang Village are lined with workshops and there is small-scale industry everywhere, most of the roads have yet to be paved and some of the shacks still lack electricity. Zhejiang Village is situated to the south of the city of Beijing and extends across 26 former natural villages. The area has a thriving economy based largely on garment manufacture. At present it supplies clothes not only to the markets of Beijing, but also to those of north and northeast China. Most of its production is of cheap, rather low quality garments, but its small businesses have earned considerable success by their quick response to changes in fashion. They have even developed an export trade. Buyers from Russia and Eastern Europe who come to Beijing via the trans-Siberian railway now find their way to Zhejiang Village to buy leather jackets and other garments.

Migrants are in the majority in this area. Its population of 110,000 is made up of 14,000 locals and 96,000 migrants (Xiang forthcoming). Among the migrants, over 50,000 come from Zhejiang Province and of these 75 per cent come from Yueqing county and 20 per cent from Yongjia county. Both these counties are in Wenzhou Prefecture in the east of the province, famous for highly developed rural industrialisation and for a high level of commercialisation. The remaining 40,000 migrants come from Hubei, Anhui and Hebei Provinces.

There are significant differences between the Zhejiang migrants and those from other provinces. The great majority of the Zhejiang migrants either run small businesses or are the dependants of small businessmen. Migrants from Zhejiang who work for someone else tend to see the job as a stepping stone towards becoming self-employed. When they have acquired the necessary skills, contacts and capital they set up their own businesses. Almost all the Zhejiang migrants have a network of friends, relatives and fellow villagers in the Beijing settlement on which they rely for raising capital, sharing business information and doing deals. Such networks smooth the path for young migrants newly arrived from Zhejiang. The migrants from other provinces who live in Zhejiang Village resemble other rural migrants in the urban areas. Many are employed by the Zhejiang businesses, others are self-employed, scraping a living within the informal sector. Lacking the social networks and the entrepreneurial skills of the Zhejiang migrants, they cannot compete with them in business.

Wenzhou has a long tradition of migration which seems to have contributed to the remarkable success enjoyed by Wenzhou migrants in Zhejiang Village. Of the male employers over 30 years old in Zhejiang Village, over 60 per cent migrated to other provinces before coming to Beijing. The Wenzhou tradition of migration was interrupted in the late 1950s and 1960s but resumed during the Cultural Revolution when the control of population movement broke down. Zhejiang people had high levels of skill in crafts such as tailoring and carpentry. They used contacts made through rusticated Red Guards and other 'official migrants' to move about the country selling these skills. As they did so they began to amass capital, which they were able to invest in trade and business as restrictions were increasingly relaxed in the early 1980s.

When they began to sell garments in Beijing, the Zhejiang migrants used some stalls rented from the local authorities and counters leased in state shops but also they set up unofficial stalls. At first these were frequently closed down by the police, but later migrants managed to negotiate toleration and even registration for their own stalls. When those who had begun as tailors became busy with trade they needed more garments than they could make. They sent for young friends and relatives from home to come to Beijing as partners or workers. As so many people with tailoring skills had left Wenzhou, tailoring classes were organised to train new hands.

After a few years in Beijing most Wenzhou migrants would try to become independent traders with employees of their own. This created an ever-expanding market for migrant labour that it was difficult to satisfy from Wenzhou. Employers began to consider workers from other provinces. Tailoring workers from Hunan and

Jiangxi even travelled to Wenzhou at the time of the Spring Festival hoping to find work with entrepreneurs from Beijing's Zhejiang Village who returned home for the holiday. Both employees and employees paid labour contractors who put them in touch with each other, and the contractors sometimes paid agents to find them workers from further afield or trainers to teach tailoring skills to the new workers.

Zhejiang Village businessmen have also developed contacts in different areas of China to source their raw materials. Silk is still brought from Zhejiang, cotton comes from Shandong and leather from Hebei. There is much division of labour in this thriving and rapidly growing community. Garment-makers, embroiderers and seamers subcontract work to each other, balancing their accounts at regular intervals. Agents specialise in cloth purchase, labour recruitment, stall hire and raising investment funds. Services are supplied by private enterprise. The first private kindergarten appeared in the village in 1988 and clinics, hairdressers, restaurants and food shops are numerous.

Official policy towards Zhejiang Village has undergone considerable fluctuation. By the late 1980s, migrants were increasingly ignoring rules that required them to register for trade in both their home areas and in Beijing. Migrants were arriving in ever greater numbers. Around 1986, when the numbers from Zhejiang reached 12,000, the area began to be spoken of as Zhejiang Village. The authorities became concerned about this concentration of migrants and the problems it might pose for social order. From 1986 to 1990 each summer the authorities had clean-up drives during which thousands migrants were expelled from the Beijing area. The migrants countered by going into hiding in villages in nearby Hebei Province from where they could continue to run their businesses on a reduced scale and wait until the storm abated. After a big anti-migrant drive in 1990 intended to 'clean up' Beijing for the Asian Games, official policy changed. A developing appreciation of the commercial activities of Zhejiang Village led to a new, more constructive approach and the discussion switched to the problems of administering the area, providing premises for a wholesale market and collecting sanitation tax. The Public Security Bureau still makes periodic sweeps of Zhejiang Village, but its objectives are now to control illegal constructions, unlicensed enterprises and traffic problems rather than eliminate the settlement.

Unusually for a migrant community, Zhejiang Village has a large group of successful, well-to-do people. We know little about the means by which they negotiate with the state, but it is clear that they are well placed to obtain concessions. At an unofficial level they have the means to bribe local functionaries and thus to obtain papers such as trading licences, clearance forms and temporary residence permits promptly. The community has shown a capacity for self-organisation that reflects its maturity (Yuan 1996). Concerned that their children were not entitled to enrol in Beijing schools because they did not have urban *hukous*, people in Zhejiang Village have raised funds to start their own schools. Hospitals have also been set up. Much research remains to be done on Zhejiang Village, but it is obvious that its success in building a comparatively stable community and increasingly in winning toleration from the state arises from its extraordinary economic success.

CONSTRUCTION WORKERS

A very high proportion of male migrants are employed on construction sites. Some are hired by the day and live like other workers in the informal economy, but many are brought into the urban areas by their employers or by labour contractors with whom they sign fixed-term contracts. An enormous amount of employment has been generated by new construction because of the scale of the boom since the economic reforms and because China's building industry is still highly labour-intensive. The pace of work on building sites does not appear hard but the working conditions are. In the absence of mechanisation there is much heavy lifting and carrying. The press carries frequent reports of fatalities from site accidents.

Contract workers not only work on the sites, they usually eat and sleep there. It is not unusual to see shacks which house 50–100 workers on sites where quite modest building projects are in progress, and far larger numbers can be found. Living conditions are primitive. Usually the shacks are inhabited only by men who are single or have left their families in the villages. The floorspace of the huts is almost entirely taken up with crudely made wooden or bamboo frame beds leaving no room for any indoor activities and almost none for the storage of possessions. The men complain that they dare not purchase anything like a radio-cassette because they have nowhere safe to store it. Even the storage of gifts to be taken home to their villages poses a problem. Cooking is done on small stoves outside the huts, and bowls and chopsticks are washed in buckets. Sanitation is primitive. The workers' laundry fluttering from strings fixed up between the huts reflects a determination to stay clean even in these difficult conditions.

Leisure time is mostly spent sleeping, or sitting on the beds or on little stools outside in the sun chatting and smoking.

Of all migrant groups construction workers working under contract have the least contact with the urban population. Almost all that they need for their meagre lifestyle is provided on the site. Often they see very little of the city they are in. They fear getting lost or being cheated, or simply spending the money that they are working to save.

DOMESTIC SERVICE

There has been a large increase in the number of families employing domestic help since the economic reforms.[2] Many factors have contributed to this increase: urban prosperity, the emergence of well-to-do dual-career families, the disappearance of the political taboo on employing maids and the development of a culture of domestic comfort. Even population policy has played its part. Young parents anxious to safeguard the health of precious only children shun crèches for very young children in favour of care in the home. Women in employed in state industries, government service or education are entitled to six months' paid maternity leave if they undertake to limit themselves to a single child. For financial and career reasons most women return to their jobs after this leave so they face the problem of finding someone to care for their baby. Most favour a grandmother or the help of another family member, but when this is not available they search for a live-in help. If the family is well-to-do a live-in help may be recruited even in addition to a female relative so that one woman can devote most of her time to the baby.

The way that domestic service has developed reflects China's dual economy and the pull that the cities can exert on poor rural areas. Maids in the cities are almost exclusively recruited from the countryside. Although urban employers complain at the amount they have to pay their maids, no urban family would regard domestic work as a good opening for a daughter. The hours are too long, the opportunities for advancement zero and the job is considered demeaning. Young women from the poorer areas of China's countryside, however, see domestic service in the city as offering all sort of possibilities: the experience of city life, the chance to help their parents with money or to save for a dowry, and the opportunity to buy pretty, fashionable clothes. Domestic service is easy to enter. It does not require large sums of capital or an extensive network of urban contacts. It draws on skills in which most rural girls have acquired some grounding in their own homes.

Maids' feelings about the job are very much influenced by their treatment. Some are treated like junior members of the family and seem to perceive themselves as such, using familial forms of address to their employers. This is likely to be the case when they are in fact relatives, but also when the family still has close links with the countryside. But the nature of domestic service is changing and maids are now more and more often strangers, recruited through less personal channels. The migration of maids to some of the major cities of China is dominated by young women from Wuwei county and the surrounding area in Anhui Province. Most arrive in the city in their late teens expecting to work in families for periods of 2–3 years. At the end of this period they return to their home areas to get married, often finding a relative to take their place with the family for which they have worked.

Thus, like other migrant occupations, domestic work seem to be dominated by migrants from a particular region of China. This is certainly the case in Beijing where 33.6 per cent of all maids are said to be from Anhui Province (Zou 1996: 362). Many of the others also travel long distances to the capital: 12.8 per cent are from Sichuan and 12.4 per cent from Zhejiang. Two less distant provinces also supply significant numbers: 13.4 per cent come from Henan and 9.5 per cent from Hebei. Taken together all the other provinces supply only 17.7 per cent of Beijing's maids. This pattern is interesting because in the case of domestic service, the survival of traditional recruitment methods would lead us to expect a more even distribution of origins reflecting the origins of the permanent residents who are the employers. Some people still like to recruit maids from villages with which they have some connection or from the families of their rural relatives. This is especially the case if the maid is to be entrusted with the care of a child. However the fact that well over 80 per cent of the maids in Beijing come from only five provinces appears to indicate that other patterns of recruitment are now dominant. Many maids find their own replacement when they leave their employers. In other cases families obtain a maid through friends or relatives who ask their own maids to introduce a suitable person. Both these methods of course support the continuation and expansion of migration chains. There are also employment agencies that specialise in placing maids in families, but many people express concern about finding a maid in this way because they would 'know nothing about her'.

Traditionally in China maids lived in the family. They had lower status than members of the family but it owed them care and protection and their personal lives came under its patriarchal authority. Sometimes a maid was the daughter of her employers' tenants or she might even be a distant relative. Employer–maid relations in contemporary China are influenced both by traditional patterns and by the market. Both words commonly used for a maid in modern Chinese – *baomu*, which incorporates the character for mother, and *aiyi*, which means aunty – have familial connotations. As in the past, in contemporary urban society most migrant maids live with their employers. To some extent they share the family's living standards, eating better and staying warmer than migrants in most other occupations. Many enjoy exclusive daytime access to the family television. But these jobs have their disadvantages. Living space is very short, even in some prosperous urban homes. Maids rarely have any privacy. They may share a room or even a bed with the child for whom they care, or may sleep in a curtained off, area that is used as family space during the day. Living with the family they are constantly 'on call' except during their time off which is usually one day a week but can be as little as a half day a fortnight. Some maids live very lonely lives alone with a young child when their employers are out at work all day. This problem is especially serious in the high-rise blocks that now ring many Chinese cities. The isolated domestic life of city apartments is in sharp contrast to the social life of the village courtyards where most of the young women who work as maids were brought up.

Employers often see themselves as *in loco parentis* and allow their maids little personal freedom. They can be harshly critical of a maid's lack of appropriate domestic or cooking skills, or of unhygienic habits. They may also find fault with the girl's clothes, especially if she dresses too fashionably, and sometimes even demand the right to choose what she will wear. They are often critical or impatient of their maids' ignorance or naïveté and complain at their low standards of hygiene and the limited range of their cooking. They show little understanding of the huge culture gap that a girl from village China must traverse when she comes to live in an urban high-rise, or of the isolation that she experiences alone all day in an apartment. Above all they appear to resent the wages they pay to their maids, frequently complaining that they are not worth the money (fieldwork, Beijing, 1987, 1994, 1995).

Married women from the villages do sometimes seek jobs as maids in the cities, but tend to do so only in exceptional circumstances, such as extreme financial difficulty, marital disharmony or widowhood.

When they do become migrants, their husbands or their husbands' families may claim some right over their earnings. I interviewed one woman from Anhui who come to Beijing to flee a violent husband in Anhui. Unfortunately he had traced her there and demanded the repayment of her brideprice before he would agree to a divorce. This was going to take up six months of her wages. Single women are in the majority among live-in maids because the life is not seen as appropriate for a married woman (fieldwork, 1994).

In recent years another model of domestic service has emerged in the large cities. Women have begun to hire themselves out by the hour or the day to cook or do domestic work. Some live with their own families in the migrant settlements in and around the cities, others have rented a space to stay, usually in a peasant household in the peri-urban area. In Beijing some Anhui maids live with relatives in Anhui Village. This system of employment is preferred by slightly older women as it allows them to work clearly defined hours and to enjoy some personal or family life. By working for several different families during the week they can usually earn considerably more than they would in a live-in position.

Employers seem to have mixed feelings about hourly paid maids. They are uneasy about the changed power relationship in this system of employment. They complain that these women feel free to leave whenever they find better paid work, negotiate about jobs they will and will not do, are unwilling to stay late in the evening and are likely to pilfer food to take back to their own homes. On the other hand, many employers are glad of the privacy they gain when a maid lives out. For those who are short of space, the availability of a maid who does not need accommodation is welcome, and the possibility of employing a woman part-time enables more families to afford domestic help.

THE SPECIAL ECONOMIC ZONES

Migrant workers in the long-established towns and cities are a minority, albeit a large one, interacting with and often having a considerable impact on a settled host population. The situation in the Special Economic Zones and other newly industrialising area around them is quite different. The SEZs were set up in south China at the beginning of the economic reforms to attract in foreign investment. They offered taxbreaks and other favourable arrangements to foreign companies that wished to set up manufacturing plant. Since the early 1980s, the booming industries of these areas have drawn in capital from the outside world and labour from all over China. More areas have been allowed to offer special investment regimes to foreign capital and trade and investment regulations have been generally liberalised. Foreign direct investment into China which reached over US$3 billion in 1988 had risen to over US$30 billion in 1994. In 1995 it was over US$40 billion (SSB 1996: 554). In 1994 the SEZs had absorbed a seventh of total foreign investment into China. Guangdong Province also receives a disproportionate share of the investment but industrialisation based on foreign investment, cheap labour and booming exports has spread northward creating many new boom areas along the coast.

In the original SEZs the process of urbanisation is far advanced. City skylines are dominated by skyscrapers. Villages whose economies were based only two decades ago on rice and fish have been absorbed by urban sprawl, their paddy fields built over with factories, roads and cheap dormitory housing. Industries set up on greenfield sites have led to the development of new urban settlements where almost everyone is a migrant. It is estimated that there are over 10 million migrant workers in the SEZs of Guangdong Province alone. Most enterprises in these areas were created with foreign capital, and management practices, wage rates and working conditions are quite different from those that prevail in state enterprises.

The industries of these areas are labour-intensive and require a workforce with only moderate skills. They offer electronics assembly-line work, garment-making and shoe and toy manufacture. China has to compete for overseas investment with other Asian countries such as Sri Lanka, Thailand, Malaysia and the Philippines where bureaucracy may be less, and living conditions more attractive to foreign managers. Much of China's success is probably owed to its linguistic, cultural and sentimental attraction for Hong Kong and overseas Chinese businessmen, but the availability of cheap labour with work discipline and a decent basic education is no doubt also important.

Factory managers in the SEZs can set their own wage rates and can hire and fire at will. Wages are far below the level to be found in Hong Kong or Taiwan and wage rates can be considerably below the rates paid to urban workers in state industry in China. However, because the hours worked by factory workers in the SEZs are so long, 10–12 hours per day is normal, overtime brings up sharply the wages actually received. Most workers in the SEZs are between 16 and 25 years old. Older workers are actively discriminated against by employers and the

Shenzhen government does not permit permanent workers over 35 to work in the zone (Summerfield 1994: 729). Around 75 per cent of workers are female (Summerfield 1995: 35). Women are preferred for assembly-line work because they are considered more dextrous than men and better able to tolerate boring repetitive work. Many young women are from poor rural areas where they worked on family farms and never received an independent wage. In the SEZs they may be able to earn in one month more cash than a man in their home villages would make in a year.

Working conditions for migrants in these industries are hard, the pace of work is fierce, they are closely overseen and they do not enjoy the health and social security benefits of workers in state industry. There are many reports of industrial accidents and fires and anecdotal evidence of bullying and abuse from managers and foremen (Knox 1997). Most enterprises are large enough to make relations with the boss rather impersonal. Discipline is strict. There are fines for being late, for refusing to work overtime, for speaking at work or during meals, and even for infringements of the rules on uniform or for going to the lavatory without permission (Lee 1995: 383). Some accounts make the lives of migrants seem almost unendurable. Workers do sometimes attempt to strike for better conditions or take their griev-ances to bodies such as the Women's Federation (Zhang 1997) Some accounts imply that they are aware of what they have lost in leaving their villages. One woman worker in an SEZ said,

> although tending the field is very hard work, we have a lot of free time. When your work is done you can play with your village friends. Here you have to hold your urine until they give you the permit to go to the bathroom. (Lee 1995: 384)

But despite these hardships migrants continue to stream into the newly industrialising areas. It appears that the chance to earn a good wage is seen as compensating for everything else. The attitude of migrants is pragmatic. They believe their lives are hard, but that if they can endure the difficulties for a short time they will save or improve their prospects enough to make it all worthwhile.

I interviewed a Sichuanese woman worker on Chengdu railway station who was very certain of the advantages of work in an SEZ. She was travelling with her sister. Both were returning from visiting their sick mother in their village. The younger woman had a job in Beijing where she liked her life and conditions. Her elder sister earned more but worked much longer hours in Shenzhen. The older woman thought the younger one a fool because she would not join her in the SEZ. Like many workers in the zones, she lived in a dormitory owned and run by the factory. She shared a room with five other women. Her 'space' within it was a bunk bed on which she slept, dressed, made up her face and did her hair. She kept her possessions on it too, including a radio cassette because she liked to listen to music. The dormitory was secure and she had had nothing stolen. All the workers at the factory were from Sichuan, as was the canteen cook. This, she said, had made adjustment easier. She could eat Sichuan food every day and speak Sichuan dialect. This woman's life was like those of many workers in the SEZs. They tend to mix wherever possible with fellow provincials. This is reinforced by recruitment of workers through introductions from other workers.

The dormitory system makes it possible for the factories of these newly industrialising areas to recruit cheap female labour from the rural hinterland. The lack of accommodation felt to be suitable for young unmarried women often inhibits their migration and helps to explain why most migrants in China are males. It is significant that where employers particularly wish to attract women, as in the case of domestic service and this type of factory work, accommodation is usually part of the employment agreement. Early Japanese industriali-sation also housed a female labour force drawn from faraway villages in dormitory accommodation (Hunter 1993; Tsurumi 1990), as did some Shanghai factories in the 1920s and 1930s (Honig 1986). This was also the practice in Taiwan in the course of industrialisation (Kung 1983). The system discourages the formation of a permanent labour force for it is incompatible with marriage and family forma-tion. It suits the needs of employers who fear problems from organ-ised labour and wish to maintain a young docile labour force which can be worked extremely hard with minimal health problems. Such an employment system encourages a high turnover of labour. Many plants lose 50 per cent of their labour force every year and few workers plan to stay in this sort of employment for more than two or three years. The temporary nature of this work does not encourage training and other investment in human capital.

There is however a clear hierarchy of work in the zones and new industrial areas. The best jobs are taken either by local urban people or by urban people from elsewhere. Whereas the assembly-line workers are predominantly female, a majority of these others, the managers, technicians, supervisors and accountants, are male. Jobs in tourist and hotel services confer higher status than factory jobs and tend also to go to local people or to the best qualified of the migrants.

In the SEZs there are also differences of status dependent on registration. At the top of the hierarchy are local people who always had local registration or those who were given it as an inducement to move to the zones when they were first set up. Most of these permanent workers are older, better educated and much better paid. They tend to live in good accommodation and to enjoy various fringe benefits (Ip 1995: 280). Contract workers do not have permanent jobs but otherwise enjoy most of the same privileges as permanent workers (Ip 1995: 272). The majority of the workers in the zones have only temporary status. Most come from other areas and have a rural *hukou*. They sign a contract with an enterprise in the zone and may even do similar jobs to the contract workers. However, when the contract of a temporary worker ends, she is expected to go home unless she can find another job. Temporary workers have no right to remain in the zones once their employment is ended.

CONCLUSION

Migrants live difficult, marginalised lives everywhere in Chinese cities. The state exerts considerable pressure on them through its attempts to control their movement and occasionally even drives them out of the cities. They have fewer entitlements and privileges than other urban residents. The difference between workers with the right to reside and migrant workers is especially sharply defined in the SEZs because the rules on entry to the zones and residence within them are still strictly implemented. For a Chinese citizen to cross into Shenzhen is as difficult as crossing a national border elsewhere in world. But the differences between the migrant and the permanent worker in Shenzhen is only an extreme version of a system which operates in ordinary cities in China to exclude migrants from the better jobs, and from the security and welfare enjoyed by urban residents. Rural migrants live as second-class citizens in Chinese cities.

The extent to which migrants are ultimately able to integrate in Chinese urban areas will no doubt vary greatly according to specific local conditions. For the present, landholding under the household responsibility system, the strength of ties to the home village, and hardships and the lack of security in the destination areas prevent many individuals from settling. However, there are already exceptions to the general circulatory form of migration. Some individuals have built up businesses in the destination area or get good jobs there.

Others form attachments or feel that they have little to return to their villages for. It seems likely that as the new industrialisation becomes better established and sophisticated, the labour market will change. A high labour turnover will no longer suit the needs of the employers, at least in some sectors of the economy, and employers may seek to train and retain their young workers to a far greater extent than they do today.

China's economic performance in the last decade has been an enormous success. She has enjoyed a growth rate of over 10 per cent per annum and has greatly increased her share of world trade even during the years of international recession. Among the many factors contributing to this success has been the availability of plentiful cheap labour. Migrants have also had a positive impact on urban life through their provision of services to the urban population. Although rural migration has brought various stresses and strains, and migrants are often unpopular in the urban communities they live in, their impact on the economy has overall been positive.

7 Women and Migration

It's lonely sometimes in the factory. I miss my family. But I like
having money. I send some home to my parents so they are happy.
And I can buy clothes and have my hair fixed. I decide about those
things for myself. That's good.
(Young woman worker at Chengdu railway station on her way back
to a factory job in Guangdong Province, 1994)

Women have been discussed in all the preceding chapters of this
book. We have looked at sex ratios among migrants, at the effects of
migration on the relatives of migrants, often female, left behind in the
sending areas, and at the sexual divisions in the labour market for
migrants in the destination areas and the lives of female migrants.
This chapter will focus on women, returning to some of the gender-
specific aspects of migration already touched on in earlier chapters
and taking up others such as female autonomy, fertility, motherhood
and prostitution. Marriage migration, that is a move undertaken in
order to join a spouse in another area, is the subject of a separate
chapter, but this chapter will look at other aspects of the relationship
between marriage and migration, such as the way in which the timing
and the duration of women's migration appears to be affected first by
the need to find a partner and subsequently by being married.

MIGRANT SEX RATIOS AND THE POSITION OF WOMEN IN
CHINESE SOCIETY

Migrant sex ratios have to be understood in the context of China's
gender system. Inequality between men and women affects both their
wish to migrate and the likelihood of their being allowed or selected
to do so. We saw in chapter 2 that although there are considerable
variations in the sex ratios between different migration streams, male
migrants generally greatly outnumber female migrants, especially if
marriage migrants are omitted from the count.

The low proportion of women in most migration streams can be
attributed to various factors. All individuals in China are expected to
live within their family circle unless there is good reason for them to
do otherwise, but the feeling that this is appropriate is stronger in the

case of women. Women are considered more vulnerable and less capable of dealing with the outside world. Single women are seen as especially in need of the protection and supervision of their families, a view certainly related to the wish to preserve their virginity and thus their marriagiability. The mobility of married women too is constrained by the demand that they should live under the protection of their families. Once one woman has been allowed to migrate she may break down the barriers for others in her family and perhaps her village (Zhang 1997: 7). Hoy cites examples of women migrants in Beijing who had followed their sisters, and interviews with female migrants usually reveal that they have travelled with a relative or fellow villager or been helped by one at destination (Hoy 1996: 217). None the less, cultural reluctance to allow women to leave their families no doubt partially accounts for migrant sex ratios.

Marriage arrangements also tend to inhibit female migration. Some women migrate either to seek a partner in a wealthier area, or because they have married a man in another administrative area. This marriage migration is discussed in the following chapter. However, for labour migrants it is seen as difficult and perhaps undesirable to marry at destination. Lacking an urban *hukou*, the migrant is not an eligible partner for the urban resident, so the choice of partners open to the migrant may be poor. A marriage arranged at destination might well incur the disapproval of the migrant's family. Not only would it deprive the family of the chance to vet the match, it would tend to weaken the migrant's links with home and so reduce the chances of eventual return. Migrants therefore often go home to marry. This is more likely to curtail the migration in the case of women, who marry earlier and because once married they are less likely than men to migrate again.

The low propensity of married women to migrate reflects the way migration functions in China. As we saw in chapter 6, inadequate accommodation and the difficulty of accessing education or health facilities hamper the settlement of migrant families at destination. Although some overcome these problems and succeed in bringing up their children in the urban areas, most do not. Some female migrants who can earn good wages in the destination areas send the children back to the villages to be cared for by relatives. But in many cases, even in areas from which migration is a common choice for young people, women, once married, stay at home to look after their children in the villages. Their husbands may continue to engage in seasonal or even longer-term migration. The landholding system tends to reinforce this choice. Migrants can retain their right to a plot of responsibility land in their village if someone cultivates it for them. From the perspective of the household, it makes sense for the woman to look after the family plot, while the husband exploits his higher earning capacity in non-agricultural work. The retention of the plot is viewed as a kind of social security because it gives migrants something to come back to if things go badly for them in the destination areas.

When married women do migrate it is frequently to accompany or to join their migrant husbands. Hoy's migrant survey in Beijing (1997, 217) found that over three-quarters of the married women migrants had been accompanied on their journey by their husbands. Dependent migration is an important form of migration for women. Once married, women are less likely to migrate than married men. They may be unwilling to do so before they have given birth. Hoy's findings (1997: 317–8) seem to imply that married women migrants to Beijing had remained in their home areas until after the birth of their first child or perhaps even until they had achieved their desired family. Women whose first child was a boy had a greater propensity to migrate than those with a daughter, presumably because the latter tended to stay at home to have another child.

Another factor in women's low migration rates may be that generally speaking in China women earn less than men. When a household decides to send someone out as an investment, it will be concerned to maximise that investment, especially when travel costs are high. This will incline the household to send a man. However the relative usefulness of the household members at home may also be a factor in the equation. As we saw in chapter 5, Wan (1992) argues that one reason for high rates of female migration in Anhui is that women are not needed in the fields there. Young female hotel attendants I interviewed in Chengdu told me that as there had been no work for them in their villages their families had been happy to send them to the city where at least they could earn their own keep.

A strong demand for female labour at destination can encourage the development of a female migration stream. Female migrants who work in the new export-oriented industries of the coastal regions discussed in chapter 6 fit this pattern. Their employers deliberately seek to recruit women, sometimes even sending agents to sign them up in the origin areas and to facilitate recruitment by supplying dormitory accommodation at destination or even helping with transport. The local state also contributes. Some county governments in Sichuan province lay on coaches to Shenzhen and to other towns in Guangdong Province (fieldwork notes, 1994). The earnings of women workers in export-orientated industries are high compared to what they could earn elsewhere and may sometimes outstrip what a male migrant would receive. Once some women in an area have taken advantage of the opportunity, others hear about it and a chain develops.

THE IMPACT OF MIGRATION ON WOMEN'S LIVES

Women who live in the sending areas can be affected by migration either because they themselves migrate, or because they are left behind. In either case the impact is complex and the gains and losses are hard to assess. The effect of migration on agriculture has provoked widespread discussion in China. There is much concern that the agricultural labour force is becoming dominated by women, the old and the weak (*nühua, laohua* and *ruanhua*). As we saw in chapter 5, officials worry that changes in the structure of the labour force will lead to falls in agricultural production. This preoccupation with agricultural productivity means that the complexity of the effects of migration on the division of labour in the sending areas is often missed. Of course, women left behind when members of their families migrate are likely to take on a greater share of work. Many accounts of women left behind depict them struggling with the heaviest farmwork (Croll and Huang 1997: 143). But the type of work will depend on who has departed. If the migrants are female, the mothers, mothers-in-law, sisters or sisters-in-law they leave behind are likely to give more time to traditional women's tasks such as the preparation of food, the care of the house and of clothes, child-rearing, including caring for children not their own, and raising poultry or vegetables. If these demands are very heavy, women may actually reduce the agricultural work they do. Thus in some circumstances the traditional sexual division of labour within the household between 'inside' and 'outside' work (Jacka 1997) could be reinforced by migration.

The more usual situation is that migrants are predominantly male. If the departing man's labour was truly 'surplus' it will not need replacing. Often, however, the departure of a man does creates a shortage of male labour power within the household and thus challenges the sexual division of labour. Male kin from other households may help out, but it is likely that the women left behind will take on some work traditionally performed by men, including the heaviest fieldwork. As, in addition, they continue to be responsible for their normal tasks, the net effect is that women have to work much harder.

Research on migration in many other parts of the world has portrayed the women left behind in the sending areas as unfortunate victims of modern economic growth (Akeroyd 1991). They are left doing poorly paid, physically taxing work in the least mechanised, least productive part of the economy (Rogers 1980). Their property rights to land are often weak, or dependent on male relatives. They struggle to bring up their children alone, helped only by minimal and irregular remittances from their menfolk in the cities. Their relationships with the men come under strain and the men may start new families in the towns during their long absences.

We lack detailed survey findings on this subject in China but the picture is probably rather different. No doubt in China, as in other societies, separation in migration does place a strain on marriages. Fieldwork has shown that Chinese male migrants are suspected by their wives of starting new relationships when they are away (Wang 1997). But in general women left behind continue to receive remittances and to expect that their husbands will return. Close contact is often maintained and the absent man is still consulted about decisions at home and on the land.

A crucial variable in the impact of migration on the sending areas and on those left behind is strength of ties between the migrants and their home areas, the frequency of contact and the level of remittances and other benefits sent back by the migrant. Family ties, usually considered to be particularly strong in Chinese culture, are undoubtedly reinforced by the highly temporary nature of much Chinese migration which gives migrants a strong incentive to stay in regular contact with their families, preserving a place for the future in their villages. As Kung (1994: 112) points out in her study of female migrant workers in Taiwan, kinship bonds in Chinese society are maintained by giving and sharing. Moreover, migration, and the economic aspirations that inspire it, should be understood in the context of the household. In rural China, as in other Asian societies, the migration of one household member represents a bid by the whole household to diversify its economic activity and improve its lot. Family ties and a sense of reciprocal obligations underpin the system. A migrant's travelling expenses are often taken from household resources or raised through loans from relatives. Migrants expect and are expected to remit money, and when they are successful the whole household benefits. The biggest gainer may well be the wife. Successful migrants are able to earn more than they would do at home and to remit sums significant enough to improve the household standard of living. Gulati (1993) has shown that in Kerala women whose men have migrated own more and better clothes and jewellery than other women. The same is clearly true in China, with the families of successful migrants enjoying higher living standards than others in the village. Men who are working away from home are commonly seen as desirable marriage partners for this reason. The most obvious sign of wealth is new housing financed by remittances, but money from the earnings of migrants also used to helps to pay for consumer goods, dowries, brideprice and education. Where a household has been left labour-short by the migration of one of its members, remittances may also be used to pay for hired labour. Alternatively, a family in receipt of considerable remittances may become less dependent on income derived from farming and may rent out land to poorer families.

Greater prosperity is not the unvarying result of migration. If we analyse migration as an investment by the household, we have also to recognise that it may fail. Migration is a high-risk business. The migrant may be unable to find work, or may fail to remit money for other reasons. Many migrants suffer periods of unemployment. Poor or even dangerous living and working conditions may make them the victims of poor health or accidents. Some migrant workers simply disappear, others fall ill, are injured or even die. In such cases their families and dependants in the sending areas will obviously suffer.

MIGRATION AND FEMALE AUTONOMY

In addition to impacts on work and income, migration has other less tangible effects on women. Female migrants are profoundly affected by their experiences. While they are in the destination areas they live very different lives from their rural sisters and come under the influence of urban culture. If they return to the villages, as we saw in chapter 5, they will bring with them different expectations of women's roles and marital relations, higher demands of living standards and housing, and greater aspirations for their children. Their knowledge and savings may enable them to set up small enterprises or find new ways to make money. Historically, urbanisation brings about enormous changes in the roles and lives of women. These changes can filter down to the rural areas if urban–rural relations are close enough, but will not do so if the city and countryside operate as independent worlds. In the Maoist era, city and countryside were isolated from each other to a considerable extent. The development of circulatory migration in which migrants go backwards and forwards between their homes and the destination areas has contributed to the breaking down of this isolation.

It is sometimes argued that migration promotes female autonomy (Chant 1992; Davin 1997; Gulati 1993). No individual can have complete autonomy within the family-based society of rural China, but there is no doubt that some women do gain increased independence through migration. Mobility separates family members and thus disrupts the day-to-day functioning of the family power structure in which authority is conferred by age and sex. Among the women left behind in the rural areas, many become *de facto* heads of household. But there are limits to their independence. Some still live with their in-laws; of those who do not, most will be expected to consult their absent husband or his relatives about major decisions. None the less the change is a real one and affects decisions about a whole range of matters including work, household spending and children's education. Women who are left alone begin to deal with village officials themselves. They may be pushed into greater contact with the modern world by the need to cash money orders or open savings accounts at post offices and banks. Women's literacy becomes valued more highly as they engage in such activities and as they need to write to absent members of the household.

Like the women left behind, women who migrate alone have to begin to take many decisions for themselves, which in the past would have been shared wholly or partly by family members. They buy money orders, use savings accounts and write letters. They decide for themselves what to eat and what to wear. They receive individual earnings and work out their own budget. They associate with new people who are neither relatives nor fellow villagers. For young rural women whose position in the family is still a subordinate one, who meet few strangers and are closely controlled by senior family members, the change is especially dramatic.

It is possible to exaggerate the degree of the autonomy achieved by female migrants. They may just be exchanging one form of authority for another less personal one. Social concern about young women workers living out of the reach of family control is manifest in various attempts to impose substitute controls on young women workers. The factory dormitory described in chapter 6 serves a particular function in this regard. It is used by employers to reassure parents that their

daughters have secure accommodation, that they are properly overseen and will be looked after. The communal sleeping and living
accommodation affords no opportunity for the young women who live
in it to develop relationships with men, and long working hours and
strictly enforced curfews limit their ability to do so outside. In many
dormitories an older woman is appointed to keep an eye on the young
female workers. The dormitory system also reinforces the dependence
of young female workers on their employers, a situation that many
employers exploit. As Hoy observes,

> with many young women literally locked into factories and dormito-
> ries, bound by contracts, their wages remitted to families sometimes
> hundreds of kilometres away and used for the promotion of the
> family and individual family members other than themselves, we
> should not assume that growing numbers of women in the migrant
> labour force are always associated with a growing sense of auto-
> nomy and independence. (Hoy 1996: 355)

The many reports of very young women working extremely long hours
in terrible conditions in China's new industries, and the various
reports of tragic deaths of such workers when fires destroy jerry-built
workplaces or dormitories, make it impossible to idealise their
growing industrial experience as a liberating process (Knox 1997).

Yet the voices of these workers themselves bear witness to the fact
that many of them do feel that they are more confident and self aware.
Heather Zhang observed that 'access to paid jobs away from the
parental households gained migrant working girls a measure of personal
freedom and independence, weakening parental control over their lives
and changing familial values and norms in society at large' (H. Zhang
1997: 18). Women whom she interviewed working in foreign-owned
industries in the northern city of Tianjin insisted that the experience of
migration had tempered them, improved their abilities and independence and given them the chance to see more of the world, to read more
and to improve their literacy (Zhang 1997: 5–20). Some were even were
prepared to fight their employers for shorter hours and better conditions and to enlist the help of outside agencies such as the Women's
Federation in this struggle. They were proud that they had found jobs
and managed their lives in the cities. They harboured non-traditional
ambitions and aspirations for their futures. Some hoped to marry well
and settle in the city while others planned to use their saving to set up
businesses in the countryside. One spoke of becoming a 'career-minded
woman', or '*nüqiangren*' (literally 'strong woman').

Migration may even be used by women to buy themselves out of a situation in which they are unhappy. In 1994 I interviewed a woman at Chengdu railway station who was on her way back from her Sichuan village to a manufacturing job. She had made an arranged marriage several years before that had turned out badly. She could not get on with her husband at all, but did not want to upset her father by leaving. When her father died she had decided on divorce. Her husband kept their son but demanded that she pay over a large sum to cover the expenses of bringing him up. She had gone to Shenzhen in the first place in order to raise the money but had decided that her life there was not bad and that she would stay until she had saved enough to make a better life for herself back home (fieldwork notes, 1994). The Beijing maid whose story is told in chapter 6 obtained a divorce from her violent husband only after she had agreed to pay him a very considerable sum. She was, in effect, buying him off.

Where migrant women are employed as maids, the phenomenon of the employer replacing the authority of the family is even clearer than in the case of factory workers. A maid's free time is likely to be very limited, there will be a curfew and her employers may ask where she spends any time off. Some even expect to have a say in what television she watches or what she wears. One woman interviewee told me that she bought clothes for her maid, holding back a part of her wages to compensate (fieldwork notes, 1984). This was necessary, she explained, because the girl did not know what was appropriate for a maid to wear and might otherwise be tempted by outrageous fashions.

Maids who rent rooms from peasants on the edges of the cities, and hire themselves out to clean or cook in urban homes at an hourly rate, are challenging not only the custom that servants should live in and work full-time for one family, but the whole relationship of authority that went with that custom. They have to pay for their food and accommodation, but they earn much more than they would if they worked for a single family and enjoy much greater personal freedom. The arrangement encourages a sharper distinction between work and leisure. An hourly worker may work more intensively, but can decide the hours she will work and her free time is more truly free. Her employers lose the paternalistic power to supervise her life, and may not even know where she lives.

Without doubt migration creates challenges to traditional gender roles and the family hierarchy. Like all social change it also causes new social tensions and great stresses in individual relationships. Family separations produce sadness and regret and may be the cause of considerable disturbance to children. Parents whose son has migrated may try to assert their authority over their daughter-in-law. If she is insufficiently submissive, family quarrels result. Women may miss their husbands while they are away, but may also resent the loss of independence when their husbands come back to the village. Women migrants have many adjustments to make when they return. They may regret their lost independence, miss the bustle of the city or struggle to reaccustom themselves to village standards of hygiene like the women mentioned in chapter 6 who so disliked the village latrines when they returned to Anhui after working as maids in Beijing. Remittances are a potential area of conflict. To whom should a money draft be sent? For example, should a young married man address it to his parents or his wife? When the money is cashed, who decides how it should be used?[1] Family conflict is one of the various costs of migration in contemporary China. Its positive role is that it contributes to a shift in family structures and gender roles which still constitute such a barrier to improving women's status in rural China.

MIGRANT FERTILITY

Although, as we have seen, most migrants in China are young and single, and married migrants usually leave their families in the sending areas, it is often claimed that migrants are putting a burden on the cities by having too many children. There have recently been concerted administrative attempts in the big cities to establish a system for monitoring and controlling the fertility of migrants (Hoy 1996: 59–77). Much of the reluctance to extend the rights of temporary migrants is related to the fear that, once established, migrants will seek to bring their families to the cities. City-dwellers who see migrants as the source of disorder, dirt and crime find comfort in the idea that they will one day go home. The widespread perception of migrants as having extraordinarily high fertility contributes to generally negative attitudes. There is much reason, however, to think that this perception is mistaken and that high levels of migration will have negative impacts on fertility (Goldstein and Liu 1996).

First, those who migrate tend to marry later than those who do not. Migrants appear to postpone marriage because it is difficult to find a partner at destination and a return to the village means giving up an urban wage and lifestyle. Second, for married migrants, migration usually involves periods of marital separation and may thus be expected to depress fertility. Third, migrants may choose to have small families because their inadequate housing, long working hours and lack of family networks in the towns, make it so difficult for them to look after children there. Their exclusion as non-residents from health, childcare and educational facilities increases these problems. Fourth, opportunity costs of children for migrants are high. Migrant women who give birth will probably experience a loss of earnings or have to pay for childcare. They then face the choice of struggling to bring their children up in the urban areas, sending them home to be looked after by relatives, or returning with them to the villages to care for them there. The fertility of migrants may also be reduced by changes in their outlook. Migration brings rural people into contact with urban lifestyles and familiarises them with urban aspirations. The usual effect of prosperity, urbanisation and a more commercial lifestyle is to reduce the desired family size. It is relevant to note here that an improved standard of living for themselves and better prospects for their children come high in the declared aims of many peasants (Croll 1994: 222).

Fieldwork findings tend to confirm the common-sense assumption that the experience of migration lowers the desired family size of migrants and inclines people to have fewer children. The Hoy migration survey carried out in Beijing found that women who migrated early in their married lives had fewer children than would otherwise have been expected and that women who migrated before marriage tended to delay their marriages (Hoy 1996: 346). Hoy's study of Muslim migrants in Beijing showed that women who had migrated had a mean age at first birth two years greater than those who did not (Hoy 1996: 304). In 1994, in Guangdong, the fertility rates of the migrant population were found to be lower than those of the resident population (*Yangcheng Wanbao*, 25 June 1994). Moreover, there was evidence of migrants postponing childbearing. The childbearing of migrant mothers peaked at 26 years of age compared with 24 for the resident population. In Beijing, Hoy found high rates of contraceptive use and contraceptive knowledge among married women migrants (Hoy 1996: 254–62).

The perception by urban people that migrants have high fertility probably arises from the fact that most migrants are young, and many are in the years of peak fertility. Their fertility will inevitably appear high, unless the figures are controlled for age. Urban attitudes also reflect stereotypes about peasant family size, and a lack of understanding of fertility norms and family planning regulations in the countryside. Whereas birth planning regulations limit family size to one child in all the big cities, in some parts of the countryside women are permitted to have two or even three children. Temporary migrants are governed by the regulations of their place of origin, not by those of the area where they are staying. A migrant woman with two children would be noticed and considered by residents in Beijing to be exceeding fertility norms because the one child family is almost universal among urban residents in the capital. Yet she would not necessarily be contravening the regulations of her own place of origin, indeed she might come from a village where a family size of two was well below the mean. Intuitively, migration may also be expected to contribute to a lowering of family-size aspirations in the villages if the influence of returned migrants is strong enough (Wan 1992), but this hypothesis needs to be tested by surveys.

Official concern about migrant fertility remains strong. Migrants are seen as people beyond bureaucratic control. Anxieties focus on their fertility in general, and specifically on their comparatively high rates of pre-marital pregnancy, on the numbers of migrants who fail to register their marriages and on women who migrate because they wish to escape official attention when they have an 'out-of-plan' (non-officially sanctioned) pregnancy (Hoy 1996: 54–5). Family planning organisations that target migrants have been set up in many of the great cities ('Beijing Establishes 135 Birth-control Associations for Migrant Population', *Beijing Ribao*, 10 June 1994). Different cities and regions began to issue regulations on family planning for migrant populations from the late 1980s. In 1991 National Family Planning Regulations for the Floating Population were issued. These required migrant women to obtain a family planning card from the authorities in their home areas that recorded their marital fertility history and their current contraceptive status. All this information had to be registered with the Public Security Bureau at destination. Women were supposed to return to their place of origin to acquire a card and to go back every three years to renew it. The cards allowed women to have children in accordance with the rules in force at their place of origin. However, to obtain 'a permit to give birth' (needed by all pregnant women in China) they had to apply to the authorities at their place of origin. All migrants were supposed to show a certificate of contraceptive practice before they could be issued with residence, business or work permits. The 1994 Jiangsu regulation on the floating population forbade householders to permit the co-habitation of men and women without marriage, and several cities introduced fines for cohabiting couples at around the same time. Local governments are urged to observe the rules and issue marriage certificates while the Public Security Bureau is supposed to check marriage certificates before they issue temporary residence certificates (Hoy 1996: 55). Those who defy the regulations and fail to carry cards or those who have 'excess births' can be forced to return to their origin areas.

The national regulations on family planning for the floating population and the many regional measures for control make up part of a complex system of bureaucratic regulation of migrants other aspects of which were examined in chapter 3. It is difficult to assess the efficacy of the regulatory system. Its very complexity seems to make it likely that it might be imperfectly understood and applied. Certainly many migrants seem entirely ignorant of the detail of the regulations and some make no attempt to comply with them (fieldwork, Beijing, 1995). Others seem simply to regard the regulations as a pretext for official exactions, which is no doubt how they are often used. However, the regulations certainly have the potential to facilitate the policing of migrant fertility at destination – the purpose for which they were intended. The regulations also, of course, tend to affect women far more than men, forcing them into contact with officialdom and making them vulnerable to expulsion, or to exactions or harassment from corrupt officials.

MIGRANTS AND PROSTITUTION

In recent years there has been a considerable growth in prostitution in China. The reasons for this are complex but they no doubt include a relaxation of state control over the daily lives of the individual, widening differentials in wealth and income, and an increased commercialisation in many spheres of urban activity.[2] Newspaper articles and other popular and official discourse, often link the growth of migration and the growth of prostitution[3] (Dutton 1997: 171). The connection is worth considering.

The greater population mobility of the 1980s brought a large transient population to the cities where they lived side by side with people far more prosperous than themselves. Although the vast majority of people in China have become much better off since the economic reforms, the widening income differentials have made relative poverty a highly relevant concept. If rural migrants find jobs, they may earn much more than they would in their villages, but they earn less than urban residents whose *hukou* qualifies them for better paid permanent employment. Understandably, migrants search for ways to maximise their incomes. Female migrants who work long hours in industry or domestic service for comparatively small wages may well be tempted by sex work which could bring them a month's salary in two or three nights. A majority of prostitutes cite economic motives for their involvement in prostitution (Hershatter 1997: 403). Interestingly, prostitutes like rural migrants tend to see their work as temporary, a sacrifice made in order to amass enough money to realise an ambition. They speak, for example, of saving up to buy a taxi licence or a small business, finding a good husband and leading a happy life (Hershatter 1997: 254). For young rural women without formal qualifications who are stuck in poorly paid work, prostitution must appear a quick way to achieve such aspirations.

There is some evidence that many prostitutes are migrants from the rural areas. A survey of prostitutes held in urban re-education centres between 1989 and 1992 showed that more than a quarter were peasants. A further quarter were unemployed and may have had rural origins. These figures did not show with any certainty that women from the rural areas were over-represented. Moreover, the fact that 45.6 per cent of the women had stable urban occupations proves that it is not just migrants who are tempted by this lucrative work (Hershatter 1997: 347).

Brothels appear to be rare in China today. As prostitution is not legal, it is necessary to provide the activity with at least a small amount of camouflage. Sexual services are offered in hotels, taxis, coffee shops, karaoke bars, roadside halts, railway stations and open spaces such as parks. High-priced prostitutes whose customers are foreign or overseas Chinese businessmen operate out of hotels and charge enormous sums for an single encounter. The most fortunate obtain 'permanent contracts' from businessmen who set them up in apartments to visit whenever they are in town. Other women serve rich Chinese such as entrepreneurs or high officials. They also work from hotels or venues such as karaoke bars. At the bottom of the scale, the women who serve construction and contract workers or other transients, or people such as truck drivers whose work involves travelling, may well be peasant migrants. The migrant is at the bottom of the hierarchy in sex work no less than in elsewhere in the labour market. There are barriers to a rural migrant working from a high-class hotel. She would have neither the means nor the knowledge to dress in the way that would gain her entry to such a venue. Moreover, customers in such places prefer women of education. Surveys and anecdotal evidence indicate that the most successful prostitutes have at least secondary education and may even be graduates or have a professional background (Hershatter 1997: 355–6). Rural migrants are likely to work in the cheapest hotels and karaoke bars, at wayside halts or simply in the street.

Population mobility and the reappearance of prostitution are also associated with the development of trafficking in women. Some young women are fooled into travelling far from their homes on the promise of a job or a good husband only to find when they reach their destination that the agent who has 'helped' them in fact forces them into prostitution (Zhuang 1993). Other women are knowingly sold into prostitution by their families or abducted and taken to work in the sex trade of some big city. The development of the trade in women is dealt with at greater length in the chapter 8.

There is considerable official concern at the reappearance of prostitution in China. It is considered to be a sign of moral decadence and harmful to China's international image. However, attempts to suppress it meet with little success. High-class prostitutes earn enough to pay off officials and the police. Not only are their activities often tolerated, they may receive active protection. The Public Security Bureau and the People's Liberation Army both own karaoke bars where prostitutes operate. Yet prostitutes are often detained and sent to re-education centres. In 1993, arrests of prostitutes totalled almost 250,000 and tens of thousands of them were detained in penal reform institutions (Hershatter 1997: 330–45). The poorer prostitutes, catering to lower-class customers and lacking money and influence are most likely to be detained. Migrants like other prostitutes probably have to deal with demands for pay-offs from the police, but are doubly vulnerable because they lack residential rights and can be compulsorily returned to their native places.

The re-emergence of prostitution is part of the development of a complex marketised society in China. Greater population mobility is part of that development. Even if migrants are disproportionately involved in prostitution, migration cannot be blamed for its re-emergence. The demand for prostitutes would exist without the phenomenon of migration, and sex work is lucrative enough to draw in even urban women with regular jobs.

CONCLUSION

Women have hugely varying experiences of migration. For some young women migrants it may be a liberating experience that widens their experiences or their options in life. Others may be forced by migration into a health-destroying regime of long hours of exhausting work in dangerous conditions. Women who are left behind in the villages may suffer loneliness or grief at the departure of their husbands, but may gain in independence and confidence. They are likely to benefit financially from money sent back to them. At a structural level, because women are disadvantaged in the traditional rural society by interlinked factors such as the patrilineal family, patrilocal marriage, the sexual division of labour, access to land and son preference, change for them brings at least the possibility of gain.

8 Marriage Migration

One of my cousins was crippled so it was very hard for his family to find him a wife. They settled on a girl who lived a long way away so her family didn't realise how serious his condition was. They bought a television and all sorts of things to give to her family. When she came to our village and saw her husband, she was very upset. She never settled down, and in the end she ran back to her family. They wouldn't give the brideprice back because they said they'd been tricked. After a lot of arguing, the boy's family sent a raiding party over to get the stuff back. They did a lot of damage to the girl's family home but they knew they wouldn't have real trouble because their relative was the head of the Public Security Bureau for the county. Later they found another girl for my cousin, but they tried a new idea. They sent up into the mountains for a girl from a really poor village. They thought she would be glad to marry into a village like ours, would work hard, be obedient and not cause any trouble. This time everything worked out.

(Interview with a student from Anhui Province)

WHEN MARRIAGE MEANS MIGRATION

Marriage migration is a major form of migration in China. It is also highly gender-specific: the great majority of marriage migrants are women. A woman normally moves to her husband's village on marriage and transfers her household registration. Very rarely the man moves to join his bride. In either case, if the move is across administrative boundaries, it will show up in both the household registers and in the Census as a migration like any other. In general the study of migration tends to focus heavily on economic migration; indeed marriage migration is often omitted altogether from the literature on migration. It seems appropriate to discuss it here in some detail for several reasons. First, as we have seen in chapter 2, as migration is defined as mobility across administrative boundaries, marriage migration is included in much macro data on migration in China. The importance of marriage in female migration makes it essential to the study of women's migration and of gender differences in migration.

Finally, there is considerable evidence that a new marriage market has developed since the economic reforms, functioning over very long distances. This development in some ways parallels the development of labour migration in recent years.

In the era of collective agriculture when peasants were virtually tied to the land, marriage was the only reason for which a woman was likely to move out of the village of her birth. Men rarely moved on marriage, and in many rural communities they were therefore less mobile than women until the great increase in labour migration in the 1980s. Today, marriage is still the major cause of migration for women and it remains unimportant for men. According to the 1990 Census, marriage was the cause of only 2 per cent of male migrations whereas it accounted for 28 per cent of female migrations within the same province, and 30 per cent of female migrations between provinces (Table 8.1). Marriage was much less important as a cause of female migration to the urban areas, but where the destination was another rural area it accounted for 35 per cent of migrations within the province and 40 per cent of those between provinces. By contrast it was the cause of only 3 per cent of male migration to other rural

Table 8.1 Marriage as a percentage of all reported causes of migration by destination of migrants (1990 residence) – Census data

Intra-provincial destination	Both sexes	Men	Women
All	14	2	28
City	3	1	6
Town	8	1	15
Rural areas	19	3	35

Inter-provincial destination	Both sexes	Men	Women
All	14	2	30
City	2	1	6
Town	8	1	18
Rural areas	20	3	40

Source: Calculated from the 1990 Census, vol. IV, table 11.16.

areas. The importance of marriage migration and the way in which it has developed since the economic reforms relate is of course closely related to Chinese marriage customs and the way in which marriage partners are selected.

MATE SELECTION IN RURAL CHINA

Economic considerations have always been important in the arrangement of marriages in China (Croll 1981). The brideprice paid to the girl's family compensates her parents for the expenses of her upbringing and may finance the marriage of her brother. The bride brings with her a dowry supplied by her family. This is normally worth less than the brideprice, but is calculated to support their prestige and that of their daughter. Families use marriages to try to form useful alliances with other families who are powerful or prosperous, and equally, they are concerned not to make disadvantageous alliances. The bridegroom's family will be concerned to acquire a suitable daughter-in-law, and the bride's family will want to ensure as good a life as possible for her.

These general principles of mate selection have survived communist attempts to eliminate 'mercenary' considerations in the arrangement of marriages and to substitute free-choice marriage based on mutual attraction. There have been significant changes in the way that decisions are made. It is now unusual for marriages to be arranged without consultation with the young people who are to be married, but equally it is unusual for the young people to make their own choice without any participation from their parents. There is usually a compromise. Sometimes the parents choose, but the young people are consulted and have a chance to exercise a veto. In other cases the young people choose, but seek the consent of the parents who are then responsible for negotiating the arrangements.

Whoever makes the choice of a mate, it tends still to be based on practical considerations. Marriage in rural China remains the business of the whole family because it affects the whole family. This is especially so for the bridegroom's side. The bride will become a member of his family and will either live with them or in an independent household very close to them. The bride's qualities can influence the future prosperity and well-being of her husband's family. Men and their families want a woman who will fit in, be good-tempered, work hard and produce healthy children. Women and their families want the best standard of living possible for the bride and not too much heavy work. The customary principle of 'matching doors' (*'mendang hudui'*), that is finding someone from a family of similar economic status, still applies, although it is more important to the boy's family than to the girl's. To a peasant family, a bride from a much wealthier family would seem a risk. She might not be a hard worker or might cause trouble by complaining about privation. A bride who came from a poorer family might be tempted to smuggle gifts of food and other things back to her parents. Her family might constantly ask for help. Both practical help and cash loans can be sought from relatives by marriage if blood relatives cannot supply what is needed in times of difficulty. As marriage for both families involves a form of risk-sharing, the risks must be calculated. A girl's parents are not likely to be concerned if she succeeds in marrying up; they may even hope for some advantage. If she marries into a poorer family they will worry she may suffer and that they themselves are acquiring potentially onerous obligations.

The changing economic and social context in China has not altered this essentially practical approach to mate selection, but has produced variations in some of the criteria. In the collective period it was hard for people of 'bad class origin' to find a mate. At the time of land reform each family was allocated to a class, and the 'class label' acquired its own importance in the marriage market. Landlords and rich peasants had to marry within their own groups because no one else would accept the stigma of such a connection (Parish and Whyte 1978: 179). Cadre status or Party membership raised the value of the individual in the marriage market (Croll 1981). Men who had been accepted for army service were also desirable husbands because they earned cash wages and were likely to become cadres on their return to the village. Even being related to someone with such advantages might improve an individual's standing in the marriage market.

Social status and prospects are judged rather differently in China today. Although cadre status is still desirable, the class labels of the collective era have been abandoned. Prospective mates are still considered for their personal qualities and for the wealth and standing of their families, but energy, initiative and entrepreneurship, once characteristics that might bring political trouble, are now likely to be regarded positively.

Lavely (1991: 299) has pointed out another effect of collectivisation: land reform and the system of remuneration in collective agriculture brought about greater equality of wealth and income in the village or team. Within this small unit there was a limited form of sharing.

However, no redistributive tax or other mechanism existed to promote levelling across larger areas or regions. If an agricultural area commanded better resources, it produced more, and this was reflected in local incomes. Nor could peasants in the poorest areas move to seek a better living elsewhere. Under the household registration system, in-migrants needed the permission of the authorities in the receiving area. Where land was short and labour plentiful, as in most of rural China, this would not be forthcoming. Spontaneous economic migration between rural areas was thus impossible. Women, however, could use marriage to move up through the spatial hierarchy. Such marriages brought benefits to their families in the form of contacts in a richer area. In the post-collective era, marriage into a wealthier area remains a form of upward mobility for women.

Out-Marriage: Choices and Calculations

Village exogamy, or marrying outside the village, used to be a general rule in much of China, although the strictness with which it was observed varied considerably. The introduction of consensual marriage after 1949 appears to have increased the incidence of marriages within villages, but exogamy is still the norm. The practice is favoured by peasants for a variety of reasons. It facilitates the avoidance of same surname marriages, or marriage with close relatives from the father's side. The bridegroom's family prefers a daughter-in-law from another village because it is believed that she will 'settle better'. She cannot easily run back to her family when there are minor disputes, take them unauthorised gifts from her husband's household or work on their land instead of his. Quarrels between husband and wife are less likely to develop into feuds between the families. Both families will be happy to extend their network of contacts beyond their own villages. Relatives in other villages may supply useful information about markets or crops. They can be called on for help with housebuilding and harvesting, or loans and gifts to meet the costs of family illnesses, weddings and funerals. Fellow villagers already belong to this 'circle of obligation' so that a marriage within the village will not enlarge the network from which help can be sought (Potter and Potter 1990: 205).

The perception of marriage as risk-sharing also promotes exogamy. Chinese peasants live close to subsistence under the constant treat of crop failure, drought or flooding. State disaster aid is very limited and without insurance of social security, most peasants rely on relatives and friends to survive periods of shortage. Disasters are likely to strike whole villages simultaneously, but others, not far away, may be spared. Aware of this, peasants try to reduce their risk by extending their circle of obligation beyond the village (Ma et al. 1997).

The decision to marry out is thus based on maximising advantages to both families. Exogamy may be felt to be in the interests of the woman's family, even if the area to which she moves is not richer than their own. However, there is a clear consciousness that it may be possible to use out-marriage to ensure a woman a better life. In Zengbu brigade, in Dongguan county, Guangdong, some young women expressed a preference for marrying out in order to better themselves economically (Potter and Potter 1990: 206). A father explained that he and his wife had married their daughter into a neighbouring village because 'in Wentang, production and living standards are high – they have more land than here'.

Lavely's work on the Shifang county in Sichuan Province at the beginning of the 1980s showed that the inflow of brides to this exceptionally prosperous county far exceeded the outflow (Lavely 1991). Women from other counties were happy to marry into Shifang, but Shifang women were reluctant to marry out. The in-marrying women tended to be from low-income counties whereas women who married out went to other high income counties. In-marrying women moving up the spatial hierarchy also tended, according to Lavely, to be better educated than average, whereas those who 'married down' had fewer years of schooling. The workings of the market can be seen in other ways. Men in Shifang who married women from poorer areas had incomes lower than the average for Shifang. This presumably made them less attractive to Shifang women. It would also increasing the attraction to them of a woman from an undesirable area for the bride-price paid was only about 60 per cent of what they would pay for a local girl.

Frequently, the in-marrying brides came quite considerable distances to Shifang whereas the women who married out of the county did not go very far. The position of Shifang women in the marriage market was strong enough to allow them choice. Women normally prefer to settle in villages near to their natal homes. In this way they can visit frequently and get emotional support from their own families. Indeed, Judd has shown that in the north China villages she studied, women do not move for once and for all at the time of wedding. Instead, where possible, they divide their time between the households for a protracted time after marriage (Judd 1989). Because women value contact with their families, it might be expected that the more control they exert over the choice of marriage partner the more likely they are to marry close to home. The developing trend for long-distance marriages, however, appears to show that women (or their families) are sometimes willing to trade the advantage of proximity for the chance to move into more prosperous areas.

Lavely's study focuses on marriages in the Chengdu plain area at the beginning of the 1980s. He argues that this process of female social mobility through the marriage market had been thrown into sharp relief by the commune system, but would also have existed in traditional China. Higher female mortality and the market for women as concubines, prostitutes, maids and entertainers in the cities would always have meant a shortage of marriageable women. The absolute losers in this competitive market would not have been able to marry at all. In each community these would have been the poorest men. A larger proportion of men in poor areas remained unmarried because their communities suffered a net loss of women to the wealthier areas. Under the People's Republic, the improved provision of long-distance transport and communications may have enlarged the area over which marriage markets functioned. In discussing the prospects for the future, Lavely speculates that 'although the correspondence between marriage migration and the spatial hierarchy may wane, it is not likely to disappear' (Lavely 1991: 106).

THE SPATIAL HIERARCHY OF MARRIAGE AFTER THE ECONOMIC REFORMS

From the vantage point of the mid-1990s, it seems that the correspondence between marriage migration and the spatial hierarchy has become more significant as ever. There seems to have been a further increase in the size of the area over which the marriage market operates. Although the vast majority of marriage migrations are still over short distances, there is evidence of the existence of marriage migration chains which stretch hundreds of miles. These may be new or at least greatly expanded. Lavely's model of a spatial hierarchy within which women try to improve their positions remains very useful, but it seems that the physical size of the hierarchy within which some marriage markets operate has increased.

This development could create problems for poor communities. The sex ratio is distorted in favour of men everywhere in China because son preference, the higher status of men and their superior entitlements to food have given them better survival chances. Historically, the sex ratio has meant that a minority of men in each community were unable to marry. Poverty and a failure to marry were closely associated. The poorest men were the ones who lost out on the marriage market. A man who suffered some other handicap might have to offer a higher brideprice or accept a less eligible bride, but men without resources could not compensate for their shortcomings. Prior to the reforms, the shortage of marriageable women tended to be worse in the poorest areas. The contemporary development of large-scale marriage migration over a huge geographical area can only exacerbate and concentrate such shortages. The result could be that in the most prosperous areas even the least well-off men will be able to afford a wife from a poor area, but in the poorer areas the number of men unable to marry will increase.

There is little marriage migration from the rural areas to the towns and cities. Rural women and their families would regard an urban bridegroom as a good prospect because urban incomes are both higher and more stable than rural ones. But urban residents would be unlikely to contemplate such a match. Connections even with a well-off rural family would have little promise for them. Young urban people are likely to wish to marry other young urbanites whom they chose for themselves. Moreover urban registration cannot be acquired simply by marrying an urban resident. Often husband and wife have to live apart for many years because one has urban registration and the other does not (Ma et al. 1996). Every Chinese is aware of such cases and knowledge of the difficulties of marrying an outsider no doubt deters urban residents from considering such a course. Marriage migration is predominantly a rural phenomenon.

One form of marriage migration that has emerged in recent years is that of men from impoverished rural areas who join the families of their brides in prosperous villages in the periphery of large cities (Ji Ping et al. 1985). Here, the man is accepting the traditionally humiliating position of a married-in son-in-law in exchange for access to the economic opportunities of peri-urban residence, while the woman's family is glad to add a son-in-law to the family labour force rather than losing a daughter. This form of marriage is interesting for what it implies about the balancing of advantage and disadvantage in mate selection, statistically, however, it is unimportant. The great majority of marriage migrations involve movement by women from one rural area to another. The rapid but uneven economic growth of the 1980s created prosperity not only in the towns and cities of the eastern seaboard provinces but also in those parts of their rural areas that developed rural industries or produce lucrative cash crops. This is reflected in the inter-provincial marriage market. The national trend is for the poor inland provinces to suffer a net loss of women to the rich coastal ones. According to data from the 1990 Census, marriage accounted for 14 per cent of inter-provincial migration nationally, but for fully half of total out-migration from the poor southwestern provinces of Yunnan and Guizhou, and around a quarter of out-migration from Sichuan and Guangxi (See Table 8.2).[1] By contrast, marriage as a cause for in-migration was only 8 per cent for Guangxi, 10 per cent for Guizhou, 11 per cent for Yunnan and 15 per cent for Sichuan. The most popular destination provinces for marriage migrants were Hebei, Anhui, Jiangsu and Zhejiang. Between 25 and 34 per cent of in-migrants to these provinces were marriage migrants, compared with only between 3 per cent and 10 per cent of their out-migrants.

Table 8.2 Marriage as a reported cause of inter-provincial out-migration (%) and in-migration by province

Destination or origin	Out-migration from	In-migration to	Destination or origin	Out-migration from	In-migration to
National	14	14			
Beijing	2	6	Henan	10	15
Tianjin	7	10	Hubei	16	9
Hebei	10	34	Hunan	12	17
Shanxi	7	15	Guangdong	6	11
Neimenggu	17	16	Guangxi	27	13
Liaoning	10	10	Hainan	4	9
Jilin	12	9	Sichuan	24	15
Heilongjiang	10	11	Guizhou	50	14
Shanghai	2	3	Yunnan	51	11
Jiangsu	7	25	Tibet	2	no data
Zhejiang	3	24	Shaanxi	17	6
Anhui	10	30	Gansu	14	10
Fujian	3	23	Qinghai	7	7
Jiangxi	11	10	Ningxia	11	13
Shandong	9	20	Xinjiang	4	9

Source: Calculated from SSB 1991a, sampling tabulation of the 1990 Census.

Marriage across provincial boundaries is not necessarily long-distance marriage, and intra-provincial marriage may sometimes involve people from neighbouring villages between which a provincial boundary runs, while intra-provincial marriage could involve movement across considerable distances. None the less, it is reasonable to suppose that high rates of inter-provincial marriage indicate high rates of long-distance marriage. Increased marketisation and monetisation of the economy made possible the growth of this type of marriage in post-reform China. Transport and communications have improved knowledge of conditions and of the market elsewhere, including the demand for brides, and have made it easier to move women around physically. Increased private trade and labour migration have also contributed by facilitating the contacts necessary for the arrangement of such marriages. Traders who have brought goods from one area to another may branch out into marriage brokering when they see an opportunity. Migrants who have settled in the destination areas arrange marriages there for girls from their home areas. Like other forms of migration, marriage migration generates migration chains as successive cohorts of brides arrange matches in their husbands' villages for younger women from their old homes. On the other hand, in some areas the movement is highly commercialised: brokers recruit girls in poor villages in southwest China with promises of husbands in the rich coastal villages. They then take them down river to Jiangnan sometimes in groups as large as 10 or 15.

In China's marriage market, it has long been normal for the parents of women disadvantaged by poverty, disability, age or looks to expect a smaller brideprice or a bridegroom with some disadvantage. Men seeking a bride will similarly know that they hold a strong or a weak hand in the marriage market according to such factors as earning ability, wealth, health, connections and education. Long-distance marriage is a part of this system of balancing of disadvantages and advantages. Men who seek wives from other provinces usually do so because they have been unable to find a local bride. Their families are likely to be among the poorest in their own community, and they may be unable to afford the gifts and brideprice expected in their area. Han and Eades (1995) see this as the main factor in the demand pull in the marriage chains that have developed between Anhui (where there has been fierce inflation in brideprice in recent years) and provinces further to the west. The bridegroom may be older than average, indeed a high age at first marriage is a symptom of poverty for a rural man. He may suffer from poor health or a disability or be considered a poor worker. The bridegroom's family may wish to seek a bride from far away precisely because his disadvantages are too widely known locally. Regional disparities in wealth are so great that a poor man in a prosperous area may seem a good match to a woman from a poor area of the country (see the story with which this chapter opens). Such women from a remote part of the country will be expected to have lower aspirations and to be more inclined to settle for a man with some handicap. The man or his family may also be able to exploit the fact that it is difficult for her to change her mind once she has made the long journey.

PROBLEMS ARISING FROM LONG-DISTANCE MARRIAGE

Long-distance marriage migrations create a variety of difficulties for those who get involved in them. In a conventional match each side is trying to maximise its advantage. Both families will try to make the most of their good points and to conceal information that does not show them to good advantage. The scope for serious deception is limited where there is geographical proximity. Each family will make enquiries through a network of friends and acquaintances. It is also customary to employ the good offices of a go-between, often known to both families, whose reputation would be damaged by any extreme deception.

These traditional safeguards are not available to migrant brides. Naïve young village women being taken hundreds or even thousands of miles are vulnerable to dishonest brokers ready to marry them to the man who offers the best price. There are many anecdotes about women tricked into marriage to men who are sick, old or disabled. The vulnerability of these migrant brides continues after marriage because they are more isolated than other married women. They may arrive in their husbands' villages without friends or even acquaintances, and with little chance of appeal to their own far-distant families if they are ill-treated, abused or merely given subservient status. They are unable to use the customary stay at their mother's home (*niangjia*) if they wish to negotiate problems with their in-laws.[2] The Women's Federation in Xiao county, Anhui Province found that wives from outside provinces complained they were not allowed to stay in touch with their families for fear that they might arrange to run away (Han and Eades 1995). Not understanding the local dialect and not knowing how to cultivate the local crops were other sources of difficulty for these migrant wives. They suffered from low status because they had no network of relations on whom to call for support and could not provide their husbands with useful local connections through their relatives.

Women may also fall into the hands of traders who are in fact procuring for the sex trade. The press is full of reports of young women being tricked or abducted and sold into prostitution by agents who had promised them a good husband or a job in some wealthy area hundreds of miles from their homes.[3] Others are abducted and then sold as brides so far away from their homes that they have difficulty in contacting their relatives again. This trafficking in women appears to be astonishingly widespread. According to a Chinese source 33,000 women were abducted and sold between mid-1993 and 1995 (Evans 1997: 170–1). Another report claimed that 70,000 abductions of women and children were discovered between 1991 and 1994, leading to the arrest of 100,000 criminals. The practice is of course widely condemned in the press and by the authorities. Severe sentences have been passed on those found guilty of engaging in it. Chinese discussion of the re-emergence of these forms of the abuse of women's rights tend to focus on poverty, ignorance and the marketisation of the economy in their search for explanations. As Evans observes, it should also be recognised that such abuse is grounded in hierarchical gender structures and ideologies. It is surely only because even normal marriage arrangements are in large part economic transactions that it is possible for women to be sold by themselves, or by others, willingly or against their will, into marriage or sex work in such large numbers.

The problems must be balanced against the fact that marriage migrants are often volunteers attracted by the prospect of greater prosperity and a higher standard of living. Some Women's Federation officials offer a strong defence of marriage migration, arguing that the women are free agents and that they have a right to try to improve their lives in this way. They claim marriage migration can offer women the same chances of economic betterment that labour migration offers men.[4] In material terms this may be realistic, but in terms of the status, autonomy and control they confer, the options are not comparable.

Women are not the only victims of those who seek to make money out of brokering these kinds of marriage. Men and their families may suffer too. Their anxiety to arrange a match may make them gullible, and if the broker is not local and the bride's family is unknown to them, they will have none of the traditional sanctions against confidence tricksters. Han and Eades (1995: 861–5) were told of many cases where men had paid money to brokers for women who never appeared, or who ran away after only a short time. Some brokers apparently move from village to village extracting brideprices from ageing bachelors. The 'bride' stays in the house only a few days before running off to rejoin the broker. Han and Eades report that, 'the villagers conclude that in the post-commune market, marriages with outside wives are cheap but risky: they cost only a third or a quarter as much as marriages with local women, but there is no assurance that the woman will stay.' There is a mythical quality to some of these stories. In others, through the indignation of the narrator, one can glimpse a different version that the woman might tell.

There is official concern about the possible abuses of long-distance marriage chains. Local branches of the Women's Federation have made attempts to help migrant wives to return to their natal homes if they chose to, and to overcome the difficulties of settling in other cases (Han and Eades 1995: 860). Local birth planning officials also take a close interest in migrant wives who they fear may upset local birth planning targets. There are reports of brokers convicted of tricking, abducting or selling women being often arrested and dealt with quite harshly, but the ambiguities in these cases must make them hard to deal with. Rural people are accustomed to the idea that a man must hand over money to get a wife and that in so doing he acquires rights over her. In the rural areas, local officials themselves belong to a world where this is seen as natural. It must be very hard for them to draw the line between the payment of brideprice, which is officially discouraged but in practice tolerated, and the sale of women, which is supposed to be severely punished.

CONCLUSION

Marriage migration should be taken seriously as a form of migration. In Maoist China it was numerically the most important form of population movement. Even now it accounts for a large proportion of population movement in China, and is particularly important in female migration (see Tables 8.1 and 8.2). Unlike labour migration it normally results in permanent settlement in the destination area. Although it has its own specific dynamics, it has, like labour migration, been affected by the economic reforms and its incidence appears to have increased. For women in the poorest areas, it may seem to offer the promise of a better life but where the migration takes place across very long distances, it can isolate the woman. Like mail order brides who come to the West from areas such as the Philippines or the ex-Soviet Union, these young Chinese women are very vulnerable to abuse or simple disappointment. The migration chain is important in marriage migration as it is other types of migration. A migrant bride may try to counter her isolation by recruiting other women from her kinship circle and her natal village to join her as brides for members of her husband's family or her new neighbours. These migrating brides are permanent leavers and their natal villages tend to be unattractive to other women, the development of long-distance marriage migration could therefore have considerable impact on the sex ratios in the poorest areas, creating groups of men who will be unable to find wives.

9 Responses to Migration and the Prospects for the Future

Immigrants rarely catch buses or trains; they 'flood', 'flux', 'flow', 'surge', 'pour', 'drain'; they are ... not just a 'tide' but a 'rising' one, and one flowing into areas which are 'saturated'. Water imagery appears irresistible.

(Nigel Harris, *The New Untouchables*, 1997, p. 186)

The great increase in population mobility since the beginning of the reforms has given rise to a variety of responses. Policy changes made to deal with large-scale migration have already been reviewed in chapter 3. This final chapter looks at urban responses to migration expressed in the press. It focuses on the reaction to young rural people in the cities because neither rural to rural, nor rural to small town movements have inspired the same level or type of attention or anxiety. The reaction is considered in the context of the rural/urban divide that underpins social stratification in China and sets up the agricultural and non-agricultural populations as sharply divided interest groups. Chinese attempts to control population movement are compared to those once made elsewhere in the world. Finally, this chapter considers the prospects for migration and migration policy in China.

MEDIA IMAGES

A cursory look at the Chinese press will easily convey to the reader that the migration of rural people to the urban areas is seen as a problem in China. Headlines and news reports constantly associate migrants with overcrowding, chaos, crime, violence, high fertility and illicit sex. There are hugely varied claims about the numbers of rural migrants, but the consistent message is that their numbers are alarming. 'Currently 80 million surplus rural labourers migrate, in seven or eight years time this will reach 200 million' (*Guangming Daily*, 12 August 1993). The imagery evoked through the repetition of such words as *wave*, *tide* and *flood* is that of the uncontrollable forces of nature.

151

'Guangdong tries to manage six million migrant labourers: will tidal wave of labourers hit again?' (*Guangming Daily*, 25 December 1993) This sort of language is common to discussion of migration elsewhere in the world as the quotation at the head of this chapter shows. It is startling in the Chinese context because these migrants are Chinese, usually Han Chinese at that, moving within their own country, that is they are people who share a nationality and, perhaps somewhat more questionably, ethnicity, language and culture with the host communities in the urban areas.

Academic studies show that probably less than a third of migrants go to the big cities (Croll and Huang 1997: 128), and for the moment at least most migration is short-term: after a sojourn in an urban area most migrants return home to be replaced by a new cohort. This sort of detail is ignored in news coverage.

Links are often made between migration and urban unemployment – 'Rural migrant labourers begin to compete with enterprise employees for limited jobs in Shanghai' (*Labour News*, 15 July 1993) – and migrants are presented as threatening social stability and law and order in various ways as the following headlines show:

Beijing migrant population reaches 1.5 million, effects on urban life and security cannot be ignored. (*Beijing Evening News*, 31 August 1993)

WHO official warns China faces danger of AIDS spreading, migration leads to multiple sex partners. (*Tianjin Evening News*, 9 March 1994)

Chongqing–Guangzhou train attacked by large numbers of migrant labourers wanting to board. (*Guangzhou Evening News*, 12 August 1993)

Labour disputes increase among migrant workers for lack of knowledge of safety and contracts. (*Wenhui News*, 27 November 1993)

Crime and rising crime rates are attributed to migration and migrant communities:

Crime rate rise due to migrant population poses tough problem for the police. (*Legal Daily*, 21 July 1994)

Shanghai punishes group of violent criminals, over 70 per cent are migrants, 25 per cent have criminal records. (*Wenhui News*, 23 July 1994)

And migrants are depicted as having too many children:

Birth control impossible when farmers are on the move. (*Huashang shibao*, 18 June 1993)

More babies abandoned, cause traced to increase of migrant labourers. (*Wenhui, News*, 8 May 1994)

though the press has also reported findings that challenge these preconceptions:

Guangdong finds migrant population makes fewer babies than natives contrary to previous theory. (*Yangcheng Evening News*, 25 June 1994)

Migrants may be presented as victims in need of protection:

Private rental house fire kills 14 Sichuan migrants, Guangzhou. (*Yangcheng Evening News*, 26 October 1993)

44 migrant workers trampled to death, 43 injured on Feb. 16 at Hunan's Henyang station. (*Consumer Times*, 26 February 1994)

Many migrant labourers this year lured to the cities by bogus invitations. (*Labour News*, 27 March 1994)

But some reports seem to blame the number, stupidity or ignorance of migrants for their misfortunes:

Ignorant migrant worker falls off scaffolding and dies half a day after arriving in Shanghai. (*Labour News*, 17 March 1994)

Anhui migrant labourer electrocuted in Beijing Shijingshan trying to steal high voltage wire. (*Beijing Youth News*, 10 March 1994)

Migrant labourers ignorant of traffic rules add chaos to Beijing traffic, three hit by cars. (*Beijing Youth News*, 15 April 1994)

Positive images of migrants are less common. When they do appear, they tend to stress the indispensable role in the economy played by migrants:

'Unemployment' discovered in Beijing, concept of job opportunities differs between natives and migrants. (*Chinese Youth*, 25 August 1994)

Sichuan migrant labourers send 2.35 billion yuan back home from other provinces in first half of 1993. (*Peasant Daily*, 17 October 1993)

Beijing suburbs: farmers enter enterprise, fields contracted to migrant workers. (*Beijing Youth News*, 8 June 1993)

Migrant labourers are the garbage processors for Beijing. (*Beijing Youth News*, 29 July 1993)

Despite some sympathetic notes, the tone of coverage of migrants in the Chinese press is predominantly negative, presenting migration at best as a social problem and often as a major threat to order and progress. Obviously on most matters the Chinese media mirror the official view rather than the ideas of the 'general public'. But in the case of migration, what is written probably reflects the views of a significant part of the urban population as well. In conversation, urban residents certainly echo the concerns about migration that are expressed in the press, often in a stronger form, with complaints about migrants and their behaviour similar to those made about immigrants or 'foreigners' elsewhere in the world. The migrant cannot do right. Poor migrants are seen as failures who may resort to crime, while those who have done well, usually in trade, attract accusations of cunning, dishonesty and clannishness. The migrant seems constantly to be viewed as 'other'. Why should this be so?

RESIDENTS AND MIGRANTS – ANOTHER LOOK AT THE DIVIDE

Modern Chinese nationalism has strongly promoted the idea of a homogeneous Chinese identity. The various terms denoting 'the Chinese' – 'Children of the Yellow Emperor', 'Children of the Dragon', 'the Chinese people', the 'great Chinese People' ('*Zhonghua Minzu*' or '*Weidadi Zhongguo Renmin*') – have different political and historical resonances, but all are employed to promote a sense of community and commonality. The Chinese creation of 'imagined community', to use Anderson's (1991) terminology, has been enormously successful. Most Chinese have internalised a 'them and us' barrier, which informs and constrains their relations with foreigners. Yet the nationalist discourse should not blind us to the existence of strong regional and local loyalties, which make host communities view incomers with suspicion and lead incomers to seek solidarity with others from their home area in native place associations.

In China, as elsewhere, host communities have their own reasons for classifying people as insiders and outsiders. Emily Honig's analysis of the prejudice and discrimination against Subei people in pre- and post-liberation Shanghai argues that discrimination can be understood as a form of stratification, which the construction of ethnicity serves to strengthen and perpetuate (Honig 1990 and 1992). Thus the host community finds it convenient to define migrants as different to themselves. The long-established Subei community in Shanghai is a case in point. Labelling helps to keep Subei migrants and their descendants in their marginalised place, where they carry out the hardest, dirtiest and most poorly paid jobs, living in the worst housing with the least access to urban amenities.

Like the Subei migrants of the 1930s, migrant communities in big Chinese cities today live in substandard overcrowded housing or shacks in the poorest parts of town and do the most disagreeable or dirty jobs that no one else would want. In one significant way they are worse off than the migrants of the 1930s: not only are they discriminated against unofficially, but the state formally underpins this discrimination with regulations that effectively give them fewer rights than their urban fellow citizens. Most basically they lack the right of abode. Unemployed migrants or those without temporary permits are often rounded up and sent back to their places of origin.[1] The requirement that they must apply for and pay to obtain temporary or permanent residence certificates exposes them to official and unofficial forms of extortion[2] (Zhou 1996: 140–2).

The best jobs are formally and informally reserved for those with urban residence. Migrants have less access to medical facilities and housing than the host community. Their children may be unable to go to school in the cities or may have to make large payments to be allowed to do so. All these forms of discrimination are linked to the attempt to control population mobility.

Despite the Maoist rhetoric of bringing the city and the countryside closer together, or 'closing the scissors gap', the distance between the city and the countryside increased in the first decades of the People's Republic. Mao recognised and was critical of the growing gap, yet his notorious efforts to reverse the process, the Great Leap Forward and the Cultural Revolution, and the rustication of certain urban groups, were unsuccessful and indeed probably counter-productive. They did not challenge the most fundamental factors in the growing inequality between the urban and rural areas; a fiscal system that taxed agriculture to pay for industrialisation and urban welfare, and the household registration system that imprisoned the peasants in the villages where they were born, denying them the right to take advantage of better opportunities elsewhere. Natural flows of population towards the most rapidly developing regions were impeded, old migration chains severed, and movement and interaction between the cities and the countryside reduced.

Such population movement as took place did not necessarily contribute to closing gaps. Official images of the countryside and rural life in China during the Maoist period were rosy. Much literature presented the poorest peasants as heroic, hard-working, forward-looking and revolutionary. Urban people, especially the young, were encouraged to look up to them and urged to learn from them. However, the official message was confused. Although city people who had committed no offence were routinely sent to the countryside for political re-education, and were expected to view the experience positively, the countryside was also used as a place of exile and punishment for disgraced intellectuals, political dissidents and counter-revolutionaries. Post-reform 'wound' literature and memoirs of rural exile make it clear that whatever the reasons for their sojourns in the countryside, most urban exiles were shocked by the dirt, poverty, hardship and backwardness they encountered there, and found it impossible to integrate themselves with the peasants (Yang 1982; Liang 1983; Zhang and Sang 1986). Where necessary, they struggled hard to regain the right to urban residence. Their negative impressions of the countryside remain influential among city dwellers today.

If we turn to the reality of migrants' lives in the big Chinese cities we find further reasons for the readiness of urban Chinese to 'consume' negative images of migrants presented by the press. With the exception of traders, rural migrants are poorer than the host population. They are easily distinguishable from city people by their old-fashioned or shabby clothing, their distinctive accents and even sometimes their darker skins, different physiques and different social customs. They cluster together in overcrowded slums or shacks, frequently with no amenities. Knowing that they may be arbitrarily evicted or cleared from their housing they have little incentive to invest in improving it. They tend to be less educated and less sophisticated than the host community. It is hardly surprising if they are disproportionately involved in crime or other illegal activities. They are predominantly young, single and male – in any society the group most likely to offend against the law. Most come to the city alone and are thus without the comfort and the discipline of family life. Poorly qualified, lacking influence and facing discrimination, they are usually the worst paid group in the city. When out of work they may have no means of support. Like poor and marginalised groups elsewhere they are under pressures that may drive them into deviant behaviour such as crime and prostitution. They are easily stigmatised and make good scapegoats.

There is plenty of demand for scapegoats in contemporary urban China. Although standards of living have risen considerably in recent decades, the economic reforms have brought new anxieties. Life is more competitive, social welfare has been cut and crime is on the increase. Perhaps the greatest worry is unemployment. The 'job for life' that was the norm in the state sector in the Maoist era has gone. State enterprises are now required to run at a profit and the budgets of many government offices have been severely induced. The result has been lay-offs on a big scale. The well-qualified can generally find new employment for the economy is growing, but the less well qualified find themselves in competition with migrants who have much lower expectations of what they should earn. Anxiety about employment underlies much of the hostility to rural migrants. The authorities are clearly aware of these tensions and in the big cities especially, the official response is to reinforce discriminatory regulations. In early 1998, the *Beijing Daily* (10 February) reported new restrictions on the employment of migrants. In future only those with a Beijing *hukou* were to be allowed jobs as postal workers, machine-operators, gardeners, street cleaners or security guards in the capital. Moreover, employers were required to dismiss any migrants already in such jobs and to replace them with unemployed locals. While it is unlikely that there will be universal compliance, the existence of such discriminatory rules clearly illustrates the strength of localism in China.

FREEDOM OF MOVEMENT AND THE CONTROL OF MIGRATION

Other societies have, at various times in history, attempted to restrict freedom of movement. In settled agrarian societies, the pre-modern state and the forces it represented were often concerned about population movement and attempted to repress it. Under the Settlement Acts of 1662, in England not only paupers, but also those whom the authorities suspected might become paupers, could be forcibly returned to the parish of their birth, or, in the case of a woman, to the parish of her husband's birth (Thane 1978). This gave the authorities a powerful weapon against vagrancy which was used regularly until well into the nineteenth century. In Russia, in both the Tsarist and Soviet eras, a system of internal passports served to control population movement. Historically, in China too, the vagrant was suspect, and the Chinese state inclined towards the position that ordinary people belonged in the place they came from. This tradition was continued in Maoist China, but the apparatus of a modern state allowed far more effective control and indeed suppression of non-state sponsored population movement (Dutton 1992).

It is sometimes claimed that large-scale migration is a new phenomenon and this is used to explain the level of anxiety that it has produced. In fact there have been large-scale population movements in China in the past, to the cities and to comparatively sparsely populated areas. Migration to the northeast in the last hundred years is one obvious example (Lary 1996). However, it is true that during the three decades of Maoist rule the cities were sealed off from the countryside in a way that allowed extraordinary cultural, economic and social differentiation to develop (Smith 1996) and this has fostered the belief that large-scale migration is completely new. The alarm urban people feel about migration is certainly related to their perception of migrants as 'different' – ill-educated, dirty and lacking in culture – and to the widespread conviction, encouraged by media reports, that migration is now occurring on an unprecedented and unmanageable scale. Both migration in contemporary China and the reaction to it have roots in the suffocating hold kept over the individual and the freedom to move in the Maoist past.

In most of the modern world, restrictions on the freedom of movement are closely linked to the existence of the nation-state and its right to control population movement across its frontiers. For the citizen, freedom to enter a country at will and to move around within its borders is normally a right. In the case of aliens it is a concession that may be allowed on certain conditions, or withheld. It is worth remembering that the establishment of these norms is comparatively recent and has never been absolute. The wealthy, the highly qualified and the citizens of the most powerful countries usually enjoy a high degree of freedom of movement across national frontiers. Labour shortages in developed countries have sometimes led to an easing of restrictions or arrangements to facilitate the movement of labour from less developed parts of the world. The legal status accorded to labour migrants in the developed world varies considerably. Some have been allowed citizenship with all its attendant rights so that they have been able to bring in family members and settle. Others arrive on a limited contract and have to return to their places of origin on the completion of the contract. There is a full range of possibilities in between these two extremes.

This process of building a world of nation-states with defined borders within which economic activity could be contained and regulated was not even complete when it came under challenge from the effects of economic globalisation. First workers from the less developed parts of the world were drawn physically into the labour markets of the developed world by the pull of the demand for labour. Then manufacturers in the developed world began to export manufacturing capacity to the developing world in order to use cheaper labour close to its areas of origin. China has, of course, been deeply affected by this development.

The economic forces behind the push and pull factors that triggered internal migration in contemporary China are proving as strong as those that draw other labour forces across national frontiers. China's economic miracle is based to a considerable extent on its ability to provide industry, both Chinese and foreign owned, with cheap, well-disciplined labour. As the demand for labour is concentrated in the coastal provinces, it naturally draws people across provincial borders from the poorer hinterland. These migrant workers are prepared to work longer hours, to take more menial jobs or to accept lower pay than local people.

There is some recognition by the Chinese authorities that population and labour mobility are necessary to modernisation and are an essential part of the policies of marketisation that it has so eagerly embraced. The recognition of the benefits of migration has led to the belief that it should be managed rather than suppressed. There have been considerable increases in the freedom of movement in China in the course of the last two decades. People are now allowed to travel for trade, work, tourism, family visits and even pilgrimages in a way that would have been unimaginable in the 1960s and 1970s. On the other hand, the government clearly believes that it must keep some control over entry into and residence in the largest cities. This maintenance of some limitations on the freedom of movement should be judged not only against the historical and economic background, but also in relation to the size of China and the potential scale of population movement. We have to recall again that China contains about one fifth of the world's population, and that Chinese provinces bear comparison both in size and population to the countries of Western Europe.

However the management of internal migration in China is frequently inequitable in its design and implementation because it is based on the interests of the urban residents with little consideration of those of migrants. Much policy discussion is deeply unsympathetic to migrants.

Of course, migrants do pose problems to the urban areas where they seek their livelihoods, but these are often exaggerated. Both the problems and the urban attitudes to them reflect the divisions between the city and the countryside, or the core and the periphery, that already existed in Maoist China, and have been exacerbated by the rapid and uneven growth of the reform years. Migrants are all too often the losers in China's changing society, and they also get the blame for its ills.

There is a growing readiness to give greater rights to migrants in China as it is recognised that labour mobility is a logical part of marketisation. The relaxation of entry into the small towns and the development of a free market in food in the early years of the reform era were the first signs. This was followed by the introduction of temporary residence permits which established the right of migrants to sojourn in the urban area, though it should be noted that it simultaneously gave the authorities a means of control over them.

There is now a liberal discourse in China, especially strong among those who study migrants and their problems, that promotes the interests of migrants and argues for extending their rights (Xiang 1993; Yuan 1996; Mallée 1995–6). For example, Lu Xueyi, the director of the Institute of Sociology in the Academy of Social Sciences, has argued that migration is an inevitable outgrowth of industrialisation and that migrants benefit the development of society more than they hurt it (Lu 1995). There have been instances of migrants getting together either to obtain help from the state or to provide their own social, health and education facilities on the basis of self-help (Xiang 1993). It has recently been conceded in a statement from the State Commission for Education that the 2–3 million school age children who accompany their migrant parents should have access to education, and some action has been taken to set up provision for this (FBIS, 6 June 1996).

Yet, taken as a group, migrants in China remain systematically underprivileged. The limitations on free movement imposed by the *hukou* system disadvantage rural people far more than their urban fellow citizens ensuring that they cannot reside and work in the urban areas on equal terms with urban people. If the authorities accept the conventions of the nation-state, they must also accept responsibility for establishing freedom of movement, solving the problems of their migrant citizens and acknowledging the justice of a claim made in another headline: 'Cities don't belong only to city folk' (*China Youth*, 25 February 1994).

Notes

1 MIGRATION IN CHINA AFTER 1949

1. This figure had fallen to 8.3 million by the time of the 1990 Census thanks to relaxations in policy after 1978.

2 AN OVERVIEW OF MIGRATION IN CHINA SINCE 1978

1. Mallée provides a useful discussion of recent estimates in which he observes that while most authorities give estimates of 50–60 million, the Project Group of the Ministry for Agriculture for Research and Survey of the Roots of the Labour Migrant Wave spreads its net even wider with an estimate of 40–80 million (1995–6: 113).
2. The most important of these were a 1990 survey of 50 townships by the Ministry for Public Security, a 1993–4 survey by the Rural Development Institute of the Chinese Academy of Social Sciences and the Agricultural Bank which sampled 12,673 households in 26 provinces, and a 1994 survey of 75 villages undertaken by the Ministry of Agriculture. These surveys are discussed in detail in Hein Mallée's useful piece (modestly titled a 'research note'), 'In Defence of Migration: Recent Chinese Studies on Population Mobility' (1995).
3. These were job transfer, job assignment, work and trade, education, joining relative, retirement, moving with family, marriage and others. The reasons for migration will be discussed at greater length in chapter 4.
4. For a discussion of the economic and geographical characteristics of these regions, see chapter 4.
5. This discussion is intended only as an indication of the pitfalls of the study of urbanisation in China. For an exhaustive guide to changing definitions of urban populations and urban places, see Chan 1994: 19–51.

3 REFORM ERA POLICIES ON POPULATION MOVEMENT

1. For a useful recent selection of Chinese views on *hukou* reform, see Mallée 1996.
2. Spouse separations of many years are common due to this problem (Ma, et al. 1996).

4   WHY PEOPLE MIGRATE

1.   A classic account of the ways in which the rural migrant decides on migration and a schematic framework for analysing the migration decision can be found in Todaro 1997: 280–3.
2.   The following account relies heavily on Simon Zhao Xiaobin's insightful article, 'Spatial Disparities and Economic Development in China 1953–92', 1976.
3.   It is perhaps worth recalling that this is not an extraordinary situation in a traditional agricultural economy where rhythms of work were quite different from those in a modern wage economy. Periods of idleness were seen as compensation for busy periods. There is evidence that the seasonal pattern of work is valued by the rural labour force and relinquished with reluctance (E. P. Thompson, 'Time, Work Discipline and Industrial Capitalism', *Past and Present* 38 1967).
4.   This estimate comes from a Chinese authority, Lun Junjie, 'The Transfer of the Rural Labour Force Should be a State Policy' (*'Nongcun laoli zhuanyi ying shi yixiang guoce'*), *People's Daily*, 28 September 1986, cited in Taylor 1988. As is clear from his title, it suited the author's argument to highlight the land shortage and his figure may paint may present too bleak a picture. It is never easy to estimate the area of cultivated land. If peasants can hide some of their land, they pay less tax. They may bribe officials in order to do so. Historical fluctuations in the figures for cultivated land in earlier times in Chinese history are thought to represent fluctuations in the power of government to raise the land tax as well as real changes in the area under cultivation.
5.   Information supplied in a briefing from the Institute of Rural Development, Sichuan Academy of Social Sciences, September 1994.
6.   Information supplied in a briefing from the Institute of Rural Development, Sichuan Academy of Social Science, September 1994.
7.   This is the case in the Indian state of Kerala when married men leave their families to seek higher wages elsewhere. Male migrants to the Middle East who make regular remittances are seen as good providers and their wives are considered lucky.

5   THE IMPACT OF MIGRATION ON THE SENDING AREA

1.   Married women do migrate independently from Anhui to work as domestic servants and from various provinces to work in factories in the southeast. Presumably where female migration streams are well established, and the benefits of employment are secure and predictable, households are sometimes prepared to let married women go.
2.   Young women in Jiangsu in the 1930s were similarly drawn to work in factories in the cities because they longed for the sort of clothes they saw women migrants wearing on their visits home (Zhang and Sang 1987: 261).

6 MIGRANTS' LIVES AND IMPACTS IN THE DESTINATION AREAS

1. My description of Zhejiang visit is partly based on a visit made in 1995, but owes much to the research of Xiang Biao (1993a, b and forthcoming).
2. This section is based mainly on my own fieldwork in China in the 1980s and the 1990s and on Wan's useful work on Anhui maids in Beijing (Wan 1992). Other sources are attributed.

7 WOMEN AND MIGRATION

1. For a detailed discussion of similar tensions among the families of migrants in Kerala state in India, see Gulati 1993.
2. Hershatter provides a careful examination of the many explanations which have been advanced for the re-emergence of highly visible prostitution in post-reform China (Hershatter 1997: chs 13–15).
3. See for example an official report on crime dating from 1989 (Dutton 1997: 171) or newspaper headlines such as 'Zhuhai Sweeps out 1,600 Migrant Girls Serving in Barber Shops with Beds Upstairs' (*Xinmin Wanbao*, 20 April 1994).

8 MARRIAGE MIGRATION

1. As most marriage migration does ultimately result in a change of *hukou* for the spouse who moves, the Census should be a better source for marriage migration data than for labour migration data.The source used for calculations here is the 10 per cent. Sampling tabulation of the 1990 Population Census (SSB 1991a) because the full four-volume tabulation of the Census results used elsewhere in this book does not provide information on the causes of out-migration by province.
2. For an interesting discussion of the use of returns to the *niangjia* and for variations in the way that rural reforms have affected gender relations in the countryside, see Judd 1989 and 1994.
3. The problem of this trade in women is also being recognised and discussed in academic circles, see Zhuang Ping, 'On the Social Phenomenon of Trafficking in Women in China', translated in *Chinese Education and Society*, Summer 1993, vol. 26, no. 3.
4. Discussion with Women's Federation officials Kunming and Beijing, June 1995.

9   RESPONSES TO MIGRATION AND THE PROSPECTS FOR THE FUTURE

1.   See for example the report, 'Shanghai Putuo Sends Hundreds of Migrants Home, Dismantles 5000 square metres of Mat Sheds' (*Wenhui News*, 19 August 1994).
2.   See another report, 'Guiyang Policeman Arrested for Accepting 9000 yuan in Bribes for Issuing Residence Permits' (*Wenhui News*, 7 July 1993).

Bibliography

Akeroyd, A., 'Gender, Food Production and Property Rights', in Afshar, Haleh (ed.) *Women, Development and Survival in the Third World*. London: Longman, 1991.

Anderson, B., *Imagined Communities, Reflections on the Origin and Spread of Nationalism*. London: Verso, 1991.

Andors, P., 'Women and Work in Shenzhen', *Bulletin of Concerned Asian Scholars*, 20:3, 1998, 22–41.

Banister, J., 'China: Internal and Regional Migration Trends', in Scharping, T. (ed.) *Floating Population and Migration in China*. Hamburg: Institut für Asienkunde, 1997.

Banister, J., *China's Changing Population*. Stanford: Stanford University Press, 1987.

Bell, L., 'For Better for Worse: Women and the World Market in Rural China', *Modern China*, 20:2, 1994.

Bernstein, T. P., *Up to the Mountains and Down to the Villages: the Transfer of Youth from Urban to Rural China*. New Haven: Yale University Press, 1977.

Brookes, R., *Implementation of the New Rural Policies in China in the 1980s: the Case of the Ningxia Hui Autonomous Region*. Unpublished PhD thesis, University of Leeds, 1994.

Brown, L. A., *Place, Migration and Development in the Third World, an Alternative View*. London: Routledge, 1991.

Buck, J. L., *Chinese Farm Economy*. Chicago: University of Chicago Press, 1930.

Buck, J. L., *Land Utilization in China*. Shanghai: University of Nanking, 1937.

Byrd, W. and Lin Qingsong, *China's Rural Industries: Structure, Development and Reform*. New York: Oxford University Press, 1990.

Caldwell, J. C., *African Rural–Urban Migration: the Movement to Ghana's Towns*. Canberra: ANU Press, 1969.

Cao Jingchun, 'Lanpi lanyin hukou yinfade sikao' ('Thoughts Inspired by the Hukou with the Blue Cover and the Blue Seal'), *Population and Economics*, 5, 1993, 38–42.

CASS – Population Research Institute, Chinese Academy of Social Sciences, *Migration to 74 Cities and Towns Sampling Survey, Chinese Population Science (Zhongguo Renkou Kexue)* special issue, Beijing, June 1988.

Census of 1990, Guowuyuan Renkou Pucha Bangongshi, *Zhongguo 1990 nian renkou pucha ziliao (Tabulation of the 1990 Population Census of the People's Republic of China)*, Vols 1–1V, Beijing: Statistical Publishing House, 1993.

Census of 1990, 10 per cent sampling, Guowuyuan Renkou Pucha Bangongshi (State Council Office of the Census) *Zhongguo 1990 nian renkou pucha 10% chouyang ziliao (10% Sampling tabulation of the 1990 population census of the People's Republic of China)*. Beijing: Statistical Publishing House, 1991.

Chai Junyong, 'Liudong renkou: Chengshi guanli de yi da kunrao' ('The Floating Population: a Major Challenge to the Management of Cities'), *Shehui (Society)*, October, 1990.

Chan Kam Wing, *Cities with Invisible Walls: Reinterpreting Urbanization in Contemporary China*. Hong Kong: Oxford University Press, 1994.

Chan Kam Wing, 'Internal Migration in China: an Introductory Overview', *Chinese Environment and Development*, Spring/Summer 1996, 3–13.

Chan, Roger C. K., 'Challenges to Urban Areas: the Floating Population', in Kuan Hsin-chi and Maurice Brosseau (eds) *China Review 1992*. Hong Kong: Chinese University Press, 1992.

Chant, Sylvia (ed.) *Gender and Migration in Developing Countries*. London: Bellhaven, 1992.

Cheng Chaoze, 'Internal Migration in Mainland China: the Impact of Government Policy', *Issues and Studies*, 27:8, June 1991, 44–70.

Cheng Chaoze, 'Bashi niandai Zhongguo dalu renkou liudong wenti' ('Problems of the Floating Population of Mainland China in the 1980s'), *Zhongguo dalu yanjiu (Mainland China Research)*, no. 7, 1992.

Cheng Tiejun and Mark Selden, 'The Origins and Social Consequences of China's *Hukou* System', *China Quarterly*, 139, September 1994, 644–8.

China Population Today, 'Control Measures for the Family Planning of the Floating Population', September 1992, 1.

Christiansen, F., 'Social Division and Peasant Mobility in Mainland China: the Implications of the Hu-k'ou System', *Issues and Studies*, 26:4, April 1990, 22–42.

Christiansen, F., '"Market Transition" in China, The Case of the Jiangsu Labor Market, 1978–1990', *Modern China*, 1992.

Christiansen, F. and Zhang Junzuo, *Village Inc.: Chinese Rural Society in the 1990s*. London: Curzon, 1998.

Croll, E., *The Politics of Marriage in Contemporary China*. Cambridge: Cambridge University Press, 1981.

Croll, E., *From Heaven to Earth: Images and Experiences of Development in China*. London: Routledge, 1994.

Croll, E. and Huang Ping, 'Migration for and against Agriculture', *China Quarterly*, 149, March 1997, 128–46.

Dai Qing (ed.) *Yangzi, Yangzi! Debate over the Three Gorges Project*. London: Earthscan Publications, 1994.

Davin, D., 'Family Care and Social Security in China before and after the Reforms', in Krieg, Renate and Monika Schadler (eds) *Social Security in the People's Republic of China*, Hamburg: Institut für Asienkunde, 1994.

Davin, D., 'Affreux, sales et mechants: les migrants dans les medias Chinois', in *Perspectives Chinois*, no. 38, December 1996, 6–11.

Davin, D., 'Migration, Women and Gender Issues in Contemporary China', in Scharping, T. (ed.) *Floating Population and Migration in China*, Hamburg: Institut für Asienkunde, 1997.

Davin, D., 'Gender and Migration in China', in Christiansen, Flemming and Zhang Junzuo (eds) *Village Inc.: Chinese Rural Society in the 1990s*, 1998.

Davis, D., 'Chinese Social Welfare: Policies and Outcomes', *China Quarterly*, 119, September 1989, 577–97.

Davis, D., 'Inequality and Stratification in the Nineties', in Lo Chin Kin et al. (eds) *China Review*. Hong Kong: Chinese University Press, 1995.

Davis-Friedman, D., *Long Lives, Chinese Elderly and the Communist Revolution*. Stanford: Stanford University Press, 1991.

Day, Lincoln H. and Ma Xia (eds) *Migration and Urbanization in China*. Armonk, New York and London: M.E. Sharpe, 1994.

Document No. 1, 'Central Committee's Circular on Rural Work in 1984', Foreign Broadcast Information Service, 13 June 1984, K1–11.

Dutton, M. R., *Policing and Punishment in China*. Cambridge: Cambridge University Press, 1992.

Dutton, M. R., 'The Basic Character of Crime in Contemporary China' (translation of 1989 document), *China Quarterly*, 149, March 1997, 128–46.

Edmonds, R. L., *Patterns of China's Lost Harmony. A Survey of the Country's Environmental Degradation and Protection*. London: Routledge, 1994.

Entwisle, B. et al., 'Gender and Family Businesses in Rural China', *American Sociological Review*, vol. 60, no. 1, 1995, 36–57.

Evans, H., *Women and Sexuality in China, Dominant Discourses of Female Sexuality and Gender since 1949*. Cambridge: Polity Press, 1997.

Fawcett John T., *Women in the Cities of Asia*. Colarado: Westview Press, 1984.

Gaubatz, Piper Rae, 'Urban Transformation in post-Mao China: Impacts of the Reform Era on China's Urban Form', in Davis, D., Richard Kraus, Barry Naughton and Elizabeth J. Perry (eds) *Urban Spaces in Contemporary China*. Cambridge: Cambridge University Press, 1995, 28–60.

Goldman, M., 'The Party and the Intellectuals', in MacFarquhar, R. and J. K. Fairbank (eds) *Cambridge History of China*, vol. X1V. Cambridge: Cambridge University Press, 1987, 218–57.

Goldstein, A. and Wang Feng (eds) *China: the Many Facets of Demographic Change*. Boulder: Westview Press, 1996.

Goldstein, S., 'Urbanization in China', Papers of the East–West Population Institute no. 93, Honolulu: East–West Population Institute, 1985.

Goldstein, S. and Goldstein, A., 'Migration in China: Data' Policies and Patterns', in Nam, C., W. Serrow and D. Sly (eds) *International Handbook of Internal Migration*. Westport, Conn.: Greenwood Press, 1990.

Goldstein, S. and Goldstein, A., 'Permanent and Temporary Migration Differentials in China', in Day, Lincoln H. and Ma Xia (eds) *Migration and Urbanization in China*, Armonk, New York and London: M.E. Sharpe, 1994.

Goldstein, S., Goldstein, A. and S. Guo, 'Temporary Migrants in Shanghai Households', *Demography*, 28, 1991, 275–91.

Goldstein, S. and Gang Liu, 'Migrant–non-Migrant Fertility Differentials in Anhui, China', *Chinese Environment and Development*, Spring/Summer 1996.

Gui Shixun and Liu Xian, 'Urban Migration in Shanghai, 1950–1988: Trends and Characteristics', *Population and Development Review*, September 1992, 18:3, 533–48.

Gulati, L., *In the Absence of Their Men: the Impact of Male Migration on Women*. London: Sage, 1993.

Han Min and J. S. Eades, 'Brides, Bachelors and Brokers: the Marriage Market in Rural Anhui in an Era of Economic Reform', *Modern Asian Studies*, 29:4, 1995, 841–69.

Harris, N., *The New Untouchables: Immigration and the New World Worker*. Harmondsworth: Penguin, 1995.

Hershatter, G., *Dangerous Pleasures: Prostitution and Modernity in Twentieth-Century Shanghai*. Berkeley: University of California Press, 1997.

Honig, E., *Sisters and Strangers: Women in the Shanghai Cotton Mills, 1919–1949*. Stanford: Stanford University Press, 1986.

Honig, E., 'Invisible Inequalities: the Status of Subei People in Contemporary Shanghai', *China Quarterly*, 122, June 1990.

Honig, E., *Creating Chinese Ethnicity: Subei People in Shanghai, 1850–1980*. New Haven: Yale University Press, 1992.

Honig, E. and Hershatter G., *Personal Voices: Chinese Women in the 1980s*. Stanford: Stanford University Press, 1988.

Howe, C., *Shanghai: Revolution and Development in an Asian Metropolis*. Cambridge: Cambridge University Press, 1981.

Hoy, Caroline, *The Fertility and Migration Experiences of Migrant Women in Beijing, China*, unpublished PhD thesis, University of Leeds, June 1996.

Huang, Jean K. M., 'The Family Status of Chinese Women in the 1990s', in Lo Chi Kin et al. (eds) *China Review 1995*, Hong Kong: Chinese University Press, 1995.

Hukou Regulations, 'Regulations Governing Household Registration Passed by the Standing Committee of the National People's Congress, 9.1.1958'. English translation in H. Yuan Tien, *China's Population Struggle*. Columbus: Ohio University Press, 1973.

Hunter, J., 'Textile Factories, Tuberculosis and the Quality of Life in Industrializing Japan', in Janet Hunter (ed.) *Japanese Women Working*. London: Routledge, 1993.

Ip, Olivia K. M., 'Changing Employment Systems in China: Some Evidence from the Shenzhen Special Economic Zone, *Work, Employment and Society*, 9:2, 1995, 269–85.

Jacka, T., 'Back to the Wok – Women and Employment in Chinese Industry in the 1980s', *Australian Journal of Chinese Affairs*, 24, 1990, 1–24.

Jacka, T., *Women's Work in Rural China: Change and Continuity in an Era of Reform*. Cambridge: Cambridge University Press, 1997.

Jefferson, Gary J. and Rawski, Thomas G., 'Unemployment and Employment Policy in China's Cities', *Modern China*, 18:1, January 1992, 42–71.

Ji Dangsheng and Shao Qin (eds), *Zhongguo liudong taishe yu guanli* (Population Mobility and Regulation in China). Beijing, 1995.

Ji Ping, Zhang Kaidi and Liu Dawei, 'Beijing jiaoqu nongcun renkou hunyin qianyi qianxi' ('An Analysis of Marital Migration Among Residents of the Beijing Suburbs'), *Zhongguo shehui kexue* (*Chinese Social Sciences*), 3, 1985, 201–13.

Jie Shusen and Chen Bing, 'Exploring the Root of the Problem of the Rural Population Flow and its Solutions', *Population Research* (*Renkou Yanjiu*), 1990, no. 5, 54–60.

Judd, Ellen R., 'Niangjia: Chinese Women and their Natal Families', *The Journal of Asian Studies*, 48:3, 1989, 525–44.

Judd, Ellen R., *Gender and Power in Rural North China*. Stanford: Stanford University Press, 1994.

Kirkby, R., *Urbanisation in China: Town and Country in a Developing Economy. 1949–2000 AD*, London: Croom Helm, 1985.

Knox, A., *Southern China: Migrant Workers and Economic Transformation*. London: Catholic Institute for International Relations, 1997.

Küchler, J., 'On the Establishment of a Poverty-orientated Development Policy in China', in Delman, Jorgen et al. (eds) *Remaking Peasant China*. Aarhus: Aarhus University Press, 1990.

Kung, L., *Factory Women in Taiwan*. New York: Columbia University Press, 1983.

Lardy, N., 'Economic Recovery and the First Five Year Plan', in MacFarquhar, R. and J. K. Fairbank (eds) *Cambridge History of China*, vol. X1V. Cambridge: Cambridge University Press, 1987, 218–57.

Lary, Diana, 'Hidden Migrations: Movement of Shandong People, 1949–1978', in *Chinese Environment and Development*, vol. 7, nos 1 and 2, Spring/Summer 1996, 56–72.

Lavely, W., 'Marriage and Mobility under Rural Collectivisation', in Watson, Rubie S. and Patricia Ebrey (eds) *Marriage and Inequality in Chinese Society*. Berkeley: University of California Press, 1991.

Lee Ching-kwan, 'Production Policies and Labour Identities: Migrant Workers in South China', in Lo Chin Kin et al. (eds) *China Review 1995*. Hong Kong: Chinese University Press, 1995.

Lee Ching-kwan, 'Engendering the Worlds of Labour: Women Workers, Labour Markets, and Production Policies in the South China Economic Miracle', *American Sociological Review*, 60:3, 1995, 378–97.

Leeming, F., *The Changing Geography of China*. Oxford: Blackwell, 1993.

Li Debin, 'The Characteristics of and the Reasons for the Floating Population in Contemporary China', *Social Sciences in China*, Winter 1994, 65–72.

Li Mengbai and Hu Xin, *Liudong renkou dui dachengshi fazhan de yingxiang ji duice* (*The Influence of the Floating Population on the Big Cities and How to Deal with it*). Beijing: Economic Daily Publishing House, 1991.

Li Rongshi, 'Dangqian woguo liudong renkou de renshi he sikao' ('Perceptions of the Floating Population in Contemporary China'), *Renkou yanjiu* (*Population Research*), no. 97, 29:1, 1996, 10–14.

Li Si-ming, 'Population Mobility and Rural Development in Mainland China', *Issues and Studies*, September 1995, 37–54.

Liang Heng, *Son of the Revolution*. London: Chatto and Windus, 1983.

Liu Lang, 'Laoqu you yiqun "liushou nü"' ('Women are Left Behind in the Sending Areas'), *Funü Shenghuo* (*Woman's Life*), April 1994, no. 4, 9–11.

Lo Chin Kin, Suzanne Pepper and Tsui Kai Yue (eds) *China Review 1995*. Hong Kong: Chinese University Press, 1995.

Lu Feng, *China's Grain Imports: Policy Evolution and Determinants, 1960–1990*. Unpublished PhD thesis, University of Leeds, 1994.

Lu Xueyi, quoted in 'Thoughts that the Concentration of Migrants from elsewhere in the Country Evoke', *Liaowang* (*Outlook*), 27 November 1995, 20–3.

Ma Xia, 'Dangdai Zhongguo nongcun renkou xiang chengzhen de da qianyi' ('Large-scale Movement of the Rural Population to the Small Towns in Contemporary China'), *Zhongguo renkou kexue* (*Chinese Population Science*), 3, 1987, 7–8.

Ma Xia, 'Changes in the Pattern of Migration in Urban China', in Day and Ma (eds) *Migration and Urbanization in China*, Armonk: New York, M.E. Sharpe, 1994.

Ma Xia, 'New Trends in Population Migration in China', in Scharping, T. (ed.) *Floating Population and Migration in China*, Hamburg: Institut für Asienkunde, 1997.

Ma Xia and Wang Weizhi, *Migration of 74 Cities and Towns Sample Survey Data*. Beijing: Population Research Institute, Chinese Academy of Social Sciences, Special issue of *Population Science of China* (*Zhongguo Renkou Kexue*) June 1988.

Ma Z., K. L. Liaw and Zeng Y., 'Spousal Separation among Chinese Young Couples', *Environment and Planning*, vol. 28, 1996, 877–90.

Ma Z., K. L. Liaw and Zeng Y., 'Migration in the Urban/Rural Hierarchy of China: Insights from the Micro Data of the 1987 Migration Survey', *Environment and Planning*, vol. 29, no. 4, 1997, 707–30.

Mallée, Hein, 'China's Household Registration System under Reform', *Development and Change*, 26:1, 1995.

Mallée, Hein, 'In Defence of Migration: Recent Chinese Studies of Rural Population Mobility', in *China Information*, vol. X, nos 3–4, Winter 1995–Spring 1996.

Mallée, Hein (trans. and ed.), *Reform of the Hukou System*, Special number of *Chinese Anthropology and Sociology*, vol. 29, no. 1, 1996.

Mallée, Hein, 'Rural Household Dynamics and Spatial Mobility in China', in Scharping, T. (ed.) *Floating Population and Migration in China*, Hamburg: Institut für Asienkunde, 1997.

Mallée, Hein, 'Rural Population Mobility in Seven Chinese Provinces', in Flemming Christiansen and Zhang Junzuo (eds) *Village Inc.: Chinese Rural Society in the 1990s*, 1998.

Meng Xianfan, 'Chinese Rural Women in the Transfer of the Rural Labour Force', *Social Sciences in China*, Spring 1994, 109–18.

Messkoub, M. and D. Davin, 'Migration in China: Results from the 1990 Census', in Terry Cannon (ed.), *China: Economc Growth, Population and the Environment*. London: Macmillan, 1998.

Middelhoek, Jan, 'Recent Development of Small Towns on China', in Vermeer, E. B. (ed.), *From Peasant to Entrepreneur: Growth and Change in Rural China*. Wageningen: Pudoc, 1992.

Myers, R., *The Chinese Peasant Economy: Agricultural Development in Hopei and Shantung 1890–1949*. Cambridge, Mass.: Harvard University Press, 1970.

Nolan, Peter, 'Economic Reform Poverty and Migration in China', *Economic and Political Weekly*, No. 28, 26 June 1993, 1369–77.

ODI, 'China's Economic Reforms', *Overseas Development Institute*, Briefing Paper, London, February 1993.

Oi, Jean C., *State and Peasant in Contemporary China: the Political Economy of Village Government*. Berkeley: University of California Press, 1989.

Oshima Kazutsugu, 'The Present Condition of Inter-regional Movements of the Labor Force in Rural Jiangsu Province, China', *The Developing Economies*, 2 June 1990.

Paine, Suzanne, 'Spatial Aspects of China's Development – Issues, Outcomes and Policies, 1949–79', *Journal of Development Studies*, 17:2, 1981, 133–95.

Parish, William and Martin Whyte, *Village and Family in Contemporary China.* Chicago: Chicago University Press, 1978.

Parnwell, M., *Population Movements and the Third World.* London: Routledge, 1993.

Poston, Dudley L. and David Yaukey, *The Population of Modern China.* New York and London: Plenum Press, 1992.

Potter, S. H. and J. M., *China's Peasants: the Anthropology of a Revolution.* Cambridge: Cambridge University Press, 1990.

Qian Wenbao, *Rural–Urban Migration and its Impact on Economic Development in China.* Aldershot: Avebury, 1996.

Ren Xianliang, Tian Bingxin, Huang Guowen and Li Shengqi, 'China's "Registration Taboo"', in Hein Mallée (trans. and ed.), *Reform of the Hukou System.* Special number of *Chinese Anthropology and Sociology*, vol. 29, no. 1, 1996.

Rice, Edward, *Mao's Way.* Berkeley: University of California Press, 1974.

Riskin, C., *China's Political Economy: the Quest for Development since 1949.* Oxford: Oxford University Press, 1987.

Rogers, Barbara, *The Domestication of Women: Discrimination in Developing Societies.* London: Tavistock Publications, 1980.

Rong Zhigang and Wang Shanmai, 'The Quality and Quantity of the Population', in Wang and Hull, *Population and Development Planning in China.* Sydney: Allen and Unwin, 1991.

Salaff, J., *Working Daughters of Hong Kong: Filial Piety or Power in the Family?* Hong Kong: Oxford University Press, 1981.

SASS, Information collected by the author from briefing sessions at the Institute of Rural Development, Sichuan Academy of Social Sciences, September 1994.

Scharping, T., 'Urbanization in China since 1949: a Comment', *China Quarterly* 109, March 1987.

Scharping, T. (ed.) *Floating Population and Migration in China*, Hamburg: Institut für Asienkunde, 1997.

Scharping, T., 'Studying Migration in Contemporary China: Models and Methods: Issues and Evidence', in Scharping, T. (ed.) *Floating Population and Migration in China*, Hamburg: Institut für Asienkunde, 1997.

Scharping, T. and W. Schulze, 'Labour and Income Developments in the Pearl River Delta: a Migration Study of Foshan and Shenzhen', in Scharping, T. (ed.) *Floating Population and Migration in China*, Hamburg: Institut für Asienkunde, 1997.

Schenk-Sandbergen, L., 'Special Economic Zone: Girls Have More Chance: Women and Socialist Modernization in Xiamen', Working Paper 17, Centre for Asian Studies, Amsterdam, 1989.

Schenk-Sandbergen, L. (ed.) *Women and Seasonal Labour Migration.* London: Sage Publications, 1993.

Shen Yimin and Tong Chengzhu, *Zhongguo Renkou Qianyi* (*Chinese Population Mobility*), Beijing: Statistical Publishing House, 1992.

Sit, V.F.S., *Chinese Cities: the Growth of the Metropolis since 1949.* Oxford: Oxford University Press, 1985.

Siu, Y. M. and S. M. Li, 'Population Mobility in the 1980s: China on the Road to an Open Society', Cheng, J. Y. S. and M. Brosseau (eds) *China Review 1993.* Hong Kong: Chinese University Press, 1993.

Skeldon, R., *Population Mobility in Developing Countries: A Reinterpretation*. London: Belhaven Press, 1990.

Skinner, G. W., 'Marketing and Social Structure in Rural China', *Journal of Asian Studies*. 24, 1–3, November 1964 and February and May 1965.

Skinner, G. W., 'Rural Marketing in China: Repression and Revival', *China Quarterly* 103, September 1985, 394–413.

Smil, V., *China's Environmental Crisis: an Enquiry into the Limits of National Development*. Armonk, New York: M.E. Sharpe, 1993.

Smith, Christopher J., 'Migration as an Agent of Social Change', *Chinese Environment and Development*, vol. 7, nos 1 and 2, Spring/Summer 1996, 56–72.

Solinger, Dorothy, 'Chinese Transients and the State: a Form of Civil Society?', *Politics and Society*, 21, 1 1993, 91–122.

Solinger, Dorothy, 'The Floating Population in the Cities: Chances for Assimilation', in Davis, D., Richard Kraus, Barry Naughton and Elizabeth J. Perry (eds) *Urban Spaces in Contemporary China*, Cambridge: Cambridge University Press, 1995.

Solinger, Dorothy, 'Migrant Petty Entrepreneurs and a Dual Labour Market?', in Scharping, T. (ed.) *Floating Population and Migration in China*, Hamburg: Institut für Asienkunde, 1997.

Song, Lena, 'The Determinants of Female Labour Migration in China: a Case Study of Handan', paper prepared for the conference *Socio-economic Transformation and Women in China*, June, School of Oriental and African Studies, University of London, 1995.

SSB (State Statistical Bureau), *10 Per cent Sampling Tabulation on the 1990 Population Census of the People's Republic of China (Zhongguo 1990 nian renkou pucha 10% chouyang ziliao)*. Beijing: Statistical Publishing House, 1991a.

SSB, *China Statistical Yearbook 1990*. Beijing: Statistical Publishing House, 1991b.

SSB, *China Population Statistics Yearbook 1993*. Beijing: Statistical Publishing House, 1993.

SSB, *China: Statistical Yearbook 1994*. Beijing: Statistical Publishing House, 1994.

SSB, *China: Statistical Yearbook 1996*. Beijing: Statistical Publishing House, 1996.

SSB, *China: Statistical Yearbook 1997*. Beijing: Statistical Publishing House, 1997.

Summerfield, Gale, 'Economic Reform and the Employment of Chinese Women', *Journal of Economic Issues*, 28:3, 1994, 715–32.

Summerfield, Gale, 'The Shadow Price of Labour in the Export-processing Zones. A Discussion of the Social Value of Employing Women in Export Processing in Mexico and China', *A Review of Political Economy*, 7:1, 1995, 28–42.

Sun Changmin, 'Floating Population in Shanghai: a Perspective of Social Transformation in China', in Scharping, T. (ed.) *Floating Population and Migration in China*, Hamburg: Institut für Asienkunde, 1997.

Sun, Lena H., 'China Wallows in its Blind Flow', *International Herald Tribune*, 11 October 1994.

Taubmann, W., 'Migration into Rural Towns (*zhen*) – Some Results of a Research Project on Rural Urbanisation in China', in Scharping, T. (ed.) *Floating Population and Migration in China*, Hamburg: Institut für Asienkunde, 1997.

Tawney, R. H., *Land and Labour in China*. London: Allen and Unwin, 1932.

Taylor, J., 'Rural Employment Trends and the Legacy of Surplus Labour', *China Quarterly*, 116, December 1988, 736–66.

Thadani V. and M. Todaro, 'Female Migration: a Conceptual Framework', in Fawcett, John T., *Women in the Cities of Asia*. Colorado: Westview Press, 1984.

Thane, P., 'Women and the Poor Law', *History Workshop Journal*, no. 6, Autumn 1978, pp. 29–51.

Thompson, E. P., 'Time, Work, Discipline and Industrial Capitalism', *Past and Present*, 38, 1967.

Todaro M., *Internal Migration in Developing Countries: a Review of Theory, Evidence, Methodology and Research Priorities*. Geneva: ILO, 1976.

Todaro, Michael P., *Economic Development*. London: Longman, 6th edition, 1997.

Tsurumi, Patricia, *Factory Girls: Women in the Thread Mills of Meiji Japan*. Princeton: Princeton University Press, 1990.

Walker, K., 'Trends in Crop Production 1978–86', *China Quarterly*, 116, December 1988.

Wan Shanping, *From Country to Capital: a Study of a Female Migrant Group in China*. unpublished M.Phil. thesis, Oxford Brookes University, 1992.

Wang Jiye and Terence H. Hull (eds) *Population and Development Planning in China*. Sydney: Allen and Unwin, 1991.

Wang Weizhi, 'An Overview of the Pattern of Internal Migration and Reasons for Migrating', in Day and Ma (eds) *Migration and Urbanization in China*. New York, 1994.

Wang Yunxian, *The Household Responsibility System and Women's Position: a Case Study of Two Villages in Zhejiang Province in China*. Unpublished PhD thesis, Pathuthani, Thailand: Asian Institute of Technology, 1997.

Wu Huailian, 'The Tidal Wave of Peasants Leaving the Land in the 1980s', *Demography (Rekouxuekan)*, 1989/5, 41–9.

White, Lynn T., 'Migration and Politics on the Shanghai Delta', *Issues and Studies*, September 1994, 63–94.

Woon Yuen-fong, 'Circulatory Mobility in post-Mao China: Temporary Migrants in Kaiping County, Pearl River Region', *International Migration Review*, vol. 27, no. 3, 1993, 578–604.

Xiang Biao, 'Beijing youge Zhejiang cun' ('There is a Zhejiang village in Beijing'), *Shehuixue yu shehui diaocha (Sociology and Social Investigation)*, no. 3, 1993a, 36–9.

Xiang Biao, 'How to Create a Visible Non-state Space through Migration and Marketized Traditional Networks: an Account of a Market Community in China', 1993b, unpublished. Manuscript courtesy of the author.

Xiang Biao, 'Zhejiang Village in Beijing' in Pieke and Mallée (eds) *Chinese Migrants and European Chinese: Perspectives on Internal and International Migration*, forthcoming.

Xiong Yu and Lincoln H. Day, 'The Economic Adjustment of Migrants in Urban Areas', in Lincoln H. Day and Ma Xia (eds) *Migration and Urbanization in China*. Armonk, New York and London: M. E. Sharpe, 1994.

Yan Hao, 'Population Distribution and Internal Migration in China since the early 1950s', in Wang and Hull, *Population and Development Planning in China*. Sydney: Allen and Unwin, 1991.

Yang Jiang, *A Cadre School Life, Six Chapters*, trans. by Geremie Barme and Greg Lee. Hongkong: Joint Publishing, 1982.

Yangcheng Wanbao (*Yangcheng Evening News*, Guangzhou), 'Guangdong Finds Migrant Population Has Fewer Babies than Residents, Contrary to Previous Theory', 25 June 1994.

Yu Dechang *Quanguo baicun laodongli qingkuang diaocha ziliaoji* (*Data from the National 100 Village Labour Force Survey*). Beijing: Statistical Publishing House, 1989.

Yuan, Victor, Zhang Shouli and Wang Xin, 'Self-Organize: Finding out the Way for Migrants to Protect their Own Rights', paper presented at the International Conference on the Flow of Rural Labour in China, Beijing, June 1996.

Zhang, Heather, 'Making a Difference in Their Own Lives: Rural Women in the Urban Labour Market in North China', Leeds East Asian Papers no. 50, 1997.

Zhang Qingwu, *Basic Facts on the Household Registration System*, ed. and trans. M. Dutton, *Chinese Economic Studies*, vol. 22, no. 1, 1988.

Zhang Wenyi, 'The Mobile Population Should not have Free Rein of the Cities', in *Minzhu yu fazhi* (*Democracy and the Legal System*), 6:12, 1995, translated in FBIS, 21 March 1996.

Zhang Xinxin and Sang Ye (1986) *Beijing ren*. Shanghai Renmin chubanshe (People's Publishing House) 1986, English edition ed. W. J. F. Jenner and Delia Davin, *Chinese Lives: an Oral History of Contemporary China*. London: Macmillan 1987, Penguin, 1989.

Zhao, Simon Xiaobin, 'Spatial Disparities and Economic Development in China 1953–92 – a Comparative Study', *Development and Change*, vol. 27, no. 1, January 1996, 130–63.

Zhao Zhongwei, *Household and Kinship in Recent and Very Recent Chinese History: Theory and Practice of Co-Residence in Three Chinese Villages in Beijing Area*. Unpublished PhD thesis, Cambridge, 1992.

Zhuang Ping, 'On the Social Phenomenon of Trafficking in Women in China', *Chinese Education and Society*, vol. 26, no. 3, 1993, 33–50.

Zhou Xiao, 'Virginity and Pre-marital Sex in Contemporary China', *Feminist Studies*, 15:2, 1989, 279–88.

Zhou, Kate Xiao, *How Farmers Changed China: Power of the People*. Boulder, Colorado: Westview Press, 1996.

Zou Lanchun, *Beijing de liudong renkou* (*Beijing's Floating Population*). Beijing: Zhongguo renkou chubanshe, 1996.

Index